Footprint Spain

Mary-Ann Gallagher and Andy Symington
2nd edition

*Spain is but Spain, and belongs nowhere
but where it is. It is neither Catholic nor
European but a structure of its own,
forged from an austere reality and
rejects all shortcuts to a smoother life*

Laurie Lee, *A Rose for Winter:
Travels in Andalucía* (1955)

Spain Highlights

See colour maps at back of book

❶ Madrid
Three of Europe's top art museums, tapas bars and fun-loving Madrileños

❷ Valencia
Baroque buildings, beaches and the fiery festival of Las Fallas

❸ Barcelona
Gaudí's fairytale architecture, palm-lined beaches, and fantastic nightlife and shopping

❹ Cap de Creus
Explore Catalunya's wild, untouched coves, a hikers' and divers' paradise

❺ Fiesta de San Fermín
Pamplona goes beserk for its bull running and beer swilling festival

❻ Bilbao
From urban wasteland to buzzy cultural capital

❼ Pyrenees
Hike through the spellbinding National Park of Aigüestortes

❽ Picos de Europa
Excellent trekking across eulogized limestone massifs

❾ Salamanca
Possibly the most beautiful city in Spain, certainly the most enjoyable architecture lesson

❿ Santiago de Compostela
A magical city and final destination for thousands of Pilgrims each year

4

Contents

Madrid and around

Castilla y León

La Rioja

Aragón

Valencia and Murcia

Andalucia

Background

Footnotes

Inside front cover
Sleeping and eating
price codes

Inside back cover
Authors' biographies

Small is beautiful
The Casa de Pilatos in Sevilla has possibly the finest display of azulejos in Andalucía.

A foot in the door

Caught between Europe and Africa, with one foot in the past and the other firmly in the 21st century, humming with life and preoccupied with death, Spain conjures up stereotypes – and then shatters them all.

Flamenco and paella may be the country's de facto symbols, but the first is from Andalucía and the second is from Valencia. The Spanish themselves sometimes refer to *Las Españas*, and it doesn't take long to discover that the notion of 'Spanishness' is more complicated than you might expect. Franco's attempts to impose a single national identity were wiped out overnight after his death in 1975, as each area sought to re-establish their unique characteristics repressed under the dictatorship. The country is now divided into 17 autonomous communities, each with their own history, culture and traditions, all being triumphantly celebrated. You won't find true flamenco in Barcelona and the stately Catalan *sardana* isn't danced on the streets of Seville. This cultural disparity is echoed in other ways. While old Al-Andalus may still linger in the elaborate Moorish palaces of Granada, the pure austerity of Romanesque holds sway in the Pyrenees where the Christian Reconquest was born.

The co-existence of apparently opposing values is a peculiarly Spanish gift. More than one writer has remarked that dreamy, idealistic Don Quixote and his earthy pragmatic side-kick Sancho Panza represent two sides of the Spanish psyche – this is after all a country in which miracles still happen in one part of town while a hot, new nightclub is being toasted in another. It's partly the Spanish preoccupation with death – and not just in the bullring – which encourages them to live life with such intense energy. And however this energy is expressed – in slick new buildings projects or a rowdy carnival celebration – it's impossible not to be seduced by it.

10 Onwards and upwards

In Spain, the present is always what counts. The country is a treasure trove of remarkable architecture, stretching back for several millennia and the product of countless cultures, which has been preserved in part through neglect and poverty, but also by a healthy lack of romanticism about the past. Things have changed: preservation is now the order of the day, but only because it reflects the pride that Spain can finally afford to take in its beauty. This new found appreciation of the past has not precluded new projects. On the contrary. Every city in Europe envies the enormous expansion and attendant prosperity which Gehry's 'titanium flower' has brought Bilbao. Valencia now has its very own celebrity architect, Santiago Calatrava, who was responsible for the futuristic new City of Arts and Sciences which houses everything from a high-tech planetarium to Europe's biggest aquarium. And Barcelona has even reclaimed a vast swathe of land from the sea for its latest show, the Forum of Cultures in 2004.

Garden of Eden
Escape the crowds of the Alhambra in the shaded gardens of the Generalife, on the slopes of Cerro del Sol.

Keep the cameras rolling

After years of repression under Franco, it would appear the Spanish shook off their shackles and chains and donned something theatrical. The arts scene flourished and cinema was no exception. In 2000 Pedro Almodóvar hit the big time when he won an Oscar for *Todo Sobre Mi Madre* (All About My Mother) and then cemented his place in cinema history with another Oscar for *Hable Con Ella* (Talk to Her) in 2003. The anarchic chronicler of the mad Movida years has become the toast of the Hollywood establishment. But international success has changed opinions back home. *Hable con Ella* was not even nominated for the Foreign Film Award by the Spanish authorities – the Oscar was won for its screenplay. Young Spaniards complain that Almodóvar has lost his edge and prefer to vaunt home-grown talent like Bigas Luna, Julio Medem, and Alejandro Amenábar. Spanish audiences bay for innovation in all areas resulting in a vibrant, often bizarre, but certainly an ever-evolving arts scene.

Puppy love
Frank Gehry's daring and brilliant creation, the Guggenheim, has helped to turn one-time dirty industrial Bilbao into a vibrant, cultural capital.

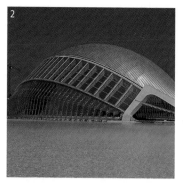

SE VENDEN
NARANJAS

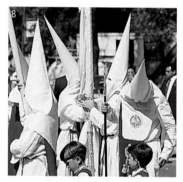

1 *From the Golden Age of Lope de Vega, to the heady days of La Movida, Madrid has delivered the best in traditional and avant-garde theatre.* ▸▸ *See page 113.*

2 *The futuristic new Ciudad de las Artes y Las Ciències in Valencia.* ▸▸ *See page 672.*

3 *Plaza Mayor, the heart of imperial Madrid, dominated by the equestrian statue of Felipe II and ringed by overpriced tapas bars, is a tourist magnet.* ▸▸ *See page 74.*

4 *Tertúlia was perfected almost a 100 years ago when contemporary artists and writers put the world to rights over brandy and coffee in boho-cafés.* ▸▸ *See page 261.*

5 *Traditional life continues in Valencia, the city much vaunted as the 'new Barcelona'.* ▸▸ *See page 666.*

6 *One-time prison for the Inquisition, the tranquil gardens of Alcázar de los Reyes Cristianos, Córdoba, are now its most arresting sight.* ▸▸ *See page 809.*

7 *Bristling with turrets and soaring spires, Segovia's fairy-tale castle, the Alcázar, provided the inspiration for Disney's Magic Kingdom, much to purists' dismay.* ▸▸ *See page 124.*

8 *In cities across Spain, the penitents, or Nazarenes, march to funereal drum beats during Semana Santa.* ▸▸ *See page 726.*

9 *One of the best times to be in Spain is during a fiesta. In Alicante, Fiesta de Moros y Cristianos, a mock battle between Moors and Christians, is spectacular.* ▸▸ *See page 686.*

10 *Rugged mountain ranges, swathes of olive trees and blood red poppies, characterize much of Jaén Province.* ▸▸ *See page 798.*

11 *The sinuous balconies and bulbous crosses of Gaudí's dream world at La Pedrera.* ▸▸ *See page 269.*

12 *The craggy beaches of the north are a far cry from the crowded costas of the south.* ▸▸ *See page 587.*

14 Where eagles dare

Spain is a paradise for walkers, climbers, nature-lovers and anyone into adventure-sports. There are a handful of stunningly beautiful national parks on mainland Spain, all of which are well worth exploring. In the Aragonese Pyrenees, there´s the Ordesan and Monte Perdido National Park; east, in Catalunya, there's the National Park of Aigüestortes and Estany Sant Maurici. Asturias has the spectacular Picos de Europa and Castilla-La Mancha boasts the important wetlands of the Tablas de Daimiel and the remote Mediterranean forest of Cabañeros. The Coto de Doñana in Andalucía has been declared a world heritage site by UNESCO and is home to endangered species like the lynx and Imperial Eagle. All the parks have cracking trails, and you'll have a good chance of spotting wildlife: vultures and chamois are a common sight, and golden eagles and massive lammergeiers sweep into sight often enough to give many a walker a thrill.

With crumbling frescoes, orange trees and an Andalucían pebble-patterned floor, this serene patio in the Hospital de San Juan de Dios is one of Granada's less-visited highlights.

For many the dusty meseta *of Castilla-La Mancha is the image of Spain. Farming isn't the only industry. Cervantes, through Don Quijote, brought tourism to the area.*

The age of revellery

If you spend any period of time in Spain, you're almost guaranteed to bump into a fiesta. Ranging in spirit from the solemnly religious to the wholly anarchic – most usually have a dose of both – local fiestas provide the focus for a range of social, cultural and sporting activity. The bull- fighting season runs to the fiesta calendar; as well as taurine activity, you're guaranteed markets, fireworks, street food, concerts and masses of revellers. The drink of choice is *calimocho*, a mix of cheap red wine and cola usually drunk out of a *cachi*, a litre-sized plastic cup. While there are better choices for taste and mornings-after, you'll certainly feel in authentic fiesta mood. There are the biggies: the running of the bulls in Pamplona; the tomato throwing frenzy of *La Tomatina*, the riotous *Carnaval* in Cádiz that even Franco failed to suppress, to name a few. Happening across a local village affair however, could turn out to be a highlight of your trip.

Feeding frenzy

Spain's passion for seafood is guaranteed to please anyone who casts hungry eyes at rock pools and goldfish bowls. Hit the Basque country for the best sauces, including the mysterious *pil-pil* and any number of fishy bartop snacks. Wash down your mussels with cider in Asturias, or head to Galicia for octopus served in oil and paprika. Paella, invented in Valencia, is where it tastes better than anywhere else, and in Cádiz you can sit out on a square with a paper cone of *pescaíto frito* – tiny fried fish caught that day. *Buen provecho*!

Out of this world
Giant boiled eggs perched on the rooftop of the Teatre-Museu Dalí in Figueres celebrate perhaps the maddest Catalan of them all.

Essentials

🔅 Footprint features

Planning your trip

Where to go

Spain is huge and incredibly diverse, both geographically and culturally. Choosing where to go will depend largely on your interests, as well as the length of time you've got, and where your point of entry is.

Up to a week

If you're on just a short break, the most convenient option might be to centre your holiday around a city, particularly one which has an international airport. Madrid has a fabulous collection of western art and the best nightlife in Spain – closely followed by its flamboyant rival, Barcelona. Barcelona's Modernista skyline, beaches and dedication to design in all its forms have made it one of Europe's hippest weekend destinations. Lesser known, but growing in the fashion stakes, is Valencia, with a beautiful Baroque core, long golden beaches, and the new high-tech City of Arts and Sciences. Bilbao was put on the map with the arrival of the stunning Guggenheim museum, but it's also home to the finest cuisine in Spain. The seaside cities of Alicante and Málaga remain refreshingly Spanish, despite the massive influx of holiday-makers every summer, but they are best enjoyed out of season. Málaga is also the gateway to Andalucía, where Moorish Al-Andalus still lingers in seductive Seville, whitewashed Córdoba, and magical Granada.

With more time at your disposal, you could base yourself in a city but explore further afield – the little-known sierras around Madrid, the scenic coastline around Bilbao, or the valleys of Romanesque monuments north of Barcelona, for example. Even in the built-up coastal regions, it won't take long to get off the beaten track and discover pristine villages and remote natural parks inland.

Two weeks

With two weeks, you can skim through some of Spain's highlights or spend time getting to know a particular corner of Spain really well. Start in Barcelona, fly to Madrid, then take the high-speed *AVE* train to Seville for a taste of three very different cities and three very distinct cultures. If you've got your own transport, a meander through the Pyrenees is rewarding whatever your interests: the stunning national park of Aigüestortes is a must for hikers, bird-watchers and anyone interested in adventure sports, but there are also countless jewels of Romanesque architecture and remote mountain villages. Around Granada, you can explore the Alhambra, take a tranquil journey through the whitewashed mountain villages of the Alpujarras, tackle the peak of Mulhacén in the Sierra Nevada, and play at Cowboys and Indians at mini-Hollywood.

For the great outdoors, the Pyrenees are an obvious attraction; you could easily spend a fortnight or more exploring the area in northern Navarra, Aragón and Catalunya. Alquézar will appeal to canyoning fans, and you can rocket down the rapids along the Noguera Pallaresa river in Catalunya. The Picos de Europa are smaller but equally picturesque. For a more out-of-the way experience, explore the Asturian forests in places like the Somiedo or Muniellos natural park, or visit the remote northern reaches of Extremadura, where waterfalls make perfect natural swimming pools in the canyons. The Sierra de Gredos and the Sierra de Guadarrama are hugely popular with Madrileño second-homers, but it's still easy to get off the beaten track for some excellent hiking, biking and climbing. Bird-lovers won't want to miss the marshlands of the Delta de l'Ebre in Catalunya, or the Coto Doñana National Park in Andalucía, which are home to hundreds of species of birds. Also in Andalucía,

If architecture is your thing, following the Camino de Santiago is a very rewarding experience, on foot of course, but even on buses or in a car. The route takes in many of the finest cathedrals of the north at León, Burgos, Jaca and Santiago itself, as well as a superb series of Romanesque churches in places like Estella and Frómista. If you're a castle fan, the Duero valley is studded with them; Peñafiel, Gormaz and Berlanga are impressive. Navarra and Aragón also have several, including superb Loarre, near Huesca. If you like beautiful brick, a Mudéjar kick could take you around the provinces of Zaragoza and Teruel. Fans of Moorish architecture should make for Andalucía, and the three great cities of Seville, Córdoba and Granada. Gaudí's delirious Modernista architecture is now internationally famous, but you'll find plenty more in Reus, Terrassa, and smaller towns across Catalunya. For modern architecture, visit Gehry's beatufiul 'titanium flower', the Guggenheim museum in Bilbao, but don't neglect Calatrava's bold new City of Arts and Sciences in Valencia.

Gourmets could consider Euskadi, with its celebrated cuisine, particularly in the lovely Belle Epoque seaside resort of San Sebastián, and the famous wine-producers of nearby La Rioja; or the fanciful Modernista *bodegas* in Catalunya, where the home-grown local fizz, *cava*, is produced.

Literary types might want to tilt at windmills along the Quixote trail in the dusty plain of La Mancha, taking in some local festivals, like the saffron festival at Consuegra, along the way. Toledo is forever linked with El Greco, who painted the city as a backdrop in many of his most famous paintings.

For lovers of sun, sea and sand, Spain offers a fabulous and richly varied coastline. Everyone has heard of the fleshpots of the various Costas which line the Mediterranean coast, but lesser known are the magnificent fjord-like *rías* of Galicia, and the remote beaches along the northwestern coast. The Costa de la Luz, which stretches south of Cádiz, is beginning to be developed but it remains one of the few places in southern Spain where you might find a place to put your beach towel in the height of summer.

One month

With three or four weeks you can combine a couple of the above itineraries. Alternatively, a good month's trip in northwestern Spain would start in the Basque country, head west along the coast, taking in the Picos de Europa on the way, and then explore Galicia. From here, head across to León, and then south to Zamora and Salamanca. Head east along the Duero Valley to Soria, then cut into Aragón and head for the Pyrenees to wash the Castilian dust off. Another option might be to follow in the footsteps of Columbus and the conquistadores, beginning in Seville, then heading down to the coast around Huelva, and slowly making your way up to Extremadura and the beautiful time-capsules of Trujillo or Cáceres, barely changed since returning conquistadores built their *palacios* with riches earned in the Americas.

When to go

Climate

The diversity of Spanish terrain is extraordinary: with the crashing Atlantic on one side and the gentle Mediterranean on the other, some of Europe's highest mountains and its only desert, dry *dehesa* and fertile farmland, and a vast central plain scattered with castles and windmills, it can feel like several countries rolled into one.

The northwestern provinces – the Basque Lands, Navarra, Asturias, Cantabria and Galicia – are generally the rainiest, but are also the least touristy during the height of the summer months when sunshine can usually be relied on. Catalunya,

Aragon and Valencia to the northeast are milder and crammed in July and August: late spring and early autumn are the best times to visit if you want to avoid the crowds. If you are interested in winter sports, Andorra and the lesser-known ski resorts of Catalunya are best in January and February when the snow can be counted on. The Pyrenees are perfect for walkers and climbers in summer, with plenty of adventure sports on offer from rafting to canyoning. The vast Castilian plain with the capital Madrid at the centre famously bakes in summer and freezes in winter, so late spring and early autumn are the best times to visit to avoid the extremes of temperature. Murcia and Andalucía are pleasantly mild in winter but searingly hot in summer, and the resorts of the Costa del Sol and the Costa Cálida teem with holiday-makers, making accommodation scarce and beach space even harder to find. But, if you avoid July and August, there's never really a bad time to visit. Extremadura, again, is just too hot in the height of summer, and is best visited in spring, when the rivers and waterfalls of the hilly north are a beautiful sight.

Public holidays

Traditionally, August is the holiday month for Spanish workers, who abandon the cities for the coast, and many shops, and restaurants – even in the capital, Madrid – close down for the whole month. If you want to party, head to the coast with them; to avoid the crowds, make for the hills.

Festivals and events

Spain has a packed calendar of festivals, see page 57, which take place throughout the year, and there is almost always something going on in even the smallest village. Some of the biggest include **Semana Santa** (Easter Week) and **Feria** in Sevilla, the **running of the bulls** in Pamplona in July, **Las Fallas** in Valencia in March, and **Carnaval** in Cádiz in February. You'll have to book accommodation months in advance for any of these.

Tour operators → Local tour operators are listed in the listings throughout the book.

General operators

In the UK and Ireland

Abercrombie and Kent, Sloane Square House, Holbein Place, London SW1W 8NS, T0845-070 0610, www.abercrombiekent. co.uk. Upmarket holidays throughout Spain.

Mundi Color, 276 Vauxhall Bridge Rd, London SW1 1BE, T020-7828 6021. Part of the Spanish airline **Iberia** and offers some moderately priced packages.

Solo's Holidays, 54-8 High St, Edgware, Middlesex HA8 7ED, T020-8951 2800, F8951 2848. Holidays for people travelling alone.

Unicorn Holidays, 2-10 Crossroad, Tadworth, KT20 5UJ, T01737-812 255. Tailor-made holidays with accommodation in small inns and paradors.

In Europe and Israel

Images du Monde, 14 rue Lahire, Paris, T014-424 8788, images.du.monde@wana doo.fr. Specialists in Spain and Latin America.

Nouvelles Frontieres, 87 Bd de Grenelle, Paris, T0825-000 825, www.nouvelles-front ieres.fr Also has offices in Belgium, Luxemburg and Switzerland and offers a wide range of holidays in Spain.

Olé Spain Tours, Paseo Infanta Isabel 21, 5ºC, Madrid 28014, T349-1551 5294, F1501 1835, www.olespaintours.com. Organize all types of tours in Spain.

In North America

Abercrombie & Kent International, 1520 Kensington Rd, Oak Brook, Illinois, IL 60521, toll free T1-800 323 7308. Glossy, upscale holidays in Europe.

Council Travel, T1-888-COUNCIL, www.counciltravel.com. Specialists in youth and budget travel.

Marketing Ahead Inc, 433 Fifth Av, New York, NY 10016, T212-686 9213, F686 02 71, www.marketingahead.com. Leading parador agents in the USA.

In Australia and New Zealand

Explore Holidays, Level 9, 234 Sussex St, Sydney NSW 2000, Australia, www.exploreholidays.com.au. Organize several northern Spanish trips.

Ibertours, 1st Floor, 84 William St, Melbourne, VIC 3000, Australia, T61-3 9857 6200, F3 9857 6271. Booking agent for many accommodation chains in Spain, including the Parador and Rusticae hotels.

Outdoor Travel, PO Box 286, Bright VIC 3741, Australia, T61-3 5750 1441, F3 5750 1020, www.outdoortravel.com.au. Affiliated to several Spanish outdoor tourism operators.

Spanish Tourism Promotions, Level 1, 178 Collins St, Melbourne, VIC 3000, T61-3 9670 7755, F3 9670 3941, www.spanishtourism. com.au. Offers all types of tours and tailor-made trips to Spain.

STA Travel, 72 Harris St, Ultimo, Sydney, and 256 Flinders St, Melbourne, T1300-360960, Australia, www.statravel aus.com.au. Specialists in student and budget travel.

STA Travel, 10 High St, Auckland, New Zealand, T09-3090458. Specialists in student and budget travel.

Timeless Tours & Travel, 2/197 Military Rd, Neutral Bay, NSW 2089, Australia, T61-2 9904 1239, F2 9904 1809, www.timeless.com.au. Specializes in tailored itineraries for Spain.

In South Africa

Azure Travel, 147th Avenue, Parktown North, Johannesburg, T011-4428044, F4428662, azuretravel@worldspan.co.za. Runs tours to Spain and help with planning itineraries, reservations, etc.

Special interest operators

Adventure

Euskal Abentura, C Salvador 16, T943214870, San Sebastián, Spain, www. ehabentura.net. An adventure company organizing a massive range of outdoor activities throughout Euskadi.

Exodus Worldwide Adventure, 9 Weir Rd, London SW12OLT, UK, T020-8675 5550, F86730779, www.exodus.co.uk. Walking and adventure tours to suit all ages and pockets.

Spirit Of Adventure, Powder Mills, Princetown-Yelverton, Devon PL20 6SP, UK T0182-2880277, F2880277, www.spirit-of-adventure.com. Adventure tours with

activities from canyoning, cycling, horse riding, to hiking and sea-canoeing.

Tall Stories, Brassey House, New Zealand Av, Walton on Thames, Surrey KT12 1QD, UK, T01932-252002, F252970, www.tallstories.co.uk. Adventure holidays.

Tura, Salvatierra, Alava, Spain, T945312535, www.tura.org. Based out of the tourist office, this is a very competent organization that arranges activities throughout Alava Province, ie walking, canyoning, abseiling, canoeing, windsurfing, paragliding and horse trekking.

Archaeology/art history

ACE Study Tours, Babraham, Cambridge, UK, T01223-835055, F837394. Covers Castilla y León, Aragón, the Camino de Santiago, etc.

Andante Travel, The Old Barn, Old Road, Alderbury, Salisbury SP5 3AR, UK, T01722-713 800, www.andantetravels.co.uk. Arranges archaeological and historical study tours of Roman Spain.

Martin Randall Travel, 10 Barley Mow Passage, London W4 4PH, UK, T020-8742 3355, F8741 7766, www.martinrandall.com. Excellent cultural itineraries accompanied by lectures.

Plantagenet Tours, 85 The Grove, Moordown, Bournemouth BH9 2TY, UK, T01202- 521 895, www.plantagenettours. com. An excellent programme of cultural tours in Andalucía and Catalunya.

Battlefields

Holts Tours, The Plough, High Street, Eastry, Sandwich, Kent CT13 0HF, UK, T01304-612248, F614 930, www.battletours.co.uk. Regular tours of the Napoleonic battlefields of northern and southern Spain.

Birdwatching

Naturetrek, Cheriton Mill, Cheriton, Alresford, Hampshire SO24 ONG, UK, T01962-733 051, www.naturetrek.co.uk. Birdwatching and botanical tours in Andalucía and Coto Doñana National Park.

Peregrine Holidays, 15 Grange Place, Bridge Street, Witney, Oxfordshire OX28 4BS, UK, T01993-849489. Birdwatching tours throughout Spain.

Spain Birds, www.spainbirds.com. Birdwatching tours and excursions all over the country.

Windrush, Coles Lane, Brasted, Westerham, Kent TN16 1NN, UK, T01959 563627, F562906, gourmetbirds@aol.com. Birdwatching tours with accommodation in paradors.

Cycling

Bravo Bike Travel, CICMA 1200, Madrid, T/F34-916401298, www.bravobike.com. Run biking tours, including wine-tasting itineraries in the Rioja and Ribera.

Cycling Through The Centuries, PO Box 529, Manitou Springs, CO 80829, USA, T1 800 473 0610, F1 719 685 9454, www.cycling centuries.com. Run guided cycling tours of the Camino de Santiago and Picos de Europa.

Irish Cycling Safaris, Belfield House, University College Dublin, Dublin 4, Ireland, T353-1 260 0749, F1 716 1168, www.cyclingsafaris.com. Irish set-up that runs some tours to Northern Spain.

Saddle Skedaddle, UK, T0191-265 1110, www.skedaddle.co.uk. Run mountain-biking and cycliing trips in Northern Spain among other places.

Disabled

Accessible City Breaks, Avionics House, Naas Lane, Gloucester, GL2 2SN, T 01452-729 739, F729 853, www.accessiblecity breaks.co.uk. Accessible city breaks for disabled travellers.

Jubilee Sailing Trust, Hazel Rd, Woolston, Southampton SO19 7GB, UK, T02380-449108, F449145, www.jst.org.uk. Tall ships running sailing journeys for disabled and able-bodied people, some around Northern Spain.

Fiestas

Travel Orb, 4629 Cass St, San Diego CA 92109, T+1 800 701 7826, www.travel orb.com. High-class tours to Pamplona.

Fishing

GourmetFly, 18 Avenue Edouard Vaillant, 92100 Boulogne, France, www.gourmet fly.com. Runs flyfishing excursions to Northern Spain.

Food and wine

Epiculinary Tours, www.epiculinary.com. A company that gets into the heart of the

San Sebastián gastronomic societies and offers lessons too.

Euroadventures, C Velásquez Moreno 9, Vigo, Spain T3498 6221 399, F6221 344, www.euroadventures.net. A range of interesting tours, for example culinary tours of the Basque region that include lessons.

Vintage Spain, C Burgos 9, 4B, 09200 Miranda de Ebro, Spain T34 699 2466 534, www.vintagespain.com. Tours in Northern Spain including wine tasting.

Winetrails, Greenways, Vann Lake, Ockley, Dorking, RH5 5NT, UK T0130-671 2111, F671 3504 , www.winetrails.co.uk. Tailor-made tours to Spanish wine regions.

Language

AmeriSpan Unlimited, PO Box 58129, Philadelphia, PA 19102-8129, T215 751 1100, USA: (800) 879-6640, www.amerispan.com.

Cactus Language, 4 Clarence House, 30-31 North St, Brighton, East Sussex, BN1 1EB. UK T0845-130 4775, USA T1-888-270-3949, www.cactuslanguage.com.

Don Quijote UK, 2-4 Stoneleigh Park Rd, Stoneleigh, Epsom, Surrey KT19 OQR, T020-8786 8081, F8786 8086. Organizes Spanish language classes and accommodation.

Enforex, Alberto Aguillera 26, 28015 Madrid, Spain, T34 91 594 3776, info@enforex.es.

Languages Abroad (CESA), Western House, Malpas, Truro, Cornwall TR1 1SQ, UK, T01872-225300, F225400. Immersion courses in cities throughout Spain.

Spanish Abroad, 5112 N 40th Street, Suite 103, Phoenix AZ 85018, USA, UK T1 602 778 6791/0-800-028-7706 (freephone); USA 1-888-722-7623 (toll free), www.spanish abroad.com. Two-week immersion language courses in Salamanca and San Sebastián.

Motorcycling

Bike and Sun Tours, 42 Whitby Av, Guiseborough, Cleveland TS14 7AN, UK, T01287-639739, F638217. Bike and motorbike tours throughout Spain.

Ride Spain, The Maltings, Knowle Hill, Hurley, CV9 2JE, UK, www.ridespain.com. Runs motorbike tours of the north, with flexible itineraries.

Walking

Alternative Travel Group Ltd, 69-71 Banbury Road, Oxford, OX2 6PE, UK, T01865-

315679, F315697, www.atg-oxford.co.uk. Walking holidays in Spain.
Pack & Pedal Europe, RR # 1 Box 35A Springville, PA 18844-9578 USA, T1 570 965 2064, F965 0925, www.tripsite.com. Walking and cycling tours in the Pyrenees and Picos.
Spain Adventures, www.spainadventures. com. Hiking and biking tours in Northern Spain.

Finding out more

Spanish tourist offices → *See individual town entries for local Spanish tourist offices.*

Spanish tourist offices can be a very useful source of information helping with both planning and booking. Details of a few of the main centres are as follows: **France:** 43, Rue Decamps, 75784 Paris Cedex 16 France, T4503-8250; **United Kingdom:** 22-23 Manchester Sq, London W1M 5AP, T020-7486 8077 and for a brochure T09063 640 630, www.tourspain.co.uk; **USA:** Water Tower Place, Suite 915 East 845, North Michigan Ave, Chicago, ILL 60611, T1 312 6421992, chicago@tourp ain.es; 8383 Wils hire Blvd, Suite 960, Beverley Hills, LA, CAL 90211, T1 213 658 7188, los angeles@ tourspain.es; 1221 Brickell Avenue, Miami, Florida 33131, T1 305 3581992, miami@ tourspain.es; 666 Fifth Avenue, New York NY 10103, T1 212 2658822, nuevayork@ tourspain.es.

Useful websites

www.okspain.org An official site with information about Spain, aimed at Americans.
www.tuspain.com A good selection of information about many aspects of Spain.
www.tourspain.es A good website run by the Spanish Tourist Board
www.red 2000.com A good introduction to the geography and culture of Spain, with some listings.
www.idealspain.com A good source of practical information.
atlasgeo.span.ch/fotw/flags/es/prov.html#map Maps of Spain by province.
horarios.renfe.es/hir/index.html Timetables and tickets for **RENFE** train network.
www.ciudadhoy.com Good Spanish-language site with fresh information about bars, restaurants, and nightclubs.
www.elpais.es Online edition of Spain's biggest selling daily paper.
soc.culture.spain The busiest newsgroup on Spain. Multilingual, ranges from the political to the everyday, and is happily snobbery-free.
www.spain360vr.com/ Pictures of locations along the Camino de Santiago.
rubens.anu.edu.au/htdocs/bycountry/spain/index1.html Good photos of many churches and buildings in Spain.
www.elpais.es Online edition of Spain's biggest selling non-sports newspaper.
www.wild-spain.com News and views on Spain's wildlife and natural parks, plus a useful directory of rural accommodation and outdoor tour operators.

Language → *See Footnotes, page 864, for some useful words and phrases.*

For travelling purposes, everyone in Spain speaks Spanish, known either as Castellano or Español. Most young people know some English, and standards are rising, but don't assume that people aged 30 or over know any at all. While efforts to speak the language are appreciated, it's more or less expected, to the same degree as English is expected in Britain or the USA. Nobody will be rude if you don't speak any Spanish, but nobody will think to slow down their speech for your benefit either. While many visitor attractions have information available in English (and sometimes French and German), many don't, or only have English tours in times of high demand.

Most tourist office staff will speak at least some English, and there's a good range of translated information available in many regions. English is widely spoken in the resorts along the Mediterranean coast.

Other languages that you'll come across include Euskara (the Basque language), Catalan (in Catalunya), Valenciano (in Valencia), Galego (Galician), Bable (the Asturian dialect), and perhaps Aragonese. Efforts to speak even a few words in these languages are usually much appreciated, and a limited knowledge of a couple of key words will be helpful for roadsigns, etc.

Disabled travellers

Spain isn't the best-equipped of countries in terms of disabled travel, but things are improving rapidly. By law, all new public buildings have to have full disabled access and facilities, but disabled toilets are rare in other edifices. Facilities generally are significantly better in the touristed south than in northern Spain. While major cities are relatively straightforward, smaller towns frequently have uneven footpaths, steep streets (often cobbled) and little, if any, disabled infrastructure.

Most trains and stations are wheelchair friendly, as are many urban buses, but intercity buses are largely not accessible for wheelies. **Hertz** offices in Madrid and Barcelona have a small range of cars set up for disabled drivers, but be sure to book them well in advance. Nearly all underground and municipal carparks have lifts and disabled spaces, as do many museums, castles, etc. An invaluable resource for finding a bed are the regional accommodation lists, available from tourist offices. Most of these include a disabled-access criterion. Many *pensiones* are in buildings

with ramps and lifts, but there are many that are not, and the lifts can be very small. Nearly all paradors and modern chain hotels are fully wheelchair-accessible, but it's best to phone. Be sure to confirm details as many hotels' claims are well-intentioned but not fully thought through.

The blind are comparatively well-catered for in Spain as a result of the efforts of **ONCE** (Organización Nacional de Ciegos de España), the national organization for the blind, which run a lucrative daily lottery. They can be found at Consejo General de la ONCE, C/José Ortega y Gasset 18, 28006 Madrid, T915773756, www.once.es. **Confederación Nacional de Sordos de España** (CNSE), www.cnse.es, has links to local associations for the deaf. **Federación ECOM**, T934515550, www.ecom.es, is a helpful Barcelona-based organization for the disabled that can assist in providing information on disabled-friendly tourist facilities throughout the country. **IMSERSO** is the branch of the Spanish ministry for social security that deals with disabled issues, including access for travellers. Theoretically, they can provide assistance and advice via email at buzon.imserso@mtas.es. **ALPE Turismo para Todos,** C/Casarrubuelos 5, Madrid, T914480864, publish a useful hotel guide which lists facilities for disabled travellers.

Organizations in the UK

Holiday Care Information Unit, 2nd Floor Imperial Buildings, Victoria Rd, Horley, Surrey RH6 7PZ, T01293-774535, F784647, Minicom: 01293 776943, www.holidcaycare.org.uk. Provides useful information on accessible hotels and attractions and activity holidays.

RADAR (The Royal Association for Disability and Rehabilitation), 12 City Forum, 250 City Rd, London EC1V 8AF, T020-7259 3222, www.radar.org.uk. Offers an array of leaflets and information on travel for the disabled.
Royal National Institute for the Blind, 105 Judd St, London, WC1H 9NE, T020-7388 1266, www.rnib.org.uk. Helpful advice,

including accommodation lists for the blind. **Tripscope**, The Vassall Centre, Gill Av, Bristol BS16 2QQ, T08457-585 641 (for calls from within the UK charged at cheap rate), T+ 44 117 939 7782 (from outside the UK), www.tripscope.org.uk. Travel advice for the elderly and the disabled.

Organizations in the USA

American Foundation for the Blind, 11 Penn Plaza, Suite 300, New York, NY 10001, T212-502 7600; toll free T800-232 5463, www.afb.org. An excellent resource for blind travellers.
Mobility International USA, PO Box 10767, Eugene, OR 97403, T503-343 1284, www.miusa.org
SATH (Society for Accessible Travel and Hospitality), Suite 610, 347 5th Avenue, New York, NY 10016, T212-447 7284, www.sath. org. For a small membership fee, SATH will provide useful information.

Gay and lesbian travellers

Homosexuality is legal, and all ages of consent have been equalized (age 13). There's a thriving pink scene in Madrid, Barcelona, Valencia and Sitges, and most other towns will have at least a few venues.

Overt displays of homophobia are rarer in the tolerant north than in the conservative south, where the spirit of *machismo* lives on and calling someone a '*maricon*' (queer) is a common insult. In general, Spaniards are not particularly gay-friendly, but the mentality is 'out of sight, out of mind', rather than downright disapproving. Same sex couples on the street shouldn't encounter any unpleasantness, at least in most of the larger cities; in rural areas amazed stares are the order of the day.

Useful websites for listings information in many Spanish cities include www.guia gay.com, www.corazongay.com, www.chueca.com, www.mensual.com (in Spanish), and www.gaywired.com, www.gay.com (in English).

Useful organizations

Casal Lambda, C/ Ample 5, Barcelona, T934127272, www.lambdaweb.org. This is a friendly, gay cultural organization which produces its own magazine (LAMBDA), and hosts all kinds of different activities.
Cogailes is a gay and lesbian organization with a handy information service on a freephone hotline, T900 601 601 (1800-2200 daily) or www.cogailes.org.
COGAM, C/Espíritu Santo 37, Madrid, T91 522 4517, T91 523 0070, is a collective of gay/lesbian organizations which encompasses several political and

social groups. It publishes a magazine (*Entiendes*), and runs an information line for visitors to Madrid.
Damron Online, www.damron.com, is a worthwhile online database of venues and travel information although most of the listings are only available via subscription.
EHGAM, Escalinatas de Solokoetxe 4, T944150719, www.geocities.com/westholly wood/1446. A good set-up whose happy folk help with any information on gay and lesbian culture and life in Euskadi.
Gehitu, C Kapitañene 13, San Sebastián, T943277638, www. gehitu.net. A gay organization covering Euskadi.

Student travellers → See Getting there, page 34, for student travel agencies.

An International Student Identity Card (ISIC), available to fulltime students, is a valuable thing in Spain. You can get one at your place of study, or at many travel agencies both in and outside Spain. The cost varies from country to country, but is generally about €6-10 – a worthwhile investment indeed, as it gets discounts of up to

20 per cent on many things. These include some aeroplane fares, train tickets, museum entry, bus tickets and some accommodation. A Euro Under 26 card gives similar discounts, and is available to anyone under 26 years of age. In Spain, the most useful travel agencies for youth and student travel are **UsitUnlimited** www.usitunlimited.es and **TIVE**.

Travelling with children

Kids are kings in Spain, and it's one of the easiest places to take them along on holiday. Children socialize with their parents from an early age here, and you'll see them eating in restaurants and out in bars well after 2400. The outdoor summer life and high pedestrianization of the cities is especially suitable and stress-free for both you and the kids to enjoy the experience.

Spaniards are very friendly and accommodating towards children, and you'll undoubtedly get treated better with them than without them, except perhaps in the most expensive of restaurants and hotels. Few places, however, are equipped with highchairs, unbreakable plates, or babychange facilities. Children are basically expected to eat the same sort of things as their parents, although you'll sometimes see a *menú infantil* at a restaurant, which typically has simpler dishes and smaller portions than the norm.

The cut-off age for children paying half or no admission/passage on public transport and in tourist attractions varies widely. **RENFE** trains let under-fours on free, and it's discount passage of around 50 per cent for under 12s. Most car-rental companies have childseats available, but it's wise to book these in advance, particularly in summer.

As for attractions, beaches are an obvious highlight, but many of the newer museums are attractively hands-on. Playgrounds and parks are common, and the Mediterranean coastline is crammed with waterparks and theme parks. The two biggest theme parks are Port Aventura in Catalunya and Warner World near Madrid. Spanish campsites are well set-up; the larger ones often have childminding facilities and activities.

Women travellers

Spain, in general, is safe for women travellers. Foreign women, particularly blondes, may attract more stares or whistles than they are used to, particularly in the south, but there is little outright harassment. While attitudes of the older generation are still prehistoric in some areas, this will rarely translate into anything less than perfect courtesy. If you go out on your own, you can expect to be chatted to (Spanish girls never do, so they'll assume you're a foreigner), but it's very rarely going to be anything more than mild flirtation. Topless sunbathing is common at most of the major beach resorts, but it's best to dress modestly in smaller towns and rural areas if you don't want to attract untoward attention.

Working in Spain

The most obvious paid work for English speakers is teaching the language. Even the smallest towns usually have an English college or two; it's taken off in a big way here. Rates of pay aren't great except in the large cities, but the cost of living is low, so you can live quite comfortably. The best way of finding work is by trawling around the schools, but there are dozens of useful internet sites; check www.eslcafe.com

www.eslusa.org or www.escapeartist.com for links and listings. There's also a more casual scene of private teaching; noticeboards in universities and student cafés are the best way to find work of this sort, or to advertise your own services.

Bar work is also easy to find, particularly in summer. Irish theme bars in the larger cities are an obvious choice, but smaller towns have plenty of seasonal work. Live-in English-speaking au-pairs and childminders are popular with wealthier city families.

EU citizens are at an advantage when it comes to working in Spain; they can work without a permit for 90 days. In theory, you are supposed to apply for a *tarjeta de residencía* after 90 days – a time-consuming process indeed, but in practice, with open borders, nobody really cares unless you give them a reason to. Non EU citizens need a working visa, obtainable from Spanish embassies or consulates, but you'll need to have a firm offer of work to obtain it. Most English schools can organize this for you but make sure you arrange this before arriving in the country.

Before you travel

Visas and immigration

Entry requirements are subject to change, so always check with the Spanish tourist board or an embassy/consulate if you're not an EU citizen. EU citizens and those from countries within the Schengen agreement can enter Spain freely. UK/Irish citizens will need to carry a passport, while an identity card suffices for other EU/Schengen nationals. Citizens of Australia, the USA, Canada, New Zealand, and Israel can enter without a visa for up to 90 days. Other citizens will require a visa, obtainable from Spanish consulates or embassies. These are usually issued very quickly and valid for all Schengen countries. The basic visa is valid for 90 days, and you'll need two passport photos, proof of funds covering your stay, and possibly evidence of medical cover (ie insurance). For extensions of visas, apply to an *oficina de extranjeros* in a major city. These are also the places to go if, as an EU citizen, you are seeking temporary residency (*tarjeta de residencía*).

Spanish embassies and consulates

Australia, 15 Arkana St, Yarralumla, Canberra ACT 2600, T733555, F733918 (embassy); Level 24 St Martins Tower, 31 Market St, Sydney, NSW: 2000, T2612433, F2831695; 766 Elizabeth St, Melbourne VIC 3000, T3471966, F3477330 (consulates).
Canada, 350 Spark St, Suite 802, Ottawa, Ontario, T2372193, F2361502 (embassy); 1 Westmount Sq, Suite 1456, Montreal, Quebec, T9355235, F9354655, 1200 Bay Street, Suite 400, Toronto, Ontario M3H 2D1, T9674949, F9254949 (consulates).
Denmark, Upsalagade 26, 2100 Copenhagen, T31424700, (embassy).
Finland, Kalliolinnantie 6, 00140 Helsinki, T17 05 05, F66 01 10 (embassy).

France, 22 Av Marceau, 75381 Paris, Cedex 08, T44431800, F47205669 (embassy); Residence du Parc, 4 Av du BAB, 64100, Bayonne, T593891, F257390, 1 rue Notre-Dame, 33000 Bordeaux, T528020, F818843, 13 Quai Kleber, 67000, Strasbourg T326727, F230717; 24 rue Marceau, 34000 Montpellier, T582021, F925218 (consulates).
Germany, Lichtensteinallee 1, D-10787 Berlin, T2616081, F2624032 (embassy); Nibelungenplatz 3, 60318, Frankfurt T596 10 41 F596 47 42 (consulate).
Ireland, 17A Merlyn Park, Ballsbridge, Dublin 4, T2691640, F2691854 (embassy).
Israel, "The Tower", Rehov Daniel Frish, N3, 16, 64731, Tel Aviv, T6965210, F6952505 (embassy); Hativat Harel 5, Sheikh Jarrah Quarter, PO Box 19/128 Jerusalem, T828006, F828065 (consulate).

Italy, Palacio Borghese, Largo Fontanella di Borghese 19-00186 Rome, T6878264, F6872256 (embassy).
Norway, Oscarsgate, 35-0258 Oslo 2, T44 71 22, F55 98 22 (embassy).
New Zealand, Mancan House, corner of Manchester St and Cambridge Pl, Christchurch, T3660244, F669859 (consulate). **Netherlands**, Spain, Lange Voorhout 50, 2514 The Hague, T3643814, F3617959 (embassy); Frederiksplein 34, Amsterdam, 1017 XN T6203811, F6380836 (consulate).
Portugal, Rua do Salitre 1, 1296 Lisbon Codex.T3472381, F3425376 (embassy).
South Africa, 169 Pine St, Arcadia, Pretoria 0083, PO Box: 1633, Pretoria 0001, T344 38 75, F343 48 91, 37 Shortmarket St, 8001 CapeTown, T222326, F222328 (both).
Sweden, Djurgardsvagen 21, Djugarden,

115 21 Stockholm T6679430, F6637965 (embassy).
United Kingdom, 39 Chesham Place, London SW1X 8SB, T020-7235 5555, F7235 9905 (embassy); 63 North Castle St, Edinburgh, EH2 3LJ, T2201843, F2264568; 20 Draycott Place, London SW3 2RZ, T020-7589 8989, F7581 7888, Suite 1A Brookhouse, 70 Spring Gardens, Manchester M2 2BQ, T0161-236 1213, F228 7467 (consulates).
USA, 2375 Pennsylvania Av, NW, Washington, DC 20037, T4520100, F7282317 (embassy); 545 Boylston St, Suite 803, Boston, Mass 02116, T5362506, F5368512; 180 North Michigan Av, Suite 1500, Chicago, Illinois 60601, T7824588, F7821635, 150 East 58th St 30th, 31 St, NY 10155, T3554080, F6443751, 1405 Sutter St, SF, California 94109, T9222995, F9319706 (consulates).

Customs and duty free

Non-EU citizens are allowed to import one litre of spirits, two litres of wine, 200 cigarettes or 250 grams of tobacco or 50 cigars. EU citizens are theoretically limited by 'personal use' only (this usually translates as 3,200 cigarettes, 200 cigars, 110 litres of beer, 90 litres of wine, 400 cigarillos, three kilograms of tobacco, 10 litres of spirits, 20 litres of fortified wine).

Vaccinations

No vaccinations are needed to enter Spain. See Health, page 64, for further information.

What to take

Spain is a modern European country, and you can buy almost everything you'll need here. If you don't know if you'll need it, leave it at home and buy it here. However, if you may struggle to explain a medical complaint to a pharmacy it is advisable to make sure that you've got an adequate supply of non-standard medications. Also, consider stocking up on tampons as they're not particularly common outside the large cities.

Make sure you're prepared for all weathers; northwestern Spain has the least predictable weather, but some of the higher regions (even those in the south) can get surprisingly cool in the evenings even in the height of summer.

Take a small torch and a penknife (make sure it's in your luggage if flying). Unless you're going to the beach or staying in hostels, you can leave the towel at home; even the most modest *pensión* will provide one with the room. Take an adaptor for any electrical goods, see Electricity below. If you are planning on hiking, visit a good map shop in your home country before coming to be sure of getting maps in English. A sleeping bag is useful in hostels and a sleeping sheet with a pillow cover will save you the cost of hiring one if you are on a tight budget.

Insurance

EU-residents are entitled to make use of Spanish state healthcare if they are in possession of a E111 form (available from major post offices, health centres and Social Security offices in the UK). But this is a complicated process and you are recommended to get private holiday insurance. Your travel agent will probably be able to advise you on the best deals. **STA Travel** and other reputable student travel organizations often offer good value travel policies. Travellers from North America can try the **International Student Insurance Service** (ISIS) which is available through STA Travel, T1-800-777 0112, www.Sta-travel.com. Some other recommended travel insurance companies in North America include: **Travel Guard** T1-800- 826 1300, www.noelgroup.com; **Access America**, T1-800-284 8300; **Travel Insurance Services**, T1-800-937 1387; **Travel Assistance International**, T1-800-821 2828 and **Council Travel**, T1-888-COUNCIL, www.council travel.com. In the UK, also worth calling for quote is **Columbus Direct**, T020-7375 0011.

Older travellers should note that some companies won't cover people over 65 years old, or may charge higher premiums. Policies for older travellers are offered by **Age Concern**, T01883 346964, though these can be expensive. Check the small print on any insurance policy you take out.

Money

Currency

At the beginning of 2002, Spain switched over to the euro, bidding farewell to the peseta in a fairly organized fashion. The euro (€) is divided into 100 centimos. Euro notes are standard across the whole zone, and come in denominations of 5, 10, 20, 50, 100, and the rarely seen 200 and 500. Coins have one standard face and one national face; all coins are, however, acceptable in all countries. The coins are slightly difficult to tell apart when not accustomed to them. The coppers are 1, 2 and 5 cent pieces, the golds are 10, 20 and 50, and the silver/gold combinations are €1 and €2. You'll still see prices in pesetas occasionally, and some people still use them verbally. The exchange rate was approximately €6 to 1,000 pesetas or 166 pesetas to the euro. So if someone says that hotel room costs '12' and it looks a flashy joint, they probably mean 12,000 pesetas; €72. In February 2003, €1 was worth £0.70, or US$1.24.

Exchange

The best way to get money in Spain is by plastic. **ATMs** are plentiful in Spain, and just about all of them accept all the major international debit and credit cards. Instructions for use are in English. The Spanish bank won't charge for the transaction, but beware of your own bank hitting you for a hefty fee: check with them before leaving home. Even if they do, it's likely to be a better deal than changing cash over a counter. To use a credit card in Spain, you'll need to show some photo ID (eg a passport), so remember to take it with you when leaving the hotel. Credit cards are accepted in most of the bigger and more expensive hotels and restaurants, but rarely in smaller places. They are also rarely accepted at sights and monuments – even the larger ones, so make sure you bring enough cash. Ticket offices in train and bus stations almost always accept credit cards, but bus drivers won't. If your card gets swallowed up or stolen, call the numbers below as soon as possible: **American Express**: T915720303. For travellers' cheques call free T900994426. **Diner's Club**: T901101011. **MasterCard**: T900971231. **Visa**: T900974445.

Banks are usually open from 0830-1400 Monday to Friday and many change foreign money (sometimes only the central branch in a town will do it). Commission rates vary widely; it's usually best to change large amounts, as there's often a minimum commission of €6 or so. Nevertheless, banks nearly always give better rates than change offices (which are fewer by the day). If you're stuck, some large department stores such as El Corté Inglés change money at knavish rates. Travellers' cheques will be accepted in many shops, although they are becoming less and less frequent since the single currency was introduced.

If you need to transfer money in a hurry, you're better off paying the premium charges at an agency like Western Union; a transfer from a British to a Spanish bank can still take upwards of a week.

Taxes

Nearly all goods and services in Spain are subject to a value-added tax (IVA). This is only seven per cent for most things, but is as high as 16-17 per cent on 'luxury' goods such as computer equipment. You're technically entitled to claim it back (on purchases costing more than €90) if you're a non-EU citizen under the Global Refund Scheme, but in practice this isn't worth the effort for small amounts. If you're buying something pricey, make sure you get a stamped receipt clearly showing the IVA component, as well as your name and passport number; you can claim the amount back at major airports on departure. For more information regarding taxes, visit www.global refund.com.

Cost of living

Spain is significantly cheaper than Britain, for example, but things aren't what they used to be. Spain's average monthly salary of €1,200 is low by EU standards, and the minimum monthly salary of some €470 is very low indeed. Buying and renting property is expensive in Spain; there's not a huge demand for rental, as many people live at home until marriage, when they tend to buy a place.

Cost of travelling

Spain is a reasonably cheap place to travel still if you're prepared to forgo a few luxuries. If you're travelling as a pair, eating a set meal at lunchtime, travelling short distances by bus or train daily, and snacking on tapas in the evenings, €40-50 per person per day is reasonable. With €80 per day and staying in a good *pensión* or *hostal* you'll not be counting pennies. With €150 per day you'll be very comfy indeed unless you're staying in four or five star accommodation when that sum won't go that far. However, if you stay in mid-range accommodation, splashing out occasionally this amount will allow you to travel in great comfort.

Accommodation is more expensive in summer than in winter, particularly on the coast. Parts of Northern Spain – the Basque lands and Catalunya in particular – are significantly more expensive year-round than much of the rest of Spain, particularly in eating and drinking. It will come as no surprise to learn that very touristy areas, like the Costas Brava, del Sol and Blanca, and the larger cities, are more expensive than rural areas. The news isn't great for the solo traveller; single rooms tend not to be particularly good value, and they are in short supply. Prices range from 60 to 80 per cent of the double/twin price; some establishments even charge the full rate. Public transport is cheap; note that buses are nearly always cheaper and quicker than trains. Note that car hire, petrol and motorway tolls are on a par with most northern European countries – which can come as a shock to North American travellers.

Getting there

Air

Spain is one of Europe's most popular holiday destinations, and there are hundreds of flights run by dozens of operators. This usually means a good deal for visitors, but you have to be prepared to shop around. Fares depend on the season, and the kind of ticket you buy. Ticket prices are highest from June to September, and around Christmas and Easter, but it's usually possible to find a reasonably-priced ticket at all times of the year thanks to the tight competition. One of the best ways of finding the cheapest offers is to look on the internet: some of the most useful websites are www.expedia.co.uk, www.cheapflights. co.uk, wwwlastminute.come-bookers.com, www.flynow.com, www.dialaflight.co.uk, www.kelcoo.co.uk and www.opodo.com (a useful new website set up by many of the larger European carriers, including **British Airways** and **Iberia**). Most airlines offer a discount when tickets are booked online.

> ✷ For the best deals, travel mid-week and note that many of the special offers require that you spend a Saturday night at the destination.

Cheap flight tickets fall into two categories: official and unofficial. Official tickets are called budget fares, Apex, super-Apex, advance-purchase tickets, or whatever each airline chooses to call them. Unofficial tickets are discounted tickets which are released by airlines through selected travel agents. They are not sold directly by airlines. Discounted tickets are usually as low or lower than the official budget-price tickets. Round-the-World (RTW) tickets for travellers flying from outside Europe can be a real bargain and may work out cheaper than a return fare, but it's probably easiest to pick up a cheap flight to Spain from London than to include it on your itinerary.

Charter flights can be incredibly cheap, and many also depart from local airports. In the UK, which has the biggest selection of charter flight operators, companies such as **Thomson, Airtours** and **Unijet** can offer return flights from as little £60. Check out your local travel agency, the weekend papers and TV Teletext.

When trying to find the best deal, make sure you check the route, the duration of the journey, stopovers allowed, any travel restrictions such as minimum and maximum periods away, and cancellation penalties. Many charter flights, for example, operate on a seven-day schedule which usually departs on a Saturday. Many of the cheapest flights are sold by small agencies, most of whom are honest and reliable, but there may be some risks involved with buying tickets at rock-bottom prices. You should avoid paying too much in advance and you could check with the airline directly to make sure you have a reservation. You may be safer choosing a well-known travel-agent such as **STA**, which has offices worldwide, or **Trailfinders** in the UK, or **Council Travel** in the USA. These and other reputable discount companies and agents are listed above.

Flights from UK and Ireland

There are scheduled and charter flights to most of the major Spanish airports from Heathrow, Gatwick, Luton and Stansted in London, and from Belfast, Bristol, Birmingham, Cardiff, Dublin, Edinburgh, East Midlands, Glasgow, Liverpool, and Manchester. The rise of the budget airlines – like **easyJet, bmi,** and **MyTravelLite** – have meant that the standard airlines have had to whittle their prices down, and there are some amazing deals to be had. Charter flights and tickets from the budget airlines can cost as little as £60 return if you book far enough in advance, but there are usually lots of restrictions. Scheduled airlines offer good deals, and you can get a return to Madrid for less than £100 in the low season, and for about £140 in high season. If you are

buying tickets at the last minute, the budget airlines are likely to cost as much as the
standard airlines. For unrestricted, fully refundable tickets with scheduled airlines,
you will could pay from £200 in the off season, and up to £500 in high season.

Airlines

Aer Lingus, T01-86 8888, www.aerlingus.ie.
From Dublin to Madrid, Alicante and Málaga
and from Cork and Shannon to Madrid.
Air Europa, T0870-240 1501,
www.air-europa.co.uk. Flights to Madrid and
Málaga from Gatwick, with onward
connections to most major Spanish cities.
British Airways, T0845-773 3377,
www.britishairways.com. Flights from
Heathrow and Gatwick to Alicante,
Barcelona, Bilbao, Madrid, Málaga, Palma,
Sevilla and Valencia. Flights from Manchester
to Madrid and Barcelona.
British Midland/bmi, T0870-607 0555,
www.flybmi.com. British Midland and its
budget carrier, bmibaby, offer flights from:
Belfast to Alicante, Madrid and Palma; Cardiff
to Alicante, Málaga and Palma; East Midlands
to Alicante, Murcia and Málaga; Edinburgh
and Glasgow to Alicante, Madrid and Palma;
Manchester to Alicante and Madrid; Teeside
to Madrid.
easyJet, T0870-600 000, www.easyjet.com.
Flights from Bristol to Alicante, Barcelona,
Málaga and Palma; East Midlands to Alicante,
Barcelona, and Málaga; Liverpool to Alicante,
Barcelona, Madrid, Málaga and Palma;
Gatwick to Alicante, Barcelona, Madrid,
Málaga and Palma; Luton to Alicante,
Barcelona, Madrid, Málaga and Palma;
Stansted to Alicante, Bilbao, Barcelona,
Málaga and Palma; Newcastle to Alicante

and Barcelona.
Flybe, www.flybe.com. Flights from
Southampton to Málaga and Murcia.
Iberia, T08705-341 341, www.iberia.com
Flights from major UK and Irish airports, to
most major Spanish cities.
MyTravelLite, T08701-564 564, www.my
travelite.com. Flights from Birmingham to
Alicante, Málaga, Murcia and Palma.
Monarch Airlines, T08700-405040,
www.monarch-airlines.com. Scheduled
flights from Gatwick to Alicante and Málaga;
Luton to Alicante, Gibraltar and Málaga;
Manchester to Alicante, Palma and Málaga.
They also offer charter flights from these
airports to Menorca, Tenerife, Lanzarote,
Almería, and Ibiza.

Travel agents

Council Travel, 28a Poland St,
London W1V3DB, T020-7437 7767,
www.destinations-group.com.
STA Travel, 86 Old Brompton Rd,
London, SW7 3LH, T0870-160 6070,
www.statravel.co.uk. They have other
branches in London, as well as in Brighton,
Cambridge, Leeds, Manchester, Newcastle-
upon-Tyne and Oxford and on many
University campuses. Specialists in low-cost
student and youth flights and tours, also
good for student Ids and insurance.

Flights from Europe and Israel

The major national carriers like **Air France**, www.airfrance.fr; **Lufthansa** www.luft
hansa.com; **KLM**, www.klm.com; **Air Portugal**, www.tap.pt and **Alitalia** www.alitalia.it
all offer flights from major cities to Madrid. Spain's own national airline, **Iberia**,
www.iberia.com, has services to all major European destinations. **Air Europa**,
www.aireuropa.com, has direct flights to Milan, Paris, Rome and Zurich. The budget
airline **Virgin Express**, www.virgin-express.com, is one of the most useful connecting
Madrid very cheaply with Brussels, Copenhagen, Geneva, Rome, Stockholm and
more. **Spanair**, T34 971745020, www.spanair.es, operate services between
Stockholm, Copenhagen, Hamburg, Frankfurt, Munich and Madrid with connections
to other Spanish cities. **easyJet**, www.easyjet.com, has flights from Barcelona to
Amsterdam and Geneva. **Iberia/El Al** fly directly from Tel Aviv to Madrid and Barcelona
in about five hours. **El Al**, www.elal.co.il, 32 Ben-Yehuda Street, Tel Aviv, T03 972
2333; **Iberia**, www.iberia.com, 78 Hayarkon Street, Tel Aviv, T03 516 1789.

There are dozens of regular flights to Spain from North America, but it might be worth checking out cheap deals to London and then getting an inexpensive onward flight from there. Other major European airlines offer competitive fares to Spain via other European capitals. For low season Apex fares, expect to pay around US$400-600 from New York and other East Coast cities and around US$600-800 from the West Coast. Prices soar to up to $1,000 during the summer months. Low season Apex fares with **Iberia** from Toronto and Montreal directly to Barcelona cost around CAN$700-900, rising to CAN$850-1000 during summer.

⬥ Most airlines fly directly from major US and Canadian cities to Madrid, with onward connections to other Spanish airports.

Airlines

Air Canada, toll-free T1-888 247 2262, www.aircanada.ca. Flights from major Canadian airports to Alicante, Barcelona, Bilbao, Las Palmas, Madrid, Málaga and Palma.
American Airlines, toll-free T1-800 433 7300, www.aa.com.
British Airways, toll-free T1-800 247 9297, www.britishairways.com. Flights via the UK.
Delta, toll-free T1-800 241 4141, www.delta.com.
Iberia, toll-free T1-800 772 4642, www.iberia.com. Iberia has direct flights from major US aiports to several Spanish destinations including Madrid, Barcelona, Málaga, Alicante and Palma.
KLM, toll-free T1-800 777 5553. Flights to Spain via the Netherlands.
Lufthansa, toll-free T1-800 645 3880, www.lufthansa.com. Flights via Germany.
Spanair, T +34 971745020, www.spanair.es. Flights from Toronto to Madrid.
TAP, toll-free T1-800 221 7370, T212 969 5775, www.tap-airportugal.us/. Flights to Spain via Portugal.
United Airlines, toll-free T1-800 538 2929.
Virgin Atlantic, toll-free T1-800 862 8621, www.virginatlantic.com. Flights to Spain via the UK or Brussels.

Flight agents

Air Brokers International, 323 Geary St, Suite 411, San Francisco, CA 94102, T1-800-883 3272, www.airbrokers.com. Consolidator and specialist on RTW fares and Circle Pacific tickets.
Council Travel, 205 E 42nd Street, New York, NY 10017, T1-8888-COUNCIL, www.council travel.com. Student/budget agency with branches in many other US cities.
Discount Airfares Worldwide On-line, www.etn.nl/discount.htm. A hub of consolidator and discount agent links.
International Travel Network/Airlines of the Web, www.itn.net/airlines. On-line air travel information and reservations.
STA travel, 5900 Wiltshire Blvd, Suite 2110, Los Angeles, CA 90036, T1-800-777 0112, www.sta-travel.com. Discount student/ youth travel company with branches in New York, San Francisco, Boston, Miami, Chicago, Seattle and Washington DC.
Travel CUTS, 187 College St, Toronto, ON M5T 1P7, T1-800 667 2887, www.travelcuts.com. Specialist in student discount fares, IDs and other travel services. Branches in other Canadian cities.
Travelocity, www.travelocity.com. On-line consolidator.

Flights from Australia and New Zealand

There are no direct flights to Spain from Australia and New Zealand; the cheapest option is usually to fly to London, Paris or Frankfurt and get an inexpensive flight from there. Some Asian airlines offer good deals, flying via their major cities.

Airlines

Air France, T02-9231 1030 (Sydney), www.airfrance.com.
Air New Zealand, T09-3573 3000 (Auckland), T02-9937 5111 (Sydney),
T03-9670 3499 (Melbourne), www.airnz.nz.
British Airways, T02-9258 3200 (Sydney), T09-3568960 (Auckland), www.british-airways.com.
Cathay Pacific, T02-9931 5500 (Sydney), www.cathaypacific.com.

Gulf Air, T02-9244 2199 (Sydney).

Japanese Airlines (JAL), T02-9272 1111 (Sydney), T09-3073687 (Auckland).

Qantas, T09-3578900 (Auckland), www.qantas.com.au.

Singapore Airlines, T02-93500100, T131011 (Sydney), T09-3793209 (Auckland).

South African Airways, T02-9223 4448

(Sydney), www.szz.co.za.

Thai Airways, T02-9251 1922 (Sydney), T09-3773886 (Auckland), www.thaiair.com.

United Airlines, T02-92924111 (Sydney); T131777 (reservations); T09-3793800 (Auckland), www.ual.com.

Virgin Atlantic, T02-9352 6199, www.flyvirgin.com/atlantic.

Flights from South Africa

There are no direct flights from South Africa to Spain, so the cheapest and quickest way is to connect via a European city: Zurich, Amsterdam, Frankfurt or London normally work out best.

Rail

Travelling from the UK to Northern Spain by train is unlikely to save either time or money; the only two advantages lie in the pleasure of the journey itself, and the chance to stop along the way. You can take the **Eurostar** (www.eurostar.com, T0870- 160 6600) to Paris, the main rail gateway from the rest of Europe to Spain, which has overnight high-speed services to Madrid and Barcelona. There are cheaper, slower trains from Paris to the Spanish border at Hendaye in the northwest or Portbou in the northeast which connect to Spanish rail services. For more information, contact www.sncf.fr (also in English), or www.raileurope.co.uk (in the UK) or www.rail europe.com (in North America). Fares vary considerably, but you can get a flexible return from London to Madrid for about £270 if you book early enough. The overnight train to Barcelona costs from €200 (return) and about €250 for a return to Madrid, but you'll need to book these fares in advance.

Rail passes

There are plenty of rail passes available but they are only worthwhile if you intend to travel extensively throughout Europe. Weigh up the options carefully and remember that rail fares are very reasonable in Spain – and local buses are often even cheaper and more convenient. If you intend to cover a lot of ground, then a rail pass might be worth considering. EU-citizens over and under the age of 26 and non-EU citizens who've been resident in Europe for six months are all eligible for InterRail passes. These are available for unlimited travel within one, two, three or four zones throughout Europe and are valid for 12 days, 22 days or one month. Prices range from £119 for 12 days travel in one zone, to £249 for one-month's travel in four zones with discounts for those under 26. *Eurodomino* pass offers three to eight days unlimited travel in first or second class within a one-month period on Spanish railways and costs between £73 (for three days travel in second class) to £207 (for eight days travel in first class). For more information, contact **Rail Europe**, T08705-848 848, www.rail europe.co.uk.

North American EurRail pass (first class only) must be bought before you leave the USA or Canada, and offers unlimited travel for periods of 15, 21, 30, 60 or 90 days and is valid in 17 countries. Some European countries including the UK and those outside the EU are excluded. A 15-day pass costs $572, a 21-day pass is $740, one-month pass costs $918, two-month passes are $1,298, three-month passes are $1,606. There are big discounts – about a third – for travellers under 26 years on these fares. A special Youth Pass gives unlimited travel for 15 or 21 days within a two-month period for $401 and $518 respectively, and is also available for longer periods (one, two and three months). Spain FlexiPass offers three to 10 days travel

within Spain during a two-month period for $155 to 365. For more information contact **Rail Europe** US, T1-800-438 7245, www.raileurope.com.

Road

Car

The main routes into Spain are the E05/E70 motorway that runs down the southwest coast of France, crossing into Spain at Irun, near San Sebastián, and the E7, which crosses the eastern Pyrenees to Barcelona. Both these motorways are fairly heavily tolled but worthwhile compared to the slow, traffic-plagued *rutas nacionales* on these sectors. Several more scenic but much slower routes cross the Pyrenees at various points. Motorways charge expensive tolls in France and Spain and ferry fares can be extremely expensive in high season. Petrol is considerably more expensive than in North America but roughly the same price in France, Spain and the UK. For information on driving through France, checkout www.iti.fr (route planner), www.autoroute.fr (for information on motorways), www.equipment.gov.fr (roads and traffic information).

All vehicles must be roadworthy, registered and insured, at least for third party. The Green Card, an internationally recognized proof of insurance, is no longer compulsory, but it is advisable to carry it all the same as it offers fully comprehensive insurance. EU driving licences are accepted throughout the European Union. For more information, contact the **AA**, www.theaa.co.uk or the **RAC** www.rac.co.uk.

In general, standard European road rules apply. The legal alcohol limit is a mere 0.05 per cent, and foreigners can get fined up to 300 euros on the spot. The speed limit in built-up areas is usually 50 km per hour, on major roads it goes up to 100 km per hour, and 120 km per hour on motorways.

Coach

Eurolines, 52 Grosvenor Gardens, London SW1, T020-7730 8235, www.gobycoach.com, run several buses from major European cities to a variety of destinations in Spain, including Barcelona, Valencia, Madrid, Bilbao, Murcia, Granada, and Seville. Fares to Madrid from London start at around £90 one-way, and £75-150 return. Peak-season fares are slightly higher, but there are good discounts for students, under-26s, senior citizens and children under 12. Journey times to Madrid are between 26 and 36 hours – considerably longer to cities in the south, and, unless you hate flying, air tickets will often work out cheaper.

Sea

P&O runs a ferry service from Portsmouth to Bilbao but in reality it's more of a cruise than a transport connection. It's a two-night trip, and cabin accommodation is mandatory. There are crossings twice-weekly except for a three-week break in January. Peak season runs from mid-July to mid-August when the return fare for an average-length car and four adults is around £1,100, including accommodation in a four-berth cabin. In winter, the price drops to around £700. Foot passengers pay around £350 return in high-season, and about half that in winter; prices include accommodation in a 2-berth cabin. Children between four and 15 years travel for just over half-price and under-4s go free. Look out for special offers. Book online at www.poports mouth.com (although it's frequently off sick) or on T0870-242 4999; Bilbao office at Cosmé Echevarría 1, 48009 Bilbao, T94-423 4477. The ferry port is at Santurtzi, 13 km from the city centre.

A cheaper and faster option is the **Brittany Ferries** service from Plymouth to Santander, 100 km west of Bilbao. These leave the UK twice-weekly, three times during high season, taking a shade under 24 hours. Book online at www.brittany ferries.co.uk or by phone T08705-360360; in Santander there's an office at the Estación Marítima, T942214500. Prices are variable but can usually be had for about £70-90 each way in a reclining seat. A car adds about £140 each way, and cabins start from about £80 a twin. The service doesn't run in winter. Cheaper offers can sometimes be had at www.ferrysavers.com, T0870-442 4223.

Touching down

Airport information → *All taxes are now paid with the relevant plane ticket.*

Spain's biggest international airports include Madrid, Barcelona, Málaga, Alicante and Bilbao. **Madrid**'s airport at Barajas, 15 km northeast of the city, is the major gateway to the country. There are currently three terminals: T1 for international flights, T2 for national and regional flights (Iberia and Air Europa also use this terminal), and T3 for the shuttle to Barcelona. A brand new terminal is due to open at the end of 2003. There are plenty of ATMS, a tourist information booth (Terminal 1), car hire offices, a post office, a free accommodation service (for mid-priced and expensive hotels only), and left luggage lockers (about €2 per day). For general airport information call T913936000; for flight information call T902353570. Shuttle buses (€2.40) depart from outside Terminal 1 for the city centre, and there are taxi ranks outside Terminals 1 and 2; count on paying between €15-20. The metro is the cheapest and most convenient option (entrance in Terminals 2 and 3), and a single ticket costs €95.

Alicante's airport is 12 km from the centre at El Altet. There is just one terminal, but, as it's a massive gateway for summer holiday-makers heading for the resorts of the Costa Blanca, there are plenty of shops, restaurants, a tourist information office, post office, ATMs, car rental offices and left luggage lockers. There are taxis (€12-15 to the centre), and buses to the the main bus centre on C/Portugal from outside the arrivals hall (*llegadas*) every 30 minutes between 0700-2200 (€1.05). There are no hotels at the airport: for accommodation in Alicante, see page 695. For airport information, call T966819000.

Barcelona's international airport is in El Prat de Llobregat, 12 km to the south of the city. Each airline is allocated to one of the two main terminals – A and B – for its arrivals and departures. There are tourist information offices in both Terminals A and B, as well as car hire agencies, ATMs, bureaux de change open 0700-2300, left luggage offices, cafés and small shops. There are trains to Plaça de Catalunya and Sants station every 30 minutes between 0608 and 2238. Single tickets cost €2.50. The A1 Aerobús (€3) departs from terminals A and B, for the Plaça de Catalunya, via Sants and Plaça d'Espanya (Monday-Friday 0530-2315 every 15 minutes; Saturday and Sunday 0600-2320 every 30 minutes). There are taxi ranks outside both terminals; it costs about €20 to get to the centre of town. Use the taxi ranks outside the Terminals rather than the touts who will approach you in the arrival halls. There is one expensive **Best Western** hotel by the airport, the **Alfa Aeropuerto**, Zona Franca, Carrer K s/n, T933362564. For airport information, call T932983828.

The principal airport for Northern Spain is **Bilbao**,10 km northeast of the centre in Sondika. There's one terminal with a couple of shops and cafés (considerably fewer once you have passed passport control), several car hire firms, a tourist information office and banks with ATMs. There are no hotels at Bilbao airport. A taxi to/from town

costs about €15. An efficient bus service (line A3247) departs from outside the terminal for central Bilbao (daily, every 30 minutes between 0630-2200). Tickets cost €0.95. For airport information, call T944869661.

Málaga, the principal airport for the Costa del Sol and Andalucía, is 8 km southeast of the city. There are two terminals, which are in the same building and linked internally, and plenty of services including shops, cafés, banks and ATMs, car hire offices, a tourist information booth, and left luggage lockers. Trains (€1.05 to Málaga, €1.70 to Fuengirola) link the airport with Málaga and resorts along the coast including Torremolinos and Fuengirola (every 30 minutes, 0545-2345) and there's a taxi rank outside the arrivals hall (about €10-12 to the city centre). City bus No 19 departs from outside the arrivals hall of Terminal 1 and outside the departures hall of Terminal 2 every 30 minutes and costs €1. For airport information, call T952048804.

Tourist information → *See individual entries for specific details of tourist offices.*

The tourist information infrastructure in Spain is organized by the regional governments and is generally excellent, with a wide range of information, often in English, German and French as well as Spanish. Most offices can provide maps of the area and towns, and lists of registered accommodation. If you're in a car, it's especially worth picking up the local booklets describing *turismo rural*, with lists of farmstay and rural accommodation. Opening hours are longer in major cities; many rural offices are only open in summer. Average opening hours will be Monday to Saturday 1000-1400, 1600-1900. Offices are often closed on Sunday or Monday, but those on the coast will usually be open at weekends during the summer. In smaller towns and villages, the information office will often be in the Ayuntamiento (town hall).

Local customs and laws

Clothing
Away from the beach and the *discoteca*, Spaniards generally cover up, but no-one in cities is going to be offended by brief clothing; the country is, however, a bit more conservative. Always consider wearing long trousers, taking off hats, and covering shoulders if you're going in to a church or monastery. Spaniards seldom wear shorts except when on holidays. Topless sunbathing is acceptable on most Spanish beaches, and there are many nudist areas along the coast.

Conduct
Spaniards – particularly those in the north – are fairly reserved, especially towards foreigners, in whom they show little curiosity. They are usually polite and courteous, but cultural differences can give first-time visitors the opposite impression. Use of 'please' and 'thank you' is minimal, but it is usual to greet and farewell shopkeepers or bartenders when entering/exiting. There's a very different concept of personal space in Spain than in northern Europe or the USA; in fact the idea doesn't really exist. People speak loudly as a matter of course; it doesn't mean they are shouting.

Most people go home for the long lunch break and may or may not have a *siesta* or snooze. Nearly all shops and sights are shut at this time (apart from large supermarkets), so you might as well tuck in yourself. Every evening, after work, nearly everyone takes to the streets for the *paseo*, a slow stroll up and down town that might include a coffee or pre-dinner drink. It's a great time to observe Spanish society at work; the ritual is an integral part of Spanish culture. Especially in summer, the whole evening is spent outdoors; friends meet by design or chance.

'Spanish time' isn't as elastic as it used to be, but if you're told something will

Touching down

Business hours Offices are usually open Monday-Friday 0800-1500. These hours might be official, but time in Spain is always fluid.

Electricity The current in Spain is 220V 50hz. North American appliances will require an adaptor, and UK plugs will need a 2-pin adaptor, available in most department stores. A few – but this very rare – of the older hotels and *hostals* still have 125V circuits which means your machines won't work, so check beforehand.

Emergencies There is now one Europe-wide emergency number for fire, police and ambulance: T112.

Telephone codes All telephone numbers listed in this book must be dialled in full. The access code to Spain from abroad is +34.

Time Local time is one hour ahead of GMT/UTC, six hours ahead of US Eastern Standard Time and nine hours ahead of Pacific Standard Time. Clocks go forward one hour on the last Sunday in March and back one hour on the last Sunday in October (as in the UK).

Toilets Public toilets are not common, although you'll find them in train stations. It's usually okay to use the ones in bars and cafés. You might have to use the bin next to the loo for your toilet paper if the system can't cope, particularly in out-of-the-way places. There are usually toilets in the big department stores, too.

Water The water is perfectly safe to drink, although it tastes odd in some places (including Barcelona and Madrid). Locals drink bottled water, and you will be given bottles in restaurants if you ask for water.

Weights and measures The Spanish use the metric system. Decimal places are indicated with commas, and thousands with points.

happen '*enseguida*' (straight away) it may take 10 minutes, if you're told '*cinco minutos*' (five minutes), grab a seat and a book. Transport usually leaves dead on time, even a couple of minutes early if the driver's in the mood.

Eating → *For more information about food and drink, see page 48.*

Spaniards eat very little for breakfast, usually just a coffee and maybe a croissant or pastry. In Madrid and central regions, they might tuck into *chocolate y churros* – thick, sticky hot chocolate with thin donut-like batter strips. They may have a quick bite and a drink in a café or bar before lunch, which is usually eaten between 1400-1530 or thereabouts. This is the main meal of the day and the cheapest time to eat, as most restaurants offer a cheap set menu (*menú del día*). Lunch (and dinner) is much extended at weekends, particularly on Sundays, when it seems to go on until the football kicks off in the evening. It's common to have an evening drink or *tapa* in a bar after the *paseo*, if this is extended into a food crawl it's called a *tapeo*. Dinner (*cena*) is normally eaten from about 2200 onwards, although sitting down to dinner at midnight at weekends isn't unusual. In smaller towns and midweek you might not get fed after 2230, so beware. Most restaurants are closed Sunday nights, and usually take a day off, either Monday or Tuesday.

Tipping

Tipping in Spain is far from compulsory, but much practised. Ten percent is considered fairly generous in a restaurant, but not excessive. It's rare for a service charge to be added to a bill. Waiters do not normally expect tips for lunchtime set meals or tapas, but here and in bars and cafés people will often leave small change, especially for table service. Taxi drivers don't expect a tip, but don't expect you to sit

around waiting for twenty cents change either. In rural areas, churches will often have a local keyholder who will open it up for you; if there's no admission charge, a tip or donation is appropriate; say €0.50-1 per head; more if they've given a detailed tour.

Religion

A huge percentage of Spaniards are Catholics, but only a third of them trouble the priest regularly, see Religion page 855. Don't wander around churches if there's a service on, and dress appropriately (see Conduct, above). Sunday is a family day, and few shops are open. Transport services are also much reduced.

Prohibitions and drugs

The laws in Spain are broadly similar to any western European country. One point to be aware of is that you are legally required to carry a passport or ID card at all times (although this is rarely an issue; hotels often hang on to them until you've paid). Smoking *porros* (joints) is widespread, although far more common in Euskadi than anywhere else (locals say the Spanish government ships the hash in to keep the Basques placid). It is technically illegal, but has been legal in the recent past. Police aren't too concerned about personal use, but don't be foolish. You'll soon work out which bars are smoker-friendly – the rolling papers on the bar are a handy sign. Use of cocaine and ecstasy is widespread but means serious trouble if caught. The Madrid city council recently banned drinking on the streets in an effort to stamp out the massive street parties or *botellónes* that were taking place in the main squares every weekend.

Responsible tourism

Responsible tourism is much to do with respect; for local people, the environment, and other travellers. While certain aspects of Spanish society may frustrate on occasion, take them in their cultural context; they're not going to change, and abusing a slow waiter in a stream of English isn't going to get you anywhere. Talking loudly about locals in English (or any other language) is a sure way to be instantly disliked, and won't do the next passing traveller any favours either. Treat people with courtesy and patience; it's very common to sit through a meal thinking the waiter is rude or ignoring you only to find he/she throws in a free coffee and liqueur at the end of dinner because he/she actually likes you.

When in the country, be aware of the environment. Stick to walking trails and carry rubbish with you, even if locals don't. If you're striking off on a seldom-used trail in the mountains, let someone know where you're going and when you expect to be back – it might save your life if the weather closes in or you have an accident, for example. Don't camp where you're not allowed to; the prohibitions are there for a good reason.

Safety

Spain is generally a safe place, with considerably less violent crime than many other European countries. However, street crime – bag-snatching and pickpocketing – in the bigger cities is on the rise, and mugging is more common than it used to be (although the statistics are negligible in comparison with London or Paris for example). Most ports – Barcelona, Bilbao and Málaga among others – have some dodgy areas that should be avoided. Don't invite crime by leaving luggage or cash in cars, and if you are parking in a city or a popular hiking zone, leave the glove box open so that thieves know there is nothing to steal. Ideally, park in a staffed underground car park, especially if you are driving a rental car; these are easily identifiable and a

magnet for thieves. The Basque separatist group ETA has been responsible for a spate of bombings in Madrid and in tourist resorts since they abandoned their ceasefire in 1999. They have pledged to continue their bombing campaign in tourist areas as a means of upsetting the Spanish economy, but in practice, it's extremely unlikely that visitors will get caught up in an attack. Be as vigilant as you would in any major European city. Foreign offices of most countries offer useful information; in the UK, www.fco.gov.uk/travel.

There are several types of police, helpful enough in normal circumstances but not the friendliest if you've done something wrong, or they think you have. Police stations are listed in phone books under *comisarías*.

Getting around

Public transport is generally good in Spain. You can expect several buses a day between adjacent provincial capitals; these services are quick, efficient, and nearly always beat the train over a given route. Once off the main routes, however, it's a different story. Don't expect to get to those picturesque rural monasteries if you're not prepared to hitch, walk, or hire a car. There is a high-speed train service, the AVE, between Madrid and Seville, and new ones planned for Madrid-Barcelona and Madrid-Valencia.

Air

Most provincial capitals have an airport that is serviced from Barcelona and Madrid at least once daily. The drawback is the cost; a full fare return from Madrid to Oviedo, for example, costs around €280. If you are fairly flexible about when you fly, **Iberia**'s last minute specials are a bit of a godsend. Every Thursday these offers are published on their website (www.iberia.es) for the following week. From the home page, go to the *entrando en pista* section (off the *Elige y vuele* menu). Plug in your point of origin and see what specials come up; a return from Madrid to the provinces can be as little as €50, but you'll be restricted as to when you can travel and return.

‡ *Offset your flight's carbon emissions by paying to have the appropriate number of trees planted in sustainable forests through Future Forests, www.futureforests.com.*

Most internal flights in Spain are operated by **Iberia**, **Spanair** and **Air Europa** also run some routes. If you're flying into Spain from overseas, a domestic leg can often be added at comparatively little cost.

If you're flying in from across the Atlantic, there is a *Visit Spain* airpass available, that has to be purchased with your international ticket. It includes three to nine flight vouchers for travel within Spain. In high season they work out at about US$100 per destination, around half that in low season. Contact T1-800-772-4642 in the US or Canada for details. **Spanair** have a Spanair pass, but you have to buy 10 vouchers – not good value at €1229. It can be bought at any *Spanair* office or travel agent and are valid for a year.

Rail

‡ *It's always worth buying a ticket in advance for long-distance travel, as trains are often full.*

The Spanish national rail network, **RENFE**, offers a bewildering variety of services. The website, www.renfe.es (also in English), has online timetables and ticketing. There's now a single phone line, T902240202, for both information and booking tickets (although there are annoying time

constraints on collecting tickets with this method). It's often possible to be passed to an English-speaking operator, but don't count on it.

Prices vary significantly according to the type of service you are using. The fastest service is the high-speed **AVE** train between Madrid and Seville via Córdoba. The journey time to Seville is a mere 2¼ hours. Another high-speed train line is planned for Madrid-Barcelona and is due for completion in 2004. The standard high-speed intercity service is called *Talgo*, while other intercity services are labelled *Arco*, *Intercity*, *Diurno*, and *Estrella* (overnight). There's a fast train service, the *Euromed*, between Murcia and Barcelona on the Mediterranean coast. Slower local trains are called *regionales*, and suburban or short-distance trains are called *cercanías*.

Allow plenty of time to queue for tickets at the station. Ticket windows are labelled *venta anticipada* (in advance) and *venta inmediata* (immediate, ie six hours or less before the journey). A better option can be to use a travel agent; the ones in town that sell tickets will display a **RENFE** sign, but you'll have to purchase them a day in advance. Commission is minimal.

On most **RENFE** trains there is first and second class and smoking/non-smoking compartments. First class costs about 50 per cent more than standard. Other pricing is bewilderingly complex. Night trains are more expensive, even if you don't take a *couchette*, and there's a system of peak/off-peak days which makes little difference in practice. Buying a return ticket is about 20 per cent cheaper than two singles, but you qualify for this discount even if you buy the return leg later (but not on every service). A useful point: if the train is 'full' for your particular destination, buy a ticket halfway (or even one stop) and let the ticket inspector know where you want to get to. You may have to shuffle seats a couple of times, but most are fairly helpful – you can pay the excess fare onboard.

The most useful of Spain's other rail services is run by **FEVE**, www.feve.es. The principal **FEVE** line runs along the north coast (*el Transcantábrico*) from Bilbao west to Santander, Asturias and as far as Ferrol in Galicia. It's a slow narrow-gauge line, but very picturesque. It stops at many small villages, and is very handy for exploring the coast. **FEVE** also operate a short narrow-gauge railway between Cartagena and Los Nietos on the coast in Murcia. Another handy network in Northern Spain is *Eusko Trenbideak*, a short-haul train service in the Basque country. It's an excellent service with good coverage of the inland towns in that region.

Discounts and railpasses

An ISIC student card or under-26 card grants a discount of between 10-20 per cent on most train services. It's worth getting the Spanish version, the *Tarjeta Joven*, which increases the discount to 50 per cent if you're travelling on off-peak 'blue days'. If you're using a European railpass, be aware that you'll still have to make a reservation on Spanish trains and pay the small reservation fee (which covers your insurance). The *tarjeta turística* is a Spanish railpass available to non-residents for period of three, five, 10, 15 or 22 days. Valid on all **RENFE** trains, it's expensive; unless you plan to travel a long distance every day, forget it.

Road

Bus

Buses are the staple of Spanish public transport. Services between major cities are fast, frequent, reliable, and fairly cheap; the four-hour trip from Madrid to León, for example, costs €17. *Supra* buses run on some routes; these are more expensive but luxurious and significantly faster. When buying a ticket, always check how long the journey will take, as the odd bus will be an 'all stations to' job, calling in at villages

that seem surprised to even see it. Tourist offices never know how long a route takes; you must ask the bus company themselves.

While some cities have several departure points for buses, most have a single terminal, the *estación de autobuses*, which is where all short and long haul services leave from. Buy your tickets at the relevant window; if there isn't one, buy it from the driver. Many companies don't allow any baggage at all in the cabin of the bus, but security is pretty good. Most tickets will have a seat number (*asiento*) on them; ask when buying the ticket if you prefer a window (*de ventana*) or aisle (*de pasillo*) seat. If you're travelling at busy times (particularly a *fiesta* or national holiday) always book the bus ticket ahead. If the bus station is out of town, there are usually travel agents in the centre who can do this for you for no extra charge.

Rural bus services are slower, less frequent, and more difficult to co-ordinate. They typically run early in the morning and late in the evening; they're designed for villagers who visit the 'big smoke' once a month or so to shop. If you're trying to catch a bus from a small stop, you'll often need to almost jump out under the wheels to get the driver to pull up. The same goes when trying to get off a bus; even if you've asked the driver to let you know when your stop comes up, keep an eye out as they tend to forget. There are hundreds of different bus companies, but most bus stations have an information window and a general inquiry line to help you out. Unfortunately, English is rarely spoken, even in the larger cities. The tourist information offices usually have timetables for bus services to tourist destinations and are a good first port-of-call before you brave the ranks of ticket windows.

All bus services are reduced on Sundays, and many on Saturdays too; some services don't run at all on weekends. Many local newspapers publish a comprehensive list of departures; expect few during *siesta* hours.

While most large villages will have at least some bus service to their provincial capital, the same doesn't apply for many touristed spots; it's assumed that all tourists have cars. Beware when a helpful tourist office employee directs you "five minutes up the road"; it probably means five minutes at 120 km/h; quite a trudge with a pack on.

Most Spanish cities have their sights closely packed into the centre, so you won't find local buses particularly necessary. There's a fairly comprehensive network in most towns, though; the travel text indicates where they come in handy.

To reach those far flung monasteries, beaches, and mountains without transport, a combination of walking and hitching usually works pretty well. The scarcity of bus services means that's what many locals do, and you'll commonly be offered a lift on country roads even if you don't have your thumb out.

Car

The roads in Spain are good, excellent in many parts. While driving isn't as sedate as in parts of northern Europe, it's generally pretty good, and you'll have few problems. To drive in Spain, you'll need a full driving licence from your home country. This applies to virtually all foreign nationals, but, in practice, if you're from an 'unusual' country, consider an International Driving Licence or official translation of your licence into Spanish. Drivers are required by law to wear seatbelts, and to carry warning triangles, spares (tyres, bulbs, fanbelt) and the tools to fit them. You may also need to fit special prisms to your headlights for driving on the right if you are bringing your car from the UK or Ireland (so that they dip to the right). Front and rear seatbelts are compulsory, and children under 10 years are not permitted to ride in the front seat. Traffic circulates on the right.

There are two types of motorway in Spain, *autovías* and *autopistas*; for drivers, they are little different. They are signposted in blue and may have tolls payable, in which case there'll be a red warning circle on the blue sign when you're entering the motorway. Tolls are generally reasonable, except in Euskadi and Catalunya, where

they are extortionate (and the locals complain bitterly). The quality of motorway is generally excellent. The speed limit on motorways is 120 kmph.

Rutas Nacionales form the backbone of Spain's road network. Centrally administered, they vary wildly in quality. Typically, they are choked with traffic backed up behind trucks, and there are few stretches of dual carriageway. Driving at *siesta* time is a good idea if you're going to be on a busy stretch. Rutas Nacionales are marked with a red N number. The speed limit is 100 kmph outside built-up areas, as it is for secondary roads, which are numbered with a provincial prefix (eg BU-552 in Burgos province), although some are demarcated 'B' and 'C' instead.

In urban areas, the **speed limit** is 50kmph. Many towns and villages have sensors that will turn traffic lights red if you're over the limit on approach. City driving can be confusing, with signposting generally poor and traffic heavy. While not overly concerned about rural speed limits, police enforce the urban limits quite thoroughly; foreign drivers are liable to a large on-the-spot fine. Drivers can also be punished for not carrying two red warning triangles to place on the road in case of breakdown.

Parking is a problem in nearly every town and city in Spain. Red or yellow lines on the side of the street mean no parking. Blue or white lines mean that some restrictions are in place; a sign will indicate what these are (typically it means that the parking is metered). Parking meters can usually only be dosed up for a maximum of two hours, but they take a *siesta* at lunchtime too. Print the ticket off and display it in the car. Underground parking stations are common, but fairly pricey; €10-15 a day is normal.

Liability **insurance** is required for every car driven in Spain and you must carry proof of it. If bringing your own car, check carefully with your insurers that you're covered, and get a certificate (green card). If your insurer doesn't cover you for breakdowns, consider joining the **RACE**, www.race.es, T902120441, Spain's automobile association, that provides breakdown cover.

Car hire in Spain is easy but not especially cheap. The major multinationals have offices at all large towns and airports; cheaper organizations include **ATESA** (government-run), www.atesa.es, which has offices at most of the larger train stations, and **Holiday Autos**, www.holidayautos.com. All major international car hire firms including **Avis**, www.avis.com; **National**, www.nationalcar.com (who often share office with *ATESA*); **Hertz**, www.hertz.com are all represented in most cities. It's also worth checking with your airline when you book your flight if they offer any special deals on car rental. Prices start at around €150 per week for a small car with unlimited mileage. You'll need a credit card and your passport, and most agencies will either not accept under-25s or demand a surcharge.

Cycling

Cycling presents a curious contrast; Spaniards are mad for the competitive sport, but comparatively uninterested in cycling as a means of transport. Thus there are plenty of cycling shops (although beware; it can be time-consuming to find replacement parts for non-standard cycles) but very few bike lanes. By far the best places to cycle are parts of the coast and the mountains, especially the Pyrenees, but trying to enjoy a Castilian highway in 40-degree heat with trucks zipping past your ears is another matter. Contact the **Real Federación de Ciclismo en España** for more links and assistance; their website is www.rfec.com.

Motorcycling

Motorcycling is a good way to enjoy Spain, and there are few difficulties to trouble the biker; bike shops and mechanics are relatively common. Hiring a motorbike, however, can be difficult; most outlets are in the major cities. **Real Federación Motociclista Española** can help with links and advice; their website is www.rfme.com.

Taxis are a convenient and reasonable option; flagfall is €2.10 in most places (it increases slightly at night) and it gets you a good distance. A taxi is available if its green light is lit; hail one on the street or ask for the nearest rank (*parada de taxis*).

Maps

The Michelin series of road maps are by far the most accurate for general navigation, although if you're getting off the beaten track you'll often find a local map handy. Tourist offices provide these, which vary in quality from province to province. The *Everest* series of maps cover provinces and their main towns; they're not bad, although tend to be a bit out of date. You can order topographical maps for hikers and mountaineers directly from **Instituto Geográfico Nacional** (IGN), C/General Ibáñez de Ibero 3, Madrid, T915333121, www.oan.es, or the **Servicio Geográfico Ejército** (SGE), C/Dario Gazapo, Madrid, T917115043, www.ejercito.mde.es/publicaciones/sge/. Good bookshops in Spain include the **Librería Quera**, C/Petritxol 2, Barcelona, T933180743, www.llibreriaquera.com, which also has an online sales service. Pick up maps in advance from **Stanford's** at 12 Long Acre, London, WC2, T020-7836 1321, www.stanfords.co.uk, or in Bristol, 29 Corn Street, T0117-929 9966, or in Manchester at 39 Spring Gardens, T0161-831 0250. In the USA, **The Traveler's Choice Bookstore**, 111 Greene Street, New York, T(212)9411535, has a good selection.

Sleeping

The standard of accommodation in Spain is reasonably high: even the most modest of *pensiones* are usually very clean and respectable. However, a great number of Spanish hotels are well-equipped but characterless places on the ugly edges of town. This guide has expressly minimized these in the listings, preferring to concentrate on more atmospheric options. If booking accommodation using this guide, always be sure to check the location if that's important to you – it's easy to find yourself a 15-minute cab ride from the town you want to be in.

All registered accommodations charge a seven per cent value-added tax; this is often included at cheaper places and may be waived if you pay cash. If you have any problems, a last resort is to ask for the *libro de reclamaciones* (complaints book), an official document that, like stepping on cracks in the pavement, means uncertain but definitely horrible consequences for the hotel if anything is written in it.

Hoteles, hostales and pensiones

Places to stay (*alojamientos*) are divided into three main categories; the distinctions between them are in an arcane series of regulations devised by the government. *Hoteles* (marked H or HR) are graded from one to five stars and usually occupy their own building, which distinguishes them from *hostales* (Hs or HsR), which go from one to three stars. *Pensiones* (P) are the standard budget option, and are usually family-run flats in an apartment block. Although it's worth looking at a room before taking it, the majority are very acceptable. *Fondas* (F) are in short supply these days, but are generally restaurants with cheap rooms available; a continuation of the old travellers' inn. The Spanish traditions of hospitality are alive and well; even the simplest of *pensiones* will generally provide a towel and soap, and check-out time is almost uniformly a very civilized midday.

Spain's famous chain of state-owned hotels, the paradors, are often set in castles, convents and other historic buildings, although there are plenty of modern ones too. Most are very luxurious, with pools, bars, fine restaurants and other fancy trimmings but standards can vary considerably. They are usually expensive, but they offer all kinds of special deals, including a youth package, which can make them surprisingly affordable. Contact one of their representatives in your own country (addresses below) or check out the website: www.parador.es.

Representatives

Ibertours Travel, Level 1, 84 William St, Melbourne, Victoria 3000, Australia, T03-9670 8388, F96708588, ibertours@bigpond.com
Keytel International, 402 Edgeware Rd, London W2 1ED, UK, T020-7616 0300, F7616 0317, paradors@keytel.co.uk.
Marketing Ahead, 433 Fifth Av, New York 10016,USA, T1-212-6869213, F6860271, toll-free T1-800-22311356, mahrep@aol.com.
PTB Hotels, 19710 Ventura Blvd, Suite 210, Woodland Hills, California 91364, USA T1-818-8841984, F8844075, toll-free T1-800-6341188, info@Taradors.com.
PTB Miami, 100 N Biscaye Blvd, Suite 604, Miami, Florida 33132, USA, T1-305-3718057, F3587003, outptbxmania@aol.com.

Rural homes

An excellent option, if you've got transport, are the networks of rural homes, called a variety of things from *agroturismos* to *casas rurales*. Although these are under a different classification system, the standard is often as high as any country hotel. The best of them are traditional farmhouses or old village cottages. Some are available to rent out whole, while others operate more or less as hotels. Rates tend to be excellent compared to hotels. While many are listed in the text, there are huge numbers, especially in the coastal and mountain areas. Each regional government publishes their own listings booklet, which is available at any tourist office in the area.

Albergues and refugios

There are a few youth hostels (*albergues*) around, but the price of *pensiones* rarely makes it worth the trouble except for solo travellers. Spanish youth hostels frequently are populated by schoolkids, and have curfews and check-out times unsuitable for the late hours the locals keep. The exception is in mountain regions, where there are *refugios*; basically simple hostels for walkers and climbers along the lines of a Scottish bothy. Some official youth hostels require an international youth hostel card, available in advance from the international Youth Hostel Associations.

Campsites

Most campsites are set up as well-equipped holiday villages for families; many are open only in summer. While the facilities are good, they get extremely busy in peak season; the social scene is good, but sleep can be tough. In other areas, camping, unless specifically prohibited, is a matter of common sense: most locals will know of (or offer) a place where you can pitch a tent *tranquilamente*.

Eating → *See Food glossary, page 869, for further details.*

Nothing in Spain illustrates its differences from the rest of Europe more than its eating and drinking culture. Whether you're halfway through Sunday lunch at 1800 in the evening, or ordering up a plate of octopus some time after midnight, or snacking on tapas in the street, or watching a businessman down a hefty brandy with his morning

revolves around food and drink.

Eating hours are the first point of difference. Spaniards don't have much more than a coffee and a pastry for breakfast most of the time, a habit described indignantly by HV Morton as "deplorable". People might sidle out from work at some point for a pre-lunch drink and tapa before the main event. Lunchtime varies slightly across Spain but is normally eaten around 1400-1530, often later at weekends. Most folk head home for the meal during the working week and get back to work about 1700; some people have a nap (the famous *siesta*), some don't. People take to the streets from about 1930 for the *paseo*, a stroll around the town often rounded off with a coffee or a drink and a *tapa*. This can turn into a *tapeo*, a crawl around various tapas bars, which are usually busiest from about 2100-2300. If people are going to eat dinner (*cenar*), they'll do it from about 2200, although it's not unusual to sit down to a meal at midnight or later. After eating, *la marcha* ("the march") hits non-food bars (*bares de copas*) and then nightclubs (*discotecas*; a *club* is a brothel...). Many of these places only open at weekends and are usually busiest from about 0300 onwards. Some don't even bother opening until 0400.

Eating and drinking hours vary from region to region. In general, people eat later and party harder in the south. Weeknights are always quieter (except along the coast in summer) but particularly so in rural areas, where many restaurants close their kitchens at 2200. The nature of barfood changes across the country, too. In the Basque country, *pintxos* are the order of the day, in Granada a free small plate of food often accompanies even the smallest drink, while in some other places you'll have to order *raciónes* (full plates of tapas).

Essentials Eating

Food → *See inside front cover for price code information.*

Cuisine

While the regional differences in the cuisine of Spain are important, the basics remain the same. Spanish cooking relies on meat, fish/seafood, beans and potatoes given character by the chef's holy trinity: garlic, peppers, and, of course, olive oil. The influence of the colonization of the Americas is evident, and the Moors left a lasting culinary legacy, particularly in the south. The result is a hearty, filling style of meal ideally washed down with some of the nation's excellent wines.

Browsing the food glossary, see page 869, will give some idea of the variety available, and regional specialities are described in the travelling text, but the following is a brief overview of the most common dishes.

Fish and seafood Even in areas far from the coast, the availability of good fish and seafood can be taken for granted. *Merluza* (hake) and by *bacalao* (salt cod) are the staple fish, while *gambas* (prawns) are another common and excellent choice. Calamari, squid, and cuttlefish are common; if you can cope with the slightly slimy texture, *pulpo* (octopus) is particularly good, especially when simply boiled *a la gallega* (Galician style) and flavoured with paprika and olive oil. Supreme among the finny tribe are *rodaballo* (turbot, best wild or *salvaje*) and *rape* (monkfish). Fresh trout from the mountain streams of Northern Spain are hard to beat too; they are commonly cooked with bacon or ham (*trucha a la navarra*).

Meat Wherever you go, you'll find cured ham (*jamón (serrano)*), which is always excellent, but particularly so if it's the pricey *ibérico*, taken from acorn-eating porkers in Extremadura. Other cold meats to look out for are *cecina*, made from beef, and, of course, sausages (*embutidos*), including the versatile *chorizo*.

Pork is also popular as a cooked meat; its most common form is sliced loin (*lomo*). The Castilian plains specialize in roast sucking pig (*cochinillo* or *lechón*),

A taste for tortilla

Tortilla is perhaps the classic dish of Spain. Served everywhere and eaten at virtually every time of the day, it is easy to prepare and can be eaten either hot or cold. Typically served as tapas or with a salad its key features are the layering of the potatoes and its rounded shape, enabling it to be eaten in slices.

Method (serves 6)

1 large frying pan for potatoes
1 small, fairly deep frying pan
6 fresh eggs
750 g of potatoes thinly sliced
half a medium onion (if desired)
enough good quality olive oil to cover the potatoes in a frying pan
salt
Total cooking and preparation time around 1 hour.

Wash and peel the potatoes then slice thinly so they are about ½ cm in thickness. Place them in a mixing bowl and sprinkle with salt ensuring that that each piece is coated with a little salt. Cut and slice the onion into small pieces about 2 cm long and add to the potatoes.

Place the salted potatoes and onions in a large frying pan and pour in enough olive oil nearly to cover the them. It is essential to use good quality oil – Spanish cooks would never dream of using inferior *aceite* for tortilla. Keep the pan at a low heat and continue to stir the potatoes regularly to ensure they do not burn. The aim is to cook the potatoes while ensuring they do not become crisp. Remove the cooked potatoes and onion from the pan and drain the oil. Total cooking time should be between 15-20 minutes depending on the thickness of the potatoes.

Mix the eggs in a mixing bowl. It is not necessary to add salt as the potatoes should have enough seasoning. Milk and pepper are rarely used in Spanish cooking but will not radically affect the taste if preferred. Prepare a new smaller pan which is deep enough to contain the egg mix and the potatoes. Place the cooked and drained potatoes in first and then add the egg mix. Fry the mixture, keeping the heat very low. When the mixture is showing signs of becoming solid remove the pan from the heat and find a plate large enough to cover the pan.

The next stage is the only tricky bit as the mixture is now to be turned over to cook the other side. Turn the solid mix on to the plate and then return it to the pan ensuring the uncooked side is facing the bottom of the pan. Continue to cook until the tortilla is solid. Total frying time should be around 10 minutes. Remove the tortilla from the pan and eat either hot or leave to cool and eat later.

usually a sizeable dish indeed. *Lechazo* is the lamb equivalent, popular around Aranda de Duero in particular. Beef is common throughout; cheaper cuts predominate, but the better steaks (*solomillo, chuletón*) are usually superbly tender. Spaniards tend to eat them rare (*poco hecho*; ask for *a punto* for medium or *bien hecho* for well-done). The *chuletón* is worth a mention in its own right; a massive T-bone best taken from an ox (*de buey*) and sold by weight, which often approaches a kilogram. It's an imposing slab of meat indeed. *Pollo* (chicken) is common, but usually unremarkable; game birds such as *codorniz* (quail) and *perdiz* (partridge) are also widely eaten. The innards of animals are popular, particularly around Madrid; *callos* (tripe), *mollejas* (sweetbreads), and *morcilla* (black pudding in solid or liquid form) are all excellent, if acquired, tastes. Fans of the unusual will be keen to try *jabalí* (wild boar), *potro* (horse), and *oreja* (ear, usually from a pig or sheep).

Vegetable dishes and accompaniments Main dishes often come without any
accompaniments, or chips at best. The consolation, however, is the *ensalada mixta*, whose simple name (mixed salad) can often conceal a meal in itself. The ingredients vary, but it's typically a plentiful combination of lettuce, tomato, onion, olive oil, boiled eggs, asparagus, olives and tuna. The *tortilla*, see box page 50, is ever-present and often excellent. Another common dish is *revuelto* (scrambled eggs), usually tastily combined with prawns, asparagus, or other goodies.

Most vegetable dishes are based around that American trio, the bean, the pepper, and the potato. There are numerous varieties of beans in Spain; they are normally served as some sort of hearty stew, often with bits of meat or seafood to avoid the accusation of vegetarianism. *Fabada* is the Asturian classic of this variety, while *alubias con chorizo* are a standard across the northern Spain. The Catalan version is *faves a la catalana*, broad beans cooked with ham. A *cocido* is a typical mountain dish from the centre of Spain, a massive stew of chickpeas or beans with meat and vegetables. Peppers (*pimientos*), too, come in a confusing number of forms. As well as being used to flavour dishes, they are often eaten in their own right; *pimientos rellenos* come stuffed with meat or seafood. Potatoes come as chips, *bravas* (with a garlic or spicy tomato sauce) or, more interestingly, *a la riojana*, with chorizo and paprika. Other common vegetable dishes include *menestra* (think of a good minestrone soup with the liquid drained off), which usually has some ham in it, and *ensaladilla rusa*, a tasty blend of potato, peas, peppers, carrots, and mayonnaise. In the north, *setas* (wild mushrooms) are a particular delight, especially in autumn, but they are rarely found in the south. See page 56 for the lowdown on eating out as a vegetarian.

Desserts and cheeses Desserts focus on the sweet and milky. *Flan* (a sort of crème caramel) is ubiquitous; great when *casero* (home-made), but often out of a plastic tub. *Natillas* are a similar but more liquid version, and *arroz con leche* is a cold, sweet rice pudding typical of Northern Spain.

Cheeses tend to be bland or salty and are normally eaten as a *tapa* or entrée. There are some excellent cheeses in Spain, however; the most famous is the dry, pungent Manchego, a cured sheep's milk cheese from La Mancha, but piquant Cabrales and Basque Idiázabal also stand out.

Regional cuisine

Regional styles tend to use the same basic ingredients treated in slightly different ways, backed up by some local specialities. Food-producing regions take their responsibilities seriously, and competition is fierce. Those widely acknowledged to produce the best will often add the name of the region to the foodstuff (some foods, like wines, have denomination of origin status given by a regulatory body). Thus *pimientos de Padron* (Padron peppers), *cogollos de Tudela* (lettuce hearts from Tudela), *alubias de Tolosa* (Tolosa beans), and a host of others.

Most of Spain grudgingly concedes that **Basque** cuisine is the peninsula's best, the San Sebastián twilight shimmers with Michelin stars, and chummy all-male *txokos* gather in private to swap recipes and cook up feasts in members-only kitchens. But what strikes the visitor first are the *pintxos*, a stunning range of bartop snacks that in many cases seem too pretty to put your teeth in, see box page 465. The base of most Basque dishes is seafood, particularly *bacalao* (salt cod; occasionally stunning but often humdrum), and the region has taken full advantage of its French ties.

Navarran and Aragonese cuisine owes much to the mountains, with hearty stews and game dishes featuring alongside fresh trout. **Rioja and Castilla y León** go for filling roast meat and bean dishes more suited to the harsh winters than the baking summers. **Asturias and Cantabria** are seafood-minded on the coast but search for more warming fare in the high ground, and Galicia is seafood heaven,

with more varieties of finny and shelly things than you knew there were; usually prepared with confidence in the natural flavours, whereas the rest of the area overuses garlic to eliminate any fishy taste.

The **Catalans** are almost as famous for their cuisine as the Basques. Seafood from the Mediterranean, rice and vegetables from the plains and meat and game from the mountains are combined in unusual ways; look out for *mandonguilles amb sèpia*, meatballs with cuttlefish, or *gambas con pollastre*, prawns with chicken. The local staple is *pa amb tomàquet*, country bread rubbed with fresh tomatoes, with a little olive oil and salt. **Valencia** is famous as the birthplace of *paella*, a surprisingly difficult dish that is often made badly elsewhere in Spain, much to the annoyance of Valencianos. The genuine article is made with starchy *bomba* rice grown in the Valencian plains, and real saffron (not yellow food colouring, which is common), which is simmered in a shallow pan with garlic and olive oil, and a mixture of meat and/or seafood (depending on the recipe – no one can agree on the ingredients of the definitive paella). The finishing touch is the *soccarat*, a crunchy crust formed by turning up the heat for a few minutes just before the paella is cooked.

Typical **Madrileño** cuisine reflects the city's land-locked status in the middle of a vast plain; hunks of roast meats and hearty stews, like *cocido*, a thick broth of chickpeas, vegetables and hunks of meat, which are cooked together and served in separate courses – often over several days. Spaniards in general, and Madrileños in particular, don't turn their noses up at any part of an animal, and another local speciality is *callos a la madrileño*, a tripe dish cooked in a spicy tomato sauce. It's not unusual to find *orejas* (pigs' ears), *sesos* (brains), *riñeños* (kidneys) and even *criadillas* (bulls' testicles) on the menu. If you head out to Segovia, be sure to try *cochinillo*, roast suckling pig, traditionally slaughtered when they are 21 days old. Ideally, it should be tender enough to cut with a butter knife.

In **Andalucia**, the Moorish inheritance is felt most strongly. The Arabs cultivated olives, saffron and almonds, which all appear in the local cuisine. There's plenty of fresh seafood along the coast, and *pescadito frito*, fried fresh fish best eaten out of a paper cone, is the specialitiy of Cádiz. Inland the emphasis is on meat and game: one of the region's best known dishes is *rabo de toro* – bull's tail slowly cooked in a rich sauce. You might already have tried *gazpacho* – a cold soup of tomatoes, onions and cucumber – but there's a delicious thicker version called *salmorejo*, usually topped with chopped ham and boiled eggs, and a white soup called *ajo blanco* in which the tomatoes have been replaced with almonds.

Extremadura is known for its *migas*, breadcrumbs fried with peppers, but it's most famous culinary export is the *jamón Ibérico*. This is the king of hams – and Spain has countless varieties – and is made from the flesh of the *pata negra* (black foot) pigs which roam the Extremaduran dehesa and are fed on acorns. Watch out, though, if you order it in a tapas bar; it's very, very expensive.

Drink

Wine

In good Catholic fashion, wine is the blood of Spain. It's the standard accompaniment to most meals, but also features prominently in bars, where a glass of cheap *tinto* or *blanco* can cost as little as €0.30, although it's normally more. A bottle of house wine in a restaurant is often no more than €2 or €3. *Tinto* is red (although if you just order *vino* it's assumed that's what you want), *blanco* is white, and rosé is either *clarete* or *rosado*.

A well-regulated system of *denominaciones de origen* (DO), similar to the French *appelation controlée*, has lifted the reputation of Spanish wines high above the party plonk status they once enjoyed. Much of Spain's wine is produced in the north, and

66 99 Wine is not there to be judged, it's a staple like bread, and, like bread, it's occasionally excellent, it's occasionally bad, but mostly it fulfils its purpose perfectly.

recent years have seen regions such as the Ribera del Duero, Rueda, Navarra, Pinedes and Rías Baixas achieve worldwide recognition. But the daddy is, of course, still Rioja.

The overall standard of Riojas has improved markedly since the granting of the higher DOC status in 1991, with some fairly stringent testing in place. Red predominates; these are mostly medium-bodied bottles from the Tempranillo grape (with three other permitted red grapes often used to add depth or character). Whites from Viura and Malvasia are also produced: the majority of these are young, fresh and dry, unlike the powerful oaky Rioja whites sold in the UK. Rosés are also produced. The quality of individual Riojas varies widely according to both producer and the amount of time the wines have been aged in oak barrels and in the bottle. The words *crianza*, *reserva*, and *gran reserva* refer to the length of the aging process (see below), while the vintage date is also given. Rioja producers store their wines at the *bodega* until deemed ready for drinking, so it's common to see wines dating back a decade or more on shelves and wine lists.

A growing number of people feel, however, that Spain's best reds come from further west, in the Ribera del Duero region east of Valladolid. The king's favourite tipple, *Vega Sicilia*, has long been Spain's most prestigious wine, but other producers from the area have also gained stellar reviews. The region has been dubbed 'the Spanish Burgundy'; the description isn't wholly fanciful, as the better wines have the rich nose and dark delicacy vaguely reminiscent of the French region.

Galicia produces some excellent whites too; the coastal Albariño vineyards produce a sought-after dry wine with a very distinctive bouquet. Pity the region's seafood is the best in the country, then. Ribeiro is another good Galician white, and the reds from there are also tasty, having some similarity to those produced in nearby northern Portugal.

Among other regions, Navarra, long known only for rosé, is producing some quality red wines unfettered by the stricter rules governing production in neighbouring Rioja, while Bierzo, in western León province, also produces interesting wines from the red Prieto Picudo grape. Other DO wines in Northern Spain include Somontano, a red and white appellation from Aragón and Toro, whose baking climate makes for full-bodied reds.

An unusual wine worth trying is *txakolí*, with a small production on the Basque coast. The most common form is a young, refreshing, acidic white which has a green tinge and a slight sparkle, often accentuated by pouring from a height. The best examples, from around Getaria, go beautifully with seafood. The wine is made from underripe grapes of the Ondarrubi Zuria variety; there's a less common red species and some rosé.

Catalan wines are also gaining increasing recognition. Best known is *cava*, the home-grown bubbly, and a night out in Barcelona should always start with a glass or two of this crisp, sparkling white wine. The largest wine-producing region in Catalunya is Penedés, which produces a vast range of reds, whites and rosés to suit all tastes and pockets, but you'll find other local specialities including the unusual *Paxarete*, a very sweet traditional chocolatey-brown wine produced around Tarragona.

One of the joys of Spain, though, is the rest of the wine. Order a *menú del día* at a cheap restaurant and you'll be unceremoniously served a cheap bottle of local red

(sometimes without even asking for it). Wine snobbery can leave by the back door at this point: it may be cold, but you'll find it refreshing; it may be acidic, but once the olive-oil laden food arrives, you'll be glad of it. Wine's not a luxury item in Spain, so people add water to it if they feel like it, or lemonade, or *cola* (to make the party drink called *calimocho*).

In many bars, you can order *Ribera*, *Rueda*, or other regions by the glass. If you simply ask for *crianza* or *reserva*, you'll usually get a Rioja. A *tinto* or *blanco* will get you the house wine (although many bartenders in tourist areas assume that visitors don't want it, and will try and serve you a more expensive kind). As a general rule, only bars that serve food serve wine; most *pubs* and *discotecas* won't have it.

Beer Spanish beer is mostly lager, usually reasonably strong, fairly gassy, cold, and good. On the tapas trail, many people order *cortos,* usually about 100 ml. A *caña* is a larger draught beer, usually about 200-300 ml. Order a *cerveza* and you'll get a bottled beer. Many people order their beer *con gas*, topped up with mineral water, sometimes called a *clara*, although this normally means it's topped with lemonade. A *jarra* is a shared jug.

Cider *Sidra* is an institution in Asturias, and to a lesser extent in Euskadi, but you'll find it in Basque and Asturian restaurants in most of the larger cities. The cider is flat, sourish, and yeasty; the appley taste will be a surprise after most commercial versions of the drink. Asturias' *sidrerías* offer some of Spain's most enjoyable barlife, see box page 565, with excellent food, a distinctive odour, sawdust on the floor, and the cider poured from above head height by uniformed waiters to give it some bounce.

Sherry If you thought sherry was for old ladies and vicars, think again. At Seville's famous *Feria*, the standard tipple is a glass of refreshing chilled *manzanilla*, a pale, dry and delicious thirst-quencher. There are dozens of other varieties including the light *fino* which is drunk young, or sweeter *amontillados* with a caramel flavour. The very sweetest are *olorosos*, a traditional dessert accompaniment. The bodegas of Jerez ('sherry' is a corruption of Jerez) offer guided visits with tastings.

> ❖ *Spirits are cheap in Spain; although EU pressure will probably change this sooner or later.*

Spirits Vermut (vermouth) is a popular pre-dinner *aperitif*, usually served straight from the barrel. Many bars make their own vermouth by adding various herbs and fruits and letting it sit in barrels: this can be excellent, particularly if its from a *solera*. This is a system where liquid is drawn from the oldest of a series of barrels, which is then topped up with the next oldest, etc, resulting in some very mellow characterful drink.

After dinner people relax over a whisky or a brandy, or hit the mixed drinks: *gin tonic* is obvious, while a *cuba libre* is a rum and coke (but can refer to vodka or other spirits). Spirits are free-poured and large; don't be surprised at a 100 ml measure. Whisky is popular, and most bars have a good range. Spanish brandy is good, although it's oaky vanilla flavours don't appeal to everyone. There are numerous varieties of rum and flavoured liqueurs. When ordering a spirit, you'll be expected to choose which brand you want; the local varieties (eg *Larios* gin, *DYC* whisky) are marginally cheaper than their imported brethren. *Chupitos* are shots; restaurants will often throw in a free one at the end of a meal, or give you a bottle of *orujo* (grape spirit) to pep up your black coffee.

Non-alcoholic drinks Juice is normally bottled and expensive, although freshly squeezed orange juice is common. It's an odd thing to order after breakfast, though. *Mosto* (grape juice; really pre-fermented wine) is a cheaper and popular soft drink in

bars. There's the usual range of fizzy drinks (*gaseosas*) available, but a popular and peculiarly Spanish soft drink is *Bitter-kas*, a dark red herby brew which tastes a bit like Campari. *Horchata* is a summer drink, a sort of milkshake made from tiger nuts which comes from the Valencia region but is popular throughout Spain. Water (*agua*) comes *con* (with) or *sin* (without) *gas*. The tap water is totally safe to drink, but it's not always the nicest.

Hot drinks Coffee (*café*) is usually excellent and strong. *Solo* is black, mostly served espresso style. Order *americano* if you want a long black, *cortado* if you want a dash of milk, or *con leche* for about half milk. A *carajillo* is a coffee with brandy, while *queimado* is a coffee heated with *orujo*, a Galician drink of ritual significance. *Té* (tea) is served without milk unless you ask; herbal teas (*infusiones*) can be found in many places. *Chocolate* is a reasonably popular drink at breakfast time or as a *merienda* (afternoon tea), served with *churros*, fried doughsticks that seduce about a quarter of visitors and repel the rest.

Eating out → *See page 48 for a fuller account of eating and drinking times.*

One of the great pleasures of travelling in Spain is eating out, but it's no fun sitting alone in a restaurant so try and adapt to the local hours as much as you can; it may feel strange leaving dinner until after 2200, but you'll miss out on a lot of atmosphere if you don't.

The standard distinctions of bar, café and restaurant don't apply in Spain. Many places combine all three functions, and it's not always evident; the dining room (*comedor*) is often tucked away behind the bar or upstairs. *Restaurantes* are restaurants, and will usually have a dedicated dining area with set menus and *à la carte* options. Bars and cafés will often display food on the counter, or have a list of tapas; bars tend to be known for particular dishes they do well. Many bars, cafés and restaurants don't serve food on Sunday nights, and most are closed one other night a week, most commonly Monday.

Cafés will normally have some breakfasty fare out in the mornings; croissants and sweetish pastries are the norm; fresh squeezed orange juice is also common. About 1100 they start putting out savoury fare; maybe a *tortilla*, some *ensaladilla rusa*, or little ham rolls in preparation for pre-lunch snacking.

Lunch is the biggest meal of the day for most people in Spain, and it's also the cheapest time to eat. Just about all restaurants offer a *menú del día*, which is usually a set three course meal that includes wine or soft drink. In unglamorous workers' locals this is often as little as €5 or €6; paying anything more than €9 indicates the restaurant takes itself quite seriously. There's often a choice of several starters and mains. To make the most of the meal, a handy tip is to order another starter in place of a main; most places are quite happy to do it, and the starters are usually more interesting (and sometimes larger) than the mains, which tend to be slabs of mediocre meat. Most places open for lunch at about 1300, and stop serving at 1500 or 1530, although at weekends this can extend; it's not uncommon to see people still lunching at 1800 on a Sunday. The quality of *à la carte* is usually higher than the *menú*, and quantities are large. Simpler restaurants won't offer this option except in the evenings.

Tapas has changed in meaning over the years, and now basically refers to all barfood. This range includes free snacks given with drinks (which is increasingly rare – although you'll still get a free tapa in León and Granada), *pintxos*, the Basque speciality which has taken off in bars all over Spain, see box page 465, and more substantial dishes, usually ordered in *raciónes*. A *ración* in Northern Spain is no mean affair; it can often comfortably fill one person, so if you want to sample a range of things, you're better to ask for a half (*media*) or a *tapa* (smaller portion, when

available). Prices of tapas basically depend on the ingredients; a good portion of *langostinos* (king prawns) will likely set you back €10, while more *morcilla* (black pudding) or *patatas* than you can eat might only be €3 or so.

Most restaurants open for dinner at 2030 or later; any earlier and it's likely a tourist trap. Although some places do offer a cheap set menu, you'll usually have to order *à la carte*. In quiet areas, places stop serving at 2200 on weeknights, but in cities and at weekends people tend to sit down at 2230 or later.

● *Better restaurants, particularly in cities, will be happy to prepare something to guidelines, but otherwise better stick*

A cheap option at any time of day is a *plato combinado*, most commonly done in cafés. They're usually a truckstop-style combination of eggs, steak, bacon and chips or similar and are filling but rarely inspiring.

Vegetarians in Spain won't be spoiled for choice, but at least what there is tends to be good. Dedicated vegetarian restaurants are amazingly few, and most restaurants won't have a vegetarian main course on offer, although the existence of *raciónes* and salads makes this less of a burden than it might be. *Ensalada mixta* nearly always has tuna in it, but it's usually made fresh, so places will happily leave it out. *Ensaladilla rusa* is normally a good option, but ask about the tuna too, just in case. Tortilla is another simple but nearly ubiquitous option. Simple potato or pepper dishes are tasty options (although beware peppers stuffed with meat), and many *revueltos* (scrambled eggs) are just mixed with asparagus. Annoyingly, most vegetable *menestras* are seeded with ham before cooking, and bean dishes usually have at least some meat or animal fat. You'll have to specify *soy vegetariano/a* (I am a vegetarian), but ask what dishes contain, as ham, fish, and even chicken are often considered suitable vegetarian fare. Vegans will have a tougher time. What doesn't have meat nearly always has cheese or egg, and waiters are unlikely to know the ingredients down to the basics.

Entertainment → *See page 64 for spectator sports.*

Bars and clubs → *Check out the website www.clubbingspain.com to get the latest info.*

Spain's nightlife is legendary, and the clubbing scene in Madrid, Barcelona and Valencia is fantastic. The *Sónar* festival, www.sonar.es, in Barcelona is massive and getting bigger every year. You won't find a cutting-edge music engineroom in many smaller towns, where *bacalao* – Spanish techno – is the standard fare. Although there's always a busy bar on every night of the week (the key is to track it down), it's Thursday to Saturday nights when things really get going; most *pubs* and *discotecas* only open at weekends. Even the smallest town will usually have some place that's packed with people dancing to Spanish pop music. Late night bars are known as *bares de copas*, and *la marcha* ('the march') doesn't usually hit them until after midnight, when people have stopped eating. These places will be at their fullest around 0100-0300, but *discotecas* (nightclubs) fill up later, and in some cities are busiest between 0400 and 0600 (the wee hours are known as the *madrugada*). *Discotecas* are often away from the centre of town to avoid council restrictions on closing hours; plenty stay open until 0900 or 1000 in the morning.

Fiestas → *Details of the major fiestas can be found in individual town and city entries and page 57.*

Even the smallest village in Spain has a fiesta, and some have several. Although mostly nominally religious in nature, they usually include the works; a mass and procession or two to be sure, but also live music, bullfights, competitions, fireworks, and copious drinking of *calimocho*, a mix of red wine and cola (not good, but not as bad as it sounds). Adding to the sense of fun are *peñas*, boisterous social clubs who patrol the streets making music, get rowdy at the bullfights, and drink wine all night

that period you're bound to run into one; expect some trouble finding accommodation.

Flamenco

The south of Spain pulses to the hypnotic rhythm of flamenco. Rarely found north of Madrid (except in a few cheesy *tablaos* laid on for tourists), flamenco's heartland and birthplace is Andalucía. Flamenco has been undergoing something of a renaissance in recent years, with flamenco performers like Joaquín Cortés touring internationally to great acclaim, and singers like Estrella Morente and José Merce bringing the art to a wider audience. Flamenco fused with folk music in the late 19th century, producing the popular Sevillanas and Malagueños which are commonly sung and danced at local fiestas. The *gitanos* (gypsies) are traditionally the guardians of the art, and there are few non-gypsy performers. While the flamenco shows or *tablaos* are fun, they rarely convey *duende*, a heart-rending, gut- searing emotion that is the essence of flamenco. To find it, seek out the local flamenco clubs or *peñas* in the inland villages, and ask what's going on: the **Flamenco Centre**, Palacio Penmartín, Plaza de San Juan 1 in Jerez, T956322711, http://caf.cica.es, is a good source of local information.

> **♥** *Often, the most authentic flamenco can be found in impromptu gatherings in the most unlikely settings.*

Cinema

Nearly all foreign films shown at cinemas in Spain are dubbed into Spanish; a general change to subtitling is strongly resisted by the acting profession, many of whom have lucrative ongoing careers as dubbers for a particular Hollywood star. Entrance to cinemas is typically about €5-6; there's often a 'cheap day', usually a Tuesday or Wednesday. When a film is shown subtitled, the term is *version original* (vo).

Museums and galleries

Spain's biggest concentration of western art is held in Madrid, but all the major cities have excellent museums and galleries. Every provincial capital will have a provincial museum. These are normally free and often full of interesting objects; their downfall is lack of context; Roman coins are often placed alongside 20th-century art. While most modern museums have multilingual information, the majority are Spanish-only, although a general leaflet might be available in English and French.

Theatre

There are theatres in almost every medium sized town upwards. They tend to serve multiple functions and host changing programmes of drama, dance, music, and cinema. There's often only one or two performances of a given show. Tickets are very cheap by European standards. The national theatre, dance and opera companies are based in Madrid, but Barcelona is better for contemporary dance and drama.

Festivals and events

Local fiestas are detailed in the travelling text, here however we list the biggest fiestas and national holiday. These can be difficult times to travel; it's important to reserve travel in advance to avoid queues and lack of seats. If the holiday falls midweek, it's usual form to take an extra day off, forming a long weekend known as a *puente* (bridge). On public holidays, many bars and restaurants close down, as do most shops. The transport system runs restricted services.

Essentials Festivals & events

5 January Cabalgata de Los Reyes (Three Kings) Throughout Spain. The Three Kings Parade in floats tossing out sweets to kids, who get Christmas presents the next day.

19 January Fiesta de San Sebastián Drummers parade through the streets at midnight in Donostia/San Sebastián.

February/March Carnaval Held in almost every town and village but the biggest and wildest party is held in Cádiz, and the parades in Sitges are also fantastic.

Mid-March Las Fallas Valencia sees massive street parades and the burning of huge papier-maché creations.

Easter Semana Santa Easter celebrations are held everywhere and parades take place in every town, particularly in the south of Spain. Seville's celebrations are particularly grand.

April Feria The traditional, light-hearted festival of music and dance takes place a fortnight after Semana Santa in Sevilla.

8-15 May Fiestas de San Isidro The second week of May is devoted to Madrid's patron saint, San Isidro, and has developed into a massive event, with live bands, parades and street parties all over Madrid. It also marks the opening of the bullfighting season, with several special bullfighting events.

End May/June Feast of Corpus Christi Held in most towns, it is celebrated with traditional dancing and parades. Toledo's processions are the grandest.

21-24 June Fiesta de San Juan, or the Midsummer's Solstice This is celebrated across Spain, often with bullfights, or with the strange custom of the 'Burial of the Sardine'.

6-14 July Los Sanfermines The famous bull-running festival held in Iruña/Pamplona.

Mid-August Mystery plays Performed in the Baroque cathedral in Elche.

September Barcelona Festes de la Mercé Huge festival with folkloric parades, fireworks, dragons and giants.

20-26 September Logroño Festival For the grape harvest in La Rioja.

31 December National Offering to the Apostle Held in Santiago de Compostela.

Public holidays

1 January Año Nuevo: New Year's Day

6 January Reyes Magos/Epifania: Epiphany; when Christmas presents are given.

Easter Jueves Santo, Viernes Santo, Día de Pascua: Maundy Thursday, Good Friday, Easter Sunday.

1 May Fiesta de Trabajo: (Labour Day).

15 August Asunción: Feast of the Assumption.

12 October Día de la Hispanidad: Spanish National Day (Columbus Day, Feast of the Virgin of the Pillar).

1 November Todos los Santos: All Saints Day.

6 December El Día de la Constitución Española: Constitution Day.

8 December Inmaculada Concepción: Feast of the Immaculate Conception.

25 December Navidad: Christmas Day.

Shopping

Spain's not as cheap as it used to be, but it remains a good place to shop. **Clothing** is an obvious one; Spanish fashion is strong and not overly influenced by the rest of Europe. While the larger Spanish fashion chains have branched out into Britain and beyond, there are many smaller stores with good ranges of gear that you won't be able to get outside the country. The big cities are the best places, but every medium-sized town will have plenty on offer. The average Spaniard is smaller than the British counterpart, so don't be fazed if you have to check a few places to find something in your size.

If you are looking for something hip and sleek for your home, don't miss Barcelona which is Spain's style capital and one of the most design-conscious cities in Europe.

Leather is another good buy; jackets tend to be priced at least 30 per cent less than their UK equivalents, although the range of styles available isn't as great. There are plenty of places

If Spaniards seem to be obsessed by **shoes**, it's because the shoe shops normally display their wares only in the window, not inside, so all the browsing is done outside in the street. Shoes are fairly well priced, and fairly unique in style, although the long-footed will struggle to find anything at all. A popular souvenir of León and Asturias is the *madreña*, a wooden clog worn over normal shoes to protect them from the muddy fields. The Catalans and Valencianos wear *espadrilles*, rope-soled shoes tied with ribbons.

Ceramics are another good choice; cheap, attractive, and practical in the most part. Úbeda in Andalucía, and Talavera de la Reina in Castilla-La Mancha are well-known, but you'll find local styles everywhere.

Local fiestas usually have one or more **handicrafts markets** attached to them; these can be excellent places to shop, as artizans from all around the region bring their wares to town; you'll soon distinguish the real ones from the samey stalls selling imported South American trend items and pseudo-Jamaican knicknacks.

An obvious choice is **food**. Ham keeps well and is much cheaper than anything you can get of equivalent quality elsewhere. Many ham shops will arrange international deliveries; for smaller quantities, El Corté Inglés department stores will vacuum pack slices for you. Chorizo is a more portable alternative. Those addictive *aceitunas con anchoa* (olives stuffed with anchovies) are a cheap and packable choice, as is the wide range of quality canned and marinated seafood. Markets are the best place to buy many of these items; don't hesitate to ask to try hams, cheeses, etc.

Spanish wine is another good purchase. Buy wine that you can't get in your home country, as the price differential isn't so huge as to make it worth lugging back bottles for only 30 per cent less than you could get them at the local bottleshop. *Vinotecas* (wine shops) are common in wine-producing areas, but elsewhere you'll find the biggest selection in department stores such as El Corté Inglés. Spirits are significantly cheaper than in most of Europe; a bottle of gin distilled in London, for example, can cost as little as 30 per cent of the price you could buy it next door to the distillery. A good and practicable souvenir is a *bota*, the goatskin winebags still used at fiestas and bullfights. Try and buy one from a *botería*, the traditional workshops where they are made, rather than at a tourist shop.

Smokers will be in heaven in Spain. Cigars (*puros*) can be as little as a tenth of UK prices, and there's a large range in many *estancos* (tobacconists). Cigarettes, meanwhile, are seriously cheap too; about €2.50 a packet for most international brands.

The annual sales (*rebajas*) are held after the 8 January and in July and August. Prices can be slashed up to 50 per cent. Most of the major department stores and some chain stores have a section devoted to *oportunidades*, where you can pick up some bargains if you are prepared to rummage.

Sport and activities → *Specialist tour operators, page 22.*

Archaeology

There are several important prehistoric monuments scattered across the Iberian Peninsula, but the most dramatic are the cave paintings at Altamira in Cantabria. Bronze Age dolmens are common in Galicia, but the dolmen-chambers at Antequera in Andalucía are the most impressive. Celtic culture is also very evident in the form of *castros*, attractive hilltop settlements composed of tightly packed round houses and a wall, found mainly in Galicia. The spectacular Roman remains at Mérida in Extremadura are the most extensive in Europe, and Tarragona (Catalunya) also has an excellent collection of Roman monuments. Other important settlements that date

back to antiquity include Itálica near Seville, and Empúries, on the Costa Brava. More examples of the famous Roman skilll in engineering include the lofty aqueduct in Segovia, and the Roman bridge in Alcántara (Extremadura). The masterpiece of Iberian sculpture, the Dama de Elche, is found at the National Archaelology Museum in Madrid.

Architecture

Spain's architectural legacy has remained remarkably intact through the centuries, and all the regions offer a wide array of distinctive architectural styles. Northern Spain is studded with Romanesque churches, like those of the Val de Boí or the Camino del Santiago, and the Gothic cathedrals in Burgos, León, Salamanca and Segovia are among the finest in Spain. In Aragón, particularly in Tarazona and Teruel, you'll find a rich concentration of the peculiarly Spanish Mudéjar style, also a feature of Toledo's diverse architecture. Castle fans are spoiled for choice; after all, Castilla is named for them. Many of the best are along the Duero Valley, but Loarre castle near Huesca, and the Templar castle of Monzón stand out among many. Extremadura is best known for the Roman remains at Mérida, but returning conquistadores built elaborate Renaissance *palacios* and churches in Trujillo and Cáceres. Madrid and the surrounding area are best known for the austere Herreran style popularized by the construction of the massive palace at El Escorial, and there is a handful of sumptuous Bourbon palaces built at the height of the giddy Baroque era. To the east, Valencia boasts a beautiful Baroque core, and Murcia has managed to hang on to its own clutch of fanciful Baroque monuments. The kingdoms of Al-Andalus bequeathed the sublime architecture of the Mezquita in Córdoba, the Alcázar in Seville, and the Alhambra in Granada.

Birdwatching → *Check out www.spainbirds.com for details of trips for birders in Spain.*

Spain is an excellent destination for birdwatchers, and where you go is largely determined by what birds you wish to observe. The Pyrenees and the Picos de Europa shelter large numbers of birds of prey, including the lammergeier (*quebrantahuesos*) and golden eagle (*aguila dorada*); other sought-after sights are the capercaillie (*urogallo*) and the wallcreeper. Spain is also an important staging-post on the migration routes between Africa and Northern Europe/Arctic, particularly the Delta de l'Ebre in Catalunya and the famous Coto Doñana national park in Andalucía. The marshlands of the Delta de L'Ebre in Catalunya are home to more than 300 species of bird, including flamingoes, herons, marsh harriers and a wide variety of ducks. The Coto Doñana national park near Huelva in Andalucía is one of Europe's best wetland reserves, and almost 400 species of bird have been recorded here. Numerous local outfits offer birdwatching tours, but one of the best guides is John Butler at **Doñana Bird Tours**, www.donanabirdtours.com.

Cycling

Many organizations run cycling trips around Spain; see page 23. It's most popular in the north. Apart from the dusty Castilian plains, the region makes for very good cycling, and it's a popular weekend activity in Navarra and Euskadi. Contact the **Real Federación de Ciclismo en España** for more links and assistance; their website is www.rfec.com.

Fishing

Spain has superb opportunities for fishing from trout and salmon fishing in mountain streams and rivers to sea fishing off the coast. It's all regulated, and you'll need a permit (*permiso de pesca*), usually obtainable from the local *ayuntamiento* or the **Delegación Agencia Medio Ambiente (AMA)**, which has offices in provincial capitals, and is valid for two weeks. A maritime recreational fishing licence (1st and 3rd Class) is required for fishing from the shore or from a boat near the coast; get it from the

in provincial capitals. Further information is available from tourist offices; the local fishing shop is, as always, the best spot to ask about what's biting where. **Federación Española de Pesca**, C Navas de Tolosa 3, Madrid, T915 328353, is another good starting point for information.

Gastronomy

Euskadi and Galicia are generally considered to produce the finest Spanish cuisine, and also boast some of the country's best wine regions. Catalunya also has an excellent reputation for dining, and some equally good regional wines. The most famous temples to the culinary art are Arzak's in San Sebastián and El Bullí in Roses: you'll have to book months in advance. Madrid, as befits a capital city, has the greatest range of national and international cuisines, and the ritual of the *cocido* is a must. Tracking down some authentic paella among all the touristy counterfeits might take some time, but you'll have your best chance in El Saler on the outskirts of Valencia.

Any wine-oriented visit should take in the Rioja, while the Ribera del Duero is also a good option, although less tourist-oriented. Most of the big *cava*- and wine- producing *bodegas* of Catalunya offer guided tours, but for the smaller ones visits need to be organized by telephone. Tourist information offices can usually help out if you don't speak Spanish. One of the biggest attractions of Jerez is a visit and tasting at one of the centuries-old *bodegas*. These are well set up for visitors but you may still need to book. Further details are in the text, while page 20 details specialist tour operators.

Golf

Golf is an increasingly popular leisure activity in Spain, with many of the courses located close to coastal tourist resorts: a third of all the golf courses in Spain are found along the Costa del Sol in Andalucía. Some hotels and specialist tour-operators are geared exclusively towards golfers. Green fees vary considerably, depending on the course, but the tourist information offices usually have details. Club hire is available at all but the most basic courses. For more information, contact the Spanish tourist office, or the **Royal Spanish Golf Federation**, C/Capitán Haya 9-5, 28020 Madrid, T915552682.

Skiing

The best Spanish and Andorran ski resorts are in the eastern Pyrenees where the most challenging pistes and best-equipped resorts can be found in Aragon (page 396), Catalunya (page 346) and Andorra (page 369). You can also ski close to Madrid in the Sierra de Guadarrama and the Sierra de Gredos, where there are three small, low-key resorts which are good for families or a day trip. The Sierra Nevada near Granada boasts Europe's most southerly ski resort where the locals like to say that they can ski in the morning and sunbathe on the coast in the afternoon. Facilities are pretty good and improving every year. For more information, contact **ATUDEM**, the Spanish ski-tourism arm, T913 591557, www.ski-spain.com. For snow conditions, call T913502020.

Walking and climbing → *Tourist offices will supply details of local routes and refugios.*

The most famous walk in Spain is probably the Camino del Santiago. Other excellent hiking routes include the trans-Pyrenean GR11 trail which crosses the Pyrenees from coast-to-coast, and there is plenty more hiking in the Picos de Europa, and the sierras of Andalucía and central Spain. There are numerous organizations offering walking-based trips in the area, see page 18. The first thing for the walker to be aware of is Spain's excellent network of marked walking trails. These are divided into *pequeño recorrido* (PR), short trails marked with yellow and white signs, and *gran recorrido* (GR), longer-distance walks marked in red and white. These take in places often completely inaccessible by car; the GR trails are planned so that nights can be spent at *refugios* (walkers' hostels) or in villages with accommodation. Detailed maps and descriptions

⁝ Man and beast

"It is extremely disgusting, and one should not write about disgusting things" Henry James
"Generally repels the northerner in the theory but often makes his blood race in the act" Jan Morris
"I would not have been displeased to have seen the spectators tossed" Admiral Nelson

Apologies to Mr James. The bullfight, or *corrida*, is an emblem of Spanish culture, a reminder of Roman times when gladiators fought wild beasts in amphitheatres. It is emphatically not a sport (the result is a given) but a ritual; a display of courage by both animal and human (there are and have been several female *toreros*, although it remains a male-dominated field). While to outside observers it can seem uncomfortably like the bull is being humiliated, that is not the way Spaniards perceive it at all. The Spanish are understandably contemptuous of the foreign anti-bullfighting lobby, whom many see as meddling hypocrites. There is significant opposition to the activity within the country, mainly in large cities, but *los toros* are destined to be with us for some time yet.

The best way to judge bullfights (and your own reactions) is to go to one. As well as being a quintessentially Spanish spectacle (count the cigars and the fans), it is all too easy to be an uninformed critic if you've never been. You may also find that you love it, although anyone with any feeling for animals is likely to find parts of it uncomfortable, even if they don't hate it outright.

The myth that bullfighting is blood-thirsty needs to be dispelled. Nobody in the crowd likes to see a *torero* hurt, a less-than-clean kill, or overuse of the *picador*. What keeps many people going is that all-too-rare sublime fight, where the matador is breathtakingly daring, and the bull strong and never-say-die.

The fighting bull is virtually a wild animal, originally bred from wild cattle, and reared in vast ranches where contact with humans is minimal. It's an aggressive beast and a majestic sight when it first charges out of the pens. They are fought when they are about four years old, and weigh about 500 kg. The age, weight, and name of the bull is displayed around the ring just before it is fought.

In a standard bullfight there are six bulls and three *matadores*, who fight two each. The fights take 15 minutes each, so a standard *corrida* lasts about two hours, usually starting in the late afternoon. The fight is divided into three parts, or *tercios*. In the first part, the bull emerges, usually a breathtaking spectacle of wild power, and is then played with by means of

of these routes can be found in good bookshops or outdoor equipment shops. For map recommendations, see page 47.

Climbers, too, will have a good time of it, with the Pyrenees, the Picos and the Sierra Nevada; depending on the time of year, there are many peaks with varying challenges; some are mentioned in the text but for more details contact the Federación Española de Deportes de Montaña y Escalada, www.fedme.es, T914451382.

Watersports

Spain's Mediterranean coastline is crammed with yacht-filled marinas, and most have sailing schools if you want to learn. Every watersport imaginable is on offer at

the cape by the *matador*, who judges its abilities and tendencies. The bull is then induced to charge a mounted *picador*, who meets it with a sharp lance which is dug into the bull's neck muscles. Although the horses are thankfully padded these days, it's the most difficult part of the fight to come to terms with, and *picadores* (under instruction from the *matador*) frequently overdo it with the lance, tiring and dispiriting the animal.

The second *tercio* involves the placing of three pairs of darts, or *banderillas*, in the bull's neck muscles, to further tire it so that the head is carried low enough to allow the *matador* to reach the point where the sword should go in. The placing of the *banderillas* is usually rapid and skilful, done on foot, occasionally by the *matador* himself.

The last part is the *tercio del muerte*, or the third of death. The *matador* faces the bull with a small cape, called a *muleta*, and a sword. After passing it a few times he'll get it in position for the kill. After profiling (turning side on and pointing the sword at the bull), he aims for a point that should kill the bull almost instantly. It unfortunately rarely happens; there are often a few attempts, and then a *descabello*, or *coup de grace*, in which the spinal cord is severed below the base of the skull using a special sword. If the poor beast is still going, someone takes a knife to it.

If the crowd have been impressed by the bullfighter's performance, they stand and wave their handkerchiefs at the president of the ring, who, based on the response, may then award one or two ears and, for exceptional performances, the tail as well. These are then chopped off the animal and paraded around the ring by the fighter, who will be thrown hats and wineskins as gestures of appreciation. These are immediately returned by his assistants. Meanwhile, the dead bull has been dragged out in a flurry of dust by mules; if it has fought the good fight, it will be applauded out of the ring.

An interesting variant is the *corrida de rejones*, where the bulls are fought from horseback; a highly skilled and often beautiful affair. Pantomime plays a part too; many fiestas are round off with a comedy bullfight.

Bullfighting is not the only bovine entertainment on offer. Less bloody affairs include *encierros*, where the bulls run through narrow streets (the most famous are the 'Running of the Bulls' at Pamplona), and *capeas*; fairly informal events where locals may practise passing bulls, or attempt to put rings on their horns. These usually occur at regional fiestas and sometimes involve not toros but *vacas*: the female of the fighting bull breed is lighter built but horned just as imposingly and no less aggressive.

most of the resorts along the Costa Brava, the Costa del Sol and the Costa Blanca. Divers favour the Iles Medes in Catalunya (although it's best to go out of season – the waters are crammed in summer), the remote paradise of the Cap de Creus, and the crystal-clear waters off the coast of Almería. Tarifa, right at the most southerly tip of Spain, is a mecca for surfers and kiteboarders, and there are good surf beaches along the northern coast too. The biggest scene is at Zarautz and Mundaka in Euskadi, while the beaches of Asturias and Galicia are more peaceful. The text details operators within the regions.

The sports daily, *Marca*, is a publication dedicated mostly to football, and is the most widely read paper in Spain. *As*, a similar publication, is well into the top ten. The conclusion to be drawn is that Spaniards are big on sport. Other popular spectator sports include road cycling, handball and basketball.

Football Spain's biggest teams are arch-rivals Real Madrid and FC Barça, but every city has its own team. Going to a game is an excellent experience; crowds are enthusiastic but well-behaved, and it's more of a family affair than in the UK. Games are usually on a Sunday evening (although there are a couple of Saturday fixtures and tickets are relatively easy to come by, with the exception of Real Madrid and FC Barça, particularly if they are playing against each other). The *taquillas* (ticket booths) are usually open at the ground for two days before the match, and for the couple of hours before kickoff. Watching the game in a bar is a Sunday ritual for many people.

Pelota There are some regional sports, of which the best known is probably the Basque game *pelota*, sometimes known as *jai alai*, which is played on a three-sided court. In the most common version, two teams of two hit the ball with their hands against the walls seeking, like squash, to prevent the other team from returning it. The ball is far from soft; after a long career players' hands resemble winning entries in a root-vegetable show. Variations of the game are *pelota a pala*, using bats, and *cesta punta*, using a wickerwork glove that can propel the ball at frightening speeds. If you want to watch it, check www.euskalpilota.com which lists matches in slightly shambolic fashion. Most courts have matches on Saturday and Sunday evenings.

Health → *See individual town and city directories for details of medical services.*

Health for travellers in Spain is rarely a problem. Medical facilities are good, and the most the majority of travellers experience is an upset stomach, usually just a result of the different diet rather than any bug. However, EU citizens should make sure they have a certified copy of the E-111 form (available from post offices in the UK) in order to prove reciprocal rights to free medical care. Non-EU citizens should consider travel insurance to cover emergency and routine medical needs; be sure that it covers any sports/activities you may get involved in. The water is safe to drink, but isn't always pleasant, so many travellers (and locals) stick to bottled water. The sun in Spain can be harsh, so take precautions to avoid heat exhaustion/ sunburn. Many medications that require a prescription in other countries are available over the counter at pharmacies in Spain. Pharmacists are highly trained but don't always speak English. In medium-sized towns and cities, at least one pharmacy is open 24 hours; this is performed on a rota system (posted in the window of all pharmacies and listed in local newspapers).

Keeping in touch

Communications

Internet → *See individual city and town directories for details of internet cafés.*
Cybercafés are very common throughout Spain. The major cities will have several, but you'll have a problem getting online in smaller towns and villages. Increasingly, hostels are offering coin-operated Internet points, and you can often find them in the

larger airports, train stations and tourist information offices. *Locutorios*, the cheap phone centres, also often have computer terminals for Internet access.

Where there is Internet access, it's normally pretty good; even the coin-operated terminals seem to have a decent connection. Access normally costs from €1.50-3 per hour, and many cybercafés are open into the early hours, although you'll have to cope with the automatic weaponfire from online games, which are very popular.

Most modern hotels above a certain standard have walljacks where you can connect a laptop. The power sockets use the standard two-pin European plug and are prone to surges; a good AC adaptor will help with this as well as voltage differences. If you need a phoneline, a fairly cheap ISP is **Spansurf** (www.spansurf.com), who use a metered system. **Telefónica** offer reasonable unlimited cable-modem access at a monthly rate.

Post

The Spanish post is still inefficient and slow by European standards. Don't post anything valuable or important unless you have to, and even then send it via the Postal Exprés system which is available at all post offices and guarantees next-day delivery to provincial capitals and 48-hour delivery elsewhere in Spain. Post offices (*correos*) generally open Monday-Friday 0800-1300, 1700-2000; Saturday 0800-1300, although main offices in large towns will stay open all day. Stamps can be bought here or at tobacconists (look for the TABAC or *estanco* sign), who will carefully wrap them in paper. A letter within the EU costs €0.50, to the USA €0.60, to Australia/NZ €0.75. The larger post offices also offer fax and poste restante services. Postboxes, marked *Correos y Telégrafos*, are yellow.

Telephone

There's a public telephone in most bars, but hearing the conversation over the ambient noise can be a hard task, and rates are slightly higher than on the street. Phone booths on the street are mostly operated by *Telefónica*, and all have international direct dialling. They accept coins from €0.05 upwards as well as phone cards, which can be bought from *estancos* (newspaper kiosks). As well as the standard *Telefónica* phone cards, you can buy international phone cards that use a scratch-off pin number system and work out considerably cheaper. A better option for international calls is to find a *locutorio*, or call centre. These are typically found in or around train stations or in the poorer end of town where people don't have mobiles or landlines. All calls are generally cheaper after 2000 and at weekends. Directory enquiries can be reached on 1003, a local operator on 1009; while 112 is the universal emergency number. For international reverse-charge calls, dial 900 99 00 followed by 44 for the UK, 15 for the USA and Canada, 61 for Australia, or 64 for New Zealand; you'll be patched straight through to an operator in the relevant country. Dialling 1008 will get you an international operator. If you want to set up a landline, **Telefónica**'s service line is 1004 (www.telefonicaonline.com), but their call charges are extortionate. Domestic landlines have nine-digit numbers beginning with 9. Although the first three digits indicate the province, you have to dial the full number from wherever you are calling, including abroad. Spain's international code is 34. All numbers given within this book must be dialled in full. Mobiles (*móviles*) are big in Spain, and coverage is very good. Most foreign mobiles will work in Spain (although most North American ones won't); check with your service provider about what the call costs will be like.

Newspapers and magazines

The Spanish press is generally of a high journalistic standard. The national dailies *El Pais* (still a qualitative leap ahead), *El Mundo*, and the rightist *ABC* are read throughout the country, but regional papers often eclipse these in readership. Overall circulation is low, partly because many people read the newspapers provided in cafés and bars. The sports dailies *Marca* and *As*, dedicated mostly to football, have an extremely large readership that rivals any of the broadsheets. There's no tabloid press as such; the closest equivalent is the *prensa de corazón*, the gossip magazines such as *¡Hola!*, forerunner of Britain's *Hello!*

English-language newspapers are widely available in kiosks in the larger towns, particularly the *Financial Times*, the *International Herald and Tribune* (which has an English-language supplement from *El País*), and the *Daily Telegraph* European editions.

Radio

Radio is big in Spain, with audience figures relatively higher than most of Europe. There's a huge range of stations, mainly on FM wavelengths, many of them broadcasting to a fairly small regional area. You'll be unlikely to get much exposure to it unless you're in a car or take your own set, however. BBC World Service broadcasts on different frequencies throughout the day. In the evenings you can find it on 12095kHz short wave.

Television

TV is the dominant medium in Spain, with audience figures well above most of the EU, and second only to Britain's. The main television channels are the state-run *TVE1*, with standard programming, and *TVE2*, with a more cultural/sporting bent alongside the private *Antena 3*, *Tele 5* and *Canal Plus*.

Regional stations also draw audiences. Overall quality is low, with lowest-common-denominator kitsch as popular here as anywhere. Cable TV is widespread, and satellite and digital are beginning to spread.

⁑ Footprint features

Introduction

Madrid is not a city of half-measures: Europe's highest, greenest, youngest, sunniest capital likes to boast Desde Madrid al Cielo ('from Madrid to Heaven') with its matter-of-fact assumption that when you've seen Madrid, the only place left is Heaven. Perversely, the city is almost as famous for what it lacks as for what it boasts – there's no great river, no architectural marvels, no immediate picture-postcard charm. But what it does have, it has in spades: a fabulous collection of western art held in the great triumvirate of the **Prado**, the **Thyssen** and the **Reina Sofía**, and an intense nightlife that makes most other cities look staid and past it.

The streets where Cervantes and Lope de Vega bickered and which later provided Goya with a backdrop for his paintings of local fiestas are still the heart of the city and remain delightfully walkable. A deliberately aimless stroll will throw up an outrageously lavish doorway, a Moorish flourish on a former belltower, or a boho-chic café set in an old pharmacy advertising laxatives in 19th-century tiles. The Spanish gift for combining tradition and modernity with such effortless aplomb reaches new heights in Madrid, a city in which miracles can still happen in one part of the city while a glossy new nightclub is being toasted in another.

And within just an hour or so drive of the capital, you can take your pick of lavish Bourbon palaces, monolithic monasteries, remote mountain villages and ancient cities. The mountains of the **Sierra de Guadarrama** are visible even from Madrid, and tucked away in their depths is Felipe II's massive palace-monastery of **El Escorial** and Franco's bombastic memorial to the fallen of the **Civil War**. The mountains also provide the backdrop for one of the most alluring cities in the area, **Segovia**, built of golden stone and crowned with a fairytale castle.

★ Don't miss...

1. **Triángulo de Arte** See some of Europe's finest art collections in Madrid's three legendary museums, page 82.

2. **El Rastro** Rummage through the bargains at this flea market, page 91.

3. **Shopping** Shop till you drop in trendy Chueca or swanky Salamanca and drool over your purchases in a hip cocktail bar, pages 92 and 96.

4. **Parque del Oeste** Picnic in the delightful rose gardens here, then head downhill to find the beautiful Goya Pantheon, page 96.

5. **Casa de Campo** On a boiling hot day, sway out in the cable car and take a stroll among the trees, page 96.

6. **El Escorial** Visit the Royal Pantheon and adjoining Rotting Room, page 119.

7. **Toledo** Follow the trail of El Greco in his adopted city, page 133.

8. **Sierra de Gredos** Explore the remote reaches of the spectacular natural park, page 129.

9. **Alcalá de Henares** Count the storks' nests in this charming Renaissance town, page 131.

10. **Cotos** Take the narrow gauge railway here for a day's skiing in the Sierra de Guadarrama, page 119.

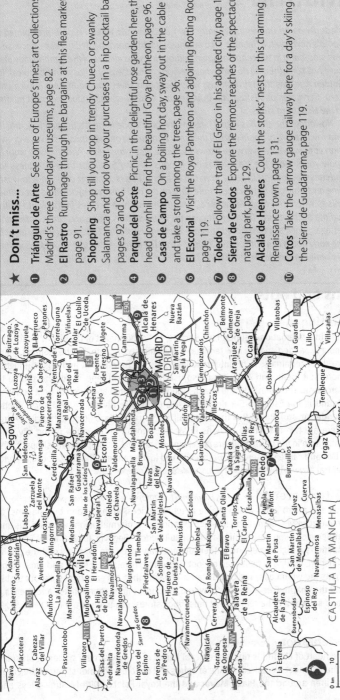

Madrid → *Colour map 5, grid A1; Population: around 5 mn.*

Madrid was an uneventful country town back in 1561 when Felipe II proclaimed it Spain's new capital. Set high on a baking plain, the city appealed to Felipe because it was slap-bang in the centre of Spain (although the excellence of the hunting may also have has something to do with what everyone agreed was an idiosyncratic choice). Its Golden Age was the 17th century, when gold and silver poured in from Mexico and Peru, Cervantes published Don Quixote, *and Velázquez was appointed court painter to the Habsburg kings.*

Nowadays the city has a split personality: on the one hand it's the political, artistic and royal centre of Spain with all the fancy trimmings; on the other, it's an overgrown market town where everyone knows everyone else's business. And they will want to know yours too – the Madrileños are famous all over Spain for their directness (or rudeness, according to some from out of town). This is simply a desire not to waste time on small talk, but to concentrate hard on the real business of having a good time. This is where the Madrileños excel, and there can be few cities in the world which radiate such vitality. There are thousands of tapas bars, flamenco clubs, cafés, and terrazas, but it's in the packed streets – especially just after El Rastro flea market, or in the early hours of a hot summer's night – that the uniquely Madrileño gift for enjoying life really shines out. ▸▸ For Sleeping, Eating and other listings, see pages 100-118.

Ins and outs

Getting there

Madrid's international airport is in Barajas, 15 km northeast of the city. It's currently being expanded and the new terminal (T4) is almost complete. For the moment, there are three terminals: T1 for international flights, T2 for national and regional flights (note that Iberia and Air Europa also use this terminal), and T3 for the shuttle to Barcelona. The main bus and coach station for national and international buses in Madrid is the Estación Sur de Autobuses, C/Méndez Alvaro, T91468 4200 (metro Méndez Alvaro). Bus 148 or the metro will link you with Plaza Colón in the city centre. There are two main train stations in Madrid: Atocha in the south of the city, and Chamartín in the north. Both are large, modern and well-equipped, with shops, cafés, ATMs and car-rental services. Both are linked to the centre of the city (Atocha is pretty central anyway) by metro. ▸▸ *For further details, see Transport page 115.*

Getting around → *The city information line (T010) will also give out transport information.*

Bus and metro plans are available at tourist offices, at metro and bus stations, or online at www.ctm-madrid.es (which also provides information on suburban bus and rail services if you are planning a day trip to Toledo or Segovia, for example). Driving in Madrid is a nightmare, and entirely unnecessary given the excellence of the public transport. Madrid is best seen on foot. The centre is relatively small and most of the sights are within easy walking distance of each other. It's easy to get lost but that is half the charm. Free maps are provided by tourist information offices, and there's a good selection of better maps at most book stores, see page 113. ▸▸ *For further details, see Transport and Activities and tours page 115.*

Orientation

The heart of Madrid is tiny, a medieval kernel of narrow streets spidering off small squares under a crooked skyline of spires and cupolas. The oldest part of the city is the area around the **Plaza Mayor** and the Royal Palace, with twisting alleys and

traditional shops and bars. To the east is the old literary barrio of **Santa Ana**, now best known for its nightlife and tapas bars, and east again is the elegant **Paseo del Prado**, where the Prado forms one point of the world-famous **Triangulo del Arte**. South of the Plaza Mayor are the shabby, bohemian neighbourhoods of **La Latina** and **Lavapiés**, and to the north is the wide, flashy **Gran Vía**, which cuts from east to west across the northern strip of the city. Madrid's trendiest neighbourhoods – **Chueca** and **Malasaña** – sit to the north of the Gran Vía. East of Chueca is the elegant 19th-century grid of **Salamanca**, Madrid's answer to London's Knightsbridge or New York's Upper West Side, and the **Paseo de la Castellana** runs north of here, lined with glassy skyscrapers and banks. Most of the sights are within strolling distance of each other, and those that aren't are easily accessibly by the cheap, efficient and easy-to-use metros and buses.

Tourist information

Madrid's tourist information offices can provide you with a basic plan of the city, and a copy of *En Madrid What's On*, a pocket-sized magazine with helpful local information and listings. Pick up the free English-language monthly newspaper *InMadrid*, with plenty of bar and club listings. There is a tourist information line, T902100007, and a city information line, T010, both of which usually have English-speaking operators. There are two official websites: www.comadrid.es, run by the regional authority, and www.munimadrid.es, run by the city.

The main tourist office is at ① *C/del Duque de Medinaceli, 2, T914293705, Mon-Fri 0900-1900, Sat 0900-1300*. Branches include: Barajas Airport ① *Terminal 1, T913058556, Mon-Fri 0800-2000, Sat 0900-1300*; Chamartín Train Station ① *Gate 16, T913159976, Mon-Fri 0800-2000, Sat 0900-1300*; Mercado Puerta de Toledo ① *Ronda de Toledo 1, T913641876, Mon-Fri 0900-1900, Sat 0930-1330*; City of Madrid office ① *Plaza Mayor 3, T913665477, Mon-Fri 1000-1400, Sat 1000-1500*.

Old Madrid

The oldest part of the Madrid lies between the Puerta del Sol on the east and the enormous Palacio Real (Royal Place) on the west surrounded with manicured gardens and graceful squares. In the middle is the Plaza Mayor, easily the grandest square in all Madrid, completely enclosed, and surrounded with elegant arcades. The Madrileños have all but abandoned it to tourists, but it's still a handsome spot for a coffee out on the terrace. The area around it is known as Habsburg Madrid, or Madrid of the Austrias, and the winding streets and passages are sprinkled with old palaces and monasteries, tiny churches and traditional shops selling handmade guitars, religious goods, or fine wines. Its proximity to the royal palace has meant that this neighbourhood has always been pretty fancy – at least until the posh families moved out to the grand new avenues of Salamanca a century or so ago – and the restaurants and smart tapas bars are a cut above the workaday places in other parts of the city.
>> *For Sleeping, Eating and other listings, see pages 100-118.*

Puerta del Sol

The 'Gate of the Sun' was once one of the entrance gates to the city back when it was still surrounded by walls. Now this elliptical square is disappointingly bland, and, although there is a constant flow of people, they are always on their way somewhere else. It wasn't always this way: the Puerta del Sol used to be the most piquant neighbourhood in Madrid, where you could pick up an assassin or a whore or just catch up with the latest gossip from the court. Even a

❗ This is the crossroads of Madrid, the meeting point of 10 major roads and shopping streets.

Madrid

Detail map
A Madrid centre, page 76.

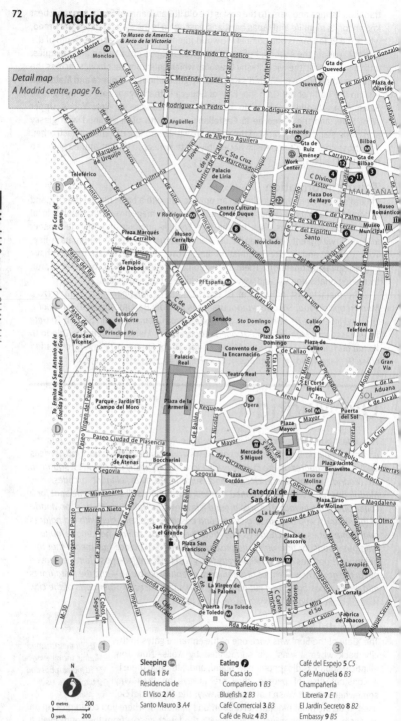

N

0 metres   200
0 yards   200

Sleeping 🛏️
Orfila **1** *B4*
Residencia de
  El Viso **2** *A6*
Santo Mauro **3** *A4*

Eating 🍴
Bar Casa do
  Compañeiro **1** *B3*
Bluefish **2** *B3*
Café Comercial **3** *B3*
Café de Ruiz **4** *B3*

Café del Espejo **5** *C5*
Café Manuela **6** *B3*
Champañería
  Libreria **7** *E1*
El Jardín Secreto **8** *B2*
Embassy **9** *B5*

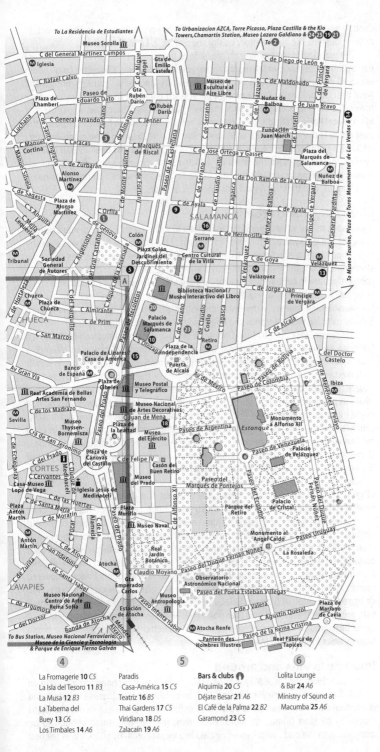

To La Residencia de Estudiantes

To Urbanizacion AZCA, Torre Picasso, Plaza Castilla & the Kio Towers, Chamartín Station, Museo Lazaro Galdiano & **24 25 19 21**

To **2**

Museo Sorolla

C del General Martínez Campos

Iglesia

Gta de Emilio Castelar

C de Diego de León

C de Maldonado

C de Miguel Ángel

C Rafael Calvo

Museo de Escultura al Aire Libre

Nuñez de Balboa

C de Velázquez

C de Juan Bravo

Paseo de Eduardo Dato

Gta Rubén Darío

Fundación Juan March

C del Príncipe de Vergara

Plaza de Chamberí

Rubén Darío

Plaza del Marqués de Salamanca

C General Arrando

C Jenner

C de Serrano

C de Padilla

C de Castelló

C de Almago

Luchana

C de Santa Engracia

C Caracas

C del Doctor

C Manuel Cortina

C de Zurbarán

C Marqués de Riscal

C de José Ortega y Gasset

Nuñez de Balboa

Paseo de la Castellana

Alonso Martínez

C de Don Ramón de la Cruz

C de Sagasta

C Orfila

C de Ayala

C de Ayala

Plaza de Alonso Martínez

C de Génova

C de Claudio Coello

C de Lagasca

C del Príncipe de Vergara

C de Nuñez de Balboa

C de General Pardiñas

Tribunal

Sociedad General de Autores

Colón

SALAMANCA

C de Hermosilla

Serrano

Plaza Colón / Jardines del Descubrimiento

Centro Cultural de la Villa

C de Goya

Velázquez

Chueca

Plaza de Chueca

C de Almirante

Biblioteca Nacional / Museo Interactivo del Libro

C de Jorge Juan

Príncipe de Vergara

C San Marcos

Palacio Marqués de Salamanca

C de Alcalá

CHUECA

Palacio de Linares / Casa de América

Plaza de la Independencia

Retiro

C del Doctor Castelo

Banco de España

Puerta de Alcalá

Paseo de Bolivia

Ibiza

Av Gran Vía

Plaza de Cibeles

Museo Postal y Telegráfico

Paseo de México

Paseo de Menéndez Y Pelayo

Real Academia de Bellas Artes San Fernando

Museo Nacional de Artes Decorativas

Sevilla

Museo Thyssen-Bornemisza

C Juan de Mena

Paseo de Argentina

Estanque

Monumento a Alfonso XII

Plaza de la lealtad

Museo del Ejército

Paseo de Venezuela

Palacio de Velázquez

CORTES

Plaza de Cánovas del Castillo

Casón del Buen Retiro

Cervantes

C de Felipe IV

Casa-Museo Lope de Vega

Iglesia Jesús de Medinaceli

Museo del Prado

Paseo del Marqués de Pontejos

Plaza Antón Martín

C de las Huertas

Plaza Murillo

Parque del Retiro

Palacio de Cristal

Antón Martín

Museo Naval

Monumento al Ángel Caído

La Rosaleda

LAVAPIES

Real Jardín Botánico

C Claudio Moyano

Museo Nacional Centro de Arte Reina Sofía

Gta Emperador Carlos

Museo Antropología

Observatorio Astronómico Nacional

Plaza de Mariano de Cavia

Estación de Atocha

Paseo del Poeta Esteban Villegas

Ronda de Atocha

Atocha Renfe

Paseo de la Reina Cristina

To Bus Station, Museo Nacional Ferroviario, Museo de la Ciencia y Tecnología & Parque de Enrique Tierno Galván

Panteón des Hombres Illustres

Real Fábrica de Tapices

To Museo Taurino, Plaza Monumental de Las Ventas & **14**

4   5   6

La Fromagerie 10 *C5*	Paradis	Bars & clubs 🎵	Lolita Lounge
La Isla del Tesoro 11 *B3*	Casa-América 15 *C5*	Alquimia 20 *C5*	& Bar 24 *A6*
La Musa 12 *B3*	Teatriz 16 *B5*	Déjate Besar 21 *A6*	Ministry of Sound at
La Taberna del	Thai Gardens 17 *C5*	El Café de la Palma 22 *B2*	Macumba 25 *A6*
Buey 13 *C6*	Viridiana 18 *D5*	Garamond 23 *C5*	
Los Timbales 14 *A6*	Zalacaín 19 *A6*		

century ago, the square's animation was legendary but now there is little to detain anyone besides the 19th-century pastry shop at No 2, **La Mallorquina**.

The grand, pinkish building on one side of the square (now government offices) has a plaque outside it which marks the very centre of Spain – **'Kilometre Zero'** – from which all distances are measured. This is also where Madrileños gather to bring in the New Year, traditionally eating one grape at each chime of the bell from the clock tower. The other famous landmark is the neon **Tío Pepe** sign, blazoned across the roof of the **Hotel Paris**, Madrid's very first luxury hotel, now down on its luck. Opposite the post office is the bronze state of Madrid's symbol, the **'bear and the madroño tree'**, which is a popular meeting place. No one quite knows how this unlikely pair came to symbolize the city, and the legends which now surround it are disappointingly prosaic – it seems most likely that the madroño tree shares the first part of its name with Madrid, and that the region was once full of bears.

Plaza Mayor and around

If you want to see what a madroño tree looks like, the council have planted several along the **Calle Mayor**, which runs off to the east of the Puerta del Sol and was once the most important street in Madrid. There's nothing much to see nowadays besides chain stores and banks, but it leads to the city's grandest square, the Plaza Mayor. This vast cobbled square is surrounded by lofty arcades and tall mansions topped with steep slate roofs. Bright and sunny, it's packed with terrace cafés, souvenir shops, and sun-worshipping tourists – the only time you might catch a Madrileño here is on a Sunday morning when a stamp and coin market is held under the arcades.

The square was built by Juan Gomez de Mora to designs conceived by Felipe II's favourite architect, Juan de Herrera. This was the ceremonial centre of Madrid, a magnificent backdrop for coronations, executions, markets, bullfights and fiestas. It is riddled with the subterranean torture chambers of the Inquisition, who used the square for *autos-da-fé* – the trial of suspected heretics. In just one day in 1680, they tried 118 prisoners here, and burned 21 of them alive. Before the square was built, a market was traditionally held in front of the **Casa de la Panadería**, the old bakery, which is now the most eye-catching building on the square. It was repainted in 1992 by Carlos Franco who covered it with a hippy-trippy fresco of floating nymphs. Opposite it stands the former butcher's market, now full of government offices and the tiny municipal tourist information office (see page 71).

Arched passages lead off the Plaza Mayor to some of the most important streets of 17th-century Madrid – Calle Toledo, Calle Mayor, and Calle Segovia – as well as several which still echo the trades which were once carried out here, like Calle Cuchilleros (the Street of the Knife-Sharpeners), which incorporates part of the old city walls. This is where you'll find the traditional *mesones*, or inns, which grew up to cater to merchants and travellers arriving at the city gates. **Casa Botín** (see page 103) opened in the 16th century and claims to be the oldest restaurant in the world. Calle Cuchilleros heads up to meet the Plaza San Miguel, with Madrid's prettiest covered market at the centre. **Mercado de San Miguel**, an airy glass and wrought-iron pavilion designed by a pupil of Gustave Eiffel, is a listed building, but it's still open for fresh fish, meat, vegetables and fruit (see page 114). There are several excellent upmarket tapas bars around the market (see page 103) – a better bet than most of the brash touristy ones in the Plaza Mayor.

Plaza de la Villa and around

Continuing down the Calle Mayor once again, there's another handsome square on the left. The small, austere Plaza de la Villa is one of the oldest squares in Madrid, and is overlooked by the **Casa de la Villa** (City Hall), which was begun in 1640 to plans drawn up by Juan Gómez de Moro. Until then, the city was small enough to be managed with the odd council meeting held in a local church. By 1640, it was felt that

something a little more imposing was in order for what was, after all, the capital of an empire. The interior can be visited as part of the guided tours run by the city council (see page 71), but there's nothing especially interesting to see besides the plush Salón de Sesiones where city matters are deliberated in a whirl of velvet and gilt.

Opposite the Casa de la Villa is the **Torre de los Lujanes**, the oldest secular building in Madrid, although it's been restored almost beyond recognition. At the corner of tiny Calle del Codo, you can just make out a Moorish archway incorporated into the walls. (If you duck down this little alley, you can pick up some cakes at the **Convento de las Carboneras**, see page 114). The handsome 16th-century palace which stands beyond the Casa de la Villa and closes off the square was home to Cardenal Cisneros, founder of the famous university in Alcalá de Henares (see page 131). Now Madrid's Mayor, José Maria Alvarez del Manzano, lives here.

Calle Arenal to the Plaza de Oriente

Another of the main roads splintering westwards from the Puerta del Sol, Calle Arenal was one of the main processional routes of Habsburg Madrid, lined with convents, palaces and churches. Now it's mainly a shopping street, with a smattering of bars, cafés and clubs. Tucked back half-way along it on the left, the **Iglesia de San Ginés** is a gloomy 17th-century church which reeks of incense, and is run by the shadowy ultra-reactionary Opus Dei. There's a version of El Greco's *Expulsion from the Temple* in a small side chapel, but it's only open during services.

Almost opposite the church, the Calle San Martín leads to the **Monasterio de las Descalzas Reales** ① *Plaza de las Descalzas Reales 3, T914548800, Metro Sol or Opera, Tue-Thu, Sat 1030-1245, 1600-1745, Fri 1030-1245, Sun and holidays 1100-1330, €4.80/3.80 concessions and free to EU-passport holders on Wed (combined ticket with the Convento de la Encarnación, see below page 80, visits by guided tour only – officially in Spanish, although guides are often multilingual).* The Royal Monastery of Poor Clares was founded by Juana of Austria, daughter of Carlos I (Charles V), who was born here in its former incarnation as a royal palace. Widowed at the age of 19, she established this convent for aristocratic nuns and widows. Thanks to its royal connections, it became one of the richest religious institutions in the kingdom, crammed with paintings, tapestries and ornaments – although most were later sold when the convent fell on hard times. There is still a community of 23 nuns here, who care for the pretty kitchen gardens and orchard which can be glimpsed from the windows. The opulent main staircase survived the transition from palace to convent, and is thickly covered in trompe l'oeil frescoes, including a delightful one of Felipe IV and his family gathered on a balcony.

> ❖ The nuns have managed to turn this monastery into an award-winning museum. It is well worth a look.

The highlight of the convent is the remarkable collection of tapestries, particularly a 17th-century series called the *Triumph of the Eucharist* which was designed by Rubens and woven in Brussels. This is where you'll find the only mirror in the whole convent, used to show off the sketch on the back of one of the tapestries. Downstairs is a recreation of a cell, complete with the spiked sandals and knotted rope which the nuns used to mortify their flesh, and some painting galleries; most are copies or minor works, but the nuns have managed to hang on to a Titian, a portrait of San Francisco by Zurbarán, and a small Virgin by Luis Morales.

Plaza de Oriente and the Palacio Real

The Calle Arenal continues westwards and widens into the **Plaza Isabel II**, a transport hub for buses and metros, which is overlooked by the imposing back entrance to the Teatro Real (see below). Pedestrian alleys on either side of the Teatro lead to the delightful Plaza de Oriente, a half-moon shaped square, with manicured gardens,

Madrid centre

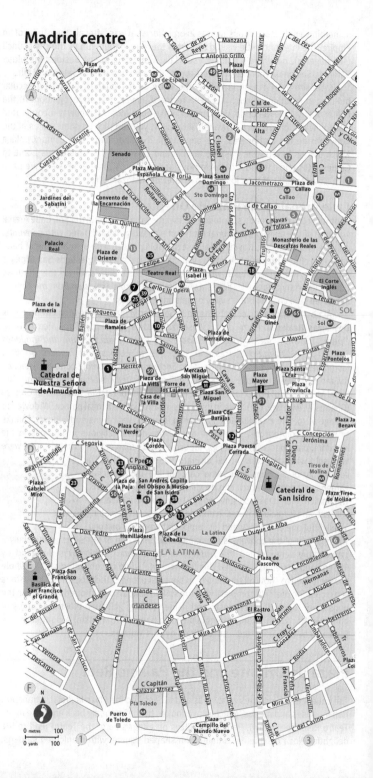

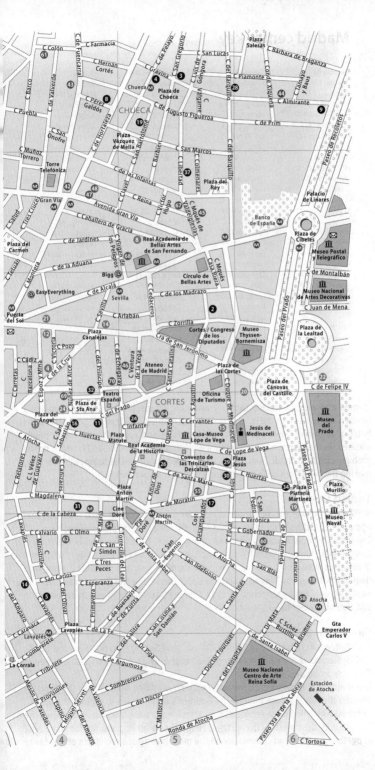

Madrid centre key

Sleeping 😴
Atlántico 1 *B3*
Emperador 2 *A2*
HH Campomanes 3 *B2*
Hostal Adriano 4 *C4*
Hostal Conchita 5 *B3*
Hostal El Barco 6 *E3*
Hostal Fonda
  Horizonte 7 *D4*
Hostal Hispano
  Argentino 8 *B5*
Hostal Las
  Fuentes 9 *C2*
Hostal Pinariega 10 *C2*
Hostal Plaza d'Ort 11 *D4*
Hostal Valencia 12 *C4*
Hostal Valencia 13 *B1*
Hostel Astoria 14 *C4*
Hostel Cervantes 15 *D5*
Hostel Jaen 16 *D5*
Hostel Lauria 17 *B3*
HsR La Coruña 18 *E6*
Mora 19 *D6*
Palace 20 *C6*
París 21 *C4*
Ritz 22 *C6*
Tryp Ambassador 23 *B2*
Tryp Reina
  Victoria 24 *D4*
Villa Real 25 *C5*

Eating 🍴
Al Norte 1 *C1*
Bar Manolo 2 *C5*
Bodegas de Ángel
  Sierra 3 *A5*
Café Acuarela 4 *A5*
Café Barbieri 5 *E4*
Café de los
  Austrias 6 *C1*
Café de Oriente 7 *C1*
Café Figueroa 8 *A4*
Café Gijón 9 *A6*
Café La Union 10 *C2*
Casa Alberto 11 *D4*
Casa Botín 12 *D2*
Casa Lucio 13 *E2*
Casa Montes 14 *E4*
Cervecería La
  Moderna 16 *D4*
Champanería
  Gala 17 *D5*
Cornucopia 18 *B2*
El Armario 19 *A5*
El Estragón 20 *D1*
El Pez Gordo 21 *A3*
Entrecajas 23 *D1*
Gula Gula 24 *D5*
Inshalá 25 *C1*
La Biotika 26 *D5*
La Carpanta 27 *D2*

La Castafiore 28 *A6*
La Dolores 29 *D5*
La Fábrica 30 *D5*
La Falsa Molestia 31 *D4*
La Luiza 32 *C4*
La Musa Latina 33 *D1*
La Platería 34 *D6*
La Taberna del
  Alaberdero 35 *B2*
Palacio de
  Anglona 36 *D2*
Sarrasín 37 *B5*
Taberna
  Almendro 38 *D2*
Taberna del
  Cruzado 39 *C2*
Taberna
  Tempranillo 40 *D2*

Bars & clubs 🍸
Baridad 41 *D2*
Café Antik 42 *B4*
Café del
  Mercado 43 *A4*
Café Oliver 44 *A6*
Camp 45 *B5*
Cardamomo 46 *C5*
Chicote 47 *B4*
Cock 48 *B4*
Coppelia 49 *A2*

Delic 50 *D1*
El 21 51 *D3*
El Bonano 52 *E2*
El Cañí 53 *C2*
El Mojito 54 *E4*
El Parnasón 55 *D5*
Flamingo/Shangay
  Tea Dance 56 *B3*
Joy Eslava 57 *C3*
Kapital 58 *E6*
Kathmandu 59 *C2*
La Divina
  Comedia 60 *E6*
La Ida 61 *A4*
La Ventura 62 *E4*
Larios Café 63 *B3*
Oui 64 *D5*
Palacio Gaviria 65 *C3*
Star's Café 67 *B5*
Suite Café-Club 68 *B5*
Villa Rosa 69 *D4*
Viva Madrid 70 *C4*
Week End/Ohm/
  Bash 71 *B3*

statues and elegant terrace cafés. It was built by Joseph Bonaparte, Napoleon's brother, who was given the nickname *El Rey de Plazuelas* (King of the Squares) for his habit of knocking down jumbles of old buildings and replacing them with public squares. In the centre is a 17th-century equestrian statue of Felipe IV, which posed problems for its sculptor, Petro Tacca, until Galileo suggested he balance the horse by making the back from solid bronze and keeping the front hollow.

Teatro Real

ⓘ *Plaza de Oriente s/n, T915160660, open for guided visits Tue-Fri at 1300, Sat, Sun and public holidays 1130-1330, closed Aug, €3. For box office info, see page 112.*

The Royal Theatre, Madrid's beautiful opera house, flanks one side of the square. Completed in time for Isabel II's 20th birthday celebrations in 1850, this is where the Madrileños were introduced to the works of Verdi, Wagner and Stravinsky, along with daring new ballets by Diaghilev and the Ballet Russe. But the theatre was closed in 1925 and only finally reopened in 1997 after a massive facelift which included the addition of state-of-the-art technology.

Palacio Real

ⓘ *C/Bailén s/n, T915420059, Metro Opera, Mon-Sat 0930-1700, Sun and public holidays 0900-1400, €6/6.90 with guided tour in English, €3 concessions, free to EU-passport holders on Wed.*

The Teatro Real is dwarfed by the other enormous edifice which flanks the Plaza de Oriente: the Royal Palace built by the Bourbons in the 1730s to replace the *alcázar* (fortress) which had done service as a royal residence since Moorish times. When the fortress was destroyed by fire in 1734, Felipe V saw an opportunity for something altogether grander, and commissioned the most prestigious architects of the day to

create this monumental pile. Built on a staggering scale – thankfully, earlier plans for a palace four times the size of the current one were rejected – it's undoubtedly imposing, but it's no surprise that Juan Carlos I and his family have chosen to live in the more modest surroundings of the Palacio de Zarzuela on the outskirts of Madrid.

The visit begins with Francisco Sabatini's icy staircase of pale marble which leads up to the main floor and the Salón de los Alabarderos (Hall of the Halbardiers), where there's a magnificent ceiling fresco by the Venetian painter, Tiepolo, who came to Madrid at the age of 62. The most sumptuous room in the palace is the Throne Room, finished in 1772, and densely upholstered in deep red velvet and gold, with Tiepolo's last masterpiece, *The Majesty of the Spanish Monarchy*, spreading dramatically across the vast ceiling. Many of the chambers are lined with tapestries made in the Real Fabrica de Tapices but most of the paintings are copies – the originals, including Goya's portraits of Charles IV and his wife María Luisa, are exhibited at the Prado. One of the most eye-popping rooms is the Porcelain Room, encrusted with 134 oriental porcelain panels and silk hangings. Other highlights include the exceptional collection of musical instruments in the Stradivarius room – some dating back to the 17th century, many with exquisite decorative detail – and the collection of royal porcelain and crystal from the royal factories in the Buen Retiro and elsewhere.

> ❗ *The Royal Palace is still used for official functions and can be closed at short notice – if two flags are flying instead of just one, the King is at home and you won't be allowed in.*

Plaza de la Armería
Off the enormous Plaza de la Armería are two small royal museums (admission included in entrance ticket); the most entertaining is the **Royal Armoury**, where El Cid's legendary sword is given pride of place. There is a huge selection of armour – including armour for horses and even an elegant outfit for Carlos I's (Charles V) hunting dog. Across the square, the **Royal Pharmacy** has a recreated 19th-century pharmacy complete with porcelain jars and fittings.

Palace gardens
The palace gardens are a good place to recover from the excess of gilt and marble: the largest is the **Parque-Jardín El Campo del Moro** ⓘ *Paseo Virgen del Puerto s/n, El Campo de Moro, Mon-Sat 1000-1800, Sun and public holidays 0900-1800, free,* which spreads downhill to the Manzanares River, but you'll have to walk all the way around to the entrance on the Paseo Virgen del Puerto to get in. They offer spectacular views up to the palace. Equally lovely and more easily accessible are the **Jardins del Sabatini** to the north of the palace, which are very small but beautifully laid out with fountains and shady paths.

Catedral de Nuestra Señora de la Almudena
ⓘ *C/Bailén, T915422200, Metro Opera, Mon-Sat 1000-1330, 1800-2000, Sun 100-1400, 1800-2045, free. Mass is held daily at 1000 and 1200, Sun 1030, 1200, 1800, and 1900.*
Right opposite the entrance to the Royal Palace, there's no missing the huge concrete lump which is the Catedral de Nuestra Señora de la Almudena, Madrid's first cathedral. Right up until 1993, when it was opened amid much pomp and ceremony (and a shower of confetti made with telephone directories) by Pope John Paul II, Madrid was part of the diocese of Toledo and had no cathedral to call its own. Plans for converting the former church of Our Lady of the Almudena into a cathedral were drawn up in the 1870s, but, despite more than a century of work, the finished product is banal. Much more atmospheric is the crypt (entrance around the corner on Calle Mayor), which was the first part to be completed, and has a creepy charm of its own.

Convento de la Encarnación

① *Plaza de la Encarnación 1, T914548800, Metro Opera. Visits by guided tour only (Spanish only, 20 mins) Tue-Thu, Sat 1030-1245, 1600-1745, Fri 1030-1245, Sun and holidays 1100-1345, €3.50/2.70 concessions (combined ticket with Monasterio de las Descalzas Reales €6/4.80 concessions, see above.*

A two-minute stroll north of the Plaza de Oriente, is another of Madrid's quirky convents – the Convento de la Encarnación – which opened its doors to the public in the 1980s. Like other religious institutions, it has had to find new ways of funding itself in post-Franco Spain. The convent was commissioned by Margaret of Austria, consort to Felipe II, and was once connected to the Royal Alcázar (which preceded the present Royal Palace, see above) by a long corridor. It looks modest enough on the outside, but parts of the predominantly Baroque interior are still fit for kings. The highlight of the tour is the final room, the Reliquario, a subterranean, dimly lit room lined with cabinets stuffed with the relics of thousands of saints – nails, skulls, hair, crumbling bones, and phials of blood all wrapped in garlands and displayed in intricate cases. Madrid's most famous relic is housed here, a tiny flask containing the blood of San Pantaleón which miraculously liquefies each year on the day of his martyrdom, 27 July. According to legend, if it liquefies at any other time, the country is in danger.

Plaza de Santa Ana and around

Just behind the Puerta del Sol is the enticing web of streets around the Plaza Santa Ana, an engaging neighbourhood of blind alleys, leaning houses and old-fashioned shops which attracts twice as many tourists as locals. It's always been the entertainment district – now it's the bars and restaurants which draw the crowds, but once it was theatres and whorehouses. On the fringes of this bohemian barrio is the decidedly un-bohemian Cortes (Parliament) and the sticky-sweet delights of some of Madrid's oldest patisseries. ▸▸ *For Sleeping, Eating and other listings, see pages 100-118.*

Plaza Santa Ana

Plaza Santa Ana, surrounded by bars, restaurants, theatres and hotels, has been the heart of this neighbourhood for centuries. It's been overhauled a dozen times, and is currently shrouded in scaffolding from its latest incarnation – which looks set to continue Madrid's infuriating tradition of banalising all its public squares. It may not be pretty, but it's a crowd-pleaser all the same; the pavements are lined with terraces from the dozens of bars, many of which are filled with tiles and turn-of-the-century fittings, and it's one of the most popular places in Madrid for the *tapeo* (a pub crawl from tapas bar to tapas bar). The square is overlooked by the **Teatro Español**, an 18th-century theatre which has seen some important premieres, including the first rowdy production of Lorca's *Yerma* in 1934, when the outraged audience screamed out 'queer' and 'whore' throughout the performance.

Opposite the theatre is the Belle Epoque-style **Gran Hotel Victoria**, a favourite with bull-fighters, which has a plaque to Manolete, perhaps the most famous *torero* of all time, just outside the entrance.

Ateneo Artístico, Científico y Literario de Madrid

① *T913906000, C/Prado 21, Metro Antón Martin or Sevilla, Mon-Sat 1000-2300, Sun and holidays, 0900-2200, free.*

A stroll down the Calle del Prado from the Plaza Santa Ana passes the entrance to **Calle Echegaray**, named for an almost-forgotten Nobel prize-winner, which is crammed with old-fashioned bars tiled from floor to ceiling. Further down on the left

you'll find the Ateneo Artístico, Científico y Literario de Madrid, which was established in 1820 as a patriotic society for the advancement of arts, literature and sciences, and so naturally it was almost immediately closed down by the repressive King Ferdinand VII who mistrusted anything which smacked of Liberalism. On Ferdinand's death in 1835, it reopened in the Calle del Prado which was then lined with cafés popular with writers and intellectuals, and has been housed in this elegant late 19th-century building since the 1880s. Officially it's only open to members but it's occasionally possible to sweet-talk the doormen into letting you in to see the glorious old library, one of Spain's finest, which exudes a dusty, tranquil air of scholarship. Another draw is the very reasonably priced cafeteria downstairs.

Casa-Museo Lope de Vega

ⓘ *C/Cervantes 11, T914299216, Metro Antón Martín, Tue-Fri 0930-1400, Sat 1000-1400, closed Sun, Aug, holidays, tours by guided visit only (Spanish) €2/1.50.*
The neighbourhood's literary tradition stretches back several centuries before the arrival of the Ateneo. One of Spain's best-known writers is Lope de Vega, whose house, the Casa-Museo Lope de Vega, has been opened to the public around the corner on Calle Cervantes (walk down Calle Léon and then take a left). Lope de Vega (1562-1635) was one of the most prolific and charismatic writers of Madrid's Golden Age. He churned out thousands of plays, poems and satires, poked fun at all his rivals (especially Cervantes) and still found time to lead a stormy love life which scandalized and enthralled Spanish society. Vega bought this house in 1610 and lived here until his death in 1635; he loved his new home ('my little house, my tranquillity, my little plot, my study' he wrote not long after moving in) and it is now a delightfully intimate and serene museum. At the back is a peaceful, enclosed garden which was Vega's pride and joy and has been beautifully restored to look much as it would have when he would sit here and read five centuries ago (the staff are happy to let visitors do the same now).

Vega fared better than his arch-rival Cervantes, whose former home – just up the street at the corner of Calles Léon and Cervantes – was demolished in the early 19th century despite a loud chorus of public outrage. The site is now marked with a plaque.

Calle Huertas and Calle Atoche

On the corner of Calle Léon and Calle Huertas is the **Real Academia de la Historia** ⓘ *Calle Léon 21, T914290611, open by appointment to researchers*, which is housed in an imposing, if dour, 18th-century building by Juan de Herrera, originally designed as a shop for the monks of El Escorial who wanted a place to flog their rosary beads and bibles. **Calle Huertas** was once known as the street with 'more whores than doors', but now the brothels have made way for bars, restaurants, and jazz cafés. Beyond the main entertainment strip is the forbidding, walled complex of the **Convento de las Trinitarias Descalzas** (not open to visitors), which was founded in 1612, and once housed the daughters of Lope de Vega and Cervantes who both became nuns. Cervantes was buried here, but, in inimitable Madrileño fashion, his bones – like the bones of most of the city's most celebrated citizens – have been lost. A memorial mass is still held here on the anniversary of his death.

Calle Atocha runs more or less parallel with Calle Huertas: noisy, slightly seedy and lined with cheaper *pensiones* and *hostales,* it's one of the main arteries of central Madrid. Just off Plaza Antón Martín at the top of the street is Madrid's most delightful cinema, the Art Deco **Cine Doré** which is now the *Filmoteca Nacional* (see page 110). It has a very pretty café and terrace, too.

Carrera de San Jerónimo

The Carrera de San Jerónimo leads down from the Puerta de Sol to the Cortes (Parliament), and is lined with showy banks and fancy offices. It's a dull street, but

worth a visit to pick up some *túrron* (nougat) at the **Casa Mira** at No 31 or peek in at the most famous gourmet institution in all Madrid: **Lhardy** at No 8, where you can still help yourself to consommé from a silver samovar or dine upstairs in the panelled dining rooms where the nymphomaniac Queen Isabel II used to entertain her lovers.

Cortes

ⓘ *Plaza de las Cortes, C/San Jeronimo, T913906525, Metro Banco de España or Sevilla, Sat 1000-1300, closed Aug, photo ID required, free, guided tours every 30 mins.*

Continuing down the Carrera de San Jerónimo, you could easily walk past Spain's **Cortes** (Parliament) and dismiss it as another boring bank. It's a dreary greyish neo-building guarded by a pair of bronze lions. Inside, things liven up and it looks much more suited for the serious business of governing the country, with plenty of 19th-century plush red velvet, stained glass, and enormous chandeliers. Back in 1981, Spain's fledgling democracy came under threat when Colonel Tejero and his troops stormed the main assembly hall, firing off shots (the bullet holes can still be seen, but you have to ask discreetly), and took the Cortes hostage for more than 24 hours. The nation, listening to the drama on the radio, held its breath, but democracy finally won out when leaders of all political parties banded together in a mass demonstration through the streets of Madrid.

Around the Cortes

Opposite the Parliament is the **Hotel Palacios**, a big cream cake of a hotel with liveried footmen and enormous chandeliers. The Calle del Duque de Medinaceli next to it leads to an ugly modern church, the **Iglésia Jesús de Medinaceli**, built to house a much-revered 16th-century statue of Jesús de Medinaceli. According to legend, the statue was stolen by pirates who demanded its weight in gold as ransom. But when the exchange took place and the statue was placed on the scales, it was miraculously found to weigh only as much as a single coin. On the first Friday of each month, queues snake endlessly around the church, waiting patiently to touch the statue and beg for miracles. Just across the small square outside the church is one of Madrid's most emblematic tiled bars, the **Taberna Dolores** (see page 102).

Prado and Triángulo del Arte

Three of Europe's most important art museums – the Prado, the Thyssen-Bornemisza and the Reina Sofía – are all happily nudged up within strolling distance of each other (although only the most fanatical art-buff would consider visiting all three in a single day). Each of the three corners of the so-called 'Triángulo del Arte' has a particular strength: the Prado is famous for its magnificent collection of Spanish masterpieces from the 12th to the 19th centuries including works by Velázquez, Zurbarán and Goya; the luminous Reina Sofía continues the thread, displaying works spanning the last 100 years or so, including Picasso's celebrated Guernica; and the Thyssen- Bornemisza perfectly complements both collections, plugging the gaps left by the Prado with its vast collection of western European art spanning eight centuries, and offering a dazzling selection of early 20th-century masters from Braque to Kandinsky to whet your appetite for the Reina Sofía. There are a smattering of smaller museums in the quiet streets behind the Prado, and then there's the cool, green expanse of the Parque del Retiro to get lost in afterwards.

▸▸ *For Sleeping, Eating and other listings, see pages 100-118.*

Museo del Prado

ⓘ *Paseo del Prado s/n, T913302800, http://museoprado.mcu.es, Metro Banco de España, Tue-Sat 0900-1900, closed Mon, 1 Jan, Good Friday; 1 May and 25 Dec, €3/1.50 concessions.*

The Prado houses one of the world's greatest art collections, a dazzling display of European art spanning seven centuries. When it opened in 1819, it was one of the very first public art museums, infused with the spirit of the Enlightenment, and shored up by royal whim (the Queen had been impressed with the Louvre and wanted one for Spain). The collection is enormous; today, it holds several thousand works of art and has long outgrown Juan de Villanueva's severely elegant neoclassical building. Plans are afoot for a major expansion by architect Rafael Moneo which is scheduled for completion in 2005. The Cáson del Buen Retiro, which holds the museum's collection of 19th-century art, is currently closed indefinitely for reconstruction.

‡ *The sheer scale can make it daunting; it is wise to pick out some highlights or favourite painters and make a beeline for them before museum fever sets in.*

Carlos I began the royal collection, his son Felipe II expanded it, but it was Felipe IV who turned it into the most important art collection of his age. It still reflects the idiosyncratic tastes of the kings and queens who formed it, and is uneven in parts – some major Spanish artists like Ribera or Murillo are barely featured, for example.

Ground floor

The ground floor holds the earliest works in the Prado's collection. The collection of medieval art is thin but includes some gilded retablos, and the haunting murals from the Hermitage of Santa Cruz de Maderuelo. Among the works from 15th-16th century Flanders are Van der Weyden's moving masterpiece, the *Descent from the Cross*, some sharply observed portraits by court painter Antonio Muro (originally from Utrecht), and the crowd-pleasing, nightmarish visions of Breughel the Elder and Bosch. There isn't much from the Italian Renaissance, but what there is is exquisite: Fra Angelico's *Annunciation*, Raphael's *Fall on the Road to Calvary*, and a series of beautiful panels by Botticelli depicting a story from the Decameron. Dürer's self-portrait is the highlight of the collection of 15th- and 16th-century German art, but don't miss the luminous panels depicting *Adam and Eve*. El Greco's paintings, with their dazzling colours, and surging, elongated forms, are given a room of their own (fans should visit Toledo, see page 133) and Titian, a favourite with Carlos I (Charles V) and Felipe II, is extremely well represented, along with his fellow Venetian painters, Veronese and Tintoretto. This floor also contains the museum's collection of classical sculpture.

First floor

The excellent collection of French, Dutch and Italian paintings from the 17th and 18th centuries may be the envy of art museums around the world, but they are still completely overshadowed by the Prado's greatest treasure, its huge collection of works by Diego Velázquez (1599-1660), court painter to Philip IV. The most famous paintings are gathered under the glass dome at the very centre of the building, including *Las Meninas*, the subtle, sublime portrait of the Infanta Margarita and her maids-in-waiting, and an acutely observed portrait of *Felipe IV* himself. The celebrated painting of *The Surrender of Breda*, and the equestrian portraits painted for the Salon de los Reinos (in the present Army Museum) may one day be returned to their original setting (see below). There are some stark, brilliantly lit paintings by Zurbarán, a handful of fluffy saints by Murillo, and some dark, intense

‡ *This is where the cream of the Prado's collection is held and where the crowds are inevitably thicker.*

Madrid & around   Prado & Triangulo del Arte

⠿ Prado's best

Prado
Ground floor

Murals from the Hermitage of Santa Cruz de Maderuelo (room 51c); Self-Portrait, Albrecht Dürer (room 49); Annunciation, Fra Angelico (Room 51b); Descent from the Cross, Roger van der Weyden (room 58); The Triumph of Death, Breughel the Elder (room 56a); The Garden of Delights, Bosch (room 58); Annunciation, El Greco (room 61a); Titian portraits (room 61b).

First floor

Artemisia, Rembrandt (room 7); Velázquez's masterpieces in room 12, especially Las Meninas, The Surrender of Breda (room 16); Santa Isabel de Portugal, Zurbarán (room 18a), The Three Graces, Rubens (room 9), El Martiro de San Felipe, Ribera (room 26), El Tres de Mayo, Goya (room 39); Goya's Pinturas Negras (room 34-38).

Second floor

The Nude Maja and The Clothed Maja, Goya (room 89).

Thyssen-Bornemisza
Second floor

Annunciation Diptych, Van Eyck (room 3); Madonna and Child Enthroned, Van de Weyden (room 3); Portrait of Giovanna Tornabuoni, Ghirlandaio (room 5); Portrait of Henry VIII, Holbein (room 5); Jesus Among the Doctors, Dürer (room 8); Annunciation, El Greco (room 11); The Garden of Eden, Jan Breughel I (room 19); The Toilet of Venus, Rubens (room 19).

First floor

Family Group, Hals (room 22); Pierrot Content, Watteau (room 28); Asensio Julià, Goya (room 31); Portrait of a Farmer, Cézanne (room 33); Houses Next to the River, Shiele (room 35); Quappi in a Pink Sweater, Beckmann (room 39).

Ground floor

The Staircase (second state), Leger (room 41); New York City, New York, Mondrian (room 43); Harlequin with a Mirror, Picasso (room 45); Reclining House, Klee (room 45); Catalan Peasant with a Guitar, Miró (room 45); Green on Maroon, Rothko (room 46); Brown and Silver I, Pollock (room 46); Hotel Room, Hopper (room 47); Last Portrait, Freud (room 47); Woman in a Bath, Lichtenstein (room 48).

Reina Sofía
Second floor

The Gathering at the Café del Pombo, Solana (room 2); The Singer, Gris (room 4); Great Prophet, Gargallo (room 5); Guernica, Picasso (room 6); Constellation, Calder (room 9); Portrait of Joella, Dalí and Man Ray (room 11); Woman, Miró (room 15).

Fourth floor

Homage to Mallarmé, Oteiza (room 20); Reclining Figure, Bacon (room 24); Spatial Concept, Hope, Fontano (room 26); Man and Woman, Lupez (room 31); Seven Chairs, Tàpies (room 35); Buen Retiro Ducks, Schnabel (room 40); The Spirit of the Birds, Chillida (room 41).

depictions of martyrs by José de Ribero. Rubens is well represented, because the Flemish painter was in the service of the Habsburg court, and visited Madrid several times. Finally, there are a series of rooms devoted to Franciso Goya y Lucientes (1746-1828), court painter to Carlos IV. On this floor you'll find the grim works painted after the anti-French uprisings of 1808 (see page 95), and the horrifying Black Paintings (Pinturas Negras), dark, hallucinatory pieces which were painted after the strange illness which left him deaf. (If you want to keep things strictly in chronological order, head upstairs to see his earlier, lighter paintings and leave the Pinturas Negras until last).

Second floor

A whole wing of this floor is devoted to **Goya**. Before war and sickness plunged Goya into depression, his works were characterized by joyful scenes and vivid colours. The early tapestry cartoons sparkle with life, but Goya's most famous works are the mysterious *Clothed* and *Nude Maja*, daringly modelled, some say, on Goya's beautiful, and unconventional patron, the Duchess of Alba.

Basement

Down in the basement, you'll find the **Dauphin's Treasure**, a dazzling collection of jewelled Renaissance and Baroque tableware and glassware, which originally belonged to Louis de Bourbon, son of Louis XIV. It's one of the most remarkable collections of its kind in the world; a single goblet is encrusted with 23 emeralds, plus plenty of cameos and cornelians. The café-restaurant is also tucked away down here, too – but there's not a jewel-encrusted salt cellar in sight.

Museo Thyssen-Bornemisza

ⓘ *Paseo del Prado 8, T913690151, www.museothyssen.org, Metro Banco de España, Tue-Sun 1000-1900, closed 1 Jan, 1 May and 25 Dec, €4.80/2.40 concessions, family days at weekends.*

The Museo Thyssen-Bornemisza is housed in an elegant palace just across the road from the Prado. When the Thyssen-Bornemisza collection was bought by the Spanish state in 1993, it proved an uncannily neat complement to the works held in the Prado and the Reina Sofía. It fleshes out the collections of medieval Flemish and Italian art held at the Prado, and adds an international dimension to the 20th-century art at the Reina Sofía.

Second floor

The visit begins on the second floor with the Thyssen's exceptional collection of medieval art. It opens with the luminous works of the Italian Primitives, followed by some glittering, highly decorative paintings in the International Gothic style which swept across Europe in the early 15th century. Van der Weyden, Van Eyck and Campen are among the early Dutch and Flemish masters, and there are some beautiful Renaissance portraits, including Holbein's celebrated portrait of Henry VIII. Moving into the 17th and 18th centuries, the bold energy of the Venetian colourists – there are stunning works by Titian, Veronese and Tintoretto – is echoed in El Greco's swirling, vibrant paintings, and there's a gaudy selection of sentimental 17th-century Baroque art from England, Flanders and Italy. There are several fleshy pieces by Rubens, hung beside Breughel's glowing *Garden of Eden*, and Bruggen's compelling depiction of *Esau Selling his Birthright*.

> ‡ *Unlike the other two corners of the 'Triangulo del Arte', the Thyssen works from the top down; head to the second floor for the earliest art.*

First floor

Downstairs on the first floor, there are dozens of examples of Dutch genre painting – a bit on the dull side at first, but strangely absorbing when you look at them more closely. Architecture, everyday objects and landscapes were becoming increasingly important, and would pave the way for the Golden Age of Dutch art a few decades later. Two galleries are devoted to 19th-century North American art, rarely seen in European museums, including some beautiful light-drenched pieces by John Singer Sargent. There are a couple of late Goyas, some wistful, bucolic scenes by Corot, and a small collection of Impressionist and post-Impressionist works which include

Degas' delightful *Swaying Dancer*, a couple of swirling Van Gogh's, and Cézanne's richly textured *Portrait of a Farmer*. A gallery is devoted to the dazzling colours of the Fauvists, but the highlight of this floor is the collection of Expressionist painting, with works by Shiele, Munch, Kandinsky, Macke, Otto Dix and Max Beckmann.

Ground floor

On the ground floor, the blazing colours and wheeling forms of the experimental artists of the early 20th century seem to leap from the walls: Picasso's splintered *Man with a Clarinet*, Léger's weaving *The Staircase (second state)*, or Mondrian's obsessively geometric *New York City, New York*. These galleries are a roll-call of the biggest names in 20th-century art – Picasso, Miró, Kandinsky, Pollock, Rothko, Dalí are just some of the artists featured. Lichtenstein's knowing cartoonish *Woman in a Bath*, and a distorted portrait by Francis Bacon are among the most recent works.

Museo Nacional Centro de Arte Reina Sofía

ⓘ *C/Santa Isabel 52, T914675062, www.museoreinasofia.mcu.es, Metro Atocha, Mon, Wed-Sat 1000-2100, Sun 1000-1430, €3.01/1.50 concessions, free Sat afternoon and Sun, free guided visits Mon, Wed at 1700, Sat at 1100, audioguide e2.40/1.20 for students, giftshop and café.*

The third corner of the Triangulo del Arte is tucked away at the bottom of the Calle Atocha, a 10-minute walk away from the Prado. It's housed in a former hospital, which has been beautifully remodelled to hold the nation's collection of 20th-century art. It's a graceful, light-filled building set around a quiet, interior courtyard, with a pair of panoramic glass lifts which are almost an attraction in themselves. The second and fourth floors are devoted to the permanent exhibition, and the first and third floors are used for temporary exhibitions which are usually excellent.

Second floor

The artworks on the second floor trace the development of Spanish art from the turn of the twentieth century to the conclusion of the Civil War in 1939. José Solana's *The Gathering at the Café del Pombo* reflects the intensity of intellectual life in Madrid's cafés, but it was the Basques and the Catalans who were creating the most innovative work in painting and sculpture; Isidre Nonell's haunting studies of gypsies in the streets of Barcelona profoundly influenced Picasso's Blue period. At the start of the 20th century, Paris was the mecca of the art world, and Spanish artists soaked up the Avant Garde art movements; Juan Gris developed his personal interpretation of Cubism, and Pau Gargallo's whiplash, wrought-iron sculptures treated space in an entirely new way. Both collaborated with Picasso, whose works are displayed in a line of galleries here. At the centre is *Guernica*, his vast, anguished response to the bombing of a Basque village during the Civil War. The Picasso galleries are flanked by a succession of galleries devoted to Joan Miró, who created a personal sign language in his colourful, abstract paintings. There are some light, graceful mobile sculptures by Calder, and two rooms are devoted to Dali's surreal, melting landscapes. Finally, there's a mixed collection of sculpture, including pieces by Miró, and a lissom, suspended piece by Àngel Ferrant.

Fourth floor

You can glide up in a glass lift to the fourth floor for post-war art. Spain's artistic and cultural life was mercilessly repressed in the first years of the Franco's dictatorship. During the 1950s, some of the most interesting work was being done by the Basque sculptor, Jorge Oteiza, whose boxy, iron pieces inspired Equipo 57, a collective

committed to exploring notions of space. There is a good collection of international artists – paintings by Francis Bacon, Yves Klein's trademark brilliant blue works, a tiny, serene sculpture by Henry Moore, and slashed canvases by Lucio Fontana. Several galleries are devoted to the Catalan artist Antoni Tàpies, whose unsettling 'material paintings' are created from layers of 'found' objects. Antonio Lupez's vast sculpture *Man and Woman* is set alongside some haunting landscapes of Madrid. The Spanish collective Equipo Crónico attacked mass culture imported from the US in their Pop Art-style pieces from the late 1960s and 70s, and the most recent works include a group of severely abstract sculptures from Eduardo Chillida.

Around the Prado

Paseo del Prada

The tree-lined Paseo del Prado sweeps between the Prado and the Thyssen-Bornemisza and connects two of Madrid's best-known monuments – at least to football fans. At the top of the Paseo is the **Plaza de Cibeles**, with flood-lit fountains and an enormous statue of the goddess **Cibeles** in her chariot at its centre. Real Madrid fans launch themselves at Cibeles to celebrate victories – she lost a hand in 1994 which had to be stuck back on with a special glue, and now she gets boarded up when danger looms. Just a few hundred metres away, at the other end of the Paseo del Prado, **Neptune** and his sea horses rear out of another fountain stuck in the middle of the Atocha roundabout. Neptune gets the Atlético fans, who also now face barricades on victory nights.

Casón del Buen Retiro and Museo del Ejército

The hushed, elegant neighbourhood around the Prado is studded with smaller museums devoted to an eccentric range of special interests from pottery to plants. The Prado's annexe, Casón del Buen Retiro, is one of the few surviving buildings of the Royal Palace of the Buen Retiro which once stretched out across this whole eastern flank of the city. It's still encased in scaffolding after a seeming endless restoration (closed indefinitely).

The faded pink building just behind it is the **Museo del Ejército** (Army Museum), ① *C/Méndez Núñez 1, T915228977, Metro Banco de España, Tue-Sun 1000-1400, €0.60/0.30 concessions, free to over-65s, under 18s, Sat, closed Aug*, housed in the main surviving building of the former Royal Palace. Miraculously, the building has preserved one of the grandest ceremonial halls of the former palace, the dazzling Salón de los Reinos, blazing with the escutcheons of the 24 kingdoms which made up pain in the 17th century. Zurbarán was commissioned to paint a series of 10 canvases depicting the Labours of Hercules to adorn the hall, along with Velázquez's *The Surrender of Breda*, and several equestrian portraits of the royal family. They are all currently on display at the Prado, but it looks like the Prado has finally won a long-running battle to rehouse the army museum in Toledo and return the paintings to their original setting.

> ❦ *The museum is a popular weekend jaunt for Madrileño dads and their kids, who seem to find the vast collection of armour, uniforms and weaponry endlessly fascinating.*

Museo Naval

① *Paseo del Prado 5, T913795299, Tue-Sun 1030-1330, free, ID required.*
There's more on the military theme at the Museo Naval (Navy Museum), tucked away in the brutally ugly Ministry of Defence building a short stroll up the Paseo del Prado. The sections which deal with the Age of Discovery, when Spain ruled the seas and a great swathe of the known world, are fascinating, with maps and models showing how the 15th- and 16th-century explorers staked their claims to the New World.

Museo Nacional des Artes Decoratives

① *C/Montalbán 12, T915326499, Metro Banco de España, Tue-Fri 0930-1500, Sat-Sun, public holidays 1000-1400, €2.40/1.20, free to over-65s, Sun.*

At the other end of the spectrum, just around the corner on Calle Montalbán, there's the National Museum of Decorative Arts, stuffed with furniture, porcelain, tapestries and tiles from all over Spain. Highlights include a pair of winsome Hansom cabs from the 17th-century, an elaborately tiled 18th-century Valencian kitchen, and a delightful collection of 19th-century dolls houses, complete with gilded wall paper and chandeliers. Several galleries are devoted to ceramics and porcelain, including the shimmering platters and vases typical of Manzes.

Real Jardín Botánico

① *Plaza de Murillo 2, T914203017, Metro Atocha, 1000-sunset daily.*

When museum fatigue sets in, head for the languid Real Jardín Botánico, which sits next to the southern entrance to the Prado on Plaza Murillo, and is cross-crossed with leafy paths and sprinkled with fountains. Established in the 16th century and given this elegant new home in the 18th century, there are now more than 30,000 plants on display including the Madrone or Strawberry Tree which has become the city's symbol.

Parque del Retiro

① *C/Alfonso XIII. Palacio de Velázquez and Palacio de Cristal, Parque del Retiro, T915736245, Metro Banco de España or Retiro, Mon-Sat 1100-1800, Sun 1100-1600, closed Tue, prices vary. Observatorio Astronómico Nacional T915270107, Metro Atocha, Mon-Thu 0900-1300, free.*

Madrid likes to boast is that it is the greenest city in Europe, and one of its largest and loveliest parks extends for several hundred breezy acres behind the Prado. This dreamy expanse of manicured gardens, lakes, shady woods and pavilions once surrounded the royal palace of the Buen Retiro and were handed over to the public in the 19th century. They've been enjoyed ever since, and the sandy paths are crammed on Sundays with families enjoying a stroll, or sitting at a lake-side café to enjoy the breeze.

The main entrance is next to the **Puerta de Alcalá**, a huge, triumphal arch topped with monstrous cherubs which was built in 1778 for no particular reason, and which has, inexplicably, become one of the city's favourite symbols. A sandy avenue leads to the Retiro's centrepiece, a stately *estanque* (lake) surrounded by columns and overlooked by a ridiculous statue of Alfonso XII. The lake used to be the scene of royal regattas, when galleons would set sail in mock-battles performed to entertain the court, but the closest you'll get nowadays is to hire a rowboat. This is the busiest section of the park, packed with buskers, fortune tellers, poets and tango dancers but you can easily find a quiet spot among the trees for a snooze or a picnic.

Just south of the lake are two beautiful pavilions, the **Palacio de Velázquez** and the ethereal **Palacio de Cristal**, now used by the Reina Sofía (see above) for temporary contemporary art exhibitions. At the southern end of the park, take a peek at the bizarre **Angel Caído** (Fallen Angel), one of only three monuments in the world to Satan, caught mid-way in his fall from Paradise.

Just by the southern entrance to the park, Juan de Villanueva's charming neoclassical **observatory** sits on a little hill overlooking the Retiro, and houses a dusty collection of old telescopes, sundials and sextants. Just beyond the park exit here is the Calle (usually called Cuesto) Claudio Moyano (heading downhill to Atocha train station), which is lined with a pretty row of wooden stalls piled high with second-hand books.

Estacíon Atocha

The area around Madrid's train station in the south of the city is as banal as most city suburbs, with its dull blocks of flats and busy main roads. But there are a few unusual

sights tucked away in its depths, from freakishly tall skeletons to tropical gardens. The **tropical garden**, perhaps unexpectedly, is hidden inside Atocha train station. When the station was massively expanded in 1992 for the high-speed AVE trains to Seville, the original station with its graceful 19th-century wrought-iron and glass frame was converted into a hazy oasis complete with lofty palm trees and terrapins – perfect for a coffee on a wintry day. The big roundabout outside the station is home to a **statue of Neptune**, see page 87, overlooked by a very fanciful 19th-century building topped with fabulous creatures which looks like it should be something more exciting than the Ministry of Agriculture but isn't.

Museo Nacional Ferroviario and around
On the other side of Atocha train station is the National Train Museum ① *Paseo de las Delicias 61, www.museodelferrocarril.org, Tue-Sun 1000-1500, €3.50/2*, where a vast collection of steam engines and model railways are held in a 19th-century train station with a wrought-iron canopy. Next to it is the entirely missable **Museo de la Ciencia y Tecnología** (Museum of Science and Technology) ① *Tue-Sat 1000-1400 and 1600-1800, Sun 1000-1430, free*, which the interactive revolution seems to have passed by. You'll find more up to date attractions in the large, modern **Parque de Enrique Tierno Galván** (a 10-minute walk south) which has a **Planetarium** and an **IMAX**.

Museo Antropología
① *C/Alfonso XII 68, Metro Atocha, Tue-Sat 1000-1930, Sun 1000- 1400, €2.40.*
Opposite the Neptune statue is the Anthropology Museum, a dusty old-fashioned museum with a rag-bag assortment of artefacts gathered from around the world. The nucleus of the collection was gathered by the eccentric Dr Pedro González Velasco, who famously embalmed his daughter and could be seeing driving around in his carriage with her body propped up beside him. A small room off the ground floor galleries contains the bizarre corpse of an extremely tall man – 2.35 m – who sold his body to science before his death.

Panteón des Hombres Illustres
① *C/Julien Gayarre, Metro Menéndez Pelayo/Atocha. Apr-Sep Tue-Fri 0900-1900, Sat-Sun 0900-1600, Oct-Mar Tue-Fri 0930-1800, Sat-Sun 0900-1500, free.*
Head down the big, noisy Avenida de la Ciudad which flanks the train station to find more old bones in the Pantheon of the Illustrious Men. Madrileños have lost the bones of most of their famous inhabitants from Cervantes to Velázquez and erected this Moorish-style pantheon in the 19th century in an attempt to rectify this habit – the names of its current inmates have long faded from memory.

Real Fábrica de Tapices
① *C/Fuentarrabía 2, T914340550, Metro Menéndez Pelayo, Mon-Fri 1000-1400, guided visits only, €2.*
Almost opposite the Pantheon, with a discrete entrance on Calle Fuentarrabía, is the Royal Tapestry Factory, where tapestries have been woven for Spain's draughty royal palaces for several hundred years. You can watch the vast hangings being threaded by hand on enormous 18th-century wooden looms, a fascinating glimpse of a dying art.

La Latina and Lavapiés

The traditionally working-class neighbourhoods of La Latina and Lavapiés spread steeply downhill south of the Plaza Mayor. Known as los barrios bajos ('low neighbourhoods') as much for their position on the social ladder as their

geographical location, they have traditionally been home to Madrid's poorest workers, smelliest industries, and most desperate immigrants. The latest wave of immigrants are more likely to be from North Africa or Latin America than Andalucía or Galicia, and the sinuous sounds of Arabic pop songs or Dominican salsa tunes regularly float above the rooftops. La Latina and Lavapiés are rapidly becoming Madrid's most multicultural neighbourhoods, and young artists are also moving in to add to the mix, bringing trendy bars, cafés and vintage clothes stores in their wake. The Sunday morning flea market El Rastro is a classic: follow it in true Madrileño style with a tapas crawl around the local bars. ‣ *For Sleeping, Eating and other listings, see pages 100-118.*

La Latina

Plaza de la Paja and around

The heart of La Latina is the Plaza de la Paja. This was once the most important square of medieval Madrid, but, until very recently, it was sadly neglected. Newly spruced up, it has become one of the prettiest in Madrid, and the best example of the neighbourhood's continuing regeneration. Some of Madrid's hippest bars have opened their designer doors around the square and, on summer evenings, it teems with Madrid's fashionable youth. Cut off from traffic, and scattered with a few trees and some benches, it is ringed with restored 19th-century palaces and overlooked by the handsome **Iglesia de San Andrés** ① *open for mass only*. The boring interior was almost completely destroyed in the Civil War, but the adjoining **Capilla del Obispo** (Bishop's Chapel) is a Renaissance gem which has been under restoration for years and is still closed to visitors.

The Plaza de la Paja is linked to the **Plaza de la Humilladero**, **Plaza de San Andrés** and **Plaza de los Moros,** which all form one large, pedestrian space on the other side of the San Andrés church. This is the place to come after the Rastro (see below), when everyone spills out of the surrounding tapas bars, kids run around with their footballs, and musicians play their bongos and guitars out in the sunshine. It's also the home of one of the newest city museums, the **Museo de San Isidro** ① *Plaza San Andrés 2, T913667415, www.munimadrid.es/museosanisidro, Metro Latina or Tirso de Molina, Tue-Fri 0930-2000 (until 1430 in Aug), Sat-Sun 1000-1400, free*. The museum is dedicated to Madrid's patron saint, San Isidro, and housed in an immaculate former palace which has been completely rebuilt by the city council. According to legend, Isidro and his equally saintly wife, Santa María de la Cabeza once lived here as servants to an aristocratic family. Countless miracles have been attributed to the saintly duo, but one of the most celebrated is the story of their drowned child, who fell down the well. The couple prayed and prayed and finally the well filled up and overflowed, disgorging their son, who was found to be perfectly fine. This very same well (honestly) has been incorporated into the building, along with the 17th-century Capilla de San Isidro, given a layer of Baroque frilliness in the 1790s, which is where the saint supposedly died. A section of the museum is devoted exclusively to the life and times of San Isidro and Santa María, another is devoted to the history of the city and features excellent temporary exhibtions, and there's also a garden which has examples of some of the trees to be found in medieval Madrid.

Catedral de San Isidro

① *C/Toledo 37-39, T913 692310, Metro La Latina, Mon-Sat 0830-1230, 1830-2030, Sun and holidays 0900-1400, 1730-2030, free.*

San Isidro's bones are kept in the Catedral de San Isidro, an enormous twin-towered Baroque church, was once the headquarters of the Jesuits in Madrid until their expulsion from Spain in 1767. The church was promptly altered to expunge all trace of

66 99 'Rastro' refers to the sticky trail of blood left when the meat carcasses were hauled through the streets.

the austere Jesuit style, the frothy Churrigueresque façade was added, and it was rededicated to San Isidro who had been canonized in 1622. The remains of San Isidro and his wife were moved here from the church of San Andrés (to the fury of the local priest) and it served as the Madrileño cathedral until the Catedral de Nuestra Señora de la Almudena was completed in 1993.

Basílica de San Francisco el Grande

① *Plaza de San Francisco, T913653800, Metro La Latina, summer Tue-Sat 1100-1300, 1700-2000, winter 1100-1300, 1600-1900, admission by guided tour in Spanish, € 1.*
Larger, grander and even gloomier than the Catedral de San Isidro, the Basílica de San Francisco el Grande (head west down Carretera de San Francisco from the Plaza Puerta de Moros) lives up to its name with a massive dome spanning more than 100 foot. It was built between 1762 and 1784 on the ruins of a hermitage supposedly founded by Saint Francis himself. It's in the middle of a lengthy restoration project and much of it is wrapped up in scaffolding and nets. Look out for Goya's early painting of San Bernadino de Siena in the chapel dedicated to the saint.

Puerta de Toledo and around

This pompous gateway was erected in 1817 as a celebration of Ferdinand VI's return to the throne after Joseph Bonaparte's brief government. Equally unattractive is the **Mercado de Toledo**, a modern development just off the roundabout, which houses an assortment of antique and craft shops; it has never really taken off (the disgruntled shop-keepers blame the city council for advertising it so poorly) and is usually deserted. There are some excellent vintage clothes stores on Calle Mira el Rio Alta and Calle el Rio Baja just to the northeast. On Calle de la Paloma, you'll find the lovely neo-Mudéjar **Iglesia de la Virgen de la Paloma**, the focus of a delightful pilgrimage and festival in early August (see page 110).

Lavapiés

El Rastro

① *Metro Tirso de Molino or Puerta de Toledo.*
Madrid's famous flea market takes place every Sunday morning. Stalls wind all the way up Calle Ribera de Curtidores and sell everything from tacky clothes and souvenirs to leather goods, underwear, arts and crafts, and kites. The street name means *Tanner's Alley* and recalls the pungent trades which took place down here out of sight (and smell) of the smart neighbourhoods at the top of the hill. 'Rastro' refers to the sticky trail of blood left when the meat carcasses were hauled through the streets. The neighbourhood is still a little shabby and run-down, although it's in the process of regeneration and half the streets seem to have been dug up, but the leather trade is now a thing of the past. The surrounding shops are mainly devoted to antiques and bric-a-brac, although you'll still find plenty of leather goods here too. Most shops are open all week, including Sunday mornings, but the days of a bargain are long gone. Watch out for your bags – the Rastro is notorious for pickpockets. The atmosphere is wonderful, and carries on long after the stall-holders have packed up, when everyone heads to the surrounding bars for some tapas and a well-earned cold beer.

Being Madrileño

Few Madrileños can boast four Madrileño grandparents. Like most capital cities, it's a big melting pot for people from all over the country as well as a liberal sprinkling of immigrants from further afield. But being Madrileño is still a matter of pride, wherever your family once came from.

The *barrios bajos* are traditionally the most *castizo*, which literally means simply 'from Castile', but has come to mean authentically Madrileño. The inhabitants used to be known as *Manolos* or *Manolas*), so called because the converted Jews who once lived here commonly named their eldest son 'Manolo'. They were known for their sharp tongues and their sharp dress sense; the men rejected French fashions for the classic Spanish cape and hair net, and the women famously tucked daggers in their stockings. Generations of travellers trawled the streets hoping for a glimpse of these romantic characters, but they had all but died out by the 19th century. Goya's *Majos* and *Majas* – similar in dress and attitude to the *Manolos* – live on in his cheerful depictions of 18th- century pilgrimages and festivals.

La Corrala
ⓘ *Corner of Calle Méson de Paredes and Calle Tribulete, Metro Lavapiés.*
Most of the tenement buildings thrown up in the late 18th and early 19th centuries to provide homes for the workers in the surrounding factories and slaughterhouses have been destroyed; this is a lone survivor, which dates back to 1790. It's been given a lick of ochre paint and has undergone several restorations since the city authorities took it over in 1981, although inhabitants still complain of cracked ceilings and damp walls. The name corralas was given to these buildings because they were usually set around a communal courtyard (*corral*), where families would have to come to collect their water. The original courtyard has now disappeared but the square in front of the Corrala is sometimes used for traditional *zarzuela* performances in summer (see the tourist information offices for details). Don't miss it if you get the chance.

Fábrica de Tabacos
ⓘ *Calle de Embajadores, Metro Lavapiés.*
At the height of its production, the enormous Royal Tobacco Factory employed 3,000 women, the original Carmens, sharp-tongued beauties who were as famous for their solidarity as they were for their feistiness. They formed a powerful union and fought for an improvement in working conditions, including the establishment of schools, nurseries and pensions. By the early 20th century, mechanisation had taken its toll, and the once-grand factory now stands forlorn and empty.

Gran Vía, Chueca and Malasaña

The broad sweep of the Gran Vía was created at the dawn of a new age, wide enough for motor cars and lined with the city's first skyscrapers and cinemas (many of which preserve the old tradition of using handpainted billboards). Now a busy, traffic-clogged shopping street, it's looking a bit down-at-heel but it's brash, larger-than-life appeal still lingers. To the north of the Gran Vía are two formerly run-down neighbourhoods which have become the focal point of the city's heady nightlife: Chueca and Malasaña, which have both been dramatically cleaned up in the last

decade. Chueca is the focal point of Madrid's gay community and Malasaña has a youthful, bohemian edge, but both are packed with some of the city's best cafés, most fashionable clubs, and trendiest shopping. Parque del Oueste runs along the north west of the city: this is where the cable car leaves for the wild expanse of the Casa del Campo (with its zoo and funpark), and where you'll find the path to Goya's beautiful pantheon. ➤ For Sleeping, Eating and other listings, see pages 100-118.

Gran Vía

Calle Alcalá

① Metro Banco de España. Calle Alcalá is a swaggering introduction to the Gran Vía, with which it connects on the eastern side of the city. It's lined with flamboyant Belle Epoque buildings, like the glamorous Casino (members only, unless you can sweet-talk the doormen into giving you a glimpse of the billowing staircase), and the **Art Deco Circulo de Belles Artes** ① Tue-Fri 1700-2100, Sat-Sun 1100- 1400, café Mon-Thu, Sun 0900-1400, Fri-Sat 0900-0400, now an excellent café-bar and cultural centre.

Plaza de la Lealtad

The creamy curves of the **Hotel Ritz** overlook the circular garden of the Plaza de la Lealtad (Loyalty Square). The obelisk and eternal flame flickering in the middle of the garden commemorate the victims of the uprising on 2 May 1808, see page 95.

Real Academia de Bellas Artes de San Fernando

① C/Alcalá 13, T915240864, Tue-Fri 0900-1900, Sat-Mon and holidays 0900-1430, guided visits Oct-Jun 1700 (Spanish only), € 2.50/1.25 concessions, free on Wed.

The Royal Academy of Fine Arts has barely changed since Dalí was a student here in the 1920s – before he was expelled for questioning his professors' competence – and there's a lingering sense that the appreciation of art is a solemn business and any frivolity will be frowned on. Nonetheless, the Academy houses a rich and surprisingly extensive collection of paintings and drawings (many of which were appropriated after the Jesuits were expelled from Spain in 1767) including works by El Greco, Velázquez, Zurbarán, Ribera, Murillo, Veronese, Titian, Rubens, Fragonard, and Van Dyck. The Academy is most proud of its large collection of paintings by Goya, including several of his later works which are all imbued with an unsettling undercurrent: even the apparently innocent festival being celebrated in the Burial of the Sardine hints at something sinister in Goya's portrayal.

Museo Calcografia, on the first floor of the same building, has a formidable collection of drawings and engravings but opening hours are erratic.

Torre Telefónica

① Gran Vía No 28, entrance around the corner on Calle Fuencarral 3, T915226645, Metro Gran Vía.

This was Spain's first skyscraper, a slick, 29-storey art deco construction which was built in 1929 to house an American telephone company. As the most instantly recognisable landmark in the city centre, it was targeted by Franco's forces during the Civil War, and kids used to collect the still-hot shrapnel embedded in its smooth façade. Spain's former national telephone company **Telefónica** own the building now, and have invested some of their billions in an exhibition space.

Plaza del Callao

This circular square is filled with bus fumes and chaos but it's overlooked by one of the prettiest of the Gran Vía's art deco cinemas, the **Cinesa Capitol**, one of the few which can still be counted on to erect a huge hand-painted advert for forthcoming attractions.

Plaza de España

Plaza de España is a large, sandy square with a pair of huge ornamental fountains, and a couple of grassy areas usually colonized by picnicing office-workers and the odd tramp sleeping off a hangover. At the centre, Don Quixote and Sancho Panza sally forth on their next adventure, while Cervantes looks on gloomily. The square is overshadowed by a pair of bombastic skyscapers – the **Edificio de España** (1948) and the **Torre de Madrid** (1957).

The delightful **Sabatini Gardens** (see page 79) and the **Templo de Debod** (see page 96) are a very short stroll from the Plaza de España – both much prettier places to sunbathe or picnic.

Museo Cerralbo

ⓘ *C/Ventura Rodríguez 17, T915473646, Tue-Sat 0930-1430, Sun 1000-1400, €2.40/ 1.20 concessions, free on Sun and Wed.*

This beautiful 19th-century palace belonged to the 17th Marqués de Cerralbo, who crammed it with treasures picked up on his many travels. On his death in 1922, he bequeathed the palace and its contents to the state, with the stipulation that nothing was to be moved. As a result, it's delightfully, eccentrically cluttered, with Roman busts rubbing shoulders with Flemish tapestries, and paintings by Ribera, Murillo, and Zurbaran jostling up together in unfashionable proximity. The palace is fitted with breath-taking opulence; even the bathrooms are works of art, with pretty shell-shaped sinks and porcelain loos. The chandelier collection is extraordinary – don't miss the ultra-kitsch pink and blue one in the Music Room – but the highlight is the magnificent ballroom surrounded with huge gilded mirrors and festooned with garlands and swarms of cherubs.

Chueca

Plaza de Chueca

Chueca is the heart of gay Madrid but it's also where most of the nightlife is concentrated. This square, with its terrace cafés and bars, may be quiet and nondescript by day, but livens up dramatically at night and is a great place to start the night.

Museo Municipal

ⓘ *C/Fuencarral 78, T915888672, Metro Tribunal, Tue-Fri 0930-2000, Sat-Sun 1000-1400.*

Madrid's town museum boasts one of the most extraordinary doorways in the city, a gushing Churrigueresque fantasy sculpted by Pedro de Ribera in the 17th century. Inside, there are plenty of plans and models, including Teixera's famous map made in 1656, a huge wooden model of early 19th-century Madrid which gets a room to itself, and some delightful models of the mock-battles which some used to take place on the Retiro lake (see page 88). Upstairs there are more furnishings, a huge collection of porcelain from the long-demolished Royal Factory of the Buen Retiro, and a series of otherwise indifferent paintings which are fascinating for the glimpses they give of the way Madrid used to look. Goya's famous *Allegory of Madrid* takes pride of place. When it was first painted (1810), the frame held by the female figure contained a portrait of Napoleon, but when the French were being beaten back a few years later, the offending portrait was painted over. Then Bonaparte came back into power and the painting had to be retouched – again. The uncertain political climate meant that the painting was eventually 'adjusted' seven times. Finally it was decided to paint it over with the words 2 de Mayo (Second of May) as a reminder of the uprising against the French occupiers (see box page 95).

El Dos de Mayo

In early 1808, Napoleon's armies marched into Madrid with the co-operation of the cowardly Spanish king, Carlos IV. On May 2, a carriage containing the royal family slipped out of the palace gates. Unfortunately, a local locksmith saw them and immediately assumed that the Napoleonic armies were spiriting them away. A crowd gathered yelling "death to the French" and the city erupted into revolt. There are dozens of tales of heroic deeds, but none more so than the seamstress Mañuela Malasaña, after whom this neighbourhood is named who was shot by the French soldiers after attacking them bravely with her scissors. Goya's celebrated works in the Prado – El Dos de Mayo 1808 and El Tres de Mayo 1808 – were painted six years later to immortalize the heroism of the Madrileños against the French troops.

Museo Romántico

ⓘ C/San Mateo 13, T914481045, Metro Chueca, Tue-Sat 1000-1500, Sun 1000-1400, closed Aug, €2.40.

This palace is crammed with folk art, period furniture and minor paintings by Zurbarán, Goya and Sorolla, but its most obvious association with the Romantic movement is the collection of memorabilia belonging to Mariano José de Larra A brilliant satirist and Romantic whose weekly newspaper column took a pitiless view of Madrid society, Larra shot himself (with the pair of duelling pistols on display) at the age of 28 over an unhappy love affair.

Sociedad General de Autores

ⓘ C/Fernando VI 4. Metro Alonso Martínez.

It took a Catalan, Grases Riera, to built this voluptuous, art nouveau beauty in the middle of Madrid. The creamy undulations of the Palacio Longoria are now the property of the General Society of Authors, who might let you in to peek at the flowing staircase with its delicate floral ironwork and rainbow-coloured stained glass ceiling.

Malasaña and around

This square is named for the famous uprising against the French in 1808 (see box page 95) and is the focal point of Malasaña's excellent nightlife, with plenty of terrace cafés, clubs and bars. It used to be the scene of a huge botellón every weekend, when a sea of teenagers would descend, clutching their plastic bottles of booze (hence the name). But Madrid has cracked down firmly on the botellón, and cleaners stand by with hoses to make sure that the kids don't come back. Just off the square is **Calle San Vicente Ferrer**, which is sprinkled with old tiled shopfronts (including a pharmacy with a memorable advert for a laxative). At night this street is crammed pierced navel to pierced navel with hip students and teenagers queuing for the endless line of bars.

Centro Cultural Conde Duque

Plaza Conde Duque 9-11, T915885834, Metro Noviciado. Tue-Sat 1000-1400 and 1730-2100, Sat 1030-1330, free.

This cultural centre puts on excellent temporary shows and is also the home of the city's large collection of contemporary art. Just to the north is the sunny **Plaza de Comendadoros**, with a handful of hip terrace cafés, a good place for a drink.

Parque del Oeste

ⓘ *C/Ferraz s/n, T917651008, Metro Ventura Rodriguez, Apr-Sep Tue-Fri 1000-1400 and 1800-2000, Oct-Mar 0945-1345, 1615-1815.*

The cool, shady Parque del Oeste spreads along the western flank of the city just a few minutes stroll north of the Plaza de España and west of Malasaña. One of its most surprising sights is a 2,000-year-old temple, the **Templo de Debod**, a gift from the Egyptians, perched on a low hill and reflected in a still pond in the south of the park. The surrounding peaceful gardens are very popular on Sunday mornings, when the benches are filled with locals reading their newspapers.

Ermita de San Antonio de la Florida y Goya Pantheon

ⓘ *Glorieta de la Florida 5, T915420722, Metro Príncipe Pío, Tue-Fri 1000-1400, 1600-2000, Sat-Sun 1000-1400, €1.80/1.90 concessions, free Wed and Sun.*

You can walk downhill – along C/Francisco y Jacinto Alcántara – towards a pedestrian bridge which crosses the train tracks and leads to the Museo Pantéon de Goya. Goya was commissioned to decorate a new hermitage sheltering a cult statue of St Antony of Padua in 1798. He worked rapidly, completing the frescoes in just 120 days and utterly transforming the simple chapel. In the cupola, St Antony raises a murdered man to life, in order to exonerate his own father who had been unjustly accused of the crime. Around him swirl Goya's famous '*angelitas*', the plump, rosy-cheeked '*majas*' of La Latina and Lavapiés who appear in his joyful paintings of local festivals – this time they have been transformed into angels. Goya's remains were brought here in 1919, and the chapel was closed for worship a decade later. The replica chapel directly opposite is used for services and is still the focus of a popular pilgrimage each year on 13 June.

Téléferico and the Casa del Campo

Madrid's cable carⓘ *Paseo Pintor Rosales s/n, T915417450, Metro Argüelles, Mon-Fri 1200-2000, Sat-Sun and holidays 1100-2030, one-way €2.80, return €4*, sways giddily across the city and out to the vast Casa de Campo, a huge and beautiful park full of shady walks and cycling paths. There's a lake at the centre (you can't miss the huge jet of water at the centre) with a few cafés and a lively trade in prostitution which doesn't seem to faze anyone. There's a park information centre close to the lake which can give you information on the special botanic walks and some of the plants and wildlife that you might encounter. Also in the park are Madrid's **zoo-aquarium** and **Parque de Attraciones** (theme park).

Museo de América

ⓘ *Avda Reyes Católicos 6, T915492641, Metro Moncloa, Tue-Sat 1000-1500, Sun and holidays 1000-1430, €3/1.5 concessions, free Sun.*

This handsome, red-brick Art Deco museum displays Spain's collection of booty from the Americas, and tries to explain what Spain was doing there in the first place. It's large, extremely well-laid out, and there's plenty to amuse kids, from shrunken heads and mummies, to slide shows and special family events. The highlights include The Treasure of the Quimbayas, the most important collection of pre-Columbian gold in the world, and an extremely rare Mayan Codex (13th-16th centuries) which recounts the arrival of the Spanish.

❧ *There's an excellent giftshop and café, and right opposite is the Faro de Madrid, a glassy observation tower.*

Salamanca

It's easy to feel overwhelmed in this part of the city; the 19th-century entrepreneurs built their broad avenues and flashy palaces here, and the 20th-century

wheeler-dealers added a string of high-tech skyscrapers along the brutal Paseo de la Castellana with its constantly whizzing traffic. Salamanca has been a rich neighbourhood since the Marqués de Salamanca urged all his aristocratic friends to buy into his new development on the northeastern fringe of the city at the end of the 19th century. They came in droves, happy to escape the insanitary medieval jumble of old Madrid for this elegant grid of broad avenues and well-equipped mansions complete with flush toilets.

The neighbourhood is still Madrid's smartest district, home to los yuppís, and their glossy offspring (pijos or pijas). Salamanca is definitely the place to come if you want to exercise your plastic; the streets – particularly Calles Serrano, Goya and Velázquez – are lined with designer boutiques (see page 100), swanky bars (see page 110) and chic restaurants (see page 106). The string of terrazas (bars and clubs with terraces) along the Paseo de la Castellana are still a fashionable spot to see and be seen, but if you choose to party here, make sure you can hold your own against the perfectly groomed locals. ▸▸ *For Sleeping, Eating and other listings, see pages 100-118.*

Paseo de Recoletas

Palacio de Linares and Casa de América
ⓘ *Times and prices vary according to the exhibitions. Paseo Recoletos 2, T915954800, Metro Banco de España.*

A century ago, everyone who was anyone wanted a mansion along the aristocratic Paseo de Recoletos. This is one of the few survivors, an elegant palace set in handsome gardens which was built by the Marqués de Linares in the 1890s. According to urban myth, the palace is still haunted by the Marqués and his wife. The Marqués defied his family and married a commoner, only to discover that she was his half-sister. The unhappy couple were forced to divide the palace into two apartments and live separately until their deaths, and they still wail about their miserable fate on stormy nights. The Palace has been sympathetically converted into the Casa de America, a cultural centre which hosts temporary exhibitions, film events, lectures and concerts with a Latin American theme.

Palacio Marqués de Salamanca
ⓘ *Paseo Recoletos 10, not open to visitors.*

This is the most flamboyant of the surviving palaces on the Paseo Recoletos, and was built for the Marquis de Salamanca – the entrepreneur behind the construction of the whole Salamanca district. An extravagant, larger-than-life character who made and lost three fortunes, he lived here with his remarkable art collection and Spain's first private bathroom until the loss of his final fortune forced him out to the suburbs where he died abruptly in 1883. Appropriately, it has been the headquarters of a Spanish bank for most of the last century.

Opposite the palace is the legendary **Café Gijón** (see page 107), one of the most famous literary cafés at the turn of the 20th century.

Centro Cultural de la Villa
ⓘ *Times and prices vary according to the exhibitions, Plaza de Colón s/n, T915756080, Metro Colón.*

Madrid's subterranean cultural centre is built beneath the modern Plaza de Colón, and hosts an impressive range of theatre, music and dance events (it is one of the main venues for the city's excellent dance festival, Madrid en Danza, see page 110). Plaza de Colón and the adjoining Jardines de Descubrimiento are dedicated to Christopher Columbus (Colón is a variation of his name), with a monument to the explorer formed from vast blocks of sandstone surrounded by illuminated sheets of water.

Biblioteca Nacional Museo Interactivo del Libro
① *Paseo Recoletos 20, T915807759, Metro Serrano, Tue-Sat 1000-2100, Sun 1000-1400, free.*

The largest and grandest building on the Paseo de Recoletos is the florid pompous National Library, built in the 19th century under Isabel II. It contains every book printed in Spain since 1712, plus a collection of illuminated manuscripts, drawings by Goya and Velázquez, and the first book of Castillian (Spanish) grammar. Many of the library's treasures are too fragile to be handled, but the library has circumvented this problem and offers an engaging history of the library and its valuable collection in the adjoining Interactive Book Museum.

Museo Arqueológico Nacional
① *C/Serrano 13, T915777912, www.man.es, Metro Serrano, Tue-Sat 0930-2030, Sun 0930-1430, €3, free on Sat afternoon and Sun.*

Madrid's enormous, gloomy archaeological museum is the most comprehensive in Spain, with a vast collection spanning several millennia. It shares the same building as the Biblioteca Nacional (see above) but the entrance is around the back on Calle Serrano. Although it's a tad old-fashioned and the labelling is exclusively in Spanish, there is plenty to keep your attention. Highlights include an excellent reproduction of the Altamira caves in Cantabria, discovered in 1879 but thought to have been painted around 8,500BC, in which bison, stags, and boars career across the walls with astonishing realism – one boar even scuttles by on several feet, obviously painted in order to create the illusion of rapid movement. The most important and most famous piece in the whole museum is the Dama de Elche, see also page 693, thought to have been sculpted around 500BC, a mysterious bust of a woman whose enigmatic expression almost outdoes the Mona Lisa. Very little is known about the Iberian culture which was wiped out when the Romans conquered the Iberian Peninsula, and the Lady of Elche has perplexed archaeologists since her discovery in 1897. The museum also houses a fine collection of Roman mosaics including a wonderful depiction of *Bacchus and His Train* from Zaragoza; a heavily jewelled collection of Visigothic crowns and crosses from Toledo; intricate Islamic art including a precious ivory casket which belong to Caliph Al-Hakam in the 10th century; and some stunning examples of Gothic *artesonado* ceilings from Seville and Toledo.

Paseo de la Castellana

Museo de Escultura al Aire Libre
The Paseo de la Castellana is not a thing of beauty; streams of cars constantly roar up it and it's lined with monstrous, glassy buildings. The Museum of Outdoor Sculpture comes as a particularly welcome oasis in this inhuman landscape – even if it is tucked underneath a flyover. There are about a dozen large works by some of Spain's best known sculptors, including Eduardo Chillida, Joan Miró and Julio González.

Urbanizacíon AZCA and Torre Picasso
Just to the north of the grim, grey slabs of the Nuevos Ministerios (which house government buildings) is the Urbanizacíon AZCA, a glittering, glassy complex of skyscrapers including Madrid's largest, the Torre Picasso which was designed by Minori Yamasaki, architect of New York's Twin Towers. Besides offices, it houses a huge shopping centre and dozens of bars and cafés.

Plaza Castilla and the Kio Towers
Madrid's most unusual contemporary buildings overlook the modern Plaza de Castilla – you may have noticed them on your way into the city from the airport. The

twin towers of the Puerta de Europa (still better known as the KIO towers even though KIO were unable to raise the finance to complete them) lean in towards each other at an alarming angle, and were completed in 1996.

Museo Lázaro Galdiano
ⓘ C/Serrano 122, T915616084, Metro Rúben Darío.

Don José Lázaro Galdiano amassed one of the most extraordinary private art collections in Madrid, which he bequeathed to the state on his death in 1942. It is displayed in the very elegant surroundings of his Italianate home in a quiet leafy corner of Salamanca. The collection is astonishingly eclectic and includes archaeological artefacts, paintings, sculptures, armour, furniture, jewellery and one of the finest collections of enamels and ivories in existence. Among the paintings are works by Bosch, Rembrandt, Zurbarán, Velázquez, El Greco and Goya.

Museo Sorolla
ⓘ C/General Martínez Camps 37, T913101584, Metro Rúben Darío, Tue-Sat 0930-1500, Sun and holidays, 1000-1500, €2.40/1.20 concessions, free on Sun.

This is one of Madrid's most delightful small museums, devoted to the Valenciano painter Joaquín Sorolla who lived here until his death in 1923. He enjoyed considerable success both internationally and among Madrid's new bourgeoisie at the end of the 19th century. His luminous paintings borrowed some of the techniques of French Impressionism, but his figures and landscapes are modelled with a sharp clarity. The upper galleries display his light-filled, happy paintings of children and pretty country scenes and seascapes while the lower floor has been left intact to give some insight into the artist's everyday life. Sunlight streams in from the huge skylights in his studio, and the living areas display his collection of popular jewellery, a mixed bag of ear-rings, religious medals and other odds and ends collected on his travels. The house stands in a tiny Moorish-style garden, deliciously cool in summer, with palms, tiles, fountains.

La Residencia de Estudiantes
ⓘ C/Pinar 23, T915636411, Metro Gregorio Marañón, times and prices vary according to the exhibitions, closed Sat afternoon and Sun.

The Students' Residence (usually known simply as 'el resi') was completed in 1915, and rapidly became one of the most influential and dynamic institutions in Spain. Famously, it was here that Lorca, Dalí and Buñuel met and became friends in the 1920s, developing their ground-breaking theories about art and literature. After the Civil War, the Residencia stultified under Franco's repressive regime, but it is now undergoing a dramatic refurbishment (most of which is now complete) and hosts some of the most stimulating temporary exhibitions in Madrid.

Fundación Juan March
ⓘ C/Castelló 77, T914354240, Mon-Sat 1000-1400, 1730-2100, Sun and holidays 1000-1400, free.

This cultural centre was established by the Catalan tycoon Juan March in the 1950s (before he got banged up for cooking the books in the 1970s). It hosts excellent temporary exhibitions and major retrospectives and also offers a regular programme of music concerts.

Ventas

There's nothing to see out in the mainly residential neighbourhood of Ventas except Madrid's bullring. The 'Cathedral of Bullfighting', as it is often called, is the largest

bullring in Spain, built in the 1930s, with capacity for 22,300 spectators. **Bullfighting Museum** ① *C/Alcalá 237, Plaza de las Ventas, Patio de Caballos, T917251857, Metro Ventas, Tue-Fri 0930-1430, Sun and bullfight days 1000-1300, free,* is at the back, near the horses' stables, with portraits of famous bullfighters, costumes, 'banderillas' (the plumed daggers used to slow down the bull) and the stuffed heads of famous bulls. Most gruesome of all are the bloodstained clothes which belonged to some of the *toreros* who met their deaths in the bullring; one of the most recent was 'Yiyo' who died here in 1985, who is commemorated by a statue outside the ring.

✦ *The first 'arm-to-arm' blood transfusion took place in the Plaza de Toros Monumental de las Ventas; celebrated bull-fighter Manolete, died here in August 1947.*

⊕ Sleeping

Finding accommodation in Madrid is not as easy as it once was. Book well as far in advance as possible. For the best deals, look on the internet; many hotels, especially the chain hotels which deal with business clients, offer good weekend deals, although this practice isn't as common as it once was. Note that many smaller *hostales* and *pensiones* are closed in Aug, the traditional holiday month. Strangely, Madrid has few hotels which are truly charming, and even fewer which offer charm at an affordable price. Exterior rooms are usually sunnier and noisier, while interior rooms are stuffier but a bit quieter. Ear plugs are pretty much essential.

In general, most moderate to inexpensive accommodation is clustered in the nightlife areas around the Plaza Santa Ana, or north of the Gran Vía in Chueca and Malasaña. Smart Salamanca has the upmarket business hotels and a few chi-chi little boutique hotels, and the area around the Plaza Mayor and the Royal Palace mainly offers traditional hotels in the moderate to expensive price range. La Latina and Lavapiés have little in the way of accommodation as yet, but now that gentrification has well and truly set in, it can only be a matter of time.

Old Madrid *p71, map p72 and p76*

C HH Campomanes, C/Campomanes 4, T915488548, www.hhcampomanes.com. A far cry from the pseudo-rustic decor of most small hotels; this boasts ultra-slick throughout, charming staff, perfect central location, and a very reasonable price.

A highly recommended option.
C Hospedaje Madrid, C/Esparteros 6, T915220060, www.hospedajemadrid.com. To the east of the Plaza Mayor, this friendly, welcoming *hostal* has been completely overhauled and now offers modern, attractive rooms decorated with pine or wrought iron furniture. En suite bathrooms with hairdryers, a/c, and TVs.
D Hostal Las Fuentes, C/ Las Fuentes 10, T915421853, reserva@hostallasfuentes.com. This opened a couple of years ago and everything is still nice and new; the best rooms overlook the street and have little balconies. The is fairly typical – chintz and dark wood – and the service is friendly.
D Hostal Valencia, Plaza de Oriente 23, T915598450. Incomparable views over the Plaza de Oriente towards the Royal Palace, and a charming welcome from the owner, an ex-ballerina. Rooms are basic, with old-fashioned decor, but spotlessly clean.
E Hostal Conchita, C/Preciados 33, T915224923, and **Hostal Conchita II**, C/Campomanes 10, T915475061. Recently completely refurbished, both these *hostales* offer remarkably good value for money. Rooms are equipped with bathrooms and fridges, and are very centrally located. An excellent choice for budget travellers.
E Hostal Pinariega, C/ Santiago 1, T629351554, pinariega@hostalpinariega. com. This gem of a *hostal* is tastefully decorated with antiques and unusual artworks. Rooms with and without

● *For an explanation of sleeping and eating price codes used in this guide, see inside the* ● *front cover. Other relevant information is found in Essentials, see pages 47-56.*

bathrooms and charming service. Excellent value, too.

E Hostal Valencia, C/Espoz y Mina 7, T915211845. Small, extremely friendly *hostal* which is geared towards younger travellers and has extras like a fridge and washing machine available for guests. All rooms are en suite and brightly decorated.

Plaza de Santa Ana and around *p80, map p72 and p76*

LL Hotel Palace, Plaza de las Cortes 7, T913608000, www.palacemadrid.com. Dripping with chandeliers and crawling with liveried footman, this sumptuous Belle Epoque style offers luxury on a grand scale. It's perfectly located for the three big museums of the Paseo del Arte.

LL Tryp Ambassador, Cuesta de Santo Domingo 5, T915416700, ambassador@tryp net.com. A chain, but set in the magnificent former palace of the Duques de Granada; many of the original fittings have been retained, although the well-equipped rooms are blandly decorated in universal chain hotel style.

LL Villa Real, Plaza de las Cortes 10, T914203767, www.derbyhotels.es. Chic boutique-style hotel, with large, ochre-painted rooms decorated with a stylish mix of antiques and modern art and sculpture. Two fine restaurants (East 47 does excellent gourmet tapas), a sauna and gym. Suites are available with jacuzzis.

L Tryp Reina Victoria, Plaza de Santa Ana 14, T915314500, F915220307. A famous Belle Epoque-style hotel which looks like it should be by the seaside. Historically, bullfighters have always stayed here and there is a plaque to Manolete at the entrance.

D Hostal Adriano, C/Cruz 26, T/F912090207, www.hostaladriano.com. Newly opened *hostal* which offers fantastic amenities for budget travellers; free internet access from all rooms (with your own laptop), as well as phones, and fridges. Sunny rooms with cheerful, brightly painted walls and modern furnishings. Highly recommended.

D Hostel Astoria, C/Carrera de San Jerónimo 30-32, T914291188, info@hostal-astoria.com. High up on the 5th floor of a lovely 19th-century building, this is a very comfortable *hostal* with attractive rooms

decorated with light floral prints, en suite bathrooms with hairdryers, efficient staff.

D Hostel Cervantes, C/Cervantes 34, T914298365, www.hostal-cer vantes.com. This *hostal* is a big favourite because the friendly owners have succeeded in making it feel like a home away from home. There's a cosy lounge, each room has been decorated with pretty blue prints and have en suites.

D Hostel Jaen, C/Cervantes 5, T914294858, www.hjaen.com. This hostel is a little plusher than the usual barebones style and the owners are extremely helpful. It's located on a quiet street and, best of all, it offers 3 apartments at very good rates (apartments from €60 per night).

D Hostal Plaza d'Ort, Plaza del Ángel, 13, T914299041, info@plaza dort.com. Right next door to the bigger and better known **Persal**, this good-value *hostal* makes a point of offering exceptionally good service in order to compete. Rooms are decorated in typical hostal chintz, but they are very well-equipped with internet access, TV and video, and a/c.

F Hostal Fonda Horizonte, C/Atocha 28, 2ºB, T913690996, www.hostalhorizonte.com. Run by a delightful brother and sister team, Julio and María-Begoña, this is a friendly little *hostal*, offering charming rooms with and without bathrooms. The nicest is sunny room 8, which has a plant-filled balcony; No 15 is quiet, and has a wonderful canopied bed and a large bathroom.

Prado and Triangulo del Arte *p82, map p72 and p76*

D Hotel Mora, Paseo del Prado 32, T914200564, F914291569. Simple hotel which is much sought-after for its perfect location just opposite the Botanic Gardens and the Prado. Rooms were renovated a couple of years ago and are clean and bright.

E HsR La Coruña, Paseo del Prado 12, T914292543. Closed Aug. Tiny, friendly little *pensión* within a stone's throw of the Prado. 6 spotless rooms sharing 2 bathrooms.

Gran Vía, Chueca and Malasaña *p92, map p72 and p76*

LL Hotel Atlántico, Gran Vía, 38, T915226480, F915310210. This large hotel is set in a 19th-

century mansion slap bang in the middle of the Gran Vía. Each room is individually decorated and staff are very attentive.
LL Hotel Emperador, Gran Via 53, T915472800, hemperador@sei.es. A very popular, centrally located hotel with elegant original fittings and a stunning rooftop pool.
LL Hotel Ritz, Plaza de la Lealtad 5, T9170-16767, www.ritz.es. Madrid's Grande Dame of the hotel world, this lavish, creamy confection has a wonderful setting right by the Prado. Pure luxury, with a fine restaurant and chic cocktail bar which was a favourite with Dalí. The leafy terrace with thickly cushioned wicker chairs is a delight in summer.
D Hostal Hispano Argentino, Gran Vía 15, 6th floor, T915322448, info@hispano-argen tino.com. Stuffed with knick-knacks and plants, this cheerful *hostal* is located in a beautiful 19th-century building on the Gran Vía. Rooms have bright bed covers plenty of prints and dried flowers. Triples are also available. Very helpful staff.
D Hostel Lauria, Gran Vía 50, T915419182, hostallauria@eresmas.com. Friendly staff and a great location – the views from the sitting room are amazing. The best rooms (all with bathrooms) face out and also have extraordinary views.

La Latina and Lavapiés *p89, map p72 and p76*

E Hostal El Barco, C/Mesón de Paredes 9, T915398066. A small, perfectly adequate cheapie tucked away on a quiet street.

Rooms are basic but clean – the nicest have balconies overlooking the street. Good for the alternative nightlife of La Latina and Lavapiés.

Salamanca *p96, map p72 and p76*

LL Hotel Orfila, C/Orfila 6, T917027770, www.hotelorfila.com. Converted from a luxurious 19th-century mansion, the **Hotel Orfila** offers discreet 5-star luxury (it's part of the prestigious **Relais** and **Chateaux** group) and has just 28 rooms and 4 suites, all decorated individually in a modern take on 19th-century style. There's a beautiful, flower-scented terrace, a charming *salon de té*, and a renowned restaurant. One of the most charming hotels in the city.
LL Hotel Santo Mauro, C/Zurbano 36, T913196900, www.ac-hoteles.com. This is a favourite with visiting celebrities who want to avoid the public gaze. Each room in this charming 19th- century mansion has been individually decorated, many in a slick minimalist style. Beautiful public areas with plump sofas and antique fireplaces, tree-filled gardens and a large pool. There's a handsome restaurant set in the former library.
B Residencia de El Viso, C/Nervión 8, T915640370, F915641965. This is pretty, pink hotel built in the 1930s and set in a quiet residential area. There are just 12 rooms, which have all been completely modernized and are simple, if a little small. There's a delightful garden and a fine restaurant.

🍴 Eating

Madrid, as you would expect from a major European city, offers a huge choice of eateries from Argentine steaks to Japanese sushi. Reservations are essential for virtually every restaurant featured, especially at weekends. Madrileños eat breakfast on the run, usually a milky coffee and a pastry at around 0730 or 0800. They might leave the office for a plate of *churros* (curls of fried donut-like batter) dipped in a thick hot chocolate at around 1000. Lunch is eaten late, usually around 1430, with perhaps some tapas after work at around 1900 or 2000. Dinner is rarely eaten before 2200.

Old Madrid *p70, map p72 and p76*

Restaurants
€€€ **Al Norte**, C/San Nicolás 8, T915472222, metro Opera. Closed Sun night. Ultra-modern, sleek new restaurant, serving specialities from Spain's Atlantic coast, with plenty of deliciously fresh seafood and vegetables. *Menú del día* at around €12, and a fine wine list. There's a shady terrace, too.
€€€ **La Taberna del Alaberdero**, C/Felipe V, T915415192, metro Opera. Open daily 1300-1600, 2100-2400. Just off the Plaza del Oriente, with a small *terrazza* in summer, this

celebrated restaurant serves exquisite Basque cuisine; splash out on the 5-course *menú del degustación*. A wide variety of tapas and *raciones* are available in the bar.

€€**Casa Botín**, C/Cuchilleros 17, T013664217, metro Sol. This rambling, stone-built restaurant tucked into what was once the city walls is the oldest restaurant in Madrid (founded in 1725). It's touristy, but it's still one of the best places to try the Madileño speciality of *cochinillo* – roast suckling pig.

€€**Casa Paco**, Plaza Puerta Cerrada 11, T913663166, metro La Latina. Closed Sun and Aug. A resolutely old-fashioned tiled bar with a restaurant at the back. Dignified waiters in long aprons serve traditional sizzling grilled meats, accompanied by a good selection of Spanish wines. Black and white photographs show the founder posing with everyone from Catherine Deneuve to the King of Spain. Simple tapas are available at the bar.

€€**Cornucopia**, C/Flora 1, T915476465, metro Opera. Closed Mon and for a fortnight in Aug. Tucked away in an old mansion, this colourful, quirky restaurant is a real find: sunshine-yellow walls, a deep blue ceiling, changing art exhibits, crisp white tablecloths, and fresh flowers on the tables. It's Spanish-American owned, and serves modern European food (and always a vegetarian choice), and sublime desserts – don't miss the strawberry mousse. *Menu del día* at €10.

Tapas bars and cafés

Recently, a number of smart tapas bars offering a range of gourmet tapas have sprung up, particularly in the Los Austrias.

Café de los Austrias, Plaza de Ramales 1, T915598436, Mon-Thu 0900-0130, Fri-Sat 0900-0230, Sun 0900-2400, metro Opera. Large, old-fashioned café-bar with marble columns and mirrors which is very popular with locals. Perfect spot to while away an afternoon or three.

Café de Oriente, Plaza Oriente 2, T915413974, daily 0930-0130, until 0230 on Fri and Sat, metro Opera. Famous, chic café with a large terrace overlooking the square and the royal palace. There's an expensive restaurant, too, if you want to splash out for a special occasion.

Café La Union, C/Union 1, T915425563. 1700-0300, until late on Fri and Sat, Sun

1700-0130, metro Opera. Stylish, airy café with changing art exhibitions, friendly staff and a mellow atmosphere – great place for a chat at any time. Fantastic *mojitos* – among the best in Madrid.

Inshalá, C/Amnistía 10, T915482632, 1200-until 0300 on Sat. Closed Sun. Metro opera. Trendy, mellow Moroccan-style tearoom and bar with mosaiced tables, wall hangings, lanterns and candles, and cushioned benches. Delicious cous cous dishes, as well as a special from a different country each day. Live music on Fri. *Menú del día* for €7.50.

Taberna del Cruzado, C/Amnistía 8, T915480131, daily 1300-1600, 2000-2400, until 0030 on Fri and Sat, closed Tue evening. Metro Opera. This has a beautiful carved wooden bar, dark red and cream walls, and charming staff. Among the unusual tapas are fried oyster mushrooms served with aioli, a kind of creamy garlic dip.

Plaza de Santa Ana and around *p80, map p72 and 76*

Restaurants

€€€**Champanería Gala**, C/Moratín 22, T914292562, metro Antón Martín. Valencian rice dishes including fantastic paella, served in a beautiful, glassy patio filled with plants and flowers. *Menú del día* is excellent value.

€€€**Gula Gula**, C/Infante 5, T914202919. Hip, modern restaurant tucked down a sidestreet serving buffet-style lunches plus à la carte options in the evening. The food is great and reasonably priced, but it's the crazy drag-queen cabaret acts in the evenings which are the big draw. (There's another, larger branch at Gran Vía 1.)

€€€-€**El Txoko**, C/Jovellanos 3, T915323443, Tue-Sat 1200-2300, Sun 1200-1500. Food served from 1400. Behind Cortes. Basque cuisine is celebrated throughout Spain, and the basement of the Euskal Etxea (Basque Cultural Centre) is a great place for a delicious, budget lunch (*menú del día* €8), or some *pintxos* – pieces of French bread with toppings – at the bar. For a real splurge, go to the 1st-floor restaurant **Erroto-Zar**.

€**La Biotika**, C/Amor de Dios 3, T914290780, metro Antón Martín. Bright and airy café serving tasty vegetarian food, with

plenty of dishes featuring seitan and tofu. *Menú del día* at just €7.50.

Tapas bars and cafés

The tapeo – a kind of bar crawl from tapas bar to tapas bar – is an institution in Madrid. **Bar Manolo**, C/Jovellanes 7, T915214526, daily except Sun and Mon evening 0830-2400. This old- fashioned local just behind the Cortes and in front of the Teatro de Zarzuela is a big favourite with local politicians and journalists, who huddle together in the little dining room at the back. The big thing here is *croquetas* – they are among the best in the city.

Casa Alberto, C/Huertas 18, T914299356, www.casaalberto.es. Open 1300-2400. Established in 1827, nothing much has changed at this steadfastly traditional tapas bar and restaurant. Friendly waiters in long white aprons scuttle efficiently between low wooden tables, and the walls are covered in kitsch paintings and old black and white photos of football teams and matadors. The house speciality is *cazuela rabo de toro* – ox tail stew, and the albondigas (meatballs) also come highly recommended.

Cervecería La Moderna, Plaza Santa Ana 12, T914201582, metro Sol. Mon-Thu 1200-2430. Most of the bars around here cultivate an 'olde worlde' charm, but La Moderna is unabashedly bright and modern. A great selection of wines and tasty, high quality tapas – try the marinated artichokes, or the platter of farmhouse cheeses. Summer terrace overlooking the square.

La Dolores, Plaza de Jésus 4, T914292243, open until 0100. Beautiful, century-old tiled tapas bar – one of the most *típico* in the city, and always jam-packed.

La Fábrica, C/Jesús 2, T913690671, 1100-0100. A cheerful, down to earth locals' bar with bright orange walls and a massive range of tapas. The counters groan with a dizzying array of canapés – slices of French bread loaded with all kinds of toppings from smoked salmon to cheese and quince jelly – and an octopus steams away on top of the counter.

La Luiza, Plaza Santa Ana 2, T915210811, metro Sol, Mon-Thu 0700-2400, Fri-Sat 0800-0200, Sun 0800-2400. Delightful, old-fashioned pastry shop with just a few tables. A great place for breakfast – a creamy

café con leche and a sweet croissant or *ensaïmada*.

Las Bravas, C/Espoz y Mina 13, T915322620. This is the home of *patatas bravas* – fried potatoes served with a (patented) sickly pinkish sauce. Neon-lit and garish, it's strictly for fast-food lovers -but the elderly waiters in their orange overalls are a cheerful bunch. Four branches, all within a few metres of each other.

Prado and Triangulo del Arte *p82, map p72 and p76*

Restaurants

€€€ **Viridiana**, C/Juan de Mena 14, T915234478, metro Banco de España. Closed Sun, holidays and Aug. A survivor from the Movida years, this is one of Madrid's chicest and slickest restaurants – with prices to match. Abraham García's imaginative Spanish cuisine is justly renowned, as is the excellent wine list.

Tapas bars and cafés

Hotel Ritz, Plaza de la Lealtad 5, T9152-12857, metro Banco de España. Treat yourself to tea at the Ritz; sink into a plush wicker chair in the enclosed gardens and forget the hoi polloi outside.

La Platería, C/Moratín 49, T914291722, metro Atocha or Banco de España. Open til 0200. A relaxed, stylish tapas bar right across from the Prado, which overlooks a small square. It's enormously popular so get there early if you want a seat on the shady terrace.

La Latina and Lavapíes *p89, map p72 and p76*

Restaurants

€€€ **Casa Lucio**, Cava Baja 35, T913653252, metro La Latina, closed sat lunchtimes and Aug. Celebrated, typically Madrileño restaurant which is so popular, it's had to open another dining area across the street. The original space is the most atmospheric; this is the place to try madrid-style tripe, or *cocido*.

€€ **Palacio de Anglona**, C/Segovia 14, T913663753, metro La Latina. Fashionable, very reasonably priced restaurant set in a 19th-century palace, but with sleek,

pared-down decor. Grilled meats, pasta dishes and unusual salads.

€ **El Estragón**, Plaza de la Paja 10, T913658992, metro La Latina. Friendly, pretty vegetarian restaurant set over several levels overlooking one of Madrid's loveliest squares. The food is very creative, using unusual combinations of ingredients.

€ **Entrecajas**, C/Moreria 11, T913651214, metro La Latina, Tue-Sun 1300-late. Cool, minimalist decor with plenty of dark wood and chrome; attentive, friendly staff and excellent Mediterranean food (plenty for vegetarians) including fantastic salads and scrumptious desserts. Very good value.

€ **La Falsa Molestia**, C/Magdalena 32, T914203238, metro Antón Martín, www.lafalsamolestia.com. Closed Mon and Tue. Slick, arty café-restaurant-bar serving light, fresh Italian dishes and delectable home-made desserts. Unusually, they feature a water list as well as a wine list. Good music, charming (and preternaturally handsome) Italian staff, and excellent coffee – perhaps the best place to chill in the city.

€ **La Musa Latina**, Costanilla de San Andrés 12, T913540255, metro La Latina, open Mon-Wed 0900-2400, Thu 0900-0100, Fri and Sat 1300-0200. This newly opened huge, stylish restaurant-café-tapas bar is right on Plaza de la Paja. New York loft meets the Far East in the decor, and the food is equally eclectic and extremely good. There's an excellent *menú del día* at €8.

Tapas bars and cafés

Café Barbieri, C/Ave Jesús María 45, T915273658, metro Lavapiés. Sun-Thu 1500-0200, Fri-Sat 1500-0300. Oozing turn-of-the-century charm, and filled with burnished mirrors and battered wooden tables. The classical music and sheaf of newspapers make it the perfect spot to while away the afternoooon.

Casa Montes, C/Lavapies 40, T915270064, metro Lavapiés. Daily 1200-1600, 1930-2400, Sun 1200-1600. Closed Mon and Aug. Tiny neighbourhood bar which hasn't changed in decades; excellent range of wines served with tasty tapas like cured meats and farmhouse cheeses. In summer, people spill out onto the square.

Champañería Libreria, Plaza Gabriel Miró 1, Las Vistillas, T913662370, metro La Latina. This relaxed café-bar is decked out like an old Parisian café, with a little 'library' in one section, complete with sofa, standard lamp and piano. It gets livelier at night.

Ciné Doré, C/Santa Isalel 3, T913694923, metro Antón Martín. 1600-2400, closed Mon. This pretty café attached to the art deco cinema has a terrace where films are shown on summer evenings. Good salads and snacks.

La Carpanta, C/Almendro 22, T913665783, metro La Latina. Closed Mon and Tue am in summer, open until 0130, 0230 on Fri and Sat. Stylish, hugely popular tapas bar with a dining area at the back, quirky wooden furnishings, paddle fans and old brick walls. Run by a famous Madrileño family of actors.

Taberna Almendro, C/Almendro 13, T913654252, metro La Latina. 1300-1600 and 1900-1200. Old-fashioned, friendly spot with ochre walls hung with wooden racks full of sherry glasses and oak barrels for tables; house specialities include roscas (a kind of round, well stuffed sandwich) and, more surprisingly, egg, bacon and chips (a great hangover cure). Excellent olives, too.

Taberna Tempranillo, Cava Baja 38, T913641532, closed Holy Week and Aug, metro La Latina. 1200-1600 and 2000-0100. A paddle fan flaps lazily, and there's a vast wall of wine bottles behind the bar. An excellent selection of wines, including weekly specials, and a good (if pricey) menu of cured meats and regional cheeses, including a contender for smelliest cheese ever – La Perbal from Asturias.

Gran Vía, Chueca and Malasaña *p92, map p72 and p76*

Restaurants

€€€ **El Armario**, C/San Bartolomé 7, T915328377, metro Chueca. Excellent cuisine, kinky decor and drag shows. Mainly gay clientele. Good-value lunch menu, but prices are more expensive in the evenings.

€€€ **La Castafiore**, C/Barquillo 30, T915322100, metro Chueca. Elegant and traditional, but entirely unstuffy, this charming restaurant features Basque cuisine; the food is excellent but the real draw is the

Madrid & around Eating

● *For an explanation of sleeping and eating price codes used in this guide, see inside the*
● *front cover. Other relevant information is found in Essentials, see pages 47-56.*

waiters, who break into snatches of opera and *zarzuela* at weekends.

€ **Bluefish**, C/San Andres 26, T914486765, metro Bilbao. Tue-Sat 1300-0100, Sun 0100-1800. A zinc counter curves around the deep blue and scarlet bar, and the candle-lit lounge area at the back has deep, comfy seats. Delicious food, an excellent value 3-course *menú del día* (around €8), and US-style brunches at weekends. A very hip crowd come for the excellent cocktails in the evenings.

€ **La Isla del Tesoro**, C/Manuel Malasaña 3, T915931440, metro Bilbao. Closed Sun and lunchtimes during holidays. Exotic bamboo screens, sea shells and deep blue walls make this a wonderfully romantic spot; it's vegetarian, and the well-priced *menú del día* (€8.50) features the cuisine of a different country each day.

€ **Sarrasín**, C/ Libertad 8, T915327348, metro Chueca. Closed Mon. Welcoming, stylish gay-run café and restaurant , which is very popular for its set priced menus which are available at lunchtimes and in the evenings. Book in advance.

Tapas bars and cafés

Bar Casa do Compañeiro, C/San Vicente Ferrern 44, T915215702. Home to Alberto the parokeet, this is a tiled, slightly battered old tapas bar run by a friendly Galician family. There's plenty of *pulpo* (octopus) and other fish on the menu, and they also serve crisp, cold *vermut* from the barrel.

Bodegas de Ángel Sierra, C/Gravina 11, T935310126, metro Chueca. 1030-1600 and 1900-2300. Ancient, delightfully old-fashioned bar with battered dark wooden fittings and a marble counter; *vermut* on tap, perfectly accompanied with a *tapa* of anchovy and olive.

Café Acuarela, C/Gravina 10, T915222143, metro Chueca. Nymphs, cherubs, candle light and candelabra; great cocktails. Get there early to get a seat. Gay-run with a mixed gay/straight crowd.

Café Comercial, Glorieta de Bilbao 7, T915215655, metro Bilbao. Daily 0730-0100 until 0200 Fri and Sat. Huge, famous, scruffy old café with outdoor tables in summer, mirrors and marble-topped tables; there's an internet area upstairs, too.

Café de Ruiz, C/Ruiz 11, T914461232, metro

Bilbao. 1230-0230. A local institution, set in a series of small salons, with plush sofas, low lighting and dark wooden fittings. Good for cakes, coffee and cocktails.

Café Figueroa, C/Augusto Figueroa 17, T915211673. Til 0230 at weekends. An elegant 19th-century café which has become a classic on the gay scene – a great first-stop in Madrid.

Café Manuela, C/San Vicente Ferrer 29, T915317037, metro Tribunal. Mon-Thu 1800-0200, Fri-Sun 1600-0230. Large, lush Art Nouveau-style café, live music, story-telling nights, poetry readings and *tertulias*.

El Jardín Secreto, C/Conde Duque 2, T915418023, metro Plaza de España. Mon-Thu 1730-0100, Fri-Sat 1800-0230, Sun 1700-2400. Magical, tranquil café with rattan furniture and a scattering of shells, candles, and hazy drapes. Occasionally marred by terrible music.

El Pez Gordo, C/Pex 6, T915223208, metro Noviciado. Mon-Sat 2000-0130, until 0230 Fri and Sat. Fat Fish (which in Spanish means something like our the Big Cheese) is a fairly ordinary tapas bar made extraordinary by its delicious food and its entertaining and very theatrical clientele.

La Musa, C/Manuela Malasaña 18, T91487558, metro Bilbao. Hugely popular with a young, lively crowd, this cellar tapas bar serves up excellent and very imaginative tapas and *raciones*.

Salamanca *p96, map p72 and p76*

Restaurants

€€€ **Zalacaín**, C/Alvarez de Baena 4, T915614840, metro Gregorio Marañón. Closed sat lunchtimes, Sun, holidays, Holy Week, Aug. Madrid's most celebrated restaurant, holder of all kinds of stars and awards. Chef Benjamín Urdiaín can't put a foot wrong, it seems; cuisine, service and decor ooze elegance and assurance.

€€ **Paradis Casa-América**, Paseo de Recoletos 2, T915754540, metro Banco de España, closed Sat lunchtimes, Sun and holidays. Located in the Palacio de Linares, this attractive tiled restaurant with a leafy summer terrace is a favourite with businessmen at lunchtimes, when it serves a good-value *menú del día*. Rice dishes are the house speciality.

€€ **Teatriz**, C/Hermosilla 15, T915775379, metro Serrano. Philip Starck and Javier Mariscal famously converted this theatre during the last years of La Movida and it's still a place to see and be seen. Regardless of all the hype, the Italian food is very good.

€€ **Thai Gardens**, C/Jorge Juan 5, T915778884, open until 0100 at weekends. Beautiful, deeply romantic restaurant decorated with traditional Thai crafts and silks; the finest Thai food in Madrid.

€ **La Fromagerie**, C/Salustiano Olózaga 5, T914319519, metro Retiro. Closed Aug, evenings, and weekends. Typical, old-fashioned basement Madrileño bar, serving a good value *menú del día* to local workers.

Tapas bars and cafés

Café del Espejo, Paseo de Recoletos 33, T913082347, metro Colón. 1030-0100, closed Sat lunch. It may look the part, but this café is in fact a recent arrival. The art nouveau-style swirls may be fake, but it's still a beautiful.

Café Gijón, Paseo de Recoletos 21, T915215425, metro Banco de España. One of the oldest and loveliest cafés in Madrid, still haunted by the ghosts of 19th-century *tertulias*. Tapas, *raciones* and meals are also available.

Embassy, C/ Castellana, 12, T915756633, metro Colón. 0930-0100. This chi chi delicatessen also has a delightful café where you can tuck into cakes with the ladies who lunch.

La Taberna del Buey, C/General Pardiñas 7, T915781154, metro Serrano. 1300-16000 and 1930-2400. Swish, upmarket bar serving high-quality Basque tapas including *pinxos* – bread with toppings – and oxtail *albóndigas* (meatballs). There's also a dining area.

Los Timbales, C/Alcalá 227, T917250768, metro Ventas. Crammed with bull-fighting memorabilia, this is the classic stop-off before or after a *corrida*. Good tapas, including the house speciality, *timbales* or pies stuffed with meat or cheese, and a terrace in summer.

🍷 Bars and clubs

Madrid's legendary nightlife may have gone off the boil since the giddy days of La Movida, but it's still among the best in Europe. The club scene is raging, with international DJs as well as plenty of homegrown ones, and there's something for everyone. The city council have been doing their best for the last few years to stamp out the so-called 'after hours' clubs which carried on when the regular clubs were closing their doors at dawn, but it's still perfectly possible to start dancing on Fri night and not stop until Mon morning. Most of the really big clubs can be found along the Gran Vía and the Paseo Castellano, but Madrid also has hundreds of *discobares*, bars with DJs and small dance floors, spread all over the city.

To get the latest, visit www.clubbingin spain.com, which has listings for upcoming events and club nights.

Old Madrid *p71, map p72 and p76*

El 21, C/Toledo 21, T913662859, metro Sol. Dusty old-fashioned bar with fading bullfighting posters and a crowd of elderly regulars. It's become an institution with

bright young things getting ready for the long night ahead.

El Cañi, C/Santiago 11, T915411255. Metro Opera. Fantastic, super-friendly neighbourhood bar, crammed with paintings and cartoons by the charismatic owner Julio. It's the kind of bar where anything can happen – an impromptu flamenco performance, a tap dance, or a sing-along session. Great fun.

Joy Eslava, C/Arenal 11, T913663733. Metro Opera. This converted theatre became one of the biggest clubs of the Movida years. The fashion pack have moved on but it's still fun for an over-the-top night out.

Kathmandu, C/Señores de Luzón 3, T9163-44201. Metro Sol and Opera. Great funk, friendly crowd, and cool DJs at this groovy, red-painted subterranean bar and club.

Palacio Gaviria, C/Arenal 9, T915266069, metro Opéra. A stunning palace with several high-ceilinged salons, dripping in frescoes and cherubs, each devoted to a different kind of music. Dance music and go go dancers at weekends, but each week night has a different speciality – tango Wed.

⁝ One-stop-shop…

Some of the hippest new places on the Madrid scene are the slickly designed restaurant-bar-club combos. These are some of the best:
Suite Café-Club, C/Virgen de los Peligros 4, T91521 4031. Metro Sevilla. Plenty of film stars at this favourite with the so-cool-it-hurts crowd; sharp 70s-style decor, good global fusion cuisine in the restaurant, cool ambient sounds on one dance floor and deep house on the other.
Larios Café, C/Silva, 4, T915479394. Metro Santo Domingo or Callao. Gorgeous, award-winning art deco-esque interior; Cuban food in the restaurant and salsa, flamenco and funk on the dancefloor.
Lolita Lounge And Bar, C/Manuel Falla 3, T913441156, www.lolita lounge.net. Metro Santiago Bernabeu. Sushi bar, cocktails and two floors of dance music – everything from 70s classics to UK and Spanish house and garage. Worth dressing up for.
Alquimia, C/ Villanueva 2, T915772785. Metro Retiro. Lounge about in deep leather sofas, or dine in faux-Gothic splendour. Wear your Manolos.

Plaza de Santa Ana and around *p80, map p72 and p76*

Cardamomo, C/Echegaray 15, T913690757, metro Sevilla, daily 2100-0400. Despite its dated look – all vintage posters and fake memorabilia – this is a cool spot which offers regular live music, including some excellent jazz, flamenco and salsa.
El Parnasón, C/Moratín 25, T914201975, metro Anton Martín. Dim, tiny, deeply romantic bar crammed with bizarre bric-a-brac; there's a red velvet salon at the back and the fantastic cocktails are served in goldfish bowls (well, nearly).
Oui, C/Cervantes 7, T915218415, metro Antón Martín. Closed Mon, Tue. Laid-back, low-lit lounge bar where you can chill out with a cocktail on a cushioned banquette. Regular DJs at weekends, when the bar is crammed.
Villa Rosa, Plaza Santa Ana 15, T915213689. Metro Sol or Sevilla. Closed Sun. Former flamenco tablao is covered in colourful tiles inside and out. Mixed, fun crowd and eclectic music.
Viva Madrid, C/Fernandez Gonzalez 7, T915213640, metro Sol or Sevilla. Huge, beautifully tiled bar on 2 levels, with paddle fans, some simple tapas, and DJ sessions at weekends. An ex-pat favourite, with a summer terrace and pricey drinks.

Prado and Triangulo del Arte *p82, map p72 and p76*

Garamond, C/Claudio Coello 10, T91578-1974. Metro Retiro. A favourite with thesps and TV celebrities, this is a chi chi cocktail bar and disco, with occasionally live music.
Kapital, C/Atocha 125, T914202906, metro Atocha, Fri-Sun and public holidays 1730-2300, 2400-0600. Huge, fun, mega-club on 6 floors, with a roof-top *terraza* (and cinema and karaoke bar). Early sessions are aimed at teens.
La Divina Comedia, C/Almaden 14, closed Mon, Tue. Metro Atocha. Cool, candle-lit bar with lamps made from popcorn boxes and deep ochre walls. The Mexican owner mixes a mean margarita.

La Latina and Lavapiés *p89, map p72 and p76*

Bar Baridad, Costanillo de San Pedro 7, T913641882. Metro La Latina. Tiny, delightfully quirky café-bar with lamps made from buckets, and a skeleton under the floor.
Danzoo (at Maximes), Puerta de Toledo 1, Fri and Sat only. Hugely popular club night – mainly electronica sounds, friendly up-for-it crowd and plenty of room.
Delic, Costanilla de San Andrés, Plaza de Paja 14, T913645450. Metro La Latina. Closed Sun, Mon. This retro-looking spot is a relaxing

café by day and a busy, very stylish bar by night.

El Bonnano, Plaza Humilladero 4, metro La Latina, T913666886. There's always a trendy young crowd propping up this little bar overlooking the wide square. Bright modern art hangs on the walls, some basic snacks and a mellow soundtrack.

El Mojito, C/Olmo 6, metro Lavapiés. Excellent music, lively gay/mixed crowd, a popular spot with the fashion pack.

La Falsa Molestia, C/Magdalena 32, T9142-03238, metro Antón Martín, www.lafalsa molestia.com. Closed Mon and Tue. Quirky, ultra-stylish bar and restaurant, with extremely charming staff and mellow music.

La Ventura, C/Olmo 31, T914680454, metro Antón Martín. You'd never think it from the outside, but this is one of the best places to hear Madrid's top DJs spinning drum 'n' bass, electronica and trip hop. The word is out, and it's always packed with a mixed international crowd.

Gran Vía, Chueca and Malasaña p92, map p72 and p76

Café Antik, C/Hortaleza 4, T915222143, metro Gran Vía. This flamboyant, quirkily decorated cocktail bar is painted in eye-popping colours and specializes in Caribbean cocktails like caipirinhas and mojitos.

Café del Mercado, C/Fuencarral 43, metro Tribunal. Young trendies pack out this bar in the basement of the Mercado de Fuencarral shopping complex (see p100). Great sofas.

Café Oliver, C/Almirante 12, T915217379. Metro Banco de España. Upstairs is a chic French bistro, downstairs is the lounge bar, full of beautiful people sipping expertly mixed cocktails.

Camp, C/Marqués de Valdeiglesias 6, T915319215, metro Chueca. Closed Sun-Thu. Superbly chic, glassy café-bar full of self-consciously beautiful people reclining on 70s style furniture. Attracts a mixed crowd.

Chicote, Gran Vía 12, T915326737. Metro Gran Vía. Closed Sun. The grandaddy of all Madrileño cocktail bars, famously a favourite with Ava Gardner and Frank Sinatra. Chicote has preserved its stunning art deco decor and its impossibly glamorous air. Lounge music after midnight – more info at www.tripfamily.com.

Cock, C/Reina 16, T915322826. Begun by a bar tender trained at Chicote, Cock is equally glamorous and chi chi. Order the speciality of the house – an exquisite gin fizz.

Coppelia, Plaza Mostenses 11 (corner of Gran Vía 68), T915475711. Fri and Sat only. Buzzing club playing deep house and techno on the main dance floor, with trancier sounds in a smaller room. Excellent resident DJs who know how to work the crowd.

El Café de la Palma, C/Palma 62, T915225031, www.cafedelapalma.net. Metro Noviciado. Excellent chill-out area at the back, comfortable booths in the main area and regular live gigs. Café and bar.

Flamingo/Shangay Tea Dance, C/Mesonero Romanos 13, T915321524. Metro Callao or Gran Via. Flamingo has some of the best club nights in Madrid, including the gay/drag Shangay Tea Dance. Don't miss the Goa after hours club which runs from 0600-1030 on Sat and Sun mornings.

La Coctelería, C/Minas 1, metro Noviciado, open 1800-0200. Thrift-store chic, excellent cocktails and a mellow, loungey soundtrack at this stylish hang-out.

La Ida, C/Colón 11, T915229107, metro Tribunal. Relaxed, arty little café-bar which serves fantastic tea and cakes by day, and gets packed out in the evenings and at weekends.

Ministry of Sound at Macumba, Plaza Estación de Chamartín, metro Chamartín. Once a month, Thu 2400-0600. The Ministry of Sound's glamorous, once-a-month party has become a massive hit on the Madrileño dance scene.

Star's Café, C/Marqués de Valdeiglesias 5, T915222712, www.starscafedance.com. Closed Sun. Metro Chueca. Glitzy, gay-friendly and muy fashionable bar-café-restaurant with live music during the week and hugely popular guest DJs at weekends.

The Room at Stella, C/Arlabán 7, T915327833. Fri, Sat only. Metro Noviciado and Plaza de España. This massively popular club night is held in Stella, one of the big stars of the Movida, which has just been dramatically refurbished. One of the best nights out in the city.

Week End/Ohm/Bash, Plaza Callao 4, Metro Callao. Same place, different club nights. One of the best venues in Madrid, with pumping

music, go go dancers, and a gay/mixed, slickly dressed clientele.

Salamanca *p96, map p72 and p76*

Déjate Besar, C/Hermanos Bácquer 10, T915625485. Closed Sun, Sun-Wed in Aug.

Metro Núñez de Balboa. Flashy decor with leopard skin sofas and movie star paraphernalia, a mixed crowd, and excellent music.
Teatríz, C/Hermosilla 15, T915775379, metro Serrano. Philip Starck's and Mariscal's designer bar set in a converted theatre. One of the best-known in the city.

🍸 Entertainment

The weekly guide *La Guia del Ocio* (Spanish only) is available from kiosks and has extensive theatre, music and opera listings. It's pretty good for live music too, but downright rubbish when it comes to clubs and bars. For what's going on in Madrid's ever-changing nightlife, get flyers from the Mercado del Fuencarral (see below) or pick up a copy of the English-language monthly newspaper InMadrid which reviews bars and clubs in English. The free *What's On* guide from the tourist office has some cultural listings in English. On Fridays, *El Mundo* and *ABC* both produce entertainment supplements which can be useful, and you can pick up the freebie *LaNetro* in most shops (all in Spanish).

Cinemas

The cinema is cheap by most European standards, and is cheaper still on the *día del espectador* ('spectator's day'), usually Mon or Wed.
Cinesa Capitol, Gran Vía 41, T902333231, metro Callao. One of several beautiful old cinemas from the beginning of the 20th century. Come to admire the handpainted billboards but films are usually dubbed.
Filmoteca Nacional, Cine Doré, C/Santa Isabel 3, T91549 0011, metro Antón Martín. Ticket office open 1600-2245, bookshop open 1700-2230, bar-restaurant 1600-2400. The home of the National Film Institute, this endearing art deco cinema puts on a varied programme of classics, foreign-language films and film festivals. Outdoor screenings on the roof terrace in summer.
Pequeño Cine Estudio, C/Magallanes 1, T9153163 61, www.pcine studio.com. Metro Quevedo. Art-house cinema mainly showing the classics from Hollywood's Golden Age.

Classical and contemporary dance

As a major European capital, Madrid hosts the finest dance companies from around the world and you might also get a chance to see the Madrid-based Ballet Nacional de Espanya (Spanish National Ballet), or the more contemporary Compañía Nacional de Danza. The annual **Madrid en Danza festival** (see p110) is a good time to check out up-and-coming dance groups.
Centro Cultural de la Villa, Plaza de Colón s/n, T915756080, metro Colón. Madrid's main municipal arts centre, with an interesting programme of dance, music, and drama. It regularly hosts *zarzuela* during the summer, and is one of the main venues for Madrid en Danza.
Sala Cuarto Pared, C/Ercilla 7, Arganzuela, T915172317, metro Embajadores. This is one of the best venues in Madrid for contemporary dance, and is also a good place to find experimental drama productions.
Teatro Real, Plaza de Isabel II, T915160660, metro Opera. Madrid's beautifully restored opera house (see p78) provides an opulent venue for opera and ballet.

Fiestas

5 Jan Cabalgata de Los Reyes (Three Kings): in all Spanish towns, the Three Kings parade in floats tossing out sweets to children.
Feb Carnavales: plenty of dressing-up, floats, parades and street parties. The festivities finish up with the Burial of the Sardine (Entierro de la Sardina) to mark the end of winter.
Feb La Alternativa: an alternative theatre and dance festival held at venues throughout the city. It's held some time in Feb or Mar – check at the tourist office for exact dates.

Zarzuela

Zarzuela is Madrid's very own light operetta. It got its name from the Palace de la Zarzuela (on the outskirts of Madrid) where the earliest performances were created for the Philip IV and his court. The stories were usually sugary and sentimental, sometimes spiced up with a little contemporary gossip based on local events – one even describes the grand opening of the Gran Vía. They were hugely popular right up until the Civil War, but only just made it through the repressive years of Franco's dictatorship. Still, *zarzuela* has been enjoying a bit of a revival over the past couple of decades.

In summer, try and catch an outdoor performance at La Corrala (see page 92), or at the Jardines de Sabatini (see page 79). The delightful Teatro de la Zarzuela (C/Jovellanes 4, T915245400, metro Banco de España) holds performances year-round.

Madrid & around Entertainment

Feb ARCO: massive, month-long, contemporary art fair.

Easter Semana Santa: Holy Week is celebrated with solemn processions and masses. Venerated statues are paraded through the streets by the different confraternities in their strange pointed hoods.

2 May Fiesta del dos de Mayo: celebrates its uprising against the Napoleonic forces with bands in the Plaza del Dos de Mayo, and events in the cultural venues.

8-15 May Fiestas de San Isidro: festivities for Madrid's patron saint, San Isidro, with parades. It also marks the opening of the bullfighting season, with several events.

May-Jun Madrid en Danza: international Dance Festival held in venues across the city.

Jun Fiesta de San Antonio de la Florida: Street party near the hermitage of San Antonio de la Florida, which is decorated with Goya's frescoes.

Jun Festimad, www.festimad.es: outdoor music festival held in the suburb of Mostoles.

Mid-Jun to mid-Jul PhotoEspaña: international photography festival, exhibitions, workshops and talks.

24 Jun Día de San Juan: this midsummer festival is not such big news in Madrid as it is elsewhere in Spain, but there are fireworks and musicians in the Parque del Buen Retiro.

Jul-Sep Veranos de la Villa (Summers in the City): the largest city-sponsored arts festival in Madrid, with a range of activities spanning theatre, dance and music.

6-15 Aug Verbenas de San Cayetano, San Lorenzo and La Paloma: these colourful, traditional street festivals take place in the old neighbourhoods of La Latina and Lavapiés.

Late Sep to Nov Festival de Otoño: the Autumn Festival focuses on the performing arts.

Oct (throughout) Festival de Jazz de Madrid: Madrid's International Jazz festival draws some big names and is very enjoyable.

9 Nov Fiesta de la Virgen de la Almudena: Mass is held in the Plaza Mayor for the city's female patron saint.

Dec Feria de Artesania (Craft Fair): the shops fill with traditional decorations for crib scenes and there's a huge craft market held in the Recoletos.

31 Dec Noche Vieja (New Year): everyone piles into the Puerta del Sol where it's traditional to eat a grape for luck at each chime of the clock.

Flamenco

Madrid's flamenco scene is as vibrant as anywhere in Spain; there are dozens of places to hear and see flamenco in all its styles, from the most traditional to the latest trends.

Candela, C/Olmo 2, T914673382, metro Antón Martín. A celebrated flamenco bar which hosts occasional performances and is very popular with flamenco artists and those who come to gawp at them. The atmosphere gets better as it gets later.

Casa Patas, C/Cañizares 10, T913690496, metro Antón Martín. The stage is in a

shadowy, intimate little room at the back of the bar-restaurant area; it's small enough to feel the sweat of the performers as they whirl about the stage, and no one can help joining in with the odd 'olé'. The flamenco performances are among the best in the city.

La Soleá, Cava Baja 27, T913653308, metro La Latina. Anything can happen at this famous flamenco bar where guitarists and singers gather for semi-impromptu performances. You won't be alone – the bar is propped up mostly by 'guiris' (young foreigners) nowadays – yet it still retains a magical atmosphere.

Las Carboneras, Plaza del Conde de Miranda 1, T915428677, metro Sol. Flamenco tablao, which has breathtakingly skilful dancers, musicians and singers, but is slightly lacking in atmosphere.

Peña Chaquetón, C/Canarias 39, T916712777, metro Palos de la Frontera. Performances on Fri nights only, but get there early or you won't have a hope of getting in. It may be basic, but this is generally considered to be one of the very best flamenco venues in the city.

Music

Contemporary

Café Central, Plaza del Angel 10, T91369-4143. One of Madrid's loveliest jazz venues, set in an elegant, art deco café. Local and international groups play in the evening, but even if you don't catch a live show, it's the perfect place to while away an afternoon.

Café del Mercado, Puerta de Toledo s/n, T913658739, metro Puerta de Toledo. Despite being tucked away in the ill-starred Mercado de Toledo development (see p91), this is a very popular salsa bar and club with regular live gigs.

La Coquette, C/Hileras 14, no Tel, metro Opéra. Tiny underground blues bar which fulfils every cliché in the book – smoky, louche and loud. Fab. Live blues Tue-Thu.

La Riviera, Paseo Bajo Virgen del Puerto s/n, Puente de Segovía, T913652415, metro Puerta del Angel. Beautiful art deco-style concert venue near the river with a retractable roof. Mainly rock, indie and pop acts on the programme, but it has hosted some big international names. It doubles as a club, too.

Populart, C/Huertas 22, T914298407, metro Antón Martin. Hugely popular, lively club featuring live jazz and blues, with occasional appearances by Latin and world music bands. It's got a great reputation and pulls in some well-known bands, but it's best during the week – weekends can get too crammed.

Sala Clamores, C/Albuquerque 14, T914457938, metro Bilbao. Very popular jazz and world music venue.

Siroco, C/San Dimas 3, T91 593 3070, metro Noviciado. All kinds of home-grown rock, indie and alternative bands show up on the programme of this laid-back music venue – which doubles up as an excellent little club.

Suristán, C/Cruz 7, T915323909, metro Sevilla. This is a great place to catch all kinds of world music, from Latin rhythms to African jazz. It attracts a more diverse crowd than many of Madrid's nightspots, especially at weekends. When the bands are done, DJs keep the party going until late.

Classical and opera

Auditorio Nacional de Música, C/Príncipe de Vergara, T9133- 70100, www.auditorio nacional.mcu.es. Metro Cruz de Rayo or Prosperidad. Home of Spain's national choir and orchestra, and Madrid's main venue for classical music. Tickets available at the box office, or through Caja Madrid, T902488488.

Fundación Juan March, C/Castelló 77, T914354240, metro Núñez de Balboa. This exhibition space hosts regular chamber concerts and recitals, including lunchtime concerts which are usually free.

Teatro Real, Plaza de Isabel II, T915160660, metro Opera. Madrid's beautifully restored opera house provides an opulent venue for opera and ballet, see also p78.

Spectator sports

Bullfighting

Plaza de Toros Monumental de las Ventas, C/Alcalá 237, T913562200, www.las-ventas. com. Metro Ventas. The bullfighting season runs between Apr and Sep; tickets are cheaper when booked at the bullring rather than through an agency.

Football

Estadio Santiago Bernabeu, Paseo de la Castellana 104, T913984300, www.real

madrid.es/. Metro Santiago Bernabeu. Real Madrid's stadium.

Estadio del Rayo Vallecano, Arroyo del Olivar 49, T914782253, www.rayovalle cano.es/. Metro Portazgo. Rayo Vallecano's home stadium.

Estadio Vicente Calderón, T913664707, www.clubatleticodemadrid.com/. Metro Pirámides. Atlético de Madrid play here.

Theatre

Madrid's theatrical tradition stretches back to the Golden Age of Lope de Vega, Calderón and Tirso de Molina, and the city is strewn with dozens of venues featuring all kinds of work from the traditional renditions of the classics to avant garde contemporary performances. The most prominent classical theatre companies Centro Dramático Nacional and Compañia Nacional de Teatro Clásico, based at Teatro María Guerrero and Teatro de la Comedía respectively. For the most interesting contemporary perform-ances, check out what's on at the **Sala Cuarto Pared** (listed above under Dance), the **Mirador** or the **Circulo de Bellas Artes**.

Circulo de Bellas Artes, C/Marqués de Casa Riera 2, T915324437 (info), T902422442 (tickets), metro Banco de España. This art deco exhibition space and café regularly hosts innovative performances.

Teatro de la Comedía, C/Principe 14, T915214931, metro Sol. Another grand theatre, this also hosts classical performances and is home to the Compañia Nacional de Teatro Clásico.

Teatro Español, C/Príncipe 25, T914296297, metro Sol. Classical Spanish drama.

Teatro María Guerrero, C/Tamayo y Baus 4, T913194769. Metro Colon or Chueca. Just west of the Paseo de Recoletos, this beautiful old theatre is home to the Centro Dramático Nacional.

O Shopping

As Spain's capital, Madrid contains every kind of shop imaginable from excellent fresh food markets like the lovely Mercado de San Miguel (see p114), to tiny old-fashioned shops which haven't changed in decades, and glitzy shopping malls where you can get everything. It's also kitsch-lovers heaven with a dazzling array of fabulous tack. You can find almost anything you want in the streets around C Preciados in the centre – department stores, chain stores, individual shops selling everything from hams to traditional Madrileño cloaks. The northwest neighbourhoods of Argüelles and Moncloa, particularly C Princesa, are also good for department stores and fashion chains. The kiosks on Puerta del Sol have newspapers. Smart Salamanca has plenty of designer fashion boutiques and interior decoration shops at prices to make you gasp. Chueca is full of hip, unusual fashion and music shops as well as shoe-shoppers' heaven, the C Augusto Figeroa.

Books and newspapers

Fnac, C/Preciados 28, metro Sol or Callao. Massive store packed with books, DVDs, CDs, videos and electronic goods. There's also a travel agency, a newspaper shop (with not much in English), and a concert ticket agency.

Pasajes International Bookshop, C/Génova 3, metro Alonso Martínez. Friendly bookshop with a useful notice board (jobs or long-term accommodation) and a good range of titles in English.

Department stores and shopping centres

ABC Serrano Centro Comercial, C/Serrano 61, metro Serrano. Shopping centre housed in the former ABC newspaper building. The usual array of fast food outlets and chain stores plus a smattering of upmarket shops selling household goods and fashion.

El Corte Inglés, C/Preciados 2-3, metro Sol. One of several branches of Spain's biggest department store: fashion, toys, electrical goods, and souvenirs plus a basement supermarket and gourmet shop. Other services include a cafétería, bureau de change, travel agency, and ticket outlet. There are 2 stores devoted respectively to

books and music at the corner of Calle Preciados and the Puerta del Sol.

Fashion and accessories

Camper, C/Preciados 75, metro Argüelles. There are branches of this popular shoe store all over the city. Bright, comfortable, and playful, much cheaper than outside Spain.

Loewe, C/Serrano 34, metro Serrano. Luxury leather goods, and ultra-fashionable clothes for men and women who don't have to look at price tags. One of several luxury labels re- presented on this street and those around it.

Mango, C/Arenal 24, metro Opera. Another runaway Spanish chain, Mango offers the latest women's fashions and accessories in decent fabrics.

Marmota, C/Rio Baja 13, metro Puerta de Toledos. There's a clutch of fabulous vintage clothes' stores in this street and around; this one has the best prices.

Mercado de Fuencarral, C/Fuencarral 45, metro Gran Vía. All kinds of small boutiques on two floors selling alternative clothes, accessories and underwear for young hipsters. Don't miss Divina Providencia on the top floor – heavenly, really original dresses and bags. There's a very popular basement bar too.

Zara, C/Gran Vía 32, metro Callao. You are never far from a branch of this fashion chain which is the best bet for stylish clothes, shoes and accessories at really low prices. Real bargain-hunters should head next door to the Zara seconds shop.

Food and drink

Mantequerías Gonzalez, C/León 12, metro Antón Martín. Fabulous range of gourmet deli items (and a very pleasant little bar area at the back to try some of them out). Wines, olive oils, luxurious tins and jars of anchovies and other delicacies (good presents) and a great range of cheeses and cured meats. Very friendly staff.

Casa Mira, C/San Jerónimo 30, metro Sol. Lovely, old-fashioned baker which sells all kinds of goodies, displayed on a revolving glass stand. It's the place to buy turrón, a delicious honey-flavoured soft nougat, which is traditionally eaten around Christmas.

Convento de las Carboneras, C/Codo, metro La Latina or Sol. This is a little hard to find, tucked down a small passageway just off the Plaza del Villa. Press the buzzer marked *monjas* (nuns) and you will ushered down a corridor and given a list of *dulces* (sweet things) to choose from. The money is put into a revolving drum, and your cakes and change will come out the other side.

Markets

Cuesta de Claudio Moyano, metro Atocha. Second-hand book stalls line this pretty street near Atocha station. Most are open daily and the stalls are always good for a rummage.

El Rastro (see p91). Madrid's legendary Sunday morning flea market.

Mercado de San Miguel, Plaza de San Miguel, metro Sol. Set in a turn-of-the-century listed building, this is probably Madrid's prettiest market. Dozens of stalls sell all kinds of very fresh produce from fish to cheese with a fantastic array of cured meats.

Mercado de Sellos y Monedas (stamp and coin market), metro Sol. Plaza Mayor on Sun mornings.

Souvenirs and unusual shops

Belsol, C/Travesia de Belen 3, metro Chueca. Exquisite, hand-made and very original lampshades in silk, paper and other fabrics. They can convert any object you choose into a lamp.

Casa Seseña, C/Cruz 23, metro Sol. This delightful old shop is the only place left in Madrid which still makes the traditional Madrileño cloaks. Current window displays show photographs of Hilary Clinton wearing her Seseña cloak.

El Flamenco Vive, C/Conde de Lemos 7, metro Opera. Specialist flamenco shop with a fantastic range of books and CDs. This is also the place to come to find out what's really going on in the flamenco scene, with lots of flyers and posters.

La Tienda de Real Madrid, Centro Comercial La Esquina del Bernabéu, C/Concha Espina 1. A mecca for football fans – strips, scarves, caps and a whole host

of other memorabilia emblazened with Real Madrid's logo.

Maty, C/Maestro Victoria 2, metro Opera. Packed with flouncy flamenco dresses, shoes, hair-combs, clackable castanets and various other accessories. The tiny dresses for little girls are adorable.

▲ Activities and tours

Municipal Tourist Office, p71, has a full list of sightseeing tours available and organizes its own walking tours and coach excursions to towns outside Madrid.

Bus tours

Madrid-Visión, T917791888, www.trapsa. com/mvision. A popular hop-on, hop-off double-decker bus which offers three routes around Madrid. Prices are around e10 for adults, e5 for children and seniors.

Madrid Tour, T902101081, www.citysight seeing-spain.com. Another of the hop-on, hop-off services, with similar prices and routes to Madrid-Visión (see above).

Juliatur, Gran Vía 68, T915599605. Tours around Madrid, including night-time tours, plus excursions to the towns around the city. Prices vary according to the tour.

Pullmantour, Plaza de Oriente 8, T915411805. Also offer a wide selection of tours, both within the city centre and further afield. Prices vary.

Cycling tours

Bravo Bike.com, Av Menorca, 2 E, 28230 Las Rozas, Madrid, T916401298, www.bravo bike.com. A very friendly outfit which will collect you from your hotel and provide all equipment. A range of bicycle tours (with multilingual guides), in Madrid and around (El Escorial, Segovia and La Granja, Chinchón and Aranjuez, mountain-biking in the Sierras.

Esto es Madrid, C/ Torpedero Tucumán 18, T91350 1160, www.estoesmadrid.net. A wide range of mountain-biking tours including women only.

Jogging

Jardin Retiro (see p88) are the shadiest and most attractive area to jog in the city centre. **Casa de Campo** (see p96) has acres of unspoilt woodland. Also well known for prostitution, but this tends to take place close to the roads.

Sports centres

The following municipal sports centres all have outdoor pools, gyms, tennis courts and other sports: **Barrio del Pilar**, Ave de Monforte de Lemos, s/n, T913147943, metro Barrio del Pilar or Begoña; **Casa de Campo**, Avenida del Angel, s/n, T914630050, metro Lago or Puerta del Ángel; **La Elipa**, Prolongación de O'Donnell, s/n, T914303511, metro La Estrella.

Walking

Municipal Tourist Office, see p70, offers a vast array of walking tours, outlined in a free booklet called *Descubre Madrid*.

Yoga

Centro de Yoga Avagar, C/Bravo Murillo 243, 1st floor, T915797282.

Yoga Center, www.yogacenter.es, C/Lagasca 32, 1st floor, T915751542. Hatha, Iyengar and Ashtanga Vinyasa yoga.

☺ Transport

Air

Most services are in Terminal 1, which has ATMs, bureaux de change, car hire services, a post office, tourist information desks, a free accommodation service (for mid-priced and expensive hotels), left luggage lockers (about €3 per day). Airport information,

⁞ Arriving late at Madrid Barajas

If you arrive at Madrid airport in the middle of the night, few services will be open. The cafeteria in Terminal 1 closes at 2330, and the shops, post office and information desks usually close at around 2200 or earlier.

If you have pre-booked a car, some car hire representatives will meet your flight whenever it arrives, but you should check this in advance.

There are a couple of expensive business hotels close to the airport. The metro runs until about midnight during the week or 0100 at weekends, and the airport bus runs until 0145. Taxis can be found outside the arrival halls; if you can't see one, call Radio Taxis on T915478500/915478600.

If you haven't booked accommodation, your best bet is to head for an area hostels clustered on one street (like Calle Hortaleza in Chueca, or the streets around the Plaza Santa Ana, see Madrid Sleeping). If you are completely skint, you'll have little choice but to wait it out at the airport until 0445 when the buses start running into the city again. Still, the airport is clean and safe, and there are snack and drink machines to keep you going.

T913936000. Flight information, T902353570.

Airline offices
Air Europa, Barajas Airport, T902401501; **Air France**, C/Princesa, 1, T915419681; **Air Lingus**, Gran Vía, 88, T915414216; **American Airlines**, C/Pedro Texeira 8, T915970739; **British Airways**, C/Serrano 60, T915778489; **Iberia**, C/Velázquez, 130, T914111155.

Transport to and from Madrid
Bus Shuttle buses depart every 15 mins between 0445 and 0145 from Terminals 1 and 2 for the Plaza de Colón in the centre of town. Tickets cost €2.40 (one way). Journey times vary from 20 to 50 mins depending on the traffic. *Metrobús* ticket is not valid here.
Metro This is the cheapest way to get into the city; a single ticket costs just €90. Journeys to the centre take roughly 40-50 minutes. Get a *Metrobús* ticket (10 rides for €5) if you think you'll be using public transport during your stay.
Taxi There are taxi ranks outside all arrival halls. Should cost between €15-20.

Bus and metro

Bus and metro plans are available at tourist offices, at metro and bus stations, or online at www.ctm-madrid.es (which also provides information on suburban bus and rail services if you are planning a day trip to Toledo or Segovia, for example). A single ticket for one trip by bus or metro costs €0.95, or you can get a *Metrobús ticket* (which can be shared) for €5 which is valid for 10 journeys on the bus or metro. Buy single tickets at metro and bus stations, and the *Metrobús* ticket is also sold at tobacconists (*estancos*).

Car

Be aware, cars with foreign number plates or Spanish rental cars are prime targets for thieves. Consider hiring a car to explore the surrounding area, but note car hire and petrol are expensive. The best deals are usually online, and you should find out if the airline you fly with offers special car rental deals.

Offices of the major car rental companies can be found at the airport, and the 2 main train stations, Atocha and Charmartín.

Details as follows: **Avis**, T902135531, www.avis.com; **Budget**, T913937216, www.budget.es; **Europcar**, T913937235, www.europcar.com; **Hertz**, T913938265, www.hertz.com; **National** (which is a partner of the Spanish car hire firm, **Atesa**), T902100101, www.national.com; **All Inclusive Car Hire**, www.all-inclusive -car-hire.com.

Cycling

Cycling in the city centre is only for the brave, although it can be fun to cycle around parks like the Buen Retiro or the huge Casa del Campo. For bike tours, see p115. There's some excellent mountain-biking in the Sierras around the city, see p120.

Taxi

There are plenty in Madrid. White with a red stripe on the front doors, they can be hailed at the Puerta del Sol or near the metro station at Opera. Prices are reasonable, but there are supplements for luggage, pets, and after 2200 and at weekends.

Train

Regional trains (*cercanías*) usually call at both Atocha and Chamartín stations, but note that the high-speed *AVE* trains for **Sevilla** and **Córdoba** leave from Atocha. See under individual town entries for details of train services.

❶ Directory

Banks and ATMs

Banks and ATMS (look for a sign saying '*telebanco*') are everywhere. You'll find several banks on the Puerta del Sol, the Gran Vía and around the Plaza España.

Embassies

Australia, Paseo de la Castellana, 143, 28046 Madrid, T915790428, www.embaustralia.es.
Canada, C/Nuñez de Balboa, 35, 28001 Madrid, T914314300, www.canada-es.org/.
Ireland, C/Claudio Coello, 73, 28001 Madrid, T915763500, F914351677.
New Zealand, Plaza de la Lealtad, 2, 3. 28014 Madrid, T915230226, F915230171.
United States, C/Serrano, 75, 28006 Madrid, T915774000, www.embusa.es/.
UK, C/Fernando el Santo, 19, 28010 Madrid, T913190200, F913190423.

Hospitals

Dr Enrique Puerta Scott, C/San Francisco de Sales 36, T915345811.
Dr Niko Mihic, C/Lagasca 104, T617041936, mihic@spainmeds.com.
Hospital Clinico Universitario San Carlos, C/Profesor Martin Lagos, s/n, T913303000, www.msc.es/insalud/hospitales/hcsc, 24 hrs.
Hospital General Gregorio Marañon, C/Dr. Esquerdo, 46, T915868000, www.hggm.es. Metro O'Donnell.
Hospital La Princesa Del Insalud, C/Diego De Leon, 62, T915202200, www.hup.es, Metro Diego de León. English-speaking.

Internet

Bigg, C/Alcalá 21, www.bbbigg.com. Huge internet café with prices which fluctuate according to demand; €1 will get you about 30-40 mins.
EasyEverything, 10 C/Montera, T915232944, metro Sol. Prices fluctuate according to demand; between €1.50/3 an hr. Open 24 hrs.
Work Center, 1 C/Albert Aguilera, T9144-87877. Metro Arguelles. Facilities include photocopying, faxing, scanning, printing, photo development. Internet access €6 for 1 hr. Macs and PCs. Open 24 hrs.

Language schools

Acento Español, C/Mayor 4, 6º9, T915213676, acentoes@teleline.es. Intensive and general courses, preparation for official DELE exam. Can arrange accommodation.
CEE Idiomas, C/Carmen 6, T915220472, cee1@arrakis.es. Courses for all levels, preparation for DELE, cultural activities.

Laundry

Ondablu, C/León, www.ondablu.com. Metro Antón Martín. Launderette, offering service washes or do-it-yourself. There are also internet terminals for while you wait.

Post

The main post office is the **Palacio de Comunicaciones**, Plaza de Cibeles,

T915216500, information T902197197, www.correos.es. Mon-Fri 0830-2130, Sat 0930-2130, Sun 0830-1400. Postboxes, marked *Correos y Telégrafos*, are yellow. Most tobacconists (*estancos*, marked with a brown and yellow symbol) sell stamps. You can send or receive faxes from any post office.

Pharmacies

Pharmacies have a list of the 24-hr pharmacies in their windows. The following are open 24 hrs: **Real Botica de la Reina Madre**, C./ Mayor 59, T915480014, Metro Opera; **Farmacia de la Paloma**, C/ Toledo 46, T913653458, Metro La Latina; **Farmacia del Globo**, C/Atocha, 46, T3692000, Metro Antón Martín; **Farmacia Goya 89**, C./ Goya 89, T914354958, Metro Goya.

Telephone

Most public payphones (which you'll find on almost every street corner) will accept coins and pre-paid telephone cards: most

newsagents, post offices and tobacconists sell pre-paid phone cards in denominations of €5, 10, 15 and 20. Calls are cheaper after 2200 during the week and all day at weekends. Phones in bars and cafés usually have more expensive rates than public payphones. Phone centres (*locutarios*) are the cheapest method for calling abroad; you'll find them in the Atocha and Chamartín train stations, and several smaller ones dotted throughout Chueca and Lavapiés.

Useful addresses and numbers

Emergency There is a single number in Madrid for all emergency services, T112.
Police Each district has its own station or *comisaría*. You have to report crimes or accidents for insurance purposes, but it's painfully slow and few speak English. Central stations: Comisaría Centro, C/Leganitos 19, T915487985. Comisaría Fuencarral, C/Gonzo de Limio 35, T913782460. Comisaría Retiro, C/Huertas 76, T913223400.

Around Madrid

Madrileños abandon the capital at weekends for their second homes in the pretty mountain villages of Navacerrada and Cotos, where there is plenty of hiking, climbing and even skiing. Backed by a startling mountainous backdrop, Segovia is one of the loveliest cities in Spain, famous for its sturdy Castillian cuisine and the vast Roman aqueduct. Ávila, known as the 'City of Saints and Stones', is quieter and more contemplative, hemmed in by a remarkable ring of medieval fortified walls. Behind it stretches the wild and remote Sierra de Gredos, a spectacular mountain range with tiny stone villages and excellent hiking trails.

When the kings and queens of Spain wanted respite from the capital's burning heat, they took themselves off to palaces and hunting lodges: the Habsburgs preferred the sombre austerity of El Escorial, but the Bourbons built fanciful Baroque extravaganzas at La Granja de San Ildefonso and Aranjuez, and surrounded them with exquisite gardens. The extensive gardens of Aranjuez are especially beautiful, a rare and refreshing oasis of green in the burning Castillian plain.

The ancient university town of Alcalá de Henares was the birthplace of Cervantes, whose home has been converted into an engaging little museum, but the old streets are still smattered with magnificent Renaissance architecture. The hilltop city of Toledo remains the most popular day-trip from Madrid and with good reason: Romans, Visigoths, Muslims, Jews and Christians have all left their mark on this famously tolerant and cultured city and the tiny streets and passages which twist around the enormous cathedral are still redolent of the city's glorious past. ➤➤ *For Sleeping, Eating and other listings, see pages 139-146.*

Ins and outs

Some of the towns and villages described in this chapter fall into the province of the Comunidad de Madrid, which forms a donut-shaped ring around the capital city, but many of them don't: Ávila, Segovia and the villages of Sierra de Gredos are in Castilla y León (see page 129), perfect stopping points on the way to the castles and wine-regions of Northern Spain; Toledo is in Castilla-La Mancha (see page 633), close to Don Quijote territory for anyone who wants to follow the footsteps of Spain's most famous literary figure.

El Escorial and the Sierra de Guadarrama

→ *Colour map 4, grid B6.*

The spiky peaks of the Sierra de Guadarrama are visible even from Madrid. This is where Felipe II chose to build his vast, forbidding palace-monastery, in a crook in the hills 42 km northwest of Madrid. A couple of kilometres away is Franco's own burial place and monument to the fallen of the Civil War (close enough to the Royal Pantheon to satisfy any ego). The villages of the Sierra are stuffed full of Madrileño second homes, and are good bases for walking, mountain-biking and even skiing.

→ *For Sleeping, Eating and other listings, see pages 139-146.*

Real Monasterio de San Lorenzo el Real de El Escorial

ⓘ *www.patrimonionacional.es, Apr-Sep Tue-Sun 1000-1800, Oct-Nov 1000-1700, €6/6.90 including guided visit/concessions €5.10. Audioguide in English €1.80. Cloakroom €1. Café and shop. The information office opposite the monastery entrance has details on trekking, horse riding and balloon rides in the area.*

The lugubrious monastery is enormous and chilly, even in the height of summer. Few admit to liking it – the 19th-century French writer Théophile Gaultier went so far as to say that its visitors could amuse themselves for the rest of their lives with the thought that they could be in El Escorial but were not – but none can fail to be impressed by the staggering proportions: 16 patios, 15 cloisters, nine towers, 1,200 doors and 2,600 windows.

‡ *The town is also an attractive base if you want to do some walking in the surrounding Sierra de Guadarrama (see below).*

The tour begins at the **Bourbon apartments** in the northeast section of the palace. Gloomy El Escorial was far too depressing for the frivolous Bourbons who spent little time here, but their apartments contain some beautiful tapestries by Goya. Two museums are housed in the cellars beneath these rooms: the Museo de Pintura, with works by Veronese, Titian, van Dyck, Rubens, van der Weyden and Ribera, among others; and the Museum of Architecture, which shows the original plans for the monastery along with some of the equipment used for hauling the huge hunks of granite.

The **Habsburg apartments** are unexpectedly intimate, prettily decorated with blue and white tiles. You can see the specially designed chair in which gout-ridden Felipe II was carried by his long-suffering servants, who had to put up with the stench of their master's gouty leg as well as his manic eccentricities, and the bed in which he died in 1598, carefully placed so that he could hear mass from the basilica directly below.

When Felipe died, he was buried in the **Panteón de los Reyes** (Royal Pantheon), where a dozen Spanish monarchs are buried in a flurry of gold and marble. Next to the pantheon is the **Rotting Room** (sealed off, thankfully), where the bodies of dead monarchs were left to rot and dry out before being placed in the Pantheon.

The **Salas Capitulares** (Chapter Halls) contain more of El Escorial's enormous art collection, gathered underneath elaborately painted 16th-century ceilings. The Basilica is the very heart of the complex, repressively dark, cold and gloomy. It contains 43 altars so that several masses could be held simultaneously – just two chapels, right at the back, were for commoners.

Around the monastery

After staggering out of the monastery, most visitors want to make for the nearest bar. **Calle Floridablanca** is one of the most animated streets, with several tapas bars and restaurants, and the added delight of the **Real Coliseo**, a charming little theatre built for Carlos III. There are two small palaces downhill towards El Escorial proper, both plush Bourbon fripperies: the **Casita del Príncipe** (or the Casita Abajo) ① *guided tours Apr-Sep Sat, Sun and public holidays 1000-1300 and 1600-1830 (must be booked in advance on T918905902), €3.45 per person*, surrounded by lush gardens, and the delightfully frivolous **Casita del Infante** (or the Casita Arriba) ① *open Holy Week and Jul-Sep Tue-Sun 1000-1845, €3*.

There's a very popular picnic area at the top of the **Monte de la Herrería**, where Felipe II would take a break from his hunting, but you'll probably have to share your spot with coachloads of weekending Madrileños in summer. The tourist office has information on walking trails from the town itself.

Valle de los Caídos (Valley of the Fallen)

① *Tue-Sun Apr-Sep 0930-1900, Oct-Mar 1000-1800; €3, free Wed with EU-passport.*
In 1940, work began on a monument to 'the fallen' of the Civil War. Despite the neutral title, its true purpose was the glorification of Franco and his regime and the labourers were Republican prisoners, leftists and anyone who criticized the new government. The setting – a craggy mountain valley with endless views across the plain and down to Madrid – is beautiful, but the monument itself is pompous, overblown and brutally ugly. The vast basilica is built into the rock and topped with an outsized cross (supposedly the largest in the world), visible even from Madrid. Franco is buried by the altar, and the monument has become a focal point for a rally on the anniversary of his death.

Sierra de Guadarrama

Since the narrow-gauge railway between Cercedilla and Cotos was opened almost 50 years ago, the Sierra de Guadarrama has become a popular playground for weekending Madrileños, many of whom have second homes here. The Sierra de Guadarrama is not as dramatic or as well known as the Sierra de Gredos to the west, but it's conveniently close to Madrid and offers some spectacular walking, climbing (the peaks of La Maliciosa and La Pedriza) and skiing in winter.

Cercedilla and Cotos The best and most convenient base for hiking in the Sierra de Guadarrama is **Cercedilla**, a rapidly expanding mountain town of chalet-style houses about 70 km from Madrid, which is easily accessible by public transport and stuffed full of bars, shops and restaurants. There's an information centre on the edge of town (just off the main M-966 road from Madrid) which has leaflets describing walking trails around the Valle de la Fuenfría, and is the starting point for a number of excellent hikes.

From here, the narrow gauge railway makes a spectacular journey up to the pretty mountain town of **Cotos**, a small ski resort and hiking centre. It's one of the three small ski resorts in the Sierra de Guadarrama (see page 120), and is about a 20-minute walk from the slightly better slopes of the Valdesquí resort almost on the border with Segovia.

Navacerrada and around The immaculate village of Navacerrada is another big weekend destination for Madrileños. It has a beautiful mountainous setting on the side of a reservoir, and there are a couple of attractive churches and a buzzy little town square, with a handful of terrace bars and restaurants. But the main attraction is the network of walking trails which lead up into the mountains; the best lead from the information centre at the Puerto de Navacerrada, T918539978, on the road to **Manzanares La Real**, another modest village. It's set on a lake (private, so you can't reach it) and backed by impressive jagged peaks, but the new housing developments detract from the charm of the old village, with its pretty square and church. There's only one sight: a stubby much-renovated 15th-century castle, which is now a small ethnographical museum, but the views from the top of the keep are wonderful.

Buitrago de Lozoya In the northern reaches of the Sierra de Guadarrama, the attractive town of Buitrago de Lozoya still retains a battered fortress and the defensive walls built by the Moors in the 12th century. During the 15th and 16th centuries, noble families built mansions and fine bridges and the town retains the slightly haughty air of a dowager down on her luck. Look out for the handsome Mudéjar **church of Santa María**, and the unexpected collection of Picasso-related memorabilia in the town hall. The collection was donated by Eugenio Arias, a local barber, and charts his friendship with Picasso with a series of autographed sketches, lithographs, ceramics and postcards. Buitrago is a good starting point for some excellent hikes in the hills and forests of the northern sierra, and the nearby reservoir is good for a swim on a hot summer's day.

Segovia and around → *Phone code: 921; Colour map 2, grid C2; Population: 54,754; Altitude: 1,002 m.*

Segovia is one of the most alluring cities in central Spain, built of golden stone, capped with a fairytale castle and set against the dramatic peaks of the Sierra de Guadarrama. It's almost as famous for its sturdy Castillian cuisine as it is for the enormous Roman aqueduct which has stood here for two millennia. It's the perfect place to relax (although perhaps not at weekends when everyone else is here doing it too) and, if you decide to spend more than the day here, there are gentle walks along the river Eresma, or tougher treks among the surrounding peaks. Close by are two royal residences: the extravagant Bourbon summer palace of La Granja, and the more modest hunting lodge of Riofrío.➤ *For Sleeping, Eating and other listings, see pages 139-146.*

Ins and outs
Getting there and around There are regular buses and trains from Madrid. Segovia station is about 2 km from the town centre; take local bus No 3 from outside the station. Most of the sights are clustered in the old city, which is easy to get around on foot.➤ *For further details see Transport, page 145.*
Best time to visit Segovia is especially lovely in early spring, when there's still a slight chill in the air and the mountains are still capped with snow. It can get a little crowded at weekends, particularly during the summer, so try and come off-season or during the week if possible.
Tourist information ① *Plaza Azoguejo 1, T9214614, segoviaturism@interbook.net, Plaza Mayor 10, T9214603 34.*

History
Segóbriga was an important military settlement when the Romans built their enormous aqueduct 2,000 years ago. In the early Middle Ages, the Arabs introduced the cloth-manufacturing trade, which would ensure Segovia's prosperity long after

the Reconquista. Segovia was doing very nicely when Carlos I (Charles V) tried to impose harsh taxes, and revolted against the king. The uprising, known as the Comunero Revolt, was viciously put down and the leaders decapitated in Segovia. Like most of Spain, it went into decline in the 18th century when a seemingly endless series of wars began. It emerged as a popular tourist destination in the 20th century, and is also a big culinary capital well known for its traditional Castilian cuisine.

Sights

The Aqueduct Segovia's most famous sight is at its most dramatic just outside the city walls on the Plaza Azoguejo (where the tourist information office is located). Nothing holds together the 25,000 stones of this soaring two-storey aqueduct which stretches for 760 m and arches a giddy 29 m above the square. The tallest surviving Roman aqueduct, it was still carrying water to the city right up until a generation or two ago, but pollution and traffic vibration have taken their toll in recent years.

Plaza Azoguejo to Plaza Mayor From the Plaza Azoguejo, at the foot of the aqueduct, the busy shop-lined **Calle Cervantes** leads up into the centre of the old city.

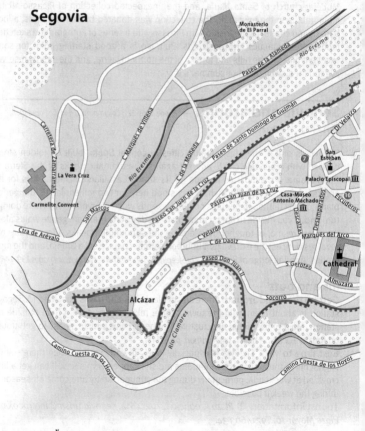

Segovia

Sleeping	Infanta Isabel 6	Eating
Camping Acueducto 1	Los Linajes 7	Casa Duque 1
Hostal Don Jaime 3	Las Sirenas 8	Cueva de San Esteban 2
Hostal Fornos 4	Parador de Segovia 9	El Bernadino 3
Hostal Juan Bravo 5	Pension Ferri 10	La Barcaza 4

At the point where it turns across the old city walls, you can't miss the knobbly 15th-century **Casa de los Picos** (House of the Spikes), which got everyone talking when it was first built thanks to its unusual façade of diamond-shaped jutting stones. It's now a cultural and exhibition centre, and you can step in to admire the graceful patio. The elegant mansion covered in swirling *esgrafado* tucked away close by is the **Palacio de los Condes de Alpuente,** and below it is the former corn exchange (**Alhondiga**), a Gothic building with an Arabic name which was built under the Catholic Kings. Continuing along Calle de Cervantes, the softly rounded Romanesque church of **San Martín**, with its covered portico and Mudéjar belltower, overlooks a peaceful square with a statue of Juan Bravo, the leader of the Comunero Revolt (with a name like that, he was bound to be a folk hero).

Close by is one of Segovia's newest museums, the **Museo de Arte Contemporáneo Esteban Vicente** ① *Plaza de Bellas Artes, T91462010, Tue-Sat 1100-14000 and 1600-1900, Sun 1100-1400; €2.40/1.20*, devoted to the Segovian painter Esteban Vicente (1903-2000). He spent most of his life in New York, but made provisions in his will for his art to be returned to his native city and his vivid paintings are now housed in the handsomely restored 15th-century Palacio de Enrique IV.

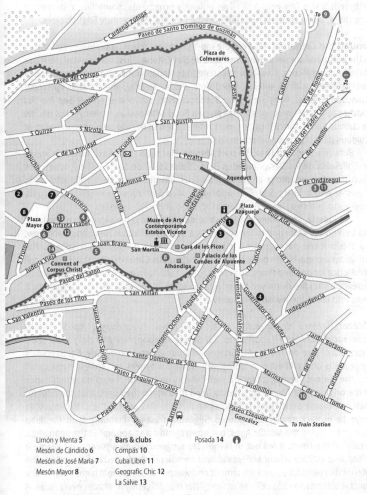

Madrid & around Segovia & around

Limón y Menta 5	**Bars & clubs**	Posada 14
Mesón de Cándido 6	Compás 10	
Mesón de José Maria 7	Cuba Libre 11	
Mesón Mayor 8	Geografic Chic 12	
	La Salve 13	

Calle Juan Bravo links the Plaza San Martín with old Segovia's main square, the wide, appealing **Plaza Mayor**, full of terrace bars and restaurants and the heart of the city's nightlife. There's a small bandstand in the centre, where concerts are occasionally held in summer.

Cathedral ① *Mar-Oct daily 1000-1830, Nov-Feb daily 1000-1730; €2/1.20, museum closed Sun am.* Rising serenely above the Plaza Mayor, Segovia's cathedral was built between 1525 and 1590 in what is probably the latest example of the Gothic style in Spain. The original cathedral was destroyed by Carlos I (Charles V) during his vicious repression of the Comunero Revolt (see History above), but he must have had a guilty conscience because he provided the funds for a replacement. Designed by Juan Gil de Hontañón, it is fashionably austere in the way the Spanish liked their churches in those days, but the soft golden stone of the exterior manages to counteract its harshness. Inside there is some elegant vaulting in the chapels surrounding the ambulatory, but little else to see. The cloister was all that remained of the original cathedral and was brought here brick by brick. Just off the cloister is the Sala Capitular, where the cathedral's scant treasures are gathered; just a few gold and silver religious ornaments, some fine 17th-century tapestries, and a curious, but rather pretty, painted 16th-century English clock.

Around the Cathedral Many of the most important religious buildings connected to the cathedral are set around the Plaza de San Esteban, just northeast of the Plaza Mayor. A magnificent, six-storey Italianate tower looms above the delicate **church of San Esteban**, with a striking Crucifixion inside. Nearby, the **Palacio Episcopal** (Episcopal Palace), ① *15 Sep-15 Jun Sat 1000-1800, Easter and 1 Jul-15 Sep Tue-Sat 1000-1430 and 1600-1930, €2*, was given a florid 18th-century makeover but retains its curious Renaissance façade – more interesting that the old-fashioned museum of religious paintings and statuary inside.

Between 1919 and 1932 the poet **Antonio Machado** stayed in a boarding-house on Callejuela de los Desamparados (just off the Plaza de San Esteban), which has been transformed into a engaging little museum dedicated to his life and work. ① *Easter and 1 Jul-15 Sep Tue-1600-1930, Wed-Sun 1000-1400 and 1600-1930, 1100-1400 and 1630-1900 Wed-Sun 1100-1400 and 1630-1900, €1.50.*

The **Judería**, once home to a Jewish community before the expulsion of the Jews, sits behind the cathedral to the south. It's a slightly run-down neighbourhood now, but the crooked passages and leaning houses make it quietly atmospheric. The former synagogue is now part of the **convent of Corpus Christi** ① *Plaza del Corpus, call in advance for opening times, T921463429*, and although much of it is a 19th-century recreation after fire destroyed the original building, it's worth a visit for the glimpse it gives into life in the Jewish community.

Alcázar ① *Plaza de la Reina Victoria Eugenia, T921460759, Apr-Sep daily 1000-1900, Oct Mon-Fri 1000-1800, Sat-Sun 1000-1900, Nov-Mar daily 1000-1800 €3.10/2.20; free on Tue for EU citizens with passports, audioguide €3.* Segovia's Alcázar sits on a cliff edge, bristling with storybook turrets and spires. Purists sniff that the current version, a fanciful 19th-century restoration, bears no resemblance to the original, but Disney apparently liked it so much they used it as a model for their first theme park. The first fortress on this site was built in the 12th century, in order to protect newly reconquered Segovia. It was a favourite with Castilian monarchs during the Middle Ages, but when Madrid was appointed the permanent capital of the court, it fell out of favour. No longer used as a palace, it became a prison and military school and was almost completely destroyed by fire in 1862. The interior has been fitted out with armour and weapons, but the real highlights are the spectacular artesonado ceilings which glitter magnificently in almost every room. A

useful plan and explanatory leaflet (which remains coy on the issue of what's authentic and what's not) is included in the admission price. There's a 144-step hike up the old watchtower for stupendous views out across the lovely old city to the mountains, still snow-capped in late spring.

Outside the city walls Segovia is stuffed full of beautiful churches. One of the loveliest, the little 13th-century **Iglesia de la Vera Cruz** (Church of the True Cross), is also built with Segovia's warm, honey-coloured stone, and sits just outside the city walls. It's constructed on a polygonal plan typical of Templar churches, and the double-chamber at its heart was used for the Order's secret rituals. Its fortunes have declined in the past few centuries and even the sliver of the True Cross which gave it its name has gone to another local church. Don't miss the fabulous views across Segovia from the belltower ① *Apr-Sep Oct-Mar Tue-Sun 1030-1300 and 1530-1800, €1.50.*

The remains of Saint John of the Cross are buried in an elaborate early 20th-century mausoleum in the nearby Carmelite convent hidden behind massive walls ① *Mon 1530-1800, Tue-Sun 1000-1330 and 1600-1900, until 2000 in summer, free but donations welcome.*

Segovia has some excellent gentle walking and you can take a peaceful stroll through the valley of the Río Eresma to the luminous **Monasterio de El Parral** ① *C/del Marqués de Villena, T921431298, 15 Sep to 1 Jul Mon-Sat 1000-1230, 1630-1830, Sun 1000-1130, 1630-1830, 1 Jul-15 Sep, Wed 1600-1930, Thu-Sun 1000-1430, 1600-1930, free but donations accepted.* The quiet church contains the alabaster tombs of the Villena family and a fine 16th-century retablo, a beautiful backdrop to mass held in Gregorian chant on Sundays at midday, and during the week at 1300.

Around Segovia
① *Both palaces open 26 Mar-7 Oct Tue-Sun 1000-1800, 8 Oct-25 Mar Tue-Fri 1000-1330, 1500-1700, Sat-Sun 1000-1400, visits by guided tour only (in several languages); €4.81 (to each palace)/3.91 concessions, free on Wed to EU-passport holders, www.patrimonionacional.es.*

There are two sumptuous royal palaces close to Segovia; **La Granja de San Ildefonso** is a 10-minute bus ride away, but you'll need your own transport to get to the former hunting lodge at **Ríofrío**. La Granja, a frothy Italian-style palace built for the Bourbon monarchs, is surrounded by magnificent gardens, famous for their fountains and sculptures. Unfortunately, you can only see the fountains in all their glory on two days a year, normally 25 July and 25 August (they turn on a few on Wednesdays and weekends to whet your appetite). The palace was destroyed by fire in 1918, but it has been carefully restored and the royal apartments are now a magnificent evocation of the opulence of the 18th-century Spanish court. Entry to the adjoining **Museo de Tapices** (Tapestry Museum) and the Collegiata (where Felipe V and his wife and son are buried surrounded by a macabre collection of relics and old bones) are both included in the ticket price. If you've been dazzled by the gorgeous crystal chandeliers, you can find out how they were made at the museum set in the former **Real Fábrica de Cristales** (Royal Crystal Factory).

The palace at Ríofrío is difficult to get to without your own transport, and is much lower key. It is beautifully set among forests and woods and attracts considerably fewer visitors than La Granja, which can be a charm in itself. Despite its grand scale, Ríofrío was merely a hunting lodge, and now half of it has been given up to a bizarre museum of hunting, complete with row upon row of stuffed heads. It's surrounded by a deer park (inaccessible on foot, although you can drive through it).

Ávila → *Phone code: 920; Colour map 4, grid C3; Population: 46,259; Altitude: 1,128 m.*

The austere mountain town of Ávila is set on a windswept plateau, surrounded by the chilly granite peaks of the Sierra de Gredos. The reddish-brown tangle of medieval mansions and Romanesque churches is completely enclosed by magnificent medieval walls, studded with towers and crenellations. This 'city of saints and stones' is the birthplace of Santa Teresa, the 16th-century mystic, visionary and writer, and is still a major pilgrimage centre. It remains a hushed and contemplative city, but if it all gets too much, you can easily escape to the surrounding mountains, scattered with attractive old villages, and a paradise for hikers and climbers. While you are here, try some yemas, a delicious sticky sweet made of egg yolk and sugar, traditionally made by Ávila's nuns. ⏩ *For Sleeping, Eating and other listings, see pages 139-146.*

Ins and outs

Getting there and around There are regular bus and train connections with Madrid, Salamanca and Segovia, as well as other major cities in Castilla y León. The old walled city of Ávila is small and easy to get around on foot. → *For further details, see Transport, p146.*

Best time to visit Late spring and early autumn are the best times to visit Ávila and the Sierra de Gredos, when the temperatures are mild and the streets and hiking trails empty. The city is chilly in winter, although the surrounding mountains are especially beautiful covered in snow.

Tourist information ① *Plaza de la Catedral 4, T921211387, www.avila.net.* The tourist office has an excellent leaflet describing a walk around the old city which takes in the best of the palaces.

Ávila

Sleeping
Gran Hostal Segundo **1**
Hostal Alcántara **2**
Hostal El Rastro **3**

Hostería de
Bracamonte **4**
La Sinagoga **5**
Las Cancelas **6**

Palacio de los Velada **7**
Parador de Ávila **8**

History

According to legend, Ávila was founded by Hercules himself. The famous walls were initiated under Alfonso VI in the 11th century, when the city was in the front line of the Reconquista. And yet Ávila was famous for its learning and religious tolerance, and the city never really recovered economically after the expulsion of the Jews in 1492 and then the Moriscos in 1609. In the 16th century, the city produced two outstanding religious figures: Teresa of Ávila and St John of the Cross, who were canonised and subsequently declared Doctors of the Church. The cult of Saint Teresa, in particular, is still very strong and she is co-patron saint of Spain, see box above.

Sights

Muralla de Ávila ① *Entrance at the Puerta de Catedral, T920102121, Tue-Sun 1100-2000 (last entrance at 1915), guided visits in Spanish only at 1115, 1215, 1315, 1715, 1815, 1915, €3.50/2 concessions.* A visit to the city should begin at Ávila's famous **walls**. Constructed in the wake of Alfonse VI's victory in Toledo, these massive walls were erected to ensure that the Arab armies couldn't re-take the city. Some 12 m high, 3 m thick, and studded with nine gates and 88 towers, they became legendary even as they were being built. A short section has been made into a panoramic walkway, with views out over the old city, and up to the peaks of the Sierra de Gredos.

> **‡** *For the very best views of the walls themselves, head to the little shrine at Cuatro Postes just outside town on the Salamanca road.*

Cathedral and around ① *Plaza de Catedral, T920211641, Apr-May Mon-Fri 1000-1900, Sat 1000-1900, Sun and holidays 1200-1900, Jun-Oct Mon-Sat 1000-2000, Sun and holidays 1200-2000, Nov-Mar Mon-Fri 1030-1330 and 1530-1730, Sat 1000-1730, €2.50.* As the massive city walls were being erected to defend the city from the Moors, the cathedral was slowly rising to take its place in the struggle for souls.

It was incorporated into the walls to become a literal and metaphorical bastion, and the austere façade betrays its dual function as a fortress and place of worship. The interior is surprisingly lovely, with its lofty Gothic nave made of rosy stone, and magnificent Plateresque stalls and retrochoir all gently illuminated by stained glass windows. One of Ávila's most famous medieval bishops is buried in an extravagant alabaster sarcophagus behind the altar; his dark skin earned him the nickname 'El Tostado' – 'the toasted'. The cloister, attractively rumpled and overgrown, is home to several storks' nests; just off it is the cathedral museum, with a rather disappointing collection of paintings, religious ornaments (including Juan de Arfe's massive Monstrance) and vestments.

Ávila once contained so many aristocratic palaces that it was known as 'City of the Nobles'. One of the grandest, the 16th-century **Casa de los Velada** which overlooks the Plaza de la Catedral has lodged Carlos I (Charles V), Isabel la Católica and Felipe II. Opposite the

Eating 🍴
Bodeguita de San Segundo 1
Casa Patas 2
Copacabana 3
Fogón de Santa Teresa 4
La Casona 5

Something in the air

Teresa de Cepada y Ahumada was born to an aristocratic family on 28 March 1515. At the age of seven she ran away to be martyred by the Moors (her family caught up with her just outside town, and a small stone cross marks the spot) and then joined the Carmelites at the age of 18. More than 20 years passed before she had the first of her famous visions, in which an angel pierced her heart with flaming arrows. In the second, the Virgin instructed her to remove her shoes and reform the Carmelite order, which had drifted away from its original vows of poverty and simplicity. Teresa embarked on a journey around Spain, urging reform and founding the Discalced – 'shoeless' – Carmelites, but her success aroused jealousy and suspicion within the Church. She and her confessor, Juan de Yepes, were both imprisoned in Toledo, where Teresa wrote The Inner Castle, a classic mystical text describing the journey of a Bride of Christ, and Juan wrote the poetic Dark Night of the Soul. Teresa died in 1582 when her writings were still regarded with suspicion by the Church, who then did a strange about-face and canonised her in 1622. Juan de Yepes died miserably, persecuted to the last, but was also canonised as Saint John of the Cross in 1726.

Teresa and Juan were not the only spiritual writers to emerge from the city. The 13th-century Jewish cleric Mose Ben Shemthom, author of the Book of Splendour (Seger-ha-Zohar) one of the most important Hebraic texts, was also from Ávila, and Mancebo de Arévalo's Tafçira was one of the last Islamic spiritual texts to come out of Spain before the expulsion of the Moors.

cathedral, C/de los Reyes Cátolicos leads to the **Plaza del Mercado Chico**, originally the site of the Roman forum and still the heart of the old city. It's flanked on one side by the 19th-century Ayuntamiento (Town Hall) and on the other by the church of **San Juan**, where Santa Teresa was baptised. The font has been preserved and the church can be visited before and after mass.

Convento de Santa Teresa ① C/La Dama, T920211030, Apr-Oct 1000-1400 and 1600-1900, Nov-Mar 1000-1330 and 1530-1730, €2. Also known as the Convento de la Santa, this convent was founded in 1636 on the site of the Cepeda mansion where Teresa of Ávila was born. The Baroque convent contains a flamboyant chapel to Saint Teresa, and several statues by Gregorio Fernández. A new **museum** devoted to the life of the saint has been established around the corner on Calle La Dama; the setting, a stone cellar, is attractive, but the exhibits are extremely dull. There are plenty of dire portraits of the saint, a few old documents, a reproduction of her cell, and a collection of her works in different languages. The most interesting section is at the end, where 'before' and 'after' (as in 'before taking Holy Orders') photographs of more recent Carmelite saints are displayed, including one of Edith Stein (later Santa Teresa Benedicta de la Cruz) who died in Auschwitz.

More mansions Old Ávila is a strange little time capsule, with a rich collection of noble mansions and churches that have survived through neglect rather than any concerted efforts at preservation. Most of its modern inhabitants live in the convenient new housing developments outside the city walls, leaving the quiet streets of the old town to pilgrims and visitors. Many of the best surviving mansions (all private) are concentrated on the southern side of the city, including the elaborate

palace-fortress of the **Dávila** on Calle de Cepadas, which incorporates four houses dating back to the 13th century. There is another clutch of palaces in the northeastern corner of the city; look out for the **Mansión de los Verdugo** and the nearby **Palacio de los Águila**, on Calle López Nuñez, both typically fortified aristocratic palaces with a wealth of elaborate Renaissance detailing.

Outside the city walls Many of Ávila's finest churches are located just outside the city walls; one of the oldest is the simple Romanesque **Iglesia de San Pedro** which overlooks the arcaded **Plaza de Santa Teresa** (known locally as the Plaza Grande). It's a handsome, bustling square (although it's currently being dug up for a new underground car park) edged with arcades containing plenty of shops and bars. The **Museo Provincial** is held in the Palacio de los Deanes and the nearby Romanesque church of Santo Tomé el Viejo① *Tue-Sat 1000-1400 and 1630-1930, Sun 1000-1400, €1.20, free on Sat and Sun*, just off the Plaza de Italia, and contains an odd but appealing assortment of ceramics, archaeological findings, religious art and traditional costumes and furnishings.

The finest Romanesque church in Ávila is the **Basílica de San Vicente**, to the north of the museum on the Paseo Humilladero. San Vicente's life and martyrdom is depicted in grisly detail on a 12th-century sepulchre, and the subterranean crypt contains the slab on which he, along with his two sisters, was martyred at the hands of the Romans. The crypt is also an important stop on the pilgrimage trail, as it was here that Saint Teresa had the second of her visions and where, according to tradition, she took off her shoes in answer to the Virgin's request for reform of the Carmelite order. Teresa spent almost 30 years in the **Convento de la Encarnación** ① *C/Encarnación, T920211212, Tue-Fri 0930-1330 and 1530-1800, Sat 1000-13000 and 1600-1800, €1.20*, which now contains a small museum of her life.

The most important monument outside the city walls is the Dominican **Monasterio Réal de Santo Tomás** ① *T920220400, 1000-1300 and 1600-2000, free entry into the church, €1 to visit cloisters and choir*, a good 15-minute walk from the old city. It's set around three cloisters and was established at the end of the 15th century by the Catholic kings. It did service as their summer residence, and was also the seat of Ávila's university. But its glory days have long gone, and grass sprouts through the cracks in the paving stones of the first and smallest cloister, the Cloister of the Noviciate. The second cloister, the Cloister of Silence, is larger, grander, and handsomely decorated with engravings on the upper gallery. The third and grandest cloister is the Cloister of the Kings, but it's also the least atmospheric. Back in the Cloister of Silence, a small staircase leads up to an exquisitely carved Gothic choir which gives a beautiful bird's-eye-view of the elegant Gothic church. The sumptuous alabaster tomb behind the main altar belongs to Don Juan, the only son of the Catholic kings. His premature death had far-reaching consequences for the country, and the Catholic kings were succeeded by Carlos I (Charles V), Spain's first Habsburg ruler. Torquemada, the notorious inquisitor, is buried in the Sacristy.

Sierra de Gredos → *Colour map 4, grid B3/4.*

The Sierra de Gredos is the westernmost region of the Sistema Central, the spiky range which, with the Sierra de Guadarrama, forms Spain's craggy backbone. It's a beautiful region of forested peaks and stone villages, and it offers excellent opportunities for hiking, fishing, hang-gliding, horse riding, mountain biking and other sports. Not surprisingly, it has become a popular refuge for stressed-out city-dwellers who have bought up holiday homes, but there's still not a great deal of accommodation in the region and it's worth checking out the *casas rurales* (see below).

▶▶ For Sleeping, Eating and other listings, see pages 139-146.

Madrid & around Sierra de Gredos

Getting there and around Public transport is restricted to sporadic and infrequent services from Madrid and Ávila, so consider renting a car.

Tourist information There is no visitors' centre within the limits of the Parque Regional de la Sierra de Gredos. You can get information on accommodation and activities from the Centro de Información Sobre Turismo Rural Gredos Norte – Alberche ① *C/Comandante Albarrán 8, T920221430*. There are lists of *casas rurales* online at www.casasgredos.com and more information on www.gredos.com. Local tourist information offices have some details of walking routes, but you should pick up detailed walking guides and maps in advance from bookshops in Madrid or Ávila.

Arenas de San Pedro

Arenas de San Pedro is one of the largest and most accessible towns in the region, a popular weekend retreat crammed with craft shops and second homes. Sights include the sturdy 15th-century **Castillo de la Triste Condessa** (Castle of the Sad Countess), named for the unfortunate Juana Pimental who was beheaded by Juan II of Castille, a **Gothic church** which contains the tomb of San Pedro de Alcántara who died here in 1562, and the simple **Puente Romano** (which is actually medieval). There is a traditional pilgrimage to the **Santuario de San Pedro**, 3 km from the town, in mid-October when the local festival is celebrated with bullfights and plenty of carousing on the streets. The tourist office (① *Plaza de San Pedro s/n, T920372368, www.aytoarenas.com*) has details of walking routes throughout the Sierra, but the string of delightful tiny villages – **Guisando**, **El Arenal**, and particularly **El Hornillo** – a few kilometres north of Arenas make better bases for hikers, with several routes splintering off into the mountains.

Hoyos del Espino and Navarredonda de Gredos

These unassuming villages have a spectacular setting in the northern foothills of the Sierra de Gredos, and are good bases for circular walks. A 12-km asphalt road leads from Hoyos (there's another from Navarredonda) to the **Plataforma de Gredos**, where there's a *hostal* (T920349023). From here, it's a spectacular two-hour trek on a well-marked reasonably easy path to the **Laguna Grande** in the **Circo de Gredos** at the centre of the park. The lake, a glowing, unearthly emerald, reflects the granite bulk of the **Pico del Almanzor** (2593 m), the highest peak of the Sierra de Gredos. There's another *hostal* here (T920348047), with an adjoining camping area. There are tourist offices in Navarredonda and Hoyos (① *Plaza de Calvo Sotelo 1, T920349001 and Cruce de la Ctra de la Plataforma de Gredos, T920349035 respectively*).

Piedrahíta and El Barco de Ávila

Piedrahíta, 60 km southwest of Ávila, is a handsome town with a smattering of noble mansions and a porticoed main square. The 18th-century **Palacio de los Duques de Alba** is surrounded by gardens designed in imitation of those at La Granja (see page 125), although they are not as manicured or well kept. The nearby **Puerta de la Peña Negra** is popular with hang-gliders from all over Spain. Piedrahíta's tourist information office is in the Ayuntamiento ① *Plaza de España 1, T920360001*.

Some 20 km further west, heading towards the Valle de la Vera in Extremadura (see page 640), is El Barco de Ávila, one of the loveliest towns in the region, with an incomparable setting on the edge of the Sierra de Gredos and overlooked by a ruined castle. It also has a fine Plaza Mayor – officially the Plaza de España – and a serene Gothic church with a pretty belltower. El Barco de Ávila's tourist information office is only open in July and August ① *Plaza de España 4, T920340888*.

Alcalá de Henares and around → *Colour map 5, grid A1. For*

Sigüenza and Cuenca, northeast of Alcalá, see Castilla-La Mancha, page 625.

An engaging, quietly affluent city, Alcalá de Henares is scattered with plenty of opulent reminders of the glory days of the 16th and 17th centuries. Set 35 km east of Madrid (on the main motorway route to Zaragoza), it's an easy day trip from the capital but, if you've got more time, you could make a diversion to the unusual 18th-century planned town of **Nuevo Báztan**. ▶▶ *For Sleeping, Eating and other listings, see pages 139-146.*

History

Alcalá de Henares' claim to fame was its university, which was established by Cardinal Cisneros (confessor to Isabel II) in 1498, and which came to rival even that of Salamanca as the intellectual centre of Spain. Named the Complutense after the Roman name for the town, Complutum, the university produced the world's first polyglot bible (you can see an example of it in the Ayuntamiento/town hall) but it's most famous as the birthplace of Cervantes. He wasn't the only famous resident: Calderón de la Barca, Lope de Vega and Ignatius Loyola all studied here during Spain's Golden Age. The university moved to Madrid in the 19th century and the city went into decline – which has been dramatically reversed since the university's return to Alcalá in 1977.

Sights

The centre of Alcalá is the **Plaza de Cervantes**, a long formal square edged with arcaded narrow mansions, and shaded by plane trees. There are plenty of bars and restaurants with tables spilling out on to the square, and a small bandstand for concerts on warm summer nights. Cervantes was baptised in the rosy 15th-century **Capilla del Oidor** that stands at the top of the square, and has a slim, graceful belltower, and the 17th-century **Teatro de Cervantes**, which is believed to be the oldest surviving public theatre in Europe, was discovered under the square in 1980. Restoration work has been ongoing for some considerable time.

Most of the major university buildings are clustered near here, including the striking **Colegio Mayor de San Ildefonso** (1537-1553) ① *T91885400, guided depart hourly 1130-1330 and 1700-1900, more frequently at weekends, €2.10*, which overlooks the Plaza de San Diego just to the east of the Plaza de Cervantes. The spectacular Plateresque façade is the work of Rodrigo Gil de Hontañón, and the well at the centre of the finest of the three internal patios is sculpted with swans (*cisnes*), in a neat reference to Cardinal Cisneros, the founder of the university. Admission is by guided tour only (although you can usually peek into the main patio) and includes entrance to the Parainfo, a sumptuous hall with a magnficent coffered ceiling, where the award ceremony for Spain's most prestigious literary prize, the Premio Cervantes, is held annually on 23 April. The Capilla de San Ildefonso is equally dazzling, a glittering mix of Gothic, Mudéjar and Renaissance styles, with plenty of gleaming white stucco ornamentation and an exquisite coffered ceiling. Many of the university's most influential associates are buried here, including Felipe II's physician, El Divino Vallés, and Antonio de Nebrija. The creamy, ornately carved alabaster tomb of Cardenal Cisneros doesn't actually contain his mortal remains, which were buried instead in the cathedral.

The delightful **Calle Mayor** runs down from the Plaza de Cervantes and is still overhung with crooked medieval houses. Once the main market street of the Judería or Jewish Quarter, it's still lined with the porticoes which would once have sheltered stall-holders and market traders. Now it's become a rather chic shopping area, with plenty of cafés and bars for a break. On the right, Cervantes' birthplace has been

converted into a charming museum, **Casa-Museo de Cervantes** ① *Tue-Sun 1015-1330 and 1600-1815, free*. The house is set around a patio, now glassed over, and contains typical period furnishings, including a recently discovered Renaissance mural in one room. Downstairs are the social and public rooms, including a sturdy Castillian kitchen and a special area for women with a raised platform known as the *estrado de los damas*, a Muslim tradition that found its way into Spanish culture. Upstairs, one room has been devoted to dozens of editions from around the world and across the centuries of Cervantes' famous work, Don Quixote, and there's also a sweet little children's room with toys and books. Cardinal Cisneros is buried in the early 16th-century **cathedral of Saints Just and Pastor,** which commemorates the two child saints who were martyred on this spot according to legend. To the west, the **Archbishop's Palace** dates back to the 13th century and is topped with an untidy fringe of storks' nests. For a glimpse into Alcalá's Roman past, visit the former **Convento de la Madre de Dios** next door, which has been converted into an **archaelogy museum** ① *Tue-Sat 1100-1900, Sun and hols 1100-1500, free*, and is largely devoted to the discoveries made in the Roman settlement of Complutum just outside Alcalá.

Around Alcalá de Henares

Nuevo Báztan, 20 km from Alcalá, is a sort of 18th-century Milton Keynes. Juan de Goyeneche commissioned the celebrated Baroque architect José Benito de Churriguera to create a purpose-built town which was to include a palace for himself, a church, and homes and workshops for the community of craftspeople whom he hoped to encourage to live there. He named it after his home village in Navarra. The project attracted a great deal of enthusiasm at the beginning but it wasn't long before the excitement fizzled out; everything looked fabulous but nothing seemed to work. Even the new glass factory, established by Felipe VI, was forced to close because of fuel problems. Nuevo Báztan became a ghost town. Recently, it's become popular with developers, who are throwing up new homes for Madrid commuters at a frightening pace. You can still visit the palace and church, built as a single unit and the centrepiece of Nuevo Báztan, but much of it is now sadly dilapidated.

Aranjuez

Lush Aranjuez, about 45 km southeast of Madrid, is a rare oasis of green in the sun-baked Castillian plain. It's famous throughout Spain for its asparagus and strawberries, and is a very popular weekend outing for Madrileño families. ➤➤ *For Sleeping, Eating and other listings, see pages 139-146.*

Sights

The Bourbons built an extravagant Versailles-inspired **palace** ① *Oct-Mar 1000-1715, Apr-Sep 1000-1815, €4.81/3.91, free to EU-passport holders on Wed*, to escape Madrid's searing summer heat, and surrounded it with spectacular gardens. Destroyed by fire in 1727, it had barely been rebuilt before another fire ripped through it in 1748. It has been beautifully restored and filled with original furniture and vast crystal chandeliers; highlights include the spectacular Salón de Baile, an enormous ballroom with wonderful views of the gardens, and the Salón de Porcelana, in which every inch is encrusted with porcelain chinoiserie in the purest rococo style. The dramatic throne room has blood red velvet walls and an elaborate allegory of the monarchy on the ceiling. Downstairs, the quirky **Museo de La Vida** has a motley collection of fans, military uniforms, kitchen utensils and all kinds of other odds and ends. Best of all is the bizarre early portable gym, and the collection of toys which includes a mini-Hansom cab, a tiny bicycle with an enormous front wheel, a doll's house and miniature uniforms and guns.

Aranjuez is most famous for its exquisite **gardens** ⓘ *Oct-Mar 0800-1830, Apr-Sep 0800-2030, free*, which provide delightful relief from the scorching summer heat. Behind the palace are the manicured, elegant Jardines de la Isla and the Parterre, which combine elements of Italian, French, Dutch and Islamic garden design. The most extensive gardens are the **Jardínes de la Princípe**, vast, cool and shady, which stretch along the river bank. At the furthest end of these gardens, Carlos IV's whimsical summer pavilion, the **Casa del Labrador** ⓘ *T918910305, Oct-Mar 1000-1715, Apr-Sep 1000-1815, admission by guided visit only (call well in advance to book) €3/2.25, free to EU-passport holders on Wed*, is now a delightful museum and perhaps even more opulent than the royal palace itself. Stuffed full of silken tapestries, fine porcelain, ornate clocks, Roman statuary, and paintings, a tour through the sumptuous apartments is a dizzying experience – and as far from the home of an ordinary labourer (*labrador*) as one could possibly get.

Down by the river, the royal boathouse has been converted into a fascinating little museum of royal barges, the **Museu de Faluas Reales** ⓘ *Jardínes del Príncipe, T918912453, Oct-Mar 1000-1715, Apr-Sep 1000-1815, €3/2.25, free to EU-passport holder on Wed*. Gawp at the ornate craft used to transport languid Royals downriver, from the gorgeous 17th-century Venetian barge covered with gilded nymphs and garlands, to Isabel II's sumptuous barge inlaid with mahogany and gold silk. For the tourist office ⓘ *Plaza de San Antonio 9, T918910427*.

Chinchón

Chinchón, a charming hill town about 50 km southeast of Madrid, is set around a famously lovely Plaza Mayor. So famous, in fact, that your chances of getting a table at one of the square's equally famous *mesónes* on a Sunday, are virtually nil. Even Orson Welles fell under Chinchón's spell, and filmed parts of *Chimes At Midnight* and *An Immortal Story* here. The dramatic connection is apt; the square is a perfectly preserved example of an early *corral de la comedias*, an outdoor theatre which was also used for bullfights, hangings, and markets and all manner of public entertainment. The elegant tiers of wooden galleries still offer a perfect view of the action below during local fiestas when *corridas* are still held. Chinchón is also known for the production of *anís*, a pungent aniseed-flavoured liqueur, which you can buy from the scores of distilleries and souvenir shops that dot the town. Better yet, come for the annual **Fiesta del Anís y Vino** in mid-April (if you don't mind the crowds) when you can sample the stuff to your heart's content. The town is also known for the Easter passion plays, enacted by the locals. Chinchón's tourist information office is in the town hall ⓘ *Plaza Mayor, T918940084.* ▸▸ *For Sleeping, Eating and other listings, see pages 139-146.*

Toledo → *Phone code: 925; Colour map 4, grid B6; Population: 70,500; Altitude: 529 m.*

Toledo was an captivating city of shadowy streets, sitting on a hilltop above the River Tajo and less than an hour's drive from Madrid. Famously one of the most learned and tolerant cities of medieval Spain, its once-glorious past is recalled in the magnificent palaces, mansions and churches that cram the maze of narrow passages. Unsurprisingly, then, it's also a tourist honeypot, stuffed full of coaches, souvenir shops, and restaurants with laminated menus in a dozen languages. Come in the off-season, or stay overnight if you can: when the day-trippers are gone and quiet falls on the ancient town, it remains one of the most beguiling cities in Spain. ▸▸ *For Sleeping, Eating and other listings, see pages 139-146.*

● Next door to Casa-Museo de Cervantes is the hospital where Cervantes' father worked as a
● blood-letter – it's Spain oldest continually functioning hospital.

Getting there Toledo is served by regular trains and buses from Madrid. The train station is a gorgeous neo-Mudéjar fantasy, about a 20-minute walk from the city centre. The bus station is about 10 minutes. ▶▶ *For further details, see Transport page 146.*

Getting around Take bus No 5 or 6 to get to the Plaza de Zocodovar in the city centre from the train station. There are several local bus services from the bus station. Once you've made it inside the walls, you can walk everywhere – Toledo's narrow streets were not designed for cars or buses.

Orientation The old walled city sits on the top of a hill in a loop in the River Tajo, with the newer neighbourhoods spreading out beyond the walls. Once in the maze of streets of the *casco histórico*, you will certainly get lost (enjoy it, everyone does) but somehow all streets seem to lead back to the massive cathedral in the centre.

Best time to visit The religious processions for Corpus Christi are famous throughout Spain. It gets very, very packed in the summer – spring and autumn are best for escaping the crowds.

Tourist information ① *Puerta de Bisagra s/n, T925220843, ww.jccm.es, Mon-Fri 1000-1800, Sat 0900-1900, Sun and holidays 0900-1500. Ayuntamiento, Plaza de Ayuntamiento, T925269700, Mon 1030-1430, Tue-Sun 1030-1430 and 1630-1900.*

History

Toledo has been an important settlement long before the Romans conquered it in the second century BC, and succeeding waves of conquerors and settlers have all left their mark here. During the Middle Ages, it gained a formidable reputation for learning and religious tolerance, and Muslims, Jews and Christians lived together in comparative harmony: after the Reconquest, Toledo's new ruler Alfonso VI gave himself the title 'Emperor of the Three Religions'. Cultured, prosperous Toledo was in the running for capital, but when Madrid won the race in 1561, it lost most of its influence and became a quiet backwater. El Greco retired here after refusing to butter up his royal patrons in Madrid, and the city holds an extensive collection of his works. Always in the shadow of Madrid, it wasn't until the Civil War that Toledo re-entered the history books with the famous Siege of the Alcázar in 1936, when more than a thousand Nationalist soldiers and their families held out while the fortress was bombed to smithereens around them.

Sights

Catedral de Toledo ① *C/Cardenal Cisneros s/n, T925222241, Mon-Sat, 1000-1830, Sun 1400-1800; €4.80 (includes entrance to Treasury, Choir, Sala Capitular, and the Sacristy Museum).* Toledo's vast cathedral, a suitably magnificent home for the Primate See of all Spains, is caught in the bewildering net of narrow streets twisting around its bulk. As a result, it's impossible to see in its entirety, and yet there are tantalizing glimpses of its ancient walls, gates and domes down every tiny passage and square. Begun in 1227 and completed in 1493, it's a complicated mish-mash of Gothic styles, confusing and flouncy on the outside, but exceptionally fine within.

The huge interior, with five broad naves supported by ranks of sturdy columns, is surprisingly light, and the 15th- and 16th-century stained-glass windows are among the finest in Spain. In the middle of the central nave is the elaborate Gothic **Choir**, divided into two tiers of seats. Those on the lower level are intricately carved with scenes from the conquest of Granada, each seat depicting the fall of a different city, and those on the upper levels are etched with biblical stories from the Old Testament and a menagerie of fantastic creatures. The choir is enclosed by a lacy grille originally made of gold, which was given an iron coating to protect it from the pillaging Napoleonic armies; unfortunately, the iron won't come off. The **main altar** is equally flamboyant, with an immense polychrome retablo soaring up to the gilded ceiling, presided over by a 15th-century silver statue of the Virgin. In the ambulatory behind

the main altar is an enormous, fluffy **Transparente**, a circular roof opening pierced by theatrical shards of sunlight, surrounded by saints and angels oozing from clouds of plaster. Visit at midday to get the full effect of its kitsch Baroque magnificence, strikingly at odds with the Gothic sobriety of the rest of the church. Below it, a tatty scrap of fabric hangs next to an urn; in fact it's a cardinal's hat, one of several dotted around the cathedral, which mark the burial places of Spanish cardinals who are allowed to choose where they want to be laid to rest. There are dozens of small chapels set into the walls around the cathedral, but the finest is the **Mozarabic chapel** beneath the dome, where mass is still held according to ancient Visigothic rites daily at 0930 (the only time you'll be able to enter it).

The admission ticket includes entrance to the **Treasury**, with a spectacular artesonado ceiling which looks like a melting honeycomb and a 10-ft-high 16th-century silver monstrance used in the annual Corpus Christi processions. The **Sacristy** and adjoining rooms contain the cathedral's paintings, notably El Greco's magnificent *El Expolio* (Disrobing of Christ), and works by Rubens, Zurbarán, Titian, Raphael and Caravaggio, as well as a collection of religious ornaments and embroidered vestments dating back to the 15th century. Finally, the **Sala Capitular** contains a blazing scarlet and gold carved ceiling and trompe l'oeil frescoes; in the second hall, there is a series of portraits of the Archbishops of Toledo, the last few all uncannily alike, beneath another gilded ceiling.

On the trail of El Greco The Plaza de Ayuntamiento flanks the eastern side of the cathedral and is overlooked by the 17th-century **Ayuntamiento** (town hall), a restrained, graceful building designed by El Greco's son, Jorge Theotocópulos. Just beyond it is the 16th-century **Convento de Saint Ursula**, on the little square of the same name, where you can buy some sweet treats from the nuns, and admire the sadly dilapidated Mudéjar carved ceilings (admission €1).

Calle Santo Tomé leads to the **Iglesia Santo Tomé** ① *Plaza del Conde s/n, T925256098, www.santotome.org,1000-1845, €1.20/.90*, which contains El Greco's masterful *El Entierro del Conde de Orgaz* (The Burial of Count Orgaz), a massive canvas which established El Greco's reputation once and for all as a spiritual painter par excellence. González Ruiz de Toledo, the fourth Count of Orgaz and tutor to Alfonso XI, was a devout man, and according to legend, Saints Augustine and Stephen miraculously appeared to aid at his burial in this chapel in 1312. The tomb was lost, and remained undiscovered until early 2001. Now the count's bones sit beneath El Greco's solemn, moving depiction of the scene, painted around 1586. The saints, dressed in elaborate robes, are lifting the count into his coffin, while behind them stand a group of influential Toledans in contemporary dress, including, just above St Stephen's head, a self-portrait of El Greco himself. The young boy on the left of the picture is El Greco's beloved son, Jorge, gazing out steadily and inviting the onlooker's participation in the scene. Above the sombre group is a swirl of angels and saints, culminating in the figure of Christ Universal bathed in golden light at the very top. The plain little church contains nothing else of note, besides the tombs of the counts of Fuensalida, whose palace sits opposite the church.

Next door to the Palace of the Counts of Fuensalida is the **Taller de Moro** ① *C/Taller del Moro s/n, T925224500, Tue-Sat 1000-1400 and 1600-1800, Sun and holidays 1000-1400, €1*, a series of rooms in a Mudéjar palace which were used as an atelier for masons working on the cathedral. Much of its original brickwork and decoration have survived, a striking backdrop for a collection of artworks from the period.

Tiny Calle San Juan de Dios, a typical Toledan street lined with an uninterrupted string of souvenir shops, runs down from the church to the **Casa-Museo de El Greco** ① *C/Samuel Leví s/n, T925224046,Tue-Sat 1000-1345, 1600-1745, Sun 1000-1345; €3/1.50 concessions*. It seems unlikely that El Greco ever actually lived here, but it remains a beautiful example of a 16th-century Toledan mansion, with a recreation of

Toledo

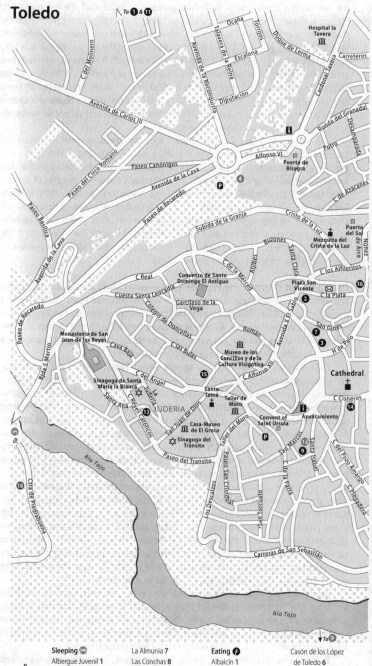

N

| 0 metres | 50 |
| 0 yards | 50 |

Sleeping
Albergue Juvenil **1**
Alfonso VI **2**
Camping El Greco **3**
Hostal Cardenal **4**
Hostal Centro **5**
Hostal Madrid **6**

La Almunia **7**
Las Conchas **8**
Parador Conde
de Orgaz **9**
Pensión Castilla **10**
Pensión Segovia **11**
Santa Isabel **12**

Eating
Albaicín **1**
Art-Café **2**
Asador
Adolfo **3**
Bar Esteban **4**
Casa Ludeña **5**

Casón de los López
de Toledo **6**
Cervecería Adolfo **7**
El Trébol **8**
El Tropezón **9**
La Abadía **10**
La Cepa Andaluza **11**

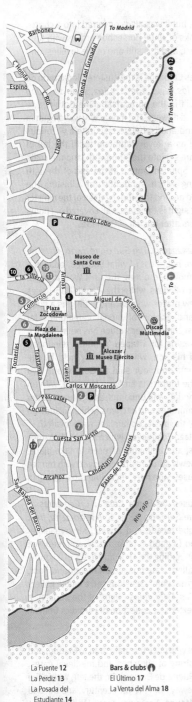

El Greco's studio on the upper floor (currently closed for restoration). The adjoining museum displays several of El Greco's masterpieces, including a magnificent *View of Toledo* (1610-1616) in a small chapel with a richly gilded artesonado ceiling. There is a gallery of portraits, a series of haunting, melancholy saints, and a room devoted to the works of the Madrid school (which you might happily skip) and another to the Sevilla School, where you'll find a beautiful depiction of the *Tears of St Peter* by Zurbarán (circa 1630-1640).

The Judería This tight spiral of streets around the Casa-Museo de El Greco was once the heart of the Jewish Quarter, or *Judería*. Before the Jews were expelled from Spain in 1492, Toledo had the largest Jewish community on the Iberian peninsula – more than 12,000 Jews lived here, and worshipped at ten synagogues. Only two survive and both were converted into churches when the Jews were forced into exile. The **Sinagoga del Tránsito** was built in the 13th century with money raised by Samuel Leví, treasurer to Pedro the Cruel (before he lived up to his name and had Samuel executed), and boasts some of the most opulent Mudéjar decoration in all Toledo. There's a magnificent artesonado ceiling carved from cedarwood, and the upper walls are adorned with a series of graceful arches and Hebraic inscriptions, thickly encrusted with elaborate mosaics and stucco designs. The annexe, once a house a convent, has been converted to the fascinating **Museo Sefardí**, ⓘ *C/Samuel Levi s/n, T9252 23665, Tue-Sat 1000-1400, 1600-1800, Sun 1000-1400, €2.40*, a museum of Sephardic Jewish culture, with tombs, columns, clothing and books.

The second surviving synagogue is almost next door, just around the corner on C/Reyes Católicos (ironically named for the monarchs who ordered the expulsion of the Jews). At the end of the 12th century, the **Sinagoga de Santa María la Blanca** ⓘ *1000-1345 and 1530-1745 (winter) 1000-1400 and 1530-1900 (summer)*, was the most

important place of worship in Jewish Toledo, but it was also converted into a church on the departure of the Jews. The serene ranks of white horseshoe arches with their pale, intricate decoration have survived intact, and it is still one of the loveliest and most contemplative corners of the city.

At the northeastern end of the Calle Reyes Católicos is the austere **Monasterio de San Juan de los Reyes** ① *Plaza San Juan de los Reyes, T925223802, 1000-1345 and 1530-1745, until 1845 in summer, €1.20*, built in the purest Isabelline Gothic style around a pretty cloister full of orange trees and flowers. The monastery was begun in 1476 by order of the Catholic Kings, Ferdinand and Isabel, to celebrate a victorious battle against the Portuguese and to serve as a Royal Pantheon (until the fall of Granada changed their plans). Their initials are set into the stonework, and the coats of arms of all the kingdoms making up the Spanish Empire at the end of the 15th century are set into the artesonado ceiling which surrounds the cloister. The gargoyles and grotesquerie which are massed around the upper gallery of the cloister were a 19th-century addition, but the oddest sight is the great wall covered in chains struck from prisoners released from the Moors after the fall of Granada.

Alcázar and around ① *Cuesta de Carlos V, T925221673, Tue-Sun 0930-1400, €2*. The Alcázar or fortress sits right on the top of the hill; most of what you see today is a reconstruction, as it was almost entirely demolished during the Civil War. In 1936, almost 1200 Nationalists holed up here for 68 days while the Republican forces bombarded the fortress. This is one of the few places where Franco still gets a good press, with plenty of patriotic plaques, and photos of medal ceremonies for siege-survivors. Most bizarrely, the Nationalist commander's office has been left as it was at the end of the siege to provide a setting for a taped 'genuine' telephone conversation between the commander and his son, who was being held by the Republicans. The Colonel tells his son "Commend your soul to God, shout Viva España, and die like a patriot". The rest of the fortress is an Army Museum, with an enormous collection of weaponry, models, medals and uniforms, and you can potter about in the cavernous cellars, where the dormitories and kitchens (which include an oven ingeniously powered by a motorbike) of the besieged families were located.

The transport hub of the old city is the **Plaza Zocodovar**, which means 'livestock market' and is where the markets, hangings, and bullfights all used to take place. Now it's an elegant, if rather bland, square, newly spruced up and edged with terrace cafés and cake shops. Almost all the local buses stop here, including those going to and from the train and bus stations.

Almost opposite the square is the **Museo de Santa Cruz** ① *C/Cervantes 3, T925221036, Mon 1000-1400, 1600-1830, Tue-Sat 1000- 1830, Sun 1000-1430, free*, a former hospital with a dazzling Plateresque façade and a wide, sunny cloister embellished with creamy Mudéjar decoration (a good spot for lazing and reading). The basement contains prehistoric artefacts including the skull and tusks of a couple of mammoths. The painting and sculpture galleries are housed on the ground floor, and include a mixed collection of 16th- and 17th-century religious art, a whole gallery of El Grecos, and the magnificent *Tapis de los Astrolabios* (Signs of the Zodiac), a 15th-century Flemish tapestry. Upstairs is an extensive collection of ceramics from all over Spain.

Puerta de Bisagra and around **Calle Armas** was once the main road to Madrid, and curves down from Plaza Zocodovar past a string of churches and medieval gates, before reaching the entrance to the city, the Puerta de Bisagra. On the left, within the city walls, the **Puerta del Sol** is a Mudéjar gateway from the 14th century, and beyond it stands the Mudéjar church of **Santiago El Mayor**. A steep passage leads up to the **Mezquita del Cristo de la Luz**, a 10th-century mosque which was converted into a church in the 13th century, making it possibly the first example of Mudéjar art in

Spain. According to legend, Alfonso VI rode into the city on El Cid's horse which suddenly knelt in front of the mosque and refused to take another step. Inside the mosque, a statue of Christ was discovered, illuminated by a lantern which had remained steadily alight for more than three centuries of Moslem rule. The legend gave the church its name – Christ of the Light.

Piercing the city walls is the flamboyant **Puerta Nueva de Bisagra**, still the main entrance to the city from Madrid, which replaced the modest Arabic gateway (still standing next to it) in the mid-16th century, and is topped with the imperial coat of arms of Felipe II. Beyond the gate, outside the city walls and reached through shady gardens with outdoor cafés, is the **Hospital de Tavera** ① *C/Cardenal Tavera 2, T925220541, 1030-1330 and 1530-1800, €3*, founded in the 16th century, and restored by the Duchess of Lerma after the Civil War. It's now a quiet and little visited museum, with sumptuous 17th-century apartments hung with paintings by El Greco, Ribera (including the wonderful *Lady with a Beard*), Tintoretto and Zurbarán.

Other churches and museums Toledo is crammed with churches and small museums. **Iglesia de San Román** is one of the oldest churches in Toledo, built with the recycled remnants of Roman columns and Visigothic capitals. It's now the **Museo de los Concilios y de la Cultura Visigótica** ① *Plaza San Román s/n, T925227872, Tue-Sat 1000-1400 and 1600-1830, Sun 1000-1400, €60*, scattered with Visigothic stonework and jewellery from the fifth and seventh centuries, and still bearing the faded remains of medieval murals on most of the exposed brickwork.

Nearby, on a quiet, dusty square, is the **Convento de Santo Domingo El Antiguo** ① *Plaza Santo Domingo El Antiguo s/n, T925222930, Mon-Sat 1100-1330 and 1600-1900, Sun 1600-1900, €1.20*. Designed by Herrera in the 16th century, the church is starkly whitewashed which only serves to highlight the beauty of the retablo above the main altar. The panels were painted by El Greco, whose tomb is in the church crypt, and visible through a cracked glass floor. The nuns will let you into the choir to admire their battered collection of religious art – mostly sentimental Baroque bits and bobs – and to pick up some of their famous cakes.

Around Toledo

From Toledo, you can head for the remote hills of the **Montes de Toledo** (see page 634), pick up pottery from the modern ceramic-producing town of **Talavera de la Reina**, or tilt at windmills like Don Quijote in **Consuegra**. These are all described in the Castilla-La Mancha chapter, page 621 .

⊜ Sleeping

El Escorial *p119*
El Escorial is an easy day-trip from Madrid, but there are a few options for staying if you want to explore the mountains. There are a couple of youth hostels, but they are only open in summer and are almost always full of school groups.
AL Hotel Victoria Palace, C/Juan de Toledo 4, T918969890, www.hotelvictoriapalace. com. The plushest place in town, with views of the monastery and the surrounding mountains, as well as a pool and fine, expensive, restaurant.
C Parrilla Principe, C/Floridablanca 46, T918901611, F918907601. Modest, family-

run hotel in a converted 18th-century mansion, with simple but well-equipped rooms and a popular local, mid-range priced restaurant.
D Cristina, C/Juan de Toledo 6, T918901961, F918901601. Right by the smart **Hotel Victoria Palace**, this hotel is set in another converted townhouse and offers the same views at a budget price.
E Hostal Vasco, Plaza de Santiago 11, T918901619. A good budget option; some rooms have balconies overlooking the plaza.
G Camping El Escorial, Ctra de Guadarrama km 14.8, T918902412. Well-equipped campsite with pools, tennis courts and laundry (nearest bus stop is 500 m).

For information on the mountain refuges in the Sierra de Guadarrama, consult the information centre. In Cercedilla, with so many second homes, there are few accommodation options.

B La Barranca, in a spectacular and secluded mountain setting, with a pool, tennis, terrace bar and mid-range priced restaurant.

C Las Postas, Ctra N-601 km 10.20, Navacerrada, T918560250, www.hotelas postas.com, is set in a former stage post and has a good bar and mid-range priced restaurant. Comfortable.

D El Aribel, Cercedilla, T918521511, F918521561, recently renovated has simple en suite rooms with pine furniture, an inexpensive restaurant, and sunny terrace.

D-E Hostal Madrid París, Ctra de Burgos Km 75, Buitrago de Lozoya, T918681136, is one of only a few options. Simple rooms and a decent restaurant.

E Hostal Mayte, Avda de Madrid, T918560297, functional and spotless, this is a decent budget option in the town centre.

E There are a couple of **youth hostels** further up the village of Cercedilla (La Dehesas, T918520135, and Villacastora, T918520334), but they are only open in summer and are almost always booked up by school groups.

Segovia and around *p121, map p122*

L Hosteria Ayala Berganza, C/Carretas 5, T921461300.

AL Parador de Segovia, Ctra Valladolid s/n, T921443737, segovia@parador.es. Bright, modern and well-equipped parador overlooking a lake, about 2 km outside Segovia, with pool, and fine restaurant. There are fabulous views of Segovia, but you'll need your own transport.

A Los Linajes, C/Doctor Velasco 9, T921460475, F921460479. Occupies part of an 11th-century mansion next to the city walls, but the interior has been over-renovated and rooms are a little sterile.

B Infanta Isabel, Plaza Mayor s/n, T921461300, www.hotelisabel.com. Perfectly placed in a restored 19th-century mansion overlooking the Plaza Mayor, the rooms are large and well-equipped, and the best have balconies on the square. Ask about weekend discounts.

B Las Fuentes, C/Padre Claret 6, San Ildefonso de la Granja, T921471024, F921471741, the prettiest option in La Granja set in a 19th-century mansion surrounded by manicured gardens, with a good mid-range priced restaurant.

C Las Sirenas, C/Juan Bravo 30, T921462663, hotelsirenas@terra.es. A classic hotel built in the 1950s with spacious antique-decorated rooms, a café-bar, and even a gym, in the centre of the old city.

D Hostal Don Jaime, C/Ochoa Ondátegui 8, T921444787. Right next to the aqueduct (the best rooms overlook it) and furnished with chintzy fabrics and dark wood.

D Hostal Fornos, C/Infanta Isabel 13, T921460198. A small, pretty *hostal* just off the Plaza Mayor, with charming rooms decorated with wicker furniture.

E Hostal Juan Bravo, C/Juan Bravo 12, T921463413. A good, central budget choice, with spotless rooms (with or without bath) and friendly owners.

E Pensión Pozo de la Nieve, C/Baños 4, San Ildefonso de la Granja, T921470598. Simple, small, a good budget bet.

F Pension Ferrí, C/Escuderos 10, T921460957. Basic *pensión* with small, clean rooms at a rock-bottom price close to the Plaza Mayor.

G Camping Acueducto, Ctra L-601, T921425000. About 2 km outside town, this is still the closest campsite to Segovia. Take bus No 6 from the centre of town. Open Easter-Sep.

Ávila *p126, map p126*

L Palacio de los Velada, Plaza de la Catedral 10, T920255100, F920254900. A luxurious 4-star hotel set in a magnificent 16th-century mansion close to the cathedral with a beautiful patio. It does excellent weekend deals – as low as €87 for a double room – if you book early enough.

AL Parador de Ávila, C/Marqués de Canales y Chozas 2, T920211340, avila@parador.es. One of the very best paradors, this is housed in a spectacular Renaissance palace and offers lots of luxury trimmings including antique-decorated rooms and a good restaurant. Prices drop a category in low season.

B Hostería de Bracamonte, C/Bracamonte 6, T920251280, F920253838. Another fine

mansion in the old city which has been attractively converted into a hotel, this has handsome, airy rooms and Ávila's finest restaurant (popular with politicians and celebrities).

C La Sinagoga, C/Reyes Católicos 22, T920352321, F920353474. A former 15th-century synagogue in the heart of the old city with some original fittings including delicate brick archways. Tasteful, individually decorated rooms, and a good café-restaurant and pretty interior patio.

C Las Cancelas, C/Cruz Vieja 6, T920212249, www.avilaservicios.com/can celas. Some of the rustically decorated rooms at this 15th-century inn still contain original fireplaces, and there's an excellent restaurant and tapas bar in the charming patio.

D Hostal Alcántara, C/Esteban Domingo 11, T920225003. Large, comfortable rooms on a quiet street in the old city.

E Gran Hostal Segundo, C/San Segundo 28. A simple *hostal* in a turn-of-the-century building just outside the city walls; the best rooms have balconies with fantastic views of the cathedral. There's an Italian restaurant and a tapas bar downstairs.

E Hostal El Rastro, Plaza del Rastroo 1, T920211218, F920251626. A good budget option in an old mansion within the city walls, with old-fashioned rooms and a good restaurant and tapas bar attached.

Sierra de Gredos *p129*

There is plenty of accommodation in Arenas de San Pedro and plenty of luxury accommodation in Navarredonda.

AL Parador de Gredos, Navarredonda, T920348048, gredos@parador.es. Set in pine forest just outside the village.

B La Casa Grande, C/de la Cruz, Navarredonda, T920348024, a sumptuous 17th-century mansion surrounded by gardens.

C Casa El Canchal, C/La Fuente 1, Arenas de San Pedro, T920370958, with a handful of tasteful rooms in a 17th-century mansion. Good value.

C La Casona, Piedrahíta, T920360362, in a 17th-century stone mansion with an excellent mid-range restaurant.

C Manila T920340844. One of a couple of 3-star hotels on the edge of town. Otherwise, you'll need to check out the *casas rurales*.

D Hostelería los Galayos, Plaza Condestable Dávalos 2, Arenas de San Pedro, T920371379, near the castle which has a solid mid-range priced restaurant and popular tapas bar.

E Fonda Goya, Piedrahíta, T920360720. Very simple.

E Hostal Isabel, El Arenal, T920375148. Friendly.

E Hostal Los Galayos, Guisando, T920374242. Simple and small.

F La Taberna, C/Carrellana 29, Arenas de San Pedro, T920370395, with a good cheap café-bar.

G Youth hostel, Navarredonda, T920348005, and **El Almanzor**, Ctra el Barco km 38, Navarredonda, T920348477, which is prettier inside than you'd expect from the gloomy exterior.

Toledo *p133, map p136*

L Parador Conde de Orgaz, Cerro del Emperador s/n, T925221850, toledo@parador.es. Just outside the city, this luxurious parador has fantastic views of Toledo from the pool and terrace, old beamed ceilings and antique-filled rooms. The restaurant serves good Toledan specialities including stewed partridge.

A Alfonso VI, C/General Moscardó 2, T925222600, F925214458. The plushest option inside the city walls, this is a vigorously converted mansion right on the Plaza Zocodovar with all the trimmings including a restaurant and tapas bar.

B Hostal Cardenal, Paseo de Recaredo 24, T925224900, www.cardenal. asernet.es. Formerly the home of Cardinal Lorenzana of the Inquisition, this magnificent stone palace is set in shady gardens in the heart of old Toledo. The rooms are traditionally decorated with carved wooden beds and old prints, and the restaurant (**La Antigua Casa del Sobrino de Botín** or 'the old restaurant of Botín's nephew', Botín being the name of Madrid's oldest tavern) is one of the best in the city.

B La Almunia, C/ San Miguel12, T925257772, www.la-alm unia.com. An immaculately restored 17th-century mansion close to the Alcázar, complete with wooden beams and interior patio. Rooms are handsomely furnished with antiques, and there's a terrace in the attic with stunning views. Families or groups might be

interested in the apartment with three double bedrooms, a kitchen and sitting room (€180).

C Hotel Las Conchas, C/Juan Labrador, T925210760, F925224271. A central, three-star option set in a converted townhouse in the heart of the Judería, with large well-equipped rooms and a restaurant.

D Hostal Centro, C/Nueva 13, T925257091, F925257848. Probably the best budget option in Toledo, this offers sparkling new rooms with a/c in a great location just off the Plaza Zocodovar.

D Hotel Santa Isabel, C/Santa Isabel 24, T925253120, F925253126. A central, much-modernized townhouse down a quiet street close to the cathedral, with large slightly antiseptic rooms and tiled patios. The rooms in the new annexe, another modernized old mansion with beams, are the best.

E Hostal Madrid, C/Marqués de Mendigorria 7, T925221114, F925228113. Simple, central and popular, this good-value *hostal* has great views from some rooms.

F Pensión Castilla, C/Recoletos 6, T925256318. Tucked down a tiny passage, this old-fashioned friendly *pensión* with a tiled entrance offers basic rooms at a basic price.

F Pensión Segovia, C/Recoletos 2, T925211124. A simple but spotless *pensión*, with 8 very basic rooms and shared bathrooms.

G Albergue Juvenil, Castillo San Servando, T925224554, F925267760. Set in a wing of a 14th-century castle with beautiful views of the city, this youth hostel fills up quickly. Note that it closes from mid-Aug until mid-Sep.

G Camping El Greco, Ctra Toledo-Puebla Montalbán km 0.7, T/F925220090. The best of the 3 campsites near Toledo, this is a good 30-min walk away from the town centre, but has a pool, laundry, pizzeria and good views of the city.

● Eating

El Escorial *p119*

€€ **Charolés**, C/Floridablanca 24, T918905975. This is El Escorial's most celebrated restaurant; the Wed *cocido* is an institution. Terrace in summer.

€€ **Fonda Genara**, Plaza San Lorenzo, T918904357. Tucked between 2 squares, this

traditional, inexpensive restaurant serves home-cooked dishes.

€ **La Cueva**, C/San Antón 4, T918901516. Another popular spot, **La Cueva** is a delightfully rickety old inn set over 3 floors which offers tapas in the bar or tasty, cheap, local dishes in the dining area.

Sierra de Guadarrama *p120*
See Sleeping above.

Segovia and around *p121, map p122*

Segovia's legendary speciality is *cochinillo asado* (roast suckling pig), traditionally slaughtered at just 21 days old. The expensive restaurants at the **Hosteria Ayala Berganza** and the **parador** (see p140) are also recommended.

€€€ **Méson de Cándido**, Plaza Azoguejo 5, T921428103. The late Señor Cándido was a legend, and his restaurant, picturesquely huddled under the aqueduct arches, is papered with photos of famous clients. Now run by his son, its reputation has palled slightly, but it's still a memorable spot.

€€€ **Mesón de José María**, C/Cronista Lecea 11, T921466017. Cándido's former pupil José María has been making a very big name for himself at his own *méson*, which is rated as one of the very best restaurants in Segovia and is a great place to try *cochinillo*. There's a lively bar area for tapas if you don't want a big meal.

€€ **Casa Duque**, C/Cervantes 12, T921462487. Another local institution, with an excellent reputation for traditional Segovian cuisine. It's generally considered to make the best *cochinillo asado* in Segovia, and the *judiones* (another local dish of beans cooked with pork) are also very tasty.

€€ **El Bernardino**, C/Cervantes 2, T921462474. A classic Castillian restaurant which is popular with local business people, and does an excellent *menú del día*. Try the amazing *sopa de chocolate* for dessert.

€€ **Dólar**, C/Valenciana 1, T921470269. Traditional Castillian cuisine in San Ildefonso de la Granja.

€€ **Riofrío**. The restaurant at the palace is surprisingly good, open lunchtimes only when you can tuck into *sopa castellana* or roast suckling pig.

€ **Cueva de San Estabán**, C/Valdeláguila 15, T921460982. This cavernous bar-restaurant

just off the Plaza San Esteban is a big favourite with locals. Good tapas and a reasonably priced *menú del día* – going a la carte will up the prices considerably.

€ **Mesón Mayor**, Plaza Mayor 3, T921460915. The best of the restaurants on the Plaza Mayor, you can tuck into roast meats or fill up on good tapas.

Tapas bars and cafés
In San Ildefonso de la Granja there are many tapas bars clustered on the Plaza de los Dolores. The following are all in Segovia.
La Barcaza, C/Gobernador Fernández Jiménez 22. A quiet spot for some tasty tapas including fish with wild mushrooms, and local *morcilla* (blood sausage).
Limón y Menta, C/Infanta Isabel 3, T921444002. A friendly little café serving good *bocadillos* and pastries that won't break the bank.
Taberna del Trovator, Paseo Ezequiel González, 42. A relaxed local bar which claims to make the 'best tortilla in the world'.

Sierra de Guadarrama *p120*
In Buitrago de Lozoya, the Plaza de la Constitución, just outside the old walls, is lined with restaurants and bars, most of which have terraces out on the square in summer. See Sleeping for other options.

Ávila *p126, map p126*
The restaurants at the **parador**, the **Hostería de Bracamonte**, **Las Cancelas** (all €€€-€€) and the **Mesón del Rastro** (€€-€) are all recommended (see above). It's worth noting that they all serve an excellent value *menú del día* at lunchtimes – often for less than €15.
€€ **Copacabana**, C/San Millán 9, T920211110. A handsome old restaurant (which bears no resemblance to anywhere in Brazil) serving classic local cuisine, including particularly good roast lamb and suckling pig.
€€ **Fogón de Santa Teresa**, Plaza de la Catedral, T920211023. Sturdy Castillian favourites made with the freshest local produce. This is a good place to try *perdiz* (partridge), a local speciality and apparently one of Saint Teresa's favourites.
€ **Casa Patas**, C/San Millán 4, T920213194. A local stalwart, this old-fashioned bar serves good tapas and simple meals.

€ **La Casona**, Plaza Pedro Dávila, T920256139. Small, family-run local, serving big portions of good home-cooking.

Tapas bars and cafés
Bodeguita de San Segundo, C/San Segundo 19. A smart tapas and wine bar which attracts a well-heeled crowd and gets packed out in the evenings.

Aranjuez *p132*
€€€ **Asador Palacio de Osuna**, C/Principe 21, T918924215. One of the best restaurants in town. Specializes in grilled meats and is set in a wing of a palace which once belonged to the Duke of Osuna.
€€ **La Rana Verde**, C/Reina 1, T918913238, you'll get reasonable, if unexceptional, food but a lovely riverside setting. The local specialities are strawberries and asparagus – if you arrive on the strawberry train, they'll serve you local strawberries on the way.

Chinchón *p133*
Good traditional *mesónes* on the Plaza Mayor include €€ **Mesón de la Virreina**, T918940015, and €€ **La Balconada**, T918941303.
€€ **Mesón Cuevas de la Vino**, C/Benito Hortelano 13, T918940206, is set in a former olive oil mill and has a particularly good, mid-range priced wine list.
€ **Mesón Chinchón**, C/José Antonio 12, T918940859, which does a great *menú del día* for less than €10.

Toledo *p133, map p136*
€€€ **Asador Adolfo**, C/La Granada 6, T925337321. This is the most celebrated restaurant in town, with a sumptuous dining room serving excellent regional dishes, particularly good roast meats, accompanied by an equally fine wine list.
€€€ **Casón de los López de Toledo**, C/Silleria 3, T925254774. A charming, beautifully renovated old mansion, serving sturdy *manchega* dishes and regional wines.
€€ **La Abadía**, C/Nuñez de Arce 3, T925251140. This restaurant and bar is enormously popular with locals who spill out on the street with their drinks. Excellent tapas and a good value *menú del día*.
€€ **La Perdiz**, C/Reyes Católicos 7, T925214658. The speciality here is, of course,

pheasant, served in a dozen different ways.

€ **Casa Ludeña**, Plaza de la Magdalena 13, T925223384. A very friendly, old-fashioned restaurant serving Toledano classics like partridge or *cuchifritos* (lamb cooked in sauce of tomatoes, egg, wine and saffron). Good value *menú del día*.

€ **El Tropezón**, Travesía Santa Isabel 2. A simple restaurant with a handful of tables in a patio, or a small bar serving tapas. Good, cheap food and an excellent *menú del día* at less than €7.

€ **La Posada del Estudiante**, Callejón de San Pedro, T925214734. This serves the cheapest *menú del día* in the city, and is always packed with hungry students tucking into lamb chops and tasty stews.

€ **Mille Grazie**, C/Cadenas 2, T925254270. A good option for veggies, this is the best of Toledo's Italian restaurants, with tasty pizzas, Italian cured hams – and long queues at weekends.

Tapas bar and cafés

Albaicín, Plaza de Cuba s/n. Tiny bar in the new part of town, serving tasty *pintxos* – chunks of baguette with all kinds of toppings.

Art-Café, Plaza San Vicente 6. This laid-back café is a good place to relax over a magazine or newspaper, with good tapas and pastries and changing art exhibitions every month.

Bar Esteban, Av Santa Barbara 31. A relaxed neighbourhood bar on the Plaza Santa Barbara, good for coffee, breakfast or a beer.

Cervecería Adolfo, C/Nuncio Viejo, 1. Attached to the celebrated restaurant, this offers high-quality tapas at a price to match.

El Trébol, C/Santa Fe 5. Buzzy lively little bar, which also does a fantastic range of tapas and raciones, including the house specialities – *bombas*, stuffed baked potatoes.

La Cepa Andaluza, C/Méjico, 11. A small, local bar serving fantastic frituras de pescado, tasty fried fish in the Andaluz style.

La Fuente, Avda Santa Bárbara, 97. Good fresh juices and an assortment of pastries make this a good bet for a leisurely breakfast. For something less healthy, try the *churros y chocolate*.

La Ría, Callejón de Bodegones s/n. An old-fashioned tavern serving traditional Gallego tapas like classic *pulpo gallego*,

octopus in a spicy tomato sauce, washed down with crisp white wine.

◐ Bars and clubs

Segovia and around *p121, map p122*
C/Infanta Isabel has got so many bars that it's known locally as **Calle de los Bares**. There are dozens to choose from: try the popular **Geografic Chic**, at No 13, which is decorated with comic-book characters, then make for **La Salve**, a club which is decorated like a medieval castle. **Compás**, at C/Santo Tomás 1, and **Cuba Libre** at C/Ochoa Andoátegui 8 are both good for cocktails, and the **Posada**, tucked away in the Judería (just off C/Real) does good tapas and has a buzzy bar with a juke box.

Ávila *p126, map p126*
Ávila isn't a great city for nightlife, but there are plenty of bars and cafés around the Plaza de la Victoria, and the Plaza de Santa Teresa and the streets which lead off them.

Toledo *p133, map p136*
Toledo's nightlife is pretty low-key for a student city of its size, and the *tapeo* is more of an institution than serious drinking or clubbing sessions – except in summer when everyone piles down to the big outdoor discos by the river, or along the Paseo del Miradero at the northern end of town. There are bars and clubs to suit most tastes in Toledo's *casco histórico*, and there are plenty more in the streets around the Plaza Cuba in the new part of town – **Albaicín** and **Trebol** (see above) are both good for a chilled beer on a hot night. For alternative, studenty bars, try the Callejón Sillería and around – **TBO** is always a good bet – and for jazz and blues, head for **El Último** on Plaza Colegio Infantes 4, T925212236, which has occasional live music. **La Venta Del Alma**, just outside the city walls at Carretera de Piedrabuena 35, T925254245, has great views of the old city and a beautiful outdoor patio surrounded by wooden galleries.

✺ Festivals and events

Segovia and around *p121, map p122*
There's usually something going on in Segovia.

Nearest Sun to **5 Feb** Fiesta de Santa **Águeda** when Segovian women take over the city for a day to celebrate this festival.
Holy Week A big event with plenty of processions.
24-29 Jun Fiestas of San Juan and San Pedro are celebrated with street parties and parades.
Jul A classical music festival.

Ávila *p126, map p126*
Unsurprisingly, Ávila's festivals are more serious than most.
Oct Santa Teresa is remembered with pilgrimages, *verbenas* and other religious ceremonies, floods of pilgrims descend on the city.
Easter week A big event.
Jul A festival of organ music.

Toledo *p133, map p136*
Late May or early Jun Corpus Christi is Toledo's most important festival with a spectacular, solemn procession through the streets. **Holy Week** is also an important event.

O Shopping

Toledo *p133, map p136*
Toledo has long been famous for its steel, and particularly for its knives. The city has dozens of gift shops selling armour, swords, etc: particularly in Calles Commercio and Ancha around the cathedral. If you like kitsch, these shops are definitely worth a rummage for quirky souvenirs. Try **Hija de José Martín**, C/Comercio 66.

You'll find ceramics and Jewish-related souvenirs in the Calle Santo Tomé and around, and you can pick up some of the city's famous *mazapan* sweets in the convents, or, more mundanely, in one of the delicious cake shops on the Plaza Zocodovar; **Santo Tomé**, at No 11, is regarded as the finest.

▲ Activities and tours

Sierra de Guadarrama *p120*
There are 3 small low-key ski resorts less than 70 km from Madrid: none is particularly high, and the slopes are short and not very demanding, but at least you can easily get

there just for the day. *Tren de la Nieve* ('Snow Train') runs between Cercedilla and the slopes of Navacerrada and Cotos-Valdesquí.
Puerto de Navacerrada, info in Madrid: C/Casado de Alisal, 7, T912305572. 60 km north of Madrid with 12 slopes, 5 chair lifts, 6 ski lifts and 1 children's ski lift. Shuttle buses leave regularly from Navacerrada for the ski station.
Valcotos, info in Madrid: C/Felipe IV, 12, T 912397503. 70 km north of Madrid, with 10 slopes, 2 chair lifts and 6 ski lifts. Considered to be the prettiest resort.
Valdesqui, info in Madrid: C/San Ramón Nonato 1, T912155939. 73 km north of Madrid, with 8 slopes, 2 chairlifts, 6 ski lifts and 2 children's ski lifts. The slopes here are the most demanding of the 3 resorts.

Sierra de Gredos *p129*
Grecaba, Navarredonda, T920348010, runs hikes into the Sierra.
Gredos Rutas a Caballo, T920348110, organizes horse-riding expeditions from Hoyos del Espino.
Turactiv Gredos, T920348385, www.turactiv.com. Offers all kinds of activities from rafting to hang-gliding.

⊖ Transport

El Escorial and the Sierra de Guadarrama *p119*
San Lorenzo de Escorial is reached by regular buses (**Herranz**, T918969028) and trains (from Atocha) from Madrid. One bus daily leaves from El Escorial for **Valle de los Caidos** at 1515, returns at 1730. **Cercedilla** and **Cotos** (for the **Parque Natural de Peñalara** and the ski station at **Puerto Navacerrada**) are also on the regional train line (C9 and C8b from Chamartín station in Madrid). Bus 724 leaves from the Plaza Castilla in **Madrid** for **Manzanares el Real**. There are daily direct buses to **Buitrago de Lozoya** from Madrid's Estación de Sur bus station (with **Continental**, T915330400).

Segovia and around *p121, map p122*
Bus is the most convenient way to reach Segovia. There are regular services (every 30 mins) with **La Sepulvedana**, T91547261, from Paseo de la Florida 11, Madrid (metro Principe Pío);1½ hrs journey time, €6.

There are local (6 times daily) buses from Segovia to **La Granja**, but you'll need your own transport to get out to **Riofrío**, which is about 10 km south of Segovia.

Trains depart every 2 hrs from Atocha; 2 hrs journey time, €5.50.

Ávila *p126, map p126*
Buses leave every 2 hrs from the Estación Sur in Madrid with **Larrear** (T915304800); 1¾ hrs, €7. Trains take 1½ hrs and cost €6.50. There are about 4 buses daily to **Salamanca**;1½ hrs, €5 and up to 7 buses daily for **Segovia** (1 hr, €4).

Train services are frequent to **Chamartín** and **Atocha** in Madrid, as well as connections to Salamanca, Valladolid, Medina del Campo and El Escorial.

Sierra de Gredos *p129*
Buses from Madrid (4 times daily) and Ávila (1 daily) to **Arenas de San Pedro**, with once-daily connections to Guisando, El Arenal and El Hornillo on weekdays. There are 3 buses daily from Ávila to **Piedrahíta** and **El Barco**, T920220154.

Aranjuez *p132*
There are regular buses to Aranjuez from **Madrid**'s Estación Sur (**Automnibus Urbanos**, T915304606); 1 hr. Trains run every 10 mins on the Guadalajara line from Atocha; 45 mins. In summer, the *Tren de la Fresa* ('Strawberry Train') steams to **Aranjuez** from Atocha station on summer weekends from late Apr until mid-Oct. For more information, T90228822, www.aranjuez.net

Toledo *p133, map p136*
Bus services with **Galiano Contintental**, T9174563 00 to **Madrid** every hour, with an express service every 90 mins. Various companies run services to **Cuidad Real**, **Cuenca**, **Albacete**, **Alcázar de San Juan** and there are local buses to **Orgaz**, **La Puebla de Montalbán**, and **Talavera de la Reina** (which has onward connections to **Extremadura**). For bus information, call T925215850.

Trains run frequently to **Aranjuez** (up to 9 daily, 45 mins) and **Madrid** (9 daily, 1¾ hrs).

● Directory

Segovia and around *p121, map p122*
Banks and **ATMs**   There are plenty around the Plaza Mayor. In Piedrahíta, there are plenty of banks and ATMS, especially around the Plaza de Santa Teresa. **Internet**   Kitius, Avda Fernández Ladreda 28. **Post office** Plaza de los Huertos 5. The main post office in Piedrahíta is on the Plaza Catédral 2.

Toledo *p133, map p136*
Banks   You'll find plenty of banks throughout the city, but there are dozens of ATMs on and around the Plaza Zocodovar. All the banks have bureaux de change. **Internet**   **Discad Multimedia**, C/Miguel de Cervantes 17, has a range of multimedia services. Many *locutarios* – cheap phone centres – also have internet access. You'll find a couple around the Plaza Magdalena. **Post office**   The main post office is in the centre of the old city on Calle de la Plata 1.

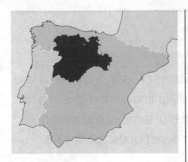

Castilla y León

Introduction

For many people, Castilla is the image of Spain; a dry, harsh land of pious cities, ham, wine and bullfighting. Visitors love or hate the dusty meseta with its extremes of summer and winter temperatures; it's a bleak, almost desert landscape in parts.

Castilla has much more to offer than faded reminders of past glories. The cities of **Southern Castilla** are all interesting: Romanesque **Soria** glows in the evening light, busy **Valladolid** preserves an imperial air, **Zamora** is a model for sensitive modern architecture, and **Salamanca** is a stunningly beautiful ensemble of Renaissance architecture. Castilla is named for its huge number of castles, many of them found in the Duero Valley. Lonely **Gormaz**, narrow **Peñafiel** and proud **Berlanga**; rich ground for exploration. Two of Spain's best wine regions also sit here. **Ribera del Duero** reds have a stellar reputation worldwide, while the lemony whites of **Rueda** are perfect for a typically hot summer's day.

Northern Castilla comprises the provinces of **Burgos** and **Palencia**, both of which stretch north from their meseta origins into some attractive valleys and uplands in the feet of the Cordillera Cantábrica range. The major attraction of Northern Castilla is its architecture; few places in the world have such a rich heritage of buildings. The main route to Santiago crosses the heart of the region and there are numerous churches and monasteries in superb Romanesque or Gothic style.

Despite being amicably joined with Castilla, the province of **León** is culturally, geographically and socially quite distinct. A vibrant city, rich in ancient and modern architectural attractions, León draws the crowds to its sublime Gothic cathedral.

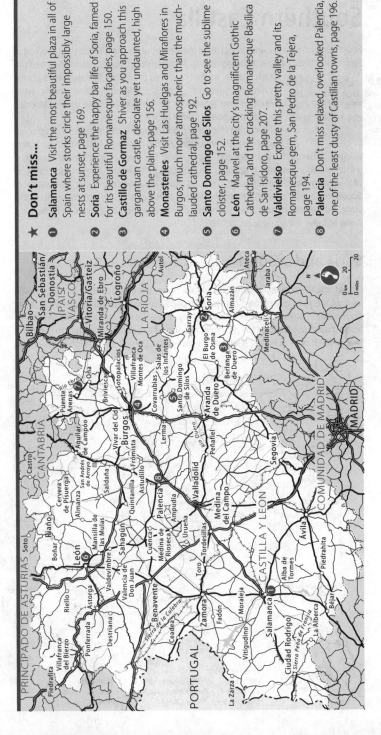

★ Don't miss...

❶ Salamanca Visit the most beautiful plaza in all of Spain where storks circle their impossibly large nests at sunset, page 169.

❷ Soria Experience the happy bar life of Soria, famed for its beautiful Romanesque façades, page 150.

❸ Castillo de Gormaz Shiver as you approach this gargantuan castle, desolate yet undaunted, high above the plains, page 156.

❹ Monasteries Visit Las Huelgas and Miraflores in Burgos, much more atmospheric than the much-lauded cathedral, page 192.

❺ Santo Domingo de Silos Go to see the sublime cloister, page 152.

❻ León Marvel at the city's magnificent Gothic Cathedral, and the cracking Romanesque Basílica de San Isidoro, page 207.

❼ Valdivielso Explore this pretty valley and its Romanesque gem, San Pedro de la Tejera, page 194.

❽ Palencia Don't miss relaxed, overlooked Palencia, one of the least dusty of Castilian towns, page 196.

Southern Castilla

Southern Castilla is the long front where the Reconquista, the Christian Reconquest of Spain, was lost and won. Pushing rapidly from the north, the Christians reached the Duero Valley, where they faced the Moors for many years from a series of muscular castles. Long-abandoned towns were resettled and gained in wealth and prestige as the Moorish kingdom began to fold in on itself.

❧ The region's cuisine tends to be more suited for winter; big roasts of pork and lamb are the order of the day.

Crossing the dusty plains today, it can be difficult to imagine just how prosperous this region once was. Places that are barely villages these days were once thriving centres; the town of Medina del Campo, a minor railstop, enjoyed a spell as one of Europe's leading commercial cities; a 16th-century Zürich or Frankfurt. This, as much as anything, is the fascination of Southern Castilla: read a little of the history of Imperial Spain and the names ring large; wander the narrow streets today and let imagination do its work. ➡ For Sleeping, Eating and other listings, see pages 175-186.

Soria and around → Phone code: 975; Colour map 2, grid C4; Population: 34,640.

One of Spain's smallest provincial capitals, Soria, the city, bosses a province that's incredibly empty, one of the most sparsely populated in Spain. Although much of it is dry Castilian plains, the Duero River gives it the fullest attention, carving a big horseshoe shape through the province, although it's certainly in no hurry to get to the sea, which it does in Portugal (where it's named the Douro). In the north of the region

Castilla y León Southern Castilla

Soria

Soria detail

Sleeping 🛏
Casa David 1
Hostal Viena 2
Hostería Solar de Tejada 3
Parador Antonio Machado 4
Pensión Carlos 5

Eating 🍴
El Mesón de Isabel 1
Mesón Castellano 2

0 metres 100
0 yards 100

are some craggy hills and tranquil hilly forests, but few trees remain in the south, for centuries a battleground between Christian and Moor. Dozens of castles are testament to this, as are the gracefully simple Romanesque churches built by the eventual victors. As the Reconquista progressed, however, Christian settlers moved south in search of less thirsty lands, leaving the province a little denuded.

Soria is little known in the travel community but is worth a day or two of anyone's time, particularly for its outstanding Romanesque architecture centred on its cheerful street life. ▶▶ *For Sleeping, Eating and other listings, see pages 175-186.*

Ins and outs

Getting there and around Soria is well connected by bus to other major cities in Northern Spain. The bus station is a 10-minute walk northwest from the centre of town. A yellow bus runs from Plaza Ramón y Cajal by the tourist office to the train station, a couple of km south. The old town, where most things of interest are, is easily walkable, tucked between two attractive parks, the hilltop Parque el Castillo, and the more formal Alameda de Cervantes. The pedestrianized main street changes name a couple of times but runs the length of the area. There are adequate bus and train services to towns and villages around Soria. ▶▶ *For further details, see Transport page 184.*

Tourist information Feel sympathy for Soria's tourist office ⓘ *daily 0900-1400, 1700-2000*, housed in a lowly shack on Plaza Ramón y Cajal. There's still plenty of reasonable information though.

History

Although nearby Numancia was an important Celtic settlement, Soria itself didn't really get going until the Middle Ages, when it achieved prosperity as a wool town until its relative isolation (plus the fact that the sheep ate all the grass) led to its decline, along with the rest of Castilla. Once the coast was under central control, there

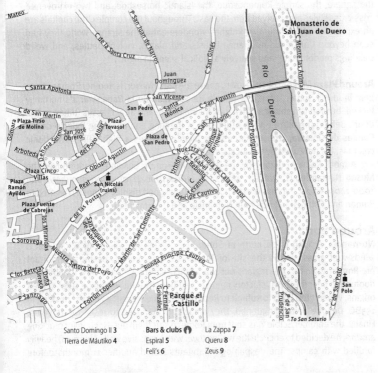

Santo Domingo II **3**
Tierra de Máutiko **4**

Bars & clubs 🎵
Espiral **5**
Feli's **6**

La Zappa **7**
Queru **8**
Zeus **9**

was no percentage left in towns like Soria; the conditions that led to its rise ceased to exist once the Moors were driven out. The cabeza (head) de Extremadura became just another decaying provincial town. Happily, this meant that there wasn't enough money to meddle with its Romanesque architectural heritage too much, a fact that the city is surely grateful for today.

Sights

Iglesia de Santo Domingo

On the northern edge of the old town, by the main road through Soria, is the Santo Domingo church, built of beautiful pale pink stone, and possessing one of the loveliest Romanesque façades in Spain. The interior is simple; barrel-vaulted, and with several interesting capitals that can be a little hard to inspect in the gloom. The portal is the highlight though; with ornately carved bands depicting a number of Biblical scenes in loveably naïve sculpture. A small guide inside the doorway helps to identify the scenes; including the visitation of the angel to the Magi. The three seem more saucy than wise, all very cosy in bed under a single duvet.

> ‡ Be sure to visit in the late afternoon, when the façade seems to glow in the setting sun.

Monasterio de San Juan de Duero

ⓘ Jun-Aug 1000-1400, 1700-2100, Apr/May, Sep/Oct 1000-1400, 1600-1900, Nov-Mar 1000-1400, 1530-1800, closed Mon all day and Sun pm, €0.60. Not far from the Iglesia de San Pedro, just on the other side of the river, is Soria's best sight, the monastery of San Juan de Duero. Although it started as a humble church, a group of Hospitallers of Saint John of Jerusalem (later known as the Knights of Malta) set up base here on their return from the crusades. The simple church, damaged by fire over the years, preserves some excellent capitals, and has decent Spanish display panels on the Romanesque in general. The cloister outside is a strange and striking sight. The knights blended four different types of arch around the square, the simple Romanesque, the Islamic horseshoe, and two extroverted criss-cross styles also derived from the east. Throughout the complex, the capitals are an expression of the returning knights' wonderment at the strange world they had seen beyond Christendom; strange beasts and plants, violent battles, and weird buildings predominate, and scarcely a Biblical scene in sight.

Around Plaza Mayor

Back in town, above the Plaza Mayor, is another Romanesque gem in lovely Sorian stone, the **Iglesia de San Juan de la Rabanera**. It's normally locked, but you can sneak a quick look inside before and after masses (times on the door). Behind the plaza on the other side is the long and imposing **Palacio de los Condes de Gómara**, whose Plateresque façade features a high gallery with Ionic columns, it's now used by the local government.

A mock-Roman building by the lovely Alameda de Cervantes park houses the **Museo Numantino** ⓘ Tue-Sat 1000-1400, 1600-1900 (1700-2000 summer), Sun 1000-1400, €1.20, information in English. The very good display is mostly devoted to Roman and Celtiberian finds from Numancia and the province.

Around Soria

Numancia

Around 6 km north of Soria, just outside the village of Garray, on a windswept grassy hill is the site of Numancia. It is one of the most important pre-Roman towns of the region, but not a must see these days. The inhabitants, doomed to bear the unsatisfactory name of Celtiberians until we can be surer of their origins, weren't too keen to submit to Republican Rome when they came knocking in 153BC. Despite being outgunned, they amazingly managed to resist for 25 years. Finally, the enforcer Scipio was sent from Rome to sort them out. Not one for mucking around, he decided to encircle the walled town with a massive wall of his own, heavily fortified with camps. The despairing inhabitants lasted another 11 months before

Antonio Machado

"Fuera pastor de mil leones/y de corderos a la vez"
"He was shepherd of a thousand lions, and also of lambs",
Ruben Dario

Tu mano y paseemos.
Por estos campos de la tierra mía,
Bordados de olivares polvorientos,
Voy caminando solo,
Triste, cansado, pensativo y viejo.

Along with García Lorca, Antonio Machado was Spain's greatest 20th-century poet. Part of the so-called 'Generation of 98' who struggled to re-evaluate Spain in the wake of the loss of its last colonial possessions in 1898. Born in 1875 in Seville, Machado lived in many places in Spain, including Soria, where he is a local hero. His poetry is simple and profound; many examples are redolent of the landscapes of Castilla:

Over there, in the high lands, where the Duero traces its crossbow's curve around Soria, between leaden hills and splashes of threadbare ilex, my heart is roaming, dreaming…
Do you not see, Leonor, the river willows with their branches frozen still? Watch the blue and white Moncayo, give me your hand and we'll stroll.
In the fields of my land, embroidered with dusty olive trees, I am walking alone, sad, weary, pensive, and old.

Allá en las Tierras Altas
Allá, en las tierras altas,
por donde traza el Duero
su curva de ballesta
en torno a Soria, entre plomizos cerros
y manchas de raídos encinares,
mi corazón está vagando, en sueños…
¿No ves, Leonor, los álamos del río con sus ramajes yertos?
Mira el Moncayo azul y blanco; dame

Machado was a staunch defender of the Republic and became something of a bard of the war. Forced to flee with thousands of refugees as the Republic fell, he died not long after in a *pensión* in southern France; his will to live dealt a bitter blow by the triumph of fascism, and his health badly damaged by the trying journey.

succumbing. The Romans built their own town on the site, but many years later the Numancian resistance became a powerful symbol of Spanish heroism, ironically even used by Franco, who surely would have better identified himself with the Romans. Even Soria's football team is named for the town.

The ruins include foundations of roads, houses, public baths, and a large public building; more approachable are the reconstructed Celtiberian and Roman dwellings. A couple of monuments from 1842 and 1904 commemorate the long-dead heroism of the siege.

Numancia is 500 m up a road on the right after passing the centre of the village. There's one bus a day from Soria to Garray, which isn't convenient; some Logroño-bound buses will drop you off, but otherwise it's not too much in a taxi; about €8-10 each way. Without your own transport you might be better confining yourself to a visit to the museum in Soria.

Almazán Desperately in search of ugly Castilian towns? Almazán will be another disappointment then; a tranquil, friendly, furniture-making centre with attractive preserved sections of walls overlooking the Duero, and a couple of Romanesque churches. Ascending from the bus station or the main road, you'll pass through an

attractive arch and find yourself in the main plaza. The tourist office can be found here, as can the sober **Palacio de los Hurtado de Mendoza**. More striking is the Romanesque **Iglesia de San Miguel** ① *Tue-Sun, 1100-1400, 1700-1900, free*, slightly strangely capped with a brick belltower in Mudéjar style. Inside, it's cool and pleasant. A sculptural relief, sadly badly damaged, depicts the murder of Thomas Becket in Canterbury Cathedral.

In the middle of the square is a statue of Diego Laynez, one of the founding Jesuits, born here in 1512. Head out of the plaza via the road by the side of the *palacio*. Shortly you'll reach another Romanesque church, **Iglesia de San Vicente**, dating from the 12th century; it's now a cultural centre and isn't usually open until *paseo* time. Behind the church starts the path along the walls, which watch over the sluggish green Duero, still with a long way to run to its mouth at Porto in Portugal.

Medinaceli This modern roadside town is a curious place which moved away from its roots – the attractive, but somewhat unreal, old town sits atop a hill a couple of kilometres away. Although some people live here (half of them in a retirement home); hotels, restaurants and craft shops are the only things open, and the whole place has the feel of an open-air museum. Still, it's very picturesque. **Colegiata de Santa María la Mayor Nuestra Señora de Asunción** ① *Tue-Sun 1100-1400, 1700-1900, free*, is a slightly forsaken 16th-century affair. The tall gilded retablo is fronted by a figure of Christ wearing a kimono.

As well as a number of stately houses and *palacios*, also worth noting is a Roman **triumphal arch** dating from the second century AD, probably wondering where the rest of the Roman town got to.

Along the Duero

Roughly, travelling west from Soria along the Duero River you follow the longtime frontline of the Reconquista. There are more castles than you could poke a battering ram at, although many are ruinous. The land is dry and sunbeaten except along the riverbanks, which give their name to one of Spain's best wine regions, the Ribera del Duero. Peñafiel, with its fine Mudéjar architecture and vibrant festival, makes the best base for exploring the Duero region. Within easy reach of Berlanga is one of Castilla's more remarkable monuments, the Ermita de San Baudelio. Further west, one of the oldest dioceses in the peninsula, dating from at least 598, El Burgo de Osma, once an important Castilian town, makes a worthy stopover, while nearby, the castle of Gormaz stands proud and forlorn on a huge rocky hill. ⤻ *For Sleeping, Eating and other listings, see pages 175-186.*

Berlanga de Duero → *Colour map 2, grid C3.*

Dominated by its impressive castle, Berlanga stands on a slope above the town, which is a likeable jumble of narrow lanes and old buildings set around an attractive plaza. In the centre is the reasonably interesting late-Gothic **Iglesia de Colegiata de Santa María**.

The **castle** ① *Tue-Sat 1100-1400, 1600-1930, Sun 1100-1400, €1*, originated as an Arab fortress, although most of it was built in the 15th and 16th centuries. The walls are preserved in a reasonable state, but little remains of the castle buildings or the elaborate gardens that once surrounded them. It is nevertheless picturesque.

Ermita de San Baudelio

Some 8 km south of Berlanga, is one of Castilla's more remarkable monuments. On a hillside, that until the 19th century was covered in oak forest, the little chapel, Ermita de San Baudelio ① *Wed-Sat 1000-1400, 1600-1900, Sun 1000-1400, €0.60*, was

66 99 Castilla continues to depend greatly upon its climate, to the degree that if the Castilian sky appears so lofty, it is probably because the Castilians have raised it, from having contemplated it so much.
(Miguel Delibes)

constructed at the beginning of the 11th century. It was close to the border that separated Muslim and Christian lands, and the design is a superb example of Mozarabic architecture. A horseshoe arched doorway leads into an interior dominated by a central pillar that branches into extravagant ribs that recall a palm grove. There's even a tiny gallery, reached by an unlikely-looking stair. Even more inspiring is the painted decoration, added a century-and-a-half later. Although, incredibly, an American art dealer was permitted to remove most of it in the 1920s (what he took is mostly now in the Metropolitan Museum, New York, although some has been repatriated to the Prado in Madrid), there's still enough left to excite: an Islamic hunting scene on the bottom half of the walls sits below a Biblical cycle; both preserve radiant colours and elaborate, sharp, imagery.

El Burgo de Osma → *Colour map 2, grid C3.*

El Burgo de Osma grew up in the Middle Ages, and a large stretch of the wall is still well preserved; a vigilant sentinel on this wall almost changed the course of world history when he lobbed a boulder at a passing shadow one night in 1469. He narrowly missed killing the young prince Ferdinand, rushing by night to his furtive wedding with Isabella in Valladolid. It's far from a major player these days but still has enough to make an interesting stop.

The **cathedral**, ① *Tue-Sun 1000-1300, 1600-1900, €2.50*, was started in the 13th century but has been sorely afflicted by later architects who just couldn't leave well alone, and added chapels left, right, and centre, as well as an ugly appendix that houses the sacristy. The interior is richly decorated; the retablo is a good piece by Juan de Juni, much of whose other work can be seen in Valladolid's sculpture museum. A guided tour will take you to the cloister and museum, the highlight of which is a superb ornately illustrated manuscript, a copy of the *Codex of Beatus de Liébana* dating from 1086, that has been described as "one of the most beautiful books on earth". A recent replica on the book collectors' market will set you back a cool €5,000. The beautiful tomb of San Pedro de Osma, who raised the Romanesque edifice, is also memorable.

The large **Plaza Mayor** has an impressive old building, a former hospital, that now houses both the tourist office, and **Antiqua Osma** ① *summer Tue-Sun 1000-1400, 1800-2000, rest of the year Sat/Sun only 1000-1400, 1700-1900*, a fun little archaeological museum with finds and reconstructed scenes from the Iberian and Roman town of Uxama, whose fragmentary ruins can still be seen to the west of town.

A more earthy note is struck by the **Museo del Cerdo** (Museum of the Pig) ① *C Juan Yagüe, 1200-1400, 1630-1900*, run by a local restaurant. The western part of Soria province is anything but New Age; stag-hunting is a popular pastime, and the eating of vegetables frowned upon. In February and March pigs are ritually slaughtered and feasted upon; this practice was probably once a way of resoundingly affirming Christian Spanishness in case any lurking inquisitors suspected you of being an unconverted Jew or Muslim.

Castillo de Gormaz

One of the 'front teeth' defending Al-Andalus from the Christians, 15 km south of El Burgo de Osma, Gormaz castle, built by the Moors around AD 950, is about the oldest, and certainly one of the largest, castles in western Europe. While not a lot remains inside them, it's well worth a visit just for its walls, which are nearly 1 km in length and utterly commanding, visible for miles around. The Muslim origin of the citadel can be seen in the Caliph's gate, an ornate horseshoe portal. Although it seems totally impregnable even today, it was taken barely a century after being built, by Alfonso VI. He promptly gave it to El Cid; never let it be said that old Alfonso wasn't good to his friends.

The castle is little visited, and is permanently open (and free). If you haven't got your own transport buses run from El Burgo de Osma to Quintanas de Gormaz, from where it's the best part of a one-hour walk, including the lengthy climb. There's a good *casa rural* in Quintanas, see page 176.

Aranda de Duero

"That's red Aranda. I am afraid we had to put the whole town in prison and execute very many people." Remark made by the Conde de Vallellano to Doctor Junod, Red Cross representative in Spain during the Civil War.

A cheerful and solid Castilian working town, Aranda was spared the decline of the region by its location on the main road north from Madrid. It's a busy place set on a junction of rivers that still functions as a market town and supply centre for the surrounding area. Aranda's pride is roast lamb, for which it is famous throughout Spain; every eatery in town seems to be an *asador*, and the smell of garlic and cooking meat pervades the air. Aranda's annual fiesta is in the second week of September, a cheerful drunken affair.

The main sights are two attractive churches. **Iglesia de Santa María** has a superb portal still preserving some colour from the original paint job; scenes from the Virgin's life are portrayed, including the Nativity and the Adoration of the Magi. Nearby, the **Iglesia de San Juan** has a striking, many-layered portal set around Christ and, appropriately enough, a lamb. The tourist office ① *Plaza Mayor, Tue-Sat 1000-1400, 1600-1900 and Sun 1000-1400.*

Peñaranda

East of Aranda is the sweet little town of Peñaranda, all cobbled streets and elegant buildings. There's a 14th-century **castle** on the hill above town, while in the heart, on the **Plaza Mayor**, the hulking **Iglesia de Santa Ana** isn't particularly loveable, but the **Palacio de Avellaneda** ① *Oct-Mar 1000-1400, 1500-1800, Apr-Sep 1000-1400, 1600-1930, tours on the hour,* opposite is more stylish. Topped with a bust of Hercules, it was built by the counts of Miranda in the 16th century. The Plateresque façade is suitably grand, and attractively topped by a carved wooden roof. Inside there's an elegant galleried patio, and salons and stairways decorated in rich style. There's a tourist office in the centre ① *Tue-Sun 1000-1400, 1700-2000.*

Ribera del Duero → *Colour map 2, grid C2.*

Peñafiel The square-jawed castle that sits on the hill above Peñafiel was one of the Christian strongholds that flexed its muscles at the Moorish frontline, and the town grew up around it, although the settlement of Pintia nearby had been important in pre-Roman times. It's now an attractive place by the river; there are even some trees; rare enough sights in the Castilian *meseta*. Nicknamed 'the Ark' because it resembles a ship run aground, Peñafiel was an important citadel, occupying a crucial strategic ridge above the Duero.

The **castle** ① *Easter-Sep Tue-Sun 1130-1430, 1630-2030; Oct-Palm Sun Tue-Fri 1130-1430, 1630-1930, Sat/Sun 1130-1430, 1630-2030, €2 castle tour, €5 castle tour*

plus museum, €7 tastings, is long and thin, so narrow as to almost resemble a film set cut-out until you get close and see how thick the curtain walls are, reinforced with a series of bristling towers. It's in very good condition but inside there's disappointingly little medieval ambience, for it now holds the **Museo de Vino**, a modern display covering all aspects of wine production in a slightly unengaging way. Tastings are available at weekends but overpriced; you'd be better off buying a bottle from a local *bodega* and drinking it with some ham and cheese by the river. Part of the castle has been left untouched, however, visitable only by guided tour (in English if there's enough demand).

The castle isn't Peñafiel's only point of interest. Down in the town, have a look at the excellent **Plaza del Coso**, a square still used for markets and bullsports. With its beautiful wooden buildings and sand underfoot, it's an unforgettable sight. The town's major fiesta is superb, running from 14-18 August (see page 183). Another highlight is the beautifully ornate brick Mudéjar exterior of the **Iglesia de San Pablo** ⓘ *Mon-Sun 1200-1330, 1730-1830, €2*. Converted from fortress to monastery in the 14th century, the interior is in contrasting Plateresque style. The tourist office on Plaza del Coso organizes walking tours.

Wineries Although it's far from being a new wine region, the Ribera del Duero has come to the world's attention in recent years, with its red wines winning rave reviews from experts and public. The wines are based on the Tempranillo grape, although here it's called *Tinta del País*. Many consider the region's top wines superior to anything else produced in the country; the best-known wine, *Vega Sicilia's Unico*, has for many years been the tipple enjoyed by the royal family, and is Spain's most expensive label. Dealing with the cold Castilian nights give the grapes more character, while traditionally a long period of rotation between oak barrels and larger vats has been employed. Ribera soils are also characteristic, and probably responsible for the wines' very distinctive soft fruity nose.

The excellent Pesquera is produced by **Bodegas Alejandro Fernandéz** in the village of Pesquera de Duero west of Peñafiel. Visits need to be arranged a week in advance by calling T983870037. In Pedrosa de Duero near Roa, the tiny **Hermanos Pérez Pascuas**, T947530100, makes the excellent Viña Pedrosa. **Condado de Haza**, T947525254, another quality producer, are in an attractive building at the end of a long driveway between Roa and La Horra. Most of the wineries in the region can be visited providing this has been arranged in advance.

Valladolid

→ *Phone code: 983; Colour map 2, grid B/C1; Population: 318,293; Altitude: 690 m.*

Valladolid, the capital of the large Castilla y León region, is not outstandingly beautiful but is a pleasant Spanish city with a very significant history; it was the principal city of Spain for most of the early 16th century and its streets are redolent with the memories of important people who walked them and events that took place in them. These days it's still an administrative centre, but a fairly relaxed and friendly one; perhaps it looks down the road to sprawling Madrid and breathes a small sigh of relief, as it must have been odds-on favourite to be named capital at one time. ▸▸ *For details of Sleeping, Eating and other listings, see pages 175-186.*

Ins and outs
Getting there Valladolid is a major transport junction, and only two hours from Madrid by road and rail. As the capital of Castilla y León, it has excellent connections within that region, as well as with the rest of Northern Spain. The bus and train stations are close together, to the south of the centre, about a 20-minute walk. They

can be reached by local buses 2 and 10 from Plaza de España, or 19 from Plaza Zorrilla.
▸ *For further details, see Transport page 184.*

Getting around Valladolid's old centre is compact and easily walked, situated on the east bank of the Pisuerga. At the southern end of this part, the large park of Campo Grande is flanked by two long avenues, Paseo de Zorrilla and Avenida Recoletos; these are the main arteries of the new town. Nearly everything of interest is

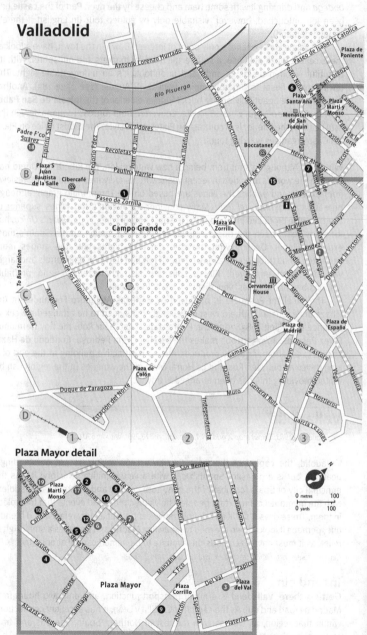

Valladolid

Plaza Mayor detail

Tourist information The narrow office is on ⓘ *C Santiago 19, T983344013, Mon-Sun 0900-1400, 1700-2000 (1900 winter)*. It's a little difficult to spot, but is fully equipped with information about most of Northern Spain. Their pamphlet on Valladolid comes in a variety of languages and details several walks around the city.

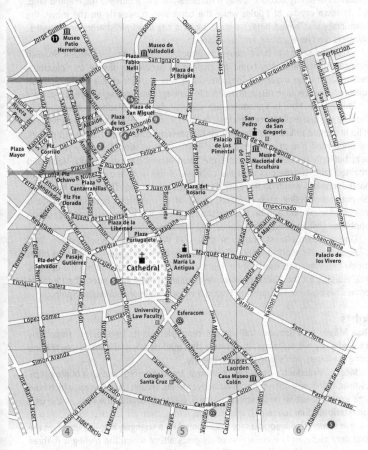

Sleeping
Amadeus **1** *C3*
El Nogal **2** *B4*
Hostal del Val **3** *detail map*
Hostal Los Arces **4** *B5*
Hostal Zamora **5** *C4*
Hostería La Cueva **6** *detail map*
Imperial **7** *detail map*
María Cristina **8** *B4*
Olid Meliá **9** *B5*

Eating
Caravanserai **1** *B1*
Don Claudio **2** *detail map*
El Figón de Recoletos **3** *C2*
Fátima **4** *detail map*
La Criolla **5** *detail map*
La Parrilla de San Lorenzo **6** *A3*
La Parrilla de Santiago **7** *B3*
La Tahona **8** *detail map*
Lion D'Or **9** *detail map*
Mar Cantábrico **10** *detail map*
Patio Herreriano **11** *A4*

Santi I **12** *detail map*
Sol **13** *C2*
Taberna El Pozo **14** *detail map*
Tea Room **15** *B3*

Bars & clubs
El Soportal **16** *A5*
La Comedia **17** *detail map*
Paco Suárez **18** *B1*
Tintín **19** *detail map*

A site of pre-Roman settlements, Valladolid's profile grew with the Reconquista; it was well placed on the frontline to become an important commercial centre, driven in part by the Castilian wool trade. Although Ferdinand and Isabella married here in 1469; a secret ceremony that profoundly changed the course of world history, it was in the 16th century that Valladolid became pre-eminent among Spanish cities. With a population of nearly 40,000, it was a massive place in a hitherto fragmented land, and de facto capital of Spain; while the court was constantly on the move, the bureaucracy was based here. As now, it was a city of administrators and lawyers: "courtiers died here waiting for their cases to come up".

Valladolid seems to have played an important part in most significant Spanish historical events, and was home for periods to people as diverse as Columbus, Cervantes, and the inquisitor Torquemada. It was a major centre of the Spanish Inquisition, see box page 161; *auto de fe's* and burnings were a regular sight in the plaza.

Philip II was born in Valladolid, but surprisingly chose Madrid as his capital in 1561. The city lost importance after that, but had a brief reprise; a scheming adviser of Philip III wanted to keep him away from the powerful influence of his grandmother, and persuaded him to move the capital northwards in 1601. The glory years were back, but only for five years before the court moved back to Madrid. Valladolid remained fairly prosperous until the collapse of the wool and grain markets, but enjoyed renewed wealth in the early part of the 20th century. The Falange held their first national meeting here in March 1934; when war broke out, and Valladolid became an important and brutal Fascist stronghold; it is estimated that over 9,000 Republican civilians were shot here behind the lines.

One of Spain's most important post Civil War writers, Miguel Delibes, is a *Vallisoletano*. His work deeply reflects the Castilian landscape but is also often bitingly anti-Francoist; much of his journalistic life was spent battling the censors while working for the liberal *El Norte de Castilla*, the regional paper. *The Hedge* is perhaps his best-known translated work; a vicious satire on totalitarian Spain.

Sights

Plaza Mayor and around Valladolid's centrepiece is its large plaza, attractively surrounded by red buildings. It was here that *auto de fe*'s and burnings were done during the Inquisition's long tenure in the city.

Most of Valladolid's buildings of interest are to the north and east of the plaza. However, to the west are a series of attractive streets around Calle Correos which hold some excellent eating and drinking options. Beyond, towards the river, is the ugly **Monasterio de San Joaquin** ① *Plaza Santa Ana 4, Mon-Fri 1000-1330, 1700-1900 (2000 in summer), Sat 1000-1430, free,* fronted by a strangely hag-like Virgin. In the monastery museum is a collection of religious art, of which the highlight is three Goyas in the church itself. Just north is the new **Museo Patio Herreriano** ① *C Jorge Guillén 6, T983362908, Tue-Sun 1100-2000 (2200 Tue, Thu, Sat), €6, €3 after 1900 on late-opening days and after 1400 on Wed*. A large and excellent display of Spanish contemporary art, the focus is refreshingly on the innovative; among high-profile artists such as Arroyo, Chillida and Oteiza are many younger names for the future.

Cathedral and around Topped by a statue of Christ standing tall above the city, the ecathedral seems a little crowded-in. The façade is Baroque, the interior fairly bare and disappointing. However, the **museum** ① *Tue-Sat 1000-1330, 1630-1900, Sun 1000-1400, €2.40,* is worthwhile with some excellent carved tombs among the usual assorted saints and Virgins.

● *In 1558, two members of the aristocracy turned up in Valladolid in a litter; the royal cat and parrot, sent back to the city by their loving owner Charles V, who had just died at his monastery retreat of Yuste.*

🎗 Grand Inquisitor

"the hammer of heretics, the light of Spain, the saviour of his country" Sebastián de Olmedo

Born in 1420, Tomas Torquemada entered a Dominican monastery in his youth and was appointed as Grand Inquisitor in 1483. He pursued his tasks with considerable energy both reforming the administration of the Inquisition and giving it its uniquely Spanish direction.

Founded by Fernando and Isabel in 1478, the Spanish Inquisition was unusual in that it did not report directly to the Pope but followed a more nationalistic course. Under Torquemada there was a paranoid obsession that the conversions of Muslim and Jewish *conversos* had been insincere; this was to dominate the Inquisitions activities.

Given a remit to extract confessions under torture, the Inquisition was initially content to seize the estates of those Jewish *conversos* it consided to be insincere. This enabled it to quickly build up considerable resources. Later it employed the full range of punishments available including execution by public burning following a theatrical *auto de fé* or trial of faith. It is estimated that during Torquemada's direction there were around 2,000 executions,

the overwhelming majority of them of Jewish *conversos*.

He was instrumental in ensuring that the Jews were expelled completely from Spain in 1492. It is reputed that when he found Fernando in negotiations with Jewish leaders over a possible payment to the Crown in order to remain, he compared Fernando's actions with those of Judas. The Jews were duly expelled with disastrous long term results.

Torquemada's pursuit of Jewish *conversos* was largely responsible for the development of the cult of *sangre limpia* or pure blood that was to continue to obsess Spain throughout the 16th century. Based on the idea that only those of pure Christian blood could participate fully in the state, it was to cost Spain the services of most of its intellectual class debilitating its development for centuries.

Torquemada stepped down from his role in the Inquisition in 1497. After his directorship it began to diversify into other areas including the maintenance of doctrinal purity and a concern with private morality. It was to retain a formidable grips over Spanish life until its formal abolition at the beginning of the 19th century. Torquemada retired to a monastery where he kept a unicorns horn close at hand as an antidote to any attempt at poisoning him. He died of natural causes in 1499.

Behind the cathedral stands the Gothic **Iglesia de Santa María la Antigua**, slightly down-at-heel but sporting an attractive tower. Also nearby is the **Pasaje Gutiérrez**, a belle époque shopping arcade with some attractive extravagant decoration, if a little care worn. The **university** law faculty, also next to the cathedral, is worth a look for its camp Baroque façade guarded by strange monkey-like lions on columns. Across the road, it's faced by a friendly-looking Cervantes. Another university building is the lovely **Colegio de Santa Cruz** a block away, with an ornate Plateresque door; it boasts an attractive central patio with the names of honorary graduates painted on the walls.

Along the Calle las Angustias North of the cathedral, along this street, is an interesting collection of buildings. **Palacio de los Pimentel** was the building that saw

the birth, in 1527, of Philip II, likely to have been a serious little child. His statue faces the palace from across the square, which also holds the **Iglesia de San Pedro**, with a very tall and ornate Gothic façade; the level of intricacy in the stonework is stunning.

Following the pedestrian street at the side of the San Pedro church, you'll soon come to an even more amazing façade. Looking like a psychedelic fantasy in stone, it's a fantastically imaginative piece of work. A pomegranate tree perhaps represents knowledge, while some hairy men represent nature and hermitity. Like much sculpture from centuries ago, it's impossible to really unlock its meaning, but it's certainly a step away from the typical. It belongs to the **Colegio de San Gregorio**, a building commissioned by Fray Alonso de Burgos to house the college he founded, and also to house him after his demise. The building is under intensive restoration until at least 2005, but the chapel is still open for visits (with a ticket from the sculpture museum opposite); it features an ornately carved wooded choirstall, and a couple of nobles' tombs.

Museo Nacional de Escultura and around Due to San Gregorio's restoration, the Museo Nacional de Escultura ① *Tue-Sat 1000-1400, 1600-1800, Sun 1000-1400, €2.40, good information sheets in English*, has moved across the way to the Palacio de Villena. It's a fairly specialized collection, excellent in its field, which is basically Spanish religious sculpture from the 16th to 18th centuries. In the first gallery is a portrait of an appropriately brooding Juana I as well as an excellent retablo of St Jerome, the highlight of which is the tiny lion; the painter obviously had only a limited notion of what they were like. An excellent collection of polychrome wooden sculptures by Alonso Berruguete show his mastery at depicting real emotion in that difficult medium, while a curious Zurbarán painting, *La Santa Faz*, displays that superb artist's passion for white cloth. Further highlights include a very creepy *Death* by Gil de Ronza, a range of Mannerist sculpture in alabaster, a gory martyrdom of St Bartholomew, and a Rubens painting of Democritus and Heraclitus, who resembles a retired fairground boxer. A couple of interesting pieces round the visit off; an ensemble depicting all the events of a bullfight, and an amazing assembly of Neapolitan dolls, forming a 620-piece Nativity scene.

Other buildings of note in this part of town are the **Palacio de los Vivero**, where Ferdinand and Isabella married in 1469, having only set eyes on each other four days before. It now holds an archive and the university library, and isn't hugely interesting. Beyond here is the **Casa Museo Colón** ① *Tue-Sat 1000-1400, 1700-1900, Sun 1000-1400, free*, a replica of Columbus's son's house, where the explorer is said to have died, far from the sea and a discontented man. The museum displays a lot of pre-Hispanic American material as well as various displays on his seafaring exploits.

Campo Grande and around On the western side of the city is the **Plaza de Zorrilla**. It was named after José Zorrilla, a 19th-century poet born in the city, although he spent much of his life in Mexico, and has an energetic fountain. On the other side of the plaza stretches the pleasant and busy park of Campo Grande. Numerous pro-Republican civilians were shot here during the Civil War, many dying with "Long live the Republic" on their lips.

Cervantes spent three years living in Valladolid, some days of it at his Majesty's leisure on suspicion of being involved in a murder. What was probably his house, on **Calle Miguel Iscar** ① *Tue-Sat 0930-1500, Sun 1000-1500, €2.40*, a pretty vine-covered building, is nearby; it contains a museum, part of which recreates the living conditions of the day, and part of which holds a reasonably interesting collection of 19th- and 20th-century Spanish painting and sculpture.

⁝ 'The Mad'

There are few more tragic figures in the turbulent history of Spain than Queen Juana, who has gone down in history with the unfortunate but accurate name of 'the Mad'. The daughter of the Catholic monarchs Fernando and Isabel, she was sent off in style from Laredo in a fleet of 120 ships bound for Flanders and marriage to Philip, heir to the throne. Philip was known as 'the Fair' and Juana made the unthinkable mistake of falling in love with her arranged husband. He didn't feel the same way, making it clear he intended to spend his time with mistresses. This sent Juana into fits of 'amorous delirium' and hunger strikes; Philip complained that she refused to leave him alone.

When she was 27, her mother Isabel died and Juana inherited the throne of Castilla. Her husband died shortly after their arrival in Spain, and this pushed the queen over the edge. She took possession of the corpse and had it embalmed, refusing to let it be buried or approached by women. She roamed the countryside for years with Philip, whom she occasionally put on a throne. Deemed unfit to rule, she was finally persuaded to enter a mansion in Tordesillas, where she was locked up, with her not-so-fair-nae-more husband with her. Her daughter Catalina was another unfortunate companion – Juana refused to let her be taken from her; when she was rescued, her mother went on a hunger strike to ensure her return. The wretched Juana lived in rags for 47 years in Tordesillas; she had occasional lucid moments and was a constant focus for those dissatisfied with the new "foreign" monarchy of the Habsburgs. Many historians (largely Protestant) have implied that her incarceration was a conspiracy, but there can be no doubt that she was mentally unfit to rule the nation. In 1555 she finally passed away at the age of 76; rarely does death seem such a blessing. She is buried in Granada alongside the husband that she loved, not wisely but too well.

West of Valladolid

Wandering the arid plains and dusty towns of western Castilla these days, it seems difficult to believe that this was once a region of great prestige and power. In the 15th and 16th centuries, towns like Tordesillas and Toro were major players in the political and religious life of the country, while Medina del Campo was a huge city for the time and one of Europe's principal trading towns, a sort of Singapore of the *meseta*. Times have changed, and these places are backwaters. Poke about their streets with a rudimentary idea of Spanish history and you may well find them surprisingly rewarding. The excellent dry whites of Rueda or the hearty reds of Toro will banish any remaining dust from the journey across the scorched plains. ▸▸ *For Sleeping, Eating and other listings, see pages 175-186.*

Tordesillas → *Colour map 1, grid C6.*

Continuing west from Simancas is the town is Tordesillas. Apart from its imposing Mudéjar monastery, there's really little to see here, although it is a very pleasant town to wander around; the Plaza Mayor is a nice arcaded 17th-century affair that would look a lot nicer if it weren't used as a car park.

Tordesillas does however have an interesting history. In 1494 it was the location for the signing of a famous **treaty** between Spain and Portugal, two major maritime powers at the time. The treaty itself was signed in a building where the tourist office

(① *Tue-Sat 1030-1400, 1700-2000, Sun 1000-1400, closed Tue in winter*) now stands. Columbus had just got back from the Americas, and things needed to be sorted out. The 1494 treaty between Spain and Portugal was basically designed to leave Africa for Portugal and the Americas for Spain, but the canny Portuguese suspected or knew of the location of what is now Brazil, so they pushed the dividing line far enough over to give them a foothold in South America. The whole thing had to be re-evaluated within a lifetime anyway, but the very idea of two countries meeting to divide the world in two gives some idea of their control over the Atlantic at the time. Not too long afterwards, Tordesillas gained an unwilling resident in **Juana La Loca**, see box page 163, who was imprisoned here, along with her daughter, and the embalmed corpse of her husband. She remained an icon of Castilian sovereignty, and it was due to her presence that Tordesillas became the centre of the *comunero* revolt against the reign of her son Charles in the early 16th century. The town was viewed with suspicion thereafter, and quickly became the backwater that it remains today.

Real Monasterio de Santa Clara ① *Oct-Mar Tue-Sat 1000-1330, 1600-1745, Sun 1030-1330, 1530-1730, Apr-Sep Tue-Sat 1000-1330, 1600-1830, Sun 1030-1330, 1530-1730, €3.46 (free Wed to EU citizens), baths Tue, Thu-Sat 1000-1200, 1600-1700 (1600-1615 Oct-Mar), Sun 1030-1200, 1530-1600, €2.25,* is an excellent construction, built in Mudéjar style, still home to a community of Clarist nuns. It was originally built as a palace by Alfonso XI, and he installed his mistress Doña Leonor here. After the king died of plague, Leonor was murdered on the orders of Pedro (the Cruel), the new king. After the deaths of Pedro's longtime mistress as well as his son, he ordered his illegitimate daughter to convert the palace into a convent in their memory. The Mudéjar aspects are the most impressive: a chapel with superb stucco work and attractive scalloped arches, and especially the small patio, an absolute gem with horseshoe and scalloped multifoil arches. Another chapel, the Capilla Dorada, also has a fine Mudéjar interior. The cloister is neoclassical in appearance. The high chapel has a very elegant panelled Mudéjar ceiling. Some fine alabaster tombs in late Gothic style can be seen in the Saldaña chapel, built by the state treasurer of John II and holding his remains, his wife's, and possibly Beatriz of Portugal, Pedro's daughter, who carried out the conversion of palace to convent. Access to the convent is by guided tour only; there are some English-speaking guides at weekends.

Medina del Campo → *Colour map 4, grid A5.*

It's the early 16th century, and you're on your way to one of the biggest cities in Spain to see the queen. Where are you off to? Here, where massive trade fairs drew the leading merchants from around Europe in their droves. Medina, 25 km south of Tordesillas, was originally an important centre for the export of Castilian wool, but diversified to become, for a while, the pre-eminent commercial city of Spain. Queen Isabella often ran Castilla from here, and in fact died in a house overlooking the square. In the *comunero* uprising of 1520-21 Medina was burned to the ground after some houses were fired by attacking royalist forces. The town's fairs recovered from this setback, but as financial activity began to surround the court once it was settled in Madrid, Medina lost influence. The commerce was greatly harmed by the royal bankruptcies of the late 16th century, and Medina drifted into obscurity. Today, there are a few remnants of Medina's past glories. The massive plaza is one of them, and there are some beautiful *palacios* around. The modern town, however, is ramshackle and poor.

One of the nicest of the many palaces is the Renaissance **Palacio de los Dueñas** ① *Mon-Fri 0900-1445, closed for part of Jul-Aug,* with a beautiful patio and staircase adorned with the heads of the monarchs of Castile.

Castillo de la Mota ① *Mon-Sat 1100-1400, 1600-1900, Sun 1100-1400, free,* is an impressive Mudéjar castle across the river from town. Its muscular brick lines are

⁞ Fighting bishop of Zamora

In an age which saw the central state increase its power over the individual, Antonio de Acuña , Bishop of Zamora during the comunero revolt , stands out as a swaggering medieval individualist whose complete lack of self awareness led to him becoming a central figure of resistance to Charles V . Born to a wealthy Castilian family who were used to dispensing patronage Acuña had come to the attention of Fernando and Isabel, who appointed him their ambassador to Rome in 1506.

After Isabel's death, Acuña saw an opportunity to further his own interests and deserted Ferdnando in preference for Philip the Fair. By pledging his absolute loyalty to the Pope he was able to secure his appointment to the Bishopric of Zamora despite the opposition of top local bigwig Rodrigo Ronquillo whose objections were brushed aside when Acuña seized the Bishopric by force. His Triumph of the Will style antics saw him temporarily in charge but at the expense of making a host of powerful enemies.

Although his appointment was eventually confirmed by Fernando, Zamora became a centre of intrigue with Acuña at its centre. When he was eventually expelled from the city at the start of the comunero revolt, he raised an army of 2,000 men and found himself on the side of the rebels while his implacable enemy Ronquillo was a leading royalist commander. He conducted a series of daring but essentially meaningless campaigns in the *meseta* around Valladolid before deciding in 1521 to march on Toledo where in a great display of showmanship he persuaded the populace to declare him Bishop.

It soon became apparent that his individualistic acts of empire building were no substitute for an effective political and military strategy and after the defeat of the comuneros Acuña was forced to flee and patriotically attempted to ingratiate himself with the French then busy invading Navarre. However he was captured and held captive in Simancas Castle where Charles hoped he would be quietly forgotten about.

Obscurity was not something Acuña could tolerate and in 1526 he attempted to escape. During the escape attempt he unchristianly killed one of his gaolers and Charles seeing an opportunity to put an end to a high profile enemy appointed the prelate's nemesis Ronquillo as custodian of Simancas Castle. He wasted no time in settling old scores and sentenced the erstwhile Bishop to be tortured and executed. His body was then displayed from the castle walls as warning to others who thought they could challenge royal power.

Although the Pope went through the motions of complaining about this breach of protocol in reality he recognised that Acuña was a son of the Church who had signally failed to bring any credit or advantage to the Papacy. Eventually the whole matter was quietly forgotten about.

Castilla y León West of Valladolid

solid in the extreme. While you can walk around inside the walls, there's not much to see inside the building itself, which holds some municipal offices.

The new **Museo de las Ferias** ⓘ *C San Martín 26, T983837527, Tue-Sat 1000-1330, 1600-1900, Sun 1100-1400, €1.20*, is situated in an old church and has an interesting look at the commerce of the great trade fairs and how they influenced the art and politics of the period. There's a large collection of documents and art relating to the period.

Heading north from Tordesillas, off the N-VI motorway that runs to Benavente, are some excellent, little visited attractions. Some 4 km from the N-V1 motorway, and not served by buses, is this small gem of a town. It's the sort of place that ought to be flooded with tourists, but is comparatively unknown. The fantastic walls that surround the village are the main attraction; their jagged teeth and narrow gateways dominate the plains around; on a clear day you can see a frightening number of kilometres from the sentries' walkway along the top.

Around a kilometre below the town is a lovely Romanesque **Iglesia de Nuestra Señora de la Anunciada**, unusually built in the Catalan style. The distinguishing feature of this style is 'Lombard arches', a decorative feature that resembles fingers traced around the apses. The key for the church is held in the tourist office in town.

Toro → *Colour map 1, grid C5.*

Toro sits high above the Duero River, west of Tordesillas on the way to Zamora (from which it makes a good day trip). Its name might mean 'bull', but its emblem is a stone pig dating from Celtiberian times, which sits at the eastern gate to the city. These days Toro is famous for wine. Its hearty reds don't have the complexity of the Ribera del Duero wines from further up the river, but some of them are pretty good indeed. Toro wines received D.O. (denomination of origin) status in 1987.

There are several churches in town with Mudéjar and Romanesque elements, but the highlight is the **Colegiata** ① *near the Plaza Mayor, Mar-Sep Tue-Sun 1000-1300, 1700-2000, Oct-Feb 1000-1400, 1630-1830, €1 for sacristy and Portada.* The interior is graced by a high dome with alabaster windows and a Baroque organ, but the real

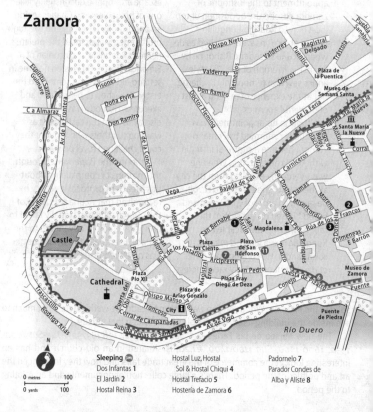

Zamora

N
0 metres 100
0 yards 100

Sleeping
Dos Infantas **1**
El Jardín **2**
Hostal Reina **3**

Hostal Luz, Hostal
  Sol & Hostal Chiqui **4**
Hostal Trefacio **5**
Hostería de Zamora **6**

Padornelo **7**
Parador Condes de
  Alba y Aliste **8**

highlight is the Portada de la Majestad, a 13th-century carved doorway decorated with superbly preserved (and well-restored) painted figures in early Gothic style; the character expressed through such apparently simple paintwork is remarkable. In the sacristy is a celebrated painting, *La Virgen de la Mosca* (the Virgin of the Fly); the insect in question is settled on her skirts.

Overlooking the river is the **Alcázar**, a fort dating from the 12th century built on a Moorish fortification. Juana, pretender to Isabella's Castilian crown, resisted here for a while; she must have enjoyed the views, which stretch for miles across the *meseta*.

There are plenty of **wineries** within easy reach and the tourist office will supply a list. Most wineries are happy to show visitors around, but all need to be phoned beforehand. In terms of wine quality, one of the best is **Bodegas Fariña**, Camino del Palo, T980577673, www.bodegasfarina.com, who market their wine as Colegiata and Gran Colegiata. **Covitoro**, Carretera Tordesillas, T980690347, www.covitoro.com, are the local wine co-operative, and also produce some good bottles, with Gran Cermeño particularly recommendable. They're a short walk along the main road east of town.

Zamora → *Phone code: 980; Colour map 1, grid C5; Population: 65,633.*

Like so many other towns along the Duero River, Zamora was a fortress of the Reconquista frontline, although originally it was a Celtic, Carthaginian, then Roman settlement. In the Middle Ages, the city was formidably walled and famous for its resilience during sieges; the saying "A Zamora, no se ganó en una hora" (Zamora wasn't taken in an hour) dates from these times and is still used widely.

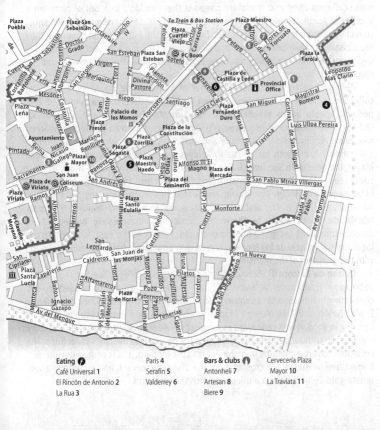

Eating		Bars & clubs	
Café Universal 1	París 4	Antonheli 7	Cervecería Plaza
El Rincón de Antonio 2	Serafín 5	Artesan 8	Mayor 10
La Rua 3	Valderrey 6	Biere 9	La Traviata 11

Today the city is a relaxed and peaceful provincial capital famous for ceramics and antiques. The centre is attractive, with, incredibly, a couple of dozen Romanesque churches, which are at ease with some very harmonious modern urban architecture. The city still preserves large sections of its walls around the old centre, which perches high on the rocky bank of the Duero. ▸▸ *For Sleeping, Eating and other listings, see pages 175-186.*

Ins and outs

Getting there and around The train and bus stations are inconveniently situated a 20-min walk to the north of town. Rickety local buses run to the bus and train station from Plaza Sagasta near the Plaza Mayor, or it's a €3-4 cab fare. Nearly all the sights of interest are within the walled old town, of elongated shape but still walkable. ▸▸ *For further details, see Transport page 185.*

Tourist information The city tourist office is at the cathedral end of town and is very helpful ① *Plaza Arias Gonzalo, 1000-1400, 1600-1900 (1700-2000 Mar-Sep)*. There's also a provincial office ① *C Santa Clara 20*.

Sights

The city's **walls** are impressive where they are preserved, and worth strolling around. There are a few noble entrances preserved around its perimeter. The western end of the walled town is narrow and culminates in the city's **castle**, founded in the 11th century, which looks the goods from the outside but is modern inside and holds a college.

Nearby, Zamora's **cathedral** ① *Tue-Sun 1100-1400, 1600-1800 (1700-2000 Apr-Sep), €2*, is an interesting building, especially its dome, which is an unusual feature, with scalloped tiling and miniature pagodas that wouldn't look out of place on a southeast Asian temple. The highlight, however, is the **museum** and its small collection of superb Flemish tapestries. Dating from the 15th and 17th centuries, they are amazing for their detail, colour and size (some of them are around 35 sq m). They depict scenes from antiquity; the conquests of Hannibal, the Trojan war, and the coronation of Tarquin.

Zamora has an extraordinary number of Romanesque churches, a pleasing collection, particularly as several of them avoided meddlesome architects of later periods. **Iglesia de La Magdalena** ① *Tue-Sun Mar-Sep 1000-1300, 1700-2000, Oct-Dec 1000-1400, 1630-1830, free*, is one of the nicest, with an ornate portal carved with plant motifs. Inside, it's simple and attractive, with a high single nave, and a 13th-century tomb with an unusually midget-like recumbent figure. In the Plaza Mayor, the **Iglesia de San Juan** ① *Tue-Sun Mar-Sep 1000-1300, 1700-2000, Oct-Dec 1000-1400, 1630-1830, free*, constructed in the 12th and 13th century, has a thistly façade and a big gloomy interior with unusual arches that run the length of the nave, rather than across it. The alabaster windows are an attractive feature. The pretty **Iglesia de Santa María la Nueva** is increasingly inaccurately named as its Romanesque lines are going-on 900 years old. Further to the east, look out for the façade of the **Palacio de los Momos**, carved with penitents' chains seemingly at odds with the grandeur of the mansion.

Museo de Zamora ① *Plaza de Santa Lucía 2, T980516150, Tue-Sat 1000-1400, 1600-1900 (1700-2000 in summer), Sun 1000-1400, €1.20*, is housed in two connecting buildings; a 16th-century *palacio*, and a modern construction designed by Emilio Tuñón and Luis Moreno Mansilla, which has won many plaudits since its opening in 1998. It was conceived as a chest that would hold the city's valuables; it's imaginative without being flamboyant, and fits quietly into the city's older lines. The collection covers everything from the Celtic to the modern, and is of medium interest; Roman funeral stelae, gilt crosses from the Visigothic period, and especially a very ornate gold Celtic brooch are things to catch the attention.

Salamanca → *Phone code: 923; Colour map 4, grid A4; Population:156,368; Altitude: 780 m.*

Salamanca has a strong claim to being Spain's most attractive city. A university town since the early 13th century, it reached its apogee in the 15th and 16th centuries; the 'golden age' of imperial Spain. The old town is a remarkable assembly of superb buildings; a day's solid sightseeing can teach you more about Spanish architecture than you may have ever wanted to know; Plateresque and Churrigueresque were more or less born here. By night, too, it's a good spot; today's university students just don't seem to tuck up in bed with a candle, hot milk, and a theological tract like they used to, and bar life is busy seven days a week, bolstered by the large numbers of tourists and foreign students learning Spanish. If you can handle the heat and the crowds, there are few better places in Spain to spend a summer evening than the Plaza Mayor, the most attractive plaza in all of Spain; sit at an outdoor table and watch storks circle architectural perfection in the setting sun. ▸▸ *For Sleeping, Eating and other listings, see pages 175-186.*

Ins and outs
Getting there Salamanca is about 200 km west of Madrid, but don't you dare consider the words 'day trip'. The bus station is west of town along Avendia Filiberto Villalobos. There are plenty of buses from Madrid, Valladolid, and other Castilian cities. If you're in a car, the straight *meseta* roads make easy driving; it's well under one hour south of Zamora, for example. There are several train connections. ▸▸ *For further details, see Transport page 185.*

Getting around You won't have much cause to stray from the old town, which is very walkable indeed. The bus and train stations are also within a 10-minute stroll of the centre.

Best time to visit If you visit in summer you are guaranteed heat, tourists, circling storks, and outdoor tables. In many ways this is the nicest time to visit, but the students aren't about (although there are always plenty of American language students) and the nightlife correspondingly quieter. As does the rest of Castilla, Salamanca gets cold in winter, but never shuts down and accommodation is cheap.

Tourist information There are two handy tourist offices ⓘ *Plaza Mayor, T923218342, 0900-1400, 1630-1830*, and ⓘ *Rúa Antigua 70, Casa de las Conchas, T923268571, Mon-Fri 1000-1400, 1700-2000, Sat 1000-1400*. The former has more information on the city, the second is better for information on the rest of Castilla y León. A few summer-only kiosks are scattered about, notably at the transport terminals. Regular walking tours of the city run from the tourist office on the Plaza Mayor.

History
Salamanca's history is tied to that of its university, see box page 172, but the town itself was founded in pre-Roman times. An Iberian settlement, it was taken by Hannibal (pre-elephants) in 218BC. The Romans later took it over but, as with most cities in these parts, it was abandoned later and only resettled during the Reconquista. The university was founded in 1218 and rapidly grew to become one of Europe's principal centres of learning. Flourishing particularly under the Catholic Monarchs, the city became an emblem of imperial Spain; the thinktank behind the monarchy that ruled half the world. Salamanca's decline in the 18th and 19th centuries mirrored that of its university and indeed the rest of Castilla. The city suffered grievously in the Napoleonic wars; the French general Marmont destroyed most of the university's buildings before his defeat by Wellington just south of the city in 1812. In the Civil War, Major Doval, a well-known butcher, cracked down fiercely on Republican sympathizers after the coup. The city was the conspirators' command centre for a while, and Franco was declared as *caudillo* in a cork grove

just outside the town. In 2002 Salamanca revelled in its status as joint European Cultural Capital, and the city can only benefit from the success and infrastructural improvements.

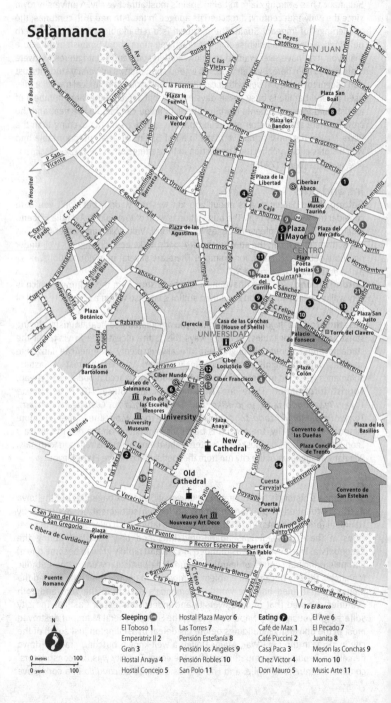

Salamanca

Sleeping		Eating	
El Toboso 1	Hostal Plaza Mayor 6	Café de Max 1	El Ave 6
Emperatriz II 2	Las Torres 7	Café Puccini 2	El Pecado 7
Gran 3	Pensión Estefanía 8	Casa Paca 3	Juanita 8
Hostal Anaya 4	Pensión los Angeles 9	Chez Victor 4	Mesón las Conchas 9
Hostal Concejo 5	Pensión Robles 10	Don Mauro 5	Momo 10
	San Polo 11		Music Arte 11

N

0 metres 100
0 yards 100

"A square like a stone-built living room." C. Nooteboom

Plaza Mayor Among strong competition, Salamanca's main square stands out as the most harmonious plaza in Spain. Built in the 18th century by Alberto Churriguera, it has nothing of the gaudiness of the style to which he and his brother unwittingly lent their names. Paying over the odds for a coffee or a vermouth at one of its outdoor tables is still a superb option; there can be fewer nicer places to sit, especially on a warm summer's evening with storks circling their nests above. Around the perimeter are medallions bearing the heads of various illustrious Spaniards; the more recent additions include Franco and King Juan Carlos ('JC'), and there are plenty of blank ones for new notables.

University and around Rúa Mayor links the plaza with the cathedral and the old buildings of the university. It's lined with restaurants that take over the street with tables for pleasant overeating and drinking in the summer sun. On the right about halfway down is the distinctive **Casa de las Conchas** (House of Shells), named for the 400-odd carved scallop shells of its façades. Now a library (with occasional exhibitions), its nicest feature is the courtyard, graced by an elegantly intricate balcony and decorated with well-carved lions and shields.

Leave the Clerecía on your right and take the second left to reach the **Patio de las Escuelas**, a small square surrounded by beautiful university buildings. In the centre stands Fray Luís de León, see box page 172. He faces the edifice where he once lectured, the main **university** building. Its incredible façade is an amazing example of what master masons could achieve with soft Salamanca sandstone. The key for generations of students and visitors has been to spot the frog; if you manage to do it unguided, you are eligible for a range of benefits; good exam results, luck in love, and more. If you don't need any of these, it's on the right pilaster; at the top of the

Peccata Minuta 12
Sakana 13
Victor Gutiérrez 14

Bars & clubs
Abadia 15

De Laval Genovés 16
El Savor 17
Gaia 18
La Fábrica 19
Paco's Cantine 20
Potemkin 21

A centre of learning

Founded in 1218, Salamanca is the second-oldest university in Spain (after Palencia). The patronage of kings allowed it to grow rapidly; in 1255 it was named by the Pope as pre-eminent in Europe, alongside Paris, Oxford and Bologna. It was the brains behind the golden age of Imperial Spain; it's Colegios Mayores, or four Great Colleges, supplied a constant stream of Spain's most distinguished thinkers, and exerted plenty of undue political influence to get their own graduates appointed to high positions. The university had in excess of 10,000 students in its pomp and was forward thinking, with a strong scientific tradition and a female professor as early as the late 15th century.

Spain's closed-door policy to Protestant thinkers was always going to have a bad effect, and Salamanca declined in the 18th century; Newton and Déscartes were considered unimportant, the chair of mathematics was vacant for decades, and theologians debated what language was spoken by the angels. The Peninsular War had a terrible effect too; French troops demolished most of the university's colleges. But the university is thriving again: although not among Spain's elite, it has a good reputation for several disciplines, and the student atmosphere is bolstered by large numbers of foreigners who come to the beautiful city to learn Spanish.

Among many notable teachers that have taught at Salamanca, two stand out; Miguel de Unamuno, see box page 460, and Fray Luís de León. Born to Jewish conversos (converts), at 14 he came to Salamanca to study law; he soon moved into theology, becoming a monk of the Augustinian order. In 1560 he was appointed to the chair of theology. Well-versed in Hebrew, Fray Luís continued to use Hebrew texts as the basis of his Biblical teaching; he was responsible for many translations of the Testaments and scriptures from that language into Spanish. Enemies and anti-Semites saw these actions as being in defiance of the Council of Trent, and on 27 March 1572 Fray Luís was arrested mid-lecture by the Inquisition and imprisoned in Valladolid, where he was charged with disrespect and imprudence. After a five-year trial he was sentenced to torture by the rack; the punishment was, however, revoked. Returning to Salamanca, he famously began his first lecture to a crowded room with Dicebamus hesterna die ("As we were saying yesterday…"). He maintained his firm stance, and got into fresh trouble with the Inquisition five years later. He was made provincial of the Augustinians and died in 1591.

Apart from his theological writings, he was an excellent poet, one of the finest in Spain's history. His verses bring out the deep feelings of a man known to be severe and sardonic, understandably given the religious hypocrisy that he struggled against.

second tier you'll see three skulls; the frog perches on the left-hand one. It's rather underwhelming if you've just spent a couple of hours searching it out.

The interior of the university ① *Mon-Fri 0930-1330, 1600-1930, Sat 0930-1330, 1600-1900, Sun 1000-1330, €4/2 students*, is interesting, but not nearly as impressive. There are several impressively worked ceilings though. The old halls radiate around the courtyard; the largest, the Paraninfo, is hung with Flemish tapestries. One of the halls is preserved as it was in the days when Fray Luís lectured here, while upstairs, the impressive library is a beautiful space, lined with thousands

of ancient texts; the old globes are particularly interesting. Fray Luís's remains are in the chapel. The museum is housed around a patio on the other side of the square, the Escuelas Menores. The patio is attractively grassed behind its Plateresque portal. The arches, looking a little like devils' horns, are typical of Salamanca, an exuberant innovation of the 15th century. There's a reasonable collection of paintings and sculptures, the best by foreign artists resident in Salamanca in its glory years, but the highlight is the remaining part of the fresco ceiling painted by Fernando Gallego. It illustrates the signs of the Zodiac and various constellations; a Mudéjar ceiling in one of the rooms for temporary exhibits is also well worth a peek.

Catedral Nueva ① *1000-1730 (1930 in summer)*. Unusually for Spain, Salamanca's new cathedral is built alongside, rather than on top of, its Romanesque predecessor. It's a massive affair that dominates the city's skyline from most angles. While the later tower is unimpressively ostentatious, the western façade is superb; a masterpiece of late Gothic stonework, with the transition into Plateresque very visible. The sheer number of statues and motifs is what amazes more than the power of any particular scene. The central figure is of the Crucifixion, flanked by Saints Peter and Paul. Around the corner to the left, the façade facing the Plaza de Anaya is also excellent. The door is named Puerta de las Palmas for the relief carving of Jesus entering Jerusalem on Palm Sunday, but take a look at the archivolts on the left-hand side; an astronaut and an imp with a large ice-cream are entertaining recent additions.

Inside, the new cathedral impresses more by its lofty lines than its subtlety. It's a mixture of styles, mostly in transitional Gothic with star vaulting and colourful, high Renaissance lantern. The coro is almost completely enclosed; the stalls were carved in walnut by the Churriguera brothers. At the back, in a capilla of the squared apse, the bronze figure of the Cristo de las Batallas is said to have been carried into war by the Cid.

Old cathedral ① *1000-1730 (1930 in summer)*, €3. Accessed from inside the new one, this is a much smaller, more comfortable space. It dates mostly from the 12th century; while the design is Romanesque, the pointed arches anticipate the later Gothic styles. On the wall by the entrance are wall paintings from the early 17th century; they depict miracles attributed to the Cristo de las Batallas figurine. The *retablo* is superb, a colourful ensemble of 53 panels mostly depicting the life of Christ. Above, a good Last Judgement sees the damned getting herded into the maw of a hake-like monster. In the transepts are some excellent coloured tombs, one with its own vaulted ribs.

Around the cloister are several interesting chambers. Capilla de Santa Barbara is where, until 1843, the rector of the university was sworn in. It was also where the students used to take their final exams; if they failed, it was straight across the cloister and out via the opposite door, and thence no doubt to the nearest boozer.

Convento de San Esteban ① *Tue-Sat 0900-1300, 1600-1800 (2000 in spring and summer), Sun 0900-1300*, €1.50. Not far from the cathedrals, the convent is slightly cheerless but worth visiting. Its ornate Plateresque façade depicts the stoning of Esteban himself (Saint Stephen); the door itself is also attractive. Entry to the church is via the high cloister, which has quadruple arches. The top deck, floored with boards, is the nicest bit; it would cry out for a café-bar if it weren't in a monastery. There's a small museum with various Filipino saints, a silver reliquary in the shape of a sombrero, and a couple of amazing early Bibles. One of them, dating from the late 13th century or so, is so perfect it's almost impossible to believe that it was handwritten. The church is dominated by its retablo, a work of José Churriguera. A massive 30 x 14 m, it's well over the top, but more elegant than some of the style's later examples.

Convento de las Dueñas ① *1030-1300, 1630-1730, €1.50*. Opposite Convento de San Esteban this convent also houses Dominicans, this time in the shape of nuns who do a popular line in almond cakes. The irregular-shaped cloister is open for visits and it's beautiful, with views of the cathedral in the background. Dating from the first half of the 16th century, its lower floor is fairly simple compared with the top level, decorated with busts and shields, as well as ornate capitals of doomed souls and beasts.

Museo Art Nouveau y Art Deco ① *C Gibraltar 14, T923121425, www.museocasalis. org, Apr-mid Oct Tue-Fri 1100-1400, 1700-2100, Sat/Sun 1100-2100, mid Oct-Mar Tue-Fri 1100-1400, 1600-1900, Sat/Sun 1100-2000, €2.10*. If you fancy a break from sandstone and Plateresque, head for the **Museo Art Nouveau y Art Deco**. It's superbly housed in the **Casa Lis**, an art nouveau *palacio* built for a wealthy Salamancan industrialist; there's a particularly good view of the building from the riverbank. The collection of pieces is very good; you're sure to find something you love and something you can't stand. Representative of the traditions of many countries, there are porcelains, sculpture, glassware, ceramics, Fabergé jewelling, and dolls. The stained-glass ceiling is particularly impressive too. If you've ever been confused about the differences between arts nouveau and deco, this place should help.

Nearby, check out the pretty **Puente Romano**, a bridge over the Tormes with Roman origins.

Around Salamanca

The mountains in the southernmost portion of Salamanca province make an excellent destination, although some areas can get uncomfortably crowded in summer, as holidaymakers leave baking Madrid in droves. La Alberca and Candelario are particularly attractive mountain villages with good accommodation options, while close to the Portuguese border, Ciudad Rodrigo is a very likeable walled town and a centre of pig-rearing. ▸▸ *For Sleeping, Eating and other listings, see pages 175-186.*

Alba de Tormes → *Colour map 4, grid A4.*
Some 15 km southeast of Salamanca, and connected with it by hourly buses, the town of Alba de Tormes seems an unlikely place to have given its name to the most powerful of Spanish aristocratic lines, the dukes and duchesses of Alba. It also has another big claim to fame as the resting place of Santa Teresa de Avila, Spain's top 16th-century mystic, but it's a small, not especially engaging place, although it is prettily set on the Tormes, which is crossed by an attractive bridge.

A 16th-century keep ① *1130-1300, 1630-1800*, is all that remains of the dukes' castle; there's nothing remotely grand about it now, although there's some noble Mudéjar brickwork. Santa Teresa founded the **Convento de Carmelitos** here in 1571. It's not especially interesting; there are some well-carved tombs, paintings of her life and doings, and a reconstruction of a nuns' cell of the time. The saint's ashes are in an urn in the middle of the retablo; it's not all of her though, for Franco used to keep one of her mummified hands next to him as he planned his next stagnations.

Béjar and Candelario → *Colour map 4, grid B3.*
Further south from Alba de Tormes, Béjar, a textile town, isn't particularly attractive in itself, but enjoys a picturesque position at the base of the Sierra de Gredos. The **Iglesia de Santa María La Mayor** has a pretty Mudéjar apse, but the biggest building in town is the former ducal palace, now a public building. Pop in to check out its pretty patio if it's open. You'd do better, however, to head 4 km up into the mountains to Candelario, a pretty, steep village with attractive houses designed to combat the fierce winter cold and spring thaw.

Sierra Peña de Francia → *Colour map 4, grid A3.*

Heading west from Béjar into the sierras of Béjar then Francia is an attractive journey through some very unCastilian scenery of chestnut groves and small herds of cattle. There are some pretty villages to stop at; **Miranda del Castañar** is one of the nicest; and **Mogarraz** is devoted to tasty ham and sausage production from the bristly pigs that are kept thereabouts. Both have accommodation and eating options, but the gem of the area is undoubtedly **La Alberca**, despite the high tourist levels in summer.

La Alberca is built directly onto bedrock in some places and has a collection of unusual stone and wood buildings, giving it a distinctly Alpine feel. Some say, indeed, that the original settlers came here from Swabia. As well as being a pretty place in itself, it makes a good base for walking in the sierra. The attractive village is centred around its main Plaza Pública, which slopes down to a stone Calvary and fountain.

South of La Alberca, the road rises slowly to a pass then spectacularly descends towards Extremadura through a region known as **Las Batuecas**, a dreamy green valley that's worth waiting for a ride for, or wearing away some brake pads. North of La Alberca, the road towards Ciudad Rodrigo runs close to **La Peña de Francia**, the highest peak in the region (1,732 m). It's a pretty drive or climb to the top and the views on a clear day are spectacular. There's a monastery at the top with a restaurant and rooms.

Ciudad Rodrigo → *Colour map 4, grid A2.*

Southwest from Salamanca, a busy road crosses bull-breeding heartland on its way to Ciudad Rodrigo and the main Portuguese border in these parts. Ciudad Rodrigo is a lovely place with a turbulent past; as a fortified border town it was constantly involved in skirmishes and battles involving Castilla and Portugal. Most famously, Cuidad Rodrigo figured prominently in the Peninsular War. The French besieged the town and finally took it, despite heroic Spanish resistance under General Herrasti. In January 1812 Wellington, aware that French reinforcements were fast approaching, managed to take the town in a few hours; the French general, Marmont, was flabbergasted, describing the action as "incomprehensible". Both sides plundered the town when in possession; Wellington was appalled at how low his troops could stoop.

> ❖ *Relaxed, elegant Cuidad Rodrigo is a great alternative to staying in Salamanca.*

The town's principal sight is its cathedral and the rest of the town is dotted with attractive buildings. The town **walls** and **ramparts** are also particularly impressive; one of the entries to the town is via a tunnel through the wall, with large wooden doors still ready to be bolted shut to repel invaders. You can climb the wall in some places and get good views over the surrounding plains at weekends when open. The **cathedral** ① *1000-1300, 1600-1900, €1.20*, is an attractive mixture of Romanesque and Gothic in golden sandstone. Inside, the carved wooden *coro* is elegant, and the cloisters are an interesting blend of styles. The cathedral's tower still is pockmarked from cannonfire, and you can see one of the two breaches by which Wellington's forces entered the city. Among the other noteworthy buildings in the town, the **castle** is now a parador, and the **Plaza Mayor** is graced by the graceful Renaissance Ayuntamiento (Town Hall). The tourist office ① *Mon to Fri 1000-1400, 1700-1900 (2000 in summer), weekends 1100-1400, 1630-2030*, is opposite the cathedral.

● Sleeping

Soria *p150, map p150*

A Parador Antonio Machado, Parque del Castillo s/n, T975240800, www.parador.es. Soria's parador is an attractive modern building peacefully set at the top of a park-covered hill above town. It's named for the famous poet, and selections of his work line the walls. The nicest rooms are suites that overlook the river and don't cost a great deal more, but it's all very comfortable, and not particularly expensive for what you get.

C **Hostería Solar de Tejada**, C Claustrilla 1, T/F975230054, solardetejada@wanadoo.es. A great place to stay in Soria's heart. Original decoration is backed up by warm-hearted service. The rooms, all different, are attractive and brightly coloured, and a solar and lunar theme runs through the place. Recommended.

E-F **Hostal Viena**, C García Soler 1, T975222109. A short walk from the centre, this *hostal* has decent management and peaceful rooms with or without bathroom.

F **Casa David**, C Campo 6, T975220033. Don't be put off by the scruffy bar that this *pensión* is run from, the rooms are spacious and reasonably pleasant, although quite noisy in the mornings.

G **Pensión Carlos**, Plaza Olivo 2, T975211555. A good option, predictably basic but clean, reasonably quiet, and right in the heart of things.

Around Soria *p152*
There are many options in Medinaceli should you want to stay.

C **La Cerámica**, C Santa Isabel 2, Medinaceli, T/F975326381, is a good choice behind the church. The rooms are very attractive with tiled floors and dark, wooden beamed ceilings, and it's heated (a vital blessing any time outside summer); there's also good rustic Castilian food on offer.

D **Puerta de la Villa**, C Arco de la Villa 5, Almazán, T975310415, with decent ensuite rooms just down from the square and a cheap restaurant.

D **Tirso de Molina**, Plaza Mayor s/n, Almazán, T975300416, a nice new *hostal* above a mediocre café-restaurant on the main square;

F **El Arco**, C San Andrés 5, T975310228, Almazán, with shower and washbasin.

Along the Duero *p154*
Nearly all Aranda's accommodation is set away from the centre on the main roads. The ones we list below are exceptions. Disappointingly there's currently no accommodation in the old centre of Peñafiel, although nowhere's very far away.

A **Hotel II Virrey**, C Mayor 4, El Burgo de Osma, T975341311, www.virreypalafox.com. A plush but courteous hotel in traditional Spanish style. Facilities on offer include gym

and sauna, and the rooms are comfortable enough, although some are pokier than the grand decor would suggest.

B **Posada del Canónigo**, C San Pedro de Osma 19, El Burgo de Osma, T975360362, www.posadadelcanonigo.es. An excellent place to stay, just inside the southern gate of the city wall. Decorated with care and style, the *posada* also has an excellent restaurant.

B **Ribera del Duero**, Av Escalona 17, Peñafiel, T983881616, F983881444. A large but attractive hotel cleverly converted from an old flour mill. Some of the rooms have good views of the castle, and there's a well-priced restaurant.

C **Casa Grande**, Castillo de Gormaz, T9753 40982, with a cheerful coloured interior inside a spick 'n' span yellow mansion.

D **Hostal Pili**, Ctra Valladolid s/n, Peñafiel, T983880213. On the main road, a 5-min walk from the centre, are standard, slightly overpriced doubles with or without bath.

D **Hotel Fray Tómas**, C Real 16, Berlanga de Duero, T975343033. Named after the town's most famous son, a missionary priest, it's got nice enough rooms, though a little staid and dull; the restaurant is good however. It is the only accommodation in town.

D **Hotel Julia**, Plaza de la Virgencilla s/n, Aranda de Duero, T947501250, F947500449, a comfortable place full of interesting old Spanish objects.

D **Posada Ducal**, Plaza Mayor s/n, Peñaranda, T947552347, is a good choice, on the main square, with attractively rustic decoration and a decent restaurant too.

D **Señorío de Velez**, Plaza Duques de Alba 1, Peñaranda, T947552201, is a decent place to stay in the heart of town. In an attractive stone and adobe building, the rooms are clean and acceptable, if a touch overpriced. There's a nice terraced restaurant too.

D-E **Riberduero**, Av Polideportivo s/n, Peñafiel, T983881637. A holiday-village style campsite with bungalows available.

E **Hostal Campo**, C Encarnación Alonso s/n, Peñafiel, T983873192. Comfortable and clean brandnew rooms in an unappealing location near the sugar refinery. Run out of the **dive-y Bar** Campo on the Carretera de Pesquera, it's only a short stroll from the centre.

E **Hostal San Roque**, C Universidad 1, El Burgo de Osma, T677431246. A grubby exterior conceals a decent option on the

main road through town. There are rooms with or without bath available; you'll likely have to call when you arrive, as the owner lives elsewhere.

E Pensión Sole, C Puerta Nueva 16, Aranda de Duero, T947500607, with good clean rooms with TV and optional bathroom, in the older part of town.

Valladolid *p157, map p158*

L Olid Meliá, Plaza San Miguel 10, T983357200, www.solmelia.com. Well-located hotel with plenty of facilites and occasional attractive discounts. The rooms are spacious and the bathrooms modern. Gym facilities and parking available.

AL Hotel Amadeus, C Montero Calvo 16-18, T983219444, www.hotelmozart.ne. A recently opened modern hotel on a central pedestrian street, smartly catering mostly for business travellers. All the facilities, big comfy beds.

A Hotel Imperial, C Peso 4, T983330300, F983330813. Located in a 16th-century *palacio* in the heart of the old town, this has considerable old-Spain charm. The bedrooms are very attractive, and there's a stiff bar/lounge with a pianist.

B Hotel El Nogal, C Conde Ansúrez 10, T983340333, www.hotelelnogal.com. An intimate modern hotel near the old market. A nice choice.

E Hostería La Cueva, C Correos 4, T983330072. Small, attractive rooms above a restaurant on Valladolid's nicest little street.

E-F Hostal Del Val, Plaza del Val 6, T983375752. Another good option. Very close to the heart of town, and decent rooms with shared bathrooms. There are cheaper but scruffier rooms in another building on the same plaza.

E-F Hostal Los Arces, C San Antonio de Padua 2, T983353853, benidiopor@terra.es. An excellent budget option, with large (if somewhat noisy) rooms, comfortable beds, and a good atmosphere. Shared bathrooms and ensuites available.

E-F Hostal Zamora, C Arribas 14, T983303052. Right by the cathedral, this place has colourful little rooms with bathroom and television; there are some cheaper ones with shared facilities.

F María Cristina, Plaza de los Arces 3, T983356902. Two neighbouring *pensiones*,

both clean, attractive, and well located. Rooms are comparatively quiet, and come with a washbasin.

West of Valladolid *p163*

Medina appeals as a day trip from Valladolid, but there are many places to stay. There are a few good sleeping options in Toro too.

A Palacio de Salinas, Ctra de Salinas s/n, Medina del Campo, T983804450, www.palaciodelassalinas.es. The most opulent choice is set in the massive palace, 4 km west of town. Set in huge gardens, it's also a spa hotel and has plenty of comfort for a relaxing stay.

A Parador de Tordesillas, Ctra Salamanca 5, Tordesillas, T983770051, www.parador.es. Although this isn't the most characterful of its ilk in Spain, it is still a good lodging option. It is located outside the town in a large mansion surrounded by pine trees. The rooms are attractive, and there's a peaceful swimming pool.

B Juan II, Paseo Espolón 1, Toro, T980690300, F980692376, is on the edge of the old town above the cliff dropping down to the river. The rooms are comfortable, and there's some good old-fashioned Spanish hospitality in the air.

C María de Molina, Plaza San Julián 1, Toro, T/F 980691414, h.molina@helcom.es. A well-priced hotel, modern but attractive, with spacious climatized rooms that lack nothing but hairdryers and minibar.

D Hostal San Antolín, C San Antolín 8, Tordesillas, T983796771, is another good choice, just down from the Plaza Mayor. The restaurant underneath is also one of Tordesillas's best, an attractive place with a good traditional *menú* for €10.

E Hostal Plaza, Plaza Mayor 34, Medina del Campo, T983811246. On the huge main square in town with well-priced, spacious floorboarded rooms with ensuite.

E Villalbín, Ureña, T983717470. This *casas rurales* is a lovely, simple house just outside the walls.

F Doña Elvira, C Antonio Miguelez 47, Toro, T980690062, on the main road at the edge of the old town, is the best budget option, with clean ensuite rooms at a pittance.

F Pensión Galván, Ctra Madrid-Coruña Km 182, Tordesillas, T983770773. One of the closer budget options to the interesting bits.

F **Villa de Urueña**, C Nueva 6, Urueña, T983717063. This *casas rurales* is run out of the restaurant of the same name on the square, and has simple doubles in a house inside the walls.

G **La Castilla**, Plaza de España 19, Toro, T980690381, is basic but cheap and well placed in the town's centre.

Camping

Camping El Astral, Camino de Pollos 8, Tordesillas, T983770953, is a decent campsite by the Duero across the bridge from town (follow signs for the parador). There's a swimming pool on the site.

Zamora *p167, map p166*

AL **Parador Condes de Alba y Aliste**, Plaza de Viriato 5, T980514497, www.parador.es. A great place to stay, in a noble palace built around a beautiful courtyard. The rooms are large and attractively furnished in wood, while the pool out the back helps with the summer heat.

A **Dos Infantas**, Cortinas de San Miguel 3, T980509898, F980533548. A modern and stylish option in the centre of town, with surprisingly reasonable rates for their well-equipped rooms.

A **Hostería Real de Zamora**, Cuesta de Pizarro 7, T980534545, F980534522. Cheaper than the parador, but just as atmospheric, set in a typical old *palacio* with attractive courtyard and good rooms.

D **Hostal La Reina**, C Reina 1, T980533939. Superbly situated behind San Juan on the Plaza Mayor, this cheery option has very good rooms with or without bathroom. Very cheap in winter.

D **Hostal Luz** and **Hostal Sol**, C Benavente 2, T980533152. Two *hostales* in the same building, run by the same management. Both are clean and modernized, with reasonably quiet rooms with bathrooms.

D **Hostal Trefacio**, C Alfonso de Castro 7, T980509104. Good option, with standard modern rooms with decent bathrooms in the heart of the town.

E **Hostal Chiqui**, C Benavente 2, T980531480. In the same building as the Luz and Sol, this is a cheaper but still acceptable.

F **El Jardín**, Plaza del Maestro 8, T980531827. Some of the cheapest beds in town above a busy tapas bar; simple but clean.

G **Padornelo**, C del Aire 4, T980532064. It ain't the Ritz, but it's quiet and warm.

Salamanca *p169, map p170*

LL **Gran Hotel**, Pl Poeta Iglesias 5, T9232 13500, F923213501. Salamanca's grandest choice is overpriced but doesn't lack comforts, and is very near the Plaza Mayor.

AL **Hotel Las Torres**, C Concejo 4, T923212100. At the back of the main square, this is an excellent option, a modern place that lacks for little.

A **Hotel San Polo**, Arroyo de Santo Domingo 2, T923211177. Excellent modern hotel, attractive and nicely situated near the river, although on a busy intersection.

C **Hostal Concejo**, Plaza de la Libertad 1, T923214737. A well-placed option, this friendly hotel has blameless modern rooms around the corner from the Plaza Mayor.

C **Hostal Plaza Mayor**, Plaza Corrillo 19, T923262020. Though not quite on the square that it's named for, it's only a few paces away and has excellent modern rooms at a very fair price.

C **Hotel El Toboso**, C Clavel 7, T923271462, F923271464. Value-packed choice in the heart of things, with very pleasing decor in an attractive stone building.

C **Hotel Emperatriz II**, Rúa Mayor 18, T923219156. Though the rooms can get stuffy in summer, this hotel couldn't be better placed, on the main pedestrian street through the old centre. Underground parking available.

D **Hostal Anaya**, C Jesús 18, T923271773. Very central with attractive and spacious modern rooms and friendly management.

E **Pensión Los Angeles**, Plaza Mayor 10, T923218166. The nicest rooms in this decent spot naturally overlook the Plaza Mayor, but there are also cheap no-frills options (G) often booked out by foreign students.

F **Pensión Estefanía**, C Jesús 3, T923217372. A very cheap and handy option in the centre of Salamanca. Though the welcome is hardly effusive, the rooms are good value, at least in summer (no heating).

F **Pensión Robles**, Plaza Mayor 20, T923213197. The best reason to stay at this basic but clean place is that some of its rooms overlook the beautiful plaza, but the price is good too.

Around Salamanca *p174*

A **Hotel Doña Teresa**, Carretera Mogarraz s/n, La Alberca, T923415308, F923415309, is the most luxurious, but attractive and relaxing with it.

A **Parador Enrique II**, Plaza del Castillo 1, Ciudad Rodrigo, T923460150, ciudadrodrigo@parador.e. The top accommodation option in Ciudad Rodrigo. Attractively set in the grounds of a 15th-century castle with good views out over the walls and a nice restaurant.

B **Las Batuecas**, Av de las Batuecas 6, La Alberca, T923415188, lasbatuecas@tele line.es. A reasonable option with a nice terrace, garden, and big lounge.

C **Hotel Colón**, C Colón 42, Béjar, T923400650, is a large but pleasant enough modern hotel.

D **Artesa**, C Mayor 57, Candelario, T923413111, F923413087, is a good *casa rural* in the heart of the village, attractively rustic and decorated with some flair; they also put on decent meals.

D **Hostal Arcos**, C Sánchez Arjona 2, Ciudad Rodrigo, T923480749. Clean and bright spot right on the Plaza Mayor. All rooms with bath. Prices rise (**B**) during Holy Week.

E **Casa Pavon**, Plaza Mayor 3, Béjar, T923402861. Satisfactory.

E-G **Pensión Madrid**, C Madrid 20, Ciudad Rodrigo, T923462467. A good cheapie near the square; the ensuite doubles are much nicer than the slightly poky ones that share a bathroom.

F **Café El Candil**, has cheap beds just off the plaza.

F **Hostal Balsa**, C La Balsada 45, La Alberca, T923415337, is a decent cheap choice in the village.

Camping

E-F **Al-Bereka**, a campsite not far away from La Alberca, the , T923415195, open from Mar-Oct.

🍴 Eating

Soria *p150, map p150*

Much of Soria's eating and drinking is focused around Plaza Ramón Benito Aceña, at one end of C Mayor. Plaza San Clemente has a few foody cafés too, while C Zapatería has a number of bars that go late at weekends.

€€€ **Mesón Castellano**, Plaza Mayor 2, T975213045. And Castilian it certainly is, with large portions of heavy dishes such as roast goat, balanced by a decent house salad and some good Ribera del Duero reds.

€€ **El Mesón de Isabel**, Plaza Mayor 4, T975213041. An offshoot of the restaurant next door, but with more interesting and delicate dishes. The stuffed vegetable dishes are good to start off with, and the ambience is relaxed and pleasant, with a large number of clocks.

€€ **Santo Domingo II**, Plaza del Vergel 1, T975211717. An elegant wood and curtains type of Spanish restaurant, with mixed Basque and Castilian fare. There are *menús* for 2 or more, which are good at €16.20 and €22.84, otherwise it'll be about €20-25 a head before drinks. There's a bust of a grumpy Antonio Machado outside.

€€ **Tierra de Máutiko**, C Diputación 1, T975214948. Opposite the church of San Juan, this is one of Soria's best, with elegant new-style cuisine. An unusual speciality is sweet-and-sour boar with a mushroom mousse. Closed Sep.

Around Soria *p152*
See Sleeping above.

Along the Duero *p154*
In Aranda de Duero, there are lots of places to try the local speciality, roast lamb. See also Sleeping.

€€€ **Virrey Palafox**, C Universidad 7, El Burgo de Osma, T975340222. This restaurant is run by the same management as the **Hotel Virrey**, and is unashamedly devoted to meat, which is superbly done. On Feb and Mar weekends, the **Fiesta de la matanza** takes place; pigs are slaughtered, devoured in their entirety, and perhaps digested.

€€€ **El Burgo**, C Mayor 71, El Burgo de Osma, T975340489. Only open at weekends, this restaurant is a temple to meat. The food is good, but some of the steaks are laughably large, so be firm with the pushy owner who is sure he knows what you want.

● *For an explanation of sleeping and eating price codes used in this guide, see inside the*
● *front cover. Other relevant information is found in Essentials, see pages 47-56.*

€€ **El Lagar**, C Isilla 18, Aranda de Duero, T947510683, is another good place, set in an old wine *bodega*, dozens of which are dug out under the town.

€€ **Mesón El Roble**, Plaza Jardines de Don Diego s/n, Aranda de Duero, T947502902, has one of the best reputations, and indeed is part of a chain that has spread Aranda's lamb to cities across Spain.

€€ **Molino de Palacios**, Av de la Constitución 16, Peñafiel, T983880505, is a lovely *asador* set in an old watermill on the river. The speciality is predictable, namely roast lamb, but there's also plenty of game and wild mushroom dishes.

€ **Bar La Salon**, C Aceite, Aranda de Duero, is a lively drinking option.

€ **Café 2000**, Plaza Mayor s/n, El Burgo de Osma. A good cheap place to eat and snack, with a terrace on the main square, and a decent €7 *menú*.

€ **El Tomoten**, Plaza Mayor 14, Aranda de Duero, is a good tapas bar

€ **Restaurante María Eugenia**, Plaza España 17, Peñafiel, T983873115. Friendly family-run place decorated with heavy Spanish furniture and decent landscapes. Good seafood and comedy-large steaks.

Valladolid *p157, map p158*

€€€€ **El Figón de Recoletos**, Av Recoletos 5. A sleek and fairly posh *asador* with a good range of meat and fish on offer.

€€ **Fátima**, C Pasión 3, T983342839. An original restaurant best visited in autumn, as the undisputed speciality is the variety of dishes created using wild mushrooms. Portions are on the smallish size, but the creative flair more than makes up for it.

€€ **La Criolla**, C Calixto Fernández de la Torre 2, T983373822. A likeable restaurant with an attractive interior adorned with quotes from *vallisoletano* writers. The fare is based around simple traditional dishes, which have been given an attractive modern boost.

€€ **La Parrilla de San Lorenzo**, C Pedro Niño 2, T983335088. An atmospheric meaty restaurant in a vault in the depths of a convent building. Closed Jul.

€€ **La Parrilla de Santiago**, Atrio de Santiago 7, T983376776. Simple but tasty *raciones* and grilled meat. There's a small terrace outside in good weather, but beware the mark-up.

€€ **La Tahona**, C Correos 9, T983344793. An unassuming bar and restaurant with an excellent selection of wines and *raciones*. *Riñones de lechazo* (lamb kidneys) are superb.

€€ **Mar Cantábrico**, C Caridad 2. A laid-back restaurant serving some good seafood and snacks, including tasty *empanada*.

€€ **Santi I**, C Correos 1, T983339355. Superbly situated in the courtyard of an old inn, named **El Caballo de Troya** for its large painting of the same, although the Trojan horse looks surprisingly sprightly. The restaurant serves good quality Castilian fare; there's also a *taberna*, which is an atmospheric place for a drink; avoid the food.

€€ **Taberna El Pozo**, C Campanas 2. A cheery and basic restaurant with some decent *raciones*. They do a mean prawn.

€ **Caravanserai**, Paseo de Zorilla 4, T983375822. A relaxed café with window seats to watch the world go by; *pintxos*, sandwiches, and tofu burgers.

€ **Don Claudio**, C Campanas 4, T983350756. A friendly and traditional Spanish restaurant with painted walls and good service. The grilled sardines are recommended when they're available.

Tapas bars and cafés

Lion d'Or, Plaza Mayor 4, T983342057. A lovely old café in the main square, complete with fireman's poles and popular with people of a certain age and social class.

Patio Herreriano, C Jorge Guillén s/n. An attractive and stylish café by the modern art museum, with a peaceful terrace, nice morsels, and steepish prices.

West of Valladolid *p163*

€€ **Juan II**, see Sleeping above, Toro. The best meal in town can be found here, which, to its infinite credit doesn't feel at all like a hotel restaurant, and is priced very fairly.

€€ **La Kapilla**, Ronda de Santa Ana s/n, Medina del Campo, is a good bar set in an old *palacio*.

€€ **Pago de Marfeliz**, C Generalísimo 8, Urueña, T983717042, is a good option serving generous portions of Castilian food at moderate prices.

€€ **Palacio del Corregidor**, C San Pedro 14, Tordesillas, T983771496, specializes in good paella. There are a range of *menús* on offer.

€€**Mónaco**, Plaza Mayor 26, Medina del Campo, T983810295, is a lively bar that has some great *pintxos*, and an upstairs restaurant with some excellent, rich, meaty plates and a good *menú* for €8.

€€**San Antolín**, Tordesillas, see Sleeping above, is a good eating option too.

€**Carpe Diem**, Plaza de España s/n, Toro, is a good bar with original church-based decor.

€**La Bodeguilla del Pillo**, C Puerto del Mercado 34, Toro, is a local-style bar with nearly every Toro wine available by the glass.

€**Restaurante Castilla**, Plaza de España 19, Toro, T980690381, has decent hearty Castilian cuisine and tapas.

€**Villa de Urueña**, Plaza Mayor 6, Urueña, T983717063, is a hearty option.

Zamora *p167, map p166*

€€€**El Rincón de Antonio**, Rua de los Francos 6. Attractive modern restaurant with a stone interior and a big glassed-in terrace. The cuisine is innovative and excellent; the *mollejas* (sweetbreads) come recommended, as does the *rodaballo* (turbot).

€€**La Rua**, Rua de los Francos 19, T980534024. A good solid restaurant for a range of choices, with simple *platos combinados*, a good *menú del día* for €10.85, and some good *zamorano* cuisine. The speciality of the house is a paella-like rice with lobster, *arroz con bogavante*.

€€**Paris**, Av de Portugal 14, T980514325. Good classy Zamoran fare, although the service varies in courtesy.

€€**Valderrey**, C Benavente 9. A slightly sombre but satisfactory restaurant with generously proportioned *raciones* of traditional Castilian fare, and some very good main courses.

€**Artepan**, C Lope de Vega 2, T980512340. A good pastry shop with a top range of *empanadas* and other goodies.

€**Café Universal**, Plaza de San Martín. A good choice in summer, with a popular terrace out the front for cheap food, coffees, or evening drinks.

€**La Traviata**, Rua de los Nobiles 1. Attractive café near La Magdalena church.

€**Serafín**, Plaza Maestro Haedo 10, T980531422. Good hearty Zamoran and Castilian fare at reasonable prices, with a pleasant terrace outside.

Some of the places around the Plaza Mayor and Rúa Mayor are a bit tourist-trappy, but it's hard to beat their terraces for alfresco dining. There are plenty of cheap options in the city.

€€€**Chez Victor**, C Espoz y Mina 26, T923213123. Surprisingly reasonably priced for its reputation, this spot deals in rich creations from traditional Spanish ingredients with a definite Gallic influence.

€€€**El Pecado**, Plaza Poeta Iglésias 12, T923266558. A classy upstairs restaurant lined with books. The *menú del día* is the price-conscious way to appreciate its charms at €18.

€€€**Victor Gutiérrez**, C San Pablo 82, T923262975. A smart modern restaurant with nouvelle Spanish cuisine as well as heartier, traditional fare.

€€**Casa Paca**, Plaza del Peso 10, T923218993. Big portions of hearty Castilian dishes are this attentive restaurant's stock in trade.

€€**Don Mauro**, Plaza Mayor 19, T923281487. A quality modern restaurant with a small but attractive selection of meats and salads.

€€**Mesón Las Conchas**, Rúa Mayor 16, T923212167. A top choice for a main street bite, with excellent *raciones* and tasty *pintxos* to accompany a drink, as well as fuller choices.

€€**Momo**, C San Pablo, T923280798. A stylish modern restaurant and bar with some excellent classy *pintxos* and a range of innovative modern Castilian cuisine downstairs. The *menú del día* is good for €12.

€€**Sakana**, C San Justo 9, T923218619. Rare for Northern Spain, this is a Japanese restaurant, pretty good too, although often booked out by tourist groups.

€**El Ave**, C Los Libreros 26, T923264511. Cheap and cheerful place serving up decent snacks and *platos combinados*; there's also a lunchtime menú for €8.

€**Peccata Minuta**, C Franciso Vitoria 3, T923123447. A very pleasant café/restaurant with a range of good tapas – the prawns are particularly good – as well as friendly service and a generous line in rum 'n' Cokes.

Tapas bars and cafés
Café de Max, C Toro 22. A nice spot for breakfast in a little courtyard off C Toro.

Café Puccini, C La Latina 9. A popular student café and bar.

Juanita, Plaza de San Bual 21. An attractive café in this nice corner of town.

Music Arte, Plaza Corrillo 20. An excellent place for breakfast, a friendly and stylish café near Plaza Mayor.

Around Salamanca *p174*

€€ **Asador La Fuente**, C Tablao 8, La Alberca, T923415043, is a decent option, with good meat dishes and several *menús*.

€€ **Hotel Doña Teresa** and **Las Batuecas**, see Sleeping above, La Alberca, both hotels have good restaurants

€ **La Artesa**, Rúa del Sol 1, Ciudad Rodrigo, T923481128, is a good place to eat, set on the plaza, with a variety of *menús* and some nice salads.

ⓐ Bars and clubs

Soria *p150, map p150*

Espiral, C Zapatería 20. The place to go for loud Spanish rock.

Feli's, Plaza Ramón Benito Aceña s/n. A small bar with nice fishy snacks and bullfighting memorabilia.

La Zappa, C Zapatería 38. A quirky and cool bar open all week.

Queru, Plaza Ramón y Cajal s/n. A popular bar with Soria's alternative youth.

Zeus, Plaza Ramón Benito Aceña s/n. A smart café/bar on 2 floors, appropriately decorated with Greek scenes on the walls.

Along the Duero *p154*

Bar Veray is a friendly place on Plaza de España, Peñafiel, with an upstairs that opens at weekends.

Café Judería, Peñafiel, nicely set in the park of the same name by the river, this is a relaxing place for a coffee or drink.

La Charca, Derecha al Coso 33, Peñafiel, is also a popular choice, as is **Al Dos**, Peñafiel, at number 38.

Valladolid *p157, map p158*

There are various zones of bars in Valladolid; some around Plaza Martí y Monso, known as La Coca, some smartish ones around Plaza San Miguel, and several *discotecas* on and around C Padre Francisco Suárez, between Paseo Zorrilla and the river.

El Camarote, C Padre Francisco Suárez. A step ahead musically of most Valladolid bars, this late-opening bar has a DJ who plays a mixture of jungle and drum 'n' bass. There's a Sunday afternoon session too.

El Soportal, Plaza San Miguel s/n. A modern, dark and moody bar with a horseshoe bar and plenty of seats. Open very late.

La Comedia, Plaza Martí y Monso 4. A good lively bar with outdoor seating. Open until fairly late and decorated with past stars of the silver screen.

Paco Suárez, C Padre Francisco Suárez 2, T983812085. Cocktails and unchallenging house music until the sun is well over the yardarm.

Tintín, Plaza Martí y Monso 2. A *discoteca* and pub with happy but average Spanish and international music.

Zamora *p167, map p166*

The zone for weekend revelry is C de los Herreros, which is densely packed with bars; take your pick.

Antonheli, C Arcipreste 2. A dark café-bar with a quiet and friendly atmosphere, as well as a small terrace.

Biere, C Benavente 7. A good modern café/bar in an old building. Stylish and cheerful.

Cervecería Plaza Mayor, Plaza Mayor s/n. Solid bar in the heart of town with a terrace and good fresh lager on tap.

Salamanca *p169, map p170*

When the students are in town, Salamanca's nightlife can kick off any night of the week. *Lugares* is a free monthly paper with listings of events and what's going on in bars and clubs; you can pick it up in cafés. There's a zone of student bars around C Libreras and C La Latina, but the main night owl area is on Gran Vía and around; Plaza de Bretón and C Varillas have a high concentration of spots.

Abadia, C Francisco Vitoria 7. An atmospheric bar near the cathedral, with faux-medieval decor and a lively crowd.

De Laval Genovés, C San Justo 27. One of Salamanca's best gay choices, with a spacious interior and cool decor that has earned it the nickname 'El Submarino'.

El Barco, Puente Principe de Asturias s/n. It's hard to beat dancing on a boat at 0900. Moored in the river near the Puente Principe

de Asturias bridge, this goes late from Thu-Sat and has a pretty happy atmosphere.
El Savor, C San Justo 2, T923268576. A stylish bar for dancing salsa and other Latin American rhythms. Free dancing classes at 2300 on Thu and Fri.
Gaia, Plaza Comillo 18. A cellar bar with frequent live music and a slightly serious student crowd.
La Fábrica, C Los Libreros 49. A large and popular bar with fresh draught beer consumed liberally by a studenty crowd.
Paco's Cantine, C San Justo 27, T661068291. A friendly and grungy little bar popular for its €1 shooters.
Potemkin, C Consuelo. Another late opener in the Salamanca zone.

🎭 Entertainment

Valladolid *p157, map p158*
Cinemas Coca, Plaza Martí y Monso, T983330290. A very central cinema.
Cines Casablanca, C Leopoldo Cano 8, T983398841. An arthouse cinema that usually uses subtitles rather than dubbing.
Cines Roxy, C Mario de Molina 6, T9833-51672. A small but handy art deco cinema.
Sala Borja, C Ruiz Hernández 12. Frequent theatre performances, less traditional than the Lope de Vega or Calderón.
Teatro Calderón, C Las Angustias s/n, T902371137, www.tcalderon.org. The main theatre, with mainstream drama and dance.
Teatro Lope de Vega, C Mario de Molina 12. A lovely tiled theatre built in 1861 with regular drama, opera, and concerts.

Salamanca *p169, map p170*
Bretón, Plaza Bretón 12, T923269844. Generally shows an interesting selection of cinema, occasionally in original version.
Multicines Salamanca, C Vázquez Coronado, T923266468. A convenient central cinema.
Teatro Liceo, Plaza de Liceo s/n, a modernized theatre near the Plaza Mayor.

🎉 Festivals and events

Soria *p150, map p150*
In late **Jun**, Soria's main festival is the **Sanjuanes** with an array of bullfights, processions, fireworks and wine-drinking.

On **2 Oct**, the feast day of **San Saturio** takes place, a big event.

Along the Duero *p154*
On **14-18 Aug** in Peñafiel there are *encierros*, where bulls run through the streets; these are followed by *capeas* in the plaza, which is basically bull-dodging, sometimes with the aim of slipping rings over the horns. The homeowners sell off balcony seats, but interestingly some families still have hereditary rights to seats during the fiesta, even if the house isn't theirs.

Valladolid *p157, map p158*
Valladolid has some good festivals, particularly its fairly serious **Semana Santa** (Holy Week), when hooded brotherhoods parade floats through the streets to the mournful wailing of cornets and tubas. In **early Sep** is the feast of the **Virgen de San Lorenzo** when the streets are full of stalls selling wine and tapas and there are bullfights, concerts, etc.

West of Valladolid *p163*
Mid-Sep is when Tordesillas's fiesta is held. It includes the **Toro de la Vega**, where a bull is released in the open woodlands near the town and the people start running and dodging.

Zamora *p167, map p166*
Semana Santa (Holy Week) is one of the most famous and traditional in Spain. Book a room well in advance if you fancy a visit. Although there's plenty of revelry in the bars and streets, the main element is the serious religious processions of hooded *cofradias* (brotherhoods) who carry or accompany giant floats; it's effectively a weeklong series of funeral processions; they are very atmospheric and traditional, although the mournful music can get a bit much after you've seen a couple of them.
At the end of **Jun** is the main fiesta is **San Pedro**, with the usual streetlife, fireworks and bullfights. At the same time, the Plaza de Viriato holds an important **ceramics fair**; a picturesque sight indeed with thousands of vessels of all shapes and sizes arranged under the trees; they range from traditional plain earthenware to imaginatively painted decorative pieces.

Salamanca's major fiesta kicks off on
7 Sep; a 2-week binge of drinks, bullfights
and fireworks. There always seems to be
some type of fiesta at other times; different
student faculties combine to make sure
there's rarely a dull moment.

Around Salamanca *p174*
In Cuidad Rodrigo, 6 weeks before Easter, is
Carnaval – a celebration the city is famous
for. It incorporates masquerades, all manner
of bull sports and general wildness. It's well
known so you'll need to book a place to
sleep well in advance, and be prepared to
pay a little more.

O Shopping

Valladolid *p157, map p158*
Valladolid's main shopping area is between
Plaza Mayor and Plaza Zorillo, particularly
along C Santiago.
Oletum, C de Teresa Gil 12, large selection of
books. Also an English language section.

Zamora *p167, map p166*
Zamora is full of interesting shops dealing in
antiques and ceramics; there are also
characterful touristy shops along the main
pedestrian streets.

Salamanca *p169, map p170*
A good thing to buy in Salamanca is ham.
La Despensa, Rúa Mayor 23. A convenient,
if slightly overpriced ham shop which has a
good selection of all things piggy.
The market just below the Plaza Mayor is a
good spot for food-shopping.
Librería Cervantes, Plaza de Santa Eulalia
s/n, is one of many bookshops in this
university city.

▲ Activities and tours

Valladolid *p157, map p158*
Real Valladolid is the city's football team,
who dress in slightly tasteless purple-striped
tops. They've spent about half their life in the
Primera division, where they currently are,
but have never excelled; 4th place is their
highest finish. Their stadium is to the west of
town, **Estadio José Zorilla**, Av Mundial 82
s/n, T983360342.

⊖ Transport

Soria *p150, map p150*
Bus There are 7 daily buses to **Madrid**, 5 to
Logroño, 6 to **Zaragoza** (a couple of them
via Agreda and Tarazona), 3 to **Berlanga** and
Burgo de Osma, a couple to **Burgos**, 3 to
Aranda del Duero and **Valladolid**, 4 to
Pamplona via **Tafalla**, and 1 to **Barcelona**.
There are hourly buses to **Almazán**, and 7 to
Medinaceli, and 4 to **Arcos de Jalón**.
Two buses daily service the **dinosaur
country** stops of **Yanguas**, **Enciso**, and
Arnedillo.
Train Apart from Almazán, easily accessed
by bus anyway, the only rail destination of
interest is **Madrid**, serviced via **Guadalajara**
4 to 5 times a day.

Around Soria *p152*
There are buses from **Soria** to **Almazán**
more or less hourly, and several trains daily.
Both bus and train station are handy for the
old town of Almazán.
 There are 7 or so buses daily connecting
Soria and **Medinaceli**, which only stop in
the new town. It's the old town that merits
a visit, so if you're coming by public
transport you'll have a bit of a walk ahead.
It's either 3½ km by road, or you can strike
at the hill directly, more strenuous but
potentially quicker and more interesting.
Medinaceli is accessible by train from
Zaragoza and **Madrid**.

Along the Duero *p154*
There are regular buses from Soria to
Berlanga de Duero. In El Burgo de Osma,
the bus station is on the main road; there are
3 services to **Soria** and 3 to **Aranda** de
Duero; 1 only on Sun. **Aranda de Duero** has
good transport connections. The bus and
train stations are across the Duero from the
old part of town. Four buses a day go to
Madrid and **Burgos**. There are 6 a day to
Valladolid, 2 to **El Burgo de Osma**, 3 to
Soria, 2 to **Roa**, and 1 to **Almazán**. Regular
trains go to **Madrid**, **Valladolid**, and **Burgos**.
There are 6 buses a day from **Peñafiel** to
Valladolid and **Aranda de Duero**.

Valladolid *p157, map p158*
Air Valladolid's airport, T983415500, 8 km
north west of town, is connected with

Barcelona, Vigo, Paris, the Balearics, and the Canaries.

Bus Intercity buses serve **Madrid** hourly, **León** 8 times daily, **Barcelona** 3 times daily, **Segovia** almost hourly, **Zamora** 7-10 times a day, **Palencia** hourly, and **Zaragoza** via **Soria** 3 times daily. Other destinations include **Aranda** (5), **Roa** (2), **Medina del Campo** (8), **Rueda** (7), **Medina de Rioseco** hourly, **Simancas** half-hourly, **Tordesillas** hourly.

Train Services run to **Madrid** via **Medina del Campo** very regularly, to **Palencia** more than hourly, and less frequently to most mainline destinations.

West of Valladolid *p163*

For **Tordesillas**, bus services running between **Valladolid** and **Zamora** stop at the bus station, just north and west of the old town. There are 7-10 on weekdays, and 3-4 at weekends.

For Medina del Campo, there's a bus terminal next to the train station, most buses to **Madrid** and **Valladolid** leave from outside a bar called Punto Rojo on Calle Artilleria near the Plaza Mayor. There are about 15 departures for **Valladolid** daily and 5 for **Madrid**. Medina is a major rail junction, and there are many trains to **Madrid**, **Valladolid**, **Palencia**, and **Salamanca**, as well as 3 a day to **León**, and 1 to **Lisbon**.

For Toro, services running between **Valladolid** and **Zamora** stop on the main road, a handier option. There are 7-10 a day on weekdays, and 3-4 at weekends. The railway station is by the river, not particularly convenient for the town far above.

Zamora *p167, map p166*

Bus Some 7 buses a day run north to **León** via **Benavente** (4 at weekends); 7 run to **Valladolid** via **Toro** and **Tordesillas** (3 at weekends); 6 service **Madrid**; a massive 13 cruise south to **Salamanca** (6 on Sun), 5 go to **Oviedo**, 1 to **Bilbao** via **Palencia** and **Burgos**, and 2 to **Barcelona** via **Zaragoza**. There's a bus to **Bragança** in Portugal 3 times a week (currently Mon, Wed, Sat at 1600, but phone the bus station on 980521281 for current information).

Train A few; 3 a day run to **Madrid**; more go to **Medina del Campo**, but you're better off with the buses.

Salamanca *p169, map p170*

Bus The bus station is west of town along Av Filiberto Villalobos. Within the province, there are buses hourly to **Alba de Tormes**, 13 a day to **Béjar** and to **Ciudad Rodrigo**, 2 to **Ledesma** (1 on Sat, none on Sun), and 6 to **Peñaranda**. Further flung destinations include **Avila** (4-6 weekdays, 2 at weekends), **Madrid** hourly, **Oviedo/Gijón** (4), **León** (4), **A Coruña** (3), **Bilbao/San Sebastián** twice, Seville (4), **Santiago/Orense** (2), **Zaragoza/Barcelona** (2), **Zamora** (more than hourly), **Valladolid** (6), **Segovia** (2), and **Cáceres** (10).

Train The train station is north of town and poorly served. There's an early morning train to **Lisboa** and **Porto**, 4 daily to **Burgos**, 6 to **Avila** via **Peñaranda**, and 9 to **Valladolid**.

Around Salamanca *p174*

From **La Alberca**, there are 1 or 2 buses daily to **Salamanca**.

For **Cuidad Rodrigo**, 13 buses a day travel to and from **Salamanca**. They leave from the bus station just east of the walled town.

❻ Directory

Soria *p150, map p150*

Internet **Merlin Center**, C Santa Luisa de Marillac s/n. An internet centre with good connections if there aren't too many online gamers in the house.

Along the Duero *p154*

Internet Access at **Ciberlibro**, Plaza Mayor 19, Aranda de Duero, Mon-Fri 1000-1400, 1730-2030, Sat 1000-1400.

Laundry **Reyna** is at C Postas 22, Aranda de Duero.

Valladolid *p157, map p158*

Hospital Hospital Universitario, T983420000, emergency T112.

Internet **Bocattanet**, C Mario de Molina 16, an internet café serving food not far from the tourist office. **Cartablanca**, C de Colón 2, is an option in the university district.

Cibercafé, Paseo de Zorrilla 46, has several coin-op terminals in a stuffy café; €2.50 per hr. **Esferacom**, C Ruiz Hernandez 3, also a *locutorio*, and fastish Internet connection.

Post The main post office is on Plaza de la Rinconada near the Plaza Mayor.

Laundry On C Embajadores in the *barrio* of Las Delicias, a trek away on the other side of the railway line in the south of town. Bus number 6 will take you there from C Vicente Moliner, near the Plaza Mayor.

Useful addresses and numbers
For the **police** phone T092 in an emergency.

West of Valladolid *p163*
Internet Access is available at **Cyber Mundo Net**, C La Antigua 23, Toro.

Zamora *p167, map p166*
Internet Plaza Viriato, Plaza Viriato s/n, is a cybercafé opposite the parador. **PC Boon**, Plaza del Cuartel Viejo s/n, has access during business hours. **Recreativos Coliseum**, C Ramos Carrión, is a gaming arcade with Internet terminals.

Laundry A friendly no-name laundry on the corner of C de Balborraz and C San Andres just off the Plaza Mayor (look for the *Tintoreria* sign) will do a service wash and dry for about €6.

Useful addresses and numbers Police station, Plaza Mayor in the old town hall.

Salamanca *p169, map p170*
Hospital Hospital Clínico, Paseo de San Vicente 58, T923291100.
Internet There seems to be an Internet café on every corner in Salamanca. **Ciber Locutório Jesús**, C Jesús 10, T923281571, has good rates for international calls and decent Internet access at €1.20 per hr. **Ciberbar Abaco**, C Zamora 7. Access at €1.20 per hr. **Ciber Francisco**, C Francisco Vitoria 5. Not the fastest, but handily close to the cathedral. **Ciber Mundo**, C Librerías 20.
Post office The main post office is on Gran Vía 25 near Plaza de la Constitución.
Language schools Apart from the university itself, which has a highly-regarded Spanish language programme, there are several smaller schools: **Letra Hispánica**, C Librerías 28, has a reasonable reputation, as does **Eurocentres**, C Vera Cruz 2.
Laundry Coin Laundry, C Azafranal 26. A self-service laundromat in an arcade.
Useful addresses and numbers
Police, call T092 or T923194433. The handiest police station is on the Plaza Mayor.

Northern Castilla

If the dust and vast expanses of dry, harsh land get too much, head north. Gradually pictureque valleys and the Cordillera Cantábria come into view. Most visitors come for the extraordinary rich collection of architectural offerings. Burgos gets most of the admirers mostly due to its stunning cathedral, while laid-back, unassuming Palencia is often overlooked. ➤ For Sleeping, Eating and other listings, see pages 202-207.

Burgos ➔ *Phone code: 947; Colour map 2, grid B2; Population 166,251; Altitude: 860 m.*

"They have very good houses and live very comfortably, and they are the most courteous people I have come across in Spain." Andres Navagero, 1526

The Venetian traveller's comment on Burgos from the 16th century could equally apply today to the city where courtliness still rules the roost. Formerly a pre-eminent and prosperous trading town, Burgos achieved infamy as the seat of Franco's Civil War junta and is still a sober and reactionary town, the heartland of Castilian conservatism. Burgos's collection of superb Gothic buildings and sculpture, as well as its position on the Camino de Santiago, make it a popular destination, but the city copes well with the summer influx. Just don't come for spring sunshine; Burgos is known throughout Spain as a chilly city, epitome of the phrase "nueve meses de invierno, tres meses de infierno"; nine months of winter, three months of hell. ➤ For Sleeping, Eating and other listings, see pages 202-207.

Getting there Burgos is roughly in the centre of Northern Spain and easily accessed from most parts of the country by bus or train. There are regular services from Madrid and the Basque country as well as Santander and all Castilian towns. ▸▸ *For further details, see Transport, page 206.*

Getting around As usual, the old centre is compact, but you may want to use the local bus service to access a couple of the outlying monasteries and the campsite.

Best time to visit Burgos has a fairly unpleasant climate with short hot summers and long cold winters (it often snows) punctuated by the biting wind that "won't blow out a candle but will kill a man". The most moderate weather will be found in May/June and September.

Tourist information The handiest is opposite the cathedral ① *Plaza del Rey San Fernando, daily 1000-2000.* Also ① *Paseo Espolón, Mon-Sat 1000-1400, 1700-2000, Sun 1000-1400* and *Plaza Alonso Martínez daily 0900-1400, 1700-2000.* There are tours and a tacky summer tourist train that rolls around the sights for €1.80, leaving from outside the cathedral square tourist office.

History

Burgos is comfortably the oldest city in Europe, if you count the nearby cave-dwellers from Atapuerca, who were around 500,000 years ago. That aside, the city's effective foundation was in the late 9th century, when it was resettled during the Reconquista. Further honours soon followed; it was named capital of Castilla y León as early as the 11th century.

The city's position at the northern centre of the Castilian plain, near the coastal mountain passes, made it a crucial point for the export of goods. The city flourished, becoming a wealthy city of merchants and beasts of burden; in the 16th century its mule population often exceeded the human one, as bigger and bigger convoys of wool made their way over the mountains and by ship to Flanders.

The Consulado of Burgos, a powerful guildlike body, was created to administer trade, and succeeded in establishing a virtual monopoly; Burgos became one of three great 16th-century trading cities, along with Seville and Medina del Campo. The strife in Flanders hit the city hard though and other towns had broken into the market. Burgos's population declined by 75 per cent in the first half of the 17th century, and the city lapsed into the role of genteel provincial capital, apart from a brief and bloody interlude. During the Civil War the Nationalist *junta* was established here; the city had shown its credentials with a series of atrocities committed on Republicans after the rising.

Sights

Cathedral ① *Mon-Sat 0930-1300, 1600-1900; Sun 0930-1145, 1600-1900, €3.60, some chapels are only accessible on guided tours, guides are independent and prices vary.* This remarkable Gothic edifice, whose high hollow spires rise over the city, is not a lovable place but the technical excellence of its stonework can only be admired, and it also houses a collection of significant artwork. The current structure was begun in 1221 over an earlier church by Ferdinand III and his Germanic wife, Beatrice of Swabia, with the bishop Maurice overseeing things. Beatrice brought him with her from Swabia, and the Northern influence didn't stop there; Gil and Diego de Siloe, the top sculptors who are responsible for many masterpieces inside and throughout the province, were from those parts, while the towers were designed by masterbuilder Hans of Cologne, a city whose cathedral bears some resemblance to this.

Entering through the western door, under the spires, one of the strangest sights is in the chapel to the right. It's reserved for private prayer, but the figure you see through the glass is the Christ of Burgos. Made from buffalo hide and sporting a head of real hair, the crucified Jesus wears a green skirt and looks a little the worse for wear.

The limbs are movable, no doubt to impress the 14th-century faithful with a few tricks; apparently the Christ was once so lifelike that folk thought the fingernails had to be clipped weekly. Opposite, high on the wall, the strange figure of Papamoscas strikes the hours, the closest thing to levity in this serious building.

> ‡ To get inside the coro and a couple of the other side chapels, first buy a ticket for the museum, then find an attendant to let you in.

Like in many Spanish cathedrals, the *coro* is closed off, which spoils any long perspective views. Once inside, admire the Renaissance main retablo; it's dedicated to Mary and sports a silver icon of her. Underfoot are the bones of El Cid and his wife Doña Jimena, underwhelmingly marked by a dour slab. The remains were only transferred here in 1927 after being reclaimed from the French, who had taken them from the monastery of San Pedro de Cardeña. They lie under the large octagonal tower, an elaborate 16th-century add-on. The wooden choir itself is elegant and elaborate. Other side chapels hold various tombs, retablos, and tapestries, but the most ornate is at the very far end of the apse, the Capilla de los Condestables. The Velasco family, hereditary Constables of Castile, were immensely influential in their time, and one of the most powerful, Don Pedro Fernández, is entombed here with his wife. The alabaster figures

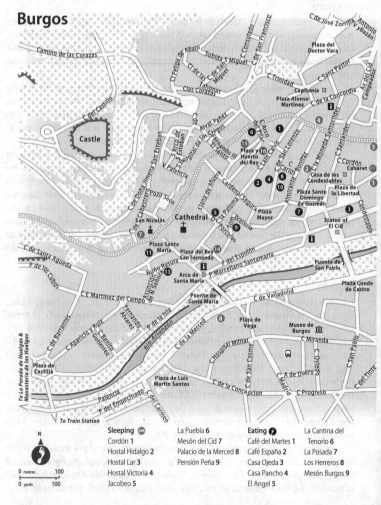

Burgos

on the sepulchre are by another German, Simon of Cologne, and his son; few kings have lain in a more elaborate setting, with a high vaulted roof, much garnishing, and three retablos, the middle of which is especially ornate and depicts the purification of Mary. The most accessible sculpture, however, is just outside, around the ambulatory, a series of sensitive alabaster panels depicting Biblical scenes.

The **museum**, set around the sunken cloister, is reasonably interesting, despite the pompous security system. The first room has a series of pieces, including some good late 15th-century Flemish paintings – the mob mentality of the Crucifixion is well portrayed. There are several reliquaries holding various bits of saints (including Thomas Becket) and nothing less than a spine from the crown of thorns. A *retablo* depicts Santiago in Moor-slaying mode.

A 10th-century Visigothic Bible is the highlight of the next room, as well as the Cid's marriage contract, the so-called Letter of Arras. In another room, high on the wall, hangs a coffer that belonged to him; possibly the one that was involved in a grubby little deed of his, where he sneakily repaid some Jews with a coffer of sand, rather than the gold that he owed them. In the adjacent chamber is a pretty red Mudéjar ceiling.

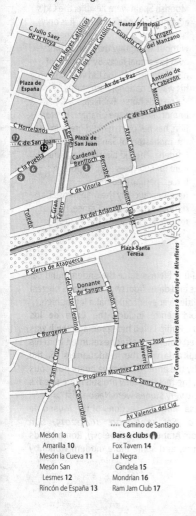

Mesón la
Amarilla **10**
Mesón la Cueva **11**
Mesón San
Lesmes **12**
Rincón de España **13**

Bars & clubs 🎵
Fox Tavern **14**
La Negra
Candela **15**
Mondrian **16**
Ram Jam Club **17**

•••• Camino de Santiago

Iglesia de San Nicolás ① *Jun-Sep Mon-Fri 1000-1400, 1630-1900, Sat/Sun 1000- 1200, €1, free Mon, currently only open for services in winter.* This small church above the cathedral is a must-see for its superb retablo, a virtuoso sculptural work, probably by Simon and Francis of Cologne. It's a bit like looking at a portrait of a city, or a theatre audience, so many figures seem to be depicted in different sections. The main scene at the top is Mary surrounded by a 360-degree choir of angels. The stonework is superb throughout; have a look for the ship's rigging, a handy piece of chiselling to say the least. There's also a good painting of the Last Judgement in the church, an early 16th-century Flemish work, only recently rediscovered. The demons are the most colourful aspect; one is trying to tip the scales despite being stood on by Saint Michael.

Around the old town The old town is entered over one of two main bridges over the pretty Arlanzón river, linked by a leafy *paseo*. The eastern of the two, the **Puente de San Pablo**, is guarded by an imposing mounted statue of El Cid, looming Batman-like above the traffic. The inscription risibly dubs him "a miracle from among the great miracles of the creator". The other, **Puente de Santa María**, approaches the arch of the same name, an impressive if pompous gateway with a statue of a very snooty

⦂ One man and his horse

Although portrayed as something of a national hero in the 12th-century epic *El Cantor de mio Cid* (The Song of the Cid) the recorded deeds of Rodrigo Díaz de Vivar actually suggest a degree of ambiguity in the fight for places in the pantheon of Spanish heroes. Born in a village just outside Burgos in 1043, El Cid (the Boss) was in fact a mercenary who fought with the Moors if the price was right.

His ability to protect his own interests was recognized even by those who sought to idolize him. The Song of the Cid recounts that on being expelled from Burgos the great man wrapped up his beard to protect it from being pulled by irate citizens angry at his nefarious dealings.

Operating along the border between Christian and Muslim Spain, the Cid was a man of undoubted military guile who was able to combine a zeal for the recoquista with an equal desire to further his own fortune. The moment when he swindled two innocent Jewish merchants by delivering a chest filled with sand instead of gold is celebrated with gusto in Burgos cathedral where his mortal remains now lie.

Banished by Alfonso VI for double dealing, his military skills proved indispensable and he was re-hired in the fight against the Almoravids. The capture of Valencia in 1094 marked the height of his powers and was an undoubted blow to the Moors. If having his own city wasn't reward enough the Cid was given the formidable Gormaz castle as a sort of fortified weekend retreat.

By the standards of his own time where the boundaries, both physical and cultural, between Christian and Moorish Spain were flexible, the Cid's actions make perfect sense. It is only later ages preferring their heroes without ambiguity that had to gloss over the actual facts. By the time of his death in 1099 the Cid was well on his way to national hero status.

The Cids horse, Babieca, immortalized in the Charlton Heston film, has her own marked grave in the monastery of San Pedro de Cardeña. The Cid himself was buried here for 600 years until Napoleon's forces, perhaps fearing a re-appearance by the man himself, removed the body to France. He was reburied in Burgos in the 1930s.

Charles V. East of here is the **Plaza Mayor,** fairly lifeless since the underground car park went in. The **Casa Consistorial** has marks and dates from two of Burgos's biggest floods; it's hard to believe that the friendly little river ever could make it that high.

Other interesting buildings in the old centre include the **Casa de los Condestables,** with a massive corded façade. Philip I died here prematurely; it was also here that the Catholic monarchs received Columbus after he returned from his second voyage. The ornate **neogothic Capitanía** was the headquarters for the Nationalist *junta* in the civil war. Still used by the army, the façade bears pompous plaques to the memory of Franco and Mola; the fact that they are still there speaks much about conservative Burgos, where "the very stones were Nationalist".

Attractively set around the patioed **Casa Miranda**, sections of the **Museo de Burgos** ⓘ *Tue-Fri 1000-1400, 1600-1930, Sat 1000-1400, 1645-2015, Sun 1000-1400, €1.20,* have prehistoric finds from Atapuerca (see below), Roman finds from Clunia, religious painting and sculpture, and some more modern works by Burgalese artists.

66 99 Burgos is comfortably the oldest city in Europe, if you count the nearby cave-dwellers from Atapuerca, who were around 500,000 years ago. ..

Monasterio de las Huelgas ① *Tue-Sat 1000-1315, 1545-1745, Sun 1030-1415, €4.81.* A 20-minute walk through a posh suburb of Burgos, the monastery still harbours some 40 cloistered nuns, heiresses to a long tradition of power. In its day, it wielded enormous influence. The monastery was founded by Eleanor of England, daughter of Henry II and Eleanor of Aquitaine, who came to Burgos to marry Alfonso VIII in 1170. The Hammer of the Scots, Edward I, came here to get hitched as well; he married Eleanor, Princess of Castile, in the monastery in 1254. Las Huelgas originally meant 'the reposes', as the complex was a favourite retreat for the Castilian monarchs. Here they could regain strength, ponder matters of state, and perhaps have a bit on the side; several abbesses of Las Huelgas bore illegitimate children behind the closed doors.

The real attractions are on the nuns' side of the barricade. The church contains many ornate tombs of princes and other Castilian royals. These were robbed of much of their contents by Napoleon's soldiers. All were opened in 1942 and, to great surprise, an array of superb royal garments remained well preserved 700 years on, as well as some jewellery from the one tomb the French had overlooked. In the central nave are the tombs of Eleanor and Alfonso, who died in the same year. The arms of England and Castile adorn the exquisite tombs. They lie beneath an ornate Plateresque retablo which is topped by a 13th-century crucifixion scene and contains various relics.

Around a large cloister are more treasures; a Mudéjar door with intricate wooden carving, a Moorish standard captured from the famous battle at Navas de Tolosa in 1212, and a postcard-pretty smaller cloister with amazing carved plasterwork, no doubt Muslim influenced. For many, the highlight is the display of the clothing found in the tombs; strange, ornate, silken garments embroidered with gold thread; the colours have faded over the centuries, but they remain in top condition, a seldom-seen link with the past that seems to bring the dusty royal names alive. Buses 5, 7 and 39 run there from Avenida Valladolid across the river from the old town.

Cartuja de Miraflores ① *Mon-Sat 1015-1500, 1600-1800, Sun 1120-1230, 1305-1500, 1600-1800, free.* This former hunting lodge is another important Burgos monastery, also still functioning, populated by silent Carthusians. John II, the father of Isabella, the Catholic monarch, started the conversion and his daughter finished it. Like so much in Burgos, it was the work of a German, Hans of Cologne. Inside, the late Gothic design is elegant, with elaborate vaulting, and stained glass from Flanders depicting the life of Christ. The choirstalls are sculpted with incredibly delicacy from wood, but attention is soon drawn by the superb alabaster work of the retablo and the tombs that lie before it. These are all designed by Gil de Siloe, the

Castilla y León Burgos

● *Above the town, a park covers the hilltop and conceals the remains of a castle, which was*
● *blown up by the French in the Napoleonic Wars.*

Gothic master and they are the triumphant expression of genius. The central tomb is starshaped, and was commissioned by Isabella for her parents; at the side of the chamber rests her brother Alonso, heir to the Castilian throne until his death at the age of 14. The retablo centres on the crucifixion, with many saints in attendance. The sculptural treatment is beautiful; expressing emotion and sentiment through stone. Equally striking is the sheer level of detail in the works; a casual visitor could spend weeks trying to decode the symbols and layers of meaning. To get here catch bus 26 or 27 from Plaza de España and get off at the Fuente del Prior stop; the monastery is a five-minute walk up a marked side road. Otherwise, it's a 50-minute walk through pleasant parkland from the centre of town.

Excursions

Atapuerca ① *Summer Wed-Sun 1000-1400, 1600-2000 (except last weekend of the month), visits at weekends the rest of the year by appointment, T947421462, www.pale orama.es.* A short way east of Burgos, an unremarkable series of rocky hills were the site of some incredibly significant palaeontological finds. The remains of *homo heidelbergensis* were discovered here; dating has placed the bones from 500,000 to 200,000 years old. It's a crucial link in the study of hominid evolution; Neanderthals seemed to evolve directly from these Heidelbergers, but there's not a huge amount to see. There's a small hall displaying some of the finds, and some walkways around the excavation sites. The site is just north of the N120 east of town, crudely signposted near the village of Ibeas de Juarros.

Monasterio de San Pedro de Cardeña ① *Mon-Sat 1000-1315, 1555-1800, Sun 1615-1800, wait in the church for a monk to appear, admission by donation.* Close to the city, at a distance of some 10 km, the monastery is worth a visit, especially for those with an interest in the Cid. The first point of interest is to one side in front of the monastery where a gravestone marks the supposed burial site of the Cid's legendary mare, Babieca. The monastery has a community of 24 Cistercians; a monk will show you around the church, most of which dates from the 15th century. In a side chapel is an ornate tomb raised (much later) over the spot where the man and his wife were buried until Napoleon's troops nicked the bones in the 19th century; they were reclaimed and buried in Burgos cathedral. The Mudéjar cloister dates from the 10th century and is the most impressive feature of the building, along with a late Gothic doorway in the *sala capitular*. Accommodation is available in the monastery.

Around Burgos Province

While the barren stretches to the east and west of the city of Burgos are dull and relentless, there are some very worthwhile trips to be made to the north and south, where the country is greener and hillier. To the south, the cloister of the monastery of Santo Domingo de Silos is worth a journey in its own right, but there's more to see. To the north are quiet hidden valleys, and one of Northern Spain's most lovable Romanesque churches, the Iglesia de San Pedro de la Tejera. ▶▶ *For Sleeping, Eating and other listings, see pages 202-207.*

Covarrubias → *Colour map 2, grid B2.*

This attractive village, 37 km south of Burgos, gets a few tour coaches but hasn't been spoiled. Its attractive wooden buildings and cobbled squares make a picturesque setting by the side of a babbling brook. Its impressive 10th-century tower stands over the big town wall on the riverbank; it's a Mozarabic work that's said to be haunted by the ghost of a noble lady who was walled up alive there. Behind

❖ *The village has several places to stay and makes a relaxing stop.*

it is the Colegiata, a Gothic affair containing a number of tombs of fatlipped men and thinlipped ladies, including that of Fernán González, a count of these lands who united disparate Christian communities into an efficient force to drive the Moors southwards, thereby setting the foundations of Castile. Opposite the church is a statue of the Norwegian princess Kristina, who married the former archbishop of Seville here in 1257; her tomb is in the 16th-century cloister ① *Wed-Mon 1030-1400, 1600-1900, €3 guided tour*.

Monasterio de Santo Domingo de Silos → *Colour map 2, grid B3.*
① *Tue-Sat 1000-1300, 1630-1800, Sun/Mon 1630-1800, €2.40 includes admission to a small museum of musical instruments in the village.*
A monastery whose monks went platinum in the 1990s with a CD of Gregorian chant, Santo Domingo is a must for its cloister, the equal of any in the peninsula. Started in the 11th century, the finished result is superb, two levels of double-columned harmony decorated with a fine series of sculptured capitals. It's not known who the artist was, but their assured expertise is unquestionable. Most of the capitals have vegetable and animal motifs, while at each corner are reliefs with Biblical scenes. Curiously, the central column of the western gallery breaks the pattern, with a flamboyant twist around itself, a humorous touch. The ceiling around the cloister is also superb; a colourful Mudéjar work. A cenotaph of Santo Domingo, who was born just south of here, stands on three lions in the northern gallery.

Another interesting aspect is the old pharmacy, in a couple of rooms off the cloister. It's full of phials and bottles in which the monks used to prepare all manner of remedies; even more fascinating are some of the amazing old books of pharmacy and science that fill the shelves. Other rooms off the cloister hold temporary exhibitions. Next door, the monastery church next door is bare and uninteresting.

Lerma → *Colour map 2, grid B2.*
Although Lerma was a reasonably important local town beforehand, what we see today is a product of the early 17th century, when the local duke effectively ruled Spain as the favourite of Philip III. He wasn't above a bit of porkbarrelling, and used his power to inflict a massive building programme on his hometown. Six **monasteries** were built for different orders between 1605 and 1617, but the **Palacio Ducal** tops it all; a ridiculously large structure that achieves neither harmony nor elegance; the "I'm the most important man in the village" syndrome taken to a laughable extreme. It resembles Colditz castle in some ways; there's certainly a martial aspect to both it and the parade-ground style square that fronts it. There's a tourist office ① *C Audiencia, Tue to Sun 1000-1400, 1600-1900, until 2000 in summer*, close to Ducal Palace.

Vivar del Cid and Sotopalacios → *Colour map 2, grid B2.*
Around 8 km north of Burgos is the town of Vivar del Cid, where the man himself was born. There's no reason to come here other than to say you've been; the only conclusion to be drawn is that he must have been pretty happy to leave. A small monument commemorates the man, but there's little else here. A couple of kilometres further on, Sotopalacios is a fairly unappealing centre for *morcilla* making; if you're motorized, drop in to have a look at its picturesque creeper-draped castle, a private residence.

‡ *The land to the north rises into the Cordillera Cantábrica. There are some excellent, little-visited places to explore, but don't go in winter – temperatures can drop well below zero.*

El Gran Cañon del Ebro → *Colour map 2, grid A2.*
From Sotopalacios, the N623 continues, through more and more mountainous terrain, finally descending to the coast and Santander on the other side of the range. The Ebro, near its source here, has carved a picturesque canyon into the rock; it's a

lovely cool valley full of trees and vultures. A marked trail, El Gran Cañon del Ebro, can be walked, starting from the spa village of Valdelateja; the whole trail is a six-hour round trip.

Valdivielso Valley

Puente Arenas and around Accessible via a windy road via the village of **Pesquera**, is a quiet little gem; the Valdivielso Valley. It's a wide green curve, also made by the Ebro, and makes a very relaxing retreat. Green (or white in winter), pretty, and reasonably isolated, the valley is perfect for walking, climbing, or even canoeing, but it also has several buildings of interest. As an important north-south conduit it was fortified with a series of towers; one of the better examples is at the valley's northern end, in the village of **Valdenoceda**.

Above the pretty village one of the finest Romanesque churches you could want to see, the **Iglesia de San Pedro de la Tejera** ① *on private property but you can visit after phoning T947303200, €1.50*. It is a beautiful little structure overlooking the valley. It's in superb condition, built in the 11th and 12th centuries. The façade is fantastic, beautifully carved with various allegorical scenes, including a lion eating a man. Around the outside are a series of animal heads in relief. The sunken interior features more carvings of animals, musicians, and acrobats as well as an impressively painted Mudéjar gallery, installed in the 15th century. The simple apse is harmonious; it's the beautiful Romanesque proportions as much as the carvings that make this building such a delight.

Oña A tiny, slightly depressing town at the southern end of the Valdivielso Valley, Oña is worth a visit anyway for its monuments; the massive **Monasterio de San Salvador** ① *guided visit only Tue-Fri 1030, 1130, 1245, 1600, 1700, 1815, Sat/Sun 1030, 1130, 1230, 1315, 1600, 1700, 1815, €2*. It is an attractive former fortified monastery that seems bigger than the rest of the town put together. It's now a mental hospital but its quite remarkable church can still be visited. The royals of the Middle Ages always favoured burial in a monastery; they shrewdly figured that the ongoing monkish prayers for their souls (after a sizeable cash injection of course) lessened the chance of being blackballed at the Pearly Gates. A number of notable figures are buried here in an attractive pantheon; foremost among them is the Navarran king Sancho the Great, who managed to unite almost the whole of Northern Spain under his rule in the 11th century. The main pantheon is in Gothic style, with Mudéjar influences, and sits at the back of the church; there are lesser notables buried in the harmonious cloister, a work of Simon of Cologne.

Botas are the goatskin winebags still used to drink from at fiestas and bullfights but formerly an essential possession of every farmer and shepherd who couldn't return to their village at lunchtime. Drinking from them is something of an art; it's easy to spray yourself with a jet of cheap red that was meant for the mouth. On the main road through town is a traditional little *botería*, one of the few left of a formerly widespread craft. Have a look even if you don't want to buy one; the process hasn't changed much over the years, although the premium models now have a rubber interior to better keep the wine. There's a small tourist office in the square outside the church.

East of Burgos → *Colour map 2, grid B3.*

The N120 crosses wooded hills on its way to Logroño, while the N1 makes its way to Miranda de Ebro and the Basque hills. This is one of the most unpleasant roads in Spain, a conga-line of trucks enlivened by the suicidal overtaking manoeuvres of impatient drivers. If you're driving, it's well worth paying the motorway toll to avoid it.

San Juan de Ortega Some 4 km north of the N120, peaceful San Juan de Ortega is the last stop before Burgos for many pilgrims on the way to Santiago. In the green

foothills, it's nothing more than a church and *albergue*, and has been a fixture of the Camino ever since Juan, inspired by the good works of Santo Domingo de la Calzada down the road, decided to do the same and dedicate his life to easing the pilgrims' journey. He started the church in the 12th century; the Romanesque apse survives, although the rest is in later style. It's a likeable if unremarkable place, and it's a good advertisement for sainthood, conferred on a real man who helped others, perhaps a more appropriate target for veneration than Santiago, who supposedly fought the Moors 900 years after his death, or San Miguel, never of this earth at all. San Juan is buried here in an ornate Gothic tomb. Pilgrims stay at the hospital that he founded.

Alcocero de Mola Further along towards La Rioja, Villafranca Montes de Oca is an unremarkable pilgrim stop with a small *ermita* in a green valley. North of here, just off the N1, is an unlikely picnic spot. The hamlet of Alcocero de Mola, 2 km from the main road on the BU703, bears the name of the general who masterminded the Nationalist rising. He was killed before the end of the Civil War in a plane crash, probably to Franco's relief. Three kilometres up a neglected side road from Alcocero is a massive concrete monument to him, on the wooded hilltop where the plane hit, with good views across the plains. All of 20 m high and completely forgotten, it's in characteristically pompous Fascist style; an intriguing reminder of a not-long-gone past. The concrete's in decline now, and weeds carpet the monumental staircase; take a torch if you want to climb the stairs inside.

Briviesca East of Alcocero de Mola, Briviesca is a sizeable service town, which seems to have beaten the decline that afflicts so many towns of Castile. The tree-lined plaza is pleasant and shady; on it stands the nicest of the three big churches, with a damaged Renaissance façade. The tourist office is on the square too. The town is famous for its almond biscuits.

Beyond here, the main road passes through a dramatic craggy pass at Pancorbo, which would be a nice hiking base were it not for the trucks thundering through. This is geographically where Castile ends; the *meseta* more or less gives way here to the Basque foothills.

Miranda de Ebro This hardbitten town is where Castile officially ends. The Basques were historically rampant smugglers of goods across from France; in a bid to stop this, the Basque lands were made a duty-free zone and tax only had to be paid once goods were brought into Castile. Miranda became the point for administering this, and grew large as a result.

While, like any Spanish town, it has some attractive parts, they are few; the rest of the sizeable town is a depressing, dusty, and full of big boulevards where nothing much happens. The only reason to come here is to change bus or train; by all means take a stroll down the pretty river, but don't miss your connection.

Southwest from Burgos: the Pilgrim Route

Sasamón West of Burgos, the principal branch of the Camino de Santiago tracks southwest to the bleak town of Castrojeriz. A more interesting, if slightly longer route would take the pilgrim through Sasamón, just north of the main Burgos-León road. Among the hard-bitten towns on this stretch, it stands out like a beacon. **Iglesia de Santa María la Real** ① *1100-1400, 1600-1900 (ask in the bar opposite if shut), €1.25 includes a helpful explanation by the knowledgeable caretaker*, is its very lovely church in light honey-coloured stone. It was originally a massive five-naved space, but was partitioned after a fire destroyed half of it in the 19th century. The exterior highlight is an excellent 13th-century Gothic portal featuring Christ and the Apostles, while the museum has some well-displayed Roman finds as well as a couple of top-notch pieces; a couple of Flemish tapestries featuring the life of Alexander the

Great, and a Diego de Siloe polychrome of San Miguel, the pretty boy bully. It's fairly unadorned, a reflection of the Inquisition passing into irrelevance. In the church itself, two works of the German school stand out; the ornate pulpit, from around 1500, and a large baptismal font. A 16th-century Plateresque retablo of Santiago is one of many that adorn the building, so monumental for such a small town.

A statue of **Octavian** stands in a square nearby. The Celtiberian town of Segisama was used as a base in 26 BC for his campaigns against the Cantabrians and Asturians. The inscription reads *Ipse venit Segisamam, castro posuit*, "then he came to Segisama and set up camp".

Don't leave town without checking out the **Ermita de San Isidro**, dominated by a massive 6-m carved crucifix that once would have stood at a crossroads to comfort weary souls. Under Christ is the Tree of Knowledge, Adam, Eve, Cain, and Abel. It dates from the 16th century and is a lovely work. Atop it is a nesting pelican; it was formerly believed that if a pelican was short of fish to feed the kids, it would wound them in its breast and let them feed on its own blood. This became a metaphor for Christ's sacrifice; pelicans are a reasonably common motif in Castilian religious sculpture. There's a tourist office in the Plaza Mayor, but the church warden knows all there is to know about the area.

Palencia → *Phone code: 979; Colour map 2, grid B1; Population: 80,836; Altitude: 740 m.*

"Nice Castilian town with good beer", Ernest Hemingway

Although its population surpasses a healthy 80,000 never a sentence seems to be written about Palencia without the word 'little'. And it's understandable; on some approaches to the provincial capital, it seems that you're in the centre of town before even noticing there was a town. Hemingway's quote holds true – it is a nice place – quiet and friendly, bypassed by pilgrims, tourists, and public awareness of its presence. This is partly an accident of geography – Palencia sits in the middle of a triangle of more important places, Valladolid, Burgos, and León – but also one of history. Palencia sits on the Carrión, so limpid, murky, and green it surely merits mangroves and crocodiles. The old town stretches along its eastern bank in elongated fashion. It is studded with churches, headed up by the superb cathedral.
►► *For Sleeping, Eating and other listings, see pages 202-207.*

Ins and outs

Getting there and around The train and bus stations are just beyond the northern end of C Mayor, a pedestrian street stretching the length of the old town. Palencia's main sights are all within easy walking distance of each other, concentrated in the old town area. ►► *For further details, see Transport page 207.*

Tourist information The city's tourist office is at the southern end of C Mayor and has a big range of information on the city, the province, and the rest of Castilla y León.

History

Like many towns in Castilla, Palencia has a proud past. Inhabited in prehistoric times, the local villages resisted the Romans for nearly a century before Pompey swept them aside in 72 BC and set up camp here. Pliny the Elder cited Palencia as one of the important Roman settlements of the 1st century AD. It wasn't until the 12th century that the city reached its zenith, however; *fueros* (legal privileges) were granted by Alfonso VIII, and Spain's first university was established here. In 1378 the city became legendary for resisting a siege by the Duke of Lancaster, fighting for

● *It was in the city of Palencia that the legendary El Cid in a rare free moment from military*
● *activities tied the knot, at the Iglesia de San Miguel.*

Pedro I. The defences were mounted by the Palentine women, as the men were off fighting at another battleground. But things turned sour in the *comunero* revolt, a Castilian revolution against the 'foreign' regime of Charles V, which became an anti-aristocratic movement in general. The *comuneros* were heavily defeated in 1521 and Palencia suffered thereafter, as Castilian towns were stripped of some of their privileges and influence.

Sights

Palencia's scenic highlight is its superb **cathedral** ① *Mon-Sat 0900-1330, 1630-1930, Sun 0900-1330; regular guided visits, €3*, known as 'La Bella Desconocida', the unknown beauty. Built in the 14th century on Visigothic and Romanesque foundations, it's a massive structure, although it hardly dominates the town, tucked away somewhat on a quiet square. The massive retablo paints the story

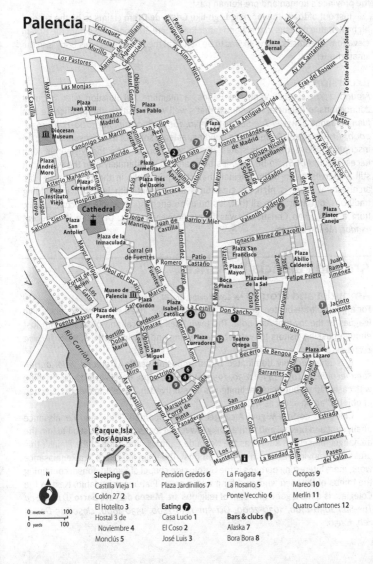

Palencia

0 metres 100
0 yards 100

of Christ's life; it's a work of the Flemish master Jan of Flanders, who also painted an attractive triptych on one side of the choir. The city's patron, the Virgen de la Calle, sits on a silver coffer in the ambulatory, while there's an amusing sculpture of lions eating a martyr at the back end of the *coro*. There's a painting by El Greco just off the cloister, but this and the Visigothic/Romanesque crypt are only accessible on the guided tours. Similarly annoying is the lighting system; to see all the impressive works of art around the building will cost you a small fortune in euro coins.

Further south, the Romanesque **Iglesia de San Miguel** is a knobbly affair with an alarmingly hollow tower. It's fairly unadorned inside, with elegant vaulting. There's a small gilt retablo of the saint, and fragmentary wall paintings.

Nearby, the **Museo de Palencia** ① *Tue-Sat 1000-1400, 1700-2000, Sun 1000 -1400, free*, sits in an attractive building on Plaza del Cordon, named for the sculpted cord that is tied around the doorway. It's a good display with plenty of artiefacts from the province's Roman and pre-Roman past.

Just out of town, the looming Lego-like **Cristo de Otero** claims to be the second highest statue of Jesus in the world (after Rio). There are good views from the 850-m elevation. The artist's last wish was to be buried at the statue's feet; his body is in the small chapel.

Excursions

Around 2 km east of Venta de Baños, a mainline rail junction with frequent connections to Palencia, is a church that's well worth visiting, the **Basílica de San Juan de Baños** ① *winter Tue-Sun 1030-1330, 1600-1800, summer 1000-1330, 1630-2000, €1 (Wed free)*. A pretty little building, at least some of it is awesomely old; an inscription above the altar states that it was founded by the Visigothic king Recesvinth in AD661. To be sure, it's been altered substantially over the years, but still preserves much of its original character, principally in the central aisle. It's architectural value is high, as clear links are evident with late Roman building traditions, but apart from all that, it's quite an enchanting simple structure, a relic from a time when Christianity was (comparatively) young. Opposite is a decent *asador*, **Mesón El Lagar**.

Around Palencia Province

Ampudia and around → *Colour map 2, grid B1.*

For a good off-the-beaten track Castilian experience, head west from Palencia five leagues to the town of Ampudia. The town itself is typical and pleasant, with just enough passing visitors to warrant a few eating and staying options. ▶▶ *For Sleeping, Eating and other listings, see pages 202-207.*

It is unexpectedly dominated by an imposing **castle** ① *guided visits during summer only Sat 1030-1430, 1830, 1930, Sun 1200, 1300, €3*. It's in top nick, bristling with castellation, but visits are limited as it's still lived in. There's an ornate collection of objets d'art on show as well.

Colegiata de San Miguel Arcángel is a floorboarded Gothic and Renaissance affair, light and breezy, and with a spiky tower that looks ready to blast off to join the archangel himself. Its known as the Novia de Campos, 'the Bride of the Plains'; this area of the province is known as 'los Campos'. The main altarpiece is a Renaissance work; more interesting perhaps is the Gothic side chapel of San Ildefonso, containing the tombs of the men who paid for it and a pretty Plateresque retablo. Next to the Colegiata is quite a good museum of religious art, **Museo del Arte Sacro** ① *May-Sep Tue-Sun 1030-1400, 1630-2000, Oct-Apr 1130-1400, 1530-1800, closed 15 Dec-15 Feb, €2.50.*

Villalba de los Alcores → *Colour map 2, grid B1.*

If you've got a car, head west from Ampudia to the village of Villalba de los Alcores. On the way, you'll pass the ruins of the 12th-century **Monasterio de Santa María de Matallana** ① *T983427100, Sat/Sun 1000-1400, 1700-2000, Mon-Fri by appointment 1000-1400*, equipped with a hotel, visitors' centre dedicated to the area's fauna and flora, and archaeological displays.

Villalba is isolated enough to feel like a real frontier settlement, which historically it was, as part of the Christian frontline that faced the Moors across the arid Castilian wastes. The village is littered with dilapidated remains of walls and other fortifications, most notably a stern fort. Built by the Knights of Saint John, its visitors included Juana La Loca, who spent some time here chatting with her husband's corpse, and two unfortunate French princes whom Charles V locked up here for a time. Now chickens peck in the courtyard around the tumbled masonry, although the bulk of the castle stands desolate yet all undaunted, waiting out the centuries in vain hope that it might be needed again.

In contrast is the village's church, an exquisitely pretty little thing that seems to be crying out for a garden path and some geraniums in windowboxes. The plaque to the Falangist dead still sparkles outside with a sinister brightness. The keyholder of the church will happily open it up for you (phone T686494074). He may also be able to track down keys to the castle gate, which is often locked.

Frómista → *Colour map 2, grid B1.*

In northern Palencia, Frómista, as well as lying on the Camino de Santiago, seems to be a compulsory stop on the Romanesque circuit; for a tiny town it gets its share of tour buses. The reason is the **Iglesia de San Martín** ① *winter 1000-1400, 1530-1830, summer 1000-1400, 1630-2000, €1, €1.50 with San Pedro*, a remarkable 11th-century Romanesque church, one of the purest and earliest, derived almost wholly from the French model that permeated the peninsula via the pilgrim route. From the outside it's beautiful, an elegant gem standing slightly self-satisfied in the sunlight. The church happily managed to survive the Gothic and Baroque eras without being meddled with, but a late 19th-century restoration brought mixed benefits. While the building owes its good condition to it, the restorers somehow managed to strip the edifice of its soul. Lacking the weathered charm that makes the Romanesque dear to modern hearts, it seems a little dishonest, like a solarium tan. That said, the purity of its lines make it well worth a visit. Inside, it's the capitals of the pillars that attract the attention. While some were sculpted during the restoration (they are marked with an R, with creditable honesty), the others are excellent examples of Romanesque sculpture. There are no Biblical scenes – many of the motifs are vegetal, and some are curious juxtapositions of people and animals, particularly lions and birds. The church is crowned by an octagonal tower as well as two distinctive turrets. ▶▶ *For Sleeping, Eating and other listings, see pages 202-207.*

> ▌ *There are better towns to spend time in when in the province of Palencia but there are a few sleeping options should you need to stay.*

Astudillo → *Colour map 2, grid B1.*

East of Frómista, the town of Astudillo is a beautiful little place. All that remains of its medieval walls is the **Puerta de San Martín**, a striking gateway. The central square is an attractive tree-lined affair, and there are several noble *palacios* and mansions. On the small hill above town is a castle; the hill itself is honeycombed with old wine *bodegas*.

La Olmeda and Quintanilla → *Colour map 2, grid B1.*

① *All 3 villas are open Tue-Sun Apr-mid Oct 1000-1330, 1630-2000, mid Oct-Mar 1030-1330, 1600-1800; closed Christmas and Jan.*

Castilla y León Around Palencia Province

West of Carrión are two of the little-known highlights of Palencia Province, the Roman villas of La Olmeda and Quintanilla. The former, near the town of Saldaña just outside Pedrosa de la Vega, is slightly more impressive than the latter. Dating from the late Roman period, the villa is set around a large central courtyard. The numerous small rooms around it are decorated with geometrical and vegetal mosaic flooring, but in a larger room is a superb mosaic with Achilles & Ulysses as well as a hunting scene, with all manner of beasts in a flurry of complex activity.

Quintanilla, just off the N120 west of Carrión, has a similarly large villa, also featuring some excellent mosaics as well as a hypocaust underfloor heating system for the cold Castilian winters. In Saldaña itself, an attractive if hard- bitten *meseta* town, some of the finds from the two villas have been assembled in a museum set in an old church; it's well worth visiting, as there are some excellent pieces, particularly those found at a funerary complex by the Olmeda villa. Buses run to Saldaña from Palencia, Burgos, and León.

North towards Santander

The northern part of Palencia Province is an incredible haven of Romanesque architecture; every little village seems to have a round-arched gem tucked away. Fans of the style could spend many happy days exploring the area, based at Aguilar de Campóo. The Department of Tourism have a number of useful booklets and pamphlets on the subject, which they rightly regard as the province's chief attraction. Most of the facilities we list in for this section are found in the main town, Aguilar de Campóo. ▶▶ *For Sleeping, Eating and other listings, see pages 202-207.*

Canal de Castilla

North of Frómista, the road heads north towards Santander. Alongside it stretches part of the Canal de Castilla. A major work, it was started in 1749 with the aim of transporting goods from the interior to the coast more easily. In those times of war and political turmoil it took over a century to complete. One branch begins at Valladolid, one at Medina del Rioseco, and they meet and continue north to Alar del Rey, from where the mountains made a continuation impossible and goods once again were put to the road. It was a significant engineering feat for its time but sadly saw only 20-odd years of effective use before it was rendered redundant by the railway. Long stretches of it have a canalside path to walk, and there are a couple of information centres along the way. Take insect repellent if planning a stroll or a hike.

Monasterio de San Andrés de Arroyo → *Colour map 2, grid B1.*
ⓘ *Tours daily at 1000, 1100, 1200, 1300, 1600, 1700, 1800, 1845, 30 mins, €1.50.*
Make every effort to get to San Andrés de Arroyo, south from Aguilar de Campóo, and some 8 km west of Alar del Rey. A working monastery populated by Cistercian nuns, it boasts a superb late 12th-century cloister, which you will be shown around by a friendly inhabitant. The cloister is double-columned and features some incredibly intricate work, especially on the corner capitals. How the masons managed to chisel out the leaves and tendrils is anybody's guess. The far side of the cloister is more recent but features equally ornate work. The Sala Capitular is a Gothic affair with an ornate tomb supported by lions, in which rest the mortal remains of Doña Mencia Lara, a powerful local countess in her day. Traces of paint remain, a useful reminder that the bare Gothic style that we admire was often probably rather garishly coloured. The centrepiece of the cloister is a Moorish fountain originally from Granada.

Closer to the main road, 2 km east, is the crumbly red Romanesque monastery **Iglesia de Santa María de Mave**. The keys are in the *hospedería* that's built into the monastery. it's a very peaceful place to stay, apart from the odd goods-train rattling by.

⁑ Mad about buscuits

For years Aguilar de Campóo has been known for biscuit-making; the rich smells wafting through the streets make a visitor permanently peckish. Two of Spain's major biscuit brands, *Fontaneda* and *Gullon*, are from here, but in 2002, clouds were on the horizon. *Fontaneda*, founded by a local family in 1881, were bought by *Nabisco* in the late 1990s. In 2002, their subsidiary arm, *United Biscuits*, decided to close the Aguilar factory and increase production in two other factories in Navarra and Euskadi. The closure was fiercely opposed; every building in town bore the message "Fontaneda es de Aguilar", even the church and the castle. The implications of the closure of the factory for a small town like Aguilar could have been nothing other than disastrous. The massive campaign finally worked – *United Biscuits* agreed to sell the Aguilar part of their operations to the *Siro Group*, who pledged to keep the factory open with minimal staff cuts.

Aguilar de Campóo → *Colour map 2, grid A2.*

The lovely town of Aguilar sits where the Castilian plain gives way to the northern mountains of the Cordillera Cantábrica. Chilly, even snowy, in winter, its pleasant summer temperatures make it a place of blessed relief from the *meseta* heat. It makes an excellent base for exploring the area's Romanesque heritage.

Aguilar is named for its 'eagle's nest', a slightly exaggerated description of the modest hill capped by a castle that overlooks the town.

The town sits on the Río Pisuerga and is centred on the long **Plaza de España**, which is where most things go on. At one end of the plaza is the **Colegiata de San Miguel**, which conceals a Gothic interior behind its attractive Romanesque façade. Inside, there's a big dusty retablo, a scary sleeping Christ with real hair, and a small museum ⓘ *museum summer 1030-1330, 1700-2000, T979122231, guided tours Mon-Sat 1100, 1200, 1700, Sun 1300, €1.60.*

A number of **gateways** remain from the walls; that on Calle Barrio y Mier has a Hebrew inscription, a legacy of the once substantial Jewish population, while the one behind the church is topped by griffins.

Across the river, **Monasterio de Santa Clara** ⓘ *visits daily between 1200 and 0100, and 1800-1900,* is home to a community of nuns that follow the Assisi saint. Appropriately in this town, baking is one of the principal activities here; the delicious pastries can be bought inside. **Museo Ursi** ⓘ *C Tobalina s/n, 1300 and 1900 Tue-Sat, Sun am only,* is the workshop of the sculptor Ursicino Martínez, whose work, mostly from wood, is a blend of the sober, the abstract, and the light-hearted.

Worth looking at is the Romanesque **Ermita de Santa Cecilia**, a chapel with a leaning tower on the hillside below the castle. You'll have to get the key from the priest's house (the tourist office will direct you). The interior is simple; the highlight is a superb capital showing the Innocents being put to the sword by chainmailed soldiers. Above, up a path, little remains of the castle but its walls; the view is good, but the town looks better from lower angles.

On the road to Cervera, 1 km west is the **Monasterio de Santa María la Real** ⓘ *summer Mon-Sun 1030-1400, 1600-2000 (guided visits 1100, 1230, 1630, 1800), winter Tue-Fri 1600-1900, Sat/Sun 1030-1400, 1630-1930, museum €1.80.* The cloister is attractive enough, although bound to be disappointing after San Andrés de Arroyo, which is similar. The columns are doubled, but many of the capitals are missing (some are in Madrid). The Sala Capitular features clusters of multiple columns, their capitals impressively carved from a single block of stone. **Museo Románico**, housed in the

monastery, is a little disappointing. Perhaps useful for planning a Romanesque itinerary as it contains many models of churches in the province, there is no information on the history or features of the style. The tourist office ① *Plaza de España, 1-hr guided walks leave Tue-Sun 1100, Tue-Sat 1700*, is helpful.

Cervera de Pisuerga → *Colour map 2, grid A1.*

Some 25 km northwest of Aguilar is the quiet town of Cervera de Pisuerga, set in the foothills of the Cordillera Cantábrica. It's not a bad base for outdoor activities; walkers will have a good time of it, at least as long as it's not quail season. The town's highlight is the Gothic **Iglesia de Santa María del Castillo** ① *May-Jun Sat/Sun 1030-1330, 1700-2000, Jul-Sep daily 1030-1330, 1700-2000*, €1, imperiously enthroned above the town. It's not of massive interest inside, but worth checking out is the side chapel of Santa Ana, with polychrome reliefs adorning the walls above the retablo. There's also a small **Museo Etnográfico** ① *summer Tue-Sat 1100- 1400, 1700-2000, winter Sat/Sun 1100-1400, 1700-2000*, €2, in the town, of moderate interest. The tourist office ① *Parque El Plantio s/n, T979870695*, on the edge of town, has plenty of information on driving and walking routes.

● Sleeping

Burgos *p186, map p188*
L Palacio de la Merced, C La Merced 13, T947479900, www.nh-hoteles.com. Attractively set in a 16th-century *palacio*, this hotel successfully blends minimalist, modern design into the old building, whose most charming feature is its cloister in Flamboyant Gothic style. The rooms are comfortable and attractively done out in wood.
AL Hotel Cordón, C La Puebla 6, T947265000, hotelcordon@cyl.com. A reasonable option in the centre, geared up for business travellers. There's nothing particularly stunning about the rooms, but there are decent weekend rates if you book ahead.
AL Hotel Mesón del Cid, Plaza Santa María 8, T947208715, F947209460. Superbly located opposite the cathedral, this hotel/restaurant is an excellent place to stay, with spacious, quiet, and modern rooms and helpful staff.
A Hotel La Puebla, C La Puebla 20, T947200011, www.hotellapuebla.com. An intimate new hotel in the centre of Burgos with classy modern design, good facilities, and comfortable furnishings. Parking available for €7.
C Jacobeo, C San Juan 24, T947260102, F947260100. Smallish central hotel, well managed, featuring good ensuite rooms with comfortable new beds.

D Hostal Lar, C Cardenal Benlloch 1, T947209655, F947209655. Decent ensuite rooms with modern facilities. Cheaper rooms upstairs as well.
E Hostal Victoria, C San Juan 3, T947201542. A good choice with friendly management. Central and relatively quiet, and the rooms with shared bath are comfortable and fairly spacious.
F Hostal Hidalgo, C Almirante Bonifaz 14, T947203481. A nice quiet *pensión* on a pedestrian street. Clean, neat, and friendly.
G Pensión Peña, C Puebla 18, T947206323. An excellent cheapie, well located and maintained. Unfortunately, it tends to be permanently full, so don't hold your breath.

Camping
Camping Fuentes Blancas, Ctra Burgos-Cartuja s/n, T947486016, F947486016. A nicely situated campsite in woody riverside parkland about 4 km from the centre. Take bus number 26 or 27 from Plaza de España (not terribly frequent).

Around Burgos Province *p192*
A Posada del Balneario, Camino del Balneario s/n, near El Gran Cañon del Ebro, T947150220, a big attractive *casa rural* by the river with a high level of comfort and service. A nice place to stay.
B Tres Coronas de Silos, Plaza Mayor 6, Monasterio de Santo Domingo de Silos, T947390047, F947390065, is attractive and

comfortable, set in a solid stone mansion just across from the monastery. The rooms are rustic and charming.

C Hotel Arlanza, Plaza Mayor 11, Covarrubias, T947406441, is a good option on the main square set attractively in a stately old house.

D Arco de San Juan, Pradera de San Juan 1, Monasterio de Santo Domingo de Silos, T/F947390074, is a hotel and restaurant peacefully set by a stream just past the monastery. The rooms are quiet and clean, and there are some nice terraces to relax on.

D El Zaguán, Calle Barquillo 6, Lerma, T947172165, F947172083, Monasterio de Santo Domingo de Silos. The nicest place to stay, a welcoming *casa rural* with attractive stone walls and interesting furniture.

D Los Castros, C Los Castros 10, Covarrubias, T947406368, is a very cosy *casa rural* with a comfy lounge and 5 excellent doubles.

E Casa de Lolo y Vicent, C Callejón 18, near El Gran Cañon del Ebro in the village of Escalada further up the road from Posada de Baleneario, T947150267, a *casa rural* set in a restored 15th-century house offering a good welcome and pretty views.

E Casa Tipi, Ctra Quecedo s/n, Puente Arenas in Valdivielso Valley, T947303130, a small *casa rural*.

E Hostal El Parque, C Francisco Cantera 1, Miranda, T947331383, a good place with clean rooms opposite a pleasant park named after the Sorian poet Antonio Machado.

F Hostal Once Brutos, C del Pan 6, Oña, T947300010, a dark but clean place just off the square that also provides simple meals - this is the best place to stay and eat.

F Pensión Galin, Plaza Doña Urraca 4, Covarrubias, T947406552, offers cheap and decent rooms above a bar.

G Fortu, C Marqués de Torresoto 11, Briviesca, T947590719, with simple but clean rooms. The restaurant downstairs does cheap but good food.

Camping

Camping Covarrubias, Covarrubias, T947406417, on the road to Hortiguela, close to town and has some bungalows available.

Palencia *p196, map p197*

Accommodation is very reasonably priced.

A Castilla Vieja, Av Casado del Alisal 26, T979749044, F979747577. Uninteresting hotel but with decent facilities and on the edge of the old town.

C Hotel Monclús, C Menéndez Pelayo 3, T979744300, F979744490. A slightly stuffy hotel in the middle of town. The rooms are comfortable but kitted out in sombre brown. Quiet and central, and parking is available.

D Hotel Colón 27, C Colón 27, T979740700, . A nice hotel with spacious rooms and a welcoming attitude in the heart of town. Good value for the price, although there's some morning racket from the school opposite.

D Hotel Plaza Jardinillos, C Dato 2, T979750022, F979750190. A hotel with a bit of character, with interesting prints on the walls and helpful staff. Recently renovated, and offers breakfast and parking.

E Hostal 3 de Noviembre, C Mancornador 18, T979703042. With surely the smallest lobby of any Spanish hotel, this is a good Palentine choice. Doubles are all exterior and comfortable, although the singles are predictably cramped (though cheap). Parking available. Reception only present 1900-2330, so phone at other times.

F El Hotelito, C General Amor 5, T979746913, hotelito@yahoo.com. Small but decent rooms, which offer fine value above a bar at the southern end of the old town.

F Pensión Gredos, C Valentín Calderon 18, T979702833. A friendly and good-standard little place with clean doubles with shared bath, not far from C Mayor.

Around Palencia Province *p198*

A Casa del Abad de Ampudia, Plaza Gromaz 12, Ampudia, T979768008, www.casadelabad.com. This is an excellent accommodation and eating option set in a beautiful originally renovated 16th-century abbot's house in the main square. A riot of colour and subtle beauty, every room is different and comfortable. There's even a gym and sauna. The meals are delicious and the wines superb.

D Atienza, C Duque de Alba 3, Ampudia, T979768076, a *casa rural* in an old workers' cottage with a restored wine *bodega*. The rooms are charming, meals are served, and there's Internet access.

D Hostal San Telmo, C Martin Veña 8, Frómista, T979811028, is a large, light and tranquil *casa rural* with a large garden/ courtyard.

F Pensión Marisa, Plaza Obispo Almaraz 2, Frómista, T979810023, is a simple and welcoming choice on the main square.

North towards Santander *p200*

A Parador Fuentes Carrionas, Ctra de Resoba s/n, Cervera de Pisuerga, 2 km above the town, T979870075, www.parador.es. This large pinkish parador has great views from all the balconied rooms, particularly those in the front, which overlook a lake. It's a lovely peaceful spot, where cows graze quietly in the grounds.

C Hotel Valentín, Av Ronda 23, Aguilar de Campóo, T979122125, www.hotelvalentin. com. A slightly larger-than-life complex on the edge of town, with disco, restaurant, shops and a hotel that actually manages to be quite calm and pleasant, large light rooms.

C Posada Hostería El Convento, in the grounds of Monasterio de San Andrés de Arroyo T979123611. Very peaceful.

D La Galería, Plaza Mayor 16, Cervera de Pisuerga, T979870568, with nice rooms on the pretty square.

E Casa Goyetes, C El Valle 4, Cervera de Pisuerga, T979870234, opposite the church, an attractive wood-beamed *casa rural* that makes a relaxing and comfortable base.

F Hostal Siglo XX, Plaza España 9, Aguilar de Campóo, T979126040, F979122900. A good choice, with cosy rooms with TV and shared bath above a restaurant. Try and grab one of the front rooms, which have access to enclosed balconies overlooking the square.

Hostels and camping

Albergue Nido de las Aguilas, C Antonio Rojo 2, Aguilar de Campóo, T979128036, www.albergueaguilas.com. The official hostel is a friendly place, which organizes several outdoor activities. Doors close between 2400 and 0730.

Camping Monte Royal, Av Virgen del Llano s/n, Aguilar de Campóo, T979123083. Near the lake to the west of town, this is a campsite with all the trappings.

❼ Eating

Burgos *p186, map p188*
Burgos is famous for its morcilla, a tasty black pudding made with plenty of onions.

€€€ Casa Ojeda, C Vitoria 5, T947209052. One of Burgos's better-known restaurants, backing on to Plaza de la Libertad. The cuisine is traditional and on the heavy side, but very well done. Oven-roasted meats are the pride of the house.

€€€ El Angel, C Paloma 24, T947208608. A smart newish restaurant near the cathedral with a range of succulent dishes like wild turbot as well as Castillian specialities.

€€ Mesón Burgos, C Sombrerería 8, T947206150. One of Burgos's better tapas bars downstairs is complemented by a friendly upstairs restaurant with good, if unexceptional fare.

€€ Meson La Cueva, Plaza de Santa María 7, T947205946. A small dark Castilian restaurant with good service and a traditional feel.

€€ La Posada, Plaza Santo Domingo de Guzmán 18, T947204578. A nice restaurant with comforting home cooking. There's a *menú* for €11.

€€ Rincón de España, C Nuño Rasura 11, T947205955. One of the better of the terraced restaurants around the cathedral, this is no stranger to tourism but does good fish and roast meats; à la carte is much better than the set menus.

€ La Cantina del Tenorio, C Arco del Pilar 10, T947269781. This bar is a buzzy and cosy retreat from the Burgos wind. A range of delicious fishy bites and small rolls is strangely complemented by baked potatoes, given a Spanish touch with lashings of paprika.

€ Mesón La Amarilla, C San Lorenzo 26, T947205936. A good sunken bar serving some decent tapas, some seeming to use a whole jar of mayonnaise. There's a good cheap restaurant upstairs too.

€ Mesón San Lesmes, C Puebla 37. Cheerful cheap eats in a gregarious downmarket bar.

Tapas bars and cafés

See above for eateries with tapas bars and restaurants.

Café del Martes, C Laín Calvo 31. A good café with plenty of seats and a chessboard.

Café España, C Laín Calvo 12, T947205337. Warm, old-style café specializing in a range of liqueur coffees. Friendly and featuring a summer terrace.

Casa Pancho, C San Lorenzo 13. Another good option on this street, despite the bright lights. Good *pintxos* and some hit and miss tapas; prawns or mushrooms are redoubtable choices.

Los Herreros, C San Lorenzo 20, T947202448. Excellent tapas bar with a big range of hot and cold platelets for very little; its popularity with Burgos folk speaks volumes.

Around Burgos Province *p192*

For more options, see Sleeping, above.
€€ **Casa Brigante**, Calle Luís Cervera Vera 1, Lerma, T947170594, a good *asador* on the giant Plaza Ducal.

Palencia *p196, map p197*

€€ **Casa Lucio**, C Don Sancho 2, T979748190. A brightly traditional bar and restaurant dealing in standard Castilian fare with a spring in its step (or was that the garlic?). Good value.

€€ **La Fragata**, C Pedro Fernández de Pulgar 8, T979750129. 2 options are on offer here; well-prepared fish and seafood in the restaurant, or cheap *raciones* and *platos combinados* in the bar on the corner.

€€ **La Rosario**, C La Cestilla 3, T979740936. A staid and typical Spanish restaurant, which still relies on the good old typewriter to produce the menu (although they have noticed the peseta's demise). The *pimientos rellenos* are the house speciality, and live up to their billing; there are also some good wines on offer.

€€ **Ponte Vecchio**, C Doctrinos 1, T979745215. Atmospheric Italian restaurant located near no bridge but opposite San Miguel in a lovely stone building. The food is upmarket and excellent.

€ **El Coso**, C Dato 4. A characterful and colourfully-tiled café, which does a range of cheap meal options.

€ **José Luis**, C Pedro Fernández de Pulgar 11, T979741510. A varied range of cheap and hearty *menús* are on offer at this decent, no-frills restaurant.

Around Palencia Province *p198*

See also Sleeping above.
€€ **Hotel San Martín**, Plaza Obispo Almaraz 7, Frómista, T979810000, serves decent meals although service can border on the hostile.

€ **Bar Garigolo**, around the corner from San Martín, has an Internet terminal.

North towards Santander *p200*

€€ **El Barón**, C El Pozo 14, Aguilar de Campóo, T979123151, F979125430. An excellent restaurant attractively set in an old stone building, and atmospherically decorated. There's a good menú for €15, and a lunch option for €9. Recommended.

€ **Al Socano**, C Puente s/n, Aguilar de Campóo. A bar with a good riverside beer garden.

€ **Café El Pueblo**, Paseo la Cascajera s/n, Aguilar de Campóo. A friendly café on a small plaza by the river.

€ **Gasolina**, Cervera de Pisuerga, T979122900, serves cheap and simple, but hearty, food in an old stone building near the plaza; there's some lovely chunky wooden furniture outside.

€ **Siglo XX**, Plaza España 9, Aguilar de Campóo, T979126040. Inside, there's a restaurant of good quality, while in the bar (and outside, weather permitting), a range of *raciones* and snacks are available.

ⓞ Bars and clubs

Burgos *p186, map p188*

During the week, nightlife is poor but it picks up at weekends on C Huerta del Rey.
La Negra Candela, C Huerta del Rey 20. One of the best options in this busy weekend drinking zone, warm and attractively dark.

Mondrian, C Huerta del Rey 25. Another popular Fri night spot.

Ram Jam Club, C San Juan. A popular basement bar with a good vinyl collection, mostly playing British music from the 1970s.

The Fox Tavern, Paseo del Espolón 4, T947273311. Impossible to miss, this is a decent pub which doesn't push the Irish theme too far. Comfy seats including a terrace; the food is OK but overpriced.

Alaska, C Mayor 24. A tiny café/bar bedecked with massive paintings a terrace, and a toilet accessed by a tight spiral staircase.

Bora Bora, C Maura 9. "It's a Samoan pub". Well, OK, French Polynesian then, but the cocktails are as frilly as anything you'd find in *Lock, Stock, and Two Smoking Barrels.*

Bar Mareo, C La Cestilla 5. A trendy modern bar with chrome furniture and red walls that packs in a busy night crowd.

Cleopas, C Pedro Fernández de Pulgar 9. A cheery bar popular for evening drinks with the Palentine young.

Cuatro Cantones, C Mayor 43, T979700463. A loveable, old-style Spanish café, all tiles and ornate light fittings, a top place for a coffee or a *coñac.*

Merlin, C Conde de Vallelena s/n. One of many bars around this block, where the weekend evenings kick on late.

North towards Santander *p200*
Al Aire, C Licenciado Fraile de la Hoz, Cervera de Pisuerga, a pretty little courtyard bar.

☻ Entertainment

Burgos *p186, map p188*
Teatro Principal, Paseo del Espolón s/n, is Burgos' main theatre, on the riverbank.

❀ Festivals and events

Burgos *p186, map p188*
At the end of **Jun**, Burgos' main festival takes place, **San Pedros**. On **30 Jan**, it also parties for the feast of its patron saint, **San Lesmes**. **Semana Santa** (Holy Week) processions are important, but have a fairly serious religious character.

Palencia *p196, map p197*
Palencia seems to have a large number of fiestas, but the main one held in the **first week of Sep** is San Antolín. While hardly over-the-top by Spanish standards, there are plenty of markets, street stalls, bullfights, fireworks and concerts.

Around Palencia Province *p198*
Ampudia's fiesta is the **first weekend of Sep**, when there are even bullfights.

✪ Shopping

Burgos *p186, map p188*
Burgos is a fairly upmarket place to shop; focused on the old town streets.
Sedano, Paseo del Espolón 6, T947202220. A small bookshop with a good range of maps and travel guides.
La Vieja Castilla, C Paloma 21, T947207367. A tiny but excellent shop to buy ham and other Castilian produce.
Luz y Vida, C Laín Calvo 38. A decent bookseller's spread over 2 facing shops.

⛰ Activities and tours

Burgos *p186, map p188*
Viajes Burgos, C Miranda 1, T947256445, organizes day and half-day trips to interesting towns and sights in the country around Burgos, including the Cartuja de Miraflores, San Pedro Cardeña, Covarrubias, and Santo Domingo de Silos, leaving from the cathedral square.

⊖ Transport

Burgos *p186, map p188*
Burgos is a transport hub, with plenty of trains and buses leaving to all parts of the country.
Bus The bus station is handily close to town, on C Miranda just across the Puente de Santa María. The trains stop a 5-min walk west of here. All buses run less often on Sun. Local services include **Aranda de Duero** 8 a day, **Miranda** 3 a day, **Santo Domingo de Silos** 1 a day, **Roa** 1 a day, **Sasamón** 2 a day, **Castrojeriz** 2 a day, **Oña** 3 a day. Long distance services include **Madrid** hourly, **Bilbao** 7 a day, **León** 1 a day, **Santander** 5 a day, **Logroño** 7 a day, **Valladolid** 5 a day, **Zaragoza** 4 a day, **Barcelona** 4 a day.

Around Burgos Province *p192*
There are 3 buses a day to **Covarrubias** from **Burgos** (none on Sun).

To **Santo Domingo de Silos**, there's a bus from **Burgos** at 1700 (1400 on Sat, none on Sun; 2 hrs), returning in the morning.

There are many buses and the odd train make their way to **Lerma** from **Burgos** and to a lesser extent **Madrid**.

To reach **Puente Arenas**, catch the Oña service (best option for getting up here by public transport as it is connected 3 times daily with Burgos by bus via Briviesca).

From **Burgos** take a bus to **Oña** or the BU629 north of **Sotopalacios**, a strange road that crosses a sort of Alpine plateau. A series of large stone waymarkers irregularly dot the route marking the road that Charles V used on entering Spain to claim the throne.

Briviesca is visited by 7 daily buses from **Burgos**; there are also a few trains.

Miranda is well connected by bus and train to most major cities in Northern Spain, particularly **Bilbao**, **Vitoria**, **Burgos**, **Logroño** and **Madrid**.

Palencia p196, map p197
Bus There are hourly buses to **Valladolid**, 4 a day to **Burgos** and **Madrid**. Within the province, there are 4 a day to **Aguilar de Campoo** via **Frómista** and **Osorno**, hourly buses to **Dueñas** via **Venta del Baños**, 2 daily to **Ampudia**, 2 to **Cervera**, 2 to **Astudillo**, and 3 to **Saldaña**.
Train Palencia is on the main line, and is very well served by rail. There are heaps of trains to **Frómista**, **Osorno**, **Aguilar de Campoo**, **Dueñas**, **Venta de Baños**, **Madrid**, **Valladolid**, **Bilbao**, and other destinations in Northern Spain.

Around Palencia Province p198
There are 2 buses daily to and from **Palencia** to **Ampudia**, and 1 to **Valladolid**.

There are regular buses and trains to **Frómista** from **Palencia**.
To **Astudillo** there are 2 buses to **Palencia**.

North towards Santander p200
Bus The bus station in Aguilar de Campóo, is in the heart of town next to the **Hotel Valentín**. There are regular services to **Palencia**, **Santander**, **León** and **Burgos**, as well as **Cervera**.
Train RENFE station in Aguilar de Campóo, is to the east of town and has frequent trains to **Palencia**, **Santander**, and **Madrid**.

❻ Directory

Burgos p186, map p188
Internet Ciber Ocio, Parque del Manzano, open 1100-1400, 1700- 2300; **Colón 11 net**, C Colón s/n, Mon-Sat 1100-1400, 1700-2000; **Cabaret**, C La Puebla s/n, quite a cool bar with Net access, Mon-Thu 1600-0200, Fri/Sat 1600-0400, Sun 1700-0200.
Post office The main office is just across the river from the old town on Plaza Conde de Castro.

North towards Santander p200
Internet Playnet, C Comercio 8, Aguilar de Campóo, has Internet access amidst bursts of gunfire from online gamers. Open 1200-1400, 1700-2230, €2/hr.
Laundry **Salmar** is a laundry at Av Ronda 16, Aguilar de Campóo, open Mon-Fri 0930-1400, 1630-2000, Sat 1030-1400.

Castilla y León León Province

León Province

Although joined in semi-autonomous harmony with Castilla, the province of León is fairly distinct, and offers a different experience to the vast Castilian plain. In fact, it's got a bit of everything; a look at the map confirms that it's part meseta, part mountain, and part fertile valleyland.

León was an important early kingdom of the Christian Reconquest, but soon lost ground and importance as the battlegrounds moved further south and power became focused around Valladolid and then Madrid. Mining has been a constant part of the area's history; the Romans extracted gold in major operations in the west of the province, while coal, cobalt and copper are all still extracted, although with limited future. This region of hills and valleys is known as El Bierzo. It's a busy rural zone of grapevines and vegetables, as well as mines; further exploration reveals superb natural enclaves and vibrant local fiestas.

The pilgrim route crosses León Province, stopping in the towns of Sahagún, Astorga, Ponferrada, and Villafranca del Bierzo as well as the capital; good places all

to regain lost strength for the climb into Galicia and the last haul of the journey. León itself is an excellent city; one of the few in Spain to combine a beautiful old town with an attractive new one. It's famous throughout Spain for three things; its superb Gothic cathedral, the free tapas in its myriad bars, and its freezing winters. ▸▸ *For Sleeping, Eating and other listings, see pages 221-226.*

Sahagún → *Colour map 1, grid B6.*

Travelling westwards into León, Sahagún is one of those rare towns whose population is only a quarter of that it housed in the Middle Ages. These days Sahagún is a likeable-enough place, wandering its dusty streets it's hard to imagine that it was ever anything more than what it is today – an insignificant agricultural town of the thirsty *meseta*. Sahagún's main attraction is its collection of Mudéjar buildings. These differ somewhat from Aragonese Mudéjar and are to some extent Romanesque buildings made of brick. ▸▸ *For Sleeping, Eating and other listings, see pages 221-226.*

> ‡ *Sahagún is best seen as a day trip from León, but there are decent places to stay.*

History

The area around Sahagún was settled by Romans and the town is named for an early Christian basilica dedicated to a local saint, Facundo (the Latin name was Sanctum Facundum). The town began to thrive once Santiago-fever began, and gained real power and prestige when king Alfonso VI invited a community of Cluny monks to establish the Roman rite in the area. They built their monastery, San Benito, on the site of the old Visigothic church; once Alfonso had granted it massive privileges and lands, it became one of the most powerful religious centres of Spain's north.

Its population of some 3,000 is much reduced from the 12,000 inhabitants that called the place home in the Middle Ages. The cost of Spain's imperial ambitions bled San Benito dry of money, and by the time the place was almost wholly destroyed in an 18th-century inferno, its power had long since waned. Sahagún's most famous son was a 16th-century Franciscan missionary to the Americas, Friar Bernardino, a remarkable figure. His respect for Aztec culture made him a controversial figure at the time; he mastered the language and wrote texts in it. He is commemorated in his hometown by a small bust near the Plaza Mayor.

Sights

Iglesia de San Lorenzo is the most emblematic of Sahagún's Mudéjar buildings; a church dating from the early 13th century and characterized by a pretty belltower punctured with three rows of arches. The interior is less impressive, remodelled in later periods. It's worth climbing the tower if restoration work permits.

Iglesia de San Tirso ① *Tue-Sat 1000-1400, 1600-1800, Sun 1000-1400, free (tours to the Santuario leave at 1200 and 1700, free but donations are badly needed for restorative work)*, dates from the 12th century and is broadly similar, with a smaller but still pretty tower. The interior has suffered through neglect, but it's worth popping in to see the floats from Sahagún's well-known **Semana Santa** celebrations, as well as a well-carved 13th-century tomb, later reused. Two visits run from here daily to another church on the hill, **Santuario de la Virgen Peregrina**, formerly a Franciscan monastery. The interior is again sadly in need of restoration, but the point of the visit is to see a little chapel at the back of the church, where fragments of superb Mozarabic stucco work were found when the plaster that covered them began to flake off in the mid-20th century. The chapel was commissioned by a local noble in the 15th century to house his own bones.

By the church is what's left of the **Monasterio de San Benito**; a clocktower and a Gothic chapel. The portal also survived and has been placed across the road behind the building; it's an ornate Baroque work from the 17th century with impressive lions. Nearby, in the still-active **Monasterio de Santa Cruz** ① *1000-1300, 1615-1830, €1.20*, is a small museum of religious art which also has architectural and sculptural fragments from the burned monastery.

Around Sahagún

If your legs aren't weary from peregrination, or if you've got a car, there's a good excursion from Sahagún. It's an hour's walk south to the **Convento de San Pedro de las Dueñas**, which preserves some excellent Romanesque capitals and attractive Mudéjar brickwork. Just as interesting is the good cheap lunch on offer, with filling dishes prepared and wheeled in on trolleys by incredibly aged nuns. The keyholder is a strange old bloke named Pablo; if he doesn't appear, seek him out in the house below the castle by the main road.

Head east from the convent for around half an hour to **Grajal de Campos**, with an excellent castle of Moorish origin but beefed up in the 15th and 16th centuries. It's a very imposing structure indeed. There's not a great deal to see inside, but it's fun to climb the crumbling stairs and walls. While you're in town, have a look at the nearby *palacio*, which has seen better days but preserves an attractively down-at-heel *patio*. From Sahagún it's an hour's walk to Grajal, visible to the north. Doing the walk whichever way round will get you to San Pedro at around lunch time.

Beyond Sahagún, the pilgrim trail continues to **Mansilla de la Mulas**. There are few mules around these days, and what remains of its once proud heritage are the ruins of its fortifications. Some 8 km north, however, is the lovely Mozarabic **Iglesia de San Miguel de Escalada** ① *Tue-Sat 1000-1400, 1600-1800 (1700-2000 from May-Sep), Sun 1000-1500*. Dating from the 10th century, it was built by a group of Christian refugees from Córdoba. There's a pretty horseshoe-arched porch; the interior is attractively bare of ornament; the arches are set on columns reused from an earlier structure, and are beautifully subtle. A triple arch divides the altar area from the rest of the church. It's a lovely place, well worth the detour and perhaps a picnic in the surrounding meadows.

León → *Phone code: 987; Colour map 1, grid B5; Population: 130,916; Altitude: 820 m.*

León is one of the loveliest of Northern Spain's cities, with a proud architectural legacy, an elegant new town, and an excellent tapas bar scene. Once capital of Christian Spain, it preserves an outstanding reminder of its glory days in its Gothic cathedral, one of the nation's finest buildings. After crossing the dusty *meseta* from Burgos, pilgrims arriving here should put their feet up for a couple of days and enjoy what León has to offer. ➼ *For Sleeping, Eating and other listings, see pages 221-226.*

Ins and outs

Getting there and around León's bus and RENFE train stations are close to each other just across the river from the new town, a ten-minute walk from the old town. The bus station, which is blessed with an excellent cheap restaurant, is the best option for getting to and from León. ➼ *For further details, see Transport page 225.*

Best time to visit Like Burgos, León's high altitude results in cold winters and roasting summers; spring and autumn are good times to visit, as there's little rain.

Tourist information León's cheerful tourist office is opposite the cathedral ① *Plaza de la Regla, Mon-Fri 0900-1400, 1700-1900 (2000 in summer); Sat/Sun 1000-1400, 1700-2000.*

León was founded as a Roman fortress in AD 68 to protect the transport of gold from the mines in El Bierzo. It became the base of the *Legio Septima*, the seventh legion of Imperial Rome; this is where the name originates (although León means 'lion' in Spanish). The city was Christianized in the third century and is one of the oldest bishoprics in western Europe. After being reconquered in the mid-eighth century, León became the official residence of the Asturian royal line in the early 10th century. The city was recaptured and sacked several times by the Moors until it was retaken for the final time by Alfonso V in 1002. León then enjoyed a period of power and glory as the centre of Reconquista pride and prestige; the city flourished on

León

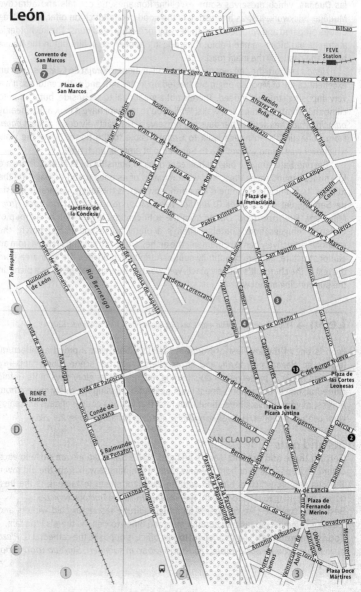

protection paid from the fragmented *taifa* states. In 1188 there was a meeting of nobles and ecclesiasts that set the pattern for what was later to become the system of *cortes*, regional quasi-parliaments that kept Spanish kings on a tight leash. As the Reconquista moved further south, however, León found itself increasingly put in the shade by the young whippersnapper Castilla. In 1230 the crowns were united, and León is still bound to Castilla to this day, a fact bemoaned by many. When the Flemish Habsburg Charles V took the throne of Spain, León feared further isolation and became one of the prime movers in the *comunero* rebellion. A Leonese named Gonzalo de Guzmán declared a "war of fire, sack, and blood" on the aristocracy. The rebellion was heavily put down, and León languished for centuries.

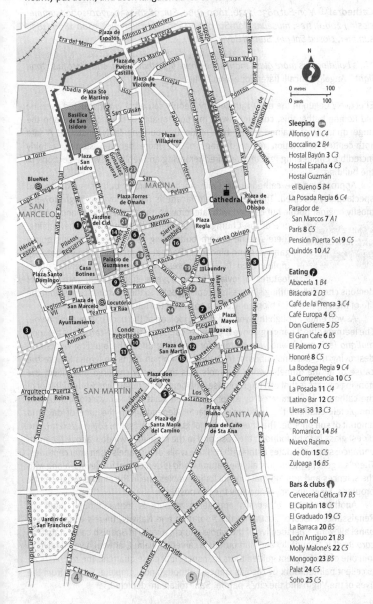

Sleeping 🛏
Alfonso V 1 *C4*
Boccalino 2 *B4*
Hostal Bayón 3 *C3*
Hostal España 4 *C3*
Hostal Guzmán
  el Bueno 5 *B4*
La Posada Regia 6 *C4*
Parador de
  San Marcos 7 *A1*
París 8 *C5*
Pensión Puerta Sol 9 *C5*
Quindós 10 *A2*

Eating 🍴
Abacería 1 *B4*
Bitácora 2 *D3*
Café de la Prensa 3 *C4*
Café Europa 4 *C5*
Don Gutierre 5 *D5*
El Gran Cafe 6 *B5*
El Palomo 7 *C5*
Honoré 8 *C5*
La Bodega Regia 9 *C4*
La Competencia 10 *C5*
La Posada 11 *C4*
Latino Bar 12 *C5*
Lleras 38 13 *C3*
Meson del
  Romanico 14 *B4*
Nuevo Racimo
  de Oro 15 *C5*
Zuloaga 16 *B5*

Bars & clubs 🍸
Cervecería Céltica 17 *B5*
El Capitán 18 *C5*
El Graduado 19 *C5*
La Barraca 20 *B5*
León Antiguo 21 *B3*
Molly Malone's 22 *C5*
Mongogo 23 *B5*
Palat 24 *C5*
Soho 25 *C5*

The region's coal provided some prosperity in the 19th century, but it has really only been relatively recently that the city has lifted itself from stagnating regional market-town to what it is today; a modern and dynamic Spanish city.

Sights

León's **old town** is to the east of the river Bernesga and surrounded by the boulevards of the newer city. Walk up the pedestrianized Calle Ancha and prepare to be stunned by the appearance of the white Gothic cathedral, a plump jewel in Spain's architectural crown.

Cathedral ① *Mon-Sat 0830-1330, 1600-1900, Sun 0830-1430, 1700-1900 (summer closing 2000), free; museum Mon-Sat 0930-1300 (1330 summer), 1600-1800 (1830 summer, closed Sat pm, Sun all day in winter), €2.50.*

"This building has more glass than stone, more light than glass, and more faith than light." Angelo Roncalli (later Pope John XXIII)

Effectively begun in the early 13th century, León's cathedral is constructed over the old Roman baths; this, combined with the poor quality of the stone used and the huge quantity of stained glass, has made the building fairly unstable. A late 19th-century restoration replaced many of the more decayed stones, a fairly incredible engineering feat that required removing and replacing whole sections of the building.

Approaching the cathedral up Calle Ancha, its broad bulk is suddenly and spectacularly revealed. The main western façade is flanked by two bright towers, mostly original Gothic but capped with later crowns, the northern (left hand) one by one of the Churriguera brothers. Walking around the outside, there's some superb buttressing as well as numerous quirky gargoyles and pinnacles. Back at the main door, investigate the triple-arched façade, expressively carved. The central portal features a jovial Christ above a graphic Hell, with TV-chef demons cheerfully stuffing sinners into cooking pots. To the right are scenes from the life of the Virgin; a brief biography of her son is on the left side.

‡ *León's cathedral is one of the most lovable of Spain's grand buildings.*

As you enter through the wooden doors, look up at the back corner behind you. The leathery object hanging above the door is supposed to be the carcass of the *topo maligno* (evil mole) who was blamed for tunneling under the building works and destroying the masons' labours. In reality, the Roman baths underneath were the cause of all the tunnels; while the mole was apparently captured and killed, the hanging carcass is that of a large tortoise. The beautifully untouched Gothic interior of the cathedral is illuminated by a riot of stained glass, a patchwork of colour that completely changes the building's character depending on the time of day and amount of sun outside. The sheer amount of glass is impressive; some 1,700 m². The oldest glass is to be found in the apse and in the large rose window above the main entrance; some of it dates to the 13th century, while other panels span later centuries. There's a general theme to it all; the natural world is depicted at low levels, along with the sciences and arts; normal folk, including nobles, are in the middle, while saints, prophets, kings and angels occupy the top positions.

Another of the cathedral's appealing attibute is that, although there's a Renaissance *trascoro* illustrating the Adoration and Nativity, there's a transparent panel allowing a perspective of the whole church, a rarity in Spanish cathedrals. The *coro* itself is beautifully and humourously carved of walnut, although you'll have to join one of the frequent guided tours to inspect it at close quarters. The *retablo* is an excellent painted work by Nicolás Francés, although not complete. Scenes from the lives of the Virgin and the city's patron, San Froilán are depicted.

Much venerated is the 13th-century statue of the Virgen Blanca, in one of the apsidal chapels; there's also a replica of the elegant sculpture in the portal. Inside the north door of the cathedral is another Virgin, also with child; she's known as the Virgin of the Die, after an unlucky gambler lobbed his six-sider at the statue, causing the Christ-child's nose to bleed. Also worth a peek are two excellent 13th-century tombs in the transepts. Holding the remains of two bishops involved in the cathedral's construction, they are carved with scenes from the prelates' lives; although heavily damaged, the representations are superb.

The **cathedral museum** is housed in the cloisters and sacristy. Most of the cloister is Renaissance in style, with several tombs of wealthy nobles and frescoes; note too the star vaulting. The museum, part of which is accessed up a beautiful Plateresque stair, is a good collection, with many notable pieces. Standout items include a Mozarabic bible dating from the 10th century, fragments of stained glasswork, and a superb crucifixion by Juan de Juni, portraying a twisted, anguished Christ. An Adoration by Campaña seems to portray the wise men as gibbering fools; an old man by an unknown Venetian artist is superb.

Basílica de San Isidoro ⓘ *Mon-Sat 1000-1330, 1600-1830, Sun 1000-1330 (open Mon-Sat 0900-2000, Sun 0900-1400 in Jul/Aug), €3.* Not only does León have a wonderful Gothic Cathedral, it also has a cracker of a Romanesque ensemble in the Basílica de San Isidoro. Consecrated in the 11th century over an earlier church, it was renamed in 1063 when Ferdinand I managed to get that learned saint's remains repatriated from Seville, see box, page 817.

The complex is built into the medieval city walls, much of which are preserved. The façade is beautiful, particularly in the morning or evening light; it's fairly pure Romanesque in essence, although the balustrade and pedimental shield were added, harmoniously, during the Renaissance. Facing the building, the right hand doorway is named the Puerta del Perdón (Door of Forgiveness); pilgrims could gain absolution by passing through here if they were too infirm to continue their journey to Santiago. The door is topped by a good relief of the Descent from the Cross and Ascension.

To the left is the Puerta del Cordero (Door of the Lamb) with an even more impressive tympanum depicting Abraham's sacrifice. Atop this door is the Renaissance pediment, decorated with a large shield surmounted by San Isidoro in Reconquista mode (like Santiago, this bookish scholar made surprise horseback appearances to fight Moors several centuries after his death). The interior of the church is dark and attractive, with later Gothic elements in accord with the Romanesque; large multifoil arches add a Moorish element. The retablo dates from the 16th century and surrounds a monstrance in which the Host is permanently on display (the basilica is one of only two churches in Northern Spain to have been granted this right). Below is a casket containing the remains of Isidore himself, or whoever it was whose bones were found in Seville long after the saint's burial place had been forgotten.

The real treasure of San Isidoro lies through another exterior door which gives access to the **museum**. On entering, the first chamber you are given access to is the Panteón Real, an astonishing crypt that is the resting place of eleven kings of León and their families. The arches, the ceiling, and some of the tombs, are covered with Romanesque wallpainting in a superb state of preservation (it's barely needed any restoration). There are scenes from the New Testament as well as agricultural life; if you're at all jaded with religious art and architecture, this sublime space will fix it. The short columns are crowned with well-carved capitals, most vegetal, but some with Biblical scenes or motifs derived from Visigothic traditions.

The next stop on the visit is the first of the two cloisters, above which rises the emblematic **Torre del Gallo** (Tower of the Cock), topped by a curious 11th-century gold-plated weathercock that wouldn't look out of place at White Hart Lane.

The treasury and library is the other highlight of the visit to the Museum. Although the complex was sacked and badly damaged by French troops in the Napoleonic Wars, most of the priceless collection of artifacts and books survived. More remains of San Isidoro reside in an 11th-century reliquary beautifully decorated in Mozarabic style; another reliquary is equally finely carved from ivory. The ornate chalice of Doña Urraca is made from two Roman cups and studded with gems. The library contains some beautiful works, of which the highlight is a 10th-century Mozarabic Bible.

Convento de San Marcos León's other great monument is the San Marcos convent by the river. It's now divided between the Museo de León and a sumptuous parador. Not a bad place to stay, you might think; so, no doubt, did generations of pilgrims who laid their road-dusted heads down here when it was administered as a monastery and hostel by the Knights of Santiago.

The massive façade is the highlight. It postdates the pilgrim era and is 100 m long, pure Plateresque overlaid by a Baroque pediment, and sensitively dignified by a well-designed modern plaza. The church itself is attractive but unremarkable, but the adjoining provincial **museum** ① *Tue-Sat 1000-1400, 1630-2000 (1700-2030 summer), €1.20*, is well worth visiting. The cloister is attractive, with the arches adorned with figures, and the collection of art has some excellent pieces. The Cristo de Carraza is a superb 11th-century ivory crucifix, while in the elegant sacristy are further good artefacts, including some by the excellent Valladolid Renaissance sculptor Juan de Juni.

Drop into the parador too; there are daily tours, but it's not too difficult to take a stroll around the ground floor areas (ask first); the bar and lounge are attractive and open to the public. Next to the parador on the riverbank a crowd gather at weekends and on some weekday evenings to watch the curious game of *bolos*, in which old men throw wooden hemispheres at skittles, aiming to describe a particular trajectory between them.

Other sights in the old town Three notable buildings stand around the main entrance to the old town. **Casa Botines** is a *palacio* built by Gaudí in subdued fairytale style. It now functions as an exhibition centre, but the top floors are a bank. If you ask at the information desk, they're usually happy for you to go up and have a look; watching executives trying to look corporate while working in a pointy turret is an amusing sight. The building's façade features St George sticking it to a dragon; a bronze sculpture of Gaudí observes his creation narrowly from a park bench outside. Next door is the elegant **Palacio de los Guzmanes**, a 16th-century Renaissance palace with a fine façade and *patio*. Across the square, the old Ayuntamiento is from the same period; next to it is the fine tower of **San Marcelo**.

Wandering around León's old quarter will reveal many time-worn architectural treasures and hidden nooks. The area north of Calle Ancha contains several such, but the area south is the most interesting. This is the **Húmedo**, the 'wet' *barrio*, named for its massive collection of tapas bars, the most popular of which are around Plaza de San Martín, which hums with life most evenings and explodes at weekends. Near here is the beautiful **Plaza Mayor**, an extremely elegant porticoed 18th-century design which holds a good Wednesday and Saturday morning fruit and veg market. Delve a little further into the area and you'll come to the **Plaza de Santa María del Camino**, popularly known as Plaza del Grano ('grain square') for its one-time wheat exchange. It's a lovely timeworn space with rough cobbles, wooden arcades and a pretty Romanesque church.

Excursions

An excellent lunch or dinnertime excursion is to head out to **Valdevimbre**, an historic winemaking village with spacious *bodegas* dug into the hills. Several of these have been converted into atmospheric restaurants with fine, well-priced food.

Two of the best are in mid-range price category: **Cueva San Simón**, T987304096, a spacious warren of a place with the main dining area in the chimneyed fermentation chamber; try the *solomillo a la brasa*, morsels of tenderest steak that you rapidly cook on a sizzling grate that's brought to the table; **La Cueva del Cura**, T987304037, has an Indian/Islamic theme despite being called 'priest's cave' and similarly excellent food. Valdevimbre is some 20 km south of León. If you are driving turn off the N630 18 km south of León. Public transport isn't great, but you can hop off a Zamora/Benavente bound bus at the turnoff, from where it's a half hour walk. A taxi from León costs about €14.

North of León

The mountainous northern reaches of León province are little known except by locals but merit plenty of exploration. It's a favourite destination of cavers and rockclimbers from the city. A series of spectacular mountain passes join the province with neighbouring Asturias; these are often snowbound in winter. A car is the best way to nose around the area, although the odd bus makes its way out from León to many outlying villages in the zone. ▶▶ *For Sleeping, Eating and other listings, see pages 221-226.*

Las Hoces and the Cuevas de Valporquero → *Colour map 1, grid B6.*

A good day out from León could see you head north to the region of Las Hoces, two narrow gorges carved from the grey stone. Take the LE-311 which follows the course of the Torio river and continue past Matallana de Torio up the first of the gorges, **Las Hoces de Vegacervera**. The villages in this area continue much as they have done for years, pasturing sheep in the summer and grimly hanging on through the cold winters. Look out for *madreñas*, a wooden clog worn over the shoes when tramping around the muddy fields. Take warm clothing, non-slip footwear and some sort of waterproof, as it can get pretty wet if the rain's been falling.

Off the road through the gorge are the stunning limestone caves of Valporquero ①*Jun-Sep daily 1000-1400, 1600-1900, Oct-mid Dec and Apr-May Fri-Sun 1000-1700, €4.20.* Much of which remains to be discovered; some of the chambers are amazingly large, and there is an underground river plunging into the depths, as well as the fascinating limestone sculpture.

Beyond the turn off for the Valporquero cave turn off, take a right-turn up the LE-313 through the other gorge, the **Valdeteja**. Before you reach the turn is the hamlet of **Getino**, which has an excellent place to eat, the **Venta de Getino**. Continuing through the gorge, take another right just after Valdeteja itself on the LE-321. About 6 km down this road, look out for a small paved area on the right. A path leads to a spectacular waterfall pounding through a hole in the rocky hill. The road ends at the village of **La Vecilla**, 4 km from the waterfall and serviced several times daily by FEVE trains from León. There are several accommodation options in this region. See Sleeping.

From Piedrafita to Asturias

An alternative to turning up the LE-313 is to continue; the road leads up to the Piedrafita pass into Asturias (not to be confused with the one of the same name leading into Galicia in the west of the province). The road isn't passable by normal traffic but there's some spectacular walking to be done beyond the village of Piedrafita itself. To get to Asturias, turn left at Cármenes; this leads to the main N-630 road into Asturias, a spectacular route in itself that crosses the border at the Puerto de Pájares, where there's a hotel and restaurant.

The motorway from León to Oviedo scythes through some spectacular country west of here; the pretty **Embalse de los Barrios de Luna** is an artificial lake beyond the friendly mining village of **La Magdalena**, which has some good bars and eating places.

Further west, **Villablino** is the main service centre of northwestern León province. Near here, the **Puerto de Somiedo** leads into a spectacular part of Asturias; the Leonese side is beautiful too, with green meadows and waterfalls in an Alpine landscape. If you want to stay in this region, there's a simple, friendly *pensión* in the hamlet of **Vega de Viejos**.

To the Picos → *For the Leonese Picos, see page 536.*

The northeastern section of León province is isolated and fairly poor, climbing steadily towards the Picos de Europa. Formerly a significant coalmining region, little of that goes on here now; farming and sausage making are the mainstays of the small towns in the area. **Vegaquemada**, a small village on the way to Boñar, has nothing of interest except a strange church in an Italianate style, with an ornate layered belltower and a porch with filigreed ironwork. **Boñar** itself is liveliest in winter; there's a ski resort nearby. It's a somewhat bleak place like much of this region, but there are a couple of decent accommodation options.

Forgive **Riaño** its slightly ugly, gawky appearance overlooking an often empty lake; the construction of the controversial dam and reservoir forced the town to reluctantly relocate to the top of the hill in the 1980s. Although it's the southern gateway to the Picos, not an awful lot goes on here except hunting and people passing through.

If you're wanting to explore this side of the range, **Posada de Valdeón** makes a smaller but more inviting and convenient base, see page 536. There's a small tourist kiosk at the entrance to the town, a couple of banks, a service station, and a handful of accommodation and eating options.

South to Zamora

The chief attraction in the small town of **Valencia de Don Juan** is its weird, twisted ruin of a castle, with strange shaped battlements rising above green grass. It was built in the 15th century; a more modern but equally strange construction seems to be falling in on itself – solutions on a postcard please. The pretty bullring is also worth a look; it sees taurine action in late September. Buses run here from León six times a day.

The villages nearby are warrened with curious tomb-like *bodegas* burrowed into the hills; they produce a slightly effervescent rosé wine.

South from Valencia is **Toral de los Guzmanes** with a massive adobe palace. The road continues south of here into Zamora province.

León to Astorga

Virgen del Camino and around

The road west from León is a depressing one, especially for the pilgrims tracking across the dull plain towards Astorga, a long walk indeed but worth doing in one hop, for there's little of interest in between. León's urban sprawl has caught the village of Virgen del Camino, where a modern church houses a statue of Mary that's much respected in these parts. If you ever meet a Spaniard called Camino, it's a good bet she's from León.

Hospital de Órbigo and around

The village of Hospital is a reasonably attractive little place, and the best place for pilgrims to stop over between León and Astorga; the *albergue* is a friendly spot with a nice *patio*. Nearby, a bridge was the scene of a curious event in 1434. A local noble, iron chain around his neck and doubtless suffering some form of insecurity, decided to take up residence on the bridge for the fortnight leading up to the feast day of Santiago. Passing pilgrims were forced to either declare his chosen lady the most beautiful in Christendom or have a joust with the knight or one of his heavies. The event became known as the *Paso Honroso*; how fair the fights were is not known, but the knights unhorsed over 700 weary pilgrims, killing one and wounding several more.

Astorga → *Colour map 1, grid B5.*

While Astorga is a small town with an interesting history, nothing much goes on here now. In fact, the Leonese are fond of saying that "in Astorga there are only priests, soldiers, and whores" – but it's a nice place with some attractive buildings and a relaxed atmosphere. Astorga and its surrounding villages are particularly famous for being the home of the Maragatos, a distinct ethnic group that for centuries were considered the bravest and most trustworthy of muleteers and guides. ►► *For Sleeping, Eating and other listings, see pages 221-226.*

History

As a major Roman centre for administering the goldmining region further to the west, Astorga was known as Asturica Augusta, having been founded by Augustus during his campaigns against the never-say-die tribes of the northwest of the peninsula. Astorga was one of the earliest of Christian communities in Spain; the archbishop of Carthage, San Cipriano, wrote a letter to the presbyter and faithful of the town as early as 254. After the disintegration of the Empire, the area was settled by the Sueves who made the journey from Swabia, now in southwest Germany. They made Astorga their capital and fought constantly with the Visigothic rulers until Astorga finally fell for good in the sixth century.

The Maragatos

"They are the lords of the highway, being the channels of commerce in those parts where mules and asses represent railway luggage-trains. They know and feel their importance, and that they are the rule, and the traveller for mere pleasure is the exception."

The matter of origin of the Maragatos has provoked much scholarly and unscholarly debate. They have been variously touted as descendants of Moorish prisoners, Sueves, Visigoths and Phoenicians, but no-one is really sure. Until fairly recently they kept pretty much to themselves; it is still common to see them in their characteristic national dress. The men wear a red waistcoat, bowler-style hat and a black tunic, while the women have a shawl and headscarf.

The Maragatos are famous for their *cocido*; usually served in reverse (i.e. the broth follows the main portion of the stew on to the table). The meal starts with the stewed meats; usually a bit of everything, chicken, lamb, sausage and chunks of pork. The chickpea and cabbage part of the stew follows on a separate plate, and is washed down by the broth after. There are many restaurants in Astorga serving it up, but some of the best are to be had in the small villages of the *maragatería*, the surrounding district.

Astorga's premier sight is its **cathedral** ① *0930-1200, 1630-1800, museum 1100-1400, 1530-1830, €2.50 including Palacio Episcopal,* on which construction began in the 15th century. The best view of the cathedral is to be had from below it, outside the city walls. Most of it is in Late Gothic style, but the façade and towers are later Baroque constructions and seem overlarge and ornate for the comparatively small town. The sculptural reliefs depict events from Christ's life, and are flanked by numerous cherubs and flights of Churrigueresque fancy. Inside, the marble retablo is impressive, while the highlight of the **Diocesan Museum** are the paintings of the temptations and trials of St Anthony, who is bothered during his hermitage by some memorable demons.

Next to the cathedral, the **Palacio Episcopal** is something of a contrast. In 1887 a Catalan bishop was appointed to Astorga. Not prepared to settle for a modest prefab bungalow on the edge of town, he decided that his residence was to be built by his mate Gaudí. The townsfolk were horrified, but the result is a fairytale-style castle with pointy turrets. Little of the interior was designed by the man, as he was kept away by the hostility of the locals, but there are a couple of nice touches, notably in the bishop's throne room and chapel. Much of the (chilly) interior is taken up by the **Museo de los Caminos** ① *Tue-Sat 1100-1400, 1600-1800, Sun 1100-1400, €2.50 including Museo Diocesano,* a collection of art and artifacts relating to the pilgrimage to Santiago. The garden is guarded by some scary angels.

Astorga's **Plaza Mayor** is attractive, and notable for the figures of a Maragato man and woman that strike the hour on the town hall clock. Some of the city's Roman heritage can be seen at the **Museo Romano** ① *Tue-Sat 1100-1400, 1600-1800 (1500-2000 summer), Sun 1100-1400, €1.50,* constructed over some of the old forum by the Ayuntamiento. Finds from many of the archaeological excavations around the town are on display. There are many **Roman remains** of some interest around the town; the tourist office will provide a map of the *Ruta Romana;* guided tours of the series run in summer. Another museum is the **Museo de Chocolate** ① *1030-1400, 1600-2000, €0.60,* where you can learn how chocolate was, and is made, and how it can be purchased. Astorga's tourist office is opposite the Palacio Episcopal.

Excursions

Some 5 km from Astorga, **Castrillo de los Polvazares** is slightly touristy, but it's still one of the most attractive of the Maragato villages, see page 217. Built of muddy red stone, it's been attractively restored, and you still expect the rattle of mulecarts down its cobbled streets. There are many other less-developed **Maragato villages** around that are worth checking out if you've got transport. There are around 40-50 of them; some of the nicest are Murias de Rechivaldo, Luyego, and Santiago Millas. There are great places to stay around here too.

El Bierzo → *Colour map 1, grid B4.*

The lands immediately west of Astorga mainly consist of low scrubby hills. There's little of interest until the Bierzo region in the west of the province. Bierzo is criss-crossed by middling mountain ranges and pretty valleys. The Romans mined gold and other metals here, and some coal mines are still creaking on towards their inevitable closure, but it's now mainly famous for red wine and vegetables; its peppers have DO (*denominación de origen*) status and are famous throughout Spain. There are numerous hidden corners of the region to investigate; it's one of Northern Spain's least known and most interesting corners. All the listings are for Ponferrada.

▸▸ *For Sleeping, Eating and other listings, see pages 221-226.*

Although afflicted by demoralizing urban sprawl, industrial Ponferrada has a small, attractive old centre above the river Sil. The town has a major munitions factory and a massive prison, a chilling sight in the bleak hills a few kilometres from town. The main feature of the centre is a superb **Templar castle** ① *Tue-Sat 1030-1400, 1600-1900, Sun 1100-1400, €2,* low but formidable, with a series of defensive walls and a steep underground passage descending to the river.

Some lovely buildings are preserved; check out the small lanes around the Plaza de Ayuntamiento, a pretty space in itself. Nearby, a pretty clocktower arches across the street. **Basílica de la Virgen de Encina** sits in another square and is an attractive building, despite the pious dedication on the gatepost. **Museo de Bierzo** ① *Tue-Sat 1100-1400, 1600-1900 (1700-2030 summer), Sun 1100-1400,* set in an old *palacio* in the centre, is a good display, with items of interest from the region's Celtic cultures as well as the Templar period. There's a nice patio and cobbled courtyard. There's also a small **railway museum** on the edge of the new town, with several lovable old locomotives. The tourist office is by the castle walls.

Valley of Silence

"De el valle de silencio. Salen canciones" From the valley of silence. Rise songs.

One of the most charming spots in Northern Spain is this hidden valley south of Ponferrada. The treeless plains of Castilla seem light years away as you wind through grape vines into the narrow valley carved by the River Oza. Chestnuts and oaks, as well as abundant animal and bird life accompany the cheerful stream through villages that are utterly tranquil and rural. ▸▸ *For Sleeping, Eating and other listings, see pages 221-226.*

Valdefrancos

This village is one of the prettiest in the valley, with a stone bridge that should be censured for picturesqueness, and villagers going about their business as if the passing centuries are curious but inconsequential things. There's a small bar here, but no accomodation. Further along the valley floor is a campsite and *refugio*, **El Molino de San Juan**, with a restaurant.

Peñalba

Perched above the hamlet of Montes del Monasterio is (how did you guess?) a monastery, mostly in ruins but of a venerable age. The road ends at Peñalba de Santiago, but don't be too harsh on it; it's done well to get this far. Peñalba is a pearl, a village of slate where three mountain ranges meet that has eked out an existence on chestnuts for centuries. Although in good modern repair, it's a grey beauty, with wooden balconies and an ends-of-the-earth feel.

The centrepiece of the village is a 10th-century Mozarabic church which belies its harsh exterior with elegant horseshoe arches inside, as well as many fragments of wall painting. Have a coffee or tapas at Cantina opposite the church, a bar steeped in tradition and the focus of village life. There are two accommodation options, both *casas rurales* available only to rent as a whole. Both need to be booked in advance, see page 222.

> ❂ *A circular walk around the valley, waymarked PR L-E 14, is an excellent way to spend a day; it takes about six hours.*

There are two buses a month from Ponferrada up the valley to Peñalba, which run on the first and third Wednesday of the month. They run twice on both days, leaving Ponferrada at 0800 and 1330. They are principally to allow carless villagers to do the monthly shopping, etc. A better option is to hitch; there are few cars, but a high lift

percentage. Best of all is the walk, about a three- to four-hour stroll through beautiful surroundings; much of the distance is a marked trail that follows the river.

Las Médulas and around

The Romans found gold all over Bierzo, but here at Las Médulas they had to perform engineering wonders to get as much as possible of it. Mining open-cast, they diverted river waters in elaborate ways and employed thousands of labourers in what was a massive ongoing operation. Las Médulas are the eerie and surreal remains of their toil, a large stretch of terrain sculpted into strange formations and criss-crossed by paths and tunnels, some of which are amazingly extensive. The best viewpoint in the area is near the village of **Orellán** not far away; from here there's an amazing vista over the tortured earth. Pliny described one of the mining techniques as *ruina montium* (the destruction of a mountain); vast quantities of water were suddenly channelled through a prepared network of wells and sluices, literally blowing the whole hillside out and down the hill to the panning areas below. A few hills survived the process; these stand forlorn, sharp little peaks red among the heathery valleys. Near the *mirador* is a network of galleries to explore; ponder Pliny's account of the labour as you walk through them:

"The light of day is never seen for months at a time. The galleries are prone to collapse without warning, leaving workers buried alive. Any rocks that blocked their passage were attacked with fire and vinegar, but the smoke and fumes often choked people in the caves. So they were broken into smaller pieces with blows from iron mallets and carried out on shoulders day and night, handing them along a human chain in that infernal darkness."

The incomprehensible thing is that these mines were by no means lucrative; recent estimates put the annual production of gold at around 25 kg; extraordinarily low from such a vast operation. The area is 20 km southwest of Ponferrada; drop in at the visitors' centre in Las Médulas to get an idea of the layout of the place.

Villafranca del Bierzo

West of Ponferrada, the Camino de Santiago heads west to Galicia and the road leads into dark wooded uplands. The next stop for most Santiago-bound walkers is Villafranca del Bierzo. An attractive town, it's a nice spot to gather strength and spirit before the long ascent into Galicia. In medieval times, many pilgrims were by this stage not physically capable of continuing into the harsher terrain and weather conditions. That being the case, if they reached the church here, they were granted the same absolutions and indulgences as if they had completed the whole journey to Santiago.

Iglesia de Santiago is where they had to go, at least from when it was built in the late 12th century. Although Romanesque, it's unusual in form, with a cavernous, barnlike interior with a calming feel. There's a crucifixion above the simple altar, with Christ looking very old and careworn; the side chapel is a more recent affair with an 18th-century retablo. The side door, the Puerta del Perdón, is what the pilgrims had to touch to receive all the benefits of their journey. It has some nice capitals around it, including one of the three wise men cosily bunked up in a single bed.

Nearby, the foursquare **castle** has big crumbly walls as well as a restored section. It's still lived in and therefore can not be visited. There's a late **Gothic Colegiata** with some local architectural influences; near here make a point of walking down Calle del Agua, a superbly atmospheric street lined with old buildings. Villafranca's has a helpful tourist office ⓘ *1000-1400, 1600-2000*.

Towards Galicia

Beyond Villafranca things get more serious for pilgrims' thigh muscles and cars clutches as the road winds up towards the pass of Piedrafita in Galicia. You may well look up and wonder how they built the motorway, which crosses the valleys on

viaducts that seem impossibly high. If you fancy a stop before you get to the top, Vega
de Valcarce is an attractive option, with a strange stuccoed church and a ruinous
castle nearby. The church's honey colour is appropriate, as much of the stuff is
produced from hives in these parts.

● Sleeping

DLa Codorniz, C Arco , T987780276,
F987780106, is a comfortable place opposite
the tourist office. The rooms are unremarkable but fine, and the restaurant is decent,
decked out in Mudéjar brick.
EHostal Ruedo II, Plaza Mayor 1,
T987780075, is a good choice on the
plaza with clean modern rooms above
an *asador*.

León *p209, map p210*
LParador de San Marcos, Plaza San Marcos
7, T987237300, www.parador.es. One of
Spain's most attractive hotels, housed in the
former monastery and pilgrim hostel of San
Marcos. The furnishings are elegant but not
over the top, and the building itself is a
treasure. The rooms are comfortable and
attractive, even if they don't quite live up to
the rest of the building. For what you get,
the price is knockdown.
ALAlfonso V, Av Padre Isla 1, T987220900,
F987221244. Attractively stylish hotel with all
modern trimmings, well-located at the edge
of the old town.
ALa Posada Regia, C Regidores 9,
T987218820, F987218821. A superb,
characterful place to stay in León's old
quarter. Just off busy pedestrian Calle Ancha,
this 14th-century building has superb rooms
with floorboards, pastel shades and many
thoughtful touches. The restaurant (see
below) is excellent, and there's underground
parking very close by.
BHotel Quindós, Gran Vía de San Marcos
38, T987236200, www.hotelquindos.com.
Very pleasant modern hotel near San
Marcos, with inventively chic , good rooms
and an excellent restaurant.
BHotel Paris, Calle Ancha 18, T987238600,
F987271572. Bright modern hotel on the
main pedestrian street near the cathedral.
The rooms are very comfortable for the price.
CBoccalino, Plaza de San Isidoro 9,
T987223060, F987227878. Attractive, homely
rooms in a top location opposite San Isidoro.

DHostal Guzmán el Bueno, C López
Castrillon 6, T987236412. A good choice in
the old town, with attractive woody rooms in
a spruce old building in the *barrio* of the Cid.
F Hostal Bayón, C Alcázar de Toledo 6,
T987231446. Excellent budget option, with
comfy rooms with shared bath in a friendly
pensión. There's sometimes nobody in at
lunchtime, but it's worth the wait.
FHostal España, C Carmen 3, T987236014.
Another decent budget option just off
elegant Avenida Ordoño II. Clean and quiet.
GPensión Puerta Sol, Puerta del Sol 1,
T987211966. It's all about location here; the
rooms are clean and decent enough, but it's
hard to beat the setting on the Plaza Mayor.
At weekends, if you're not carousing all
night, you'll be kept awake by those that are.

South to Zamora *p216*
CEl Palacio, C Palacio 3, Valencia de Don
Juan, T987750474, is set in a beautiful old
mansion and has friendly management and
a good restaurant.

Astorga *p217*
BHotel Gaudí, C Eduardo de Castro 6,
Astorga, T987615654, F987615040. Opposite
the Palacio Episcopal, this is one of Astorga's
best, a beautiful and stylish place with a
good restaurant and café.
CCuca la Vaina, C Jardín s/n, T987691078, is
a top base in the village of Castrillo de los
Polvazares, with a lively bar and excellent
restaurant. Beautiful, rustic rooms and
much-needed heating in winter. The
mid-range restaurant naturally serves a
good *cocido*; there's also a *menú* for €14.
CGuts Muths, Santiago Millas, El Bajo s/n,
Astorga, T987691123, is a superbly peaceful
and welcoming place run by a Dutch expat;
the rooms are decorated by art students and
are out-of-the-ordinary, to say the least.
DHostal La Peseta, Plaza San Bartolomé 3,
Astorga, T987617275, F987615300. Good
rooms above what is widely considered
Astorga's best restaurant.
DEl Molino de Arriero, Av Villalibre 5,
Luyego, T987601720, www.molinodel

Castilla y León León Province: listings

arriero.com, is another welcoming *casa rural* managed by a Russian and serving good cheap meals.

F Pensión García, Bajada Postigo 3, Astorga, T987616046, is a cheap but not particularly appealing choice.

North of León *p215*

C-D Hotel Presa, Av de Valcayo 12, Riaño, T987740637, F987740737, is the nicest, with views across the lake and mountains, a good restaurant, and cosy if frilly rooms.

D El Negrillón, Plaza El Negrillón s/n, Boñar, T987735164, is the nicest, a cosy wood-lined *casa rural* on the square by the church.

E Hostal El Pescador, Felmín s/n, T987576623, is just beyond the Valporquero cave turn off and has good views over the mountains.

E Hostal Ines, Av Constitución 64, Boñar, T987735086, does decent food

El Bierzo *p218*

The accommodation listed is situated in Ponferrada. Few are in the old town; nearly all are in the sprawl across the river.

A Hotel Temple, Av Portugal 2, T987410058, F987423525. The town's top hotel is set in a large stone building with pseudo-Templar furnishings; it doesn't lack comfort, although still has plenty of "big hotel" impersonality.

C Hotel El Castillo, Av del Castillo 115, T987456227, elcastillo@picos.com. Just across from the castle, the slightly noisy rooms are modern with good bathrooms. There are numerous basic *pensiones* in the new town.

E-F Santa Cruz, C Marcelo Macias 4, T987428351, is a cut above with good-value rooms with or without bath.

Valley of Silence *p219*

There are several good places to stay in Villafranca and a couple of good casa rurales in Peñalba. Book in advance for the latter. The whole house must be rented out in each case.

AL Parador Villafranca del Bierzo, Av Calvo Sotelo- Constitución s/n, T987540175, www.parador.es. This cheerful cottagey affair, draped in creepers has all the comfort and style associated with the chain.

C Hostal San Francisco, Plaza Mayor/Generalísimo 6, T987540465, F987540544, is a solid option on the attractive main plaza. Right in the centre,

D Hospedería San Nicolás, Travesía de San Nicolás 4, T987540483, is located in a 17th-century Jesuit college and pilgrims' rest and has excellent rooms and a very good restaurant.

G Hostal Comercio, Puente Nuevo 2, T987540008, is attractively set in an old stone building and offers fairly basic comfort at bargain rates.

Casas rurales

Casa Elba, Arriba de la Fuente 2, Peñalba, T988322037, is very cosy, with 3 twin rooms, kitchen, balcony, heating and lounge with log-fire. If there are a few of you, it's a bargain at €91 a day or €505 for a week.

Turpesa, Plaza de la Iglesia s/n, T987425566, isn't quite as cosy but still a good deal for €75 a day (minimum stay 3 days). It sleeps 3 to 4.

● Eating

Sahagún *p208*

Sahagún is famous for its *puerros* (leeks), and the best place to try them is in this following restaurant.

€€ Restaurante Luís, Plaza Mayor 4, T987781085, a great restaurant with a log fire, courtyard and a large fresco depicting market day. There's a *menú* for €10.80 at lunchtimes.

León *p209, map p210*

Eating in León is a pleasure. Nearly all the tapas bars give a free snack with every drink; it's standard practice to order a *corto* (short beer) to take full advantage – these cost €0.60 or so. The most concentrated tapas zone is around Plaza San Martín in the Barrio Húmedo; for a quieter scene, head across C Ancha into the Barrio Romántico. There are also lots of modern tapas bars near the river on Av de los Reyes Leoneses and, near El Corté Inglés department store to the south of the old town. The student zone around Av San Juan de Sahagún north of the old town also has a few low-key choices.

● *For an explanation of sleeping and eating price codes used in this guide, see inside the*
● *front cover. Other relevant information is found in Essentials, see pages 47-56.*

€€€**Bitácora**, C García I 8, T987212758. One of León's top restaurants, this specializes in beautifully prepared seafood; the *arroz con bogavante* (rice dish with lobster) is superb, and there's a decent wine list.

€€€**Mesón del Románico**, C Ordoño IV 12, T987231559. A new restaurant with attractive modern design along with some Romanesque-looking statues in the window. The cuisine is typically Leonese in parts, but also borrows seafood dishes from the north coast. There's a *menú del día* for €15.

€€**El Palomo**, C Escalerilla 8, T987254225. A good little restaurant in the Húmedo area, with a cheap evening *menú*. Friendly.

€€**La Bodega Regia**, C Regidores 9, T987213173. A warm rustic restaurant with wooden beams, in which all care is taken in the service and preparation of the food. Part of the old Roman wall features.

€€**Nuevo Racimo de Oro**, Plaza San Martín 8, T987214767. Beautiful *comedor* tucked above and behind a popular tapas bar. The food is rich but excellent.

€€**Restaurante Zuloaga**, C Sierra Pambley 3, T987237814. Very original modern restaurant set in a large space with a pretty courtyard in an old mansion, with surprisingly large tables. The dishes are prepared with some French influence and a lot of originality, and the service is warm. Highly recommended.

€**Café de la Prensa**, C Burgo Nuevo 10, T987213857. Attractively decorated in wood, this is an unpretentious place serving a decent *menú del día* and a limited range of evening food.

€**Don Gutierre**, Plaza Don Gutierre, T987. One of the city's nicest places to eat, with superb *raciones* at very low prices, an outdoor terrace heated in winter, and top service. Highly recommended.

€**La Competencia**, C Conde Rebolledo 17/ C Matasiete 9, T987212312/987849477. Very good pizzas in two locations in the heart of the Barrio Húmedo. Serve late at weekends.

€**La Posada**, C la Rúa 33, T987258266. A lovely cosy family-run place serving a range of simple and tasty fare with a welcoming smile. Recommended.

€**Lleras 38**, C Burgo Nuevo 48, T987205163. A popular lunch stop for its €8 *menú*, which is also available in the evening. The paellas here are excellent also.

€**Restaurante Honoré**, C Serradores 4, T987210864. A welcoming place to eat with some superb choices at very low prices. The *solomillo al foie* is the tenderest of steaks, and comes smothered in rich sauce.

Tapas bars and cafés

Boccalino, Plaza de San Isidoro 9, T987223060. Great outdoor terrace facing beautiful San Isidoro. The restaurant upstairs does good pizzas and fish dishes.

Café Europa, Plaza la Regla 9, T987256117. Great location looking up at the cathedral, relaxed atmosphere, and a good range of coffees and teas.

El Gran Café, C Cervantes 9. Popular and atmospheric spot for a coffee, with a beautiful upstairs *sala* above the busy downstairs.

Latino Bar, Plaza de San Martín 10, T987262109. One of Northern Spain's better tapas bars, always busy and cheerful, with excellent free snacks.

Museum, Av Reyes Leoneses 14, T9872-79402. A bright new tapas bar near the government building complex. Good food and smart atmosphere. Prices reasonable too.

El Bierzo *p218*

€€**Las Cuadras**, Trasero de la Cava 2, Ponferrada, T987419373, is a good dark Spanish restaurant with gutsy fishes and meats and a good set lunch for €10.

€€**La Fonda**, Plaza del Ayuntamiento 10, Ponferrada, T987425794, with a nice covered terrace and excellent *alubias* (stewed beans) and generous meat dishes.

Tapas bars and cafés

Edesa, Plaza de la Virgen de Encina s/n, Ponferrada, is a good café with occasional live drama and poetry.

Maes de Flandes, Paseo San Antón 1, Ponferrada, specializes in good Belgian beers.

Astorga *p217*

€€**Hostal Peseta**, see Sleeping above. The best place to eat serving the best *cocido* in town.

€€**La Maruja**, on the main street, C Real 24, T987691065, serves the best *cocido* in Castrillo de los Polvazares in a beautiful little house with a warm welcome and filling

meal. Reservations are essential.
Closed Sep.

€€€ **Parrillada Serrano**, C Portería 2,
T987617866, is spacious and cosily stylish;
there's a big range of mid-range priced
dishes (including an excellent fish soup), and
a *menú del día* for €8.40.

€ **Pizzeria Venezia**, C Matías Rodríguez 2,
T987618463, is an inexpensive option with
poor service and excellent pizza.

Valley of Silence *p219*
€€ **Viña Femita**, Av Calvo Sotelo-
Constitución 2, Peñalba, T987542409, is
worth a look just for its massive chimney,
proudly emblazoned with the word
'ALCOHOL'. The reason is that it's a former
distillery. The restaurant, mid-range, serves
up solid mountain fare and has several
menús and a terrace in summer.

€ **Mesón Don Nacho**, C Truqueles s/n,
Peñalba, T987540076, has good hearty
portions of tapas and stews.

Bars and clubs

Sahagún *p208*
Temple, Av de la Constitución 87. The
busiest bar in town.

León *p209, map p210*
The Barrio Húmedo is the best place for
concentrated action, but by law it shuts at
0400 (although lock-ins are common). For
later dancing and drinking, head for the zone
between Av Lancia and C Burgo Nuevo in
the new town. When the students are in
town, there's always something going on.
Abacería, C Ruiz de Salazar 14. Excellent
shop and wine bar with classy produce from
all around the region.
Bar Montecarlo, C San Juan 9, T987255025.
An unusual one; the bar is typically Spanish,
totally unglamorous, and filled with old men
grumbling about football and interminable
games of cards and *parchís*. But they make
the best cocktails in León behind the bar.
Cervecería Céltica, C Cervantes 10,
T987230774. Big bright bar with an excellent
range of Belgian beers.
El Capitán, C Ancha 8, T987262772. A
reliable standby which ranges from quiet

candlelit spot for quiet chat to a pumping
party den. Open every night until after 0200.
More of a mixed crowd than many in León.
El Graduado, C La Paloma 3. One of the
latest-opening of the bars in this part of
town. Doesn't get busy until after 0200.
La Barraca, C Fernando González Regueral.
A small bar with a lesbian scene.
León Antiguo, Plaza Ordoño IV s/n. A good
bar with a friendly vibe and a nice outdoor
terrace in the quieter part of the old town.
Molly Malone's, C Varillas s/n. There are
many better bars in León, but if everywhere
else is dead, you can guarantee a happy
crowd in here; Tue seems to be one of the
biggest nights.
Móngogo, C Serranos 11. This self-styled
'trash bar' is marked only by a 'pub' sign and
is devoted to 70s and 80s rock and indie
culture and music. There's also good
Tex-Mex food.
Oh! León, Av Alcalde Miguel Castaño s/n. On
the edge of town, this *discoteca* is accurately
named but goes very late. Music tends to
change in the evening from Spanish pop
through to harder dance beats later on.
Palat, C Pozo s/n. One of the city's better
pink choices, with a gay-mixed crowd and
decent music.
Soho, around the corner, is run by the same
management and can also have a good buzz.

North of León *p215*
Cervecería Sierra, Ctra Cisuterna 11, Boñar,
is one of the better spots for a drink.

Astorga *p217*
Café Kavafis, C Enfermeras 3,
T9876-15363, is a cosy little place with
internet access. It transforms itself into
a *discoteca* at weekends.
Taberna Los Hornos, Plaza del Ayuntamiento
s/n, is a good bar for snacking and drinking.

Festivals and events

León *p209, map p210*
León's major fiestas are during the last
10 days of **Jun**, covering the feasts of **San
Juan** (24th) and **San Pablo** (28th). There's a
good range of activities, including bullfights,
concerts and high alcohol consumption.

● *A throwback to Christian Spain's dark past is that in León going out to drink a few is
traditionally known as* matar judios *('kill Jews').*

The first weekend of **Oct** is the fiesta of San Froilán, the city's patron; there's a Moorish/medieval market, processions and dances; there's also a good Celtic music festival. **Semana Santa** (Holy Week) is a very traditional, serious affair, with heaps of mournful processions by scary hooded *cofradías* (religious brotherhoods). Every man in town seems to take part, and women have recently been allowed to participate too). Relief comes in the form of *limonada*, a *sangría*-like punch.

Astorga *p217*

In **Aug** there's a **Roman festival** with togas and all that.

O Shopping

León *p209, map p210*

The main shopping street is Av Ordoño II in the new town; more quirky shops can be found in the old town.
Don Queso, C Azabachería, is a good cheese shop.
Near **Don Queso** is a shop that sells all the necessary to make your own sausages and *chorizo*.
Iguazú, C Plegarias 7, T987208066, is a good place to go for maps, guides and other travel literature.

O Transport

Sahagún *p208*

Bus A few buses stop in Sahagún but they are significantly slower than the train.
Train There are a dozen or so feasible daily trains linking **León** and **Sahagún**, a journey of half an hour. Some of the trains continue to **Grajal**, 5 mins away.

León *p209, map p210*

Bus Local services, within the province include: **Astorga** is served hourly, **Sahagún** several times daily, **Riaño** 3 times, **Posada de Valdeón** once, **Ponferrada** hourly, and **Villafranca** 3 times. Long distance: There are 10 to 12 departures for **Madrid** via Valladolid, a similar number north to **Oviedo** and **Gijón**, 5 to **Benavente** and **Zamora**, 2 to **Salamanca**, 4 to **Barcelona**, 1 to **Palencia**, 3 to **Burgos**, and 3 into **Galicia**.

Train From the RENFE station, trains run to **Madrid** 8 times a day, north to **Oviedo** and **Gijón** 7 times, east to **Barcelona** twice daily via **Palencia**, **Burgos**, **Logroño**, **Vitoria**, **Pamplona** and **Zaragoza** and westwards to **A Coruña** and **Santiago** twice. A dozen trains run east to Sahagún, and several daily go west to **Astorga** and **Ponferrrada**. The FEVE station is on Av Padre Isla, northwest of the centre. While the FEVE line currently only runs as far as Guardo, northeast of León, it is due to be extended to Bilbao by the middle of 2003, providing a slow but scenic link with the coast. The luxury train service, the *Transcantábrico*, will follow this route and onwards to Santiago, see p59.

North of León *p215*

Boñar is served by buses from **León**, but also has a train connection to **Santander** on the private FEVE network. From Boñar, the quickest route to the peaks is east via Sabero, a coalmining town amid low mountains that look to be melting.

There are 3 buses daily (only one on Sun) from **León** to **Riaño**. The 1830 bus continues to **Posada de Valdeón** in the heart of the Leonese Picos. On Fri/Sat there's an additional bus running between León and Santander that passes through Riaño.

Astorga *p217*

There are 15 daily buses from **León** to Astorga. There are a few trains too, but the station is inconveniently situated 20-mins' walk from the centre.

El Bierzo *p218*

Ponferrada's bus and train stations are across the river from the old town; the bus station is a bit of a trudge, but there are frequent city buses crossing the river. Many buses go to **León**, several a day go on west to **Villafranca**, and several continue into **Galicia**, mostly to **Lugo** and **Santiago**. Trains run east to **León** via **Astorga** 6 times a day, and some go west to **A Coruña**, **Ourense** and **Vigo**.

Valley of Silence *p219*

Villafranca is served by ALSA buses from **León** and **Ponferrada**. Many buses continue into **Galicia**.

Directory

León *p209, map p210*

Hospital Hospital Virgen Blanca, C Altos de Nava, T987237400. Call T112 in an emergency.

Internet BlueNet, C Lope de Vega 7, has a good number of terminals and a good connection speed; **Cibercentro**, C Emilio Hurtado 7, T987242311, is another one of many choices; **Locutório La Rúa**, C La Rúa 8, T987230106, internet access and reasonably-priced phone calls.

Laundry La Paloma, C Paloma 6, near the cathedral.

Post office The main post office is on Plaza de San Francisco and open continuously from 0800-2000 Mon-Fri and 1000-1400 Sat.

Useful addresses and numbers

Police, Paseo del Parque s/n, T987255500. Call T092 in an emergency.

❖ Footprint features

Introduction

The province of La Rioja is known above all for its **red wines**, although part of the wine denomination falls in Euskadi. **River Ebro** runs down a shallow valley of enormous fertility, which also produces an important cereal, fruit, and vegetable crop. The region was well known by the Romans, who produced and exported much of the good drop here; they referred to it as Rioiia; the name comes from the Río Oja, a tributary of the Ebro.

La Rioja is Spain's smallest mainland region, given **semi-autonomous** status for the same political reasons as Cantabria: it was felt that if it was just one more province of Castilla, the people would be easier swayed by whisperings from separatist movements in Euskadi and Navarra; of which the territory historically was a part. In truth, though, it feels very conservative and Spanish, particularly when the summer sun sends temperatures soaring over 40ºC. Pity the pilgrims walking through this furnace en route to Santiago.

The **cuisine** is wholly unsuited to the summer sun, being designed more for the chilly winters. Riojan dishes par excellence are hearty stews of beans, or large roasts of goat and lamb, perfect with a bottle of the local.

The southern part of the province is hillier and has an excellent attraction in its multitude of **dinosaur footprints** hardened and fossilized in the Mesozoic mud. **Logroño** is a peaceful base for exploring the area's wineries, as is **Haro**, the effective grape capital.

La Rioja

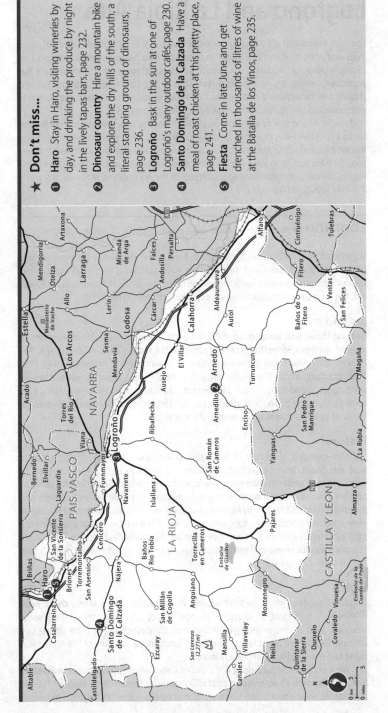

★ Don't miss...

1 Haro Stay in Haro, visiting wineries by day, and drinking the produce by night in the lively tapas bars, page 232.

2 Dinosaur country Hire a mountain bike and explore the dry hills of the south, a literal stamping ground of dinosaurs, page 236.

3 Logroño Bask in the sun at one of Logroño's many outdoor cafés, page 230.

4 Santo Domingo de la Calzada Have a meal of roast chicken at this pretty place, page 241.

5 Fiesta Come in late June and get drenched in thousands of litres of wine at the Batalla de los Vinos, page 235.

Logroño and La Rioja Alta

Logroño, the capital of La Rioja province, is a pleasant small city with plenty of plane trees and opportunities for leisurely outdoor life. If you've got transport it makes an excellent base for exploring the area's bodegas, although the town doesn't feel particularly winey. It's also an important stop on the Camino de Santiago. Fashion fascists will be appalled and amused in equal measure to discover that Logroño enjoys undisputed status as the mullet capital of the peninsula.

If you're on the trail of the good drop, you'll want to either want head north from Logroño to Alava (see page 474), or stay in La Rioja and head northwest towards Haro, the wine capital of the Rioja Alta. It's a pleasant place to stay and definitely the best base for wine tasting in Rioja Province, but if you're mobile explore the villages of the region, pretty spots with looming mountains in the background. ▸▸ *For Sleeping, Eating and other listings, see pages 233-236.*

Logroño → *Phone code: 941; Colour map 2, grid B4; Population: 131,655; Altitude: 379 m.*

Logroño's Casco Antiguo sits on the south bank of the Ebro, while the newer town's boulevards stretch west and south to the train station, a 10-minute walk away. Centred around its elegant Renaissance cathedral, not all the old town is actually very old, but it's a pleasant space with arcades and outdoor tables.

Ins and outs

Getting there and around Logroño is a good transport hub, with connections to most of Northern Spain. Bus services run from the station on Avenida España. The train station is just south of the bus station. ▸▸ *For further details, see Transport page 235.*

Tourist information The tourist office ① *Central Parque Espolón, winter Mon-Sat 1000-1400, 1630-1900, Sun 1000-1400, summer Mon-Fri 0900-2100, Sat 1000-1400, 1700-2000, Sun 1000-1400.* Guided tours of town leave Monday to Friday at 1200 from behind the tourist office (€3).

History

Logroño emerged in history in Visigothic times, and later, along with much of Northern Spain, became part of the Navarrese kingdom until it was annexed by Castilla in 1076 under the name *illo gronio*, meaning 'the ford'. The town prospered as pilgrims flooded through on their way to Santiago, but the city's development was plagued throughout history by fighting over it; the rich agricultural lands of the region were a valuable prize. The city's name rose when it mounted a legendary defence against a French siege in 1521 and it became an important tribunal of the Inquisition. In more peaceful times, and with Riojan wines drunk all over the world, it can't help but prosper.

Sights

Logroño's outdoor life is centred around its cathedral, **Santa María de la Real**, ① *Mon-Sat 0800-1300, 1830-2045, Sun 0900-1400, 1830-2045, free*, a handsome structure, with a very ornate gilt retablo and elaborate vaulting. The impressive Baroque façade still has a faded inscription proclaiming the glory of the Nationalist rising and the Caudillo, Francisco Franco.

West of the cathedral, along the arcaded Calle Portales, you'll come to **Plaza de San Agustín**, with its impressive post office and the **Museo de la Rioja** ① *Tue-Sat 1000-1400, 1600-1900 (2100 summer), Sun 1130-1400, free*. It's a typical provincial

museum, the usual mixed bag of archaeological finds and art; the highlight here is a portrait of Saint Francis by El Greco.

Iglesia de Santiago is a bare and atmospheric Gothic edifice with a massive retablo of carved polychrome wood. There's an inscription outside to the Falangist leader José Antonio Primo de Rivera, but the front is dominated by a massive statue of Santiago Matamoros trampling some Muslim heads onboard a massive stallion. **Iglesia de San Bartolomé** is worth a visit for its intricate Gothic portal and Mudéjar-influenced tower.

Wineries

One of the closest *bodegas* to Logroño is **Marqués de Murrieta de Ygay** ① *Ctra Zaragoza Km 5, T941271370, 45 mins' walk or €7 in a taxi, prior appointment only Mon-Thu 1000-1200, 1600-1800, Fri 1000-1200 (closed Aug)*. An attractive traditional winery, Murrieta has one of the best reputations for quality in the entire region. Its reds, though complex, are remarkably smooth for a wine with such lengthy ageing potential.

A little closer to town, **Ontañon** ① *T941234200, free tour Mon-Fri at 1100 and 1700*, is just a bottling and ageing point; the actual winemaking is done elsewhere. The Bacchanalian sculptures and paintings by a local artist are impressive, but there's no sound of corks being pulled.

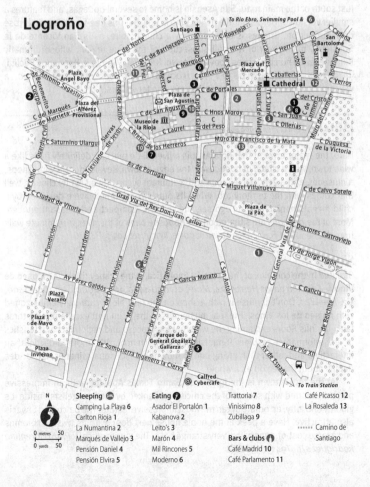

Logroño

N

0 metres 50
0 yards 50

The wine route to Haro

Fuenmayor, Cenicero and Torremontalbo

On the road to Haro, first stop is **Fuenmayor**, 16 km out of the capital. A pleasant place with a square and a couple of *pensiones*, it would make a quiet base for visiting wineries if you've got a car.

Cenicero is given over completely to wine, with several *bodegas* and the mansions lived in by those who own them. As with all these towns, the backdrop is the mountains of the Sierra de Cantabria to the north, rising sharply from the Riojan plain. Although it sounds mellifluous in English, *Cenicero* actually means 'ashtray'; don't worry, it's really rather nice. Cenicero is on the train line; if you want to stay there's a swish hotel/restaurant in town. Wineries here include **Marqués de Cáceres**, ⓘ *T941455064*, who don't particularly encourage visitors but will show you around, and they do make decent wine. **Torremontalbo**, between Cenicero and Briones, is home to **Bodegas Amezola de la Mora** ⓘ *T941454532*. They make their very tasty wines in a small castle.

San Asensio, Briones and San Vicente

Just south of the main road, **San Asensio** is home to several bodegas, and features a smaller version of Haro's **Batalla de los Vino** in July, but this free-for-all is strictly rosé only. Further on, **Briones** is dominated by a church spire, as is **San Vicente de la Sonsierra**, main town of a small subsection of the wine region, whose dramatic Romanesque church perches above the town. Near San Vicente is **Hermanos Peciña**, ⓘ *T941334366, Mon-Fri 0830-1330, 1500-1900, Sat 1000-1400, 1600-2000*, a welcoming winery likely to splash out some *vino* for visitors.

Haro → *Colour map 2, grid B3.*

Haro, the major town of the Rioja Alta, is a lively little place. It definitely feels like a wine town, with a clutch of *bodegas* on the edge of town, several decent wine shops, a museum, and a very active tapas and restaurant scene. If it's slightly cliquey, well that comes with the territory too. While its outskirts apparently were designed by a child megalomaniac with a Lego set, the centre is compact and pleasant enough. Most of the *bodegas* are situated on the opposite bank of the river, a 15-minute walk from the centre. ➤➤ *For Sleeping, Eating and other listings, see pages 233-236.*

Sights

Situated in the complex of the **Estación Enológica**, is the grapey thinktank **Museo de Vino** ⓘ *C Bretón de los Herreros 4, Mon-Sat 1000-1400, 1600-2000, Sun 1000-1400, €2, free Wed.* Don't confuse it with a shop on the next block cunningly emblazoned with **Museo de los Vinos**. The real museum is to the point and excellent, with three fairly no-frills floors explaining the winemaking process and regional characteristics in an informative fashion (Spanish, English, French). It's more didactic than interactive, and rather than giving information about individual wineries, it provides details about the region as a whole.

At the top of town is the **Iglesia de Santo Tomás Apostol**, with an impressive portal decorated with scenes of the crucifixion flanked by the Evangelists. Inside it's gloomy and lofty; an ornate organ the most impressive feature. The balconied tower is also attractive. Have a peek at the noble house next door, with its twisted columns and a large coat-of-arms with a very strange base. The tourist office ⓘ *Plaza Florentino Rodríguez s/n, T941303366.*

There are several wineries clustered around the far bank of the river, a 15-minute stroll from town. One of the best wineries to visit is **Bodegas Muga** ① *T941310498, Muga run an English language tour Mon-Fri at 1100 and a Spanish one at midday costing €2 with a tasting session at the end.* Founded in 1832, the firm relocated here in 1969; it's an attractive and traditional-style *bodega*. There's a firm commitment to time-honoured processes, so everything is fermented and aged in wood; there's no stainless steel in sight. Even the filtration uses actual egg-whites, painstakingly separated, rather than the powdered albumen favoured by most operators. Most interestingly, Muga make their own barrels on site; if the cooperage is working, it's fascinating to see. The wines are of very good quality; an appley white takes its place along a full range of aged reds. Near to Bodegas Muga is the **Bodegas Bilbaínas** ① *T941310147, 0930-1330 Mon-Fri.*

For a further list of *bodegas*, ask the tourist office for both their pamphlet *Rutas del Vino de la Rioja* and a list of opening hours. Most require a prior phone call, but many are beginning to realize the potential value of tourism and tastings.

⬤ Sleeping

Logrono *p230, map p231*
AL **Hotel Carlton Rioja**, Gran Vía 5, T941242100, hotelcarlton@pretur.es. Logroño's best hotel is smart, clean, and vaguely minimalist. The rooms are spacious without being amazing. Service is good.
B **Marqués de Vallejo**, C Marqués de Vallejo 8, T941248333, F941240288. A comfortable central hotel with slightly stuffy albeit a/c rooms. Pleasant TV and breakfast lounge.
D **La Numantina**, C Sagasto 4, T941251411. A slightly tacky and faded place but with plenty of comfort in its way, in ensuite doubles in the heart of town.
E **Pensión Daniel**, C San Juan 21, T941252948. Very good value, this pensión: it's in the heart of things and offers considerable comfort. If it's full, try the Sebastián in the same building.
E **Pensión Elvira**, Av República Argentina 26, T941240150. A smartish pensión with good value rooms, neat as a new pin.

Camping
Camping La Playa, T941252253. By the River Ebro on the opposite bank from town, this is a good place to stay, and relatively handy for town.

The wine route to Haro *p232*
A **Ciudad de Cenicero**, C La Mojadilla s/n, Cenicero, T941454888, a swish option in an alternative area.
E **Mozart**, Cenicero, T941454449, on the main square, a *pensión*.

Camping
There's also a good campsite by the riverjust out of the town of Fuenmayor, T941450330.

Haro *p232*
A **Los Agustinos**, C San Agustín 2, T941311308, F941303148. A peaceful place set in a beautiful old monastery with a cloister-cum-patio as its focus, this is Haro's best choice.
C **Hostal Higinia**, Plaza Florentino Rodríguez s/n, T941304344, F941303148. With a little viney terrace outside, this is a cool and comfortable option in the heart of town run by the same management as **Los Agustinos** opposite. Open Apr-Dec only.
E-F **Pensión La Peña**, C Arrabal 6, T941310022. A rock-solid option with sound management and very attractive rooms with or without bathroom, close to where it all happens in town.
F **Pensión Aragón**, C La Vega 9, T941310004. Slightly taciturn but oddly likeable place with decent rooms with shared bathrooms. The mattress springs gave up the ghost years ago.
F **Pensión El Maño**, Av de la Rioja 27, T941310229. A fine option for the price, between the bus station and the old town.

Camping
Camping de Haro, Av de Miranda s/n, T941312737. Only a 10-min walk from town across the river, this is a good campsite with some shady spots and facilities.

❼ Eating

Logroño *p230, map p231*

As well as the main arcaded C Portales, it's well worth checking out C Laurel for tapas; it proudly claims to have the highest concentration of bars per sq m in Northern Spain (there are a few pretenders to this title however).

€€€**Marón**, C Portales 49, T941270077. A smart modern restaurant with French-inspired cuisine that's more delicate than your average Riojan fare. On weekdays you can enjoy the €25 *menú de degustación* that comes with the works. One of the best wine lists in town is another reason to turn up.

€€€**Zubillaga**, C San Agustín 3, T941220076. A wide mix of Northern Spanish cuisine, with many tasty fish dishes – try the *merluza con setas*, a tasty dish of hake and wild mushrooms.

€€**Asador El Portalón**, C Portales 7, T941241334. While this *asador* does excellent heavy roast meat, it also has a very nice line in salads to balance out a meal.

€€**Kabanova**, C Benemérito Cuerpo de la Guardia Civil 9. Despite the Francoist street name, this is a stylish but surprisingly reasonable restaurant with interesting nouveau Riojan cuisine, a welcome change if you've overdone it on the heavy food.

€€**Leito's**, C Portales 30, T941212078. Stylish and rich Riojan cuisine, with surprises on the menu. There's a set lunch/dinner for €12 or €16, both of which are superb value.

€**Mil Rincones**, C Menéndez Pelayo 5. A character-packed new town eatery, stuffed with curios and with a menu derived from different corners of the world.

€**Moderno**, Plaza Martínez Zaporta 7, T941220042. A very sound local place with a good *menú del día* and tapas centred around fried cheesy morsels.

€**Trattoria**, C Bretón de los Herreros 19, T941202602. Don't be fazed by the bizarre drive-by shooting style glass frontage, this is an excellent Italian restaurant with a split-level interior.

€**Vinissimo**, C San Juan 25. A good choice, with a €9 *menú*. There's a slightly North African flavour here, with dishes like couscous and tajine featuring on the menu.

Tapas bars and cafés

See the section above for tapas bars situated within a restaurant.

Café Madrid, C Bretón de los Herreros 15. Many of Logroño's young and smart meet here for an evening coffee.

Café Parlamento, C Barriocepo s/n. Lively café opposite the Riojan parliament filled with a young crowd.

Café Picasso, C Portales 4, T941247992. Cool café with imported beers fronted by a sleek grey parrot whose daily diet includes fingers.

La Rosaleda, Parque Espolón s/n. An outdoor café with heaps of tables in the park.

Haro *p232*

€€€**Mesón Atamauri**, Plaza Gato 1, T941303220. A top-grade stone restaurant specializing in fish, prepared with a *finesse* that belies the inland location. Richer offerings include some delicious *tournedos* and more traditional Riojan dishes. Excellent *pintxos* in the bar too.

€€**Asador Fharo**, Plaza San Martín 6, T941311203. A friendly, family-run place with a decent *menú* for €15, although à la carte won't push you much further.

€€**Beethoven I & II**, C Santo Tomás 3 & 10, T941310018. A pair of facing establishments, the first a spacious place with comfy wooden furniture serving tapas and *raciones* based around ham and seafood, the latter a smarter restaurant with a very complete menu of all things fishy and meaty, as well as an excellent house salad (closed Tue). There's now a third one opposite the Santo Tomás church.

€€**Terete**, C Lucrecia Arana 17, T941310023. Founded in 1877, this is a mainstay of the Riojan eating scene. Lamb is the speciality here; any bit of one from half a head to a massive roast. There's a reasonable €9.10 *menú* and a good selection of cheap *raciones* and desserts. The wine list is no disappointment either.

€**Mesón Los Berones**, C Santo Tomás 24. A good and popular bar serving inexpensive portions of Riojan food in a warm, friendly atmosphere.

€**Vega**, Plaza Gato 1, T941312205. A friendly and decent place for an inexpensive bite or a drink.

● *For an explanation of sleeping and eating price codes used in this guide, see inside the*
● *front cover. Other relevant information is found in Essentials, see pages 47-56.*

❶ Bars and clubs

Logroño *p230, map p231*
Fax Bar, Plaza San Agustín s/n. Although the days of curling thermal paper will soon be a distant memory, this is a good dark little bar with a mixed crowd. Its best feature is the summer terrace outside.

❷ Entertainment

Logroño *p230, map p231*
Cines Moderno, Plaza Martínez Zaporta, is a central cinema.
Teatro El Bretón, C Bretón de los Herreros, T941207231, is a theatre but also occasionally shows *versión original* (ie subtitled not dubbed) English-language films.
Viajero, C Sagastay s/n, is a smart cabaret venue just west of the old town.

❸ Festivals and events

Logroño *p230, map p231*
The most enjoyable time to be in the Rioja is during harvest time. On **21 Sep** is the **harvest festival** coinciding with the feast-day of **San Mateo**.

Another good fiesta, held on **11 Jun**, is **San Bernabé**, used to commemorate the town's defence against the French. Free fish and wine are given out to the multitudes.

Haro *p232*
On **29 Jun** is Haro's best-known and messiest festival, the **Batalla de los Vinos** (yes that does mean Battle of the Wines). Taking place at the Riscos de San Bilibio a couple of km from town, it has its origins in a territorial dispute between Haro and Miranda del Ebro for the area, where there was a medieval castle. The mayor climbs the hill where it used to be to symbolize Haro's possession of the area, there's a mass in the chapel, a lunch, and then all hell breaks loose, with thousands of litres of red wine being sprayed, poured, and thrown over anyone and everyone. Not a little disappears down throats too.

On **21 Sep** is the **grape harvest** celebration with floats and dancing.

⊙ Shopping

Logroño *p230, map p231*
Vinsa, C Canalejas s/n (cnr C Marqués de Murrieta). One of the better places to buy wine in town.

Haro *p232*
Vinícola Jarrera, C Santo Tomás 17, T941303778, is one of the better places to buy wine. Owned by the Muga family, there's a big range of Riojas, including some very old examples. While most prices here are good compared with the competition, some of the rarer wines are alarmingly overpriced, so shop around a bit before splashing out. Open daily 1000-2200; tapas and tastings available. Case discounts.

▲ Activities and tours

Logroño *p230, map p231*
If the summer heat is too much, head across the river to Las Norias, a sports complex with an outdoor pool. There's a small admission charge.
Rutas Rioja, C Hermanos Moroy 18, T941244230, organize tours of the region and its wineries, as do **Guía Trip Rioja**, based above the bus station.

⊖ Transport

Logroño *p230, map p231*
Bus Within the region, 20 a day go to **Nájera**, 2 to **San Millán de Cogolla**, 6 to **Calahorra**, 7 to **Haro**, 3 to **Ezcaray**, 6 to **Arnedo**, and 6 to **Oyón** in Alava. Longer routes include **Pamplona** (5 daily), **San Sebastián** (5), **Vitoria** (6), **Zaragoza** (6), **Valencia** (2), **Barcelona** (4), **Bilbao** (5), **Burgos** (7), **Madrid** (6), and **Miranda del Ebro** (4).
Train Services include **Haro, Zaragoza**, and **Bilbao**, but it's not as useful a service as the buses.

Haro *p232*
Bus Haro's bus station is situated in the Casa de Cune, former home of the main wine co-operative, currently being refurb- ished. There are services to **Logroño, Burgos**, and

La Rioja Logroño & La Rioja Alta: listings

Santander as well as **Miranda del Ebro**, **Vitoria**, **Bilbao**, **Santo Domingo de la Calzada**, **Nájera**, and **Laguardia** in **Alava**. **Train** Services are few, and the station is a fair walk from town, but there are trains to Logroño and Bilbao.

❶ Directory

Logroño *p230, map p231*
Internet Café **Picasso** (see above) has 2 coin-op terminals for €2.40; **Café Parlamento** also offers access but doesn't

open until 1530 (closed Sun). **Cálfred II**, C Menéndez Pelayo 11, T941247195, is a more conventional cybercafé open Mon-Sat 1100-2200.

Post office The main office is a pretty affair on Plaza San Agustín, next to the Museo de la Rioja.

Haro *p232*
Internet Access can be had at 2 neighbouring establishments on C La Vega, **BeMax** at No 42, and **Beep** at No 40.

Calahorra and La Rioja Baja

Calahorra is the major town of the Rioja Baja, the province's eastern portion. Wine lovers won't find this as good a base as Haro, although there are plenty of producers around. Although it's a pleasant enough place, there's little reason to stay unless you're parador-hopping; if you want to check it out, you might be better off making it a day-trip from Logroño. The Rioja Baja east of Logroño is a land where wine isn't the be-all and end-all; it's a fertile country (at least near the river), and produces large quantities of high-grade vegetables and cereals. In the southeast, the main attraction is dinosaurs; 100 million years ago (and between 1936-1975) prehistoric beasts roamed the land, leaving numerous footprints all across the region. ➤➤ *For Sleeping, Eating and other listings, see pages 238-239.*

Calahorra → *Colour map 2, grid B5.*

The town is of Roman origin – its fertile riverside situation was what attracted them, and it remains a prosperous agricultural market town. The **old centre** is on a hillock above the river; some of the sloping paths still seem medieval, with chickens running among broken stones and weeds on the side of the hill. The **cathedral** is by the river, noticeable for its ornate white sculpture on a sandy façade, a side doorway depicting the Assumption, and a tiled turreted belltower. Next to it is the similarly hued **Palacio Episcopal**, but the centre of town is the **Plaza del Raso**, down by the square **Iglesia de Santiago**, a church that seems to want to be a town hall. The tourist office is just off Plaza del Raso, next to the town museum.

There are **Roman ruins**, but they are so fragmentary as to be almost invisible, although it was once an important town, with a circus for chariot-racing. It was the home of the Roman Christian poet Prudentius; the city was one of three in Spain mentioned by the geographer Strabo in the early 1st century AD. Some of the remains can be found in the **Museo Municipal** ① *Plaza del Raso, C Angel Olivan, Tue-Sat 1200-1400, 1800-2100, Sun 1200-1400.*

Dinosaur country

The southern part of La Rioja province feels a bit left out, with few grapevines and less arable soil. There's a major attraction however; the area's former residents, namely stegosaurs, iguanodons, and the like, lived in considerably wetter conditions and left

Tracked down...

In the early Cretaceous period, about 120 million years ago, what we now see as hot, dry, craggy hills was a flat place with dense vegetation, marshes, and lagoons. Herbivorous dinosaurs were drawn here by the abundant plant life, carnivorous ones by the plump prey on offer. While most of the tracks the dinosaurs left in the mud were erased, some hardened in the sun and, over time, filled with a different sediment. This eventually turned to stone, making the footprints clearly distinguishable as the layers eroded again over 10s of millions of years.

There are 20-odd marked sites (*yacimientos*) in the region. Just across the river from Enciso is the site of Virgen del Campo, a large flat bed of rock with a confusing mixture of trails and fossilized mudslides and ripple patterns. One intriguing set of tracks seems to show an iguanodon being run down and attacked by an allosaurus. The road east from here has a great variety of sites, with fossilized trees, footprints of the massive brachiosaurus, tracks of whole herbivore families, and more. Six kilometres north of Enciso, in the village of Munilla, a shocking dirt road leads a couple more kilometres around the hills to the excellent sites of Barranco de la Canal and Peña Portillo. The former has a long trail of 33 clear iguanodon footprints, while the latter has a number of well-preserved tracks, including some posited to be those of a stegosaur dragging its tail. Other beds include one half-an-hour's walk above Arnedillo, and several over the border in Soria province (needless to say, there's no cooperation between the two authorities). The sites are enlivened by decent life-size models of the beasts, with frighteningly pitiless eyes.

La Rioja Dinosaur country

footprints wherever they trod. Some of these tracks have been extraordinarily well preserved. A hundred-odd million years on, it's an unforgettable and slightly eerie sight. Heading into the area south of Calahorra, you hit **Arnedo**, a major Riojan town nestling among rust-red hills. It's a nice enough place, but there's better further on, in the heart of dinosaur country.

Arnedillo, 12 km beyond Arnedo, makes a good base. It sits in a gully carved by the Tiver Cidacos. Compared to many other Spanish villages, it's upside-down – the church is at the very bottom of town, and the main road at the top of the steep streets. Half a kilometre from town is a **spa**; there's a large array of treatments and courses available, and it draws a good number of (mostly elderly) visitors. From here a path follows the banks of the river as far as Calahorra; it's named the **Via Verde**. There's a small unofficial information centre in Arnedillo on the main road opposite the turn-off down to the spa.

Enciso, some 10 km further on the road to Soria, is set in the heart of things Cretaceous. Some of the best sites are within a short walk of here, and the village houses the **Centro Paleontológico** ① *Jun-mid Sep daily 1100-1400, 1700-2000; mid Sep-May Mon-Sat 1100-1400, 1500-1800, Sun 1100-1400, €2.40.* It's worth stopping here before you go off looking at footprints. There's a decent audiovisual display (in Spanish) and some average exhibits; the overviews of the different sites are the most valuable.

Beyond Enciso, the road continues into Soria Province, and to the city itself. **Yanguas** is a delightfully homogeneous town of stone buildings and cobbled streets on the road between Soria and Arnedo. It's got a very unspoiled feel, and those in need of a quiet stop could do little better. There's a fairly ruinous castle at the eastern

end of town that used to house the local lairds; work is in progress to spruce it up a bit. A kilometre north of the town is another reminder from days when these places were thriving; Yanguas actually had a suburb, **Villaviejo**, but it's now in ruins apart from a church, **Iglesia de Santa María**, in rapid decline but still a pretty sight with its curious cupola.

● Sleeping

Calahorra p236

A Parador Marco Fabio Quintiliano, Era Alta s/n, T941130358, www.parador.es. Calahorra's modern parador sits on the edge of town overlooking the plains below. The Roman remains around can accurately be described as ruins, but the rooms are (of course) a/c, a prerequisite in the baking Riojan summers.

B Ciudad de Calahorra, C Maestro Falla 1, T941147434. A good, comfortable option in the heart of town. The rooms lack for nothing save character.

E Hostal Teresa, C Santo Domingo 2, T941130332. A clean and tidy place not far from the old town with singles and doubles with bathroom.

F Fonda Paca, C Angel Olivan 5. A very basic but cheap option near the tourist office.

Dinosaur country p236

B Hospedería Las Pedrolas, Plaza Félix Merino 16, Arnedillo, T941394401, laspedrolas@telefonica.net. This is by far the best in Arnedillo and indeed one of the nicest places to stay in this part of Spain. Set opposite the church, the place has been decorated in smart yet welcoming white. The atmosphere is homelike and the rooms are large and superbly comfortable. Breakfast included.

D El Rimero de la Quintana, C La Iglesia 4, Yanguas, T975185432, on the plaza in the heart of the little town. The most atmospheric of a couple of casas rurales here. Good meals are also served.

D La Tahona, C de Soria 4, Enciso, T941396066, a friendly casa rural on the main road, with appropriate displays of local fossils, welcomingly rustic rooms, and a big terrace by the river. They also rent mountain bikes for €9 a day; the perfect way to get around the footprint sites.

D-E Hostal Parras, Av Velasco s/n, Arnedillo, T941394034, by the spa, is a well-priced hotel. Spacious rooms with or without bathroom are available, and there's an attractive bar/café as well as a restaurant.

F Camas Teresa, Av de Cidacos 39, Arnedillo, T941394065, which is clean and good.

F Posada de Santa Rita, C de Soria 7, Enciso, T941396071, is another good option.

❼ Eating

Calahorra p236

€€ Casa Mateo, Plaza del Raso 15, T941130009. A smart restaurant with heavy Riojan cuisine, a good spot for lunch on a day-trip if you can handle the jowly men flashing their bulging wallets.

€€ Taberna Cuarta Esquina, C Cuatro Esquinas 16, T941134355. Tucked away in the back streets, another good bastion of Riojan cuisine with a friendly atmosphere.

€ El Mesón, C de los Monetes s/n, T941148056. Up an arcade off C Ipatro, this asador does sizeable roasts and has a menú del día for a paltry €6.60.

Dinosaur country p236

Eating options abound in Arnedillo, but be aware that late nights aren't their forte; many kitchens close shortly after 2200.

€€ Casa Cañas, Av del Cidacos 23, Arnedillo, T941394022, spreads over 2 floors and is best for meat and game, which are prepared with Riojan pride.

€€ La Fábrica, C de Soria 2, Enciso, T941396051, open weekends, likeable set-up in an old flour mill. There are a few other options for weekday visits here.

€ Mesón de los Cazadores, Av del Cidacos 25, T941394138, homely with a good lunch menú for €9.

❶ Bars and clubs

Calahorra p236

There are also a couple of nightspots on Paseo del Mercadal, among them **Oasis**, a bar at No 25.

🎵 Entertainment

Calahorra *p236*
Lope de Vega, on the main square, a cinema doubles up as a *discoteca* at weekends.

🛍 Shopping

Calahorra *p236*
Porqus Porqus, C Cuatro Esquinas 9. A hearty shop to try and buy *jamones*.

Dinosaur country *p236*
Arnedillo has a good wine shop, the **Vinoteca Elias**, Av Cidacos 36, T941394010, which has a comprehensive range of Riojas.

▲ Activities and tours

Dinosaur country *p236*
Hotel El Olivar, T941394000, www.balneario arnedillo.com, if you want to take the waters this operation offers the most comprehensive range of services: various 2- to 6-day programmes as well as one-off sessions.

🚌 Transport

Calahorra *p236*
The bus station is convenient, and connects the town more frequently with **Logroño**. Buses also run to **Zaragoza**, **Pamplona**, **Soria**, and **Vitoria**. It's a weary uphill trudge from the train station with heavy bags, and there's no *consigna* there.

Dinosaur country *p236*
Three buses a day (1 on Sun) run from **Calahorra** via **Arnedo** to **Arnedillo** and **Enciso**; 1 continues to **Soria** (and vice versa).

Pilgrim route to Santiago

For those heading to Santiago, the stretch from Logroño is often completed under baking sun, but there are a couple of characterful towns in which to stop. Nájera and Santo Domingo are nice places, and the imposing monasteries of San Millán merit a detour. The area prides itself on being the birthplace of the Spanish language; the earliest known texts in that idiom derive from here. ▶▶ *For Sleeping, Eating and other listings, see pages 242-243.*

Nájera → *Colour map 2, grid B4.*

After passing through the rosé wine centre of Navarrete, the town of Nájera is the first major stop for pilgrims on the road from Logroño to Burgos. It doesn't seem as large as its population of 7,000 would suggest; most are housed in the modern sprawl close to the highway, leaving the river and care-worn, but attractive, old town in relative tranquillity. The town and area is renowned for wooden furniture, which involves a sizeable portion of the workforce. The town's name derives from an Arabic word meaning 'between rocks', referring to its situation, wedged among earthy crags. These are riddled with caves, some of which were used extensively in medieval times, and were dug through to make a series of interconnecting passageways, some of which can be accessed to the south of the town's imposing highlight, the Iglesia de Santa María de la Real.

History

In former times Nájera was an important medieval city and a capital of many Navarran kings; under Sancho the Great in the early 11th century most of Northern Spain was ruled from here. In the 14th century, Nájera was the site for two important battles of the Hundred Years War, both won by Pedro the Cruel, while a famous short-term resident was Iñigo de Loyola, waiting on the Duke of Navarra during the period

immediately before his wounding at Pamplona and subsequent conversion from dandy to saint.

Sights

The impressive **Iglesia de Santa María la Real** ① *Mon-Sat 0930-1300, 1600-1900, Sun 1000-1230, 1600-1830, €2*, is a testament to this period's glories. It was originally founded by Sancho's eldest son, King García, who was out for a bit of falconry. His bird pursued a dove into a cave; following them in, García found them sitting side by side in front of a figure of the Virgin Mary with a vase of fresh lilies at her feet. After his next few battles went the right way, he decided to build a church over the cave; the rest, as they say, is history. Today the figure is in the main *retablo*, still with fresh lilies at her feet, and the cave holds a different Virgin. Today's structure is a much-altered Gothic construction, which was heavily damaged during the Peninsular War and later, when much looting followed the expulsion of the monks by government order in 1835. Heavy investment in restoration has restored many of its glories. The cloister is entered via an elaborate door crowned by the coat of arms of Carlos V, who donated generously to monastery building projects. Above is an elaborately painted dome. The cloister itself is pleasant, although many of the artistic details have been destroyed. The church itself is a fairly simple three-naved affair. The retablo features the statue of Mary; to either side kneel King García and his queen. Most impressive is the rear of the church, where elaborately carved tombs flank the entrance to the original cave. The tombs hold the mortal remains of several 10th to 12th-century dukes, kings, and other worthies, but were made several centuries later. The exception is the sepulchre of Doña Blanca, a beautifully carved Romanesque original with Biblical reliefs and funerary scenes. Above in the gallery the *coro* (choir), although damaged, is a superb piece of woodwork, an incredibly ornate late Gothic fusion of religious, naturalistic, and mythological themes adorning the 67 seats.

Round the corner is the moderately interesting **Museo Arqueológico** ① *Plaza Navarra, Mon-Sat 1000-1400, 1700-2000, Sun 1000-1400, €1.20*, with a range of finds from different periods mostly garnered from volunteer excavations. The area was inhabited by prehistoric man, and later by a succession of inhabitants, including Romans, Visigoths, and Moors.

Iglesía de Santa Cruz is smaller and simpler than La Real and dates from the 17th century. It seems to be the preferred home for the town's stork population, which have built some unlikely nests in its upper extremities.

A half-hour walk from Nájera takes you to **Tricio**, famous for its peppers and the **Ermita de Santa María de Arcos** ① *Mon-Sun 1000-1300, 1600-1930*, which is worth a look. Built over extensive Roman remains, some of it dates to the fifth century AD; it's a curious architectural record and a peaceful little place.

The tourist office ① *C Constantino Garrán 8*, will provide a map of the town, but they're currently good for little else.

San Millán de Cogolla

Some 18 km into the hills is the village of San Millán de Cogolla, which grew up around its two monasteries ① *both open winter Mon-Sun 1030-1300, 1600-1800, summer 1030-1330, 1600-1830, guided tour only €2*. The original is the **Monasterio de Suso**, tucked away in the hills a kilometre or so above town. It was started in the sixth century to house the remains of San Millán himself, a local holy man who lived to be 101 years old. It feels an ancient and spooky place, with low arches and several tombs. Mozarabic influence can be seen in the horseshoe arches and recessed chapels. The saint himself was buried in a recessed chapel off the main church but was dug up by Sancho the Great, who built a solemn carved cenotaph in its place. The

❚ Chickens in church

Santo Domingo's claim to fame concerns something that the 'santo abuelo' (holy grandpa) achieved after his death. A buff 18-year-old German backpacker by the name of Hugonell was heading for Santiago with his parents in the Middle Ages when they stopped here for the night.

The barmaid in the inn liked what she saw but got a terse "nein" from the boy. In revenge she cunningly replaced his enamel camp-mug with a silver goblet from the inn and denounced him as a thief when the family departed. Finding the goblet in his bags, the biz took him to the judge, who had the innocent teenager hanged outside town.

The parents, grief-stricken, continued to Santiago.

On their way back months later, they passed the gallows once again, only to find Hugonell still alive and chirpy; the merciful Santo Domingo had intervened to save his life.

The parents rushed to the judge and told the story, demanding that their son be cut down. The judge laughed sardonically over his dinner and said "Your boy is about as alive as these roast chickens I´m about to eat". At that, the chickens jumped off the plate and began to cluck. The boy was duly cut down; the waitress was hopefully on the dole queue shortly thereafter.

bones were taken down the hill and had another monastery built around them, **Monasterio de Yuso** (the word means 'low' in a local dialect; *Suso* means 'high'). The current structure is on a massive scale and is a work of the 16th century, far more ornate and less loveable than *Suso*. Still an active monastery, the highlight is the galleried library, an important archive, some of whose volumes can barely be lifted by one person. San Millán finds himself in an ivory-panelled chest in the museum; this ascetic hermit would also be surprised to see himself depicted over the main entrance door astride a charger with sword in hand and enemies trampled underhoof. There's also a tourist office in the grounds of Yuso.

Santo Domingo de la Calzada → *Colour map 2, grid B2.*

Santo Domingo is a lovely town, worth a stop for anyone passing through the area. This is a town with a curious history behind it, mostly connected with the man for whom it is named. Born in 1019, Domingo dedicated his young life to the pilgrims who were passing through the area. He built a hospice, a bridge, and generally improved the quality of the path; it's no wonder he's the patron saint of roadworkers and engineers in these parts. He made himself a simple tomb by the side of the camino before dying at the ripe old age of 90, but admirers later had him transferred to the cathedral, which was built in the town that grew up around his pilgrims' rest.

The **cathedral** ① *0900-1330, 1600-1830, €1.80,* with its ornate freestanding tower is the town's centrepiece. Time and the elements haven't quite rubbed off the Fascist slogans on the façade, but inside it's pleasant and light. There's much of interest after you've made it through the officious bureaucracy at the entrance. Santo Domingo himself is in an elaborate mausoleum with a small crypt underneath it.

● *Monasterio de Yuso has styled itself the 'birthplace of Spanish', as the first known scribblings in the Castilian language were jotted as marginal notes by a 10th-century monk in a text found in Yuso's library. A couple of centuries later, the nearby village of Berceo produced a monk, Gonzalo, who penned the first known verse to have been written in the language.*

Around it are votive plaques and offerings from various engineering and roadworking firms. An attractive series of 16th-century paintings tell some incidents from the saint's life. In memory of this event a cartwheel is hung in the cathedral every 11 May. The chooks are the main attraction in their ornate coop, punctuating the pious air with the odd cock-a-doodle-doo. There's a 16th-century retablo with a few nasty fleshy relics of various saints in small cases, and a museum around the cloister. Climb onto the roof for some fresh air and a view over the narrow streets below.

There are several admirable buildings in the old town, which basically consists of three parallel streets; pilgrims who have passed through Puente de la Reina may experience a bit of dejà vu. The northwest section of the old walls is still intact. The tourist office ① *C Mayor 70*, *T941341230*, *1000-1400*, *1700-2000*, is near the cathedral on the main street.

● Sleeping

Nájera *p239*
Places to stay are currently limited.
C Hotel San Fernando, Paseo San Julián 1, T941363700, F941363399, across the river from the old town. This is the best option. It's quite a charming place, and the doubles offer good value. There's even a replica British telephone box in the lobby.
E Hostal Hispano II, C La Cepa 2, T941362957, is characterless but clean; it's run out of a nearby restaurant.
F María Emilia del Rey, Flat 5E, C Espadaña 1, T941360808. You can stay at this home, just around the corner from the post office. The buzzer (top right) is unmarked, but you'll get a chatty and warm-hearted welcome.

San Millán de Cogolla *p240*
AL Hostería de San Millán, T941373277, F941373266, www.sanmillan.com. A swish option set in a wing of Yuso monastery offering excellent comfort amid a slightly starchy decor.
E Posada de San Millán, C Prestiño 3, T941373209 is a peaceful place set in the former gardens of the monastery; there's also a café doing decent *raciones*.

Santo Domingo de la Calzada *p241*
AL Parador de Santo Domingo de la Calzada, Plaza del Santo 3, T941340300, www.parador.es. Right next to the cathedral, this mostly modern parador is built around the saint's old pilgrim hospital and is an attractive place with facilities and charm, backed up by a decent restaurant.

A Hotel El Corregidor, C Mayor (Zumalacárregui) 14/Av Calahorra 17, T941342128, F941342115. Bright and breezily decorated modern hotel (although the pink curtains in the rooms are a bit sugar-sweet) in the old town; a friendly spot to stay.
D-E Pensión Miguel, C Juan Carlos I 23, T941343252. On the main road through town, the rooms are noisy but not overly so. The ensuite ones are significantly nicer than the ones without bathroom, although all are reasonable.
F Hostal Rio, C Etchegoyen 2, T941340277. Faded rooms above a restaurant, run by cheerful management. Decent budget option.

❷ Eating

Nájera *p239*
€ **El Buen Yantar**, C Mártires 19, T941360274, this *asador* does a very good *menú* for €8.50, with hearty Riojan bean dishes washed down by tasty grilled meat and decent house wine.
€ **El Trinquete**, C Mayor 8, T941362564, where you can try fried sheep's ears, a waste-not-want-not Riojan speciality.
€ **Las Ocas**, C Descampado 4, T941362985, a *cervecería* specializing in portions of grilled meat. Good *raciones*.
€ **Rio**, Hotel San Fernando's restaurant, also does a good set meal for both lunch and dinner, €9.30.

Santo Domingo de la Calzada *p241*
There's good cheap eating to be done in Santo Domingo; although it might be wise to keep off the roast chicken.

● *For an explanation of sleeping and eating price codes used in this guide, see inside the*
● *front cover. Other relevant information is found in Essentials, see pages 47-56.*

€€ **Mesón El Peregrino**, C Mayor 16/Av Calahorra 19, T941340202. A cavernous eating barn doing some standard Riojan food very well. The *menú del día* for €9 is hearty, filling, and good.
€€ **El Rincón de Emilio**, Plaza Bonifacio Gil 7, T941340527. Tucked away in a tiny plaza off the main road, this is a charming chessboard of a place with good Riojan stews and meats.
€ **Rio**, C Etchegoyen 2, T941340277. A cheerful place with a huge range of cheap and homely dishes, including plenty of fish.

🄰 Bars and clubs

Nájera *p239*
Bar Choquito, C Mayor 23, sell good fried fish snacks.
La Piedra, C San Miguel 2ª, a place for rock fans to go with their air guitar.

⊛ Festivals and events

Santo Domingo de la Calzada *p241*
The town celebrates the anniversary of the saint's death in style, with a series of processions for a couple of weeks prior to the fiesta on **12 May**.

⊖ Transport

Nájera *p239*
Frequent services run from the spangly new bus terminal by the Hotel San Fernando to **Logroño** and **Santo Domingo**, and 3 or 4 daily go to **Burgos** and **Zaragoza**. There are 2 daily to **San Millán**, leaving at 0720 and 1320, returning at 1500 and 1945; and 2 to **Haro** and **Ezcaray**.

Santo Domingo de la Calzada *p241*
Buses leave from Plaza Hermosilla just south of the old town. There are regular buses to **Logroño**, stopping in **Nájera**; to **Burgos**; and to **Bilbao** via **Haro** and **Vitoria**.

⊙ Directory

Nájera *p239*
Internet Head for **Cybercom**, C Mártires 7, who charge €1.80 per hr for good access.
Laundry There's a *lavandería* at Ribera del Najerilla 5.

Santo Domingo de la Calzada *p241*
Internet There's free access for pilgrims in the Ayuntamiento Mon-Fri 0900-1300, 1500-1900. Non-pilgrims might be able to negotiate something.

La Rioja Pilgrim route to Santiago: listings

Barcelona

⁝ Footprint features

Introduction

Barcelona really has got it all. Just for starters, there's the location: the city dips its toes in the Mediterranean, leans back against the Pyrenees, and basks in year-round sunshine. Then there is the skyline: this is Gaudí's city after all, and his buildings seem to have erupted magically between Gothic spires and glassy 21st-century design. Add to that a fantastic and varied nightlife, a discerning cuisine which prides itself on being the finest in Spain, and a nose for the latest and best in fashion and design, and it's hardly surprising that Barcelona has become the most popular city in Europe.

But underneath the flirty, glamorous exterior lies a city that had to work to get attention. A couple of decades ago, the creamy stone of Gaudí's La Pedrera was black with grime, and a bingo parlour held court on the first floor, parts of the city were too dangerous to walk through at any time of day, and the spectacular legacy of the Modernistas was slowly disintegrating. The 1992 Olympics changed all that; with breathtaking energy the city reinvented itself, demolishing and reconstructing great swathes of land, and unfurling itself along the long-ignored Mediterranean. This dynamism is still blazing a trail: Barcelona's big chance to get the world's attention is the 2004 Universal Forum of Cultures, held in a new complex created on reclaimed land in the once-shabby worker's neighbourhood of Poble Nou.

★ Don't miss...

❶ Mercat de la Boquería Have a counter-top breakfast at the colourful market, page 254.

❷ Plaça Reial Sit out on the buzzy square and watch the (weird) world go by, page 254.

❸ Sardana dancing Join in some sardana dancing in front of the Gothic cathedral, page 255.

❹ El Born Go shopping at the trendy boutiques of this district and follow it up with a tapas crawl, page 262.

❺ Palau de la Musica Catalana Be dazzled by the fabulous Modernista concert hall, page 264.

❻ El Raval Rummage through the vintage clothes on the Riera Baixa in El Raval, then check out the ultra-hip bar scene, page 265.

❼ Casa Batlló Gaze at Gaudí's shimmering dragon house, page 268.

❽ La Pedrera Enjoy a cocktail and live music on the undulating rooftop of this building, page 269.

❾ Barceloneta Rent a sun-lounger on the beach and top up your tan, page 277.

Barcelona

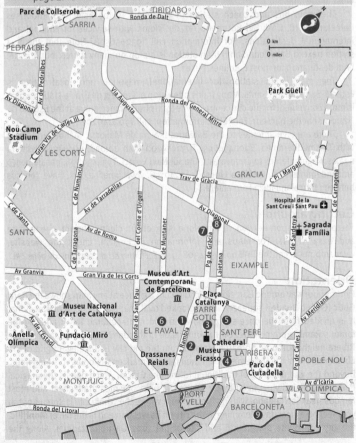

Ins and outs → *Colour map 3, grid B5; Populaton: around 1 625 000.*

Getting there

Barcelona's international **airport** is in El Prat de Llobregat, 12 km to the south of the city. Airlines are allocated to one of the two main terminals – A and B – for arrivals and departures. Both terminals have tourist information booths, car hire offices, ATMs, bureaux de change (0700-2300), cafés and a few shops. There are left luggage facilities in Terminal B (€4.50 for 24 hours). Flight information: T932983838, www.aena.es. To reach the centre Airport trains (€2.25) travel to Plaça de Catalunya and Estació de Sants every 30 minutes from 0608 to 2238. The journey takes about 25 minutes. A1 Aerobús (€3.50) departs from both terminals for the Plaça de Catalunya, with stops at Estació de Sants and Plaça d'Espanya (daily 0600-2400 every 12 minutes).There are taxi ranks outside both terminals; count on paying €17-20 to the centre of town. Fares rise after 2200 and at weekends and there are supplements for luggage and pets. Use the taxi ranks outside the Terminals rather than the touts who will approach you in the arrival halls. The budget flight hub of Girona airport is 90 minutes from Barcelona by train. Ryanair run a bus service in addition to this, €15.80 return.

If arriving by **car**, the main access road into Barcelona is the A-7 autopista, which crosses the eastern Pyrenees and runs down past Girona and Figueres. The tolls are high, which means that the other main access road, the N-II, is clogged with traffic most of the time.

The main **bus and coach** station in Barcelona is the Estació d'Autobuses Barcelona-Nord, C/Ali Bei 80, metro Arc de Triomf, with services for national and international destinations. For information call T932656508. Note that the bus station next to Barcelona-Sants train station is a stop on many routes, but it is the final destination for most Eurolines buses.

The main **train** station for international, regional, and local trains is Estació-Sants, metro Sants. Many trains often stop at Passeig de Gràcia station which is more convenient for the city centre. Some trains from France arrive at the Estació de Francia near the harbour. For RENFE information, call T902240202.

There are regular ferries to the Balearics (Palma de Mallorca, Máhon, and Ibiza) with **Trasmediterránea**, T902454645, T932959100 from abroad, www.trasmediterranea.es. Regular ferries to Genova with **Grandi Navi Veloci**, T934439898, pasaje.bcn@amcondeminas.com. **Umafisa Lines**, T932210156, www.umafisa.com, have services between Barcelona-Ibiza-Formentera.

Getting around

The public transport network in Barcelona is excellent: clean, efficient, cheap, safe and easy to use. For maps and information in English, check the website, www.tmb.net or call the TMB on T934430859. ►► *For further details, see Transport page 298.*

Orientation

Finding your way around Barcelona isn't difficult; a glance at any map shows the **Barri Gòtic** (Gothic Quarter) squeezed into a crooked oval shape at the heart of Barcelona. It is divided from the once-sleazy, now hip and multi-cultural, **Raval** area by the famous **Rambla** promenade. On the other side of the Barri Gòtic is the fashionable **Ribera** neighbourhood. Spreading inland from the old city is the elegant grid of the **Eixample,** where the Modernistas left their fanciful mark on the bourgeois mansions. Beyond the grid lie a ring of traditional towns like **Gràcia,** which boasts the magical Park Güell. The city is ringed by the Collserola hills, of which the highest and most famous peak is **Tibidabo**, with its funfair, from where the whole city is spread out at your feet on a clear day. Hemming in the city on its western end is the hill of **Montjüic**, the city's favourite playground and site of the 1992 Olympic stadium. Along the

❗ Just the ticket

Barcelona Card Offers unlimited public transport plus more than 100 discounts at shops, restaurants and museums. It is available for 1, 2 or 3 days and costs between €17 for a 1-day pass and €27 for a 5-day pass. Discounts include 50% off the Museu d'Història de la Ciutat and the Museu Picasso; 30% off the temple de Sagrada Família; 20% off La Pedrera, MNAC, MACBA, CCCB, Fundació Miró and Fundació Tàpies; 20% off zoo, Poble Espanyol and 10% off Aquarium and IMAX cinema.

Ruta del Modernisme This ticket is available from the Centre del Modernisme in the Casa Amatller, Passeig de Gràcia 41, T93 488 0139, www.rutamodernisme.com. It costs €3 and offers half-price admission at four Modernista attractions: Palau de la Música Catalana, Fundació Antoni Tàpies, Museu d'Art Modern, and the Museu de Zoologia. The ticket includes a free guided visit of the façades of the Manzana de la Discòrdia (in English at 10.15, 1200, 1300, 1500, 1600 and 1800).

Art Ticket The Art Ticket offers free entrance to six of Barcelona's best art museums: the Museu Nacional d'Art de Catalunya (MNAC); Fundació Joan Miró; Fundació Antoni Tàpies; Centre de Cultura Contemporània de Barcelona (CCCB); Centre Cultural Caixa Catalunya (La Pedrera); Museu d'Art Contemporani de Barcelona (MACBA). It costs €15 and is available from tourist offices, and participating museums.

Montjuïc Card This is a brand new discount card for Montjuïc. It costs €20, and offers free rides on the Montjuïc Tourist train (a summer only service) and cable car; free bike rental; free entry to many museums and attractions including: the Fundació Miró, the Pavelló Mies Van der Rohe, the Galeria Olímpica, the Jardí Botanic, MNAC, the Museu D'Arqueologia de Catalunya, the Institut Teatre, Museu Etnologica, Museu Militar, Poble Espanyol and the Caixa Forum. It also includes free admission to the Bernat Picornell and Montjuïc swimming pools and a performance at the Teatre Lliure or the Mercat de les Flors theatres.

seafront are the spanking new developments of the **Port Vell** and the **Port Olímpic**, crammed with beaches, restaurants and bars. It's an engagingly walkable city, but if you get footsore, the bus system and the metro are clean, safe and easy to negotiate, and you can swing up to Montjuïc in a cable car or take a vintage tram to Tibidabo.

Tourist information

The tourist information services in Barcelona are excellent. The **main tourist office** on the Plaça Catalunya also has a bureau de change, an accommodation-booking service, and a gift shop. You can book tours here and buy the various discount cards (see below). There is plenty of information on the excellent websites www.barcelonaturisme.com and www.bcn.es. For telephone information, call T906 301 282 within Spain, or T+34 933 689 730 from abroad. Main office ① *Plaça Catalunya, daily 0900–2100.* Branches ① *Plaça Sant Jaume (in the corner of the Ajuntament/City Hall). Mon–Fri 1000–2000, Sat 1000–2000, Sun and hols 1000–1400; Estació Barcelona-Sants. winter Mon–Fri 0800–2000, Sat, Sun and hols 0800–1400, open daily in summer 0800–2000. Palau de Congressos (Trade Fair office), Avinguda Reina Maria Cristina, Montjüic. Open during trade fairs only. Airport (Terminals A and B), 0900–2100. Palau Robert, 107 Passeig de Gràcia, T932384000, www.gencat. es/probert. Open Mon–Fri 1000–1900, Sat 1000–1430.* This has information on all of

Barcelona

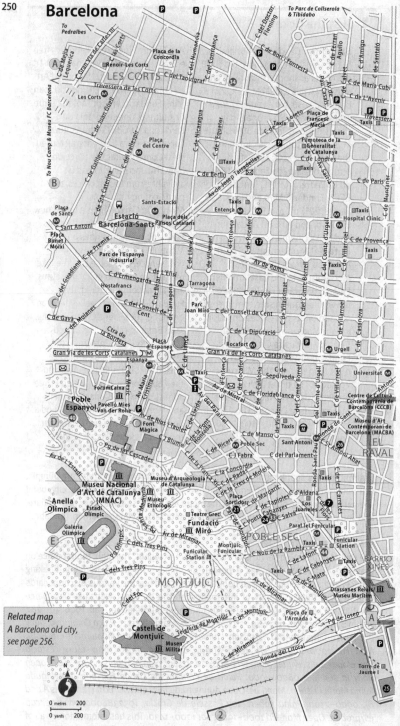

To Pedralbes

To Parc de Collserola & Tibidabo

LES CORTS

Plaça de la Concòrdia

Travessera de les Corts

Les Corts

To Nou Camp & Museu FC Barcelona

Plaça de Sants

Estació Barcelona-Sants

Plaça del Centre

Sants-Estació

Plaça dels Països Catalans

Plaça de Francesc Macià

Filmoteca de la Generalitat de Catalunya

Taxis

Entença

Hospital Clínic

Taxis

Plaça Bonet i Moixí

Parc de l'Espanya Industrial

Hostafrancs

Tarragona

Parc Joan Miró

C de la Diputació

Rocafort

Urgell

Universitat

Gran Via de les Corts Catalanes

Espanya

Gran Via de les Corts Catalanes

Taxis

ForumCaixa

Poble Espanyol

Pavelló Mies Van der Rohe

Font Màgica

Pg. de les Cascades

Centre de Cultura Contemporània de Barcelona (CCCB)

Museu d'Art Contemporani de Barcelona (MACBA)

EL RAVAL

Poble Sec

Sant Antoni

Museu Nacional d'Art de Catalunya (MNAC)

Anella Olímpica

Estadi Olímpic

Galeria Olímpica

Museu d'Arqueologia de Catalunya

Museu Etnològic

Teatre Grec

Fundació Miró

Plaça Sortidor de Margarit

POBLE SEC

Juaneles

BARRIO XINES

Av de Miramar

Montjuïc Funicular

Funicular Station

Paral·lel Funicular

Funicular Station

MONTJUIC

Drassanes Reials/ Museu Marítim

Related map
A Barcelona old city, see page 256.

Castell de Montjuïc

Museu Militar

Plaça de l'Armada

Torre de Jaume I

0 metres 200
0 yards 200

Barcelona map key

Sleeping 🛏
Actual 1 *B5*
Arts Barcelona 2 *F6*
Claris 3 *C5*
Ginebra 4 *D4*
Hostal Edén 6 *C4*
Hostal Windsor 7 *C4*
Paseo de Gràcia 8 *B4*
Pensión Abete 9 *B4*
Pensión Rondas 10 *D5*
Ritz 11 *D5*
Sea Point Hostal 12 *F5*

Eating 🍴
Agua 1 *F6*
Antigua Casa Solé 2 *F5*

Bar-Restaurant del
 Teatre Lliure 3 *A5*
Beltxenea 4 *C5*
Botafumeiro 5 *B4*
Bracafé 6 *D4*
Ca L'Isidre 7 *E3*
Casa Calvet 8 *D5*
Domèstic 9 *C4*
El Cangrejo Loco 10 *F6*
El Japonés 11 *B4*
El Roble 12 *B4*
Els Pescadors 13 *F6*
Flash Flash 14 *B4*
Hivernacle 16 *E5*
Jaume de Provença 17 *B2*
La Bodegueta 18 *C4*

Laie Llibreria Café 19 *D4*
La Taverna de
 Cel Ros 20 *F6*
La Tomaquera 21 *E2*
L'Hostal de Rita 22 *C4*
L'Olivé 23 *C4*
Quimet & Quimet 24 *E2*
Rúccula 25 *F3*
Sésamo 26 *D3*
Sol Solet 27 *B5*
Taira 28 *E5*
Taverna Can
 Ramonet 29 *F5*
Torre d'Alta Mar 30 *F4*
Tragaluz 31 *B4*
Xiringuito Escribá 32 *F6*

Bars & clubs 🍸
BCN Rouge 33 *E2*
Bikini 34 *A2*
Café del Sol 35 *B5*
La Fira 38 *B4*
La Pedrera de Nit 39 *B4*
La Terrazza 40 *D1*
Mirablau 42 *A4*
Mond 43 *B5*
Nitsa (Sala Apollo) 44 *E3*
Razzmatazz 45 *D6*
Row Club (at Nick
 Havanna) 46 *B4*

Catalunya, including plenty about Barcelona. Centre d'Informació de la Virreina, ⓘ *Palau de la Virreina, La Rambla 99, T933017775, Mon-Sat 1000-2000, Sun 1100-1500, ticket sales Tue-Sat 1100-2000, Sun 1100-1430*. This is the information service for the Generalitat's culture department, with details of concerts, exhibitions and festivals throughout the city.

History

The first known settlers in the Barcelona area were the Laetani, followed by Greek and Phoenician traders from the eighth century BC onwards. Around 15BC, a fully-fledged Roman colony called Barcino was established, but it was still a backwater, outshone by Tarragona and Empuries which had better ports. Still, the next wave of invaders, the Visigoths, liked it well enough to name it a capital of one of their kingdoms in the fifth century AD. The Arabs occupied it briefly, before being expelled by the Franks from north of the Pyrenees. Wilfred the Hairy (Guifré el Pilos) united the earldoms of the area which was becoming known as Catalunya under the House of Barcelona, a dynasty which was to last 500 years.

The 12th to the 14th centuries were Barcelona's Golden Age: the city prospered as the Catalan empire began to expand, and a network of profitable trade routes was established around the Mediterranean. But, by the 15th century, with the marriage of Ferdinand of Aragon and Isabella of Castile, the balance of power shifted from Catalunya to Castile, and Barcelona was sidelined as Madrid emerged as the new political centre of Spain. Worse was to come: as Europe was ravaged by war during the 17th and 18th centuries, Barcelona always seemed to pick the losing side and was viciously punished in consequence. Revolt against the repressive Castilian regime was followed by siege and vicious reprisal in 1640 and again in 1714; despite defeat, the Catalans named their national anthem after the heroic protestors of the 1640 rising, *Els Segadors* (the Reapers), and 11 September, the day the city fell to the Castilian armies in 1714, is now celebrated as Catalunya's National Day.

By the early 19th century, however, Barcelona was getting back on its feet thanks to the opening up of the trade routes with the Americas. It prospered, largely thanks to the cotton trade, and the city began to grow rapidly as factories and housing proliferated for the vast flood of workers. This was also the age of the *Renaixença*, a profound cultural revival which transformed the Catalan arts, particularly architecture: flamboyant Modernista buildings sprang up throughout the new extension (*Eixample* in Catalan) to the old city, and none were more magical than the dreamy palaces and mansions created by Antoni Gaudí. The Universal Exhibition of

1888 was held to bring Barcelona to the world's attention, and the city was transformed for the event (a harbinger of the Olympics over a century later). But the good times didn't last: ignominious defeat in the Spanish-American war of 1898 meant the loss of Spain's last remaining colonies and the trade routes. Barcelona's factory workers, crammed into slums and working in unspeakably miserable conditions, were becoming increasingly politicized. Tensions finally boiled over on the streets of Barcelona in 1909 in the *Setmana Tragica* – a week of carnage and destruction which left 116 people dead and 80 buildings torched. In 1923 Primo de Rivera suspended the constitution and declared himself Dictator. He resigned, exhausted, seven years later and finally the country was swept up into the Spanish Civil War (1931-1936). Under Franco's repressive regime, the city suffered through the 'years of hunger', but the surge of tourism in the 1960s and 70s ushered in a new period of prosperity. Every cava bottle in the city was popped at the news of Franco's death in 1975, and in 1980, the Catalan government (*Generalitat*) was finally reinstated under Jordí Pujol. The city was utterly transformed for the 1992 Olympic Games which really put it on the international map, and its next chance to show off is at the 2004 Universal Forum of Cultures in Poble Nou.

Sights

La Rambla and down to the sea

Almost inevitably, everyone's first glimpse of Barcelona will be the Rambla, the city's most famous promenade, a mile-long ribbon shaded with plane trees which meanders down to the sea. Caught somewhere between banality and beauty, it's a strange and oddly appealing mixture of the picturesque and the tacky: almost lost among the fleets of 'human statues' are pretty turn-of-the-century kiosks overflowing with flowers and songbirds, fast-food outlets are squeezed between crumbling theatres and mansions, and banks pop up in whimsical Modernista houses. It's at its best early in the morning and especially on Sunday lunchtimes, when families stroll among the flower kiosks and couples amble towards the seaside.

Plaça Catalunya

The mouth of the Rambla, and the inevitable starting point for a stroll, is the Plaça Catalunya, a huge square which links the old city with the new, dotted with fountains and benches. It's the main transport hub of the city, where buses and trains converge, disgorging endless crowds on to the Rambla. The Rambla looks like one street, but in fact it is five, all placed end-to-end in a seamless progress down to the harbour and referred to as La Rambla or Las Ramblas with equal ease by locals.

Las Ramblas

Each section has its own name and its own characteristics. The first stretch of the five adjoining Ramblas is the **Rambla de las Canaletes**, named for the **Font de las Canaletes**, a florid 19th-century fountain which is where fans of **FC Barça** come to celebrate victories. Drink from this fountain, a legend says, and you'll return to Barcelona.

Next up is **La Rambla dels Ocells**, the Rambla of the Birds, and it won't take long to work out why: the kiosks along this section sell cages full of parrots, canaries and even a few scraggy chickens, and you can hear the clamour for miles.

Rambla de las Flores is the prettiest and most sweet-smelling section of the street, with dozens of kiosks spilling over with brightly coloured bouquets. Set back

∎ Crazy Catalans

You won't find flamenco, paella or any of the other stock clichés about Spain in Barcelona – for the very good reason that Barcelona isn't properly part of Spain at all. It's the capital of Catalunya, a proud nation with its own language, customs and traditions and a fiercely democratic history. The Catalans are supremely proud of their *seny*, a deep-rooted natural wisdom which is treated with pious reverence. But *seny* is only half the Catalan story – the other half is *rauxa*, an outburst of uncontrollable emotion or just plain old craziness. *Rauxa* is what is going on when demons charge down narrow streets spitting flames and surrounded by leaping devils; when ice-cream houses undulate wildly to the sky without a straight line in sight; or when thousands of sweating bodies converge on the beaches for parties which might stop at dawn or maybe next week. The Catalans believe, with characteristic good sense, that a touch of madness will keep them sane.

on the right is the elegant **Palau de la Virreina**, which houses the city's cultural information offices, and a small temporary exhibition space.

Further down on the right is the colourful Mercat de Sant Josep, affectionately and more usually known as **La Boquería**, capped with a lacy wrought-iron roof and a Modernista sign in bright jewel colours in 1914. Inside are piles of gleaming produce and there's a liberal sprinkling of tiny bars for a coffee or some oysters. Dive straight to the back of the market to avoid tourist prices and to enjoy better its unique atmosphere.

Back on the Rambla, there's a large colourful pavement mosaic by Miró, overlooked by the delightful **Casa Bruno Quadros**, formerly a Modernista umbrella shop, with a Chinese dragon supporting an umbrella. Stop off for cakes in the Modernista **Antigua Casa Figueres**, now an outpost of the famous Escribà patisserie (see page 284). There are pleasures of a different kind to be had at the **Museu de l'Eròtica** ① *La Rambla 96, T933189865, Jun-Sep 1000-2400, Oct-Mar 1000-2200. €7.50/6.50, www.erotica-museum.com, Metro Liceu, Bus 14, 38, 51, 59, 91,* but it's all rather dull.

Rambla de los Caputxins is named after a Capuchin monastery which was destroyed in 1835. A new opera house, the **Liceu** ① *La Rambla 51-59, T93 485 99 14, www.liceubarcelona.com. Open for visits daily 1000-1300, guided visits at 1000. Metro Liceu. Bus 14, 38, 51, 59.*, was built in its place and has become one of Barcelona's best-loved institutions (making tickets very hard to come by). It's had its share of disasters since it first opened in 1847, and has burned down twice (rumours of a curse persist). This latest incarnation dates from 1999 and, while faithful to the original in terms of decoration, it's now equipped with the state-of-the-art technical improvements. There are tours around its opulent interior, with marble staircases and nymphs floating across the ceilings. Look out for the contemporary fresco in the main auditorium by one of Catalunya's best known contemporary artists Perejaume, which has transformed the Liceu's trademark velvet chairs into a series of gentle mountain peaks, fading softly into the distance. Buy tickets for guided visits in the excellent new shop and café in a modern annexe next door called *L'Espai de Liceu*.

Beyond the opera house, the grandeur fizzles out into the shabby genteel kind pretty quickly. Once-grand theatres and hotels struggle gamely to keep up appearances despite their ageing façades, while life on the street below carries on cheerfully oblivious. On the left, a pair of tall arches leads into the **Plaça Reial**, a grand 19th century square with neoclassical arcades and lofty palm trees. The fountain of

the Three Graces is flanked by twin lamp posts designed by Gaudí for his first municipal commission. Until recently, the square was well known for its squatters, prostitutes and drug-sellers. Some still linger in the corners, but it's now a tourist favourite, not least for the dozens of terrace cafes. Explore the tiny passages which lead off the square to discover some of the best nightlife in the city.

The last stretch of the Rambla, called the **Rambla de Santa Monica** after another convent, is still the shabbiest despite ongoing restoration: for a long time it got the spillover from the surrounding red light districts, but that's almost a thing of the past now. Cafés sprawl across the pavements, and there is a daily craft market. Tucked down an alley off the Rambla is the city's waxwork museum, the **Museu de Cera** ① *Passatge Banca 7, T933172649, Oct-Jun 1000-1330 and 1400-1930 Mon-Fri, 1100-1400 and 1600-1930 weekends and hols, Jul-Sep 1000-2200 daily, €6.65, Metro Liceu, Bus 14, 36, 38, 57, 59, 64, 91.* Guided night tours for groups €12, begun 100 years ago by the city executioner. The dummies of international criminals have been augmented by Hollywood stars, Royals and the 1992 Olympic mascot, Cobi.

It's also worth taking a peek across the Rambla at the **Centre d'Art Santa Monica** (CSAM) ① *Rambla de Santa Mònica 7, T93 316 28 10, Tue-Sat 1100–2000, Sun 1100-1500, free, Metro Liceu Bus 14, 36, 38, 57, 59, 64, 91,* a gleaming modern building which incorporates the ruins of the old convent and which sometimes has interesting temporary exhibitions.

Almost at the harbour, the Rambla opens out into the **Plaça Portal de la Pau** (Gate of Peace), where the **Monument a Colom** ① *Plaça Portal de la Pau, Oct-May Tue-Sat 1000-1330, 1530-1830, Sun 1000-1900, Jun-Sep daily 0900-2030, €2 /1.30 . Metro Drassanes, bus 14, 36, 38, 57, 59, 64, 91,* the world's largest statue of Christopher Columbus, enjoys a bird's eye view of the city. The statue was erected in 1888 and was immediately popular thanks to the unusual addition of an interior lift which still swoops visitors up to a viewing platform.

Barri Gòtic

The Rambla marks the southern boundary of the Barri Gòtic (The Gothic Quarter); the heart of the city for more than 2,000 years. It is one of the best preserved Gothic quarters in Europe, a dizzy maze of palaces, squares and churches piled on top of the remnants of the original Roman settlement. But the Barri Gòtic is no picture-perfect tourist-museum – the Barcelonans have always been too pragmatic to pickle their city for posterity and the old city is a noisy, chaotic maze packed with shops, bars and clubs which cater for every possible taste, and where the streets are just as crowded at midnight as they are at midday.

Cathedral of La Seu and around
① *Pla de la Seu s/n, T93 310 25 80, cathedral Mon-Fri 0800-1330 and 1600-1930, Sat-Sun 0800-1330 and 1700-1930, free; lift and choir daily 1000-1330 and 1600-1800, €2 each; Museu de la Catedral, T93 310 25 80, 1000-1300 and 1600-1830 daily, €1 , Metro Jaume I, Bus 17, 19, 40, 45.*
It's impossible to miss the dramatic spires of the Gothic cathedral of La Seu soaring above the old city. The main entrance overlooks the wide Plaça Nova; from here you'll get the full effect of the fairytale façade which was actually stuck on in the 19th century. The main cathedral dates back to the 13th century, and the interior is magnificent, suitably dim and hushed, with soaring naves supported by heavily decorated Gothic cross vaults. Underneath the main altar lie the remains of the city's patron saint, Santa Eulàlia, in a 14th-century alabaster sarcophagus adorned with grisly depictions of her martyrdom. It's an operatic setting; to get the full effect, put a coin in the slot and watch the whole thing light up. Behind the altar, a lift just off the

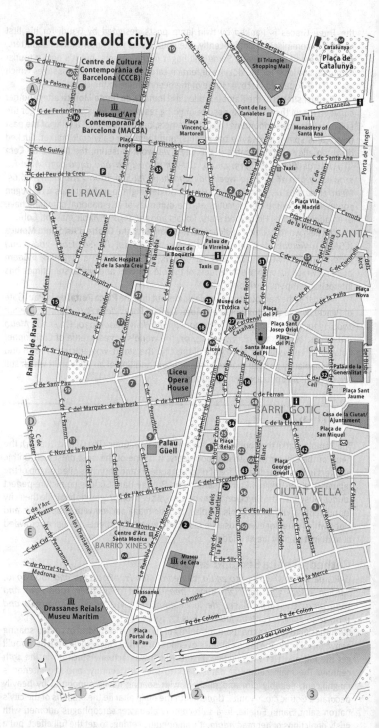

Barcelona old city

C del Tigre
C de la Paloma
C de Ferlandina
Centre de Cultura Contemporània de Barcelona (CCCB)
C de Montalegre
C dels Tallers
C de Bergara
El Triangle Shopping Mall
Plaça de Catalunya
Catalunya
C de Valldonzella
Museu d'Art Contemporani de Barcelona (MACBA)
Plaça Angels
C de Guifré
C del Peu de la Creu
EL RAVAL
C d'Elisabets
C del Notariat
Plaça Vincenç Martorell
Font de les Canaletes
C Fontanella
Taxis
Monastery of Santa Ana
Porta de l'Àngel
C de Santa Ana
C de Bertrellans
C de les Ramelleres
C de Xuclà Fortuny
C del Pintor
C del Carme
C de Angels
C del Doctor Dou
La Rambla dels Estudis
La Rambla de les Flors
Plaça Vila de Madrid
C de Canuda
Prge del Duc de la Victoria
SANTA
C d'En Bot
Palau de la Virreina
Mercat de la Boqueria
Taxis
C de Portaferrissa
C del Duc de la Victoria
C de Petritxol
C de Pi
C de la Palla
Plaça Nova
Antic Hospital de la Santa Creu
C de Hospital
C de Jerusalem
C de la Riera Baixa
C de les Floristes de la Rambla
C d'En Roig
C de les Esplugues
C de Sant Rafael
C del Robador
C de Sant Josep Oriol
C de la Cadena
C de St Josep Oriol
C de Sant Pau
Museu de l'Eròtica
Plaça del Pi
Plaça Sant Josep Oriol
Plaça del Pi
Santa Maria del Pi
C del Cardenal Casañas
Liceu
C de Boqueria
Banys Nous
EL CALL
C de Sant Domènec del Call
C del Bisbe
Palau de la Generalitat
Plaça Sant Jaume
Rambla de Raval
C de Junta de Comers
Liceu Opera House
C de les Penedides
C de la Unió
C d'En Xuclà
C de les Carretes
La Rambla dels Caputxins
C d'En Arihau
C Quintana
C d'Avinyó
BARRI GÒTIC
C de Ferran
C de la Lleona
Casa de la Ciutat/Ajuntament
Plaça de San Miquel
C del Marqués de Barberà
Palau Güell
C Nou de la Rambla
C del l'Est
C de Guàrdia
C de Lancaster
Plaça Reial
C Nou Zubano
C dels Escudellers Blanc
Plaça George Orwell
CIUTAT VELLA
C d'Atauir
Palau
C de l'Arc del Teatre
Av del Teatre
Av de les Drassanes
C del Cid de Peracamps
BARRIO XINES
C de Sta Mònica
Centre d'Art Santa Mònica
C de l'Arc del Teatre
C dels Escudellers
Prge dels Escudellers
C d'En Rull
Nou de Sant Francesc
C dels Còdols
C d'En Serra
C d'En Carabassa
C d'Avinyó
C d'Atauir
Museu de Cera
Prge de la Pau
C de Sils
C de la Mercè
C de Portal Sta Madrona
Drassanes
Drassanes Reials/Museu Marítim
Plaça Portal de la Pau
C Ample
Pg de Colom
Pg de Colom
Ronda del Litoral

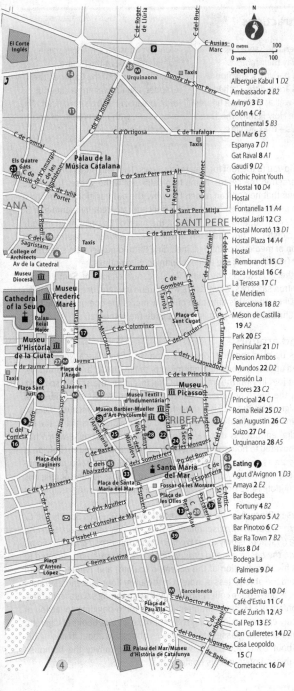

N

0 metres 100
0 yards 100

El Corte Inglés

Urquinaona

C de Roger de Llúria

C del Bruc

C Ausiàs Marc

Taxis

Ronda de Sant Pere

C de les Jonqueres

C d'Ortigosa

C de Trafalgar

C de Comtal

Taxis

Els Quatre Gats

Palau de la Música Catalana

C de Sant Pere mes Alt

C d'En Monec

C de N'Amargós

C de les Magdalenes

Montsió

C de Julià Portet

C de Ripoll

ANA

C de Sant Pere Mitja

SANT PERE

C de Sant Pere Baix

C dels Sagristans

Taxis

College of Architects

Av de la Catedral

Museu Diocesà

Museu Frederic Marès

C de Jaume Giralt

C dels Metges

Av de F Cambó

C de Gombau

C d'En Tantarantana

Cathedral of the Seu

Palau Reial Major

Museu d'Història de la Ciutat

C de Jaume I

Plaça de l'Àngel

Taxis

Plaça Sant Just

C de Jaume I

Museu Tèxtil i d'Indumentària

Museu Barbier-Mueller d'Art Precolumbí

Museu Picasso

LA RIBERA

Via Laietana

C dels Mercaders

Plaça de Sant Cugat

C de Colomines

C dels Carders

C dels Assaonadors

C de la Princesa

Montcada

C dels Flassaders

C del Rec

C de les Mosques

Plaça dels Traginers

C del Cometa

C dels Abaixadors

C de Basea

C dels Sombrerers

Pg del Born

Santa Maria del Mar

C del Sots-tinent Navarro

C de Banys Vells

C de la Seca

Plaça de les Olles

Plaça de Santa Maria del Mar

Fossar de les Moreres

Plaça de les Olles

C de A J Baixeras

C de la Fusteria

C dels Agullers

C del Consolat de Mar

Pg d'Isabel II

Plaça d'Antoni López

C Reina Cristina

Palau del Mar/Museu d'Història de Catalunya

Plaça de Pau Vila

Barceloneta

C del Doctor Aiguader

C del Doctor Aiguader

C de Balboa

4

5

Barcelona Barri Gòtic

Faecal attractions

During the Feria de Santa Llúcia, artisans display their *santons* (collection of nativity scene figures) in the streets around the Cathedral of La Seu. As well as the usual figures – the crib, the Holy Family, the Three Kings, animals – the Catalans wouldn't consider a manger scene complete without the bizarre, squatting figure of the Cagoner, the Crapper, usually wearing a cheerful red Catalan cap and an entranced expression, with his little pile of poo beneath him.

ambulatory will whip you to the roof for staggering views. The delightful cloister has a lush palm-filled garden in the centre, home to a colony of white geese. They have lived here for so long that no one can remember why. The old tradition of dancing a hollow egg (known as the *l'ou com balla*) on the delicate 15th-century fountain of St George was recently revived, and takes place on the feast of Corpus Christi in early June. Just off the cloister, a tiny **museum** in the *Sala Capitular* (Chapter House) displays a collection of medieval paintings, including Bartolomé Bermejo's beautiful retablo of *La Pietat* (1490), one of the earliest Spanish oil paintings.

Next door to the museum is the plain Romanesque chapel of **Santa Llúcia**, dedicated to the patron saint of seamstresses who queue up here for her blessing on the saint's day, 13 December. This date also officially marks the opening of the **Feria de Santa Llúcia**, a Christmas fair which is held outside the cathedral.

Plaça Nova and around

The cathedral rises up over the dull, concrete expanse of the Plaça Nova. In the evenings it's livened up with the odd flame-thrower or tango dancer and on Sundays, from noon, you can join in with the traditional Catalan dance, the stately *sardana*. Across the square, the frieze of *sardana* dancers blazoned across the **College of Architects** was designed by Picasso, but executed by a Norwegian because Picasso refused to set foot in his homeland while it remained under a dictatorship. To the left of the main cathedral entrance is the Pia Almoina, a Gothic almshouse which has been beautifully renovated to hold the **Museu Diocesà** (Diocese Museum) ① *Av de la Catedral 4, T93 315 22 13, www.arquebisbatbcn.es, Tue-Sat 1000-1400 and 1700-2000, Sun 1100-1400, €2*, Metro Jaume I, Bus 17, 19, 40, 45, a goldmine of religious treasures from the Middle Ages onwards, including several shimmering retablos by Bernat Martorell.

Behind the Museu Diocesà is the **Museu Frederic Marés** ① *Plaça Sant Iu (off C/ des Comtes), T93 310 58 00, www.museumares.bcn.es, Tue-Sat 1000-1900, Sun and hols 1000-1500, €3 (first floor is only open Wed, Fri and Sun; second and third floors are Tue, Thu and Sat, the basement and ground floors are always open)*, devoted to the obsessive, patchwork collection of the eccentric sculptor and painter who had obviously never heard the phrase 'less is more'. On the lower floors are endless ranks of tiny Iberian ex-votos and a huge collection of sculpture spanning several centuries. The upper floors contain the Museu Sentimental, with a mind-boggling collection of 18th- and 19th-century ephemera, including 108 snuffboxes, 1,295 books of cigarette papers, and 158 pairs of opera glasses (Marés was as obsessive about itemising his finds as he was about collecting them), which eloquently convey the hothouse atmosphere of a 19th-century bourgeois home.

Plaça de St Jaume

Plaça de St Jaume would be more impressive if a street (the busy Carrer Ferran) didn't cut straight through it. Still, it's grand enough, thanks to the presence of the medieval

palaces of the Generalitat (Catalan parliament) and the Ajuntament (City Council), which have been struggling for control of the city for centuries and glower at each other like two dowagers at a tea party. The square abandons its gravitas annually on 23 April – a kind of Catalan Valentine's Day, when couples exchange the traditional gifts of books and roses, and flower-sellers and book stalls fill the square in a flutter of petals.

Palau de la Generalitat ① *C del Bisbe, guided visits only on second and fourth Sun of the month 1000-1400, arrive early to sign up for the English tour and bring ID*, has housed the Catalan parliament since the early 15th century, when Mark Safont designed its graceful inner courtyard and the sumptuous Chapel (1432) on the first floor. The Pati dels Tarrongers (Courtyard of Orange Trees), with its pink marble columns, was begun a century later. The Golden Room, named for its 16th-century gilded ceiling, is purely ceremonial, and the assembly prefer the modern Sala Antoni Tàpies to conduct business, blazoned with the eponymous artist's four-part series of medieval chronicles of Catalunya.

Facing the main façade of the Palau de la Generalitat is the late 14th century Casa de la Ciutat, which contains the offices of the **Ajuntament** ① *Sun 1000-1400, free*. The sumptuous Staircase of Honour leads up to the Saló de Cent, the core of the old Gothic palace. Designed by Pere Llobet, the hall was inaugurated in 1373, a masterpiece of monumental simplicity. On the other side of the Saló de Cent is the Saló de les Cróniques, awash with Josep María Sert's dramatic sepia murals depicting Catalan victories in Greece and Asia Minor during the 14th century.

Plaça del Rei

Plaça del Rei (King's Square) is a tiny, exquisite square just off the Plaça Sant Jaume. The rulers of Catalunya held court for centuries in the austerely beautiful **Palau Reial Major** which closes off the square, and prayed in the adjoining Royal Chapel with its dainty belltower. Incredibly, the astonishingly intact remnants of the Roman city of Barcino were unearthed beneath this square a century or so ago.

The fascinating **Museu d'Història de la Ciutat** ① *Plaça del Rei s/n, T93 315 11 11, www.museuhistoria.bcn.es, Oct-May Tue-Sat 1000-1400 and 1600-2000, Sun and hols 1000-1400, Jun-Sep Tue-Sat 1000-2000, Sun and hols 1000-1400, €4 (ticket includes audio-visual), Metro Jaume I, Bus 16, 17, 19, 40, 45*, reveals the history of the city layer by layer. The deepest layer contains the Roman city of Barcino, established here more than 2000 years ago. Tacked on to it are Visigothic ruins which were built during the 5th and 6th centuries and built on top of the whole lot are the palaces and churches of the middle ages which still enclose the Plaça del Rei.

A glass lift glides down a couple of millennia to the subterranean excavations of Roman Barcino. A vast swathe of the Roman city survives, an astonishing stretch of walls, watchtowers, baths, temples, homes and businesses, founded two thousand years ago and discovered by chance less than a century ago. Glass walkways lead over the ruins, where you can peer into the old wine vats or stroll along the top of a fortified wall. Still underground but heading steadily towards the site of the present cathedral, the Roman ruins become interspersed with the remnants of Visigothic churches which date back to around the 5th century. Stairs lead up to the Gothic Royal Palace and you enter the next layer of the city's history, the Golden Age of the medieval period. The echoing throne room, the Saló de Tinell, was built in 1359 and is a masterpiece of Catalan Gothic. Seven solemn arches succeed each other in great broad arcs, creating an overwhelming impression of space and grandeur. Next to the throne room is the Royal Chapel of Saint Agatha, with a single graceful nave and a dazzling polychrome ceiling supported by diaphragm arches. It was built at the beginning of the 14th century, and topped with a whimsical octagonal belltower in the form of a crown. The glittering 15th-century retablo of the *Epiphany* is by Jaume Huguet, and is considered one of the finest examples of Catalan Gothic painting. A stairway leads to the Mirador del Rei Martí, an old watchtower with fabulous views.

Jews in Barcelona

No one really knows when the first Jews settled in Barcelona but by 694 they had established a large enough presence for the Visigoths to find them threatening and decree that all Jews become slaves. However, the community was thriving by the 11th century, and many Jews worked for the king as advisers and translators, especially to the Arab courts. Yet, although the kings marginally improved their status, the community was taxed heavily and given no civil rights. In 1243, by decree of Jaume I, El Call became a ghetto: Jews were forced to remain within its walls (bounded by Carrer Banys Nous, Carrer el Call, and the wall of the Generalitat building) between dusk and dawn and identify themselves with capes and hats. The Jews suffered increasing persecution: bitter jealousy of their influence at court erupted in sporadic attacks on the ghetto from the end of the 13th century. Hundreds of inhabitants were massacred in a vicious pogrom in 1391; Jewish synagogues and cemeteries were suppressed throughout Catalunya a decade later; and finally, in 1424, Jews were expelled from the city, a harbinger of the expulsion of all Jews from Spain in 1492. Jews didn't return to the city until the early 20th century, and, soon after, the triumph of Franco resulted in another exodus. It wasn't until 1948 that a Jewish synagogue opened again in the city.

Plaça del Pi and around

The pretty Plaça del Pi is named for a glade of pine trees which once stood here, their memory recalled now by a single pine. The hulking 15th-century Gothic church of Santa Maria del Pi is now solely remarkable for its enormous rose window, the biggest in Europe, as looters burnt the interior to a crisp during the Civil War. Plaça del Pi and the adjoining Plaça Sant Josep Oriol and miniature Plaçeta del Pi are now great spots for an evening copa out on the terrace, with plenty of wandering musicians for entertainment. On the first Friday and Saturday of the month, a market selling local cheeses, honey and *embutits* (cured meats) sets up its stalls, and on Thursdays there's a regular antiques market. Plaça Sant Josep Oriol has artists of dubious quality most weekends, and an art market on the first weekend of each month.

El Call

Carrer Banys Nous, off Plaça Sant Josep Oriol, marks the boundary of the old Jewish Quarter, known as El Call from the Hebrew word *quahal*, meaning 'meeting place'. There is virtually no trace of what was once the most important Jewish population in medieval Spain – just a faded stone with a Hebrew inscription from 1314 which was erected at the corner of Carrer Arc de Sant Ramon de Call and Carrer Marlet in the 19th century. The quarter, a shadowy maze of twisting passages and overhanging buildings, is now mainly known for its antique shops, see page 295, and is a delightful place for a wander or a good rummage.

Barrio de Santa Ana

North of the Plaça Nova is the unassuming district of Santa Ana, with few eye-catching monuments or museums, but plenty of opportunities to shop. The two main shopping streets of the Barri Gòtic meet here: the **Carrer Portaferissa**, with lots of trendy fashion stores, and the **Avinguda del Portal de l'Àngel**, with several of the major chains and a branch of El Corte Inglés. Avinguda del Portal de l'Àngel, the main artery of this neighbourhood, links the Plaça Nova with the Plaça Catalunya. The area is known as

‖ The art of conversation

The Spanish gift of the gab is legendary and they like to boast that they have elevated their daily orations to an art form. The *tertúlia*, an almost untranslatable term for discussion, was perfected a hundred years ago when writers gathered daily at celebrated cafés and expounded at length over coffee and brandies. The *tertúlia* became an essential thread in the cultural revival which some compared to the Golden Age of Cervantes and Velázquez – and some of the old cafés, like the elegant Café Gijon in Madrid, or Picasso's old haunt, the

Els Quatre Gats, still survive. The fundamental criteria for a *tertúlia* are that it should have no purpose save that of the sheer joy of conversation, and that the group should meet regularly and be composed of roughly the same people. They are still as much of a fixture as ever, and you'll regularly see signs in café windows advertising them – sometimes even in English. It's the perfect place for Spain's budding authors to daydream of becoming the next José Jiménez Lozano or Manuel Vázquez Montalbán.

the Barrio de Santa Ana after the simple, Romanesque **Monastery of Santa Ana** (just off the Calle de Santa Ana) which was founded by the Knights Templar in the early 12th century. South of the Calle de Santa Ana is the **Plaça Vila de Madrid**, a wide square which has been mostly dug up in archaeological excavations. In a grassy corner, you can peer down into a Roman sepulchural way, a series of simple funerary monuments lined up beside one of the smaller Roman access roads into the city.

On the other side of the Avinguda del Portal de l'Àngel, the famous **Els Quatre Gats** tavern has been faithfully recreated at No 3 Calle Montsió. Unfortunately, it is now just a pretty tourist trap. Els Quatre Gats began life here in 1897, when the painters Ramon Casas and Santiago Rusiñol, along with Miquel Utrillo and Pere Romeu, nostalgic for their old stomping ground of Montmartre, opened the tavern in order to provide a meeting place for all their friends. The tavern survived just six years, but was a roaring success among its varied clientele of artists, intellectuals, and bohemian hangers-on. It produced its own review, held concerts, poetry readings and art exhibitions and encouraged protegés, including Picasso who designed the menus and held his first exhibition here.

La Ribera

The old artisans' district of La Ribera is a funky, fashionable neighbourhood with some of the city's trendiest bars, restaurants and shopping, as well as its most popular museum (the Picasso Museum), its most beautiful church, and a string of elegant palaces along the Carrer de Montcada.

Carrer Montcada and the Museu Picasso

Carrer Montcada was the swankiest address in the city during the 12th century, when affluent merchants lined it with beautiful mansions set around elegant patios. Now it's one of the most popular streets in Barcelona, mainly thanks to the pulling power of its biggest attraction, the Museu Picasso, which draws more visitors than any other museum in the city except FC Barça museum, see page 278 – get here early to avoid the crowds.

● El Quatre Gats was partly inspired by the celebrated Parisian café Le Chat Noir, alluded to
● in the name which also means a 'handful of friends' in Catalan slang.

① *C/Montcada 15-23, T933196310, www.museupicasso.bcn.es, Tue-Sat 1000-2000, €5, Metro Jaume I, Bus 14, 17, 19, 39, 40, 45, 51, 59.*

The Museu Picasso draws more visitors than any other museum in the city except the FC Barça museum, see page 278, and it is well worth getting here early to avoid shuffling along behind the crowds. The collection includes few of Picasso's most famous paintings, and focuses instead on the early works, particularly those created by the young artist in Barcelona. The early selection of works includes some of the chilly paintings of his Blue Period, like the stricken mother and child of *Desamperados* (The Despairing, 1904). Picasso was partly influenced by the grim studies of gypsies and beggars painted by Isidro Nonell, who also frequented the tavern of **Els Quatre Gats** (see page 261) for which the young Picasso painted the menu (you can see it here). The works of his Rose Period are well represented but there is almost nothing, just a small *Head* (1913), from the Cubist years, and a single *Harlequin* (1917), from the celebrated series. From 1917, there's another leap in time, this time to the extraordinary series of 44 paintings and drawings based on Velázquez's *Las Meninas*, which Picasso painted in a single concentrated burst over six months at the end of 1956, and in which every detail of Velázquez's masterpiece has been picked out, pored over and reinterpreted.

Museu Tèxtil i d'Indumentària ① *C/Montcada 12-14, T933104516, www.museutex til.bcn.es, Metro Jaume, Tue-Sat 1000-1800, Sun and holidays 1000-1500, €3.50, free first Sat of the month from 1500.* Opposite, in more converted palaces at Nos 12-14, is one of two museums (see below) sharing an airy courtyard with a fashionable, laid-back café out on the terrace. This textile museum is a fashionista's dream, with a collection of historic fashions from the 16th to the 20th centuries.

Museu Barbier-Mueller d'Art Precolumbi ① *C/Montcada 12-14, T93 310 45 16, www.barbier-mueller.ch, Tue-Sat 1000-1800, Sun and hols 1000-1500, €3, Metro Jaume I, bus 14, 17, 19, 36, 39, 40, 45, 51.* Next door, this was established when the Swiss museum of the same name offered to lend Barcelona 170 pieces from their collection on a rotating basis. The city spent millions expensively converting another of Carrer Montcada's palaces to exhibit them, and now three millennia of art treasures – encompassing powerful sculpture, jewellery and ceramic ware from the ancient civilizations of Central and South America – are theatrically arranged on spotlit plinths.

Església de Santa Maria del Mar

① *Plaça de Santa Mara del Mar, Metro Jaume I, 0900-1330 and 1630-2000, free.*

The loveliest church in all Catalunya sits at the bottom of the Carrer Montcada: the church of Santa Maria del Mar. Construction began in 1329 and was completed in just 54 years – record speed for the era – which meant that other styles and forms couldn't creep in as successive architects took over the job. As a result, the church is considered one of the finest and purest examples of Catalan Gothic. The hulking exterior, built to withstand wind and storms, gives no hint of the spellbinding interior, a soaring central nave flanked with supporting columns of ethereal slimness. The ornate fittings accumulated over centuries were lost when the church was gutted during the Civil War; only the stained glass windows, some dating back to the 15th century, were spared. Regular concerts are held here; the city cultural office at the Palau de la Virreina (see page 254) can provide details.

Passeig del Born and around

Passeig del Born begins at the side entrance to the church of Santa Maria del Mar. Once a theatre for medieval jousting tournaments and carnivals, nowadays the fiesta continues at the string of ultra-trendy bars and clubs which line the street. This is one

⁞ Picasso's Barcelona

In 1895, Picasso and his family moved from Málaga to Barcelona, where his father took up a post as professor of fine arts at the Academia Provincial de Bellas Artes.

In 1897, the famous tavern Els Quatre Gats (see page 261) was inaugurated and quickly became the heart of the city's avant garde, and Picasso designed its menus and held impromptu exhibitions. In 1899, Picasso shared a studio just off the Carrer Avinyò, a street famous for its brothels, which gave him the inspiration for his celebrated painting Les Demoiselles d'Avignon (it was also here that he contracted gonorrhoea). The following year, one of his paintings was chosen to be exhibited at the Universal Exhibition in Paris, and he travelled to what was then the mecca of the art world with Carlos Casegamas. Casegamas, troubled and addicted to drink and drugs, killed himself the following year, and Picasso returned to Barcelona. This time, he was able to afford a studio by himself at Carrer del Comerç 28, where he created many of the haunting works of his Blue Period, using the beggars, prostitutes and gypsies of the streets as his models.

of the hippest neighbourhoods in Barcelona, known simply as 'El Born', and the narrow streets which splinter off the Passeig are packed with slick tapas bars, restaurants and stylish interior design and fashion shops.

Just off the Passeig is the **Fossar de les Morares** (Mulberry Cemetery), the burial place of the martyrs of 1714, who defended the besieged city against the Bourbon armies; they are remembered here annually on 11 September, Catalan National Day.

Just around the corner is one of the city's newest museums, the **Museu de Xocolata** (Chocolate Museum) ① C/Comerç 26, T93 268 78 78, www.museudel xocolata.com, Mon and Wed-Sat 1000-1900, Sun and hols 1000-1500, €3.60, Metro Jaume I, Nus 14, 16, 17, 19, 36, 39, 40, 45, 51, 57, 59, 69, tucked away in the old convent of San Agustín on Carrer Comerç, which describes the histories and legends behind chocolate and – best of all – does tastings.

Parc de la Ciutadella

This is one of Barcelona's most popular parks, a quiet oasis in the heart of the city with a clutch of small museums, shady walkways and fountains, and a cramped zoo (due to move to the new complex in Poble Nou in 2004, see page 276). The park was originally the site of an enormous star-shaped citadel, built after Barcelona fell to the Bourbon armies in 1714. It became the most hated building in the city, and was torn down in 1869. The park was laid out in the late 19th century by a team which included the young Gaudí, and expanded again for the Universal Exhibition of 1888 – Barcelona's first taste of what an international show could do to change the face of a city.

At the centre of the park is the delightful **Museu d'Art Modern** ① T933195728, Metro Arc de Triomf or BarcelonetaTue-Sat 1000-1900, Sun 1000-1430, €3. It's not much of an obvious crowd-pleaser, concentrating almost exclusively on Catalan art from the mid-19th to the early 20th centuries, but this means it is usually enjoyably quiet. Among the earlier paintings are Marià Fortuny's enormous Battle of Tetuan (1863), and the works of Santiago Rusiñol and Ramon Casas (owners of the Els Quatres Gats tavern, see page 261). There's plenty of fabulous Modernista sculpture, but the real treat is the furniture and fittings, which include several fine pieces by Gaudí, and a stunning chapel studded with elaborate stained glass. NB In late 2004 it is moving to the MNAC (see page 272).

The **zoo**ⓘ *Parc de la Ciutadella s/n, T93 225 6780, daily Nov-Feb 1000-1700, Mar and Oct 1000-1800, Apr and Sep 1000-1900, Jun-Aug 0930-1930, €12.90/8.30 for children aged 3-12, metro Ciutadella*, takes up half of the park, but it's still not enough for the poor animals cramped into small concrete enclosures. The highlight for many years for Snowflake (Copito de Nieve), the only albino gorilla in captivity, who died in late 2003. Things will hopefully improve when the zoo moves to roomier quarters in the new complex created in Diagonal Mar for the Universal Forum of Cultures 2004.

Domènech i Montaner's **Castell dels Tres Dragons** sits in one corner of the park, the most daring of the new buildings created for the Universal Exhibition of 1888. It's one of the earliest Modernista edifices, and is now home to the dull and dusty **Museu de Zoologia** ⓘ *Parc de la Ciutadella s/n, T93 19 69 12, www.bcn.es/museuciencies, Tue, Wed, Fri-Sun 1000-1400, Thu 1000-1830, €3 (includes entrance to Museu de Geologia), metro Arc de Triomf and Jaume I. Bus 14, 39, 40, 41, 42, 51, 141.*

Nearby is the **Museu de Geologia** ⓘ *Parc de la Ciutadella s/n, T93 19 69 12, Tue-Sat 1000-1400, until 1800 on Thu, €3 (includes Museu de Zoologia, above). Metro Arc de Triomf and Jaume I, bus 14, 39, 40, 41, 42, 51, 141*, the oldest museum in the city, opened in 1882. It hasn't changed much since, and is only for dedicated fossil fans. Next to the museum is the charming **Hivernacle** (winter greenhouse), a glassy pavilion with a great café (see page 285). In the opposite corner of the park is the extravagant **Cascade**, a flamboyant fountain said to have been designed by Gaudí. It overlooks a small **boating pond**, a popular Sunday picnic spot for Barcelonan families.

Just to the north of the park is the **Passeig de Lluís Companys**, a pedestrian promenade which was designed as a spectacular entrance to the site of the Universal Exhibition (1888) in the Parc de la Ciutadella. The main gateway is the huge red-brick neo-Moorish **Arc de Triomf**, topped with a gracious figure representing Barcelona handing out gifts. Now the Passeig is a temporary home to the Mercat Santa Caterina and a popular spot for skateboarding teenagers.

Sant Pere

The neglected neighbourhood of Sant Pere sits quietly across the Carrer Princessa, a wide road which divided Sant Pere from La Ribera a century ago. These two *barrios* may be neighbours but they have nothing in common: fashionable La Ribera is a world away from humble Sant Pere where life continues much as it has done for decades. Nonetheless, Sant Pere does boast one important monument, the opulent Modernista Palau de la Musica Catalana.

Palau de la Musica Catalana

ⓘ *C/Sant Pere mes Alt s/n, T93 295 72 00, www.palaumusica.org, daily 1000-1530, visits by guided tour only, booking in advance is advisable. Tours depart every 30mins in English, Castilian, and Catalan and last 50mins including a 20-min video, closed Aug, €7, metro Urquinona.*

The Palau was built between 1905 and 1908 as a new home to the Orfeò Català, the first and biggest of the choral societies which sprang up during Catalunya's *Renaixença* (cultural renaissance) a century ago. It was designed by Domenech i Muntaner, who collaborated with many of Catalunya's most celebrated craftsmen and artists. The extraordinary sculpted façade is a hymn to music and Catalanism, and beneath it is a dense forest of floral columns, sprouting multi-coloured flowers of broken tiles. The main auditorium is spell-binding: rainbow-coloured light streams in through the vast stained glass ceiling of flowers and musical angels. Galloping winged horses bearing

❦ *The best way to see the Palau is to come for a concert, but tickets are hard to come by.*

The Palau won the Building of the Year award in 1908, but just two decades later it was being sneeringly referred to as the Palace of Catalan Junk by architects who thought it thoroughly old-fashioned. And whatever the punters thought of the , no one argued about the appalling acoustics. The glass walls may have allowed the sunlight to flood in – but with it came all the street noise. Concerts were regularly punctuated by church bells and warbling ladies catching up on their housework. It barely escaped demolition. After decades on the sidelines, interest in the building was revived: Oscar Tusquets extended and remodelled the building in the 1980s and made a largely unsuccessful attempt to improve the terrible acoustics. He's about to get another chance, as work is underway to add a 600-person choral hall to the building.

El Raval

The Raval area is now one of the hippest neighbourhoods in the city, packed with slick clubs, bars, shops and restaurants, but just a century or so ago it was a miserable slum. The streets nearest the port formed the most notorious red light district on the Mediterranean, filled with whorehouses, seedy bars, and music halls. Nicknamed the Barri Xinès after San Francisco's vice-ridden Chinatown, its heyday was in the 1920s and 1930s. Like New York's Harlem, tourists flooded in to slum it at the bars and cabaret halls until Franco put an end to the party.

> ‡ Despite the improvements, you should watch out for your bags and don't walk the streets alone late at night, especially those nearest the port.

By the 1970s, the arrival of heroin was causing serious problems and the city hall eventually stepped in to begin the latest regeneration project: rotting tenements have been replaced with new apartment blocks, bars and bordellos have been closed down, and a brand new promenade, the Rambla de Raval, slices through its heart. It's still poor, but the construction of the glossy new Museu d'Arte Contemporani has brought in trendy new galleries, fashion shops and arty bars, and, with the arrival of immigrants particularly from north Africa and Pakistan, it's also becoming multicultural, with halal butchers and curry houses rubbing shoulders with old-fashioned haberdasheries and grocers.

The establishment of MACBA and the CCCB, see below, has drawn a glamorous crowd of art galleries, restaurants, bars and clubs – with more springing up almost daily. Many are clustered along **Carrer Carme**, **Carrer Doctor Dou**, and there's another string of great bars along **Carrer Joaquim Costa**. It's also a good place for shopping, with plenty of hip little designer boutiques and a whole street – the **Carrer de la Riera Baixa** – full of vintage fashion and music shops.

Museu d'Art Contemporani de Barcelona (MACBA)

① *Plaça dels Angels. T 93 412 08 10. www.macba.es. 26 Sep-24 Jun Mon, Wed-Fri 1100-1930, Sat 1000-2000, Sun 1000-1500; 25 Jun-25 Sep Mon, Wed-Fri 1100-2000, Sat 1000-2000, Sun 1000-1500. €7 , prices vary for temporary exhibitions. Metro Universitat. Bus 9, 14, 16, 17, 22, 24, 38 41, 55, 58, 59, 66, 91, 141.*

Richard Meiers' huge, glassy new home for MACBA was built in 1995, a symbol of the city's dedication to urban renewal and a monument to its preoccupation with contemporary design. It overlooks a wide, modern square, which has become a huge favourite with skateboarders.

Although the museum's permanent collection officially begins after the Civil War, there are some earlier pieces by Alexander Calder, Paul Klee and Catalan artists like Leandre Cristòfol, Joan Ponç and Àngel Ferrant. The collection is loosely

structured around four periods; the first, which roughly covers the 1940s to the 1960s, is represented by artists like Antoni Tàpies, Joan Brossa, and Antoni Saura. These artists were members of the *Dau al Set* ('seven spot die' in Catalan) group, a loose collection of writers and artists who were influenced by the surrealists, and particularly by Joan Miró, and whose works marked an end to the torpor which had settled on the cultural life of Spain after Franco's victory in the Civil War. Popular and consumer culture had more of an impact on the art of the 1960s and 1970s: there are several fun, kitsch pieces from Carlos Pazos, including the mocking *Voy a hacer de mí una estrella* (I'm going to make myself a star, 1975), a series of pouting, celebrity-style photographs. The 1980s and early 90s are marked by a return to painting and its forms of expression; among Catalan artists, Miquel Barceló's paintings and Susana Solano's stark metal sculptures reflect this return to traditional forms. There are also several excellent photographic pieces from this period, including works by Anselm Keifer, Jeff Wall, and Suzanne Lafont. Many of the usually excellent temporary exhibitions focus on the latest digital and multi-media works. MACBA has a great bookshop and an attractive café-bar which shares a square with the CCCB (see below) around the corner.

Centre de Cultura Contemporània de Barcelona (CCCB)

ⓘ *Metro Universitat, 9 Sep-May Tue, Thu-Fri 1100-1400 and 1600-2000, Wed and Sat 1100-2000, Sun and holidays 1100-1900, Jun-8 Sep Tue-Sun 1000-2000, €5.50/4.* The excellent Contemporary Culture Centre (CCCB) sits behind MACBA and is the second prong of the city's institution for contemporary culture. It's set in the former Casa de la Caritat, a hospice for pilgrims established in the 16th century which has undergone dramatic remodelling. The CCCB hosts wide-ranging and eclectic exhibitions on all aspects of contemporary culture not covered by MACBA, as well as running several community-based projects and dozens of other activities, including the Sonar music festival and an alternative film festival (see Festivals, page 294).

Antic Hospital de Santa Creu

ⓘ *La Capella Tue-Sat 1200-1400 and 1600-2000, Sun 1100-1400.* An anachronistic leftover in the heart of this fashionable neighbourhood is the Antic Hospital de Santa Creu (on Carrer de Hospital), a hulking stone complex built in 1402 which comprised an orphanage, leper hospital and wards for the city's sick and dying. These vaulted Gothic wards now contain the National Library of Catalunya (entrance only to members but you can try begging for a peek), as the hospital was moved in 1926 to Domenech i Muntaner's Modernista pavilions. One of its last patients before the move was Gaudí, brought here after he fell under the wheels of a tram in 1926; he was so shabby – even his shoes were kept on his feet with elastic bands – that everyone took him for a tramp. The former chapel holds regular workshops, commissions pieces from local artists, and holds excellent shows of contemporary works from up-and-coming Barcelonan artists.

Palau Güell and around

ⓘ *C/Nou de la Rambla 3, T93 317 3974, open for guided tours only Mon-Sat 1000-1330 and 1600-1830, tours fill up quickly – book in advance in summer €2.50, Metro Liceu, bus 14, 38, 51, 59.* Palau Güell on Carrer Nou de la Rambla was Gaudí's first major commission for the man who was to become his most important patron, Eusebi Güell. Both men were intensely Catalanist and intensely religious, and these themes are replayed throughout the tall, narrow mansion. The small visiting room off the long glass vestibule (which Güell's horrified wife thought looked like a barber's shop) boasts a spectacularly ornate carved ceiling in which tiny spyholes were carved so that the Güells could overhear their guests' private conversations. The main salon

is overwhelming, a lofty hall topped with an arched cosmic dome covered with deep blue honeycombed tiles; thin shafts of light entering through tiny windows symbolise the stars circling the moon. This is the heart of the house, with all the rooms organised around the central hall in the Mediterranean fashion, and surrounded by a series of galleries and miradors. Behind the salon is the family's dining room and private sitting room, with stained glass windows featuring historical Catalan heroes, and there's a small terrace which allows you to see the lovely tribunal which juts out at the back. Despite the sumptuousness, this was never a comfortable palace and the Güells always preferred their main residence in Pedralbes (see page 278): the dim lighting, the heavy religious solemnity and the weight of historical references combine to make it a sombre, gloomy experience (Antonioni used it as the setting for his unsettling thriller *The Passenger* in 1977). But the rooftop is its antithesis: a rippling terrace with a playful forest of swirling, trencadi-covered chimneys, surrounding a lofty central spire topped with a wrought iron bat, a legendary guardian of Catalan heroes.

Raval de la Rambla and around

In 2000, a great swathe of rundown tenement houses in the heart of the Raval were torn down and replaced with a new promenade, the palm-studded Raval de la Rambla. Still too new and shiny to have much atmosphere, it does have a sprinkling of cafés, and occasionally hosts outdoor concerts in summer. Just off the Rambla, the Carrer de Sant Pau runs down to the tiny, delightful church of **Sant Pau del Camp**, ① *C/Sant Pau s/n. Metro Paral.lel, Wed-Mon 1120-1300 and 1800-1930, Tue 1130-1230, free,* the most important surviving Romanesque church in the city. The tranquil cloister has Moorish-inspired arches and simple columns carved with a menagerie of mythical creatures.

Drassanes Reials

Almost at the harbour, in the southernmost tip of the Raval, are the magnificent Drassanes Reials, the vast medieval shipyards built at the height of the Catalan empire. Begun in 1243, the shipyards form the largest and most important civil Gothic structure in the world, and were eventually capable of accommodating 40 galley ships. Now they contain the excellent and entertaining **Museu Marítim** (Maritime Museum) ① *Av Drassanes s/n, T933429920, www.diba.es/maritim, Metro Drassanes, 1000-1900 €5.40,* and the star exhibit is a monstrous galley ship, a replica of the Royal Galley of John of Austria which was built to lead the Holy Alliance against the Turks in the Battle of Lepant in 1571. There's also a fine series of ship figureheads, and an absorbing collection of beautifully illuminated medieval maps. There's more to come in the interactive 'Great Adventure of the Sea', a favourite with kids; get caught in a storm in Havana, wander through a huge ocean liner, or investigate one of the world's first submarines, the *Ictíneo*, invented by Narcís Monturiol in 1859. Down in the Port Vell, the museum has recently renovated a beautiful turn-of-the-century sailing ship, the *Santa Eulàlia*, which is also part of the visit.

Barrio Xinès

The dark, narrow web of streets in this southern section of the Raval are still the poorest (and most intimidating at night), but it's also here that a glimmer of the old Barrio Xinès can still be found in a handful of old-fashioned bars – like the **Kentucky**, the **London** and **Bar Marsella**, see page 289, which haven't changed in decades. A small square is named after Jean Genet, whose novel *Journal de Voleur* (Thief's Journal) viscerally describes how he scraped a living as a rent boy and thief in these streets in the 1920s and 1930s.

Eixample

The Eixample (pronounced *Ai-sham-play*) is Barcelona's most upmarket neighbourhood, with its finest restaurants and designer boutiques, and one of the greatest concentration of Modernista monuments in Europe. Ironically, this elegant and ultra bourgeois district was created by a utopian socialist, Ildefons Cerdà, who won the commission to create a new extension (which is what 'Eixample' in Catalan) in the 19th century. Cerdà envisioned a modular city of regular blocks formed around airy central gardens in which workers and the bourgeoisie would live harmoniously side by side, but his original design was rapidly undermined by greedy speculators who filled up all the communal spaces with more houses. The poor couldn't afford to move anyway, but the rich rushed out to the new district, commissioning the greatest Modernista architects – Gaudí, Domènech i Montaner, Puig i Cadafalch and others – to create trophy mansions which would dazzle their neighbours.

Passeig de Gràcia

Passeig de Gràcia is the heart of the Eixample, a glossy boulevard of chic boutiques lined with plane trees and twirling wrought-iron lampposts. It's overlooked by an eclectic mix of spiky neo-Gothic castles, pompous neoclassic insurance offices, and fairy-tale Modernista mansions thickly encrusted with stucco flowers.

The most famous stretch of the Passeig de Gràcia is the block between Carrer Consell de Cent and Carrer d'Aragó, where flamboyant mansions designed by the three most famous Modernista architects – Gaudí, Domènech i Montaner, Puig i Cadafalch – are nudged up against each other. It's known as the **Mansana de la Discòrdia** (Block of Discord), the 'discord' arising from their dramatically different styles. The architects were independently invited by three of the city's most influential families to entirely remodel existing buildings. The first, at the corner of Carrer Consell de Cent, is the **Casa Lleo i Morera**, which was built in 1864, and transformed by Domènech i Montaner in 1902. Sadly, much of the beautiful façade was destroyed by the luxury leather goods shop, Loewe, who ripped out the original ground floor windows and stripped it of much of the original sculptural decoration. The surviving nymphs bearing symbols of the new age – electric light, photography, the telephone and the phonograph – flit across the façade, thickly clustered with garlands of flowers oozing like piped icing.

Casa Amatller, three doors up at No 41, was the first of the three major remodellings. Antoni Amatller's fortune was built on chocolate and Puig i Cadafalch built him a fairytale castle, with a stepped gable covered with shimmering polychrome ceramics which almost look good enough to eat. The Casa Amatller functions as the Centre del Modernisme where you can get information on the Ruta del Modernisme (see page 249), and which offers free guided tours of the three façades of the Mansana de la Discòrdia (the Casa Batllò was opened to visitors as part of the special activities which marked Gaudí Year 2002 but usually the interiors of all three mansions are closed to visitors).

Next door to the Casa Amatller is the fantastical **Casa Batlló** (1904-1906), unmistakably the work of Antoní Gaudí: covered with shimmering, multi-coloured trencadis (broken tiles) and culminating in an undulating scaly roof, it gleams like an underwater sea dragon. All kinds of theories about the symbolism of the façade have been thrown up, but the story of St George and the dragon seems to fit most neatly. The rippling waves of tiny ceramic tiles and the bone-white pillars which support the balconies evoke the curling dragon, his scaly back formed by the swaying roof ridge, and St George is represented by the bulbous cross erupting from a thick column, or lance, spearing the dragon from on high. The spiky, trencadi-covered, chimney is the final flick of the dragon's tail. The fibia-like columns of the lower façade gave the building its popular nickname 'the house of the bones'.

66 99 Eixample was Gaudí's playground, and his delirious imprint is everywhere, from the creamy La Pedrera apartment building to the looming, still unfinished spires of the Sagrada Família.

One of Gaudí's most famous buildings is a little further up the Passeig de Gracia, the **Casa Milà** ① *C/Provença 261-265, T 902 400 973, www.caixacatalunya.es, daily 1000-2000, last admission 1930. €7, free admission to temporary exhibitions. Metro Diagonal. Bus 7, 16, 17, 22, 24, 28*. Better known as **La Pedrera** ('the stone quarry'), the building rises like a creamy cliff draped with sinuous wrought iron balconies. The first occupants of the apartment building moved in around 1911, and there's a recreation of an apartment from the era on the top floor. There isn't a straight line anywhere, with the walls, ceilings, doorways and windows flowing around the interior patios. Many of the fittings in the apartment are original, including the elegant bedroom suite with its pretty polychrome floral motif which was designed by the celebrated craftsman Gaspar Homar (whose work is also in the Museu d'Art Modern, see page 263). The attic now houses L'Espai Gaudí, a slick museum providing a systematic overview of the architect's life and works in the city with models, photos, drawings, and video installations. A spiral staircase leads up to the climax of the visit, the sinuous rooftop terrace which curls around the patios like a dreamscape studded with fantastical bulbous crosses, and plump *trencadi*-covered towers, Gaudí's magical response to the building's prosaic need for chimneys, air vents and stairwells. On summer weekends, you can enjoy live music on the rooftop (see page 290).

Museums around Passeig de Gràcia

Just off the Passeig de Gràcia in Carrer Valencia is the **Museu Egipci de Barcelona** ① *C/València 284, T934480188, www.fundclos.com, Mon-Sat 1000-2000, Sun 1000-1400, €5.50, Metro Passeig de Gràcia, Bus 7, 16, 17, 20, 22, 24, 28, 45, 47*, with an excellent selection of artefacts spanning more than three millennia. Among the most interesting exhibits are the sarcophagi; the earliest are made of terracotta moulded vaguely into the form of the body within, but they grow steadily more elaborate. Burial scenes are dramatically recreated, with cult chapels, mummies – including x-rays of mummified animals – and tombs. There is also a rich collection of ceramics, some dating back to 3,500BC, and jewellery – gold and silver, glittering with lapis lazuli and cornelian for the rich, painted glass paste for the poor – revealing the astonishing level of craftsmanship that the early Egyptians attained.

Another of the city's fine, privately owned museums is on the first floor of the building next door, the **Fundació Francisco Godia** ① *C/València 284, T932723180, www.fundacionfgodia.org, Mon, Wed-Sun 1000-2000, €4.20, metro Passeig de Gràcia, bus 7, 16, 17, 20, 22, 24, 28, 45, 47*. Francisco Godia (1921-1990) was an odd combination: a successful racing driver for more than three decades, he also found time to acquire a dazzling collection of painting, medieval sculpture and ceramics. There's a mesmerising gathering of polychrome, gilded statues from the 12th century onwards, and among the ceramics are lustrous 15th-century pieces from Manises. Godia also collected turn-of-the-century art, including Ramon Casas' *At the racecourse* (circa 1905) and Isidre Nonell's haunting study, *Gypsy Woman* (1905). Godia's daughters are expanding the collection by adding works from the later 20th century and some contemporary art.

⦂ Never-ending story

The Sagrada Família had a gloomy start. It was commissioned by a reactionary organization known as the Josephines, who wanted an expiatory temple where the faithful could go to beg forgiveness for the depravity of the modern age. The first architect quit after a year and Gaudí, aged just 31, was given the job in 1883.

The project became an obsession and after 1914 he devoted himself solely to its construction, spending the last two years of his life living ascetically in a shack on the building site. In June 1926, he was crushed under a tram and died two days later. Some 10,000 mourners followed his coffin to its burial place in the crypt of the Sagrada Família but even so, by this time, Gaudí, his architecture and his ultra-conservative brand of Catholicism were thoroughly out of fashion. Work limped on for a few years but came to an abrupt halt with the start of the Civil War, when anarchists attacked the crypt destroying every plan, model and sketch that they could find in an attempt to ensure that it would never be completed. The temple languished for decades until finally, in 1952, a group of architects decided to continue the work by raising money through public subscription.

Japanese corporations are currently the highest contributors; Gaudí-mania was big in Japan long before it really took off Europe.

In the absence of detailed plans and records, the architects are being forced to conjecture what Gaudí might have envisioned and it this which has caused such controversy: purists argue that it is simply impossible to guess Gaudí's intentions as he was infamous for his lack of reliance on plans and his buildings changed shape even as they were being constructed.

The current team is directed by Jordí Bonet, the son of one of the temple's original architects, and the sculptor Josep Subirachs. The Passion façade on the Carrer de Sardenya is now complete, but has aroused equal amounts of scorn and praise for the distinctly un-Gaudíesque sculptures which adorn it. Gaudí, in the meantime, looks set to become a saint. The Vatican announced that it would consider the case for his beatification in 2000 and the Association for the Beatification of Antoní Gaudí, founded in 1992 by architects, admirers, and artists, are getting down to the business of finding out the particulars of his miracles.

On the other side of the Passeig de Gràcia, down Carrer d'Aragó, you can't miss the extraordinary red-brick building topped with what looks like a huge cloud of barbed wire, a vast sculpture entitled Nuvol i Cadira (*Cloud and Chair*) by Antoni Tàpies, probably Spain's best-known living artist. The building, known as the Editorial Montaner i Simon, was built in 1880 by Domènech i Montaner for the family publishing house and is one of the earliest Modernista monuments. It now houses the **Fundació Antoni Tàpies** ① *C/Aragó 255, T934870315, www.fundaciotapies.org, Metro Passeig de Gràcia, Tue-Sun 1000-2000, €4.20*, which holds one of the largest collections of Tàpies' works in the world. There are interesting temporary exhibitions by contemporary artists, often featuring video and installation work, and at least one floor usually shows a selection of works by Tàpies himself. In 1948, he became part of the Dau al Set ('seven-spot die' in Catalan) group, a gathering of writers and artists whose works were the first sign of cultural revival in Spain after the grim 'hunger years' which succeeded Franco's victory. He is most celebrated for his 'material

innovative techniques and media, particularly the use of found objects.

Sagrada Família

① *C/Mallorca 401, T932080414, daily Oct-Mar 0900-1800, Apr-Sept 0900-2000, €8, www.sagradafamilia.org, Metro Sagrada Familia, Bus 19, 33, 34, 43, 44, 50, 51.*

Gaudí's unfinished masterpiece, the Templo Expiatorio de la Sagrada Família (Expiatory Temple of the Sagrada Família), is undoubtedly the most emblematic and most controversial monument in Barcelona: Evelyn Waugh found it so depressing he refused to leave his cab to visit it, but Jean Cocteau, like most people, couldn't get his head around it: 'It's not a skyscraper, it's a mindscraper'. Love it or hate it, it's impossible to ignore: the completed towers stand at almost 100 m, and the central spire, when finished, will soar 180 m into the sky. Gaudí designed three façades: Nativity and Passion on either side of the nave and Glory as the magnificent main entrance. Only one façade was completed by the time of his death in 1926: the craggy Nativity

> ⁑ *As the biggest tourist attraction in Catalunya, the constant bustle of crowds and tour buses inhibit any sense of religious awe as you jostle through the iron gates.*

Façade surmounted with a green cypress tree flecked with white doves of peace. Many of the thickly clustered statues were made from life casts – including, apparently, the donkey. Inside, you'll find a building site where work has begun on the construction of four huge columns which will eventually support the enormous domed roof. The Passion façade flanks the other side of the church: the antithesis of the joyful Nativity façade, this is supposed to represent death and sacrifice, but Josep Subirachs' grim, lifeless sculptures are entirely devoid of any emotion or vitality, veering in a mechanical sequence from the Last Supper at the bottom left, to Christ's burial in the top right. The temple is supposedly set for completion in 2026, the anniversary of Gaudí's death, but this seems increasingly unlikely in view of the technical problems surrounding the construction of the vast central tower which still need to be resolved.

There's a lift (with long queues) up the towers and the very brave can climb even higher into the blobby spires for an uncanny sensation of stepping out into space, and descend by the tight spirals of the vertiginous staircase. Underneath, the Crypt contains Gaudí's tomb and a newly expanded interactive museum devoted to the history of the temple, with drawings, models, and photographs.

Hospital de la Sant Creu i Sant Pau

The pedestrian Avinguda Gaudí sweeps up to the other enormous Modernista project of this neighbourhood, the Hospital de la Sant Creu i Sant Pau (1926-30), a fairytale assembly of delightful ceramic-covered pavilions ingeniously linked by underground passages and encrusted with mosaics. It's still a working hospital, but visitors are invited to wander freely around the grounds and admire the magical turrets and spires – it's particularly lovely, if ghostly, at dusk. Sadly, the squat pre-fab additions to the gardens are a sign of the lack of space which is forcing the hospital to consider new premises once again.

Montjüic

The ancient promontory of Montjüic rises up above the sea to the west of the city. A green, park-filled oasis, it's undergone a series of dramatic face lifts in the last century or so: palaces, museums and gardens were constructed for Barcelona's International Exhibition of 1929, and the upper reaches were entirely revamped to create the Olympic Ring, a string of dazzling sports complexes used during the 1992 Olympics. The next phase of improvements, including a lake and more parklands on the hill's scrubby southern side, is set to be completed this year for the Universal Forum of

Cultures (see page 277). Despite all the development, in some ways nothing much has changed: it's still a popular weekend destination for locals, who come to wander through the parks and gaze down across the city from the hilltop castle.

Plaça d'Espanya to the Museu Nacional d'Arte de Catalunya

The circular **Plaça d'Espanya**, now a big, busy thoroughfare surrounded by whizzing traffic, was built for the International Exhibition of 1929. The Avinguda Maria Cristina, flanked by a pair of grim towers, leads to the **Font Màgica**① *Metro Espanya. Bus Nos 9, 13, 30, 50, 55, 23 Jun-3 Sep fountain 2000-400, music shows Thu-Sun and holidays 2130-2330*, a completely over-the-top fountain which is best appreciated during the fabulously kitsch sound and light shows in which jets of fruity-coloured water leap and dance to music.

Close by is the sleek **Pavelló Mies Van der Rohe** ① *www.miesbcn.com, Metro Espanya, Nov-Mar 1000-1830, Apr-Oct 1000-2000, €3*, a cool, glassy reconstruction of Ludwig Mies Van der Rohe's monument to rationalist architecture which was built for use as the German pavilion during the 1929 International Exhibition. Largely misunderstood at the time, it was dismantled at the close of the exhibition, but rebuilt on the same site in 1986 and is now home to the Mies Van der Rohe foundation, which hosts conferences and exhibitions.

Just across from the Mies Van der Rohe pavilion is one of Barcelona's newest museums, the **ForumCaixa** ① *Av Marquès de Comillas 6-8, T934768600. www.funcadion.lacaixa.es, Tue-Sun 1000-2000, free, metro Espanya, bus 9, 13, 30, 50, 55*, a Modernista textile mill which has been slickly redesigned to house an excellent permanent collection of contemporary art and exhibition halls. Pick up a brochure for details of seasonal events, which hosts include concerts, dance performances and other cultural events.

The dour Palau Nacional which looms from the hilltop houses the **Museu Nacional d'Art de Catalunya** ① *Palau Nacional, T93 622 03 60, www.mnac.es, Tue-Sat 1000-1900, Sun and hols 1000-1430, €4.80, temporary exhibitions €4.20, combined entry €6, metro Espanya, bus 9, 13, 30, 50, 55*. Devoted to Romanesque and Gothic art, there's an utterly spell-binding array of Romanesque murals gathered from the tiny churches of the Catalan hinterlands, hauntingly lit and displayed on reconstructed church interiors. The stars of the exhibition are the murals from the Boí Valley, which was designated a World Heritage Site in 2000 for the richness of its Romanesque heritage. Some of the most important come from the Church of Sant Climent in Taüll, which features a huge resplendent Pantocrater with a serene, hypnotic gaze. The paintings from the parish Church of Santa Maria (also in Taüll) are the most complete set in the museum, a blazing, richly coloured series which reaches its apotheosis in the splendid depiction of Mary as the Seat of Wisdom in the apse. The Gothic collection is less magical than the Romanesque, but equally magnificent. The 13th to the 15th centuries were Catalunya's glory years, when her ships ruled the seas and the arts flourished. Rooms 11 and 12 are devoted to one of the most brilliant periods in Catalan art and the three outstanding painters of the time: Bernat Martorell, Lluís Dalmau and Jaume Huguet. Tacked on at the end is a small collection of works from the 15th to the 18th centuries, including a couple of striking pieces from Zurbaran, a fleshy Allegory of Love by Goya, and a swirling portrait of John the Baptist and St Francis of Assisi in the desert by El Greco. By 2004 (when the Universal Forum of Cultures will be held), the holdings of the Museu d'Art Modern, currently in the Parc de la Ciutadella (see page 263) are set to join the rest of MNAC's collection in newly refurbished galleries, allowing visitors to see the best of Catalan art in one setting.

Poble Espanyol

① *Avda Marquès de Comillas s/n, T935086300. Sep-Jun Mon 0900-2000, Tue-Sat 0900-0200, Sun 0900-2400; Jul-Aug Mon 0900-2000, Tue-Thu 0900-0200, Fri-Sat*

0900-0400, Sun 0900-2400. €7/3.90 . Guided visits in Catalan, Castillian, English
and French every hour, €2. metro Espanya, bus 9, 13, 30, 50, 55. (Take a bus up the hill
if you don't want to face a long walk from the metro.).

After all the high art at MNAC, there's the pure kitsch of the Poble Espanyol (on Avda Marqués de Comillas) to look forward to. The 'Spanish Village' was also built for the 1929 Exhibition, a gloriously tacky collection of traditional architectural styles from around the country. The entrance way is marked by a couple of fake medieval-style copies of the towers in the Castilian town of Avila, which were turned into the most over-the-top designer bar in Barcelona by Alfredo Arribas and Javier Mariscal in the 1980s. Inside, there's an arcaded Plaça Mayor, a pretty little Barrio Andaluz, a Catalan village, and streets copied from villages all over Spain, from Extremadura to the Basque lands, all lined with scores of souvenir and craft shops, cafés, galleries and restaurants.

Anella Olímpica (Olympic Ring)

ⓘ *Museum, Passeig Olimpic s/n, T934269200, www.fundaciobarcelonaolimpica.es, entrance by prior booking, Mon-Fri 1000-1300 and 1600-1800, €2.50, Metro Espanya, then bus 61.*

The new stadia and other buildings erected for the 1992 Olympics are strung along the Avingud de l'Estadi, half-way up the hill. The main stadium (estadi) was originally built in 1929 (the Catalans beat Bolton Wanderers in the inaugural football match), but only the external structure of the stadium was retained during the radical alterations necessitated by the 1992 Olympics. The stadium contains the Galeria Olímpica, a museum devoted to the Games, where you can relive the highlights through videos, photos and displays.

Fundació Miró

ⓘ *Parc de Montjüic s/n, T934439470, www.bcn.fjmiro.es, Oct-Jun Tue-Wed and Fri-Sat 1000-1900, Thu 1000-2130, Sun and holidays 1000-1430, Jul-Sep Tue-Wed and Fri-Sat 1000-2000, Thu 1000-2130, Sun and holidays 1000-1430, €7.20, temporary exhibitions €3.20.*

Further down the Avinguda de l'Estadi is the fabulous Fundació Miró, set in a white, light-drenched building designed by Josep Lluís Sert. The Foundation was established in 1971 and contains the most important and comprehensive gathering of Miró's works in the world. The opening rooms hold some of Miró's huge tapestries, including one created specially for the Foundation (Tapestry of the Foundation, 1979), with a huge figure of a woman dancing ecstatically beneath a star and moon.

During the war years, a growing colony of exiled artists brought new stimuli to local painters, including Miró, who began to experiment; *Carrer de Pedralbes* (1917), a skewed, glowing street, shows him dabbling with Cubism, and *Chapel of Sant Joan d'Horta* (1917), with its rich colouring and broad brushstrokes, is Fauvist in inspiration. Increasingly, objects float weightlessly in space – as in *The White Glove* (1925) and *The Music-hall Usher* (1925) – as Miró stripped away the unnecessary in pursuit of the essence.

He never forgot his earthy Catalanism; *Man and Woman in front of a pile of excrement* (1935), has two figures, enormous feet planted firmly on Catalan soil, gesturing lewdly with their bulging genitalia in front of a turd raised up as though looking on with interest. He was completely fascinated by hair, which sprouts on snakes, in stars, on genitalia throughout his works. In 1937, war broke out in Spain and Miró was devast-ated. He took his family to Normandy, where his work began to reflect his 'profound desire to escape...night, music and the stars began to play an increasing role'. The poetic series of *Constellations*, of which the Foundation holds one, *Morning Star* (1940) date from this period. Delicate lines trace between the floating symbols, suggesting an interconnectedness between the earth and the sky, flooded with wheeling stars.

The constant themes of the post-war years were woman, birds and stars – as in *Woman dreaming of escape* (1945), and *Woman and birds at daybreak* (1946). His sign language was being constantly refined and stripped and his paintings became increasingly gestural and impulsive – like the *Woman in a pretty hat* (1960), in which there are just two isolated spots of colour, and the *Figure in front of the sun* (1968). This Zen-like urge to strip things to their essence is beautifully illustrated in the series of paintings he made after a visit to Japan, including the spare, luminous *The Day* (1974). There are some spectacular sculptures from this later period, including the soaring white *Solarbird* (1968), blazing against a brilliant blue background, and more in a sculpture terrace on the roof.

Castell de Montjüic

ⓘ *T933298613, Nov to mid-Mar 0930-1630, mid-Mar to Oct 0930-1930, €2.50 for admission to castle and museum, €1 for admission to the castle only.*

Just beyond the Fundació Miró is the funicular station which trundles down to the Paral.lel, and which is also the starting point for the cable car ride up to the castle at the top of Montjüic. At the brow of the hill, is the Castell de Montjüic, formerly a prison and torture centre, which is now the city's dull **Museu Militar** with a collection of weaponry and lead soldiers and a new gallery devoted to Catalan art. The castle ramparts (separate admission) is worth a visit for the stunning views.

Other musems and the Ciutat del Teatre

At the bottom of Montjüic is a cluster of less visited museums in a crop of fanciful pavilions left over from the 1929 Exhibition. The best is the **Museu d'Arqueologia de Catalunya** ⓘ *Passeig Santa Madrona 39-41, www.mac.es, Metro Espanya, Bus No 55, Tue-Sat 0930-1900, Sun and holidays 1000-1430, €2.50*, which opens with copies of early cave paintings, dramatic hunting and battle scenes, discovered in the Pyrenenean regions. There's a whole gallery devoted to the findings from the Greek colony of Empuriés on the Costa Brava, an extensive collection of Roman artefacts, and a reconstruction of a magnificent palace room in Pompeii.

Just across the road is another revamped pavilion from the 1929 Exhibition. The former Palau de l'Agricultura is the new home of the prestigious **Teatre Lliure**, and forms part of the new **Ciutat del Teatre** (Theatre City). Behind it is the **Mercat de las Flors**, a former flower market now transformed into a performance space (see page 293). These buildings look inward on to the pretty Plaça Margarida Xirgù, now dominated by the spanking new, glassy building for the **Institut del Teatre and the museum of Performing Arts** ⓘ *T932273900, www.diba.es/iteatre, Metro Espanya, Tue-Sat 1000-1300 and 1700-1930, Sun and holidays 1000-1400*. It now hosts excellent temporary exhibitions.

Close by is the **Museu Etnològic** ⓘ *Passeig Santa Madrona s/n, T934246807, www.museuetnologic.bcn.es, Metro Espanya, Tue and Thu 1000-1900, Wed, Fri-Sun, holidays 1000-1400, €3*, with extensive holdings from Africa, Oceania, Asia, South America and Spain. They are shown on a rotating basis – there is simply too much to show at one time – but the short, temporary exhibitions are usually the most interesting. Below the museum, steps lead down to the **Teatre Grec**, an amphitheatre inspired by a model of Epidaurus and built over an old quarry for the 1929 Exhibition. It's the main venue for the Grec Festival, the city's main performing arts festival, which is held in June and July (see page 294).

Gràcia and Parc Güell

Gràcia was an independent town until 1897 when it was dragged, under protest, into the burgeoning city of Barcelona. The 'Liberation for Gràcia' movement hasn't quite died out, with the occasional T-shirt and graffited scrawl demanding freedom from

identity. In the 19th century, Gràcia was a hotbed of radicalism, but now it has largely settled down to its role as a mildly bohemian, traditional neighbourhood of narrow streets and charming squares far from the flashiness and pace of the Diagonal which divides it from the Eixample. Gràcia's unique identity is best expressed in the Festa Major (held in August) which turns the streets into a riot of streamers, stars and balloons, as everyone vies for the prize of best-decorated street. On the edge of Gràcia is Gaudí's magical Park Güell, a dreamy wonderland which looks over the whole city and out to sea.

Squares, markets and Modernista mansions

The centre of Gràcia has no really big sights or monuments; its distinctive charm is best appreciated with a stroll, especially in the evening, when the names of streets and squares – the **Mercat de la Libertat**, the **Plaça de la Revolució** – evoke its fiercely liberal past. **Plaça de Sol** is the hub of the area's nightlife, with dozens of bars and cafés. A couple of blocks away is the **Plaça de la Virreina**, a quiet attractive square lined with a row of simple cottages and a pretty church. The oldest section of Gràcia is squeezed between the broad avenues of the Carrer Gran de Gràcia and the Via Augusta; at the heart of the district stands the neighbourhood's oldest market, the pretty Modernista **Mercat de Libertat**. Two streets to the north is the delightful **Rambla de Prat**, with a cluster of Modernista buildings showing off their swirling façades. Dedicated Gaudí fans should make a pilgrimage to the Carrer de Carolines, the site of Gaudí's first major architectural project in Barcelona, the neo-Mudéjar **Casa Vicens** (1883-1888), designed for the ceramics manufacturer Manuel Vicens, whose business was advertised by the eye-popping proliferation of sea-green and white tiles.

Parc Güell

① *C/Olot 7, T934132400, Nov-Feb 1000-1800, Mar and Oct 1000-1900, Apr and Sep 1000-2000, May to Aug 1000-2100, free, Metro Lesseps, then a 10-min walk, or bus 24 to the gate; Casa Museu Gaudí Oct-Mar 1000-1800, Apr-Sep 1000-1900, €3.*

The whimsical turrets, fabulous *trencadi*-covered creatures, floating balconies and sloping parklands of the Parc Güell are perhaps the most delightful and varied of Gaudí's visionary creations. It wasn't originally designed as a park: it was meant to be an aristocratic housing estate. Gaudí's benefactor and friend, Eusebi Güell, had visions of an exclusive garden city, modelled on the English fashion (which is why the Park is spelt with an English 'k' and not a Catalan 'c'), but it never took off and the empty grounds passed to the city for use as a public park in 1922.

Two fairy-tale **pavilions**, with their swirling roofs and shimmering coats of multi-coloured *trencadis* guard the entrance to the park, from which sweeps up the multi-coloured **dragon** which has become one of Barcelona's most well-known and best-loved symbols. (So beloved, in fact, that your chances of pushing past the coach parties of Japanese tourists and school kids getting their picture taken are pretty slim.)

The steps culminate in the **Sala Hipóstila,** also known as the Hall of a Hundred Columns for the forest of thick, Doric columns which support its undulating roof. Gaudí's talented collaborator, the architect and mosaicist Josep Maria Jujol, was given free reign to colour the vaulted ceiling with elaborate whimsy; look carefully and you'll see the designs are made of smashed china, ceramic dolls heads, wine glasses, and old bottles.

More steps lead up from the Hall to the **main square** which offers beautiful views of the city below. The endless bench which snakes around the square is thickly encrusted with *trencadis*, which shimmer and change colour in the sunlight like the scales of a monstrous dragon. This, too, is the product of Gaudí's collaboration with Jujol, a dazzling collage of bizarre symbols, fragments of text, stars, butterflies, moons and flowers which presaged Cubism and Surrealism.

Surrounding the square are **porticoes and viaducts**, which hug the slopes and stretch for more than 3 km. The arches and columns are made from unworked stone quarried *in situ*, which seem to erupt organically, swooping overhead like cresting waves.

Just off the main esplanade is the modest, pink Torre Rosa, Gaudí's home for the last twenty years of his life. It's now the **Casa Museu Gaudí,** a delightful little cottage covered in creamy swirls and topped with a *trencadí*-covered spire surmounted with a cross. Inside, the modest rooms are filled with plans and drawings, examples of Gaudí's furniture designs for the grand mansions of the Eixample, and a sparse collection of his few personal possessions. His bedroom, which has been conserved much as he left it, contains a narrow bed, a copy of his prayer book and his death mask.

Port Vell, Barceloneta and Vila Olímpica

The seafront in Barcelona was the main focus for the frenzy of construction and redevelopment which heralded the 1992 Olympic Games. The brash, glistening development of the Port Olímpic was erected in all its towering, neon-lit splendour, and the old port was utterly transformed: now, yachts and gin palaces bob in the harbour, and smart restaurants have spread their awnings on to broad boulevards. Behind all the tourist gimmicks and laminated menus of the Port Vell sprawls the old fishermen's neighbourhood of Barceloneta, a shabby, old-fashioned district of narrow streets and traditional bars serving fresh seafood tapas. Beyond Barceloneta stretch the city's six beaches, not especially lovely, but buzzy and always packed in summer. They edge past the glitzy new Port Olímpic and culminate at the seafront of another quiet old worker's district, Poble Nou, which has been totally revamped to host the city's Universal Forum of Cultures in 2004, Barcelona's next excuse to dress itself up and show off.

Port Vell

Port Vell ('old port'), once a grimy working port, was transformed beyond recognition for the 1992 Olympics. The port's activity was shunted down the coast to an industrial zone, and the docks and warehouses were demolished or restored to house elegant restaurants, shops, a marina, and a string of glittering new tourist attractions. Designed with tourists in mind, it's pretty rare to find any Barcelonans here.

Now the crowds sweep down from the Rambla and across the undulating **Rambla de Mar,** a floating wooden walkway which leads to the Maremagnum shopping centre, the IMAX cinema, and the aquarium. The glassy **Maremagnum** building is stuffed full of shops, bars and restaurants, many with terraces overlooking the yacht-filled harbour, as well as a couple of popular (touristy) clubs. **IMAX** ① *Moll d'Espanya-Port Vell, T902400222, 1200-0030, consult film listings (cartelera) in listings magazines for shows and times, €7 for a single session,€10 for a double session, Metro Barceloneta, Bus 14, 17, 19, 36, 39, 40, 45, 57, 59, 64 and 157*, offers everything from dinosaurs to dolphins in 3D and surround sound. (but in Catalan and Castilian only) Next door at **L'Aquàrium** ① *T932217474, Jul and Aug 0930-2300, Jun and Sep 0930-2130, Oct-May Mon-Fri 0930-2100 Sat-Sun 0930-2130, €11/7.70 for children*, you can see the real thing (well, dolphins anyway). This is the largest aquarium in Europe, with dozens of exhibits and special interactive centres for kids, but the highlight is still the enormous central tank, which you can coast through gently on a conveyor belt to a schmaltzy sound-track as sharks and glinting shoals of silvery fish wheel overhead.

The old dockside access road is now the **Passeig Joan de Borbó,** an elegant promenade overlooking the marina. A former warehouse complex has been carefully renovated to become the Palau del Mar, which houses a string of elegant restaurants

as well as the engaging **Museu d'Història de Catalunya** ⓘ *Plaça Pau Vila 3,* *T932254758, www.mac.es, Metro Barceloneta, Tue-Sat 0930-1900, Sun and holidays 1000-1430, €3,* devoted to the story of Catalunya's fortunes from prehistory to the present with plenty of interactive toys and gimmicks. The rooftop café has fantastic harbour views.

Passeig Joan de Borbó culminates in the scruffy little Plaça del Mar, overlooked by the Torre de Sant Sebastià, where cable cars begin their terrifying journey over the harbour, see page 298, and up to Montjüic with a stop at the World Trade Center in the middle. The tower now holds a very slinky designer restaurant, see page 288, with more fabulous views.

Barceloneta

While tourists sit under canvas umbrellas and sip their cocktails in between visits to the beach, the shabby little neighbourhood of Barceloneta just behind it goes about its business undisturbed. The pre-Olympic reforms only touched the fringes of the old neighbourhood, leaving its unassuming, down-to-earth heart intact. The best time to appreciate it is during the **Festa Major de Barceloneta**, see page 294, at the end of September, when the lumbering figure of Bum Bum careers down the narrow streets popping off a cannon and showering sweets on to the children, and fireworks fly in the evenings, watched from boats in the harbour. There are no sights or monuments, but it's a great place for an evening wander when you'll discover scruffy little bars serving up wine from the barrel and freshly fried sardines.

The **beaches** which extend for several kilometres from the Platja Sant Sebastià at the end of Passeig Joan de Borbó in Barceloneta all the way to the Platja Nova Mar Bella near the Besos River, are not the most beautiful nor the cleanest on the Mediterranean, but they are fun, easy to get to, and conveniently lined with cafés and snack bars. You can rent a sun-lounger for about €3 if you want to work on your tan for a while, but if you'd prefer something more active, stroll along to Mar Bella beach where you can get sailing and wind-surfing lessons, or hire snorkelling equipment, see page 297. The crowds thin out slightly the further you walk.

Vila Olímpica

Until Barcelona was nominated to host the 1992 Olympic games, the city's seafront was a vast conglomeration of docks, warehouses, and slums linked by a grimy railway track. This unglamorous stretch of land became the site of the city's biggest and most ambitious architectural project: the Vila Olímpica (Olympic Village). Although the city's finest architects were commissioned for the project, the result is a sterile mini-city of boxy, uninspired buildings. Do as everyone else does and head straight for the beach by the **Port Olímpic**. This neon-lit development is the undisputed success of the Olympic Village and encompasses a marina, sailing school and leisure complex stuffed with cafés, restaurants and shops. Above it flaps Frank Gehry's enormous shimmering copper fish.

Diagonal Mar and the Universal Forum of Cultures 2004

ⓘ *Metro El Maresme i Forum, bus 7.*

Barcelona's new project for getting the world's attention is the Universal Forum of Cultures in 2004. The Exhibitions of 1888 and 1929, and the 1992 Olympics were all used as a means of underpinning grandiose regeneration schemes for the less salubrious sections of the city, and the city's latest scheme for the run-down area of Poble Nou is no different. The Universal Forum of Cultures takes place between 9 May and 26 September 2004 and aims to promote cultural diversity, world peace and a

sustainable urban environment with a dizzying array of activities from debates and lectures to concerts and circus acts (more information at www.barcelona2004.org). The glistening modern park which will host the Forum is being partly constructed on reclaimed land and some of the buildings will use solar power, in order to press home the environmental theme, and a Virtual Forum linked with points all over the world will celebrate the spirit of cultural diversity. The whole project is five times as a big as the Olympic Village – almost 3 km of coastline has been covered.

Tibidabo and the outlying districts

There are plenty of things to do around the edge of the city centre in Barcelona. Few attractions – besides the giddy peak of Tibidabo with its funfair and the huge Nou Camp stadium in Les Corts – are on the tourist trail but some lesser known sights, like the quiet monastery of Pedralbes which holds part of the fabulous Thyssen-Bornemisza art collection, are worth the trek. Sloping up the hills which circle the city are some of its loveliest parks, including the delightful wilderness of the Parc de Collserola.

Nou Camp Stadium

ⓘ *Museu FC Barcelona, C/Aristides Maillol 7-9, T934963608, www.fcbarcelona.es, Mon-Sat 1000-1830, Sun and hols 1000-1400, €5, €9 with guided tour of stadium. Metro Collblanc. Bus 15, 52, 54, 56, 57, 75.* The Nou Camp stadium is one of the largest in Europe, built to accommodate 120,000 fans, and yet getting tickets for a match – particularly with arch-rivals Real Madrid – can be unbelievably tough. If you can't get into a game, a visit to the **Museu FC Barcelona** is a worthy substitute, and holds holds an evocative collection of mementoes, cups and footballing paraphernalia which recount the Club's fortunes over the past century. The highlight for many fans is the European cup, won at Wembley in 1992.▶▶ *For information on getting tickets, see page 297.*

Pedralbes

North of the western end of the Avinguda Diagonal is the plush, affluent suburb of Pedralbes, spilling down the once-wooded slopes of Collserola. Just off the Diagonal is the stately mid-19th century Palau Reial de Pedralbes, originally built for the Güell family, Gaudí's benefactors. It now houses two quiet museums in separate wings; on the right is the **Museu de les Arts Decoratives** ⓘ *Av Diagonal 686, Metro Palau Reial, T932805024, www.museuartsdecoratives.bcn.es, Tue-Sat 1000-1800, Sun and holidays 1000-1500, €3.50, free on the first Sun of the month*, with an eclectic selection of furniture, tapestries, glasswork and jewellery dating back to the Middle Ages.

The opposite wing of the palace holds the charming **Museu de Ceràmica** ⓘ *www.museuceramica.bcn.es, Tue-Sat 1000-1800, Sun and holidays 1000-1500, €3.50, free on the first Sun of the month*, with an exceptional collection of pieces from the most important Spanish ceramics manufacturers stretching back over the last millennium. There's a small gallery with works by Picasso, Miró and the Catalan sculptor Josep Llorens Artigas, who gave Miró his first ceramics lessons.

At the top of Avinguda Pedralbes is the lovely 14th-century **Monestir de Santa María de Pedralbes**. The convent still houses a small community of Poor Clares, but a section of it is open to the public as the **Museu Monastir Pedralbes** ⓘ *T932039282, www.bcn.es/museus, Tue-Sun 1000-1400, €3.50, free first Sun of the month, combined ticket with Col.lecció Thyssen-Bornemisza.* The unusual three-tiered Gothic cloister, one of the best preserved in Europe, is a still, contemplative arcade of slender columns, surrounding groves of cypress trees, rose gardens and a small pond. The former nuns' dormitories have been remodelled to hold the excellent **Col.lecció Thyssen-Bornemisza** ⓘ *T932801434, www.museothyssen.org, Metro*

⁙ Temptation of Christ

According to legend, this is where the Devil is supposed to have shown Christ the world's treasures spread out at his feet, and tempted him with the words *'haec omnia tibi dabo si cadens adoraberis me'* – All this will I give you if you will fall down and worship me. Not even this vision of the city curled around the sea in one direction, and the Collserolas undulating gently inland towards Montserrat and the Pyrenees were enough to tempt Christ, but the name stuck, and the views are usually tremendous – at least when a salty blast of sea air lifts the smoggy pall.

Maria Cristina, Tue-Sun 1000-1400, €3, free first Sun of the month, a selection of works prised from the Thyssen bequest held in Madrid. There's a shimmering collection of gilded medieval paintings and sculpture, which includes Fra Angelico's lovely masterpiece, the glowing, rosy-cheeked Madonna of Humility, works by Tintoretto, Titian, Veronese, Rubens, and Tiepolo, and among the Spanish artists are portraits by Velázquez and Zurbarán.

Parc de Collserola

The most unexpected delight in Barcelona is this beautiful natural park, which stretches for more than 6,500 hectares across the undulating Serra de Collserola, the ring of hills which contain the sprawling city. Despite being hemmed in by towns on all sides, it's still possible to forget completely the existence of the bustling city, and stroll, ride or mountain bike through wooded paths, between old farmhouses (*masies*), ancient chapels and half-forgotten springs. For maps and information on the various activities, visit the helpful park information office ① *T932803552, www.parccollserola.amb.es, 0930-1500.*

Tibidibo, the highest peak of the Collserola hills which surround Barcelona, is the city's mountain of fun. At the summit, reached by a rickety tram and a funicular railway, is a bizarre (but dull) church and a great old-fashioned **funfair** ① *FGC to Av Tibidabo on Plaça John F. Kennedy where the Tram Blau leaves for the Plaça Dr Andreu, where a funicular railway makes the final ascent, late Mar-Apr, Fri-Sun 1200-1900; May, Thu-Sun 1200-1900; Jun, Wed-Sun 1200-1900; Jul and Aug, Mon-Thu, Sun 1200-2200; Fri-Sat 1200-0100; early Sep, Mon-Thu 1200-2000, Fri-Sat 1200-2200; late Sept, Sat-Sun 1200-2000; entrance and 6 rides €8, free to children under 1m 10 cm, or €15 for a day pass offering unlimited rides, €4.50 to children under 1 m 10 cm.* The ferris wheel, dodgems and other rides are great for little kids. The views across the city can be breathtaking on a clear day.

From up here (or pretty much anywhere, for that matter) you can't miss the needle-like **Torre de Collserola** ① *Ctra Vallvidrera-Tibidabo, T934069354, Sep-May Wed-Fri 1100-1430 and 1530-1900, Sat-Sun 1100-1900; Jun-Aug Wed-Fri 1100-1430 and 1530-2000, Sat-Sun 1100-2000, €4.60, www.torredecollserola.com,* which spikes the horizon. A glass lift will whoosh you up to the mirador, with panoramic views stretching for miles in all directions. A free 'mini-train' plies between the funfair and the tower in summer; otherwise you can walk, or take the T2 or 211 bus from outside the main entrance to the funfair.

At the bottom of Tibidabo is the **Museu de la Ciència** ① *T932126050, www.fundacio.lacaixa.com, Tue-Sun and holidays 1000-2000, €5, discounts for kids, free first Sun of the month, bus 17, 22, 58, 60, 73.* This is a big touchy-feely museum and planetarium set in an old Modernista asylum. Most of the descriptions are in Catalan or Castilian, but there are enough gadgets to keep kids occupied for hours;

best is a wonderful exhibit called *Toca, toca!* (touch touch) which shows kids how to pick up all kinds of peculiar Mediterranean creatures, from sea anemones to starfish.

🛏 Sleeping

Barcelona is one of the most popular weekend destinations in Europe and finding a place to stay can be a nerve-shattering experience. The city is hoping to double the number of beds it currently offers in time for the 2004 Forum but, for the moment at least, it's a test of endurance. Book as early as possible and never just turn up and hope to find something. Note that many of the really cheap places will only take reservations on the day you want to arrive, but call early. Check out online deals, and if all else fails, get an agent to find you a bed (see below).

Most of the cheaper places can be found in the old neighbourhoods in the centre of the city (the Barri Gòtic, La Ribera, and the Raval) which are also the noisiest places to stay. The smartest (and quietest) places are generally concentrated in the Eixample. There are relatively few places near the seaside, although that will undoubtedly change after 2004, and you might want to think about staying in Gràcia to get a feel for Barcelona without the tourists. There are no campsites close to the city centre - the nearest is 7km away.

La Rambla *p253, map p256*

LL Le Meridien Barcelona, Ramblas 111, T933186200, www.lemeridien-barcelona. com. Before the **Hotel Arts** (see p282) stole its thunder, this was Barcelona's swankiest hotel. It's still a favourite with visiting opera stars thanks to its superb location right on the Ramblas, and there's a fine restaurant and all the luxury trimmings.
B Continental, Rambla 138, T933012570, www.hotel continental.com. George Orwell wrote some of the pages of *Homage to Catalonia* between the walls of this welcoming, century-old hotel. It's surprisingly good value for the location and outer rooms have balconies overlooking the Ramblas.
C Hotel Roma Reial, Plaça Reial 11, T933020366, F933011839. A bright, friendly hotel in the corner of the buzzy Plaça Reial, this offers decent rooms, and a bar with

terrace on the square. Like all the accommodation on the square, it's best for night owls who won't mind the noise.
D Pensión Las Flores, Ramblas 79, T933171634. This tiny *pensión* is hidden up a narrow staircase off the Rambla. The rooms are spotless, but can get very stuffy in summer. Some have bathrooms, and those at the front have balconies overlooking the prettiest, flower-filled section of the Rambla.
E Pensión Ambos Mundos, 10 Plaça Reial, T933187970, F934122363. This attractive little *pensión* is situated above the laid-back bar of the same name on the square; there are a dozen pleasant, tiled rooms with bathrooms, and some have balconies looking out over the square.
G Albergue Kabul, 17 Plaça Reial, T933185190, F933014034. Right on the Plaça Reial, the Kabul offers dorms and rooms sleeping from 2 to 12 people. It's noisy, but the once-rundown rooms are being refurbished and you can't get any closer to the action. Facilities include TV and video and laundry.

Barri Gòtic *p255, map p256*

LL Colón, Av de la Catedral 7, T933011404, www.hotel colon.es. A discreetly luxurious hotel in a fantastic location facing the Gothic cathedral, the aristocratic Colón has all the amenities including piano bar and restaurant; the upper rooms have terraces, and all are decorated with classic elegance. Cheaper rooms are available in a less atmospheric annexe around the corner.
AL Suizo, 12 Plaça del Angel, T933106108, www.gargallo-hotels.com. This is a dignified, traditional hotel handily placed for the main sights of the Barri Gòtic. It faces the noisy Via Laietana but the nicest rooms overlook the narrow passage called Baixada Llibreteria.
C Hostal Jardí, Plaça de Sant Josep Oriol 1, T933015900, F933183664. Book well in advance if you want to get a room at this extremely popular *hostal*; the nicest rooms overlook the leafy Plaça del Pi, one of the

main hubs of the old city. The simpler, less expensive rooms at the back look out onto a patio. It's just emerged from a thorough refurbishment, reflected in the higher prices.
D Hostal Rembrandt, C/ Portaferrisa 23, T/F933181011. Spotless, good-sized rooms decorated with 70s wicker furniture and prints, many with balconies overlooking the busy shopping street (so nice and quiet by night).
F Avinyó 42, C/Avinyó 42, T933187945, www.hostelavinyo.com. Very plain, very basic and very cheap, this is an excellent budget choice close to the art school, right on a hip, narrow little street of fashion boutiques and bars. Rooms with and without bathrooms.
G Itaca Hostel, C/Ripoll 21, T933019751, www.itacahostel.com. A bright, friendly new *hostal* with colourful murals and laid-back owners. Dormitory accommodation in large rooms all with balconies, plus one twin room with en suite bathroom. Facilities include a lively café-bar and internet.

La Ribera and Sant Pere
p261, maps p250 and p256

AL Hotel Park, 11 Av Marquès de l'Argentera 11, T933196000, www.parkhotelbarcel ona.com. Built in the early 1950s by the celebrated architect Antoni de Moragas, the **Hotel Park** was renovated in 1990 by Moragas' son using the original plans. It's a narrow, slim hotel with good-sized balconies looking out towards Barceloneta, an exquisite interior wraparound staircase and comfortable, well-equipped rooms.
B Hotel Urquinaona, Ronda de Sant Pere 24, T932681336, www.barcelonahotel.com/ urquinaona. This is a friendly, well equipped little hotel, offering lots of unexpected extras like internet access. The rooms all have satellite TV and a/c, and the prices are reasonable for the standard of the facilities. Triples also available.
D-E Hostal Fontanella, Vía Laietana 71, T933175943. This cosy little *hostal* is located very close to the Plaça Urquinaona. The traffic can be a bit of a problem, but the owner is very welcoming and looks after her guests very well. The rooms are clean and simple, and come with all kinds of bathroom

goodies. Rooms without bathrooms drop a price category.
F-G Gothic Point Youth Hostel, C/Vigatans 5, T932687808, www.gothicpoint.com.
New hostel (opened 2001) which has neatly sussed out what budget travellers really want. The dormitories (all with heating and a/c) are split into 'modules', each with their own light and side table and the reasonable prices include breakfast. Facilities include bike hire, Internet access and a big terrace. They also run the Sea Point Hostel (see below).

El Raval *p265, maps p250 and p256*

LL Hotel Ambassador, C/ del Pintor Fortuny 13, T934120530, F933027977. A graceful, modern hotel with a piano bar and rooftop terrace with garden and swimming pool. The rooms are quietly elegant, although those on the upper floors are sunnier.
AL Gaudí, 12 C/ Nou de la Rambla, T933179032, www.hotelgaudi.es. This has a Gaudiesque fountain of broken tiles just inside the door, but you can get a glimpse of the real thing from the top-floor rooms which overlook the Palau Güell (see p266) opposite. Service is frosty.
AL San Agustin, Plaça Sant Agustí 3, T933181658, www.hotelsa.com. One of the city's oldest hotels, this graceful, apricot-coloured building overlooks the pretty Plaça Sant Agustí. Top floor rooms have wooden beams and wonderful views.
A Méson de Castilla, C/ de Valldonzella 5, T933182182, www.husa.es. A chain hotel with a family feel. Breakfast is served out on the pretty interior patio garden, and rooms are furnished in warm colourful fabrics and wicker. They also have some good-sized family rooms.
B España, C/ de Sant Pau 9-11, T933181758, hotelespanya@tresnet.com. The España is marked on every tourist map thanks to Domènech i Montaner's stunning murals and swirling wooden fittings on the ground floor. Disappointingly, rooms are grimly functional although some at least open out onto a delightful interior terrace, and the service can be surly.
B Peninsular, C/ de Sant Pau 34-36, T933023138, F934123699. **Peninsular** is a

For an explanation of sleeping and eating price codes used in this guide, see inside the front cover. Other relevant information is found in Essentials, see pages 47-56.

good moderately priced choice set in an old convent almost opposite the **Hotel España**. There's a charming interior patio filled with plants and greenery and the rooms are comfortable and good value.

C Principal, 8 C/ Junta de Comerç, T933188970, www.hotelprincipal.es. The nicest of several cheaper *hostales* along this street, the Principal is possibly the most eccentric, with florid rooms decorated with a mixture of antiques, and nick-nacks. The friendly owners also run the **Joventut** (up the street at No 12 with the same email and website).

D Gat Raval, C/Joaquin Costa 44, T934816670, hostelgatraval@gataccommodation.com. A hip new *hostal* painted in black, white and lime green and set on one of the Raval's funkiest streets. The modern rooms are bright, clean and well-equipped, but they haven't quite got their internet booking system to work yet, so call to confirm.

E La Terassa, 11 C/ Junta del Comerç, T933025174, F933012188. This is a very popular *pensión* run by the same people as the *Jardí*; some of the nicer rooms have balconies overlooking the street, or the pretty interior patio where breakfast is served in summer.

Eixample *p268, map p250*

LL Claris, C/ de Pau Claris 150, T934876262, www.derbyhotels.es. Set in an old palace, this is currently one of the most fashionable and stylish hotels in the city. Art, antiques and the latest design are mixed with impeccable taste, and there's a Japanese garden and a rooftop pool.

LL Ritz, 668 Gran Vía des les Corts Catalanes, T933185200, ritz@ritzbcn. Classic luxury, with all the Belle Epoque trimmings. **Ritz** opened in 1919 and has hosted everyone from Ava Gardner to Salvador Dali (who holed up in room 110). The bathrooms are magnificent; marble, Roman-style baths, and walls inlaid with *Sevillano* tiles. There's also a very fine restaurant, the **Diana**, which is open to non-residents.

L-AL Actual, C/Rossello 238, T935520550. €138. Brand new trendy hotel which is fashionably decorated in the slickest

minimalist style, with plenty of white marble and dark wood.

B-C Hostal Plaza, C/Fontanella 18, T/F933010139, www.plazahostal.com. Run by a very friendly and welcoming family, the *Plaza* is a gem – complete with disco ball and pictures of Marilyn Monroe. All the simple rooms have showers and fans, TV room, fridge and freezer and a laundry service.

B-C Hotel Paseo de Gràcia, Passeig de Gràcia 102, T932155824, F932150603. A simple, friendly modern hotel in a superb location. The rooms are basic but all have phones and TVs and the staff are very helpful. Doesn't ooze charm, but prices are exceptionally good value.

C Hotel Ginebra, Rambla de Catalunya 1, 3°, T933171063, F933175565. A friendly, cosy hotel in a graceful old building just off the Plaça Catalunya: rooms are double-glazed and well-equipped and some have balconies with views across the square. Excellent value.

D Hostal Edén, C/ Balmes 55, T934547363, hostaleden@hotmail.com. A fantastic little *pensión* in a rambling old Eixample building. Rooms have unexpected amenities – fridges, whirlpools and tiny terracotta patios.

D Hostal Windsor, Rambla de Catalunya 84, T932151198. A very popular *pensión*, with good sized rooms decked out in pure 70s , this offers good value and a quiet location on the leafy Rambla de Catalunya.

E Pensión Rondas, C/ Girona 4, T/F932325102. A delightful little *pensión* run by a friendly brother and sister with spotless, if basic, rooms and a wonderful wooden lift which looks like a museum piece.

Gràcia and Parc Güell
p274, map p250

B Pensión Abete, C/ Gran de Gràcia 67, T/F932185524. A simple, family-run *pensión* with basic, pleasant rooms which don't quite match up to the prices. Still, it's a good place to escape the crowds in the centre.

Port Vell, Barceloneta and Vila Olímpica
p276, maps p250 and p256

LL Arts Barcelona, C/ Marina 19-21, T932211000, F932211070. Easily the most glamorous hotel in the city, set in one of the enormous glassy towers at the entrance to

the Port Olímpic. Inaugurated in 1992, it offers 33 floors of unbridled luxury, including an indoor and outdoor pool, a piano bar overlooking the gardens and the sea, a fine restaurant, sauna, gym and beauty centre. **B Hotel Del Mar**, Pla Palau 19, T933193302, www.gargallo-hotels.com. This hotel doesn't have much in the way of charm – although set in a listed building – but it's got a great

location by the harbour and the nightlife of La Ribera. Very well-equipped for the price. **G Sea Point Hostel**, www.seapoint hostel.com. Right next to the San Sebastian beach in Barceloneta, this opened in summer 2002 and offers all kind of amenities including internet access and bike hire. Breakfast is included in the price. Dorms for 4, 6 or 8, all with heating and a/c.

🍴 Eating

The Catalans are renowned for their cuisine. The dishes are often simple, and rely on the freshness of the local ingredients. The Catalan staple, for example, is *pa amb tomàquet*, bread rubbed with fresh tomatoes, drizzled with olive oil and salt. With extra toppings (like ham or cheese) it becomes a *torrade*.

Meat and fish are often served simply grilled, or cooked slowly in the oven (*al horno*) in a tomato-based sauce. There are some delicious vegetable dishes – like the refreshing *escalivada*, a salad of roasted aubergine, peppers and onions, or *espinacas a la catalana*, spinach cooked with pine nuts and raisins.

Rice dishes are also popular, with variations on the famous Valencian dish *paella* like *arros nègre*, rice cooked slowly with squid ink and shellfish, or *fideuà*, which is made with tiny noodles cooked in with meat and fish. The most popular Catalan dessert is *crema Catalana*, a local version of crème brûlée, or you could finish up with local curd cheese drizzled with honey, *mel i mató*.

There are plenty of old-fashioned bars near the harbour which offer fresh seafood tapas – like *sardines* (grilled sardines) – but the most common Catalan tapas are *truita*, thick omelettes (*tortilla*) or platters of cheeses or *embutits* (charcuterie). Don't forget to wash them all down in style with Catalan wine, or the local *Estrella* beer.

La Rambla *p253, map p256*

€€€ **Rúccula**, World Trade Centre, Moll de Barcelona, T935088268, 1300-1600 and 2030-2345, closed Sun night, metro Drassanes. Fabulous views over the Mediterranean, and adventurous, exquisite Catalan cuisine are pulling in the crowds at this glossy new restaurant in the World Trade Centre.
€€ **Amaya**, La Rambla 20, T933021037, daily 1300-1700 and 2030-2400, metro Drassanes. Despite its unprepossessing exterior, **Amaya** is an excellent Basque restaurant which is popular with everyone from local businessmen to opera stars from the Liceu. Terrace on the Rambla in summer.
€ **Egipte**, La Rambla 79, T933179545, daily 1300-1600 and 2000-2400, metro Liceu. A great budget choice with a wide choice of popular Catalan dishes including pigs' trotters stuffed with prawns.
€ **Les Quinze Nits**, Plaça Reial 6, T933173075, daily 1300-1545 and 2030-2330, metro Liceu. Those long queues snaking across the Plaça Reial are for this good-value restaurant, which serves up simple, fresh Catalan dishes in coolly modern surroundings. No bookings, so be prepared to wait.

Tapas bars and cafés
Bar Pinotxo, Mercat de la Boquería 66-67, T933171731, Mon-Sat 0600-1700, metro Liceu. The best-known and most well-loved counter bar in the market, serving excellent, freshly prepared food – don't miss the tortilla with artichokes.

● *For an explanation of sleeping and eating price codes used in this guide, see inside the front cover. Other relevant information is found in Essentials, see pages 47-56.*

Café Zurich, Plaça Catalunya, T933179153, daily Jun-Oct 0800-0200, until 2300 on Sun; Nov-May Mon-Thu, Sun 0800-2300, Fri-Sat 0800-2400, metro Catalunya. When the new **El Triangle** shopping mall was built, the infamous old **Café Zurich** was swept away. This new version doesn't have the same charm, but it's got a fine location at the top of the Rambla.

El Café de l'Opéra, La Rambla 74, T933177586, Mon-Thu and Sun 0800-0215, Fri-Sat 0800-0300, metro Liceu. Sitting right on the Rambla opposite the Liceu Opera house, this is the perfect café for people-watching. Original Modernista-style fittings and an Old World ambience add to its charm.

Escribà, La Rambla de les Flors 83, T933016027, 0830-2100. A delightful outpost of the mouth-watering patisserie set in a gilded Modernista shop.

Barri Gòtic *p255, map p256*

€€€ **Agut d'Avignon**, C/Trinitat 3, just off C/de Avinyó, T933026034, daily 1300-1530 and 2100-2330, metro Jaume I. A very fine, traditional Catalan restaurant with comfortably old-fashioned decor reminiscent of an old farmhouse. Try the *farcellets de col* – stuffed cabbage leaves or the succulent roast meats.

€€ **Café de l'Acadèmia**, C/Lledó 1, T933198253, Mon-Fri 0900-1200 and 1330-1600 and 2045-1130, metro Jaume I. An elegant and romantic restaurant just off the lovely Plaça Sant Just, with torch-lit tables out on the square in summer. Classic Catalan cuisine – try the *rossejat* (rice cooked in fish broth).

€€ **Can Culleretes**, C/d'en Quintana 5, T933173122, Tue-Sat 1330-1600 and 2100-2300, Sun 1330-1600, metro Liceu. This is the city's oldest restaurant, founded in 1786, with a series of interconnected, wooden panelled and beamed rooms papered with pictures of celebrity visitors. Great desserts.

€€ **Slokai**, C/ Palau 5, T933179094, Mon-Fri 1300-1600 and 2100-2400, Sat 2100-2400, metro Jaume I. A very fashionable, minimalist white restaurant with extraordinary sculptures and art, with projections and screenings on Fri and Sat evenings.

There's a lunchtime salad buffet and the main menu leans slightly towards fish – sea bass with a piquant sauce, for example.

€ **La Fonda**, C/Escudellers 10, T933017515, 1300-1545 and 2030-2330, metro Liceu. Wooden floors, lots of plants and modern lighting are a perfect setting for the simple Catalan cuisine at good prices. No bookings are taken, so you'll have to queue.

€ **La Veronica**, C/de Avinyó 30, T934121122, Tue 2000-1330, Wed-Sun 1200-0130, metro Jaume I. A bright, sleekly contemporary space with a terrace out on the Plaça George Orwell in summer. Bold red and white and great pizzas with imaginative toppings and an interesting range of starters.

€ **Zoo**, C/Escudellers 33, T933027728, daily 1800-0200, until 0230 Fri and Sat, metro Liceu. This is a funky, very popular place decorated with toy animals and all kinds of kitsch. The dishes are simple, mostly variations on very substantial toasted sandwiches, which arrive overflowing with fillings. Good salads plus a couscous of the day and a few daily specials.

Tapas bars and cafés

Bliss, Plaça Sants Just i Pastor, T932681022, Mon-Sat 1330-1530, 2030-2315, closed Aug, metro Jaume I. A small, cosy café, with a couple of leopard-print sofas to sink into. Delicious homemade quiches, salads and cakes. There are tables out on a pretty little square by the church in summer.

Café d'Estiu, Plaça Sant Iu 5, T933103014, Easter to Sep Tue-Sun 1000-2200, metro Jaume I. This is prettily set among the orange trees in the courtyard outside the Museu Frederic Marés. Simple snacks, pastries and cakes are on offer.

Juicy Jones, C/Cardenal Casañas 7, T933024330, daily 1300-2400, metro Liceu. A brightly-lit juice counter with a small vegetarian restaurant downstairs, painted with big bold flowers. Good value set menu (from the lentil school of cookery) and organic beers and wines, as well as the delicious, freshly made juices and smoothies.

La Pallaresa, C/ Petritxol 11, T933022036, www.lapallaresa.com. Sat, Sun 0900-2200, Mon-Fri 0900-2100, metro Liceu. This is where to get your *chocolate con churros* in the morning – locals swear it's the best *xocolatería* in the city. It's still got the lino,

formica tables and waiters in dicky bows.

La Vinateria del Call, C/de Sant Domènec del Call 9, T933026092, open 1900-0100 metro Liceu. Down a tiny side street, this is a dark, wooden-panelled bar with very friendly and knowledgeable staff. Excellent, very fresh tapas (choose from the menu) – platters of cheese or cured meats, *pa amb tomaquet*, and a fine wine list featuring local wines. It's so popular that it has 2 sittings at weekends (2100-2300 and 2300-0100).

Venus, C/ Avinyó 25, T933011585, 1200-2400, metro Liceu. A deli-style café on a very fashionable street, Venus manages to be cool without being pretentious. Wooden tables, mellow music and lots of newspapers and magazines make it a very welcoming spot.

La Ribera and Sant Pere
p261, maps p250 and p256

€€€ **Hofmann**, C/de l'Argenteria 74-78, T933195889, closed Sat and Sun, metro Jaume I. Outstanding cordon bleu cuisine impeccably served in a series of charming, plant-filled dining rooms. The menu focuses on modern Mediterranean dishes: try the roast lamb and the mouth-watering *fondant de chocolat* which is served warm.

€€€ **Taira**, C/Comerç 7, T933196614, Tue-Sun 1300-1600 and 2100-2430. This is the latest designer creation of Otto Zutz; it's a slick Japanese restaurant-bar-club with even slicker New York-style decor which has become extremely popular with the local fashionistas, so don't bother to turn up without a reservation.

€€ **Cometacinc**, C/Cometa 5, T933101558, Tue-Thu 2000-0100, metro Jaume I. A very stylish restaurant set in an old 19th-century mansion, this is elegantly and simply furnished with whitewashed walls, and wooden tables and chairs. Relaxed jazz and excellent fusion cuisine accompanied by a very decent wine list.

€€ **La Flauta Magica**, C/Banys Vells 18, T932684694, daily 1330-2400, metro Jaume I. Friendly mainly vegetarian restaurant, with soft peach and violet walls and lots of dim lighting and candles. Daily specials are on offer at lunchtimes.

€€ **Salero**, C/del Rec 60, T933198022, Mon-Thu 0845-1730 and 2000-0100, Fri 0845-1730 and 2000-0300, Sat 2000-0300,

metro Jaume I. An ultra-stylish cool white New-York style restaurant in the heart of the Born district, serving creative Mediterranean-Japanese cuisine at surprisingly low prices. Good breakfasts too.

€€ **Senyor Parellada**, C/de l'Argenteria 37, T933105094, daily except Sun 1300-1530 and 2100-2330, metro Jaume I. Set in a magnificent 18th-century building, this is a stylish, buzzy restaurant. The menu concentrates on modern Catalan dishes using the freshest market produce; try the *papillotte* of French beans with mushrooms or the delicious sole cooked with almonds and pine nuts.

€ **Comme Bio I**, Via Laitana 28, T933198968, Mon-Fri 1300-1600 and 2000-2330, Sat 1300-1600 and 2030-2400, Sunday 2000-2300, metro Jaume I. Big, stylish vegetarian restaurant and shop with a buffet, and a good lunchtime menu, and all kinds of organic goodies. No smoking during the week. There's another branch in the Eixample at Gran Via 603, T933010376.

Tapas bars and cafés
Cal Pep, Plaça Olles 8, T933107961, daily 1300-1645 and 2000-2400, evenings only on Sun and Mon, metro Barceloneta. A classic: there's a smart, brick-lined restaurant at the back, but it's more entertaining to stand at the bar as charismatic Pep grills fish and steaks and holds court at the same time. Refreshing house *cava*.

El Xampanyet, C/ Montcada 22, T933197003, Tue-Sat 1200-1600 and 1830-2330, Sun 1200-1600, metro Jaume I. A classic little bar with old barrels and colourful tiles, serving simple tapas like salt cod and anchovies and tortilla washed down with a delicious house *xampanyet* – poor man's *cava*.

Euskal Etxea, Plaçeta Montcada, T933102185, bar Tue-Sat 0900-2330, Sun 1245-1530, restaurant Tue-Sat 1330-1530 and 2100-2330, metro Jaume I. Where better to tuck into Basque *pintxos* than the recently revamped Basque cultural centre. Get a plate from the bar staff, help yourself and then count up the cocktail sticks at the end.

Hivernacle, Parc de la Ciutadella, T932954017, 1000-0100, metro Arc de Triomf. A beautiful, relaxing café-bar set in an elegant iron and glass pavilion built for the 1888 Universal Exposition; lots of shady

palms, a terrace, changing art exhibitions and weekly jazz concerts in summer.

La Vinyor del Senyor, Plaça Santa Maria 5, T933103379, Tue-Sat 1200-1330, Sun 1200-1600, metro Jaume I. This features a fine selection of wines, *cavas* and sherries accompanied by excellent tapas (in minuscule portions). A summer terrace faces the beautiful church of Santa María del Mar.

S:Pic, C/Ribera 10, T933101595, metro Barceloneta. Funky cellar bar lit with weird projections. Good tapas (in odd categories like 1980s tapas and 1090s tapas) and a very fashionable, clubby crowd.

Tèxtil Cafè, C/Montcada 12, T932682598, Tue-Sun 1000-2345, metro Jaume I. Set in the graceful courtyard by the Textile Museum (see p262), this is a delightful café with a good range of snacks and pastries.

El Raval p265, maps p250 and p256

€€€ **Casa Leopoldo**, C/ Sant Rafael 24, T934413014, 1330-1600 and 2130-2300. Closed Mon night and Sun, metro Liceu. This classic, family-run restaurant has been going since 1939 and not much has changed since – you'll still find solid wooden tables and chairs, dark beams and tile-covered walls. Hearty Catalan dishes using the freshest market produce are on offer, like an excellent *sopa de pesca* (fish soup) and perfectly grilled seafood and meat.

€€ **Mamacafé**, C/Doctor Dou 10, T933012940, 1300-0100, until 1700 on Sun and Mon. Food served 1300-1730, and 2100-2330. Closed Aug, metro Catalunya. Bright colours, bold design and great music have made the **Mamacafé** a stylish hang out in El Raval: the menu offers a selection of dishes from around the world including several vegetarian options.

€€ **Silenus**, C/dels Angels 8, T933022680, Mon 1300-1600, Tue-Sat 1300-1600 and 2100-2345, metro Catalunya. A coolly arty restaurant serving top-notch international and Catalan dishes. It's a long narrow space with pale walls lined with comfy sofas and dotted with changing art and projections.

€ **Elisabets**, C/Elisabets 2-4, T933175826, Mon-Thu and Sat 1300-1600, Fri 1300-1600 and 2100-2330, metro Catalunya. Classic neighbourhood restaurant catering to locals and serving up tasty Catalan

dishes at very low prices. The *menú del día* usually offers several choices and is very good value.

€ **Imprévist**, C/Ferlandina 34, T933425859, daily except Mon 1230-2430, metro Universitat. This cool café-bar, with funky industrial-style decor, is relaxed and arty. It serves good light dishes – salads, pasta and noodle dishes, falafel platters – and there are sometimes poetry readings, or performances.

€ **Pla dels Àngels**, C/Ferlandina 23 (opposite MACBA), T933294047, 1300-1500, 2030-0030, metro Universitat. Bright, modern decor, dark blue walls, this is a large, popular restaurant which serves well priced dishes (salads, meats, pastas). Good service and excellent wine – try the fantastic *Tinto Artesano*.

€ **Sésamo**, C/Sant Antoni Abat, T934416411, open 1100-0100, closed Mon night and Tue, metro Sant Antoni. This is a new, laid-back, tiny organic restaurant serving tasty vegetarian dishes. Service is friendly, and prices are very low.

Tapas bars and cafés

Bar Bodega Fortuny, C/Pintor Fortuny 31, T933179892, Tue-Sun 1000-2400, metro Catalunya. A colourful conversion changed this old-fashioned bodega into a perennially popular hang-out for arty locals. It opens up on to the street in summer, and there are delicious snacks and light meals are on offer all day and evening.

Bar Kasparo, Plaça Vincent Martorell 4, T933022072, 0900-0100 in winter, until midnight in summer, metro Catalunya. A popular, Australian-run café-bar overlooking the playground in the square (it's a good place to bring your kids). Tasty sandwiches and hot dishes; friendly but unhurried service.

Bar Ra Town, Plaça Gardunya 7, T933014163, Mon-Sat 0930-0230, metro Liceu. Friendly, hip little bar-café just behind the Boquería market offering tasty breakfasts out on the terrace, and a wider night-time menu with Thai, Mexican and Mediterranean influences. Audiovisuals, DJs and a clubby feel from Thu-Sun nights.

Eixample p268, map p250

€€€ **Beltxenea**, C/Mallorca 275,

T932153024, 1330-1530 and 2100-2300, closed Sat lunch and Sun, metro Diagonal. A grand restaurant overlooking an immaculately manicured garden which has a romantic terrace in summer. The Basque cuisine is every bit as magnificent as the surroundings, featuring Basque classics like *merluza koskera a la vasca*, a delicate dish of hake cheeks simmered with clams and parsley. A real treat.

€€€ **Casa Calvet**, C/de Casp 48, T934134012, Mon-Sat 1300-1530 and 2030-2300, metro Urquinaona. Gaudí designed the building (for which he won an award in 1900) and it retains some beautiful Modernista touches inside, including exquisite stained glass windows. Fresh, modern Catalan cuisine is on offer; try the smoked foie gras with mango sauce, and the fabulous desserts.

€€ **L'Olivé**, C/Balmes 47, T934521990. Closed Sun eve, metro Hospital Clínic. A popular, lively restaurant, this serves traditional Catalan dishes, using the freshest market produce. Try the *rap amb all cremat* – monkfish with roasted garlic, or the *calçots*, when in season.

€€ **Tragaluz**, Passatge de la Concepció 5, T934870621, 1330-1600 and 2030-2430, until 0100 Thu, Fri and Sat, metro Diagonal. In a very pretty side street off the Passeig de Gràcia, this is a very stylish, fashionable restaurant on 2 levels with a huge glass skylight (*tragaluz*), which slides open in summer. The food is fresh, simple Mediterranean-style fare, and the downstairs bar has tapas and light snacks all day. They also run a slick Japanese restaurant across the street, **El Japonés**, T934872592.

€ **Domèstic**, C/Diputacio 215, T934531661, 1830-0230 (kitchen open until 0100), until 0300 Fri and Sat, metro Universitat. Welcoming hip bar and restaurant with a resident Brazilian DJ playing mellow sounds. An excellent, highly creative menu combining unusual ingredients to great effect, and a fantastic red-painted bar area with sofas to sink into.

€ **L'Hostal de Rita**, C/d'Aragó 279, T934872376, daily 1300-1545 and 2030-2330, metro Passeig de Gràcia. Another branch in the popular chain which includes La Fonda, see p284, and Les Quinze Nits, see p283. Again, they don't take booking and

there are always long queues. The food, good simple Catalan favourites and stylish, understated decor draw big crowds of tourists and locals.

Tapas bars and cafés
La Bodegueta, Rambla de Catalunya 100, T932154894, Mon-Sat 0800-0200, Sun 1830-0100. A charming, old-fashioned little cellar bar lined with bottles, which serves a selection of excellent tapas and does a very good value fixed price lunch

Laie Llibreria Café, C/ Pau Claris 85, T933027310, Mon-Fri 0900-0100, Sat 1000-0100, metro Urquinaona. Barcelona's original bookshop café, with comfy armchairs, magazines to flick through, and a good range of tasty snacks and light meals including a good value *menu del dia*.

Bracafé, C/ Casp 2, T933023082, 0700-2230, metro Plaça Catalunya. This is a very busy café just around the corner from the Plaça Catalunya; it has tables outside in summer and has a cosy little glassed-in area in winter.

Montjüic *p271, map p250*

€€€ **Ca L'Isidre**, C/Flors 12, T934411139, Mon-Sat 1330-1600 and 2030-2330, metro Paral.lel. This celebrated family-run restaurant proudly displays a photograph of the owners posing with King Juan Carlos, who is said to be a big fan of the classic Catalan cuisine on offer. Try the *cabrit*, goat marinaded and roasted slowly in a wooded oven, or the succulent loin of lamb.

€ **La Tomaquera**, C/de Margarit 58, no tel, Tue-at 1330-530 and 2030-2330, metro St Antoni or Paral.lel. A resolutely no-nonsense restaurant serving up great grilled meats with garlic sauce, *torrades* with different toppings, and home made desserts. Much of the appeal of the place comes from the owner-chef – he refuses to have a telephone installed, and won't serve Coca Cola.

Tapas bars and cafés
Quimet & Quimet, C/ Poeta Cabañas 25, T934423142, Tue-Sat 1200-1600 and 1900-2230, Sun 1200-1600, metro Paral.lel. A small, traditional bodega usually packed with crowds; it's got one of the best selection of wines in the city, and a range of excellent tapas to match.

€€€ **Botafumeiro**, C/Gran de Gràcia 81, T932184230, daily 1300-0100, metro Fontana. An outstanding Galician seafood restaurant, with a stunning array of sea creatures on the menu; the excellent value *menu de degustación* is highly recommended. They also run the tavern next door which serves fresh oysters among the tapas.

€€€ **Jaume de Provença**, C/Provença 88, T934300029, 1330-1530 and 2030-2300, closed Sun night and Mon, metro Entenç. The decor may be verging on the austere but the cuisine is emphatically the opposite: chef Jaume Bargués is renowned for his adventurous and imaginative Catalan cuisine – like the lobster tempura served with a poached egg and truffle sauce.

€€ **Bar-Restaurant del Teatre Lliure**, C/Montseny 47, T932186738. Attached to the prestigious Catalan theatre, this large, airy restaurant is very popular with locals and serves excellent, highly imaginative regional cuisine at very reasonable prices. Some tables sit out on the balcony overlooking the narrow street. Highly recommended.

€ **Flash Flash**, C/Granada del Penedès 25, T932370990 daily 1300-0130, bar daily 1100-0200, FGC Gràcia. Classic 1970s black and white decor with white leatherette seating and black silhouettes on the walls. Best known for its excellent selection of tortillas, it also does great burgers and steaks and attracts a trendy uptown crowd.

Tapas bars and cafés

El Roble C/ Lluis Antúnez, T932187387, 0700-0100, closed Sun, metro Diagonal. This is a roomy old-fashioned tapas bar which hasn't changed in decades. There's a rickety, yellowing old sign showing what's on offer, or you can go and inspect the dishes lined up along the counter. Long-aproned waiters dash about the place, and it's a big favourite with locals.

Sol Solet, Plaça del Sol 21, T932174440, Mon and Tue 1900-0200, Wed and Thu 1500-0200, Fri and Sat 1200-0300, Sun 1200-0300, metro Fontana. One of the prettiest bars in Gràcia, this has marble-topped tables, old tiles and paddle fans, and looks out on to the square. An excellent range of unusual tapas are on offer, including several vegetarian options.

Port Vell, Barceloneta and Vila Olímpica *p276, maps p250 and p256*

€€€ **Antigua Casa Solé**, C/Sant Carles 4, T932215112, Tue-Sat 1300-1600 and 2000-2300, metro Barceloneta. This is a very pretty restaurant set in a 19th-century building with breezy blue and white tiles and lots of flowers. The local fish stew *sarsuela* was invented here and it's still a great place to try traditional Catalan fish recipes.

€€€ **Els Pescadors**, Plaça Prim 1, T932252018, daily 1300-1545 and 2000-2400, metro Poble Nou. A charming whitewashed restaurant with a terrace overlooking a magical square surrounded by tumble down buildings and shaded by two huge mulberry trees. It's way off the beaten track, but has a fine reputation for its seafood dishes.

€€€ **Torre d'Alta Mar**, Paseo Joan de Borbó 88, T932210007. This is the latest of Barcelona's designer restaurants, and one of the most unusual: it's set in the cable car terminal and has 360° views of the city and the Mediterranean. The slightly retro decor has caused almost as much of a stir as the much-vaunted cuisine: try the *suquet de pescadors*, a delicious fish stew.

€€ **Agua**, Paseig Marítim 30, T932251272, 1330-1600 and 2030-2430, until 0100 Thu, Fri and Sat, metro Barceloneta. A slick, stylish restaurant with tables overlooking the sea, this specializes in rice dishes, often with an unusual twist but there are plenty of good meat and fish dishes.

€€ **El Cangrejo Loco**, Moll de Gregal 29, T932210533, daily 1300-0100, metro Ciutadella-Vila Olímpica. The 'Crazy Crab' offers excellent, very reasonably priced paellas and other seafood dishes. The *menú de degustación* is a bargain. It's a big, bustling cheerful place on two levels with a terrace right by the shore, but it's always full and you may wait a while for service.

€€ **Set Portes**, Passeig de Isabel II 14, T933193033, daily 1300-0100, metro Barceloneta. A very famous old restaurant, with frilly net curtains, a piano and aproned waiters, the 'Seven Doors' has been dishing up traditional Catalan cuisine since 1836. The clientele is now fairly touristy, but the food

retains its excellent reputation, particularly the house speciality, *paella de peix*.

€ **La Taverna de Cel Ros**, Moll de Mestral 26, T932210033, daily except Thu 1300-1700 and 2000-2400, metro Ciutadella-Vila Olímpica. A very unpretentious place in the midst of the bustle of the Port Olímpic, this is popular with local sailors and port workers. There's a good value lunch menu too.

Tapas bars and cafés

Taverna Can Ramonet, C/ Maquinista 17, T933013064, 1000-1600, 2000-2400, closed Aug, metro Barceloneta. This is the oldest

tavern in Barceloneta, set in a pretty pink two-storey house covered in flowers. Wine from the barrel accompanied by tasty seafood tapas, or there's a smart (expensive) seafood restaurant at the back.

Xiringuito Escribá, Platja de Bogatell, Tue-Thu 1300-1600 , Fri-Sun 1300-1600 and 2100-2300 in winter, Tue-Sun 1100-0100 in summer, metro Ciutadella-Vila Olímpica or Llacuna. This is run by the celebrated *Escribá* confectioners, and serves delicious seafood tapas and main dishes followed by truly mouth-watering desserts. Book well in advance.

Bars and clubs

La Rambla *p253, map p256*

Boadas, C/Tallers 1, T933188826, Mon-Thu 1200-0200, Fri-Sat 1200-0300, metro Catalunya. Elegant, classy art deco cocktail bar which began life in 1933; celebrity drinkers, including Miró, have left sketches and mementoes along the walls.

Café Royale, C/ Nou de Zurbano 3, T933176124, Tue-Thu 1100-0230, until 0300 on Fri and Sat, metro Liceu. A very hip, sleek bar and club just off the Plaça Reial, with big sofas to lounge in, and two dance floors playing the best in soul, jazz and funk. (Does great breakfasts, too). Gets uncomfortably mobbed at weekends.

Jamboree, Plaça Reial 17, T933017564, www.masimas.com, daily 2230-0530, metro Liceu. This jazz club (see p292) becomes a night club when the sets end: after about 0100, the crowds pour in to enjoy the R&B, soul and funk which plays until dawn.

Barri Gòtic *p255, map p256*

Dot, C/ Nou de Sant Francesc 7, T933027026, daily 2200-0230, until 0300 on Fri and Sat, metro Drassanes. One of the trendiest (and smallest) clubs around, **Dot** has a minuscule dance floor, with groovy lighting, cult films and wall projections. The varied line up of DJs provides the latest sounds from across the spectrum of dance music.

La Macarena, DJ Zone, C/Nou de Sant Francesc 5, daily 2300-0400, until 0500 on Fri

and Sat. Small, intimate club playing jazzy electronica beloved by DJs from around the world. Buzzy, upbeat and very cool.

Malpaso, C/ Rauric 20, T934126005, daily 2130-0230, until 0300 Fri and Sat, metro Liceu. Just down an alley behind the Plaça Reial, this is a groovy, red-painted little bar with decks playing an eclectic range of music, and a few punters dancing under the revolving disco ball.

Pilé 43, C/ N'Aglà 4, T933173902, daily 1900-0200, until 0300 on Fri and Sat, metro Liceu. A brightly-lit, fashionable bar filled with retro furniture, lights and knick-knacks – everything you see and sit on is for sale.

La Ribera and Sant Pere
p261, maps p250 and p256

Astin, C/ Abaixadors 9, T933010090, www.nitsa.com/astin.htm, Thu-Sat 2230-0330, metro Barceloneta/Jaume I. A small, chrome-filled, ultra-hip bar and club run by the **Nitsa** (see p291) crew, playing the very latest pop, house and breakbeat. Guest DJ sessions and concerts.

Gimlet, C/ Rec 24, T933101027, 2000-0300, closed Sun. Metro Arc de Triomf. Classic, very stylish cocktail bar which draws the fashion crowd as well as plenty of celebrities (not that anyone would deign to notice).

Pitin Bar, Pg/ del Born 34, T933195087, daily 1200-0300, metro Barceloneta. **Pitin** has been going for years and years, unaffected by changes in fashion, and yet managing to

stay cool without any effort. It's a split level bar with a tiny spiral staircase, decorated with all kinds of junk and lit with fairy lights. **Ribborn**, C/ Antic de Sant Joan 3, T9331-07148, Wed-Sat 1900-0200, until 0300 on Fri and Sat, Sun 1800-0300, metro Barceloneta. A relaxed, thoroughly unpretentious bar with simple tapas and a small stage for live music, usually jazz, funk and blues.

El Raval p265, maps p250 and p256

Benidorm, C/Joaquim Costa 39, T933178052, Mon-Thu, Sun 1900-0200, Fri-Sat 1900-0230, closed Aug. This is a tiny, funky little space decked out with eccentric furnishings – a baroque bench, 1970s wall paper – and has a miniature dancefloor complete with disco ball.

Bongo Lounge at La Paloma, C/Tigre 27, T933177994, Thu 0100-0500 and Fri 0230-0500, metro Universitat. Twice a week the ballroom dancers make way for clubbers at this old-fashioned, much-loved dance hall; the **Bongo Lounge** is one of the best nights out in the city, with resident DJs spinning a funky mix of electronica and Latin sounds.

El Café Que Pone Muebles Navarro, Carrer de la Riera Alta 4-6, T907189096, Tue-Sun 1700-0100, until 0200 on Fri-Sat, metro Universitat. A New York-warehouse-style café-bar set in a converted furniture shop with a mellow retro air and a fashionable, arty crowd.

La Ruta dels Elefants, C/ Hospital 48, no phone, 2000-0200 daily, metro Liceu. Very close to the Plaça San Augustin, this is a popular, laid-back bar with African art all over the walls, an upbeat, friendly atmosphere and live music most nights – you never know what you might get, from old fashioned cabaret to teenage rock or reggae.

Lupino, C/ Carme 33, T934123697, 0900-0300. This new 'restaurant-lounge-cocktail club' is ultra-stylish in a fashionably minimalist way. The music is laid back and loungey, and the Mediterranean menu is very decent. Mobbed by the fashion pack at weekends.

Marsella, C/ Sant Pau 65, T934427263, Mon-Thu 2200-0230, metro Liceu. The big, dusty, bottle-lined **Marsella** was started by a homesick Frenchman more than a century ago. The smell of absinthe hits you as soon as you walk in; get there early to grab a battered, marble-topped table under the lazy paddle fans and soak up the atmosphere.

Eixample p268, map p256

La Fira, C/ Provença 171, no phone, Mon-Thu 2200-0300 until 0430 Fri and Sat, metro Hospital Clínic or FGC Provença. One of the most original bars in town, this cavernous 'bar-museum' is stuffed with old fairground memorabilia; sit in a Dodgem sipping a beer or find a swing at the bar. Raucous weekend parties.

La Pedrera de Nit, C/ Provença 261-265, tickets through Tel-Entrada T902101212, Fri and Sat 2100-2400 in July and August, metro Diagonal. Sip a cocktail and check out the live music and stunning views across the city from the undulating rooftop of La Pedrera. A hundred tickets are sold in advance (€10) – bag one or be prepared for long queues.

Row Club (at Nick Havanna) , C/ Roselló 208, T932156591, 2300-0400, until 0500 on Fri and Sat, metro Diagonal. This regular Thu night club is hosted by the organizers of the Sonar festival (see p294) and the music runs from house and techno to the latest experimental sounds. A great night out.

Montjuic p271, map p250

BCN Rouge, C/ Poeta Cabañas 21, T934424985, 2300-0300. Ring for entry to this intimate and very slick chill-out bar, with lots of big sofas and tables (everything is red, of course). Bizarrely, it turns into a football bar on Sun nights.

La Terrrazza Discothèque, Poble Espanyol, T934231285, www.nightsungroup.com, May-Oct only Thu-Sun and days before bank holidays 2400-0600, metro Espanya. The biggest summer party in the city, La Terrrazza is a hugely popular and posey outdoor venue, where you can chill out under the pine trees or prance on the podiums to excellent dance music played by an impressive list of guest DJs. Massive queues and a strict door policy. When the temperatures drop, the party at Terrrazza comes indoors and calls itself **Discotheque**.

Nitsa, C/ Nou de la Rambla 113, T934414001, www.nitsa.com. Fri-Sat 2430-0600, metro Paral.lel. The club takes over when the gigs have ended at the **Sala Apolo** (see below), another converted ballroom; this big weekend party is very popular so be prepared for massive queues. The main dance floor features hard techno, breakbeat and house, but the two smaller rooms off the upper gallery are mellower.

Gràcia and Parc Güell *p274, maps p250 and p256*

Café del Sol, Plaça del Sol 16, T934155663, 1300-0200, until 0230 Fri and Sat, metro Fontana. This is a very mellow spot during the day, with creamy white walls showing changing art exhibitions. There's a good selection of tapas on Sun mornings and a delightful terrace out on the square in summer. DJ sessions on Fri and Sat nights. **Mond Bar**, Plaça del Sol 29, T934573877, daily 2100-0230, metro Fontana. A small, slinky bar on the lively Plaça del Sol, with soft lighting, plush sofas, chilled out house, lounge and trance and a friendly, laid-back crowd.

Port Vell, Barceloneta and Vila Olímpica *p276, map p250*

Razzmatazz/The Loft, C/ Almogàvers 122, T933208200, Fri and Sat 0100-0500, metro Bogatell, www.salarazmatazz.com. **Razzmatazz** is a popular party spot at weekends with 3 spaces catering to all musical tastes: pop, rock and techno in the Razz Club; and house, electronica and DJs in the trendy Loft.

Tibidabo and the outlying districts *p278, map p250*

Bikini, C/ Deu i Mata 105, (in *L'Illa* shopping centre), T933220005, www.bikinibcn.com. 2400-0430, until 0530 on Fri and Sat, closed Sun and Mon, metro Les Corts. The original legendary **Bikini** was bulldozed to make room for the **L'Illa shopping centre**. The club has been recreated in the shopping centre and offers 3 different spaces, hosting everything from live gigs (very big names) to Latin sounds and lounge.
Mirablau, Pza Dr Andreu s/n, T933528746, 1100-0500, FGC Avinguda del Tibidabo then taxi uphill. Plaça Dr Andreu is where the Tramvia Blau stops and the funicular climbs up Tibidabo. The bar is a swanky, elegant spot with a terrace overlooking the whole city, perfect for a cocktail or some tapas.

🎭 Entertainment

For comprehensive, up to date information, see the cultural agenda section of the city's website, www.bcn.es

The weekly listings guide *La Guia del Ocio* (€90), www.guiadelocio.com, is on sale at most news kiosks (in Spanish with an English-language spread at the back). *LaNetro*, www.lanetro.com, is a comprehensive listings freebie (distributed in hotels and shops), but it's in Spanish only. You'll also find entertainment supplements in Fri day or Saturday editions of newspapers like *El Pais* or *El Mundo*. The quarterly bilingual style magazine/bible *b-Guided* (which includes a map) is on sale at some kiosks and distributed free in some bars and restaurants. There are dozens of free, usually very glossy and stylish, magazines distributed in bars and music shops: among

them are *AB*, *Go Mag*, *Punto H*, *Venus* and *Mondo Sonoro*. For information on theatre, classical music and opera, visit the very helpful Palau de la Virreina (see p254) and pick up the free leaflets.

Cinemas

Filmoteca de la Generalitat de Catalunya, Cinema Aquitania, Avda Sarrià 31-3, Eixample, T934107590. The Catalan government funds the **Filmoteca** which offers an overview of the history of cinema, with a constantly changing series of films devoted to themes, directors or countries.
Renoir-Les Corts, C/Eugeni d´Ors 12, Les Corts, T934905510, www.cinesrenoir.com. A well-equipped 6-screen cinema which offers at least 2 films in English. It also offers

the best facilities for disabled people.
Verdi, C/Verdi 32, T932370516 and **Verdi Park**, C/Torrijos 49, T933287900, www.cinemes-verdi.com. Both in Gràcia. Two cinemas in Gràcia showing international and Spanish art and independent films.

Contemporary music

There's always plenty going on in Barcelona, from impromptu performances in shabby bars to huge concerts with all the big names.

The **Sonar festival** of multimedia music and art is fantastic (see p294), and the **BAM festival** which runs at the same time as the **Festa de la Mercé** (see p294), is a great way to catch some alternative sounds. Jazz is traditionally very strong in the city, and the Andalusian immigrants and their children ensure that the flamenco scene retains its energy.

Clubs like **Jamboree** and **Luz de Gas** (see above) offer a real mixed-bag of musical styles, and are always worth checking out. There are plenty of venues covering everything else, from tiny, ultra-hip bars with the latest in electronica to huge crowded *salas* with mainstream rock and pop. Pick up flyers at music shops to discover some of the less well-known venues.
Bikini, C/ Deu i Mata 105, T933220005, metro Les Corts. See Bars and clubs above.
Harlem Jazz Club, C/Comtessa de Sobradiel 8, T933100755, metro Jaume I. One of the most dynamic jazz clubs in the city, small but atmospheric, with very creative programming.
Jamboree, C/Plaça Reial 17, T933017564, metro Liceu. Hugely popular and always packed. The programme includes jazz, blues, funk and hip-hop and the Sunday night blues nights is the best way to finish up the weekend. After performances, the club opens up to become a late-night club.
Jazz Sí Club, C/Requesens 2, T933290020, metro Universitat. Impromptu performances from students of the music school who run the place, as well as a diverse programme of live music each night, ranging from Cuban folk to soul, and jazz to rock.
Luz de Gas, C/Muntaner 246, T932097711, FGC Muntaner. A stunning turn-of-the century music hall, with a wide selection of live music: everything from soul, jazz and

salsa to rock and pop.
Razzmatazz, C/Almogavers 122, T933208200. See Bars and clubs above.
Sala Apolo, C/ Nou de la Rambla 113, T934414001, metro Paral.lel. One of the best-known live music venues in the city, with a varied programme of concerts including pop and rock, reggae and world music.

Dance

Barcelona's contemporary dance scene is the best in Spain, with dozens of innovative dance groups producing some of the most striking and exciting dance in Europe. Names to look out for include **Cesc Gelabert**; **Danat Dansa**; **Mudances**, founded by Angels Margarit; and **La Fura dels Baus**. Andalucian immigrants have kept the flamenco tradition alive, and there's a **Flamenco Festival** in early May and it's often possible to see some great visiting performers. The *tablaos* (flamenco shows) are touristy, but can be fun. Watch out for special events at some of the museums and cultural institutions like the **CCCB** and **MACBA** (see p266), and try to catch the 3-day dance festival (see p294) in mid-Sep or the dance programme *Dansa + a prop*, which offers a range of dance performances in several venues every 3 months. There are always dance events in the summer **Grec Festival** (see p294), which usually feature the best of local talent.
L'Espai de Dansa i Música, Travessera de Gràcia 63, Gràcia, T934143133, www.cultura.gencat.es. Advance sales also from *Servi-Caixa*. One of the few venues in the city with a dedicated dance slot; contemporary dance and music.
The following theatres regularly host dance events: **El Mercat de les Flors**, the **Teatre Nacional**, **Teatre Lliure** and the Sala Beckett (details below under theatres).

Classical music

The city's churches often offer concerts, particularly in the summer (details from the Palau de la Virreina, see p254). The church of Santa Maria del Mar is one of the loveliest, with perfect acoustics, but the cathedral of la Seu, the churches of Santa Maria del Pi, Santa Anna, Sant Felip Neri and the Monastery in

Pedralbes all offer a sporadic programme of concerts. **Festival de la Música Antigua** (see p294) is not to be missed, with early music in some of the city's most beautiful venues, like the *Saló de Tinell* in the Palau del Rei. Many of the museums also offer concerts: it's always worth checking out what's on at the **CCCB** (see p266) and the Fundació Miró, and there is a series of concerts in the city parks during the summer.

Gran Teatre del Liceu, La Rambla 51-59, T934859900, www.liceubarcelona. com, Metro Liceu. The (almost) faithful reincarnation of the celebrated opera house has become extremely popular, so getting hold of tickets can be difficult. There's now a subterranean extension which offers recitals, talks, children's puppet shows and other events, usually related to the main programme.

Palau de la Música Catalana, C/Sant Francesc de Paula 2, Barri Gòtic, T932957200, www.palaumusica.org. The acoustics may be terrible, but the triumphant Modernista setting makes any performance worthwhile (see p264).

Flamenco

Barcelona can't compare with Madrid, Seville or Granada on the flamenco front, but there are a few decent choices if you want to catch an act.

El Tablao de Carmen, Poble Espanyol, Montjüic, T933256895. Set inside the 'Spanish village', this is a pricey flamenco joint geared towards coachloads of tourists, but features very high-class acts, and if you book in advance you won't have to pay the entrance fee into the Poble Espanyol.

Los Tarantos, Placa Reial 17, Barri Gòtic, T933183067. Popular, touristy flamenco *tablao*, but this venue has the added attraction of a late-night club and other performances.

Theatres

Barcelona's theatrical tradition is both accessible and highly innovative, with several experimental theatre groups demonstrating the city's flair, verve and innovation. The widespread use of multi-media, mime and choreography

means that theatre in the city can cross any linguistic barriers.

The latest project in the city's ambitious drive for redevelopment is the **Ciutat de la Teatre**, which opened in 2001, and offers theatres, student spaces, a museum of theatre, the Theatre Institute and the Mercat de las Flors theatre.

Institut del Teatre, Plaça Margarida Xirgú, T932273900, www.diba.es/iteatre. Student productions in Barcelona's theatre school, which has been given elegant new premises in the Ciutat del Teatre. The work is always interesting and very inexpensive.

Mercat de les Flors, C/Lleida 59, Montjüic, T934261875, www.bcn.es/icub/mflorsteatre. This beautifully converted flower market has become one of the main venues for the **Grec Festival** (see p294) and puts on productions from some of the city's most innovative performers. Excellent contemporary dance as well as cutting edge drama.

Sala Beckett, C/Alegre de Dalt 55 bis, T932845312, www.teatral,net/beckett. Founded by the **Teatro Frontizero** group, which includes the eminent contemporary playwright José Sanchis Sinistierra. Interesting new theatre and contemporary dance.

Teatre Lliure, C/Montseny 47, T932189251, www.teatrelliure.com. One of the most prestigious theatres in Catalunya which has produced some of its leading actors and directors. It has a brand new outpost in the refurbished Palau de l'Agricultura in Montjüic, part of the city's Ciutat del Teatre complex.

Teatre Nacional de Catalunya (TNC), Plaça de les Arts 1, Eixample, T933065707, www.tnc.es. Inaugurated in 1997, this Ricardo-Bofill designed building is the flagship of the city council's efforts to smarten up the grim Glories district. Performances range from high quality drama to contemporary dance.

Spectator sports

Basketball Basketball is massively popular throughout Spain. Barcelona's 2 biggest teams are **FC Barça** and **Club Joventut Badalona**. The season runs from Sep-May.
FC Barcelona Palau Blau Grana (next to Camp Nou stadium), Avda d'Arisitides Maillol, metro Collblanc, T934963675, tickets

from €5-25, www.fcbarcelona.com, **Club Joventut Badalona**. C/Ponent 143-161, Badalona (on the outskirts of the city), T934602040, metro Gorg, tickets from €15-20, www.penya.com.

Bullfighting The *corrida* season runs from April to September. Children under 14 are not admitted.

Plaza de Toros Monumental, 749 Gran Via de les Catalanes 749, T932159570, metro Monumental. Tickets from €15-90.

Football The city has 2 first-division clubs: **FC Barcelona** and **RCD Espanyol**. Getting tickets for the Camp Nou stadium is difficult, but you stand a chance of seeing **Espanyol** play. The season runs from late Aug-May.

FC Barcelona Camp Nou, Avda d'Arisitides Maillol, metro Collblanc, T934963600, ticket hotline: T934963702, tickets from €20-90,

www.fcbarcelona.com. An online ticket sales service is on the way, but for now you'll have to buy tickets from the stadium ticket office, available 2 days before a match. **RCD Espanyol**, Estadi Olimpic, Pg. Olimpic, 17-19, Montjüic, metro Paral.lel then funicular, or metro to Plaça Espanya then shuttle bus (match days only), www.rcdespanyol.com. Tickets for Barcelona's less famous team can be purchased near the stadium entrance.

Tennis Barcelona Open, a prestigious 10-day international tournament, takes place at Barcelona's smartest tennis club during the last week of Apr.

Reial Club de Tennis Barcelona-1899, C/ Bosch i Gimpera 5-13, T932037852, bus 63, 78, tickets €20-60. Bono-tickets give you admission to all 10 days and are better value, www.rctb1899.es.

☻ Festivals and events

Contact the Palau de la Virreina (see p254) for information on cultural festivals.

1 Jan Cap d'Any/Noche Vieja: Street parties and carousing to bring in the New Year. Big club nights – with high prices.

5 Jan Cavalcada des Reis: The Three Kings parade through the city throwing sweets to the kids.

Feb/Mar Carnestoltes/Carnaval: Carnival is not such a big event as in other parts of Spain, but there's a great party atmosphere all the same.

23 Apr Sant Jordi: Big celebration for the festival of the patron saint of Catalunya. Lovers traditionally exchange gifts on this day – books for men and roses for women (nowadays it's often the other way around).

Holy Week Semana Santa: Parades and religious processions.

Late Apr/Early May Feria de Abril: Andalucian-style flamenco and carousing.

11 May Festa de Sant Ponç: A street market on Carrer Hospital (Raval) to honour of the patron saint of beekeepers and herbalists.

May Festival de Flamenco and Festival de Música Antigua: Festivals of flamenco and early music.

May/Jun Corpus Christi: See the 'ou com balla' (egg dancing on a fountain) in the cathedral cloister.

Jun Trobada Castellera: The casteller

groups build human castles in the Plaça Sant Jaume.

Early Jun Marató de l'Espectacle: Non-stop alternative performances at the Mercat de les Flors (see Theatres above).

21 Jun Festa de la Música: City-wide free concerts on the streets.

23 and 24 Jun Festa de Sant Joan: The most exuberant festival in the Catalan calendar: bonfires, fireworks, demons and *cava*.

28 Jun Dia per l'Alliberament Lesbià i Gia: Gay pride parade though the city.

Jun/Jul Sónar Festival of Multimedia and Music: www.sonar.es.

Jun/Jul Classics als Parcs Classical: Concerts in the city's parks, www.bcn.es /parcsijardins.

Jun/Jul Festival del Grec: The city's biggest performing arts festival.

Mid-late Aug Festa Major de Gràcia: Gràcia's neighbourhood festival.

11 Sep Diada National de Catalunya: Catalan National Day.

Mid-Sep Dies de Dansa: 3-day festival of dance.

24 Sep Festes de la Mercè: A massive week-long celebration, with dragons, fatheads, human castles, fire-running and fireworks, all kinds free events, a swimming race across the harbour, as well as concerts and the BAM alternative music festival.

End-Sep Festa Major de la Barceloneta: Barceloneta's neighbourhood festival.
Oct-Dec International Jazz Festival.
1 Nov Tots Sants (Castanyada): All Saints Day; people visit family graves and eat traditional foods.
1-22 Dec Fira de Santa Llúcia: The feast day of Santa Llúcia marks the beginning of the Christmas season and the Christmas market.

25-26 Dec Nadal and Sant Esteve: Christmas and the Catalan equivalent of Boxing Day are low-key family affairs, with big family lunches; kids beat the Christmas Log, shouting '¡Caga Tio¡ ¡Caga¡' – Shit, log! Shit! The log bursts open to reveal a small gift. The main present giving doesn't happen until 6 Jan.

O Shopping

The designer shop Vinçon on the Passeig de Gràcia used to have the slogan 'I shop therefore I am' blazoned across its packaging. No other city makes shopping so easy, with more shops per capita than anywhere else in Europe. They range from tiny old-fashioned stores which haven't changed at all in decades, to grand glitzy shopping malls where you can get everything you could possibly want under one roof.

Bookshops, newspapers and magazines

The stalls along the Rambla all have a good selection of foreign newspapers and magazines and occasionally even a few novels in English.
Altaïr, C/Balmes 69-71, metro Passeig de Gràcia. A travel and sailing specialist with a good selection of books, guides and maps, many in English.
Fnac, El Triangle, Plaça Catalunya 4, metro Catalunya. Enormous store with books, music, a concert ticket service, and an international news-stand and café on the ground floor.

Department stores

El Corte Inglés, Plaça Catalunya 14, www.elcorteingles.com, metro Catalunya. This huge department store is part of a vast Spanish chain. There's a basement supermarket and delicatessen, plus fashion, leathergoods, toiletries, electrical goods, and souvenirs. There's a café on the top floor with fabulous views, and look out for the 'Opportunidads' or bargains on the 8th floor. There's another branch just down the

road at Avda Portal de l'Àngel which has books, music and DVDs.

Design, decorative arts and household goods

BD Edicions de Disseny, C/ Mallorca 291, metro Passeig de Gràcia. Set in a stunning Modernista mansion, the **BD** group was founded in 1972 by the prestigious architect Òscar Tusquets among others. Exquisite, expensive furniture – both reproduction Modernista and contemporary designs – and other household goods.
Galeries Vinçon, Passeig de Gràcia 96, www.vincon.com, metro Diagonal. The best-known and most influential design emporium in the city, located right next to La Pedrera, with everything for the home from furniture and lighting to kitchenware and table accoutrements.
Ici et Là, Plaça Santa Maria del Mar 2, www.icietla.com, metro Jaume I or Barceloneta. Affordable, unusual creations for the home from around the world.

Fashion

Barcelona has an excellent reputation for cutting edge design; there are hundreds of boutiques offering the unusual work of local designers, as well as plenty of others which feature the latest from the big international fashion houses. Carrer Portaferrissa in the Barri Gòtic is lined with young fashion shops, and there are several new designers popping up almost daily in the trendy Born area. The Raval has lots of clubwear and vintage fashions, and the big, international fashions (**Chanel**, **Prada** and **Gucci** et al), can be found up in the Eixample, particularly along the Diagonal.

Bad Habits, C/València 261, metro Passeig de Gràcia. Strikingly original, often androgynous designs from Mireya Ruiz.

Camper, El Triangle, C/Pelai 13, www.camper.es, metro Catalunya. Trendy, comfortable shoes at a reasonable price.

Forum Ferlandina, C/Ferlandina 31, www.forumjoies.es, metro Universitat. This original jewellers, just around the corner from MACBA, has a range of unusual contemporary designs in everything from gold to plastic.

Furla, Plaça Francesc Macià 5, metro Les Corts, FGC Gràcia. Flagship store offering very stylish bags and shoes in unusual colours and designs.

Giménez & Zuazo, C/ Elisabets 20, metro Catalunya. Ultra-hip women's fashions from this Raval-based designer shop. Bright colours and prints feature in their latest collection, and you'll also find their BoBa t-shirts.

Jean-Pierre Bua, Avda Diagonal 469, metro Diagonal. The original and best-known designer fashion shop, with the latest from names like **Jean-Paul Gaultier**, **Vivienne Westwood** and **Dries Van Noten**. There is also a selection of unusual, stylish bridal wear.

Mango, Passeig de Gràcia 65, www.mangoshop.com, metro Passeig de Gràcia. Catwalk fashion at affordable prices, with ranges for work, evening and casual wear, including shoes and accessories. Several branches.

Mies & Felj, C/ Riera Baixa 5, metro Liceu or Sant Antoni. A great selection of second-hand jackets, dresses, hats, bags and t-shirts.

Tribu, C/Avinyó 12, metro Jaume I. One of several slick fashion boutiques on this street. Trendy outlet for designers like **D&G**, **E-Play**, **No.L.Ita**, and **Diesel Style** as well as their own label. Look out for guest DJ nights.

Zara, C/Pelai 58, metro Catalunya. Great fashion – clothes and accessories – for men, women, teenagers and kids at very low prices. Check fastenings, etc, before you buy.

Food and wine

Casa del Bacalao, C/Comtal 8, metro Urquinaona. This ancient, delightful little shop sells nothing but dried and salted cod. They will pack it specially if you want to take it home.

Escribà, Gran Via de les Cortes Catalanes 546, metro Urgell. Chocolate heaven, and it's worth coming just to see the incredible window displays. Wonderful cakes and beautifully packaged chocolates.

Queviures Murrià, C/ Roger de Llúria 85, metro Passeig de Gràcia. This old-fashioned grocery store is set in a beautiful old Modernista premises. You'll find a range of farmhouse cheeses, excellent hams, and a good selection of wines and cavas.

Vila Viniteca, C/Agullers 7-9, www.vilaviniteca.es, metro Jaume I. This is a family-run wine store, with a dizzying selection of wines and cavas from all over Catalunya and Spain.

Malls

El Triangle, C/Pelai 39, www.triangle.es. Metro Catalunya. This gleaming mall contains an enormous **Fnac** (books, music and concert tickets), **Habitat**, **Sephora** (perfumes and cosmetics), a **Camper** shoe store and several other smaller fashion shops.

L'Illa, Avda Diagonal 545-557, www.illa.es. Metro María Christina. The largest mall in the city, this has all the fashion chains there are along with a **Fnac**, **Decathlon** sports shop, and several upmarket fashion boutiques.

Markets

Els Encants, Plaça de las Glòries Catalanes, metro Glòries. A sprawling flea market; get there early if you want a bargain and keep a close eye on your belongings.

La Boquería, La Rambla 91, metro Liceu. Barcelona's best loved food market with hundreds of stalls. Stalls at the front have tourist prices – be prepared to browse and price check.

Mercat de Sant Antoni, C/Comte d'Urgell 1, metro Sant Antoni. Another wrought-iron Modernista market, the fresh produce stalls are replaced by a second-hand book and coin market on Sun.

Plaça del Pi, metro Liceu. Plaça del Pi hosts several markets. On the first Fri and Sat of the month, there's a honey market, when you'll also find other things like cured hams and farmhouse cheeses for sale. There's an antiques market on Thu, and art is for sale

on weekends in the adjoining **Plaça Josep Oriol**.

Music

Discos Castelló, C/Tallers 3, www.discoscast ello.com, metro Catalunya. There are several branches of this music shop; this one specializes in classical music. For Spanish and international dance music, go to C/Nou de la Rambla 15.
Etnomusic, C/Bonsuccés 6, www.etnomusic. com, metro Catalunya. Well-known world music shop with helpful staff.

Sports goods

Nus Esports de Muntanya, Plaça Diamant 9, metro Fontana. A mecca for mountaineers or anyone interested in adventure sports.
Tactic Surf Shop, C/Enric Granados 11, metro Universitat. Clothes and equipment for surfers, windsurfers, snowboarders and skateboarders.
Tomás Domingo, C/ Rocafort 173, metro

shops in the city, with a wide range of models and accessories.

Unusual shops

Almacenes del Pilar, C/Boquería 43, metro Liceu. A stunning selection of traditional fringed Spanish silk shawls and elaborate fans.
El Ingenio, C/Rauric 6, metro Liceu. This magical old shop was founded in 1838. Inside you'll find everything you need for a fiesta – puppets, masks, carnival and fancy dress outfits.
El Rei de la Màgia, C/Princesa 11, ww.arrakis.es/~reimagia. Metro Jaume I. An extraordinary shop devoted to magic and magicians, with walls papered with photographs of celebrated magicians.
Kitsch, Placeta de Montcada 10, metro Jaume I. A virtually life-sized papier mache model of a grinning gipsy sits at the entrance to this extraordinary shop; inside are even wilder creations.

▲ Activities and tours

Barcelona Sports Information Centre: Servei d'Informació Esportiva, Avda de l'Estadi 30-40, Montjüic, T934023000. Leaflets and information on local sports centres.

Golf

Club de Golf El Prat, El Prat de Llobregat, T933790278. Daily 0800-2200. This club is out near the airport (get a taxi). In past years, this club has been used for the **Spanish Open**. You must be a member of a federated club to play.
Club de Golf Sant Cugat, C/de la Villa s/n, Sant Cugat del Vallès, T936743958, FGC from Plaça Catalunya to Sant Cugat. Open daily 0800-2200. 18-hole course with a bar, restaurant and pool.

Gyms and fitness clubs

Centres de Fitness DiR. There are seven well-equipped (pools, saunas, weight rooms, etc) DiR fitness centres in the city; for

location information call T901304030 or check out www.dirfitness.es. Bring your passport to sign up.

Jogging

Best places to jog include the boardwalk from Barceloneta to Mar Bella – run early before the crowds come. Parc de Collserola is another great place for a run (see p279). The park information centre has maps. There are fantastic views along Carretera de les Aigüess at the top of Av Tibidabo in the Collserola.

Sailing and watersports

Base Nàutica de la Mar Bella, Avda de Litoral (between the beaches of Bogatell and Mar Bella), T932210432. Daily winter 0930-1730, summer 0930-2100. Windsurf rentals, boat rentals, Snorkelling equipment rentals and a wide range of courses. There's also the added bonus of DJ sessions in summer.
Centre Municipal de Vela, Moll de Gregal,

Port Olímpic, T932211499, www.vela-barcelona.com. Mon-Fri 0900-2100, Sat and Sun 0900-2000, office open daily 1000-2000. Sailing courses for all levels.

Swimming

Club de Natació Barceloneta/Banys de Sant Sebastià, Plaça del Mar 1, T932210010, www.cnab.org, metro Barceloneta. Jun to mid-Sep Mon-Sat 0700-2300, Sun 0800-200, mid-Sep to Jun Mon-Sat 0700-2300, Sun 0800-1700. Very close to Barceloneta beach. Indoor and outdoor pools, gym, sauna, restaurant and café.

Piscina Bernat Picornell, Avda de l'Estadi 30-40, T934234041, www.picornell.com, metro Paral.lel then funicular, or metro to Plaça Espanya then bus no 61. Mon-Fri 0700-2400, Sat 0700-2100, Sun 0730-1600 (until 2000 Jun-Sep). Magnificent pools used in 1992 Olympics. Indoor and outdoor pools, gym/weights room.

Tennis

Centre Municipal de Tennis Vall d'Hebron, Psg de la Vall d'Hebron 178-196, T934276500, metro Montbau. Mon-Sat 0800-2300, Sun 0800-1900. 17 clay courts, 7 asphalt courts and 2 open-air pools.

Yoga

Happy Yoga Centre, Rambla de Catalunya 7, T93 318 11 07. Metro Catalunya. This occasionally offers classes in English. Call for times and more information.
Centre de Ioga Iyengar de Barcelona, C/ Pelai 52-3, T 93 318 35 33. Metro Catalunya. Pure Iyengar yoga in a convenient, central location.

🚇 Transport

Air

Air France: T933797463, www.airfrance.com.
British Airways: T902111333, www.british-airways.com.
Delta: T901116946, www.delta-air.com.
easyJet: T902299992, www.easyjet.com.
Iberia: T902400500, www.iberia.com.
For further information, see p248.

Bus

The main hub for buses is the Plaça Catalunya. The bus stops display clear, user-friendly bus maps listing the stops made on each route. Single tickets cost €1.10. Buses on most routes usually run from Mon-Sat 0600-2230, with a less frequent service on Sun. The night bus (*nit bus*) service runs from 2230-0400 daily and covers 16 routes. Most pass through Plaça Catalunya, and arrive roughly every half hour. The discount passes like the **T-Dia** or the **T-10** are not valid; you must buy a single ticket (€1.10), or invest in the 10-trip night bus *targeta* which costs €7. These are only available on board the bus. The local bus routes are clearly marked at bus stops, and the TMB and tourist offices have a useful transport map. It's unlikely that you'll need buses to get around the old city, but useful bus routes for tourists are: Nos 50 and 61 for Montjüic; No 24 to the gate of the Parc Güell; No 63 for the Palau Reial de Pedralbes and the Monestir de Santa Maria de Pedralbes; Nos 14, 17, 19 and 36 for Barceloneta. Bus Nos 14 ,38, 51 and 59 run the whole length of La Rambla.

Car

Driving in Barcelona is not to be recommended: the streets are small and always clogged and parking spaces are difficult to find. Cars with foreign plates or hire cars are prime targets for thieves so don't ever leave anything valuable in them and use monitored underground car parks when possible.

Offices of the major car rental companies can be found at the airport, and at Barcelona-Sants train station. The best deals are almost always available online, and you should find out if the airline you fly with offers special car rental deals.

❖ Arriving late in Barcelona

Trains and buses from the airport stop at around 2330. After this, you'll have to get a taxi. Call one of the following if there are none at the taxi ranks, Fono-Taxi T93300 1100; Ràdio Taxi T932250000; Taxi Ràdio Móbil T933581111. Note that few drivers speak English.

There are a couple of expensive business hotels near the airport (like the Best Western Alfa Aeropuerto, T933362564, which will collect guests) but budget travellers should make for the Barri Gòtic where most of the cheaper hostels are. Try Carrer

Boquería just off the Rambla which has dozens of places. If you can't get anywhere to stay – more than likely in the height of the season – you may as well find a bar or a club and hang out there until the morning. Again, most bars and clubs are concentrated in the Barri Gòtic in the centre of the old city. You can get some breakfast at La Boquería market which opens around 0500 and is just off the Rambla. Sleeping outdoors or on the beach is not advisable – there have been reports of thefts and attacks.

Avis, T902135531, www.avis.com.
Europcar, T934914822, www.europcar.com.
National (a partner of the Spanish car hire firm, **Atesa**), T902100101, www.national. com, www.atesa.es.
Vanguard, T934393880, C/Villadomat 297, www.vanguardrent.com. Local car hire firm, which also rents out motorbikes and scooters.

Cycling

There are very few cycle lanes in Barcelona, and cycling through the maze of narrow streets in the old city isn't very practical. However, if you're happy to brave the kamikaze drivers on the roads in the Eixample, bikes can be a practical way of seeing the sights which are more spread-out. Bikes are great if you want to do some off-road cycling in the wonderful Parc de Collserola (see p279) behind Tibidabo. Cycling along the seafront, from Barceloneta, along the Port Olímpic and out to the beaches of Mar Bella is a great way to spend an afternoon. The tourist information centre at the Plaça Catalunya has a free cycling map of the city.
Al Punt de Trobada, C/ Badajoz 24, T932250585, www.lasguias.com. Bike (including tandems) and roller-blade rental. They also offer guided tours by arrangement.

Biciclot-Marítim, Pg. Marítim, Platja de Barceloneta, www.biciclot.net. Bikes and

tandems for rent – great location on the beach front if you want to cycle along the boardwalk.
Scenic, C/ Marina 22, T932211666, www.gdesigners.com/scenic. Bike and roller-blades for sale or rental. They can also organize day or night-time excursions.
Un Cotxe Menys, C/ Esparteria 3, T932682105. 'One car less' (in Catalan) do bike rentals, and offer guided tours.

FGC trains

Some city and suburban destinations are served by FGC trains (Ferrocarrils de Generalitat de Catalunya), which are run by the Catalan government. They are mainly useful for getting to the less central sights like Gràcia or Tibidabo.

Metro

There are six metro lines (Mon-Thu 0500-2300, Fri-Sat 0500-0200, Sun 0600-2400) identified by number and colour. A single ticket costs €1.10 or you can get a T-Dia for €4.60 which allows unlimited transport on the bus, metro and FGC trains for 1 person during 1 day, or a T-10, which offers10 trips on the bus, metro and FGC trains for €6 and can be shared.

Taxi

City taxis are yellow and black, and easily

Barcelona Transport

available. There's a taxi stand on the Plaça de Catalunya, just across the street from the main tourist information office. To call: **Barnataxi**, T933577755; **Fono-Taxi** T933001100; **Ràdio Taxi** T932250000.

Teleféric/cable cars

Telefèric de Monjüic The cable car from Avda Miramar swings up to the castle at the top of the hill. Open Jun-mid-Sep, daily 1115-2100; mid-Sep-mid-Nov daily 1100-1915; mid-Nov-mid-March weekends only 1100-1915; mid-March-mid-Jun daily 1100-1915. Open daily over New Year and Easter holidays. Tickets cost €3.60 single and €5 return.

Telefèric de Barceloneta The cable car journey across the bay is one of the most thrilling rides in Barcelona, and definitely not for people suffering from vertigo. It closes intermittently for works. It runs from the Miramar station at the end of Avda Miramar on Montjüic down to Passeig de Joan de Borbo in Barceloneta, via the tower near the new World Trade Centre. Open daily mid-Oct-Feb 1030-1730, March-mid-Jun and mid-Sep-mid-Oct 1030-1900, mid-Jun-mid-Sep 1030-2000. Ticket prices are hefty: €9 return.

Tram and funicular

Tramvia Blau/Blue Tram A refurbished antique tram which is the first part of the journey up Tibidabo. It runs every 15-30 minutes between from Plaça Kennedy (near

FGC train station Avda del Tibdabo) to the Plaça Andreu (tickets cost €2 single and €2.90 return) where it joins the funicular (see below). Runs 1000-1805, weekends only in winter (mid-Sep to mid-Jun) and daily in summer and over Easter.

Tibidabo funicular Take the funicular from the Plaça Andreu to the top of Tibidabo. Single €2, return €3. Open end-Sep-early Jun Sat, Sun and public hols1030-1930; in May also Thu and Fri 1000-1800; Jun-Aug Mon-Fri 1030-2230, Sat and Sun 1030-1330.

Montjüic funicular Departs Paral.lel metro station and heads up to Avda Miramar, close to the Fundació Miró. Metro tickets and passes are valid, or a single ticket costs €1.10. Open spring and summer 0900-2200, autumn and winter 0900-2200. It connects with the telefèric/cable car to the top of Montjüic (see below).

Walking

Barcelona is a delightful city to walk around, and seeing it on foot is definitely the best way to appreciate its charms. The sights of the old city are all within easy walking distance, but those of the Eixample are quite spread out. There are free maps provided by the the the big department store **El Corte Inglés**, but it's worth investing in the slightly better tourist office map (€1.5). There's also a great interactive Barcelona street map at www.bcn.es/guia.

Directory

Cultural centres

British Institute, C/Amigó 83, T932096090. English lessons, library, and a noticeboard full of accommodation ads.
North American Institute, Via Augusta 123, T932405110. Useful reference library.

Dentist

Centre Odontològic de Barcelona, C/Calabria 251, Eixample, T934394500, metro Entença.

Embassies and consulates

There's a full list of embassies and consulates in the phone book under Consolats/ Consulados.
Australia, Gran Via Carles III 98, metro Maria Cristina, T933309496, www.spain.embassy. gov.au.
Canada, C/Elisanda de Pinós 10, FCG Reina Elisanda, T932150704, www.canada-es.org.
Ireland, Gran Via Carles III 94, metro Maria Cristina or Les Corts, T934519021, F934112921.

New Zealand, Travessera de Gràcia 64, FGC
Gràcia, T932090399, www.nzemb.org.
UK, Avda Diagonal 477, metro Hospital
Clinic, T933666200, www.ukinspain.com.
USA, Psg Reina Elisenda 23, FCG Reina
Elisenda, T932802227, www.embusa.es.

Hospitals

Centre d'Urgències Perecamps, Avda
Drassanes 13-15, T934410600, metro
Drassanes or Paral.lel. This clinic deals with
less serious emergencies and injuries.
Hospital Clínic, C/ Villarroel 170,
T932275400, metro Hospital Clinic.
Hospital de la Santa Creu i Sant Pau, Avda
Sant Antoni María Claret 167, T932919000,
metro Hospital de Sant Pau.

Internet

Bcnet-Internet gallery Café, C/ Barra de
Ferro 3, T932681507, www.bcnetcafe.com.
Daily 1000-0100. Relaxed little internet café
in a cool brick vaulted space, just down a
side street close to the Picasso museum. It's
very friendly and has its own decks playing
soothing music, as well as regularly
changing art exhibitions on the walls.
Rates are from €1.50 for 30 mins.
EasyEverything, Ronda Universitat 35,
T932448080, and La Rambla 41. Both
branches open 24 hrs. The monster of the
internet cafés, there are 300 terminals in the
Eixample branch and 450 at the branch on
La Rambla. Prices depend on demand, but
€1 will get you about 30 mins at peak times
(lunchtimes and early evening) and up to 3
hrs early in the morning.
Idea, Plaça Comercial 2, T932688787,
www.ideaborn.com. Mon-Thu 0830-2400, Fri
0830-0300, Sat 1000-0300, Sun 1000-2300.
Delightful bookshop, café and internet
centre, with comfy chairs, reading areas,
books for sale or loan, magazines to flick
through with your coffee. Prices start at
€1 for 30 mins.

Pharmacies

Farmàcia Alvarez, Passeig de Gràcia 26,
T933021124, metro Passeig de Gràcia. 24-hrs.
Farmàcia Clapés, La Rambla 98,
T933012843, metro Liceu. 24-hrs.

Post offices

Correos (postboxes) marked Correos y
Telégrafos, are yellow. Most tobacconists
(estancos, marked with a brown and yellow
symbol) sell stamps. You can send or receive
faxes from any post office. The main office is
on Plaça d'Anton López (at the port end of
Vía Laietana), T934124166, Mon-Sat
0830-2130, Sun 0900-1400.

Telephones

Public payphones will accept coins and
pre-paid telephone cards (available from
tobacconists). Phone centres (locutarios) are
the cheapest way for calling abroad; there's
one in the Plaça Catalunya RENFE station,
another in the Estació del Autobuses del
Nord, and another in Sants station.

Useful addresses

Emergency numbers There is one
number for all the emergency services
(ambulance, fire and police): T112.
To contact the emergency services directly,
call: Ambulance/Ambulància T061; Fire
service/Bombers/Bomberos T080; National
Police/Policia Nacional T091; Municipal
Police/Policia Municipal T092.
Police station The most central
comisarías (police stations) are at C/Nou de
la Rambla 76-80, T932904849 and C/Bosch
4-8, T932903087. If you have to report a
crime, go immediately to the Turisme Atenció
station on the Rambla (La Rambla 43,
T933019060 or T933441300, open daily
24 hrs), a special police service for assisting
tourists, with multi-lingual staff.

❖ Footprint features

Introduction

Catalunya packs a lot into a small space. Bounded by the Pyrenees to the north and the Mediterranean coast to the east, the Catalan interior veers dramatically from endless wetlands to sudden volcanic eruptions, or waterfall-studded cliffs. Its attractions are as diverse as its geography: from seaside holiday towns to remote mountain villages, Romanesque churches to Modernista bodegas, and chic ski resorts to wild natural parks.

Barcelona, Catalunya's proud, flamboyant capital, shouldn't be missed, but the rest of the region boasts a dazzling array of attractions. The Belle of the Catalan coast is **Sitges**, a fun-loving town which goes wild during **Carnaval**. The southern tip of Catalunya is swallowed up by the haunting flat wetlands of the **Delta de l'Ebre**.

To the north of Barcelona is the the wild, remote **Cap de Creus** which Dalí made his home. **Girona**, Catalunya's second city, has a beautiful medieval core barely touched by time, and a lively nightlife. The **Pyrenees** are wilder, craggier and altogether less civilized. Trek across the hauntingly beautiful **Parc Nacional Aigüestortes** or snowboard at one of a dozen resorts. West of Barcelona are the eerie jagged peaks of Montserrat, Catalunya's holy mountain, with great hiking and climbing. More medieval monasteries dream silently in the quiet villages of **Poblet** and **Santa Creus**, and in **Villafranca de Penedès**, you can taste the local fizz, cava.

The tiny Principality of **Andorra**, wedged between Spain and France and deep in the Pyrenees, is best known for its duty-free shopping and winter sports. Avoid the brash capital and head into the hills.

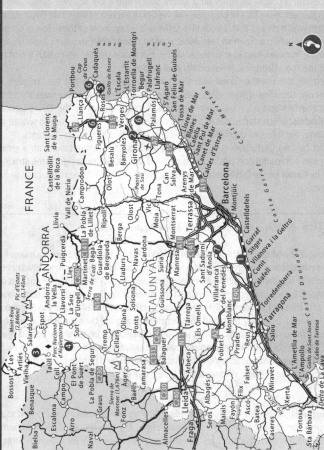

FRANCE

ANDORRA

CATALUNYA

Barcelona

Tarragona

Costa Brava

Costa del Maresme

Costa Daurada

Costa Garraf

N

0 km 20

0 miles 20

Catalunya & Andorra

★ Don't miss...

① **Sitges** Visit this gorgeous seaside party town, stuffed full of reminders of Modernista painters and home of crazy nightlife, page 306.

② **Girona** Explore the Jewish ghetto in Girona, a shadowy maze of narrow stone passages steeped in history, page 339.

③ **Vall de Boí** Contemplate the Romanesque churches and frescoes of this valley, page 360.

④ **Parc Nacional d'Aigüestortes** Trek across this magnificent park, one of the most beautiful regions of Spain, page 359.

⑤ **Cadaqués and Cap de Creus** Hire a boat in pretty whitewashed Cadaqués and explore the wild, remote Cap de Creus, page 329.

⑥ **Dalí triangle** Follow in Dalí's footsteps and take in the 'Dalí triangle': the museum in Figueres, page 343, his home in Port Lligat, page 329, and the castle in Púbol, page 344.

⑦ **Sant Sadurní d'Anoia** Taste Catalunya's famous fizz, *cava*, at one of the ornate, Modernista *bodegas* in Sant Sadurní d'Anoia, page 308.

South of Barcelona

The beaches south of Barcelona are long and golden. The prettiest seaside town is Sitges, which also has the wildest and most outrageous nightlife. The buzzy, easy-going city of Tarragona is crammed with Roman ruins, but also has a clutch of good beaches, and a port full of great seafood restaurants. The resorts of the Costa Daurada aren't for everyone, but fine if you are just looking for sun, sea and sand. At the southernmost tip are the wild, empty wetlands of the Ebre Delta, a paradise for bird-watchers. Inland, there are Modernista bodegas for trying out local wines and cava, the spectacular medieval monasteries of the 'Cisterican Triangle' and a smattering of fine old medieval towns and villages with some fantastic local festivals. ►► *For Sleeping, Eating and other listings, see pages 317-323.*

Costa Garraf

Almost in the suburbs of Barcelona are a couple of cheerful, if undistinguished resorts, which have almost been swallowed up in Barcelona's sprawl, but they are still good for a couple of hours on a sandy beach and a big seafood dinner. Most foreign tourists make for the big resorts of the Costa Brava and the Costa Daurada, in the north which means that, although relatively low-key, most of these towns closer to Barcelona retain a Spanish feel. Most coastal resorts offer excellent facilities for everything from sea-kayaking to water-skiing, but Castelldefels, which had a part to play in the 1992 Olympics, is especially well equipped.

Leaving the city the Garraf Massif drops dramatically into the sea, creating a spectacular coastline of steep cliffs overlooking tiny coves. Beyond the massif stretch sandy beaches and a couple bustling seaside towns known as the Costa Garraf. **Castelldefels**, which started out as a tourist resort, has effectively become a suburb of Barcelona, but it has long golden beaches and some fine seafood restaurants.

Just beyond Castelldefels is **Garraf**, a quietly pretty seaside town with a great beach and a colourful port packed with seafood *tascas*. Gaudí designed the striking **Celler de Garraf** for the Güell family in 1888, a pointy, fairytale *bodega* attached to an old keep.

Sitges → *Phone code: 938; Colour map 3, grid B4; Population: 19,583.*

The Belle of the whole coastline south of Barcelona is undoubtedly Sitges, a beautiful whitewashed town clustered around a rosy church out on a promontory, which gets packed with hip Barcelonans on summer weekends. Strictly speaking, it's not part of the Costa Daurada proper (which begins a few miles down the coast) but it does have some of the finest long sandy beaches on the coast. No one really comes to Sitges for the museums; beaches, bars and the certainty of a good time are what draw the hordes of trendy Barcelonans. Since the 1960s, it's also become a hugely popular gay resort who put the kick into its famously over-the-top celebrations for Carnival in early spring. The long sandy beaches are invariably crowded, and right at the westernmost end are a couple of pretty wild nudist beaches, one of which is gay.

Sights
Cau Ferrat ① *C/Fonollar s/n, T938940364, 15 Jun-15 Sep 1000-1400 and 1700-2100, 16 Sep-14 Jun Tue-Fri 1000-1330 and 1500-1830, €3, free first Wed of the month, combined ticket available to Sitges' three museums at €5 – valid for 1 month.* Sitges

⁝ He says plaça and I say plaza

Catalunya doesn't feel like the rest of Spain – probably because it doesn't really consider itself Spanish. Now an autonomous community, the Catalans are too pragmatic to contemplate a complete break with Spain, but they still consider themselves a nation apart. Post-Franco Catalunya has vigorously encouraged the re-emergence of its national language, traditions and culture, and Catalan, rather than Castellano, is the *lingua franca*.

has a big reputation for partying, which began when the Modernista painter Santiago Rusiñol (one of the founders of **Els Quatre Gats** in Barcelona, see page 261) set up home here in the 1890s. Two little fishermen's cottages leaning over a sheer cliff in the heart of the old town were expensively and flamboyantly renovated, the walls painted a glowing azure blue and hung with paintings by all Rusiñol's friends including Picasso, and then the place was crammed with a fantastical hoard of Catalan ironwork; he called it the Cau Ferrat –'Den of Iron' – and it is now a fascinating museum. Rusiñol made the top floor into one huge neo-Gothic hall, which looks like a cross between a cathedral and a junkshop: it's stuffed full of ironwork, bric-a-brac, paintings and bits of ancient pottery and glass which Rusiñol dug up himself. There are also two minor paintings by El Greco, which were the star attraction of the 1894 Festa Modernista (Festival of Modernism), when they were brought from Barcelona by train and then hoisted aloft by four artists and taken in a solemn procession to their new home in the Cau Ferrat – for years, the residents of Sitges thought Señor El Greco was one of Rusiñol's relatives. Rusiñol's home was always filled with artists, musicians and writers, and he organised five Modernist Festivals between 1892 and 1899 to celebrate the new ideas that were being expounded – the wild antics which accompanied these festivals gained the town a heady reputation for bad behaviour which it has been cultivating ever since.

Museu Marice ⓘ *C/Fonallar s/n, T938940364, 15 Jun-15 Sep Tue-Sun 1000-1400 and 1700-2100, 16 Sep-14 Jun Tue-Fri 1000-1030 and 1500-1830, Sat 1000-1900, Sun 1000-1500, €3, free first Wed of the month, see also combined ticket above.* Next door to the Cau Ferrat the Museu Maricel has a collection of art from the medieval period to the early 20th century displayed in a light-filled old mansion hanging over the sea. On the top floor there's a small naval museum with models and plans.

Museu Romàntic ⓘ *C/Sant Gaudenci 1, T938940364, 15 Jun-15 Sep Tue-Sun 1000-1400 and 1700-2100, 16 Sep-14 Jun Tue-Fri 1000-1330 and 1500-1830, Sat-Sun 1000-1900, guided tours every hour, €3, free first Wed of the month, see also combined ticket above.* The third of Sitges' museums is tucked away in a small street in the centre of the old town, set in an elegant townhouse and recreates the life of an affluent Sitges family at the end of the 19th century. Stuffed with knick-knacks, engravings, and period furniture and carriages, it also has a large collection of working musical-boxes and another of antique dolls.

Vilanova i la Geltrú → *Colour map 3, grid C4.*

Further down the coast and resolutely down-to-earth after flamboyant Sitges, Vilanova i La Geltrú is a busy working port with a large fishing fleet. The palm-lined

Passeig Marìtim is crammed with restaurants where you can taste the day's catch, and there are two good beaches – the nicest is at the end of the Passeig Marìtim. There is also a handful of museums to keep you occupied on a rainy day. ►► *For Sleeping, Eating and other listings, see pages 317-323.*

Right by the train station is the **Museu del Ferrocarril** ① *Costat de l'estació, T938158491, www.ffe.es/vilanova, 15 Jul-15 Sep Tue-Fri 1100-1430 and 1700-200, closed Mon from Jul-Sep, 16 Sep-14 Jul Tue-Fri and Sun 1030-1430, Sat 1030-1430 and 1600-1830, €2,* where fans of old trains can potter about steam engines and play with model railways.

Nearby there's the **Biblioteca Museu Balaguer** ① *Av de Victor Balaguer s/n, T938154202, Jun-Sep Tue-Sat 1000-1330 and 1630-1900, until 2030 on Wed, Sun 1000-1330, Oct-May Tue-Sat 1000-1330 and 1600-1830, Sun 1000-1330, €2,* with a surprisingly good collection of artworks including a couple of fine El Grecos and some pieces on loan from the Prado.

Museu Romàntic Can Papiol ① *C/Major 32, T938930382, Tue-Sat 1000-1300 and 1600-1800, Sun 1000-1400, €2,* is linked to the Sitges Romantic museum (see above), and is housed in another fine mansion with an equally florid collection of 19th-century fripperies. The tourist office ① *C/Torre de Ribarroges, T938 154 517.*

The Wine Route

Catalan cava, the delicious home-grown bubbly, is mostly produced in the valleys of the Alt Penedès region, just southwest of Barcelona and a short trip inland from Sitges. Well over half the land is given over to vines, which snake trimly across the hills as far as the eye can see. Many *bodegas* are open for visitors, but you'll have to check with the tourist offices in Sant Sadurní d'Anoia (the main centre of cava-production) or in Villfranca de Penedès for opening hours and times. Most *bodegas*, besides the really big producers like Freixenet, prefer visits to be arranged in advance. The hills become increasingly rugged beyond Falset, another big wine-producing town, and, lost among them, are some tiny medieval villages overlooked by ruined castles and monasteries. The tourist office ① *Plaça del Ajuntament 1, T938910325, st.sadurnia@diba.es,* has a complete list of wineries.

Sant Sadurní d'Anoia

① *Codorniu, T938183232, www.codorniu.es, Mon-Fri 0900-1700 and Sat-Sun 0900-1300; Freixenet, T938917000, www.freixenet.es, guided tours Mon-Thu 1000, 1130, 1530, 1700, Fri 1000 and 1130. Weekends only in Nov and Dec by prior arrangement.* The main centre for cava production is Sant Sadurní d'Anoia, where the two giants of the cava world, Freixenet and Codorniú, have flung open their swirling Modernista doors for slick and professional tours and tastings.

Vilafranca de Penedès

This is the centre for the region's still-wine production and there are some interesting excursions around the town with dozens of small *bodegas* tucked away in the surrounding hamlets. Vilafranca de Penedès itself is a relaxed market town with a smattering of Modernista mansions and the odd Gothic church or townhouse, Vilafranca de Penedès is the perfect setting for an old-fashioned slap-up lunch on a square. In the centre of the old town, there's a delightfully eccentric wine museum ① *Plaça Jaume I 1-5, T938900582, Oct-May Tue-Sat 1000-1400 and 1600-1900, Sun 1000-1400, Jun-Sep, Tue-Sat 0900-2100, €2.50 (includes small tasting),* set in a Gothic palace which gives an overview of the history of wine-making in the area, with old-fashioned dioramas, ancient equipment, racks of *porróns* (Catalan wine jugs), and a queasy collection of local art and stuffed birds on the top floor. At the end of the

⁞ Plonk

Catalunya has been making wine since the fifth century BC. The Romans thought of it as plonk (although it was popular in all corners of their empire) and it took almost 2,000 years for its reputation to improve. Now Catalunya is one of the most up-and-coming wine-producing areas in Spain, with a very wide variety of red, white, and rosé wines. But of course it's best known for the sparkling wine, *cava*, produced locally by the *methode champenoise*.

There are eight main wine-growing area which have been designated as Denominació d'Origen (DO) like the French and Italian models, each producing distinctive wines. The Alella region makes mostly very good dry and sweet whites, but also some delicious reds. The Conca de Barbarà region produces excellent cava and whites. In the Ampurdan region on the Costa Brava, you'll find simple reds and rosés. Around Costers del Segre, they produce a bit of everything – red, white, rosé and cava. Tarragona is known for its red and white wines, but it also has something unusual: Paxarete, a very sweet traditional chocolate-brown wine. The wines of the Priorato D.O. are unusual and pricey, reflecting the difficulty of cultivating the hilly land, while the wine of the Terra Alta is usually light and fresh.

Undoubtedly the best-known wines come from the Penedès region, the largest and most important wine-producing area in Catalunya. These include the vast range of wines made by the enterprising Torres family.

visit, head for the recreated *bodega* downstairs to try a couple of the local wines, which should put you in the mood for lunch. The tourist office ① *Carrer Cort 14, T938920358*, has a list of *bodegas* which run tours and tastings.

Olèrdola

A couple of kilometres towards the coast, the Iberian-Roman ruins of Olèrdola ① *16 Jun-15 Sep Mon-Fri 1000-1400 and 1630-2030, Sat-Sun, 1000-1400, 16 Sep-15 Mar 1000-1400 and 1500-1800, Sat-Sun 1000-1400 and 1600-1800, 16 Mar-15 Jun 1000-1400 and 1500-2000, Sat-Sun 1000-1400 and 1600-2000, €2*, are clustered on a windswept hilltop which has been inhabited since around 1800 BC. Right at the top, a ghostly ancient church is still surrounded by strange body-shaped stone tombs dating back a thousand years. There is some fine, easy walking in the surrounding forested hills – the visitor's centre at Olèrdola has a map.

Falset

Modernista architecture is not confined to the cities in Catalunya; many of the old *bodegas* were designed by fashionable architects at the end of the 19th century and most wine villages boast a an extravagant Modernista wine cellar or two. These villages are hidden in the folds of steep hillsides thickly laced with vines that produce some notoriously strong wines. The largest of the wine-producing towns of the Priorat is Falset, which has a swirling Modernista *bodega* by César Martinell, one of Gaudí's acolytes, which is known as the 'Catedral del Vino', and the ruins of an ancient castle.

Prades Mountains

Wines were first produced in this region by the monks of the Cartoixa d'Escaladei (Charterhouse of Scala Dei), 25 km away in the Prades Mountains, who established

the first **Carthusian monastery** ① *Camí de la Cartoixa s/n, Escaladei, T977827006, Oct-May Tue-Sat 1000-1330 and 1500-1730, Jun-Sep Tue-Sat 1000-1330 and 1600-1930, Sun 1000-1330, €2.40/1.80*, in the Iberian peninsula in the 12th century. Little remains of the monastery's former splendour, but the ruins are hauntingly set just beneath the peak of Montsant, where there's some excellent walking.

Close to Montsant are several striking villages: tiny **Siurana**, with just 30 inhabitants, is dominated by the imposing ruins of an Arab fortress perched on the edge of a vertiginous cliff. It's a densely packed village of winding streets with ancient houses lined by stone archways, overlooked by a Romanesque church. Tourists, mainly Catalans, pile up here in the summer, but out of season it's very quiet and there is some very attractive walking in the surrounding area. **Prades**, a walled medieval city built of warm, rosy stone, has another ruined Arab castle, and an arcaded central square overlooked by the 13th-century Església de Santa María built in the transitional style between Romanesque and Gothic. Another little charmer is **Poboleda** with its rather grand 17th- and 18th-century mansions lining the pretty streets.

Tarragona → *Phone code: 977; Colour map 3, grid C3; Population: 110,947.*

Tarragona, imposingly perched on a rocky outcrop overlooking the sea, is one of the oldest cities in Spain and one of the most important in Catalunya. It's a brisk, industrious city with a shadowy, picturesque old quarter curled around the unusual Gothic cathedral, and a busy working harbour lined with great seafood restaurants.

Ins and outs

Getting there Tarragona is well connected by train and bus to most Spanish cities and to inland cities. The train station is at the bottom of the hill, with the harbour located down the coast to the south. ▶▶ *For further details, see Transport page 322.*

Getting around You won't need to use the local buses for getting around most of the main sights which are mainly located in the old quarter. To get to the (slightly) less crowded beaches along the coast, take buses 1 or 9 from the Rambla Vella.

Orientation Tarragona is easy to negotiate on foot: right on top of the hill is the old quarter with the cathedral, where most of the sights are concentrated. The old quarter is divided from the newer extension which spreads downhill by the parallel avenues of the Rambla Vella and the Rambla Nova, two long avenues where many of the shops are located.

Tourist information The tourist office is near the cathedral ① *Carrer Mayor 39, T977245064.*

History

The Romans established a military base here at the end of the third century BC which played an important role in the conquest of the Iberian peninsula. They liked it so much that they decided to make Tarraco the capital of Hispania Citerior, and built temples, baths, an amphitheatre, a circus and a forum, bequeathing a spectacular series of Roman monuments which are among the most extensive in Spain and were declared a World Heritage Site by UNESCO in 2000. St Paul is said to have preached here and it became an important bishopric under the Visigoths in the fifth century AD. Like most of Catalunya, its fortunes peaked in the middle ages, but it suffered once power was transferred from Catalunya to Castille and it became a backwater. Severely repressed after the Catalan rebellion of 1640, and then sacked by the French in 1811, the city sank into decline. That all changed in the 20th century, thanks to the growth of the wine and tourist industries, and Tarragona has finally re-emerged as one of Catalunya's most dynamic and prosperous cities.

Cathedral and the Old City ① *Plaça de la Seu, T977238685, 16 Mar-May Mon-Sat 1000-1300 and 1600-1900, Jun to 16 Nov Mon-Sat 1000-1900, 17 Nov-15 Mar Mon-Sat 1000-1400, closed Sun and religious holidays, €2.40/1.50.* At the heart of the old city stands the austerely beautiful Cathedral. Construction began at the end of the 12th century and was completed in 1331, and the cathedral is a perfect example of the transition from Romanesque to Gothic. A wide staircase sweeps up to the main façade with an imposing Romanesque portal surrounded by 13th-century sculptures of the Virgin and the Apostles surmounted by a vast rose window. The cloister has delicately carved pinkish columns featuring a world of fabulous creatures, including one which depicts the 'Procession de las Ratas' – the story of the clever cat who outwitted the mice by playing dead and leaps up from his own funeral to gobble them up (get a custodian to point it out). Hidden in the medieval gloom of the church is a magnificent 15th-century alabaster altarpiece by Pere Joan, and the entrance ticket includes a visit to the small Museu Diocesano, with a dusty collection of

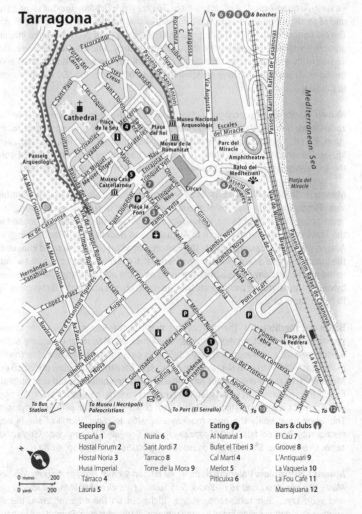

Tarragona

Catalunya & Andorra Tarragona

Sleeping 🛏		Eating 🍴	Bars & clubs 🍸
España **1**	Nuria **6**	Al Natural **1**	El Cau **7**
Hostal Forum **2**	Sant Jordi **7**	Bufet el Tiberi **3**	Groove **8**
Hostal Noria **3**	Tarraco **8**	Cal Martí **4**	L'Antiquari **9**
Husa Imperial	Torre de la Mora **9**	Merlot **5**	La Vaqueria **10**
Tárraco **4**		Piticuixa **6**	La Fou Café **11**
Lauria **5**			Mamajuana **12**

0 metres 200
0 yards 200

ecclesiastical treasures (including a reliquary containing St John the Baptist's finger) and a 15th-century tapestry of medieval life, La Bona Vida.

Carrer de Cavallers ⓘ *C/Cavallers 14, T977242752, Jun–Sep Tue-Sun 0900-2100; Oct-May Tue-Sat 0900-190, Sun 1000-1400, €1.87.* The main street of the old city, the Carrer Major, heads down from the cathedral; off to the right is the Carrer de Cavallers where sounds of pianos, opera singing and trumpets from the Conservatory of Music float across it. This was the city's most aristocratic address during the medieval period. A former mansion which dates back to the early 15th century has been beautifully refurbished to hold the Museu Casa Castellarnau with a graceful Gothic courtyard and rather patchy exhibits outlining the city's history. The second floor has retained its opulent 18th-century fittings, with vast chandeliers dripping from frescoed ceilings, and preserves the interior of a pretty 18th-century pharmacy, moved here when the original premises just down the street collapsed.

Passeig Arqueològic ⓘ *Av Catalunya s/n, T977245796, Oct-May Tue-Sat 1000-1330 and 1630-1830, Sun 1000-1500, Jun-Sep Tue-Sat 0900-2100, Sun 1000-1500, €1.87.* The old Roman walls which still ring much of the old city have been converted into an attractive walkway known as the Passeig Arqueològic which winds between the Roman walls and a stretch of 18th-century walls built by the British during the War of the Spanish Succession. There are stunning views out across the plains and around to the sea.

Museu Nacional Arqueològic ⓘ *Plaça del Rei 5, T977236209, Jun-Sep Tue-Sat 1000-2000, Sun and holidays 1000-1400, Oct-May Tue-Sat 1000-1330 and 1600-1900, €2.40.* On the edge of the old town, just off the Plaça del Rei, the huge, airy Museu Nacional Arqueològic holds an excellent collection of artefacts gathered from the archaeological sites which provide a vivid picture of life in Imperial Tarraco.

Museu de la Romanitat ⓘ *Entrances on Plaça del Rei, or via the Circus on Rambla Vell, T977241952, Jun-Sep Tue-Sun 1000-2100, Oct-May Tue-Sat 0900-1900, Sun 1000-1500, €1.87.* Next to the archaeological museum, this museum is housed in the Praetorium tower, once home to Augustus and Hadrian, and later the Kings of Aragón who built a castle on top of the Roman ruins. Computer-generated images of the Roman city give a sense of its magnificence two millennia ago. A glass lift swoops to the roof for dizzying views across the rooftops of the old town, and it is also linked by vaulted underground passages to the Circus, which was built in the first century AD to hold chariot races.

Balcó del Mediterrani The old city lies north of the Rambla Vell, a handsome promenade which culminates in the famous Balcó del Mediterrani (Balcony of the Mediterranean), a mirador with beautiful views over the amphitheatre, the town's main beach (the Platja del Miracle) and out to sea. Take the path below the Balcó del Mediterrani to reach the ancient Amphitheatre, where gladiators and wild animals fought to the death. Three Christian martyrs were tortured to death here in AD 259, and a basilica was erected to them in the sixth century on the site of their martyrdom. The lower town holds the busy modern extension to the city, full of shops and restaurants. **Parc del Miracle** ⓘ *T977242579, Jun-Sep Tue-Sat 1000-2000, Sun 1000-1400, Oct-May Tue-Sat 1000-1300 and 1600-1700, Sun 1000-1400, €1.87.*

Museu I Necròplois Paleocristians ⓘ *Av Ramón y Cajal 80, T977211175, Jun-Sep Mon-Sat 1000-1300 and 1630-2000, Sun 1000-1400, Oct-May Mon-Sat 1000-1330 and 1500-1730, Sun 1000-1400, €2.40.* Right out on the edge of town, there's another fascinating collection of Roman remains at this museum. Roman law forbade

and inscribed tablets, was established well outside the ancient city. It was used for pagan and Christian burials, and the museum currently houses an extensive collection of sarcophagi and glimmering mosaics gathered from the site. It is being refurbished to house a new Early Christian Museum, in recognition of the importance of the city where St Paul is said to have preached.

Port and Tarragona's beaches A good 20-minute walk from the old city is Tarragona's port, El Serrallo, a busy harbour crammed with fishing boats and densely packed with seafood restaurants. They are all good, and crowded at weekends, but it's worth heading into the streets behind the seafront to get a better deal. The Platja de Miracle, the city's main beach, falls short of its fancy name: it's a perfectly decent city beach but it can get very crowded. There are better, quieter beaches north of the city – such as Arrabassada – which you can reach by taking bus No 1 or 9 from the Rambla Vella, about 4 km from the centre, or Sabinosa (another kilometre beyond Arrabassada), which is for nudists at its northern end.

Excursions

There are plenty more Roman ruins scattered across the plains around Tarragona, including the spectacular aqueduct, better known as the **'Devil's Bridge'**, which brought water to the Roman city all the way from the Río Gayo, about 32 km away. The aqueduct is about 10 minutes outside the city; take bus number 5 from Avenida Prat de la Riba. West of the city at **Centcelles** near the small town of Constantí, is the most important Paleo-Christian monument in Spain, a resplendent Roman villa which, during the fourth century, was converted into a basilica ① *T977523374, Jun-Sep Tue-Sun 1000-1330 and 1600-1930, Sun 1000-1400, Oct-May Tue-Sun 1000-1330 and 1500-1730, Sun 1000-1400, €1.80.*

Other Roman sights are scattered along the coast along the ancient Vía Augusta but they are pretty much impossible to reach without your own transport; about 6 km northeast is the **Torre dels Escipions**, a massive 10 m-high funerary monument probably dedicated to the Scipio brothers who died in battle against the Carthaginians, and 2 km further north is the **Pedrera del Mèdol**, a Roman stone quarry with an impressive 'needle'. Near the town of Altafulla (see below), the triumphal **Arc de Bera** stands astride the ancient road, in memory of some long-forgotten battle.

Costa Daurada

The 'Golden Coast' has been popular with visitors since the Romans ruled half of the Iberian peninsula from their base at Tarragona. It hasn't been developed quite as intensively as parts of the Costa Brava, but nor is it as striking, although the broad, sandy beaches still attract millions of families every summer. ►► *For Sleeping, Eating and other listings, see pages 317-323.*

Resorts north of Tarragona

The northernmost resorts of the Costa Daurada – **Cunit**, **Calafell** and **Torredembarra** – are low-key collections of seaside villas with decent beaches but little else. Lively **Altafulla** has an a picturesque walled old quarter tucked back from the sea which is dominated by a sturdy castle, spectacularly floodlit at night, and a handsome 17th-century church. There are more good, if busy, beaches along the modern seafront, and plenty of bars and restaurants. Nearby **Tamarit** has another castle out on a small promontory jutting into the sea. On the outskirts of Altafulla at Els Munts, a magnificent Roman villa ① *Barri Marítim d'Altafulla, T977562806 Jun-Sep Tue-Sun 1000-1330 and 1600-1930, Sun 1000-1400, Oct-May Tue-Sun 1000-1330 and*

1500-1730, Sun 1000-1400, €1.87, has been discovered; it probably belonged to a prominent official from Roman Tarraco who spared no expense on the fine mosaics and elegant decoration.

Salou and around

Just southeast of Tarragona, **Salou** is the Costa Daurada's main resort, a cheerful, neon-lit mini-Benidorm with high-rise developments, fish and chip shops and cafés advertising 'tea just like your mum makes'. Between Salou and Tarragona is **Port Aventura-Universal Mediterranea** ① *T902202220, www.portaventura.es, winter 1000-2000, summer 1000-2400, 1-day admission €31 for adults, €23 for juniors, night entrance is cheaper (€22 and €16)*, a massive theme park with heart-stopping rollercoasters like the Dragon Khan (the biggest in Europe), log flumes and a great virtual underwater ride called the Sea Odyssey. It's popular enough to have its own train station – and if you show your theme park entrance ticket, you can get discounts or free admission to many of the museums in Tarragona. In 2002, it also opened the **Costa Caribe** ① *T902202220, €14 for adults, €10.50 for juniors*, a gigantic water park. Port Aventura has its own train station, and you can get discounts or even free transport when you buy an admission ticket in advance.

Cambrils, just down the coast from Salou, is smaller and less hectic. It's an unassuming resort town set back from a large harbour which still has a working port and an excellent selection of seafood restaurants. Cambrils has an excellent gastronomic reputation. The award-winning **Can Bosch**, is one of the finest restaurants in Catalunya, see Eating page 320.

If you want a break from the beach, spend a day in Reus, which is just a couple of miles inland and stuffed with Modernista mansions and plane-shaded squares. It was the birthplace of Antoní Gaudí, but he never designed any buildings for his home town. Many of the finest houses in Reus were designed by Domènech i Montaner – who built the Palau de la Música in Barcelona, see page 264 – including the resplendent Casa Navàs (a private house, admission by guided tour only, see below) which overlooks the arcaded Plaça del Mercadal. The tourist office has a useful map marked with all the Modernista highlights, and offers guided tours around the city which are often the only way to see the interiors. Reus makes a less hectic base than the coastal resorts.

Costa Daurada is easy to get to by public transport. There's a regular local train service between Barcelona, Tarragona and all the other resorts, €8 return.

Parque Natural Delta de l'Ebre → *Colour map 3, grid C2/3.*

At the southernmost tip of Catalunya are the wide, flat marshlands of the Delta de l'Ebre, where the huge River Ebre finally meets the sea. The area has been designated a natural park in order to protect the 300 species of bird which have made these wetlands their home, including flamingoes, herons, marsh harriers and a wide variety of ducks. There's a spellbinding if harsh beauty in the immense expanse of wetlands, the vast sky, and the wild beaches scattered with driftwood, and even in the height of summer you are almost guaranteed to find yourself alone. One of the best ways to see it is to rent a bike, but it's important to stick to the marked trails – the birds won't return to their nests if they are disturbed. The trails and birdwatching hides are marked out on a map available from the park information office. Boat-trips down the river and out to sea are offered from Amposta and Deltelebre. Amposta, the largest town in the region, is also the least attractive but it's a hub for local bus routes: quiet little Deltelebre or seaside Sant Carles de la Ràpita make more attractive bases. There's a park information office and a small eco-museum ① *C/Dr Martí Buera 20, Deltelebre, T977489679.* Tourist information office ① *Sant Carles de la Ràpita.*

Up the Río Ebre

Tortosa

Just inland, the fortified city of Tortosa straddles the River Ebre, surrounded by lush farmland. It's southern Catalunya's largest town and main transport hub. It was in the front line for several months during the Civil War, until the Republicans were ousted in a bloody battle that cost 35,000 lives and is commemorated by a monument by the river. War took its toll and Tortosa's medieval streets suffered extensive damage. Among the survivors are the Gothic cathedral, built on the site of a mosque, which has a delightful cloister, and a rich collection of Modernista townhouses which are sprinkled throughout Tortosa's Eixample and are marked on the tourist office map. The most spectacular sight is the lofty Arab fortress, La Zuda, which bristles from the highest point in the town; it's now a luxurious parador, but you can still stroll around the ancient walls for wonderful views across the plains.

Miravet

There's another castle upriver at Miravet; built by the Arabs, it was given to the knights of the Templar by Ramon Berenguer IV in 1153 after the reconquest of Catalunya. The fortress is balanced heartstoppingly on a cliff above the Río Ebro, reached by a steep, narrow path. It's a quiet, even ghostly, spot, not least in the Patio de la Sang (Patio of Blood) where the last Templars of Miravet were beheaded in 1308. A winding staircase leads to the top of the tower for far-reaching views along the river and down to the pretty village beneath.

Cistercian Triangle

Lost in the barely-visited expanses of southern Catalunya, the three medieval monasteries of the Cistercian Triangle offer a tranquil alternative to the giddy social life of the coastal resorts. The most important is Poblet, which inspired Gaudí, and is surrounded by beautiful forest with some great walking trails. Santes Creus and humble Vallbona de las Monges are both close to quietly charming villages which rarely see visitors. ▸▸ *For Sleeping, Eating and other listings, see pages 317-323.*

History

The Monestir de Santa María de Poblet was founded in 1151 by Ramon Berenguer III in gratitude for the success of his campaign to rid Catalunya of the Moorish invaders. Poblet and its sister monasteries Santa Creus and Vallbona de las Monges became known as 'the Cistercian Triangle', imposing reminders of the power of Christianity and the sovereign. From the 16th century, their influence waned and the final blow was struck in 1835, when the Mendizabel laws were enacted, depriving the Church of vast swathes of its land and properties. All three suffered attacks, but Poblet, the first and most important of the three, was suspected of harbouring Carlist sympathisers, and an angry mob rampaged through its halls, destroying everything they could find and torching its celebrated library. The ruins mouldered for decades, but became a haunting symbol of an empire lost to the romantic innocents of the late 19th century. Gaudí was one of many who dreamed of its reconstruction, which was finally carried out after the Civil War.

Monestir de Santa María de Poblet and around

ⓘ *T977870089, Tue-Sun 1000-1230 and 1500-1730, until 1800 in summer, €3, a combined ticket to all 3 monasteries of the Cistercian triangle is available for €6, entrance by guided tour only.*

The monastery is spectacularly set in a tranquil, golden valley, a vast complex sprawling behind glowering battlements and fortifications. The main entrance into the Monastery is through the Puerta Dorada (Golden Gate) where kings would dismount to kneel and kiss the crucifix proffered by the Abbot, and above it is the sumptuous 14th-century Gothic palace. It was a favourite retreat and resting place of a long line of count-kings, many of whom were buried here; Alfonso II was the first, as early as 1196, but the monastery was officially declared a Royal Pantheon in the 14th century. A community of monks now live here, and one of them will guide you around the monastery's stirring collection of beautifully renovated buildings.

At the heart of the complex is the peaceful Romanesque cloister, rimmed with delicate arcades and the stone tombs of long-forgotten monks, and containing an octagonal pavilion with a huge stone fountain. Leading off the cloister is an echoing vaulted Gothic chapter house with the tombs of the monastery's abbots laid into the stone-flagged floor, the library with its brick parabolic arches which must have inspired Gaudí, an enormous wine cellar, the old kitchens lined with copper pots and pans, and the austere wood-panelled refectory. Steps lead up to the vast dormitory, with a screen behind which the present-day monks have their humble cells, and you can look down over the cloister from the upper gallery. The glorious main church is austerely unadorned in the Cistercian tradition apart from a tremendous Renaissance alabaster retablo which fills the apse behind the main altar. But the prize here is the collection of royal tombs exquisitely wrought in alabaster which flank the altar; they were desecrated by the rampaging mob in 1835, but Frederic Marès, the eccentric sculptor and obsessive collector, see page 258, was responsible for their reconstruction in 1850.

Behind the monastery, Poblet forest stretches up to the peaks of the Prades mountains, a craggy, wild landscape where eagles wheel overhead. There are some beautiful walking trails, including a scenic route up to the Pic de l'Aliga (1,052 m), which begins and ends in the tranquil village of Poblet (information on the trails from Poblet tourist office, by the monastery gates). The delightful town of L'Espluga de Francoli makes a good base for walkers and vists to the monastery. There are tourist offices ① *L'Espluga de Francoli, Torres Jordi 16, T977871220*, and ① *Poblet monastery, Passeig Abat Conill 9, T977871247.*

Montblanc

Montblanc, about 5 km from Poblet, is an enchanting medieval town completely encircled by turreted walls which time, and tourists, seem to have passed by. Montblanc prospered during the Middle Ages, when it had a substantial Jewish community who lived in the tangle of streets between the grand Gothic **Església de Santa Maria** and the humble little Romanesque **Església de Sant Miquel** lower down the hill. The best time to come is during the **Setmana Medieval**, which kicks off on the feast day of Sant Jordi (23 April) and is a week-long festival of medieval song and dance. Plaça Major is always busy, particularly during the evening *paseo*, when families gather at the lively cafés spilling out on to the square. **Museu Frederic Marès** ① *Jun-Sep Tue-Sat 1000-1400 and 1600-2000, Sun 1000-1400, Oct-May, Sat and Sun only, free*, holds a typically eccentric selection of painting and sculpture from the 13th to the 19th centuries, including some beautiful carved polychrome statues from the 14th century.

Monestir de Vallbona de les Monges

① *T973330266, Tue-Sat 1030-1330, 1600-1845, 1730 in winter, Sun 1200-1330, €2.* Almost 30 km north of Poblet, the humblest of the three Cistercian monasteries is the Monestir de Vallbona de les Monges, which has housed a community of nuns for eight centuries. Catalan queens made it a place of retreat and some, including the Violant of Hungary, wife of Jaume I, are buried here. There's a delightful Romanesque

cloister with prettily carved capitals covered in vines and flowers and the church is a fine example of the Transitional style between Romanesque and Gothic. It was built between the 13th and 14th centuries, and is quiet, contemplative and almost unadorned but for Violant's tomb and a stone Virgin. You will need your own transport. The tourist office ① *Passeig Montesquiu s/n, T973330567.*

Monestir de Santes Creus

① *T977638329, Mid-Sep to mid-Jan Tue-Sun 1000- 1330 and 1500-1730, mid-Jan to mid-Mar Tue-Sun 1000-1330 and 1500-1800, mid-Mar to mid-Sep Tue-Sun 1000-1330 and 1500-1900, €4.* Like Poblet, the monastery of Santes Creus has had a colourful history; the favourite of many of the Catalan count-kings, both Pedro the Great and Jaume II chose to be buried in its magnificent church. After 1835, the monks were ousted and the monastery's buildings were sacked, only to suffer further ignominy when the Tarragon prison was shifted here for fear of the plague in 1870, finishing off the job begun in 1835. The honey-coloured village grew up when locals moved into the abandoned monks' residences in the early 19th century, and is surrounded by ancient fortified walls. Visits to the monastery now begin with an audio-visual presentation which gives a 3D- glimpse into the life of a medieval monk, after which visitors can wander around the semi-ruined complex. The highlight is the lacy Gothic cloister with its tracery and carved capitals, which was created by the English master mason Reinard de Fonoll, and contains an elaborate Gothic stone fountain. There's a small tourist office ① *Santes Creus in the Plaça Sant Bernat s/n, T977638141.*

Valls

The nearest town of any size to Santes Creus, Valls doesn't look much on the outskirts but contains a neat little medieval hub, with crooked streets and a fine old Gothic church. It's famous for two things, both close to the Catalan heart; the daring of its castellars (it has the best regarded team of human castle builders in Catalunya, Els Xiquets de Valls – see page 321) and the tastiness of its calçots. The castellers are commemorated with a huge statue in the centre of town which shows a complicated human tower presided over by the anxenata, the nimblest, littlest kid who waves from the top. Calçots are a kind of onion, a cross between a shallot and a spring onion, which are roasted on a charcoal grill and served with a piquant romesco sauce. They are traditionally accompanied by lamb cutlets, and are a favourite springtime dish when every bar and restaurant hangs out a sign advertising the '*calçotada*'. The tourist office ① *Plaça del Blat 1, T977601950.*

● Sleeping

Sitges *p306*
Sitges plenty of good accommodation options oozing character. That said, there never seem to be enough rooms to go round in the high season or over Carnaval, so book well in advance. Sitges also gets very crowded in Jul and Aug, when finding accommodation is virtually impossible.
LL Hotel Antemare 'Novo Dimensió', Avda de Mare de Deu de Montserrat 48-50, T938947000, www.antemare.com. A huge hotel with a spa and thallassotherapy centre, with all kinds of treatments on offer including an 'Anti-Stress' course. It's spread

over 6 buildings, all surrounded by thickly forested gardens, and offers 2 pools, gym, sauna and jacuzzi.
AL Estela Barcelona (Hotel del Arte), Avda Port d'Aiguadolç s/n, T938114545, www.hotelestela.com. Harbourfront hotel, with expansive rooms filled with art works from famous Catalan artists.
A Hotel Celimar, Passeig de la Ribera 20, T938110170, F938110 403. A pale, creamy Modernista mansion right on the seafront, with elegant rooms just 20 m from the beach.
B Hotel Romàntic, C/Sant Isidre 33, T938948375, F938948167. Set in a graceful 19th-century mansion with a garden terrace, this is one of the most popular hotels in

Sitges, particularly with gay visitors, and gets booked up very quickly.
B La Pinta, Passeig de la Ribera 52, T938940999, F938947871. Run by same owners of **Santa Maria**, more modern.
B Santa Maria, Passeig de la Ribera 52, T938940999, F938947871. Bright, modern rooms in a 19th-century mansion right on the seafront; there are 2 good, busy seafood restaurants downstairs with a pavement terrace.
C El Xalet, Isla de Cuba 33-35, T938110070, F938945579. Delightful quirky hotel set in a Modernista villa, with a garden and pool. Rooms are surprisingly simple, but always booked up well in advance.
D Hostel Mariangel, C/de les Parellades 78, T938948375. A reliable budget choice.

Camping

There are a few campsites in Sitges.
El Garrofer, T938941780, which has shady sites off the main road into Sitges.
El Rocà, T938940043, just north of the town but close to the beach.

Vilanova i la Geltrú *p307*

A-C César, C/Isaac Perel 4-8, T938151125, F938156719, www.hotelcesar.net. Best place to stay. Unusual extras are provided, like a china tea service and Earl Grey tea. It's good value most of the year, but prices leap a couple of categories in Jul and Aug. The **C-E Hotel Ricard**, Passeig Maritim 88, T938157100, F938159957, is a classic little resort hotel close to the beach. It's cheap unless you come in Jul and Aug.

Camping

There are 3 campsites in Vilanova i la Geltrú; the best is **Platja Vilanova**, T938950767, right on the beach, which also rents bungalows.

The Wine Route *p308*

AL Domo, C/Francesc Maciá 4, Vilafranca de Penedès, T938172026, www.domohotel. com. 4-star comforts including jacuzzi, sauna and pool.
C Sol I Vi, Ctra San Sadurni, Vilafranca km 4, T938993204, F938993204. This is best place

to stay. Set in a beautifully converted stone farmhouse, 4 km outside Sadurni, it has a pool and friendly owners who can organize tours to the surrounding vineyards.

Tarragona *p310, map p311*

L Husa Imperial Tárraco, Paseo de las Palmeras, 43000, T977233040, www.husa.es. Magnificent panoramic views from the 'balcony of the Mediterranean' are the principal attraction of this large, modern hotel with pool, tennis, and restaurant.
C Hotel Nuria, T977235011, F977244136. A large modern hotel next to the Arabassada beach, with a café downstairs. It's also a 5-min bus journey (No 1 or No 9) to the city.
C Hotel Sant Jordi, Via Augusta 185, T977207515, F977207632. One of several large, modern hotels lining the busy N-340, this one offers spacious rooms with large terraces and is just a short walk from the Sabinosa beach, popular with Tarragona's trendy crowd. It's a 5-min bus journey (take the No 1 or the 9) into the city.
C Lauria, Rambla Nova 20, T977236712, www.hlauria.es. Accommodating staff, and a central location close to all the sights of the old city, plus a pool and café.
D Hotel España, Rambla Nova 49, T977232707. Small and modern with unexceptional rooms but a good central location.
E Hostal Forum, Plaça La Font 37, T977231718. On the corner of the delightful Plaça la Font, the Forum has basic en suite rooms at a bargain price.
E Hostal Noria, Plaça La Font 53, T977238717. Set in a narrow, creaky house overlooking one of the prettiest squares in old Tarragona, this has small, but attractive, rooms and a busy (and noisy) bar downstairs. Upper floors are quietest.

Camping

There are plenty of campsites on the coast.
Tarraco, T977 239 989, closest to the city centre, right by Arabassada beach (bus No.1 or No.9 from the Rambla Nova).
Torre de la Mora, Ctra N-340, T977651277, www.fut.es/camtmora, further up the coast, right by the sea, but far enough away from

📍 *For an explanation of sleeping and eating price codes used in this guide, see inside the*
● *front cover. Other relevant information is found in Essentials, see pages 47-56.*

the coastal train line to guarantee a good night's kip. Count on around €18-22 per night for 2 people plus a car and tent for both.

Costa Daurada *p313*
B Hotel Gaudí, C/ Arabal Robuster 49, Reus, T977345545, central, recently refurbished
E Hostal Santa Teresa, C/Santa Teresa 1, Reus, T977316297, a simple, family-run *pensión* on a little pedestrian street.

Parque Natural Delta de l'Ebre *p314*
C Delta Hotel, Av del Canal, Camino del Illeta s/n, T977480046, www.dsi.es/ delta-hotel. A traditional local house, set in wilderness in the middle of the natural park, which can organize different excursions and rent out bikes. It's also got one of the best restaurants, mid-range priced, in the area.
C Juanito Platja, Passeig Marítim s/n, Sant Carles de la Ràpita, T977740 462, F977742757, a welcoming, low-key resort hotel close to the beach.
D Hotel Rull, Av del Canal, T977487728, right by the park information office, this new hotel offers large, comfortable rooms and a restaurant.

Camping
There are 2 official campsites in the Delta de l'Ebre.
L'Aube, Urbanització Riumar, T977 445 706, **Riomar**, Urbanització Riumar, T977267680, slightly more expensive and better equipped than **L'Aube**, has a launderette and rents bungalows. Both have pools.

Up the Río Ebre *p315*
AL Parador de Tortosa, Castillo de la Zuda, Tortosa, T977444450, tortosa@parador.es. The huge 10th-century fortress is now a beautifully appointed parador with gardens, a pool and a good, but expensive, restaurant (open to non-residents).

Cistercian Triangle *p315*
C Masia del Cadet, Les Masies de Poblet, T977870869, masiadelcadet@eresmas.com. A beautifully renovated 15th-century farmhouse in a hamlet outside Poblet, with a fine, mid-range, restaurant and welcoming owners. There's a small, cheap family-run restaurant with a terrace, the Hostal Fonoll, right opposite the monastery entrance,

T977870333, which offers a good menú del día at less than €10.
D Del Senglar, Plaça Montserrat Canals, L'Espluga de Francoli, T977870121, www.hostaldesenglar.com. A real charmer, with old wooden beams and a garden with a pool. The restaurant is excellent, and they hold barbecues on Saturday evenings in Aug.
D Hostal Grau, C/Pere III, Monestir de Santes Creus, T977 638 311, just outside the old walls. Welcoming and traditional. Also has a restaurant.
E Hostal dels Àngels, Plaça Angels, Montblanc, T977860173. An attractive little *pensión* in the heart of the town, with a reasonably priced restaurant.
F Torreblanca, Cra del Pla de Santa Maria 86, Valls, T977601022, F977606323, which offers good-value en suite rooms.

🍴 Eating

Costa Garraf *p306*
€€ **Las Botas**, Avda Constitución 326, Castelldefels, T936651824. A good, traditional roadside restaurant serving typical Catalan dishes. Just outside town.
€€ **Xiriniguito del Garraf**, Platja de Garraf s/n, Garraf, T936320016, a classic, beachside restaurant, with fresh fish and other local dishes. Cheaper dishes too. Recommended.

Sitges *p306*
If you've got the money, there's plenty to choose from in Sitges, including good seafood restaurants and lots of places to pose. Unfortunately, cheaper places are few and far between.
€€€ **Maricel**, Passeig de la Ribera 6, T938942054, www.maricel.es. Probably the best seafood restaurant in town; right on the beachfront with a pale, elegant dining room full of floral prints and oil paintings. Closed Tue and second two weeks in Nov.
€€ **El Celler Vell**, C/Sant Bonaventura 21, T938111961. Good Catalan food and a laid-back atmosphere. The *menú del día* is good value at less than €15.
€€ **El Velero**, Passeig de la Ribera 38, T938942051. Another classic seafood restaurant on the main drag, with a loyal, local clientele and an excellent menú degustación (tasting menu) for €23.

Pizzeria Cap de la Villa, Cap de la Villa 3, T938941091. There's not much in the way of budget food in Sitges, but the pizzas here are pretty good and very reasonable.

Vilanova i la Geltrú

€ **Celler del Racó**, C/Jacint Veraguer 18, Cubelles, T983952914, a popular local *bodega* with excellent tapas and a great selection of local wines (5 km from Vilanova).
€ **La Fitorra**, C/Isaac Peral 4, T938151125, is a pretty, cheap restaurant serving big portions of fine fresh fish and you can try the *menú degustación* (tasting menu) for just €15.

The Wine Route *p308*

€€ **Cal Ton**, C/Casal 8, T938903741, you can try hearty, expensive, traditional Catalan cuisine accompanied by an extensive wine list.
€€ **C Pedro III El Grande**, Plaça del Penedès 2, Vilafranca de Penedès, T938903100, recepcion-h.pedro3@ctv.es. Reasonable and central but a bit dour.
€€ **El Cairat**, C/Nou 3, Falset, T977830481. You can enjoy more classic, moderately priced, Catalan cooking (including homemade pasta) a welcoming spot which uses the freshest local produce.
€€ **Fonda Neus**, C/Marc Mir 15-16, Sant Sadurní d'Anoia, T938910365, you can try some serious country cooking here and wash it down with local wines.
€ **Casa Joan**, Plaça Estació 8, T938903171, has simple, inexpensive dishes from all over Spain and friendly staff.
€ **El Pigot de Arbolí**, C/Trinquet 7, T977816063. In Arbolí, close to Siurana, is this friendly and cheap restaurant. The staff are happy to recommend dishes.

Tarragona *p310, map p311*

€€ **Belle Epoque**, C/Mare de Deu de la Mercé 1, T977238055. Sumptuous Modernista style and excellent Catalan cuisine accompanied by an extensive wine list.
€€ **Cal Martí**, C/Sant Pere 12, T977212384. One of the best of several seafood restaurants on this street in Tarragona's port: try the suquet, or the oven-baked fish.
€€ **Merlot**, C/Cavallers 6, T977220652. Chic, fashionable restaurant in a Modernista townhouse, serving contemporary French and Mediterranean cuisine with a

well-deserved reputation for excellence.
€€ **Piticuixa**, C/Cardenal Cervantes 14, T977230649. A traditional, comfortable tapas bar with a well-heeled clientele, where you can try local cured meats, cheeses and salads and a range of regional and Spanish wines.
€ **Al Natural**, C/Arquitecte Rovira 3, T977216454. A friendly vegetarian restaurant with a buffet-style lunch menu with soup, salads, a hot dish and a dessert for €8. Everything is fresh and tasty. Open lunchtimes and Fri and Sat night.
€ **Bufet el Tiberi**, C/Martí d'Ardenya 5, T977235403, www.eltiberi.com. Stuff yourself Roman style for around €9.

Costa Daurada *p313*

€€€ **Can Bosch**, Rambla Jaume I, Cambrils, T977360019,award-winning, this is one of the finest restaurants in Catalunya. It offers 3 fixed-price menus (at €30, €39 or €48) with a range of local delicacies including *arroz negre*: try the fabulous *carpaccio de gambas* if it's on the menu

Parque Natural Delta De l'Ebre *p314*

Plenty of restaurants offer rice dishes made with rice grown in the Delta.
€€ **Casa Ramon Marines**, C/Arsenal 16, T977742358, family run, this has been going since 1948 and serves excellent seafood.
€€ **Desembocadura Riu Ebre**, in Delta de l'Ebre, T977267503. Right at the mouth of the river, offers particularly good local dishes.
€€ **Varadero**, Av Constitució 1, T977741001. A good option in Sant Carles de la Ràpita, is the elegant **Varadero**. Offers a good value *menú* and a *menú degustación* to try out the local delicacies.

Up the Río Ebre *p315*

See also Sleeping.
€€ **Berenguer IV**, C/Cervantes 23, T977249580, F977449589. Reasonable.

Cistercian Triangle *p315*

See also Sleeping.
€€ **El Molí de Mallol**, Muralla Santa Anna 2, near Montblanc, T977860591. One of the best places to eat, a converted watermill clinging to the ancient walls serving delicious, traditional dishes.
€€ **Masia Bou**, Ctra Lleida km 21.5, Valls, T977600427, known as the 'Palace of

⁝ Giants, dragons and castles in the air

After years of repression during the Franco era, Catalunya is celebrating its traditional festivals with ever-greater verve and exuberance, resuscitating centuries-old customs and traditions in an outpouring of national pride and optimism. These are some of the most popular traditions, which you'll almost certainly see at any village 'festa'.

Correfoc

'Fire-running' goes back hundreds, if not thousands, of years. Parading drummers beat a pulse-quickening march through the streets, heralding the arrival of *dracs* (dragons), surrounded by leaping *demonis* (demons) setting off fireworks. Youths step out from the crowd to prevent the dragons passing, standing or kneeling in their path and getting showered with sparks as they shout ¡No pasaran¡ (You will not pass). Fire-running can be dangerous, and the tightly packed mass of the crowd means escape isn't easy – wear protective, cotton clothing if you want to join in.

Gegants and Capsgrossos

The *gegants* (giants) first appeared at Catalan festivals in the Middle Ages. They are enormous figures made of wood and papier-mâché who lumber along in the festival parades. The *capsgrossos* (fatheads) are squat leering versions, who accompany the giants on the mischievous little figures, some of the modern ones bear the faces of famous celebrities and politicians.

Castellers

The art of building human towers dates back to the 1700s, and has undergone a major revival in recent years. It's a perfect example of the civic pride which marks the Catalans, each person having an important part to play, and the whole depending on the co-operation and steadiness of each individual. The bottom layer with its central sturdy knot of people known as the pine cone or *pinya* looks like a rugby scrum, upon which, gradually, carefully, the layers are built up. An *aixedor* (child) provides the support for an *anxenata* (an even smaller child) who nimbly scampers to the top and grins like a gargoyle, waving to the crowd below.

Sardana

The grave, stately circle dance of the Catalans is a world away from the flamboyance of Andalusian flamenco. It's an ancient folkloric tradition which can be seen most weekends in towns and villages, where you will probably be encouraged to join in. But beware – it's not as easy as it looks. The *cobla* (band) strike up, and a knot of people, sometimes as few as four, will link hands and circle with slow sedate steps, interspersed with longer, rising ones. The circles get bigger and bigger as more and more people join in. True aficionados will wear espadrilles tied with coloured ribbons.

Calçotadas', is the best place to try Valls' speciality.

⊙ Bars and clubs

Sitges *p306*
You'll find dozens of bars and clubs on and around the Carrer Marqués de Montroig and the Carrer 1er de Maig – among them are **Panchito**, **Afrika**, and **Quim's** but there are dozens more – and many have small summer terraces. In the Port of Aiguadolç, there's a huge outpost of Barcelona's **Otto Zutz club** with dozens of smaller bars playing different kinds of music. In the quieter streets near the church, you'll find

less raucous bars with big terraces to kick back and relax. Most of the gay bars are concentrated on and around the Carrer Sant Bonaventura. For the best gay bars and restaurants, pick up the gay map of Sitges/ Barcelona from almost any bar in town.

Vilanova i la Geltrú *p307*

While Sitges is the main focus for nightlife on this strip of coast, there's still plenty of action on the Passeig Maritim and around.

Tarragona *p310, map p311*

Tarragona is always pretty buzzy, with plenty going on across the city.

In the old town, there's **El Cau**, C/ Trinquet Vell 2, with alternative music and live bands at weekends; **L'Antiquari**, C/ Santa Ana 3, is young, arty and trendy; **Groove**, C/Cervantes 4, in the new part of town, has jazz, blues and funk, and DJs on Fri nights; **Le Fou Café**, C/Cervantes 17, plays jazz and electronica, with acoustic sets on Thu.

There are dozens of clubs around the port, including the cheerfully tacky **Mamajuana**, Porto Deportivo, with 70s music during the week and techno at weekends, **La Vaqueria**, C/ dels Rebolledo 11, which has live jazz, blues, rock and pop as well as art exhibitions and theatre performances.

✹ Festivals and events

Sitges *p306*

There is something going on in Sitges almost every month, and the best time to visit is when a fiesta is in full swing. In **Feb/Mar** is Carnaval, among the biggest and wildest celebrations in Spain, largely thanks to the gay community who have taken the event into their own hands. In **Jun** the streets are carpeted with flowers for **Corpus Christi**, and the town's **Festa Major** dedicated to Sant Bartomeu at the end of Aug, is a riot of traditional parades with Giants, Fatheads, and Dragons, see box.

Tarragona *p310*

Between **mid-Jun and mid-Aug** is Festival d'Estiu (FET), a huge, city-wide performance arts festival featuring theatre, dance, cinema and music events, many of which are held outdoors and for free. Pick up a brochure from the tourist office. There's also the traditional **Festa de Santa Tecla** held for 10 days at the **end of Sep**, with parades featuring Catalan gegants, and popular dance and music.

Parque Natural Delta De l'Ebre *p314*

Hípica Delta, T977267646, based next to the information office in Riumar, out at the tip of the natural park. Contact if you want to see the marshes on horseback.
For information on sailing **Creuers Delta de l'Ebre**, T977481128.

⊖ Transport

Costa Garraf *p306*

There are regular local trains from **Estació-Sants** down the coast south of Barcelona but not all of them stop at **Castelldefels** and **Garraf**. For the beaches at Castelldefels, get off at Castelldefels-Platja just after the town stop.

Sitges *p306*

Sitges is on the main coastal train line between **Murcia**, **Valencia** and **Barcelona**, although not all the high-speed trains stop here. There are regular local trains between Barcelona-Sants and Tarragona. There are regular daily bus services (T939937511) to Barcelona, but the train is more reliable and the views are fantastic.

The Wine Route *p308*

There are regular local trains from Barcelona-Sants to **Vilafranca de Penedès** and **Sant Sadurní d'Anoia**. Many of the *bodegas* are scattered outside the main towns, and you'll need your own transport as few are on bus routes. There are twice-daily buses between Reus and Prades, stopping at some villages on the way. The tourist offices have details of local bus routes.

Tarragona *p310*

Tarragona is linked by bus to most major Spanish cities, including **Barcelona**, **Madrid**, **Seville**, **Alicante** and **Murcia**, and there are services inland to **Lleida**, **Reus**, **Poblet** (T977229126 for information).

There are very frequent local and express trains from **Barcelona-Sants** down the coast to Tarragona and onwards to **Tortosa**,

Valencia and Alicante. The more expensive, plusher Euromed trains are hardly any faster unless you are travelling longer distances. There are also train services inland to Lleida via L'Espluga de Francoli and Montblanc, and express services to Madrid and Seville.

Parque Natural Delta de l'Ebre *p314*
Hilario Pagò, T646069186, and Tornè, T977408017, both in the nearby village of Goles de l'Ebre, rent out bikes.

Cistercian Triangle *p315*
The nicest way to get to **Poblet** is by train from **Barcelona-Sants** to **L'Espluga de Francoli**, and walk the final attractive 3 km to the monastery. Otherwise, there are regular buses between **Tarragona** and **Lleida** which will drop you right outside the monastery gates. To **Montblanc**, trains leave **Barcelona-Sants**, from here you can pick up a bus to **Poblet**. There are infrequent local buses from **Valls** to **Santes Creus**.

Along the coast north of Barcelona

Costa Maresme → *Colour map 3, grid B5.*

Costa Maresme runs for about 50 miles north of Barcelona; despite the grand title, it's really just a string of small towns joined up by a railway. The narrow beaches, an almost unbroken sandy strip from Barcelona to Blanes (official starting point of the Costa Brava, see page 324), have the railway line running right behind them but they are hugely popular with Barcelonan day-trippers and are always packed out on summer weekends. ▶▶ *For Sleeping, Eating and other listings, see pages 330-334.*

Caldes d'Estrac

Fly past the dreary sprawl which extends northwards as far as ugly, industrial Mataró and continue on to Caldes d'Estrac (also known as Caldetes), a smart resort spread attractively over pine-forested hills which has been celebrated for its hot springs since Roman times. As a result, the streets are lined with graceful villas and it boasts fewer ugly developments than some of the concrete ex-fishing villages that sprouted like toadstools during the 1960s.

Arenys de Mar

Caldetes is joined by 4 km of sandy beaches to Arenys de Mar, which has an excellent reputation for its local cuisine and you can escape the crowds in a hill-top seafarer's cemetery, with fabulous views and some over-the-top Modernista headstones. There isn't much in the way of nightlife along this coast (with the exception of Mataró, which is packed with blaring *bacalao* discos), but Arenys has a couple of decent bars especially around the fishing harbour and around Calles Ample and D'Avall in the old part of the town.

Canet de Mar

The Modernista architects were especially fond of Canet de Mar, just up the coast, and built a smattering of summer houses there a century or so ago. Most are private but you can visit the **Casa Museu del Lluis Domènech i Montaner** ① *T937954615, Tue, Thu and Sat in summer, check times in advance*, a winsome, pointy pavilion which is stuffed full of memorabilia relating to the architect of the extraordinary Palau de la Música, see page 264, in Barcelona. Canet's beachfront is a bit more down-to-earth, with the usual souvenir shops and cafés lined up behind the long sandy beaches.

Beyond Canet is delightful Sant Pol de Mar, with a few fishing boats pulled up on to the sands and a colourful tumble of old houses (behind the inevitable apartment blocks). Easily the prettiest town on this stretch of the coast, most of the old cottages have been spruced up and belong to wealthy Catalan second-homers – it's a chi chi little spot, where even the train tracks deferentially head inland, leaving the lovely coves in peace.

Calella

The biggest resort along this strip of coast, Calella is a shrimp compared to the big boys up the coast on the Costa Brava proper, but still a sizeable tourist town, especially popular with families, with ranks and ranks of apartment buildings running along its endless sandy beaches. The tourist office ① *C/Sant Jaume 231, T937695982.*

Costa Brava

The former fishing villages of Blanes and Lloret de Mar have become two of the biggest resorts on the Costa Brava, with ever-growing suburbs of apartment blocks and long, sandy beaches which teem with crowds of northern European tourists on package holidays. If you are looking for sun, sea, sand and a decent English breakfast, this is the place to come. If not, keep heading up the coast to the resorts further north where package tourism has yet to take such a determined hold. The stretch from Sant Feliu de Guíxols to L'Estartit is one of the most varied. While there are plenty of huge, anonymous resorts, it's also possible to find some ex-fishing villages like Tamariu which, while not exactly off the beaten track, are still refreshingly low-key. There is a clutch of beautifully preserved medieval towns just inland, and the prosperous fishing town of Sant Feliu de Guíxols has a smattering of Modernista mansions and a colourful harbour. ▶ *For Sleeping, Eating and other listings, see pages 330-334.*

Blanes

The Costa Brava starts officially in Blanes, at the rock called Sa Palomera which divides its lengthy golden beach. It is the first of a string of towns devoted to package tourism on a grand scale. The small fleet of fishing boats in the harbour, a tiny old quarter of narrow streets and a lively daily produce market evoke faint memories of its former life as a prosperous fishing town, but it's the unending stretch of newly built apartment blocks, with their neon-lit bars and cafés, which bring in the business nowadays. If you aren't here for the beaches, the only other things to do are climb up to the old watchtower for stunning views, or visit the botanical garden, the **Jardí Botànic Mar i Murtra**, which has more than 7,000 species of Mediterranean and tropical plants. The gardens are located on top of the cliff at the Passatge Karl Faust 10. A special bus service leaves from the Plaça Catalunya near the tourist office if you can't face the stiff walk.

There are also a couple of pretty coves to explore, like the one at **Sant Francesc**, beyond the old watchtower, and the cove of **Santa Cristina**, with a series of well-marked botanical trails and a crumbling hermitage. There's a smart hotel and a couple of beachside cafés which are open in summer only. It's a steep walk down if you come by road but the summer boat service (from Blanes or Lloret de Mar) will take you there effortlessly.

Lloret de Mar

A few kilometres up the coast is Lloret de Mar, a brash, brassy resort dedicated wholeheartedly to package tourism. It's not for everyone, so if you're not looking for a

few days of unabashed hedonism, give Lloret a miss. The tourist information office has leaflets which mark a couple of walks and mountain-bike itineraries along the rocky coastline, passing some truly delightful coves (best, obviously, out of season). But Lloret's raison d'être is to give its foreign visitors a good time and it does a reasonable job, with its fish and chip shops, theme parks, go-kart tracks, and unapologetically tacky nightlife.

Tossa de Mar

Tossa de Mar, hugging a small cove dotted with small boats, and overlooked by the ruins of a fortified village, is generally considered to be the first truly charming town along the Costa Brava. But even Tossa has succumbed to the big bucks offered by property developers – it's worth squinting to avoid the sight of the dreary new section of the town which has taken over one end of the harbour. Despite that, the narrow streets lined with whitewashed houses and the perfectly curved bay, are still among the prettiest sights of the Costa Brava. The Villa Vella ('Old Town'), perched high on the Cap de Tossa, is the only medieval fortified village left standing in Catalunya, with a crumbling church and several old stone houses contained within an amazingly intact circle of walls and towers. In July and August, the crowds descend in droves and there isn't an inch of free sand on its beach (clamber around the headland to find less crowded bays). In summer, a glass-bottomed boat, *Fonda de Cristal*, makes a tour of the surrounding coves. From the 1930s, Tossa began to draw a stream of artists including Marc Chagall who described it as a 'blue paradise' and the **Municipal Museum** ⓘ *Plaça Roig i Soler 1, T972340709, Jun-Sep Tue-Sun 1000-2100, Oct-May 1000-1330 and 1600-1900 €1.80*, was inaugurated to house some of their works along with a collection of archaeological findings gathered over the centuries.

> ❖ *The town is quieter, prettier and infinitely more atmospheric out of season.*

Sant Feliu de Guíxols and around

Sant Feliu de Guíxols is a pleasant old port with a long sandy beach and a handsome Passeig Marítim dotted with the odd Modernista mansion. Sant Feliu made its fortune in the cork industry in the 19th century and still has an agreeable air of doing-very-nicely-thank-you. The town has managed to keep the worst excesses of the tourist industry at arm's length, and the harbour hasn't yet been blighted by high-rise apartment blocks. The narrow streets of the old town make a delightful stroll, skirting the 10th-century **monastery**, an endearingly lop-sided mix of Romanesque, Gothic and Baroque. It now contains an equally quirky and eclectic local **history museum** ⓘ *C/Abadia, T972821575, Jun-Sep Tue-Sat 1100-1400 and 1700-2000, free*, with exhibits on the cork and fishing industries, and some archaeological finds from the area.

Overlooking the town is the little hermitage of **Sant Elm**; it's a stiff climb up but worth it for the fantastic views. The tourist office has information on various walking and biking itineraries in the area, including one which leads past several dolmens. The tourist office ⓘ *Plaça de Monestir, T972820051, www.guixols.net.*

S'Agaró to Palamós

There is a string of big, beach resorts north of Sant Feliú de Guíxols; first up is **S'Agaró,** the smallest and prettiest with a fine, shallow beach spread around a horseshoe-shaped bay. **Platja d'Aró** is neon-lit and very built-up with dreary apartment blocks, but it's worth exploring the little coves outside the town to the north. Platja d'Aró was the port for the medieval town of **Castell d'Agaró**, a couple of kilometres inland, with a much-restored castle and a handsome late-Gothic church. **Calonge** is even lovelier, a dense medieval town of narrow streets twisted tightly around another church and castle. Its port, now another bland resort spread around a small bay, is **Sant Antoni de Calonge**. The monster along this part of the coast is

Palamós, which still has a busy, colourful harbour full of fishing boats at one end, but has otherwise been swallowed up in a grim sea of apartment blocks overlooking the long, sandy beaches.

Palafrugell

A lively cork-manufacturing town, with a slew of **Modernista buildings**, Palafrugell has a little 16th-century **church** and a colourful **Sunday market**. Set a couple of kilometres back from the sea, it's not over-run with tourists and retains a refreshingly authentic Catalan village atmosphere. There's an engaging little museum to the cork industry, **Museu del Suro** ① C/de la Tarongeta 31, T972303998, summer Tue-Sat 1000-1300 and 1700-2100, Sun 1030 and 1330, winter Tue-Sat 1700-2000, €2, which is more interesting that it sounds. Palafrugell has only a handful of hotels and restaurants, but it makes a nicer base than the overcrowded resorts in summer and you can take the bus (from the SARFA bus terminal, C/de Torres Jonama 69, on the outskirts of town) down to the beach with the locals for about €1 although the last buses back are surprisingly early.

Villages around Palafrugell

This is one of the prettiest and least spoiled stretches of the Costa Brava. From Palafrugell, there are frequent bus connections to a handful of fishing villages which have grown into bustling resorts squeezed between some delightful coves. This charming stretch of the coastline is a favourite with wealthy Barcelonans, whose villas and seaside apartments line the bays. There are plenty of foreign visitors too, but, so far at least, these seaside towns are still unblighted by concrete monstrosities. In whitewashed **Calella de Palafrugell**, a former fishing village which still has a harbour full of brightly painted boats, you can listen to the old sea shanties (*havaneras*) brought back from Cuba, and try *cremat*, coffee flambéed with rum and spices. Little **Tamariu**, tucked around a tiny bay, is a favourite with families and sufficiently cut off to feel undiscovered (at least in Costa Brava terms), unless you are here in July or August. **Llafranc** is larger, a chic resort set around a yacht-packed marina, surrounded by pine forests and gleaming villas. There are great views from the Sant Sebastià lighthouse, which you can reach on foot from Llafranc or Tamariu.

Villages inland

To escape the coastal fleshpots, head inland to these relatively unspoiled villages and market towns with a clutch of historical attractions. Lofty **Begur**, with its fancy mansions built by local boys who made good in the Americas (known as *Indianos*) and its old walls studded with grim stone keeps, is set just inland. It's a stiff, steep climb down to the beaches and there's no public transport. Just north is the striking fortified village of **Pals**, with spectacular views across the surrounding countryside and an over-preserved old quarter known as El Pedró which has been colonised by snooty second-homers. Despite the obvious prettification, it's hard not to be charmed by the warm stone houses spilling over with flowers. The nearby beaches are among the least known on the coast – although don't expect them to be empty: **Sa Riera** has broad sands and good views across to the Illes Medes (see below), and little **Sa Tuna** has been saved from package tours because of its remote, pebbly cove.

The unfinished Gothic castle of Montgrí stands in ruins on a hillside above **Torroella de Montgrí** ① C/Major 31, Mon-Sat 1000-1400 and 1800-2100, winter 1700-1900, Sun 1000-1400, free, which has a decent local museum devoted to the history of the area. The tranquil, arcaded Plaça de la Vila is the setting for concerts during the annual **International Music Festival** held in July and August.

Northwest, **Verges** is famous for its unsettling medieval Dansa de la Mort (Dance of Death) performed in the narrow streets the night before Good Friday, and Foixà has a magnificent medieval castle. Ullastret, with a neat winding medieval hub, has a

small museum (part of the Museu de Arqueologia de Catalunya) ① *Puig de Sant Andrau s/n, T972179058, Tue-Sat Jun-Sep 1000-2000, Oct-May 1000-1400 and 1500-1800, €2/1,* devoted to the remains of the ancient Iberian city (third-fourth century BC) discovered in its outskirts in the 1940s, and still being excavated.

Charming **Peratallada**, one of the most attractive and least visited of these villages, boasts its own fine collection of sturdy medieval buildings, and is famous for its local pottery. It's also close to the little village of **Púbol**, home to the third point of the so-called Triangle Dalinià (Dalí Triangle). Dali gave the **Castell de Púbol** ① *T972488655, 15 Mar-14 Jun and 16 Sep-1 Nov 1030-1800 daily except Mon, 15 Jun-15 Sep 1030-2000, €5.50/4,* also known as the Castell Gala Dalí, to his wife and muse Gala, who would frolic here with her young lovers and demand that her husband made appointments to see her. The castle houses a collection of the paintings and drawings which Dalí gave Gala to decorate it, and there's a selection of Gala's haute couture finery upstairs. The beautiful gardens are filled with elephant sculptures, another gift from Dalí to his wife.

There are tourist offices in most of the villages including Begur ① *Av Onze de Setembre s/n, T972624020,* and Pals, *C/Major 7, T972636161;* both have information on the numerous excellent walks in the area, including parts of the GR92.

Golfo de Roses → *Colour map 3, grid B6.*

The huge, curving bay of the Golfo de Roses stretches for about 25 km, tipped at both ends with a craggy cape. In the middle is a vast expanse of flat wetlands, part of which have been set aside as the Parc Natural dels Aiguamolls de l'Empordà, a paradise for birdwatchers. This area was among the first to be settled on the Iberian peninsula when Greek and Phoenicians established trading posts along the coast more than two and a half thousand years ago. The remains of one of the most important Greek settlements have been found near Empúries. Just off the southern cape is another natural park, the tiny islands of the Illes Medes, a very popular diving destination, and the Gulf is rounded off with Roses, a family resort lined with long sandy beaches.
▶▶ *For Sleeping, Eating and other listings, see pages 330-334.*

Illes Medes and L'Estartit

The small archipelago of the Illes Medes was once a haven for pirates and smugglers; now a marine reserve with a wealth of aquatic creatures living in and around the rare coral. It hit the news in 2002, when a group of Catalans 'took' the island for Catalunya: the leader called himself 'Pere Gil', a tongue-in-cheek reference to the island of Perejil which was briefly occupied by the Moroccans and caused a furore in Spain. The islands have become very popular – perhaps too popular – for water sports, and there are several diving companies based in the mainland resort of L'Estartit. L'Estartit is well known for its preserved anchovies, jars of which are sold in every shop in town. This area is the heartland of the Empordà region, well known for its fine regional cuisine which often combines meat and seafood in unusual ways – pig trotters stuffed with prawns is a local favourite.

The tourist office in L'Estartit ① *Passeig Marítim 47-50, T972751910, otestar@ddgi. es.* Illes Medes park information office ① *Edificio Medas Park, C/Ibiza, T972751103, Jun-Sep.* A list of the dozens of diving companies which offer trips and diving courses around the Illes Medes is available. It's best to come in the off season – May or September – when the waters aren't so crowded.

L'Escala and Empúries

L'Escala was home to Caterina Albert (1869-1966), the author of *Solitude*, a novel published under a *nom de plume* in 1905 which scandalised the public with its frank

portrayal of female sexuality. Nowadays, there isn't a whiff of decadence in this comfortably low-key seaside resort, which is popular with Spanish families and renowned for its excellent seafood, still brought in each day by the small fishing fleet.

Close by L'Escala are the ancient ruins of Empúries, founded around BC 600 and possibly the first and certainly one of the most important Greek colonies in Iberia. The first settlement was built on what was then a small island, now the site of the small, walled village of **Sant Martí d'Empúries** (now a pretty village tucked behind crumbling medieval walls which gets over-run with tourists in the summer), where the Greeks erected a temple to Artemis, the goddess of the moon and hunting. They built a new city ('Neapolis') on the mainland, where you can stroll among the old market, streets, cisterns and temples clustered along the shore. The Roman town established a couple of centuries later just inland has been excavated, and you can visit two fine **Roman villas** with beautiful mosaics floors, and the remnants of the forum and amphitheatre. Many of the artefacts discovered on the site are displayed in the small **museum** ① T972770208, www.mac.es, Jun-Sep 1000-2000, Oct-May 1000-1800, €2.50, but most of the important ones have been taken to the Museu d'Arqueologia in Barcelona. There's a wild expanse of sand dunes to stretch out on after a visit.

Parc Natural dels Aiguamolls de l'Empordà to Roses

When the Greeks were around, much of the land curving around the Golf de Roses was marshy and waterlogged, popular with birds but no use to the human population, who subsequently drained much of it to grow rice and other crops. Another chunk was drained when the mad scrabble for holiday properties erupted in the mid-20th century, but finally sense prevailed and the remaining marshlands with their important bird and animal life were given legal protection and became the Parc Natural dels Aiguamolls de l'Empordà. These wetlands are home to about 330 species of birds (and mosquitoes – don't forget repellent) and there are plenty of walking trails and hides for bird or animal watching, along with Spain's only **Butterfly Theme Park**.

Squeezed between the two protected sections of the marshes is another theme park, this time devoted to yuppiedom: **Empuriabrava** is a kind of posh, watery Milton Keynes, an overgrown housing estate with canals instead of roads and its own airport, nightclubs and shopping malls. A couple of miles inland, **Castelló d'Empúries** makes a much nicer base and has a vast Romanesque-meets-Gothic church known as the 'Cathedral of the Empordà', with an accomplished sculptural *Adoration of the Kings* around the door. The biggest town on the Golf de Roses is **Roses** itself, big, blowsy and overpriced, but with an interesting *ciutadella* (fortress) to stroll around, and a fine, sandy beach which is crammed in summer. The next little bay is **Cala Montjol**, home to one of Spain's most celebrated restaurants, **El Bulli**, see below. Kids will enjoy **Aqua Brava** ① Bahi de Roses, Ctra de Cadaqués,T972254344, www.aquabrava.com, a brand new water park with the biggest wave pool in Europe. Park information office ① El Cortalet, T972454222.

Cap de Creus to the French border

The Cap de Creus is one of the wildest and most beautiful stretches of coastline in Catalunya. A narrow road twists across the cape and out to whitewashed Cadaqués, spilling prettily down to a curving bay right out on the tip of the cape. The Cap de Creus has also been designated a natural park, and offers some spectacular hiking and diving. More whitewashed fishing villages dot the coast all the way to Port Bou on the French border, but only Llança can lay claim to being a sizeable resort. If you've got your own transport, finding a quiet beach should be pretty straightforward but public transport can be sketchy.»» *For Sleeping, Eating and other listings, see pages 330-334.*

66 99 It's a strange, haunting region, brooding, insular, and still strewn with forgotten dolmens, shepherds' huts and ancient ruins...

Cap de Creus Natural Park

Behind Roses, the flat wetlands of the Empordà suddenly rear up into the jagged peaks of the Cap de Creus, formed by the final thrust of the Pyrenees, its slopes narrowly ridged with olives, corktrees and low stone walls which once supported rows of vines. The cape, severe, wild and beautiful, has been designated a natural park and offers a variety of activities from hiking and scuba diving to fishing and birdwatching: artificial platforms have been introduced to try to coax back the ospreys which vanished two decades ago, but there are plenty of other species – more than 200 – of bird life to enjoy. From the Verdera watchtower at the tip of the peninsula, there are stunning views back over the Cap's twisted rocks stripped of plants and moulded into surreal shapes by the winds. The park information office is in the Monestir de Sant Pere de Rodes ⓘ *El Port de la Selva, T972193191.*

Cadaqués and Port Lligat

The sheer inaccessibility of remote, arty Cadaqués, and the fact that the determined residents wouldn't allow massive building projects, means that it has managed to hang on to its old-fashioned charm. Steep crooked streets lined with gleaming whitewashed cottages meander down to the bay, and it's stuffed full of smart restaurants, art galleries and craft shops. A simple white church seems to float above the highest part of the old town, where there's a small square which offers beautiful views across the bay. The town was once known as the St Tropez of the Costa Brava and you can see why. Nearby is Cadaqués' quirky **municipal art museum** ⓘ *C/Narcís Monturiol 15 (behind the church), T972258877, 1100-1330, 1600-2030, €2,* with works by Picasso and Dalí. The tourist office ⓘ *C/Cotxe 2, T972258315.*

Cadaqués is an excellent base for exploring the remote coves and walking trails of the Natural Park, and the magnificent trans-Pyrenean walking trail, the GR11, begins here too. Hire a boat to find a tiny, pebbly bay all for yourself around the cape: the water is so clear that the starfish creeping along the sea bed 50 ft below are clearly visible. There's a celebrated classical music festival in the summer.

The tiny bay of Port Lligat, a mile or so around the cape from Cadaqués, is where the area's most famous resident, Salvador Dalí, chose to settle during much of his life at **Casa-Museo Salvador Dalí** ⓘ *T972251015, www.salvador-dali.org, 15 Mar-14 Jun and 16 Sep-6 Jan 1030-1710, 15 Jun-15 Sep 1030-2010, €8.* Long abandoned but now partly refurbished, it can be visited in small groups but you must reserve in advance. The house is a surprise; furnished mainly by Gala, his wife and muse, it is a very private series of simple, whitewashed rooms and terraces linked with stairways. It was obviously conceived as a refuge and doesn't even have a spare bedroom. There are some touches of Dalí's imperious surrealism, like the enormous stuffed polar bear dripping with medals and jewellery which greets visitors at the main entrance, but these are largely confined to the entranceway and swimming pool – the most public areas of the house. In private Dalí was obviously less of showman than might have been expected, but he did insist that Gala's private boudoir was to be constructed in the same shape as a sea urchin. The bizarre acoustics mean that even the dullest conversation is given a purring, sensuous edge. The swimming pool is shaped like a keyhole, overlooked by surreal artworks including a statue of the Michelin man, and there's a fat, stuffed boa over the canopied seating area.

Around the coast, comfortable whitewashed Port de la Selva is refreshingly humble after all the glitz of Cadaqués. A twisting road winds up and up to the lofty **Monastir de Sant Pere de Rodes** ① *T972387559, Oct-May Tue-Sun 1000-1730 Jun-Sep 1000-2000*, clamped grimly against the mountainside and often lost in wreaths of mist. When the Moors were finally driven back, the lands were distributed between the victors and the Church; this was once a Dominican monastery with lands stretching across the whole peninsula and beyond during the height of its influence in the 13th century. An entire town grew up on the outskirts of the monastery but nothing remains besides the graceful, ruined church of Santa Helena resting on the horizon. A thousand years ago, the monks who lived among these lonely peaks began to cultivate grapes; the vines eventually covered the entire region, until phylloxera killed them off in the 19th century. These narrow walls snaking palely across the slopes are all that remain. Try to come in the morning when the sun is on the monastery; it can be cold and gloomy in the afternoon.

There is some excellent walking to be had around the complex; a twenty-minute scramble up the steep hillside will take you to the solid remnants of the **Castle of Sant Salvadera de Verdera**, commanding the highest peak and offering more breathtaking views, or there are more extensive hikes around the Cap de Creus natural park (the information office, with a book shop selling maps and guides, is in the monastery).

Llança to Port Bou

Next up on the coast from Port de la Selva is Llança, a cheerful harbour town which is the nearest this stretch of coast has to a full-blown resort, but is often overlooked in the charge towards better-known Cadaqués. It's popular with Spanish and French families, and there are plenty of wild beaches to be discovered close by. Then comes **Colera**, another small-scale resort, overlooked by the romantic ruins of a Romanesque Benedictine monastery Santa Qirze de Colera. Right on the border (3 km from Cerbere in France) is **Portbou**, which at first glance seems to be nothing more than a massive railway station, but is trying very hard to get in on the tourist game now that its former raison d'etre as a border town has been taken away by the Schengen agreement. And it's done a pretty good job, too: hidden behind the mass of train tracks is an agreeable little town, with narrow plane-shaded streets, a handful of good but reasonably priced seafood restaurants, and a small promenade around a tiny, pebbly bay.

● Sleeping

Costa Maresme *p323*

C Fonda Manau Can Raimón, C/Sant Josep 11, Caldes d'Estrac, T937910459, in a 19th-century mansion with a beautiful patio.

D Hostal Mar Blau, Canet de Mar, C/Sant Domenec 24, T937940499, close to the beach.

D Hostalet I, C/Manzanillo 9, Sant Pol de Mar, T937600605, is a welcoming, old-fashioned *pensión*. Good value.

D Hotel Rocatel, Av del Maresme 1, Calella, T937940350, most accommodation is uniformly bland in Calella. This is a good choice, with a pool.

F Mitus, C/Riera de la Torre, Canet de Mar, T937942903, a basic cheapie.

F Pensión Pinzón, C/el Callao 4, Caldes d'Estrac, T937910051, friendly, simple.

Costa Brava *p324*

LL Mas de Torrent, Alfueras de Torrent s/n, Torrent (just outside Pals), T972303292, www.mastorrent.com. This stunning 18th-century country house, set in gardens, has an award-winning restaurant, an outdoor pool, and all kinds of activities on offer including mountain-biking or a ride in a hot-air balloon.

AL Hotel de la Gavina, Plaça de la Rosaleda s/n, S'Agaró, T972321100, www.iponet.es/gavina. For a real treat stay here. The perfect setting for an Agatha Christie novel, **Gavina** has antique-furnished rooms, a stunning

seawater pool, 2 excellent restaurants (expensive and mid-range) and superb facilities. Closed 13 Oct-Easter.

AL Parador Costa Brava, Platja d'Aiguablava, in Aiguablava, T972622162, aiguablava@parador.es. Surrounded by woods and gardens right out on the cliffs, there is also an excellent restaurant and bar, open to non-residents.

AL Vilar del Mar, C/de la Vila 55, Lloret de Mar, T972349292, is one of several luxury hotels in town, but it has a bit more charm than most and boasts lots of extras including a pool, tennis courts and gym.

B Hotel Sant Roc, Plaça Atlàntic 2, Calella de Palafrugell, T972614250, F972614068, is a fabulous place to stay, surrounded by gardens with a panoramic terrace overlooking the bay. Prices jump dramatically in Aug. Closed Nov-Mar.

B-C Hotel Diana, Plaça d'Espanya 6, Tossa de Mar, T972341116, www.hotel-diana.com. The nicest accommodation option in Tossa, a 19th-century mansion with some original Modernista decor, including a fireplace designed by Gaudí, the Diana offers great discounts out of season, but book well in advance. Closed mid-Nov to Mar.

C Hostal Sa Tuna, T972622198, Playa Sa Tuna, www.hostalsatuna.com. This cosy, family-run hotel has an excellent, mid-range seafood restaurant.

C Hotel Plaça, Plaça de Mercat 22, Sant Feliú de Guíxols , T972325155, www.hotelplaza. org, with an excellent restaurant.

C La Marina, C/Ciutat de Palol 2, Platja d'Aró, T972817182, has a pool and modern rooms, and the family-run.

D Hostal Celimar, C/Carudo 12, Llafranc, T972301374, with small but attractive rooms, some with balconies.

D Hotel Rosa, C/San Pedro Martin 42, Blanes, T972330480, a modern hotel not far from the beach with a pool.

D Pensió Cap d'Or, Passeig del Mar 1, Tossa de Mar, T972340081, friendly, this is right on the seafront, and has spotless, if simple, accommodation but book rooms with sea views weeks in advance. Closed Oct-Feb.

D Planamar, Paseo del Mar 82, Platja d'Aró, T972817177, www.planamar.com, on the beach, has excellent watersports facilities.

D Residencia Reina Isabel, C/Venècia 2, Lloret de Mar, T972364121, a modest but welcoming budget choice, close to the beach.

D Rosa, Carrer Forga i Puig 6, Begur, T972623015, hotelrosa@hotmail.com, friendly, family run, where prices drop considerably out of season.

D Sa Barraca, Ctra de Fornells, Begur, T972623360, where each room has a terrace with views over the bay.

E Fonda L'Estrella, C/ de les Quatre Cases 13, Palafrugell, T/F972300005, just off the Plaça Nova, popular budget option offering simple rooms around a sunny courtyard. More upmarket, but not as charming.

F Hostal Kiku, C/Sant Andreu de Sa Palomera, Blanes, T972332727, right by the beach and the rock of Sa Palomera, and has a very decent, cheap restaurant.

F Pensió Gas Vell, C/Santa Magdalena, Sant Feliú de Guíxols , T972321024, pristine but very basic.

G Fonda Can Lluna, C/Roqueta 20, Tossa de Mar, T972340365, is the best budget choice, tucked in a narrow street in the old quarter. Rooms are small, but made up for by the fabulous roof terrace. Full or half board only in Jul and Aug. Book in advance and confirm 2 weeks before arrival. Closed Nov-Apr.

Camping

G Camping Moby Dick, C/Costa Verde 16-28, Calella de Palafrugell, T972614307, with shady sites just 100 m from the beach. (About e10 for 2 people plus tent.).

G Camping Pola, Ctra de Sant Feliu, Tossa de Mar, T972341050, 4 km out of town, is the best campsite, with a pool, supermarket and other facilities. Take the bus for Sant Feliu and ask them to drop you off.

G Camping Santa Elena Ciutat, T972364079, one of several in the area. This has shady sites, a pool, and Playa de Fenals on the doorstep.

Golfo de Roses *p327*

AL Almadraba Park, Platja de Almadraba, Parc Natural dels Aiguamolls de l'Empordà to Roses, almadrabapark@almadrabapark.com, T972256550, perched on a cliff above an excellent beach. Glitzy and modern.

C Hotel Ampurias, L'Escala and Empúries, T972770207, is right on the beach by the archaeological site of Empúries. Bland and rather over-priced.

D El Roser, Plaça Església 7, L'Escala and Empúries, T972770219, www.elroser.com. This attractive, old-fashioned hotel has a popular restaurant and during the summer you can join in the *sardana* dancing on the seafront on Wed evenings.

D Hotel les Illes, C/Illes 55, T972751239, Illes Medes and L'Estartit, is a modern hotel near the port which is geared towards divers.

D Hôtel-Restaurante La Cala, C/Sant Sebastià 61, Parc Natural dels Aiguamolls, T972256171, down-to-earth comforts, simple rooms and a good Catalan restaurant. Prices drop out of season.

Cap de Creus to the French Border *p328*

There are plenty of places to stay in Cadaqués.

C Hotel Masia, Paseo de la Sardana 1, Port Bou, T972390372, the best rooms have views across the bay.

D Hostal Cristina, C/Riera 1, T972 258 138. One of the nicest places to stay in Cadaqués. On the beach. Best rooms have a terrace.

D Hostal Maria Teresa, C/Pintor Terruella 22, Llança, T972380125, surrounded by olive trees between the old town and the beach.

D Hostal Marina, C/Riera 3, next door from Cristina, T972159091, closed Jan-Mar. The other nicest place to stay in Cadaqués, also on the beach.

E Hostal La Tina, C/Sant Baudil 16, T97238149, in Port de la Selva is this family run affair.

E Pensión Vehi, C/Església 5, Cadaqués T9722 58470, with simple rooms in the old town near the church, and a very decent and cheap restaurant.

⊙ Eating

Costa Maresme *p323*

€€€Portinyol, Puerto de Arenys s/n, Arenys de Mar, T937920009. Good place to splash out on some fine dining: beautiful sea views and food.

€€€ Sant Pau, C/Nou 8-10, Sant Pol de Mar, T937600662. One of the most acclaimed restaurants in the area.

€€ Marola, Paseo del Anglesos 6, Caldes d'Estrac, T937910700, great local seafood which has been going since the 1940s.

€ Emma, Baixada de l'Estació 5, T93791305, with a very cheap *menú del día*. Family run.

€ Plenty of cheap, if more or less indistiguishable places, around the buzzy harbour in Arenys de Mar.

Costa Brava *p324*

The food is pretty ordinary in all these resorts unless you've got money to burn. In Palafrugell you'll find plenty of places around the Plaça Nova. For eateries in the villages around Palafrugell look around the port and harbour areas and note that many of the hotels have very decent restaurants which offer good value *menús*.

€€€ Ca L'Antoni, C/Carles Riba 36, Lloret de Mar, T972369370, one of the finest and most exclusive seafood restaurants in the region, with prices to match.

€€€ Es Molí, C/Tarull 5, Tossa de Mar, T972341414, is an elegant restaurant serving up imaginatively prepared Catalan cuisine. There are excellent home-made desserts, and a beautiful patio surrounded by citrus trees. Fixed price *menús* start at around euro21, but choosing from the *carta* is considerably more expensive. Closed mid-Oct–Mar.

€€€ The Big Rock, Barri de Fanals 5, S'Agaró to Palamós, T972818012, is the most renowned restaurant of the area, with expensive prices to match, set out in a rural farmhouse near Platja d'Aró (and if you can't make it home, there are 5 suites (**AL**) and a swimming pool). Closed Sun nights, Mon and all Jan.

€€ Can Flores II, Esplanada del Port s/n, Blanes, T972332633, is a classic, over-bright, 60s-style restaurant which makes up for what it lacks in atmosphere with excellent seafood. The house speciality is fish baked in a salt crust, and the paellas are also good.

€€ Can Toni, Carrer Garrofers 54, Sant Feliu de Guíxols, T972321026, good, well known for its mushroom (*bolets*) dishes in season.

€€ Fonda Caner, Carrer Pi i Ralló 14, T972622391, which is a great place to try local Empurdan specialities – local game like rabbits and partridge, snails and dishes made from locally grown rice.

€€ Maribú Grill, Paseo del Mar 35, Sant Feliu de Guíxols, T972321023, for freshly-caught-sardines and also does a *menú del día* for €15.

€€ Restaurant El Far, next to the Faro de Sant Sebastià, Calella de Palafrugell,

T972301639, offers excellent seafood and is attached to a sumptuous hotel (**AL**).

€ **Can Claver**, C/Joan Maragall 18, Sant Feliu de Guíxols, T97 82 0486, home-cooking at a good price, has a *menú* at around €7 and tasty *bocadillos*.

€ **Casa Andrés**, Av da la Palma 19, Tossa de Mar, T972341909, which serves a good value fixed price *menú* at lunchtimes and evenings (e10) which includes wine. You can eat out on the pretty flower-filled terrace.

€ **El Sorrall**, Passeig de S'Abanell 6, Blanes, T972333420, a good bet in the new part of town, serving local dishes, and offering a good value menú del día.

€ **Els Patis de Begur**, C/Pi i Ralló 9, Begur, T972623741, a cheap lunchtime *menú* in this delightful little restaurant with terrace.

€ **Pomodoro**, Paseo de Sa Caleta, Lloret de Mar, T972369023, serves great, cheap, oven-baked pizzas right by the seafront.

€ **Taverna de Mar**, C/Pescadors 5, Lloret de Mar, T972464090, is popular with locals, and serves delicious tapas and seafood dishes; try the tasty *fideuá*, the Catalan version of paella.

€ **Tragamar**, Playa de Candell, Calella de Palafrugell, T972615189, does great tapas (including, amazingly, guacamole).

Golfo de Roses *p327*
See also Sleeping above.
€€ **El Bullí**, Cala Montjol, Parc Natural dels Aiguamolls, T972150457, www.elbulli.com. This legendary restaurant regularly wins plaudits from chefs all over the world, and enjoys a magnificent setting looking out over the Mediterranean; you should book months in advance. Open Apr-Oct.

Cap de Creus to the French Border *p328*
€€€-€€ **Casa Nun**, Plaça Port Ditxos (at the end of Passeig Marítim), Cadaqués, T972258856, housed in a romantically rickety, narrow old house, which serves some of the freshest and tastiest sea food on the coast as well as heavenly homemade desserts (menus at €34 and €13).

€€ **Bodegón Casa Anita**, Cadaqués, T972258471, for tapas or good home-cooking, crammed with locals.

€€ **La Vela**, Av Pau Casals 23, Llança, T972380475, a classic from the 1960s which has a big reputation for its seafood.

€ **Restaurante L'Àncora**, Paseo de la Sardana 3, T972390025, in Port Bou, which has freshly caught seafood to go with the sea views.

○ Bars and clubs

Costa Brava *p324*
In Blanes, there are dozens of bars and clubs along the Paseo Marítimo; try **La Carpa** and **Illegal** for drinks, and finish up at the **Sant Trop** disco.

Cap de Creus to the French Border *p328*
There's plenty of nightlife in Cadaqués, at least during the summer. You can get cocktails invented on the spot at **Bar 57 c**, right on the harbour front just beyond the casino (also a good spot for a coffee while you watch the old men fleece each other at cards). **Es Purró**, just behind the church, is the current clubbers' favourite, although there are a couple of popular spots, like **L'Hostal**, on the Passeig Marítim as well.

⊛ Festivals and events

Costa Brava *p324*
In Blanes in the summer (usually **late Jul**), the town explodes for the stunning International **Fireworks Festival**.

▲ Activities and tours

Costa Brava *p324*
Lloret is well set up for activities.
Centro BTT, Av Rieral s/n, Urb. El Molí, T972371149, for bike rental.
Club Hípic Lloret, Sant Pere del Bosc, T972368615, horse riding.
Nauti Sub Lloret, C/ Europa 16, T972372641, for diving lessons.

Cap de Creus to the French Border *p328*
Boats and Bikes Cadaqués, T972258027. To rent a zodiac, scooter or kayac.
Creuers Cadaqués, T972159462, offers cruised around the cape which leave from the harbour (€9 per adult, for 1½ hrs around Cap de Creus).
Els Caials, T972258841, rent diving and snorkelling equipment.

❂ Transport

Costa Maresme *p323*

Regular buses leave from the Estació d'Autobuses **Barcelona-Nord** for most resorts. *Cercanías* (local trains) depart very regularly (at least every 30 mins) from **Estació-Sants** via Plaça Catalunya, for all the coastal towns north of **Barcelona** to **Blanes**. Return fares to Blanes: around €7; Barcelona to Castelldefels: €3.50.

Costa Brava *p324*

Bus SARFA, T902302025, run a regular bus service from **Girona** to most coastal resorts including **Blanes**, **Lloret de Mar** and **Tossa de Mar**. Tossa doesn't have its own train station; take a bus from Blanes, or from Girona. There are at least 10 departures daily. Teisa, T972200275, also runs a bus service between **Sant Feliu de Guíxols** and **Girona**.
Boat Crucetours, T972372692, run a summer boat service between **Blanes**, **Lloret de Mar**, **Tossa de Mar**, **Sant Feliu de Guíxols** and **Palamós** (it also makes stops at smaller villages and coves).
Car If you are driving, the coastal road is beautiful but expect long, delays in summer.
Cycle You can rent bikes at **Bicis Costa Brava**, C/Girona 20, T972322998.
Train There are regular *cercanías* from **Barcelona's** Plaça Catalunya station to **Blanes**; the station is 2 km out of town, and

services are met with buses to Blanes proper and **Lloret de Mar**.

Golfo de Roses *p327*

SARFA, T902302025, run regular bus services to **Roses**, **Castello de Empuriés** and **L'Estartit** from **Figueres**. There are also less frequent services to **L'Estartit** and **Roses** from **Barcelona**, but it's usually quicker to get the train to **Figueres** and take a bus from there. There are also bus connections with L'Escala and Empúries via **Toroella de Montgri** from **Palafrugell**.

Cap de Creus to the French Border *p328*

Bus SARFA, T972674298, run infrequent (3 times daily except Sun) services to **Cadaqués** from **Figueres**; €8 return, a daily service from **Girona** (weekdays only), and a twice-daily service from **Barcelona**. There are buses from **Llança** to **Port de la Selva**, but none between **Cadaqués** and **Port de la Selva**: there's a beautiful coastal hiking trail (part of the GR11) or you could call a minibus taxi in **Cadaqués** on T972258771 (Pepe, the driver, also gives guided visits and is very knowledgeable about the park and local history); around €40-50 from Cadaqués to Port Bou.
Train There are regular trains from **Barcelona**, **Girona** and the French border at **Cerbere** to **Llança** and **Port Bou**.

Inland Catalunya

This area contains some of the most visited and least visited attractions in all of Spain. The haunting monastery at Montserrat is the most popular day trip from Barcelona with many visitors arriving via the knee-trembling cable car ride. Further north in Figueres is the Teatre-Museu Dalí, a museum as flamboyant and bizarre as one would expect from the master of the absurd, which attracts the most visitors in Spain with the exception of the Prado. However, lurking further inland are isolated corners well worth exploring: the rugged landscape of Parc Natural Albera and the lava-stripped cliffs of La Garrotxa, for example, are both wonderfully remote. ▸▸ *For Sleeping, Eating and other listings, see pages 348-354.*

Terrassa → *Phone code: 937; Colour map 3, grid B4; Population: 172,807.*

Terrassa, on the way to Montserrat, is a strikingly unattractive industrial city wreathed in puffs of acrid smoke. The Japanese once voted it the 'Ugliest City in Europe', but they obviously didn't get past the outskirts because the centre has managed to hang on to a

Sights

A walk down the Carrer de Sant Pau will give you a taste of Terrassa's Modernista heritage; the former **Teatre Principal** is a frilly, domed confection with plenty of murals and stained glass, and nearby is a covered market, and the grandiose **Institut Industrial** in a former wool warehouse with a huge glass dome. There are also three delightful **Modernista shops** at Nos 17, 11 and 9, including one built by Domènech i Montaner (No 11).

Terrassa was at the forefront of Spain's industrial revolution in the mid-19th century and there are a couple of museums dedicated to its unique industrial heritage. The excellent and slickly designed **Museu Nacional de la Ciència i de la Tècnica de Catalunya** (MNACTEC) ① *T937368966, www.museu.mnactec.com, Tue-Fri 1000-1900, Sat and Sun 1000-1430, Jul and Aug Tue-Sun 1000-1430 only, €3/1.50, free first Sun of the month*, is set in a stunning Modernista 19th-century fabric factory and features all kinds of interactive gizmos. **Museu Textil** ① *C/Salmerón 25, www.cdmt.es, 0900-1800, Thu 0900-2100, Sat and Sun 1000-1400, closed Mon and holidays, €3/1.50*, has a vast collection of fabrics, clothing and original designs.

Out in the **Parque del Vallparadis**, on the edge of the city, there's a remarkable complex of pre-Romanesque churches set in quiet gardens which were built on top of the old Roman settlement of **Egara**. The largest, the Església de Sant Pere, has a Romanesque sarcophagus pressed into service as a font, and some Byzantine-inspired murals. **Iglesia de Santa Maria** has a glittering retablo by Jaume Huguet, and the smallest church, **Església de Sant Miquel**, was begun in the fifth-century using Roman columns, and odds and ends, found on the site to prop up the dome. The park has a boating lake and swimming pool, especially popular at weekends.

Excursion

Astonishingly close to industrial Terrassa, it's possible to lose yourself completely in the forests, jagged peaks and narrow ravines of **Sant Llorenç del Munt i l'Obac** (the park information office ① *T937433020, pstllorenc@diba.es*, and starting point for most of the trails, is near Matadapera, down a small track leading off the main road from Terrassa to Talamanca Km10.8). There are well-marked walking trails for people of all fitness levels, including a wonderful circular walk which passes over the peak of La Mola and through the ravine of Santa Agnès (about four hours).

Montserrat → *Phone code: 938; Colour map 3, grid B4.*

One of the most popular day trips from Barcelona (about 40 km) is the Monastery of Montserrat, clamped high to a dramatic reddish massif (Montserrat means 'jagged mountain') and home to a miraculous statue of the Virgin known as La Moreneta ('the little brown one'). The Montserrat mountains erupt surreally from the surrounding plain, as unreal as a painted backdrop. The most dramatic way to arrive is by cable car which sways on a tiny thread across the valley and up to the monastery. The area around the monastery itself gets unpleasantly crowded, but you can escape to the surrounding Parc Natural Montserrat which offers fantastic hiking trails linking tiny half-forgotten hermitages. ▸▸ *For Sleeping, Eating and other listings, see pages 348-354.*

Ins and outs

Getting there The monastery is easily accessible from Barcelona. A daily bus departs from Sants, or a more adventurous train/cable car route. Good value all-inclusive tickets are available. ▸▸ *For further details, see Transport page 353.*

Best time to visit Montserrat is a hugely popular pilgrim destination, and it's always packed at weekends and in July and August. It's less crowded on weekdays in spring or autumn. The biggest annual pilgrimage takes place on 27 April and there's another on 8 September. Try to catch the children's choir in the basilica.

Tourist information ① *Plaça de la Creu, T938777724, www.abadiamontserrat.net.* They can provide information on accommodation, as well as plans and walking itineraries of the natural park of Montserrat. You can buy a detailed guide to the park, *Guide Officiel de Montserrat*, from any of the souvenir shops by the monastery.

History

The mountain of Montserrat has long been sacred to Catalans: there were already five hermitages tucked between its peaks by the ninth century, and monks would hole themselves up in remote caves to fast and pray. The Benedictine monastery clamped daringly beneath a peak was established in the 10th century, but was largely demolished during the Napoleonic wars and most of the current grim, prison-like building was erected in the 19th and 20th centuries. The monastery vied with Santiago de Compostela as a place of pilgrimage during the middle ages, thanks to the sacred statue of *La Moreneta* (The Brown One), the miraculous polychrome wooden statue of the Black Virgin and Child which still presides over the altar of the basilica and is Catalunya's Holy of Holies. Legend has it that it was carved by St Luke and that St Peter later hid the statue in a cave, where it was discovered by shepherds in 880. Floods of pilgrims, particularly newly-weds, still pour in to touch the statue, and, even now, Montserrat is one of the most popular names for a girl in Catalunya.

Sights

Basilica ① *0800-1030 and 1200-1830, free.* The heart of the monastery complex is the gloomy basilica, built in the last century, and very dark and gloomy. A passage on the right (with flashing neon-lights) leads to the statue of La Moreneta encased in glass above the altar, and you can join the queue to touch it and pray for a miracle. The Escolania, one of the oldest children's choirs in Europe, sings daily at 1300 and 1910 in the basilica. The monastery's **museum** ① *Plaça del Monestir, T938350251, Summer 1030-1400 and 1530-1800, winter 1030-1400 and 1500-1800, €3*, is divided into three sections, which displays a dull collection of Catalan art from the 19th and 20th centuries, a more interesting selection of Spanish, Flemish and Italian Old Masters, and a collection of archaeological treasures from Mesopotamia, Egypt and Palestine. An audio-visual display offers a glimpse into the daily life of the community of monks who still live here.

Parc Natural de Montserrat The bus-loads of tourists, jostling crowds, souvenir stalls and 1960s cafeteria have largely stripped the area around the monastery of any sense of spirituality or contemplation. If you head out from the monastery into the surrounding natural park it doesn't take long to lose the crowds. There are two funiculars: the funicular Sant Joan heads up to the top of the massif for spectacular views, and another drops down to the tiny chapel of Santa Cova, built to celebrate the discovery of La Moreneta. Trails of various lengths and difficulties lead from both of them and wind across the park (maps and information available from the tourist information office); one visits each of the abandoned 13 hermitages and chapels which are scattered around the mountain. Experienced rock climbers can tackle some of the sheer cliffs.

● *The peculiar silhouette of the Monserrat Mountains inspired Gaudí's designs for the*
● *Sagrada Família and Wagner envisioned Sir Parsifal discovering the Holy Grail in their secret hollows.*

Vic and the Parc Natural de Montseny

→ *Phone code: 938; Colour map 3, grid B5; Population: 30,739; Altitude: 484 m.*

The handsome market town of Vic is set on a plain just 70 km from Barcelona, and surrounded by the gentle mountains of Montseny. The old town is curled around one of the largest and finest squares in Catalunya, where twice-weekly markets are still held in a tradition which dates back several centuries. Vic may have lost the political prominence it boasted back then, but it remains a prosperous and genial town with a smattering of decent museums and vestiges of its Roman past. ▸▸ *For Sleeping, Eating and other listings, see pages 348-354.*

Ins and outs

Getting there and around Vic is accessible from Barcelona by train and there are several bus connections to other local villages, but it is difficult to explore fully the region without your own transport. The town itself is small and easy to get around on foot. ▸▸ *For further details, see Transport page 353.*

Tourist information The tourist office ① *just off the Plaça Major at C/ de la Ciutat 4, T938862091, www.victurisme.com*, provides a useful map marked up with a 'tourist itinerary' and has a list of multilingual guides offering tours in the town and region. There are several information offices for the Parc Natural de Montseny, but the main one ① *Vall de Santa Fe, T938475113, montseny@diba.es*. Guided tours of the park are available and information is provided on the hiking trails, as well as opportunities for birdwatching, balloon rides, and horse riding.

Vic

Vic's famous markets still take place on Tuesdays (a small version) and Saturdays (huge) beneath the arcades of its grand old **Plaça Major**. Stalls are piled high with the local embutits, cured meats made from local pork, which are considered among the finest in Catalunya. If you miss the market, there are plenty of shops devoted to them lining the narrow streets. To see the sausage in its original incarnation, come during the week before Easter, when the traditional livestock market, the Mercat del Ram, is held. The buildings which surround the square are mainly Baroque or Modernista, some with curly sgraffito and wide, elegant façades.

❖ *There are plenty of cafés around the Plaça to sit back and enjoy the scene.*

Back when the Romans were in charge, at least nominally, they built a temple at the city's highest point, the ruins of which were discovered more than a century ago in the rubble of a 12th-century castle built by the ruling Montcada family. Since the sixth century, the town has been a bishop's see but much of its original Romanesque **cathedral** ① *Plaça Catedral s/n, T938864449, 1000-1300 and 1600-1900, free*, was destroyed during a banal neoclassical refurbishment during the 18th century: the Romanesque crypt, the original belltower and fragments of the original cloister (which was shifted during the refurbishment) are still on view. Other highlights include a monumental Gothic alabaster altarpiece and colourful murals in the nave by the Barcelonan artist Josep María Sert. **Museu Episcopal** ① *Plaça Bisbe Oliba 338869360, informacio@museuepiscoplavic.com, Apr-Sep Tue-Sat 1000-1900, Sun 1000-1400, Oct-Mar Tue-Fri 1000-1300 and 1500-1800, Sat 1000-1900, Sun 1000-1400, €1.50/2*, holds an excellent collection of Romanesque murals and artworks gathered from rural churches and has just moved into brand new premises.

All these sights, as well as the Romanesque Porta de Queralt and the sturdy remnants of the city walls raised under Pedro III the Ceremonious, form part of a useful 'tourist route' marked out on a map by the tourist office which is clearly signposted around the town.

Catalunya & Andorra Vic & Parc Natural de Montseny

Northeast of Vic, heading deeper into the mountains along the C-153, lies the region known as Les Guilleries with a string of especially lovely villages; surrounded by rolling hills, cliffs and secret waterfalls, this is a landscape to linger in, although you'll only manage it with your own transport as bus services are pretty sketchy and infrequent.

Closest to Vic is **Tavèrnoles**, with a Romanesque church and the remnants of a medieval castle; then there's Tavertit, a minuscule and perfectly preserved 17th-century village of less than 200 souls (outside the tourist season) clinging to the edge of the mountain; and finally Rupit, so picture-postcard-perfect that it was reproduced in the Poble Español in Barcelona, see page 272. They are all best visited during the week, particularly in spring and autumn, when you can enjoy them in peace.

Some 15 km east of Vic is the **Pantà de Sau**, an attractive lake surrounded by forested hills where you can rent boats or swim. When the lake was dammed, the little village of Sant Romà de Sau was abandoned to the waters and the top of an old belltower sometimes appears when the water levels are low.

Parc Natural de Montseny and spa towns

The Vic area, particularly the charming spa town of Viladrau, is a handy starting point for the Parc Natural de Montseny which has a particularly rich diversity of flora and fauna thanks to the range of habitats it offers and provides excellent opportunities for walking (GR4 and GR5 cross the park) and horse riding as well as balloon tours. Spring and autumn are the best times to visit the park.

More spa towns are dotted around the hills to the east: Sant Hilari Sacalm, perched on a hilltop, is a prosperous little town where the pace of life is pleasingly slow. It's well known for its Easter passion plays (Via Crucis Vivent), some of the oldest and most dramatic in Spain. Southeast of Montseny lie the densely forested peaks of the La Selva region, brooded over by the immense Gothic ruins of Montsoriu castle. There are a host of villages lost in its folds, from Breda with its long tradition of ceramic-production and lofty Romanesque belltower to Arbúcies, dreaming on a mountain top. Hostalric, on the southern edge of the natural park, is just off the main A-7 motorway to France; it's corseted with a ring of ancient houses squeezed against the remarkably intact city walls.

Cardona

If you are looking for a place to break your journey to the Pyrenees, medieval Cardona, piled up on a rock in the middle of a plain, isn't a bad option if only for its famous parador. This is set in a spectacular castle clamped to the very top of the hill and was founded in 789 by Louis the Pious. Cardona is known as the 'Capital of Salt', for its nearby Salí, a ghostly mountain of pure salt that sits beside the river and has been mined since Roman times. It's easiest to get to Cardona by bus from Manresa (on the train line).

Solsona

West of Cardona is another fortified medieval town, Solsona, tightly packed behind a ring of walls studded with crenellated towers and topped with a ruined castle. It's an elegant town, packed with noble mansions dating back to the 16th and 17th centuries, and the cathedral houses a much-venerated 12th-century Virgin made of black stone. **Museu Diocesà i Comarcal** ① *Plaça Palau 1, T973482101, Jun-Sep 1000-1300 and 1630-1900, Oct-May 1000-1300 and 1600-1800, €2*, is housed in the archbishop's palace and contains some mesmerising frescoes from the Romanesque church of Sant Quirze de Pedret.

Girona → *Phone code: 972; Colour map 3, grid B5; Population: 74,754.*

Girona, Catalunya's second city, is an unexpected charmer, sprawling languidly around the confluence of the Rivers Ter and Onyar. The expansive modern city, with its leafy avenues lined with galleries and a handful of Modernista mansions, lies on the west side of the Onyar; on its eastern bank is the shadowy huddle of the ancient city which grew up around an early Iberian settlement. A ribbon of yellow-, orange- and ochre-painted houses, once attached to the city walls, hang over the river and behind them lies a medieval web of crooked alleys and narrow passages built on top of the Roman colony. A long-established university town, the big student population means the city's nightlife is almost as buzzy as Barcelona's, and the arcaded streets and placid squares of the old city are lined with trendy shops, bars and restaurants.
▶▶ *For Sleeping, Eating and other listings, see pages 348-354.*

Ins and outs

Getting there Girona's airport is 12 km from town; for airport information, call T972186600. There's an hourly bus service from the airport with TEISA, T972 204 868, from outside the terminal to the bus station. Taxis (from outside the arrivals hall) cost around €5. Girona is very well served by buses and trains from Barcelona; for general bus information, call T972212319. ▶▶ *For further details, see Transport page 353.*

Getting around The bus and train stations are next to each other, 10-minutes walk from the old city where you'll find most of the sights. If driving, note that much of the old city is pedestrianized, so you'll have to park in the new part and walk. You won't need to use the bus system in Girona as the sites are all together in the old part of the city by the banks of the river.

Best time to visit Girona keeps a very full festival calendar (see below) so there's something going on for most of the year. The city's biggest festival is the Festa de Sant Narcis held at the end of October or beginning of November, when devils, dragons and giants parade though the streets. The old stone streets are always cool, even in the height of summer.

Tourist information The helpful tourist office ① *Rambla de la Llibertat 1, T97222 6612 (T972216761 for English speakers), www.girona-net.com*, has informaton on guided walks around the Call (Jewish Quarter). They can also provide a leaflet on the 40 km-long former railway line which has been converted into a walking/biking path between Girona and Sant Feliu de Guíxols.

History

An Iberian settlement, then a Roman colony and eventually a Moorish city for almost two centuries, Girona was also the medieval centre of one of Spain's largest and most influential Jewish communities. An important school of Jewish mysticism, the *Cabalistas de Girona*, was established during the 12th and 13th centuries, and the undisputed master of the Cabala was Moses Ben Nahman, or Nahmanides, who was born in Girona in 1194 and became the Grand Rabbi of Catalunya. The Jews suffered increasing persecution throughout the 14th century; 40 inhabitants were killed during the pogrom of 1391, and the Jewish quarter, or Call, was gradually sealed off and became a ghetto. Finally, by decree of the Catholic Kings, all Jews were expelled from Spain in 1492. The city's strategic location at the confluence of three rivers meant that it would always be in the front line of the seemingly endless wars which ripped across Europe and divided Spain for much of the following three centuries: by the time Napoleon's armies came south of the Pyrenees in 1809, it had already been besieged

● *Girona has regained its former prosperity as well as its reputation for learning; many*
● *publishing houses and prestigious academic institutions are based here, and Girona has quietly become Spain's richest city.*

more than 20 times. It held out against the French for nine months, gaining the nickname 'The Immortal'.

Sights

El Call: The old Jewish Quarter The old core of Girona has barely changed in centuries. **Carrer de la Força** follows the line of the Vía Augusta, and was the main artery of the medieval Jewish quarter, or Call, which remains astonishingly intact. Halfway up it, the Centra Bonastruc Ça Porta is built around the old Synagogue of Girona which is being painstakingly restored. It houses an institute of Jewish learning, as well as the fascinating **Museo de los Judeos en Catalunya** ① *T972216761, May 15-Nov 14 Mon-Sat 1000-2100, until 1800 in winter, Sun and holidays 1000-1400, €2*, which describes the development of the Jewish community from the first mention of

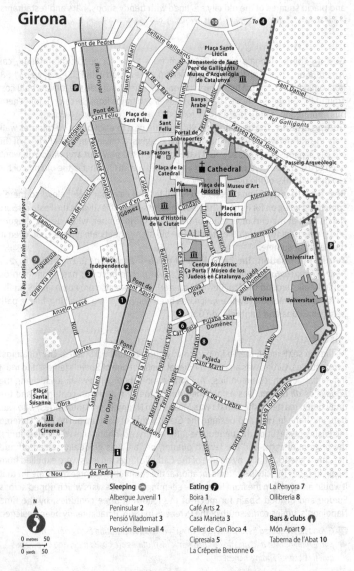

Girona

Sleeping 🛏	Eating 🍴	La Penyora **7**
Albergue Juvenil **1**	Boira **1**	Ollibreria **8**
Peninsular **2**	Café Arts **2**	
Pensió Viladomat **3**	Casa Marieta **3**	Bars & clubs 🍸
Pensión Bellmirall **4**	Celler de Can Roca **4**	Món Apart **9**
	Cipresaia **5**	Taberna de l'Abat **10**
	La Crêperie Bretonne **6**	

N

0 metres 50
0 yards 50

Further up, the **Museu d'Història de la Ciutat** ① *C/de la Força 27, T972222229, museu@ajgirona.org, Tue-Sat 1000-1400 and 1700-1900, Sun 1000-1400, closed Mon except holidays, €2*, is housed in a sturdy 18th-century mansion with well laid out exhibits documenting the history of the city from prehistoric times to the introduction of electricity and the computer age. The most gruesome sight is the Capuchin cemetery (just inside the entrance on the right); the Capuchins dissected the bodies of dead monks on perforated benches and buried them in vertical tombs.

Cathedral and around Just beyond the museum, the street opens up on to the lovely **Plaça de la Catedral**, flanked by the 18th-century Casa Pastors (law courts) and the imposing Gothic Pia Almoina (almshouse). A broad flight of steps sweep up to the Cathedral ① *Plaça de la Catedral s/n, T972214426, www.lacatedraldegirona.com, Jul-Sep 1000-2000, Oct-Feb 1000-1400 and 1600-1800, Mar-Jun 1000-1400, free, admission to the museum and cloisters €3*, one of the grandest in Catalunya, with an elaborate Baroque façade topped with a frilly belltower. The present cathedral was begun in 1312, but a century later Guillem Bofill added a single, daring nave in defiance of a committee of architects who swore it wouldn't work; it's the largest in Europe, with an audacious 23-m span. The delicate Romanesque cloister with its intricately carved capitals was left over from the previous cathedral which occupied the spot, as is the Romanesque belltower, the Torre de Carlemany which was incorporated into the new construction as a buttress. **Museu Capitular** holds a fine collection of religious art, including a powerful 12th-century tapestry of the Creation (the best preserved Romanesque tapestry in Europe), and the *Còdex del Beatus* exquisitely illuminated by Mozarabic miniaturists during the 10th-century.

The former Episcopal Palace tucked behind the cathedral now houses Girona's excellent **Museu d'Art** ① *T972209536, www.ddgi.es/museu, Mar-Sep Tue-Sat 1000-1900, Sun 1000-1400, Oct-Feb 1000-1800, Sun 1000-1400, €2*, an eclectic collection of painting, sculpture, furniture, glass and gold and silver-work from the Visigothic period until the 19th century, displayed in cavernous vaulted halls. There are two notable Gothic *retablos*, including a particularly fine piece from Bernat Martorell, and paintings from Joaquim Vayreda of the Olot school and the bohemian dandy, Santiago Rusiñol.

Beyond the Portal de Sobreportes Below the cathedral is the Portal de Sobreportes, the ancient Roman entrance to the city, and the final exit for condemned prisoners who went to their deaths in the square beyond. To the left stands the **Església de Sant Feliu** which was built over an old Christian cemetery where legend has it that the city's martyred patron saint, Sant Narcís, met a sticky end and contains some finely carved Roman and paleochristian sarcophagi. The Gothic belltower had its spire blasted off by a bolt of lightning in 1581, but still manages to poke its head above the red-tiled rooftops.

Behind the church of Sant Feliu are the **Banys Àrabe** ① *C/Ferran El Catòlic, T972213262, Apr-Sep Tue-Sat 1000-1900, Sun 1000-1400, Oct-Mar Tue-Sun 1000-1400, €1.50*, which were built on a Roman model, perhaps by Moorish craftsmen in the 13th century, and are among the most well preserved in Spain. The loveliest area is the *frigidarium* (cold water pool), which is subtly illuminated by a skylight supported by a ring of slim columns. The niches are filled with changing contemporary art exhibitions and there's a little walkway across the rooftop.

Across the empty riverbed of the tiny Riu Galligans is **Monesterio de Sant Pere de Galligants** ① *Plaça de Sant Llúcia, T972202632, Jun-Sep Tue-Sat 1030-1330, 1600-1900, Oct-May 1000-1400, 1600-1800, €1.80/1.35*, a sober 12th-century monastery with an unusual octagonal belltower and a fine cloister, which now houses

an outpost of the Museu d'Arqueologia de Catalunya. The holdings date from the Paleolithic to the medieval period, attractively displayed in the former church and scattered around the overgrown cloister, and include Roman monuments and everyday objects like lamps and vases, a lead plaque inscribed with Iberian writing, and Iberian and Greek memorial stones. From here, you can climb up to the Passeig Arqueòlogic for a panoramic stroll across the top of the old city walls ① *1000-2000, free*, with sweeping views out across the rooftops and the Ter Valley.

Museu del Cinema ① *C/Sèquia 1, T972413047, Tue-Fri 1000-1800, Sat 1000-2000, Sun 1100-1500, €3*. Over on the other side of the river, in the 19th-century extension to old Girona, this lively museum with an excellent collection of film memorabilia gathered by local film-maker Tomas Mallol: the 25,000 exhibits cover everything from 15th-century shadow puppets and magic lanterns to a rare piece of original film by the Lumiere brothers.

Excursions

There are a couple of popular excursions from Girona: you could escape the heat of summer out at the lake of Banyoles, where local families come to eat picnics and mess about in boats, or visit nearby Besalú, an immaculate, perfectly preserved medieval town.

Banyoles Some 18 km north of Girona, Banyoles is a quiet town sitting peacefully beside a placid lake full of plump carp. Chosen to host the rowing competitions during the 1992 Olympics which sparked a host of new developments along the lake side. The new areas are not particularly attractive – although you can hire a boat, take a cruise, or potter about in a pedalo – but the old town has remained largely unspoilt, and there is some pleasant walking around the lake to pretty villages.

The hub of the old town (called the Vila Vella) is the arcaded **Plaça Major**, an agreeable leafy square with plenty of cafés, where a lively local market (on Wednesdays) has been held for almost a thousand years. The maze of narrow streets which surround the square still contain some fine medieval buildings, including the **Pia Almoina** (Almshouse) on the Plaça del Font which is now the local **Museu Arqueològic** ① *Jul-Aug 1100-1330 and 1600-2000, Sep-Jun 1030-1400 and 1600-1830, Sun and holidays 1030-1400; combined entrance ticket with the Museu Darder d'Historia, €3*. The museum's prize exhibit, the famous Banyoles jawbone, has been replaced with a replica but the original dates back to the paleolithic period, and is a reminder that this region is where the earliest human remains have been found. **Museu Darder d'Historia Natural** ① *same hours and price as the Museu Arqueològic above*, has a limp display of flora and fauna.

The town first grew up around the **Monesterio de Sant Esteve** which was established in 812; now sadly neglected on the eastern edge of town, it is rarely open, but if you manage to get in, it has a peaceful cloister and a remarkable 15th-century retablo. There's another attractive Romanesque church at the nearby village of Porqueres, an enjoyable half-hour walk around the lake.

Besalú Some 14 km north of Banyoles, Besalú is a perfectly preserved medieval town with a handsome 11th-century bridge complete with fortified gatehouse; so artful are its immaculate streets lined with impossibly picturesque houses that it looks suspiciously like a stage set. No matter who was invading or ruling Catalunya, Besalú seemed to prosper, even briefly becoming the seat of a small independent principality. Its fortunes declined from the 14th century, when it sank into genteel obscurity before being 'discovered' by zealous excursionists a century ago. Like Girona, Besalú also had an important Jewish community, and the most substantial relic of their time here is the **Miqwé**, or bath house,

❧ *Tour buses disgorge visitors by the hundreds in the height of the season when it's worth staying overnight to enjoy the town in peace.*

near the river (you may need to get the key from the tourist office, €1) which was once attached to a synagogue. Cobbled streets meander prettily between medieval squares, overlooked by Romanesque churches like the handsome 11th-century **Monesterio de Sant Pere**, and the more elaborate 12th-century **Església de Sant Vicenç**, which overlooks a flower-filled square.

Figueres and around

→ *Phone code: 972; Colour map 3, grid A6; Population: 34,573.*

Figueres is a likeable, down-to-earth provincial town which would be entirely unremarkable but for its most famous son: Salvador Dalí, who was born here at No.6 C/Monturiol on 11 May 1906. Thanks to its links with the celebrated artist, and the spectacular Teatre-Museu Dalí which he established in the centre of the city, it has become one of the most popular tourist destinations in Spain. Few visitors, however, make it to the dusty, windswept corner of Catalunya north of Figueres, strewn with dolmens and home to the endangered Mediterranean tortoise beautiful. There are unspoilt villages to discover as well as excellent hiking in the wilds of the Albera Natural Park on the eastern end of the Pyrenees. ▶▶ *For Sleeping, Eating and other listings, see pages 348-354.*

Ins and outs

Getting there and around Frequent bus and train services travel to Figueres from Girona and Barcelona. You'll need your own transport if you are exploring the Albera and around, as most of the region is covered by buses that only make the trip to the bigger towns on market days. ▶▶ *For further details, see Transport page 353.*

Tourist information The tourist office ① *Plaça del Sol s/n, T972503155, www.figueresciutat.com*, has plenty of maps and guides to the area, and they offer guided walks of the town, including a two-hour guided walk of Dalí's Figueres. Outside Figueres, there are tourist offices in Maçanet de Cabrenys ① *T972 544 297*, and in Sant Llorenç de la Muga ① *T972569167*; both provide a leaflet called *Turisme Actif* (also available in English) which has lists of walks, nature trails, watersports and other activities in the Albera region.

Teatre-Museu Dalí

① *T972501666. www.salvador-dali.org, Jul-Sep Tue-Sun 0900-1915, Oct-May Tue-Sun 1030-1715, Jun daily 1030-1715, night visits in Aug only, €7.50/5.50.* Dalí's bizarre Teatre-Museu Dalí strikes a flamboyant pose in the centre of the city. Other Catalans have always suspected that the Tramontana wind which rages through the city has affected the Figuerans in the head, but Dalí was undoubtedly the battiest of them all. The Teatre-Museu is topped with a huge glass latticed dome like a fly's eyeball, and surrounded by giant boiled eggs and leaping figures; the walls are covered in squidgy protuberances, which, from a man who had a special toilet installed in order to better inspect his excrement and then wrote a book about it, can only be turds. His scatalogical obsessions have their roots in the earthy Catalan culture which puts a *Cagoner* ('Crapper', see page 258) just downwind of the manger in the traditional Nativity scene which decorates good Catalan homes at Christmas.

Inside, the museum twists around a central courtyard strewn with old bones and skulls, in which a naked singing diva sprouts out of a Cadillac with a snake and a thorny rose; rooms and passages lead off into unexpected dead ends, and recesses hold classical statues with drawers for stomachs, or a velvet curtain providing a lush backdrop to an old fish skeleton. Surrealism demanded the participation of its viewers, and Dalí delighted in optical tricks; in the **Mae West room**, a sofa and a fireplace suddenly melt into the features of the great screen actress when viewed

through a special eye-piece (suspended over a ladder supported by a plastic camel). In the **Palau del Vent**, a vast ceiling fresco depicts the ascension of Dalí and Gala (his adored wife and muse) into heaven, their enormous feet flapping as their bodies disappear into clouds. Dalí retired to the **Torre Galatea** (attached to the museum) at the end of his life and died here in 1989; he is buried behind a granite slab, so plain and simple that it's impossible not to suspect some kind of trick.

Dedicated Dalí fans will want to make the trip to the other two corners of the Dalí Triangle: his whitewashed house overlooking a beautiful little cove near Cadaqués, page 329, and Gala's former home at the Castell de Púbol (Castell Gala Dalí), near Peratallada, page 327.

Other sights

Museu de L'Empordà ① *Rambla 2, T972502305, info@museuemporda.org, Tue-Sat 1100-1900, Sun 1100-1400, closed Mon except holidays, €2/1, free with ticket for Dalí museum*. The Teatre-Museu Dalí may be the top crowd-puller in Figueres, attracting almost as many visitors as the Prado in Madrid, but there are a couple of other museums which are worth a glance on a rainy day. The Museu de l'Empordà has a collection of Roman artefacts, ceramics from the monastery of Sant Pere de Rodes and a surprisingly good collection of 19th- and 20th-century art, including works by Sorolla, Nonell, Vayreda and Tàpies, as well as pieces by Dalí himself.

Museu del Joguet de Catalunya ① *C/Sant Pere 1, T972504 585, www.mjc-fig ueres.com, Jun-Sep Mon-Sat 100-1300 and 1600-1900, Sun and holidays 1100-1330 and 1700-1930; Oct-May Tue-Sat 1000-1300, and 1600-1900, Sun and holidays 1100-1330, €4.70/3.80*. This privately owned (and expensive) museum has more than 4,000 delightfully old-fashioned toys – including some owned by Dalí, Miró and Lorca – from train sets and Meccano, dolls and doll houses, to balls and spinning tops.

Castell de Sant Ferran ① *Jun-Sep 1030-1900, Oct-May 1030-1400, free*. To the north of the city is the huge 18th-century Castell de Sant Ferran which is still owned by the military but you can walk around the star-shaped walls and bastions. It was the last stronghold of the Republicans during the Civil War, and used as a barracks for new recruits to the International Brigade before they were sent to Barcelona.

Around Figueres

Sant Llorenç de la Muga Northwest of Figueres is this peaceful fortified village overlooking the River Muga and close to the **Pantà de Boadella**, a large reservoir surrounded by forest, good hiking and mountain-biking trails. There's an excellent trail skirting the western edge of the reservoir which leads to the handsome medieval town of **Maçanet de Cabrenys**, with a maze of lively, narrow streets. Close by is **Darnius**, quieter and altogether less charming thanks to haphazard modern developments, but at least it's handily placed for the Club Nàutic which offers a range of watersports on the Pantà de Boadella.

Parc Natural Albera The rugged landscape northeast of Figueres forms part of the Albera, the easternmost Pyrenean range, a wild and sparsely populated region scattered with dolmens and menhirs which is still home to the Mediterranean tortoise, or Herman's tortoise. There's a Conservation Centre ① *Santuari del Camp, Garriguela, T972552245, 1000-1300, 1600-1900, closed Nov-May*, near Garriguela, where an audio-visual account is given of the birth and development of these highly endangered creatures. Heading north towards the French border is the little stone village of **Espolla**, which is where the park information office ① *Parc Natural Albera, Centre d'Informació del Paratge Natural, C/Amadeu Sudrià 3, 17753 Espolla, T972545079*, is located with plenty of maps and leaflets on the various activities in and around the park. The

millennia or more; the most important is the **Dolmen de la Barranc**, 3 km from the village, which is the only carved tomb as yet found in the region.

Olot and La Garrotxa

→ *Phone code: 972; Colour map 3, grid B5; Population: 26,713.*

Olot is a surprisingly vibrant market town lined with handsome mansions from the 18th and 19th centuries. It's also the main town and transport hub of the Garrotxa region, a strange landscape pocked with peculiar stubby eruptions. These are the grassy craters of long-extinct volcanoes, now part of the Parc Natural de la Zona Volcanical de la Garrotxa. Olot makes a good base for hiking and horse riding in the natural park, with plenty of bars, shops and restaurants on hand. The park is at its best in spring, when the streams are full and the woods are full of flowers, or in autumn, when the leaves change. Your own transport is pretty much essential for exploring the surrounding area.▶ *For Sleeping, Eating and other listings, see pages 348-354.*

Sights
Jardí Botànic The information office ⓘ *Ctra de Santa Coloma, T972266202, www. garrotxa.com*, for the Parc Natural de la Garrotxa is set in a tranquil mansion in a pretty duck-filled Jardí Botànic on the edge of town. It has plenty of maps and information on the walking trails which criss-cross the forested park. Medieval Olot was flattened by a volcano in the 15th century, and you can relive it in a dramatic audio-visual display at the excellent little **Museu de Volcans** ⓘ *Jun-Sep Mon, Wed-Sat 1000-1400 and 1700-1900, Sun and holidays 1000-1400, €2*, at the information office.

Museu Comarcal de la Garrotxa ⓘ *C/Hospici 8, T972279130, Mon, Wed-Sat 1100-1400, 1600-1900, Sun 1100-1400, €1.80*. The surrounding, hazy landscape of forested, misty cliffs and green fields edged with neat stone walls inspired the 19th-century artists of the Olot School, and you can check out their work at this excellent museum. The founder of the movement was Joaquim Vayreda i Vila (1843-1894), who visited Paris in 1871 and was spellbound by Millet's celebrations of rural life and scenery. On his return to Olot he began to paint lyrical landscapes suffused with a soft green light and developed an important following of painters and sculptors including Modest Urgell, Josep Armet and Joan Llimona. The collection is not entirely restricted to the works of the Olot school; one of the most dramatic paintings here is Ramon Casas' powerful *La Carga* (The Charge, 1899), in which mounted policemen viciously charge at a crowd of fleeing workers.

The museum also runs the **Casa-Museu Can Trinchería** ⓘ *C/Esteve 29*, which belonged to an aristocratic family in the 18th century. Filled with period furniture and decorations among them a very enthusiastic cagoner, see box page 258.

Excursions
Close to Olot is the sleepy medieval town of **Santa Pau**, tucked behind crooked walls. Narrow streets hung with flower-filled balconies lead to the arcaded Plaça Major, overlooked by the Romanesque church of Santa María. There's a gentle walking path (about three hours) through the beautiful **Fageda d'en Jordà beech forest** from Olot and plenty more easy trails in the surrounding area. Information on walking trails can be obtained from the Park Information office in Olot, see above.

La Garrotxa
The villages scattered in the wilder reaches of northern Garrotxa are perfect bases for trekking among the lava-striped cliffs. Medieval **Castelfollit de la Roca** is perched on a

sheer cliff overhanging the river Fluvià, and boasts the only museum ⓘ *C/Girona 10, T972294463, Mon-Sat 0930-1330 and 1600-2000, Sun 0630-1400 and 1630-2000, free*, in the world devoted to sausages.

Just west is **Sant Joan les Fonts**, ringed by shabby industrial development, but with a handsome medieval bridge and an interesting Romanesque monastery. Just below the walls, a path leads to spectacular waterfalls cascading powerfully over a dam – the perfect spot for a dip.

Ripoll → *Phone code: 972; Colour map 3, grid B5; Population: 11,334; Altitude: 691 m.*

Ripoll is now a nondescript little town west of Olot where nothing seems to happen; quiet during the week, it is absolutely dead at the weekends, when everyone leaves for their second homes in the mountains. And yet it has a legendary place in Catalunya's history: this was the heart of the original Pyrenean fiefdom of Guifré el Pilos (Wilfred the Hairy), who slayed dragons, saved damsels, and created the foundations of modern Catalunya. He is buried in the Monestir de Santa María de Ripoll, which he founded in the ninth century, and which survives – at least in part – in the centre of the town. The portal is one of the finest examples of Romanesque sculpture in Catalunya. The pretty stone village of Gombrén, about 15 km from Ripoll, is worth a visit. ▶▶ *For Sleeping, Eating and other listings, see pages 348-354.*

Sights

Monestir de Santa María de Ripoll ⓘ *Plaça Abat Oliba, 1000-1300 and 1500-1900, €1*, was once a supremely important centre of learning, with one of the finest libraries in the world, but the whole thing went up in flames in 1835. The irreplaceable library, luckily, was saved and so too was the magnificent 12th-century portal, one of the most sublime works of the Romanesque period. A dense profusion of exquisitely wrought sculptures fan out from the doorway and on to the surrounding walls: Christ in Majesty presides at the highest point over the door, guarded by the Evangelists, and accepting the homage of the Ancients of the Apocalypse and saints. A host of biblical events, from the decapitation of Sant Paul to Jonah being swallowed by the whale, are played out in gory detail on the panels below. Around the door, the passing seasons are marked by charming depictions of the month's tasks: harvesting wheat in June; grape-picking in September, slaughtering a pig in November, and enjoying the sausages in December. Much of the delicate two-storeyed cloister also survived the fire, with more intricate carving around the capitals. After the fire of 1835, the church was restored to late 19th-century tastes, and is hideous and gloomy. Lost in the shadows you'll find the tombs of Berenguer III and Wilfred the Hairy.

Next door to the monastery is the little **Museu Etnogràfic** ⓘ *Plaça Abat Oliba, Jul-Sep Tue-Sun 0930-1900, Oct-Jun Tue-Sun 0930-1330 and 1530-1800, €2.50*, set in part of the winsome 14th-century church of Sant Pere. Most of the church is closed, but, if you are lucky, one of the museum custodians might let you in. The museum itself is small and rather endearing, with exhibits covering everything from cooking pots to guns. Elsewhere, there's nothing much to detain you, although the tourist map does point out a Modernista church and mansion built by one of Gaudí's disciples.

Northeast of Ripoll to the French border

Beyond Ripoll, the Pyrenees begin to loom dramatically. The mountain towns are stuffed full of Romanesque churches and monasteries, and make good bases for hikers in summer and skiiers in winter. ▶▶ *For Sleeping, Eating and other listings, see pages 348-354.*

A few kilometres northeast of Ripoll, Sant Joan de les Abadesses grew up around another monastery founded by Wilfred the Hairy, who shrewdly learned to get the Church on his side early on. The old train line between Ripoll and Sant Joan has been tarmaced over to create an easy and enjoyable walk (the 'Ruta del Ferro') through the countryside. A fine Gothic bridge spans the Riu Ter, but, like Ripoll, Sant Joan's days of glory are long gone. Unlike Ripoll, however, Sant Joan has become an attractive, relaxed market town with some gently worn old stone houses; the 15th-century bishop's palace which houses the tourist information office is especially pretty and has a peaceful cloister.

Close to San Joan, the hulking Romanesque **monastery** ① *Plaça de la Abadia s/n, T972722353, Mar-Jun and Sep-Oct daily 1000-1400 and 1600-1900, Jul-Aug daily 1000-1900, Nov-Mar Mon-Fri 1000-1400, Sat-Sun 1000-1400 and 1600-1800, €2,* built to withstand earthquakes, was established by Wilfred as a gift to his daughter Emma who was the first abbess here. Inside, it's a shadowy, cavernous space, which, on a dark afternoon before the lights are switched on, is still charged with the awe it must have inspired in medieval worshippers. The church's sole adornment is a sublime 12th-century wooden Descent from the Cross, a group of seven almost life-size figures; in 1256 a miraculously uncorrupted host was discovered inside the head of Christ and the statue has been an object of veneration ever since. The monastery museum (included in entrance ticket) has a rich collection of ecclesiastical treasures dating back a millennia, including gilded Gothic retablos, and jewel-encrusted chalices.

There are more Romanesque churches scattered around the countryside. The tourist office has a leaflet describing a stiff but enjoyable walk, Sender de les Quatre Ermites, PRC60, to a few of them which joins up with the GR1.

Camprodon

Beyond Sant Joan de les Abadesses is the little mountain town of Camprodon, which straddles the confluence of two rivers, the Ter and the Ritort, and is prettily criss-crossed with stone bridges, including the sturdy 12th-century Pont Nou, still guarded by a tower. A century ago, this was a popular weekend excursion for affluent Barcelonans who would arrive here by train (sadly, long defunct) and stroll along the leafy promenades beside the river. It's a prosperous town, with bustling streets crammed with old-fashioned shops selling embutits (local cured meats) and leather crafts, a neglected Romanesque monastery tucked behind the showier parish Església de Santa Maria, and ornate townhouses boasting a Modernista flourish or two.

The composer Isaac Albéniz (1860-1909) was born in Camprodon and led a spectacularly adventurous life: he gave his first piano recital aged three, ran away from home aged nine, and, after touring Spain as a musical prodigy, stowed away on a boat heading to Port Rico. He is commemorated with an annual music festival and a chubby bust on the Plaça de Santa María.

North to the French Border

Twisting roads follow the river valleys northwards from Camprodon: the Ritort heads into France through a relatively bleak valley, but it's worth turning off to see the medieval monuments in the nearby villages of **Beget** and **Rocabruna**: Beget's church, with its lofty belltower, is especially handsome, and Rocabruna is overlooked by a crumbling castle. Neither town has anywhere to stay.

The local road which curves through the prettier **Ter Valley** culminates at the **Vallter 2000** ski resort which is surrounded by a glacial cirque reaching 2,702 m (8,865 ft) ensuring snow well into April. There's no public transport directly to the resort – it's best to get a package with a Barcelona travel agency. Vallter 2000 has 12 pistes and a slalom course and there are several hotels and restaurants in nearby

Setcases. The excellent website, www.acem-cat.com, has complete information on all the facilities available in all Catalan ski resorts, as well as snow reports, news and a calendar of events.For information and to book accommodation in Vallter 2000 call T972136057, www.vallter2000.com.

Villalonga, a few kilometres from Camprodon, is a pleasant, down-to-earth town with another sturdy Romanesque church overlooking the main square, but just beyond it is tiny **Tregurà**, perched winsomely on a hillside and the starting point for some excellent hikes. Just beneath Vallter 2000 is the picturesque town of **Setcases**, but unfortunately its glossy reputation as a beauty spot has meant that most of its attractive stone houses have been snapped up by weekending Barcelonans.

● Sleeping

Terrassa p334

Terrassa is too close to Barcelona to make staying overnight a particularly attractive option and most hotels are expensive and geared towards business travellers anyway.
A-B Don Candido, Rambleta Pare Alegre 98, T937333300, F937893062. The best choice is this modern, classy hotel which offers 4-star comforts including a pool and gym for a surprisingly reasonable price.

Montserrat p335

There are two options (with the exception of the *refugio*), both run by the monks at the monastery.
C Abat Cisneros, T938350201, is where newly-weds stay on a visit to get La Moreneta's blessing.
E El Monestir, T938350201. The monks also have this cheaper *hostal*.
F Refugio de Monastère de Santa Cecilia, T938350566, near the monastery of the same name. Best *refugio* of the three here.

Camping

G Camping de Sant Miguel, accessible on foot, down the path between the funiculars, T938777777, which has a terrace and costs around €8-10 for 2 people and a tent.

Vic and the Parc Natural de Montseny p337

Note that much of the accommodation in the spa towns is only open in summer. If you fancy a visit to a spa – check out the website www.bal neario.org or email info@bal neario.org for lists of spas and their facilities.
L Parador de Vic-Sau, Paraje El Bac de Sau, Vic, T938122323, vic@parador.es. The plushest place to stay, is set in a luxurious stone farmhouse with beautiful views overlooking the Pantà de Sau (see below), 15 km from Vic. There's an excellent restaurant, a pool and facilities for watersports, horse riding, trekking, and mountain biking.
A Hotel Sant Bernat, Ctra de Sta María de Palautordera a Seva km 20.7, T938473011, Hsantbernat@husa.es. This traditional, stone hotel in the heart of the natural park has beautiful views over the wooded hills from the terraces and good hiking and mountain-biking on the doorstep.
A Hotel Urbisol, about 20 km southwest of Vic in the little town of Calders, T938309153, www.hotelurbisol.com. A beautifully converted farmhouse set in rolling hills. The ultra-chic interior is filled with sleek minimalist decoration, and each room has wooden floors, exquisitely simple wooden furniture, and beautiful views. There's also a gym, jacuzzi, outdoor pool and a fine restaurant, and the owners can arrange mountain-bike trips, horse riding and balloon rides. A real treat.
B Hotel Balmes, C/Francesc Pla 6, Vic, T938891272, balmesvic90@hotmail.com. A modern hotel on the edge of town with functional but bright rooms and friendly service.
C Hostal Torras, Plaça Gravalosa, Sant Hilari Sacalma, a reasonable option that is open all year and has a decent restaurant.
C Mas Banús, 1 km outside Tavernoles, T938122091, is set in a gorgeous 16th-century farmhouse with lush gardens and a pool.
D Estrella, Plaça Bisbe Font I, Rupit, T938522005, is a friendly *hostale* with an old-fashioned bar and inexpensive restaurant.
D La Riba, Vilanova de Sau, T938 847 023, a family-run place with pretty rooms, an excellent restaurant and a swimming pool.

D Masia del Montseny, Pg de la Pietat 14, Viladrau, T938848014, which has just 10 simple rooms.

D Parador Nacional Duques de Cardona, Cardona, T938691275, cardona@parador.es. This dramatic parador has antique-furnished rooms in an eighth-century castle. There's also a good, expensive restaurant serving local specialities.

E Hostal Osuna, C/Remei 3, Vic, T93883245, is a good, if bland, budget option with very plain rooms and a central location.

E Pensió Sant Roc, T973480827, Solsona, is a good, central budget option and has a small, cheap restaurant.

Girona *p339, map p340*

B Mas Salvanera, Beuda (8 km from Besalú), T972590975, www.salvanera.com. A lovely 17th-century stone farmhouse on a sunny hillside with just 8 thoughtfully decorated rooms and a pool.

C Hotel Peninsular, C/Nou 3, T972203800, F972210492. A modern hotel close to the river with well-equipped rooms (no a/c, though, which can be a problem in summer) at a reasonable price.

C Mirallac, Paseo Darder 50, Banyoles, T972571045, hrmirallac@terra.es. Located right on the lake with large bright rooms and a pool (prices jump a category in summer).

C Pensión Bellmirall, C/Bellmirall 3, T972204009, www.grn.es/belmirall. One of the nicest places to stay in Girona and almost always booked up as it has just 7 rooms: behind the cathedral, the artist owner has filled the medieval stone house with all kinds of knick knacks and plants. Rooms without bathrooms are cheaper. Closed Jan-Feb.

D Hotel Siqués, Av President Companys 6-8, Banyoles, T972590110, F97259 0110. A large, traditional stone guesthouse on the edge of town with a pool and an excellent restaurant. Best budget choice.

D Pensió Viladomat, C/Ciutadans 5, T972203176. Call ahead to get rooms at this friendly little pensión, which is perfectly located in the old town.

E Fonda Comas, C/ Canal 19, Banyoles, T972 570127, which is nicely located in the old town and has a good, cheap restaurant downstairs.

E Les Turros, Gloria Mota, Argelaguer (7 km from Besalú) T972687350, F972687733. Lost in the middle of a forest, Les Turros has just 4 rooms; sit around an old wood burning stove, and enjoy a home-cooked meal.

E Pensió Marià, Plaça Llibertat 4, Banyoles, T972590106. A tiny guesthouse right in the heart of the old town. If you've got your own transport, there are a couple of delightful options out of town:

G Albergue Juvenil, C/Ciutadans 9, T972218003, www.gencat.es/catalunyajove. Well-equipped youth hostel in a great location in the old town. It functions as a university residence during the academic year, but still keeps a few rooms for visitors.

Figueres and around *p343*

There aren't too many accommodation options around the Parc Natural Albera.

C Finca Paraiso, Camí del Club Nàutic, Darnius, T/F972 535 662, a traditional, rustically decorated guesthouse set in gardens close to the Boadella lake with facilities close by for horse riding, watersports, fishing, hiking and tennis.

C Hotel Durán, C/Lasauca 5, T972501250, duran@hotelduran.com. A classic Empordan hotel with an exceptionally good, expensive restaurant specializing in regional cuisine.

C Hotel Empordà, Cra N-II, km 763, Figueres, T972500562, hotelemporda@hotelemporda.com. Lots of chintz and dowdy decor in the rooms, but it's the expensive restaurant that draws the crowds; one of the best in Catalunya.

C Mas Pau, Ctra de Figueres–Besalú km 4, Figueres, T972546154, maspau@grn.es. Four-star comfort in a converted 17th-century stone farmhouse, with lovely gardens and a pool. Doubles start at around €80.

D Hostal La Quadra, C/Rectoria 11, Maçanet de Cabrenys, T972 544 032. A delightful little hostel with rooms decorated in stylish muted colours and quirky art. It's on the edge of town with a popular vaulted restaurant in the cellar (which offers a lunchtime menú at €7.50 during the week).

D Hotel Les Angeles, C/Barceloneta 10, Figueres, T972510661. Good value, modest hotel in the centre of town with flouncy rooms equipped with TVs and phones.

Catalunya & Andorra Inland Catalunya: listings

● *For an explanation of sleeping and eating price codes used in this guide, see inside the* ● *front cover. Other relevant information is found in Essentials, see pages 47-56.*

E España, C/Jonquera 26, Figueres, T972500869. Comfortable, friendly *pensión* a little out of the centre with an old-fashioned restaurant serving good local dishes.
F Pensió La Manela, Plaça del Carme 7, Espolla, T972563065, the only place to stay, cosy and friendly with home-cooked meals.

Olot and La Garrotxa *p345*
Most of the villages in Northern Garrotxa have a few eating and sleeping options.
C Hotel Cal Sastre, C/ Cases Noves 1, Santa Pau, T972 680 049, sastre@agat.es, which is tucked into the ancient walls and surrounded by gardens. The antique-filled rooms and excellent restaurant mean it's very popular, so reserve in advance. This is one of the prettiest hotels in the Northern Garrotxa area.
D Hostal La Perla, C/La Deu 9, Olot, T972262326, F972270774. A modern hotel close to the botanic gardens with rooms or mini-apartments, some with views of the park.
E Casa Paula, Placa Santa Roc 3, Castellfolit de la Roca, T972294032, which overlooks the main square and has a nice little restaurant and bar.
E Pensión Narmar, C/Sant Roc 1, Olot, T972269807. Spotless budget rooms in the centre of town, with a good cheap restaurant and patisserie downstairs.
G Albergue Juvenil, Passeig de Barcelona, Olot, T972264200, www.tujuca.com. Set in a graceful turn-of-the-century mansion close to the centre, with newly renovated dorm rooms sleeping 4 to 10.

Ripoll *p346*
Ripoll has little to offer besides the monastery and surrounding villages like Sant Joan de las Abadesses make more attractive bases.
C Solana de Ter, T972701062, www.solana deter.com. On the outskirts of town the **Solana de Ter** has a pool, tennis facilities and even a campground. The restaurant is very good and fairly priced.
D Fonda Xesc, Plaça del Roser 1, Gombrén, T972730404. A delightful option just outside Ripoll; a picturesque stone guesthouse with an excellent restaurant.
D Hostal del Ripollès, Plaça Nova 11, Ripoll, T972700215, ramontu@intercom.es.

A well-located, reasonable *hostal* above a good pizza joint and bar.

Northeast of Ripoll to the French Border *p346*
B Hotel La Coma, Prat de la Coma s/n, Setcases, T972136073/4, hotellacoma@logic control.es. This modern chalet-style place is a fancy option with a sauna, jacuzzi, gym, swimming pool and the friendly staff will happily give you tips on on local hiking and mountain-biking trails. You won't find anything much cheaper and much the town is closed in the off season.
C Hotel Güell, Plaça d'Espanya 8, Camprodon, T972740011, F972741112, is a family-run hotel in a traditional Pyrenean stone townhouse.
D Mas Janpere, Esteve Dorca i Mara Navarro, 2 km from the centre of Sant Joan de les Abadesses, T972720366, is a traditional Catalan mas (farmhouse) with comfortable rooms and self-catering apartments. Rates vary according to season and number of occupants.
E Can Janpere, C/ Mestre Andreu 3, Sant Joan de les Abadesses, T972720077, is a modest, centrally located little guesthouse with a reasonably priced restaurant.
E Hostal Nati, C/ Pere Rovira 3, Sant Joan de les Abadesses, T972720114, is a basic *hostal* with a cheap café-bar just outside the centre.

⊘ Eating

Terrassa *p334*
There are a few pleasant cafés with terraces on the Plaça Vella in the old quarter.
€€ Hostal del Fum, Ctra de Montcada 19, T937888337, this classic restaurant on the outskirts of town, is the best. Serves traditional Catalan dishes. Closed Sun pm, Mon, and Aug.

Montserrat *p335*
Bring a picnic or pick up supplies from the small shop near the monastery. The *cafetería* food on Montserrat is dire and overpriced.

Vic and the Parc Natural de Montseny *p337*
See also Sleeping.
€€€ Jordi Parramon, C/Cardona 7, Vic, T938863815. The best restaurant in town

with a highly respected chef and very elegant surroundings. For a real blow out, choose the menú degustación (around €50)

€€ **La Taula**, Plaça Don Miquel de Clariana 4, Vic, T938863229. Closed Sun and Mon. This is a local favourite, a traditional stone-walled restaurant serving classic local dishes.

€€ **Rectoria d'Oris**, Ctra de Torrelló a St Quirze de Bisora km 83, T938590230. This converted rectory (5 km from Vic) houses a well-reputed restaurant serving the freshest cuisine made with local produce.

There are a few places to eat by the lake in summer in Pantà de Sau including:

€€-€ **Sau Vell**, next to the sailing club, T937447130, which has good fish and lighter snacks.

€ **El Basset**, C/Sant Sadurni 4, Vic, T938890212. Comfortable, traditional restaurant serving Catalan dishes and delicious nut bread. You can fill up on the lunch menú for around €10.

€ **El Peregrí**, C/Nou 21, Vic, T938864130. Closed Sat and Sun. This tiny, peaceful vegetarian restaurant offers a salad buffet and good soups. The lunch menu is good value at €7.

€ **Coqueria Cucafera**, C/Canyelles 3, Vic, T938861278. A great place for a cheap lunch, this offers the local *cocas* – bread – topped with anchovies, hams, cheese and all kinds of goodies.

Girona *p339, map p340*

€€€ **Celler de Can Roca**, Ctra Taialà 40, T972222157. You wouldn't think so from the outside, but this is one of the finest restaurants in Catalunya and a great place for a treat.

€€ **Can Ginabreda**, C/ de Mieres, Porqueres, T972574962, offers changing exhibitions by local artists, and tasty regional cuisine. Friendly.

€€ **Casa Marieta**, Plaça Independencia 5, T972201016. A classic, this traditional restaurant offers Catalan dishes prepared from seasonal ingredients.

€€ **Cipresaia**, C/General Fournas 2, T972222449. Fashionable, arty hang-out serving contemporary Catalan cuisine.

€€ **La Penyora**, C/Nou del Teatre 3, T972 218 948. Closed Sun night and Tue. This is a local favourite and with good reason: the

Catalan cuisine is excellent and the service warm and efficient. While going a la carte can push it up into the expensive category, they also do 2 *menús* (one vegetarian) for less than €10.

€€ **Pont Vell**, C/Pont Vell 28, Besalú, T972591027, set in a medieval house overlooking the old bridge this restaurant makes for a memorable evening. Dishes served are based on recipes which date back to the Middle Ages.

€€ **Quatre Estacions**, Paseo de la Farga s/n, Banyoles, T972573300, uses the freshest local produce for its excellent, Catalan cuisine. They've got a great range of local liqueurs as well.

€ **Boira**, Plaça de la Independència 10, T972203096. This bar has a perfect location on the river edge. There's a good value lunch menú and tapas or you could head upstairs for the fancy restaurant – although the food doesn't always match the views.

€ **Café Arts**, Rambla Llibertat 25. One of dozens of popular cafés on Girona's lovely, arcaded rambla. A great place to muse over a coffee on the terrace.

€ **La Crêperie Bretonne**, C/Cort Reial 14, T972218120. A good choice for veggies, this friendly, French-owned crêperie is easy to spot thanks to the old caravan at the entrance. Budding artists can draw their impression of Girona on the paper table-cloths with the crayons provided.

€ **Ollibreria**, C/Ciutadans 15, T972204818. A delightful little arty café attached to a bookshop with Internet access and good tapas which usually include hummus and other vegetarian options. There's a *menú del día* at €9.50.

Figueres and around *p343*

The most acclaimed restaurants in the region are the hotel restaurants in the **Duran** and the **Empordà** (see Sleeping) in Figueres.

€€ **La Taberna del Baron**, C/Damas Calvet 1, Figueres, T 972501868. A stylish new restaurant serving creative local cuisine in plush surroundings.

€ **El Café del Barri Vell**, Plaça de las Patates, Figueres, is a simple, laid-back, and cheap, vegetarian café on a pretty little square just behind the Dalí museum, which puts on poetry readings and concerts out on the terrace in summer.

Olot and La Garrotxa *p345*

Many *fondas* (guesthouses) and hotels in the area around Olot have good, traditional restaurants offering tasty local dishes.

€€ **El Pati**, C/Mayor 2, in the little village of Ventalló, T972793005 (open in the summer only), is a new stylish bar-restaurant set in a brightly painted cellar. The inventive dishes are served in *raciones* (large tapas), but watch out because the prices quickly do add up.

€€ **Les Cols**, Ctra de la Canya s/n, Olot, T972269209. Delightful restaurant in a traditional stone mas, with a menu based on the excellent regional produce.

€ **El Mig**, Plaça del Mig 1, Olot, T972270298. Relaxed café-bar with cheap snacks and coin-operated Internet terminals.

€ **La Terra**, C/Bonaire 22, Olot, T972274151. This friendly vegetarian restaurant is a welcome surprise; help yourself to the huge range of soups, salads and stews laid out on a big wooden table. Open lunchtimes only.

❶ Bars and clubs

Vic and the Parc Natural de Montseny *p337*

Vic's nightlife isn't exactly pumping, but there are a few good bars around the Carrer Sant Miquel de Sants.

Girona *p339, map p340*

Món Apart, C/Figuerola. Covered in brightly coloured murals, this bar has occasional live music and regular DJ sessions.

Numulit, C Nord 7-9. Buzzy club with DJs playing house on Thu and everything from funk to 80s music at weekends.

Taberna de l'Abat, Plaça Santa Llúcia 6, T972 219 704. Drinks, live music, art exhibitions, and light snacks at one of Girona's most popular night spots.

Olot and La Garrotxa *p345*

There are dozens of bars concentrated on and around the Plaça Carme; try the little **Bar Carme**, right on the square, with a small terrace.

Bar Cocodrilo, C/Sant Roc 5, T972263124. Also on the square with marble tables and a long list of cocktails.

❂ Festivals and events

Terrassa *p334*

There's an international **Jazz Festival** in **Mar**, with the city's main festival (dedicated to **San Pedro**) held on the following Sun when you'll see plenty of traditional Catalan traditions from *gegants* to human castles (Terrassa has got a couple of champion *castellar* teams).

Vic and the Parc Natural de Montseny *p337*

In **mid-Sep** is the **Music Festival** held, always a good event with bands playing on the square and in venues across the town.

Girona *p339, map p340*

In **mid-May** there's the **Festival of Flowers**; in **Jun and Jul**, there's the **Festival de Músiques Religioses**; the **Jazz Festival** and a pretty low-key **Cinema Festival** take place in **Sep**; and you can do your Christmas shopping at the traditional **Fira d'Artesans**, in **Nov** and **Dec**. The city's biggest festival is the **Festa de Sant Narcis** at the end of **Oct** to the beginning of Nov, when devils, dragons and giants parade though the streets.

Ripoll *p346*

Ripoll has a low-key **Music Festival** held on weekends during **Jul** and **Aug**, when concerts are held in the monastery and the church of Sant Pere next door.

▲ Activities and tours

Vic and the Parc Natural de Montseny *p337*

The countryside around Vic is great for riding, walking and hot-air ballooning – there are dozens of companies offering trips in hot-air balloons.

The **tourist office** has a full list of tour operators and dozens of useful leaflets, or you could contact **Baló Tour**, Bisbe Morgades 49, Vic, T934144774, www.balo-tour.com, one of the biggest companies offering balloon rides across the Vic plain.

Viatges Alemany, Placa Major 10, T938833330, central@valemany.com, for bike rentals and bike tours around the Osona region and also tours around the villages of Rupit and Esquirol.

Olot and La Garrotxa *p345*
There is plenty of walking and horse riding in this region. Olot tourist office has a list of local tour operators, or you could contact **A Peu**, Mas Collelldemunt, Ctra d'Olot a Santa Pau km 7, T972680523, www.tursimerural.net/apeu. Half- or whole-day treks are offered around the Garrotxa region, as well as guided visits to monuments and villages.

⊖ Transport

Terrassa *p334*
Frequent (at least 4 an hour) **trains** from Sants station in **Barcelona**, or **metro** from Plaça Catalunya. Return tickets on the train or metro cost less than €5. If you are travelling by **car**, take the E9 from Barcelona.

Montserrat *p335*
Bus From **Barcelona**, there's a daily Juliá bus (T934904000) to Montserrat from just outside Sants station (which usually departs at 0900 and returns in the early evening).
Train The train/cable-car option is the most thrilling; take the FGC train (line R5) from Plaça d'Espanya in **Barcelona** to **Aeri de Montserrat**, where the cable car swoops up to the monastery. There are 2 all-inclusive tickets available: the TransMontserrat (€18) which includes metro, train, cable car, and Sant Joan funicular, and the Tot Montserrat (€32) which includes metro, train, cable car, Sant Joan funicular, entrance to the museum and lunch at the self-service café.

Vic and the Parc Natural de Montseny *p337*
Vic is less than an hour away from **Barcelona** by train (trains leave half-hourly from Plaça Catalunya and Sants). Exibus, T938892577, run twice-daily services to **Lleida** and another to **Girona**.

There are infrequent local buses from **Vic** to **Viladrau**, **Sant Hilari Sacalm** and **Rupit** and infrequent buses to other local villages but the region is best explored with your own transport. Trains stop regularly at **Hostalric** (on the Barcelona-Girona line) and **Aguafreda** on the Barcelona-Puigcerdà line.

Girona *p339, map p340*
Air Girona's airport is used mainly for charter flights but **Iberia Air** (T972414192) also fly here.
Bus There are regular local buses from Girona and Figueres to **Banyoles** (very frequent in summer) and **Besalú** with TEISA, T972200275, which also runs less regular services to these villages from Barcelona. Services arrive at Girona from Estació del Nord, Barcelona. **Olot** and **Besalú** are linked with Girona by regular direct buses from Barcelona with **Garrotxa Exprés**, T902177178, and TEISA (T9722 04868). SARFA, T972201796, run services from the beach resorts of the Costa Brava.
Train Services leave regularly from Sants and Pg de Gràcia in **Barcelona**.

Figueres and around *p343*
The bus and train stations are next to each other a 10-min walk from the city centre. The Dali Museum is signposted.
Bus There are regular SARFA, T972674298, buses to **Roses**, **Cadaqués**, **Sant Feliu de Guixols** and other coastal towns. Barcelona Bus, T935931216, run daily services from **Barcelona** to **Figueres** via **Girona**, and Teisa, T972503175, run services to **Besalú** and **Olot**.
Train There are frequent (at least hourly) trains to **Figueres** via **Girona** from Estació-Sants and Passeig de Gràcia in **Barcelona**. These continue on to **Llança** and **Port Bou**.

The area around Figueres is comparatively little-visited and very difficult without your own transport. You can get a **taxi** from Figueres out to the surrounding villages or wait for the single **bus** on Thu to **Sant Llorenç de la Muga** and **Albanyá** with J.Terradas T972526170. There are daily services between **La Jonquera** and **Maçanet de Cabrenys** with David Manell, T972672853.

Olot and La Garrotxa *p345*
There are regular bus services to **Olot** from **Girona**, and twice-daily services from Barcelona via **Banyoles** and **Besalú**. There's also one bus a day from **Lloret de Mar** and one from **Ripoll**. There are bus connections from **Olot** to **Santa Pau**, which run daily in summer but only twice-weekly in winter (Mon and Wed).

Ripoll *p346*

TEISA, T972702095, has bus services between **Olot**, **Girona**, **Camprodon**, and **Sant Joan de les Abadesses**. Ripoll is on the main train line from Barcelona-Sants to Puigcerdà and the French border via Vic.

Northeast of Ripoll to the French Border *p346*

Buses between Barcelona, Olot, Girona, **Camprodon** and **Sant Joan de les Abadesses**. Buses between Camprodon and Setcases, but you'll need your own transport to reach some of the more remote villages.

Catalan Pyrenees

The Catalan Pyrenees cover a vast swathe of the region. The highest and most dramatic peaks are in the northwest corner of Catalunya, near Puigcerdà and La Seu d'Urgell. This is where you'll find the best ski resorts as well as the spectacular National Park of Aigüestortes and the Romanesque churches in the remote Vall de Boí. If you are approaching from the south, the massive Cadí range is not, strictly speaking, part of the Pyrenees proper, but still offers some demanding climbing and hiking in the Cadí-Moixeró Natural Park. One of the most popular sports in the region is white-water rafting along the powerful Noguera Palleresa river, and you can head also over the border into Andorra for some shopping and magnificent scenery.

Vall de Núria → *Colour map 3, grid A5.*

A tiny rack-and-pinion railway makes the spectacular, vertiginous journey to the Vall de Núria, set more than 2,000 m up in the Pyrenees. A low-key ski resort in winter, and hikers' favourite in summer, it's also famous for a miraculous statue of the Madonna in the ugly sanctuary which dominates the valley. The Vall de Núria can get surprisingly crowded in summer and winter but most people just come for the train ride and a picnic by the lake – so even a 20-minute walk will take you away from the hordes. ▶▶ *For Sleeping, Eating and other listings, see pages 363-367.*

La Cremallera

Heading directly north of Ripoll on the N-152 which meanders along the Freser Valley, you'll reach **Ribes de Freser**, a low-key town with a spa (Balneari de Ribes), sheep-trials every September, and a weekly market where you can pick up some of the local farmhouse pâté, *pa de fetgfe*. This is the departure point for **La Cremallera**, the last private rack-and-pinion train line in Catalunya, which makes a spectacular and magical journey through the mountains. It makes one stop, at the attractive town of **Queralbs**, a graceful huddle of stone and slate houses with an elegant Romanesque church, which hasn't quite been overwhelmed by the new developments springing up like toadstools on its outskirts. The train continues onwards and upwards across viaducts, through tunnels, past dramatic cliffs, forests and waterfalls, finally disgorging its passengers up at the Vall de Núria, 1,000 m above Ribes de Freser and more than 2000 m above sea level. The lugubrious sanctuary of **La Mare de Deu de Núria** overlooking the valley was built in the late 19th century, and looks more like a prison than a place of worship. Like Montserrat, the valley has long attracted pilgrims, who still come to venerate the 12th-century carved wooden statue of the Madonna, which is almost as famous as Montserrat's La Moreneta. The Madonna is the patron saint of shepherds, but she's also credited with helping women with fertility problems: there's a hole in part of the Choir and anyone hoping to conceive should put their head in it while the bell tolls.

There is a ski station, especially popular with families (10 ski runs, including two 355
black and two red runs), a lake where you can hire boats, horse-riding facilities, and
plenty of easy to moderate walking trails; www.valldenuria.com has all the details.

Berga and Parc Natural de Cadí-Moixeró

→ *Colour map 3, grid B4/A4.*

Berga, on a rocky slope 50 km west of Ripoll, is the capital and main transport hub of
the Berguedà *comarque* (county). The old quarter has an old-fashioned faded
charm, but the town is best known as a base for the nearby Parc Natural de
Cadí-Moixero which offers spectacular hiking and rock-climbing, including the
celebrated peak of Pedraforça. If you've got your own transport or plenty of patience
with bus schedules, there are some delightful stone villages scattered around the
edges of the park which make more attractive bases for exploring. → *For Sleeping,
Eating and other listings, see pages 363-367.*

Berga

Berga doesn't have any particular sights or monuments, and serves mainly as a base
for visits to the nearby natural park of Cadí-Moixero. The old town, shabby but still
picturesque, is a pleasant place for a stroll. During Corpus Christi, in May or early June,
the town explodes with one of Catalunya's most exhilarating festivals, the three-day
Festa de la Patum, with *gegants* (dragons spitting fire) dancing in the streets to the
sounds of strange hornpipes, plenty of carousing by red-capped Catalans, and, for a
grand finale, a wild dance by masked men covered in rushes.

Some 14 km west of Berga is the **Rasos De Peguera** ski resort, the closest to
Barcelona and a favourite for day-trippers. Small and low key, it's good for families
and beginners. For information and to book accommodation, call T9728210584,
www.ajberga.es.

Parc Natural de Cadí-Moixeró

Beyond Berga, the foothills of the Pyrenees loom with startling abruptness, pale and
forbiddingly craggy. These dramatic peaks are part of the Sierra Cadí, one of the most
spectacular sights in Catalunya, and part of the Parc Natural de Cadí-Moixeró. The sheer
Pedraforça ('stone pitchfork') peak is a serious challenge for experienced mountain
climbers, who descend in droves during the summer months.

Bagà and around The park information office is in Bagà, a few kilometres further up
the C-1411, a tranquil town with another pretty medieval core. From here, a small
paved road heads up through a valley of Alpine lushness and beauty, ringing with the
soft sounds of cow bells, climbing higher into forested peaks and finally emerging at
the heady Coll de l'Escriga. Just beyond it is the attractive hamlet of Gisclareny, a good
base for trekking.

Back a mile or two before Bagà is the dreary roadside straggle of **Guardiola de
Bergueda**, which hides the elegant Romanesque **Monestir de Sant Llorenç** – get keys
from the Ajuntament (Town Hall), mornings only – and is the starting point for the
single daily bus which heads west to the more remote, prettier villages of **Saldes** and
Gòsol. Saldes sits right at the foot of Pedraforça and is the usual point of departure for
the most difficult routes; lofty Gòsol, a dense stone warren of ancient streets, once
inspired Picasso who spent the summer of 1906 painting and walking here and is the
starting point for a number of easier, if less dramatic, trails up the back of Pedraforça.

La Pobla de Lillet East of Guardiola de Bergueda, a small road follows the thin trickle
of the Llobregat to La Pobla de Lillet, with two sturdy stone bridges straddling the river,

and an appealing old quarter to wander around. There's also a delightful garden, the **Jardí de la Font** (Spring Garden) designed by Gaudí on the bank of the river, and a couple of fine Romanesque churches on the outskirts – the **Monestir de Santa María**, and the **Santuari de Falgàs**. There are ancient churches tucked into almost every fold of these mountains; one of the loveliest is at **Sant Jaume de Frontanyà**, south of La Pobla de Lillet (get the keys from the tourist office), and there are several within a couple of miles of Berga itself, including **Església de Sant Quirze de Pedret**, a pre-Romanesque church with Moorish sides, and the humble little **Església de Sant Pere de Madrona**, clamped in a little hollow just below the shrine of Queralt.

Castellar de n'Hug and ski resorts Heading north of Pobla de Lillet, the road winds up towards Castellar de n'Hug, an ancient stone sprawl hugging the mountain which has a special place in every Catalan's heart, thanks to the Fonts de Llobregat, a spring which has famously never dried up – it's the source of the great river which meets the sea just south of Barcelona, but here it's a lazy trickle tumbling over stones and overhung with trees. The town makes a good, if touristy, base for walking and isn't too far from the ski resorts of **La Molina** and **Masella** (known collectively as **Alp2500**). La Molina has 31 pistes, with plenty for skiers of all abilities including intermediate and advanced skiiers. For information and to book accommodation call T972892031 www.lamolina .com. Masella is even bigger and offers more challenges for advanced skiiers with 37 pistes including six black and 15 red runs. For information and to book accommodation, T972144201, www.masella.com. The tourist office ① *Castellar de n'Hug's Ajuntament, T938257097*, has lists of accommodation.

Toses To the southeast of Alp 2500 on the N-152 to Ripoll, Toses stands precariously balanced high on a lofty peak and boasts the enchanting frescoed Romanesque Església de Sant Cristòfol. The original frescoes have been taken to MNAC in Barcelona but copies of the surviving fragments hint at their former splendour.

Cerdanyà Valley → *Colour map 3, grid A4.*

North of Bagà, the mountains are pierced with extraordinary tunnels – including the Tunel de Cadí, Spain's longest – which lead into the lush valley of the Cerdanya, shaped like 'the handprint of God' according to local tradition. The capital of the region is Puigcerdà, jauntily set on a promontory overlooking the valley and surrounded by snow-capped peaks. Most of its monuments were wiped out by bombing during the Civil War, but it's still got a few pretty squares which are the centre of the town's buzzy nightlife. The best times to visit depend on whether you are interested in walking, best in late spring and early autumn, or skiing, you can count on snow in January and February. ›› *For Sleeping, Eating and other listings, see pages 363-367.*

Puigcerdà

Puigcerdà was once the capital of the kingdom of Cerdanya which spread across the Pyrenees before being divided between France and Spain in the 17th century. Bombing wiped out most of its ancient monuments during the Civil War, including the Gothic church of Santa María on the main square, although its formidable belltower survived, along with the 13th-century church of Sant Domènech on the city's eastern flank. Inside, barely discernible in the gloom, there's a macabre series of murals depicting the saint's head being split in two with a sabre.

A cheerful, appealing town, Puigcerdà has plenty of bars and restaurants, and bustling squares full of outdoor cafés. In summer, you can join in with some typical Catalan sardana dancing on Wednesday afternoons, although check with the tourist office as it takes place on different squares. There are easy strolls down to a lake

where you can hire a boat and laze about among the swans and weeping willows, and the town has also got an enormous ice rink (a hangover from the Olympics) and is the capital of Spanish ice hockey.

Lliva

When the former kingdom of Cerdanya was being divided up between the French and Spanish, the French claimed the 33 villages between the Ariège and Roussillon. But after the deal was done, the Spanish triumphantly claimed Llivia by pointing out that it was a town and not a village. As a result, Llivia is now a curious Spanish colony tucked a couple of miles inside the French border. It's a tiny, attractive town, with a twisting medieval hub guarded by a fortified church ① *C/dels Forns, Jun-Sep 1000-1300 and 1500-1900, Oct-May Tue-Sun 1000-1300 and 1500-1800, free*, and a medieval pharmacy, now part of the **Museu Municipal** ① *C/dels Forns 10, T972896313, Apr-Jun Tue-Sun 1000-1800, Jul-Aug daily 1000-1900, Sep Tue-Sun 1000-1900, Oct-Mar Tue-Sun 1000-1630, €1*. The Esteva pharmacy dates back to the 15th-century, and only stopped doling out potions and unguents in 1918 – there's a collection of jars and bizarre apothecary's instruments and some delightful hand-painted herb boxes. The rest of the museum's holdings are a bit musty – Bronze Age relics and old maps – and the entrance ticket also allows admission into the 15th-century Torre Bernat de So next to the church. It's a good place for a stroll and a long, lazy lunch on one of the squares.

Bellver de Cerdanya

South of Puigcerdà lie a string of relaxed, country towns: Bellver de Cerdanya, heaped on a hill overlooking the river, is one of the largest, with a handsome porticoed square and pretty, flower-decked balconies strung along the old stone houses. The **Romanesque Església de Santa Eugènia de Nerellà** just south of the town is pierced with a peculiar leaning belltower, and has an ancient polychrome statue of the Madonna. The village is also one of the access points for the Parc Natural de Cadí-Moixeró (see above).

Strung along the main road to the west, **Martinet** is less obviously alluring, but has a good reputation for its country cooking and lies just beneath the small ski resort of **Llés**, which also has a lake, the Estany de la Pera, for messing about in boats and kayaks.

La Seu d'Urgell and Castellciutat

At the western end of the valley is La Seu d'Urgell, on the banks of the River Segre, a relaxed market town which was named for its imposing *seu* (cathedral). After mouldering away for years as a remote backwater, La Seu d'Urgell got a new lease of life when the Olympic canoeing events were held here in 1992 and it now has excellent watersports facilities. It's also the main point of access on the Spanish side of the border for Andorra (see below).

Fortunately, the new development has left the medieval centre almost untouched, and the cobbled streets linking a chain of little squares are a relaxing place to amble. The cathedral ① *T973353242, www.museudiocesaurgell.com, Jun-Sep Mon-Sat 1000-1300 and 1600-1900, Sun 1000-1300, Oct-May Mon-Fri 1200-1300, Sat-Sun 1100-1300, €1 (combined with Museu Diocesano €2.10)*, was first established in the eighth century, but completely rebuilt in 1184. There's an elegant cloister with finely sculpted capitals, and the **Museu Diocesana** holds a good collection of ecclesiastical treasures, including an illuminated copy of the *Beatus de Liébana*.

La Seu d'Urgell has one odd little curiosity; the **Cloister of Vallira**, in the park of the same name on the edge of town, was designed by Luis Racionera and, instead of the usual saints and beasts, the capitals depict 20th-century icons, from Marilyn Monroe to Picasso.

Castellciutat, up on a rock overlooking the town, is the site of the ancient settlement which was wiped out by the Moors during the eighth century; there are some scenic trails leading along the valley and up to the ruined castle which is all that remains. La Seu d'Urgell's tourist office has a range of leaflets describing walks in some of the surrounding villages, including a particularly beautiful walk to a waterfall near the tiny hamlet of Estana.

Noguera Palleresa Valley and Parc Nacional d'Aigüestortes → *Colour map 3, grid A3.*

Heading west of La Seu d'Urgell, the mountains are studded with steep valleys, ancient stone villages of slate-roofed houses and powerful rivers: the most powerful of them all is the Noguera Palleresa, which has become a paradise for rafting and adventure sports. The stunning park of Aiguestortes spreads across this northeastern corner of Catalunya, one of only 10 national parks in Spain, and certainly one of the most enchanting and beautiful regions in the whole country. ▸▸ *For Sleeping, Eating and other listings, see pages 363-367.*

Tremp and Talarn

The southernmost large town on the Noguera Palleresa Valley, Tremp is squeezed between two massive hydroelectrical plants which harness the energy of Catalunya's most powerful river. Talarn, tucked behind chunky walls on a hilltop just north of Tremp, makes a much more attractive stopover.

La Pobla de Segur and around

La Pobla de Segur was the final destination for the rafters from the Pyrenees who nudged their loads of felled treetrunks down river to the factories in an epic journey which is re-enacted annually from Sort (see below). A couple of Modernista mansions, including the Casa Mauri (now the Ajuntament, or town hall), are left over from the years of prosperity, but the town is now really a tourist and transport hub for buses into the Pyrenees.

There are some interesting, isolated villages with their own forgotten Romanesque churches nearby; **Ribert** is beautifully set in wooded countryside by the Riú Verde, and **Claverol** is topped by the ruins of an ancient castle. Heading northeast towards Sort, the road passes through a spectacular gorge, the **Desfiladero de Collegats**, pummelled by the Noguera Pallaresa in its rush from the mountains and the inspiration, some say, for Gaudí's La Pedrera. **Gerri de la Sal**, peacefully sitting by the side of the river was, as its name indicates, an important salt-manufacturing village. Salt has been gathered here since Roman times, but a flood wiped out almost all the salt flats in 1982; a small eco-museum describes the process and the history of salt-production. The town is dominated by the 12th-century **Benedictine Monestir de Santa María**, with a striking, if shabby, wall of bells looming above the entrance.

Sort

The biggest centre for rafting and adventure sports is Sort, where the pretty old town is rapidly being swallowed up by hasty development. The streets are now lined with tour-operators and outdoor kit shops, offering an incredible array of activities in the surrounding canyons and valleys. Every year in late June or early July, there's a festival of Raiers (Rafters) who scud down the river on simple rafts made of lashed-together branches just as the old timber pilots used to do.

● *'Sort' means luck, and the locals seem to have it in spades – the town has produced an*
● *extraordinary number of lottery winners.*

Llavorsí is also full of adventure tour operators offering rafting trips on the Noguera Pallaresa (it's the starting point for many of the trips), and is easily the prettiest town along this stretch. Northeast of Sort is the ski resort of Port-Ainé, a smallish ski station which has a good range of pistes suitable for intermediate and advanced skiers. For ski information and to book accommodation, T933519609.

Espot and Parc Nacional d'Aigüestortes i Estany de Maurici

Further up the valley, there's another ski resort at Super Espot above the small village of Espot which is the western gateway to the preternaturally beautiful Parc Nacional d'Aigüestortes i Estany de Maurici. This is Cata- lunya's only national park, a spellbinding but forbidding landscape of green meadows flecked with scores of crystal-clear lakes and surrounded by jagged, forested peaks. There are hikes for walkers of all fitness levels, and it's also an excellent destination for serious climbers; the park information office ① *Casa del Parc, C/Prat del Guarda, Espot, T973624036*, has maps and information on the 13 refuges scattered through the park. These are usually staffed with fulltime wardens during the summer, and it is worth calling in advance to ensure a place. Jeep taxis will drop you off at the park boundaries (or you can avoid the road and walk along the GR11), where you can make the short stroll to the Estany de Maurici, a still, clear lake of hallucinatory beauty, looked over by the strange stone eruptions of Els Encantats (The Enchanted Ones). Legend has it that two hunters and their dog sneaked off one Sunday morning instead of attending mass; they were lured deeper into the mountains by an elusive stag when a bolt of lightning shot down from the heavens and turned them into stone. For experienced walkers, there's a spectacular trek (about 10 hours from Espot to Boí) right through the park from east to west. The park information offices have details. See below for information on Boí, on the western edge of the park.

Vall d'Aran

The lush Vall d'Aran was originally part of Aquitaine, although it joined the kingdom of Catalunya and Aragon in 1389. It was often cut off entirely from the rest of the world during the winter until the massive Vielha tunnel was hammered through the Maladeta peak by Republican POWs in the 1940s. This is the only Atlantic valley in the eastern Pyrenees, drained by the River Garonne which meets the sea near Bordeaux; cooler, wetter and altogether neater than the surrounding valleys, it has preserved a distinctly French character audible in the local language, Aranès, a mixture of Gascon French, Catalan and even the odd Basque word thrown in for good measure. The valley's capital, Vielha, is a buzzy mountain town stuffed full of smart boutiques catering to the constant flow of French day-trippers. There are tourist information offices in most of the Aranese villages. ▶▶ *For Sleeping, Eating and other listings, see pages 363-367.*

Vielha

The capital of the Vall d'Aran is Vielha, which is prettier when you get off the drab main drag and wander about the narrow streets behind it. Here you'll find the distinctive Aranese stone houses, with their stepped gables, slate roofs, and carved wooden balconies. Vielha is becoming increasingly smart, thanks to the droves of French visitors who have triggered a spate of fashionable shops, galleries and restaurants, and it doesn't hurt that the Spanish royal family traditionally choose this region for their skiing holidays.

In the heart of old Vielha is the 12th-century **Església de Sant Miquèu**, with an octagonal belltower overlooking a little square. The church holds a very beautiful 12th-century sculpture of Christ de Mijaran which is one of the finest examples of

Romanesque sculpture in this region. Across the river is the tiny **Museu de la Vall d'Aran** ① *C/Major 10, T973641815, Mon-Sat 1000-1300 and 1700-2000, Sun 1000-1300, €1.50*, with a description of the butterflies unique to the valley, and exhibits relating to the history and folklore of the region.

Bacqueira-Beret and the Port de la Bonanaigua

At the eastern end of the Vall d' Aran is the ultra-chic ski resort of Baqueira-Beret, where the Spanish royal family like to belt down the pristine slopes. Their patronage has sparked a spate of chi chi development throughout the Vall d'Aran, much of it in harmony with the ancient grey-slated villages (Baqueira-Beret itself being the exception, with some eye-poppingly dreadful modern architecture). Beyond Baqueira-Beret is the dizzying pass of the Port de la Bonanaigua, which at more than 2,000 m is one of the most spectacular in the Pyrenees. Shaggy mountain horses daydream in the middle of the road and, with admirable equanimity, refuse to budge for even the biggest lorries. The Port de la Bonanaigua chair lift also runs in summer (usually July to mid-September) and there are some excellent hikes across the top of the mountains.

Salardú and Artíes

Salardú and nearby Artíes make good bases for hiking in the valley, and are delightful crooked old towns of grey stone overlooked by a pair of Romanesque churches. In Salardú, the 13th-century Església de Sant Andreu is set in its own gardens, and has an imposing carved portal; inside, the remnants of its ancient frescoes have been restored revealing a glowing Pantocrater (Christ in Majesty).

Artíes, the most attractive village in the valley, has the Església de Santa María, fortified by the Templar knights, and the small Església de Sant Joan, which now holds a small local museum.

Vall de Boí → *Colour map 3, grid A3.*

South of Vielha, the Noguera Ribagorçana river forms a natural boundary between Aragon and Catalunya. Tucked just east of the river is one of Catalunya's greatest treasures, the Vall de Boí, scattered with ancient villages crammed with so many masterpieces of Romanesque art that the whole valley was designated a World Heritage Site in 2000. The finest frescoes have been taken to MNAC in Barcelona, see page 272, in order to safeguard them from rapacious collectors who were snapping them up at an alarming rate at the turn of the last century. They have been replaced by copies, which give a glimmering sense of their original splendour. Thoughtless development and heavy tourism has taken its toll on many of the villages, but the surrounding scenery is spellbinding and the churches themselves can be magical if you get there before the crowds. Most of the villages have several tour-operators offering trekking, horse riding and mountain biking in the surrounding hills. The main tourist office for the Boí Valley is in Barruera, one of the first villages along the valley.
▶▶ *For Sleeping, Eating and other listings, see pages 363-367.*

Coll and Barruera

From El Pont de Suert, a single road winds up through the Vall de Boí, with smaller roads splintering off to the villages; the first of these turnings leads up to **Coll**, often overlooked in the charge towards the biggest prizes at Taüll, but very prettily tucked into a hillside. Its Romanesque **Església de Santa Maria de l'Assumpció** is rarely open, but it is very occasionally possible to arrange guided visits with the valley's main tourist office in **Barruera**, the large town spread along the main road further north. The tourist office is right on the main road and provides plenty of helpful maps,

① *Tue-Sat 1100-1400 and 1600-1900, Sun 1200-1400 and 1600-1900, €1*, has a peaceful setting away from the constant whizz of traffic down by the river.

Durro and Erill La Vall

A turning to the right leads to **Durro**, smaller and more peaceful, with the imposing **Església de La Nativitat de la Mare de Déu**, and a humble Romanesque monastery hidden in the mountains beyond. North of Barruera, and just before the turning for Boí, is **Erill La Vall**, a quieter base than Boí or Taüll, with a handful of good restaurants and hotels. The spick-and-span 12th-century **Església de Santa Eulàlia** ① *Tue-Sat 1100-1400 and 1600-1900, Sun 1200-1400 and 1600-1900, €1*, has been thoroughly – perhaps too thoroughly – renovated, but still boasts a soaring six-storey belltower, and the town is hoping to build a visitors' centre which will give tourists a glimpse into the Romanesque tradition.

Boí

The tiny medieval centre of Boí is corseted by a grim ring of car parks and modern developments, but it's the closest base for western access to the **Parc Nacional d'Aigüestortes i Estany de Maurici**, see page 358. The park information office is at ① *Casa del Parc Nacional d'Aigüestortes i Estany de Sant Maurici, Plaza del Treio 3, Boí, T973696189*. The town is surrounded by good walking trails to the other villages of the valley. It's about 3.5 km to the park boundaries, unless you take a jeep taxi (book at the information office), and another 3.5 km to the waterfalls of Aigüestortes ('twisted waters').

Boí's ancient **Església de Sant Joan**, dating back to around 1100, has been extensively renovated and contains a copy of the startling murals which are now in MNAC and are some of the earliest examples of Catalan Romanesque art; there's a vicious depiction of the Stoning of St Stephen, and a lurid Heaven and Hell, in which monsters taunt a soul burning in Hell. The road through the Vall de Boí peters out at the spa complex in **Caldes de Boí**, which has been famous for its waters since Roman times, and is beautifully set in dense forest.

Taüll and Boí-Taüll ski resort

The road twists upwards through Boí towards the very pretty village of Taüll, which contains the most spectacular church in the valley, the beautiful **Església de Sant Climent de Taüll** ① *summer daily 1030-1400 and 1600-2000, winter Mon-Sat 1030-1400 and 1600-1900, Sun 1030-1400, €1*, with its distinctive soaring belltower. The image of the Pantocrater (Christ in Majesty) is one of the most important elements of Romanesque art, and the Christ which looms from the apse of Sant Climent, fixing the congregation with his limpid terrible gaze, is startling in its intensity. You'll have to get there very early to enjoy it without the constant clicking of cameras and drone of tour group leaders. The views from the top of the slim belltower (included in entrance ticket but queues can take forever in summer) are breathtaking.

Taüll is a likeable little town, despite the rash of modern chalets which have sprung up in the wake of the nearby ski resort of **Boí-Taüll**, and another good base for walking in the surrounding hills. At the heart of the oldest part of the town, a stone maze of hunched cottages, is another medieval church, the **Església de Santa María** ① *1000-2000, free*, gently but determinedly subsiding and taking its belltower with it. For ski information and accommodation, T902406640, www.boitaullresort.es. The ski resort of Boí-Taüll is relatively new, but unfortunately some thoughtless modern development has already grown up around it. The resort itself has a respectable number of slopes – more than forty, including eight black and 19 red runs – and a wide range of accommodation in all price categories.

Lleida and around → *Phone code: 973; Colour map 3, grid B3; Population: 113,686.*

Cheerful, if rather nondescript, the provincial town of Lleida sits on a bump in the middle of a fertile plain close to the Aragonese border, a strategic location which led to the establishment of a Roman settlement and, later, the capital of a small Moorish kingdom. Nowadays the substantial student population gives Lleida a buzz, particularly around the lively Plaça de Sant Joan, but there are virtually no reminders of its illustrious past. It's the transport hub for bus services to the Pyrenees, with several services a day heading up the Noguera Palleresa valley. With so few monuments or obvious attractions, few visitors bother spending much time in this region, but there are some tiny villages close to Lleida which make excellent bases for some serious walking and are well off-the-beaten-track. ►► *For Sleeping, Eating and other listings, see pages 363-367.*

Ins and outs

Getting there There are regular train and bus services from Barcelona to Lleida with connections for the Pyrenees, as well as connections to Madrid and other major cities in Spain. You'll need your own transport to get to the more remote villages. For general bus information, T973268500 (am). ►► *For further details, see Transport page 367.*
Tourist information The main tourist office is at ① *Av Madrid 36, T973270997, www.turismedelleida.com.*

Sights

Lleida was once dominated by the 13th-century fortress of La Zuda, but it was virtually demolished by the Napoleonic armies in 1812, and then given a final battering during the Civil War. The remnants shelter Lleida's only remaining 'sight', the old cathedral, la Seu Vella, which can be reached by a rickety lift from Plaça de Sant Joan ① €0.50, or you can make the 20-minute slog up from the centre of town. Begun in 1203, the lofty **cathedral** ① *T972230653, Tue-Sat 1000-1330 and 1600-1930, 1730 in winter, Sun 0930-1330, €2.50, free Tue*, is an elegant example of the Transitional style from Romanesque to Gothic, with a sturdy octagonal tower and traces of Mozarabic decoration. The Gothic cloister is particularly charming, with arcades of different sizes and shapes, harmoniously knitted together with delicate stone tracery.

The old cathedral was turned into a military barracks in the 18th century, when a new cathedral, back in town on the Carrer Major, was constructed. It's a dull and uninspiring building, illuminated by narrow stained-glass windows. Around the corner on nearby Carrer Cavallers, there's a collection of art by local artists.

On the other side of the cathedral, the elegant 16th-century Hospital de Santa María houses the little-visited **Museo Arqueològic** ① *T972271500, Tue-Fri 1200-1400 and 1800-2100, Sat 1100-1400 and 1900-2100, Sun 1100-1400, free*, with a rather tired collection of Roman odds and ends. It's worth a visit for the handsome patio, where you can drowse away an afternoon over a book.

Around Lleida

Most of the towns heading towards the Segre Valley are entirely unexceptional, although **Balaguer** is worth a stop for the ruins of its medieval fortress, which was once the castle of the influential Counts of Urgell. There's another beautiful Gothic cloister in the Monestir de Santo Domingo, and the Gothic Església de Santa Maria is very appealing.

North of Balaguer, a small unnumbered road peels west off into the hills towards the **Monesterio de Santa María de Bellpuig de les Avellanes y Àger**, which was richly endowed by the Counts of Urgell who were buried here. Their sarcophogi were carried off the Metropolitan museum in New York where they are displayed in a cloister and

and down to the winsome castle-topped village of **Àger**. The original fortress was established by the Romans, then rebuilt by the Moors and finally converted into a church after the Moors were driven out of Catalanya.

Back on the main road north towards **Tremp** (C-147), a tiny road winds eastwards up to the old stone village of **Llimiana**, with another graceful Romanesque church and fine views of the surrounding almond groves, forests and the Sierra de Montsec. Below it is a lake, the **Pantà de Terradets**, where families come to windsurf and picnic at weekends.

⬤ Sleeping

Vall de Núria *p354*

C **Estación de Montaña Vall de Nuria**, T972732000, hotel@valldenuria.com. The sanctuary only looks like a prison from the outside, and inside you'll find light, attractive rooms and a good restaurant.

E **Els Caçadors**, C/Balandrau 24, Ribes de Freser, T972727006. This small hotel, close to the Cremallera train station, has a good restaurant dishing up tasty local specialities.

G **Pic de l'Àliga Youth Hostel**, Estació de Montaña Vell de Nuria, T972732048, which enjoys a spectacular setting right at the top of the ski-lift.

Camping

Up in the Vall de Núria, you can camp in a small area behind the sanctuary.

Berga and the Parc Natural de Cadí-Moixeró *p355*

B **Hotel Les Fonts**, Ctra Castellar km8, Toses, T/F938257089, lesfonts@bsab.com. The largest and best-equipped although the decor is high-kitsch with plenty of flounces.

D **Hotel Queralt**, Plaça de la Creu 4, Berga, T938211795. Centrally located, overlooks a pretty square, book weeks, if not months, in advance if you want to stay during the Festa de la Patum.

E **Estel**, Ctra Sant Fruitós, Berga, T938213463, www.hotelestel.com. Modern and accommodating on the edge of town.

E **Hostal Alt Llobregat**, C/Portell s/n, Toses, T938257074. A simple but reasonably priced pensión with a café-bar.

E **Hostal La Muntanya**, Plaça Major 4, Toses, T938257065. A delightful, cheerful guesthouse with a popular restaurant.

E **Hostal La Pineda**, C/Raval 50, Bagà, T938244515, F938244368. This is the best

place to stay in Bagà; a down-to-earth hotel just off the main shopping street.

E **Santuari de Falgars**, Poblet de Lillet, T937441095, a popular *pensión* with wonderful views.

Camping

G **Càmping Bastereny**, Bagà, T938244420; **Càmping Cadí** at Gósol, T973370134 and 2 campsites in Saldes: **Càmping Repós de Pedraforça**, T938258044 and **Càmping Mirador del Pedraforça**, T938258044.

Cerdanyà Valley *p356*

Puigcerdà has the best range of accommodation in the Cerdanyà Valley.

LL **El Castell**, Ctra N-620, Km 224, Castellciutat, T973350704, www.relaischat eaux.fr. Tucked next to the ruins of the old castle, **El Castell** is a discreetly elegant modern building with all the luxury trimmings, including a fabulous restaurant.

LL **Torre del Remei**, Camí Reial s/n, Bolvir de Cerdanyà, 5 km from Puigcerdà, T972140182, www.torredelremei.com. One of the most luxurious hotels in Catalunya. It's spectacularly set in a Modernista palace surrounded by gardens, and rooms are individually decorated with a stylish mixture of traditional and new fabrics and furniture. The restaurant has a superb reputation.

B **Avet Blau**, Plaça Santa Maria 4, Puigcerdà, T972882552, F972881212, is a good little hotel in the heart of the old town.

B **Parador Nacional de la Seu d'Urgell**, C/ Sant Domènec 6, La Seu d'Urgell, T973352000, seo@parador.es. A mix of ancient and modern, this parador is built around a glassed-over Renaissance cloister.

C **Del Prado**, Ctra de Llívia s/n, Puigcerdà, T972880400, www.cerdanya.net/hprado/. A well-equipped, chalet-style hotel close to the ice-skating rink with a pool and a very good restaurant.

D Fonda Biayana, C/Sant Roc 11, Bellver de Cerdanya, T973510853, delightfully rickety with a popular local bar and mid-range restaurant downstairs.

D Hostal Rita Belvedere, C/Carmelites 6-8, Puigcerdà, T/F972880356, is a well-kept *hostal* with some old and some modernized rooms, many with good views.

D Hotel La Glorieta, C/Afores s/n, T972351045, F973354261, is a modern hotel just outside town on the way to Castellciutat, with all mod cons including a pool and a good restaurant.

E Hostal Rusó, C/Frederic Bernades 15, Llivia, T972146264, the best budget option, set around a little courtyard in the town centre and has a decent old-fashioned and cheap restaurant.

F Internacional, C/La Baronia s/n, Puigcerdà, T972880158, is a basic but central budget choice.

F Fonda Pluvinet, C/El Segre 13, Martinet, T973515075, is an appealing stone guesthouse with a few rooms and a good, cheap little restaurant.

Noguera Palleresa Valley and Parc Nacional d'Aigüestortes *p358*

There isn't much in the way of accommodation in this area.

B Lamoga, Av Pallaresa 4, Llavorsí, T/F973622006, wel equipped.

D Hotel Solé, Avenida Estació 44, La Pobla de Segur, T973680452, F973660082, is conveniently central and perfectly comfortable.

D Roya, C/Sant Maurici s/n, Espot, T973 624 040, simple with an excellent restaurant and is close to the park information office and the jeep taxi stand.

F Pensió del Rey, Llavorsí, T973622011, standard budget option.

F Pensió La Palmira, C/Marineta s/n, Espot, T973624072, also has a cheap restaurant with a good *menú del día* for €6.

Vall d'Aran *p359*

In Salardú and Artíes there are plenty of places to stay, from super chi chi ski hotels to humble guesthouses.

LL Tryp Royal Tanau, Ctra de Beret s/n, in Baqueira-Beret, T973644446, www.solmelia.

com. This is the smartest place. There are private ski lifts to deliver you straight to the slopes, and a heated pool, Turkish baths, gym, and jacuzzi for some post-skiing pampering.

AL Parador de Arties, Carretera a Baqueira-Beret s/n, Arties, T973640801, www.parador.es. Luxurious, chalet-style parador with all kinds of extras including an outdoor pool.

B Parador de Vielha, Vielha, T973640100, www.parador.es. A modern and charmless place but has great views of the valley.

C Mont Romies, Plaça Major s/n, Salardú, T973642016. This traditional stone hotel is in a perfect location in the heart of the village. A very good choice.

C-D Hotel Aran, Avda Castiero 5, Vielha, T972 640 050, F973640053, offers pretty wooden rooms, as well as a jacuzzi and sauna to soak tired limbs. Family run. Prices leap in Aug.

D Besiberri, C/El Fuerte 4, Arties, T973640829, a delightful, family run chalet-style hotel right by a stream with flower-filled balconies and delicious breakfasts.

E Casa Vicenta, C/ Reiau 7, Vielha, T973 640 819, is a sweet little *pensión* with simple, but very cheap rooms; those without bathrooms are cheaper.

E Pensió Portolá, C/Major 21, Arties, T973640828, run by a friendly Uruguayan and his Aranese wife, with immaculate rooms decorated with flower prints and pine furniture. A good reasonably priced option.

Vall de Boí *p360*

AL Balneario El Manantial, Caldes de Boí, Boí, T973696219, a grand spa hotel with all the trimmings in a magnificent location.

C Casa Peyró, C/ Unica s/n, Coll, T9732-97002, which is a typical 19th-century stone mountain house with a wooden gallery and rustically furnished rooms. The mid-range priced restaurant is particularly good.

D Farre d'Avall, C/Major 8, Barrurera, T973694029, F973694096, is very comfortable, and has another well-reputed, mid-range restaurant but traffic noise can be a problem.

🍷 *For an explanation of sleeping and eating price codes used in this guide, see inside the*
● *front cover. Other relevant information is found in Essentials, see pages 47-56.*

D Hostal La Plaça, Unica s/n, Erill la Vall, T973696026, attractive option which overlooks the main square and has another very good restaurant.

D Pensió la Coma, C/ Unica s/n, Taüll, T973696025, is an old favourite with a cosy restaurant much loved by locals.

F Pensió Pascual, Pont de Boí s/n, T973696014, a friendly little place on the outskirts of the village by the bridge. A good budget choice.

Lleida and around *p362*

B Catalonia Transit, Plaza Berenguer s/n, Lleida, T973230008, www.hoteles-cata lonia.es. Set in a turn-of-the-century building above the train station, the rooms of this historic hotel are surprisingly crisp and modern but very comfortable.

C-D Hotel Principal, Plaça de la Paeria 7, Lleida, T973230800, principa@teleline.es. Modern, well-equipped hotel handily located just off the Plaça Sant Joan.

E Goya, C/ Alcalde Costa 9, Lleida, T973266788. Central budget hotel, with modern en suite rooms.

E Hostal Molí, C/Santes Creus s/n, Àger, T973455102, a cosy guesthouse over a popular local bar. Best choice here.

E Urgell, C/Urgell 25, Balaguer, T973445348, which is old-fashioned but impeccably kept.

❶ Eating

Berga and the Parc Natural de Cadí-Moixeró *p355*

€€ **Balcó de Catalunya**, Santuario de Queralt, Berga, T938213828. Head up here for dinner enjoying spectacular views; set in the sanctuary of Queralt on a crag overlooking the mountains.

€€ **Sala**, Paseo de la Paz 27, Berga, T938211185, rest.sala@minoriza.es. The best-known local restaurant run by a welcoming father-and-daughter team, the Sala produces excellent regional cuisine with some inspired contemporary touches.

Cerdanyà Valley *p356*

Much of what's on offer in Puigcerdà is geared towards tourists. The cafés set around the two adjoining squares of Santa María and Herois at the centre of Puigcerdà are particulary tourist orientated and,

consequently, the food here is usually overpriced and very ordinary. Those listed below are exceptions.

€€€ **La Vila**, C/Alfons I, 34, Puigcerdà, T972140804, closed Sun night and Mon and all of Jun. Rustic **La Vila** serves reliable Pyrenean and Catalan dishes to well-heeled locals. The home-made desserts are especially good – try the tiramisu.

€€€ **Torre del Remei** (see Sleeping above), Puigcerdà, an award-winning restaurant, for a special treat.

€€ **Andria**, Passeig Joan Brudeu 24, La Seu d'Urgell, T973350300, hotelandria @tecnomatic.net. This celebrated old restaurant with Modernista decor in the heart of the old town is one of the best in the town. It serves delicious, local dishes. There are a few rooms (**D**) upstairs.

€€ **Can Ventura**, Plaça Major 1, Llivia, T972895178, this delightful restaurant overlooks a lovely square and serves tasty local dishes out on the terrace in summer.

€€ **Carlit**, Avda Catalunya 68, Llivia, T972896326, a welcoming restaurant serving unusual, mid-range priced, Basque specialities.

€€ **El Galet**, Plaça Santa María 8, Puigcerdà, T972882266, a friendly, old-fashioned spot offering good Catalan food at good prices.

€ **Cal Cofa**, C/Frederic Bernades 1, Llivia, T972896500, serves succulent, cheap, grilled meats to a lively, local crowd.

€ **The Restaurante Madrigal**, C/Alfons I, Puigcerdà, is a low-key bar which has freshly made tapas and basic meals at a good price.

Vall d'Aran *p359*

There are great places to eat in the Vall d'Aran; mostly for people with deep pockets.

€€€ **Casa Irene**, C/Mayor 3, Artíes, T973644364, is one of the finest restaurants in the whole region, run by the charismatic Irene España, and well worth a splurge.

€€ **Era Mola**, C/ Marrec 4, Vielha, T973642419, is a romantic and central located restaurant, which offers delicious Aranese specialities featuring wild mushrooms and very good crêpes.

€€ **The Urtau**, Plaça Artau s/n, Artíes, T973640926, is plain but cosy, with wooden beams, whitewashed walls, and a fireplace. Excellent, local dishes, a good wine list and some of the best desserts in the Pyrenees.

Next door, they also run a noisy, buzzy bar, where you can find Basque-style tapas (*pintxos*) – slices of bread piled high with all kinds of toppings – which are tasty, filling and very cheap.

€ **Nicolas**, C/Castèth 10, Vielha, T973641820, you'll find more delicious, local specialities and rustic decor.

Vall de Boí *p360*

€€ **El Caliu**, C/Feixanes 11, Taüll, T973696212, serving elegantly prepared dishes and an array of wonderful home-made desserts. One of the best restaurants in these parts.

€€ **La Cabana**, Ctra de Taüll s/n, mid-way between Boí and Taüll, T973696213, serves tasty grilled local meat and Catalan mountain dishes.

Lleida and around *p362*

There is lots of choice in Lledia from good budget places catering to students to swish award-winning establishments for a posh night out.

€€€ **Forn del Nastasi**, C/ Salmerón 10, T973234510. One of the finest restaurants in Catalunya; elegant surroundings and classic Catalan dishes. It does a very reasonably priced *menú del día* (less than €20) at lunchtimes.

€€ **Xalet Suis**, C/ Rovira Roure 9, T973235567. Good local dishes as well as the fondues, which are delicious – there's a fabulous chocolate fondue for dessert.

€ **Cal Morell**, Passeig Estació, Balaguer, close to the station, T973448009, is a popular local restaurant with a good *menú del día* serving hearty local dishes.

€ **Casa Tiell**, Plaça Berenguer IV, T93237874. Cosy little family-run restaurant close to the train station serving 2 fixed-price lunch menus (one vegetarian) for around e7.

€ **El Portón**, C/Sant Martí 53. Stylish tapas bar with a huge range of tasty snacks.

€ **Muixi**, Plaça Sant Jaume 4, Balaguer, T973445497. Don't miss this award-winning confectioner's shop which makes delicious local cakes and other goodies.

⊛ Festivals and events

Cerdanyà Valley *p356*

There's a **Festival de l'Estany** by Puigcerdà's

lake on the last weekend in **Aug**, which culminates in a spectacular fireworks show.

▲ Activities and tours

Noguera Palleresa Valley and Parc Nacional d'Aigüestortes *p358*

Tour operators based along the Noguera Pallaresa river include:

Rafting Llavorsí, Llavorsí, T973622158, www.raftingllavorsi.com. Rafting, kayaking and hydro-speed trips are offered.

Yeti Emotions, Llavorsí, T973622201, www.yetiemotions.com, for rafting, canyoning, hydrospeed, mountain-biking and rock-climbing.

Vall d'Aran *p359*

Vielha tourist office has maps with good suggestions for walking trails close to the town. The town is also stuffed full of tour operators who can organize everything from horse riding and mountain biking to kayaking or heli-skiing.

Escuela de Equitación, Ctra Francia, T973642244. For horse riding.

Horizontes, Carretera de Francia 22, T973642967, www.horizontesaventura.com.

Deportur, Cami Paisàs s/n, further up the Vall d'Aran in Les, T972647045, deportur@arrikas.es.

⊖ Transport

Vall de Núria *p354*

There are regular trains from Barcelona-Sants via Plaça Catalunya to **Ripoll** and **Ribes de Freser**, where you join **La Cremellera**, T972732044, up to the Vall de Núria. The rack-and-pinion train runs regularly (usually between 0900 and 1800, although hours are extended in season) daily except in Nov when it is closed (€14/7.70 for a return ticket from Nuria to Ribes).

Berga and the Parc Natural de Cadí-Moixeró *p355*

This region is very difficult to explore without your own car, as buses are infrequent. There are 5 buses daily from **Barcelona** to **Berga** with ATSA, T938738008; 1 bus a day (except on Sun) to **Casteller de N'Hug via La Pobla de Lillet**.

Cerdanyà Valley *p356*
Regular bus services link **La Seu d'Urgell** with **Andorra la Vella** and other towns in Andorra. There are regular trains from **Barcelona-Sants** via Plaça Catalunya to **Puigcerdà** via **Vic** and **Ripoll**. Regular local bus services link **Puigcerdà** with **La Seu d'Urgell** via **Bellver de Cerdanya** with **Alsina Graells** (T973350020) who also run direct services to **La Seu d'Urgell** from the Estació del Nord in **Barcelona**.

Noguera Palleresa Valley and Parc Nacional d'Aigüestortes *p358*
This region is hard to explore fully without your own transport, although all the larger towns are connected by bus.
Bus The bus service is run by Alsina Graells, T973350020, who run twice-daily buses from **La Seu d'Urgell** for **Sort** and **Llavorsí**. There are daily buses from **Barcelona** and **Lleida** for **Espot**, but you'll have to ask the bus driver to let you off at the turn-off for the village and walk the last 7 km, or call a jeep taxi, T973624036. There are direct buses from **Barcelona** to **La Pobla de Segur** and **Lleida**, but you'll need your own transport to get to the more remote villages.
Train There are regular trains from **Sants** to

Lleida, where several buses depart for the Pyrenees, stopping at **Tremp**, **La Pobla de Segur**, **Sort** and **El Port de Suert**.

Vall d'Aran *p359*
There are 2 early buses from **Barcelona** to **Vielha**, one travelling via **Sort**, from the Estació del Nord with Alsina Graells (T932656592).

Vall de Boí *p360*
There's only one bus up the Vall de Boí from **El Pont de Suert** (usually runs Jun-Sep only). El Pont de Suert has twice-daily connections to **Lleida** and **Vielha** with Alsina Graells (T973274470) which are timed to connect with the Vall de Boí service.

Lleida and around *p362*
Bus There are direct buses from **Barcelona** to **La Pobla de Segur** and **Lleida**.
Train There are regular services from **Barcelona-Sants** to **Lleida**, where several buses depart for the Pyrenees, stopping at **Tremp**, **La Pobla de Segur**, **Sort** and **El Port de Suert**. There are regular trains to **Madrid** (5 per day) and **Zaragoza** (12 per day), and an early-morning train to **Seville** and **Córdoba**.

Andorra

Andorra gets a bad press, and it's sometimes hard to find reasons to defend it, particularly during the high season and at weekends, when a stream of traffic pours in to the principality to stack up on cheap goods at the ranks of hideous hypermarkets. In the unrelenting drive to plonk a resort on every mountainside, few regions have been left untouched. To find an unspoiled corner takes serious effort; you'll have to tramp your way to tranquillity whenever you come, but it's easiest during the early summer and autumn. ▶▶ *For Sleeping, Eating and other listings, see pages 369-370.*

History
The Principality of Andorra has been squabbled over by the Counts of Foix and the Archbishops of Seu d'Urgell for centuries; a treaty signed in 1278 allowed the Andorrans some autonomy but the community was obliged to pay tribute to the rulers on either side of their borders in alternate years. The remoteness of the region meant that in practice it was difficult for anyone to intervene in local affairs, and the Andorrans zealously protected their rights and privileges, even managing to maintain neutrality during the Civil War and the Second World War. Smuggling was big business during the wars, and was the basis for the legitimate tax-free business which grew up in the 1940s and 1950s. Money also began to roll in from the increasingly popular sport of downhill skiing, opening up new transport connections

and allowing an alarming rate of development. Andorra was getting richer and richer and no longer needed the help or patronage of its neighbours. Finally, in 1993, the locals voted overwhelmingly for independence and a democratic constitution to replace their ancient feudal obligations.

Andorra la Vella and around → *Phone code: outside Andorra 00 376; Colour map 3, grid A4; Population: 22,700; Altitude: 1,029 m.*

The capital of Andorra, Andorra La Vella, enjoys a spectacular setting but is an ugly modern city lined with hideous, shoddy architecture and neon-lit shopping malls. The city's raison d'etre is shopping, and there's virtually nothing else to do. Head for the hills and escape to some of the surrounding hiking trails where you can put all crowds and neon behind you.

The old quarter (Barri Antic) is worth a visit for the **Casa de la Vall** ① *Carrer de la Vall, T829129, Mon-Sat 0930-1300 and 1500-1800, Sun 1000-1400 (closed Sun between Nov and May), admission by guided tour only, reserve in advance, free*, which was the seat of the Counsell de la Tera, the representatives of Andorra's seven valleys who ruled the country until 1993, and is now the seat of the national parliament.

Heading northeast of Andorra la Vella, there's some gentle walking around the **Estany d'Engolasters**, overlooked by the Romanesque Església de Sant Miquel with a statuesque belltower. It's a suitably picture-book setting for a handful of old legends including one which states that all the stars of the sky will be so entranced by the beauty of the lake that they will fall to the bottom and stay there until the end of time.

Northeast to Pas de la Casa

The road wiggles along to the French border at Pas de la Casa, a hideous high-rise conglomeration of duty-free shops with another big ski-resort, but passes some prettier stopping points along the way. **Canillo** has not managed to survive unscarred, but the old quarter with its balconied houses is quietly attractive with its fine old Romanesque church and characteristic lofty Andorran belltower. On the outskirts of the town is one of the best Romanesque churches in Andorra, Sant Joan de Caselles, with a glittering Gothic retablo and a richly decorated wooden ceiling. The ski resort of **El Soldeu-El Tartar** is surprisingly small and unassuming, and the villages have some fantastic walking in the surrounding forests during the summer.

Northwest to Ordino

Northwest of Andorra La Vella, the other main route through the principality heads up the Ordino valley. Ordino is another good base for hiking, with some handsome old stone buildings still holding their own among the ring of modern apartments. It's also got a pair of small museums on the Carrer Major: one is devoted to a history of Andorra's postal service and the other is the **Areny-Plandolit House Museum**, which carefully recreates the life of a 19th-century Andorran merchant's family with exhibits and original furnishings.

There's also a **Nature Interpretation Centre** ① *on the outskirts of Ordino, Tue-Sat 0930-1330 and 1500-1830, Sun and holidays 1000-1400, €4/3*, which aims to show the effect mankind has on nature (you'll never forget your litter again). It's very child-friendly with plenty of touchy-feely exhibits and clever multi-media exhibits. Almost opposite is a big, modern sports' centre which has everything you can think of from a pool, gym, and squash courts to a Turkish bath and jacuzzi.

Villages north from Ordino

The string of villages which unfurls along the river further north includes **La Cortinada** and **Llorts**, which are sleepier but less over-developed. There are two more ski resorts at **Arsinal** and **Pal** to the west of Ordino; Arsinal is bigger and more dynamic, but Pal,

⁞ Slope facts

Check out the comprehensive website www.ski.andorra.com for weather reports, links, and information on all the resorts.
Val Ordino-Arcalis, www.vallordino.ad, T(00376) 739 600. The most dramatically beautiful of the ski resorts, with slopes for all levels. 26 km of runs.
Pal–Arinsal, palarinsal@palarinsal.com, T(00376) 737 000. Arinsal is a very well-equipped ski resort; Pal, close by, is smaller and surrounded by forest. 63 km of runs.

Soldeu-El Tartar, www.soldeu.ad, T(00376) 890500. Good for families and beginners, although there are sometough runs for more experienced skiers. 88 km of runs.
Pas de la Casa-Grau Roig, www.pasgrau.com, T(00376) 801060. The highest, biggest but least attractive resort. 100 km of runs for all levels.
La Rabassa, T(00376) 843452. Cross-country skiing with separate pistes for snowmobiles. Southeast of Andorra La Vella. 15 km of runs.

huddled around another Romanesque church, is smaller and prettier thanks to local planning laws which have banned ugly ferro-concrete developments. Up near the border with France, **El Serrat** sits near the Tristaina lakes and is surrounded by waterfalls; beyond it is the ski resort of **Arcalis**, which is a big favourite with British snow boarders and probably Andorra's most attractive resort.

● Sleeping

Andorra la Vella p368
Only serious shopaholics will want to use Andorra la Vella as a base, but if you get caught overnight, there are dozens of places to stay.
AL Hotel Plaza, C/Maria Pla 19-21, T879444, F879445, with gym, jacuzzi, sauna and beauty centre. One of the plushest.
C Hotel Flora, Antic Carrer Major 25, T821508, flora@andornet.ad. A central, modern hotel, and right in the heart of the shopping area, with reasonable prices, a pool and helpful staff.
D Hotel Tivoli, C/Sant Salvador 3, T804265, F820689, is central, down-to-earth, welcoming and the rooms have double-glazing.
F Hotel Racó d'en Joan, C/ de la Vall 20, T820811. A good budget choice in the old town is this friendly small hotel with a restaurant.

Northeast to Pas de la Casa p368
C Sport, Ctra General s/n, Soldeu, T870500, sporthotels@andorra.ad. The best-equipped hotel in Soldeu and the closest to the ski-lifts. Views of the slopes, a pool, sauna and gym.

D Hotel Roc Sant Miquel, Ctra General s/n, Soldeu, T851079, which has a good little restaurant and there's a great bar area where the local ski-instructors play in a band. Warm and friendly.
E Hotel Canigó, Avda St Joan de Casselles, T851024, F851824, which also has a decent, old-fashioned, cheap restaurant.

Northwest to Ordino p368
D Hotel Santa Barbara, Ordino, T837100, F837092, has spacious, immaculate rooms, some of which look out over the main square. There's a good, mid-range priced restaurant too.

❼ Eating

Andorra la Vella p368
€€€ **Chez Jaques**, Av de Tarragona, Edificio Terra Vella, T820325. One of the best, if quirkiest, places to eat in Andorra la Vella. An eccentric but delightful place to lunch (it's closed in the evenings) with just 7 tables, and a chef who serves up whatever his fancy pleases.
€€ **Borda Estevet**, Ctra de la Comella 2, T864026. A good choice, this traditional, Pyrenean restaurant specializes in delicious

grilled local meat and fish – famous all over Andorra.

€€ -€ **Don Denis**, C/Isabel Sandy 3, T820692, off the main shopping drag. An old favourite with locals which does a good value lunchtime *menú* at €10.95, but also serves some of the finest and freshest seafood in the area. Highly recommended.

Northeast to Pas de la Casa *p368*

€€ **Cort del Popaire**, Plaça de Poble, Soldeu, T851211. One of the town's best restaurants, set in a old stone barn offering friendly service and roaring fires in winter.

€ **Molí del Peano**, Crtra General, Canillo, T851258, offers local specialities like rabbit and home-made desserts. Friendly, cheap and cosy.

Northwest to Ordino *p368*

€€-€ **Topic**, Ctra General s/n, Ordino, T736 102, is an enormously popular cavernous restaurant and bar, which offers good regional specialities, as well as fondues and a huge range of international beers.

▲ Activities and tours

Andorra la Vella *p368*

Almost all the Barcelona travel agencies offer skiing packages, which include transport, lift-passes and accommodation. Check out the website www.travelski.com.

⊖ Transport

Andorra la Vella *p368*

Bus There are regular buses to Andorra La Vella with **Alsina Graells** (in Barcelona T932 65 6592, in Andorra La Vella T00376 826567) from Estació del Nord bus station, Barcelona, and buses with **Julià** (T934904000) from Estació de Sants, Barcelona. **Novatel** (T00376 803789) offer a mini-bus service from Barcelona airport if you can't wait to get on the slopes. Within Andorra, there are local bus services to **Pas de la Casa** with La Hispano Andorrana T(00376) 821372.

Train You can also take the train from Barcelona-Sants to **Puigcerdà** and get a bus from there (services are run by **Alsina Graells**).

Aragón

❣ Footprint features

Introduction

The once-mighty region of Aragón is now one of the peninsula's less known areas. It's the ruggedness of its northern and southern extremes that attract most visitors; walkers and climbers beckoned by the same remote beauty that once drew legions of monks to establish themselves in lonely corners.

Wandering the sparsely populated region, it's hard to credit that this was once a major Mediterranean power. Unification with Catalunya was a major part of that, and once the two separated, landlocked Aragón was never going to wield the same influence despite the powerful dynastic union of the Catholic Monarchs. The region saw much of the Civil War's bloodiest stalemates, exacerbated by the extremes of temperature that are a feature of the area. To this day Aragonese enjoy a reputation for stubbornness.

The region's north is taken up by a large chunk of Spain's most dramatic mountains, the **Pyrenees**, and many of the range's best spots are to be found here. Whether you're a serious climber, trekker, or skier, or you just enjoy fresh air, picturesque villages, and proud granite peaks, the area is deeply satisfying. South of here, **Zaragoza** is one of the larger of Spain's cities and the scene of yet another dubious day in the long life of St James. It's a good lively place with museums, bars, and Roman ruins enough to keep anyone happy for a couple of days. This area was the homeland of Goya, one of the world's great painters, and several of his lesser works are scattered around. The southernmost Aragonese province, **Teruel**, feels so out of the spotlight that its successful civic campaign is plaintively titled 'Teruel exists!'. The town is one of several showcases in Aragón for **Mudéjar architecture**, and bosses a province of wild hills and spectacular stonebuilt villages.

★ Don't miss...

❶ **Tarazona and Teruel** Nose around the beautiful Mudéjar brick of these two towns, pages 380 and 413.

❷ **Monasterio de San Juan de la Peña** Marvel at the sculptural skills on display at this monastery, page 399.

❸ **Pyrenees** Put on a pack and strike out on foot across the valleys, staying at convivial *refugios*, page 396.

❹ **Eastern Teruel** Wander the wild country of eastern Teruel province, page 417.

❺ **Uncastillo** or **Roda de Isábena** Get away from things in one of these remote villages, pages 382 and 393.

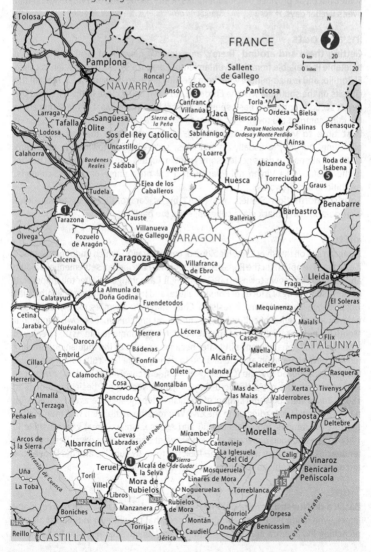

Western Aragón

Zaragoza → *Phone code: 976; Colour map 2, grid C6; Population: 610,976.*

One of Spain's larger cities, Zaragoza is the nicest of places, with an easygoing modern European feel allied to some attractive architecture and good eating options.While it's not a touristed place in other ways, thousands of pilgrims come from all over Spain to visit the Basílica de Nuestra Señora del Pilar, a massive construction that dominates the square of the same name. Formerly an important Roman city, it's now a prosperous centre which stands in stark contrast to the somewhat bleak province that it commands. It sits on the Ebro and was a port in that river's livelier days. ▶▶ *For Sleeping, Eating and other listings, see pages 383-387*

Ins and outs

Getting there and around There's an extensive network of local bus routes; a timetable is available from the Ayuntamiento. Zaragoza's busy train station is called El Portillo, and is a 20-minute walk from the old centre, to the southwest. Most of the city sits on the south bank of the Ebro; the old town being close to the river, and the newer sections spreading east, south, and west from there. Most of the sights are in the fairly compact old town. ▶▶ *For further details, see Transport page 386.*

Best time to visit In high summer the pilgrim crowds in the basilica can be offputting, but they're usually on day trips, so the rest of town is by no means cluttered, although it does get fearsomely hot in August. The week around 12 October is the Fiesta de La Virgen del Pilar, with a full programme of parties, concerts, exhibitions and fireworks.

Tourist information Stonethrowing isn't big at Zaragoza's helpful tourist office ① *1000-2000*, in a black glass cube opposite the basilica.

History

Zaragoza sits on the River Ebro, lifeblood of central Aragón, which undoubtedly made it an attractive option for the Romans, who took over the Iberian settlement of Salduie and founded their own town in 14BC, naming it Caesaraugusta after the emperor. It became something of a focus of Roman culture, and then an important Visigothic city. Taken in 714 by the Moors, it resisted Charlemagne's attempts to conquer it and enjoyed a long period of cultural and architectural pre-eminence, known throughout Moorish lands as *Al Baida*, or the 'White City'. Reconquered in 1118, it enjoyed a period of religious tolerance but later became a centre of the Inquisition. Growing tension between Aragón and Castilla led to rioting in the late 16th century, and the town was annexed by the Castilian armies; effectively the end of Aragonese independence. The city's heroic defence against Napoleon's besieging armies in 1808-1809 is still a powerful symbol of Spanish independence. Zaragoza played a full part in the tensions leading up to the Civil War too; the archbishop was murdered in 1923 by the famous anarchists Durruti and Ascaso, while a great general strike in 1933-1934 astounded observers, as workers went unpaid for 57 days. Despite these tendencies, the military rising in 1936 took the town by surprise and the Republican forces were never able to regain it despite a lengthy campaign.

Sights

Basílica de Nuestra Señora del Pilar ① *0545-2030 (2130 in summer); free.* Saint James, who might have been surprised to learn that he was ever in Spain at all, was preaching in Zaragoza in AD40 when the Virgin Mary descended from heaven on a

jade pillar to have a word in his shell-like. The pillar stayed when she disappeared
and is now enshrined in the enormous Basílica de Nuestra Señora del Pilar. Such is
the Virgin's importance that Pilar has for many centuries been a popular name for
Spanish girls. During the Civil War, the Virgin was named Captain-General of the city,
which was under attack by Republican forces. A couple of bombs landed near the
basilica but failed to explode; this was of course attributed to the Virgin's intervention
rather than the poor quality of the ordnance. The bombs are still proudly displayed in
the basilica, hopefully defused.

The basilica is one of the country's foremost pilgrim sites. The church itself is a
monumental edifice of a variety of architectural styles. It was built in the 17th and 18th
centuries on the site of an earlier church, and not actually completed until 1961.
There's a local saying that something long and drawn-out 'goes on longer than the
work on El Pilar'. The Santa Capilla chapel at the eastern end of the building houses
the pillar itself, entombed in an ornate 18th-century retablo. Round the back is a small
chink for the column to be kissed through. Nearby, two alcoves have domed ceilings
painted by the young Goya. Visitors throng the building, standing around watching
the very public masses and confessions, or lighting candles (there are even real ones
as well as LEDs!). The other item of major artistic interest is the main retablo by the
Aragonese sculptor Damián Forment, an incredibly intricate alabaster work depicting
the Assumption of the Virgin. Opposite, the impressive organ has 6,250 pipes, which
don't seem to be tuned very often.

Behind the basilica is the **Ebro**. It's a little disappointing that more hasn't been
done with the riverbanks, but it is crossed by a heavily restored 15th-century stone
bridge, attractively lioned at each end with modern bronze works.

Plaza del Pilar The basilica dominates the Plaza del Pilar, a long rectangular space
with a large population of pigeons and tourist shops; a 'find the tackiest religious
souvenir' competition could entertain for hours. The plaza's western end is given
character by the attractive modern **Fuente de la Hispanidad**, while in the east a bronze
Goya overlooks sculpted figures derived from his paintings. Next to him is the **Lonja**, a
Renaissance building that was originally the influential merchants' guild, but now
houses exhibitions in its elegant columned hall.

Plaza de la Seo At its eastern end Plaza del Pilar becomes Plaza de la Seo,
dominated by Zaragoza's **cathedral** of the same name ⓘ *winter Tue-Fri 1000-1400,*
1600-1800, Sat 1000-1300, 1600-1800, Sun 1000-1200, 1600-1800 (museum open
until 1400 but closed pm), summer Tue-Fri 1000-1400, 1700-1900, Sat 1000-1300,
1700-1900, Sun 1000-1200, 1700-1900 (museum open until 1400 but closed pm),
€1.50. Built on the site of the city's mosque, it's a curious blend of styles covering
everything from Romanesque to neoclassical. Admire the Mudéjar tiling and
brickwork on its northern side before heading inside, where the highlight is an
excellent tapestry collection; the amount of work involved in these Flemish
masterpieces can hardly be imagined.

Arco del Dean Near Plaza de la Seo, the street is crossed by the pretty Arco del
Dean. The dean didn't fancy soiling his robes in the medieval muck when travelling
between home and the cathedral, so he had an elegant overhead passage built
across the street, with ornate Gothic-Mudéjar windows.

Roman Caesaraugusta ⓘ *All Tue-Sat 1000-1400, 1700-2000, Sun 1000-1400,*
€1.90 each, €3.80 for all 3. As you stroll around the area of Arco del Dean, you're
walking over the centre of Roman Caesaraugusta. There are three underground
museums where the foundations of the Roman forum, riverport and public baths can
be investigated. The forum is probably the most interesting.

Other **Roman remains** to check out are the walls, of which an 80-m stretch is well conserved just west of Plaza del Pilar, and the theatre, which once held 6,000, but is now fairly fragmentary.

Museo de Zaragoza ① *Tue-Sat 1000-1400, 1700-2000, Sun 1000-1400, free.* The main provincial museum is divided into two sections, the more interesting of which is on the Plaza de los Sitios. This contains art and architecture sections and includes several Goyas, as well as much Aragonese religious art, and more modern works. The other section on the edge of the large Parque Grande, a long walk southwest of town, is an ethnographic musuem based on Pyrenean life. There's also an extensive pottery collection.

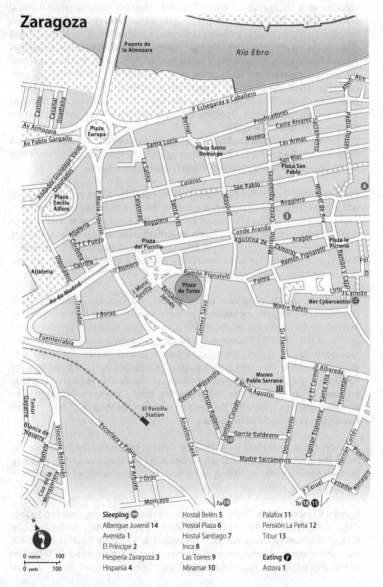

Zaragoza

Sleeping
Albergue Juvenil **14**
Avenida **1**
El Príncipe **2**
Hesperia Zaragoza **3**
Hispania **4**

Hostal Belén **5**
Hostal Plaza **6**
Hostal Santiago **7**
Inca **8**
Las Torres **9**
Miramar **10**

Palafox **11**
Pensión La Peña **12**
Tibur **13**

Eating
Astora **1**

Espacio Goya ⓘ *C San Ignacio de Loyola 16, Tue-Fri 0830-1430, 1800-2100, Sat* 377
1100-1400, 1800-2100, Sun 1100-1400, free. Located in the headquarters of a bank, Espacio Goya is a decorative 16th-century patio from a different building, around which are exhibited Aragonese paintings, including many Goyas.

Museo Pablo Gargallo This museum is set in an attractive 17th-century *palacio* in the old part of Zaragoza, and fronted by two stocky horses. It contains works by the impressive if slightly bombastic Aragonese sculptor of the same name.

Museo Pablo Serrano ⓘ *Paseo María Agustín 20; Tue-Sat 1000-1400, 1700-2000, Sun 1000-1400.* A curious bunker-like building near the train station, the Pablo

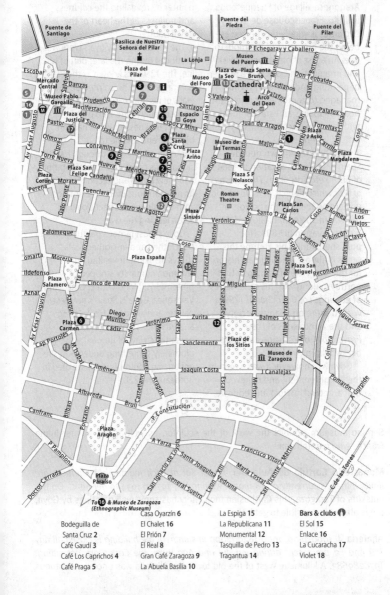

Aragón Zaragoza

		La Espiga **15**	Bars & clubs ⓘ
	Casa Oyarzín **6**	La Republicana **11**	El Sol **15**
Bodeguilla de	El Chalet **16**	Monumental **12**	Enlace **16**
Santa Cruz **2**	El Prión **7**	Tasquilla de Pedro **13**	La Cucaracha **17**
Café Gaudí **3**	El Real **8**	Tragantua **14**	Violet **18**
Café Los Caprichos **4**	Gran Café Zaragoza **9**		
Café Praga **5**	La Abuela Basilia **10**		

To ⑯ & Museo de Zaragoza
(Ethnographic Museum)

⁝ Master of Darkness

"Goya , a nightmare full of the Unknown"
Baudelaire

The man who reputedly threw a plaster bust at the Duke of Wellington for moving during a portrait sitting was born in the Aragonese village of Fuendetodos in 1746. Francisco José de Goya y Lucientes is widely recognized as being the first artist of the modern age. An artist of great technical skill and imagination Goya was a master of painting and engraving who managed to combine his role at the heart of Spain's art establishment with his own uncompromising artistic vision.

Goya became known outside Spain with the publication in 1864 of his 80 etching series *The Disasters of War* which depicts in a brutal and unyielding manner the horrors of the war in Spain that followed the French invasion of 1808. Not published during his lifetime this series is almost unique in art history for the dark view of humanity that it portrays. Along with his other series of etchings *Los Caprichos of 1799* ,a wicked satire on Spanish society, and the 18 etchings of *Los Proverbios* Goya's vision can seem overwhelmingly bleak.

Goya was however a was a man of the enlightenment and believed that art could instruct and educate.

An examination of his enormous number of paintings reveals an artist who worked on many different levels. His designs for the Royal Tapestry factory are rustic and optimistic while his portraits of the family of Charles IV shows him subverting his role as courtly painter by revealing the coldness and ugliness at the heart of the Royal Court.

The darker side of Goya's work was produced during the later part of his life. The 12 works known as the Black paintings which he painted on the walls of his house in Madrid are undoubtedly influenced by his numerous illnesses which had left him deaf and unable to communicate except through hand signals. His constant experimentation with new forms and techniques is at its most obvious in these paintings with the almost abstract *Dog on a Leash* leading the way.

Goya's most famous paintings of the clothed and unclothed Maja shows his skill in revealing our common humanity stripped of pretensions. Along with El Greco and Velásquez, Goya is Spain's greatest painter and although his paintings and etchings show at times a pessimistic view of humanity there is ultimately something undeniably life enhancing about his work. He died in Bordeaux in 1828.

Serrano museum exhibits the work of the sculptor, as well as the painter Juana Francés who married him.

Monasterio Cartuja de Aula Dei ① *Last Sat of each month, but numbers are limited; there's currently an 18-month waiting list, T976714934 to get on it*. On the outskirts of Zaragoza, this Carthusian monastery has some wall paintings by Goya, but is almost impossible to get into.

Aljafería ① *1000-1400, 1600-1830 (2000 in summer), the building is closed all day Thu and Fri pm except during Jan, Jul and Aug when the Cortes are not sitting. T976289683*. A kilometre west of the old town, the Aljafería was once a sumptuous

Muslim palace. After the city was reconquered, it was lived in by the Aragonese kings, before Ferdinand and Isabella obtained planning permission to put on a second storey. Philip II had the building converted into a military fort, building exterior walls and a moat; he was having problems with the Aragonese at the time. The most unfortunate incident in the Aljafería's history was its conversion into a barracks, which removed much of its interior character. Today the complex holds the Aragonese regional parliament. The most impressive part to visit is the Muslim courtyard, a modern reconstruction with original fragments still visible. It gives a good sense of what it must have been like, with characteristic scalloped arches and delicate carved filigree work. There's a small, ornate prayer-room; the niche is the *mihrab*, which points towards Mecca. Upstairs, little remains of the Catholic kings' palace other than some very elaborate ceilings of superb polychrome wood. As it's a parliament building, there's a scanner on the way in, so leave swords at your *pensión*.

East from Zaragoza

Due east of Zaragoza, the N-II ploughs its way to Lleida and beyond through a desolate and dry terrain. It's not an attractive route unless you happen to be an enthusiast of long-haul trucking or an aficionado of the Osborne bulls, a few of which stand undaunted on the arid hills.

While the most convenient stop between Zaragoza and Lleida is **Fraga**, it's not a particularly inviting option. Baking hot in summer and icy in winter, Fraga straddles the River Cinca, which gives some relief from the rugged and dry terrain. The old part of town is run-down but attractive – a steep array of narrow streets and raised passageways. The church, as ever, is the major structure, its tall spire topped with bricks and seasonal storks. Philip IV stopped here for three days so that Velasqúez could paint him with his favourite dwarf – an odd choice. ▸▸ *For Sleeping, Eating and other listings, see page 383-387.*

Southwest from Zaragoza

Heading southwest of Zaragoza is a dry land of eroded crags and dusty towns. It's got quite a Moorish feel, which continues into Teruel Province, see page 412. Daroca is a pretty little place, while a large lake and a monastery theme park provide some watery relief from the harsh landscape. ▸▸ *For Sleeping, Eating and other listings, see page 383-387.*

Calatayud and around → *Colour map 2, grid C5.*

Aragón's fourth-largest town, Calatayud, lies 5 km northeast from the site of ancient Bilbilis, an important Roman settlement that was the birthplace of the poet Martial. Martial was proud of his heritage and tells of swordmaking in the town, where blades were taken from the forge and plunged into the Jalón river to cool. Things seem to have taken a turn for the worse since his day; there's a distinctly desultory feel about Calatayud, although there is some noble architecture remaining.

Started in the eighth century, Calatayud's castle, known as the **Plaza de Armas**, still looms over the town, although not a great deal is left apart from two octagonal towers and some wall. Other fragmentary fortifications are scattered through town, which was an important Moorish outpost. Other things to see are the bulging **Renaissance gateway** into the former walled precinct, the graceful Mudéjar tower on the **Colegiata de Santa María la Mayor**, and the rococo **Iglésia de San Juan el Real**, with some paintings in the cupolas and in the sacristy fairly recently attributed to the young Goya. The tourist office is on Plaza del Fuerte near the river. The ruins of **Bilbilis**, 5 km to the northeast of town are pleasant to stroll around.

① *Park open winter 0900-1700, summer 0900-2000, €7.50guided visit of monastery and an audiovisual display, €4 monastery only.* This is a curious place, west of Calatayud. The monastery itself, indeed made from stone, has been converted into a smart hotel set around the cloister. The gardens around have been made into a sort of nature theme park, perhaps so the local Aragonese can experience green grass and moist soil, in short supply elsewhere in Zaragoza Province. Extensive woods are dotted with waterfalls, caves, a fishfarm and lakes; definitely a place for a stroll (helpfully marked in case you dare to stray), but you'll not be alone; it's a favourite outing spot for families at weekends. Accessible by bus from Zaragoza.

Daroca

Sleepy Daroca nestles between superb walls, which slide up and down the town's rusty crags. Its castellated towers and portals are an impressive sight and gave the city the name 'Iron Door of Aragón' for keeping out numerous Castilian sieges. Founded by Muslims, Daroca also has a **castle** at its eastern end, and seems to have an incredible number of churches for its small size, the most impressive of which is the **Basílica Menor de Santa María de los Sagrados Corporales**, a grand affair with some attractive features from different periods, including a 14th-century organ and the 'door of forgiveness', a portal around the side of the building. There's a tourist office opposite the church.

If you have your own transport, you might want to head south, where a half-hour drive will bring you to the saltwater **Lago de Gallocanto**, the largest natural lake in Spain. It's a good birdwatching spot.

Northwest from Zaragoza

The province's most interesting corner contains the superb Mudéjar brick of Tarazona which is an easy day trip from Zaragoza or Soria, but is a nice, peaceful place to stay too. ►► *For Sleeping, Eating and other listings, see pages 383-387.*

Tarazona → *Colour map 2, grid B5.*

Those who hold stone and wood to be the only noble building materials should pay Tarazona a visit. Brick can be beautiful too, as this town's many Mudéjar edifices prove. Once home to thriving Muslim and Jewish populations, Tarazona still seems to pine for its expelled, although a look at the *turiaso* faces suggests that the Catholic purists didn't come close to erasing every last drop of non-Christian blood. The best time to see Tarazona is on a summer evening, just as the sun decides it's baked the bricks enough for one day, people emerge from hiding and the buildings glow with a cheery light.

Tarazona was populated by Celto-Iberians from way back but flowered in the 13th and 14th centuries, when it sheltered a flourishing population of Jews, Muslims, and Christians. A frequent target for Castilian expansion, it suffered several sieges over the years. The Aragonese crown generally protected its non-Christian citizens from the pogroms that plagued the land in the late 14th century but once unified with Castile, the population was doomed to convert or leave.

Most of Tarazona's Mudéjar architecture is clustered on a knoll above the struggling river Queiles. The tower rising imperiously over the town belongs to the **Iglesia de Santa María Magdalena**, built in a mixture of architectural styles from the Romanesque to the Renaissance. Next to it stands the episcopal palace, formerly a residence of Muslim rulers and Aragonese kings. The ornate Plateresque façade overlooking the river suggests that the local bishops weren't exactly prepared to rough it. Descending from here, **Calle San Juan** was the centre of the *morería*, or

⁑ Much ado about Mudéjar

Mudéjar is a style of architecture that evolved in Christian Spain, and particularly Aragón, from around the 12th century. As the Reconquista took town after town from the Muslims, Moorish architects and those who worked with them began to meld their Islamic tradition with the northern influences of Romanesque and Gothic. The result is distinctive and pleasing, typified by the decorative use of brick and coloured tiles, with the tall elegant belltowers a particular highlight. The style became popular nationwide; in certain areas, mudéjar remained a constant feature for over 500 years of building.

Moorish quarter. Little remains of the *judería*, the Jewish quarter, which was clustered at the foot of the hill, overhung by houses perched above. The **Ayuntamiento** is an unusual and attractive building faced with pictures of the labours of Herakles, perhaps an attempt to flatter Carlos V, the king and emperor at the time it was built. An intriguing sculpture in front depicts El Cipotegato, a jester-like character who appears to open the town's annual fiesta on 27 August. He attempts to run from the Ayuntamiento across the town; an easy enough task apart from the minor inconvenience of the entire citizenry trying to stop him by pelting him with tomatoes.

Across the river stands the **cathedral** with an extraordinary Mudéjar brick tower. Currently closed for major renovation, it's another hotchpotch of styles; the attractive cloister is one of its best features. Nearby, the old **Plaza de Toros** is an interesting bit of civil history. Annoyed by the lack of a bullring, a group of citizens in the late 18th century decided to build their balconied houses in an octagonal arrangement that both gave them a place to live and the town a venue for tauromachy. The tourist office on the main square ① T976640074, *turismo@tarazona.org*.

Monasterio de Veruela

① *Oct-Mar, Tue-Sun 1000-1300, 1500-1800; Apr-Sep open Tue-Sun 1000-1400, 1600-1900.*

Beautifully situated in a valley to the southeast of Tarazona, is the Veruela monastery. The Cistercian order, bent on a return to traditional monastic values, found Aragón a suitably harsh terrain for their endeavours. Veruela was the first of many monasteries founded by the White Monks in the 12th century.

Its small, gardened entrance conceals the size of the complex, girt by a formidable hexagonal wall. The relatively unadorned church is a blend of Romanesque and early Gothic styles. The cloister is similarly attractive and under-stated, its capitals crowned with simple fronds and leaves. The monks still work the fields, both inside and outside the walls. During summer there are occasional classical concerts in the grounds. The romantic writer GA Becquer often stayed here with his brother; spells that inspired many of his works. The best way to get to the monastery is to take a bus from Tarazona to Zaragoza and get off at the second of the junctions for Vera de Moncayo; the monastery is a 45-minute walk from here. Be sure to prompt the driver to let you off, as they frequently forget. You'll have to signal the return bus clearly, as they tend to thunder past the crossing quite fast.

Parque Nacional Dehesa de Moncayo

The Dehesa de Moncayo national park straddles the border of Zaragoza and Soria provinces and is an attractive spot for walks, with scented pine hills and a couple of interesting sanctuaries and villages. A visitor's centre opens at weekends in spring and summer from 1000-1400, 1500-1900.

Cinco Villas → *Colour map 2, grid B6.*

North of Zaragoza in a land of harsh hills, cold winds, and beating sun are situated these five towns, granted their charter by the Bourbon king Philip V but important towns long before that. If you've got transport you might want to check out all five, but otherwise the bus connections are a bit limiting. A daily bus from Zaragoza to Cinco Villas, returns in the evening. Sos del Rey Católico and Uncastillo are the two most rewarding to visit. ▸▸ *For Sleeping, Eating and other listings, see pages 383-387.*

Sos del Rey Católico

Once just called Sos, words were added in memory of its most famous son. Not only did young Fernando become king of Aragón, he also united Spain in partnership with his wife Isabel. She was quite a catch; although she admitted to only having bathed twice in her life, that was still twice more than most people of the time, and what's more, she was heiress to the Castilian throne.

The city wall is partly intact, with houses built into it. It has become a very popular spot for summer outings and weekends but at other times of year you may have it to yourself – pace the lonely streets and plot your own Reconquista. It's the village as a whole rather than individual buildings that impress. Sos is an architectural gem of medieval streets. In the centre of town is the **Plaza de la Villa**, presided over by the decorative **Ayuntamiento**, featuring a stern warning from Ecclesiastes. The square used to be used for markets; a hole in one of the columns was for hanging a balance, and next to it is etched an official measure of length of the time, the *bara jaquesa* (Jaca bar).

Ascending from the square you'll reach the church via a haunting underpass. The high-vaulted interior is impressive, a more homely touch is provided by the colourful organ. The highlight is the crypt which preserves some excellent wall-paintings of the life of Christ and the Virgin. At the far end of the village, remains of a castle and walls are backed by the modern but sensitively constructed parador. Fernando himself was born in the Palacio de Sada, one of the largest of the town's buildings. Sos's tourist office ① *Tue-Sat 1000-1400, 1700-2100 (2000 in winter)*, run guided walks through the chruch twice a day. There are several *casas rurales* in town: the tourist office will mark them all up on a map for you.

Uncastillo

The most remote of the Cinco Villas, Uncastillo is also its most charming. The small old town is more welcoming than Sos, and is spared the steady procession of tourists. Originally fortified by Muslims to counter the Christian Reconquista, it changed hands and became an important bastion for the Navarrese king Sancho the Great, before it passed to the Aragonese monarchy. The town also had a flourishing *judería*, or Jewish quarter.

What's left of the **castle**, above the town, has been transformed into a small but excellent museum ① *summer 1100-1400, 1700-2000, €2, at other times T976679121*. The visit commences with a short audiovisual presentation (Spanish or English), which is epic enough for a David Lean feature, and then sends you up the tower where some accessible, light-handed displays give good information about the history of the town and region. The small tourist office is open all week during the summer.

Ejea de los Caballeros

The 'capital' and largest of the Cinco Villas, Ejea de los Caballeros lacks the charm of its neighbours, with a dusty feel and traffic thundering through it. The fortress-church of San Salvador is elegant and has some vestiges of colour in its portal, which depicts the Last Supper and the Nativity.

Sádaba

Scorched but pleasant, Sábada is notable for its castle standing proud to one side of the town. Built by Sancho VII of Navarra, it was incorporated into the kingdom of Aragón in the mid-13th century. When its importance faded, its outer walls were taken down to allow the town some breathing room.

Tauste

The southernmost of the Villas, Tauste is another large town, but with a pretty centre featuring a beautiful Mudéjar church.

● Sleeping

Zaragoza *p374, map p376*
There are well over 100 places to stay in Zaragoza, although many of them are clonish business hotels or functional *pensiones*.
LL Hotel Palafox, Casa Jiménez s/n, T976237700, www.palafoxhoteles.com. The most classic of Zaragoza's hotels has undergone a refurb resulting in some very attractive lighting arrangements, and much more comfortable and minimalist furnishing than is typical in this style of hotel in Spain. Free minibar is the highlight in the rooms!
L Hotel Inca, C Manifestación 33, T976390091, F976390128. A likeable and stylish small hotel in the small streets south of the basilica. The wood-floored rooms have simple elegance, and the attractive restaurant is suitably classy.
AL Hesperia Zaragoza, Av Conde de Aranda 48, T976284500, conde-aranda@adv.es. An efficient modern hotel set up for the business traveller. Less stuffy than many of its species, and reasonable value for its price bracket.
A Hotel Tibur, Plaza de la Seo 2, T976202000, F976202002. A smart place in a quiet corner of the Plaza del Pilar area. The rooms are well equipped, and are roomy and tastefully furnished. Good restaurant.
C El Príncipe, C Santiago 12, T976294101, www.hotel-elprincipe.com. A very central, quiet hotel just off Plaza del Pilar. Fairly spacious rooms and courteous management. Parking is available for €8.71 per day.
C Hotel Avenida, Av César Augusto 55, T976439300, www.hotelavenida-zara goza.com. A clean, fresh spot with mock Roman decor on the street where the old walls used to run.
C Hotel Hispania, Av César Augusto 103, T976284928, hotelhispania@terra.es. A handy, pleasant option with modern rooms with all facilities. Good value.

C Hotel Las Torres, Plaza del Pilar 11, T976394250, F976394254. Directly opposite the basilica, this is a nice old hotel run by good friendly folk. Rooms are comfortable and air-conditioned, most with views and a balcony rail. Parking available.
D Hostal Belén, C Predicadores 2, T9762-80913, hostalbelen2@hostalmail.com. In a brandnew building close to the market, with smallish but nice doubles and friendly management. Rooms have TV, a/c and heating.
D Hostal Santiago, C Santiago 3, T976394550. A well-placed warren of a hotel near the tourist office and basilica. Management is slightly strange, but it's clean, comfortable, and a/c.
E-D Hostal Plaza, Plaza del Pilar 14, T976294830. A reasonable choice with a top location opposite the basilica. Decent air-conditioned rooms with or without bathroom. Slightly wayward management style, so confirm any bookings.
F Miramar, C Capitán Casado 17, T976281094. Handy for the station, this is a good little *pensión* with a friendly attitude and clean, quiet rooms.
G Pensión La Peña, C Cinegio 3, T976299089. Simple, cheap doubles with washbasin in the old part of town.

Camping
Camping Casablanca, T976753870, F976753875. The closest campsite to town, large and fully-equipped, although only open Apr-Sep. Follow the signs off the N-II west of town, near the Km 317 marker.

East from Zaragoza *p379*
Of a number of cheap *pensións* that do little to revive a tired traveller's spirits, a couple offer a little more in Fraga, those listed.
A Casanova, Av Madrid 54, Fraga, T974471999, F974453788, a chain hotel with large, comfortable rooms.

D Trébol, Av Aragón 9, Fraga, T974471533, above a bar across a bridge from the old town, is nothing special from the outside but has pleasant enough rooms with ensuite.

Camping

Camping Fraga, Fraga, T974345212. In the crags a short walk above town is this friendly campsite. It compensates for its lack of lush green meadows with a bar/restaurant.

Southwest from Zaragoza *p379*

A Hotel Monasterio de Piedra, T976849011, hotel@monasterio piedra.com. Stay includes free park entry.

C Mesón de la Dolores, Plaza de los Mesones 4, Calatayud, T976889055, www.mesonladolores.com. Set around a charming patio in an old *palacio*. The nicest place to stay and eatin Calatayud.

C Posada del Almudi, C Grajera 5-9, Daroca, T976800606, www.staragon.com/posada delalmudi. A lovely option in the centre.

F Agiria, Ctra Sagunto-Burgos Km 218, Daroca, T976800731, unattractively located by a service station 10 mins' walk from the centre of town, but not bad value for all that.

F El Ruejo, C Mayor 88, Daroca, T976800962, with basic but acceptable rooms above a locals' bar.

F La Perla, C San Antón 17, Calatayud, T976881340, much better than the seedy choices by the train station.

Northwest from Zaragoza *p380*

C Hostal Santa Agueda, C Visconti 26, Tarazona, T976640054, www.santaagu eda.com. Well-manicured establishment, recently opened, just off the main plaza. Stylish rooms and friendly management.

C O Cubillar, Plaza de Nuestra Señora 12, Tarazona, T976641192, F976199086. Attractive and cosy rooms, decorated with a nice touch, above a good bar and restaurant.

E Palacete de los Arcedianos, Plaza Arcedianos 1/C Marrodón 16, Tarazona, T/F976642303. Good, if sometimes stuffy, rooms in a curious domed building. Bathrooms are shared. The cheapest of Tarazona's options.

Cinco Villas *p382*

A Parador de Sos del Rey Católico, C Sainz de Vicuña 1, Sos del Rey Católico, T948888011, www.parador.es. At the far end of town, this parador is mostly modern but characterful, with a nice veranda terrace and slightly sombre but comfortable rooms, and some nice mini suites.

C Casas Rurales, Plaza del Ordinario 8, Uncastillo, T976679012, one of a few in the area. This one is good, by the church and with comfy double and shared bath costing about €27.

C Hostal Las Coronas, Plaza de la Villa s/n, Sos del Rey Católico, T948888408, F948888471. In the heart of town, these doubles are slightly overpriced but equipped with TV and bathroom above a good restaurant, with rich food, snails being something of a speciality.

D-E Fonda Fernandina, C Alfaro s/n, Sos del Rey Católico, T948888120. A very good and friendly option, with simple rooms with washbasin and a bar/restaurant.

● Eating

Zaragoza *p374, map p376*

€€€ **El Chalet**, C Santa Teresa 25, T976569104. An excellent and not exorbitant restaurant run by chef Angel Conde, an avid historian of Aragonese cuisine. Although his beef dishes are sublime, the careful treatment of vegetables marks the restaurant out from most of its compatriots.

€€ **Casa Oyarzún**, Plaza Nuestra Señora del Carmen 1, T976216436. Popular with business workers for its good-quality lunchtime *menú* and sunny terrace. The cuisine is Basque in style.

€€ **El Prión**, C Santa Cruz 7. A big generous *asador* for healthy appetites only.

€€ **El Real**, C Alfonso I 40. Probably the best of the row of places opposite the basilica, but drinks on the terrace don't come cheap. Roast meats are what they do best.

€€ **La Abuela Basilia**, C Santiago 14, T976390594. A good downstairs restaurant specializing in suckling pig and milk-fed lamb cooked in their wood-fired oven. Relaxed, stylish decor.

● *For an explanation of sleeping and eating price codes used in this guide, see inside the*
● *front cover. Other relevant information is found in Essentials, see pages 47-56.*

€ **Astora**, C San Vicente de Paúl 20. An interesting little place with frequent art exhibitions. Serves cheap snacks and *platos combinados*.

€ **Bodeguilla de Santa Cruz**, C Santa Cruz s/n. Small, cosy, and popular bar serving very good tapas.

€ **La Espiga**, C Hernando de Aragón 1. A quiet little place in the business district serving decent *platos combinados* and with a good-value *menú del día*.

€ **Tasquilla de Pedro**, C Cinegio 3, T976390658. There's some good eating to be done here, with a large range of good cold tapas. Ignore the pushy owner who likes to trap tourists with an expensive 'mixed plate' and make your own selections.

Tapas bars and cafés

Café Gaudí, Plaza Santa Cruz s/n. A good summer option, with outdoor tables in a quiet square. A range of sandwiches and *bocadillos* are on offer.

Café Los Caprichos, C Espoz y Mina 25. A good little backstreet bar with a few outdoor tables in summer.

Café Praga, Plaza Santa Cruz 13, T976200251. A good spot for evening drinks, with a large terrace and good service.

Gran Café Zaragoza, C Alfonso I 25. Beautiful, traditional old Spanish café with a good range of small eats.

La Republicana, C Méndéz Nuñez 38. A cheap and cheerful little old town tapas bar.

Monumental, Plaza de los Sitios 17. A good upmarket café and tapas bar on a pleasant green square.

Tragantua, Plaza Santa Marta s/n, T976299174. Excellent little tapas bar specializing in seafood, which they do very well indeed.

Southwest from Zaragoza *p379*

€€€ **The Posada**, Daroca, has a smart restaurant, and the **Agiria**, Daroca, has a reasonable one too.

€ **El Patio**, C Mayor 94, Daroca, which is really a small shop, but does simple pizzas and some delicious marinated prawns.

Northwest from Zaragoza *p380*

€€ **Mesón O Cubillar**, Plaza de Nuestra Señora 12, Tarazon, T976641192. A sound

choice, with an attractive 1st floor restaurant, serving modern Aragonese fare and the bar downstairs dishing out inexpensive *raciones* of grilled meats.

€€ **El Galeón**, Av La Paz 1, Tarazon, T976642965. It's a fair way from the sea, but this good ship does some excellent seafood – the mussels are especially good, and available in cheap *raciones* at the bar.

€ **Amadeo I**, Paseo de los Fueros de Aragón s/n, Tarazon. A fine terraced café by the violent Rio Queiles, a spot for early evening drinks and ice-creams.

€ **Bar Visconti**, C Visconti 19, Tarazon. The place where locals eat, with a range of *raciones* and tapas, many of them fried morsels of this and that.

Cinco Villas *p382*

The restaurants in the parador are all good. See Sleeping for further options.

€€€-€€ **Hostería de Un-Castillo**, next to the tourist office, has classically hearty Aragonese meats and stews; in the expensive range, but there's a *menú* for €17.75.

€ **Bar Landa**, C Alfaro s/n, T948888158. A good place for a morning coffee, with a peaceful back terrace and inexpensive meals in the evenings.

€ **El Caserio**, C Pintor Goya s/n, T948888009. A welcoming bar serving *raciones* of ham and sausage.

€ **Vinacua**, C Pintor Goya 1, T948888071. Eschew the €14 *menú* for à la carte; it's no more expensive. Simple filling dishes and cheap wine are the order of the day.

🌓 Bars and clubs

Zaragoza *p374, map p376*

Bar El Sol, C Jerónimo Blancas 4. A big bar open nightly until 0300, popular with a young businessy set.

Enlace, Av César Augusto 45. A large bar with decent pumping house music and a dancefloor. Open very late most nights.

La Cucaracha, C Temple s/n. One of many rowdy bars on this street, with a youngish crowd.

Violet, C Fita 14. A very late opening darkwave club, cranking the doors open at 0300 Fri and Sat. One of a few similar clubs in Zaragotham.

Florida 135, Fraga, is one of the best *discotecas* in Aragón outside Zaragoza.

Southwest from Zaragoza *p379*
There's a decent bar in the courtyard next to El Ruejo, Daroca.

✪ Entertainment

Zaragoza *p374, map p376*
Cinema Filmoteca de Zaragoza, Plaza San Carlos 4, T976721853, shows excellent repertory cinema, mostly English-language films with Spanish subtitles. Admission €2. **Cines Goya**, C San Miguel s/n, T976225172, shows recent releases, as does **Cines Buñuel**, C Francisco Vitoria 30, T976232018.
Theatre Teatro Principal, C Coso 57, T976296090; **Teatro del Mercado**, Plaza Santo Domingo s/n, T976437662.

O Shopping

Zaragoza *p374, map p376*
Zaragoza is a good place to browse; most shops are around the broad avenues south of the old town.
Bacanal, near the Mercado, is an entertaining costume shop on C Manifestación.
Librería General, Paseo Independencia 22, for books.
Mercado Central, just southwest of the Plaza del Pilar, is a *modernista* market. Also worth checking out is the **flea market** on Sun morning by the bullring, and the **clothes market** on Wed and Sun mornings by the football stadium.

▲▲ Activities and tours

Zaragoza *p374, map p376*
A colourful tourist bus runs in summer around a 16-stop city route. A hop-on hop-off ticket costs €3. The tourist office also run a variety of tours of the city and province (www.turismozaragoza.com). Most of the city's sights have regular guided tours around them, €1. A tourist-taxi service is also available, with a 1- or 2-hr trip accompanied by recorded commentary (T976751515).

✪ Transport

Zaragoza *p374, map p376*
Air The city's airport is served by Iberia from **Barcelona** and **Madrid**; there are also flights to **Frankfurt**. Airport buses leave from the corner of Gran Vía and Paseo Pamplona. Airport enquiries: T976712300.
Bus There are many bus companies serving a huge variety of destinations. All unfortunately leave from different parts of town. From behind the basilica, catch a 20, 21, 22, 25, 31, 32, 33, or 36 to the station; these also pass near the Aljafería. Bus 45 runs from here to the ethnographic section of the Museo de Zaragoza on the Parque Grande. The major long-distance operators are: **Agreda**, who serve **Madrid**, **Barcelona**, **Valladolid**, **Soria** and more from a station on Paseo María Agustín 7, T976229343. **Viajes Vieca**, who run to **Bilbao**, **Vitoria**, **Santander**, **León**, **Asturias** and **Galicia**, leave from near the bullring at C Pignatelli 120, T976283100; and **Tezasa** services **Logroño**, **Burgos**, **Teruel**, and **Valladolid** from Calle Juan Pablo Bovet 13, T976229886. **La Oscense**, T976434510, run to **Huesca** and **Jaca** from Agreda's bus station (see above); this is also where to get on for **Cariñena** and **Daroca** (T976554588). **Tarazona** is served by **Therpasa** (T976300045), whose bus station is at C General Sueiro 22. **Belchite** and **Alcañiz** are reached on **Autobuses del Bajo Aragón**, leaving from Av Valencia 20, T976229886. For **Calatayud** and the **Monasterio de Piedra**, **Automoviles Zaragoza** are at C Almagro 18, T976219320. **Cinco Villas** are serviced once daily by **Automoviles 5 Villas** (Av de Navarra 81, T976333371); **Sos** can also be reached on the **Sangüesa** bus that leaves at 1900 daily from the carpark under the train station. **Autobuses Conda** also run from Avenida de Navarra (T976333372); going to **Pamplona**, **Tudela**, and **San Sebastián**. For **Fuendetodos**, hop on a Samar Buil vehicle at C Borao 13, T976434304.
Train Run 10 times daily from El Portillo to **Barcelona** and **Madrid**, and less often to **Bilbao**, **Pamplona**, **Burgos**, **Huesca**, **Jaca**, **Calatayud**, **Teruel**, **Valencia**, and more.

Southwest from Zaragoza *p379*

Calatayud is regularly served by bus and train from **Zaragoza**; the bus station is in the centre of town near the tourist office, while the RENFE station is a 10-min walk south across the river.

Northwest from Zaragoza *p380*

Therpasa buses leave from the corner of Av de Navarra and C Arenales. They service **Zaragoza** 7 times daily, and **Soria** 6-7 times daily, falling to 3-4 on Sun. **Cada** leave from Av Estación just off Carrera de Zaragoza for Tudela 6 times a day, with no service on Sun. Autobuses Iñigo stop in **Tarazona** on their way from **Soria** to **Barcelona** once a day. Their station is at the corner of C Teresa Cajal and Ronda de la Rocedo.

❶ Directory

Zaragoza *p374, map p376*
Internet CyberCentro, C Ramón y Cajal.
Laundry There's a *lavandería* on C Pedro María Ric s/n.
Medical facilities C Isabel La Católica s/n. Phone T112 in an emergency.
Telephone There is an unnamed *locutório* on C Jardel s/n by the side of the basilica.
Useful addresses and numbers Police: C Doctor Palomar 8, T976396207. Phone T092 or 112 in an emergency.

Northwest from Zaragoza *p380*
Internet and telephone There's a *locutório* at C Don Bonifacio Daz, which has a couple of slowish terminals.

Foothills of the Pyrenees

Huesca and around → *Phone code: 974; Colour map 3, grid A1; Population: 54,634.*

Huesca is in a slightly strange situation – although it's the capital of Aragón's Pyrenean province, it has been eclipsed by Jaca as 'gateway to the mountains'. Huesca's town planners need a little kick in the backside too; unlike most Spanish towns, it lacks a pedestrianized zone and a focal point for paseos or cafés. Its old town, although interesting, has been allowed to become vaguely seedy, and although the town has plenty of character, it's hard to pin down. That said, it's far from unpleasant, and if you're en route to the Pyrenees transport connections may well require a stopover. There are a few surrounding sights that are worth a visit too, not least Loarre castle – one of the finest in Northern Spain. ▶ *For Sleeping, Eating and other listings, see page s 393-396.*

Ins and outs

Getting there and around Both buses and trains run from the new combined station on Calle Zaragoza. There are frequent connections with Zaragoza and regular connections to all major cities in Spain. Huesca is small and easily traversed on foot. The old town is ringed by a road, which changes name several times; south of here is the main area for bars and restaurants, as well as the new combined bus and train station. ▶ *For further details, see Transport page 395.*

Tourist information Huesca's active tourist office is opposite the cathedral ① *Plaza de Catedral 1, T974292170, www.huescaturismo.com, Mon-Sun 0900-1400, 1600- 2000.* As well as being a good source of information, they run guided tours of the city (1100 and 1700 depending on numbers, 2 hrs, €2). A recent initiative is a vintage bus that has been beautifully restored and runs day trips into the Huescan countryside during summer. It leaves Plaza de Navarra at 0900 daily, returning around 1430. There are dozens of different excursions; it's a great way to reach some hard-to-get-to places. Booking is essential. The trip costs €5.

Aragón Huesca & around

Huesca's history is an interesting one. An important Roman town, it was known as Urbs Victrix Osca and was used by Sertorius as an education centre for Romanizing the sons of local chieftains. Taken by the Muslims, it was known as Al-Wasqa before Pedro I retook it. It became a significant bastion in the continuing Reconquista, a walled town with 90 sturdy towers that was capital of the young Aragonese kingdom for a few years. Its importance declined, along with Aragón's, after union with Castile. Republicans besieged it for a long period during the Civil War but unsuccessfully; George Orwell tells how an optimistic general's cry "Tomorrow we'll have coffee in Huesca" became a cynical joke in the loyalist lines.

Sights

Cathedral ① *museum open Mon-Sat 1000-1330, 1600-1800 (1930 in summer); €2.* Huesca's cathedral is a sober Gothic edifice that appears a touch over-restored. It has an attractive portal with characterful apostles, and a quite interesting Diocesan museum, but the highlight is a magnificent alabaster retablo sculpted by the Aragonese master Damián Forment. The vivid central pieces depict the crucifixion; the sculpture's naturalistic beauty makes the gold-painted retablos in the side chapels look tawdry.

Museo Provincial ① *Tue-Sat 1000-1400, 1700-2000, Sun 1000-1400; free.* North of the cathedral, this museum houses a varied collection, prettily set around the old royal palace and university buildings. The pieces range from prehistoric finds to Goyas and modern Aragonese art. In one of the rooms of the royal palace the famous incident of 'the bell of Huesca' took place. When his two older brothers died heirless, Ramiro II unwillingly left his monk's cell in France and took the throne. The nobles saw him as a pushover, and he was unable to exercise authority. Desperate, he sent a messenger to the abbot of his old monastery, asking for advice. The abbot said nothing, but led the messenger out to the garden, where he chopped the leaves off the tallest plants with a knife. Ramiro got the message, and announced that he was going to forge a bell, which would be heard through the kingdom. He summoned the nobles to the palace, and beheaded them as they arrived, making a circle of the heads and hanging one in the centre, thus forming the Bell of Huesca. It was an effective political manoeuvre: Ramiro's difficulties were said to be less from then on.

Iglesia de San Pedro El Viejo ① *Mon-Sat 1000-1330, 1600-1930, €2.* In the south of the old town is the church of San Pedro El Viejo, of old stock indeed, as it stands on the location of a Visigothic church, and was the place of worship of the city's Christians during Muslim rule. The current building was constructed in 1117, and features some superb Romanesque capitals in its small cloister. Featuring scenes of the Reconquista and the story of Christ's life, it's thought that the same sculptor was involved both here and at San Juan de la Peña. The plain burial chapel off the cloister houses the earthly remains of Alfonso I, and Ramiro II ('the monk'), whose tomb is faced with a panel from a Roman sarcophagus. Inside the church, the soft Romanesque lines are complemented by excellent wall paintings.

Around Huesca

Ayerbe Northwest of Huesca, on the Pamplona road, the town of Ayerbe is worth a stop. In the pleasant square, overlooked by an old *palacio* and clocktower, is a bust of Santiago Ramón y Cajal, a Nobel prize winner for his research of nerve cells in the early 20th century; a man with many streets named after him. Born just over the border in Navarra, he lived his childhood here, but showed no interest or ability at school. Despite this, he managed to become a professor at Zaragoza by the age of 25,

after a spell in Cuba. He had an interesting life, some of which is documented in a small museum ① *winter Wed-Fri 1000-1300, 1600-1900, Sat/Sun 1000-1400, 1630-1930, summer daily 1000-1400, 1600-2000*, in his childhood home. Regular buses run between Huesca and Ayerbe.

Castillo de Loarre ① *Mon-Sun 1000-1330, 1600-1900, €2 for guided tour*. First recorded in 1033, shortly after it had been built by Sancho the Great of Navarra, the

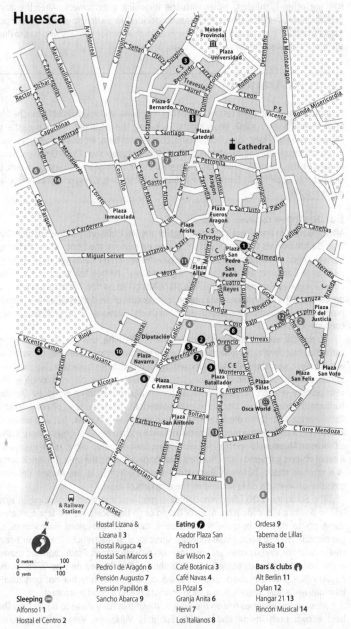

Huesca

Sleeping 😴
Alfonso I **1**
Hostal el Centro **2**
Hostal Lizana &
    Lizana II **3**
Hostal Rugaca **4**
Hostal San Marcos **5**
Pedro I de Aragón **6**
Pensión Augusto **7**
Pensión Papillón **8**
Sancho Abarca **9**

Eating 🍴
Asador Plaza San
    Pedro **1**
Bar Wilson **2**
Café Botánica **3**
Café Navas **4**
El Pózal **5**
Granja Anita **6**
Herví **7**
Los Italianos **8**
Ordesa **9**
Taberna de Lillas
    Pastia **10**

Bars & clubs 🍸
Alt Berlin **11**
Dylan **12**
Hangar 21 **13**
Rincón Musical **14**

Aragón Huesca & around

Loarre castle became an important centre, a monastery, and also briefly a royal residence, before continuing life as a stout frontier post. The design is functional, with few adornments. The towers in the wall are open on the inside, to prevent attacking enemies using them as a refuge once inside the walls. There are some unusual carvings of monkeys above the entrance, while a small dog marks the ascent from the crypt up a narrow staircase that emerges in front of the altar of the church, an unusually high Romanesque structure. The grim dungeons and remains of the royal hall are other highlights, along with the imposing watchtowers. After the early construction used limestone, the masons decided to switch to sandstone, much easier to work. This was bad news for the Muslim prisoners, however, who had to drag the blocks from 20 km away.

Eastern Aragón

An agricultural zone at the feet of the soaring Pyrenees, this region is little touched by tourism but boasts some good sights, including the excellent Templar castle of Monzón. Aragón's best wine, Somontano, comes from here, around Barbastro, which is coincidentally the spiritual home of the Catholic organization Opus Dei. If you want to stay in the area, Monzón, has more peaceful charm than Barbastro; a lack of character is endemic in Barbastro's hotels. ▸▸ *For Sleeping, Eating and other listings, see pages 393-396.*

Barbastro → *Colour map 3, grid B2.*

After enlisting in Barcelona to fight alongside the Republic Army in the Spanish Civil War, Barbastro was George Orwell's first stop en route to the front. Although things have changed since those dark days, you can still see what he was getting at when he referred to Barbastro as "a bleak and chipped town"; he had few good words to say about Aragonese towns in general. The place has taken on new life in recent years as the centre of the **Somontano wine region**, a small core of producers who have risen to prominence with modern winemaking methods allowing high production and consistent quality.

Barbastro was an important Muslim town in its time, but it's the 16th-century **cathedral** that dominates today. Built between 1517 and 1533, it's an elegant structure with a newer, separate belltower. Archaeological unearthings have revealed parts of a former church and a mosque alongside the building. The church's pride is the 16th-century retablo, sculpted from alabaster and polychrome wood by Damián Forment (whose work is also in Huesca cathedral), an Aragonese of considerable Renaissance kudos. He died before he could complete the work, but you wouldn't know – it's a remarkable piece, centred around a niched figure of Christ. There's also a **Diocesan Museum** ① *1000-1300, 1800-1930, summer 1000-1330, 1630-1930,* with a set of objects garnered from churches and chapels around the area. The brick portal is a strange touch, however. Barbastro's tourist office is in the Museo del Vino complex on Avenida de la Merced on the outskirts of town.

The Somontano DO (*denominación de origen*) was approved in principle in 1974 and in practice a decade later. Most of the 10 or so producers are modern concerns, using up to date techniques to produce a range of mid-priced wines from 12 permissible red and white grape varieties, some local, some French. The region's cold winters and hot, dry summers are ideal for ripening wine grapes. Production has soared in the bodegas; a handy achievement in a short period. **Museo de Vino** ① *above the tourist office, Mon-Sat 1000-1400, 1630-2000, free,* is an arty but not particularly informative display. There's also a shop downstairs and a good restaurant.

Most of the **wineries** are on the road to Naval relatively close to Barbastro. The best known both inside and outside Spain is **Viñas del Vero** ① *T974302216,*

Opus Dei lead the Way

It's ironic that after centuries of severe persecution of Freemasons on the grounds that they were a secretive, satanic, power-hungry cult, Spain should produce Opus Dei, a Catholic sect with marked similarities to the Lodgemen.

It was founded in 1928 by Josemaría de Escrivá, a Barbastro lawyer turned priest appalled at the liberalism prevalent in 1920s Spain. He saw Opus (the name means 'the work of God' as a way for lay people to devote their life to God; one of his favourite phrases was 'the sanctity of everyday life'. His book *The Way* is the organization's handbook, with 999 instructions and thoughts for everyday life. Members are both men and women, and though some follow a semi-monastic life, the majority continue in their worldly professions. The organization has members all around the world, identifiable by their use of Atkinson's eau de cologne, but Spain has remained its heartland. Politically and religiously conservative, Opus was a powerful peacetime ally of Franco's government, many of whom were

members. This explains part of the considerable hostility towards the sect, as does its capitalistic ventures; the group is very wealthy and owns numerous newspapers, television channels and companies worldwide.

Allegations of secrecy about Opus centre around the lack of transparency in its involvement in these enterprises as much as the private nature of personal participation. More serious, perhaps, is its backwards-looking approach to Catholicism, with holiness deemed to derive in a large part from the regular performance of the ritual of the sacraments, and the more recent dogmas of the rosary and the stations of the cross, an approach bemoaned by forward-thinking Catholic theologians. Pope John Paul II, a devoted admirer of capitalism and conservatism, unsurprisingly has a lot of time for Opus, who enjoy a privileged status within the Vatican. On 6 October 2002, Escrivá was canonized in Rome as St Josemaría; to call the event controversial risks understatement.

www.vinasdelvero.es. A 30-minute walk from the centre on this road, they're happy to show visitors around by prior appointment on weekdays and Saturday mornings. Some 5 km further on, **Bodegas Enate** ① *T974302580, www.enate.es, Mon-Thu at 1030, 1130, 1730, Fri 1030, 1130, Sat 1000, 1200*, is in a less attractive building but can be visited without appointment.

For a walk, a view, and a good lunch, head west out of Barbastro along Calle San Miguel, then take Calle Virgen del Plano until you get to the signposted GR45 trail. After an hour or so, it'll get you to the hilltop **Monasterio del Pueyo**, with a panoramic vista and well-regarded restaurant.

Monzón → *Colour map 3, grid B2.*
Though seldom visited, Monzón is one of those surprising Spanish towns that has a superb attraction, in this case its relatively unspoiled castle; an atmospheric Templar stronghold that still feels impregnable, albeit bare. The fairly populous town stretches along the river in languid fashion and mostly functions as a service centre for the surrounding agricultural area. There's not a huge amount to see; still, an overnight stay won't disappoint.

The **castle** ① *Tue-Sat 1000-1300, 1700-2000, Sun 1000-1400, €2, guided visits on Sat at 1030, 1730, Sun at 1030, 1130*, itself was fought over extensively during the

Reconquista, and changed hands several times. The mercenary El Cid came here a few times to accept contracts from Muslim governors, while his renowned blade *El Tizón* was later kept here as a relic. The Templars were given the fortress in the 12th century, and modified it to include a monastery. Mercilessly battered in several wars since then, it was still used by the military until the early 20th century. Although some reconstruction has been effected, the buildings still preserve the Templar austerity and ambience. There are several underground passageways to be explored; some are said to have originally descended right down to the river. They're blocked off now, but you'll still need a torch to explore what remains of their depths. The tourist office is in the bus station, but the admissions booth at the castle also functions as one.

Torreciudad → *Colour map 3, grid A2.*

① *0900-1900 (later in summer).* The holy shrine of Opus Dei is worth a visit if you have your own transport, but don't expect revelation: it's likely to reinforce anyone's pre-existing love or otherwise of the organization, see box page 391. In a spectacular setting on a rocky promontory amid craggy hills, it overlooks the Embalse de el Grado and Franco's dam that created it. The main building, once you're past the security guard (don't look too scruffy, although you'll make it in with shorts and a suitably serious expression), is a curious affair. Virtually windowless (who said Opus were secretive?), the brick design seems to recall the designs of both Oriental temples and Victorian power stations. Inside, the altarpiece is the main attraction, a very ornate sculptural relief. In the centre is a Romanesque statue of the Virgin – a passage behind leads to a kissable medallion.

Many Catholic theologians see Opus Dei as an organization looking backwards towards ritual piety rather than a more enlightened spirituality; the complex certainly bears this out – visitors are encouraged to seek God in the devotions of the rosary and stations of the cross in several undeniably attractive locations. The structure was conceived by Saint Josemaría himself, who was born in nearby Barbastro. He died suddenly 11 days before the official opening.

Graus → *Colour map 3, grid A2.*
"I've a brother of sorts in Torquemada." Andrew Eldritch
This small service town doesn't seem much to most who pass through it en route to higher ground. In fact, it's a town with plenty of history, an important bastion of the Reconquista, and long-time marketplace for much of the eastern Pyrenees. While there's not masses to see, what there is, is quality.

Plaza Mayor is an extravagant and beautiful square. Surrounded by beautiful mansions, the **Casa de Barrón** stands out for its red colour and two large paintings on its façade. The female forms are depictions of Art and Science, supposedly created to please the owner's Andalucian wife, perhaps longing for a touch of Mediterranean decadence in dusty Aragón. It's also been suggested, though, that there are several symbols of freemasonry in the paintings, an amusing thought in Opus Dei heartland. Another former resident of the square would not have been amused – Tomás de Torquemada, one of the masterminds of the Spanish Inquisition and scourge of the Spanish Jews, who lived here for a period, see box page 161. Not to be outdone, however, the owner of the **Casa de Heredía** did his eaves up with a series of Renaissance female figures. Unable to compete, the **Ayuntamiento** on the square is distinctly restrained by comparison.

Abizanda
Heading north from Barbastro towards Aínsa, the village of Abizanda is unmissable, with its *atalaya* or defensive tower ① *tower and museum open Jul to mid-Sep Mon-Sun 1100-1400, 1700-2100, May/Jun and mid-Sep to mid-Oct Sat/Sun only 1100-1400, 1500-1800, €1.50,* looming over the road. Turn the car or stop the bus (or

11th century but has been recently rebuilt. Typical of the area, it functioned as a watchtower, one of a chain that could relay signals up and down the valley. A series of levels (sometimes spruced up by art exhibitions) leads to a vertiginous wooden platform with views in all directions through narrow wooden slots. Adjacent is the **Museo de Creencias y Religiosidad Popular**, a small but interesting collection of pieces focusing on the local customs that were (and still are, in some villages) designed to keep evil spirits at bay.

Guara Canyons

Alquézar
The pretty town of Alquézar is a mecca for canyoning and one of the best spots in Europe for the sport. Although the town sees plenty of visitors, the surrounding region is little touristed – with patience, and preferably a car, there are many excellent villages and hidden corners to discover.

Roda de Isábena
An Aragón gem is tiny Roda, an unlikely cathedral town with a population of 36 in a valley south of the Pyrenees. Apart from the odd tourist shop, the hilltop town preserves a superb medieval atmosphere. The Romans established it as a hilltop fortification overlooking the valley, but it owes its current appearance to the powerful counts of Ribagorza, sometime troublemakers who made this a major residence.

> **❢** *It's well worth making the effort to get to Roda, which compares favourably with touristy Aínsa to the north.*

The **cathedral** ① *admission by guided tour only; 1115, 1200, 1245, 1330, 1630, 1715, 1800, 1845, €2*, claims to be the smallest in Spain, but it's no chapel. The intricate 12th-century façade (with a later porch) is the portal to several architectural and artistic treasures but is impressive in itself with columns crowned with rearing lions around a massive studded door. The delicate crypt boasts superb Romanesque wall paintings of which the best is a Pantocrator. There are more in a chapel off the cloister. The earthly remains of San Ramón are housed in an ornately carved tomb, while the 350-year-old organ still belts out a decent note. The cloister is beautiful, swathed with grass and flowers, and centred around a well.

The rest of the town invites wandering around its stone buildings and fortifications; there are several coats-of-arms for heraldists to decipher, and occasional art exhibitions and music recitals.

Benabarre
There's no flies on Benabarre, a relaxed little town at a crossroads in the middle of Aragonese nowhere. Most folk motor on through, but on the hilltop there's a castle, or what's left of one. The central hall and defensive wall are still in place, and a couple of defensive towers decided to stay on to enjoy the view.

⊜ Sleeping

Huesca and around *p387, map p389*
AL Pedro I de Aragon, C del Parque 34, T974220300, pedroprimerohuesca@ hotmail.com. Fairly typical modern Spanish hotel, with cool but dull rooms and an ugly exterior. The best feature is the swimming pool. Special offers are frequent.

A Hotel Sancho Abarca, Plaza de Lizana 13, T974220650, F974225169. A good option, with fairly stylish furnishing and smallish frilly rooms, most exterior.
D Hospedería de Loarre, Plaza Iñigo Moya 7, Loarre, T974382706, F974382713. This is the most beautiful place to stay (and eat) in town. Situated in a big stone building with commodious rooms. The major

Aragón Foothills of the Pyrenees: listings

attraction, the castle, lies 6 km above, on a rocky outcrop.

D Hostal Rugaca, Porches de Galicia 1, T974226449, F974230805. Right in the heart of things above a popular café, the rooms are simple and small but boast a/c, TV, and ensuite bathrooms. Parking is available (€6).

D Hostal San Marcos, C San Orencio 10, T/F974222931. A friendly spot in the café/bar zone, with clean rooms and attractive new wooden furniture. Breakfast served, and parking available at €6.

E-C Hostal Lizana and Lizana II, Plaza Lizana 6/8, T974220776, lizana2@teleline.es. Neighbouring places on a small square, both good value. The rooms come with or without bathroom, and are clean and comfortable.

E Hostal El Centro, C Sancho Ramirez 3, T974226823, hcentro@inicia.es. A somewhat old-fashioned establishment, featuring decent rooms with bathroom and TV.

F Alfonso I, C Padre Huesca 67, T/F9742-45454. Small but pleasant rooms with and without bathroom. Hospitable management.

G Pensión Augusto, C Aínsa 16, T974220079. Seriously cheap option, but reasonable, with friendly staff and clean rooms, although the beds aren't the most comfortable. Near to the **Casa Paco** bar on the corner.

Eastern Aragon *p390*

Although Barbastro has plenty of amenities if you are staying overnight, Monzón is a much nicer place to stay than Barbastro.

D Vianetto, Av de Lérida 25, Monzón, T974401900, vianetto@monzon.net. The best option in Monzón, with affable management and dull but comfortable doubles with a/c. The restaurant is decent too, with a *menú* for €8.88.

F Pensión El Manchego, C Antonio Torres Palacio, Monzón, T974401922. A small *pensión* just by the train station and runs out of the Tropical bar on the corner. The doubles are good for the price, but in summer the singles make the Black Hole of Calcutta seem icy.

Guara Canyons *p393*

There are several places to stay and eat in Roda, which can get busyish at summer weekends. There is also a simple option in Benabarre.

D Casa Rafel, Plaza la Catedral s/n, T974544533. Good 4-berth apartments for rent by the day.

E Hospedería Roda de Isábena, Plaza la Catedral s/n, T974544554, F974544500, virtually touches the cathedral steps, and is garlanded with grapevines. It's a very good, well-priced place to stay, despite a little snootiness. The rooms are comfortable but more atmospheric is the restaurant in the old refectory of the White Monks who founded the cathedral, or the patio overlooking the rocky valley below. See Eating.

E-F Mars Hotel, C Vicente Pirinés 22, Benabarre, T974543166, just near the small Plaza Mayor. Simple but decent.

● Eating

Huesca and around *p387, map p389*

There's not a great deal of action in the old town – most eating and drinking options are in the zone just south, around C Orencio, San Lorenzo, Padre Huesca, and Porches de Galicia. For eating in and around Loarre castle, see **Hospedería de Loarre** above.

€€€ **Café Navas**, C Vicente Campo 3, T974212825. A quality seafood restaurant with a Basque slant on things. Drinkless *menús* for €16 and €30, the latter with the best of the fresh shellfish on offer.

€€€-€€ **Taberna de Lillas Pastia**, Plaza Navarra 4, T974211691. A classy, slightly snooty restaurant in the old casino with undeniably good rich fare. A *menú* costs €24, but expect to pay over €50 a head à la carte. House speciality is *revuelto de trufas*, a delicate combination of truffles and scrambled eggs.

€€ **Asador Plaza San Pedro**, Plaza de San Pedro 5. A restaurant with a fairly simple range of meat dishes, but with good flavour and generous portions.

€€ **Hervi**, C Santa Paciencia 2, T974240333. A popular spot with an outdoor terrace and some excellent fish dishes.

€ **Bar Wilson**, C Orencio s/n. A no-frills bar with good beer, and cheap *bocadillos* and *platos combinados*.

€ **Café Botanica**, Plaza Universidad 4. A popular and attractive next to the museum.

€ **El Pózal**, Travesía de Valdés s/n. A cheery bar serving a good simple *menú del día* for €7.20, often featuring bull stew.

€ **El Rincón del Palacio**, Ayerbe, is a good, cheap, place to eat, with a *menú* and plenty of good *raciones* available in a corner of the plaza.

€ **Granja Anita**, Plaza Navarra 5, T974215712. A smart coffee spot opposite the Diputación.

€ **Los Italianos**, Cosa Baja 18, T974224539. An ice-cream parlour with some tempting pastries and coffee. Try a *pastel ruso*, a traditional Aragonese confection of almonds, meringue, and hazelnut paste.

€ **Ordesa**, C Padre Huesca 20. A decent restaurant with an interesting *menú del día* for €7.85, featuring quail and rabbit.

Eastern Aragon *p390*

€€ **El Cenador de San Julián**, Av de la Merced 64, Barbastro. A smallish and good quality restaurant on the ground floor of the Museo del Vino complex behind the tourist office. The €12 lunch is worthwhile, and there's a €18 evening *menú*, both of which can be enjoyed on the quiet terrace facing the seldom-used bullring.

€€ **Europa**, C Romero 8, Barbastro. A fairly upmarket place specializing in gourmet steaks, rabbit, and *longanizo* (an Aragonese sausage along German lines). The bar serves cheaper *platos combinados*.

€€ **La Taberna del Muro**, C Juan de Lanuza s/n, Monzón. A reasonable restaurant, frequented by Monzonese, and with public internet access.

€ **Acapulco**, Av Lérida 11, Monzón, T974400185. A café/bar on the main drag with a slightly formularized range of food, but a good place to sit out nevertheless. There's both chart and blues available in different sections for late night atmosphere.

€ **La Brasería**, Plaza Mercado s/n, Barbastro. A cheapish upstairs restaurant and downstairs bar serving *raciones* to a porticoed terrace.

€ **Mesón Muro**, C Corona de Aragón 30, Barbastro. A popular local lunching spot, with heavyish Aragonese food, and a *menú del día* for €7.81.

€ **Monzorella**, Plaza Estación s/n, Monzón. A decent and popular local pizzeria opposite the station.

€ **Stop**, C Argensola 11, Barbastro, T974314325. Good and very cheap no-frills dishes prepared with cheery know-how.

Guara Canyons *p393*

€€-€ **Hospedería Roda de Isábena**, see Sleeping above. For an atmospheric bite to eat, go to the restaurant in this hospedería.

€€ **Restaurant Catedral**, set in the building itself, just off the cloister, Roda. The cuisine is very Aragonese, with game such as partridge, rabbit, and quail featuring large, although the most unusual is certainly *jabalí al chocolate* (wild boar with chocolate). There's a reasonable *menú de la casa* for €10.50. An excellent option.

⬤ Bars and clubs

Huesca and around *p387, map p389*
Alt Berlin, Plaza de López Allue s/n, Huesca. Good beer on an attractive if faded plaza that comes to life during San Lorenzo.
Dylan, C Sancho Ramirez 4, Huesca. A homely underground bar, late at weekends.
Hangar 21, C Padre Huesca 52, Huesca. A great cartoon plane adorns the front of this busy weekend *discoteca*.

⊛ Festivals and events

Huesca and around *p387, map p389*
Huesca's big event is **San Lorenzo**, a week-long festival starting on **9 Aug**. It's got all the frills: processions of giants and bigheads, bullfights, cow-dodging in the ring, and copious partying. Like Pamplona, people dress in white, but here the scarves are green rather than red.

◯ Shopping

Eastern Aragon *p390*
Bodega del Vero, C Romero s/n, Barbastro, is a good shop to buy local wine and food.

⊖ Transport

Huesca and around *p387, map p389*
Regular buses run from Huesca to **Zaragoza** (50 mins), other major destinations include **Barcelona** (4 a day), **Pamplona** (5), **Lleida**

● *For an explanation of sleeping and eating price codes used in this guide, see inside the front cover. Other relevant information is found in Essentials, see pages 47-56.*

(6). Several buses go to **Jaca**, **Barbastro**, and **Monzón**. Three a day go to Ayerbe, 7 km from Ayerbe, (en route to Pamplona). There's 1 to 2 buses daily to Loarre, departing at 0825 (Mon-Sat) and 1330 (Mon-Fri).

There are 7 trains daily to **Zaragoza** (1 hr, €4.15), 2 to **Jaca**, and 1 to **Madrid** (5 hrs). Bus services run to **Graus** from **Barbastro**.

Eastern Aragon *p390*
Barbastro is a major transport junction for the eastern Pyrenean towns. The bus station is near the cathedral. Many buses connect with ongoing services to **Huesca** and **Zaragoza**, so you're unlikely to have to stay unless you want to. Buses to and from Barbastro include: **Barcelona** (4 daily, 3½ hrs); **Huesca** (11 daily; 50 mins); **Benasque** (2 a day; 2 hrs); **Lleida** (10 a day); **Monzón** at least hourly (15 min); **Aínsa** one at 1945 (1 hr), returning at 0700. In summer there's another at 1100, returning at 1515. For bike hire **Solo Bike**, Camino de la Barca, Barbastro, T974310409.

From **Monzón**, there are many daily buses to **Huesca** via **Barbastro**, 4-6 a day to **Lleida**, 4 to **Fraga**, and a couple to **Benabarre**. The train travels to: **Madrid** 3 a day (€31.50), **Barcelona** 7 a day (€15-21; 2½ hrs), **Zaragoza** 11 a day (1 hr).

Bus services run to **Graus** from **Barbastro**.

❶ Directory

Huesca and around *p387, map p389*
Internet Osca World, Plaza Nuestra Señora de Salas 4 (corner of C San Lorenzo), Loarre, T974226110, 1000-2400, €2.40/hr. **Osc@.com**, C Calasanz 13, Loarre, 0600-0100, €2.40/hr. There are also Internet terminals in the bus/train station.

Eastern Aragon *p390*
Internet Access can be arranged in Barbastro in the **UNED** (distance education university) building on C Argensola near Plaza Constitución.

Aragonese Pyrenees

Jaca → *Phone code: 974; Colour map 3, grid A1; Population: 14,701; Altitude: 820 m.*

A relaxed spot in northern Aragón, Jaca is far from being a large town but it ranks as a metropolis by the standards of the Pyrenees, for which it functions as a service centre and transport hub. The town has enthusiastically bid for three Winter Olympics, most recently for the 2010 event, but with no luck so far. Most visitors to this part of the Pyrenees are in Jaca at some point, and its also the major stop on the *camino aragonés* pilgrim route, so there's always plenty of bustle about the place. ➤➤ *For Sleeping, Eating and other listings, see pages 405-412.*

History
Jaca was the centre of the Aragonese kingdom in the early Middle Ages under Ramiro I and his son Sancho Ramirez, who established the *fueros*. It was a crucial base in the Reconquista after having been under Moorish control in the eighth century, and a Roman base before that. The city sits on a high plateau above the rivers Aragón and Gállego.

Sights
"It does exist, love for a building, however difficult it may be to talk about. If I had to talk I would have to explain why it should be this particular church that, when I can no longer travel, I will want to have been the last building I have seen." Cees Nooteboom, *Roads to Santiago*
Jaca's treasure is its **cathedral** ① *1000-1300, 1600-2000; museum Tue-Sun 1100-1300, 1600-1830, €2,* which is indeed lovable, a gem of Romanesque architecture

that sits moored like a primitive ship, surrounded by buildings. Neither majestic nor lofty, it was built in the late 11th and early 12th centuries, although the interior owes more to later periods. The main entrance is a long open portico, which approaches a doorway topped by lions and the Crismon symbol. The idea was perhaps that people had a few paces to meditate on their sins before entering the house of God. The cathedral is usually dark – many visitors bypass the coinbox just inside the main door. Come prepared with half-euro pieces, each of which lets there be light for five minutes. The south door has a wooden porch, and fine, carved capitals depicting Abraham and Isaac, and Balaam with the angel. These were carved by the so-called 'Master of Jaca', a coded way of saying 'we don't know anything about who did 'em but they're very good, aren't they'; they certainly are. The interior is less charming than outside. The most ornate of the chapels is that of San Miguel, which contains a fanciful 16th-century retablo and a carved portal, near which is a charming dog with

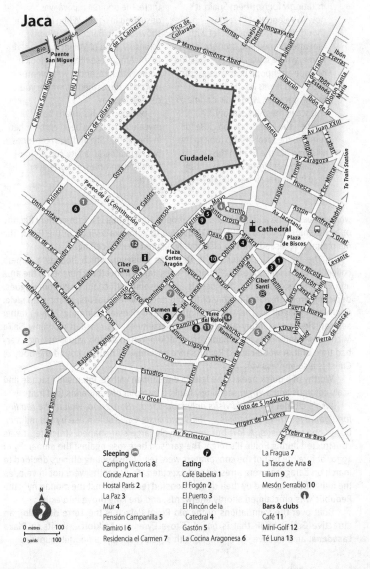

Jaca

Sleeping 🛌
Camping Victoria **8**
Conde Aznar **1**
Hostal París **2**
La Paz **3**
Mur **4**
Pensión Campanilla **5**
Ramiro I **6**
Residencia el Carmen **7**

Eating 🍴
Café Babelia **1**
El Fogón **2**
El Puerto **3**
El Rincón de la Catedral **4**
Gastón **5**
La Cocina Aragonesa **6**
La Fragua **7**
La Tasca de Ana **8**
Lilium **9**
Mesón Serrablo **10**

Bars & clubs 🍸
Café **11**
Mini-Golf **12**
Té Luna **13**

N

0 metres 100
0 yards 100

The Holy Grail

Relics have always been big in Spain. Fragments of the true cross, feathers from the archangel Gabriel's wings, half-pints of the Virgin's milk, the last breath of San Sebastián in a bottle... But the daddy of them all is the Holy Grail, the cup used to knock back the bevy at the Last Supper. Several Aragonese monasteries have held this over the years, although, irritatingly for Northern Spain, it's now in Valencia. St Peter thoughtfully took the goblet with him after dinner, and brought it to Rome, where it was in the possession of pope after pope until things got dicey, and it was handed to a Spanish soldier, who took it home to Huesca in the third century.

When the Moors got too close for comfort, the local bishop took to the hills, and hid the Grail in the monastery of Siresa. After a century or so it was transferred to safer Jaca, where it sat in the cathedral awhile before monks took it to San Juan de la Peña, where it was guarded by Templar knights. The Aragonese king Martino V thought it would look nice on his sideboard, however, and took it to his palace in Zaragoza in 1399. The monks were none too happy, but he managed to fob them off with a replica (a replica of the replica is still there; the original replica was destroyed in a fire). When he died, it showed up in Barcelona. When Alfonso V, King of Valencia, acceded to the Aragonese throne, he took it home with him, and it was eventually placed in the cathedral, where you can see it today.

Spoilsport art historians have revealed that it has been embellished in the ninth, 15th and 16th centuries, but its heart is an agate cup dating from Roman times, so you never can tell.

what appears to be a loaf of bread in its mouth. Next to this is a 12th-century figurine of a wide-hipped virgin and child, dedicated to Zaragoza's Virgin of the Pillar. The main altar is recessed, with an elaborately painted vaulted ceiling.

In the cathedral cloister is the **Diocesan Museum**, which houses a superb collection of Romanesque and Gothic frescoes, taken from other churches in the area and cleverly reconstructed. The best is an awesome 11th-century set from Bagües, depicting an abbreviated history of the old and new Testaments, comic-strip style. Another highlight is the apse paintings from Riesto, featuring some rather self-satisfied 12th-century apostles. Of the paintings, a prim and womanly Saint Michael is standing, as is his habit, on a chicken-footed demon who is having a very bad time of it. A wood-carved Renaissance assembly of figures around the body of Christ is also impressive.

Worthy of a quick peek is the **Iglesia del Carmen** with its interesting façade and scaly columns and a Virgin seemingly flanked by a pair of mandarins (not fruit).

Jaca's **citadel** ① *guided visits only 1100-1200, 1800-2000, wait at the red line for a guide to arrive, tour takes 35 mins and costs €4*, is still in use by the military, but is open for visits. A low but impressively large star-shaped structure, it was constructed during Philip II's reign. The garrison here rose against the monarchy in 1930, before the rest of the conspirators were ready. Two young officers decided to march on Zaragoza, were arrested and executed. Their deaths were not in vain, as the indignation caused by their deaths boosted feeling against the monarchy – the Republic was proclaimed shortly afterwards, and the king drove into exile.

Built over the foundations of the old Royal Palace is the **Torre del Reloj**, an attractive Gothic affair that is now HQ to a Pyrenean taskforce. It sits in **Plaza Lacadena**, an attractive spot at night, with several bars and a floodlit fountain.

Walking down **Paseo de la Constitución**, the town comes to an abrupt end in a slope down to the river Aragón. A path leads down to the river, a popular bathing spot, which is traversed by an attractive medieval bridge. The tourist office ① *Av Regimento Galicia 19*.

Monasterio de San Juan de la Peña → *Colour map 3, grid A1.*

① *€3.50 old monastery only, €5 including return bus from the parking area at the new monastery, €5.50 including an audiovisual presentation in the new monastery (ticket includes entry to the monastery at Santa Cruz de la Seros, 10 km away).*

This famous monastery allegedly came into being when a noble named Voto was chasing down a deer on horseback. The despairing creature took the Roman option and leaped to its death over a cliff. Lacking ABS, Voto's horse was unable to stop itself from following. Still in the saddle, Voto launched a quick prayer to John the Baptist and, to his amazement, landed safely outside a small cave. Investigating, he found the body of a hermit and a small shrine to the headless saint. Moved by his salvation, he decided to continue the hermitage and settled here with his brother, who was equally impressed with the tale. The monastery became an important centre on the pilgrim route to Santiago in the Middle Ages and today constitutes two separate buildings. The new monastery is an impressive brick Baroque structure currently being renovated to incorporate a *hospedería* and restaurant. It's the older monastery that draws visitors, spectacularly wedged into the cliff 1 km down the hill.

Built around bedrock, the lower part consists of a spooky 11th-century church and dormitory, with fragmentary wall paintings and the tombs of several early abbots. Upstairs is a pantheon, where nobles could (with a chunky donation) be buried; it's decorated with the characteristic *ajedrezada jaques* chessboard pattern that originated in these parts.

The high church features three apses, one of which holds a replica of the Holy Grail, see box page 398, and a martial funerary chapel that holds the remains of the Aragonese kings Pedro I and Ramiro I. It's the open remains of the cloister that inspire most awe; the columns are decorated with superbly carved Romanesque capitals under the conglomerate cliff. Scenes from the life of Christ and the book of Genesis are superbly portrayed; Cain takes on Abel with a particularly fearsome sledgehammer.

The monastery is difficult to reach without a car. You can walk the whole way from Jaca on the GR65.3.12, otherwise jump off a Pamplona-bound bus at the cruce for Santa Cruz de la Seros; the monastery is just under a two-hour walk from there.

Canfranc Valley → *Colour map 3, grid A1.*

Canfranc Valley stretches north from Jaca to the French border at Puerto de Somport. Apart from the spectacular mountains at its northernmost extremity, the valley is attractive but not breathtaking. There's not a huge amount of interest in the valley; some fine walks to be sure, but the townships seem listless most of the year, perhaps too busy anxiously scanning the skies for the first signs of snow. Pilgrims on the *camino aragonés* branch of the route to Santiago enter Spain along this valley, but the area's main source of tourist revenue is skiing, with two important resorts close to the border. ▸▸ *For details of Sleeping, Eating and other listings, see pages 405-412.*

Villanúa

The first large settlement in the Canfranc Valley is Villanúa, an uninspiring place apart from a limestone cave nearby, **La Cueva de las Güixas** ① *opening schedule is impossibly complex (the system of different coloured days would do credit to a British*

railway) but it's basically open daily in summer from 1000-1330, 1630-2000 and at weekends only the rest of the year, with a morning visit at 1230 and evening one at 1730, €3.60, the tour takes about 1 hr. Formerly a home for prehistoric man, there are some excellent calcified formations and an underground river.

Canfranc and Canfranc-Estación

The village of Canfranc was destroyed by fire in 1944 and plays second fiddle to its neighbour up the valley, Canfranc-Estación, where most of its residents settled after the blaze. Between the two is a small but impressive moated defensive tower built by Philip II. It now functions as an information centre for the Somport tunnel project, a long-running saga due to committed opposition to the project from lobbies who fear the impact on local wildlife.

Canfranc-Estación's main feature is, sure enough, its railway station, inaugurated in 1928 in a spirit of Franco-Hispanic cooperation. A massive edifice with a platform of prodigious length, it will look familiar to fans of the film *Dr Zhivago*, in which it featured. It's a sad place now, derelict and abandoned; France closed the rail link in the 1970s, although a couple of daily trains still roll in from Jaca. Its rehabilitation is in the pipeline, enmeshed in the tunnel debates. On Saturdays at 1030 a guided trip leaves from Jaca station up the valley to here. The tourist office ① *0900-1330, 1630-2000.*

Candanchú

The ski resort of Candanchú is amid pretty mountains, 1 km short of the border. An ugly place, it's nevertheless equipped with excellent facilities, a variety of accommodation, and a full range of runs, as well as a cross-country circuit.

Nearby, **Astún** is a smaller but equally professional centre, but lacks cheap accommodation, although it's only a 4 km trudge away.

Echo and Ansó valleys → *Colour map 2/3, grid A6/A1.*

These valleys are centres for a mountain culture known as *cheso*, with a distinctive dress and dialect that can still be heard in the villages. ⏵ *For Sleeping, Eating and other listings, see pages 405-412.*

Echo

Also referred to as Hecho, Echo is a small place popular with weekenders. There's a sculpture of a couple in traditional *cheso* costume, but it's close enough to Basque lands that there's a *frontón* for playing *pelota*. There's a small **ethnographic museum** ① *summer 1030-1330, 1800-2100 (except Mon pm), €1.20.* Behind the tourist office on the main road is a sculpture garden, a legacy of a former annual festival.

Siresa

North of Echo, the village of Siresa houses a **monastery** ① *1100-1300, 1700-2000, €0.50,* that was another stop on the long journey of the Holy Grail, see box page 398. A blocky Romanesque construction, it dominates the surrounding hillside. There are a few places to stay, including a youth hostel, which rents bicycles and provides information about walking in the area. Further up, the valley becomes more spectacular; the most popular spot for starting a hike is 11 km north at **Selva de Oza**, where there's a campsite and a bar.

Ansó

Overlooking a river, Ansó is a characterful town. Belying its chunky exterior, the church houses a massive retablo and several large gold-framed paintings as well as a small **ethnographic museum** ① *€2.*

Tena Valley → *Colour map 3, grid A1.*

While not as spectacular as the valleys to the east and west, the Tena Valley is pretty and accessible. It holds two ski resorts, Panticosa and Formigal, and sees most action in winter; during summer it seems a little bit ill at ease without a coating of snow. ►► *For Sleeping, Eating and other listings see pages 405-412.*

Sabiñánigo

The town at the head of the valley is Sabiñánigo, a fairly dull and uninteresting place useful only for transport connections, see Transport page 411. On the edge of town is a good **ethnographic museum**, worth a visit if you're stuck here for a few hours. West of here, the semi-abandoned villages of the Serrablo region are worth exploring with time and a car; there are numerous small Romanesque gems scattered through the near-deserted land.

Biescas

Moving on into the valley, next comes Biescas, a nice quiet little place divided by a pebbly river. There's a road from here leading to Torla and the Ordesa valley, with occasional buses plying the route. There's not a lot going on in Bielsa, but it's a more authentic place than anywhere else further up the road. The tourist office ① *1000-1330, 1700-2030,* in Biescas is above the main square by the river.

La Cuniacha

If you've got a car, you may want to drop into La Cuniacha, an open-plan wildlife park/zoo ① *up a side road 5 km north of Biescas, winter 1000-1600, summer 1000-2000, €7.21, children 5-12 €4.40, under 5 free.* It's a good chance to see some of the Pyrenean animals and plant species, although some are a little reclusive.

Panticosa

Around 10 km beyond Biescas, a road branches right to the ski resort of Panticosa. It's not a bad town, although the odd shop and restaurant break the symmetry of the hotels lining the streets. A cablecar takes skiers up to the chairlift 800 m higher; it also runs in summer, when most visitors are using the town as a base for walks in the area.

Balneario de Panticosa

Further up the narrow valley of the river, 8 km from Caldarés, is an old spa resort, Balneario de Panticosa. It's a bit like Hyde Park in the mountains, with a small lake, rowboats, and a tourist train. Although it's in a pretty location there are three reasons, and only three, to visit; hiking, young children, or rheumatism. **Bar Arlequin** does a decent lunch at a reasonable price. There is a refugio which enables expeditions further up the valley.

Sallent de Gállego and around

Back on the main road through the valley, the destination of choice for many middle-class Spaniards is Sallent de Gállego, still bravely trying to be pretty through the mushrooming clusters of hotels that surround it. There are several easy walks in the area, detailed by the tourist office, but the main attraction outside skiing season is the **Pirineos Sur** world music and culture festival, with high-quality international performers and a market selling more interesting stuff than is the norm at Spanish fiestas ① *runs for 3 weeks from mid-Jul, T974294151, www.pirineos-sur.com.* The tourist information is unfailingly friendly ① *1000-1300, 1700-2000,* and is set in a square with a curiously attractive sculpture.

One of the positives to spring from the festival has been the rebirth of the town of **Lanuza**, a couple of kilometres away, on the shore of an *embalse*.

Formigal

The ski resort of Formigal, 4 km above Sallent, enjoys a bleak but spectacular mountain setting, but is by no means attractive. There's absolutely no reason to come except for winter sports, or to stop for the last drops of Spanish petrol before hitting pricier France. The skiing is good, however, with dozens of runs – although the wind can bite as it sweeps over the bare hills.

Benasque and around → *Colour map 3, grid A2.*

One of the major towns of the Aragonese Pyrenees, Benasque is a relaxed resort dedicated to outdoor pursuits. Although some of the modern development is reasonably tasteful, it has buried the old centre, which was outgrown by the massive surge in Pyrenean tourism in the years since Spain's return to democracy. It's unquestionably a good base – there's plenty of accommodation, though few beds come cheap, several restaurants and bars, and resources for guides, tours, information, and equipment. ▸▸ *For Sleeping, Eating and other listings, see pages 405-412.*

Ins and outs

The intelligent and helpful tourist office ① *just off the main road, opens 1000-1400, 1600-1900 (2100 in summer)*, is more than adequate for most needs, but for more detailed information about the main attraction of the area, the Parque Nacional Posets Maladeta, go to the visitors' centre about 1 km from Benasque off the road to Anciles ① *daily in summer1000-1400, 1600-2100 and weekends only the rest of the year.* There's also a small exhibition.

Sights

The main attraction in the area is the **Parque Nacional Posets Maladeta**, named after the two highest summits in the Pyrenees, which it encompasses. It's a terrain of valleys gouged by glaciers that extends well into Catalunya. Wild and high, the park includes seven summits over 3,000 m. The Maladeta's highest peak, **Aneto**, is the Pyrenees' highest at 3,404 m – it's climbable from the **Refugio de Rencluso**, T974552106, 45 minutes beyond the bus-stop at La Besurta, see Transport page 411, but only fully equipped, even in summer: not for nothing is the chain known as the 'Cursed Mountains'. On the other side of the main road, to the east, the dark summit of Posets is of a similar difficulty level. There are several marked trails and *refugios* around it – one of the most used is the new **Refugio Angel Oíns in Eriste**, T974344044. It's worth checking out some of the area's glaciers, the southernmost in Europe, sadly rapidly diminishing; some estimates give them less than 30 years of life. The park imposes summer restrictions on vehicles in the park; you're better off using the bus services provided from Benasque.

There's much scope for shorter walks in the area, around the **Hospital La Besurta**, and the **Vallibierna Valley** (also accessible by bus), which is traversed by the GR11 long-distance path. There are several mountain biking routes recommended by the Benasque tourist office.

Some 6 km above Benasque stands the village of **Cerler**, which purports to be the highest place in Aragón to be inhabited year-round. It's dominated by a ski resort of average quality but with plenty of runs. There's no shortage of sleeping and eating options, although it lacks the atmosphere of Benasque.

Further up the valley, **Baños de Benasque** is another example of the enduring popularity of spa towns in Spain; there's a hotel here with various regimes targeted at

potential as the mineral composition of the water. Above here is the former pilgrims' rest, the **Hospital de Benasque**, founded in the 12th century. There's now an excellent *hospedería* on the site, where archaeological investigation has revealed a large set of remains from different periods.

Aínsa/L'Aínsa → *Colour map 3, grid A2.*

Characterized by its hilltop location and spectacular mountainous backdrop, tourists flock to Aínsa. Although authentic, the medieval quarter can feel like a theme park during summer, when throngs of travellers amble through the streets and seem to vaguely wonder why they're there. Come the evening, though, you'll have a freer run, and the sleeping and eating options are good. It is an important service town for some of the high Pyrenean villages. ▶▶ *For Sleeping, Eating and other listings, see pages 405-412.*

Sights

The 12th- to 13th-century **old town** stands proud high above the gravelly junction of the Cinca and Ara rivers. From the entrance portal, two narrow streets lead past beautifully preserved houses to the massive cobbled main square, lined with arcades. Every odd year on 14 September there's a play performed here, with most of the town participating – it tells of the defeat of the Moors in 724. Legend has it that García Jimenez, attacking the Muslim town with 300 men, was facing defeat. He called on God, and a glowing red cross appeared on a holm oak tree; heartened, the Christians won. The top left corner of the Aragonese coat of arms refers to this event.

At the other end of the square is what's left of the **castle** ① *summer 1030-1400, 1700-2030*, basically just the still-impressive walls and a reconstructed tower, home to an exhibition of Pyrenean ecology. Back in the narrow streets, there's a better museum ① *summer 1000-1400, 1600-2100, €2.40*, devoted to traditional Pyrenean art. The Romanesque **church** is Aínsa's other highlight, although the jukebox-style Gregorian chant removes some of the atmosphere. There's a strange-shaped cobbled cloister, frequently hung with the work of local artists. The semi-crypt behind the altar has a small view out the window, while the tower, when open, offers excellent vistas.

The tourist office is on the main crossroads below the old town; guided tours of the town run in summer.

Bielsa and around → *Colour map 3, grids A2.*

Bielsa

One of the most peaceful centres in the Aragonese Pyrenees, Bielsa sees most action during the day at weekends, when French Pyreneans nip over the border to secure stashes of cheap whisky and cigarettes. Although the setting isn't as dramatic as Benasque or Torla, it's beautiful here, and the rather unspoiled village atmosphere makes this one of the nicest places to hang out in the area.

> ⁝ *You may end up staying longer than you meant to – it's easy to miss the only bus out at 0600.*

Bielsa was mostly destroyed in the Civil War; a posse of determined Republicans held the town against the Fascist advance before finally retreating up the valley and across the border. The artillery in the car park, however, is used for a less destructive purpose, to trigger avalanches in controlled conditions. **Plaza Mayor** houses the tourist office and a small ethnographic exhibition; nearby is the simple but attractive 15th-century church. ▶▶ *For Sleeping, Eating and other listings, see pages 405-412.*

Valle de Pineta

Beyond Bielsa the main road makes its way into France via a long tunnel. Above the town, a side road winds over a hill and into the Valle de Pineta, a 15-km stretch of road that admits defeat when confronted with the imposing bulk of Monte Perdido. The car park at the road's end is the start or finish for a number of trails, one heading across the Ordesa national park towards Torla. There's also a parador here, as well as a small chapel with a local Virgin.

Some 2½ km short of the car park, you'll see a sign to **Collado de Añisclo**, a tiring but spectacular ascent of the mountain across the valley. Allow eight hours for a return trip in summer – at other times you'll be after snow gear to reach the top.

Cañon de Añisclo

South and west of Bielsa, a small, slow, and scenic route links the village of Escalona with Sarvisé near Torla (there's a quicker way through Aínsa). The road becomes one-way, snaking along a pretty gorge before arriving at a car park, about 12 km from the main road. This is the head of the Cañon de Añisclo, a small-scale but beautiful gorge with a popular path running down it. Some sections wind easily through oak and beech forest, but other sections are slightly precipitous one one side, although the path isn't steep. Most day trippers walk as far as La Riparela, a level grassy plain about three hours from the car park (the return is slightly quicker). It's difficult to get to the canyon without your own transport or a tour from Bielsa or Torla, but it's possible to walk in on the GR15 path, staying at one of the two good refugios in tiny Nerín, a hamlet with a view. If you're in a car, the return road to Bielsa takes you back a different way, over the top of the hills, while the other option is to continue on to Sarvisé.

Torla → *Colour map 3, grid A2.*

Although touristy, there's still something magical about Torla, the base most people use to reach the **Parque Nacional Ordesa**. As such it's well equipped with places to stay, eat, and stock up on supplies and gear for trekking. In town however, Torla's sober square grey belltower stands proud in front of the soaring background massif of Mondarruego (2,848 m). The beautiful church houses a small **ethnographic museum** with a small display of traditional working and domestic life – apart from that it's the great outdoors that beckons. The tourist office ① *Plaza Mayor, 1000-1400, 1700-2000.*

Further down the valley, **Broto** and **Sarvisé** are pleasant little villages with a good range of facilities, but lack the convenience of the Torla shuttle bus that goes to the national park so are only handy if you've got transport. Even better is the tiny village of **Oto**, a 10-minute walk from Broto, and featuring some excellent medieval buildings; there's also a good campsite here, and a couple of *casas rurales*.

Parque Nacional Ordesa y Monte Perdido

→ *Colour map 3, grid A2.*

From Torla you can spot the beginning of the Ordesa valley, taking a sharp right in front of the bulk of Mondarruego. It's the most popular summer destination in the Aragonese Pyrenees, and understandably so, with its dramatic sheer limestone walls, pretty waterfalls, and good selection of walking trails. The number of visitors to the park is restricted to 1,800 at any one time, but even in the height of summer you shouldn't have to wait long, if at all.

The valley was formed by a glacier, which chopped through the limestone like feta cheese, albeit over many thousands of years. Beyond the end of the valley looms

Monte Perdido (3,355 m); it's not recorded who managed to lose it, but it must have been a misty day. The valley and national park is an important haven for flora and fauna – the latter have retreated further into the hills as the stream of visitors became a torrent. You'll likely spot griffon vultures, choughs, and wild irises even from the most-used trails, and you may see isard (Pyrenean chamois) and the massive lammergeyer (bearded vulture). Access to the park is usually confined to the shuttle bus from Torla in summer, see Transport page 412. There's also a very pleasant two-hour walk starting from the bridge on the main road in town. ▸▸ *For Sleeping, Eating and other listings, see pages 405-412.*

Hiking in the park

Most trails start from La Pradera car park where the bus stops. There's a bar/restaurant here, as well as meteorological information (an important consideration for longer walks even in summer).

The most popular route is an easy four-hour return up and down the valley, passing the pretty waterfalls of **El Estercho** and **Gradas de Soaso** before arriving at the aptly named **Cola de Caballo** (horse's tail). It climbs gently most of the way before levelling and widening out above the **Gradas**.

A much better option, if more strenuous, is to head across the bridge from the car park, following signs for the **Senda de los Cazadores**. As long as the weather is clear, don't be fazed by the danger sign – the trail has been much improved, although not recommended if you don't have a head for heights. After

> ● *Hit the ground running when you get off the bus to avoid the crowds on the popular trails.*

crossing the bridge, you're straight into a steep ascent 650 m up the valley walls to the small shelter of **Calcilarruego**, where there's a viewing platform. The worst is over; it's flat and gentle downhills from hereon in. The path spectacularly follows the *faja* (limestone shelf) along the southern edge of the valley, with great views north to the Brecha de Roldán, a square-shaped pass on the French border. If you think it looks man-made, you may be right – Charlemagne's knight Roland is said to have cleared the breach with one blow of his sword Durandal. The path continues through beautiful beech and pine forest until you slowly descend to the **Cola de Caballo** waterfall (3-3½ hours after starting). From here it's a two-hour stroll back down the valley floor.

For attempts on **Monte Perdido** (hard on the thighs but no technical experience required in summer), continue up another hour or two to the **Refugio de Góriz**, usually quite full and fairly unwelcoming. From here, you can continue east towards the **Pineta** valley and **Bielsa**, or north towards **France**.

● Sleeping

Jaca *p396, map p397*

Cheap places are available but not plentiful. For someone on their own, it can be expensive as many of the hotels don't have singles.

A **Hotel Conde Aznar**, Paseo de la Constitución 3, T974361050, F974360797. A charming hotel with an excellent restaurant that generally only accepts guests on a half-board basis. The rooms are comfortable and attractively old-fashioned with modern conveniences.

C **Hotel La Paz**, C Mayor 41, T974360700, F974360400. Decent place run by decent folk. The rooms are standard modern

Spanish, with TV, tiled floors, and bathrooms. **Residencia El Carmen** (see below) is also run out of here.

C **Hotel Mur**, C Santa Orosia 1, T974360100, hotelmur@hotmail.com. Historic Jaca hotel with a good feeling about it. Bedrooms are airy and have full facilities; the best overlook the citadel, so you can overlook the top-secret manoeuvres of the Spanish army.

C **Ramiro I**, C del Carmen 23, T974361367, F974361361. Middle of the road hotel with courteous management and fairly simple but spacious enough rooms. The restaurant is uninspired but decent value.

E **Pensión Campanilla**, C Mayor 42-44 (arcade), T974361448. Very acceptable

doubles with bathroom, run out of a bar nearby.

F **Hostal Paris**, Plaza San Pedro 5, T974361020. A good option near the cathedral with clean doubles with shared bathroom. The doors are locked until about 0700, so be sure to make some arrangement if you've got an early bus.

F **Residencia El Carmen**, Pasaje Carmen s/n, T974360700. A student residence, frequently unavailable, but a very good option for the solo traveller. Adequate rooms cost €12. It's an unmarked brown building next to a clothes shop, but first enquire in the **Hotel La Paz**, see above. Noisy, if there's a school group in.

Camping

Camping Victoria, Ctra Jaca-Pamplona, T974360323. A year-round site with less campervan traffic than many, and only 15 mins' walk from town.

Canfranc Valley p399

B **Hotel Candanchú**, Candanchú, T974373025, www.hotelcandanchu.com, is one of the more characterful of the hotels, with views and a terrace.

D **Faus-Hütte**, Ctra de Francia s/n, Villanúa, T974378136, is a welcoming spot, full of good advice about walks in the area that transcends the town's torpor.

F **Pepito Grillo**, T974373123, Canfranc-Estación, friendly management, dorm beds, and simple ensuite doubles. The best of one of the several *albergues* in Canfranc-Estación.

G **Pensión Somport**, Candanchú, T974373009, is simple and cheap and consequently solidly full all winter, although they're reluctant to take bookings.

Echo and Ansó valleys p400

There are some cheaper *casas rurales* in Echo in addition to the recommended option, **Casa Blasquico**. In Ansó there are several places to stay in the old town, the nicest of which is:

C **Posada Magoria**, C Milagros 32, Ansó, T974370049, a very homely *casa rural* run by welcoming folk.

D **Casa Blasquico**, Plaza Palacio 1, Echo, T974375007, and its restaurant **Gaby**, with charming rooms, good hospitality and great food. THE place to sleep and eat.

Tena Valley p401

The hotels are fairly cheap in Panticosa – the skiing is low-key compared to Formigal. There are tons of places to stay in Sallent. The hotels are predictably pricey in Formigal – most are €100 a night or more for a double room – if you're planning to ski, you are better off either basing yourself further down the valley or booking a package.

A **Almud**, C Espadilla 3, Sallent, T/F9744-88366, hotel-almud@ctv.es. A welcoming and elegant place, full of antique furniture. The nicest room is at the top, with a *mirador* to sit and admire the view over the lake.

B **Tirol**, T974490377, tirol@arrakis.es. One of the cheapest in Formigal.

D **Casa Ruba**, C Esperanza 18, Biescas, T/F974485001.

D **La Rambla**, Las Ramblas de San Pedro 7, Biescas, T/F974485177, larambla@publiciber caja.es.

E **Albergue Foratata**, C Francia 17, Sallent, T974488112. The cheapest place in Sallent.

E **Navarro**, Plaza de la Iglesia s/n, Panticosa, T974487181.

E-F **Habitaciones Las Heras**, C Agustina de Aragón 35, Biescas, T974485027, a friendly sort of place with some recently renovated rooms with or without bath.

Benasque and around p402

All those listed are situated in Benasque.

A **Hotel San Marsial**, Av Francia 77, T9745-51616, sanmarsial@pirineo.com. The classiest option of Benasque, although often beset by package tourists. They organize several activities. Elegant hunting-lodge style decor.

C **Casa Mariano**, C Única s/n, Eresué, T974553034, casamariano@imaginapunto. com. A top spot for people who want a base in the great outdoors in a village 10 km southeast of Benasque. This *casa rural* is very homely, with 2 large bedrooms and excellent home-cooked meals. One of the owners is a mountain guide and will happily help organize activities and give advice.

C **Hotel Ciria**, Av Los Tilos s/n, T974551612, www.hotelciria.com. Very nice balconied rooms on the main street with cheerful fittings and many facilities. There are also suites with hydromassage units to soothe those muscles ailing from hiking or skiing.

C-E **Hostal Valero/Hotel Aneto**, Ctra de Anciles s/n, T974551061, F974551509.

⁞ Take refuge

If you spend time walking in the Pyrenees, you're likely to want to use a refugio, comradely places which are essentially mountain hostels along Scottish "bothy" lines. The word can mean anything from a one-person lean-to upwards, but the better ones have cosily packed dormitories where wet socks are hung from every available nail, and most of the staffed ones offer meals at good rates; the communal atmosphere is usually excellent. It's always worth booking in summer; no-one is usually turned away, but you might find yourself on the floor or outside. The staff are usually knowledgeable about the area; it's a good idea to inform them if you're climbing a peak so they can give advice and alert emergency services in case of trouble. Most also have a book where walkers and climbers write hints, routes, warnings and advice.

A large complex across the main road from the town centre. There's a huge variety of rooms and prices, as well as some apartments. The service and staff are helpful and welcoming.

D Hospital de Benasque Hospedería, Llanos de Hospital, T974552012, www.llanos delhospital.com. With a variety of rooms, this remote inn offers every comfort. There's a welcoming bar and restaurant, but come prepared to stay a while in winter – every now and then it gets cut off by snowfalls.

D Hotel Avenida, Av Los Tilos 14, T9745-51126, www.h-avenida.com. A friendly family-run concern in the heart of Benasque, with spotless rooms overlooking the main street and nice terrace restaurant downstairs.

D-F Hostal Solana, Plaza Mayor 5, T/F974551019. Good clean rooms above an unmemorable but bustling bar/restaurant. The without-bath option is about the best value in town, but make sure they charge according to the rate-sheet.

E Fonda Vescelia, C Mayor 5, T974551654. Dormitory accommodation and some doubles at most un-*fonda* like prices. Decent bar downstairs, and a shop downstairs that offers massages.

Hostels and camping

Camping Aneto, Ctra Francia km100, T974551141. Several facilities as well as some simple bungalows.

Camping Los Baños, Ctra Francia s/n, T974344002, F974551263. A busier campsite with more facilities.

Refugio La Rencluso, T974551490. Run by the **Hotel Avenida**, this is the best base for climbing Aneto.

Aínsa/L'Aínsa p403

Many of Aínsa's options are unattractive in the new town. Budget accommodation is in short supply in summer.

B Hotel Posada Real, C de las Escalaretas s/n, T974500977, www.posadareal.com. An establishment run out of the **Bodegón de Mallacán** restaurant, this stately place has an odd mixture of the old and new, with 4-poster beds side by side with modern tiling and art. Still, it's a very comfortable place to stay just off the plaza.

D Casa del Marqués, Plaza Mayor s/n, T974500977. Another arm of the Bodegón de Mallacán restaurant on the plaza, this stone house has rustic and attractive wooden furnishings and a terrace with a view.

E Casa El Hospital, C Santa Cruz 3, T/F9745-00750. A good *casa rural* in a stone house next to the church, charming doubles at a very good price.

Bielsa and around p403

A Parador de Bielsa, Valle de Pineta, T974501011, bielsa@parador.es. At the end of the Valle de Pineta road, under looming Monte Perdido, this makes an excellent base for walks in the area. Modern but sensitive construction, recently renovated.

E Marboré, Av Pineta s/n, T974501111. Another good option, with comfy rooms with television, run by identical twins.

E Valle de Pineta, C Los Ciervos s/n, T974501010, www.monteperdido.com/ hotelvalle. Reasonably priced rooms, some overlooking the river valley. Get your 15 mins of fame by eating in the pleasant restaurant; diners are telecast onto a screen in the street.
E-F Vidaller, C Calvario 4, T974501004. One of the best places to stay in Bielsa, with pleasant top-value rooms with and without bathroom above a small and friendly shop.

Hostels

Añisclo Albergue, Nerín, T974489008. This *refugios* is a good place to stop if you're heading for the Cañon de Añisclo on foot. A top situation, with great valley views, dorm beds, and simple but happy meals.

Torla *p404*

There are several *refugios* in the park.
C Villa de Torla, Plaza Nueva 1, T974486156, villadetorla@staragon.com. The best place to stay in Torla; although the rooms are nothing to write home about, there's a terrace with great views, a swimming pool, good eating, and it's in the heart of town.
D Edelweiss, Ctra Ordesa s/n, T974486168. The best of the cluster of main road hotels, with good ensuite rooms, many with balconies and views.
E Casa Frauca, Ctra de Ordesa s/n, Sarvisé, T974486182. A faded but quite charming old inn, with characterful and unusual bedrooms with bathroom, and a decent restaurant.

Hostels and camping

Camping Rio Ara, T974486248. A peaceful campsite in the river valley below Torla. Access by car is 1½ km beyond town, but there's a quicker footpath.
Camping/Refugio Valle de Bujaruelo, T974486348. A well-equipped and beautiful site further up the valley, open Apr-Oct.
Refugio de Góriz, T974341201. A crucial *refugio* despite frequent shortages of berths and cheerfulness. Book ahead if you don't want to camp out.
Refugio L'Atalaya, C Ruata 1, T974486022. Although the manager rubs people up the wrong way, the rest of the staff and the decor are welcoming. The bar/restaurant is great, but the 2 dorms are cramped.
Refugio Lucien Briet, C Ruata s/n, T974486221, reflucienbriet@eresmas.com.

The roomier of the 2 *refugios* in town, with a couple of doubles too. Good restaurant, and board rates offered.

Eating

Jaca *p396, map p397*
Jaca has many good options. C Ramiro I is best for tapas, while C Gil Berges is the domain of several late-night bars.
€€€ El Fogón, C del Carmen s/n, T974363892. An old-fashioned Spanish restaurant with a vaulted chamber. Jaca's proximity to France shows in the careful preparation, but local favourites are the staples, particularly the large tender steaks, succulent venison, and native Pyrenean kangaroo.
€€€ La Cocina Aragonesa, Paseo de la Constitución 3, T974361050. One of Jaca's best, a friendly spot serving up Aragonese cuisine with a distinctly French touch. Part of the Hotel Conde Aznar. There's a *menú del día* for €12, but it's not really representative of the quality on offer.
€€ El Rincón de la Catedral, Plaza de la Catedral. The place to sit and admire the soft Romanesque lines of the cathedral. Large range of meals, salads, and delicious *montaditos*.
€€ Gastón, Av Primer Viernes de Mayo 14, T974361719. This upstairs establishment offers a €12 *menú* that features good homestyle cooking. On the *carta*, the *lenguado* (sole) in cava is excellent.
€€ La Fragua, C Gil Berges 4, T974360618. A good hearty *asador*, popular with locals at weekends for its excellent *chuletón de buey* oxsteaks.
€€ Lilium, Av Primer Viernes de Mayo 8, T974355356. On the main street, this spot has a covered terrace and an artistic touch that is manifest in its beautifully presented Pyrenean cuisine.
€€ Mesón Serrablo, C Obispo 3, T974362418. An attractive and delicious restaurant in an antique-y stone building. Two levels, and a good weekend *menú* for €15.50.
€ Café Babelia, C Zocotin 11, T974356082. Not far from the cathedral, this zappy modern café-bar does some excellent and inventive salads as well as other food. Terrace prices add a hefty kick onto the bill.

€ El Puerto, C Bellido 6, T974356336. A doughty little place serving decent *raciones*, particularly seafood and fish. The *caballa* (mackerel), if they have it, is an excellent choice.

€ La Tasca de Ana, C Ramiro I 3. An indispensable stop on the Jaca food trail with a very large variety of quality hot and cold tapas, great salads, good wine, and more.

Echo and Ansó valleys *p400*
See Sleeping above.

Tena Valley *p401*
There are many places to eat in Sallent.

€€€-€€ Hotel Villa de Sallent, the best place to eat in Formigal, run by a well-known Spanish chef.

€€ La Rambla and **Casa Ruba** in Biescas, see Sleeping, have good restaurants – well known in these parts – which makes it tricky to get a table at weekend lunchtimes without a reservation.

€€-€ Martón, Plaza Valle de Tena s/n, Sallent, T974488251, has a quiet riverside terrace and cosy interior serving cheap dishes, including good roasts cooked in an open brick oven.

€ Manél, Panticosa, a stone café/restaurant with a shady terrace; they do a solid *menú del día* for €12. A nice place to eat.

Benasque and around *p402*
€€€ Ixeia, C Mayor 45, T974552875. The smartest restaurant in Benasque with some very classy food. The general tenor is Aragonese, with a variety of meats carefully prepared with local Pyrenean fare: forest fruits and mountain herbs.

€€ El Pesebre, C Mayor 45, T974551507. A dark stony traditional restaurant with a small terrace, serving traditional Aragonese food, with plenty of lamb and game.

€€ La Sidrería, C Los Huertos s/n, T974551292. An excellent restaurant run by welcoming Asturians. Cider is the obvious choice but there are several good wines to accompany the delicious food. If there's some homemade cheesecake around, grab a slice – it's a short-priced favourite for the best dessert in Aragón.

€€ Restaurant La Parrilla, C Francia s/n, T974551134. A spacious and smartish restaurant dealing in well-prepared steaks –

eat 'em rare if you want to do as the Aragonese do. There's a *menú del día* for €12.84.

€€ Sayó, C Mayor s/n. A cheery big stone place with good homestyle mountain comfort food and a *menú* for €11.

€ Hostal Pirineos, Ctra Benasque s/n, T974551307. A couple of kilometres back down the valley on the main road, this terrace is a nice place to sit and enjoy simple but well-done food and wine. There's good rooms available too.

Aínsa/L'Aínsa *p403*
€€€ Bodegas del Sobrarbe, Plaza Mayor 2, T974500234. A high-class restaurant with the best of Pyrenean cuisine, based around game. Last count featured 11 different land-based creatures on the menu, but vegetarians can be consoled by the excellent wild mushrooms. There's a *menú* for €19.26, but it doesn't feature the best on show.

€€ El Portal, C Portal Bajo 5, T974500138. Just about the first building you pass in the old town, this restaurant has some great views over the rivers below and *menús* for €9.60 and €13.50.

Bielsa and around *p403*
€ El Chinchecle is an excellent place in a small courtyard serving homemade liqueurs to the sound of traditional music. Also serves some very nice *cecina de ciervo* (cured venison), and put on one or two nightly dishes for some excellent simple eating.

€ La Terrazeta, C Baja s/n, T974501158. Well set with a dining room overlooking the valley, this is one of Bielsa's better options in summer or winter. There's a *menú* for €9.40 (excluding drinks), but à la carte isn't too pricey either.

€ Reyna's Bar, Av Pineta s/n, T974501084. A people-watching spot with outdoor seats, and a good value *menú del día* and snacks.

Torla *p404*
€€ El Rebeco, Plaza Mayor s/n. Not the friendliest of places, but there's a good restaurant upstairs, as well as two terraces, one shady, one sunny. It's named for the isard/Pyrenean chamois, which thankfully doesn't feature on the menu, although it's a traditional local dish.

€€ L'Atalaya, C Ruata 1, T974486022. Funky bar and restaurant doing a range of

quality dishes in a colourful atmosphere. *Menú del día* for €9, and a drinkless evening *menú* for €13. The bar does *tapas* and *platos combinados*.

€ **A'Borda Samper**, C Travecinal s/n, T974486231. One of the nicest places to eat in Torla – a great range of simple *tapas* in a welcoming family atmosphere, and a good upstairs restaurant.

€ **El Taillón**, C Ruata s/n, T974486304. A no-nonsense bar featuring a lawn terrace with superb views of Mondarruego. The good-value restaurant upstairs does cheap and filling *menús*.

€ **La Brecha**, C Ruata s/n, T974486221. Friendly upstairs restaurant doing a good set *menú* for €10.20; a rare exception to the 'don't eat where they photograph their food' rule.

🍷 Bars and clubs

Jaca *p396, map p397*
Café, Plaza de Lacadena s/n. And this is the best, at least for those who believe that the world's greatest music came out of the decade between 1979 and 1990 from places like Manchester, Berlin, Leeds and Bucharest. Superb collection of vinyl and a good vibe to boot.

Mini-Golf Bar, Gran Hotel, above tourist office. Go on, you know you want to.
Té Luna, Pasaje Dean s/n. A very cosy little tea bar tucked away near the cathedral.
Viviana, Plaza de Lacadena s/n. With a mixed selection of Asian prints on the walls, a pool table, and drum 'n bass sounds, this is one of Jaca's best bars.

Tena Valley *p401*
Bar Casino, Sallent, if you've never had a beer in a town hall before, head here.

Benasque and around *p402*
Petronilla, C San Marcial 8. A warming resort-style bar that packs a crowd around its pool and football tables.

🛒 Shopping

Jaca *p396, map p397*
Librería La Unión, C Mayor 34, T974355273. A reasonable bookshop with a selection of maps and travel books.

Benasque and around *p402*
Alvi, Edificio Ribagorza, C Francia. A supermarket.

🏔 Activities and tours

Jaca *p396, map p397*
Jaca has several tour operators who offer activities throughout the Aragonese Pyrenees.
Alcorce Pirineos Aventura, Av Regimiento Galicia 1, T974356437, www.alcorceaven tura.com. Specialize in mountains, particularly skiing, trekking, climbing, and caving.
Aragón Aventura, C Mayor 2, T974485358, www.aragonaventura.es. Skiing and canyoning experts, but also cover other activities.
Deportes Goyo, Av Juan XXIII 17, T974360413, hire mountain bikes.
Pirineo Aragonés Aventura, Av Premier Viernes de Mayo 14, T974356788, www.pirineoaventura.com. Primarily a summer operator, running, climbing, canyoning, and canoeing trips among other things.

Tena Valley *p401*
Escuela de Esquí de Formigal, T974490135, www.valledetena.com/eef, has a monopoly on skiing courses in Formigal.
Sport Panticosa, Panticosa, rents bikes to explore the countryside.

Benasque and around *p402*
Barrabés, C Francia s/n, T974551056. Run a series of alpine, rock climbing, rafting, and canyoning activities for all levels. Their massive shop is full of equipment and maps.
Casa de la Montaña, Av Los Tilos s/n, T974552094. A similar range on offer.
Centro de Formación de Benasque, Campalet s/n, T/F974552019, fedmeben@sct.ictnet.es. Serious mount-aineering, canyoning, and skiing courses throughout the year; from 3-5 days, book well in advance. Part of the Escuela Española de Alta Montaña, a reputation for excellence.
Centro Ecuestre Casa Palo, C La Fuente 14, Cerler, T974551092. Horsey trips into the valleys.
Compañia de Guías de Benasque, Av de Luchón 19, T974551336, www.guiasben

asque.com. Organize all sorts of mountainous activities in the area.

Escuela Español de Esquí, Centro Cerler, Cerler, T/F974551553. Run skiing and snowboarding courses.

La Garahola, C San Pedro, Edificio San Pedro, T974551360. Run a number of fishing courses and excursions in the Benasque area.

Radical Snowboard, Edificio Ribagorza 10, T974551425. Snowboard hire and instruction.

Aínsa/L'Aínsa p403

Aguas Blancas, Av Sobrarbe 4, T974510008, www.aguasblancas.com. Run whitewater rafting and canoeing expeditions.

Ignacio Gabás, in the Bodegón de Mallacán restaurant, organizes scenic flights over the Pyrenees.

Torla p404

The 2 major operators in Torla for excursions in the area are **Compañia Guías de Torla**, C Ruata s/n, T/F974486422, www.guiasde torla.com, and **Aragón Aventura**, C Ruate s/n, T974486455, www.aragonaventura.es. **Center Aventura**, Av Ordesa s/n, T974486337, has a good supply of trekking equipment and maps. **Casa Blas**, in Sarvisé, T974486041, run all manner of equine activities.

⊙ Transport

Jaca p396, map p397

Jaca's bus station is conveniently located on Plaza Biscos in the centre of town.

Bus There are 4 buses daily to **Lourdes** in France via **Canfranc**, **Pau**, and **Tarbes**. These reach the frontier in 1 hr. There are 1 or 2 buses daily head for **Pamplona** (1 hr 40 mins), and 6 buses make for **Huesca**, with a connection for **Zaragoza**. **Alosa** run buses from **Jaca** via **Sabiñánigo** up the valley as far as **Sallent de Gállego** and **Formigal**, detouring to **Panticosa** on the way. They depart from Jaca at 1015 and 1815, arriving at Sabiñánigo 15-30 mins later, and **Sallent** after 90 mins. The 1015 bus goes all the way to **Formigal** and returns at 1545, arriving in **Jaca** at 1715. The 1815 bus stops in **Sallent** and doesn't run on Sun – it leaves for Jaca again at 0700. In Jul and Aug the 1015 bus has a companion that runs all the way up to

Balneario de Panticosa, returning from the spa town at 1730.

Train The train station is neither as handy nor as useful and is to the east of town. A shuttle bus links to it from outside the bus station. There are 2 trains that head up the **Canfranc Valley** daily as far as the massive station at **Canfranc-Estación**. There are 2 trains that go the other way, from Jaca down to **Huesca** and on to **Zaragoza**.

Canfranc Valley p399

Bus There are 4 buses daily from **Jaca** to **Lourdes** in France via **Canfranc**, **Pau**, and **Tarbes**. These reach the frontier in 1 hr. From Canfranc-Estación there are regular buses running across the frontier.

Train Two trains daily head up the **Canfranc Valley** as far as the massive station at **Canfranc-Estación**. Two trains go the other way, from **Jaca** down to **Huesca** and on to **Zaragoza**.

Echo and Ansó valleys p400

There's a daily bus to **Echo** and **Ansó** from **Jaca**.

Tena Valley p401

Bus Alosa run buses from **Jaca** via **Sabiñánigo** up the valley as far as **Sallent de Gállego** and **Formigal**, detouring to **Panticosa** on the way. They depart from Jaca at 1015 and 1815, arriving at Sabiñánigo 15-30 mins later, and Sallent after 90 mins. The 1015 bus goes all the way to **Formigal** and returns at 1545, arriving in **Jaca** at 1715. The 1815 bus stops in **Sallent** and doesn't run on Sun – it leaves for **Jaca** again at 0700. In Jul and Aug the 1015 bus has a companion that runs all the way up to **Balneario de Panticosa**, returning from the spa town at 1730.

Benasque and around p402

Bus There are buses departing **Benasque** for **Barbastro** at 0645 and 1500 (2 hrs), which connect directly with buses to **Huesca**, **Lleida**, and **Zaragoza**. For **Parque Nacional Maladeta**, a bus runs from Benasque to the trailhead of **La Besurta**, leaving 0430, 0900, and 1300, returning at 1400, 1830, 2130. The bus also runs to **Vallibierna**, and shuttles between **La Besurta** and the **Hospital de Benasque**.

Cycling El Baul, C Francia s/n, hire bikes from €13 a day, as do **Ciclos A Sanchez**, Av del Luchón s/n.

Aínsa/L'Aínsa *p403*

A bus line runs between **Barbastro** and **Aínsa**, leaving **Barbastro** Mon-Sat 1945 (1hr), and leaving **Aínsa** at 0700. In Jul and Aug a second bus runs, leaving **Barbastro** Mon-Sat 1100, and leaving **Aínsa** at 1510. A bus leaves **Aínsa** for **Bielsa** at 2045 Mon, Wed, Fri (Mon-Sat in Jul and Aug). The return bus leaves **Bielsa** at 0600. The service connects with the **Barbastro** bus. A daily bus runs from **Aínsa** to **Sabiñánigo** via **Torla** and **Biescas**, leaving at 1430.

Bielsa and around *p403*

Services run from **Bielsa** to **Aínsa** at 0600 Mon, Wed, Fri (Mon-Sat in Jul and Aug), with a connection to **Barbastro**. The bus into town leaves **Aínsa** at 2045.

Torla *p404*

Torla is accessed by bus from **Aínsa** once daily at 1430 (1 hr), the return bus leaves **Torla** at 1200. 2 buses a day arrive from **Sabiñánigo**, via **Biescas**; they return at 1530 and 1945.

From Jul to Oct (and Easter) a shuttle bus runs from the parking lot at **Torla** to **La** Pradera, in the valley of Ordesa. Leaving every 15-20 mins from 0600-1900, the last return bus leaves the park at 2200. A return trip costs €2.70; outgoing buses stop at the park's visitors' centre **El Parador**. This bus is often the only way to reach the park by road, as private vehicle access tends to be cut off. Parking in Torla costs €0.50 per hr or €5.50 per day, but there are other places to park.

⊙ Directory

Jaca *p396, map p397*

Internet Ciber Civa, Av Regimiento Galicia, is 3 doors from the tourist office and charges €1.90 per hr for a reasonable connection. **Ciber Santi**, C Mayor 42-44 (in arcade), charges €2 per hr.

Post office C de Correos s/n, on the corner of Av Regimiento Galicia.

Benasque and around *p402*

Internet Coin-operated terminal in the tourist office, and **Bar Surcos** also has a computer, available from 1900-2300.

Laundry Lavandería Ardilla, Cn, T974551504.

Aínsa/L'Aínsa *p403*

Internet Bar Abrevadero, C Portal Bajo s/n.

Teruel Province

The southern Aragonese province of Teruel is one of the least known and least visited in Spain. Undeservedly; as it's a wild and spectacular place. The provincial capital is a cheery little town, but it's the soul-stirring uplands around it that provide the best reason for a visit. The province is a mountainous one, largely covered by the Sistema Ibérico range and studded with beautifully unspoiled villages, almost every one of them a gem. There's a significant prehistoric heritage, with dinosaur fossils and cave art; there's good walking in summer and a couple of decent ski resorts for the winter months. The towns of Albarracín and Alcañiz are both worth a visit.

The area east and northeast of Teruel has some of Spain's finer landscapes; a network of sparsely shrubbed hills that have been morphed by wind, water and geological pressure into a series of unusual shapes in gold and grey stone. The comparatively unknown areas of Maestrazgo and Sierra de Gúdar worth exploring; the region is a great idea for anyone who won't be put off by lack of trees and water features. In winter it is seriously cold, and many passes may be snowbound.

There are few settlements, but those that brave the heat and cold are nearly all appealing little villages, with noble Aragonese architecture; several perch dramatically on clifftops or windswept brows of rocky hills. There are two modern ski-resorts in the region; in spring and autumn it's an excellent place for hiking and cycling.

Coming from Zaragoza, you reach Teruel Province after passing Daroca and the Laguna de Gallocanta (see above). There's not a great deal of interest until you reach Teruel itself, but a couple of towns are worth looking at. **Calamocha** is a ham-producing place with a number of stately mansion houses and an attractive church, the **Iglesia de Santa María La Mayor**. South of here, **Monreal de Campo** is known for production of saffron, and has a small museum dedicated to that prized spice.

Teruel → *Phone code: 978; Colour map 5, grid A4; Population: 31,158.*

"Teruel exists!" is the plaintive slogan of the citizenry of this oft-forgotten Aragonese town. And indeed it does. Spain's smallest provincial capital is remote and hard to reach, but rewards the effort with a relaxed atmosphere and an excellent collection of Mudéjar buildings. ▶ *For Sleeping, Eating and other listings, see pages 420-423.*

Ins and outs
Getting there and around Teruel is poorly served transport-wise. The bus station is conveniently close to the old centre while the **train** station is just below town. ▶ *For further details, see Transport page 413.*
Best time to visit In winter temperatures several degrees below zero are not uncommon. The summers are baking hot, so spring and autumn are the least extreme.
Tourist information Teruel's office isn't exactly eager to please ① *C Tomás Nogués 1, Mon-Sat 0900-1400, 1700-1930, Sun 1000-1400, 1700-1930.* Free guided tours of the city at 1030, 1200, and 1730 leaving from the town hall, 15 bookings minimum.

History
While the area was occupied by Iberians, then Romans, what we now know as Teruel has its origins as a Muslim settlement governed from nearby Albarracín. Reconquered in 1171, the city became one of the places where multi-culturalism thrived. Ordnances from the provincial archives attest to the liberal and tolerant atmosphere in which the Jewish, Muslim and Christian populations lived; the city's Mudéjar architecture is further evidence of cultural interchange. Teruel's geographical isolation was bound to tell in the end, and the city became one of Spain's poorest, exacerbated by civil strife during the Carlist wars of the 19th century. Further damage occurred in the Civil War, see box page 416, and the city and province were largely neglected during the dictatorship and since. ¡Teruel Existe! is a community initiative aimed at redressing what the turolenses see as unequal treatment by the national and provincial governments. It's had some success, and the city is beginning to appear quite a prosperous little place.

Sights
Cathedral ① *1100-1400, 1600-2000, €1.20, €2 guided tour.* Teruel has an excellent collection of Mudéjar towers, the most spectacular of which graces the cathedral. The tower dates from the mid-13th century and is adorned with colourful glazed ceramic tiles and cylinders; it's a powerful statement of the relative harmony of mixed-creed turolense society in the post-Reconquista years. The cathedral itself mostly dates from the 16th century and isn't as impressive. The interior features a big wooden retablo with scenes from the crucifixion; a side chapel contains a painted 15th-century altarpiece with much more character in its depiction of the Assumption. The jewel, however, is the ceiling, a superbly ornate Mudéjar work from the 13th century. Covered for many years, it features intricate geometrical motifs as well as scenes from

the life of the court. The best view is to be had from the gallery, but you'll need to take the guided tour to get access to it.

Museo Diocesano ① *Mon-Sat 1000-1400, also 1600-2000 in Jul/Aug, €0.60.* Next door to the cathedral, this museum is housed in the former residence of the bishop. It's an attractive building with an elegant Aragonese patio. The collection has been garnered from around the province and isn't especially impressive. There's a range of stuff, including glazed ceramics from the cathedral façade, processional crosses, and several religious sculptures, of which the most impressive is a 14th-century wooden Calvary.

Mudéjar towers There are three other Mudéjar towers around the old town. The elegant **Torre de San Martín** dates from the early 14th century; its ceramics are green and white, typical of the province. The latest and most impressive is the **Torre de El Salvador** ① *1100-1400, 1630-1830, €1.50,* finished in the mid-14th century. It's been carefully restored and well-worth visiting, both for the views and the interior architecture. It's a curious design, as there are actually two concentric towers; the stairs and corridors occupy the space between them.

Iglesia de San Pedro and the Museo de los Amantes ① *Museo de los los Amantes: daily 1000-1350, 1700-1930, €0.60.* Iglesia de San Pedro's campanile dates from the 13th century; the church itself has some Mudéjar features too, including the cloister (although it's been tampered with). Teruel's most famous legend is that of Los Amantes, the 'lovers of Teruel', whose embalmed bodies were allegedly discovered in the 16th century along with a summary of the story, which has been the subject of numerous romances in Spanish history. The lovers are now in a small chapel next to the Iglesia de San Pedro, the Museo de los Amantes, and they are a popular attraction.

Legend has it that in the 13th century, Isabel de Segura, daughter of a noble family, was wooed by Diego Martínez de Marcilla. Her family didn't feel he had the cashflow required, so he was given five years to boost his credit rating. Heading off to the Reconquista wars, he returned to Teruel after that period, only to find that Isabel has been betrothed against her will to a local lord. Diego stole into her room and begged her for a final kiss. She refused and he died heartbroken at her feet. His funeral was the next day; in the middle of the service Isabel entered, dressed in mourning garb. She drew near the body, gave Diego the kiss he had desired, then died by his side. Stunned by the display of love, the townspeople buried them together. The tiny room is curtained, domed, and completely filled by large statues of Diego and Isabel, a work of Juan de Avalos from 1953. They're a little unnerving as they lightly touch stone hands, but to dispel the slightly brash sentimentality, take a look underneath at the mummies. There's another sculptural representation of the lovers on the attractive stairway leading up to the town from the railway station.

Museo Provincial ① *Tue-Fri 1000-1400, 1600-2100, Sat/Sun 1000-1400, free.* This museum is an interesting collection housed in a beautiful Renaissance civic building. There's an ethnographic section with traditional costumes, farming implements, and craft tools and a summary of the many sites in the province with Neolithic and Palaeolithic cave art, and Bronze Age skulls. Cat-lovers might baulk at the catskin purse, but conveys a desperately poor and underdeveloped region until frighteningly recently. The upper floors contain a good collection of ceramics from different periods; the Iberian examples from the first millennium BC are of especially high quality.

Plaza Carlos Castel and Plaza de San Juan Plaza Carlos Castel is almost universally known as Plaza del Torico, referring to the tiny bull that sits atop an oversized column in

its centre. It's the old town hub, and focus of the annual fiesta. There are some excellent Modernista façades on the square. The larger Plaza de San Juan is characterized by a black pyramid and dignified buildings, including the casino.

Los Arcos A beautiful piece of Renaissance architecture is the narrow aqueduct of Los Arcos. Built in the 16th century, it carried both water and people across the valley on its two levels of arches.

Dinópolis At the edge of town, by the Valencia highway, the brand new Dinópolis ⓘ *Jun-Sep daily 1000-2000 (Jul/Aug 0900-2200), rest of year Thu-Sun 1000-2000, last entrance 2 hrs before closing, €16 (€13 for under-12s)*, is an interactive-style modern museum dealing with the giant saurians but mainly aimed at young kids. There are dozens of skeletons and plasticky-looking replicas as well as a 3D cinema and playground area; the whole place is kitted out as a Jurassic forest. There's a frustrating lack of detailed information about the creatures on display, but the real

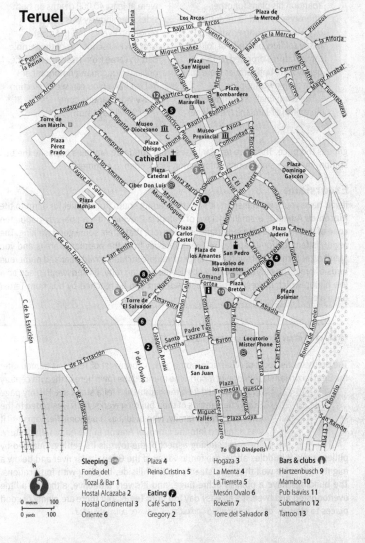

Teruel

Aragón Teruel

Sleeping ⬤	Plaza 4	Hogaza 3	Bars & clubs ◉
Fonda del	Reina Cristina 5	La Menta 4	Hartzenbusch 9
Tozal & Bar 1		La Tierreta 5	Mambo 10
Hostal Alcazaba 2	Eating ◉	Mesón Ovalo 6	Pub Isaviss 11
Hostal Continental 3	Café Sarto 1	Rokelin 7	Submarino 12
Oriente 6	Gregory 2	Torre del Salvador 8	Tattoo 13

To ⑥ & Dinópolis

⁞ Battle for Teruel

One of the bleakest and bloodiest episodes of the Spanish Civil War was the battle for Teruel in the winter of 1937-38. The Republicans were well on the way to defeat by this stage, but, in a last throw of the dice, moved on Teruel in December 1937. They quickly took much of the town, but resistance continued for weeks, courageously marshalled by the Nationalist commander Col Rey d'Harcourt. Franco decided to abandon his plans for other offensives in a bid to recapture the city. Heavy fighting ensued and many soldiers perished of cold as temperatures dropped to 18°C below zero; both armies were cut off from their own supplies.

The town finally surrendered on the eighth of January; the colonel and the bishop were taken prisoner and later shot. But Republican delight was short-lived as the Nationalist armies moved in once the blizzards had stopped. They recaptured the city in February after brutal fighting and two months later Franco reached the coast, breaking the Republic's main territory in two; the final blow. The International Brigades were involved in the Teruel campaign; it is estimated that there were at least 40,000 deaths on both sides. Hemingway was there to report on events, but the most evocative descriptions of the terrible battles came from the camera of the brilliant Hungarian photographer Robert Capa (you can see a selection at www.barranque.com/guerracivil/capa.htm).

gripe is the price. There are regular buses from Ronda de Ambeles opposite the bus station; there's a small tourist information kiosk open in summer.

Excursions

If you have your own transport, it's worth heading south from Teruel for a trip to the **Rincón de Ademuz**, a small enclave of Valencia Province. It's a sparsely populated zone of arid hills and wild indentations in the rock that offers some good walking. The region is famous for its apples but venture away from the populated areas and you stand a good chance of spotting a range of wildlife including wild boar and numerous birds of prey. The only place of any size is **Ademuz**, a pretty, if windswept, place on a low hilltop which makes the best base. Ademuz can be reached by bus from Teruel once a day.

Albarracín → *Colour map 5, grid A4.*

The pretty tourist town of Albarracín, some 38 km northwest of Teruel, is named after the Beni Razin family, Almoravid Moors who founded the town here in the 11th century

⁞ *If you want to go for a stroll, there's a good riverside walk below the town.*

and developed it as the capital of a taifa state, see History page 814. Little remains of their building works, for it was ceded to the Christian Azagra family, who held it as a personal fiefdom until it was annexed into the crown of Aragón in the early 14th century. The most striking aspect of the town is its setting. Guarded by pitiless rock, it huddles above the fertile valley of the Guadalaviar river and below a mighty defensive wall that runs steeply up the hillside, bristling with fortifications. The buildings have a pinkish ochre tinge, and it's very attractive, although a little overtouristed and twee. It's an easy day trip from Teruel, but there are plenty of good places to stay. ⤍ *For Sleeping, Eating and other listings, see pages 420-423.*

Sights

The nicest thing to do in Albarracín is to wander the narrow streets and climb up to the top of the imposing ramparts, but it's also worth dropping into the **cathedral** and, particularly, its museum. The cathedral, imposing from the outside and sporting a colourfully-roofed tower, is small and relatively unadorned inside. The star vaulting is a good piece of workmanship, and there is some wallpainting flanking the large coat-of-arms at the back of the coro. The Baroque organ is also a highlight. **Museo Diocesano** ① *1030-1400, 1600-1800, €1.80, the ticket is a joint one with 2 other attractions: Museo de Albarracín (a scant collection of historical odds and ends) and the Torre Blanca (a refurbished tower on the edge of town)*, has an undisputed highlight in its Flemish tapestries, a series depicting the life of Gideon and dating from the 16th century. The tourist office is just off the main square.

A torture and witchcraft exhibition at the **Torre Blanca** ① *Mon-Fri 1200-1400, 1700-2000, Sat/Sun 1100-1400, 1600-2000, €2*, gives an interesting, if predictably gruesome, overview of belief and punishment in the Middle Ages and later. Some 4 km from town, near the hamlet of **Rodeno de Albarracín**, is a good ensemble of *pinturas rupestres*, prehistoric art dating from the Neolithic period and depicting a range of animals over a number of adjacent sites.

Excursions

Beyond Albarracín is a large expanse of pineforest, originally planted for resin. It covers a range of low but intriguing mountains, with good walking and picnicking. At the far corner of the province, the small town of **Orihuela del Tremedal** has cobbled streets and an attractive Baroque church, **Iglesia de San Millán**; a good quiet little base for walking in the western hills of Teruel.

Sierra de Gúdar → *Colour map 5, grid A5.*

The Sierra de Gúdar is a high land of mesas and gullies where erosion seems to have acted with playful artistry. The region is notable for its architecture; the villages are filled with noble *palacios* in typical Aragonese style; these have three floors, the top one of which has an open gallery. Outside the towns are *masías*, chunky stone farmhouses originally designed with defence as well as homemaking in mind. These are beautiful buildings solildy built from the orange-gold stone of the region, but many are now derelict; the unsustainability of much of the farmland has exacerbated the population drain to the cities. Two of the area's most attractive towns are extremely confusingly named **Mora de Rubielos** and **Rubielos de Mora**. ▶▶ *For Sleeping, Eating and other listings, see pages 420-423.*

Mora de Rubielos

Some 30 km east of Teruel, Mora de Rubielos, has some imposing mansions and a superb 13th- to 14th-century **castle** ① *Sat/Sun 1030-1400, 1630-2030, Jul/Aug every day*, an outstanding piece of architecture and lord of all it surveys. Although suitably bristly and warlike outside, the interior is more comfortable than most citadels, with an attractive arched patio. There's a small **ethnographic museum** in the basement; there are also summer musical festivals held in the castle.

The Gothic **Iglesia de Santa María** dates from the 14th century and is also very harmonious, with intricate stonework detail. There's a small tourist office ① *Diputación 2, open year-round*.

Rubielos de Mora

Near to Mora de Rubielos, Rubielos de Mora is as gallant a village as anywhere in Aragón. The old part is entered via one of the stone-arched gates. In the plaza is the

huge **Casa del Marqués de Villasegura**, a late 17th-century structure typical of the region and massive in size. There's an imposing door, but the highlight is the superbly carved wooden eaves. After the marquises' financial demise, the building was used as a tile factory. Opposite the palacio is the **Ayuntamiento**, a 16th-century beauty with a dark, columned interior patio. **Plaza del Carmen** is another pretty part of the village; a plaque commemorates Franco's stay during the Civil War. **Iglesia del Carmen** is an unusual exuberant church; the nearby **Colegiata de Santa María** is a 17th-century affair with a colourful turret and 19th-century façade; the retablo inside portrays the life of the Virgin. The tourist office ① *Plaza Hispano América.*

Northern Sierra de Gúdar

If you're touring the region, head north from Rubielos de Mora through some of the Sierra de Gúdar's most spectacular country. **Noguereuelas** is another nice village on a hilltop with a couple of *hostales*; beyond here, through a region studded with golden farmhouses, you reach **Linares de Mora**, which has a large Baroque church and a small ruined castle perched on a rock.

Best reached via Mora de Rubielos, the village of **Alcalá de la Selva** has a haughty castle and a 16th-century church, **Iglesia de San Simón y San Judas**. The nearby **Sanctuario de Virgen de la Vega** is a popular pilgrimage spot. There's a year-round campsite with excellent bungalows there, **Los Alamos**, with some good walking in the immediate vicinity. North of Linares is the ski resort of **Valdelinares**, a smallish but decently equipped station with eight runs (no blacks) and some cheap *pensiones*.

Moving on from Linares de Mora, the cheerful windy town of **Mosqueruela** is worth a stop for its collection of stately *palacios*. **Iglesia de La Asunción**, is much modified but preserves its Gothic façade. The stone here is different to further back in the Sierra de Gúdar, a more sombre grey replacing the warm honey; the hills hereabouts are heavily terraced, but the centuries have not made farming here any better a prospect. Continuing on this road, you'll enter Castellón Province briefly before turning left into the heart of the Maestrazgo.

El Maestrazgo → *Colour map 5, grid A5.*

El Maestrazgo is named after its *maestros*, or masters; much of the land was claimed and ruled by campaigning knights of various orders during the Reconquista. One of them was El Cid, who inflicted several minor defeats on the Moors in this region. Like the Sierra de Gúdar, it's an area of strange and bare rocky hills cut by often-dry streams and narrow ravines. ▸▸ *For details of Sleeping, Eating and other listings, see pages 420-423.*

La Iglesuela del Cid

The first major village you reach if coming from Mosqueruela is La Iglesuela del Cid, named after the man himself, who is venerated in a small chapel 3 km out of town. The Templars founded La Iglesuela; what was once their castle is now the late Gothic Ayuntamiento, which preserves the 13th-century tower from the original structure; the **Torre de Nublo**. The church dates from the 16th century but was heavily modified in the 18th; the Plateresque façade survived.

Cantavieja

Northwest from La Iglesuela, Cantavieja is something of a must-see; a perfect but not prettified ensemble of Aragonese Gothic dramatically covering a ridge from where cliffs drop sharply into the gullies on either side. The nicest spot is the tiny porticoed plaza that separates the large porch of the **Iglesia de la Asunción** and the **Ayuntamiento**; a third side gives onto a terrace looking down into the ravine below. As well as its atmospheric architecture and location.

Mirambel

Beyond Cantavieja, Mirambel has been named 'the most beautiful village in Spain' by none other than the Queen, Reina Sofía. The village has a superb assemblage of historical harmony but doesn't have that lived-in feel that makes the other settlements in the area so attractive. That said, it's worth a look for its elegant mansions, cobbled streets and walls, once protected by a moat. The portal at the eastern end of town is particularly attractive, with a wooden gallery above decorated with ornately carved grille-work. There are some typical Aragonese seigneurial houses too, with their elaborate wooden eaves and top-floor galleries; note the metal shelves at the base of the doors to keep out the water when rain floods the stony streets.

Bajo Aragón and around

From Teruel to Bajo Aragón

From Teruel en route to Bajo Aragón, you pass through the mining region of **Las Cuencas**, also popular for caving. In the town of **Escucha**, the **Museo Minero** ① *Tue-Fri 1100-1400, 1600-1900, Sat/Sun 1000-1400, 1600-2000*, is an excellent coalmining museum housed in a real mine 200 m underground. In the northeast, beyond El Maestrazgo, **Bajo Aragón** has been dubbed the 'land of the drums' by the tourist board for its deafening Easter fiestas.

Molinos to Calanda

Near the town of Molinos, in the northern tip of El Maestrazgo, are a series of beautiful caves, **Las Grutas de Cristal**, with amazingly delicate formations as well as a range of spectacular stalactites and stalagmites. East of here, **Castellote** has a castle improbably set high above it on a rock. **Embalse de Santolea**, nearby, has a nice spot to swim in summer. There's some excellent walking and climbing; the GR-8 long-distance path crosses the area. Beyond here, the town of **Calanda** is famous as the birthplace of the filmmaker Luís Buñuel. There's a good *refugio* in the hamlet of Ladruñán at the far end of the *embalse*, **Refugio Crespol**, T978723060, that also serves good meals. By the *embalse*, **Camping Castellote**, T978887576, offers six-person bungalows for €57.

Alcañiz

The **castle** of Alcañiz' was once the Aragonese home of the Knights of Calatrava and is now a parador. Even if you're not staying it's worth going up for the views and the fortified approach. There are still some knightly elements though; the Gothic chapel is attractive, and there's a honeycomb of underground passages in the rock. The grassed inner courtyard is particularly pleasant too. Below in the lively town, the **Colegiata de Santa María** is massive in scale, including its Churrigueresque-style façade. The interior is lofty but not especially remarkable. The building also has a late Mudéjar tower. The town's best sight is below the **Colegiata** in the Plaza España, where the grandiose arched Gothic porch of the *lonja* (market, now a music school) abuts the typical Aragonese ayuntamiento with its noble eaves.

Valderrobres

East of Alcañiz, it's worth heading to lovely Valderrobres; a web of narrow streets leads to the river from its beautiful castle and elegant Gothic church with a rose-window above its layered portal. This corner of the province is beautifully unspoiled, with fairly lush green valleys and good walks.

● The village of Mirambel looks a little like a film-set; so much so that Ken Loach chose to
● make part of his movie Land and Freedom here in the mid-1990s.

Aragón Bajo Aragón & around

● Sleeping

Teruel *p413, map p415*

AL Hotel Reina Cristina, Paseo del Ovalo 1, T978606860, www.gargallo/hoteles.com. A smart option looking out from the bottom of the old town. Nice views and peaceful location.

A Parador de Teruel, Ctra Sagunto-Burgos s/n, T978601800, www.parador.es. Not the nicest of the paradores, this modern rendition sits on a hill 2 km to the west of town and boasts a tennis court among other amenities.

A Hotel Plaza, Plaza Tremedal 3, T978608655, hotelplaza@teruel.org. Well-located just by the Plaza San Juan.

B Hotel Oriente, Av Sagunto 5, T978601550, F978601567. A good option just across the bridge from the old town. Clean, efficient and modern facilities.

E Casa Garrido, C Solano 6, Ademuz, T963614472, www.ademuzaventura.com. Outside of the Teruel, this friendly *casa rural* with a generous restaurant is a nice place to stay. It's in the heart of town and the owners also run a tour company running excursions into the hidden corners of the enclave.

E Fonda del Tozal, C Rincón 5, T978601022. A lovely option in an old inn that dates back to the 16th century. The bedrooms are characterful and clean, and the management friendly, but you may have to remind them to turn the heating on.

E Hostal Alcazaba, C Joaquín Costa 34, T978610761, F978610762. In the heart of things, this *hostal* has clean modern rooms with bathroom.

F Hostal Continental, C Juan Pérez 9, T978602317. Unremarkable but clean, decent place close to the cathedral, with simple rooms with shared bathrooms.

Albarracín *p416*

Most of the several accommodation choices in the old town are pretty well-priced.

B La Casona del Ajimez, C San Juan 2, T978710321, www.casonadela jimez.arra kis.es. An excellent choice with highly original decor in an old townhouse. The rooms are all different and themed on the 3 cultures of Christianity, Islam and Judaism that once coexisted here. Two are split-level, while another features a 4-poster bed.

C-E Posada del Adarve, Portal de Molina 23, T978700304, is a very attractive old building with tastefully furnished rooms with varying degrees of luxury (and price) and a relaxing atmosphere.

F Hostal Palacios, C Palacios 21, T978700327, www.montepalacios.com. Attractive heated rooms, views a decent restaurant, and a terrace. Excellent value. Recommended.

G Bar Orijola, Plaza José Antonio s/n, Orihuela del Tremedal, T978714 016. A cheap option out of town.

Sierra de Gúdar *p417*

B Hotel Los Leones, Plaza Igual y Gil 3, Rubielos de Mora, T978804477, is a welcoming, friendly option in a *palacio* in the heart of the pretty town; its restaurant is also excellent.

B Jaime I, Plaza de la Villa s/n, Mora de Rubielos, T978800092, F978800067, right in the centre of town, with modernized rooms with most conveniences and a decent restaurant. Best place in the town.

B-C Hotel de la Villa, Rubielos de Mora, in the centre this stylish converted mansion is a great option.

E Tres Hermanos, C Renajo 14, T978802127 and **F La Venta**, C El Regajo 13, T978802018, both in Linares de Mora, are good places to stay and eat in this quiet hamlet, around which are several good walks.

El Maestrazgo *p418*

AL Hospedería de Iglesuela del Cid, C Ondevilla 4, La Iglesuela del Cid, T964443476, F964443461, is a luxurious option in a lovely restored *palacio*.

C Hotel Balfagón, Av Maestrazgo 20, Cantavieja, T/F 964185076, mabalgas@arrak is.es. An excellent hospitable country hotel with a good restaurant. They also hire dirtbikes for exploring the hills .

F Casa Amada, C Fuente Nueva 10, La Iglesuela del Cid, T964443373, offers good-value beds, with nice food in the downstairs restaurant.

F Fonda Guimera, C Agustín Pastor 28, Mirambel, T964178269, F964178608, a sensitively-constructed modern stone building with excellent rooms; make sure you get one of the heated ones in winter. Very low price for the quality.

G Pensión Julián, García Valiño 6, Cantavieja, T964185005. Very basic clean rooms, housed in a cracking old stone building, and good meals.

Bajo Aragón and around *p419*
L Torre del Visco, T978769015, F978769016, lies isolated, 12 km from Valderrobres (signposted near Fuentespalda). Lovingly restored, this farmhouse sits on wooded slopes above a pretty valley, perfect for walking. Its English owners have designed the place for total relaxation with attractive furnishings, log fire, many books, and excellent meals (half-board compulsory).
AL Parador de Alcañiz, Castillo de los Calatravos, Alcañiz, T978830400, is an obvious choice, housed in the castle compound with an elegant courtyard garden and great views. Alcañiz makes a decent base for a night.

🍴 Eating

Teruel *p413, map p415*
Teruel is full of shops selling Denominación de Origen ham, which is tasty if not extremely subtle.
€€€ La Menta, C Bartolomé Esteban 10, T978607532. One of Teruel's best options, a cheerful choice with class but no snobbery. The food lives up to the atmosphere, with the salads particularly good.
€€€ La Tierreta, C Francisco Piquer 6. A stylish, modern restaurant with an innovative takes on Aragonese cuisine and plenty of Mediterranean influence.
€€ Mesón Ovalo, Paseo del Ovalo 2. A good restaurant offering *turolense* (from Teruel) cuisine, with plenty of vegetable and fish dishes.
€€ Torre del Salvador, C Salvador 20. A popular local with a summer terrace, known in Teruel for its stuffed peppers and aubergines. Tapas and bigger meals available.
€ Café Sarto, C Joaquín Costa 12, T978602039. A good place for breakfast or a snack, with croissants and tapas.
€ Gregory, Paseo del Ovalo 6. Nice tapas bar with a summer terrace. Plenty of local specialities as well as good *pulpo* (octopus).

€ Hogaza, C Bartolome Esteban 8. Good place for cheap salads and rolls.
€ Rokelin, Plaza Carlos Castel. You can't miss this name intown; they're in the ham business, and this is the best of their bars. The food is cheap and plentiful.

Albarracín *p416*
There are a number of dark wooded bars and restaurants in town.
€€ Restaurante Aruila, Plaza José Antonio s/n, an attractive modern bar in Orihuela del Tremedal that serves tasty mountain food.
€€ Rincón del Chorro, C Chorro 15, T978710112, characterfull with a deserved reputation for its traditional fare including *rabo de toro* (stewed bull's tail) and *cabrito asado* (roast goat).

Sierra de Gúdar *p417*
See also Sleeping above.
€€ La Cazuela, C Aduana 2, Rubielos de Mora, T978804416, is another good eating option near the Ayuntamiento.

Bajo Aragón and around *p419*
€€ Guadalope, Plaza de España 8, T978830750. A lively bar serving good snacks and a good upstairs restaurant.

🍸 Bars and clubs

Teruel *p413, map p415*
Fonda del Tozal, C Rincón 5, T978601022. The bar in this historic fonda is big, busy, and characterful. There's frequent live music.
Hartzenbusch, C Salvador 20. A 1st floor bar by the Torre del Salvador. Good relaxing spot with frequent live jazz.
Mambo, C Commandante Fortea 16. A cheerful Caribbean sort of bar with palm trees and cocktails; they make a decent *caipirinha* with lemons.
Pub Isaviss, Plaza de Carlos Castel 14. A dark pub which expands onto the square in summer. Good hangout for winter whiskies to keep the cold at bay.
Submarino, C Santos Martir 6. A popular bar with mixed crowd and nautical decor.
Tattoo, C San Andrés 4. Teruel's most popular *discoteca*, open Thu-Sat nights with

● *For an explanation of sleeping and eating price codes used in this guide, see inside the*
● *front cover. Other relevant information is found in Essentials, see pages 47-56.*

La Rioja

Spain's most famous wine-producing area is confusingly not solely located in the province of the same name, but extends into Basque Álava and even a small part of Navarra, a small hop from Aragón. The Ebro Valley has been used for wine production since at least Roman times; there are numerous historical references referring to the wines of the Rioja region.

In 1902 a royal decree gave Rioja wines a defined area of origin, and in 1926 a regulatory body was created. Rioja's D.O. (denominación de origen) status was upgraded to D.O.C. (denominación de origen calificada) in 1991, with more stringent testing and regulations in place to ensure the high quality of the wine produced. Wine was formerly produced in cellars (bodegas) dug under houses; the grapes would be tipped into a fermentation trough (lagar) and the wine made there; a chimney was essential to let the poisonous gases created escape. Techniques changed with the addition of French expertise in the 19th century, who introduced destalking and improved fermentation techniques.

Nowadays, the odd wine is still made in the old underground bodegas, but the majority of operations are in large modern buildings on the edges of towns.

Although Rioja's reputation worldwide had sunk by the second half of the 20th century, it picked up in the 1990s and is now thriving. Sales are around the 220 million litre mark, about a quarter of which is exported, mostly to the UK, USA, Germany, Scandinavia, and Switzerland.

By far the majority of Riojas are red (85-90%); white and rosé wines are also made. There are four permitted red grape varieties (with a couple of exceptions), these being Tempranillo, which is the main ingredient of most of the quality red Riojas, Garnacha (grenache), Mazuelo, and Graciano. Many red wines are blends of two or more of these varietals, which all offer a wine something different. Permitted white varieties are Viura (the main one), Malvasia, and Garnacha Blanca.

The region is divided into three distinct areas, all suited to producing slightly different wines. The Rioja Alavesa is in the southern part

---

frequent promotions and very late closing. Good fun.

⊕ Entertainment

Teruel *p413, map p415*
Cines Maravillas, C San Miguel s/n, which shows more interesting fare than some.

⊛ Festivals and events

Teruel *p413, map p415*
Teruel's major fiesta is known as **La Vaquilla** and is celebrated around the 2nd Sun of **Jul**. One of the major events sees a bull led through the crowded streets on a rope.

El Maestrazgo *p418*
La Iglesuela del Cid's lively fiesta takes place in the first week of **Sep**.

⊖ Transport

Teruel *p413, map p415*
Bus Within the province, there are buses to **Alcañiz** 5 daily, **Albarracín** twice, **Ademuz** once, the towns around **Rubielos de Mora** once on weekdays (1430), and **Mosqueruela** (1630). There are long distance services to **Valencia** 5 times a day, **Zaragoza** 10 times, **Madrid** 4 times, **Barcelona** once, **Daroca** once, **Cuenca** once, and **Castellón** once.
Train Connections with **Valencia** 3 times a day, and **Zaragoza** 3 times a day.

of Euskadi and arguably produces the region's best wines, somewhat lighter and better balanced than some of the others. The Rioja Alta is in the west part of Rioja province and its hotter climate produces fuller-bodied wines, full of strength and character; parts with chalkier soil produce good whites. The Rioja Baja, in the east of Rioja province, is even hotter and drier, and favours Garnacha; wines from here don't have the same longterm ageing potential. Most of the best Rioja reds are produced from a combination of grapes from the three regions.

Oak aging has traditionally been an important part of the creation of Rioja wine; many would say that Riojas in the past have been overoaked but more care is taken these days and younger styles are more in fashion. The quality of individual Riojas varies widely according to both producer and the amount of time the wines have been aged in oak barrels and in the bottle. The words crianza, reserva, and gran reserva refer to the length of the aging process (see below), while the vintage date is also given. Rioja producers store their wines at the bodega until deemed ready for drinking, so it's common to see wines dating back a decade or more on shelves and wine lists.

Riojas are classified according to the amount of ageing they have undergone. A joven or cosechero wine is in its first or second year, and is typically fresh and fruity; many are made using the whole-grape carbonic maceration technique, giving a more complex, slightly bitter flavour, and a slight effervescence. A crianza is a wine at least two years old, with 12 months of life spent in oak casks (six for whites). A reserva is a wine at least three years old, of which 12 months at least must have been in oak (two years old and six months in cask for whites); while a gran reserva has spent at least two years in oak and three in bottle; these last two are only selected from good vintages.

Many of the bodegas accept visitors, but be sure to arrange the visit beforehand. The best places for winery visiting are Haro in the Rioja Alta, and beautiful Laguardia in the Rioja Alavesa.

Aragón Teruel Province: listings

Albarracín *p416*
There are 2 buses daily to **Albarracín** from **Teruel**.

Bajo Aragón and around *p419*
Five buses run daily between **Alcañiz** and **Teruel**.

There are 2 daily buses from **Alcañiz** to **Valderrobres**.

Directory

Teruel *p413, map p415*
Internet Ciber Don Luís, Plaza de la Catedral 4, and also at **Locutorio Mister**.
Post office C Yagüe de Salas s/n.
Telephone C San Andres 19, which also has decent rates for international telephone calls.

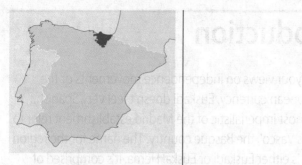

El País Vasco

✷ Footprint features

Introduction

Whatever your views on independence movements or the single European currency, Euskadi doesn't feel very Spanish. Even the most imperialistic of the Madrid establishment refer to it as 'El País Vasco', the Basque country. The name for the region in Euskara is either Euskadi or Euskal Herría. It's comprised of three provinces, Guipuzkoa (Guipúzcoa), Bizkaia (Vizcaya), and Áraba (Álava). Things are certainly different here; there's a strange language on road signs, weird sports are played to packed houses, it rains an awful lot, and there's a subtle vibrancy that infects even the most mundane of daily tasks.

Bilbao, has managed to superbly reinvent itself from declining industrial dinosaur to optimistic European city. **Guggenheim Museum** is a world-class building, but it's the vision and spirit that put it there that is even more invigorating. **San Sebastián** is perennially popular for its superb natural setting, and **Vitoria**, the peaceful Basque capital, is also very appealing. If one thing apart from the Guggenheim is guaranteed to delight first-time visitors, it's the food, or more accurately the food culture. From about 1900 in the evening until midnight or so, everyone lives in the street, walking, talking, drinking, and eating pintxos.

Euskadi isn't very large, which means that most of the rural areas are within easy reach of the three cities. The rugged coast has a few excellent **beaches**, and some very personable **fishing towns** that historically defined the Basque nation with the daring maritime expeditions they mounted in search of whales, cod, or glory. Inland, medieval towns still preserve an excellent architectural heritage, while **Laguardia**, is both one of the most attractive walled towns in Northern Spain and an important centre of the **Rioja wine region**. Outside the towns, the green hills and rocky peaks of this corner of the peninsula are an invitation into the open air.

★ **Don't miss...**

❶ **Bilbao's Casco Viejo** Snoop around Bilbao's Casco Viejo; it's tiny, but you get lost in it, page 455.

❷ **Guggenheim** Go to the Guggenheim either as a cynic or breathless with anticipation. It's good, page 459.

❸ **Laguardia** Stay in this beautiful hilltop village thoughtfully placed in some of Spain's top wine country, page 480.

❹ **San Sebastián** Eat out in San Sebastián; blow the bank on a Michelin constellation, eat your fill of *pintxos*, page 436.

❺ **Ondarroa or Lekeitio** Get to know Basque culture in a fishing town, all are very characterful places, pages 446 and 447.

❻ **Basque hill country** Check out the Basque hill country, go walking, and visit the great modern monastery of Arantzazu, page 441.

❼ **Vitoria** Vitoria's festival of the Virgen Blanca is one of Spain's liveliest parties, page 483.

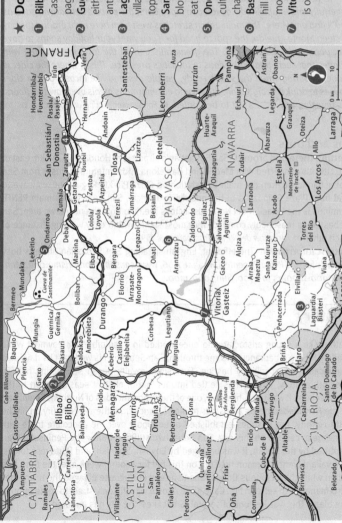

El País Vasco

San Sebastián/Donostia

→ *Phone code: 943; Colour map 2, grid A5; Population: 181,064.*

The sweep of La Concha bay and the hills overlooking it draw inevitable comparisons with Rio de Janeiro. Considered by many to be one of the peninsula's most beautiful cities, it's a place with a light and leisurely feel, and draws throngs of holiday-makers. With a superb natural setting, lovely sandy beaches, top restaurants, and a regular influx of international stardom during its film festival, it's a relaxed and enjoyable place that has recently been invigorated by the addition of a couple of excellent museums and a piece of world-class modern architecture in the Kursaal auditorium.

The pedestrianized old town lies at the foot of the Monte Urgull hill, and is cheerfully and unabashedly devoted to tapas bars; the pintxos here are as good as you'll find anywhere. The main beach stretches west from here right around the bay to steep Monte Igueldo, the spot to head for if you want your holiday snaps to have that panoramic postcard feel. The green hills behind the town are studded with villages that seem totally oblivious to the city's presence. This is where the cider is made; in spring when the stuff's ready, people descend like locusts on the cider houses to drink it straight from the vat and eat enormous meals over sawdust floors. It's amazing any cider's left to be bottled. ▶▶ *For Sleeping, Eating and other listings, see pages 435-439.*

Ins and outs

Getting there and around San Sebastián's airport is at Hondarribia, 20 km east of the city. It's connected with Madrid and Barcelona. Most interurban buses from San Sebastián leave from the main bus station on Plaza Pio XII. Regular buses leave to and from Plaza Guipúzcoa to the outerlying districts. San Sebastián's main RENFE terminus is the Estación del Norte just across the river from the new town area. San Sebastian is reasonably compact with most sights within easy walking distance of each other. ▶▶ *For further details, see Transport page 439.*

Tourist information The efficient, English-speaking San Sebastián office is busy but helpful ① *C Reina Regente 3, T943481166, www.sansebastianturismo.com, Mon-Sat 0900-1400, 1530-1900, Sun 1000-1400.*

History

Rather like a young aristocrat who once worked in a 'suitable' employment while waiting for the inheritance to come through, San Sebastián is well past its days as a significant port or military bastion. Ever since royalty began summering here in the 19th century, the city has settled into its role of elegant seaside resort to the manner born. It was once, however, one of the important ports of Northern Spain, part of the *Hermandad de las Marismas* trading alliance from the 13th century on. In the 18th century, the Basques established a monopoly over the chocolate trade with Venezuela, centred on this city. San Sebastián suffered during the Peninsular War; captured by the French, it was besieged by English, Spanish, and Portugese forces. The valiant French garrison held out on this hill for another week after the town had fallen while the victorious British, Spanish, and Portuguese pillaged the town; they also managed to set it on fire. Calle 31 de Agosto was the only street to come through the blaze. This was just one of several 'Great Fires' the city has endured.

A bright future...

It's difficult to exaggerate the flowering that has taken place since the return to democracy here. The Basque language, banned during Franco's dictatorship and in danger of a lingering death, has been pounced on by the young and is now spoken widely and ever-increasingly in the streets. There's a touching and understandable feeling that everything Basque is good: to walk into a bookshop and see Tintin and Captain Haddock foiling villains in streams of Euskara gives an idea of how things have changed in quarter of a century.

Despite the Basque authorities' best effort, terrorism still grabs more column inches in the foreign press than any other issue. It's a serious business but shouldn't cloud visitors' judgement. ETA is alive, active, and focused, but harming tourists in the Basque region is in complete opposition to their agenda; nearly all of their actions are targeted at the Madrid government in some way, or at Basques who are seen as collaborators. A huge majority of Basques deplore terrorism, but this doesn't mean that they don't feel strongly about independence: many do, and they shouldn't be confused with *etarristas*. For further inform-ation on ETA, see page 826.

Sights

The most lively part of San Sebastián is its old section at the eastern end of the bay. Although most of it was destroyed by the 1813 fire, it's still very characterful, with a dense concentration of bars, *pensiones*, restaurants, and shops. Protecting the narrow streets is the solid bulk of Monte Urgull, which also shelters the small harbour area.

Parte Vieja (Old Town)

El Muelle Beyond the town hall, San Sebastián's small fishing and recreational harbour, El Muelle is a pleasant place to stroll around. There's a handful of cafés and tourist shops, and you can see the fishermen working on their boats while their wives mend the nets by the water. Halfway round the harbour is a monument to "Aita Mari" (father Mari), the nickname of a local boatman who became a hero for his fearless acts of rescue of other sailors in fierce storms off the coast. In 1866 he perished in view of thousands attempting yet another rescue in a terrible tempest.

Motorboats to Isla Santa Clara in the middle of the bay leave from here, as do boats offering cruises round the harbour.

Museo Naval ⓘ *Paseo del Muelle 24, T943430051, Tue-Sat 1000-1330, 1600-1930, Sun 1100-1400, €1.20,* is a recently opened harbourside museum, which unfortunately succeeds in making a potentially intriguing subject slightly dry and lifeless. While there's plenty of information about Basque seafaring, the interesting aspects are hurried over, and there's little attempt to engage the visitor. Descriptions are in Spanish and Euskara only.

San Sebastián's **aquarium** ⓘ *Plaza Carlos Blasco de Imaz s/n; T943440099; www.aquariumss.com, Tue-Thu 1000-1900 (2100 in summer), Fri-Sun 1000-2000 (2200 in summer), €8, sharks fed at 1100 and 1600,* isn't bad at all, despite the high entry fee. The highlight is a massive tank brimming with finny things; fish, turtles, and rays, plus a couple of portly sharks to keep the rest of them honest. There's a good perspex tunnel through the tank, which can also be viewed from above. Viewing space can get crowded, particularly around shark-feeding time, which isn't quite as dramatic as it sounds.

El País Vasco San Sebastián/Donostia

Monte Urgull The bulk of Monte Urgull is one of several Donostia spots to climb up and appreciate the view. An important defensive position until the city walls were taken down in 1863, it saw action from the 12th century onwards in several battles, wars, and skirmishes. The hill is topped by a small fort, the **Castillo de la Mota** ① *Mon-Sun 1100-1330, 1700-2000, summer only*, once used as the residence of the town's alcalde and as a prison. It's got a small collection of old weapons, including a sword that belonged to the Moorish king Boabdil. There's also a large statue of Christ, the Monumento al Sagrado Corazón, which is not the only Rio-like aspect of San

San Sebastián

San Sebastián detail

Iglesia de Santa María del Coro In the heart of the old town, and with a façade about as ornate as Spanish Baroque ever got, the church of Santa María del Coro squats under the rocks of Monte Urgull and faces the newer cathedral across the city. After the exuberant exterior, the interior can seem a bit oppressive with low lighting, heavy oil paintings, and the numbing scent of incense. Above the altar is a large

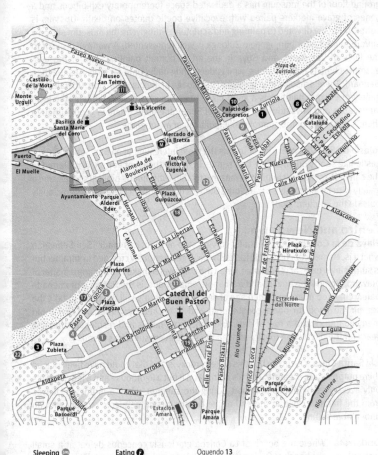

depiction of the man the city was named for, unkindly known by some as the 'pincushion saint' for the painful way he was martyred. Facing him at the other end of the nave is a stone crucifix in the unmistakable style of Eduardo Chillida, the late Basque sculptor, see box page .

Museo de San Telmo ① *Plaza Zuloaga 1, T943424970, Tue-Sat 1030-1330, 1600-1930, Sun 1030-1400, free.* The museum, set in a 16th-century Dominican convent, is worth a visit if only for its perfect Renaissance cloister set around a green lawn. The ground floor of the museum has a dedicated space for temporary exhibitions and a series of grave markers paired with evocative poetic quotes on death. Upstairs is currently mostly devoted to painting and sculpture. Fittingly, as the museum sits on a square named after him, Ignacio Zuloaga is well represented. A worthy sucessor to the likes of Velazquez and Goya in the art of portrait painting, one of the best examples here is his Columbus, who is deep and soulful (and far more Basque than Genoan). There's also a small memorial to Zuloaga in the plaza outside. Upstairs, the gallery of Basque painting is a good place to get an idea of how different the local landscapes and physiques are to those of Spain; the quality here is good, although there's not a sniff of the controversial, political, or avant-garde.

Iglesia de San Vicente This church is the most interesting of all San Sebastián's; a castle-like sandstone building that squats in the northeast of Parte Vieja. Started in the early 16th century, it features a massive retablo with various biblical scenes, and a gallery with an impressive organ. Jorge Oteiza's fluid, modern Pietá stands graciously outside the southern door.

Centro and New Town

Playa de la Concha This beautiful curving strip of sand, has made San Sebastián what it is. Named *concha* (shell) for its shape, it gets seriously crowded in summer but is surprisingly quiet at other times, when the chilly water makes swimming a matter of bravado. Behind the beach, and even more emblematic, is the Paseo, a promenade barely changed from the golden age of seaside resorts. It's still the place to take the sea air (so good for one's constitution) and is backed by gardens, a lovely old merry-go-round, and a row of desirable beachfront hotels and residences that still yearn for the days when royalty strolled the shore every summer season.

Isla Santa Clara Out in the bay this a pretty rocky island that could have been placed there purposely as a feature. There's nothing on it but a lighthouse and a jetty, and it's only accessible by public transport during the summer, when a motorboat leaves from the harbour close to the end of the beach. It is prime picnic territory with an unbeatable setting.

Ondarreta Where the beach of La Concha graciously concedes defeat at a small rock outcrop, the beach of Ondarreta begins. It is a good place to stay in summer, with less hustle and bustle than in the centre. Atop the rock sits the Palacio de Miramar; commissioned by the regent María Cristina in the late 19th century, it would not be out of place offering selective bed and breakfast in an English village.

The beach of Ondarreta gazes serenely across at the rest of San Sebastián from beyond the Palacio de Miramar. It's a fairly exclusive and genteel part of town, appropriately overwatched by a statue of a very regal Queen María Cristina. The beach itself feels a bit more spacious than La Concha and at the end the town gives way to the jagged rocky coastline of Guipúzcoa again. Integrating the two is **El Peine del**

● *Chillida asked to borrow helicopters from the US embassy to help place the sculpture, El Peine del Viento. They refused, and the sculptures were finally erected using a specially designed floating bridge.*

⁑ Bitter and twisted

You can't go far in the Basque lands without coming across a hauntingly contorted figure or sweep of rusted iron that signals a creation of Jorge de Oteiza or Eduardo Chillida. The powerful and original work of these two Basque sculptors is emblematic of the region, but the product of two very different men.

Jorge de Oteiza, forthright and uncompromising well into his 90s, was born in Orio in 1908. After ditching a medical career in favour of sculpture he taught in South America before his big breakthrough came when commissioned to create pieces for the façade of the visionary new monastery at Arantzazu in the early 50s. With his grey beard, leather jacket, beret, and thick glasses, Oteiza cut quite a figure on site, but the anguish and power he managed to channel into his Apostles and Pietá was something extraordinary. The Vatican prevented the erection of the 14 apostles for 18 years. Although he gave up sculpture for a long period, Oteiza has continued to strive for something beyond: he is preoccupied with relevance, famously saying that "a monument will be no more than a pile of stones or a coil of wire if it does not contribute to the making of a better human being, if it is not… the moulded key to a new kind of man".

Eduardo Chillida was born in 1924 in San Sebastián and in his youth appeared between the sticks for Real Sociedad before a knee injury. A sculptor of huge world renown, the spaces he creates within his work are as important as the materials that comprise it. Peine de los Vientos at San Sebastián and the Plaza de los Fueros in Vitoria are designed to interact dynamically with their setting, while his exploration of oxidised iron as a medium is particularly appropriate for Euskadi, built on the glories of a now-faded iron industry. Softer work in alabaster and wood is less confronting, but evokes the same theme of space. His recently opened museum outside San Sebastián houses a large cross-section of his massive output. Many view him as the world's greatest living sculptor.

The two were on bitter terms for many years; Oteiza, perhaps jealous of Chillida's rising profile, held the view that he had 'sold out', refused to use his name, and criticized him bitterly in public. Over the years there were accusations of plagiarism from both sides. Oteiza eventually had a change of heart, and after many peaceful overtures were rejected, they finally buried the hatchet in 1997 with the 'Zabalaga embrace' and, it would seem, that before Chillida's death, aged 78, in August 2002, they had become firm friends.

Viento, The Comb of the Wind, one of sculptor Eduardo Chillida's signature works. It consists of three twisted rusty iron whirls that at times do seem to be struggling to tame the ragged breezes that can sweep the bay.

Above Ondarreta rises the steep **Monte Igueldo** ① €1.10, which commands excellent views of all that is San Sebastián. It's not a place to meditate serenely over the panorama – the summit of the hill is capped by a luxury hotel and a slightly tacky fun-fair. The view makes it special though, and unforgettable in the evening, when the city's lights spread out like a breaking wave below. There's a funicular ① *runs 1100-2000 €0.80/1.50 return*, running up and down from a station behind the tennis club at the end of the beach. Otherwise it's a walk up the winding road beside it, which gives occasional views both ways along the coast. To reach Ondarreta and the funicular, walk or take bus number 16 from Plaza Guipúzcoa hourly/half-hourly in summer.

434 **Catedral de Buen Pastor** This simple and elegant neo-Gothic cathedral is light and airy with an array of geometric stained glass, but in reality, there's little to detain the visitor – it's more impressive outside than in. Students of poor-taste works of art will, however, have a field day – the Christ with sheep above the altar is upstaged by the painted choirboy with donation box in hand.

Gros

A bit more down-to-earth and relaxed than the rest of San Sebastián, Gros lies across the river and backs a good beach, which sees some decent surf. It's dominated by the Kursaal, but is also worth exploring for its *pintxos*.

Kursaal ① *Av Zurriola 1, T943003000, www.kursaal.org, guided tours €2 at 1330 weekdays, weekends 1130, 1230, 1330.* In a space derelict for three decades since the old Kursaal was demolished, these two stunning glass prisms opened their doors in 1999. Designed by Navarran architect Rafael Moneo to harmonize with the rivermouth, the sea, and 'communicate' with the hills of Uría and Urgull to either side, the concert hall has inspired much comment. The architect fondly refers to his building as 'two stranded rocks' – critics might agree – but the overall reaction has been very positive, and in 2001 the building won the European Union prize for contemporary architecture. The main building hosts concerts and conventions, while its smaller sidekick is an attractive exhibition centre. It's also the new home of the **San Sebastián Film Festival** and also houses an attractive café and an upmarket modern restaurant.

> **!** *The Kursaal looks at its most impressive when reflecting the setting sun, or when lit up eerily at night.*

Excursions → *See page 440 for trips further afield.*

→ *See page 440 for trips further afield.*

Museo Chillida-Leku

① *Bº Jauregui 66, T943336006, 1000-1500 Wed-Mon (summer 1900).* Museo Chillida-Leku is a very relaxing place to spend a few hours out of the city. The late Basque sculptor Eduardo Chillida, see box page , gracefully restored a 16th-century farmhouse with his own concepts of angles and open interior space. The lower floor, lit by a huge window, has a selection of large pieces; upstairs is some of his smaller, earlier work, as well as preparatory drawings. Around the house is a large park, which has 40-odd of his larger sculptures (these are changeable depending on exhibition commitments). It's a very peaceful place and shady place to stroll; the organized should pack a picnic.

Cider-houses

In the hills around Hernani and Astigarraga a short way south of town, apples are grown among stunning green hills. Although it's not hugely popular as a day-to-day drink in San Sebastián these days, cider has an important place in Guipúzcoan history. It's nothing like your mass-produced commercial ciders, being sharpish, yeasty, and not very fizzy. It's best drunk fresh, poured from a height to give it some bounce after hitting the glass. The cider is mostly made in the hills near San Sebastián in a great number of small *sagardotegiak*, or *sidrerías*. When it's ready, in early January, cider houses stoke up their kitchens, dust down the tables, and fling the doors open to the Donostian hordes, who spend whole afternoons eating massive traditional cider-house meals and serving themselves freely from taps on the side of the vats. It's an excellent experience even if you're not sold on the cider itself. Tradition has it that this lasts until late April or so, although several are now open year-round.

> **!** *The tourist office in San Sebastián has a map and list of the cider-houses; several in very picturesque locations with walking trails through the hills and valleys.*

The typical meal served starts with *tortilla de bacalao* (salt-cod omelette), continues with a massive slab of grilled ox, and concludes with cheese, walnuts, and *membrillo* (quince jelly, delicious with the cheese). The best of the places are the simpler rustic affairs with long, shared, rowdy wooden tables and floors awash with the apple brew, but these tend to be harder to get to. Expect to pay from €15-30 for the *menú sidrería*, which includes as much cider as you feel like sticking away.

😴 Sleeping

San Sebastián *p428, map p430*
Parte Vieja is the best spot for budget accommodation; there's also plenty in Centro around C San Martín.
LL Hotel María Cristina, C Oquendo 1, T943437600, www.westin.com. Tiny riverfront hotel that's difficult to spot – if you're in orbit. Taking up an entire block, its elegant sandstone bulk has cradled more celebrities than you could drop a fork at. All the luxury and class you'd expect, and prices that boot other 5-star hotels into the campsite class.
L Hotel Londres y Inglaterra, C Zubieta 2, T943440770, www.hlondres.com. Grand old beachfront hotel that is an emblem of the city's glory days. Great location and good service – if royalty don't drop by as often as they once did, no one's letting on.
AL Hotel Monte Igueldo, Paseo del Faro 134, T943210211, www.monteigueldo.com. It's all about location at this place at the top of Monte Igueldo; most of the rooms offer a spectacular view one way or another. It's hardly a peaceful retreat though, as the summit of the hill is shared with a tacky amusement park.
A Hotel Ezeiza, Av Satrustegui 13, Ondarreta, T943214311, www.hotelezeiza. com. Nicely situated at the peaceful western end of Ondarreta beach, this is a welcoming place with the added attraction of an excellent terrace bar.
A Hotel Niza, C Zubieta 56, T943426663, www.hotel niza.com. Slap bang on the beach, this hotel is an odd mixture of casual seaside and starchy formality. About half the rooms have views – some are better than the others, and some are noisy.
B Hostal Alemana, C San Martín 53, T943462544, www.hostalalemana.com. That rarest of beasts: an efficient modern hotel with warm personal service. Excellent

value for what's on offer, which is all the conveniences plus some nice views and a pretty breakfast room.
C Pensión Aida, C Iztueta 9, T943327800, aida@pensionesconencanto.com. Another good place to stay in Gros, and convenient for the station. The gleaming rooms are appealing, and breakfast in bed is a great way to start the day.
C Pensión Gran Bahía, C Embeltrán 16, T943420216, www.paisvasco.com/ granbahia. Very attractive luxury *pensión* convenient for both beach and Parte Vieja. The comfy beds sport leopard-print covers and the rooms are extremely quiet. Immaculately maintained, the place is run in belle-époque style by the *dueña*. Non-smoking.
C Pensión Kursaal, C Peña y Goñi 2, T943292666, www.pensionesconen canto.com. A good place to stay just across the river in Gros, and very near the beach. Big windows in attractive rooms with bathrooms and TV. Internet access. Recommended.
D Pensión Anne, C Esterlines 15, T943421438, www.pensionanne.org.es. Behind an imposing wooden door is a spotlessly new *pensión*. All the rooms are exterior and come with heating, TV, and optional bathroom.
D Pensión San Martín, C San Martín 10, T943428714. One of the better of the host of choices on this street. The rooms are good and comfy, and have bathrooms and TV. Very handy for the train station/heavy bags combination.
E Pensión Amaiur, C 31 de Agosto 44, T943429654, amaiur@telefonica.net. Situated in the oldest surviving house in the Parte Vieja (few others survived the 1813 fire), this is one of the best budget options in town. Lovingly decorated and sympathetically run, there are a variety of smallish but homely, carpeted rooms, most

El País Vasco San Sebastián/Donostia: listings

🔴 *For an explanation of sleeping and eating price codes used in this guide, see inside the*
⚫ *front cover. Other relevant information is found in Essentials, see pages 47-56.*

with satellite TV and some with balconies. Guests have free use of the pretty (stoveless) kitchen, and there's coin-operated high-speed Internet access. Highly recommended.

F **Pensión Aussie**, C San Jerónimo 23, T943422874. Long-established favourite of backpackers, particularly from south of the equator. Rooms vary in size and are run on the hostel principle by the unpredictable boss, inevitably nicknamed Skippy.

F **Pensión San Lorenzo**, C San Lorenzo 2, T943425516, www.infonegocio.com/pensionsanlorenzo. A friendly star of the old town near the Bretxa market. Admirably, the well-priced rooms are not only brightly decorated but come with TV, fridge, kettle and piped radio. Some rooms come with shower and basin only, others with full bathroom. Internet access for €2/hr with 15 mins complimentary. It's a quiet place and is highly recommended, but fills very fast.

Camping
Camping Igueldo, Paseo Padre Orkolaga 69, T943214502, F943280411. Open all year, this big San Sebastián campsite is back from Ondarreta beach behind Monte Igueldo.

---

❶ Eating

San Sebastián *p428, map p430*
San Sebastián has a strong claim to the title of gourmet capital of Spain, with some seriously classy restaurants dotting the city and the hills around. It's also a great place for crawling around bars eating *pintxos* ; the best zone for this is the Parte Vieja. Gros is a quieter but equally tasty option.

€€€ **Casa Nicolasa**, C Aldamar 4, T943421762. This simple and gracious second-floor dining room is the seat of one of the city's best restaurants. The emphasis is on seafood – the *almejas* (small clams) with trout roe are superb – and the service is restrained and attentive.

€€€ **Kursaal Restaurant**, Av Zurriola 1, T943003162. One of several restaurants overseen by the top local chef Martín Berasategui, this is attractively set in the Kursaal and features the most modern of Basque *nouvelle cuisine*. For the quality on offer, it's not too dear; you can eat well for €50 odd a head, and there are *menús de*

degustación for €32.45 and €40.90 (no drinks), as well as a daytime one for €33.05 all inclusive.

€€€ **Panier Fleuri**, Paseo Salamanca 2, T943424205. A bright and airy split-level restaurant with a French-inspired menu and an emphasis on fresh market produce and charcoal grilled meats.

€€€ **Zuberoa**, Bº Iturriotz 8, T943491228, closed Sun night and Mondays. Outside San Sebastián, near the town of Oiartzun/Oyarzun is the lair of top chef Hilario Arbelaitz and his brothers. Actually it's far from being a lair, rather an attractive stone farmhouse with a wooden porch and terrace. Arbelaitz combines an essential Basqueness with a treatment inspired by the very best of French and Mediterranean cuisine. Everything is delicious, from a typical fish soup to the sort of thing not even dreamed of elsewhere, such as a grapefruit, spider crab, and trout roe jelly with potato and olive oil cream. For a real gastronomic experience, order the €73 *menú de degustación*, a once-in-a-lifetime 7-course sonata of a meal.

€€ **Barbarin**, C Puerto 21, T943421886. A well-priced restaurant specializing in local seafood. The *rollitos de txangurro*, fried crab rolls, are especially tempting.

€€ **Oquendo**, C Oquendo 8, T943420932. A good, fairly formal restaurant near the Hotel Maria Cristina, serving a range of fresh fish around €18 a plate. The front's got some good bartop eating, and the photo wall from the San Sebastián Film Festival is great for testing your silver-screen knowledge.

€€ **Restaurante San Martín**, Plazoleta Funicular, T943214084. Next to the Igueldo funicular, this pretty house-on-a-hill is a restaurant specializing in fish and the odd game-bird. Outdoor eating and some great views from the dining room.

€€ **Sansonategi**, Bº Martindegi s/n, T943553260. One of the few cider-houses to be open for meals year-round. Rates about midway on the authentic scale, and offers the traditional *menú sidrería* for €24, as well as good à la carte choices.

€ **Casa Marita**, C Euskal Herría 7, T943430443. Fairly touristy restaurant with good wholesome roasts, some decent seafood and a *menú* for €15 in the evenings. Intriguing horsey fresco work.

⦂ Secrets and pies

Eating is a large part of life all through the Basque country, but San Sebastián is the food capital of the region, perhaps because people seem to have more time and cash on their hands. In the city and the hills around are several of the best restaurants in the business, and modern Guipúzcoan chefs are making waves around the world.

A more unusual aspect is the *txokos*, or gastronomic societies. While these exist all across the region, Donostia is their spiritual home. The vast majority are private, and with an all-male membership. The three key parts of a *txoko* are a members' lounge, a dining room, and a vast kitchen. The members gather to cook, swap recipes for sauces, and prepare massive gourmet meals which are then devoured by the men, friends and family. There's no way for the casual tourist to access this scene except by invitation, see page 61; the best bet is to make friends with a member; look around San Sebastián for tubby men with a twinkle in their eye.

A similarly social but more inclusive scene can be found at the *sagardotegiak*, or *sidrerías*, the cider-houses that speckle the hills to the south of the city. The apples are harvested in autumn and when the cider is ready, the cider houses fling their doors open to the public who gather in the large sawdust-covered rooms to eat and drink massively. The cider is flat and sourish, and you pour your own directly from the huge kegs in the room. The more height you get on the pour, the better, as it gives the drink some fizz, and it should be poured in small amounts and downed immediately. The traditional meal served at these places starts with *tortilla de bacalao*, cod omelette, which is backed up by a massive *chuletón* (T-bone steak), and followed by cheese, *membrillo* (quince jelly), and walnuts. Most of the *sagardotegiak* are only open during March and April, although some are year-round. The best time to go is Saturday or Sunday lunch. The more traditional ones are more fun than the frilled-up restaurant-like ones.

€ **Txalupa**, C Calbetón 3, T943429875. The restaurant under this bar does a decent *menú del día* for €9.50, which rises to €12 at weekends. Standard but tasty Basque fare.

Pintxo bars and cafés

Bar Ondarra, Av de la Zurriola 16. Opposite the Kursaal exhibition centre in Gros, this is a decent bar with a small street level and an underground den featuring regular live jazz and soul. Good *pintxos*.

Bar Garriti, C San Juán 8. An unglamorous bar with a mighty impressive spread of *pintxos* during the day and early evening.

Café de la Concha, Paseo de la Concha s/n, T943473600. A pretty place to stop for a coffee or a glass of wine during a stroll along the beach. Decent restaurant, good views.

Casa Gandarias, C 31 de Agosto 25, T943428106. A busy bar near the Santa María

church with a pricey adjoining restaurant. The *pintxos* are good, but you virtually need a retina scan to use the bathroom.

Ganbara, C San Jeronimo 21, T943422575. A fairly upmarket bar and *asador* with a worthwhile array of *pintxos* to accompany the cheerfully poured wine.

Garbola, Paseo Colon 11, T943285019. A local legend in its own *pintxo* -time for its scrumptious mushroom creations and *caipirinhas*, this Gros bar also offers more unusual snacks, such as kangaroo and shark.

Kursaal Café, Av Zurriola 1, T943003162. The café is an excellent spot for an early evening *pintxo* and drink, with superb views over the rivermouth and sea.

La Cepa, C 31 de Agosto 7, T943426394. Perenially and deservedly popular bar lined with hams and featuring the head of a particularly large *toro* on the wall. Good

atmosphere and *pintxos* and *raciones* to match.

La Cuchara de San Telmo, C 31 de Agosto 28 (back), T943420840. An extraordinary bar up the side of the museum. The kitchen serves made-to-order gourmet dishes in miniature, which cost €1.50-2.50. Original and inspiring!

⊙ Bars and clubs

San Sebastián *p428, map p430*
Parte Vieja has many options, and the cross made by Calles Larramendi and Reyes Católicos near the cathedral is full of bars. There's studenty nightlife around Calle San Bartolomé just back from the beach

Altxerri Bar, C Reina Regenta 2. An atmospheric cellar bar that regularly showcases live jazz and other acts. Draws an interesting crowd and is worthwhile even if there's nothing on.

Bataplán, Playa de la Concha s/n, T943460439. San Sebastián's most famous *discoteca*, right on La Concha beach. Open Thu-Sat for a smart young crowd from midnight on. The music is pretty much what you'd expect for a resort club; mostly club anthems and pop crowd pleasers. Rises to prominence during the film festival when it hosts various after-parties. €12-15 entry.

Bideluze, Plaza Guipúzcoa 14, 2 floors of eccentric furniture on the south side of Plaza Guipúzcoa, serving some food downstairs.

El Nido, C Larramendi 13, A sizeable pub that fills after work and doesn't empty again until late. Friendly crowd and board games.

Garagar, Alameda del Boulevard 22, T943422840. Slightly overpriced pub at the edge of the Parte Vieja with some comfy booths. Keeps 'em pouring until 0200 most nights (0400 at weekends), and it's much more relaxing than some of the other tourist-oriented late-openers. DJ at weekends.

Kandela, C Escolta Real 20, Antiguo. This bar in the suburb of Antiguo usually features live bands from Thu-Sun. It ranges from rock to pop and usually kicks off at about 2300. €6 entry includes a drink.

Komplot, C Pedro Egaña 5, T943472109.

Small and *à la mode* club featuring probably the best house music in San Sebastián.

Ku, Monte Igueldo s/n. Atop the Igueldo hill at the end of Ondarreta beach is one of the city's more glamorous discos, with a smart mixed crowd. Usually goes later than anywhere.

Rotonda, Playa de la Concha 6, T943429095. Another club on La Concha beach and open very late weekend nights. The music hovers around popular dance, with some salsa and reggae thrown in as required.

Soma 107, C Larramendi 4, T943468810. Every facet of this remarkable bar is devoted to making the smoking of *porros* as chilled as possible. It's almost a dope centre rather than a mere bar, with internet, books, food, and two levels of seating sensitively decorated with cool murals, graffiti and paintings.

⊙ Entertainment

San Sebastián *p428, map p430*
Bullfighting Near the stadium is the brand new bullring, Illumbe, which was inaugurated in 1998 and includes a massive cinema complex. The city had been without a bullring since 1973, when the famous **El Chofe**, in Gros, was demolished.

Football Estadio de Anoeta is the home of **Real Sociedad**, the city's football team. Given the title 'Real' (Royal) in 1910 by the king, who spent much time in the city, the club is one of comparatively few to have won the Spanish league title, which it managed twice running in 1981 and 1982. Paseo de Anoeta 1, T943462833, www.real-sociedad-sad.es. Tickets €24-39 (sold at the stadium from the Thu afternoon before a game to the Sat evening, then 2 hrs before the kick off on Sun).

⊛ Festivals and events

San Sebastián *p428, map p430*
19-20 Jan, **Tamborrada** is the day of the 'pincushion saint' celebrated with a deafening parade of drummers through the streets from midnight on the 19th.
Week before 15 **Aug**, the **Aste Nagusia** or 'big week' kicks off in San Sebastián with world-renowned fireworks exhibitions.
On third week of **Sep** is the **International Film Festival**.

O Shopping

San Sebastián *p428, map p430*
La Bretxa, Plaza de Bretxa, San Sebastián.
Market complex in the old town.
Solbes, C Aldamar 4, San Sebastián.
A delicatessan and wine shop with a
high-quality line-up that isn't
particularly cheap.

▲ Activities and tours

San Sebastián *p428, map p430*
Barco de Ocio runs trips around the bay,
half-hour duration, Sat and Sun am and
pm hourly departures, €5.50 leaves from
half-way along aquarium wharf.
There's a sightseeing bus that runs: Mon,
Wed, Thu 3 times a morning; Fri-Sun 3 times
a morning, 2 times an afternoon. Ticket (€9)
valid for 24 hrs, hop-on, hop-off system.
There's also a small tourist 'train' running
around streets. It leaves every hour from
Teatro Victoria Eugenia.

⊖ Transport

San Sebastián *p428, map p430*
Bus Local buses (no 92) go travel to **Museo
Chillida-Leku** from C Oquendo every 30
mins on the half-hour. Other shorter-haul
buses to Guipúzcoan destinations leave from
the central Plaza Guipúzcoa. Destinations
include **Zumaia**, **Zarautz**, **Azkoitia**, **Tolosa**,
Oiartzun, **Hernani**, **Astigarraga**, all with
very frequent departures. There are buses to
Bilbao from the bus station every 30 mins
weekdays, every hour at weekends operated
by PESA and ALSA, 1 hr 20 mins, €5.93 and
to **Vitoria**, 7 buses a day with ALSA, 1¾ hrs,
€6.55. There are services to **Madrid**
(**Continental**), and most major Spanish cities.
The company offices are on Paseo Vizcaya
and Av Sancho el Sabio on either side of the
bus bays.
Cycle hire **Bici Rent Donosti**, Av de la
Zurriola 22, San Sebastián, T943279260.
Open from 0900 till 2100 every day, this shop
on Gros beach rents bikes by the hour and
by the day. They're not cheap at €18 per

day, but there's a decent range, and the staff
will help with planning trips, etc.
Train Euskotren connects the city with
other Basque destinations on the coast and
inland: its hub is Amara, on Plaza Easo in the
south part of the new town. **Bilbao** is served
hourly via the coast (2¾ hrs, €5.50). There
are 11 trains a day for **Vitoria**. There are
several mainline train departures to **Madrid**
and other Spanish cities, as well as **Hendaye**
in France.

❶ Directory

San Sebastián *p428, map p430*
Hospital Hospital Nuestra Señora de
Arantzazu, Av Doctor Begiristain 115, San
Sebastián, T943007000.
Internet **Click in D@ House**, C San Martín
47, San Sebastián, 0930-1400, 1600-2130,
Sun 1030-1400, 1600-2130,€3/hr.
Zarranet, C San Lorenzo 6, San Sebastián,
T943433381. A good place to get online,
with a fast connection at €3 per hr. Open
1000-2200 daily.
Donosti-Net, C Embeltrán 2, San Sebastián,
C San Jerónimo 8, T943429497. An internet
café in the heart of the old town, which also
offers a left-luggage service. Open
0900-2300 daily. €3.30 per hr.
Ciber Sare, C Aldamar 3, San Sebastián,
T943430887. Another good internet option
with heaps of terminals. Open Mon-Fri
1030-1400, 1500-2300, Sat 1030-1400,
1600-2200, Sun 1630-2200. €0.05 per min.
Laundry **Lavomatique**, C Iñigo 4, San
Sebastián. Self-service laundry in the Parte
Vieja open Mon-Fri 0930-1300, 1600-1930,
Sat 1000-1400. Also does a drop-off service.
Wash'n Dry, C Iparragirre 6, San Sebastián,
T943293150. This Aussie laundromat across
the river in Gros offers self-serve and drop-off
facilities. The friendly owner is a mine of
information about the city. Typical wash 'n'
dry €10, service wash €14.
Post Paseo de Francia s/n.
Useful addresses and numbers
The emergency number for all necessities is
T112, while T091 will take you to the local
police. Policia Municipal San Sebastián, C
Larramendi 10, T943450000, police station.

Around San Sebastián

Guipúzcoan Coast

Crossing the French border, the first stretches of Spain are well worth investigating, starting with the very first town. Hondarribia is a very beautiful walled place completely free of the malaise that seems to afflict most border towns; if you don't mind a few day-trippers, this is one of the most beautiful towns in Euskadi. It's a good place to stay, but is easily reached as an excursion from San Sebastián too. ⏵ *For Sleeping, Eating and other listings, see pages 444-446.*

Hondarribia/Fuenterrabia → *Colour map 2, grid A5.*
This old fishing port sits at the mouth of the river Bidasoa looking directly across at France, a good deal more amicably now than for much of its history. The well-preserved 15th-century walls weren't erected just for decoration, and the city has been besieged more times than it cares to remember. Hondarribia's tourist office ① *C Ugarte 6, www.bida soaturismo.com.*

❖ There are some very nice walks around the river and in the hills above, including some marked trails; ask at the tourist office for further details.

Although there's a fishing port and a decent beach, the most charming part of Hondarribia is the walled part, a hilly grid of cobbled streets entered through arched gates. The stone used for many of the venerable old buildings seems to be almost luminous in the evening sun. The hill is topped by a plaza and a 16th-century palace of Charles V, now a parador; its imposing bulk is offset by a very pretty courtyard. Nearby, the Iglesia de Santa María de Manzano is topped by a belltower and an impressive coat-of-arms. In 1660, María Teresa, daughter of Philip IV, married Louis XIV of France, the Sun King, here.

Plaza Guipúzcoa is even nicer than the main square, with cobbles and small but ornate buildings overhanging a wooden colonnade. Outside the walls, there are two ports, an old and a new. Near the new one is the cala asturiaga, where there are a few remnants of a Roman ship and anchorage.

West of Hondarribia
From Hondarribia, the GI-3440 rises steeply towards the east, resulting in some fantastic views over a long stretch of coastline. Before reaching San Sebastián, it's worth stopping at **Pasaia/Pasajes**, the name given to all the towns that cluster around a superb natural harbour 6 km east of San Sebastián.

Inland from San Sebastián

Guipúzcoa is crisscrossed by valleys that are lush from rainfall and dotted with small towns, some agricultural centres for the surrounding farmland, some seats of heavier Basque industry such as cement or paper manufacture. In many ways this is the 'real' Basqueland, and the smaller, poorer communities are still where separatism flourishes. The valleys also conceal beautiful churches (as well as the massive Loiola basilica), and plenty of walks and picnic spots. Due to Euskadi's good transport connections, many of these places are within easy daytrip range of both San Sebastián and Bilbao, but there are good accommodation options, especially in *casas ruralesor agroturismos*, usually Basque farmhouses with good welcoming accommodation in the heart of the countryside. ⏵ *For Sleeping, Eating and other listings, see pages 444-446.*

① *Mon-Sun 1000-1300, 1500-1900.* This is a strange one. A massive basilica, not quite St Peter's or St Paul's but not very far off, standing in the middle of Guipúzcoan pasture land. All is explained by the fact that St Ignatius, founder of the Jesuits, see page 442, was born here. The house where he first saw daylight has bizarrely had the basilica complex built around it; it's now a museum.

The most arresting feature of the basilica from a distance is the massive dome, which stands 65 m high. Designed by Carlo Fontana, an Italian architect from Bernini's school, it's topped by an ornate cupola. Lavish is the word to describe the rest of the decoration of the church; Baroque haters and minimalist gurus will probably drop dead on the spot. The building is designed to be viewed from a distance – this is the function of the formal promenade in front of it – and, as the visitor approaches, the intricacy of the decoration becomes apparent. Inside, the Baroque style verges on (to some, far surpasses) the pompous, with a silver-plated statue of Iñigo himself gazing serenely at somevery elaborate stonework and massive slabs of marble.

> ⁑ *The best time to visit is during the week, when hordes of elderly pilgrims descend to pay their respects to the saint or the grandiosity of the building.*

Oñati and Arantzazu → *Colour map 2, grid A4.*
The town of Oñati is one of the most attractive in the region and has a proud history as a university town and, until the mid-19th century, as a semi-independent fief of the local lord. Universidad de Sancti Spiritus was established in 1540 and is a beautiful example of cultured Renaissance architecture with an attractive colonnaded quadrangle. The stately red-balconied Casa Consistorial overlooks the main square where the two principal pedestrian streets, Calles Zaharra and Barria, meet. These streets are the centre of the lively weekend nightlife as well as being the town's major axes. Oñati's tourist office is on Plaza de los Fueros. There's some excellent walking to be done in this area, with views of one of the most beautiful parts of Euskadi.

Sanctuario de Arantzazu
Some 9 km south of Oñati is the Franciscan Sanctuario de Arantzazu, perching on a rock in a valley of great natural beauty.The basilica, built in the 1950s, is one of the most remarkable buildings in Euskadi. Incredibly avant-garde for the time, its spiky stone exterior is a reference to the hawthorn bush; according to tradition, a statue of Mary was found by a shepherd in 1468 on the spines of a hawthorn. A tinkling cowbell had led him to the spot, and the discovery ended years of war and famine in the area. The statue now sits above the altar, surrounded by the visionary abstract altarpiece of Luzio Muñoz. Although it appears to be made of stone, it's actually treated wood, and 600 sq m of it at that. Above the iron doors, sculpted by Eduardo Chillida, are Jorge Oteiza's fluid apostles and Pietá. He created great controversy by sculpting 14 apostles; for years they lay idle near the basilica as the Vatican wouldn't permit them to be erected. In the crypt, the impressive paintings of Néstor Basterretxea also caused problems with the church hierarchy. He originally painted the crucifixion backwards; when this was censured, he agreed to repaint it but with an angry Jesus. He succeeded – his powerful red Christ is an imposing figure.

West from San Sebastián

The coast west of San Sebastián is characterized by some fairly muscular cliffs placated by a few excellent beaches, a popular summer playground. As with Vizcaya, the area's history is solidly based on the fishing of anything and everything from anchovies to whales. While Zarautz's aim in life seems to be to try and emulate its big

Army of Christ

There can be few organizations that have had such an impact on all levels of world history than the Society of Jesus, or Jesuits. Their incident-filled five centuries of existence matches the strange life of their founder, Iñigo de Loiola, a Basque from a small town in the valleys of Guipúzcoa.

Born in 1491 to a wealthy family, he was the youngest of 13 kids. Sent as a pageboy to the court of Castile, he embarked on the life of a dandy, gambling, womanizing and duelling. Joining his brother in attempting to relieve the French siege of Pamplona, he managed to persuade the garrison commander to continue the defence of what was already a lost cause. The few men held out for several days, but finally the defences were blown apart. Iñigo, ready to die with sword in hand, was badly wounded in the legs by a cannonball. After being taken prisoner and operated on, he was sent home on a stretcher by the French, who admired his courage. His leg didn't heal, however, and it had to be rebroken and set. Although near to death several times, the bones eventually healed, but the vain Iñigo realized to his horror that a knob of bone still protruded from his leg, which had become shorter than the other. Desperate to once again strut his stuff as a dashing courtier, he ordered the doctors to saw the bone off and lengthen the leg by repeated stretching. He took some time to recover from this agonizing procedure (without anaesthetics).

During his boredom and pain, he began to read the only books at hand, the lives of the saints and a book on Jesus. Finally recovered in 1522, he set off on a journey, hoping to reach Jerusalem. Not far from home, riding muleback, he came across a Moor, with whom he argued about the virginity of Mary in her later life. When they parted company at a fork in the road, Iñigo decided that if his mule followed the Moor, he would kill him, and if it went the other way, he would spare him. Luckily the mule went the other way.

After further enlightening experiences, and a spell in jail courtesy of the Inquisition, Iñigo ended up in Paris, meditating on what later became his Spiritual Exercises. His sceptical roommate was Francis Xavier, another Basque, whom Iñigo eventually won over. He and some companions travelled to Rome and, with the Pope's blessing, formed the Society of Jesus.

Iñigo died in 1556 and was canonized along with Francis Xavier in 1609. Since then the Jesuits, 41 saints on, have shared his passion for getting the hands dirty, being involved in education, charity, and, more sinister, politics. They are a favoured target of conspiracy theorists, who see them as the real power behind the Vatican – the top Jesuit, the Superior General, is often called the 'Black Pope'.

For many centuries, however, the Jesuits were the prime educational force in western Europe and the New World: they have been called the 'schoolmasters of Europe'. The reducciones, communities of native Amerindians that they set up in Paraguay and Argentina were a brave and enlightened attempt to counteract slavery. These efforts, made famous by the film The Mission, were lauded by Voltaire as "a triumph of humanity which seems to expiate the cruelties of the first conquerors". As a direct result of these works they were expelled from South America and Spain. In more recent times, the Jesuits have again courted the displeasure of western powers by advocating human rights in South America, a so-called liberation theology seen as a grave danger to US musclepower in the region.

brother Sebastián just along the coast, Getaria is a particularly attractive little port. A further 5 km along, Zumaia may lacks the charm of its neighbour, but has the worthwhile Museo Ignacio Zuloaga to see. ▸▸ *For Sleeping, Eating and other listings, see pages 444-446.*

Zarautz → *Colour map 2, grid A4.*

While similarly blessed with a beautiful stretch of sandy beach and a characterful old town, like its neighbour San Sebastián, Zarautz has suffered from quick-buck beachfront high-rise development, which seems to appeal to the moneyed set who descend here by the thousand during the summer months. Nevertheless, despite the rows of bronzed bodies and the prudish but colourful changing tents, it can be quite a fun place. There's a good long break for surfing – one of the rounds of the world championship is often held here, and there's scope for more unusual water sports such as windboarding.

The old town is separated from the beach by the main road, giving Zarautz a slightly disjointed feel. There are a few well-preserved medieval structures, such as the Torre Luzea, and a handful of decent bars. Zarautz is known for its classy restaurants; after all, there's more to a Basque beach holiday than fish 'n chips. The tourist office is on the main street through town.

Getaria/Guetaria → *Colour map 2, grid A4.*

Improbably perched on a hunk of angled slate, Getaria is well worth a stop en route between Bilbao and San Sebastián. Despite being a large-scale fish cannery, the town is picturesque with cobbled streets winding their way to the harbour and, bizarrely, through an arch in the side of the church. Getaria gets its fair share of passing tourists, which is reflected in the number of *asadors* that line its harbour and old centre. For an unbeatable authentic feed, grab a bottle of sprightly local *txakoli* and wash it down with a plate of grilled sardines – you'll turn your nose up at the canned variety for ever more.

Iglesia de San Salvador is intriguing, even without the road that passes under it. The wooden floor lists at an alarming angle; to the faithful in the pews the priest seems to be saying mass from on high.

You won't stay long without coming across a statue of **Juan Sebastián Elkano**, winner of Getaria's most famous citizen award for 480 years running, although fashion designer Cristobal Balenciaga has come close in recent times. Elkano, who set sail in 1519 on an expedition captained by Magellan, took command after the skipper was murdered in the Philippines. Sailing into Seville with the scant remnants of the expedition's crew, he thus became the first to circumnavigate the world. Not a bad finish for someone who had mutinied against the captain only a few months after leaving port.

Beyond the harbour, the wooded hump of San Antón is better known as **El Ratón** (the mouse), and it certainly does resemble that rodent. There are good views from the lighthouse at its tip; if the weather is clear you can see the coast of France arching northwards on the horizon.

Zumaia/Zumaya → *Colour map 2, grid A4.*

Some 5 km further along, Zumaia is not as attractive, but has the worthwhile **Museu Zuloaga** ① *Carretera San Sebastián-Bilbao, T943862341, Wed-Sun 1600-2000 Apr to Sep only.* Ignacio Zuloaga, born in 1870, was a prominent Basque painter and a member of the so-called 'Generation of 98', a group of artists and thinkers who symbolised Spain's intellectual revival in the wake of the loss of the Spanish-American War, known as 'the disaster'. Zuloaga lived in this pretty house and garden, which now contains a good portion of his work as well as other paintings he owned, which include some Goyas, El Grecos, Zurbaráns and others. Zuloaga is

most admired for his expressive portraiture, with subjects frequently depicted against a typically bleak Spanish landscape. In the best of his work, the faces of the painted have a deep wisdom and a deep sadness that seems to convey both the artist's love and hatred for his country. The museum is a 15-minute walk on the Getaria/San Sebastián road from the centre of Zumaia.

⊕ Sleeping

Guipúzcoan Coast *p440*

For paradors, go to www.parador.es.

AL Parador de Hondarribia, Plaza de Armas 14, Hondarribia, T943645500, F943642153. Originally constructed in the 10th century, then reinforced by Carlos V to resist French attacks. Behind the beautiful martial façade is a hotel of considerable comfort and delicacy, although the rooms don't reach the ornate standard set by the public areas, which are bristling with reminders of the military function of the fortress. A pretty courtyard and terrace are the highlights of a relaxing hotel.

A Hotel Obispo, Plaza del Obispo s/n, Hondarribia, T943645400, www.hotelobispo. com. The old archbishop's palace is another ultra-characterful place to stay; it's a beautiful building and features some nice views across the Bidasoa. The rooms are well-equipped although aren't quite up to the standard of the gorgeous façade.

C Hotel San Nikolas, Plaza de Armas 6, Hondarribia, T943644278. Also attractively set on the main square, this hotel offers reasonable and colourful rooms with TV and bathroom. Slightly overpriced, but it ain't a cheap town.

D Hostal Alvarez Quintero, C Bernat Etxepare 2, Hondarribia, T943642299. A tranquil little place with a distinctly old-fashioned air. The rooms are simple but not bad for this price in this town. It's a little difficult to find: the entrance is through an arch on the roundabout by the tourist office.

E Hostal Txoko-Goxoa, C Murrua 22, Hondarribia. A pretty little place on a peaceful, sunny street by the town walls. The bedrooms are smallish but homely, with flowers in the windowboxes.

Camping

Camping Faro de Higuer, Paseo del Faro 58, Hondarribia, T943641008. One of 2 decent campsites, slightly closer to town on the way to the lighthouse.

Inland from San Sebastián *p440*

There are a couple of hotels and bars in Arantzazu but, happily, nothing else. The cheaper beds in Oñati tend to fill up quickly at weekends.

B Hotel Loiola, Av de Loiola s/n, Loiola, T943151616. Although the building itself won't win many prizes for harmonious rural architecture, it's handy for the basilica, and reasonable value. The rooms are a touch dull but don't lack conveniences.

C Ongi, C Zaharra 19, Oñati, T943718285, F943718284. A new hotel on the main pedestrian street. Well-decorated snug rooms and family-run.

E Arregi, Ctra Garagaltza-Auzoa 21, T943780824. An excellent *agroturismo* a couple of kilometres from Oñati. A big farmhouse in a green valley with beautiful dark-wood rooms, a ping-pong table, and good folk running it. Recommended.

E Goiko Venta, Arantzazu 12, T943781305, F943780321, is up the hill in Arantzazu and has good rooms, some with a great view of the valley.

E Hospedería de Arantzazu, Arantzazu 29, Arantzazu, T943781313, ostatua@arantza zu.org. Right next to the basilica and offers fairly simple rooms in a slightly pious atmosphere.

E Laja Barrio, Santa Cruz, Azkoitia, T943853075. A good choice on the edges of Azkoitia that offers homecooked meals and good-value rooms in striking distance of the basilica.

F Echeverria, C Barria 15, Oñati, T943780460. A cheap *pensión* not far from the main square. Its clean rooms are good value but it's definitely worth ringing ahead at weekends.

West from San Sebastián *p441*

There's plenty of accommodation in Zarautz.

D Gure Ametsa, Orrua s/n, T943140077. Off a backroad between Zumaia and Getaria, this friendly farmhouse is in a superb location with hilly views over the sea. There are also cheaper rooms without ensuite.

D **Pensión Iribar**, C Nagusia 34, Getaria, T943140406, iribar@iname.com. Clean and comfy little rooms around the back of the restaurant of the same name, right in the narrow heart of the old town.

D **Pensión Txikipolit**, Plaza Musica s/n, Zarautz, T943835357, www.euskalnet.net/txikipolit. Very well located in a square in the old part of town, with comfy and characterful rooms. This is the best budget option.

E **Hostal Itxas Gain**, C San Roque 1, Getaria, T943141033. Lovely place overlooking the sea (that's what the name means). Warm-hearted and open place with some lovely rooms with impressionists on the walls. On the top floor there's a suite with a spa-bath. There's also a garden, which is a top place to chill in hot weather, and a friendly dog. Recommended.

Camping

Gran Camping Zarautz, Zarautz, T943831238, is a massive campsite with the lot, open all year round but depressingly packed in summer's dog days.

🍴 Eating

Guipúzcoan Coast *p440*

The town is notable for its excellent restaurants; the standard no doubt kept high by the visiting French.

€€€ **Sebastián**, C Mayor 9, Hondarribia, T943640167, is attractively set in a dingy old grocery packed with interesting aromas. The food goes beyond the humble decor: this is known as one of the better restaurants in Euskadi. There's a good value *menú de degustación* for €38.

€€ **Medievo**, Plaza Guipúzcoa 8, Hondarribia, T943644509, is an intriguing newish restaurant decorated in 21st-century medieval style. It may sound debatable, but it works, and so does the imaginatively prepared food. Try the venison with prunes. *Menú del día* for €9. À la carte, €30 a head.

Inland from San Sebastián *p440*

€€ **Kiruri**, Auzoa 24, Loiola, T943815608. Directly opposite the basilica, this restaurant is the best option. Does some good traditional plates. Hugely popular with families and wedding parties at weekends

and not averse to the odd coachload of pilgrims.

€ **Arkupe**, Plaza del los Fueros 9, Oñati, T943781699. A good eating option is this bar/restaurant on the main square, with a variety of cheap *raciones* and *platos*. Also a focus of the early evening outdoor drinking scene.

West from San Sebastián *p441*

€€ **Asador Mayflower**, C Katrapona 4, Getaria, T943140658, is one of a number of *asadors* in this attractive harbour town, with the bonus of an excellent *menú del día*. Grilled sardines are a tasty speciality.

€€ **Kaia**, C Katrapona Aundia 10, Getaria, T943140500. The best and priciest of Getaria's restaurants with a sweeping view over the harbour and high standard of food and service. Whole fish grilled over the coals outside are a highlight, as is the exceptional and reasonable wine list.

€€ **Kulixka**, C Bixkonde 1, Zarautz, T943831300, is a welcoming waterfront restaurant with an unbeatable view of the beach. Good seafood as you'd expect, and a decent *menú del día* for €8.

€ **Politena**, Kale Nagusia 9, Getaria, T943140113, is a bar fairly oriented towards weekend visitors from Bilbao and San Sebastián. A very enticing selection of *pintxos*, and a €12.50 'weekend' *menú*, which isn't bad either.

€ **Txalupa**, C Herrerieta 1, Getaria, T943140592, is a great place to buy or taste the local fish and *txakolí* in a hospitable bar, which offers *pintxos* as well as *cazuelitas*, small portions of bubbling stews or seafood.

🍸 Bars and clubs

Guipúzcoan Coast *p440*

Bar Itxaropena, C San Pedro 67, Hondarribia, T943641197, is a good bar in the new town offering a variety of cheap foodstuffs and plenty of company at weekends.

Inland from San Sebastián *p440*

For later action in Arantzazu, head for one of the bars on C Zaharri, such as **Bar Irritz**, a late opener with popular techno and a friendly scene at weekends.

▲ Activities and tours

West from San Sebastián *p441*
K-Sub, C Trinidad 2, Zarautz, T/F943132472, ksub@euskalnet.net, run PADI scuba courses, and also hire out diving equipment and give advice on good locations.

⊖ Transport

Guipúzcoan Coast *p440*
To **Hondarribia**, there are buses to and from Plaza Guipúzcoa in **San Sebastián** every 20 mins. Boats run across the river to the French town of **Hendaye**; there are also a few buses. The most common way of crossing the border is by the *topo* train that burrows through the mountain from between ugly **Irún** and **Hendaye**. There are frequent buses linking **Hondarribia** with **Irún**, just a few kilometres down the road.

Inland from San Sebastián *p440*
You can reach **Loiola** by bus from **Bilbao's**

bus station (3 a day), and from **San Sebastián** (destination marked for both is Azpeitia).

Oñati is accessed by bus from **Bilbao's** bus station with **Pesa** once daily Mon-Fri, otherwise connect with local bus from **Bergara**. There's no public transport from **Oñati** to **Arantzazu**; a taxi costs about €10 each way. Walking from **Oñati** takes about 2 hrs, but the return trip downhill is much less. There's plenty of traffic, and it's easy to hitch a ride.

West from San Sebastián *p441*
Zarautz is serviced by Euskotren hourly from **Bilbao's** Atxuri station and San Sebastián's **Amara** station, also regularly by bus from **San Sebastián** bus station.

Zumaia is serviced by **Euskotren** trains hourly from Bilbao's Atxuri station and San Sebastián's Amara station. Fairly regular buses connect the 2 towns.

Getaria also is serviced by bus from San Sebastián bus station with Euskotren.

Vizcayan Coast to Bilbao

The Vizcayan section of the Basque coastline is some of the most attractive and dramatic of Northern Spain; cliffs plunge into the water around tiny fishing villages, surfers ride impossibly long breaks, and the towns, like spirited Ondarroa, are home to a convivial and quintessentially Basque social scene. The easternmost section is the most rough-edged, with stirring cliffs and startling geological folding contrasting with the green foliage. The major town of this stretch is Lekeitio, one of Euskadi's highlights. A small way inland is Guernika, a city shedding off the weight of its past, and some nearby worthwhile trips: caves home to prehistoric man and a tranquil pine forest which has served as an artists' canvas. ▶ *For Sleeping, Eating and other listings, see pages 435-439.*

❧ *Fishing is god on this coast; some of the small villages are far more accessible by sea than by land.*

Ondarroa → *Colour map 2, grid A4.*

The friendliest of towns, Ondarroa marks the border of Vizcaya and Guipúzcoa. Situated at the mouth of the Artibai River, the town is straddled by two bridges, one the harmonious stone Puente Viejo, the other a recent work of Santiago Calatrava, which sweeps across with unmistakable panache. Although low on the glamour ladder and short on accommodation, Ondarroa could be worth a stop if you're exploring the coast, particularly on a Friday or Saturday night, when the nightlife rivals anywhere in Euskal Herría. Music has long been a powerful vehicle of Basque expression, and in Ondarroa the bars pump not with salsa or bacalao but nationalist

⦂ Cod, whales and America

The Basques are understandably proud of their maritime history. The traditional industries of fishing and shipbuilding are still crucial parts of the region's economy today but there was a time when the Basques were the foremost seagoers of the world.

In former times whales were a common species off the northern coast of Spain. The Basques were among the first to hunt whales, which they were doing as far back as the seventh century. It became a major enterprise, and, as the whales grew scarcer, they had to go further afield, venturing far into the North Atlantic. It's a good bet they reached America in the 14th century at the latest, signing the native Americans' visitors book under the Vikings and the shadowy, debatable scrawl of St Brendan.

The whaling expeditions provisioned themselves by fishing and preserving cod during the trip. The folk back home got a taste for this bacalao, and they still love it, to the bemusement of many tourists. Meanwhile, Elkano added to the Basques' seafaring CV by becoming the first man to circumnavigate the globe, after the expedition leader, Magellan, was killed in the Philippines after miscalculating some early gunboat diplomacy with the locals.

Basque whalers established many a settlement along the coast of Labrador and around during the 16th century, starting a love affair with the continent that reached epidemic proportions in the 19th and 20th centuries. Basques left their homes in droves for the promise of the New World, and Basque culture has been very significant in the development of the USA, particularly in some of the western states, as well as in Argentina and Chile.

rock. "Bacalao (salt cod) is for eating, not for listening to", said one group of locals. Ondarroa is a centre of Basque nationalism, and if you're against the concept it might be worth not letting on.

Lekeitio → *Colour map 2, grid A4.*

Along the Basque coastline, Lekeitio stands out as one of the best places to visit and stay. Its fully functioning fishing harbour is full of cheerfully painted boats, and the tall old houses seem to be jostling and squeezing each other for a front-row seat. Once a favourite of holidaying royalty, the town is lively at weekends and in summer, when it's a popular destination for Bilbao and San Sebastián families. There are two beaches – the one a bit further from town, across the bridge, is nicer. Both look across to the pretty rocky islet of the **Isla de San Nicolás** in the middle of the bay, covered in trees and home only to goats. The countryside around Lekeitio is beautiful, with rolling hills and jagged cliffs. The emerald green colour unfortunately doesn't come for nothing though – the town gets its fair share of rainy days.

There's not a great deal to do in the town itself however, the narrow streets backing the harbour conceal a few well-preserved medieval buildings, while the harbour itself is, of course, lined with bars. **Iglesia de Santa María de la Asunción** is definitely worth a visit. Lauded as one of the best examples of Basque Gothic architecture, it seems to change colour completely from dull grey to warm orange depending on the light. The retablo is an impressive ornate piece of Flemish work, while, if you ever wondered what a flying buttress was, take a look at the exterior.

The tourist information office ⓘ *C Independencia s/n, T946844017*, has a very good selection of information and is very helpful.

Guernica/Gernika → *Colour map 2, grid A4.*

A name that weighs heavy on the tongue, heavy with blood and atrocity, is Gernika. The symbol of Basque Nationalism, this thriving town has moved on from its tragic past, and provides the visitor with a great opportunity to experience Basque culture. Gernika sits at the head of the estuary of the Oka River, and the Biosphere Reserve of Urdaibai and the cave of Santamamiñesare within easy reach and well worth a day trip.

"...*the concentrated attack on Guernica was the greatest success*", from a secret memo to Hitler written by Wolfgang von Richthofen, commander of the Condor Legion and cousin of the 'Red Baron' First World War flying ace.

History

During the Spanish Civil War, in one of the most despicable planned acts of modern warfare there has ever been, 59 German and Italian planes destroyed the town in a bombardment that lasted three gruelling hours. It was 26 April 1937, and market day in Gernika, which meant that thousands of villagers from the surrounding area were in the town, which had no air defences to call on. Three days earlier a similar bombardment had killed over 250 in the town of Durango, but the toll here was worse. Splinter and incendiary bombs were used for maximum impact, and fighters strafed fleeing people with machine guns. The deaths caused were about 1,650.

> ‡ *Gernika's English-speaking tourist office is at Artekale 8; Guided tours of the town leave here daily at 1100.*

Franco, the head of the Nationalist forces, simply denied the event had occurred; he claimed that any damage done had been caused by Basque propagandists. In 1999 Germany formally apologized for the event, making the Spanish conspicuous by their silence. Apart from a general wish to terrorize and subdue the Basque population, who were resisting the Nationalist advance on Bilbao, Gernika's symbolic value was important. For many centuries Basque assemblies had met here under an oak tree – this was common to many Vizcayan towns but the Gernika meetings became dominant. They were attended by the monarch or a representative, who would solemnly swear to respect Basque rights and laws – the *fueros*. Thus the town became a powerful symbol of Basque liberty and nationhood. The first modern Basque government, a product of the Civil War, was sworn in under the oak only six months before the bombing.

One of the most famous results of the bombing was Picasso's painting named after the town. He had been commissioned by the Republican government to paint a mural for the upcoming World Fair, and this was the result. It currently sits in the Reina Sofia gallery in Madrid although constant Basque lobbying may yet bring it to Bilbao. A ceramic copy has been made on a wall on Calle Allende Salazar. Picasso commented on his painting: "By means of it, I express my abhorrence of the race that sunk Spain in an ocean of pain and death".

Sights

Today, thankfully, Gernika is anything but a sombre memorial to the devastation it suffered. While it understandably lacks much of its original architecture, it's a happy and friendly place, which merits a visit. Its Monday morning market is still very much in business and entertaining to check out. **Casa de Juntas**, symbolically placed next to the famous oak tree, is once again the seat of the Vizcayan parliament. The highlight of the building itself is the room with a massive stained glass roof depicting the oak

tree. The tree itself is outside by the porch, while part of the trunk of an older one is enshrined in a slightly silly little pavilion. Behind the building is the **Parque de los Pueblos de Europa** ① *1000-1400, 1600-1800 (winter), 1000-1400, 1600-1900 (summer), free*, which contains sculptures by Henry Moore and Eduardo Chillida. Both recall the devastated buildings of the town and are dedicated to peace.

Museo Gernika ① *Plaza Foru 1, T946270213, F946257542, Mon-Sat 1000-1400, 1600-1900, Sun 1000-1400, no lunchtime closing in summer, free*, is a comprehensive collection of documents about the Civil War and Gernika's role in it. Valuably, there are many descriptions from eyewitnesses, as well as recreations of the bombing. To place Gernika in context, there's a section on other cities destroyed by bombardment; the aerial assault here served as a template for similar raids in the Second World War and since.

Cueva de Santamamiñe

The cave of Santamamiñe is well worth a visit. It was an elegant and spacious home for thousands of generations of prehistoric folk, who decorated it with an important series of paintings depicting bison, among other animals. The chamber with the paintings is now closed to protect the 12,000-year-old art from further deterioration. The cave itself is fascinating nonetheless, winding deep into the hillside and full of eerily beautiful rock formations. The cave is a short climb up stairs from the car park. There is a bus from Gernika to Lekeitio which runs approximately every two hours which will drop you at the turn-off just before the town of Kortezubi. From there it's about a half-hour walk. Hitching is easy. Tours are free but limited to 15 people on a first-come, first-served basis. They run each weekday at 1000, 1115, 1230, 1630 and 1715.

Bosque Pintado de Oma

Near the caves is an unusual artwork: the Bosque Pintado de Oma. In a peaceful pine forest on a ridge Agustín Ibarrola has painted eyes, people, and geometric figures on the tree trunks in bright, bold colours. Some of the trees combine to form larger pictures – these can be difficult to make out, and it doesn't help that most of the display panels have been erased. Overall, it's a tranquil place with the wind whispering through the pines, and there's a strangely primal quality about the work. It's hard not to feel that more could have been made of the original concept though.

It's open 24/7 and free. A dirt road climbs 3 km to the wood from opposite the **Lezika** restaurant next to the Santamamiñe caves. It's a nice walk. If you are on foot, it's worth returning another way. Take the path down the hill at the other end of the Bosque from the entrance. After crossing a couple of fields, you'll find yourself in the tiny hamlet of Oma, with attractive Basque farmhouses. Turning left along the road will lead you back to the caves. It is also accessible by car.

Mundaka and Bermeo → *Colour map 2, grid A4.*

From Gernika, following the west bank of the estuary takes you back to the coast. A brisk half-hour's walk is all that separates the fishing towns of Bermeo and Mundaka, but they couldn't be more different. Mundaka is petite and, these days, slightly upmarket as visitors come to admire its beautiful harbour. Bermeo puts it in the shade in fishing terms: as one of the most important ports on this coast some of its boats seem bigger than Mundaka's harbour. There's a good atmosphere though, and an attractive old town.

While **Mundaka**'s still got its small fishing fleet, it's better known as a **surfing** village. It claims to have the longest left break in the world; whoever officially verified that had a pretty acceptable line of work. A left break, by the way, is a wave that breaks from right to left, looking towards the beach. When the wind blows and the big waves roll in, a top surfer can jump in off the rocks by Mundaka harbour and ride a wave right across the estuary mouth to Laida beach, a couple of kilometres away. After the long paddle back it might not seem like such a good idea the next time. Apart from surfers, Mundaka gets its fair share of visitors attracted by its bonsai harbour and relaxed ambience. The village itself is a small maze of winding streets and an oversized church. There are some good places to stay or camp here, and it's within easy striking distance of several highlights of the Basque coast. In summer boats run across to Laida beach, which is the best in the area. The *tigres* at the small bar on the estuary are almost worth a trip alone. There's a small tourist office in Mundaka by the harbour.

Bermeo is a bigger and more typical Basque fishing town with a more self-sufficient feel. One of the whaling towns that more or less pioneered the activity, Bermeo has a proud maritime history documented in its museum. The ships for Columbus's second voyage were built and largely crewed from here. There's much more action in the fishing harbour here than peaceful Mundaka. The old town is worth wandering through. There's a cobbled square across which the church and the Ayuntamiento vie for power; the latter has a sundial on its face. There's a small chunk of the old town wall preserved, with a symbolic footprint of John the Baptist, who is said to have made Jonathan Edwards weep by jumping from here to the sanctuary of Gaztelugatxe in three steps. **Museo del Pescador** ① *Plaza Torrontero 1, T946881171, Tue-Sat 1000-1330, 1600-1930, Sun 1000-1330, free*, is set in a 15th-century tower and is devoted to the Basque fishing industry and the various members of the finny tribes. Bermeo's tourist office is opposite the station.

Sanctuario de San Juan de Gaztelugatxe

West of Bermeo, some 6 km from town is the spectacular sanctuary of San Juan de Gaztelugatxe. Sancho the Great, King of Navarra, was in Aquitaine, in France, in the early 11th century when a surprising gift was presented to the local church hierarchy; the head of John the Baptist, which had mysteriously turned up a short while before. The membership database of the cult of the Baptist received an understandable boost, and many monasteries and sanctuaries were built in his name, including several in northeastern Spain, with the express encouragement of the impressed Sancho. San Juan de Gaztelugatxe is one of these (although the church dates from much later). A rocky island frequently rendered impressively bleak by the coastal squalls, it's connected by a bridge to the mainland, from where it's 231 steps to the top. Apart from the view, there's not a great deal to see, but the setting is spectacular. The island is a pilgrimage spot, particularly for the feast of St John on 24 June, and also on 31 July. From Bermeo, buses run about every two hours along the coast road to Bakio.

● Sleeping

Ondarroa *p446*
If you're staying, there are two accommodation options.
C-E Arrigorri, Arrigorri 3, T946134045, www.arrigorri.net. A good choice across the river from the centre, right on the beach. There are a variety of rooms with differing prices; the best have a full bathroom and views over the sea. Friendly and comfortable. Breakfast included.
F Patxi, Arta Bide 21, T609986446, is an exceedingly low-priced *pensión*, comfortable rooms with a basic shared bathroom.

Lekeitio *p447*
Lekeitio has some very inviting accommodation options, though none is really in the budget category.

C **Emperatriz Zita**, Santa Elena Etorbidea s/n, T946842655, www.saviat.net. This slightly odd-looking hotel was built on the site of a palace where Empress Zita had lived in the 1920s. The hotel is furnished in appropriately elegant style and is also a thalassotherapy (sea water) and health centre. The rooms are very pleasant and well-priced for the location and quality, as is the restaurant.

C **Hotel Zubieta**, Portal de Atea, T946843030, www.hotelzubieta.com. A superbly converted coachhouse in the grounds of a *palacio*. Considering its surprisingly low prices, this is one of the best places to stay in Euskal Herría, with friendly management, a lively bar, and cosy rooms with sloping wooden ceilings. Definitely one to pre-book at weekends. Highly recommended.

D-E **Piñupe Hotela**, Av Pascual Abaroa 10, T946842984, F946840772. The cheapest place in town, and a sound choice. The rooms have ensuite, phone, and TV and are plenty more comfortable than the bar downstairs would indicate.

E **Hotel Zubieta** (see above) has reasonably priced 2- and 4-berth apartments attached to the hotel in Lekeitio.

Guernika *p448*

B **Hotel Gernika**, C Carlos Gangoiti 17, T946254948, www.hotel-gernika.com. Gernika's best hotel is nothing exceptional, with uninteresting rooms in an ugly brick building on the edge of town. There's a bar and café, and the service is helpful.

B **Hotel Katxi**, Morga/Andra Mari s/n, T946270740, www.katxi.com. A few kilometres west of Gernika in the hamlet of Morga is this excellent rural hotel. The rooms, some much larger than others, are extremely comfortable, and there's a friendly lounge area. It's a great place to get away from things a little in a warm atmosphere. The same owners run a good *asador* next door so you won't go hungry.

D **Hotel Boliña**, C Barrenkale 3, T94625 0300, F946250304. In the centre of Gernika, this hotel has some good value doubles with TV and telephone. Can be stuffy in summer.

E **Pensión Akelarre**, C Barrenkale 5, T9462-70197, www.akelarre.euskalnet.net. Funky little rooms with TV and varnished floorboards. There's a terrace to take some sun and it's in the heart of the pedestrian area.

E **Pensión Madariaga**, C Industria 10, T946256035. Very attractively furnished little place with rooms with TV, bathroom, and welcoming furniture for not much cash.

F **Pensión Iratxe**, C Industria 6, T946253134. A simple and cheap *pensión* run out of the Bar Frontón a few doors down the street.

F **Ugaldeberri**, T/F 946256577, elenaelan@euskalnet.net. Located north of Gernika on the eastern side of the estuary, with superb views over the reserve, this big farmhouse has 3 doubles that make an excellent place to stay if you've got a motor. Guests can use the kitchen.

Bosque Pintado de Oma *p449*

E **Bizketxe**, Oma 8, T9462 54906, anidketxe@terra.es, is an excellent place to stay if you've got transport. Lovely rooms in a traditional farmhouse, with or without bath. Recommended.

Mundaka and Bermeo *p449*

Accommodation in Mundaka isn't cheap.

B **Hotel Atalaya**, C Itxaropen 1, Mundaka, T946177000, www.hotel-atalaya-mundaka.com. The classier of the town's options, with a summery feel to its rooms and café. Garden and parking adjoin the stately building. Very nice breakfasts.

C **Hostal Torre Ercilla**, C Talaranzko 14, Bermeo, T946187598, fbarrotabernav@nexo.es. A lovely place to stay in Bermeo´s old town, between museum and church. The rooms are thoughtfully designed for relaxation, with small balconies, reading nooks, and soft carpet; there's also a lounge, terrace, chessboard, and barbecue among other comforts. Recommended.

C **Hotel El Puerto**, Portu Kalea 1, Mundaka, T946876725, hotelelpuerto@euskalnet.net. Perhaps the best value of Mundaka's 3 hotels, this is set right by the tiny fishing harbour and has cute little rooms, some overlooking the harbour (worth paying the few extra euros for). The bar below is one of Mundaka's best.

El País Vasco Vizcayan Coast to Bilbao: listings

● For an explanation of sleeping and eating price codes used in this guide, see inside the
● front cover. Other relevant information is found in Essentials, see pages 47-56.

C **Hotel Mundaka**, C Florentino Larrinaga 9, Mundaka, T946876700, www.hotelmund aka.euskalnet.net. Decent option with a garden and a bar with Internet access at €3/hr. The accommodation is irreproachable, but lacks some of the charm of the other 2 hotels in town.

Camping
Camping Portuondo, 1 km out of Mundaka on the road to Gernika, T/F9946877701, www.campingportuondo.com. Sardined during the summer months, this is a well-equipped campsite with a swimming pool, cafés and laundry. There are several bungalows that sleep up to 4, but are not significantly cheaper than the hotels in town with only 1 or 2. They do come with kitchen, fridge, and television though.

● Eating

Ondarroa p446
€€ **Eretegia Joxe Manuel**, C Sabino Arana 23, T946830104. Although it does a range of other appetising dishes, the big charcoal grill outside this restaurant caters to carnivores with large appetites. Forget quarter pounders; here the steaks approach the kilogram mark and are very tasty.
€€ **Sutargi**, Nasa Kalea 11, T946832258. A popular bar with a good-value restaurant upstairs with main dishes around €9-10. For this reason, it's difficult to get a table at weekends.

Lekeitio p447
Despite the busy summer scene, there are lots of fairly traditional places to eat and drink.
€€€ **Oxangoiti Jauregia**, C Gamarra 2, T946843151. A fairly expensive restaurant in an historic building next to the Ayuntamiento. Smart wooden interior, a craft shop, and tasty seafood (how did you guess?) at fairly stiff prices.
€€ **Emperatriz Zita**, Santa Elena Etorbidea s/n, T946842655. The restaurant in this seafront hotel is well-priced and of good quality in a rather grand dining room.
€€ **Hotel Beitia**, Av Pascual Abaroa 25, Lekeitio, T946840111. The restaurant is a much better bet than the hotel it lies in, with high-quality seafood and a pleasant patio.

€€ **Kaia**, Txatxo kaia 5, T946840284. One of the many harbourside restaurants and bars, this serves fairly upmarket but tasty fish.
€ **Hotel Zubieta**, Portal de Atea, T946843030. The lively café bar in this beautifully restored coachhouse is an excellent spot for a chat and a beverage in uplifting surroundings.

Guernika p448
€ **Arrien**, C Eriabarrena 1, T946258551. Overlooking the flowery Jardines de El Ferial, this terraced restaurant/bar has a very acceptable *menú del día* for€7.21 and various other set meals from €10 as well as à la carte selections.
€ **Foruria**, C Industria 10, T946251020. A good option for a cheapish meal, with a selection of hot dishes around the €9 mark as well as a wide selection of *jamón, chorizo*, and cheese for cold platters.

Cueva de Santamamiñe p449
€€ **Lezika**, Cuevas de Santamamiñe, Kortezubi (by the Cuevas de Santamamiñe). The whole of Vizcaya seems to descend on the beer garden here at weekends with kids and dogs in tow; the restaurant is worthwhile as well, and better value than the meagre *raciones* on offer at the bar.

Mundaka and Bermeo p449
€€ **Asador Bodegon**, Kepa Deuna 1, Mundaka, T946876353. Mundaka's best restaurant, despite a slight air of 'we know what the tourists want'. Meat, and, especially, fresh fish are grilled to perfection over the coals. Try the home-made *patxarán*, a liqueur made from sloe berries.
€€ **Ereperi**, while in Bermeo have lunch here, overlooking the sanctuary with a superb terrace and a cheap lunch *menú*.

● Bars and clubs

Ondarroa p446
Ondarroa's nightlife scene revolves around the main streets of the old centre The music school, on the corner of Iñaki Deunaren and Sabino Arana (Arana'tar Sabin), often has live Basque alternative rock on Fri or Sat nights – it's usually free. Nasa Kalea is well-stocked with bars, many of which are temples to Basque rock, which is

heavily identified with the independence movement. Two worth dropping in on are **Apallu**, at No 30, and **Sansonategi**.

Ku-Kua, Kanttoipe Kalea s/n, is a very lively bar that gets very full and goes on very late.

Lekeitio *p447*

Talako Bar, above the fisherman's co-operative on the harbour, is a great spot for one of Lekeitio's rainy days, with a pool table, board games, and a 180° view of the harbour, town, and beaches.

Txalupa, Txatxo kaia 7, Lekeitio. While Lekeitio isn't as out-and-out Basque as Ondarroa, this bar keeps the Basque rock pumping, and does a range of simple snacks.

Guernika *p448*

Arrana, C Juan Calzada 6. A vibrant Basque bar with a lively young crowd spilling outside at weekends.

Metropol, corner C Unamuno and Iparragirre. A cavernous and comradely bar, open later than anywhere and then some.

✹ Festivals and events

Lekeitio *p447*

In a land of strange festivals, Lekeitio has one of the strangest, the **Fiesta de San Antolín** on **5 Sep**. It involves a long rope, a few rowing boats, plenty of able-bodied young folk, and a goose. Thankfully these days the goose is already dead. The hapless bird is tied in the middle of the rope, which is stretched across the harbour and held at both ends. Competitors take turns from rowing boats to grab the goose's head

(which has been liberally greased up) under their arm. The rope is then tightened, lifting the grabber into the air, and then slackened. This is done until either the goose's head comes off, or the person falls into the water.

◉ Transport

Ondarroa *p446*

Ondarroa is served by Pesa from **Bilbao** and **San Sebastián** bus stations 4 times a day.

Lekeitio *p447*

Bizkaibus hourly from Calle Hurtado Amezaga by Abando train station in **Bilbao**; Pesa 4 times daily from the bus station in **San Sebastián**.

Guernika *p448*

There are hourly trains to Gernika from **Bilbao**'s Atxuri station, and buses half-hourly from C Hurtado de Amezaga next to Abando station.

Mundaka and Bermeo *p449*

Hourly trains run to Mundaka and Bermeo from Bilbao's Atxuri station. Buses half-hourly with **Bizkaibus** from the station next to the Bilbao main tourist office.

❶ Directory

Guernika *p448*

Internet Aramu Sarea, C Miguel Unamuno 1, T946258522. €2.50.

Lekeitio *p447*

Internet **Gozamen**, C Gamarra 10, T946841448.

Bilbao/Bilbo → *Phone code: 944; Colour map 2, grid A3; Population: 353,943.*

In an amazingly short time this once dirty industrial city that has successfully transformed itself into a buzzy cultural capital, without losing sight of its roots. The Guggenheim Museumis the undoubted flagship of this triumphant progress, a sinuous fantasy of a building that literally takes the breath away. It inspires because of what it is, but also because the city had the vision to put it there. While the museum has led the turnaround, much of what is enjoyable about modern Bilbao was already there. Bustling bar-life, harmonious old and new architecture, a superb eating culture, and a tangible sense of pride in being a working city are still things that make Bilbao a little bit special, and the exciting new developments can only add to those qualities. ▸▸ *For Sleeping, Eating and other listings, see pages 462-470.*

Ins and outs

Getting there

Bilbao's airport is the only international one in Euskadi, and a good gateway to Northern Spain. It's served from several European destinations, including London Stansted by the budget operator easyJet, as well as British Airways and Iberia from Heathrow and Gatwick. There are many domestic flights from Barcelona and Madrid, as well as other cities. There's a ferry service from Portsmouth, which is cruise-like in style and pricing. Bilbao is well served by buses from the rest of the nation. It's exceedingly well connected with Vitoria, San Sebastián, and smaller destinations in Euskadi. There are a few train services to other Spanish cities. ▸▸ *For further details, see Transport page 468.*

Getting around

Bilbao is a very walkable city, as are cities all in Northern Spain. The Guggenheim Museum, as far afield as many people get, is an easy 15 minutes along the river promenade from the old town. For further-flung parts of Bilbao, such as the beach or the bus station, or to save tired legs, the Metro is an excellent service. It runs until about midnight Sunday-Thursday, until about 0200 on Friday, and 24 hours on Saturday. A single fare costs €1, while a day pass is €3. There's one main line running through the city and out to the beach suburbs, while the recently opened second line will eventually reach the coast on the other side of the estuary. Although there's a reasonable network of local bus services in Bilbao, they are only generally useful for a handful of destinations; these are indicated in the text. There is also a tram service.

Best time to visit

Bilbao's summers are warm but not baking. This is the best time to visit, but be sure to book ahead during the boisterous August fiesta, see Festivals page 468. At other times of year, Bilbao is a fairly wet place, but never gets especially cold. The bar life and museums provide more than ample distraction from the drizzle.

Tourist information

Bilbao's main tourist office ① *Paseo del Arenal 1, T944795760, bit@ayto.bilbao.net, Mon-Fri 0900-1400 and 1600-1930, Sat 0900-1400, Sun 1000-1400*, is excellent. There's also a smaller office by the Guggenheim Museum ① *Abandoibarra Etorbidea 2, Tue-Sat 1100-1400 and 1600-1800, Sat 1100-1400 and 1700-1900, Sun 1100-1400.* The tourist office supplies a good free map of the city; for more detail there's a bigger one on sale for €2.50. Basque Industrial Development Agency ① *Gran Via, 35-3A, 48009 Bilbao, T944037070, F944037021.* The city's website, www.bilbao.net, is also a good source of information.

History

In 1300 the lord of the province of Vizcaya, Don Diego López de Haro V, saw the potential of the riverside fishing village of Bilbao and granted it permission to become a town. The people graciously accepted, and by the end of the 14th century history records that the town had three parallel streets: Somera, Artekale, and Tendería (Street of Shopkeepers). These were soon added to: Belostikale, Carnicería Vieja, Barrenkale, and Barrenkale Barrena came to the party; these are the Siete Calles, the seven original streets of the city. It was a time of much strife, and the fledgling town

● *The city's coat of arms features two wolves; these were the family symbol of Don Diego–*
● *his surname López derives from the Latin word* lupus, *wolf.*

Bilbao suffered during the first Carlist war in the 19th century, when the liberal city was besieged (ultimately unsuccessfully) by the reactionary Carlist forces. The one bright spot to emerge was the invention of bacalao al pil-pil, now the city's signature dish, but originally devised due to lack of any fresh produce to eat. Not long after the war, Bilbao's boom started. The Vizcayan hills harboured huge reserves of haematite, the ore from which the city's iron was produced. In the middle of the century, it soon became evident that this was by far the best ore for the new process of steelmaking. Massive foreign investment followed, particularly from Britain, and the city expanded rapidly as workers flooded in from all parts of the peninsula. The good times didn't last, however; by the early 20th century things were looking grimmer. Output declined, and dissatisfied workers sunk into poverty. The Civil War hit the city hard too; after the Republican surrender, Franco made it clear he wasn't prepared to forgive the Basques for siding against him. Repressed and impoverished, the great industrial success story of the late 19th century sunk into gloom, only relatively recently lifted. The dictator's death sparked a massive reflowering of Basque culture, symbolized by the bold steps taken to revitalize the city. The Guggenheim's opening in 1997 has confirmed Bilbao's newly won status as a cultural capital of Northern Spain.

Sights

Casco Viejo, the old town, still evokes a cramped medieval past. Along its web of attractive streets, designer clothing stores occupy the ground floors where families perhaps once huddled behind the city walls. The Ensanche, the new town, has an elegant European feel to it. The wealth of the city is more evident here, with stately banks and classy shops lining the planned avenues. The riverbank is the most obvious beneficiary of Bilbao's leap into the 21st century: Calatrava's eerily skeletal bridge and Gehry's exuberant Guggenheim bring art and architecture together and make the Nervión River the city's axis once more. It doesn't stop there, as ongoing work aims to further soften the remaining industrial edges.

Casco Viejo

Bilbao's old town is a good place to start exploring the city. This is where most of the budget accommodation and bar life is based. Tucked into a bend in the river, it's the most charming part of town, a lively jumble of pedestrian streets that has always been the city's social focus. There's something of the medina about it; on your first few forays you surely won't end up where you might have thought you were going.

Siete Calles The parallel Siete Calles (seven streets) are the oldest part of town, and even locals struggle to sort out which bar is on which street. While there aren't a huge number of sights per se, there are dozens of quirky shops and some very attractive architecture; leisurely wandering is in order. The true soul of the Casco emerges from early evening on, however, when Bilbaínos descend on the Casco like bees returning to the hive, strolling the streets, listening to buskers, debating the quality of the *pintxos* in the myriad bars, and sipping wine in the setting sun.

Mercado de la Ribera By the river where stallholders used to come for the weekly market, the art deco Mercado de la Ribera is a permanent market of ample size. With over 400 stalls on three floors of fruit, veggies, meat, and fish, it's the major centre for fresh produce in Bilbao. Come in the morning if you want to get the true flavour; the afternoons are comparatively quiet. Skip the meat floor if you don't want to see pigs' heads and horse butchers.

Catedral de Santiago In the centre of the market area is the Catedral de Santiago, whose slender spire rises high above the tight streets. A graceful Gothic affair, it was mostly built in the late 14th century on the site of a previous church, but was devastated by fire in the 1500s and lost much of its original character. Two of its best features are later additions: an arched southern porch (it seems a pity that it's fenced off from the street), and a small but harmonious cloister (if it's locked, the attendants are happy to open it). Promoted to cathedral in 1950, the building has benefitted from recent restoration work.

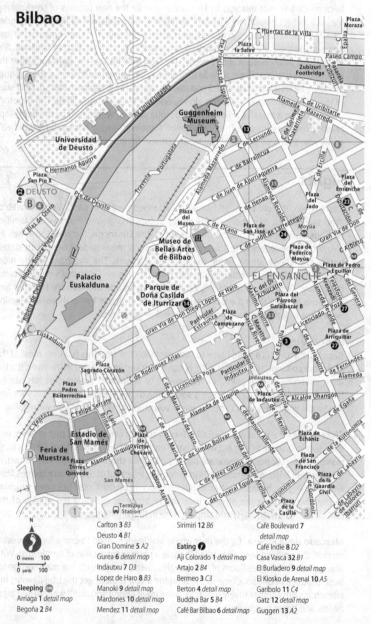

Bilbao

Sleeping			
Arriaga 1 *detail map*	Deusto 4 *B1*	Sirimiri 12 *B6*	Café Boulevard 7
Begoña 2 *B4*	Gran Domine 5 *A2*		*detail map*
	Gurea 6 *detail map*	**Eating**	Café Indie 8 *D2*
	Indautxu 7 *D3*	Aji Colorado 1 *detail map*	Casa Vasca 32 *B1*
	Lopez de Haro 8 *B3*	Artajo 4 *B4*	El Burladero 9 *detail map*
	Manoki 9 *detail map*	Bermeo 3 *C3*	El Kiosko de Arenal 10 *A5*
Carlton 3 *B3*	Mardones 10 *detail map*	Berton 4 *detail map*	Garibolo 11 *C4*
	Mendez 11 *detail map*	Buddha Bar 5 *B4*	Gatz 12 *detail map*
		Café Bar Bilbao 6 *detail map*	Guggen 13 *A2*

0 metres 100
0 yards 100

Plaza Nueva The 'New Square', one of a series of similar cloister-like squares in Euskadi, was finished in 1849. Described by Unamuno as "my cold and uniform Plaza Nueva", it will particularly appeal to lovers of geometry and symmetry with its courtly neoclassical arches, which conceal an excellent selection of restaurants and bars, with some of the best *pintxos* in town on offer. In good weather, most have seating outside in the square.

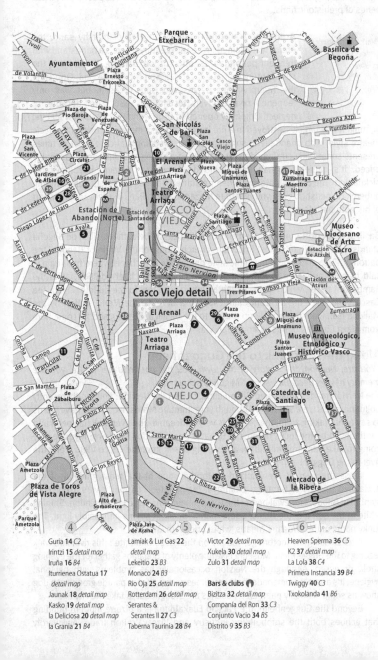

Casco Viejo detail

Guria 14 *C2*
Irintzi 15 *detail map*
Iruña 16 *B4*
Iturrienea Ostatua 17
  detail map
Jaunak 18 *detail map*
Kasko 19 *detail map*
la Deliciosa 20 *detail map*
la Grania 21 *B4*

Lamiak & Lur Gas 22
  detail map
Lekeitio 23 *B3*
Monaco 24 *B3*
Rio Oja 25 *detail map*
Rotterdam 26 *detail map*
Serantes &
  Serantes II 27 *C3*
Taberna Taurinia 28 *B4*

Victor 29 *detail map*
Xukela 30 *detail map*
Zulo 31 *detail map*

Bars & clubs 🍸
Bizitza 32 *detail map*
Compania del Ron 33 *C3*
Conjunto Vacio 34 *B5*
Distrito 9 35 *B3*

Heaven Sperma 36 *C5*
K2 37 *detail map*
La Lola 38 *C4*
Primera Instancia 39 *B4*
Twiggy 40 *C3*
Txokolanda 41 *B6*

Museo Arqueológico, Etnológico y Histórico Vasco ① *Plaza Miguel de Unamuno 4, T944155423, www.euskal-museoa.org, Tue-Sat 1100-1700, Sun 1100-1400, €3 (free on Thu).* Near the Plaza Nueva, this museum is attractively set around an old Jesuit college and houses an interesting if higgledy-piggledy series of Basque artefacts and exhibits covering thousands of years. There's a fascinating room-sized relief model of Vizcaya on the top floor, a piece of one of the Gernika oak trees, and some good displays on Basque fishing, as well as a decent but poorly presented series of prehistoric finds.

> ❦ The Arenal by the river is a busy nexus point for strollers, lovers, demonstrators, and dogwalkers.

Arenal and around Formerly an area of marshy sand, the Arenal was drained in the 18th century. There's a bandstand with frequent performances, often of folk dancing. Next to it is the 18th-century Baroque façade of San Nicolás de Bari. Opposite, the Teatro Arriaga seems very sure of itself, but was only reopened comparatively recently in 1986, after decades of neglect. Originally opened in 1890 with miraculous new electric lighting, it was largely destroyed in a fire in 1915. It's very much in plush *fin de siècle* theatre style, with chandeliers, soft carpet, and sweeping staircases, but at times presents some fairly cutting-edge art, usually of a strong standard and reasonably priced. It's named for Juan Crisóstomo de Arriaga, a Bilbaíno boy inevitably nicknamed 'The Spanish Mozart' when he started dashing off octets before hitting puberty. He perished even younger than Mozart, dying in Paris in 1826, 10 days short of his 20th birthday.

Basílica de Begoña Atop a steep hill above the Casco Viejo, the Basílica de Begoña stands, and is, Bilbao's most important church, home of the Virgin of Begoña, the patron of Vizcaya. It's built in Gothic style on the site of a chapel where the Virgin is said to have appeared in former times. The cloister is a later addition, as is the flamboyant tower, which gives a slightly unbalanced feel to the building. From the Casco Viejo, take the lift from Calle Esperanza or leave the Metro station by the Mallona exit. From there, walk up the hill to the basilica. Buses 3 and 30 come here from Plaza Circular, or bus 41 from Gran Vía.

Along the riverbank to the Guggenheim
"You are, Nervión, the history of the town, you her past and her future, you are memory always becoming hope." Miguel de Unamuno

The Nervión made Bilbao, and Bilbao almost killed the Nervión: until pretty recently pollution levels were sky-high. Although your immune system would still have words to say about taking a dip, the change is very noticeable. The riverbank has been and continues to be the focus of most of Bilbao's beautification schemes; if you're only going to take one stroll in Bilbao, an evening *paseo* from the Casco Viejo along the river to the Guggenheim is it.

Cross the river at the Zubizuri footbridge, one of the most graceful of the acclaimed bridges of Santiago Calatrava. Inaugurated in 1994, it was a powerful symbol of Bilbao's renewal before the Guggenheim was close to completion. Shining white in the sun like the ribs of some marine beast, it seems impossibly light. The funky name of the structure means 'white bridge' in Euskara.

After crossing the footbridge, you are on the Paseo Uribitarte ; this riverside walk leading to the Guggenheim Museum is where plenty of Bilbaínos gather for the evening stroll, or *paseo*. Although the Nervión occasionally has problems with personal hygiene, it's a lovely promenade that sometimes seems like the parade ground at a dog show as some seriously pampered pooches are brought out to take the city air.

Beyond the Guggenheim, the **Palacio Euskalduna** is a bizarre modern building that echoes both the shipbuilding industry and Vizcaya's iron trade. Awkwardly

situated, hemmed in by a busy bypass, it's a building that leaves many people cold, although it is impressive in a clumsy kind of way. Particularly interesting are the coathanger 'trees' out the front. It's now a major venue for conferences and concerts, particularly classical. More *simpático* is the covered Euskalduna bridge nearby, which sweeps into Deusto in a confident curve.

Guggenheim Museum

① *Abandoibarra Etorbidea 2, T944359000, www.guggenheim-bilbao.es, Tue-Sun 1000-2000, Jul/Aug only Mon-Sun 0900-2100, €7, audio tour €3.61, guided tours free at 1130, 1230, 1630, 1830 (Spanish, English, and Euskara). Metro: Moyúa, buses 13, 27, 38, 46, 48 stop a block away on Alameda Recalde.*

"The idea was that the building had to be able to accommodate the biggest and heaviest of contemporary sculpture on the one hand, and a Picasso drawing on the other hand. In the first sketch I put a bunch of principles down, then I become self-critical of those images and those principles, and that evokes the next set of responses...and those evolve, and at some point I stop, because that's it... ". Frank Gehry

More than anything else, it is this building that has thrust Bilbao so firmly back on to the world stage. Daring in concept and brilliant in execution, the Guggenheim Museum has driven a massive boom in the local confidence as well as, more prosaically, economy; its success has given the green light to further ambitious transformation of the formerly industrialized parts of the city.

It all started when the Guggenheim Foundation, strapped for cash (or something like that...), decided to build a new museum to enable more of their collection to be exhibited. Many cities around the globe were considered, but Bilbao were keenest and the Basque government were prepared to foot the US$100 million bill for its construction.

Exterior Frank Gehry was the man who won the design competition and the rest is the reality of what confronts visitors to Bilbao today; a shining temple of a building that completely fulfils the maxim of 'architecture as art'. Gehry's masterstroke was to use titanium, an expensive soft metal normally reserved for Boeing aircraft and the like. Gehry was intrigued by its futuristic sheen and malleable qualities; the panels are literally paper-thin. The titanium makes the building shimmer: it seems that the architect has managed to capture motion. The exuberant curves recall the fish, one of Gehry's favourite motifs; the structure could almost be a writhing school of herring or salmon.

One of the most impressive features of the design is the way it interacts with the city. One of Bilbao's enjoyable and surprising experiences is to look up when crossing a street in the centre of town and see the Guggenheim perfectly framed, like some unearthly craft that's just landed. Gehry had to contend with the ugly bulk of the Puente de la Salve running through the middle of his site, yet managed to incorporate the bridge fluidly into his plans. The raised tower at the museum's eastern end has no architectural purpose other than to link the building more effectively with the town upriver; it works.

The building also interacts fluidly with the river itself; the pool at the museum's feet almost seems part of the Nervión, and Fuyiko Nakaya's mist sculpture, when turned on, further blurs things. It's entitled FOG, which also happen to be the architect's initials...

A couple of creatures have escaped the confines of the gallery and sit in the open air. Jeff Koons's giant floral sculpture, Puppy, sits eagerly greeting visitors. Formerly a

There's also a spot reserved for Picasso's Gernika, which the Basque government persistently try and prise away from the Reina Sofía gallery in Madrid.

El País Vasco Bilbao/Bilbo

⁞ Philosopher's Last Stand

One of Bilbao's most famous sons was Miguel de Unamuno, poet, philosopher, and academic, born in 1864 on Calle Ronda. One of the 'Generation of '98', a new wave of artists and thinkers emerging in the wake of the Spanish-American war of 1898, Unamuno, who spoke 15 languages, was a humanist and a catholic with an idealistic love of truth. This made him enemies in a Spain where political beliefs tended to come first. To this day, many Basques have mixed feelings about 'Don Miguel', who, although proud of being Basque, wasn't pro-independence and deplored some of the myths created in the name of nationalism.

Unamuno became rector of the university at Salamanca but after criticizing the dictatorship of Primo de Rivera, he was imprisoned in the Canary Islands, from where his rescue was organised by the editor of the French newspaper Le Quotidien. In Salamanca when the Civil War broke out, Unamuno, previously a deputy in the Republic, had supported the rising, but grew more and more alarmed with the nature of the Nationalist movement and the character of the war.

On 12 October 1936 he was presiding over the Columbus day ceremony at the university which rapidly degenerated into a fascist propaganda session. A professor denounced Basque and Catalan nationalism as cancers that fascism would cut out. General Millán Astray, a war veteran with one eye, one arm, and missing fingers on the other one continued with more empty rhetoric, and the hall resounded to the popular Falangist slogan "long live death".

Unamuno rose to close the meeting. "At times to be silent is to lie", he said. "I want to comment on the speech – to give it that name – of the professor. Let's ignore the personal affront implied. I am a Basque from Bilbao. The bishop (pro-fascist) next to me is Catalan, from Barcelona". He then moved on to Astray, whom he harshly criticised, and who responded by crying "Death to intellectuals". Guns were pointed at the 72 year old, who went on: "You will win, because you have the brute force. But you will not convince. For to convince, you would need what you lack: reason and right in the struggle". At the end of his speech, he was ushered out of the hall by Franco's wife to safety. Under house arrest, he died a couple of months later, it was said, of a broken heart. On the day of his death, his two sons enlisted in the anti-fascist militia.

touring attraction visiting the city for the opening of the museum in 1997, he couldn't escape the clutches of the kitsch-hungry Bilbaínos, who demanded that he stayed put. On the other side of the building, a sinister spider-like creature guards the waterside approach. Entitled *Maman*, we can only be thankful that sculptor Louise Bourgeois's mother had long since passed away when it was created. It's a striking piece of work, and makes a bizarre sight if approached when the mist is on.

So much for the exterior, which has met with worldwide acclaim. What about the inside? It is, after all, an art museum.

Interior Gehry's idea was that there would be two types of gallery within the building: "galleries for dead artists, which have classical [square or rectangular] shapes, and galleries for living artists, which have funny shapes, because they can fight back". The embodiment of the latter is the massive Gallery 104, built with the

realization that many modern artworks are too big for traditional museums. Central to this space is Richard Serra's *Snake*, whose curved iron sheets will carry whispers from one end to another. A hundred feet long, and weighing 180 tonnes, it's meant to be interactive – walk through it, talk through it, touch it.

This, however, is one of only a few pieces that live in the museum; the rest are temporary visitors, some taken from the Permanent Collection of the Guggenheim Foundation, others appearing in a range of exhibitions. This, of course, means that the overall quality varies according to what's on show.

Architecturally, the interior is a very soothing space, with natural light flooding into the atrium. It's a relief to realize that this isn't one of those galleries that you feel you'll never be able to see everything without rushing about; it's very uncluttered and manageable. In the atrium is Jenny Holzer's accurately titled *Installation for Bilbao*, an arresting nine-column LED display that unites the different levels of the building. The effect created is a torrent of primal human sentiment expressed simply in three languages. There are three floors of galleries radiating off the central space.

For a look at some smaller-scale Frank Gehry work, drop into the reading room on the ground floor, furnished with his unique cardboard chairs and tables, which are surprisingly comfortable and solid. The cafés also feature chairs designed by him. The museum has an excellent modern art bookshop.

Deusto

Across from the Guggenheim is Deusto, a university district abuzz with alternativity and purpose. Sometimes described as a republic, it developed separately from Bilbao for much of its history and still has a different vibe.

> If you want that postcard-perfect snap of Frank Gehry's masterpiece, this is the place to come, particularly in the evening light.

Universidad de Deusto The 'republic of Deusto' is a lively university district worth exploring for its barlife and different vibe. Bilbao's principal university was founded in 1886 by the Jesuits, who felt that the Basque community needed such a centre of learning. It now counts over 20,000 students and staff among its several buildings. While the academic standard of the university has traditionally been very high, it has also played an important role in Basque nationalism. After the Civil War, Franco banned public universities from the Basque country as he feared they would breed opposition to his regime. Deusto, being privately run by the Jesuits, remained and became, along with the economics college down the road at Sarriko, an important centre of radical opposition to the dictatorship. Texts and music written in the Euskara language, still outlawed by Franco, circulated clandestinely around the campus, and illegal lessons were given outside of class time. The refined neoclassical main building is on the river opposite and slightly downstream from the Guggenheim.

El Tigre On Deusto's waterfront, a large stone lion defies the sky. This building was originally a pavilion to house the small workshops of local tradespeople but is now abandoned, pending conversion into luxury flats. Bilbaínos perversely name it 'El Tigre' (the tiger).

El Ensanche

The residents of old Bilbao had long been crammed into the small Casco Viejo area when the boom came and the population began to surge. In 1876 the Plan de Ensanche (expansion) de Bilbao was approved, and the area across the river was drawn up into segments governed by the curve of the Nervión. The Ensanche quickly became Bilbao's business district, and it remains so today, its graceful avenues lined with stately office buildings, prestige shops, and more than a few bars to which to adjourn at knock-off time.

El País Vasco Bilbao/Bilbo

Although you can stride across its width in a quarter of an hour, it's divided into barrios too; the studenty Indautxu, the besuited *Abando*. At weekends there's a different vibe, as patrolling families roam the shops by day and the bars and *discotecas* crank up for all-night action later on.

Museo de Bellas Artes ① *Plaza del Museo 2, T944396060, www.museobilbao.com, Tue-Sat 1000-2000, Sun 1000-1400, €4.50, €10 with Guggenheim, €2 audio guide, Metro Moyúa.* Not to be outdone by its titanium colleague, the Fine Arts Museum has tried to keep up with the times by adding a modern building of its own on to the existing museum. Opened in November 2001, the result is a harmonious credit to its architect, Luis Uriarte, who seamlessly and attractively fused new to old. Similarly, the collection is a medley of modern (mostly Basque) art and older works – there's also a new space for temporary exhibitions. The Basque sculptors Eduardo Chillida and Jorge de Oteiza are both well represented, but the museum confidently displays more avant-garde multimedia work by young artists too. Among the portraits, the jutting jaw of the Habsburg kings is visible in two famous works. The first, of a young Philip II, is by the Dutchman Moro, while the Philip IV, attributed to Velasquez, and similar to his portrait of the same king in the Prado, is a master work. The decline of Spain can be seen in the sad king's haunted but intelligent eyes, which seem to follow the viewer around the room. A lighter note is perhaps unintentionally struck by the anonymous Temptations of St Anthony, who is pestered by a trio of colourful demons. Among other items of interest is a painting of Bilbao by Paret y Alcazar. Dating from 1793 and painted from the Arenal, it looks like a sleepy riverside village.

Plaza de Toros de Vista Alegre ① *www.torosbilbao.com for details of corridas and ticketing, museum at C Martin Agüero 1, T944448698, Mon-Fri 1030-1300, 1600-1800, €1.50, Metro Indautxu.* Bilbao's temple of bullfighting, sees most action during Semana Grande in August, when there are *corridas* all week. The locals are knowledgeable and demanding of their matadors, and the bulls they face are acknowledged to be among the most *bravo* in Spain. Tickets to the spectacles don't come cheap, starting at about €30 for the cheapest seats. The ring also hosts occasional concerts. The bullring is also home to a museum dedicated to tauromachy; there are displays on the history of the practice, as well as memorabilia of famous matadors and bulls.

Estadio de San Mamés ① *C Felipe Serrate s/n, Metro: San Mamés, T944411445, www.athletic-club.es.* The stadium is at the far end of the new town. Few in the world are the football teams with the social and political significance of Athletic Bilbao, see box page 467; support of the team is a religion, and this, their home stadium, is known as the Cathedral of Football. Services are held fortnightly, usually on Sundays at about 1700. The Basque crowd are fervent but good-natured. It's well worth going to a game during the season; it's a far more friendly and social scene than the average match in the rest of Europe. The Monday papers frequently devote ten pages or more to Athletic's game. Tickets for games usually go on sale at the ground two days before the game. On match days, the ticket office opens two hours before kick-off. Athletic are building a museum in the stadium, but it will be some time before this is opened. There's currently no access to the ground itself except during game.

● **Sleeping**

Bilbao *p453, map p456*
Finding accommodation is frequently difficult; it's worth phoning ahead, although some of the *pensiones* won't take

reservations. Most budget accommodation is in or near the Casco Viejo, while the classier hotels are spread through the new town.
LL Hotel Carlton, Plaza Moyúa 2, T944162200, carlton@aranzazu-hoteles.com. Metro Moyúa. Set on noisy Plaza Moyúa, it is

considerably more luxurious inside than out. Its refurbished neoclassical ambience has colonnaded Einstein, Lorca, and Hemingway among other notables.

LL Hotel Ercilla, C Ercilla 37-39, T944705700, www.hotelercilla.es. Metro Indautxu. Well located on the city's main shopping street, this large 4-star hotel has a cheerful entrance and helpful service. It's undergoing a gradual renovation, and the rooms in the newer section are much the better for it. There are excellent weekend rates here, with savings up to 40%. Check the website for current offers. The hotel restaurant, the **Bermeo**, see Eating below, is excellent.

LL Hotel Lopez de Haro, C Obispo Orueta 2, T944235500, www.hotellopezdeharo.com. Metro Moyúa. A modern but still characterful 5-star hotel in classic style. While there are better hotels at this price, it's popular for its genuinely helpful service and excellent restaurant.

L Gran Domine, Alameda Mazarredo 61. Metro Moyúa. This just-opened 5-star hotel is directly opposite the Guggenheim and has been designed by innovative Basque architect Iñaki Aurrekoetxea. The original façade of the building consists of 48 mirrors at slightly different angles, while the interior is dominated by a large central atrium.

L Hotel Nervión, C Paseo Campo Volantín 11, T944454700, hotelbcnervion@barcelo clavel.com. Metro Casco Viejo. The cavernous lobby of this modish luxury hotel includes a piano, which is the focus of a weekly jazz session. The well-designed rooms offer the expected comforts, including the business traveller's delight, PlayStation. Some rooms have good river views.

L Hotel Indautxu, Plaza Bombero Etxariz s/n, T944211198, www.hotelindautxu.com. Metro Indautxu. Behind a mirrored façade which bizarrely dwarfs the older building in front, are comfortable executive-style rooms, set on a comparatively quiet square. There's a terrace, and pianists make the odd scheduled appearance in the bar. More character than many in this category and cheerful to boot.

A Hotel Deusto, C Francisco Maciá 9, T944760006, F944762199, Metro Deusto. This colourfully decorated hotel is an enjoyable place to stay on this side of the river. The large rooms, featuring minibar, safe, PlayStation and inviting beds are offset by an attractively arty bar and restaurant downstairs.

B Hotel Arriaga, C Ribera 3, T944790001, F944790516. Very friendly hotel with a garage and some excellent rooms with floor-to-ceiling windows and views over the theatre. Plush, formal-style decoration and fittings. Good value. Parking underneath for €10.80 per night. Recommended.

B Hotel Sirimiri, Plaza de la Encarnación 3, T944330759, www.hotelsirimiri.com. Named after the light misty rain that is a feature of the city, this is a small gem of a hotel in a quiet square. The genial owner has equipped it with a gym and sauna, and there's free parking at the back. Rooms come with TV, a/c, and phone. Recommended.

C Hostal Begoña, C Amistad 2, T944230134, www.hostalbegona.com. Metro Abando. A recent refit has transformed the Begoña into a welcoming modern hotel packed with flair and comfort. From the inviting library/lounge to the large chalet-style rooms and mini-suites at very reasonable prices, this is an excellent option. The hotel also offers free Internet access, and can organize a range of outdoor activities. Highly recommended.

C Iturrienea Ostatua, C Santa María, T944161500, F944158929. This beautiful *pensión* is caringly lined in stone, wood, and ideosyncratic objects. With delicious breakfasts and homely rooms, you might want to move in. Recommended.

C-E Hostal Mendéz, C Santa María 13, T944160364. Dignified building with castle-sized doors and an entrance guarded by iron dogs. The 1st floor has *hostal* -grade rooms with new bathrooms, while the 4th floor is *pensión* -style accommodation, simpler, but still very adequate, with many rooms with balconies.

E Hostal Gurea, C Bidebarrieta 14, T944163299. Carefully refurbished and well-scrubbed establishment on one of the Casco Viejo's principal axes. Welcoming and cheerfully vague about bookings. Usually request a 0100 curfew. Recommended.

El País Vasco Bilbao/Bilbo: listings

For an explanation of sleeping and eating price codes used in this guide, see inside the front cover. Other relevant information is found in Essentials, see pages 47-56.

E **Hostal Mardones**, C Jardines 4, T944153105. Run by a welcoming and chatty owner and very well situated in *pintxo* heartland. Entered by the side of a newsstand, the *pensión* is fitted in attractive dark wood, and both exterior and interior rooms are pleasant, light, and airy.

F **Pensión Ladero**, C Lotería 1, T944150932. Across the road from the Roquefer, this small and welcoming option has cork tiles, good shared bathrooms, and very well-priced rooms, with TV, some of which are reached by a tiny spiral staircase. Can be noisy in the mornings. Recommended.

F **Pensión Manoli**, C Libertad 2, T944155636. In the heart of the Casco Viejo with some good value exterior rooms with balcony and shared bathroom. Bright and well looked-after.

G **Albergue Bilbao Aterpetxea**, Ctra Basurto-Kastrexana 70, T944270054, www.albergue.bilbao.net. Bus 58 from Plaza Circular and the bus station. Bilbao's cheerful HI hostel is a block-of-flats-sized structure by a motorway on the outskirts of Bilbao. Despite its inconvenient location, it does have good facilities (including bike hire), although it may well be flooded with school groups. It's just about the cheapest bed in town for single travellers, but couples won't save much, and the 0930 check-out is a shock to the system when the rest of the nation runs with midday. There's a dining room with full meal service, but no kitchen facilities. Around €12.50 per person depending on season.

❶ Eating

Bilbao *p453, map p456*
Bilbao's Casco Viejo is undoubtedly the best place to head for *pintxos* and evening drinking, with the best areas being the Plaza Nueva and around the Siete Calles. There's another concentration of bars on Av Licenciado Poza and the smaller C García Rivero off it. The narrow C Ledesma, a street back from Gran Vía, is a popular place to head for after-work snacks and drinks. There are some good restaurants in the Casco Viejo, but also plenty of options scattered through the New Town and Deusto.

€€€ **Bermeo**, C Ercilla 37, T944705700. Metro Indautxu. Although it's the restaurant of the **Hotel Ercilla**, this stands on its own feet as one of the best places to dine in Bilbao. Specializing in seafood, which is done in both typical Basque style and some innovative modern styles.

€€€ **Guggenheim Restaurant**, Av Abandoibarra 2, T944239333. Metro Moyúa. A good all-round option in the museum. The restaurant is administered by one of San Sebastián's top chefs, and has the quality and prices to match, but also offers a *menú del día* for €12.39, which is first-rate. The furniture is Gehry's work, but the view over the car park is disappointing. No bookings are taken for the *menú*, which is served (slowly) from 1330 on a first-come basis. Both the cafés do a fine line in croissants, coffee, and *pintxos*; the one-off Gallery 104 has more seating and a nice view over the river.

€€€ **Guria**, Gran Vía 66, T944415780. Metro San Mamés. One of Bilbao's top restaurants with a sombrely elegant atmosphere. Its stock-in-trade, like many of its counterparts, is *bacalao*. After tasting it here, you may forgive the codfish all of the bad dishes that have been produced with it in other kitchens and factories around the world; if not, you can write *bacalao* off for good. There are *menús de degustacíon* for €41 and €59, and a *menú del dia* for €28.40. Outwith these, count on €60 a head minimum, more if you forsake the fish for the meat, which is tender and toothsome.

€€€ **Victor**, Plaza Nueva 2, T944151678. A quality upstairs restaurant with an elegant but relaxed atmosphere. This is a top place to try Bilbao's signature dish, *bacalao al pil-pil*, or the restaurant's variation on it, and there's an excellent wine selection. Conforms to the general Iberian rule of decreasing vegetables with increasing price. Recommended.

€€ **Aji Colorado**, C Barrencalle 5, T944152209. A small and friendly Peruvian restaurant in the heart of the Casco Viejo. Discover the taste of ceviche, delicious seafood 'cooked' by being marinated in lemon or lime juice – flavour and then some.

€€ **Casa Vasca**, Av Lehendakari Aguirre 13-15, T944483980. A Deusto institution on the main road – the front bar has a good selection of posh *pintxos* and a couple of comfortable nooks to settle down with a

⁝ Pile it high

Wherever you go in the Basque country, you'll be confronted and tempted by a massive array of food across the top of bars. Many bars serve up very traditional fare: slices of *tortilla* (potato omelette) or *pulgas de jamón* (small rolls with cured ham). Other bars, enthused by 'new Basque' cuisine, take things further and dedicate large parts of their day to creating miniature food sculptures using more esoteric ingredients – *pintxos*. The key factor is that they're all meant to be eaten. You can ask the bartender or simply help yourself to what you fancy, making sure to remember what you've had for the final reckoning. If you can't tell what something is, ask *de que es?* Pintxos usually cost about €1 to 1.20 depending on the bar.

slightly pricey drink. Behind is a restaurant that serves pretty authentic Basque cuisine in generous portions.

€€ **Kasko**, C Santa María, T944160311. With funky decor inspired by the fish and high-class new Basque food, this is one of the Casco Viejo's best restaurants, and has a very reasonable evening *menú* for €16.60, which is sometimes accompanied by a pianist. Recommended.

€€ **La Deliciosa**, C Jardines 1, T944163590. Modern decor and contemporary Basque cuisine in a new restaurant whose bright interior contrasts with the dark Casco Viejo alleys. The set dinner at €16 is good value. One of the few in the Casco to be open for Sun and Mon dinner.

€€ **Serantes and Serantes II**, C Licenciado Poza 16 and Alameda Urquijo 51, T944102066. Metro Indautxu. These *marisquerías* are not as pricy as their high reputation would suggest, with fish dishes around the €18 mark. It´s all very fresh, and the chefs have the confidence to let the flavours of the seafood hold their own. Go with the daily special – it's usually excellent, or tackle some *cigalas*, the 4WD of the prawn world, equipped with pincers (sometimes called Dublin Bay prawns in English).

€ **Buddha Bar**, C Ayala 1, T944157136. Metro Abando. Tucked away behind El Corte Inglés is this modern Asian fusion restaurant.

€ **Garibolo**, C Fernández del Campo 7, T944273255. Metro Moyúa. While at first glance Bilbao doesn't seem large enough a Spanish city to sustain a vegetarian restaurant, the colourful Garibolo packs 'em in, particularly for its €9 lunch special.

€ **Guggen Restaurant**, Alameda Recalde 5, T944248491. Metro Moyúa. Despite its name and its proximity to the museum, this restaurant is a fairly authentic workers' lunch den with an unspectacular but enjoyable *menú del día* for €6.15, and an upgraded version for those who don't want to pay as little as that.

€ **Rio Oja**, C Perro 4, T944150871. Another good option on this street, specializing in bubbling Riojan stews and Basque fish dishes, most of which are in big casseroles at the bar.

€ **Rotterdam**, C Perro 6. Small and uncomplicated Casco Viejo restaurant with a *simpático* boss. Decent lunch menú for €7.

Pintxo bars and cafés

Artajo, C Ledesma 7, T944248596. Metro Abando. Uncomplicated and candid bar with homely wooden tables and chairs and good traditional snacks of *tortilla* and *pulgas de jamón*. Famous for its *tigres*, mussels in spicy tomato sauce.

Bar Irintzi, C Santa María 8. *Pintxos* are an art form in this excellent bar; there's a superb array of imaginative snacks, all carefully labelled, freshly made, and compassionately priced.

Berton, C Jardines 11, T944167035. The hanging *jamones* and bunches of grapes define this cheerful bar, which has top-notch hammy *pintxos* and *raciones* and some quality wines by the glass. Packed at weekends.

Café-Bar Bilbao, Plaza Nueva 6, T944151671. A sparky place with top service and a selection of some of the better *pintxos* to be had around the old town.

El País Vasco Bilbao/Bilbo: listings

Café Boulevard, C Arenal 3, T944153128. Fans of art deco will not want to miss this refurbished defender of the style, which appears unchanged from the early 20th century, when it was Bilbao's beloved 'meeting place'.

Café Iruña, Jardines de Albia s/n, T944237021. Metro Abando. This noble old establishment on the **Jardines de Albia** is approaching its century in style. Well refurbished, the large building is divided into a smarter café space with wood panelling in neo-Moorish style, and a tiled bar with some good *pintxos* – including lamb kebabs sizzling on the barbie in the corner.

Café La Granja, Plaza Circular 3, T944230813. Metro Abando. Another spacious old Bilbao café, opened in 1926. Its high ceilings and long bar are designed to cope with the lively throng that comes in throughout the day. Plenty of attractive art nouveau fittings and good food. Closes fairly early.

Café Lamiak, C Pelota 8, T944161765. A relaxed 2-floor forum, the sort of place a literary genre, pressure group, or world-famous funk band might start out. Mixed crowd.

El Kiosko del Arenal, Muelle del Arenal s/n. Metro Casco Viejo. Elegant and cool café under the bandstand in the Arenal. Plenty of outdoor tables overlooking the river.

Gatz, C Santa María 10, T944154861. A convivial bar with some of the Casco's better *pintxos*, which are frequent contenders in the awards for such things. Happily spills on to the street at weekends.

Jaunak, C Somera 10. One of quite a few earthy, friendly Basque bars on this street, with a huge range of large *bocadillos* at about €3.50 a shot.

Lekeitio, C Diputación 1, T944239240. Metro Moyúa. An attentive bar with a fanstastic selection of after-work eats. The variety of fishy and seafoody *pintxos* are good, as is the *tortilla*.

Okela, C García Rivero 8, T944415937. Metro Indautxu. A modern bar popular with the office crowd and dominated by a huge signed photo of the footballer Joseba Etxebarria in full stride for Athletic Bilbao. Nice *pintxos*.

Oriotarra, C Blas de Otero 30, T944470830. A classy *pintxo* bar in Deusto that has won an award for the best bartop snack in Bilbao.

A round of applause for the pig's ear mille feuille.

Taberna Taurina, C Ledesma 5. Metro Abando. A tiny old-time tiles 'n' sawdust bar, which is packed top to bottom with bullfighting memorabilia. It's fascinating to browse the old pictures, which convey something of the sport's noble side. The *tortilla* here also commands respect.

Xukela, C Perro 2, T944159772. A very social bar on a very social street. Attractive *pintxos*, some good sit-down food, and a clientele upending glasses of Rioja at competitive pace until comparatively late.

❶ Bars and clubs

Bilbao *p453, map p456*
Bilbao doesn't go particularly late during the week – although there are always options – but makes up for it at weekends, when it doesn't stop until well after dawn.

Bars

Compañia del Ron, C Máximo Aguirre 23. Friends of Ronald will be happy here, with over 100 rums at the disposal of the bar staff, who know how to handle them. Despite the chain-pub feel, this is a good early-evening spot in the heart of the new town.

Bizitza, C Torre 1. Very chilled predominantly gay bar with a Basque political slant. Frequent cultural events.

Heaven, C Dos De Mayo 4, Bilbao. Metro Abando. A men-only gay bar with loud dance music that goes late. There's a lounge area and *cuarto oscuro* (backroom) behind the main bar.

K2, C Somera 10. One of the last to shut in the Casco on weeknights, this is quite a big bar with seating, a varied set of folk and exhibitions on the walls.

Luz Gas, C Pelota 6, T944790823. A beautiful mood bar with an Oriental touch. Sophisticated but friendly, and you can challenge all-comers to chess or **Connect-4**.

Primera Instancia, Alameda Mazarredo 6, T944236545. Metro Abando. Buzzy modern bar that's upmarket but far from pretentious. Small restaurant section with a €19.90 *degustacíon* menu. Check out the snazzy umbrella wrapper by the door.

Sperma, next door to **Heaven**, is a small and stylish option.

: Livin' la vida boca

So this Bilbaíno is in a bar chatting with a friend and asks him:
Did you hear that they've spent 100 million on El Guggenheim?
The friend thinks for a while:
Well, as long as he bangs in a few goals that's not too bad…
Rarely is a football team loved as deeply as Athletic Club are by Bilbao. A Basque symbol in the same league as the ikurriña or the Gernika oak, the team, as a matter of principle, only fields Basque players. Astonishingly, they have remained very competitive in the strongest league in the world and have never been relegated. To date, they have won the championship 8 times, more than any other club bar the two Madrid giants and Barcelona, and have won 24 Spanish Cups.

Athletic Club grew out of the cultural exchange that was taking place in the late 19th century between Bilbao and the UK. British workers brought football to Bilbao, and Basques went to Britain to study engineering. In the early years, Athletic fielded many British players, and their strip was modelled on that of Sunderland, where many of the miners were from. Jose Antonio Aguirre, who led the Civil War Basque government so nobly, had been a popular player up front for the club.

Games are usually on Sundays at 1700, see San Mamés page 462. The Monday papers usually devote at least 10 pages to the deeds of the previous day.

Twiggy, Alameda de Urquijo 35. Psychedelic colours and a sixties feel characterize this bar in one of the busiest weekend hubs.
Zulo, Barrenkale 22. A tiny nationalist bar with plenty of plastic fruit and a welcoming set who definitely don't follow the Bill Clinton line on non-inhalation. The name means 'hole' in Euskara.

Clubs

Many clubs are busiest around 0400 or 0500 in the morning.
Café Indie, C Doctor Areilza 34. Trendier and sleeker than the name might suggest. Sofas downstairs, and a bar and dancefloor upstairs. At weekends this makes some of the other clubs look empty, with both music and crowd that are suspiciously on the mainstream side of indie. British retro gets some play too.
Conjunto Vacío, C Muelle de la Merced 4. Empty by name and packed by nature, at least from about 2 on Friday and Saturday nights. The music is fairly light *bakalao*, the crowd mixed and good-looking, the drinks horrendously expensive, but the entry free.
Cotton Club, C Gregorio de la Revilla 25. Live music venue with a relaxed atmosphere and lined with characterful trappings from the world of showbiz. Music ranges from rock to jazz.
Distrito 9, Alameda Rekalde 18. Still probably the best spot in Bilbao for house music. Goes very late and is quite a dressy scene. Drag shows and a €10 cover.
La Lola, C Bailén 10. Decorated in industrial style with sheet-metal and graffiti, this is a good Saturday night club that varies in character from fairly cheesy dance to pretty heavy garage. Open until 0600, and then runs as a Sun day club from 1130. €5 at the door.

Entertainment

Bilbao *p453, map p456*
For footy and bullfighting, p438 and p462.
Cinema Cines Avenida, C Lehendakari Aguirre 18, T944757796. Metro Deusto. In Deusto, this is one of the better cinemas around, which tends to show a few lower profile releases and artier films, as well as some Basque pictures.
Music venues Bilbo Rock, Muelle de la Merced s/n, T944151306. Atmospheric venue in a converted church that is now a temple of live rock with bands playing most nights of the week at 2100 or 2200.

El País Vasco Bilbao/Bilbo: listings

Kafe Antzokia, C San Vicente 2, T944244625, www.kafeantzokia.com. An ex-cinema fast becoming a Bilbao icon, this is a live venue for anything from death metal to Euskara poetry, and features two spacious floors with bars that go late and loud at weekends. **Palacio Euskalduna**, C Abandoibarra 4, T944310310. Euskotren Abandoibarra, Metro San Mamés. Top-quality classical performances from the symphonic orchestras of Bilbao and Euskadi, as well as high-profile Spanish and international artists.

Theatre **Teatro Arriaga**, Plaza Arriaga 1, T944792036. Metro Abando/Casco Viejo. Bilbao's highest profile theatre is picturesquely set on the river by the Casco Viejo. It's a plush treat of a theatre in late 19th-century style, but the work it presents can be very innovative. The better seats go for €25 and above, but there are often decent pews available for as little as €4-5.

✹ Festivals and events

Bilbao *p453, map p456*
Aste Nagusia is Bilbao's largest festivals. Following on from those in Vitoria and San Sebastián to make a whole month of riotous partying. It starts on the Saturday after 15 Aug, and is a boisterous mixture of everything; concerts, *corridas*, traditional Basque sports, and serious drinking.

◎ Shopping

Bilbao *p453, map p456*
Bilbao is the best place to shop in Northern Spain. The majority of mainstream Spanish and international clothing stores are in the Ensanche, particularly on and around C Ercilla. The Casco Viejo harbours dozens of quirkier shops.

▲ Activities and tours

Bilbao *p453, map p456*
Barco Pil-Pil, Bilbao, T944465065. Trips Apr-Oct Sat/Sun, Jul/Aug Tue-Sun, €9.30, 1-hr trip and drink. Dinner and dance cruises, 4 hrs, all year Fri/Sat, €49.50, book in advance as the meal is pre-prepared by caterers. Leaves from a jetty not far from the Guggenheim Museum.

Bilbao Paso a Paso, T944730078, bilbao.pap@euskalnet.net, run knowledgeable tours of Bilbao and the whole of Euskadi that can be tailored to suit. **Eroski Bidaiak**, C Licenciado Poza 10, T944439012; **Viajes Ecuador**, Gran Vía 81, T902207070, both offer tours, bookings.

◎ Transport

Bilbao *p453, map p456*
Air The cheapest direct flights from the UK are with the budget operator **easyJet**, www.easyjet.com. Bilbao is also served from **London** by **Iberia** and **British Airways** and directly connected with several other European cities, including **Frankfurt**, **Zürich**, **Brussels**, **Paris**, **Milan**, and **Lisbon**, and has frequent domestic connections with **Madrid**, **Barcelona**, and other Spanish cities operated by **Iberia** and **Spanair**. Airlines offices contact details: **Iberia**, C Ercilla 20, Bilbao, T944245506, www.iberia.es; **Spanair**, Aeropuerto de Bilbao, T944869498, www.spanair.com; **British Airways**, Aeropuerto de Bilbao, T944710523, www.british-airways.com.

Bilbao's brand new **airport** is in Sondika, 10 km north east of the centre. It's a beautiful building designed by Santiago Calatrava, seemingly in homage to the whale. A taxi to/from town costs about €15-20. There's an efficient bus service that runs to/from Plaza Moyúa in central Bilbao. It leaves from outside the terminal and takes 20-30 mins. From airport Mon-Fri every 30 mins at 15 and 45 mins past the hour, Sat hourly at 30 mins past. From Plaza Moyúa Mon-Fri every 30 mins on the half-hour, Sat hourly on the hour. One-way €0.95.

Boat P&O run a ferry service from **Portsmouth** to Bilbao but in reality it's more of a cruise than a transport connection. The ship, the *Pride of Bilbao*, is the largest ferry operating out of the UK and has several restaurants, a cinema, pool, sauna and casino. None of which comes cheap. It's a 2-night trip, and cabin accommodation is mandatory; look at £400-500 return with a car. Boats leave Portsmouth at 2000, Tue and Sat, except during winter, when there are few crossings. The return ferry leaves Bilbao on Thu and Mon at 1230. Many passengers don't even get off. Book online at

www.poportsmouth.com or on 0870 242 4999. The ferry port is at Santurtzi, 13 km from the city centre, accessible by **Euskotren**.

Bus The majority, but by no means all, of Bilbao's interurban buses leave from the **Termibus** station near the football stadium (Metro San Mamés). All long-haul destinations are served from here, but several Basque towns are served from the stops next to Abando station on C Hurtado Amezaga or by the tourist office on the Arenal.

Bilbao to **San Sebastián**: buses from the **Termibus** station every 30 mins weekdays, every hour at weekends, operated by **PESA**. Also trains from Atxuri station every hour on the hour, 2 hrs 39 mins, €5.50.

Bilbao to **Vitoria**: buses from the **Termibus** station about every 30 mins with **Autobuses La Union**, 55 mins, €4.50.

Car hire The usual assortment of multinationals dominate this cut-throat trade. The process is fairly painless, and national driving licences are accepted.

Atesa, C Sabino Arana 9, T944423290; Aeropuerto de Bilbao, T944533340, www.atesa.es. State-run and cheaper but less efficient than the multis.

Avis, Av Doctor Areilza 34, T944275760; Aeropuerto de Bilbao, T944869648; www.avis.com.

Hertz, C Doctor Achucarro 10, T944153677; Aeropuerto de Bilbao, T944530931; www.hertz.com.

Cycle hire Bilbao currently has a notable lack of cycle hire. The youth hostel and the **Hotel Nervión** both hire bikes, but normally only to guests, although they might be persuaded.

Metro Greater Bilbao, long and thin as it follows the river valley down to the sea, was much in need of an efficient public transport system when it commissioned Norman Foster to design an underground in 1988. In November 1995 the line was opened and the Bilbaínos were impressed with the Mancunian's work. Foster's design is simple, attractive, and, above all, spacious; claustrophobes will be able to safely banish Bakerloo line nightmares. Many of the stations are entered through *fosteritos*, distinctive transparent plastic tubes nicknamed for the architect.

Train Bilbao has 3 train stations. The main one, Abando, is the terminal of **RENFE**, the national Spanish railway. It's far from a busy network, and the bus usually beats it over a given distance but it's the principal mainline service. Abando is also the main terminus for **Euskotren**, a handy short-haul train network, which connects Bilbao and **San Sebastián** with many of the smaller Basque towns as well as their own **outlying suburbs**. The other Bilbao base for these trains is Atxuri, situated just east of the Casco Viejo, an attractive but run-down station for lines running eastwards as far as San Sebastián. These are particularly useful for reaching the towns of **Euskadi's coast**. **Gernika** is serviced every hour (18 mins past, 53 mins) and on to**Mundaka** and **Bermeo**. Trains to **San Sebastián** every hour on the hour (2 hrs 39 mins) via **Zarautz**, **Zumaia**, **Eibar**, **Durango**.

Private FEVE trains connect Bilbao along the coast to **Santander** and beyond. They are slow but scenic and leave, unsurprisingly, from the Estación de Santander just next to Bilbao's main Abando railway station.

❶ Directory

Bilbao *p453, map p456*

Consulates Britain T944157600; Eire T944912575; France T944249000; Germany T944238585; Portugal T944354540; South Africa T944641124. The nearest consular representative of the USA is at the embassy in Madrid, T915872200.

Doctors Clínica San Sebastián, C Rafael Ibarra 25.

Hospitals Hospital de Basurto, Av Montevideo 18, T944006000, T944755000. Metro San Mamés.

Internet **Laser Internet**, C Sendeja 5, T944453509. Mon-Fri 1030-0230; Sat/Sun 1100-0230, €0.05 per min. Photocopier and fax services also. Handy and pretty quick. **El Señor de la Red**, Alameda de Rekalde 14, T944237425. €2 per hr. **Ciber Bilbo**, C Pablo Picasso 7, T944218176. Internet and *locutório*. **Web Press**, C Barrancua 11, Mon-Sun 1000-2230.

Language schools Language Schools Instituto Hemingway, C Bailén 5, T944167901, www.institutohemingway.com.

Laundry Laundry Tintoreria Lavaclin, Campo de Volantín 15, T944453191. Bag wash for €10.

Library Biblioteca Municipal, C Bidebarrieta 4, T944156930. Mon-Fri 0930- 2100, Sat 0930-1400. Beautiful library in the Old Town.

Police The emergency number for all necessities in 112, while 091 will take you to the local police. Main police station is Policia Municipal Bilbao, C Luis Briñas 14, T944205000.

Post Bilbao main post office: Alameda Urquijo 19. Casco Viejo branch: C Epalza 4 (opposite Arenal).

Useful addresses and numbers The emergency number is 112. Dialling 091 will patch you through to the local police force, while 085 will get an ambulance.

Around Bilbao

The seaside suburbs, once reached by hours of painstaking river navigation by sweating steersmen, are now a nonchalant 20 minutes away by Metro. Fashionable Getxohas a relaxed beachy atmosphere while, across the estuary, Portugaletestill seems to be wondering how Bilbao gets all the credit these days: for hundreds of years it was a far more important port. Much of inland Vizcaya is fairly industrial, but the mountains are green and craggy, and there are several smaller towns worth visiting. ›› *For Sleeping, Eating and other listings, see pages 472-474.*

Bilbao's seafront

At the mouth of the estuary of the Nervión, around 20 km from Bilbao, the fashionable barrio of Getxo is linked by the improbably massive Puente Vizcaya with the grittier town of Portugalete, in its day a flourishing medieval port. On a nice day, it's a great day trip from Bilbao; the fresh air here is a treat for tired lungs, and not far from Getxo stretch the languid beach suburbs of Sopelana, Plentzia, and Gorliz.

Getxo → *Colour map 2, grid A3.*

Very much a separate town rather than a suburb of Bilbao, Getxo is a wealthy, sprawling district encompassing the eastern side of the rivermouth, a couple of beaches, and a petite old harbour. It's home to a good set of attractive stately mansions as well as a tiny but oh-so-pretty whitewashed old village around the now disused fishing port-ette. There's a very relaxed feel about the place, perhaps born from a combination of the relaxed seaside air and a lack of anxiety about where the next meal is coming from.

Playa de Ereaga is Getxo's principal stretch of sand, and location of its tourist office and finer hotels. Near it, the Puerto Viejo is a tiny harbour, now silted up, and a reminder of the days when Getxo made its living from fish. The solemn statues of a fisherman and a *sardinera* stand on the stairs that look over it, perhaps mystified at the lack of boats. Perching above, a densely packed knot of white houses and narrow lanes gives the little village a very Mediterranean feel, unless the *sirimiri*, the Bilbao drizzle, has put in an appearance. There are a couple of restaurants and bars to soak up the ambience of this area, which is Getxo's prettiest quarter.

Further around, the **Playa de Arrigunaga** is a better beach flanked by crumbly cliffs, one topped by a windmill, which some days has a better time of it than the shivering bathers. A pleasant, if longish, walk leads downhill to the estuary end of Getxo, past an ostentatious series of 20th-century *palacios* on the waterfront, and a monument to Churruca, whose engineering made the estuary navigable, making Bilbao accessible to large vessels; a vital step in its growth.

Passing the hulking modern **Iglesia de Nuestra Señora de las Mercedes**, which contains some highly-regarded frescoes, will bring you to the unmistakeable form of the Puente Vizcaya and the trendy shopping area of Las Arenas (Areeta). Tourist information ① *Playa de Ereage s/n, T944910800.*

Puente Vizcaya

① *1000-sunset, €0.24 per person, €1 per car, walkway €3, Metro Areeta.*
A bizarre cross between a bridge and a ferry, the Puente Vizcaya was opened in 1893, a time when large steel structures were à la mode in Europe. Wanting to connect the esturay towns of Getxo and Portugalete by road, but not wanting a bridge that would block the *ría* to shipping, the solution taken was to use a 'gondola' suspended by cables from a high steel span. It's a fascinating piece of engineering – the modern gondola fairly zooms back and forth with six cars plus foot passengers aboard. You can also ascend to the walkway 50 m above. You'll often see the bridge referred to as the Puente Colgante (hanging bridge).

Portugalete

On the other side of the Puente Vizcaya from Getxo is Portugalete, a solid working-class town with a significant seafaring history. In former times, before Churruca did his channelling work, the Nervión estuary was a silty minefield of shoals, meanders, and sandbars – a nightmare to navigate in anything larger than a rowing boat. Thus Bilbao was still a good few hours' journey by boat, and Portugalete's situation at the mouth of the ría gave it great importance as a port. Nowadays, although from across the water it looks thoroughly functional, it preserves a characterful old town and attractive waterfront strollway.

Above the waterside the old Casco is dominated by the **Iglesia de Santa María**, commissioned by Doña María the Kind at the time of the town's beginnings, although the current building, in Gothic style, dates from the early 16th century. There's a small museum inside. Next to it, the **Torre de Salazar** is what remains of the formidable compound built by Juan López de Salazar, a major landowner, in about 1380. The main living area was originally on the second floor – the first was a prison – and the tower was occupied until 1934 when a fire evicted the last residents. One of the Salazar family who lived here, Luís García, was one of the first chroniclers of Vizcaya. He had plenty of time to devote to his writings, as he spent the last few years of his life locked up by his loving sons.

Inland Vizcaya

Markina → *Colour map 2, grid A4.*

This village in the Vizcayan hills is set around a long leafy plaza. Not a great deal goes on here but what does is motivated by one thing and one thing only: *pelota*. Many *hijos de Markina* have achieved star status in the sport, and the *frontón* is proudly dubbed the 'university of pelota'. As well as the more common *pelota a mano*, there are regular games of *cesta punta*, in which a long wicker scoop is worn like a glove, adding some serious velocity to the game. Games are usually on a Sunday evening, but it's worth ringing the tourist office, or checking the website www.euskalpilota.com.

The hexagonal chapel of **San Miguel de Arretxmago** is a 10-minute stroll from the plaza on the other side of the small river. The building itself is unremarkable but inside, surprisingly, are three enormous rocks, naturally balanced, with an altar to the saint underneath that far predates the building. According to local tradition, St Michael buried the devil here; a lingering odour of brimstone would tend to confirm this. This is the place to be at midnight on 29 September, when the village gathers to perform two traditional dances, the *aurresku*, and the *mahai gaineko*.

A half-hour walk from Markina is the hamlet of Bolibar, which features a museum dedicated to a man who never set foot here. Simón Bolivar, El Libertador (the Liberator) to half of South America, was born in Caracas to a family who originally came from here. The museum ① *Tue-Fri 1000-1300, Sat/Sun 1200-1400. Open afternoons 1700-1900 in Jul and Aug, free*, documents some of the family's history as well as the life and career of the man himself. There's a summer tourist office in a palace across the iron footbridge over the river.

Elorrio → *Colour map 2, grid A4.*

The most Basque of places, this inland Vizcayan community is highly recommended for a peaceful overnight stay. Overwatched by some rugged peaks, it's a small valley town and one of the few places where you might hear as much Euskara spoken on the street as Spanish. The small and appealing old town is centred around the church, which has a beautiful belltower and looks a treat floodlit at night. The church is set on a shady plaza, also home to the Ayuntamiento, which sports an old sundial and a couple of finger-wagging quotes from the Bible.

In the streets around the plaza are many well-preserved buildings, including the attractive vine-swathed Palacio de Zearsolo, dating from the 17th century. Families of Elorrio must have been keen on one-upmanship – dozens of ornate coats-of-arms can be seen engraved on façades around the town. There's a spirited Basque feeling about the place with plenty of posters, flags, and bars making the local position on independence, torture of Basque prisoners, and Basqueness in general very clear. When the wind blows the wrong way down the valley, another typically Basque sensation can be detected; the smell of the pulp and paper mills around Durango.

An energetic walk is to climb the mountain of **Udalaitz/Udalatx** (1,117 m), the most distinctive of the peaks visible from the town. The mountain is accessible off the Bl632 about 7 km from town, on the way to Mondragón or, more easily, off the Gl3551 outside of that town. The climb isn't as steep as it looks, but it's still a good workout.

● Sleeping

Bilbao's seafront *p470*
Staying here is a good alternative to the city; there are plenty of options.

A **Gran Hotel Puente Colgante**, C María Díaz de Haro 2, T944014800, www.granhotel puentecolgante.com. Euskotren Portugalete, Metro Areeta. Very recently opened in a reconstructed 19th-century building with a grand façade, this upmarket modern hotel is superbly situated right next to the Puente Vizcaya on the waterfront promenade. All the rooms face outwards, and the hotel has all the facilities you come to expect.

A **Hotel Igeretxe**, Playa de Ereaga s/n, T944910009, F944608599. Metro Neguri. Shaded by palms, this welcoming hotel is right on Ereaga beach, Getxo's main social strand. Formerly a *balneario*, the hotel still offers some spa facilities, as well as a restaurant overlooking the slightly grubby sand. Breakfast included.

D **Pensión Usategi**, C Landene 2,

T944913918. Metro Bidezabal. Well placed on the headland above pretty Arrigunaga beach, the rooms are clean and cool, and some have great views.

E **Pensión Areeta**, C Mayor 13 (Las Arenas), T944638136. Metro Areeta. Near the metro of the same name and a iron bar's throw from the Puente Vizcaya, this is a good place in the heart of the trendy Las Arenas district of Getxo.

Camping
Camping Sopelana, Ctra Bilbao-Plentzia s/n, T946762120. Metro Sopelana. Very handy for the Metro into Bilbao, this is the most convenient campsite within range of the city. Well equipped with facilities, and in easy range of the shops, it's right by the beach too. Bungalows available, which are reasonable value.

Inland Vizcaya *p471*
B **Hotel Elorrio**, Bº San Agustín s/n, Elorrio, T946231555, hotelelorrio@wanadoo.es. A

short walk from the centre on the Durango road, this modern hotel is not the prettiest but has some good views around the valley and a decent restaurant. As its primary function is for business, it's a fair bit cheaper come the weekend. The rooms are attractive, airy, and light.

D Berriolope, in the hamlet of Berrio, T946820640, is the most luxurious of the three *agroturismos* near Elorrio, with 6 attractive doubles with bathroom in a vine-covered stone building.

D-E Hotel Vega, C Abasua 2, Markina, Bolibar, T946166015, is a sleepy place on the square that makes a relaxing base and has rooms both with and without bathroom.

G Pensión Nerea, C Pio X 32, Elorrio. A budget traveller's dream with perfectly adequate rooms with shared bathrooms for a pittance. If no one's about, go to the *tintorería* at C Labakua 8.

● Eating

Bilbao's seafront *p470*
Some of Bilbao's best dining can be done out here.

€€€ Cubita Kaia, Muelle de Arriluze 10-11, T944600103. Metro Neguri. A highly acclaimed restaurant with views over the water from Getxo's marina. People have been known to kill for the *cigalas* (Dublin bay prawns) turned out by young modern chef Alvaro Martínez. Not to be confused with another restaurant named Cubita next to the windmill above Arrigunaga beach.

€€€ Jolastoki, Av Leioa 24, T944912031. Metro Neguri. Decorated in classy but homely country mansion style, Jolastoki is a house of good repute throughout Euskadi. Definitely traditional in character, dishes such as *caracoles en salsa vizcaína* (snails) and *liebre* (hare) are the sort of treats that give Basque cuisine its lofty reputation.

€€ Karola Etxea, C Aretxondo 22, T944600868. Metro Algorta. Perfectly situated in a quiet lane above the old port. It's a good place to try some fish; there are usually a few available, such as *txitxarro* (scad) or *besugo* (sea bream). The *kokotxas* (cheeks and throats of hake in sauce) are also delicious.

€ Restaurante Vegetariano, Algortako Etorbidea 100, T944601762. Metro Algorta.

A good vegetarian option with a salad buffet, a *menú del día* for €8, and an upbeat attitude.

Pintxos bars and cafés
Zodiako's, C Euskal Herria s/n (corner of Telletxe), T944604059. Metro Algorta. This squiggly bar in the heart of Getxo is one of the area's best, with a terrace, *pintxos*, and service with a smile. There's a *discoteca* underneath.

Inland Vizcaya *p471*
Pintxos bars and cafés
Parra Taberna is a peaceful bar in Elorrio with tables on the main square and a beautiful glass and stone interior.

▲ Activities and tours

Bilbao's seafront *p470*
Getxo Abentura is an initiative of the Getxo tourist office. They'll organize just about any outdoor activity you can think of in the Getxo area, from caving to canoeing, provided there are enough people to make a go of it (usually 4 for group-style outings).
Maremoto Renting, Puerto Deportivo de Getxo, T650439211, rental of jet-skis, sailboards, run trips.
Náutica Getxo, Puerto Deportivo de Getxo, T609985977, nauticagetxo@terra.es. On the jetty at the end of Ereaga beach, this company hires out yachts with or without a skipper. Sailing knowledge isn't really required as the boats come with auxiliary power, but if you want to learn to sail, these guys can teach you that too.

● Transport

Bilbao's seafront *p470*
For **Getxo**, Metro stops Areeta, Gobela, Neguri, Aiboa, Algorta, and Bidezabal. Buses 3411 and 3413 run from Plaza Moyúa every half-hour. The beaches further on can be accessed from Larrabasterra, Sopelana, and Plentzia metros. **Tsunami**, at the marina in Getxo, T944606503, rent bicycles but charge an outrageous €31 for a day.
For **Portugalete** Euskotren from Abando (Santurtzi line) every 12 mins weekdays, less frequently at weekends, 20 mins.
Metro Areeta (across bridge), bus 3152 from the Arenal bus station in Bilbao (Mon-Sat).

Markina is serviced by the bus company Pesa which run a bus 4 times daily from Bilbao bus station (which continues to Ondarroa), also by Bizkaibus every half-hour (slightly slower).

ⓘ Directory

Bilbao's seafront *p470*
Internet Net House, Plaza Villamonte 5 Getxo, below Algorta metro, T944319171. €2.70 per hr, 1000-2200 daily.

Alava

The province of Alava is something of a wilderness compared to the densely settled valleys of Vizcaya and Guipúzcoa. It's the place to come for unspoiled nature; there are

❣ *If you venture off the main roads in Alava you'll feel like an explorer; the tourist count is low in Alava, even in high summer.*

some spots of great natural beauty, and plenty of scope for hiking and other more specialized outdoor activities. The capital of Euskadi, Vitoria/Gasteiz, makes a pleasant base for exploring the region. The attractive walled town of Salvatierra is worth a visit and a base for exploring the area. The southern part of the province drops away to sunny plains, part of the Rioja wine region. Laguardia, the area's main centre is not to be missed.

Vitoria/Gasteiz → *Phone code: 945; Colour map 2, grid A4; Population: 218,902.*

Vitoria is the quiet achiever of the Basque trio. A comparatively peaceful town, it comes as a surprise to many visitors to discover that it's the capital of the semi- autonomous Basque region. A thoughtful place, it combines an attractive old town with an Ensanche (expansion) designed to provide plenty of green spaces for its hard-working inhabitants. While it lacks the big-city vitality of Bilbao or the languid beauty of San Sebastián it's a satisfying city much-loved by most who visit it. Perhaps because it's the political centre of the region, the young are very vocally Basque, and the city feels energized as a result. ▸▸ *For Sleeping, Eating and other listings, see pages 481-484.*

Ins and outs

Getting there Victoria bus station is just east of town on C Los Herrán. There are frequent connections with Bilbao. Vitoria's RENFE station is south of the centre at C Eduardo Dato and has better connections with Spain than Bilbao.▸▸ *For further details, see Transport page 483.*

Getting around Vitoria is a good two-wheel city with more planned cycle ways and green spots than in busier Bilbao. Vitoria train station to the Basilica at Armentia, €5. Vitoria is easily walkable on foot with C Dato the focus of the evening *paseo*.

Tourist information Head for either the efficient city tourist office ⓘ *C Eduardo Dato 11, Mon-Sat 1000-1900, Sun 1100-1400*, or the Basque government office ⓘ *southwestern corner of Parque de La Florida, Mon-Sun 0900-1300, 1500-1900*. Both are helpful.

Background

Vitoria's shield-shaped old town sits on the high ground that perhaps gave the city its name; beturia is an Euskara word for hill. After having been a Basque settlement, then a Roman one, Vitoria was abandoned until being refounded and fortified by the kings of Navarra in the 12th and 13th centuries. An obscure Castilian town for much of history, Vitoria featured in the Peninsular War, when, on Midsummer's Day in 1813, Napoleon's forces were routed by the Allied troops and fled in ragged fashion towards home, abandoning their baggage train, containing millions of francs, which was

gleefully looted. "The battle was to the French", commented a British officer sagely, "like salt on a leech's tail". Vitoria has thrived since being named capital of the semi-autonomous Basque region, and has a genteel, comfortable air, enlivened by an active student population.

Sights

Casco Medieval Calle Cuchillería, and its continuation, Calle Chiquita, is the most happening part of the old town, with several impressive old mansions, a couple of museums, dozens of bars, and plenty of pro-Basque political attitude. Like several in the Casco Medieval, this street is named for the craftspeople who used to have shops here; in this case makers of knives. Walking along this street and those nearby you can see a number of old inscriptions and coats of arms carved on buildings.

Housed in a beautiful fortified medieval house on Cuchillería, the unusual **Museo Fournier** ① *Tue-Fri 1000-1400, 1600-1830, Sat 1000-1400, Sun 1200-1400, free*, is devoted to the playing card, of which it holds over 10,000 packs. Diamonds might be a girl's best friend, but there aren't too many on show here – the cards are mostly Spanish decks, with swords, cups, coins and staves the suits. The corner of the old town at the end of Calle Chiquita of is one of Vitoria's most picturesque. **Casa del Portalón**, now a noted restaurant, is a lovely old timbered building from the late 15th century. It used to be an inn and a staging post for messengers. Across from it is the **Torre de los Anda**, which defended one of the entrances in the city wall. Opposite these is the 16th-century house of the Gobeo family that now holds the **archaeology museum** ① *Tue-Fri 1000-1400, 1600-1830, Sat 1000-1400, Sun 1100-1400, free*. The province has been well occupied over history, and the smallish collection covers many periods, from prehistoric through Roman and medieval. There are three floors of objects, of which arguably the most impressive is the so-called Knight's Stele, a tombstone carved with a horseman dating from the Roman era.

Iglesia de San Miguel stands like one of a series of chess pieces guarding the entrance to the Casco Medieval. Two gaping arches mark the portal, which is superbly carved. A niche here holds the city's patron saint, the Virgen Blanca, a coloured late Gothic figure. On the saint's day, 5 August, a group of townspeople carry the figure of Celedón (a stylized farmer) from the top of the graceful belltower down to the square.

Los Arquillos is slightly strange series of dwellings and covered colonnades was designed in the early 19th century as a means of more effectively linking the high Casco Medieval with the newer town below, and to avoid the risk of the collapse of the southern part of the hill. It leads up to the attractive small Plaza del Machete, where incoming city chancellors used to swear an oath of allegiance over a copy of the Fueros (city statutes) and a machete, in this case a military cutlass. The postcardy Plaza de España (Basques prefer to call it Plaza Nueva) was designed by the same man, Olaguíbel, who thought up the Arquillos. It's a beautiful colonnaded square housing the town hall and several bars with terraces that are perfect for the morning or afternoon sun.

Her Gothic majesty **Catedral de Santa María** ① *Tours at 1100, 1400, 1700, and 2000, but check with the tourist office or www.catedralvitoria.com for the current situation*, is undergoing a long-term renovation. While this is taking place, the massive 14th-century structure is closed to passing visitors. However, guided tours of the renovation works are being run when the state of play allows. The tours are interesting: the project is a massive one and involves considerable ingenuity and expertise.

New Town Vitoria's new town isn't going to blow anyone's mind with a cavalcade of Gaudí-esque buildings or wild street parties but it is a very satisfying place: a planned mixture of attractive streets and plenty of parkland. It's got the highest amount of greenery per citizen of any city in Spain and it's no surprise that it's been voted one of the best places to live in Spain. With the innovative Artium in place, the mantle of

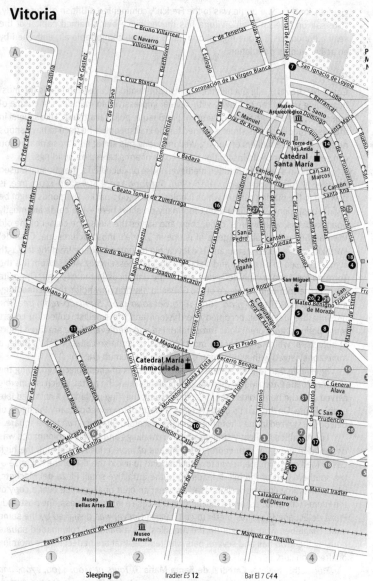

N

| 0 metres | 100 |
| 0 yards | 100 |

Sleeping

Achuri *E5* **1**
Almoneda *E3* **2**
Amarica *E3* **3**
Canciller Ayala *E3* **4**
Casa 400 *E5* **5**
Ciudad de Vitoria *E1* **6**
Dato *E4* **7**
Desiderio *C5* **8**
Hostal Eguileta *C5* **9**
Hostal Florida *E5* **10**
Hostal Nuvilla *E5* **11**

Iradier *E5* **12**
La Bilbaína *C5* **13**
Páramo *E4* **14**
Pensión Antonio *C4* **15**
Pensión Araba II *E4* **16**
Pensión La Paz *E4* **17**
Pensión Zuriñe *E4* **18**

Eating

Antiguo Felipe *D5* **1**
Arkupe *D4* **2**
Asador Matxete *D4* **3**

Bar El 7 *C4* **4**
Baztertxo *D4* **5**
Café Jai Alai *D5* **6**
Café Los Angeles *A4* **7**
Café Moderno *D4* **8**
Cafeteria Marañón *D4* **9**
Cuatro Azules Florida *E3* **10**
Dos Hermanas *D1* **11**
El Jardín de Amarica *E4* **12**
Eli Rekondo *D3* **13**
Hala Bedi *B4* **14**
Ikea *F1* **15**

The shiny new **Atrium** ① *C Francia 24, T945209020, www.artium.org, Tue-Fri 1100-2000, Sat/Sun 1030-2000, €3, Wed 'you decide',* (opened April 2002) is Vitoria's answer to Bilbao's Guggenheim and San Sebastián's Kursaal. It's an exciting project, which features some excellent contemporary artwork and many exhibitions, some of which incorporate some of the older buildings in Vitoria's Casco Medieval. Shiny and white, the visitor's attention is taken immediately by the building's confident angles and Javier Pérez's *Un pedazo de cielo cristalizado* (A crystallized piece of heaven), a massive hanging glass sculpture in the atrium. The galleries are accessed down the stairs. The work by contemporary artists, mostly Basque, is backed up by some earlier 20th-century pieces by Miró, Dalí, and Picasso, among others. The cool little café is also a good place to hang out.

There's no missing the new **Catedral de María Inmaculada**; built in the 20th century in neo-Gothic style; its bulk looms attractively over this part of the town. Built in authentic medieval style, it now houses the **Museo Diocesano de Arte Sacro** ① *Tue-Fri 1000-1400, 1600-1830, Sat 1000-1400, Sun 1100-1400, free.*

The gorgeous **Parque de la Flórida** is an excellent retreat right in the heart of Vitoria. Cool and shady, the park has a number of exotic trees and plants and a couple of peaceful cafés. You can watch old men in berets playing *bolas* (boules), and there's an old bandstand with Sunday concerts, guarded by statues of four ancient kings. If you see anyone taking things too seriously, they're probably politicians – the Basque Parliament stands in one corner of the park.

It's well worth the half-hour walk or the bus ride to see **Basílica de San Prudencio** in the village of Armentia, now subsumed into Vitoria's outskirts. The village is supposedly the birthplace of San Prudencio, the patron saint of

El País Vasco Vitoria/Gasteiz

Alava province, and the church was erected in his honour. It was rebuilt in the 18th century, but still has some excellent features from its Romanesque youth, such as a harmonious round apse and the carvings above the doors, one of Christ and the apostles, the other of the Lamb and John the Baptist. To reach Armentia on foot, continue past the Museo de Bellas Artes on Paseo Fray Francisco de Vitoria, then turn left down Paseo de Cervantes when you reach the modern chapel of La Sagrada Familia. The basilica is at the end of this road.

Western Alava → *Colour map 2, grid A3.*

West of Vitoria the green pastures soon give way to a rugged and dry terrain, home of vultures, eagles, and spectacular rock formations. The area is fairly well served by bus from Vitoria. ▶▶ *For Sleeping, Eating and other listings, see pages 481-484.*

Salinas de Añana

This hard-bitten half-a-horse village has one of the more unusual sights in the Basque lands. The place owes its existence to the incredibly saline water that wells up from the ground here, which was diverted down a valley and siphoned into any number of *eras* or pans, flat evaporation platforms mounted on wooded stilts. It's something very different and an eerie sight, looking a little like the ruins of an ancient Greek city in miniature. As many as 5,500 pans were still being used by the 1960s but nowadays only about 150 are going concerns. The first written reference to the collection of salt in these parts was in AD822, but it seems pretty likely the Romans had a go too.

During **Semana Santa** Salinas itself comes to life; Judas is put on trial by the villagers. It's something of a kangaroo court though; the poor man is always convicted and then burned.

Cañon de Delika

To the west beyond Salinas, and actually reached via the province of Burgos, is this spectacular canyon that widens into the valley of Orduña. The river Nervión has its source near here and when running, it spectacularly spills 300 m into the gorge below: the highest waterfall in Spain. There's a good 1½-hour round walk from the car park. Follow the right-hand road first, which brings you to the falls, then follow the cliffs along to the left, where vultures soar above the valley below. When you reach the second mirador, looking down the valley to Orduña, there's another road that descends through beech forest back to the car park. Near the car park is a spring, the Fuente de Santiago. Legend has it that St James stopped here to refresh himself and his horse during his alleged time in Spain. Access the site from a car park, which is about 3 km from the main road, the 2625 (running from Orduña in the north to Espejo in the south and beyond, turn-off is signposted Monte Santiago and is about 8 km south of Orduña).

Eastern Alava → *Colour map 2, grid A4.*

The eastern half of the Alava plain is dotted with interesting villages, churches, and prehistoric remains. The town of Salvatierra is the most convenient base for exploration. At the northern fringes of the plain, the mountains rise into Guipúzcoa. Part of the Camino de Santiago passes through the natural tunnel of San Adrián here, and there's some scenic walking to be done. ▶▶ *For Sleeping, Eating and other listings, see pages 481-484.*

Salvatierra/Agurain

The major town in eastern Alava is the not-very-major Salvatierra, a well-preserved, walled medieval town with some interesting buildings. Around Salvatierra there's plenty of walking, canyoning, and abseiling to be done, while further afield canoeing, windsurfing, paragliding, and horse trekking can be arranged. The sleeping and eating possibilities are nothing to write home about, but there are a couple of pensiones, both attached to restaurants.

Túnel de San Adrián and around

One of the most interesting walks starts from the hamlet of Zalduondo, 8 km north of Salvatierra. A section of the Camino de Santiago, part of it follows the old Roman/medieval highway that effectively linked most of the peninsula with the rest of Europe. It's about 5½ km from Zalduondo to a small parking area named Zumarraundi. From there, the track ascends through beech forest to the Túnel de San Adrián. Shortly after meeting the old stone road, there's a right turn up a slope that's easy to miss: look for the wooden signpost at the top of the rise to your right. The tunnel itself is a spectacular natural cave cutting a path through the hill. It now houses a small chapel, perhaps built to assuage the fears of medieval pilgrims, many of whom thought that the cave was the entrance to Hell. After the tunnel, the trail continues into Guipúzcoa, reaching the attractive town of Zegama about 90-minutes' walk further on.

Zalduondo and Eguliaz

The area around Zalduondo and Salvatierra is also notable for its prehistoric remains; in particular a series of dolmens. Near the village of Eguilaz three-quarters of an hour's walk from Salvatierra (just off the N1 to the east) is the dolmen of Aitzkomendi, which was rediscovered by a ploughing farmer in 1830. What happened to the plough is unrecorded, but the 11 impressive stones making up the structure all tip the scales at around the 10-ton mark. It's thought that the dolmen was a funerary marker dating from the early Bronze Age.

Sorginetxe and around

On the other side of Salvatierra near Arrizala is the similarly impressive Sorginetxe, dated to a similar period. The name means 'house of the witch'; in the Middle Ages when the area was still heavily wooded, it could well have been the forest home of somebody of that profession. To the east of here, near the village of Ilarduia, is the Leze Cave, a massive crevice in the cliff face. It's 80 m high and a stream flows from its mouth, making access tricky for casual visitors. It's a good place for canyoning, organized by **Tura**, see Salvatierra page 483.

Gorbeia

North of Vitoria, straddling Vizcaya and Alava, is the massif of Gorbeia, an enticingly inaccessible area of peaks and gorges topped by the peak of the same name, which hits 1,482 m when it remembers not to slouch. It features in Basque consciousness as a realm of deities and purity. There are several good marked trails around Murguia, including an ascent of the peak itself, which, needless to say, shouldn't be attempted in poor weather.

La Rioja Alavesa → *Colour map 2, grid B4.*

Basque Rioja? What's this? The two words don't seem to associate but in fact many of the finest Riojas are from Alava province. Confusion reigns because the Spanish province of La Rioja is only one of three that the wine region encompasses. Although

it's not far from Vitoria, the Rioja Alavesa definitely feels Spanish rather than Basque; the descent from the green hills into the arid plains crosses a cultural and geographical border. As well as the opportunity to visit some excellent vineyards, the hilltop town of Laguardia is one of the most atmospheric places in Euskadi.

Laguardia/Biasteri and around

The small, walled hilltop town of Laguardia commands the plain like a sentinel, which it was; it was originally called La Guardia de Navarra – the guard of Navarra. Underneath the medieval streets, like catacombs, are over 300 small bodegas, cellars used for the making and storing of wine, as well as a place to hide in troubled times. Most are no longer used – Bodega El Fabulista is a fascinating exception. Laguardia was also the birthplace of the fable writer **Felix de Samaniego**.

All bodegas *require a phone call in advance to organize a visit; the more of you there are, the more willing most will be.*

Even if wine is put aside for a moment, the town itself is captivating. Founded in 1164, its narrow streets are a lovely place to wander. Traffic is almost prohibited due to the *bodegas* 6 m below. The impressive **Iglesia de Santa María de los Reyes** ① *weekend tours at 1730 and 1830, €2, at other times get keys from tourist office*, begun in the 12th century, has a extraordinarily finely preserved painted Gothic façade, while the former Ayuntamiento on the arched Plaza Nueva was inaugurated in the 16th century under Charles V. Laguardia's tourist office ① *Plaza San Juan, T945600845, www.laguardia-alava.net.*

Bodegas Palacio ① *Ctra de Elciego s/n, T945600057, www.cosmepalacio.com, tours Tue-Sun at 1230 and 1330, €3 (redeemable in shop or restaurant), booking essential,* is one of the handiest of the wineries, and worth seeing, is Bodegas Palacio, located just below Laguardia on the Elciego road, some 10-minutes' walk from town. The winery is modern; the older bodega alongside having been charmingly converted into a hotel and restaurant. Palacio produces a range of wines, the quality of which has increased in recent years. Their **Glorioso** and **Cosme Palacio** labels are widely sold in the UK. The winery was originally founded in 1894 and is fairly typical of the area, producing 90% red wine from the Tempranillo grape, and a small 10% of white from Viura. As well as *crianzas*, *reservas*, and *gran reservas*. Palacio also produce a red wine for drinking young, which is soft, fruity, and a nice change from the heavier Rioja styles.

Bodega El Fabulista ① *Plaza San Juan s/n, next to the tourist office, T945621192, tours daily at 1130, 1300, and 1730, €4.81,* is a massive contrast to Palacio, which produces two million bottles a year. Eusebio, the owner, effectively runs the place alone and produces about 1-50th of that amount. The wine is made using very traditional methods in the intriguing underground cellar from grapes he grows himself. The wines, marketed as Decidido, are a good young-drinking red and white. He runs three tours a day, which are excellent, and include lots of background information on the Rioja wine region and a generous tasting in a beautiful underground vault.

Herederos del Marqués de Riscal ① *C Torrea 1, Elciego, T945606000 (Mon-Fri), www.marquesderiscal.com, by prior appointment only and it's usually essential to reserve several weeks in advance,* founded in 1860, is the oldest and best known of the Rioja *bodegas* and has built a formidable reputation for the quality of its wines. The Marqués himself was a Madrid journalist who, having cooled off in France after getting in some hot political water at home, started making wine on his return to Spain. Enlisting the help of Monsieur Pinot, a French expert, he experimented by planting Cabernet Sauvignon, which is still used in the wines today. The innovative spirit continues, and Marqués de Riscal have enlisted none other than Frank Gehry of Guggenheim Museum fame to design their new visitors' complex, which will include a hotel, restaurant, and exhibition centre as well as other facilities. Due to open in late 2004, the building will be another visual treat; Gehry's design (a model of which is

visible at the bodega) incorporates ribbons of coloured titanium over a building of
natural stone. The silver, gold, and 'dusty rose' sheets are Gehry's response to 'the unbroken landscape of vineyards and rich tones'. The winery is modern but remains faithful to the bodega's rigorous tradition of quality. As well as their traditionally elegant Reserva and Gran Reserva, the more recently inaugurated Baron de Chirel is a very classy red indeed, coming from low-yielding old vines and exhibiting a more French character than is typical of the region. Buses from Vitoria to Logroño via Elciego pass through here and Laguardia, which is 7 km away.

North of Laguardia, with a waved design echoing the steep mountains behind it, is the new **Ysios bodega** designed by Santiago Calatrava, the brilliant Valencian engineer/architect who seems to have made Euskal Herría his second home. At time of writing, it wasn't yet open for visits.

The area around Laguardia also has a few non-vinous attractions. A set of small lakes close by is one of Spain's better spots for **birdwatching**, particularly from September to March when migrating birds are around. There are a series of marked walking and cycling routes in this area, spectacularly backed by the mountains of the **Sierra Cantabrica**.

⊜ Sleeping

Vitoria *p474, map p476*

L **Hotel Ciudad de Vitoria**, Portal de Castilla 8, T945141100, vitoria@hoteles-silken.com. Massive 4-star hotel situated at the edge of the centre of Vitoria, where character starts to make way for 'lifestyle'. It's airy and pleasant, with good facilities, including a gym and sauna. Chief attractions, however, are its incredible weekend rates, with doubles from €63, less than half the weekday rate.

A **Hotel Almoneda**, C Florida 7, T945154084, www.hotelalmoneda.com. Attractively situated a few paces from the lovely Parque de la Florida, this hotel has reasonable rooms with a rustic touch, much nicer than the stuffy lobby suggests. Significantly cheaper at weekends. Breakfast included.

D **Hotel Dato**, C Eduardo Dato 28, T945147230, F945232320. While it might not be to everyone's taste, this hotel is a treasury of *clásico* statues, mirrors, and general plushness, in a comfortable rather than stuffy way. Its rooms are exceptional value too; all are pretty, with excellent facilities, and some have balconies or *miradores* (enclosed balconies). Recommended.

D **Hotel Desiderio**, C Colegio San Prudencio 2, T945251700, F945251722. Welcoming hotel with comfy rooms with bathroom just out of the Casco Medieval.

E **Pensión Araba II**, C Florida 25, T945232588. A good base in central Vitoria. Clean and comfortable rooms with or with-

out bathroom. Parking spaces available (€6).

F **Casa 400**, C Florida 46, T945233887. At this price you don't expect many facilities, but this is clean, pretty comfortable, and cheerfully run.

F **Hostal Eguileta**, C Nueva Fuera 32, T945251700, F945251722. Cheap, clean, but institutional rooms run out of the **Hotel Desiderio** round the corner.

F **Hostal Nuvilla**, C Fueros 29, T945259151. Centrally located *pensión* with smallish rooms with washbasin. It's friendly and it's cheap.

G **Pensión Antonio**, C Cuchillería 66, T945268795. Cheapest place in town, with rooms at €9.70 per person, shared bathrooms.

Eastern Alava *p478*

A **Parador de Argómaniz**, Carretera N1 Km 363, T945293200, www.parador.es, 12 km east of Vitoria , is in a Renaissance palace. It's a tranquil place with some good views over the surrounding countryside. Napoleon slept here before the disastrous battle of Vitoria. A cab to/from Vitoria costs about €15.

D **Merino**, Plaza de San Juan 3, T945300052 and E **Jose Mari**, C Mayor 73, T945300042, Two unremarkable *pensiones* in Salvatierra, both offering *menús* in their restaurants.

E **Mendiaxpe**, Barrio Salsamendi 22, T945304212, is cleverly located in the wooded foothills of the Sierra de Urkilla, a superb base for walking in the area.

La Rioja Alavesa *p479*

There are some excellent places to stay in Laguardia.

A Castillo El Collado, Paseo El Collado 1, Laguardia, T945621200, F945621022. Decorated in plush style, this mansion at the north end of the old town is comfortable and welcoming and has a good, reasonably priced restaurant.

A Posada Mayor de Migueloa, C Mayor 20, Laguardia, T945621175, F945621022. A beautifully decorated Spanish country house, with lovely furniture and a peaceful atmosphere. The restaurant is of a similar standard.

B Hotel Antigua Bodega de Don Cosme Palacio, Carretera Elciego s/n, Laguardia, T945621195, antiguabodega@cosmepalacio. com. A wine-lover's delight. The old Palacio bodega has been converted into a charming hotel and restaurant, adjacent to the modern winery. The sunny rooms are named after grape varietals, and come with a free half bottle. Air-conditioned to cope with the fierce summer heat, most rooms feature views over the vines and mountains beyond. The rates are reasonable too.

C Hostal Biazteri, C Berberana 2, Laguardia, T941600026, biazteri@jazzfree.com. Run by the bar on the corner, this is a very airy and pleasant place to stay, newly fitted and furnished. Breakfast included.

E Larretxori, Portal de Páganos s/n, Laguardia, T/F945600763, larretxori@ euskalnet.net. This comfortable *agroturismo* is just outside the city walls and commands excellent views over the area.

❶ Eating

Vitoria *p474, map p476*
Eduardo Dato and the streets crossing it are excellent for the early evening *pintxo* trail.

€€€ **Arkupe**, C Mateo Moraza 13, T945230080. A quality restaurant with some imaginative dishes, such as a tasty squid 'n' potato pie, and some inspiring salads. There's a *menú degustación* for €27.35.

€€€ **Dos Hermanas**, C Madre Vedruna 10, T945132934. One of Vitoria's oldest restaurants, and certainly not the place to come for nouvelle cuisine, with generous, hearty, and delicious traditional dishes.

€€€ **Ikea**, Portal de Castilla 27, T943144747. Lovers of homely Swedish furniture will be disappointed to find out that this is in fact one of Vitoria's best restaurants. It is mainly French in style, but there are a few traditional Basque dishes on the agenda too.

€€ **Asador Matxete**, Plaza Machete 4, T945131821. A stylish modern restaurant harmoniously inserted into this pretty plaza above Los Arquillos. Specializing in large pieces of meat expertly grilled over coals.

€€ **Izago**, Tomás de Zumárraga 2, T945138200. Excellent eating is to be had in this fairly formal restaurant in a smart stone building. The focus is on seafood, but there are plenty of other specialities – such as duck's liver on stuffed pig's ear, and some sinful desserts.

€ **El Jardín de América**, C América 3, T945135217. Set on a square just off C Florida, you can sit outside and pick from a range of carefully prepared dishes in the €5-10 range. Good value.

€ **Restaurante Zabala**, C Mateo Moraza 9, T945230099. Although you wouldn't know it from the basic decor, this is a well-regarded local restaurant. The dishes on offer, without being spectacular, are solid Basque and Rioja choices, and are priced fairly.

Pintxo bars and cafés

Bar El 7, C Cuchillería 7, T945272298. An excellent bar at the head of the Casco Medieval's liveliest street. Its big range of *bocadillos* keeps students and all-comers happy. Order a half if you're not starving; they make 'em pretty large.

Baztertxo, Plaza de España 14. A fine bar with some great wines by the glass and top-notch *jamón*. Although service can be beneath the dignity of the staff, it's a good choice nonetheless.

Café Moderno, Plaza España 4. Sunseekers should head here in the afternoon – the terrace in the postcardy arched square is perfectly placed for maximum rays.

Cuatro Azules Florida, Parque de la Florida. One of Vitoria's best spots, with lots of tables amid the trees of this peaceful park. Regular games of *boules* (check basque word) take place nearby.

Hala Bedi, C Cuchillería 98, T945260411. A late-opening Basque bar with a cheerful

---

❶ *For an explanation of sleeping and eating price codes used in this guide, see inside the* ● *front cover. Other relevant information is found in Essentials, see pages 47-56.*

atmosphere. Out of a tiny kitchen come crepes with a massive variety of sweet and savoury fillings.

Korrokon, C Cuchillería 9. Tasty cheap food can be had here al fresco courtesy of a good range of simple raciones. The *mejillones* (mussels) in spicy tomato sauce are particularly good.

Sherezade, C Correría 42, T945255868, is a relaxed café, well frequented by students, and serving up good coffee and a range of *infusiones* (herb and fruit teas).

La Rioja Alavesa *p479*

€€ **Castillo El Collado**, Paseo El Collado 1, Laguardia, T945621200. There's an excellent, well-priced restaurant in this beautiful fortified hotel at the northern end of Laguardia.

€€ **El Bodegón**, Travesía Santa Engracia 3, Laguardia, T945600793. Tucked away in the middle of old Laguardia is this cosy restaurant, with a €11 menú del dia focusing on the hearty staples of the region, such as *pochas* (beans), or *patatas con chorizo*.

€€ **Marixa**, C Sancho Abarca s/n, Laguardia, T945600165. In the Hotel Marixa, the dining room boasts great views over the vine-covered plains below and has a range of local specialities with formally correct Spanish service.

€ **Biazteri**, C Berberana 2, Laguardia, T945600026. One of the cheaper places to eat in Laguardia, this down-to-earth bar does some fine *platos combinados*.

€ **Café Tertulia**, C Mayor 70. With couches, padded booths, and a pool table, this is the best place for a few quiet drinks in Laguardia.

🌓 Bars and clubs

Vitoria *p474, map p476*

C Cuchillería has the liveliest weekend scene.

Bar Rio, C Eduardo Dato 20, T945230067, is a decent café with outdoor tables by day, and one of the last bars to shut at night, when it caters to a good-natured gay/straight crowd. Original live music on Thu nights.

Cairo Stereo Club, C Aldabe 9. Excellent club with some excellent and innovative DJs and a mixed crowd. During the week they often show cult movies or hold theme parties.

Cruz Blanco, C San Prudencio 26. This cavernous *cervecería* is a popular evening

drinking spot with several outdoor tables and decent-sized *cañas*. Handy for the cinema and theatre.

✱ Festivals and events

Vitoria *p474, map p476*

On **25 Jul** is Santiago's day, celebrated as the **Día del Blusa** (blouse day) when colour-coordinated kids patrol the streets.

On **4-9 Aug** is **Fiesta de la Virgen Blanca**, the city's major knees-up, which comes thoroughly recommended.

Vitoria is known for its spectacular full-sized Nativity scene, **Advent** , with over 200 figures.

⊙ Shopping

Vitoria *p474, map p476*

Segunda Mano, C Prudencio María Verástegui 14, T945270007. This is an amazing barn-sized second-hand shop, which literally seems to have everything. From books to grand pianos, from skis to confessionals to tractors. You name it, it might well be there.

⛰ Activities and tours

Eastern Alava *p478*

Tura, T945312535, www.tura.org, based out of the tourist office in Salvatierra, is a very competent organization that organizes a range of activities throughout Alava province.

⊖ Transport

Vitoria *p474, map p476*

Vitoria is well served for public transport. The bus station is on the eastern side of town. Buses to Bilbao run about every 30 mins with **Autobuses La Union**, 55 mins, €4.50. There are 7 buses a day to San Sebastián, as well as buses to **Logroño**, **Haro**, **Laguardia**, **Salvatierra**, **Orduña**, and other larger cities.

Train station, south of town, has regular services to **Madrid**, **Zaragoza**, **Logroño**, **Barcelona**, **Burgos**, and other destinations.

Western Alava *p478*

There are 5 buses daily from Vitoria bus station to **Salinas de Añana**.

Buses to **Orduña** for **Cañon de Delika** from Vitoria bus station with La Unión.

Eastern Alava *p478*

There are buses hourly from Vitoria's bus station to **Salvatierra**, run by Burundesa.

Five buses daily to **Zalduondo** from Vitoria/Salvatierra (destination Araia), falling to 2 on Saturday and 1 on Sunday.

For **Gorbeia** buses head to Murguia from Vitoria bus station.

La Rioja Alavesa *p479*

There are buses to **Laguardia** from Vitoria bus station. If you are arriving from Vitoria by car, it's marginally quicker and much more scenic to take the smaller A2124 rather than

the motorway. After ascending to a pass, the high ground dramatically drops away to the Riojan plain; there's a superb lookout on the road, justly known as 'El Balcón' (the balcony).

ⓘ Directory

Vitoria *p474, map p476*

Internet Link Internet, C San Antonio 31, T945130484, charge €2.10 per hr to use their machines, and are open Mon-Fri 1000-1400, 1730-2130, Sat 1030-1400.
Nirvana Net Centre, C Manuel Iradier 11, T945154043. Mon-Sat 1030-1430, 1700-2200, Sun 1700-2200, €2.10-2.40 per hr.

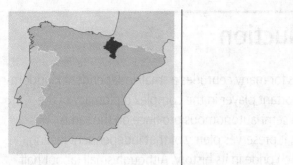

☃ Footprint features

Introduction

Navarra was for many centuries a small independent kingdom and an important player in the complex diplomacy of the period. As a semi-autonomous province on the same boundaries, it preserves plenty of that independent feeling, and has much pride in its history. Although small (about half the size of Wales), it's stuffed full of things to see from the awe-inspiring Pyrenees to dusty plains and sun-baked wine country.

Navarrese **Pyrenees** are beautiful, if not quite as spectacular as those further to the east in Cantabria. A series of remote valleys make intriguing places to explore, summer pastureland for generations of cowherds from both sides of the border.

The principal route of the pilgrims to Santiago, the **Camino Francés**, crosses Navarra from east to west and has left a sizeable endowment of some of the peninsula's finest religious **architecture**. Entering the province at **Roncesvalles**, where Charlemagne's rearguard was given a nasty Basque bite, it continues through small gems of towns like **Estella** and **Viana**. It's not all hard work; at one lunch stop there's a drinking fountain that spouts red wine.

In the midst of all is **Pamplona**, a pleasant and sober town which goes berserk for nine days in July for the Fiesta de los Sanfermines, of which the most famous event is the daily encierro, or Running of the Bulls, made famous by Hemingway and more recently by thousands of wine-swilling locals and tourists looking scared on television every year.

The south of Navarra is much more **Castilian**; sun-baked and dotted with castles, it produces some hearty **red wines** and some of Spain's best vegetables, grown around Tudela, watered by the **Ebro**, the peninsula's second-longest river.

★ Don't miss...

❶ Pamplona Go to the Fiesta de los Sanfermines, Europe's biggest party, page 488.

❷ Valle de Roncal Head to this beautiful valley for some walking or cross-country skiing, page 495.

❸ Viana Follow the pilgrim trail east from Pamplona, and relax for a couple of days at this peaceful town, page 506.

❹ Olite and Ujué Check out these medieval towns, page 509 and 510.

❺ Tudela Eat the peninsula's tastiest vegetables in Tudela, washed down by the excellent local wine, page 511.

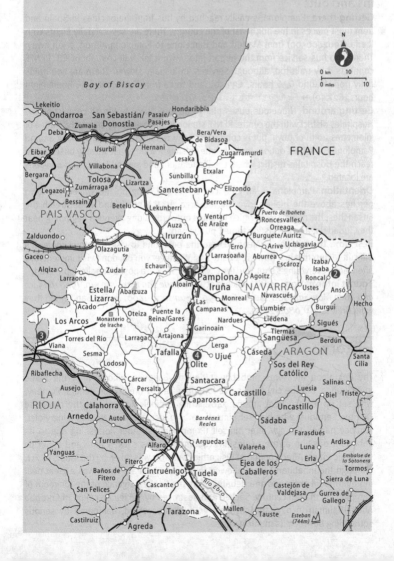

Pamplona/Iruña

→ *Phone code: 948; Colour map 2, grid B5; Population: 186,245; Altitude: 444 m.*

Pamplona, the capital of Navarra, conjures images of wild drunken revelry and stampeding bulls. And rightly so; for that is exactly what happens for nine days every July, Los Sanfermines. Love it or hate it, if you're around it's a must to check out. At other times Pamplona is quite a subdued, but picturesque city, with its high-walled old town very striking when it's approached from below. It's a good place to stop over, with plenty of good accommodation and eating options. It's also the hub for all transport in Navarra, so expect to pass through a few times if you're exploring the province by bus. ▶▶ *For Sleeping, Eating and other listings, see pages 492-495.*

Ins and outs

Getting there Pamplona is easily reached by bus from major cities in Spain and from most places in the northeast of the country. There are several daily flights with Iberia (T902400500) from Madrid and Barcelona to Pamplona airport, 7 km away. There's no bus service from the airport into town: a taxi will cost about €8. RENFE connects it by train too, although services are usually slower. There are two trains daily from Madrid (4½ hours, €33.50), and three from Barcelona (5½ hours-eight hours, €27.50). ▶▶ *For further details, see Transport page 495.*

Getting around Numerous buses plough up and down Av Pio XII connecting the Hospitales district with the centre. RENFE station is inconveniently situated a couple of kilometres north of town, but is connected every 10 minutes by bus. Walking around Pamplona is the best option; the only time you might want to use the city buses are to reach the Hospitales district where the Planetarium and several hotels and *pensións* are located.

Orientation Pamplona is an easy city to get the hang of: the walled old town perches above the plain above the Rio Arga. To the south and west stretch the Ensanches, the newer town, which radiates outwards along avenues beginning near the Ciudadela, a large bastion turned public park.

Best time to visit Los Sanfermines are the best time to visit for atmosphere: it's difficult to describe just how big a party it is. Whatever you do, don't visit immediately afterwards: everything's shut, and the city seems sunk in a post-alcoholic depression.

Tourist information Tourist office is at ① *Plaza de San Francisco s/n, T948206540, and open Mon-Sat 1000-1400, 1600-1900, Sun 1000-1400*. During San Fermín they work tirelessly ① *0800-2000*.

History

The Pamplona area was probably settled by Basques, who gave it the name Iruña/Iruñea, but the city's definitive founding was by the Roman general Pompey, who set up a base here around 74BC while campaigning against the renegade Quintus Sertorius, who had set himself up as a local warlord. No shrinking violet, Pompey named the city after himself (Pompeiopolis). After flourishing due to its important position at the peninsula's doormat, it was sacked time and again by Germanic tribes. After a period of Visigothic control, it was taken by the Moors in 711, although the inhabitants were allowed to remain Christian. There was a great deal more territorial exchange and debate before the final emergence of the Kingdom of Pamplona in the 9th century. Sacked and destroyed by the feared caliph of Cordoba Abd-al-Rahman in 924, the city only gradually recovered, hampered by serious squabbling between its municipalities.

Party animals

Better known in English as the 'running of the bulls', the nine-day Fiesta de los Sanfermínes lays a very serious claim to being the biggest party in Europe. The city goes completely loco for the whole time, with the streets and bars bursting with locals and tourists clad traditionally in white with red neckscarves, downing beer and wine with abandon while dancing to the music pumping from a dozen different sources. Imagine the world's biggest stag do meeting the world's biggest hen night and you'll have the gist of it.

It's quite possible to lose a week of your life here and never set eyes on a bull, but it's the *encierros* (bull-runnings) that add the spice. It's difficult to imagine many other countries allowing upwards of three tons of bullflesh to plough through a crowd of drunken citizens, but it happens here at 0800 every morning of the fiesta. The streets are barricaded and six bulls released to run from their *corral* to the Plaza de Toros (bullring). If they keep in formation and don't get panicked or distracted they'll only take three minutes to cover the course, but if they find a buttock or two to gore along the way, they can be on the streets for 10 minutes or more. Rockets are let off; the first is single and signals the release of the bulls, the next, a double, means that they've all left the *corral*, and the triple is fired after they've arrived at the bullring and been penned after being calmed by steers. Once everybody's in the ring and the bulls are safely away, a few cows (with covered horns) are released for good measure and general chaos. That evening the bulls are fought in the daily *corrida*.

The festival kicks off each year on 6 July at the Ayuntamiento, with El Chupinazo (rocket) fired at midday and cries of 'Viva San Fermín!'. The saint himself was a Roman convert to Christianity who became the first bishop of Pamplona. Pushing his luck, he travelled to Gaul to convert the descendants of Asterix and Obelix to the faith. They had his head, by Toutatis. The day proceeds with a procession of larger than life papier mâché headed figures (*cabezudos y gigantes*) who parade through town scaring children. The *riau-riau*, a bizarre free-for-all where local dignitaries walking to mass at the chapel of San Fermín find that the whole town is trying to physically stop them from getting there, has been banned for rowdiness. The biggest day is 7 July with the first *encierro* and the most revellers, but there arethings going on all week: heaps of live bands, processions, street performers, fireworks. Especially noticeable are *peñas*, large social clubs that travel the length and breadth of Spain to find a party. Loud, boisterous and usually equipped with their own brass section, their colourful parades through the town are a feature.

One of the nicest aspects of the festival is that, despite the tourism, it's still a fiesta with a strong local flavour. How the city keeps functioning is a mystery, as bleary bank tellers struggle to stay awake at work after being out all night. While things are busiest from 1900 onwards, it's great to wander around during the day, seeking out little pockets of good-time in the quietened backstreets. It's a time for family and friends to get together too; you'll see long tables set up in unlikely places.

The festival finally ends at midnight on 14 July, again at the Ayuntamiento, with a big crowd chanting the "Pobre de mí" (poor me), mourning the end of things until next year. If you hear a faint sigh of relief, it comes from the liver and kidney population.

Pamplona's rise to real prominence ironically came when Navarra was conquered by Castile; Ferdinand built the city walls and made it the province's capital. After a turbulent 19th century, Pamplona expanded rapidly through the 20th century, necessitating the development of successive *Ensanches* south and west of the old centre.

Pamplona

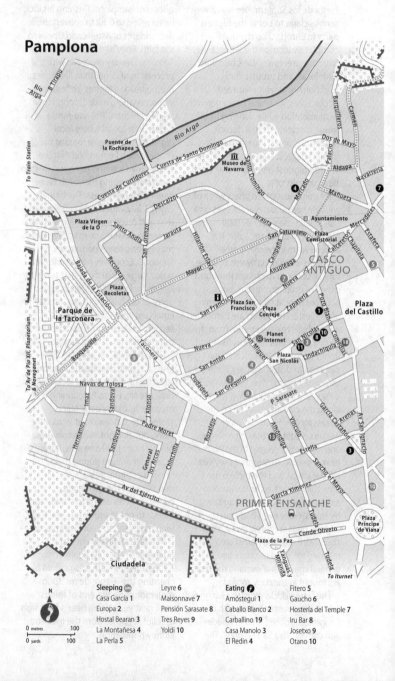

Navarra Pamplona/Iruña

Sleeping		Eating	
Casa García **1**	Leyre **6**	Amóstegui **1**	Fitero **5**
Europa **2**	Maisonnave **7**	Caballo Blanco **2**	Gaucho **6**
Hostal Bearan **3**	Pensión Sarasate **8**	Carballino **19**	Hostería del Temple **7**
La Montañesa **4**	Tres Reyes **9**	Casa Manolo **3**	Iru Bar **8**
La Perla **5**	Yoldi **10**	El Redin **4**	Josetxo **9**
			Otano **10**

Sights

Plaza del Castillo

At the southern edge of the old town is the Plaza del Castillo, centre of much social life. During excavations for a controversial underground car park, Roman remains were discovered and work came to a halted pending a decision on how to proceed.

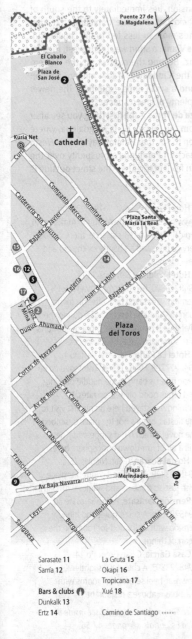

Before the Plaza de Toros was built, the bullfights were held in this square. Behind the square to the east is the famous cobbled **Estafeta**, the main runway for the bulls during San Fermín; it's lined with shops and bars.

Cathedral and around

The quiet, seemingly deserted part of town east of here is dominated by the cathedral ① *T948224667, Mon-Sat 1000-1330, 1600-1900 (1800 winter, closed Sat pm), €3.61.* Don't be daunted by the rather austere 18th-century façade, as the interior is a masterpiece of delicate Gothic work. Facing the front, the entrance is up the street to your right. First stop is the gorgeous cloister, a superb work of delicate harmony with excellent carved reliefs on some of the doorways leading off. The cathedral itself is similarly impressive, and houses the tombs of Carlos III '(the noble') of Navarra and his queen. **Diocesan museum** is located in what used to be the larder, kitchen and dining room, and holds a reasonably interesting selection of artefacts.

Behind the cathedral, past the shady **Plaza de San José**, is the tranquil corner of **El Caballo Blanco**, named after the inviting bar/restaurant that looks over the ramparts. Walking down the east wall from here you'll reach the **Plaza de Santa María la Real**, another peaceful spot, overlooked by the archbishop's palace.

Plaza Consistoria and around

The centre of town is occupied by the small Plaza Consistorial, seat of the pretty Baroque **Ayuntamiento**, where the crowd gathers to watch the start of San Fermín. Down the hill from here, near the market, is the impressive **Museo de Navarra** ① *Tue-Sat 0930-1400, 1700-1900, Sun 1100-1400;*

Map labels:
- Puente 27 de la Magdalena
- El Caballo Blanco
- Plaza de San José ②
- Ronda Obispo Barbazán
- CAPARROSO
- Kuria Net @
- Cathedral
- Curia
- Compañía
- Merced
- Dormitalería
- Plaza Santa María la Real
- Caldetería San Agustín
- Javier
- Bajada J
- Tejería
- Juan de Labrit
- Bajada de Labrit
- ⑮
- ⑯ ⑫ ⑤
- ⑰ ⑥
- Espoz y Mina ②
- Duque Ahumada
- Plaza del Toros
- Cortes de Navarra
- Av de Roncesvalles
- Av Carlos III
- Arrieta
- Olite
- Paulino Caballero
- Leyre
- Amaya
- Francisco
- Plaza Mérindades
- Av Baja Navarra
- To ⑥
- Leyre
- Vittoriada
- Av Carlos III
- Bergamín
- Sangüesa
- San Fermín

Navarra Pamplona/Iruña

restricted opening during San Fermín, €1.80, set in a stately former convent hospital. The museum contains a wide range of material, from prehistoric remains on the ground floor through to modern Navarrese art at the top. There are a few Goyas, as well as much religious art that has been gathered from the many provincial churches and monasteries.

Primer Ensanche

The Primer Ensanche, the city's earliest expansion, lies immediately to the south of Plaza del Castillo. The Avenida de San Ignacio has a statue depicting that man wounded while defending the city; the wounds more or less led to his conversion. This avenue ends at the busy **Plaza Principe de Viana**; a short way to the west, the bus station stands on the off beat **Plaza de la Paz.** Beyond the old town in the Primero Ensanche stretches the pentagonal wall of the **Ciudadela**, a low military bastion constructed by Philip II; it houses a chapel and a small arms exhibition. The newer parts of town south of here are blessed with plenty of green space.

Back on the edge of the old town, the **Plaza de Toros** is the first thing you see after winding up the Bajada de Labrit into town from the Puente de la Magdalena, where the pilgrims cross the river. It's no exaggeration to say that Hemingway's novel *Fiesta (The Sun Also Rises)* has had a massive impact on Pamplona's prosperity over the years, so it's fitting that there's a bust of him in front of the ring – the street outside is also named after him.

● Sleeping

There are scores of budget options around the old town and along Avenida Pio XII in the Hospitales district; look for signs saying Camas above bars and restaurants. Outside of Los Sanfermínes, finding accommodation is never a problem.
LL **Tres Reyes**, C Taconera s/n, T948226600, www.hotel3reyes.com. Pamplona's most stellar hotel is on the edge of the old town and predictably geared for conferences. This does mean that there are excellent facilities, plenty of staff on call, and weekend rates that are very good value, up to 50% cheaper with advance booking.
AL **Hotel Europa**, C Espoz y Mina 11, T948221800, heuropa@cmn.navarra.net. If there is a hint of the self-satisfied about this place, they do have reason. The small hotel is superbly located just off the Plaza del Castillo, and with balconies overlooking C Estafeta (the main drag of the bull-running). The restaurant is also one of the better ones.
AL **Maisonnave**, C Nueva 20, T948222600, www.hotelmaisonnave.es. A sleek but friendly modern hotel with comfortable furnishings, a decent café, and a sauna for Finnophiles. Some good out-of-season specials.

B **Hotel Leyre**, C Leyre 7, T948228500, www.hotel-leyre.com. Although furnished in typically awkward 3-star style, there's good service here and it's handy for the old and new towns.
B **Hotel Yoldi**, Av San Ignacio 11, T948224800, hyoldi@cmn.navarra.net. Hemingway stayed here after his friend Juanito Quintana lost his hotel during the Civil War. It happily offers modern comforts with surprisingly reasonable prices.
C **Hotel La Perla**, Plaza del Castillo 1, T948227706, F948211566. This faded *fin de siècle* hotel is bang in the middle of things, and offers good off-season rates. Hemingway stayed here on his first visit to the fiestas, but it's not the place described in the novel, which has disappeared. There's still a bit of run-down atmosphere here.
D **Hostal Bearan**, C San Nicolás 25, T948223428. A cosy and courteous place with just-so doubles and singles with bath.
E **Pensión Sarasate**, Paseo Sarasate 30, T948223084. A small, quiet and friendly *pensión* with well cared-for rooms in the heart of things.
F **Casa García**, C San Gregorio 14, T948223893. A cheerful if slightly down-at-heel selection of rooms with washbasin above a restaurant.

● *For an explanation of sleeping and eating price codes used in this guide, see inside the* ● *front cover. Other relevant information is found in Essentials, see pages 47-56.*

F **La Montañesa**, C San Gregorio 2, T948224380. Comfortable rooms above a restaurant on this busy evening street.

Camping
Ezcaba, Ctra N121 Km7, T948330315. The closest campsite to Pamplona, with a pool and a few caravans. On the road to Irún.

🍴 Eating

€€€ **Josetxo**, Plaza Principe de Viana 1, T948222097. One of Pamplona's most refined restaurants, with wines to match. The *txangurro* (spider crab) stuffed in its own shell is one of a number of outstanding dishes.

€€ **Amóstegui**, C Pozo Blanco 20, T948224327. An unglamorous upstairs restaurant that happens to serve some of the nicest mid-priced food in Pamplona. Try the fresh asparagus or artichokes if they're in season, but only go for the fresh foie gras if you fancy something seriously rich.

€€ **Casa Manolo**, C García Castañon 12, T948225102. A dependable 2nd floor restaurant proudly presenting Navarran specialities like *pichón estofado con pochas* (braised pigeon with beans).

€€ **Hostería del Temple**, C Curia 3, T948225171. A cosy bar and restaurant guarded by a suit of armour, and serving some reasonably priced fresh fish. Famous for its *moscovita* pintxo, a fried piece of ham, egg, and cheese invented by a bloke from Moscow who's a regular here.

€€ **Otano**, C San Nicolás 5, T948227036. Although you're sometimes left wondering whether style or substance takes precedence here, it's a nice spot, well decorated, with tables overlooking one of Pamplona's livelier weekend streets. If there's *rodaballo* (turbot) about, consider it.

€ **Carballino**, C Los Teobaldos 2. A smart modern *pulpería* serving good calamari and octopus with a minimum of fuss and a Galician flair.

€ **El Redin**, C Mercado 5. A cheap and cheerful restaurant behind the market.

€ **Sarasate**, C San Nicolás 19, T948225727. Not to be confused with its namesake, until its recent closure one of the heartiest meat restaurants in Navarra, this cheerful vegetarian restaurant will appeal to all-comers with its cheap and imaginative offerings.

Tapas/pintxo bars and cafés
Caballo Blanco, Rincón del Caballo Blanco s/n. Pamplona's nicest spot, a fantastic location tucked into a quiet corner of the city walls with views over the ramparts. The bar serves some good food in a beautiful stone building, but the beer garden is the place to hang out. Superbly peaceful.

Fitero, C Estafeta 58, T948222006. Award-winning bites on the main drag, which include an excellent spinach and prawn *croqueta*.

Gaucho, C Espoz y Mina. A buzzy little corner bar with good *pintxos* and strong coffee.

Iru Bar, C San Nicolás 25. Another bar with nice *pintxos* on this street full of such things.

Sarría, C Estafeta 52, T948227713. The sort of hammy bar that makes a heart glad. Rows of the stuff hanging from the ceiling, a cheery atmosphere, and plenty of wine.

🍸 Bars and clubs

The streets in the western part of the old town are full of bars, while Calle Calderería and around has a vibrant Basque social scene.

Dunkalk, Alhóndiga 4. They can't get enough of theme bars in this part of the world. This is the best of them, with cold beer and kangaroo *pintxos*.

Ertz, C Tejería 40, T948222362. A trendy, mixed crowd fill this place Thu-Sun nights.

La Gruta, C Estafeta 36. A well-named cellar bar, which can get mighty stuffy when a crowd's packed in.

Okapi, Plaza El Castillo 11, T948211572. A bar that serves up quiet *pintxos* and *raciones* by day and kicks off at weekend nights and during San Fermín. Regular live music.

Tropicana, Plaza del Castillo s/n. The best option on the main square, with good cold beer and down-to-earth attitudes.

Xué, C Comedias 7. Stonefronted and quite a cool bar to sip wine in, with classy *pintxos* and with-it bar staff.

Zona Limite, C Intxaurdia s/n, T948331554. Hop in a taxi for this club, which doesn't open until 2400. Loud party-time sounds.

Footprint's survival techniques

Sleeping Prices literally triple and quadruple during the fiesta. Rooms should be booked several months in advance. Having said that, there are many rooms available on an impromptu basis – check noticeboards at the bus and train stations, the tourist office and the newspaper. The official campsite is packed, but more secure than the free areas set up by the council to the east of town. If all else fails, sleep out – you'll be in good company and there are plenty of green areas to stretch out south of the centre or under the walls. It's easier to get rooms for later in the fiesta.

Eating and drinking Prices are predictably high and it can be tough to find space in restaurants without a reservation. Most people live off *bocadillos*, which are available all over the place, with proportionately decreasing prices as you move away from Calle Estafeta. Plenty of shops stay open all night selling beer, sangría, and wine; a good way to avoid the crushes at the bar.

Pitching a spot Watching the *encierro* can be a bit of an anti-climax. It's tough to get a good spot, and even if you get one, you may not see much: it's often over in a blur. The best spots are the private balconies along Calle Estafeta, but you'll have to pay – check for notices on the buildings. Otherwise, grab a seat on the wooden barriers along the course. You're not allowed on the front fence, only on or behind the second one. Get there at least two hours beforehand, and don't expect a comfortable wait.

Tickets You can buy bullfight tickets for that day and the next at the *taquillas* at the Plaza de Toros. These get snapped up very fast, so you may have to buy from scalpers, who drop their prices rapidly once the *corrida* is underway. It's worth spending up on tickets, as the cheaper seats often degenerate literally into a peanut gallery with rowdy food-fights between *peñas*.

Safety Even if you aren't going to run, come prepared to: staring down the barrel of a drink at 0400 it may suddenly seem like an excellent idea. Wear decent shoes as the cobbled streets are slippery. Walk the course beforehand, and pick a sensible place to start your run. The tight corner at the bottom of Calle Estafeta is where most carnage occurs, with bulls and people slipping. Get there well before the start. Women should keep a lowish profile, as the police still aren't too keen for non-males to run. Carry something throwable – chucking a cap or a newspaper can distract a bull if you're in trouble. Don't try and attract a bull's attention; once separated from the herd they are far more deadly. It's much better to run later in the week; on the first two days there are too many people falling over each other. Try to watch an *encierro* so you've got an idea of what goes on. Above all, respect the bulls as the large, fast, lethal animals they are. People get seriously injured all the time, sometimes fatally. Your travel insurer will likely only laugh if you try and claim medical expenses for a horn wound. Remember to San Fermín is Christmas for pickpockets and petty thieves. Don't carry a bag if you can help it, and watch your pockets in the crowds. Although the atmosphere inevitably can get volatile with all that much booze, there's remarkably little violence.

Crowds It can be overwhelming at first, and there's plenty to dislike: the stench of stale beer and urine, the crowds and inflated prices. However, enjoy the atmosphere and take breaks, it is easy to get aways from the hectic epicentre.

☺ Entertainment

Cines Carlos III, C Cortes de Navarra. The handiest cinema for the old town.
Teatro Gayarre, Av Carlos III 3, T948220139. This noble old theatre doesn't see as much action as in its heyday, but still has regular shows.

☻ Festivals and events

See the boxes.

✪ Shopping

Foto Auma, Plaza del Castillo. During Los Sanfermínes, this photography shop has excellent photos of that day's *encierro* available for €4 a shot.
Librería Abarzuza, C Santo Domingo 29, T948213213, sells decent maps of the city.

▲ Activities and tours

This list covers activities and tours for the entire province.
Bideak, Plaza del Castillo 28, T948221773, www.bideak@navarraactiva.com. An association of tour operators who will find the company that does what you want done, from architectural tours to canoeing and horse-trekking.
Ekia, Camping Osate, Ochagavia, T948890184. A friendly set-up organizing mountain activities in Navarra's eastern Pyrenees.
Roncal Escuela de Esqui, Ctra General s/n, Izaba, T948893266, www.roncaleski.com. A ski school in the Roncal valley running courses in cross-country and downhill skiing.

⊖ Transport

Bus Conda to **Artajona** Mon-Sat 0915, 1330, 1900; **Cintruénigo** and **Fitero** 0915, 1330, 1630, 2000 (0915 and 1015 Sun); **Madrid** 0730, 1530, 1830; **Olite** 7 a day; **Puente la Reina** same as Artajona; **Soria** 8 a day; **Zaragoza** 8 a day; **Tudela** 8 a day. **Alsa** to **Bilbao** 6 daily (4 Sun); **Vitoria** 11 a day (less weekends); **Altsasu** hourly. **Tafallesa** to Roncal 1700; **Barasain** 7 a day; **Roncalesa** to San Sebastian 9 a day (€5.25); **Jaca/Huesca** 0830, 1530; **Pamplonesa** to **Barcelona** 0835, 1640, 0045; **La Estellesa** to **Estella** 12 a day; **La Sanguesina** to **Elizondo** 0800, 1315, 2000.
Train 3 daily services to **Barcelona**, 2 to **Madrid**.

❶ Directory

Hospital Hospital de Navarra, C Irunlarrea s/n, T948422100 (emergencies). **Internet** Kuria Net, C Curia 15, T948223077, 1000-2200, €3 per hr; **Planet Internet**, C San Anton 7, fast; **Naveganet**, Trav de Acella 3, T948199297, Mon-Sat 1030-1330, 1530-2230, €3 per hr; **Iturnet**, C Iturrana 1, T948252820, Mon-Thu 0900-2200, Fri 0900-0000, Sat 1000-0000, €2 per hr.
Post Paseo de Sarasate s/n.
Telephone There's a friendly *locutorio* next to the bullring at Paseo Hemingway s/n, 1000-2230.
Useful addresses and numbers The main **police station** is at Calle Chinchilla. Phone 112 in any emergency.

Navarrese Pyrenees

Valle de Roncal → *Colour map 2, grid A6/B6.*

If you're only going to visit one of Navarra's valleys, make it the easternmost, the Valle de Roncal. Here the mountains of the Pyrenees are beginning to flex their muscles – it's a popular base for cross-country (and some downhill) skiing in winter. Summer, though, is when it really comes into its own, when flowers bloom from windowboxes in the lovable villages, and the cobblestones aren't icy invitations to a sprained ankle.
➤➤ *For Sleeping, Eating and other listings, see pages 500-502.*

⁞ Breach of Roland

Taking the crown of the Franks in 768 at the age of 26, Charlemagne embarked on a lifelong campaign to unite and bring order to western Europe, which resulted in an empire that included France, Switzerland, Belgium, Holland, and much of Italy and Germany, as well as the 'Spanish March', a wedge of territory stretching down to the Ebro river. Or so he thought; the local population wasn't so sure. Allowing him to pass through their territory to battle the Moors, the local Basque population were outraged at his conduct; he destroyed Pamplona's fortifications after taking it; and accepted a bribe from the city of Zaragoza to return to France. As the army ascended the Ibañeta pass above Roncesvalles on their way home, their rearguard and baggage train was ambushed and slaughtered by locals. Among the dead was Hrudoland, or Roland, governor of the marches of Brittany, and a shadowy historical figure immortalized in the later romantic account of the event, *Le Chanson de Roland*. He refuses to blow his great warhorn, Olifant, because he feels that a cry for help would shame them. He finally blows it so that Charlemagne will return to give them Christian burial, and blows it with such force that it kills him. He tries to break his sword, *Durandal*, but without success. The sword was some weapon: Roland is said to have created the Pyrenean pass, the Breach of Roland, with one swing of the blade. Not for nothing, then, did the French name an anti-runway bomb after the sword.

Izaba/Isaba

While it may be the big smoke of the valley, Izaba is not more than a village. Back from the road that winds along its length are unspoiled stony lanes where sheep are still penned on the ground floors of houses and vegetable patches are tended in the heart of town. There's lots of accommodation too, as it's a popular base for walkers, skiers and cross-border weekenders. The village **Iglesia de San Cipriano** towers fortress-like over the settlement, and there's also a local museum. Otherwise, spend a while climbing around the streets, trying to find the perfect photo-framing stone houses, geraniums and craggy peaks behind.

The valley above Izaba has such lush pastureland in summer that for many centuries French shepherds and cowherds couldn't help themselves and took their flocks over the border to get fat on Navarrese grass. After a hard winter, the shepherds in the Roncal Valley were in no mood to be neighbourly, and much strife ensued. Finally, it was agreed that the French would give a gift of three cows to the Navarrese each summer in return for incident-free cud-chewing. The mayor of Izaba, dressed in traditional conquistador-like costume, still collects on it – you can see the two parties solemnly clasp hands on the frontier stone every 13 July at midday, before the Spanish party solemnly select three cows from a frisky herd (sadly, they don't actually keep them). If you're going to the ceremony, get there early or be prepared to walk a couple of kilometres, as cars are parked way back down the road on both sides.

Roncal

Down the valley from Izaba is the village of Roncal itself, famous for its sheep's milk cheese. Its another attractive Pyrenean village with crisp mountain air that must have been a boon to its favourite son, Gayarre, a tenor from opera's golden days in the late 19th century. His tomb in the village cemetery is an ornate riot of kitsch, happily out of place amid the humbler graves of cheesewrights.

66 99 The valley above Izaba has such lush pastureland in summer that for many centuries French shepherds and cowherds couldn't help themselves and took their flocks over the border to get fat on Navarrese grass.

The valley, particularly in its higher reaches, is home to a great variety of wildlife, including rare species such as bears, boars, capercaillies, ptarmigan, chamois and a variety of birds of prey. It offers numerous opportunities for exploring. There are tourist offices in Roncal with internet access available.

Western Pyrenees

Continuing north from Roncal, the slopes of the western Pyrenees rise towards France. One of the two principal branches of the Camino de Santiago descends to Pamplona from the pass near Roncesvalles, a place of rest for millions of pilgrims over the centuries, which still retains some medieval character. Further north, the river Bidasoa runs through some attractive Basque villages, while one of its tributaries, the Baztan, runs down a peaceful valley that is also worthy of investigation. ▶▶ *For Sleeping, Eating and other listings, see pages 500-502.*

Roncesvalles/Orreaga → *Phone code: 948; Colour map 2, grid A6; Altitude: 924 m.*
On a misty evening the stern ecclesiastical complex at Roncesvalles resembles Colditz, but appearances are deceptive. It is the first night's stop for many a pilgrim following the Camino Francés into Navarra.

A **pilgrim hostel** was built in Roncesvalles in 1127. Its fame grew with the growing streams of walkers who were succoured here, aided by the discovery of the Virgin of Roncesvalles, found by a shepherd who was guided to the spot by a deer with Rudolf-style illumination. The statue is said to have been buried to protect it from Moorish raiders. In any event, the **collegiate church** that houses the silver-plated statuette is the highlight of the sanctuary, a simple and uplifting example of French Gothic architecture, with blue stained-glass windows and the Virgin taking pride of place above the altar. On her birthday, 8 September, there's a major *romería* (pilgrimage day) and fiesta here. Off the austere cloister is the burial chapel of the Navarrese king Sancho VII ('the strong'), whose bones were transferred here in 1912. He lies with his wife under a 2.25-m 14th-century alabaster statue of himself that's said to have been life size, the stained-glass depiction of him battling the Moors at the scene of his greatest triumph, Navas de Tolosa, certainly cuts an imposing figure. A **warhammer** leaning nearby is predictably said to have been Roland's. The small **museum** attached to the complex is less impressive, but has a few interesting manuscripts, as well as a blue-embossed reliquary known as 'Charlemagne's chess set'.

> ▪ *Roncesvalles is little more than the Colegiata church complex, pilgrim hostel and a couple of posadas.*

A few paces away from the church complex are two further buildings, the tiny 14th-century **Iglesia de Santiago** ① *T948790480, 1000-1400, 1530-1730 (1930 summer, morning only in Jan), €2, or €3.20 including visit to the Iglesia de Santiago*

Navarra Western Pyrenees

⁞ Points of view

While the area has been populated for millennia, the historical entity of Navarra emerged in the seventh century after periods of Basque, Roman, Visigothic, Moorish and Frankish control. The Kingdom of Navarra emerged as part of the Reconquista, the Christian battle to drive the Moors southwards and out of the peninsula. Under the astute rulership of King Sancho III in the early 11th century, Navarra was unified with Castilla and Aragón, which meant that Sancho ruled an area extending from the Mediterranean right across to Galicia; not for nothing is he known as 'the Great'. After his death things began to disintegrate, and provinces were lost. In 1200 it had roughly the boundaries it had today. In 1512, King Ferdinand of Aragón (who was still Regent of Castilla following his wife's death) invaded Navarra and took it easily. In the 19th century, after centuries of relative peace, things kicked off, first with Napoleon's invasion, then with the rise of the liberal movement and Carlism. These events were always likely to cause schisms in the province, which already had natural divisions between mountains and plains, and families who were Basque, French, or Spanish in alignment. Navarra became the centre of Carlism and suffered the loss of most of its rights as a result of that movement's defeat. During the Civil War, the Carlists, still strong, were on Franco's side; as a result the province was favoured during his rule, in contrast to the other Basque provinces, which had taken the Republican side.

Today, as a semi-autonomous province, the divisions continue; most Basques are striving for the union of Navarra with Euskadi, but the lowland towns are firmly aligned with Spain. Navarra's social and political differences are mirrored in its geography. The northern and eastern parts of the province are dominated by the Pyrenees and its offshoots, and are lands of green valleys and shepherd villages, which are culturally very Basque. The baking southern and central plains seem still to reflect the dusty days of the Reconquista and are more Spanish in outlook and nature.

and the Silo, which are otherwise kept closed, and the 12th-century funerary structure known as the 'Silo of Charlemagne', which legend maintains is built on the site where Charlemagne buried Roland and his stricken rearguard. Underneath it is a burial pit holding bones of various origins; some may well have been pilgrims for whom the hard climb over the Pyrenees had proved to be a step too far. Opposite the complex, there's a **visitors' centre**, which is half an excuse for a shop to keep the steady stream of tourists happy. There is, however, a small exhibition and audiovisual display ① *1000- 1400, 1600-1900, €1*, on Navarra and the Roncesvalles area.

Roncesvalles sits just below the Puerto de Ibañeta pass, after which the road starts descending towards **St Jean Pied de Port** in the French Basqueland.

Burguete/Auritz → *Colour map 2, grid A5.*

Some 3 km closer to Pamplona through an avenue of trees, the village of **Burguete** offers more services than the bare Roncesvalles, and has been made moderately famous by Hemingway, whose characters Jake and Bill put away several gallons of wine there on a trout-fishing expedition before descending to Pamplona in his novel *Fiesta (The Sun Also Rises)*. However, it is still an austere village whose main street is curiously flanked by drains, which give the stone cottages a fortress-like appearance.

A severe church is the town's centrepiece but it's a solid, friendly place to stay with a handful of good-value sleeping and eating options. Hemingway fans will head for the **Hostal Burguete**, which happily seems to have changed little since his day.

Puerto de Ibañeta

Not far up the road to France is the pass itself, the Puerto de Ibañeta. Here, there's a modern chapel and a memorial to Roland. Some say this is where the grieving Charlemagne buried Roland; at any rate the memorial is slightly strange, seeing as it was the Navarrese who probably did him in. A more recent and appropriate memorial in Roncesvalles commemorates his vanquishers. Continuing from Puerto de Ibañeta, the valley of **Valcarlos/Luzaide** is seen by many scholars as the most likely place for the battle itself. At the border, the town of the same name is pretty enough but overwhelmed with French hopefuls paying over-the-odds prices for Spanish ham and wine. There's plenty of accommodation here but no real reason to linger.

Bidasoa Valley

Northeast of Pamplona, the road to Irun follows the course of the salmony river Bidasoa, which divides France and Spain at the Bay of Biscay. The road itself is a nightmare of speeding trucks and smelly industry, but the valley houses several likeable villages that are very Basque indeed. Lesaka and Etxalar are charming places; further into the hills Zugarramurdi was a hotmbed of witchcraft in the 17th century, or so the inquisition thought.➤ *For Sleeping, Eating and other listings, see pages 500-502.*

Bera/Vera de Bidasoa

Closest to the coast is Bera/Vera de Bidasoa, a place where you may hear more Euskara than Spanish, and a hotbed of support for ETA. Below the imposing grey stone church is the Ayuntamiento (Town Hall), with a façade painted with female figures of Fortitude, Temperance, Justice, and Prudence, who sometimes seem to dominate this sober town. On the edge of town is the posh farmhouse where the Basque novelist Pío Baroja used to spend his summers; it's still a private home (used by his nephew) and very rarely open to the public. There's a tourist office ① *C Errotazar, T948631222.*

Lesaka

Further inland from Bera, a couple of scenic kilometres off the main road, is Lesaka, prettier and more welcoming than its neighbour. Its architectural highlights are a pair of tower-houses, but there are several impressive homes, many built by *indianos*, colonists returning with fortunes made in the New World. As in Bera, the stone church looms large over the town, but it seems more at ease amid gardens and tranquil pathways. If this was Britain, it is certain that the village would have won some sort of council award for 'best geranium window boxes of the northeast' or similar; it's a colourful place when they're in bloom.

Etxalar

Some 3 km off the main road on the other side of Lesaka is peaceful Etxalar, a stone Basque village with a very attractive pinkish church surrounded by circular Basque gravemarkers, widely thought to be a continuation of pre-Christian tradition. There are several *hostales* and *casas rurales* around here.

Zugarramurdi

From Etxalar, a deserted road leads up a spectacular valley and around a couple of hills to Zugarramurdi. On entering this spotless whitewashed village you might think

⦂ Sloe shots

One of Navarra's most emblematic products is this liqueur, usually taken as a digestivo after a meal. Although there are patxaranes made from a variety of berries and fruits, the traditional Navarrese one, which now has its own Denominación de Origen quality grading, is made from sloe berries macerated in an aniseed liquor.

Usually served on ice, the taste can range from the sweet and superbly delicate to the medicinal. The name comes from the Euskara word for sloe, basaran. Some folk like to mix it: a San Fermín is patxarán and *cava* (sparkling wine), while a *vaca rosa* (pink cow) is a blend of the liqueur with milk. Adding a few grains of cinnamon or coffee is also done.

it a place of peaceful rural life, the only corruption to be found in shifty-eyed shops selling laughably overpriced wine and ham to their fellow Basques from across the border. You'd be wrong.

The Inquisition weren't fooled in 1610 when they turned up. **Don Juan del Valle Alvarado**, sent from the tribunal at Logroño after hearing of an outbreak of witchery in the area, spent several months investigating here and found the village to be a whitened sepulchre, a seething pit of blasphemy and moral turpitude. He understandably accused over 300 villagers (men, women, and children) from the surrounding area of witchcraft, and of committing crimes including: whipping up storms to sink ships in the Bay of Biscay, eating the dead and the living, conducting black masses, indulging in various unspeakable acts with Satan in the form of a black goat, crossing the road against the lights and more. As in most of the Inquisition's investigations, denunciations by fellow villagers were the dubious source of most of the evidence. Many people turned themselves in; the punishments were far harsher if you didn't. The most heinous of these contemptible criminals were taken to Logroño and left in prison while the evidence was debated. Many died before the verdicts were announced; their effigies were burned or pardoned accordingly. A total of 12 were sentenced to death.

Some five minutes' walk from town is a large **cave complex** ① *1000-2100, €2.40*, said to have been the site for most of the diabolical activity. It certainly would make a fine spot for a black mass, with an impressive natural tunnel overlooked by a couple of viewing galleries. It may well be that various unchristian rituals were practised here: veneration of traditional Basque deities such as Mari, the mother goddess, was still alive well into the 20th century. It's said that in the year of the witch trials, the local priest came to the caves and daubed them with mustard, declaring that the witches would vanish for as many years as there were mustard grains.

Being so close to France, this whole area was (until the Schengen treaty) a nest of smuggling, and many marked walking trails in the area would have been used by moonlight. The unwritten contract between police and smugglers was that, if sprung, the smugglers would drop their booty and make themselves scarce. The law, for their part, would hold their fire and take the goods home with them.

◉ Sleeping

Valle de Roncal *p495*
There are dozens of places to stay in Izaba and around, many of them *casas rurales*.
B **Hotel Isaba**, Carretera Roncal s/n, Izaba, T948893000. A modern and friendly hotel at the edge of town. Comfy communal lounges, and happily non-standard rooms. Next to the municipal swimming pool.
E **Hostal Zaltúa**, C Castillo 23, Roncal, T948475008. A convivial inn with some faded but clean rooms that can get very noisy at weekends.

F Txabalkua, C Izargentea 16, Izaba, T9488-93083. A peaceful and pretty *pensión* in the middle of the old town, shared bathrooms.

Hostels and camping
Albergue Oxanea, T948893153, Izaba. A hostel that lives a happy life without lockouts, curfews, or meddlesome rules. The dorms are crowded but comfortable, and it's in the heart of the cobbled old town.
Refugio de Belagua, Ctra Izaba-Francia Km 19, T948394002. On the way up to the French border, this *refugio* looks like a big tent but is a warm base for skiers and walkers year round. Accommodation in huge dorms, and warming meals.
Camping Asolaze, Carretera Isaba-Francia Km 6, T948893034. This year-round campsite is 6 km from Isaba towards France. Its open all year round and gets very busy, but there's pine forest right up to the back door.

Western Pyrenees *p497*
There are plenty of *casas rurales* around Burguete should you fail to find a bed.
C Hostal Loizu, Av Roncesvalles 7, Burguete/Auritz, T948760008, hloizu@cmn.navarra.net. The most upmarket of the places to stay in this area, a decently modernized old house in Burguete with reasonable rooms with TV and heating, which can be much needed in summer and winter.
D Hostal Burguete, C San Nicolás 71, Burguete/Auritz, T948790488, F948760005. The place where Ernest used to hang out, and the base for Jake and Bill's fishing expedition in *Fiesta* (*The Sun Also Rises*). Plenty of character on Burguete's main street.
D La Posada, Roncesvalles s/n, T948760225. It feels like an old travellers' inn and it is one, dating from 1612. The best place to stay in Roncesvalles itself with snug heated rooms for when the weather comes a calling. Decent restaurant.
E Casa Sabina, Roncesvalles s/n, T948760012. While this place's main concern is feeding the pilgrims from the adjacent hostel, it has a few rooms that are nicer than the exterior might suggest.
F Juandeaburre, C San Nicolás s/n, Burguete/Auritz, T948760078. This simple summer-only *pensión* has unheated rooms

with washbasin at a good price. Fills quickly so ring ahead.

Hostels and camping
Albergue de Juventud, Roncesvalles s/n, T948760015. An official youth hostel in part of the Colegiata complex. Institutional but friendly and reasonably comfortable. It's early to bed and early to rise, but there's little going on in Roncesvalles in the way of nightlife. You might wangle a key for late entry.
Camping Urrobi, Ctra Pamplona-Valcarlos Km 42, T948760200. Just below Burguete, this campsite is reasonably equipped and also has cheap dormitory beds on offer. Open Apr-Oct.

Bidasoa Valley *p499*
C Donamaria'ko Benta, Barrio Ventas 4, Donamaria, T948450708, donamariako@jet.es An excellent place to stay for those with transport, this creeper-swathed inn 3 km from the main road beyond the town of Santesteban/Doneztebe dates from 1815. The welcoming owners rescued it from dereliction and it's now a beautiful place to stay, with rustic floorboarded rooms with no little comfort and style. The restaurant is excellent.
D Hostal Ekaitza, Plaza Berria 13, Lesaka, T948637559. Reasonable rooms above a bar in the centre, some with bath, some without. Gets noisy at weekends and during the festival.
F Domekenea, Etxalar s/n, T948635031. In Etxalar itself, this typically solid, whitewashed Basque house has a couple of comfy rooms, which are very good value with TV, ensuites, and a shared balcony.
F Matxinbeltzenea, C Arretxea 22, Lesaka, T948637796. Loads of cheap bunks in this hostel above this noisy Basque bar in Lesaka.
F Soltxagaerea, C Arretxea 14, Lesaka. A good and cheap place to stay in a beautiful Basque house with simple but acceptable double rooms. Irregular opening.

❶ Eating

Valle de Roncal *p495*
€€ **Pekoetxe**, Carretera Roncal s/n, Izaba, T948893101. An attractive and styled

For an explanation of sleeping and eating price codes used in this guide, see inside the front cover. Other relevant information is found in Essentials, see pages 47-56.

modern restaurant specializing in grilled meat and fish, but featuring a range of other local options with a touch of flair.

€**Txiki**, C Mendigatxa 17, Izaba, T948893118. A lively and atmospheric local bar and restaurant serving a *menú* for €9.70 that's got few frills but plenty of authentic Navarran taste.

Bidasoa Valley *p499*

€€ **Ansonea**, Plaza de los Fueros 1, Bera, T948631155. A well-priced place to try homely Basque specialities like *kokotxas* (hake cheeks: delicious), or red peppers stuffed with crab (*pimientos rellenos de txangurro*). There's a *menú del día* for €7.75.

€€ **Donamaria'ko Benta**, Barrio Ventas 4, Donamaria, T948450708. Excellent modern cuisine with a homely feel in one of the nicest rural hotels in the area (see above).

€ **Kasino**, Plaza Zahorra 23, Lesaka. This charming building houses a dark and homely restaurant with a small terrace. Don't be fooled by the humble surroundings; the *tortilla* here has been voted best in the land by judges in San Sebastián.

€ **Matxinbeltzenea**, C Arretxea 22, Lesaka, T948637796. A good source for cheap filling meals or a beer in a Basque atmosphere.

Western Pyrenees *p497*

€€ **Loizu**, Av Roncesvalles 7, Burguete/ Auritz. T948760008. This hotel restaurant serves up good warming mountain food with a touch of class. A *menú* for €16.90.

€ **Burguete**, C San Nicolás 71, Burguete/ Auritz, T948790488. If you've read *Fiesta* you'll be eating here of course. The piano that Bill played to keep warm is in situ in the dining room, and, while they may have forgotten how to make rum punch, there is a *menú* for €10.11 that is good value and includes trout, as it should. Pictures of the bearded writer adorn the room.

⦿ Bars and clubs

Valle de Roncal *p495*
Ttun Ttun, Barrikato s/n, Izaga. A great little bar with a terrace in the stone-housed back streets below the main road.

⊛ Festivals

Valle de Roncal *p495*
Isaba's main festival is from **25-28 Jul**, while Roncal's kicks off on **15 Aug**.

Bidasoa Valley *p499*
Lesaka is famous for its own **San Fermín, starting at the same time as the Pamplona** one. The major event is on the morning of **7 Jul**, with a dance, the *zubi gainekoa*, **performed along both sides of the river to symbolize friendship in the region. Bera's major *fiesta* starts on 3 Aug, while Zugarramurdi celebrates its witchy history on 15 Aug.**

⊖ Transport

Valle de Roncal *p495*
La Tafallesa run 1 bus daily from **Pamplona** to Roncal and Izaba, leaving at 1700. There's one bus from **Pamplona** to Ochagavía daily, leaving at 1530 Mon-Thu, 1900 Sat, and 1530 Sun. It leaves Ochagavía Mon-Sat at 0900.

Western Pyrenees *p497*
La Montañesa run one bus from **Pamplona** to Roncesvalles at 1800 Mon-Fri, 1600 on Sat, no service on Sun.

Bidasoa Valley *p499*
La Baztanesa runs a complex series of buses up and down the Bidasoa and Baztan valleys. There are effectively 3 buses to and from **Pamplona** daily, some require a change along the road. For enquiries; T948226712.

Pilgrim route to Santiago

The two main branches of the Camino Santiago, the Camino Francés, which has come through Roncesvalles and Pamplona, and the Aragonés, which has tracked through Aragón and Sangüesa, meet at Puente La Reina and continue westwards together. This

part of the province is one of Navarra's nicest, with towns such as Estella and Viana joys   503
for the traveller or pilgrim to discover. Off the main route, too, are some perfect little
villages, while, to top things off, some of Navarra's best wine is made in the area.

Sangüesa and around → Colour map 2, grid B6.

Descending from the mountains, pilgrims on the Camino Aragonés usually make
Sangüesa their first stop in Navarra. It's a fine little town with more than its fair share
of quirky buildings, and within reach are a few other interesting places – the
Monasterio de Leyre and Castillo de Javier are places steeped in religious history,
while the Embalse de Yesa reservoir offers a break from the fierce heat. Mingers will
be happy to know they can skip washing in Sangüesa; the stench from the nearby
paper mill makes all bodily odours fade into insignificance. After an hour or so, it's
actually not too bad – plenty of locals swear they love it. To the west, around the town
of Lumbier, are two gorges of great natural beauty.➤➤ *For Sleeping, Eating and other listings,
see pages 506-508.*

Sights
Iglesia de Santa María ① *T620110581, tours Mon-Sat 1230, 1330, 1630, 1730, 1830
(Wed-Sat 1030, 1130 also), €1.65 church only, €3.30 whole town.*

*"What I myself do or do not believe is immaterial: to the sculptor who transformed the
dead stone into a living, rippling stream, the scene he depicted was as clear as it is to
me today, across centuries of battles, plague and change."* Cees Nooteboom, on the
portal of Iglesia de Santa María.

Originally founded by Romans on a nearby hill, Sangüesa served its
apprenticeship as a bastion against the Moors before quieter times saw it moved
down to the banks of the cloudy green Río Aragón. First among its several impressive
structures is the Church de Santa María by the bridge. Its elaborately carved portal
takes Romanesque sculpture to heights of delicacy and fluidity seldom seen
anywhere, although some of the themes covered stray a fair way from lofty religion.
The inside is less interesting and annoyingly only accessible by guided tour (the office
is at the back of the building). This goes for most of the other buildings in town. The
tourist office is opposite the church.

Palacio de Vallesantoro Sangüesa's town hall is based in the outrageous Palacio
de Vallesantoro. The doorway is flanked by two bizarre corkscrew columns, but it's
the macabre overhanging eaves that draw even more attention. They make the
building look like a Chinese pagoda, designed after a night of bad dreams. Leering
dogs, lions and asses alternate with tortured human figures along the black overhang
– stress leave among councillors here is high.

Iglesia de Santiago ① *open for mass or on the town's guided tour.* A couple of
streets back is the church of Santiago, a late Romanesque building with an
impressive fortified tower and several good Gothic sculptures, including Saint James
himself. He also appears in colour on the building's façade, flanked by two pilgrims
who look like they might have made the journey from the Australian outback.

Around Sangüesa
Castillo de Javier ① *0900-1300, 1600-1900, last visits 1 hr before closing.* Like a
lion with its mane plaited, the castle of Javier doesn't seem as formidable as it no
doubt once was. Enough of a thorn in the side of Spain for Cardinal Cisneros (also
known as Ximenez the Inquisitor) to have commanded its partial destruction, it is

Navarra Sangüesa & around

better known as the birthplace of the missionary and founding member of the Jesuits, Saint Francis Xavier. Unlike the birthplace of Francis's former roommate Saint Ignatius, there's not too much ostentatious piety and the castle makes for a good visit. It has been heavily restored; someone foolishly backed a basilica into it in the 19th century, and more work was done in the 1950s, but there's still some feeling of what it might have been like when young Francis roamed its corridors.

Monasterio de San Salvador de Leyre ⓘ *Mon-Fri 1015-1400, 1530-1900, Sat 1015-1400, 1600-1900, €1.65*. Off the N240 northeast of Sangüesa, a road winds 4 km through fragrant hills here, a stop on the Camino de Santiago. A monastery was first founded on the spot as early as the eighth century AD – the beautiful but rugged spot (the name means 'eagerness to overcome' in Euskara) has been a favourite haunt of hermits before that. Nothing but foundations remain from that period – the older parts of today's structure date from the 11th and 12th centuries, when the Navarrese monarchs took a liking to the spot and made it the seat of their kingdom. The centre flourished with religious and secular power and became extremely wealthy before an inevitable decline. The abbey was abandoned in the 19th century after loss of monastic privileges and was not reused until 1954, when it was colonized by Benedictines from the Monasterio de San Domingo de Silos.

❧ *The monks sing in Gregorian chant at 0730, 0900, 1900, 2110 in the church.*

The church itself is of mixed styles but preserves much simplicity and tranquillity inside, above all when it's filled with the Gregorian chanting of the monks during offices. The structure is remarkably off-kilter – lovers of symmetry and proportion will be appallingly ill-at-ease. The portal is a fascinating 12th-century work, filled with Romanesque scenes. While the main groups are of the Last Judgement, Christ and the Evangelists, the sculptors let their fancy run a bit freer elsewhere – you can spot several interesting demons and nightmarish animals, Jonah getting swallowed, and some lifelike prowling lions. Inside, the centrepiece is the Virgin of Leyre, while the adult Christ is relegated to his customary Spanish place in the wings. A large chest on one wall contains the bones of no fewer than 10 Navarrese kings, seven queens, and two princes – these were exhumed and boxed in 1915 – their feelings on the matter unrecorded. A small side-chapel has a retablo in a pleasingly rustic style.

The crypt, accessed from the ticket office, is a weird space, whose stone altar and ram-horned columns suggest darker ritual purposes. The columns all vary, and are tiny – it's strange to have the capitals at waist height. Next to the crypt is a tunnel leading to an image of San Virila – a former abbot. This dozy chap wandered up to a nearby stream and was so enchanted by the song of a bird that he didn't make it back for vespers for another three centuries. If you fancy some time out too, follow his lead and head up to the spring, which is signposted five minutes' walk above the complex. If you like the spot, you might consider staying in the attached *hospedería* (see below).

Foz/Hoz de Lumbier ⓘ *€1.50*. A mile from the small town of Lumbier is the Foz/Hoz de Lumbier, a fashionably *petite* designer gorge. It's a top place, with gurgling stream (bring your swimming gear on a hot day), overhanging rock walls, and a large population of vultures that circles lazily above, in the vain hope that a tourist will drop dead from the heat. Twenty-minutes' walk from the car park will get you to the other end, where you can see the ruins of the 'Devil's Bridge', destroyed in the Peninsular War but possibly none too safe before that. Return the same way or via a longer circuit around the top of the gorge.when the ticket booth is attended.

Puente La Reina/Gares and around → *Colour map 2, grid B5.*

"*And from here all roads to Santiago become only one.*" While this is not a hundred percent true, the two principal pilgrim routes converge here just before reaching the medieval bridge that the town grew around, a long and beautiful Romanesque span that emerges from an arched entrance and speaks of many kilometres to come under a beating sun. ▸ *For Sleeping, Eating and other listings, see pages 506-508.*

Sights

The town is small, and a good place to stop for a night if you're inclined. Arriving from the east, on the outskirts, you'll see the strange monument to pilgrims, a wild-eyed and gaunt bronze figure who might provoke more anxiety than comfort in passing peregrines. The pilgrim hostel isn't much further, and stands next to the 12th-century **Iglesia del Crucifijo**. In the heart of town is another church ① *0900-1300, 1700-2030*, dedicated to Santiago himself. The so-called Matamoros ('Moor killer') might not be too impressed to notice that his doorway looks remarkably Muslim in style with its horseshoe notched recessed portal. Opposite is the fine façade of the **Convento de la Trinidad**. The peaceful centre of the town, the **Plaza** Julián Mena, houses the Ayuntamiento and tourist office ① *Tue-Sat 1000-1400, 1700- 2000, Sun 1100-1400*.

Near Puente La Reina, the medieval village of **Obanos** is famous for its biennial staging of a mystery play based on a legend of the Camino.

Estella/Lizarra and around

Sights

The major town of western Navarra, Estella is a very likeable place to stay a while. The town likes to dust off the moniker 'the Toledo of the North'; this is a little unjustified, but its crop of historic buildings are certainly interesting.

Estella's history as a town goes back to 1052 when King Sancho Ramírez, taking ruler and pencil to the burgeoning pilgrim trail, established it as a new stop on the official route. On a hill, close to the Puente de la Carcél, on the western bank, the older part of town, is the towering grey bulk of the **Iglesia de San Pedro de la Rúa** ① *apart from the guided tour (see below) the church only opens at about 1930, but you'll have to be prompt, as mass starts at 2000*, with its crusty façade and indented Romanesque portal. The highlight inside is the semi-cloister. It was here that the Castilian kings used to swear to uphold the Navarrese *fueros* after the province was annexed; it was a promise honoured in varying degrees by different monarchs.

Opposite is the **Palacio de los Reyes** ① *Tue-Sat 1100-1300, 1700-1900, Sun 1100-1300, free*, another Romanesque edifice, which now houses a museum devoted to the early 20th-century painter Gustavo de Maeztu, who was influenced by the art nouveau movement, and lived his later years in Estella. Estella's tourist office is next door, guided tours of the town depart from here.

Across the river, the **Iglesia de San Miguel** is also set above the town on a hillock. Its most endearing feature is the Romanesque portal, richly carved with a scene of Christ in Majesty surrounded by his supporting cast. It's an impressive work. Similarly to San Pedro, the church is only open by guided tour or about half an hour before 2000 mass.

The newer part of town centres around the large **Plaza de los Fueros**, overseen by the Iglesia de San Juán, a mishmash of every conceivable style. Nearby is the quiet **Plaza de Santiago**, in whose centre four 'orrible creatures spill water from their mouths into a fountain.

A couple of kilometres southwest of Estella, on the way to Ayegui on the Camino, is the **Monastery of Irache** ① *for visits Tue 0830-1330, Wed-Sun 0830-1330, 1700-1900*, the oldest of the original Navarran pilgrim refuges. It is a bit bare and down at heel these days but scheduled for some restoration work. The light and airy church features an inscrutable Virgin and a bony bit of San Veremundo in a reliquary by the altar.

The monastery is famous for its palatable red table wine, and pilgrims who love the good drop might be tempted to linger on the way here a little: there's a tap at the back of the *bodega* that spouts red wine for the benefit of travellers on the road, a sight to gladden the heart if ever there was one!

There are numerous **wineries** in the Estella area which are happy to show visitors around. One of the quality labels is **Palacio de la Vega** ① *T948527009*, in the small town of **Dicastillo**, south of Estella. The *bodega*, whose home is a striking 19th-century palace, is a modern producer that has been at the forefront of the successful establishment of French varietals like Cabernet Sauvignon and Merlot in Navarra. A more traditional producer of quality wines is **Bodegas Sarría** ① *T948267562*, based by Puente La Reina. The tourist office provides a list of *bodegas*; phone beforehand to arrange a visit.

Viana → *Colour map 2, grid B4.*

One of Navarra's loveliest towns, Viana is the last stop before the Camino descends into the oven of La Rioja. Fortified to defend the kingdom's borders against Castile, it still preserves small sections of its walls, rising above the surrounding plains. The **Iglesia de Santa María** has a monumental façade and a high Gothic interior, which seems to clash with the large numbers of grandiose retablos stuffed into every corner.

In front of the church is the gravemarker of an unexpected man; Cesare Borgia, a 15th-century Italian noble who could rightly be described as Machiavellian – *The Prince* was based on his machinations. Son of a pope, after becoming a cardinal he likely had his elder brother murdered as part of his schemes, one of a number of opportunistic assassinations he masterminded while conquering significant swathes of Italian territory. It all went pear-shaped for Borgia though, and he ended up as a minor noble in Viana. After having been imprisoned in Spain, Borgia was placed under the protection of the King of Navarra. Elected constable of the town, he was killed in a siege by Castilian forces in 1507, aged 30. The atmospheric ruined Gothic church of San Pedro sheltered French troops during the Peninsular War before it collapsed in 1844.

● Sleeping

Sangüesa and around *p503*
B **Hotel Xabier**, Plaza de Javier s/n, Javier, T948884006, www.hotelxabier.com. The nicer of the 2 hotels in the touristic zone by the castle of Javier. The old-style rooms have modern comforts, there's some cooling marbled effects, and a reasonable restaurant.
C **Hospedería de Leyre**, Monasterio de Leyre, T948884100, hotel@monasteriode leyre.com. With great views over the plains and reservoir. Some very nice walks in the scented hills, the hotel offers much more than monastic comfort, and very good meals.

D **Hostal JP**, Paseo Raimundo Lumbier 3, Sangüesa, T948871693. A clean, fresh and good option (if slightly hospital-like) just across the river from Iglesia de Santa María.
E **Pensión Las Navas**, C Alfonso el Batallador 7, Sangüesa, T948870077. Although not the most welcoming of establishments, these rooms are pretty decent value in the heart of town and equipped with bathrooms.

Hostels and camping
Camping Cantolagua, Paseo Cantolagua s/n, T948430352. A good place to stay by the riverside, swimming pool and tennis courts. There are also bungalows and caravans

Puente La Reina/Gares and around *p505*

Puente has a couple of excellent lodging choices. It's close enough to Pamplona that prices soar during **Los Sanfermines**.

AL Mesón del Peregrino, C Irunbidea s/n, T948340075, www.hotelelperegrino.com. An impressively individual and classy hotel and restaurant on the approach to town. Packed with arty objects and quirky architectural kinks, but with a comfortable stone-and-wood feeling. Lovely pool and surrounding terrace. Very high quality restaurant. Despite the name, one senses eyebrows might rise if a road-weary pilgrim with backpack and staff actually ventured inside.

C Bidean, C Mayor 20, T948341156, www.hotelbidean.com. A charming hotel in the centre of town with welcoming staff and an old-fashioned homely feel. Comfy beds.

F Fonda Lorca, C Mayor 54, T948340127. A cheery place facing the small Plaza Mena, with a balcony, reasonable home-style food, and some cheap rooms.

Estella/Lizarra and around *p505*

C Hotel Yerri, Av Yerri 35, T948546034. Unappealing modern hotel near the bullring, Estella's most upmarket option.

D Cristina, C Baja Navarra 1, T948550772. A well-positioned *hostal* in Estella's liveliest part. Nearly all the rooms have a balcony to watch the world go by; those rooms overlooking Plaza de los Fueros can get a bit noisy.

E-F Pensión San Andrés, Plaza Santiago 58, T948550448. A very good option on a quiet square, with friendly management and nice rooms with/without bath.

Camping

Camping Estella, Ctra Pamplona-Logroño Km 44. A range of accommodation options are available at this riverbank site. There's a big swimming pool on site. On the road to Pamplona a couple of kilometres from town.

Viana *p506*

E Casa Armendariz, C Navarro Villoslada 19, T948645078, is a good choice for both lodging and cheerful dining.

F Bar Pitu, C Medio San Pedro 9, T94864-5927, some rooms above the restaurant.

🍴 Eating

Sangüesa and around *p503*
See also Sleeping above.

€€€ El Pilar, C Mayor 87, Sangüesa. The posh place in town to come for a drink or a coffee.

€€ Mediavilla, C Alfonso el Batallador 15, Sangüesa, T948870212. A hospitable *asador* with filling *menús* for €17 and €22.

€ Bar Ciudad de Sangüesa, C Santiago 4, Sangüesa, T948871021. There are several bars on this street – this bar does good cheap meals and is popular with locals.

Puente La Reina/Gares and around *p505*

€ Restaurante Joaquin, C Mayor 48. Decent for lunch with a *menú del día* for €8.

€ Valdizarbe, Paseo de los Fueros s/n, T948341009. A bar doing a decent line in cheapish paella, all good carbohydrates for pilgrims.

Estella/Lizarra and around *p505*
Estella's signature dish is gorrín, another name for roast suckling pig, a heavy but juicy meal seeded with a potent dose of garlic.

€€€ La Cepa, Plaza de los Fueros 15, T948550032. One of Estella's best, this upstairs restaurant makes up for its dull decor with imaginatively prepared Navarrese dishes. There's a *menú* at lunchtimes and weekends, otherwise it's fairly pricey.

€€ Astarriaga, Plaza de los Fueros 12, T948550802. An *asador* offering a decent *menú del día* for €11.90, and doing the usual good steaks, but also some traditional Navarrese offerings. Good *pintxos* and a terrace on the square.

€ Izarra, C Caldereria 20, T948550678. The restaurant above this bar is nothing special, but does offer a *menú* for €9 day and night. The *bocadillos* and *pintxos* in the bar downstairs are more inspiring.

€ Katxetas Taberna, Estudio de Gramática 1, T948550010. This hang-out for the young Basques of the town is an excellent place, serving cheap and filling *raciones* at happy indoor and outdoor tables. Recommended.

Navarra Pilgrim route to Santiago: listings

● *For an explanation of sleeping and eating price codes used in this guide, see inside the*
● *front cover. Other relevant information is found in Essentials, see pages 47-56.*

♬ Bars and clubs

Estella/Lizarra and around *p505*
Kopa´s, C Carpintería 9. A popular modern bar. Good range of quality imported beers.
Pigor, C La Estrella 6, T948554054. A sociable and attractive bar with a range of good *bocadillos*. The music cranks up later on weekend nights.

❀ Festivals and events

Estella/Lizarra and around *p505*
Estella's fiesta starts on the first Fri in **Aug**, with *encierros*, *corridas* and more. It warms up with a **medieval week** in **mid-Jul**, with troupes of jongleurs and crumhorn-players roaming the streets, which are enlivened by flaming torches, bales of straw, and chickens and rabbits in cages.

Viana *p506*
Viana goes wild in late **Jul** for a joint fiesta of **Mary Magdalene and St James**; there are two *encierros* (bull-runnings) daily.

◉ Transport

Sangüesa and around *p503*
La Veloz Sangüesina, T948226995, runs

3 buses daily to and from **Pamplona** (only 1 on Sun).

Puente La Reina/Gares and around *p505*
La Estellesa runs frequent buses between **Pamplona** and **Logroño**, stopping at all the towns en route.

Estella/Lizarra and around *p505*
La Estellesa runs 10 buses a day to and from **Pamplona**; the journey takes 1 hr. A similar number go to **Logroño**. There are also 6 buses daily to **San Sebastián** and 1 to **Zaragoza**.

❶ Directory

Puente La Reina/Gares and around *p505*
Internet **Librería Ohiuka**, corner of C Cerco Viejo and Las Huertas, 0800-1300, Mon-Sat, 1700-2000.

Estella/Lizarra and around *p505*
Internet **Alfonso**, C De Puy 44, 1000-2200 daily but with only 2 terminals.
Ice Net, Plaza Santiago 3, Mon-Fri 1030-1400, 1630-2200, Sat/Sun 1630-2200.

Southern Navarra

Not far south of Pamplona, the land flattens and hardens as the Spanish meseta opens up. It's a land where the weather doesn't pull punches; the winters are cold, the summers can be merciless, and massive windmills put the relentless westerlies to good use: Navarra is one of Europe's leaders in this form of energy. Where there's water, corn, wheat, olives, and grapes are grown, while towns and villages stand defiantly under the big sky, seemingly defying nature to do its worst. ▸▸ *For Sleeping, Eating and other listings, see pages 511-512.*

South of Pamplona → *Colour map 2, grid C3.*

In easy reach of Pamplona, the towns of Tafalla and Olite, only 7 km apart, are cultural gems. Although overshadowed from a touristic point of view by its neighbour, Tafalla is a larger and more complete town, whose old quarter boasts an attractively run-down web of medieval streets and petite plazas centred around its impressive church. Olite stands in the middle of the baking valley like a bullfighter in the middle of the ring. Capital of the Navarrese court in its most extravagant phase, there's a Spanish feel to much of the area; perhaps it's just that the sunbaked sandstone seems in such

contrast to the softer stone and wood buildings of the Pyrenean villages. Olite's centrepiece is its magnificent castle, which sometimes seems bigger than the town itself. The surrounding area's architecture is magnificent: even the smallest village seems to have a church tucked away that would draw hundreds of visitors daily in other parts of the world. The remote areas southeast of Olite are difficult to access without a vehicle, and some of the least populated morsels in Europe.

Tafalla

The biggest town in the area, Tafalla is a busy place, an industrial and commercial centre as well as focus for the surrounding districts. Historically an important stop on the road from Pamplona to Tudela, its architectural charm is as much in the small details, an arch here, a coat of arms there, as its selection of larger monuments.

The major structure in the narrow old town streets is the **Iglesia de Santa María** (no prizes for guessing that one!). Built in the 16th century over older foundations, it's been tweaked a fair bit over the years. The façade is fairly unadorned, and curious in shape; it looks like someone's put up a lean-to along one side. The highlight for most visitors is the retablo, an ornate late 16th-century work by the hand of Juan de Ancheta. After working on it for seven years, the strain (perhaps caused by the meddling patrons) killed the maestro, and the work was completed by his colleague and pupil Pedro González de San Pedro. If you find the piece over-ornate, blame the patrons: when the work was finished, they decided it wasn't striking enough, and got a third artist to touch up some of the paintings and spraypaint the rest gold. The bottom row is a brief biography of the Virgin Mary from left to right. The piece is topped by Ancheta's sensitive crucifixion. Down the hill from the old town, the three-sided Plaza de Navarra is the town's focus these days, and has several good places to eat and drink on it and in the vicinity.

Olite

One of the oldest towns in Navarra, Olite was founded and fortified by the Romans. It wasn't until the 12th century, however, that the town began to rise to prominence within Navarra. The Navarrese monarchs had very itchy feet and were always decamping the court from one capital to the next. Olite became something of a favourite, and a **palace** was built, incorporating what remained of the Roman fortifications. This palace is now a parador.

It's the newer **castle** ① *Oct-Mar 1000-1400, 1600-1800; Apr-Sep 1000-1400, 1600-1900, Jul/Aug open until 2000, €2.50*, that turns heads though. Charles III of Navarra, 'the Noble', felt that the ambitions of a kingdom should be reflected in its buildings. Accordingly, he went for broke, building the new palace in the early 15th century. Capitalizing on a period of peace in the Hundred Years' War between England and France (which tended to unavoidably involve Navarra), Charles was determined that the palace would be a model of elegance, etiquette, and courtly splendour, and put in second-floor 'hanging' gardens, exotic trees, elegant galleries, and towers, and a population of African animals including several lions and a giraffe. The castle was unfortunately destroyed in the Peninsular War to prevent it falling into French hands, but has been faithfully restored (perhaps overly) to something like its original appearance. It bristles with towers like an extravagant sandcastle, all with flags aflutter, but the highlight is certainly the restored 'queen's garden', a beautiful green space for which Charles installed a very high-tech irrigation system for the time.

As well as several other elegant buildings from Olite's zenith, underneath the town are an intriguing series of medieval galleries ① *Oct-Mar Mon-Fri 1000-1400, Sat/Sun 1000-1400, 1600-1800, Apr-Sep daily 1000-1400, 1700-2000, €1.50*. Their origins are uncertain, but it seems likely they were created, or at least enlarged by Charles III, who extravagantly dreamed of linking the towns of Tafalla and Olite with a secret passageway for times of trouble.

"What's that gorgeous hilltop village on all the Navarrese tourist posters?" The answer is this remote spot some 17 km east of Tafalla. Perched above concentric terraces harbouring almond trees, Ugué was founded in the early days of the Navarran monarchy in the ninth century AD. The walled settlement was ennobled by Charles I, who built much of the sanctuary complex that perches atop the hill. The **Santuario de Santa María** seems part castle and part church, which it effectively was; the town was seen as an important defensive bastion. The María in question is the 'black virgin', a dusky Romanesque figure with an intense stare who refuses to shiver in the bleak stone church. King Charles II left his heart to the figure, literally; it sits in a box under the altar. How pure a heart it is, is not known: Charles was known as 'the Bad' for a number of dodgy political manoeuvres during his reign, he was imprisoned for a while by the French king John, whom history has named 'the Good'.

The most attractive part of the complex is the Paseo de Ronda, a covered walkway around the outside of the church with elegant galleries with beautiful vistas over the surrounding countryside. The road to Ujué starts from the attractive village of **San Martín de Unx**, worth a look in itself for its crypted church and noble old houses. There are no buses to Ujué or San Martín: it's a hitch or a long walk from Tafalla or Olite.

Monasterio de La Oliva

ⓘ *0930-1230, 1530-1800, admission to cloister and garden €1.50.* The isolated monastery at La Oliva (it's actually near the village of Carcastillo, but it feels in the middle of nowhere), dating from the mid-12th century, is populated by a working community of Cistercians ('white monks'). Although the monastery was only repopulated in 1927 after a century of abandonment, there's a remarkable feel of living history here: the monks farm and make wine in true Cistercian style, and the smell of the farm yard pervades the monastery air. The beautifully simple portals, long gloomy church, and supremely peaceful cloister make this a very attractive visit. Carcastillo is 18 km east of the main N121 on the NA124.

Artajona

There are not many ugly villages in Navarra, and you'll steer well clear of Artajona if you want to find one. Some 11 km northwest of Tafalla, its stunningly well-preserved walls are on a huge scale, and speak of a pride and resolve little related to the size of the village. On *fiestas*, a team of *campaneros* gathers to push the four bells in a steady rhythm until they begin swinging right around. It requires a fair bit of strength and timing: the two heaviest bells each weigh over a ton. Around Artajona are several **dolmens**, as well as the excavated Iron Age settlement of **Las Eretas** ⓘ *May-Sep Sat 1100-1400, 1700-1900, Sun 1100-1400, Jul/Aug also Tue-Fri 1100-1400, 1700-1900, T699907650 for the possibility of visiting at other times*, which consists of several houses and burials; some bits have been reproduced, and it's not badly done.

La Ribera

Tudela is Navarra's second largest city and centre of the southern region known as La Ribera, for the Ebro, the peninsula's second longest river, meanders lazily through it, giving life to the rows and rows of grapevines that stripe the area. To the west of Tudela are winemaking villages that have given Navarra's reds a very good and growing reputation, to the annoyance of some Rioja producers who, although literally in some cases next door, have to work under more stringent conditions and have limited scope for experimentation.

● *The small picturesque village of Artajona claims to be the only place in the world whose bells are rung upside down.*

Even during its chilly winters, Tudela's got a scorched sort of look, while in summer the heat radiating from the footpaths and brown brick buildings can make it feel like a kiln. Apart from this factor, there's a definite Andalucian or Middle Eastern feel to the place, so it's no surprise to find that this was a place where Christians, Moors and Jews lived in relative harmony together for centuries.

Although there had been a Roman settlement here, it was in fact the Moorish lord Amrus ibn Yusuf who founded modern Tudela in the ninth century. Tudela was a centre of learning and, at times, government during the Middle Ages but its main claim to fame these days is vegetables. Although aridity is the main feature of the area, the silty banks of the Ebro have been a grower's paradise for millennia. If you're eating *alcachofas* (artichokes) or *cogollos* (lettuce hearts) in Spain, one thing's certain: if they aren't from Tudela, they aren't the best.

Like many Spanish towns above a certain size, Tudela's outskirts look like no-man's land in a construction war and, like most Spanish towns, the centre is old and remarkably beautiful. The major sight is an example of biting the hand that feeds. After the city was taken by Christians in the early 12th century after centuries of tolerant Muslim rule, the Moors watched in dismay as their mosque was demolished and a **cathedral** erected on top of it. Despite this unchristian beginning, the cathedral is something of a masterpiece, although seemingly crowded by the surrounding buildings. The Puerta del Juicio is the finest of its entrances, and food for thought for unrepentant sinners passing under it: the Last Judgement is pretty thoroughly depicted. The high rib-vaulted Gothic interior has several elegant artistic works. There is also a **cloister museum**ⓘ *Tue-Sat 1000-1330, 1600-1900, Sun 1000-1330, €1.40.*

Nearby, the **Plaza de los Fueros**, has a cute bandstand and several terrace bars. Tudela's tourist office is next to the cathedralⓘ *Mon to Sat 1000-1400, 1600-1900, Sun 1000-1400.*

Around Tudela

The town of **Fitero** is home to a beautiful monastery ⓘ *Mon 1730-1815, Tue-Sat 1130-1215, 1730-1815, Sun 1200 for guided tours, €2*, whose charming crumbly façade fronts an cavernously attractive church, cloisters, and chapterhouse. Dating from 1140, this is the oldest of Spain's Cistercian monasteries. Less attractive, but interesting nonetheless is the memorial to the Falangist dead of the civil war. The tourist office is next doorⓘ *Mon-Fri 1100-1300, 1700-1830, Sat 1100-1300, T948776600*, who might be persuaded to arrange a visit at other times if you look keen.

On the outskirts of Fitero, **Baños de Fitero** and its adjoining Riojan village **Ventas del Baño** are spa towns in a craggy little valley. Thousands of people still come here to take the waters, which are considered beneficial for many ailments.

North of Tudela, the **Bardenas Reales** is technically semi-desert; a violently rugged expanse of white gypsum flats and scrawny sheep grazing on what little spiky foliage survives. It's a popular location for filmmaking: parts of the recent Bond film *The World is not Enough* were made here. From Tudela, Rio Alhama run buses to most of the towns in southern Navarra. If you've got a car, a few roads are drivable with two-wheel drives; otherwise take a tour.

⬤ Sleeping

South of Pamplona *p508*
Olite has no cheap places. For reasonable rates, head for Tafalla or San Martín.
AL Parador Principe de Viana, Plaza de los Teobaldos 2, Olite, T948740000, www.para dor.es. Just restored, the parador occupies

the old palace next to the flamboyant castle. It feels sober and elegant by comparison. The rooms have modern bathrooms and are centred around a lovely courtyard.
D Hotel Carlos III, R de Medios 1, Olite, T948740644, F948712467. Thankfully this place on the main square opposite the castle doesn't live up to its billing as a 'medieval

hotel'; it's not short on modern comforts. The best rooms have mock stained-glass windows looking over the square. The hearty *asador* downstairs popular with tour groups.

E-F Casa Pedro, Ctra San Martín de Unx-Ujué Km 1, T948738257, semibad@ navegalia.com. A warm, welcoming, ecological, individual place to stay, just outside the village of San Martín de Unx. Comfy and attractive doubles in a peaceful setting with home-cooked meals and a great atmosphere. Attached hostel section.

La Ribera *p510*

A Ciudad de Tudela, C Misericordia s/n, Tudela, T948402440, ctudela@ ac-hoteles.com. A stately mansion house near the Plaza de los Fueros, recently converted into a modern hotel. Good facilities, although some of the rooms are a little gloomy, with an enthusiastic attitude.
C Balneario Becquer, Fitero, T948776100, historic but not as attractive as other option.
C Virrey Palafox, Fitero, T948776275, up the hill, is more peaceful than the option above.
D Parrilla, C Carlos III 6, Tudela, T948822400, F948822545. A decent mid-priced option with restaurant attached.
E Remigio, C Gaztambide 4, Tudela, T948820850, F948824123. A cool and shady hotel just off Plaza de los Fueros, with basic but clean rooms with bath. Well-priced and popular local restaurant underneath.
F Estrella, C Carnicerías 13, Tudela, T94882 1039. A good-value set of rooms above a popular bar. Reasonable shared bathrooms and oversoft but acceptable beds.

● Eating

South of Pamplona *p508*

€€ Erri Berri, Rúa del Fondo 1, Olite, T948741116. Big chunks of chargrilled meat are very popular at this *asador*. *Chuletón de buey* is a big T-bone from a mature ox, packed with flavour and sold by weight, usually a kg, a big meal in any language.
€€ Gambarte, Rúa del Seco 15, Olite, T9487-40139. A likeable restaurant, which makes a point of doing traditional Navarrese dishes well. Try *cogollos de Tudela*, lettuce rarely reaches these heights; or the *jannete de cordero*, a herb-flavoured lamb stew that comes with plenty of bones to gnaw.

€€ Tubal, Plaza Navarra 6, Tafalla, T948700852. A Tafalla institution, and a must on any *pintxo* hopping trip in Tafalla, and does some equally tasty smart modern meals.

La Ribera *p510*

€€ Bargota, C Virgen de la Cabeza 21, T948824911. A quality place. One of the best to try the veggies, preferably in a *menestra*.
€€ Estrella, C Carnicerías 13, T948821039. A good and lively bar and restaurant with a good selection of *pintxos* and local dishes.
€€ Iruña, C Muro (also called Abilio Calderón) 11, T948821000. Smartish modern dining with a distinct Navarrese and Riojan flavour near the plaza.

● Bars and clubs

La Ribera *p510*

Bar Aragón, Plaza de los Fueros, Tudela. Bar with a shady terrace to watch things happening (or not). Good beer and snacks.
Bar José Luis, C Muro (also **Abilio Calderón**) 23, Tudela. A good, cheap place to eat withoutside tables, superb *ensaladas mixtas*.
La Parra is the best bar in Fitero, just across the bridge in La Rioja.

● Festivals and events

La Ribera *p510*

Tudela's big party is the **Fiestas de Santa Ana** from **24-30 Jul**, featuring *encierros* and general revelry. A few days before this is the **Bajada del Ebro**, a rough-house regatta.

● Transport

South of Pamplona *p508*

La Tafallesa runs regular **buses** from **Pamplona** to **Tafalla**, while **Conda** sends 7 daily to **Olite**. A handful of **trains** link Tafalla and Pamplona, but the bus is better.
Artajona has 3 buses a day from Pamplona by **Conda**. 1 bus daily from Tafalla to **Ujué**.

La Ribera *p510*

Six or 7 buses daily connect Tudela with **Pamplona**, operated by **Conda**. **Fitero** is serviced by **Conda** buses from **Pamplona** 4 times daily. From Tudela, Río Alhama run buses to most of the towns in southern Navarra.

513

Cantabria and Los Picos de Europa

🔹 Footprint features

Introduction

Genteel Cantabria is an island of reaction between the more radical Asturians and Basques. Historically part of Castilla, it prospered for many years as that kingdom's main sea access, and is still known as a well-heeled sort of place: "people are prone to go to puerile lengths in their vanity about heraldry", claimed writer Gregorio Marañon in the early 20th century.

Way back beyond then, from 18000BC onwards, a thriving stone-age population lived in the area. They've left many remains of their culture, most notably the superb cave paintings at Altamira. It's now closed to the public, but you can see a replica of their very sophisticated art; for more atmosphere, head to one of the smaller caves in the region.

Apart from the Picos, Cantabria's principal attraction is its coast. **Santander** itself has some superb beaches and great restaurants. **Santillana del Mar** is misnamed (it's not on the sea) but is within easy reach of the beaches; it's a touristy but captivating town of stone mansions and cobbled streets.

For such a small area, the **Picos de Europa** have a high reputation among visitors, who eulogize this fraction of the vast **Cordillera Cantábrica** that's blessed with spectacular scenery, superb walking, abundant wildlife and most crucially, comparatively easy access. They encompass the corners of three provinces: Asturias, Cantabria, and León and have a comparatively mild climate due to their proximity to the sea. The Picos is comprised of three main massifs of limestone cut and tortured over the millennia by glaciation, resulting in the distinctive rock formations given the adjective 'karstic'. The central part of the range is national park, expanded from the original Parque Nacional de la Montaña de Covadonga, the first such beast in Spain, denominated in 1918.

★ Don't miss...

1 Beaches of Santander Hang out on the beaches, backed by elegant mansions, page 520.

2 Santillana del Mar Stay in this gem of a town; it's amazing how attractive the pompous conceits of nobles look a few centuries on, page 524.

3 Cuevas del Castillo Visit these beautiful caves with staggeringly old paintings, page 520.

4 Bodegas of Santander Spend an evening in an atmospheric bodega, a great place to eat and drink, page 522.

5 Castro Urdiales Check out this seaside town with a relaxed feel, good food, and a nice church, page 516.

6 Puerto San Glorio Take in the superb views from this pass, page 536.

7 Fuente Dé Walk the walks in this area, page 535.

8 Cangas de Onís Enjoy the friendly Asturian atmosphere here, page 530.

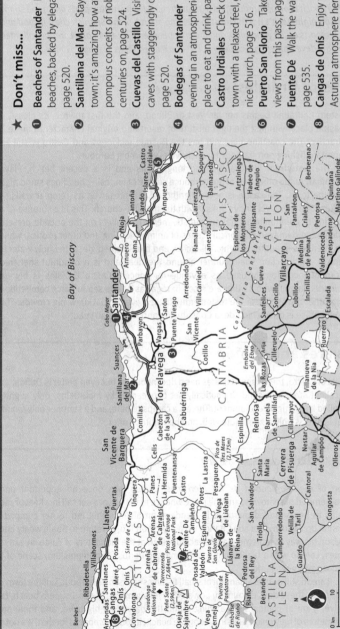

Cantabria & Los Picos de Europa

Along the coast to Santander

The eastern Cantabrian coast is a fairly uncomplicated place, with decent beaches and a sprinkling of resorts and fishing towns that attract many summer visitors from Madrid and the Basque lands. The nicest place by far is Castro Urdiales, while the large beach town of Laredo offers a great stretch of sand, watersports and good sunny season nightlife. It's not the most interesting stretch of the Spanish coast if sand and watersports aren't your thing, and the area between Santander and Laredo is blighted by ugly development. ▸▸ *For Sleeping, Eating and other listings, see pages 520-524.*

Castro Urdiales → *Colour map 2, grid A3.*

Eastern Cantabria begins not far west of Bilbao, and the first town is its nicest, a seaside place with just the right mixture of resort and original character to make it attractive. The coastline here still has the Basque rockiness and Castro is still an important fishing port (famous for anchovies) with a big harbour.

The **waterfront** is attractive and long; at its end is a decent beach, Playa Brazomar. At the other end of the harbour a couple of imposing buildings stand high over the town. The **castle** is now a lighthouse but preserves its Templar walls; a picturesque medieval bridge links it with the massive **church**. This is a surprise of a building of great architectural and artistic merit. The reliefs on the outside present strange but damaged allegorical scenes of animals kissing and other exotica, while the interior is beautifully Gothic, all arches and blue-stained glass; the holy water is kept in a giant clam shell. Further around the headland is a beautiful sheltered **rockpool**, occasionally used as a venue for concerts.Castro Urdiales is big on *traineras*, large rowboats that are raced in **regattas** on the sea in fierce competition with other towns. These are testosterone-fuelled events that draw big crowds. The tourist office is on Avenida de la Constitución and is open all year.

Islares and Oriñon

West of Castro, the village of Islares has a decent beach, but even better is Oriñon, an excellent stretch of sand dramatically set between rocky mountains, only slightly spoiled by the ugly development. There's a campsite here, and a summer-only *fonda*, but Islares is only a 20-minute walk and has more to offer.

Laredo → *Colour map 2, grid A3.*

Part of the *Hermandad de las Marismas*, Laredo was once an important port brotherhood of seatowns, and the place whence Juana La Loca set sail in a fleet of 120 ships to her arranged marriage in Flanders; an alliance that led to her complete mental breakdown. Her son Charles V used the port too, to return to Spain weary and old, on his way to retirement and peaceful death at the monastery of Yuste. In earlier times, Laredo was a big Roman seaport, named Portus Luliobrigensium, scene of a major naval engagement.

Laredo still nurses a handful of small fishing shacks in its harbour, but the town's sole focus these days is tourism, powered by its sunny climate and superb beach, **La Salvé**, 5 km of golden sand arching round the bay. It's a big town, and there are kilometres of ugly resort housing along the beach; if you're prepared for that, it's not a

bad place. The beach and **nightlife** are the reason to be here; but it's also worth
visiting the 13th-century **church**, and a tunnel carved in the 1860s through the
headland to a small harbour. The tourist office① *Alameda Miramar park, 0900-1400,
1700-1900*, is efficient .

Santander → *Phone code: 942; Colour map 2, grid A2; Population:185,231.*

Still an important Spanish port, Santander has for years encouraged visitors to turn
their attentions away from its industrial side and towards its series of superb
beaches. These gird the barrio of Sardinero, which became a genteel and exclusive
resort for the summering upper classes from the mid-19th century on. An earthier
lifestyle can be found around its old centre, which has a good collection of
restaurants and bars. Santander's ferry link to Plymouth makes it many visitors' first
point of entry into Spain; it's a relaxing and pleasant, if unexciting, introduction to the
country. ▸▸ *For Sleeping, Eating and other listings, see pages 520-524.*

Ins and outs
Getting there Santander is connected by bus and train with the rest of Northern
Spain, and by plane with Madrid and Barcelona only. Its only international ferry
service runs from the centre of town to Plymouth, operated by Brittany Ferries. ▸▸ *For
further details, see Transport page 523.*
Getting around Santander is long and thin, with its beaches a good couple of
kilometres from its old centre. Fortunately, buses are very frequent, with nearly all
lines ploughing the waterside. Taxis are fairly prevalent; a fare from Sardinero to the
centre won't cost much more than €4-5. A tourist bus plies a circular route around the
town and its beaches, with information along the way and a 'hop-on hop-off' system.
Tickets and schedules are available at the tourist office in the Jardines de Pereda near
the ferry terminal.
Best time to visit August is the best time to visit Santander, with the International
Festival in full swing and superb weather guaranteed. The downside is the number of
sunseekers, and the difficulty of finding accommodation, which increases in price.
The sea is pretty chilly, so if you're not too worried about staying out of the water,
April/May should offer decent warm weather and not too much rain; apart from Easter
week, the accommodation is a bargain outside the summer months.
Tourist information The main tourist office ① *Plaza Porticada, centre of town,
0900-1300, 1600-1900.* Sociedad Regional de Turismo de Cantabria ① *Paseo de
Pereda, 31-Entlo, E-39004, Santander, T942 31 85 79, F942 31 85 78.*

History
As the Reconquista progressed and the Moors were driven southwards, the north
coast became increasingly important as an export point for Castilian produce. The
important northern ports joined together in 1296 to form the Hermandad de las
Marismas, a sort of trading union that included Santander along with La Coruña, San
Sebastián, and nearby Laredo. Although Laredo was a more important port for much
of Spain's imperial period, Charles I picked Santander to sail home from after his
incredible Interail-like jaunt through France to Madrid in 1623.

Santander's major growth period as a port came in the 19th century; this was also
the time that it achieved fashionable status as a resort, which it has retained. Despite
the genteel feel of parts of the town, Santander was firmly in the Republican camp
during the Civil War but finally fell in August 1937. Much of the centre of town was
destroyed in a fire in 1941, which originated in the Archbishop's palace (did he burn
the toast or was he smoking in bed?). The Franco years didn't treat Santander too
badly though, and it's one of very few cities not to have changed its Fascist street

names since the return to democracy; a statue of the *caudillo* himself still sits on a horse outside the town hall, facing the industrial suburbs defiantly, with conservative Santander at his back.

Sights

In the centre, the **cathedral** ① *1000-1300, 1600-1930, crypt 0800-1300, 1700-2000*, is reasonably interesting. Largely destroyed by the 1941 fire, its church is dull although the

> ✱ *Santander's principal attraction is its excellent town beaches east of the centre.*

cloister offers a chance to relax for a moment from the city streets. The crypt, around the back, is used for masses, and is an intriguing little space, with curious stubby columns and ill-lit Roman ruins under glass. A reliquary holds the silver-plated heads of San Emeterio and San Celedonio, the city patrons.

Nearby, the **Ayuntamiento** is fronted by a statue of Franco; it says much about Santander that he hasn't dismounted and slipped away into history as he has in most other Spanish towns. Behind the building is the excellent **Mercado de la Esperanza**, with lashings of fruit, fish, meat, and deli products; the

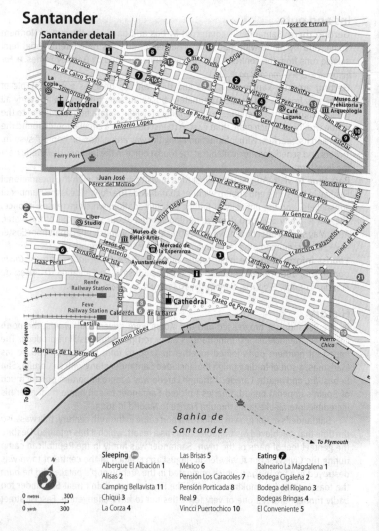

Santander

Santander detail

Bahía de Santander

▲ To Plymouth

Sleeping ⊖		Eating ⊖
Albergue El Albación 1	Las Brisas 5	Balneario La Magdalena 1
Alisas 2	México 6	Bodega Cigaleña 2
Camping Bellavista 11	Pensión Los Caracoles 7	Bodega del Riojano 3
Chiqui 3	Pensión Porticada 8	Bodegas Bringas 4
La Corza 4	Real 9	El Conveniente 5
	Vincci Puertochico 10	

0 metres 300
0 yards 300

place to buy your hams and olive oils if you're heading back home on the ferry. Not far from here is the **Museo de Bellas Artes**① *C Rubio 5, T94223948, Mon-Fri 1000-1300, 1700-2000, Sat 1000-1300; opens half-an-hour later in summer, free,* which has a fairly mediocre collection of different artworks. The undoubtable highlight is many of Goya's *Horrors of War* prints, a dark and haunted series; there's also a portrait of Ferdinand VII, which isn't one of his better works. A small Miró is also notable, as are several sculptures by the Basque Jorge Oteiza, among them an expressive Adam and Eve. Worth a noise if you have a few minutes to kill.

Other museums in town include the **Museo Marítimo** and the **Museo de Prehistoria y Arqueología**, a collection of well-presented pieces from the province's past, many of which are creations of Neanderthal and modern man, and were found in several caves around the region.

The **waterfront** is the nicest part of this area; it's a nice walk that fills with people during the *paseo*. The **Puerto Chico** is the leisure marina; after passing this you come to the huge festival centre; which is quite attractive when floodlit, see it by day, however, and it is pretty ugly.

Past the festival centre, Avenida de la Reina Victoria heads for the sands past some very flashy houses indeed; some chalets go for well over €3 million. The **Península de la Magdalena** protects the bay of Santander from the moody Atlantic and is topped by a flashy *palacio*. This was a gift from the city to the king but it now houses the renowned summer university that draws people from around the globe. Jan Morris described the building as "like a child's idea of a palace, surrounded on three sides by the sea and on the fourth by loyal subjects". A small **zoo** nearby holds marine animals.

On the bay side of the peninsula are a couple of sheltered and pretty beaches, **Playa de la Magdalena** and **Playa de los Bikinis**; just around on the sea side is the artificial Playa del Camello, named for the humped rock that sticks out of the water opposite it.

Sardinero is the centre of the sand suburbs; an attractively unmodern collection of belle-époque buildings that back two superb beaches, perceptively named **La Primera** and **La Segunda**. The Primera is the beach to be seen at; it's backed by the elegantly restored *casino* and several pricey hotels. The Segunda is less crowded and usually gets better waves, either at the far end or around the spur that divides the two. Both are kept creditably clean and have enough sand that you're never hurdling bodies to reach the water.

Excursions inland

Inland Cantabria is still a very rural area; mulecarts and cow traffic jams are still a common sight once off the main roads. The N611 and N623 forge south to Palencia and Burgos respectively through attractive countryside. The main towns in the area, Torrelavega and Reinosa, are both depressing and dull industrial centres but there are enough small attractions in the area to make a trip interesting.

Puente Viesgo, 30 km south of Santander, is a peaceful spa village long used as a weekend retreat from Santander. The waters are reportedly effective for skin disorders and rheumatism but of greater interest are the caves up on the hill above, 1½ km from town and one of the highlights of the province.

Cuevas del Castillo ① *May-Sep daily 1000-1400, 1600-2030, Oct-Feb Wed-Sun 0930-1655, entry is by guided tour in Spanish, but the guides speak very clearly and slowly and make every effort to be understood, €2, tours run roughly every hour and last 45 minutes, daily visitors have a maximum limit*, were home to thousands of generations of Neanderthal man and Cro-Magnon man (*homo sapiens sapiens*); with the earliest occupation being dated at some 130,000 years ago. Both left extensive remains of tools and weapons (Teilhard de Chardin and Albert of Monaco both got their hands dirty in the excavations here), but Cro-Magnon man did some decorating in a series of paintings that extend deep into the cave complex; these were discovered in 1903. The earliest efforts date from around 30,000 years ago and some are of several outlines of hands, created with red ochre. Interestingly, most of the prints found are of the left hand, suggesting that most folk were righties even back then. More sophisticated works are from later but still predate the more advanced work at Altamira. There are outlines of bison here too, as well as deer, and a long series of discs that has mystified theorists. Although the quality of the art is nothing to touch Altamira, it's a much more satisfying experience to see the originals here than the replicas there and atmospheric, for the caves are fantastic in themselves; the one that is open for visits is a sort of Gothic cathedral in lime.

🔵 Sleeping

Castro Urdiales *p516*
C **Pensión La Sota**, C Correría 1, T942871188, F942871284, is a good-looking place with lovely, if slightly overpriced, rooms a street back from the water.
D **Lantarón**, Playa de Arenillas s/n, Islares, T942871212, a relaxed beachy hotel right by the sands.

D-E Pensión La Mar, C La Mar 1, T942870524, F942862828, is another good bet with rooms with or without bath.

Laredo *p516*

Most places are unattractive but functional beach hotels and rentable apartments, although few are right on the sands.

A Miramar, Alto de Laredo s/n, T942610367, F942611692, has excellent views over the bay and is very well-priced off-season.

D-E Pensión Esmeralda, Fuente Fresnedo 6, T942605219, is in the old, hilly part of town and has attractive, clean doubles with bath.

E Pensión Salomón, C Menéndez Pelayo 11, T942605081, is an excellent option despite an unremarkable exterior. The nearby

F Cantabria, C Menéndez Pelayo, T942605073, is a clean choice by the market.

Camping

Several campsites at the far end of the beach.

Santander *p517, map p518*

As befits its resort status, Santander has dozens of places to stay. Many of these are in lofty price brackets, especially in the beachside *barrio* of Sardinero. There are several cheap *pensiones* around the bus and train stations, most fairly respectable if a bit noisy. All rates are significantly lower here once the summer rush is over.

LL Hotel Real, Paseo de Pérez Galdós 28, T942272550, www.husa.es. Santander's top hotel has superb views over the bay and prices to match. It's an elegant place that has seen its fair share of celebrity guests.

L Hotel Chiqui, Av García Lago 9, T902282700, www.hotelchiqui.com. Slightly snooty but very well placed hotel at the quiet end of the Sardinero beaches. The front rooms have superb views out to sea. Excellent off-season specials are offered.

L Hotel Vincci Puertochico, C Castelar 25, T942225200, puertochico@vinccihoteles.com. A good hotel right on the marina. The rooms are comfortable and modern, but the best, which overlook the water, cost up to €32 more than the ones at the back.

AL Hotel Balneario, C Manuel Pérez Mazo s/n, Puente Viesgo, T942598061, F942598261, this ugly place is the venue to take in waters effective for skin disorders and rheumatism.

A Hotel Las Brisas, Travesía de los Castros 14, T942275011, F942281173. A block back from the main Sardinero beach, this hotel is in the thick of it and has homely, characterful decor and welcoming owners.

A Hotel México, C Calderón de la Barca 3, T942212450, F942229238. One of the city's older hotels, and a good option, with attractive Modernista decor. Handy for all the transport options and close to the centre of town.

B-C Hotel Alisas, C Nicolás Salmerón 3, T942222750, F942222486. A comfortable, clean hotel, which is overpriced in Aug but reasonable at other times. Rooms are largish and come with television, direct dialling, and clean, modern bathroom.

D-E La Corza, C Hernán Cortés 25, T942212950. A very good choice right on the central Plaza del Pombo and a block from the water. The rooms are clean and spacious, and the management friendly. Recommended.

E Pensión Porticada, C Méndez Núñez 6, T942227817. Convenient for the ferry, this is a good and friendly option; the front rooms are nicer but can get very noisy.

F Pensión El Carmen, Puente Viesgo s/n, T942598141, is a homely place to stay in Puente Viesgo by the small stream.

F Pensión Los Caracoles, C Marina 1, T942212697. Simple, heated rooms in a good location close to bars, eateries, and the harbourside.

Hostels and camping

Camping Bellavista, T942391530, is a year-round campsite well located by the Mataleñas beach just north of Sardinero. Bus 9 goes to the campsite via the coastal boulevards from the Ayuntamiento.

G Albergue El Albación, C Francisco Palazuelos 21, T942217753, F942211452. A decent independent hostel, close to the centre and happily curfewless.

🍴 Eating

Castro Urdiales *p516*

Basques come here often for day trips and weekends, so the food standards are high.

€€ El Segoviano, Plaza del Ayuntamiento s/n, T942861859, serves up heavier fare, with roast meats the order of the day.

€€ **Mesón Marinero**, Plaza del Ayuntamiento s/n, T942860005, is an excellent restaurant with a terrace under the arcade in the plaza. The seafood is excellent and is allowed to stand on its own merits rather than being smothered in cheese or garlic sauces.

€ **Bodega Manolo**, C Bilbao 1, is a good little bar doing tapas.

Laredo *p516*

€€ **Mesón del Marinero**, C Zamanillo s/n. Good seafood tapas and a reasonable upstairs restaurant specializing in the ocean's harvest.

€ **El Rincón del Puerto**, Puerto Pesquero s/n. Unpretentious seafood straight off the boats.

Santander *p517, map p518*

Santander's status as elegant holiday resort as well as active fishing port assures a good selection of eating places. Top seafood restaurants compete for attention with characterful ex-wine cellars and no-frills joints doling out the best of fresh fish. Sardinero has some excellent eating options, but for concentration, head for the zone around Plaza Cañadio in the old town. Calle Peña Herbosa nearby also has a selection of cheap tapas bars.

€€€ **La Posada del Mar**, C Juan de la Cosa 3, T942215656. A fairly formal old restaurant with a formidable wine list. Although the seafood is good, it's the meat that this restaurant is known for. The *menú del dia* is good value at €18. Closed all Sep.

€€€ **Rhin**, Plaza Italia 2, T942273034 An obvious choice overlooking the Sardinero beaches, this pleasant light restaurant has excellent if conservative dishes, with seafood the definite highlight.

€€ **Balneario la Magdalena**, C La Horadada s/n. Excellently located café and restaurant on the peaceful and calm Magdalena beach.

€€ **Bodega del Riojano**, C Río de la Pila 5, T942216750. Characterful restaurant set in an old wine merchants', famous for its decoratively painted barrels. The food focuses on the sea, and is plentiful and well prepared.

€€ **La Gloria del Puerto**, C Castelar. On the main waterfront road, this restaurant has a smallish but good fish selection, and some surprisingly excellent vegetable dishes.

€ **Bodega Cigaleña**, C Daoiz y Velarde 19. Another characterful *bodega*, crammed with wine bottles, serving a good range of plates.

€ **El Conveniente**, C Gómez Oreña 9. Another atmospheric bodega by Plaza Cañadio with a spacious, beamed interior, several shiploads of wine, and a good variety of cheap food.

€ **La Colodra**, C Del Medio 11. A good place for cheap bites, with a fishing theme. There are other decent options on this street.

€ **La Gaviota**, C Marqués de la Ensenada 35. One of a series of downmarket seafood restaurants in the Barrio Pesquero, a seedy zone by the fishing harbour. Excellent grilled sardines can be had here for a pittance. Get bus 4 or 14 from anywhere on the Santander waterfront to here.

Tapas bars and cafés

Bodegas Bringas, C Hernán Cortés 47, T942362070. An excellent tapas bar, one of several set in old wine merchants' warehouses. The atmosphere is great, with wine bottles and barrels for days, and the food good and well priced.

Hijas de Florencia, Paseo de Pereda 23. A long, cavernous stone bar and wine and cheese shop with a good atmosphere and nice ham *pintxos*. Outdoor terrace overlooking the water.

La Casa del Indiano, Mercado del Este s/n. The recently renovated 19th-century market now houses a variety of specialist shops, as well as this cheerful café/bar.

Bars and clubs

Castro Urdiales *p516*

There's plenty of weekend nightlife in Castro. **Safari**, C Ardigales 26, T942863489, is good for mellow music and a happy crowd, while **Twist**, C Rúa 16, T942863489, offers some serious dancefloor action.

Laredo *p516*

A popular summer-only *discoteca* is **Playamar** on the beachfront, T942610150.

● *For an explanation of sleeping and eating price codes used in this guide, see inside the*
● *front cover. Other relevant information is found in Essentials, see pages 47-56.*

Santander *p517, map p518*

Bar del Puerto, C Peña Herbosa. Sleek and popular with the upwardly mobile apres work.

Fortumy, C Moctezuma s/n. Weird little bar!

La Cata, C Pedruca s/n. A friendly stone bar, suitable for a quiet after-dinner glass of wine.

La Floridita, C Bailén s/n. A cheerful and very lively bar, with a youngish crowd and unpretentious scene.

Naroba, C Perines. Popular with Santander's young for its large variety of beers.

Pachá, C General Mola 45, T942310067. Big 2-level *discoteca* that packs out late at weekends with Spanish top-40 hits.

Rocanbole, C Hernán Cortés 24. A late-running bar with frequent live jazz and blues.

Stylus, C Valderrana 1. As lively as anywhere, this bar has good home-made vermouth if you can make it through the crowd.

Ventilador, Plaza Cañadio s/n. A popular bar with outdoor tables on this lively night-time square. The atmosphere is a bit better in the quieter early evening.

Zona Límite, C Tetuán 32. A lively gay spot, particularly during summer.

🎭 Entertainment

Santander *p517, map p518*

Bahia Cinema, Av Marqués de la Hermida.

Palacio de Festivales, C Castelar s/n.

Gran Casino, Plaza Italia s/n. 2000-0400 (0500 in summer). Slot machine room opens at 1700. Dress code and proof of age regulations apply. €3 cover charge.

🎉 Festivals and events

Santander *p517, map p518*

The major event is its **International Festival**, held in the month of **Aug**, and featuring some top-drawer musical and theatrical performances. The liveliest street action comes at its end, which coincides with the fiesta of the city's patron saints. The province's major rowing regatta is held here on **28 Jul**.

🛍 Shopping

Santander *p517, map p518*

Santander's main shopping district is in the streets around the town hall, cathedral and to the west. **Librería Estudio**, Paseo Calvo Sotelo 19. Largish selection.

⛰ Activities and tours

Santander *p517, map p518*

Football Racing Santander yo-yo between the Primera and Segunda divisions in Spanish football. At time of writing, they were in the top flight, and entertain the likes of Real Madrid in their stadium in Sardinero. Tickets can be bought at the stadium on Fri and Sat for a Sun fixture, as well as from 2 hrs before the game.

🚌 Transport

Castro Urdiales *p516*

Bus Castro Urdiales is connected very regularly by bus with both **Santander** and **Bilbao**, which is only ½ hr away.

Laredo *p516*

There are very frequent buses connecting **Laredo** and **Santander.**

Santander *p517, map p518*

Air Iberia, Plaza Pombo s/n, www.iberia.es.

Boat Brittany Ferries run a service between **Santander** and **Plymouth**. These leave the UK on Mon and Thu mornings, taking a shade under 24 hrs. Return ferries leave **Santander** on Tue and Thu. A third one operates during the summer. Book online at www.brittanyferries.co.uk or T08705 561 600. Prices are variable but can usually be had for about £70-90 (€115-150) each way in a reclining seat. A car adds about £140 (€225) each way, and cabins start from about £80 (€130) a twin. The service doesn't run in winter.

Bus Many buses ply routes from **Santander** to other Spanish cities. Up to 6 buses a day go to **Burgos** (via **Puente Viesgo**) and on to **Madrid**, while buses east to Bilbao are almost hourly. Several a day follow the coast westwards as far as **Gijón** and **Oviedo**, while there are also buses serving **Zaragoza**, **Valladolid**, **A Coruña,** and others. Within the province, there are 8 buses a day to **Santoña**, 6 to **Reinosa**, and very frequent services to **Laredo** and to **Torrelavega**. For the **Picos de Europa**, there are 3 buses daily to **Potes** at 1030, 1245, and 1700, the last 2 with onward connections to **Fuente Dé**.

Car hire Hertz, Puerto Ferrys, T942362821; **Alesa**, C Sanz de Santuola, T942222926.

Train Santander is both on the national RENFE network and the private coastal FEVE service. The stations are next to each other (as is the bus station). RENFE runs up to 5 trains daily to **Madrid** (slower than the bus), and 7 or so to **Valladolid** and **Palencia** on the same line. There are half-hourly *cercanía* trains to **Torrelavega** and **Reinosa**. FEVE trains run east to **Bilbao** 3 times daily, and west along the coast as far as **Oviedo**, **Gijón** and **Ferrol** in Galicia twice daily. It's a fairly slow but scenic service, and invaluable for accessing smaller coastal towns.

● Directory

Santander *p517, map p518*
Internet Café Lugano, C Hernán Cortés 55, T942224280; **Ciber Studio**, C Magallanes 48; **La Copia**, C Lealtad 13, T94227680 (by cathedral).
Laundry Lavandería del Palacio, C Juan de la Cosa 15, will do a 6-kg service wash for €10.22.
Post The main post office is on C Alfonso XIII, at the corner with Av de Calvo Sotelo.
Telephone There's a *locutório* near the station at C Madrid 2, and one at C Burgos 9.

West of Santander

Cantabria's western coast is its nicest. As well as some good beaches, there are some very attractive towns; these are headed up by Santillana del Mar, a superb ensemble of stonework which also boasts the newly opened museum at nearby Altamira, the site of some of the finest prehistoric art ever discovered. Comillas will appeal to fans of Modernista architecture, and beyond, the coast continues towards Asturias, backed spectacularly by the bulky Picos de Europa mountains. ▸▸ *For Sleeping, Eating and other listings, see pages 527-528.*

Santillana del Mar → *Colour map 2, grid B5.*

Although it may sound like a seaside town, it isn't: it's 4 km inland. A cynical old saying claims that it's the town of three lies: "*Santillana no es santa, no es llana, y no hay mar*" (Santillana's not holy or flat, and there's no sea). Nevertheless, Santillana is a gem, despite the tourist hordes that wander around the place that Sartre immortalized (albeit in *Nausea*) as "the most beautiful village in Spain". While it's still a dairying region, every building within the old town is now devoted to tourism in some form. It's definitely worth staying overnight, as the bulk of the visitors are day-trippers, and the emptier the town, the more atmospheric.

Ins and outs

The tourist office ① *at the edge of the old town near the main road, 0900-1300, 1600-1900*, is understandably brusque. They supply a decent map/guide to the town in a variety of languages.

Background

Founded by monks, the town became important in the Middle Ages due to the power of its monastery, which had a finger in every pie. What the town is today is a result of the nobility wresting control of the feudal rent system from the abbot in the 15th century. Once the peasants were filling secular coffers, the landowners grew wealthy, donated money in exchange for titles, and started trying to outdo each other in ostentatious *palacio* construction. Though undoubtedly hideous, antidemocratic, and tasteless at the time, these buildings are now very beautiful, except for the ridiculously large coats of arms adorning them.

The old town is well preserved and picturesque, with rows of noble stone buildings lining cobbled streets. **Colegiata** ① *1000-1330, 1600-1930, €2.50 includes entrance to the Diocesan Museum at the other end of town*, sits at the end of the town and has a jumbled, homely façade in orangey stone. The current Romanesque building replaced a former Benedictine monastery in the 12th century. An arcaded gallery runs high above the portal, and a round belltower to the right outrages hardcore symmetry fans. Wander around the side to gain access to the church and cloister. To the latter can be applied all the adjectives normally used to describe its kind; its shady Romanesque arches also feature many different motifs on the capitals, ranging from mythological creatures to geometric figures and Biblical scenes. The church is big with impressive stone vaulting; there is some of the *ajedrezado jaqués* chessboard patterning originally used in the town of Jaca and disseminated through Northern Spain by wandering masons and pilgrims. The building is dedicated to Santa Juliana, a third-century saint for whom the town is named. She was put to death by her husband for not coming across on their wedding night (or any other night); her bones were originally brought here by the community of monks that founded the monastery and town. One of her achievements in life was the taming of a demon, whom she used to drag around on a rope (to the despair of their marriage counsellor); scenes from her life can be seen on her tomb in the centre of the church, and the retablo, a 16th-century work. There's a figure of Juliana in the centre, standing above a chest that holds various of her earthly remains.

> ❖ *You are advised to come out of season, and avoid weekends; the opening of the Altamira museum has increased the daily flow.*

The other major sight in town is the collection of grandiose *palacios* emblazoned with arms. They are concentrated down the main street, **Calle Cantón**, and around the main square. The square has two Gothic towers, one of which is an exhibition hall. In front of the church, the former **abbot's house** was later occupied by the Archduchess of Austria; further down this street note the former marquis's house (now a hotel). The **Casa de los Villa** near the main road has a façade emblazoned with a pierced eagle and the motto *un buen morir es honra de la vida* (a good death glorifies the life); a precursor to the Falangist Civil War cry ¡*Viva la muerte!*

As Santillana is a popular place to spend holidays, there's always plenty on for young and old, with frequent temporary exhibitions, craft displays and festivals. Permanent attractions include a decent **zoo** ① *0930-dusk daily*, on the edge of town, which includes a snow leopard among its constricted but cared-for captives. A **torture museum** ① *1000-2000, 2300 in summer, €3.60*, near the church has all sorts of horrible fantasies in iron. **Diocesan Museum** ① *1000-1330, 1600-1930, ticket with the church €2.50*, on the main road, which is a good example of its kind, has a large collection that includes some Latin American pieces brought back to Santillana by *indianos*.

Altamira Caves

In 1879, in the countryside 2 km from Santillana, a man and his daughter were exploring some caves only discovered a few years before when they looked up and saw a cavalcade of animals superbly painted in ochre and charcoal. The man, Marcelino Sanz de Sautuola, was interested in prehistoric art, but the quality of these works far exceeded any known at the time. Excitedly publishing his findings, he wasn't believed until several years after his death, when the discovery of similar paintings in southern France made the sceptics reverse their position. The paintings are amazing; fluid bison, deer and horses, some 14,000 years old. Understandably, they became a major tourist attraction, but the moist breath of the visitors began to damage the art and admission had to be heavily restricted; the waiting list is about three years at present. Visits are due to be entirely terminated.

Enter the **Neocueva** ① *T942818005, www.mcu.es/nmuseos/altamira, Jun-Sep Tue-Sat 0930-1930, Sun 0930-1700, Oct-May Tue-Sun 0930-1700, €2.40, cameras are prohibited*, opened in 2001 with much pomp and ceremony. It's a replica of part of the original cave and paintings and is part of a museum that puts the art in context. The exhibition begins with an excellent overview of prehistoric hominids so you can get your Neanderthals sorted from your Cro-Magnons before moving on to more specific displays about the Altamira epoch and ways of life at the time. It's a good display with information in Spanish and English.

The cave itself is accessed in groups with a guide; there can be quite a wait if the museum is busy. It's an impressive reconstruction, and the explanations are good. You can admire the replica paintings, particularly as they were probably painted from a prone position, but they lack the emotion that comes from actually feeling the incomprehensible gulf of 14,000 years. All told, it's a very good museum, and an impressive substitute for the original cave, which the government were absolutely right to protect from destruction. To apply to visit the original cave, write to the museum at Museo de Altamira, 39330 Santillana del Mar, or fax 942840157, but as of 2002, you have to have a serious scientific reason to gain admission.

Comillas → *Colour map 2, grid A2.*

A fashionable Cantabrian beach resort, Comillas is still popular with the well-heeled but is worth a visit for its architecture, out of the ordinary for a seaside summer town. Rather than drab lines of holiday cottages, it boasts some striking *modernista* buildings ostentatiously perched on the hilltops around the town. They are a legacy of Catalan architects who were commissioned by local bigwigs to create suitably extravagant residences for them.

The town's most unusual architectural flourishes are found in Gaudí's **El Capricho**, a caprice that is either loved or hated by all who visit. It's certainly imaginative, embossed with bright green tiles adorned with Mediterranean sunflowers. The best feature is a whimsical tower, an ornate Muslim fantasy with a balcony. Apart from a tourist shop with Gaudí paraphernalia, the interior is taken up by an upmarket restaurant. Next door is the **Palacio de Sobrellano** ① *Oct-Jun Wed-Sun 1030-1400, 1600-1930; Jul/Aug daily 1000-2100; Sep daily 1030-1400, 1600-1930, €2 palace, €2 chapel*, commissioned by the Marqués de Comillas, a heavy pseudo-Gothic structure full of quirky furniture. A small plot in the parish graveyard wasn't the marquis's vision of resting in peace, so he had an ornate chapel knocked up next to the family summer home to hold their showy tombs.

On the eminence opposite, the **Universidad Pontificia** was built as a theological college in similarly avant-garde style. Whether the priests-in-training were imbued with Christian humility in such a building is open to question, but in any event the college moved to Madrid in 1964. The building is now subject to various plans for its future.

The town itself has several attractive squares and mansions that seem modest by comparison. There's still a slightly twee feel to the town, but there are two good beaches a 10-minute walk from the centre. West of Comillas is a good beach, **Playa Oyambre**, with a campsite and cheap but tasty restaurant. The tourist office① *centre of town, Tue-Sat 1030-1330, 1630-1930, Sun 1030-1400*, is efficient and helpful.

San Vicente de Barquera → *Colour map 2, grid A2.*

Though pretty when backed with snowy mountains, San Vicente isn't the north coast's most inviting seaside town, although it has some appeal, mainly in its seafood restaurants. The town is a fair walk from the beach, but still functions as an

important fishing port. It is set where two rivers meet each other and the sea, but its attractive old-town streets have been surrounded by jerry-built modern developments. The architectural highlight is the Gothic **Iglesia de Nuestra Señora de los Angeles**, which has a wooden floor like a ship's deck and attractive Gothic vaulting. The church was built in the 13th century, when Romanesque was going pointy, and it's an interesting example of the transition. There are good views from here over the river estuary and the long bridge crossing it. On the same ridge, the **castle** ① *Tue-Sun 1100-1400, 1700-2000, €1.20*, is in reasonable shape but isn't especially compelling. The big tourist office is on Avenida Generalísimo.

● Sleeping

Santillana *p524*
Santillana has a good range of accommodation for all budgets. There are many hotels on the main road, or worse, in an ugly expansion on the other side of it that tried to retain that old-town look but failed, but there are enough in the old centre to get by, though you should definitely book ahead in summer. Many private homes put signs out advertising *camas* or *habitaciones* at peak time; some are very good options.
LL La Casa del Marqués, C Cantón 26, T942818888, F942818188. Santillana's priciest hotel is excellently set in a large *palacio* that belonged to the local marquis, who had to display his superior status with no fewer than 3 coats of arms, but the interior decoration and quality of service seem to be sadly lacking.
AL Parador Gil Blas, Plaza Ramón Pelayo 11, T942028028, www.parador.es, is in a modernized *palacio* on the attractive Plaza Mayor. It's named for a famous fictional character from Santillana created by the French novelist Lesage in the 18th century. There's a good restaurant, and the rooms have every comfort.
A Altamira, C Cantón 1, T942818025, F942840136, is cheaper than the parador but equally characterfully set in another sumptuous *palacio*, with appropriate decor. There's also a good patio restaurant, an excellent spot to eat or have a drink.
B Posada La Casa del Organista, C Los Hornos 4, T942840352. Set in a smaller but still impressive old home; this is a welcoming place with lovely wooden furnishings and rustic bedrooms.
E Casa Claudia, C El Río 13, T942893610, 639662734. A superb place to stay. Atmospheric beamed doubles with shared bathroom above a potters' workshop near

the church; the balconies overlooking the main street are outrageously pleasant if you can grab one of those rooms.
E Casa Octavio, Plaza de las Arenas s/n, T942818199. A peaceful and very attractive spot to find a bed in an alley off the Plaza de las Arenas by the side of the church. There's a variety of rooms on offer, but all are rustic and charming.

Camping
Camping Santillana, T942818250, 5-min walk down the main road west out of town, is a good campsite, although swarming during summer. There are bungalows available too.

Comillas *p526*
There are many places to stay, with the usual summer price hike.
A Casal del Castro, C San Jerónimo s/n, T942720036, F942720061. The nicest option in town, an attractively renovated mansion with a garden and thoughtfully homely rooms. Well priced for this coast.
B Esmeralda, C Antonio López 7, T942720097, is a good friendly choice with sharp off-season prices and a restaurant.
D Pensión Pasiegos de la Vega, Paseo del Muelle s/n, T942722102, is comfy if not stylish and overlooks the beach.
F Pensión Fuente Real, C Fuente Real 19, T942720155, is right behind **El Capricho** and its shabby but clean rooms are cheap and pretty good value for the area.

San Vicente de Barquera *p526*
There are heaps of places to stay.
D Pensión Liébana, C Ronda 2, T942710211 is in the centre of things and has decent rooms with bathroom and TV, that become very cheap once summer's over.
E Hostería La Paz, C del Mercado 2, T942710180, is another reasonable option.

● Eating

Santillana *p524*

€€ **Altamira**, C Cantón 1, T942818025. The best of the hotel restaurants, and fairly reasonably priced. Seafood here is excellent; at lunchtime you can eat in the patio.

€€ **Gran Duque**, C Escultor Jesús Otero Orena. A good restaurant, with views over the meadows outside town and much attractive seafood on the list, and a good set *menú* for €15.

€ **El Castillo**, Plaza Mayor 6, T942818377. Although in the heart of the town, this bar/restaurant is refreshingly unpretentious and does some good plates at reasonable prices. The *menú de cocido* is particularly hearty; broth followed by a big serve of chickpeas and salt pork.

Comillas *p526*

The pleasures of eating fish 'n' chips all holiday are lost on wealthy Spaniards – there are several excellent restaurants.

€€€€ **El Capricho de Gaudí**, Sobrellano s/n, T942720365. A gimmick-free restaurant in Gaudí's flight of fancy, serving excellent new Spanish cuisine with a heavy emphasis on seafood; there are some excellent fishes, such as *rodaballo salvaje con ajetes* (wild turbot with fresh garlic shoots).

€€ **Gurea**, C Ignacio Fernández de Castro 11, T942722446. A Basque restaurant that lives up to all the good things that implies.

€ **Filipinas**, C de los Arzobispos s/n. Where the locals eat; a lively bar serving good, cheap plates of fish and other bites.

San Vicente de Barquera *p526*

€€€ **Boga-Boga**, Av Generalísimo, T942710135. The food at Boga-Boga lives up to its excellent name (a type of local fish). There's a great variety of seafood and some good wines to knock back with it. There are also decent rooms upstairs.

€€ **Augusto**, C Mercado 1, T942712040, is no stranger to tourism but the quality of the seafood is undeniable. There are also plenty of mixed plates to choose from in the shiplike interior.

€ **Los Arcos**, Av Generalísimo 11. Good, cheaper plates of seafood *raciones*.

● Bars and clubs

Comillas *p526*

Pamara, C Comillas s/n, is a good summer *discoteca* with an upmarket set.

● Transport

Santillana *p524*

There are 5 daily buses (2 on Sun) running to and from **Santander**.

Comillas *p526*

There are 5 daily buses, 2 on Sun, running to and from **Santander** via **Santillana del Mar**. They continue westwards to **San Vicente de Barquera**.

San Vicente de Barquera *p526*

Five buses daily run eastwards to **Santander** via **Comillas** and **Santillana del Mar** (2 on Sun); also buses bound westwards to **Asturias**.

Los Picos de Europa

The Picos de Europa are a small area of the vast Cordillera Cantábrica blessed with spectacular scenery, superb walking, abundant wildlife, and, most crucially, comparatively easy access (but take your hat off to the engineers who built the roads). They encompass the corners of three provinces: Asturias, Cantabria, and León, and have a comparatively mild climate due to their proximity to the sea. It is this fact that probably gives them their curious name ('the Peaks of Europe'); they often would have been the first sight of land that weary Spanish sailors got on their return from the Americas.

The Picos is comprises three main massifs of limestone cut and tortured over the millennia by glaciation, resulting in the distinctive rock formations given the adjective 'karstic'. The central part of the range is national park, expanded from the original

Ins and outs

Getting there

The Picos are easily accessed from Santander or Oviedo, and slightly less so from León. The two principal towns for Picos tourism are Cangas de Onís (Asturias) and Potes (Cantabria): both make excellent bases, especially if you lack transport. Potes is serviced regularly by bus from Santander and the Cantabrian coast, while frequent buses run from Oviedo and Gijón to Cangas (see Transport, below).

Getting around

Travelling around the Picos de Europa is simple with your own transport, and time-consuming without. The Picos is basically a rectangular area with a main road running around its perimeter and several smaller roads dead-ending into the heart of the mountains from it. Buses run on the main roads, and to popular destinations like Covadonga and Fuente Dé. Fewer buses run on Sundays on routes indicated within each travelling text section; if the buses just don't get you where you need to go, taxis are a reasonable alternative, if there are two or more of you. There are also some jeep services that operate as shared taxis. Hitching is also easy in the Picos. The ideal solution for some is to walk; after all, it's only three hours through the Cares Gorge, and you've crossed the Picos from north to south; the journey wouldn't take you much less by car.

> ❖ There's a slightly different feel in each part of the Picos, and if you have time it's a good idea to visit all three provinces.

Tourist information

The Picos de Europa National Park offices run free guided tours around the Picos region during summer, an excellent service. The schedule changes each year and is organized from the three regional information centres; phone for details: Cangas de Onís, Asturias ① T985848614; Posada de Valdeón, León ① T987740549; Camaleño/ Potes, Cantabria ① T942730555. There's also a head office in Oviedo ① C Arquitecto Reguera 13, T985241412, F985273945. All the major towns have year-round tourist offices, and in addition many villages have summer-only kiosks. The best tourist information office for the Picos is in Cangas de Onís. ▸▸ See Cangas de Onís, page 539 and Potes, page 539.

Best time to visit

The best time to visit the Picos is either side of high summer; September/October and May/June are ideal, as in July and August prices are well up, and the crowds can hamper enjoyment of the natural beauties of the area. The Picos have a fairly damp and temperate maritime climate so you're never assured of clear days, but neither does it get extremely cold, at least on the north side of the range. Mists descend regularly; if you're doing any challenging walks, take a compass and check the forecast.

Asturian Picos

Asturias claims the largest slab of the Picos massif and has the most advanced environmental and tourism infrastructure of the region. The area's main town, Cangas de Onís, is an excellent place to begin a trip to the Picos, while nearby Covadonga is revered as the birthplace of Christian Spain. The area is also famous for producing the

⁝ Birds and the bears

The Picos are home to a huge variety of fauna and flora, due partly to the hugely varying climactic zones within its terrasculpted interior. Among the birds, vultures are common; rarer are eagles and capercaillies. Less glamorous species include choughs and wallcreepers. Chamois are a reasonably common sight, as are wild boar; there are also mountain cats, wolves and bears about, but they are much scarcer. A frequent and pretty sight on roads are herds of soft-eyed cows, an attractive variety from these parts. Insect and reptile life is also abundant; clouds of butterflies are about in spring and summer. The flora varies widely from the temperate to the Alpine; in spring the mountain fields are full of wildflowers.

strong blue cheese known as Cabrales after the villages it is produced in. Similar in style to Roquefort, it lends its flavour to many a gourmet dish, but is also enjoyed by the locals as a smotherer of chips. Some of the most dramatic rocky scenery of the area is accessed south of here; there are some fantastic hikes in the area around Puente Poncebos, including the three-hour gorge walk to Caín, a route that crosses the Picos from north to south.➤➤ *For Sleeping, Eating and other listings, see pages 536-540.*

Cangas de Onís

This service town is a typically cheerful Asturian centre, with plenty of places to stay, and some top *sidrerías* to drink and eat in. Its highlight is a superb medieval bridge across the Río Sella with an alarmingly steep cobbled arch. It's at its best when eerily floodlit at night; locals inaccurately name it the **Puente Romano** (Roman bridge). Also of interest is the **Ermita de Santa Cruz**, just across the other river (the Güeña), a tiny 15th-century chapel, which has fifth-century origins and was built over a dolmen; the key can be collected from the tourist office.

After his victory at Covadonga (see below), Pelayo set up base here, and Cangas proudly claims to be the first capital of Christian Spain as a result. A statue of a very rugged Pelayo stands defiantly outside the church, a 20th-century construction with *indiano* and Italian influences visible in its three-storey belltower. There are many *indiano* buildings in town; a good number of eastern Asturians left to seek their fortunes in the New World.

Cangas's tourist office ① *T985848005, 1000-1400, 1600-1900,* is the best equipped in the Picos region. It sits on the main square and has plenty of information about the whole Picos area.

Around Cangas

South of Cangas the road to Riaño soon plunges into the narrow **Desfiladero de los Beyos**. It's a popular spot for walking and salmon fishing, and vultures are a common sight. If you want to stay in the heart of the narrow gorge, north of Cangas, the town of **Arriondas** is a popular base for canoeing the Río Sella, but lacks the appeal of Cangas, which also operates canoeing trips. The descent is brisk but not too challenging; a fun introduction to the sport. A typical half-day involves transport to the launch point, descent, lunch, and return to the town, be it Cangas or Arriondas.

Covadonga and around → *Colour map 2, grid A1.*

Some 4 km east of Cangas, a side road leads a further 6 km up a wooded valley to Covadonga, a name written large in Spanish history, more for what it represented after the fact than for what it was. Thronged with Spanish pilgrims and visitors, its

main touristic interest lies in its pretty setting and in the observation of just how deep the Reconquista is embedded as the country's primary source of national pride.

The facts are few and lost in time and propaganda. What is conjectured is that Pelayo, an Asturian leader, defeated a Moorish expedition here some time around AD718. Some accounts from the Middle Ages claim that 124,000 Moors were killed here by 30 men. This is an obvious exaggeration, it would seem more likely that the force was of a small expeditionary nature, and the defeat a minor one. For the Moors, the defeat was certainly of little military significance; it was another 14 years before their serious reverse occurred at Poitiers, a good distance into France. But Spanish history has seen Covadonga as the beginning of the Reconquista, the reconquest of the Peninsula by Christian soldiers, a process that wasn't complete until 1492, nearly 800 years later. In truth, the battle may have had some effect, at least in establishing Pelayo as pre-eminent among Asturian warlords and sowing the seeds for the foundation of a Christian kingdom in the mountains, a kingdom that did play a significant role in unravelling Muslim dominance in Iberia. But it's hard to sit at Covadonga, watching the coaches roll in, and not wonder what it's all about.

The focus of Covadonga is the **cave** where the Christian reconquest of the peninsular allegedly began, a pretty little grotto in a rockface with a waterfall and a small chapel. Pelayo is buried here at the scene of his triumph, in a plain but powerfully simple sarcophagus in a niche in the cave wall. A pink **basilica** ① *Wed-Mon 1030-1400, 1600-1930, €2*, was erected in the late 19th century; it's not particularly attractive or offensive, and is surprisingly unadorned inside; the focus is on a replica of the Asturian victory cross forged by Pelayo to commemorate the victory. There's also a museum on site, which primarily displays a collection of expensive gifts lavished on the Virgin over the years.

Beyond Covadonga, a 12-km road leads further into the mountains, offering a couple of spectacular panoramas to the north. At the top are two lakes, **Enol** and **Ercina**; neither particularly appealing in themselves, but in superb surroundings bristling with peaks that are often snow-capped. From Ercina, a 10-minute walk beyond Enol, there are some good walks; one heads south up the face of the Reblagas face to an isolated *refugio*, Vega de Ario (six hours return); others head westwards and south to various viewpoints and *refugios*. A small information centre at the lake is open in summer and has reasonable maps of the area; otherwise grab them in Cangas.

Arenas de Cabrales Valley → *Colour map 2, grid A1.*

The road east from Cangas to Arenas de Cabrales is very attractive, and there are numerous hamlets both on and off the road, which offer potentially relaxing rural stays. The Arenas de Cabrales Valley and the surrounding hillsides are famous throughout Spain for the strong blue cheese made here, *cabrales*. If you've been underwhelmed by Spanish cheeses so far, you're in for a treat. Not for nothing is the stuff known as the 'Spanish Roquefort'; it shares many similarities in taste and production methods with the classic French blue cheese. It's made from cows' milk, often with a percentage of sheep or goat milk added, and is matured in damp caves, where the bacteria that give it its sharp taste and distinctive colour develop.

Arenas is a busy little place, as it's here that many people cut south into the heart of the Picos around Poncebos and Sotres. It makes a good base for the region, with banks, restaurants, shops, and plenty of hotels. There's a small tourist kiosk by the bridge.

In **Cares**, a five-minute walk south of Arenas, the **Cueva del Cares** ① *Apr-Oct daily 1000-1400, 1600-2000, Nov-Mar weekends only, €2.50*, is a small factory and cave where *cabrales* cheese is made in the traditional manner. A guided tour takes visitors through the process and finishes up with a tasting of the blue-blooded stuff.

Hiking the Cares Gorge trail An hour's walk south of Arenas, the road reaches **Puente Poncebos**, a small collection of buildings set among high, bleak mountains. There's a shared-jeep service running to here and Sotres from Arenas. The main reason people come here is to walk the Cares gorge, one of the Picos's most popular trails. It's about three hours from here to **Caín**, at the other end of the gorge; there's accommodation there, or you can continue another three hours to **Posada de Valdeón**, see Leonese Picos below, if you don't meet up with a jeep that connects those two towns. This is definitely the best direction to walk in, as the walk gets more spectacular as you go, and Posada de Valdeón is a welcoming place to finish up.

The trail is there thanks to a hydroelectric scheme, and follows the course of a small, fast-flowing canal that would itch for a fairground-style dinghy ride if it didn't plunge underground every few metres. It's not the best walk if you're not a fan of heights or enclosed spaces; there are several claustrophobic tunnels (a torch helps), and the path runs alongside steep drops to the river much of the time. It's incredibly

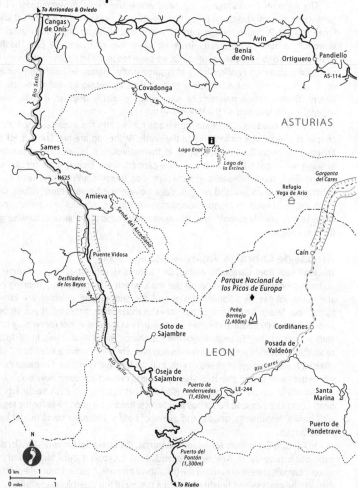

Picos de Europa

popular, so don't do it at weekends or in high summer unless you fancy a conga-line experience. From Poncebos, the trail climbs moderately for the first hour or so, leaving the river far below. If you hear jangling far above, it probably comes from belled goats, who seem to reach completely impossible locations high on the precipitous rocks.

The walk gets prettier and more dramatic as you approach the tail of the **Valdeón Valley**; the massive slabs of rock get bigger and more imposing, but provide shelter for a large range of tree and plant life. You'll probably see vultures circling lazily overhead, and you may spot wallcreepers thumbing their beaks at gravity as they hop up perpendicular stone faces. After two hours or so, you'll reach a large green bridge; the path gently descends from here to Caín, crossing the river a couple more times. There are a couple of swimming holes here to refresh you, although the water is never less than icy. See the Leonese Picos section below, for Caín and beyond.

Hiking from Poncebos to Bulnes Another walk from Poncebos is the steep hour-and-a-bit's climb to Bulnes, a remote village in the midst of lofty mountains.

Beatus and a medieval bestseller

In the middle of the eighth century when the future of Christianity in Europe was in the balance, a monk writing in the remote mountains of Cantabria produced a work which was to be the equivalent of a European bestseller for the next 400 years. Writing from the monastery of Liébana , Beatus wrote a commentary on Saint John's Apocalypse that struck a note with readers who, as well as fearing further invasions from the Moors, also believed that the approaching millennium would bring the coming of the Antichrist. Only 22 of these manuscripts still survive, nearly of them in academic libraries. Produced in various monasteries in Northern Spain, the text of each is the same, but the illustrations differ. The quality of the illustrations make these manuscripts masterpieces of medieval art. The one in Burgo de Osma has been described as "the most beautiful book in the world".

Umberto Eco used the Beatus manuscripts as the basis for his novel *In the Name of the Rose*. However if you fancy reading the original for yourself be warned. Eco describes the Beatus text as "tortuous, even to those well acquainted with medieval Latin".

Until 2001, this was the only way to get to the place, and villagers lugged their provisions up this trail as part of everyday life. There's now a funicular railway① *runs every half-hour or so and costs a massive €12 one way/€15 return unless you hold a Bulnes resident's card, in which case it's free*, in place at Poncebos, a controversial scheme that outraged environmentalists but pleased the villagers (although it certainly wasn't built for their benefit).

The walk leaves from near the car park for the Cares gorge walk, and crosses the river before zigzagging steeply up the hill. The first half is the hardest bit, but the trail continues to climb before reaching Bulnes, which is actually two separate hamlets, a higher and a lower. Most facilities are in the lower one, **La Villa** although the funicular will no doubt necessitate more options. The village's setting is superb, almost completely surrounded by threatening grey peaks, but with enough pastureland to sustain a grazing economy.

Hiking from Poncebos to Sotres From Poncebos, a spectacular road winds through the brooding mountains to the remote village of Sotres (this route is also serviced by shared jeeps in season), another walking base. Sotres is slightly on the grim side, especially in bleak weather, but there are a couple of good lodging and eating options.

Hiking from Sotres to Vego de Urriello One of the best walks from Sotres is the four-and-a-half hours to the *refugio* of Vega de Urriello (T985925200; year-round), in a grassy meadow near the signature peak of **Naranjo de Bulnes**, which is basically a massive rock jutting out apart from the massif; it's not a climb for the inexperienced. The walk to the *refugio* crosses the pass at **Pandébano**, from where there are excellent views.

Cantabrian Picos

This is the most heavily visited section of the Picos due to its easy road access and good tourist facilities. The region's main centre is the town of Potes, an attractive place that at times struggles to accommodate the numbers passing through it. The

heart of the area is the Liébana Valley, a green swathe watered by mountain streams and the Deva river. It's noted for its cheeses, its chestnuts, and its *orujo*, a fiery grape spirit that comes in original form as well as mellower flavoured varieties. A hefty shot in a cup of black coffee is another popular way of taking it. ▸▸ *For Sleeping, Eating and other listings, see pages 536-540.*

Potes and around → *Colour map 2, grid A1.*

Potes is a pretty town on the side of a hill by the river Deva, with cobbled streets and a few noble stone buildings; those that survived the Civil War damage. The most striking of these is a large tower, looking like a medieval fort, but in fact built as a mansion by the Marqués de Santillana in the 16th century; it's now the town hall. There's a tourist office on the tower side of the river, and a national park information office a couple of kilometres out of town on the Fuente Dé road.

A 45-minute walk from Potes, off the Fuente Dé road, is a monastery of great historical importance, **Monasterio de Santo Toribio de Liébana**. Although in a magnificent setting, the building itself isn't of massive interest, but makes up for it with two claims to fame. The first is that it was here that the abbot Beatus de Liébana wrote his apocalyptic commentaries on the book of Saint John; one of the superb illustrated copies of this work is kept here, far from the public gaze, see box page 534. Prints of some of the pages of this beautiful work are displayed around the cloister, and there are some good laminates on sale for €1.50 in the shop. The other item of interest here is kept locked away in a side chapel off the main church. It is nothing less than the largest fragment of the True Cross in existence, a hefty chunk of cypress wood that measures 63 x 40 cm and has one of the nail-holes. It's embedded in an ornate silver crucifix of Gothic styling.

> ❗ *Potes is a centre for tour agencies that operate activities in the mountains, see page 539.*

Fuente Dé and around → *Colour map 2, grid A1.*

The N621 follows the river Deva upstream to the west of Potes, passing through several pretty **hamlets**. It's a well-travelled route, but there are several *casas rurales* to stay just off the main road that are wonderfully tranquil.

The road stops at Fuente Dé, and it's not hard to see why; there's a massive semicircle of rock ahead; a spectacular natural wall that rises 800 m almost sheer. Named Fuente Dé for this is where the Deva springs from the ground, there's little here apart from two hotels, a campsite, and a **cablecar** station ① *1000-1800 daily, €5 one-way/€8 return.* The cablecar takes 3½ minutes to trundle to the top of the rocky theatre; it's a bad one for claustrophobes, as you're jammed with 25 or so others into the tiny capsule.

There are some superb **walks** in this area, some leaving from the top cablecar station; don't worry if you don't fancy the trip up, as there's a steep path that'll get you there eventually. At the top station, tourists mill around aimlessly; a complex is being built that will give the poor souls a focus. In clear weather the views from here are superb, with the parador hardly more than a dot below. This is the start of a jagged, rocky plateau, an Alpine landscape in contrast to the lush meadows below. Following the track from here, you'll soon leave the crowds behind and start a gentle ascent to the top of a rise. Descending downwards to the right from here, you'll come to the *Refugio de Aliva* (T942730999), a year-round hotel and *albergue* C in double rooms) with a popular restaurant (popular because there's a jeep running from the top of the cablecar station) that does a *menú del día* for €12. From here, a spectacular descent for an hour-and-a-half winds around the valley and down to its floor at Espinama, from where you can follow the river back up to Fuente Dé. The whole circuit takes about four hours and is one of the most beautiful walks in the Picos. Other walks start from the campsite and provide equally spectacular valley and mountain views.

South to León

South from Potes, the road winds through the green **Liébana Valley** for a while, then begins to ascend to the **Puerto San Glorio** and **León Province**. This stretch of road offers perhaps the best views in the entire Picos; the contrast between the lush green valley and the harsh grey mountains is superb.

Leonese Picos

Although this part of the Picos range isn't as endowed with tourist facilities as the Asturian or Cantabrian sections, it contains much of the area's most dramatic scenery, with breathtaking mountainscapes suddenly revealed as you round a bend in the path or road. While Riaño, see León page 209, is the area's biggest town, it's a bit far from the action, and not especially charming; a better bet is Posada de Valdeón, spectacularly set in a lush valley surrounded by rocky peaks. ▶▶ *For Sleeping, Eating and other listings, see pages 536-540.*

South to the Naranco Valley

The N621 running south from Potes meets León province at the spectacular **Puerto de San Glorio** pass, proposed site for a controversial ski station. Descending rapidly through dark rocks and grassy pasture, the first settlement is **Llánaves de la Reina**.

Valdeón Valley

Some 6 km further south is the turn-off for the Valdeón Valley. The road climbs to the **Puerto de Pandetrave** at 1,562 m, which suddenly reveals a superb view of the valley, dwarfed by the imposing stone masses of the Picos. The first village in the valley itself is **Santa Marina**, a very rural settlement of simple stone houses. The *Ardilla Real* on Plaza de la Esquina serves meals and has dormitory accommodation.

Around 4 km up the lovely grassy valley is the area's main settlement, **Posada de Valdeón**. This is the southern terminus for the popular walk along the Cares Gorge, see page 532, and is well-equipped for a small place, with a supermarket and bank, but no cash machine. The setting is spectacular, with the intimidating mass of **Peña Bermeja** behind it contrasting with the lush pasturelands around.

Caín

North from Posada de Valdeón, a steep and narrow road makes its way to the village of Caín, a walk of just over 1½ hours. Jeeps run a shared-taxi service between the two towns. Not far from Posada, a fantastic view opens up as the valley seems to be swallowed up by lofty mountains; it's an awe-inspiring sight in good weather. The **Mirador de Pombo** is one vantage point to appreciate the vista; it's marked by a slender chamois and a confusing diagram of the peaks around. Before you reach here is the hamlet of **Cordiñanes**, which has a good rustic *pensión*, see below.

● Sleeping

Asturian Picos *p529*

There are many places to stay in Cangas de Onís – even in summer there should be a bed or two. The tourist office have a full list.

AL Parador de Cangas de Onís, Villanueva s/n, Cangas, T985849402, www.parador.es. Set in an old Benedictine monastery 3 km north of Cangas, this new parador offers excellent comfort and some good views.

Most of the rooms are in a modern annexe; those in the original building are slightly less comfortable but more atmospheric. Well priced.

A Ciudad de Cangas de Onís, Av Castilla 36, Cangas, T985849444, www.hotelcangas deonis.com. A 5-min walk from the centre on the road to Riaño, this is a fairly stylish modern hotel with all the trimmings. €10 extra gets a spa-bath in the room; not a bad option for weary hiking legs.

A Hotel Pelayo, Covadonga s/n, Covadonga, T985846061, F985846054, is right in the middle of the complex at Covadonga, is devoid of warmth but is reasonably well equipped, with a good restaurant. The price halves off-season.

B Hotel Puente Romano, C Puente Romano s/n, Cangas, T985849339, F985947284. An authentically heavily decorated 19th-century mansion across the Sella, with courteous management and comfortable heated rooms.

B Peñalba, half-way between the main road, at La Riera, T985846100, is way overpriced in the height of summer but is a good option at other times, set in a nice roadside village by the lively Covadonga stream.

B Picos de Europa, Ctra General s/n, Arenas, T985846491, picosdeeuropa@fade.es, is a little faded but is still Arenas's grandest hotel. Swimming pool, rooms with great views, and a granary feature by the bar in the garden.

B Villa de Cabrales, Ctra General s/n, Arenas, T985846719, F985846733, in a big stone building, is a more modern affair, with smart rooms with balconies (although there's some traffic noise). The off-season rates here are appealing.

C El Texu is a cosy rural hotel in the Covadonga.

C Hotel Puente Vidosa, T985944735, slap-bang in the middle of Puente Vidosa.

C Los Robles, C San Pelayo 8, Cangas, T985947052, F985997165. A nice sunny option a street back from the main road.

C-D Hotel Los Lagos, Jardines de Ayuntamiento 3, Cangas, T985849277, loslagos@fade.es. Good hotel with a warm, professional attitude with modern, attractive and quiet rooms on the main square. Closed Nov-Mar.

D Hotel La Plaza, C La Plaza 7, Cangas, T985848308, F985848308. Simple and cheery rooms with bathroom in the heart of town. The best options have a balcony and look out towards the mountains.

E Pensión Reconquista, Av Covadonga 6, Cangas, T985848275. Modern, 6th-floor rooms with balconies overlooking the town, and that rarest of beasts, a good shower. Run out of the bar on the corner. Excellent.

F Fonda Fermín Cotera, Arenas, T985846566, has simple, clean rooms in traditional Spanish *pensión* style.

Camping

Camping Naranjo de Bulnes, Ctra Cangas-Panes Km 32.6, T985846578, is a 10-min walk east of Arenas along the main road, and is open Mar-Oct.

Covadonga, at Soto by the main road, Covadonga, T985940097. A bland campsite.

Hiking in the mountains *p532*

B El Mirador de Cabrales, T985846673, www.hotelmirador.com, is the top accommodation option in Poncebos. Although overpriced in summer, it does have a top location and good restaurant.

D Hostal Poncebos, Poncebos, T985846447, is dwarfed by mountains. Reasonable rooms and a restaurant by the chilly river Cares.

D La Perdiz, Sotres, T985945011, hotel.laper diz@terra.es, has good rooms with bath.

D-E Casa Cipriano, Sotres, T985945024, is a convivial mountain hostal, which runs many guided excursions in the area. The rooms are good, and there's a bar and restaurant.

F Bulnes, T985845934, and **Peña Main**, T985845939, *albergues* that also do meals, both in La Villa.

F Garganta del Cares, Poncebos, T985846463, is a simple *pensión* with decent, heated rooms above a bar.

F Peña Castil, Sotres, T985945049, is an albergue with a restaurant.

E Rojo, C Santiago 8, Cordiñanes, T987740523, a clean and comfortable place with an unbeatable location if you're not scared of big powerful mountains.

Cantabrian Picos *p534*

A Parador de Fuente Dé, Fuente Dé, T942736651, www.parador.es. The top place to stay is this modern but fairly sensitive construction, this is one of the cheaper paradores but loses nothing on location, particularly when the day-trippers have gone home. The rooms are spacious and attractive, most with views of some sort, and the restaurant focuses on Picos cuisine.

C Posada La Antigua, C Cántabra 9, Potes, T942730037, eltarugu@mixmail.com. A very characterful mountain inn, with beautiful wood-beamed rooms with balustraded balconies.

C Rebeco, Fuente Dé, T942736601, F942736600, which doesn't lack comforts either, and also has a bar/restaurant.

D Casa Cayo, C Cántabra 6, Potes, T9427-
30150, www.casacayo.com. A very good
option above Potes's best bar and restaurant.
The rooms are large, comfortable, and
tastefully furnished; some overlook the river.

Camping
Camping El Redondo, 5 mins' walk from
Fuente Dé, T942736699, also has bunkbed
accommodation.

Leonese Picos *p536*
C Posada El Asturiano, Ctra Cordiñanes s/n,
Posada de Valdeón, T987740, has warm and
comfortable rooms just off the square.
D Hostal Campo, Ctra Cordiñanes s/n,
Posada de Valdeón, T987740502, has big,
warm, and comfy rooms with views at a
reasonable price.

● Eating

Asturian Picos *p529*
The *sidrerías* in Cangas are a superb eating
and drinking option.
€€ El Abuelo, Av Covadonga 21, Cangas,
T985848733. A cheerful, warming restaurant
specializing in hearty stews and *fabadas*.
€€ La Panera, Arenas, T985846505, is set
away from the bustle on a terrace above the
town. It's a good spot for a quiet drink, but
the food is attractive too. There's a set *menú*,
which is reasonable for €11, and plenty of
dishes making full use of *cabrales* cheese; try
it with wild mushrooms.
€€ Sidrería Los Arcos, Av Covadonga 17,
Cangas, T985849277. A popular cider bar on
the main street, serving good Asturian food.
€ Chigre El Orboya, C Pedro Niembro,
Arenas, is a decent place to down cider and
inexpensive food.
€ El Corcho, C Angel Tárano 5, Cangas,
T985849477. Great seedy *sidrería* with fine
food; try the grilled *gambones* (king prawns).
€ El Molin de la Pedrera, C Bernabé Pendas
1, Cangas, T985849109. A smart cider bar
with some great fishy stews on offer, as
well as roast chestnuts in season. One of
Cangas's best.
€ Mesón El Puente Romano, Av
Covadonga s/n, Cangas. The chief virtue of
this bar/restaurant is its terrace looking up at
the lovely medieval bridge. The food is
simple but reasonable Asturian fare,
including *fabada*.
€ San Telmo, Ctra General s/n, Arenas,
T985846505, gets plenty of tourists on its
roadside terrace, but the food is great; try the
chicken salad, or the ultimate expression of
cabrales, chips 'n' cheese.

Cantabrian Picos *p534*
€€ El Bodegón, C San Roque 14, Potes,
T942730247. Set in a stone building off an
old-timers' bar, this restaurant lacks warmth,
but is a good place to tuck into a hearty
cocido lebaniego (the local chickpea stew
garnished with sausage and pork). *Revuelto
de erizos* (scrambled egg with sea-urchins) is
also delicious, but an acquired taste.
€€ El Fogón de Cus, C Capitán Palacios 2,
Potes, T942730060. Excellent modern
mountain cuisine, with some good wines,
and a set lunch for €7.50.
€ Casa Cayo, C Cántabra 6, Potes,
T942730150. Potes's best eating and
drinking option, very lively and cheerful. The
portions are massive, so watch out when
ordering. The *cocidos* (chickpea stews) are
good, as are the *revueltos* (scrambled eggs
mixed with anything and everything). Some
tables overlook the river.
€ Los Camachos, C El Llano, Potes,
T942732148. Cheap, decent food in a lively
Cantabrian bar that has won prizes for its
home-made *orujo*.

Leonese Picos *p536*
Asturiano, Posada de Valdeón, has a good
restaurant, but the most characterful meal in
town will be had at the **Begoña**, which does
a cheap set *menú* in traditional and delicious
no-frills mountain style. You might get trout,
which abound in the streams around here, or
stew made from a freshly-hunted wild boar,
but its bound to be hearty and good.

● Bars and clubs

Asturian Picos *p529*
César Llosa, Constantino González 2,
Cangas. A friendly bar, good for late drinks
or breakfast.

● *For an explanation of sleeping and eating price codes used in this guide, see inside the*
● *front cover. Other relevant information is found in Essentials, see pages 47-56.*

Cantabrian Picos *p534*
Bar Chente, Bajos la Plaza s/n, Potes, T942730732. A good summer terrace on the hidden square below the road. The restaurant also does good cheap meals.
Cucu, Bajos la Plaza s/n, Potes. A warren of a *discoteca* with several bars under the square by the river. Good atmosphere at weekends and in summer.

❸ Festivals and events

Asturian Picos *p529*
25 Jul is the fiesta of Santiago is celebrated with gusto at Cangas de Onís; and the **Fiesta del Pastor** is a big, sociable party with shepherds and visitors mingling on the shores of Lake Enol near Covadonga. In **Aug**, regattas down the Rio Sella from Arriondas.

Cantabrian Picos *p534*
On **2 Jul** is **Romería** (pilgrimage procession) and festival in the Liébana Valley.

Leonese Picos *p536*
On **8 Sep** is the Picos' biggest day, when **Asturias Day**, the feast of the **Virgen de Covadonga**, is celebrated with processions and partying, and the fiesta of the **Virgen de Corona** in the Valdeón Valley. First week of **Nov** is **Orujo festival** in Potes; can be messy.

❂ Shopping

Asturian Picos *p529*
La Barata, Av Covadonga 13, Cangas, T985848027. A very attractive shop dealing in all manner of Asturian handicrafts, deli produce, and souvenirs.

▲ Activities and tours

Asturian Picos *p529*
Cangas Aventura, Av Covadonga 17, Cangas, T985849261. Canoeing trips on the river and quad excursions into the mountains.
Escuela Asturiana de Piragüismo, Av de Castilla s/n, Cangas, T985841282. By the Puente Romano in Cangas, they organize canoeing trips on the Río Sella as well as horse riding and canyoning.

K2 Aventura, Las Rozas s/n, Cangas, T985849358, www.k2aventura.com. A canoeing outfit based on the river between Arriondas and Cangas. There's a bar on hand for *aprés-kayak* ciders.
La Ruta Quads, Ctra Cangas-Cabrales Km 10, T629127323. A quad tour company based between Cangas and Arenas de Cabrales.

Cantabrian Picos *p534*
Europicos, C San Roque 6, Potes, T942730724, www.europicos.com. One of several tour operators based in popular Potes, this group organize everything from quad tours to 4WD trips to paragliding. They also hire mountain bikes from €20 for a half-day.
La Liébana, C Independencia 4, Potes, T942731021, F942731000. Organize a range of activities including horse-trekking and paragliding.
La Rodrigona, Cillorigo de Liébana s/n, Tama, T615970442, F942730506. A specialist horse-trekking operator based in a village north of Potes.
Picostur, C Obispo 2, Potes, T942738091, www.picostur.com. Offers the lot. Most guides speak decent English.
Potes Tur, C San Roque 19, Potes, T/F942732164, potestur@ceoecant.es. Specialize in quad excursions into the mountains but also cover other options.

❂ Transport

Asturian Picos *p529*
Cangas de Onís is serviced very regularly by ALSA buses from **Oviedo** and **Gijón** (almost hourly; 1 hr 20 mins). From **Cangas**, 4 buses a day ascend to **Covadonga**, from where you can catch a bus up to the lakes in summer only, and 4 a day run east to Arenas de Cabrales and Panes.

From **Oviedo** and **Cangas**, 4 buses a day ascend to **Covadonga**. In summer a couple a day continue to the lakes, as do several hundred families in cars; about 4 a day continue along the AS114 to **Arenas de Cabrales** and **Panes**.

ALSA run buses from **Arenas de Cabrales** to the **Bulnes** funicular at **Poncebos**. Shared-jeep taxis also do this trip in summer, and continue to **Sotres**. 4 buses a day run between **Cangas** and **Panes**, via **Arenas**.

Cantabrian Picos *p534*

A bus service from **Santander** to **Potes** runs 3 times daily, stopping along the western Cantabrian coast, turning inland at **Unquera**, and stopping at **Panes**. This connects with 2 of 3 daily buses from **Potes** to the cablecar at **Fuente Dé**.

Leonese Picos *p536*

The southern part of the Picos is a bit more problematic in terms of transport. There's one daily **Santander-León** bus (and vice versa), which stops at **Panes**, **Potes**, **Llánaves de la Reina** and **Riaño**. Occasional buses link **Riaño** with **Posada de Valdeón**, and there's a shared taxi service from here to **Caín**, at the head of the **Cares** gorge walk.

Two buses a day hit **Riaño** from **León**. There is 1 bus daily from **León** to **Posada de Valdeón**.

❶ Directory

Asturian Picos *p529*

Laundry Higiensec, Av de Castilla 24, Cangas, T985947471. For those dirty hiking clothes. Just off the road to Riaño. Service wash at a slightly pricey €13.22.

Cantabrian Picos *p534*

Internet Ciber-Plaza, on the main street, and **Cyber-Liébana**, in an arcade, are 2 neighbouring options in the centre of Potes.

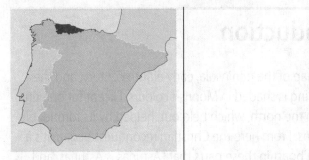

Introduction

Grab a map of the peninsula, early eighth century, and the whole thing is shaded in Moorish colours. Except for one tiny pocket in the north, which held out, helped by its formidable mountains. From here the Christian reconquest began; it's a common boast in these parts that "Asturias is Asturias, and Spain is just reclaimed land".

Asturias has had the foresight to look after its natural heritage. While the province is heavily industrialized, there are vast swathes of untouched old-growth **forest** inland that still harbour **bears** and **wolves**. A well-documented network of **trails** gives access to these places, maintained by an army of ecologists. The cities of the region are no less appealing. **Oviedo** is an elegant and beautiful capital, and claims some of the best of the ancient Pre-Romanesque architecture left by the Asturian monarchs; **Gijón** is a lively place with an excellent beach and a nightlife to match, while much-scorned **Avilés** shields a beautiful old town inside its ring of industry. Although the sea temperatures aren't exactly Caribbean, it's not hard to see why the Asturian coast is so popular; the mix of sandy beaches and pretty fishing ports is hard to beat. Hit the east coast for a developed summer scene, or the west for some more low-key places.

It's a tough, proud land that suffered greatly in the 20th century, when its radical miners were put down brutally by the army in 1934 and again in the Civil War. Franco wasn't forgiving, and the area was starved of resources during his reign; the decline of the coalmining industry didn't help. Asturias is still the most leftwing and egalitarian region in Northern Spain and, along with Euskadi, its friendliest. Wherever you head in the province you're guaranteed a gruff welcome and the sound of a cider cork popping.

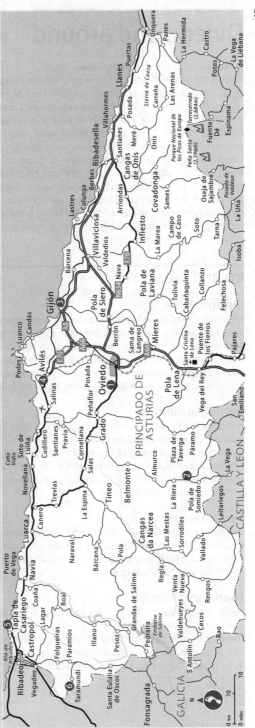

543

Asturias

★ Don't miss...

❶ **Oviedo** Explore ancient pre-Romanesque architecture, page 544.

❷ **Somiedo** Take yourself off to this national park and imagine what the rest of Spain would look like with trees and wildlife, page 548.

❸ **Gijón** Drink cider by the sea in this city, and wonder why anyone could say a word against the place, page 554.

❹ **Avilés** Go to *Carnaval* in this underrated, beautiful town, page 570.

❺ **Tapia de Casariego** Hit the west coast beaches and fishing towns, Tapia de Casariego has both, page 565.

❻ **Taramundi** stay here, explore the green hills on foot, and feel hundreds of years and miles away from 21st-century stresses, page 566.

Oviedo and around

→ *Phone code: 985; Colour map 1, grid A5; Population: 201,005.*

Oviedo, the capital of Asturias, seems to have come a long way since Clarín wrote in 1884, "he looked down on...the old squashed and blackened dwellings; the vain citizens thought them palaces but they were burrows, caves, piles of earth, the work of moles". Luckily, the description is from a novel written in a characteristic hyper-critical style. Nowadays, after an extensive programme of pedestrianization and restoration, the new town is a prosperous hive of shops and cafés, while old Oviedo is an extremely attractive web of plazas and old palaces built of honey-coloured stone. Three of the best and most accessible examples of the distinctive and beautiful Asturian pre-Romanesque style (see box page 549) are in and around Oviedo; other highlights include the cathedral, the Museo de Bellas Artes, and the never-say-die nightlife. The inland areas west of the capital are well worth exploring, and reasonably well served by public transport.➤➤ *For Sleeping, Eating and other listings, see pages 550-554.*

Ins and outs

Getting there

Asturias is served by the Aeropuerto de Ranón, on the coast west of Gijón. Most of the intercity buses are run by ALSA, www.alsa.es, an efficient service that connects Asturias with much of Spain. These connections are typically faster than the train. RENFE connects with the major cities in Northern Spain, as well as Madrid and Barcelona, while the slower FEVE network connects Oviedo with the coast eastwards and westwards to Galicia.➤➤ *For further details, see Transport page 553.*

Getting around

Buses are mostly of use to reach outlying areas – there are 12 or so routes, clearly labelled at bus stops. Taxis are easy to find, but bear in mind that, due to Oviedo's commitment to pedestrianization, many locations aren't easily accessible by car. Hemmed in by hills, Oviedo is a fairly compact city, and moving about isn't a problem. From the bus and train stations it's an easy 15-minute walk to the heart of the old town down C Uría; most accommodation is closer.

Best time to visit

Oviedo has a comparatively mild climate; neither winter nor summer usually hit uncomfortable extremes, although it is notoriously rainy in autumn and winter. Oviedo's major fiesta is in September (see below), but the *sidrerías* (cider bars) and other haunts are busy year-round.

Tourist information

Oviedo's main tourist office ① *Plaza de Alfonso II, just across from the cathedral, T985213385, Mon-Fri 0900-1400, 1630-1830, Sat 0930-1400 during Jun to Sep.* There's a smaller municipal office ① *Campo de San Francisco park, T985227586, Mon-Fri 1030-1400, 1630-1930, Sat/Sun 1100-1400.* Sociedad Regional de Turismo de Asturias ① *C/Burriana, 1 Bajo 33006, Oviedo, T985 277 870.*

History

Oviedo was born in the early years of the stubborn Asturian monarchy, when a monastery was founded on the hill of 'Ovetao' in the mid-eighth century. Successive kings added other buildings until Alfonso II saw the city's potential, rebuilt and expanded it, and moved his court here in 808. He saw it as a new Toledo (the former Christian capital having long since fallen to the Moors). It was this period that saw the consolidation of the Pre-Romanesque style, as Alfonso commissioned an impressive series of buildings. A glorious century in the spotlight followed, but Oviedo soon regressed when the court was moved south to León. Oviedo continued to grow through the Middle Ages, however; partly as a result of pilgrim traffic to Santiago. The university was founded in about 1600, which helped to raise Oviedo's profile. Real prosperity arrived with the Industrial Revolution and, crucially, the discovery of coal in the green valleys near the Asturian capital. Asturias became a stronghold of unionism and socialism, and Oviedo suffered massive damage in the 1934 revolt, and again in the Civil War, see box page 590. Franco had a long memory, and it has only been fairly recently that Oviedo has emerged from his shadow. A progressive town council has transformed the city, embarking on a massive program of pedestrianization (there are over 80 pedestrian streets), restoration, and commissioning of public sculpture. Now, painted and scrubbed, Oviedo is taking new pride in living up to its coat of arms as the "very noble, very loyal, meritorious, unconquered, heroic, and good city of Oviedo".

Sights

Cathedral

① *Mon-Sat 1000-1300, 1600-1800 (1900 in summer), admission to Cámara Santa, museum, and cloister €2.50, Cámara Santa only €1.25.*

The cathedral, a warm-coloured and harmonious construction, dominates the **Plaza de Alfonso el Casto** with its delicate and exuberant spire. While most of the building is a 14th- and 15th-century design, it contains a series of important relics of the Asturian kings in its Cámara Santa. This chamber, originally part of Alfonso II's palace, contains the Cruz de los Ángeles and the Cruz de la Victoria. These bejewelled crucifixes were gifts to the Church by Kings Alfonso II and III respectively. The former now is the symbol of Oviedo, while the latter features on the Asturian coat of arms. Also behind glass in the Cámara Santa is a silver ark said to contain relics brought from the Holy Land to Spain in the seventh century. One of the relics, supposedly the shroud of Christ, is behind a panel in the back wall – it is brought out and venerated three times a year. The relics in the ark are said to include a piece of the cross, some bread from the Last Supper, part of Christ's clothing, some of his nappies, and milk of the Virgin Mary. The cathedral also boasts an attractive cloister, and a good collection of objects in its museum; these, unfortunately, are basically left to the visitor's interpretation. Across the square from the cathedral is a statue of Clarín's La Regenta.

Museo Arqueológico

① *Tue-Sat 1000-1330, 1600-1800, Sun 1100-1300, closed Mon, free.*

Behind the cathedral, on Calle San Vicente, is the Museo Arqueológico, built around a beautiful monastery cloister. The sparsely labelled finds somehow lack context, but it's a pleasant stroll around the old building.

Oviedo

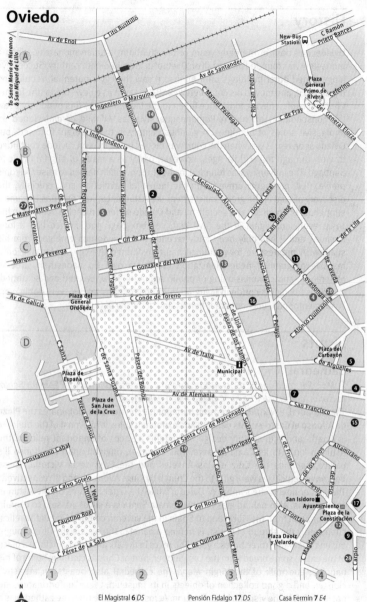

N

0 metres 200

0 yards 200

Sleeping 🛌
Alteza 1 *B2*
Casa Albino 2 *D5*
Ciudad de Oviedo 3 *C5*
Covadonga 4 *D4*
De la Reconquista 5 *C2*

El Magistral 6 *D5*
Favila 7 *B2*
Gran Hotel España 8 *D5*
Hospadaje
 Berdasco 9 *B2*
Hostal Alvarez 10 *B2*
Hostal Arco Iris 11 *B2*
Hostal Arcos 12 *F4*
Hostal Belmonte 13 *C3*
Hostal Oviedo 14 *B2*
Hostal Romero 15 *C3*
Ovetense 16 *E5*

Pensión Fidalgo 17 *D5*
Pensión Pomar 18 *D5*
Santa Cruz 19 *E2*
Vetusta 20 *C4*

Eating 🍴
Barbacana 1 *B1*
Bocamar 2 *B2*
Café Colonial 3 *C4*
Café Dólar 4 *D4*
Café Filarmónica 5 *D4*
Casa Conrado 6 *D5*

Casa Fermín 7 *E4*
El Asador
 de Aranda 8 *D5*
El Cafetón 9 *F4*
El Cogollu 10 *F5*
El Pigüeña 11 *D5*
El Raitan &
 El Chigre 12 *F5*
La Casa Real
 de Jamón 13 *C4*
La Corrada
 del Obispo 14 *F5*

Museo de las Bellas Artes de Asturias

ⓘ *Tue-Fri 1030-1400, 1630-2030, Sat 1130-1400, 1700-2000, Sun 1130-1430, free*. This museum is housed in a 17th-century palace and a grand 18th-century townhouse that are joined back-to-back. There are two entrances, one on Calle Santa Ana, and one Calle Rua. The museum has an excellent collection of 20th-century Asturian art and a good selection of Spanish masters. In the vestibule at the Santa Ana entrance hangs José Uría y Uría's evocative *Después una huelga* (after a strike). Painted in 1895, it evocatively demonstrates that the events of 1934 and 1936 were a long time in the making.

Other sights

The old town is made for wandering. The walk-through **Ayuntamiento** is on Plaza de la Constitución, as is the honey-coloured **Iglesia de San Isidoro**. Other pretty plazas include **Trascorrales**, and **Porlier**, in which is the mysterious sculpture *El regreso de (the return of) William B Arrensberg*, one of many street sculptures that invigorate Oviedo. From here, walking down Calle San Francisco (the Assisi saint passed through Oviedo on his way to Santiago) brings you to the large park of the same name. *Maternidad*, a sculpture by the Colombian Botero, is an unmissable landmark here on the **Plaza de la Escandalera**; it's irreverently nicknamed *la Muyerona* (the big woman) by locals.

Heading north of the old town, **Calle Gascona**'s sharpish slope serves to drain away all the cider spilled in its numerous and gregarious *sidrerías*. The pre-Romanesque **Iglesia de San Julián de los Prados** ⓘ *T607353999, Oct-Apr Tue-Sat 0930-1200, May-Sep also 1600-1800 guided visits, Mon 1000-1300 unguided, guided visits take half-an-hour, last entry half-an-hour before closing time, €1.20, Mon free*, was built by Alfonso II in the first half of the ninth century. Northeast of the old centre, beyond the fountained Plaza de la Cruz Roja, it now struggles for serenity beside the Gijón motorway. Designed

with the characteristic triple nave, the highlight of the church is its superbly preserved frescoes, which show interesting similarities with first-century AD Roman wall-paintings known from Pompeii.

The pre-Romanesque structures of **Santa María de Naranco** and **San Miguel de Lillo**, collectively known as Los Monumentos, overlook the city on Naranco hill to the northwest. It is a pleasant enough 30-minute walk up the hill from the railway station, otherwise buses run hourly from C Uría (No 3). There's a good view over Oviedo, which, it has to be said, isn't super-attractive but is backed by beautiful mountains.

Santa María, built as a palace by Ramiro I (1842-1850), is arguably the finest example of this architecture. The columns in the upper hall could almost be carved from bone or ivory, such is the skill of the stonework. Balconies at either end add to the lightness of the design; one contains an altar with an inscription of the king. A range of sculptural motifs, many of them depicting alarming animals, decorate the hall, and have been attributed to Visigothic and Byzantine influences. Underneath the hall is another chamber variously identified as a crypt, bathhouse, and servants' quarters.

Iglesia de San Miguel ① *Apr-mid Oct 0930-1300, 1500-1900, mid Oct-Mar 1000-1300, 1500-1700, closed Sun pm and Mon, €2.20 (guided tour only)*, a stone's throw further up the road, is a church also constructed during the reign of Ramiro I. What remains is a comglomeration of the original building, much of which collapsed in the 13th century, and later additions. The original building was undoubtedly an amazing structure for the time in which it was built. What remains is impressive, with a series of intricately carved lattices, and some remaining fresco decoration. Carved panels appear to show gladiatorial or circus scenes. It is about a 30-minute brisk walk up Avenida de los Monumentos from above and behind the railway station. Bus No 3 plies the route hourly from Calle Uría. Get off at the car park – Santa María is a five-minute walk up the hill, San Miguel a short way beyond.

New town

The elegant facades of the new town, many of them coloured, are an attractive feature. Off busy Calle Uría on Calle Gil de Jaz stands the **Hotel de la Reconquista**, see also page 550. It's worth a look for its beautiful courtyard and galleries.

Around Oviedo

"*Where there is coal, there is everything*", J Aguado, Asturian industrialist, 1842.

Iglesia de Santa Cristina de Lena

① *Tue-Sun 1100-1300, 1630-1830 (summer), 1200-1300, 1600-1700, free.*
Further south from El Entrego, overlooking the motorway near the border with León Province, it's worth making the effort to visit another excellent pre-Romanesque church, Iglesia de Santa Cristina de Lena. Dating from the mid-ninth century, it's a pretty thing on the outside, but its hauntingly beautiful interior is better. A delicately carved raised triple arch is topped by symbols of early Christianity, not without some Islamic influence. The altarstone inscriptions have clear Visigothic/Germanic parallels, and there are several stones reused from a Visigothic edifice. To reach the church take cercanía line C1 to La Cobertoria, from where it's a short walk; you thus avoid the depressing town of Pola de Lena.

Somiedo National Park → *Colour map 1, grid B5.*

Southwest of Oviedo, the national park (and UNESCO biosphere reserve) of Somiedo is a superbly high, wild area of Asturian forest, home to bears and wolves, as well as some extremely traditional Asturian villages. There are many superb walks in the park, one of the best starting from the hamlet of **Valle de Lago**, from where there's a

⦂ Beauty and the bricks

From the late eighth century, the rulers of the young Asturian kingdom began to construct religious and civil buildings in an original style that drew on Roman, Visigothic, and Eastern elements.

Some of the buildings that remain are of striking beauty. There are some 20 standing churches and halls that preserve some or many of their original features. The style was characterized by barrel-vaulted, usually triple, naves and a rectangular or cross-shaped ground plan. The roof is supported by columns, often elaborately carved with motifs derived from Moorish and Byzantine models. The transepts are wide, and the altar area often raised. A triple apse is a common feature, sometimes divided

from the rest of the building by a triple arch; the windows, too, are characteristic, divided by a miniature column. The exterior is typically buttressed; the supports line up with the interior columns.

The style progressed quickly and reached its peak in the mid ninth century under Ramiro I. From this period are the supreme examples outside Oviedo, Santa María de Naranco and San Miguel de Lillo. Other excellent example of the Asturian Pre-Romanesque style (a term coined by Jovellanos, see box page 558, are San Salvador de Valdedíos not far from Villaviciosa; San Julián de los Prados in Oviedo, and Santa Cristina de Lena, south of Oviedo on the way to León.

walk to (you guessed it) Lago del Valle, a 12-km return trip up a high grassy valley with abundant birdlife. If you're scared of dogs, take a bribe or two; they're really big softies. The trail is waymarked as PR 15.1. You can stay in Lago del Valle, or in the bigger village of **Pola de Somiedo**, a 1½-hour walk back on the main road.

West from Oviedo → *Colour map 1, grid A5.*
Although towns such as Pravia, ancient Asturian capital, and Salas, hometown of an arch-inquisitor, can be easily visited as day trips from Oviedo or Gijón, they also make good bases in themselves; there are several rewarding walks in the area. This is salmon country – in season, the rivers teem with them. It's hard to understand why they bother; the phalanxes of local and international fly-fishers make survival a dim prospect indeed. Perhaps none make it back to warn the others. One of the most typical sights in this area are the *hórreos*, wood and stone huts raised on legs for the storage of grain. Most of these are at least a century old, and many are much older. Some *hórreo* enthusiasts border on the obsessive. There's a Galician version too, which is smaller and made of stone.

Salas West of the fishing centre of Cornellana, along a valley of eucalyptus and wild deer is the town of Salas. Although it features prominently on most maps of Asturias, it is in fact a small, picturesque, and tranquil place. Salas's most famous son was Hernando de Valdés, whose formidable presence still looms large in the town over 500 years since his birth. An extremely able theologian and orator, he rapidly ascended the church hierarchy until in 1547 he became Inquisitor-General for the whole of Spain. His rule was, like the man himself, strict, austere, and inflexible. Quick to crack down on any books, tracts, or people with so much as a sniff of liberalism or reformation about them, he can be seen as a symbol of the "Spain that turned its back on Europe". Down the hill a little stands the **Colegiata de Santa María la Mayor**, where the body of the inquisitor now rests in an alabaster mausoleum. Valdés came from a notable local family, whose small castle and tower still

dominates the town. Inside is the tourist office, as well as a small museum of Pre-Romanesque inscriptions and ornamentation in the tower. ① *Tourist office and museum, T985830988. Mid-Sep to mid-Jun Mon-Thu 0930-1430, 1600-1900, Fri 0930-1430; mid-Jun to mid-Sep Tue-Sun 1030-1430, 1630-1930, Mon 1030-1430; admission €1.20.* The rest of the castle is mostly dedicated to a hotel set around the pleasing courtyard.

Pravia Little-known Pravia is another small gem in the crown of Asturias. Founded in Roman times, it was briefly the home of the Asturian court in the eighth century before being forsaken for Oviedo in 808. Now a small agricultural town, its small centre is a relaxing collage of perfect façades, which are at their best in the soft evening light. The town feels oddly South American, perhaps as a result of the large numbers of *indianos* who returned home having made their fortunes in the new colonies. Many of their houses dot Pravia and the surrounding area (as well as much of Asturias) – they are typically tall and grandiose, and often have gardens planted with palms and cactus. The centre of town is presided over by the bulky **Colegiata de Pravia** and the connected **Palacio de los Moutas**, good examples of Spanish Baroque architecture. The oldest building in the town proper is the **Casa del Busto**, a large and dignified *casona* now tastefully converted into a hotel. Built in the 16th century, it was a favourite refuge of Jovellanos, see page 558, whose sister-in-law lived here.

Santianes In the village of Santianes, the **Iglesia de Santianes de Pravia**, the oldest of the series of existing pre-Romanesque buildings of this size, is 3 km from town. It preserves little of its original character, having been substantially altered over the years, but is an attractive building nonetheless. It stands on the site of an earlier Visigothic church. Santianes is one stop from Pravia on the FEVE line, and also accessible by bus, but if you're after a nice walk on a dry day, go down Calle de la Industria from the centre of Pravia, cross the river and two roundabouts, and continue up the hill. Santianes is signposted to the right about 1½ km up this road.

⊙ Sleeping

Oviedo *p544, map p546*
LL Hotel de la Reconquista, C Gil de Jaz 16, T985241100, www.hoteldelare conquista. com. Oviedo's top hotel, fantastically built around, and faithful to, the 18th-century Hospital of the Principality. Set around galleries, courtyards, and chapels brimming with period objets d'art, the Prince of Asturias, heir to the Spanish throne, stays here when he's in town. Sensitive visitors are welcome on the ground floor – it's well worth a look. Check website for accommodation offers.
L Gran Hotel España, C Jovellanos 2, T985220596, F985222140. Typical of a certain sort of smart Spanish hotel slightly yearning for the glory days of the 1920s. Untypically, this has been sensitively renovated, and the courteous staff do justice to the plush interiors.

A Hotel El Magistral, C Jovellanos 3, T985215116, www.elmagistral.com. The steel-and-bottle glass decor gives an intriguingly space-age feel to this original establishment. The rooms are softer, with lacquered floorboards and pastel colours accompanied by the expected facilities.
A Hotel Vetusta, C Covadonga 2, T985222229, www.hotelvetusta.com. Small and welcoming central hotel; the modern design exudes warmth and personality. All rooms exterior, half come complete with a mini sauna/massage unit. Sunny café-bar downstairs. Recommended.
C Hostal Romero, C Uría 36, T985227591, hostalromero@terra.es. Big and inviting rooms, all with bathroom and TV. Welcoming and enthusiastic owners are, at time of writing, completely renovating the place. Recommended.
C Hotel Favila, C Uría 37, T985253877, F985276169. Handy for transport and

---

For an explanation of sleeping and eating price codes used in this guide, see inside the front cover. Other relevant information is found in Essentials, see pages 47-56.

> **❝❞ There are few more interesting places to have a drink than an Asturian *sidrería*, with sawdust-covered floor and streams of booze poured from alarming heights...**

situated on Oviedo's main shopping street, comfy rooms with cable TV and smart bathroom, cheery staff. Restaurant downstairs does a cheap, tasty, and filling lunchtime *menú*.

D Hostal Belmonte, C Uría 31, T985241020, calogon@teleline.es. Hospitable option, probably the best of the cheapies in this part of town. Attractively renovated, with wooden floor and a variety of rooms, all with TV. Student discount.

D Hotel Alteza, C Uría 25, T985240404, F985240408. Decent, cheap hotel with compact but snug rooms and a comfy lounge. All rooms with TV and bathroom. Warm in winter, hot in summer. Breakfast included.

D Hotel Ovetense, C San Juan 6, T985220840, www.hotelovetense.com. Prime central location and cosy rooms, which, although small, are top value. Potentially stuffy in summer, but quiet and friendly nonetheless. Pay parking available.

E Hostal Arcos, C Magdalena 3, T985214773. A very friendly place in the heart of the old town; shared bathrooms are clean and modern; 24-hr access. Recommended.

E Pensión Fidalgo, C Jovellanos 5, T985213287. Homely, welcoming, and colourful family set-up well placed between the old and new towns. Some of the rooms can be noisy; the dog is large but a soft touch. Recommended.

E Pensión Pomar, C Jovellanos 7, T985222791/985219840/630279638. Simple and pleasant *pensión* in the heart of Oviedo. Exterior rooms are light, airy, and spotless. Interior rooms quieter.

Around Oviedo *p548*
B Casa del Busto, C Rey Don Silo 1, Pravia, T985822771, www.bestwestern.es/casa delbusto.html. The use of period-style furniture perfectly sets off an already

charming building. The rooms all have individual character. Recommended.

C Castillo de Valdés-Salas, Plaza de la Campa s/n, Salas, T985832222, F985832299, hotel in the small castle, beautiful setting, rooms have more than castle-comfort but are very true to the building.

D Pensión 14, C Jovellanos 8, Pravia, T985821148. Small and welcoming *pensión* with two home-from-home rooms, lavishly appointed with stove, sink, utensils, TV, pine wood, and skylights! Recommended.

E Hotel Soto, C Arzobispo Valdés 9, T985830037, reasonable hotel in pleasant old building; best rooms overlook the back of the floodlit Colegiata.

E Mierel, Pola de Somiedo, T985763993, is a good comfy spot to sleep and refuel on hearty Asturian food.

Self-catering
The hills to the northeast of Salas have a number of good options for self-catering. One of the best, in the tiny village of Mallecina, 11 km from Salas, is **Ca Pilarona**, T629127561, www.galeon. com/capilarona. This is a series of four restored houses, modernized with excellent facilities.

🍴 Eating

Oviedo *p544, map p546*
€€€ **Barbacana**, C Cervantes 27, T985963096. Snappy modern joint in the new town, stylish and popular with business folk. Small but quality selection with fresh fish the highlight. *Menú* for €39. Closed Sat lunch and Sun.

€€€ **Casa Conrado**, C Argüelles 1, T985223917. Fairly traditional Spanish *mesón*, all dark wood and cigar smoke. A local byword for quality and elegance. Top wine list. Closed Sun.

Casa Fermín, C San Francisco 8, T985216452, specializes in high quality Asturian dishes, with *merluza a la sídra* a speciality. A hefty multi-course *menú* showcasing a range of Asturian cuisine is €35. Closed Sun.

€€ **Bocamar**, C Marqués de Pidal 20, T985271611. In the heart of the shopping district, this is a reasonably upmarket fish restaurant. Offers a good €15 *menú del dia*.

€€ **El Cogollu**, Plaza de Trascorrales 19, T985223983. Little gem of a restaurant in the southeastern corner of Trascorrales. Peaceful stone and ochre interior, imaginative Asturian cuisine, and a four course *menú* that is superb value at €18.60. Recommended.

€€ **El Pigüeña**, C Gascona 2, T985210341. For those with a largish appetite, this is an excellent choice for cider and seafood. While the à la carte fish dishes are around €16-20, *raciones* are generous here as well, and a fair bit cheaper.

€€ **El Raítan** and **El Chigre**, Plaza de Trascorrales 6, T985214218. Long a favourite for Asturian cuisine, this two-in-one establishment offers a hearty degustation *menú* for €24.64, and has other *menús* for €16.83 and €14.42. Good value.

€€ **La Corrada del Obispo**, C Canóniga 18, T985220048. Beautifully decorated, with plenty of natural light as well as chandeliers, polished wood floors, and all the trimmings. The thoughtfully prepared food matches the surroundings and feels slightly underpriced. Offer a €20 *menú* (not including drinks). Closed Sun night.

€ **La MásBARata**, C Cimadevilla 2, T985213606. Modern but casual tapas bar/restaurant specializing in rice dishes and tapas; there's a huge variety of potential and delicious accompaniments to a *caña* at the bar.

€ **La Pumarada**, C/ Gascona 8, T985200279. The outdoor tables are good spots for watching (and helping) C Gascona go wild at the weekend. A good range of seafood is on hand to wash down the cider, and there's a €12 lunchtime *menú*.

€ **Las Campanas de San Bernabé**, C San Bernabé 7, T985224931. Attractive faded façade conceals a popular restaurant with a good line in bistro-style Asturiana, seafood dishes, and rices. Deservedly busy. Recommended.

€ **R.Q.R**, C Cimadevilla 16, T985203694. Definitely long rather than wide, this bar has a day-and-night range of hot and cold sandwiches and rolls. The lunch *menú* has plenty of choices and is exceedingly good value for €7.50. Recommended.

€ **Sidrería Asturias**, C Gascona 9, T985211752. Another cheery seafood and cider specialist on the self-styled 'Boulevard of Cider', with street tables and plenty of cheap tapas options.

€ **Villaviciosa**, C Gascona 7, T985204412. A good earthy *sidrería* with hearty food typical of the region. Just don't wear your best shoes.

Tapas bars and cafés

A traditional Oviedo pastry is the *carbayón*, an eclair-like almond creation. It's named after the oak tree, the traditional centre and meeting place of Asturian villages. A large *carbayón* was controversially chopped down in Oviedo in 1879 to make more room on C Uría; a plaque marks the spot where it stood.

Café Colonial, C 9 de Mayo 2, T985210369. A good café for watching the busy human traffic from outdoor tables on a pedestrianized street.

Café Dólar, Plaza de Porlier 2. A very typical, rather than noteworthy, café with a relaxed ambience and a good location.

Café Filarmónica, C Argüelles 4, T985227251. Upmarket and popular café.

El Cafetón, Plaza del Sol 4. Pleasant place for a coffee, snack, or cheap lunch, nicely situated on a plaza.

La Mallorquina and **La Elma**, C Milicias Nacionales, two cafés opposite each other with pleasant outdoor tables, heated and covered in winter, from which to observe Oviedo's bustle.

La Paloma, C Independencia 1. Always buzzing with folk stopping by for afternoon coffees or evening vermouths.

Around Oviedo *p548*

Salas isn't bristling with places to eat.

€€ **Casa del Busto**, Pravia, attractive restaurant in the hotel with tables in the open atrium. Speciality is chicken stuffed with salmon.

€ **Casa Pacita**, in the middle of Sala, T985832279, deals in simpler fare, mostly meat, for which the region has a good reputation.

€€ **Castillo**, Sala, offers a *menú* for €9.63, and cooks up some of the local trout catch in season. The best option in town.

€ **Balbona**, C Pico de Merás 2, Pravia, T985821162. Despite the garish neon sign, this is a very acceptable choice, with Asturian cuisine enlivened with modern ideas.

€ **La Hilandera**, C San Antonio 8, Pravia, T985822051. Good-looking *sidrería* with friendly service and hearty meals and snacks.

◑ Bars and clubs

Oviedo *p544, map p546*

Be aware that many of the bars only open at the weekend. Much of Oviedo's nightlife is centred in the rectangle bounded by Calles Mon, Postigo Alto, San José, and Canóniga. Other areas are C Rosal, for a grungier scene, and, of course, the area around C Gascona and C Jovellanos.

Asturianu, C Carta Puebla 8, 985206227. While there's nothing particularly Asturian about this bar, it's super-friendly, is a monument to good beers from around the world, and is lively till very late.

Ca Beleño, C Martínez Vigil 4. Legendary Oviedo bar focusing on the Asturian folk.

El Cuelebre, C Mon 9. Chart Latin and international pop. Only open weekends, and fairly packed with a young crowd.

La Real, C Cervantes 19. Oviedo's top spot for house, with top DJs from Madrid and the UK frequently appearing. Sat nights from 0100 until 0900. €16 entry includes drink.

La Reserva, C Carpio 11. Decent indie club open at weekends.

Paddock, C Rosal 70. For those with an ear tuned to metal. Suitably dark and loud.

Planeta Tierra, C Padre Suárez and C Carta Puebla. Mid-20s crowd, 80s and 90s pop.

T.K.C, C Canóniga 12. Latino chart hits.

◉ Entertainment

Oviedo *p544, map p546*

Cajastur bank, Plaza de la Escandalera, has a programme of art house films.

Ciné Ayala, C Matemático Pedrayes 2, T985236380.

Cinés Brooklyn, C General Zubillaga 10, T985965856.

Cinés Clarín, Av Valentín Masip 7, T985243316.

Teatro Campoamor, Plaza del Carbayón, T985207590. As well as a programme of well-regarded mainstream theatre, it has a weekly Sun morning performance of Asturian folk music.

◉ Festivals and events

Oviedo *p544, map p546*

Oviedo's major festival is the **fiesta of San Mateo**, the city's patron.

The third week of **Sep** is given over to street parades, dances, bullfights, an opera season, and similar celebration.

Carnaval in Oviedo is also gaining a reputation – the main day here is **Shrove Tuesday**, 47 days before **Easter Sunday**.

◉ Shopping

Oviedo *p544, map p546*

Books La Palma Libros, C Rua 6, T985214782. A good bookshop for information on Asturias; also has a good English language section.

Librería Cervantes, C Doctor Casal and C Campoamor. Bookshop with an excellent range of English language books, as well as Asturian and Spanish literature.

Department stores El Corte Inglés, C Uría 9. A superstore with anything anybody could want.

Markets Mercado El Fontán. Just behind the Plaza Mayor, this covered central market is a good place to stock up on Asturian produce. The curious might be interested in the horse butcher.

Supercor, C Uría 21. Decent supermarket for self-catering.

◉ Transport

Oviedo *p544, map p546*

Air There are several flights daily from **Madrid** and **Barcelona** operated by Iberia and Spanair. There are also 3 **Iberia** flights weekly from both **London** and **Paris**. A bus service operates to/from **Oviedo**, **Avilés**, and **Gijón**; these are regular but infrequent – about 8 a day, scheduled to connect with outgoing flights. Iberia, Plaza de Juan XXIII 9, T985118783.

Bus Local city buses are blue and run on 12 clearly marked routes around the city. The

asic fare is €0.75. Bus No 3 runs hourly from C Uría up to Santa María de Naranco and San Miguel de Lillo. The bus station, completed in late in 2002, brings all of Oviedo's bus services to one location. There are many buses to **Gijón**, 30 mins, and many companies run services across Asturias. The major inter-city operator is **ALSA** www.alsa.es, T902422242, who connect **Oviedo** with **A Coruña** (6 hrs), **Santiago** (7 hrs), **León** (1½ hrs), **Valladolid** (3½ hrs), **Madrid** (5½ hrs), **Santander** (3½ hrs), and **Bilbao** (5 hrs). There's also a service to **London** (26 hrs, change in **Paris**).

Cycle Salvador Bermudez, C/ Postigo Alto, opposite C/Fueros, rents and repairs bicycles.

Train There is a bewildering number of short distance *cercanía* train routes around the **central valleys** of Asturias. These are run by both FEVE and RENFE out of the train station. Details of individual lines can be found in the relevant destination section. For long-distance services, **RENFE** links **Oviedo** with **León** (7 per day; 2 hrs), **Madrid** (3 per day; 6 hrs), **Barcelona** (2 per day; 12 hrs), and points in between. Note that the bus is generally quicker on these routes. FEVE's coastal network links **Oviedo** (slowly) with **Santander** (2 through trains per day; 4 hrs), **Bilbao** (1 per day; 6½ hrs), and westwards as far as **Ferrol** in **Galicia** (2 per day, 6½ hrs).

Around Oviedo *p548*
There are buses twice daily from **Oviedo** to **Pola de Somiedo**.

Cornellana and **Salas** are both well served by ALSA buses from **Oviedo**.

Pravia is served hourly by **FEVE** trains from both **Oviedo** (Line F7) and **Gijón** (Line F4), 1 hr. **ALSA** also runs buses here from **Oviedo** and **Gijón** (2 a day, 1 hr).

❸ Directory

Oviedo *p544, map p546*
Internet Café Oriental, C Jovellanos 8, T985202897. Cybercafé at €2.50 per hr.
Laser Internet Center, C San Francisco 9, T985200066, www.las.es. Internet centre open 24 hrs, €0.05 per min, another branch at C Asturias 15.
Hospital There's a large **medical centre** that deals with emergencies at C Naranjo de Bulnes behind the train station. T985286000.
Pharmacies, C Uría 16, C Uría 36 and C Magdalena 17, have a 24-hr service.
Language schools Alea, C Fontán 9, T985086349, www.mundoalea.com. A large company that organizes Spanish courses, including Oviedo. Reasonable reputation.
Laundry Riosol, C Capitán Almeida 31, T985222090.
Libraries The provincial library is on C Quintana near Plaza del Fontán, T985211397.
Post The main post office is on C Alonso Quintanilla.
Telephone There is a *locutório* (telephone centre) at C Caveda and C Alonso Quintanilla, and another at C Foncalada 6.

Gijón and the east coast

→ *Phone code: 985; Colour map 1, grid A6; Population: 269,270.*

Following what seems to be the established law for such things, there is no love lost between Gijón and Oviedo. People in Gijón, the larger of the two, feel that it should be capital of Asturias instead of Oviedo, which some consider soft and effete. Those in Oviedo aren't too bothered, but occasionally enjoy riling Gijón by referring to it, tongue in cheek, as 'our port'. Gijón is a fun city set around two beaches and a harbour. The larger and nicer of the beaches, Playa de San Lorenzo, is an Asturian Copacabana, fronting two kilometres of city blocks with a stretch of very clean sand, which almost wholly disappears at high tide and in summer, under rows of bronzing bodies. There's a fair-sized surf community here, and a thriving summer gay scene.

The coast east of Gijón is popular with Spanish summer tourists but it's always possible to get away: the sheer number of small villages and accommodation options sees to that. There are dinosaur footprints scattered around; pick up the tourist office brochure if you're interested in tracking them down. There are some

good examples, but they're nothing to touch the ones in La Rioja. ▶▶ *For Sleeping, Eating and other listings, see pages 559-562.*

Ins and outs

Getting there Gijón's bus station is on C Magnus Blikstad with regular long-distance connections to other cities in Northern Spain and local services. Services depart from the FEVE station on Plaza del Humedal. RENFE station is on Avenida de Juan Carlos I, a 15-minute walk from the old centre. ▶▶ *For further details, see Transport page 561.*

Gijón

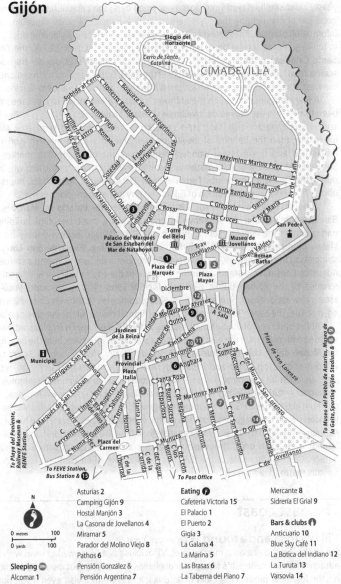

	Asturias 2	Mercante **8**
	Camping Gijón **9**	Sidrería El Grial **9**
	Hostal Manjón **3**	
	La Casona de Jovellanos **4**	**Bars & clubs**
N	Miramar **5**	Anticuario **10**
	Parador del Molino Viejo **8**	Blue Sky Café **11**
0 metres 100	Pathos **6**	La Botica del Indiano **12**
0 yards 100	Pensión González &	La Turuta **13**
	Pensión Argentina **7**	Varsovia **14**
Sleeping		
Alcomar **1**	**Eating**	
	Cafetería Victoria **15**	
	El Palacio **1**	
	El Puerto **2**	
	Gigia **3**	
	La Galana **4**	
	La Marina **5**	
	Las Brasas **6**	
	La Taberna del Piano **7**	

Tourist information The city has a municipal and a provincial tourist office. The latter, supplemented by a network of summer information booths, is very helpful, and stocks a range of literature in a various languages. Municipal office ① *Dársena Fomento pier off Av Rodriguez San Pedro, Mon-Sun 1000-1400, 1600-2000.* Provincial office ① *Jardines de la Reina park by the harbour, Mon-Fri 0900-1400, 1630-1830.*

Sights

The small old quarter, at the base of the Cimadevilla promontory, is heady with the yeasty cider smell relayed from dozens of small bars; the council has also done a good job of highlighting the city's heritage with a number of small museums and information plaques. There are also numerous small art exhibitions leading brief lives in unlikely places. At the tip of the Cimadevilla headland is a small hill, the **Cerro Santa Catalina,** at the tip of which stands Eduardo Chillida's *Elogio del Horizonte* sculpture, which has become the symbol of the town. Further around the headland to the west stands the equally-photographed *Nordeste,* a work by Vaquero Turcios.

A few blocks back through the old town's web, the birthplace of Jovellanos has been turned into the **Museo de Jovellanos** ① *Plaza Jovellanos, T985346313, Tue-Sat 1000-1300, 1700-2000 (Jul/Aug 1100-1330, 1700-2100), Sun 1100-1400, free.* More interesting than the handful of Jovellanos memorabilia are the modern works of Navascués and the massive wooden depiction of the old Gijón fish market by Sebastian Miranda, a work he patiently restarted from scratch after the first was lost during the Civil War. The nearby **Torre del Reloj** ① *Recoletas 5, T985181111, hours as above, free,* houses an exhibition of Gijón's history in a modern clock tower.

Although now a bank, the succinctly named sandstone **Palacio del Marqués de San Esteban del Mar de Natahoyo** is one of Gijon´s most beautiful buildings, particularly in the evening sun. Behind it, the Plaza Mayor leads a double life as stately municipal square and lively hub of cider drinking. **Playa de San Lorenzo** stretches to the east of here, watched over by the Iglesia de San Pedro and a statue of Augustus Caesar, who stands near the entrance to the city's moderately interesting remains of the Roman public baths ① *Tue-Sat 1000-1300, 1700-2000 (Jul/Aug 1100-1330, 1700-2100), Sun 1100-1400, €2.10, combined ticket with Campa Torres, €3, free Tue.* The beach's long boulevard is the natural choice for the evening *paséo.*

At the other end of the beach, the sluggish **Río Piles** is flanked by pleasant parks studded with palms. On the east side, about a 10-minute walk back from the beach, is the **Museo del Pueblo de Asturias** ① *Paseo del Doctor Fleming s/n, T985332244, Tue-Sat 1000-1300, 1700-2000 (Jul/Aug 1100-1330, 1700-2100), Sun 1100-1400, free,* an open-air ethnographic park with reconstructions of various examples of traditional Asturian buildings and life. If you are heading for southwest Asturias, the museum at Grandas de Salime is more engaging. Also in the complex is the **Museo de la Gaita,** devoted to bagpipes from around the world. Bagpipes have a long history in Asturias – the local type has a more austere tone than the Scottish kind. Information (audio) is Spanish only. The museum has a *sidrería*/restaurant with a pleasant terrace. On the other side of the river, by the **Sporting Gijón** stadium, is the busy Sunday **rastro** (flea market).

The east coast

Villaviciosa and around → *Colour map 2, grid A2.*
Set back from the sea on a marshy inlet, Villaviciosa is a busy market town with an attractive historic centre. It's famous for *avellanas* (hazelnuts), but more importantly, it's the foremost producer of cider in Asturias, and is worth a visit even if you don't

fancy a night on the apple sauce. The centre boasts several elegant *indiano* buildings,
as well as a church, the **Iglesia de Santa María de la Oliva** ① *Tue-Sun 1100-1300, 1700-1900*, a Romanesque building with very attractive zig-zagged portals. In a square nearby is a statue of Charles V (I) – intending to make his first entry to Spain a grand one in 1517 he limped ashore at Tazones just north of here, thus making Villaviciosa his first sizeable stop. He stayed at a *palacio* nearby, which is marked with a plaque.

> ❖ *A good time to be in Villaviciosa is Wednesday; market morning.*

A good chunk of the town's population work in the **cider factories**, some of which are open for tours, such as **El Gaitero**, a 10-minute walk from the centre. The tourist office will give details of visiting hours for this and others.

Southwest of Villaviciosa at a distance of about 10 km is the ninth-century Pre-Romanesque **Iglesia de San Salvador de Valdedios** ① *winter Tue-Sun 1100-1300, summer Tue-Sun 1100-1330, 1630-1830, €1.50*, one of the province's finest. It is believed to have been the spiritual centre of the Asturian kingdom and part of a palace complex for Alfonso III and is attractively proportioned with its typical three naves and carved windows. Plenty of paintwork remains, as well as charming leafy capitals and dedicatory inscriptions. Bat-phobes should avoid the place entirely; several of the little creatures call the dark church home.

Lastres and around → *Colour map 1, grid A6.*

Lastres is a quiet fishing port with attractive vistas over the sea and rocky coast. Its steep streets see plenty of summer action, but little at other times, when the town gets on with harvesting *almejas* (clams) and fishing. There's nothing really to see; it's a working town with some decent accommodation and makes a good, relaxing waterside stay, even when the nights are chillier and the seamist rolls over the green hills.

Some 3 km away by road (but a shorter walk) is **Playa La Griega**, an excellent beach morphed strangely by a small river. There are sets of underwhelming dinosaur prints on the southeast side and a decent campsite, see Sleeping.

Ribadesella and around → *Colour map 1, grid A6.*

Ribadesella is a town of two halves, separated by a long bridge. On the western side is the beach, a long, narrow strip of sand with plenty of accommodation and holiday homes. Across the bridge is the fishing port, a more characterful area with plenty of good eating and drinking options, particularly in the summer season. The tourist office is near the bridge on the harbourside. Rio Sella that flows into the sea here is a popular venue for **canoeing.** ▶▶ *For details of tour operators, see page 561.*

Just outside the town is a good place for a break from the beach, the **Cuevas Tito Bustillo** ① *Apr-Sep 1025-1615 Wed-Sun, groups of up to 25 people are admitted every 25 mins but there's a daily limit, so get there earlier rather than later in summer, free on Wed*, a limestone cave complex with some prehistoric art from the Magdalenian culture that created Altamira, only discovered in 1968.

Llanes and around → *Colour map 2, grid A1.*

Llanes is the most important town on this stretch of coast. Although it sees plenty of tourists, it has retained a very pleasant character around its fishing port and walled, pedestrianized medieval centre. The tourist office is located in an old tower within the walled town. There are plenty of good beaches within reasonably easy reach. Llanes was an important whaling town, and still hauls in a good quantity of fish every day; the best spot to see them is in the lonja where they are sold off every day at around midday. There's a tiny beach close to the town walls, **Playa del Sablón**, that soon fills up in summer. For more breathing room, head 20-minutes' walk east to **Playa de Toró**. Note the accent, as for some reason locals never fail to be amused by people calling it 'beach of the bull' (*toro*).

Gaspar Melchor de Jovellanos 1744-1811

It is peculiarly appropriate that Spain's greatest enlightenment reformer and author should have the same name as two of the wise men. Jovellanos was truly a figure of the enlightenment who combined careers in politics , social reform and the law. In addition he was a major literary figure who made important contributions to educational theory.

Born in Asturias in 1744 he initially trained as a priest but moved to the law and started a his career as a magistrate in Sevilla. His reputation as a man of letters is based on his multi-faceted personality which allowed him to develop a variety of writing styles. His literary works published under the name Jovino have a elegant and natural style that have secured his place in the history of Spanish literature. His best known work *Epistola de Fabio a Anfriso* (letter from Fabio to Anfriso) is both philosophical and reflective. He was also a major playwright his *El si de las niñas* introducing melodrama to the Spanish stage.

His wide ranging interests brought him to the attention of the liberal Charles III who unusually for a Spanish monarch saw Spain's forward progress as a practical matter rather than one to be based on a renewal of faith. He was commissioned to report on the condition of agricultural workers and on prisons. Both these works are consided models of their type and were the inspiration for other social reformers. His concern was the application of enlightenment principles of reason and justice as part of a strategy for bringing Spain into the modern age.

His first political career ended with the death of Charles in 1788 and the increasing reaction which followed the French Revolution forced him to return to Asturias where he investigated the conditions in the coalmining industry. Here he also started keeping his famous diary and found time to found the Real Instituto Asturiano, an important carrier of the enlightenment message to this industrial part of Spain. Much to his surprise he was appointed Minister of Justice in 1797 a post he held until 1799 when the changing political climate saw him removed from office.

In 1802 he was arrested on the instigation of the Inquisition and held on Majorca until 1808. While in exile he continued writing and was especially concerned with education. His pedagogical writings and proposed reforms are regarded as important statements of the enlightenment spirit. In 1808 with the French invasion he found himself once again in the field of action as a member of the Supreme National Junta leading resistance against Napoleon. He was declared a Padre de la Patria by the Cortes of Cadiz as the French were closing in. Forced to flee by ship to his native Asturias he became ill during the voyage and died shortly after landing at Puerto de Vega.

Towards Cantabria

The last stretch of Asturias has many beaches and pretty pastures, with looming mountains in the background. Just across in Cantabria, **Devatur** run all kinds of canoeing, rafting, and horseback activities. ▶▶ *For contact details, see page 561.*

● Sleeping

Gijón *p554, map p555*

Gijón bristles with hotels, but many are featureless cells for business travellers. Happily, there are several options with more charm.

L Parador del Molino Viejo, Av Torcuato Fernandez Miranda s/n, T985370511, www.parador.es. This parador, in a suburban setting in a duck-filled park at the eastern end of Gijon, is mostly modern but its restaurant is set within the walls of an old mill. Its next-door neighbour is the Sporting Gijón stadium.

A Hotel Alcomar, C Cabrales 24, T985357011, F985346742. Slightly starchy hotel with an excellent beachfront location. The rooms with a view are predictably lovely and light.

A Hotel Pathos, C Santa Elena 6, T985176400, www.celuisma.com. Refreshingly offbeat modern crashpad. Pop art decorates the walls and each of the small but stylish rooms is dedicated to a 20th-century icon: Jagger, Thatcher, Gandhi? Your choice. Recommended.

B La Casona de Jovellanos, Plazuela de Jovellanos 1, T985341264, hotel-lacasona@jazzfree.com. Simple, elegant rooms in an historic building with characterful wooden *objets*, including an alarming dragonboat prow on the stairs.

C Hotel Miramar, C Santa Lucia 9, T985351008. In the heart of Gijón's shopping and barhopping area, this small boutique-like hotel has just-so rooms.

D Hostal Manjón, Plaza del Marqués 1, T985352378. Very well-located hostel with benevolent management. Rooms with a view are much nicer but at weekends you're better joining the late cider-drinkers in the square rather than letting them keep you awake. Recommended.

E Pensión González, C San Bernardo 30, T985355863. Basic but wholesome option with high ceilings, wooden floorboards, and a significant population of porcelain dogs. Particularly cheap off-season.

Camping

Camping Deva, T985133848, is something of a resort 4 km from town just off the highway, and boasts a swimming pool. The better-equipped of the two.

Camping Gijón, T985365755, is well situated at the tip of the headland to the east of the Playa de Lorenzo.

The east coast *p556*

There are many places to stay in Ribadesella; along the beach is a series of upmarket hotels, while the few cheaper options are in the town. Llanes makes a pretty good base, with plenty of accommodation and eateries.

A La Posada del Rey, C Mayor 11, Llanes, T985401332, www.laposadadelrey.iespana.es. A very attractive tiny hotel near the port, decorated with *cariño* and style by an enterprising and energetic old lady. The tiny but cute bar is another highlight; off-season rooms are significantly cheaper.

A Villa Rosario, C Dionisio Ruíz Sánchez 6, Ribadesella, T985860090, www.hotel villarosario.com, is a very blue and ornate mansion on the beach that could have come out of the Addams Family; one of the best things about the interior is that you can't see the exterior, but the rooms are good, with excellent facilities, some top views and a good restaurant.

B Casa de Paloma Castillo, C Ricardo Cangas 9, Ribadesella, T985860863, is one of the nicer hotels on the beach, and close to the town end.

B Casa España, Plaza Carlos I 3, Villaviciosa, T985892030, www.hcasaespana.com. This friendly and attractively renovated *indiano*-style house has good bedrooms, modern bathrooms, and cheap off-season rates. Heart of town.

B Hotel Eutimio, C San Antonio s/n, Lastres, T985850012, is a well-maintained and modernized old *casona* with friendly staff and a good seafood restaurant.

B Hotel Las Rocas, C Canillejas 3, Llanes, T985402431. A nice, quiet place backing on to the sheltered port.

B Sablón's, El Sablón s/n, Llanes, T985400787. A well-located hotel and restaurant, with views out to sea, and perfect for dashing down after breakfast and staking a claim on the tiny beach.

C Carlos I, Plaza Carlos I 4, Villaviciosa, T985890121, F985890051, is in a smart old *palacio* in the centre of town decorated in period style with modern comfort.

C **Hotel Los Molinos**, Cotiella Bojo s/n, Llanes, T985400464. A reasonable, newish hotel, clean and quiet.

C-D **Miramar**, Bajada al Puerto s/n, Lastres, T985850120, which wins no prizes for the name , but has decent, clean, and slightly boring rooms, some with excellent views. Both hotels are much cheaper off-season.

D-E **Hotel Covadonga**, C Manuel Caso de la Villa 9, Ribadesella, T985857461. A good value and cheerful place with rooms with or without bath above a convivial bar.

D-E **Pensión La Guía**, C Parres Sobrino 1, Llanes, T985402577. A very nice central *pensión* in an old stone building. There's some noise from the road, but it's worth putting up with.

E **Pensión Puerto de Llanes**, overlooking the river in Llanes, this is a slightly shabby but well-placed option.

F **Pensión Sol**, C Sol 27, Villaviciosa, T985891130, a bit tatty but friendly and low priced.

Camping and hostels

Albergue Roberto Frassinelli, C Ricardo Cangas 1, Ribadesella, T985861380, is an official YHA hostel on the beachfront in a ramshackle old building. Reception is only open 1700-2100.

Camping Las Bárcenas, Llanes, T985402887. One of many campsites, this one not far from Toró beach. Jun-Sep.

Camping Los Sauces, Ribadesella, T985861312, near the beach, is the nicer of 2 campsites in the area. It's open from the last week of Jun to mid-Sep.

Costa Verde, T985856373, Jun to Sep, Playa La Griega, near Lastres. A decent campsite.

Ribadesella, the other near Ribadesella, T985858293, is in the small village of Sebreño 1 km inland, has more facilities (including a pool), and is open Apr-Sep.

Eating

Gijón *p554, map p555*

Gijón offers some excellent eating around the Plaza Mayor and the marina. The black spiny *ericios* (sea-urchins) are a local favourite, as are *zamburiñas* (a tasty small scallop).

€€€ **El Puerto**, Paseo de Claudio Alvargonzález s/n, T985349096. Upmarket restaurant on the jetty, whose reputation for seafood makes it a popular destination for people stepping off their yachts. Fairly dark despite the large windows.

€€€ **La Taberna del Piano**, C Cabrales 12, T985342257. Nicely set on the beachfront, with a quality range of dishes and some excellent tapas.

€€ **El Palacio**, Plaza de Marqués 3. Popular cider joint with a restaurant above.

€€ **La Galana**, Plaza Mayor 10, T985358466. Distinguished looking *sidrería* on the main square, with heavy wooden beams and a painted ceiling.

€€ **La Marina**, C Trinidad 9, T985346246. Colourful cider place with an excellent range of tapas laid out on wooden boards.

€€ **Mercante**, Cuesta del Cholo 2, T985350244. A very good harbourside option with an excellent €9 lunch *menù*. In fine weather, a popular choice is to grab a cold drink and sit on the stone wall outside. Recommended.

€€ **Sidrería El Grial**, C Melquiades Alvarez 5, T985344497. Good little basement *sidrería*, which prepares some excellent plates of shellfish, including *zamburiñas*.

€ **Cafetería Victoria**, C Magnus Blikstad 5, T985357020. Half-an-hour until the bus and not sure whether you can fit in a 4-course lunch and coffee? Let this place show you how; its €8.10 *menú* is good and served by speedy staff high on stress (or is that the other way around?).

€ **Gigia**, C Oscar Olivarriá 8 , T985344509. The crates of cider stacked in the corner give a good clue to this bar´s raison d'etre. Also does a good line in seafood.

€ **Las Brasas**, C Instituto 10, T985356331. No-frills *parilla* restaurant with a range of *platos combinados* and *menús*. The half *parilla* can comfortably feed 2 people.

The east coast *p556*

Good eating in Villaviciosa can be had all along C Generalísimo by the town hall. Apart from the hotel restaurants in Ribadesella, most of the characterful eateries and bars are in the old town.

For an explanation of sleeping and eating price codes used in this guide, see inside the front cover. Other relevant information is found in Essentials, see pages 47-56.

€€ **Covadonga**, C Manuel Cue 6, Llanes. One of Llanes's best restaurants with good meat dishes as well as the expected seafood. Book ahead in summer.

€€ **El Rompeolas**, C Manuel Fernández de Juncos 13. A massive bar and restaurant with a good range of seafood and snacks.

€€ **Hotel Eutimio**, see Sleeping, Lastres, closed Mon, good seafood restaurant.

€€ **La Terraza**, Av San Pablo s/n, Llanes. Atmospheric *sidrería* with some excellent food, but also a good place to sit in the courtyard and down cider on a hot day.

€€ **Mesón El Galeón**, C Mayor 20, Llanes. A very good seafood restaurant in the old town near the port. What's on offer encouragingly depends on the catch.

€€ **Sidrería Carroceu**, C del Marqués de Argüelles 25, T985861419. A good harbourside venue for classy seafood and cider, a typical Asturian combination.

€ **Azor**, C San Antonio 18, Lastres, is a great place to hang out with a drink, with floor-to-ceiling windows, great view, daggy 80s beach decor and a monster dog.

€ **Bar Casa del Mar**, C del Muelle s/n, Llanes. Underneath the ugly fishermen's club, this cheap place serves excellent fish to locals. *Menú del día* on offer for €7.

€ **Bar Del Puerto**, Paseo del Puerto s/n, has not a frill in sight, but their grilled sardines are a treat for €6; good range of other fish.

€ **El Cafetín**, C Pedroyes s/n, Lastres, T985850085, just above the tourist office. A decent bite can be had here though It's hardly inspired, and the wooden seats are a penance, but some of the stews and seafood are pretty good and cheap too.

€ **El Congreso de Benjamín**, C Generalísimo 25, Villaviciosa, T985891180, is good and has a *menú* for €9.65.

€ **Gran Café de Vicente**, C Malrayo s/n, Villaviciosa, does good pastries.

€ **Sidrería El Almacen**, C Posada Herrera, Llanes. Good place for fish and apple sauce.

🍷 Bars and clubs

Gijón *p554, map p555*
The small streets around C Santa Lucía are a mass of bars, many operating only at week-ends. For every bar calling last orders in the early hours, another is probably just throwing open its doors. Other places include:

Anticuario, C San Antonio 9. A popular white-collar type of bar.

Blue Sky Café, C San Antonio 6, this bar is dark, sleek, and styled.

La Botica del Indiano, Plaza Mayor. Kitted out with all manner of decoration from Old Habana, this is a convivial bar-café.

La Turuta, C Avé María 21. With posters of Ché Guevara and Bob Marley on the walls, this relaxed Cimadevilla bar has what is euphemistically called a liberal atmosphere.

Varsovia, C Cabrales 18. A grungy venue on the beachfront with live music on Fri/Sat and a quieter upstairs bar.

🎭 Entertainment

Gijón *p554, map p555*
The most convenient cinema to the centre of town is **Cines Centro**, behind Playa San Lorenzo in a shopping centre off C San Agustín; T985353757.

🥾 Activities and tours

The east coast *p556*
Llanes has a golf course east of town.
Devantur, Edificio Estación s/n, Unquera, T942717033, Cantabria.
Güe, C El Castillo s/n, T985402430, run a variety of excursions in the surrounding area, including canoeing on the Río Sella.

🚌 Transport

Gijón *p554, map p555*
Bus Local services run very regularly to **Oviedo** (30 mins) and **Avilés** (30-40 mins). Long-distance services run to **A Coruña** (6 hrs), **Santiago** (7 hrs), **León** (2 hrs), **Valladolid** (4 hrs), **Madrid** (6 hrs), **Santander** (3 hrs), and **Bilbao** (5 hrs), among many other destinations. Nearly all of these services stop at both **Gijón** and **Oviedo**.
Train Connections to **Santander** (2 through trains daily; 4 hrs), **Bilbao** (1 per day; 6½ hrs), and westwards as far as **Ferrol** in **Galicia** (2 per day, 6½ hrs). More regular services run to **Llanes**, **Cudillero**, and **Avilés**. RENFE station is west of the centre on Avda de Juan Carlos I, about 15-min walk from the old centre. RENFE links **Gijón** with **León** (7 per day; 2½ hrs), **Madrid** (3 per day; 6½ hrs), **Barcelona** (2 per day, 12½ hrs), and points in

between. The bus is generally quicker on these routes.

The east coast *p556*
From **Villaviciosa** there are several **buses** a day to **Oviedo** and **Gijón**, and some heading east to **Lastres** and beyond. **Llanes** is linked by this service too and it continues east to **Santander**. The **train** also reaches these towns, and other coastal destinations.

---

❶ Directory

Gijón *p554, map p555*
Internet **Ciber del Muelle**, on the harbour, C Claudio Alvargonzález 4, T985190252, is a

decent cybercafé, Sun-Fri 1100-2200, Sat 1100-0300; €1.50-1.95 per hr.
Post The main post office is on Plaza 6 de Agosto to the south of the centre, not far from the bus station.
Telephone There are *locutórios* in the FEVE station, and on the boulevard above Playa de San Lorenzo, at the western end.

The east coast *p556*
Internet There's internet access for €3 per hr at the **Hotel La Ría** on C Marqués de Villaviciosa 5, Villaviciosa, T985891555; **Cyberspacio**, Av de la Paz 5, Llanes. Slow Internet connection.

Avilés and western Asturias

→ *Colour map 1, grid A5.*

Like Hans Christian Andersen's ugly duckling, the reputation of Avilés is slowly changing from grim to vivid. For a long time, the only travellers to pass through this large industrial centre were businessmen under company orders. Now, having tackled its pollution problems, the city is capitalizing on its major asset, a remarkably beautiful historic centre, the quality of it's eateries, and the openness of the people.

The coast west of Asturias is a rugged green landscape, speckled with fishing villages and gouged by deep ravines. The fishing towns of Cudillero, Luarca, and Tapia bristle with character, and there are many excellent beaches, some with good surf breaks. Southwestern Asturias is something of a wilderness, where some of the steep green valleys still contain villages that are not accessible by road. It's a hillwalker's paradise: there are several good bases with a range of marked trails. In the far southwest corner of Asturias, the Parque Nacional Muniellos is worth applying to visit – its old growth European forest is home to several endangered species, including a small community of bears. ▸▸ *For Sleeping, Eating and other listings, see pages 566-570.*

Ins and outs
Getting there and around The FEVE line from Gijón and Oviedo to Galicia follows this coast faithfully, although the stations tend to be at a short distance from the town centres. In Avilés, as with the bus station, it is a 15-minute walk. ALSA buses are much more frequent. Travelling away from the coast is a different matter. It is generally The system of local buses, although slow and infrequent, has fairly good coverage. ▸▸ *For further details, see Transport page 570.*
Tourist information Avilés's tourist office ① *C Ruiz Gómez 21, T985544325, a block down from Plaza de España.*

Sights

The heart of Avilés is **Plaza de España**, from which a number of pedestrian streets radiate. One side of it is occupied by the Ayuntamiento, an attractive arched

⁝ Kiss of death

El Cambaral was the most famous of the Moorish pirates who terrorized the Cantabrian and Asturian coasts.

The scourge of local shipping, he was finally tricked by a local knight who put to sea in an apparently harmless ship bristling with hidden soldiers. El Cambaral was wounded and captured. The knight took him home, as the trial had to wait until he had healed, but foolishly let his young daughter tend to the pirate's wounds. The two predictably fell in love and decided to elope. Reaching the port, where a boat was waiting, they stopped for a kiss, thinking themselves safe, but the enraged knight had been warned. Arriving at the quay, he chopped off both the kissers' heads with one blow. Luarca remembers the ill-fated couple in the name of its bridge *El Beso* (The Kiss) and the fisherman's quarter, named El Pirata Cambaral.

building that is a symbol of the post-medieval expansion of the town. Opposite is the sombre bulk of the **Palacio del Marqués de Ferrera**, in the process of being converted into a parador.

From the Plaza de España (many locals refer to it as the Plaza Mayor), **Calle San Francisco** runs up to the **Plaza Domingo A Acebal**, where it becomes the colonnaded **Calle Galiana**. This whole area is lined with bars and cafés, several of which have tables outdoors. It's a popular and recommended evening meeting spot. Calle San Francisco is dominated by the 13th-century **Iglesia de San Nicolas de Bari** with a pretty Romanesque cloister, now partly occupied by a school. In front is the quirky **Fuente de los Caños** (fountain of the spouts), which pours water into a basin from six lugubrious bearded faces. Further up Calle Galiana, the **Parque de Ferrera** was part of the impressive backyard of the counts of Ferrera before being given over to public use. It's now a rambling network of paths filled with strolling *avilesinos*.

On the other side of Plaza de España, Calle Ferrería leads into the oldest part of town; this part of the city was originally walled. At the bottom of the street are the early **Gothic Capilla de los Alas**, and the earlier **Iglesia de los Padres Franciscanos**, a church started in the late 12th century. Its sandy Romanesque façade is appealing; inside is the tomb of a notable *avilesino*, Pedro Menéndez, who founded the city of San Agustín in Florida, which claims to be the oldest city in the USA (Saint Augustine). West of here, in the **Plaza Camposagrado**, is a statue of another famous local, the hairy Juan Carreño de Miranda, a notable 17th-century Spanish painter. He is looking more than slightly annoyed, possibly at the shabby state that the formerly elegant palace opposite him is in. A few blocks further west again, past the waterfront park of **El Muelle**, is Avilés's prettiest square, the **Plaza del Carbayo**. This is in the *barrio* of **Sabugo**, which was where the majority of Avilés fisherfolk lived. It was almost a separate town, and this was its centre, where whaling and fishing expeditions were planned. Walking back towards town along Calle Bances Candamo gives further flavour of this tiny district.

West coast Asturias

Salinas → *Colour map 1, grid A5.*

The nearby town of Salinas is a fairly bland place whose raison d'etre is its long, sandy beach, thronged in summer but quiet at other times. At its western end is one of Asturias's best restaurants (see below), and a good view can be had from the headland; there's also a vaguely surreal collection of anchors.

The houses of this small fishing town are steeply arrayed around the harbour like the audience in a small theatre. Its picturesque setting and fishing harbour small enough not to have any unsightly associated industry have made this prime outing territory during summer holidays. Entirely dormant during winter, in season Cudillero makes a good destination, having enough restaurants and bars to keep things interesting, but still a long way from being a resort. The town, called Cuideiru in Bable, effectively has just one street, which winds its way down the hill to the harbour. There's not a lot to see; the setting of the town itself is the main attraction. Most of the action takes place around the waterfront, where the smell of grilling fish is all-pervading at lunchtime.

There are some wildly shaped cliffs in this area, and while the summer sea might seem almost Mediterranean, in winter the waves give the sea wall a very healthy pounding. The village of **El Pito**, just off the main road east of town, has its own FEVE station and a few accommodation options. It's an attractive walk down into the town but a daunting return trip!

Luarca → *Colour map 1, grid A4.*

While it receives large numbers of tourists in summer, drawn by its attractive harbour and plentiful facilities, Luarca gives the refreshing impression that fishing remains its primary concern. While it has grown a little since Borrow exclaimed that it "stands in a deep hollow...it is impossible to descry the town until you stand just above it", it's still a compact place, centred around the Rio Negro, which often seems in danger of relegation to 'stream' status. Luarca was formerly a big whaling port; the whale still has a proud place on the coat of arms.

Once again, the **harbour** is the biggest attraction, filled with colourful boats of all sizes. A variety of restaurants line it; beyond them you can walk around to the sea wall and watch it take a fearful pounding if the sea is in the mood. At the other end of the harbour is the **beach**, a pretty apologetic affair with dirty grey sand and lined with changing huts. A much better beach is Playa de Tauran, a few kilometres west.

Just by the water opposite the church is the lonja, where the fresh-caught fish is sold in the middle of the day. It's decorated with tiled murals depicting the town's fishing history, one of which shows the curious custom of deciding whether to put to sea or not in bad weather. A model of a house and of a boat were put at opposite ends of a table and the fishermen lined up according to their preference. If more chose to stay home, nobody was to go to sea.

As with much of the coastline, the **tourist office** ① *T985640083, Easter-Sep, Mon-Fri 1230-1400, 1630-2100,* is only open in summer. It's by the river on Paseo del Pilarin. The library on the hill behind it usually has free maps to hand out.

Navia and around → *Colour map 1, grid A4.*

At the mouth of the river of the same name, Navia is a more commercial port than the others on this coast, with a significant boatbuilding and plastics industry. It can be a noisy place, with trucks and buses shuddering through town to and from Galicia. Unlike most of the others, Navia's charm is definitely to be found away from its harbour, in the narrow paved streets above.

The valley of the Rio Navia, winding inland to **Grandas de Salime** and beyond, is one of Asturias's natural highlights, dotted with Celtic *castros*, small hillforts, most of which are between 2,000 to 2,500 years old. While some of the remoter ones are well worth exploring with transport, the most accessible is at **Coaña** ① *4 km from Navia, Oct-Mar Tue-Fri 1100-1500, Sat-Sun 1100-1500, 1600-1900; Apr-Sep Tue-Sun 1100-1400, 1600-1900, closed Mon, €1.30.* It's an impressive, well-conserved structure commanding a spur in the valley. There's a café and a small visitor's centre. Infrequent buses run from Navia. If you want to walk, cross the bridge over the river and take the first road on the left. The fort is a short way past the village of Coaña.

⁝ Cider house rules

Wine may be Bacchus' choice of drink in the rest of Spain but in Asturias it is cider that is to found when refreshment is needed. Drunk all over the province in thousands of *sidrerías*, *sidra* has developed a complex ritual of its own that a times seems as mysterious as the Japanese tea ceremony. Ordered by the bottle, and not by the glass, Asturian cider is a medium-strength drink containing around 6% alcohol.

The most obvious aspect to the ritual is the method of pouring for which a special word escanciar has been developed. It is a case of once seen never forgotten as the waiter holds aloft the crystal-like bottle of cider and pours it from arms length into a glass without looking. This is is done not just for show but to create bubbles in the cider which are an essential part of the drinking process. The smaller the bubbles the higher the quality of the cider.

The drinker then has a small period of grace known as the espalmar during which the bubbles remain in the glass and the cider must be drunk. Normally a maximum of 10 seconds. So a leisurely sip is not the norm for Asturian drinkers who normally down the glass or culín in one. Normal practice is then to wait for the eagle-eyed master of ceremonies to refill the glass. However those feeling a little

impatient or emboldened after a bottle or two are welcome to try themselves. Just be prepared to smell of fermented apples for the rest of the evening.

The different types of cider are a result of the different blends of apples used. There are around 20 different varieties used in Asturias each one falling into a different category of sweetness. Usually the cider will be made of 80% dry and semi-dry varieties. The apples are harvested between the middle of September and mid October and important local festivals are based around the harvest. The best known one is in Villaviciosa. Another important cider festival is held in Nava on the 11 and 12 of July each year.

Not surprisingly given the importance of cider in Asturian culture it is widely used in local cooking. Most siderorías will produce there own dishes with cider added as a flavouring. For those feeling a bit jaded with classic Spanish cooking this can come as a welcome change. It is important to realize though that more than three bottles may seriously impair the dinners judgment. Local people are reported to have a number of traditional hangover cures all of which will be denied the intemperate visitor. You have been warned.

Asturias West coast Asturias

Tapia de Casariego and around → *Colour map 1, grid A4.*

Tapia, one of the most relaxed places on this coast, deserves a look. While there is a small harbour, the town's beautiful beach deservedly is the main attraction. There's a small surf community here, established by the semi-mythical Gooley brothers; two Aussies who fetched up in a camper van one day in the 1970s, and it certainly feels more like a beach town than a fishing port. The town itself is charming, with a quiet elegance radiating from its whitewashed stone buildings and peaceful plazas watched over by the dominant Christ on the church tower. Opposite the church, there's a small tourist information kiosk open in summer. Apart from Tapia, the best surf beaches are **Peñarronda** to the west, where there are two campsites, and **Frejulfe**, further east. Waves also get caught under the bridge that crosses into Galicia.

Towards the Galician border

Asturias ends at the Ria de Ribadeo, a broad estuary at the mouth of the River Eo, notable for the cultivation of shellfish. The N634 highway blazes straight on over a massive bridge into Galicia. While the main town in this area, Ribadeo, is across the water, Asturias still has a little more to offer in the village of **Castropol**, with a great setting on the estuary. This onion-like village is a peaceful and seldom visited gem. Formerly an important ferry crossing, it has been completely bypassed by the massive bridge, and now does little but cater to passing traffic on the Lugo road. If you've got a spare hour or two, it won't be wasted exploring the narrow streets of this lovely place. The central plaza contains a memorial to the Spanish-American war of 1898. The naval defeats of this war, and subsequent decline in shipping due to the loss of all Spain's remaining colonies, was a big factor in the decline of towns on this coastline.

Southwest Asturias

Taramundi and around

More easily accessed from the coast, the road to Taramundi beetles up green valleys where mules and donkeys still draw carts and herds of cows take priority over through traffic.The village itself is an earthy place, which draws its fair share of summer tourists, many of whom are attracted by its numerous knife workshops. The Taramundi blades are renowned throughout Spain; the range available runs from professional-standard kitchen knives to carved tourist souvenirs. Most of the workshops welcome visitors – there are plenty to choose from. Taramundi is only a couple of kilometres from Galicia, and the locals speak a bewildering mixture of *bable* and *gallego* that they cheerfully admit is incomprehensible to outsiders.

> There are a number of walking trails in the area, most of which are wellmarked.

In the valley around Taramundi are a number of ethnographic projects, where traditional Asturian crafts and industries have been re-established. The best of these is possibly **Teixois**, in an idyllic wooded valley with a working mill and forge powered by the stream. If there aren't many people about, it feels uncannily like you've just stepped back in time. There's a small restaurant, which cheerfully serves up simple but abundant food, much of it produced by the local projects. Teixois is about one-hour's walk from Taramundi – head straight down the hill and follow the signs. The road passes near several of the other projects en route.

Grandas de Salime → *Colour map 1, grid A4.*

This sleepy little municipal centre is notable for an excellent museum, the **Museo Etnográfico** ① *Tue-Sat 1130-1400, 1600-1830, Sun 1130-1430 (1930 in Jul/Aug, including Sun), closed Mon, €1.50,* an ambitious and enthusiastic project that seeks to recreate in one place a range of traditional Asturian crafts, industries, and daily life. Working mills, grape presses, and pedal-operated lathes are fascinatingly and lovingly put to work by the informative staff. Here you can see the making of the characteristic *madreñas*, wooden clogs worn over shoes when working outdoors, still very much in use. It's an important project and indicative of the deep pride Asturians hold for their heritage.

● Sleeping

Avilés *p562*

The most luxurious place to stay will undoubtedly be the parador in the palace on the Plaza de España. The cheapest places are inconvenient for the old centre, and are often full of longer-term residents.

B **Hotel de la Villa**, Plaza Domíngo A, Acebal 4, T/F985129704. Well-situated looking over a pleasant plaza and the church of San Nicolas de Bari. Rooms are appealing, with

dark wood floors and prints of Kandinsky and Klee.

C Hotel Don Pedro, C La Fruta 22, T985512288, donpedro@asturvia.cajastur.es. Small hotel run out of a busy café. The stone-faced rooms are charmingly grotto-like and have a slightly Arabian feel. Recommended.

D Pensión La Fruta, opposite the Don Pedro and part of it. Well-equipped *pensión* run by the friendly Don Pedro. Every room with own bathroom (either ensuite or next to room), and TV. Recommended.

West coast Asturias *p563*

Several of the hotels in Luarca shut for Jan and Feb. Places in Tapia is unremarkable but adequate. There are 2 hotels on the main road in Castropol. Unfortunately, both are uninspiring motel-style set-ups.

A-C Hotel Palacio Arias, Av Emigrantes 11, Navia, T985473675, F985473683. One of the most lavish and eccentric *indiano* constructions in western Asturias, surrounded by the trademark walled garden and furnished in period style. The hotel's modern annexe offers cheaper but less characterful accommodation. Neither section is immune from the noise of the road, widely known as Av José Antonio.

B Hotel Gayoso, Plaza Alfonso X, Luarca, T985640050. Founded in 1860 but refurbished since, this hotel offers some sharp off-season prices.

B La Casona de la Paca, Cudillero, T985591303, www.casonadelapaca.com. In El Pito, this red 3-storey house is a typical *casa de indiano* with a walled garden. Fairly formal in style, a relaxing and secluded hideaway. Turning left out of the El Pito station, it's 5-min walk on the right. Closed Jan.

B San Antón, Tapia, Plaza San Blas 2, T985628000. Uninspiring and ugly brick hotel with clean and well-appointed rooms.

C Hotel Baltico, Paseo del Muelle 1, Luarca, T985470134. Stolid but adequate hotel well situated on the harbour.

C La Casona del Pio, C Riofrío 3, Cudillero, T985591512, www.arrakis.es/~casonadepio/. Beautiful stone hotel and restaurant just off the harbour. Welcoming rooms with hydromassage mini-tubs. Warm service. Closed Jan. Recommended.

C La Colmena, C Uría 2, Luarca, T985640278, lacolmena@infonegocio.com. Smallish but

newly refurbished rooms with attractive wooden floors and furnishings and plenty of light.

C La Xungeira, Tapia, T985628213. Right by the beach, the best option in Tapia. Pastel-shaded rooms are unoriginal but blameless. Significant off-season discounts.

C Peña Mar, Carretera General s/n, Castropol, T985635481. The best of the two uninspiring motel-style options.

D Casa Vicente, opposite Peña Mar, T985635051, the other uninspiring motel.

D Hotel Arco Navia, C San Francisco 2, Navia, T/F985473495, www.hotelelarco.com. Attractive slate building by an arch on an historic medieval street. St Francis is said to have stayed in what is now the hotel's rental apartments.

D Hotel La Ruta, Av Primo de Rivera 38, Tapia , T985628138. Directly opposite and similar, with larger rooms, but a little noisier and not as hospitable.

D Hotel Puente de los Santos, Av Primo de Rivera 31, Tapia, T985628155, F985628437. On the main road, where the buses stop. You've seen it in several other beach towns, but it's friendly enough and comfy.

D Hotel Rico, Plaza Alfonso X, Luarca, T985470585. Value-packed rooms above a café with TV and ensuite. Heated debates from downstairs can echo through the building. Recommended.

D Pensión Alver, C García de la Concha 8, Cudillero, T985591528. A friendly option. Open Easter-Sep.

D Pensión El Camarote, C García de la Concha 4, Cudillero, T985591202. In the top half of the main street, an upmarket *pensión* with well-equipped rooms. Open Apr-Sep.

D-E Hotel Oria, C Crucero 7, Luarca, T985640385. Pretty good option by the river; rooms both with and without bathroom.

E Pensión Alvaro, Cudillero, T985590204. By the FEVE station in El Pito. Clean, cheap and comfortable, but not terribly convenient. Open Apr-Sep.

E Pensión Cantábrico, C Mariano Luiña 12, Navia, T985474177. Fairly large *pensión* with well-priced rooms.

E Pensión Moderna, C Crucero 2, Luarca, T985640057. A simple, old-style *pensión* with 3 spotless doubles and polished floors.

E **Pensión San Franciso**, C San Francisco s/n, Navia, T985631351. On a tiny plaza, this white-washed *pensión* is clean, simple and cool. The area around Taramundi is brimming with **casas de aldea**. Two to consider are **Freixe**, T985621215, near the village of Barcia, and **Aniceto**, T985646853, a small nucleus of houses in Bres. Pricier, but with unbeatable character and setting is **Las Veigas**, T987540593, where, as part of the ethnographic project, a deserted village has been restored to life; the two buildings of the priest's house can be rented.

Camping

Camping Cudillero, Cudillero, T985590663, is the nicer of the two (**L'Amuravela**) but both slightly inconvenient for town.
Camping Playa de Tapia, Tapia , T985472721. On the other side of the beach from town, this summer-only campsite has reasonable facilities. Road access a couple of kilometres west of town but on foot it's much quicker across the beach.
L'Amuravela, Cudillero, T985590995, boasts a swimming pool. Handy for the beach.
Playa del Tauran, Luarca, T985641272. The best campsite in this part of Asturias, on a clifftop west of Luarca with access to a small cove beach. Excellent atmosphere and facilities. Bar, shop, and cabins can all be found among the eucalyptus. It is located some 3 km from the main road, near the hamlet of San Martín. Quicker access by foot from the far end of Luarca beach. Open Easter-Sep. Recommended.

Southwest Asturias *p566*

AL **La Rectoral**, Cuesta de la Rectoral s/n, Taramundi, T985646760, F 985646777. Historic hotel housed in the 18th-century building that used to be the home of the parish priest, with superb views over a fairytale valley. Rooms of the highest comfort factor – the best have balconies overlooking the valley, as does the dining room.
D **Casa Petronila**, Calle Mayor s/n, Taramundi, T985646874, www.tara mundi.net/web/Petronila/petronila.htm. Attractive rooms in an old stone building on the main street.
D **Hotel Taramundi**, C Mayor s/n, Taramundi, T985646727, www.hoteltara mundi.com. Friendly hotel with bedrooms plum-full of homely Asturian comfort. Recommended.
E **Pensión La Esquina**, C Mayor s/n, T985646736. Cheapest beds in town in a simple *pensión* above a café. Small and comfy (except for the tall – the beds have footboards). Owner is building an annexe opposite, for rooms with more facilities.

🍴 Eating

Avilés *p562*

Avilés is an excellent place for eating out; especially C Galiana and the old streets north of Plaza de España.
€€€ **Casa Tataguyo**, Plaza del Carbayedo 6 (unsigned), T985564815. Amazing split-personality place that has been an Avilés legend for years. The front bar dishes out cheap workers' lunches at shared tables in a satisfyingly no-frills atmosphere. At the back is an expensive, attractive 2-level restaurant.
€€€ **Real Balneario**, Av Juan Sitges 3, Salinas, T985518613. One of Asturias's top restaurants, beautifully set on the beach at Salinas. Predictably specializing in seafood, the €17 lunch *menú* is definitely the most economical way to enjoy the haute cuisine.
€€ **Casa Lin**, Av de los Telares 3, T985564827. Historic *sidrería* near the station serving up excellent seafood and a well-poured apple-juice.
€€ **L'Alfareria**, C La Ferrería 25, T985546834. Restaurant in an old pottery with a pleasant conservatory-style dining area.
€€ **La Araña**, Plaza del Carbayo 15, T985562268. Dark, cave-like restaurant on this beautiful square. High quality Asturian and Castilian fare and plenty of it. Recommended.
€€ **La Serrana**, C La Fruta 9, T985565840. Spacious seafood restaurant under the **Luzana hotel** with a good-value lunch *menú* for €9.62. Bags more character than the hotel.
€ **Casa Nina**, C Del Sol 6, T985551601. Homely little 1st-floor restaurant with simple and authentic Asturian fare.
€ **La Coruxa**, Plaza del Carbayo 16, T985565381. Another restaurant on this fine square, with a small upstairs *comedor* and a bar downstairs. Unpretentious and good-quality food.

Tapas bars and cafés

Café Don Pedro, in the hotel of the same name and decorated in similar stony style. Good coffee.

Cafeteria Delfín, Plaza Domingo A Acebal 7. Does a range of rolls and snacks best consumed from its shady outdoor tables on the attractive square.

Cafetón, C Del Sol 4, cosy bar/café with board games and a happy bohemian crowd.

West coast Asturias *p563*

There are plenty of seafood 'n' cider places of varying quality in Cudillero, many featuring meet-your-meal style aquarium tanks. The majority of restaurants and bars in Tapia are huddled around the harbour. Fresh fish is understandably their stock-in-trade.

€€€ **Casa Mariño**, Concha de Artedo, Cudillero, T985590186. A couple of kilometres west of town, this cheery yellow restaurant is superbly situated on a headland overlooking the coast.

€€€ **La Barcarola**, C Las Armas 15, Navia, T985474528. Fairly upmarket restaurant in a heavy 3-storey stone building in the old part of town. Attractive interior with dark wood and soft, coloured lights. Good reputation in these parts, particularly for seafood rices.

€€€ **La Casona del Pio**, Cudillero, see Sleeping, has an excellent seafood restaurant in its slate dining room with layered wooden ceiling. The philosophy is to produce '*cocina de siempre*' with high-quality ingredients; they succeed. Lunch *menú* for €18.

€€€ **Restaurante Sport**, C Rivero 8, Luarca, T985641078. Smart harbour side joint specializing in shellfish, including river oysters from the nearby Eo.

€€€ **Villa Blanca**, Av de Galicia 25, Luarca, T985641035. The gourmet option in town, with a choice of dining rooms. The seafood is of excellent quality, as you would expect from this proud fishing town, paintings of which decorate the walls.

€€ **El Barómetro**, Paseo de la Muelle 4, Luarca, T985470662. This is an excellent seafood restaurant. Try the *oricios* (sea urchins; more usually called *erizos*), which have an unusual but acquirable taste. Recommended.

€€ **El Bote**, C Marqués de Casariego 30, in Tapia, T985628282, a thoughtful seafood restaurant with a homely feel.

€€ **El Risón**, Castropol, is best place for a meal or a drink here. A friendly and peaceful place on the water with outdoor tables looking over the oyster and clam beds of the *ria*, and over to Ribadeo in Galicia.

€€ **Meson de la Mar**, Paseo de la Muelle 35, Luarca, T985640994. Massive old stone building on the harbour with plenty of character and a big range of *menús*.

€€ **Restaurante Isabel**, C La Ribera 1, Cudillero, T985590211. Bang on the harbour with lifebuoy-and-anchor style nautical decor but top seafood.

€ **Bar Julio**, Cudillero, a good café on the harbour. Sitting on the outside terrace you can keep tabs on the whole town stretching up above you.

€ **Café Martinéz**, corner of C Mariano Luiña and Av de los Emigrantes, Navia. Good lunch option with a €6 *menú*.

€ **Café Riesgo**, C Uría 6, Luarca. Pleasant 1st-floor café with plenty of window space for contemplation.

€ **Cambaral**, C Rivero 14, Luarca, named after the swashbuckling pirate, see p563, this is another good tapas and drinks option.

€ **El Ancla**, C Riofrío 2, Cudillero, T985590023. Seafood restaurant specialising in *paella* and a mixed seafood *parillada*, but also does a range of *raciones* and tapas.

€ **El Baltico**, Paseo del Muelle 1, Luarca, T985470134. Another good option on the harbour, under the hotel. A big range of seafood with a lunch *menú* for €7.

€ **El Cuadrante**, C Rivero 10, Luarca, T985640797. Yet another harbourfront eatery cooking up the finny tribes, with a lunch *menú* for €7.50.

€ **El Sotanillo**, C Mariano Luiña 24, Navia, T985630884. Restaurant with a range of seafood with a good *menú del día*. Café upstairs does a range of snacks.

€ **La Cubierta**, C/Travesia del Dr Enrique Iglesias Alvarez, in Tapia, T985471016. A good *sidrería* with massive *raciones*.

€ **Sidrería El Ancla**, Paseo del Muelle, Luarca. This inexpensive and buzzy bar does a good range of tapas.

Southwest Asturias *p566*

See also Sleeping.

€€€ **Hotel Taramundi**, Taramundi, one of the three hotels with a restaurant, is particularly hospitable, with excellent food.

€ **Pantaramundi**, Taramundi, is a friendly café and good for snacks.

€ **Sidrería Folleiro**, Taramundi, further down the hill from **Pantaramundi**, another decent place.

🍸 Bars and clubs

West coast Asturias *p563*
El Bar de Siñe, C Las Armas 17, Navia. A good bar on one of Navia's nicest streets.
El Faro, Tapia, is a friendly bar by the harbour decorated with photos and paintings of lighthouses.
Te Beo, Av del Muelle, Navia. One of Navia's best bars, with a good range of beers.
Txomi and **La Luna**, Cudillero, are the summer nightspot options, happy places but definitely not at the cutting edge of the international music scene.

🎉 Festivals and events

Avilés *p562*
Carnaval, known as Antroxu, at **Easter** in Avilés is big and getting bigger every year. The town happily submits to a week of parties and events centred around the Plaza de España. On the Sat, C Galiana sees a riotous procession of boats on a river of foam, while the Tue hosts a more traditional, but equally boisterous, procession.
Ash Wednesday sees the traditional Burial of the Sardine. Accommodation is tight, but FEVE run trains all night from Gijón and Oviedo on the major nights.

▲▲ Activities and tours

West coast Asturias *p563*
Jatay, based 3 km west of Luarca, organizes tours on horses and quad-buggies in the area; on more of a holiday-fun than serious trekking footing. T985640433.
Valdés Aventura, Luarca, T689148295, organize more serious adventures on mountain bikes and horses.

Southwest Asturias *p566*
Ondabrava, Taramundi, T985626002, based in Castropol, organize an excellent range of activities over southwest Asturias.

◎ Transport

Avilés *p562*
RENFE, FEVE and bus stations are all together on Av de los Telares on the waterfront to the west of the old town, and about 15-mins' walk. Both RENFE and FEVE connect the town frequently with both **Oviedo** and **Gijón** (35 to 40 mins), as does the bus company ALSA. Avilés is a good point for connecting with buses for western Asturias.

West coast Asturias *p563*
Salinas can be reached by city buses 1 and 11 from Avilés bus station.
The bus station in **Luarca** is next to El Arbol supermarket on Paseo de Gómez on the river, while the FEVE station is a little further upstream, on the accurately named Avenida de la Estación, 10-mins' walk from the centre of town.
The railway station in **Cudillero** is at the top of the town, while ALSA services only stop on the main road about half-an-hour's walk away. A few make it into town; these mostly go to/from **Avilés**.
In **Navia** the FEVE station is on Av Manuel Suaréz. There are 3 services a day to and from **Oviedo** (2 of which continue to Galicia). ALSA station is on the main road, Av de los Emigrantes. **Autos Piñeiro** service the **Navia Valley** to **Grandas de Salime**.
In **Tapia** ALSA buses stop on Av Primo de Rivera in the centre of town. FEVE station is an inconvenient 20-min walk.

Southwest Asturias *p566*
Taramundi can be reached by bus from **Vegadeo**, on the N640 that links **Lugo** with the **Asturian coast**.

❶ Directory

Avilés *p562*
Internet There is a **Laser** Internet café, C Rivero 83, T985542529, charging is €0.05 per min.
Post The main post office is on Plaza Alfonso VI, just north of Plaza de España.

✸ Footprint features

Introduction

"Spaniards, strive to imitate the inimitable Galicians,"
Duke of Wellington

Remote Galicia's Celtic history can still be keenly felt in this northwestern region of Spain, about the size of Belgium. It's dotted with hill villages and dolmens, and the gaita, or bagpipe, is a strong element of Galicia's musical heritage. Another point it shares with other Celtic nations is its rainfall, which is high; in the northwest, for example, it rains 150 days of the year.

The course of Galicia's history was changed forever when the tomb of the apostle St James was allegedly discovered. Pilgrims flocked from across Europe, as they have recently started to do again, and the noble granite city of **Santiago de Compostela** that grew up around the tomb is a fitting welcome for them. Apart from religion, fishing is Galicia's main business; the ports of **Vigo** and around furnish much of Spain with its fish, and shellfish are intensively farmed in the sheltered rías (inlets).

The variety of Galicia's rural and urban landscapes make it a fascinating part of the country; the unifying factor is the seafood, which is uniformly superb, particularly the 'national' dish, pulpo (octopus), which is deliciously served in no-frills pulperías and gourmet restaurants.

Galicians have a reputation for being superstitious and introspective, not hard to understand when you've seen the Atlantic storms in full force. A Celtic melancholy known as morriña is also a feature, expressed in the poems of Galicia's favourite writer, Rosalía de Castro. To visitors, though, gallegos are generous and friendly; the region's cities are as open and convivial as anywhere in Northern Spain.

★ Don't miss...

❶ Santiago de Compostela Visit Santiago and its iconic cathedral, particularly if you've walked five weeks to do it, page 574.

❷ A Coruña Kick back here, one of the nicest cities in northern Spain, page 591.

❸ Vigo Dine on octopus and *albariño* wine in gritty, fascinating Vigo, after a day at the beautifully unspoilt Islas Cíes, page 606.

❹ Pontevedra and Ourense Probe the pretty squares of these towns, pages 605 and 616.

❺ Lugo March the walls of Lugo with a Roman soldier stance, page 584.

❻ Cabo Finisterre Gaze out at the limitless Atlantic from Cabo Finisterre, the end of the earth, page 601.

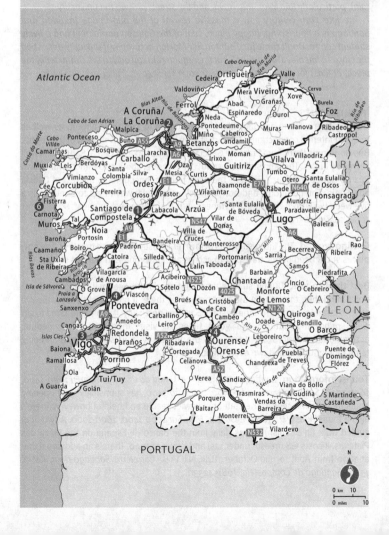

Santiago de Compostela

"The true capital of Spain", Cees Nooteboom, *Roads to Santiago*.

→ *Phone code: 981; Colour map 1, grid B2; Population: 93,381.*

Archaeologists in the ninth century weren't known for their academic rigour, so when a tomb was discovered here at that time it was rather staggeringly concluded to be that of the apostle Santiago, or Saint James. Christianity was in bullish mode at the time, and the spot rapidly grew into the biggest pilgrimage destination of Europe as thousands of people walked thousands of miles to pay their respects, reduce their time in purgatory, or atone for crimes committed. The city has transcended its dubious beginnings to become one of the most magical cities in Spain, its cathedral the undisputed highlight of a superb architectural ensemble of mossy granite buildings and narrow pedestrian lanes. Simply walking the streets is a pleasure (even in the rain), particularly Rúa Vilar, Rúa Nova, and the streets around the university.

The late 20th century saw a massive revival of the pilgrimage tradition and Santiago is a flourishing, happy place, seat of the Galician parliament and a lively student centre. Don't come for a suntan: HV Morton accurately if unkindly described the city as a 'medieval aquarium', but the regular rain can add to the character of the place, at least for the first three days or so. ▸▸ *For Sleeping, Eating and other listings, see pages 580-583.*

Ins and outs

Getting there There are daily flights from **London** to **Santiago's** airport, as well as frequent internal connections. The bus station is a 20-minute walk east of the centre. Bus No 10 runs there from Praza de Galicia via Rúa da Virxe da Cerca. Santiago is well served by buses. The train station is south of the centre, about a 10-minute walk down Rúa de Horreo (off Praza Galicia). There are trains connections to the rest of Galicia and Spain. The traditional and now increasingly popular way to get to Santiago is a five-week walk from the French Pyrenees, but there are ways to cheat. ▸▸ *For further details, see Transport page 582.*

Getting around The interesting bits of town are mostly very close together. The only places you'll need public transport to access are the airport and the bus station.

Best time to visit During summertime Santiago is thronged with tourists; if you don't mind that, this can be the best time to be there. It rains slightly less, the old town is buzzing, and there's the fiesta of Santiago on 25 July. If you're prepared to get wet, spring and autumn are good times to visit; there are fewer people, accommodation prices are down, and the university is in session, guaranteeing rampant nightlife until dawn every night.

Tourist information Santiago's tourist office ① *Rúa do Vilar 43, Mon-Fri 1000-1400, 1600-1900, Sat 1100-1400, 1700-1900, Sun 1100-1400*, has suprisingly short opening hours for a tourist centre. The staff are knowledgeable and helpful however. There's also a tourist kiosk ① *Praza de Galicia, Mon-Sat 1000-1400, 1600-1900*. A two-hour guided walk (in Spanish) leaves daily from the Banco de España on the Praza das Platerias. It costs €8 (free for under 12s) and leaves at 1200. There's an additional tour at 1800 from April to mid-October. TURGALICIA ① *Carreterra Santiago-Noia, KM 3, 15896 Santiago de Compostela, T981542530.*

History

Relics have been a big deal in Christendom since the early Middle Ages, and especially in Spain. Under Catholic doctrine, Christ physically ascended into heaven, and the Virgin was bodily assumed there too. With the big two out of the question, the apostles were the next best thing. However, the fact that few people actually believe that the bones of Saint James are, or were ever, under the altar of the cathedral is beside the point; the city has transcended its origins completely, as the number of atheist pilgrims to it attests.

After the discovery of the tomb in the early 9th century, Santiago's PR people did a good job. Pilgrims soon began flooding in, and the city had achieved such prosperity by 968 that it was sacked by none other than the Vikings, who were never averse to a long voyage for a bit of plunder. Some 29 years later Santiago had another bad day, when Al-Manzur came from the south and sacked it again. Legend says that an old monk was praying by the tomb of Saint James while chaos reigned around. The Moorish warlord himself burst in and was so impressed by the old man's courage that he swore on his honour to safeguard the tomb and the monk from all harm.

Although the city was razed to the ground, Santiago continued to flourish as Saint James became a sort of patron-cum-field marshal of the Reconquista. Pilgrims came from across Europe and the cathedral was constructed to receive them in appropriate style; they used to bed down for the night in its interior. Constant architectural modifications followed from Santiago's swelling coffers, which also paid for the 40-something churches in the small city. This restructuring reached its peak in the 17th and early 18th centuries, from which period most of the granite-built centre that exists today dates . A rapid decline followed as pilgrimage waned and A Coruña thrived at Santiago's expense. The French occupied Santiago during the Napoleonic Wars, and carried off a large amount of plunder.

The late 20th century brought a rapid revival as the age of tourism descended on Spain with bells on. Santiago is high on many visitors' lists and, unexpectedly, the Camino itself is now phenomenally popular again, with pilgrims of all creeds making the journey in whole or part on foot or bicycle saddle. Although A Coruña remains the provincial capital, Santiago is the seat of the *Xunta* (semi-autonomous Galician government established in 1982), which has provided a further boost to the town's economy.

Sights

Cathedral and around

① *1000-2030 but tourists are not allowed to wander around too much during mass, entry at these times is via the Praza das Praterías; mass for pilgrims daily at 1200 and evening mass at 1930, a 45-min service, free, apart from the museum (see below).*

The whole of Santiago's past, present, and future is wrapped up in its cathedral and its emblematic grey towers. Pilgrims trudge weary weeks to reach it, many tourists visit Galicia specifically to see it, and locals go to mass and confession in it as part of their day-to-day lives. While the original Romanesque interior are superbly preserved, what first greets most visitors is the western façade and its twin towers. Granite is the perfect stone for Spanish Baroque; its stern colour renders the style impressive rather than pompous, and it's hard enough to chisel that masons concentrated on noble lines rather than ornate frippery. It rises high above the square, the moss-stained stone towers (which incorporate the original Romanesque ones) seem to say 'Heaven this way'. The façade was added in the 18th century and is reached by a complex double staircase that predates it.

The plaza that it dominates, named **Obradoiro**, is the main gateway to the cathedral, but it's worth strolling around the building before you enter. Walking clockwise around the building, you pass the façade of the Romanesque **Palacio de Xelmírez,** which adjoins it and forms part of the cathedral museum. Turning the corner, you emerge in the **Praza da Inmaculada**, where the north façade is a slightly underwhelming 18th-century Baroque construction that replaced the earlier Romanesque portal, which, from fragments of stone and textual descriptions, was superb. It faces the **Monasterio de San Martín Pinario**, with a huge façade that's like a display of 'little man attitude' next to the cathedral; this part of it is now a student residence. The plaza used to be known as the *Azabachería*; this is where craftsmen made and sold rosaries made of jet (*azabache*) to the arriving pilgrims.

Continuing around, the **Praza da Quintana** is a curious space, with an upper and lower half; these are known as the halves of the living (the top) and the dead (below); the area used to be a cemetery. A plaque here is dedicated to the Literary Batallion, a corps of student volunteers who fought the French in the Napoleonic wars. The portal on this side is known as the Puerta Santa, or holy door. It is only opened (by the archbishop himself) on the feast day of Santiago (25 July) in a Holy Year (ie a year when it falls on a Sunday). The façade is 17th century, but contains figures salvaged from the Romanesque stone choir (see below). The 18th-century clocktower soars over the square; it's a remarkable work that seems to have borrowed ideas from several cultures.

The last square on the circuit is named **Praza das Praterías** and has an entrance to the cathedral through an excellent original portal, the oldest that remains, with scenes from the life of Christ.

Come back to the western façade and ascend the complex staircase. Once through the Baroque doorway, you're confronted with the original Romanesque façade, the Pórtico de la Gloria. Built between 1168-88 and the work of a man named Master Mateo, it is one of the finest pieces of sculpture in Spain, and a fitting welcome for weary pilgrims entering the church. Three doorless arches are intricately carved with Biblical scenes; a superb last Judgement on the right, and variously interpreted Old Testament scenes on the left. In the centre Santiago himself sits under Christ and the Evangelists, who are surrounded by the elders of the Apocalypse playing medieval musical instruments, all superbly depicted.

Upon entering the church, pilgrims traditionally queue to touch the pillar under the feet of Santiago; over the centuries five clear finger marks have been worn in the granite. Going around the other side of the pillar, carved with the Tree of Jesse, many then bump heads with the figure of Master Mateo, hoping that some of his genius will rub off. Many mistakenly butt the head under Santiago's feet: this is in fact Samson; Master Mateo faces into the church.

The interior itself is still attractively Romanesque in the main. High barrel vaulting and the lack of a *coro* in the centre of the nave give an excellent perspective down the church, although it's a pity the original stone *coro* by Master Mateo was destroyed in the early 17th century to make way for a wooden one that is no longer there.

The massive altar is over-ornate and features some particularly ridiculous cherubs on the *baldacchino* (canopy), which is topped by an image of Santiago in Moorkilling mode; the whole thing belongs on a circus caravan. Conspiracy theorists will enjoy the symbol in the cupola above. Behind the altar is the image of Santiago himself. Pilgrims ascend behind the statue and give it an *abrazo* (embrace); this, a kiss to the back of his head, and a confession below, was the symbolic end to the pilgrimage. After descending on the other side, there are more stairs down to the casket where the remains of the apostle doubtlessly lie.

On special occasions (which seem to be becoming more and more frequent), a large silver censer (*botafumeiro*) is hung from the ceiling at the crossing and slowly swung by eight men until it covers the whole length of the transept and reaches

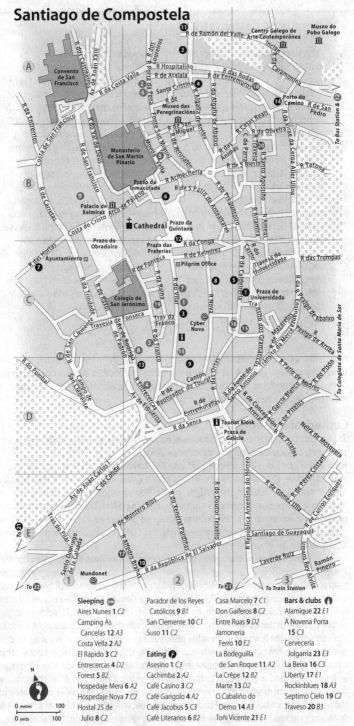

Galicia Santiago de Compostela

Sleeping 🛏
Aires Nunes **1** *C2*
Camping As
  Cancelas **12** *A3*
Costa Vella **2** *A2*
El Rápido **3** *C2*
Entrecercas **4** *D2*
Forest **5** *B2*
Hospedaje Mera **6** *A2*
Hospedaje Noya **7** *C2*
Hostal 25 de
  Julio **8** *C2*
Parador de los Reyes
  Católicos **9** *B1*
San Clemente **10** *C1*
Suso **11** *C2*

Eating 🍴
Asesino **1** *C3*
Cachimba **2** *A2*
Café Casino **3** *C2*
Café Garigolo **4** *A2*
Café Jacobus **5** *C3*
Café Literarios **6** *B2*

Casa Marcelo **7** *C1*
Don Gaiferos **8** *C2*
Entre Ruas **9** *D2*
Jamonería
  Ferro **10** *E2*
La Bodeguilla
  de San Roque **11** *A2*
La Crêpe **12** *B2*
Marte **13** *D2*
O Cabaliño do
  Demo **14** *A3*
Toñi Vicente **21** *E1*

Bars & clubs 🍸
Alamique **22** *E1*
A Novena Porta
  15 *C3*
Cervecería
  Jolgarría **23** *E3*
La Beixa **16** *C3*
Liberty **17** *E1*
Rockinblues **18** *A3*
Septimo Cielo **19** *C2*
Traveso **20** *B3*

0 metres 100
0 yards 100

Rosalía de Castro (1837-1885)

"I do not know what I am seeking, but it is something that I lost I know not when".

Born in Santiago, poet and novelist Rosalía de Castro grew up in Padrón. Although officially an orphan her mother was in fact an unmarried Galician aristocrat and her father a priest. The publication of her Cantres Gallegos (Galician songs) in 1863 is seen as marking the highwatermark of the Galician rexurdimento (renewal) movement that sought to express liberal ideas through the medium of the Galecian language.

Her marriage in 1858 to historian and Galician nationalist Manuel Murgula brought her into contact with other writers who were using the Galician language to express political ideas. Her unique achievement was to express traditional Galician tales through complex, innovative metre and in her refreshing use of pastoral imagery. Many of her poems are redolent with morriña, a particularly Galician word that refers to a melancholy longing.

Her marriage was not a happy one and for the last years of her life she struggled with chronic illness. Her ability to find a distinctive voice against such a difficult background has meant a new interest in her work from feminist critics. She continues to be a source of inspiration to many Spanish authors and in Galicia she has become something of a national icon. Her works have been translated into many languages and are widely available in English.

frightening velocities, diffusing incense and sparks all the while. It's a fantastic and unnerving thing to see, and it's only flown off twice; once in a mass celebrated for Catherine of Aragón to wish her luck on her journey to wed Henry VIII in England. It was considered a bad omen, and so it proved.

Cathedral museum

① *Mon-Sat 1000-1330, 1600-1830 (closes earlier in winter and later in summer), Sun 1000-1330, €5 includes entry to all three sections.*

Back in the Praza do Obradoiro, investigate the Romanesque crypt at the base of the main staircase. One of the three sections of the cathedral museum, it was built by Master Mateo to support the weight of his Romanesque façade above; it's an interesting space dominated by a sturdy loadbearing pillar. There are reproductions of some of the musical instruments that appear on the façade above, as well as some processional crosses and, more interestingly, the 14th-century battle-horn of Alfonso XI, made from an elephant's tusk.

The main section of the museum is accessed either from the cathedral or the Praza do Obradoiro. Entering from the square, the first rooms (although rearrangement was scheduled at time of writing) contain fragments of Romanesque sculpture, including one of the Punishment of the Damned, with two naked sinners having their sensitive bits eaten by beasts. The highlight of this section is the reconstruction of the stone *coro* by Master Mateo, which must have looked superb in the cathedral until it was unbelievably destroyed in 1603 to make way for a wooden one. Some granite slabs elegantly painted in Mudéjar style are also noteworthy. Upstairs, there's a range of sculpture in granite and wood, including a San Sebastian in gold shorts and a good Last Judgement, with a big-haired San Miguel presiding over the weighing of souls (psychostasis). There's also a wooden relief of the bells of the original church being carried back from Córdoba, where they had been taken after Al-Manzur sacked the city. They were triumphantly reclaimed during the Reconquista,

although they were allegedly found in a pantry, being used to hold olive oil. A 10th-century Moorish dirham coin is another item of interest.

The cloister is absolutely massive, and has a slightly neglected feel. The star vaulting is ornate Gothic, and the arches massive. There are several tombs and fragments around, as well as some large, 18th-century bells. A small library contains one of the ex-*botafumeiros* (see above), and there are some mediocre tapestries. Don't despair, there are some better ones upstairs, especially three depicting the life of Achilles by Rubens. Others are factory-made ones depicting rural life, some based on Goya sketches. Off the cloister is the cathedral archive; you'll need a good reason to arrange browsing rights.

Between the cloister and the cathedral is the treasury, a vulgar display of wealth donated by various bigwigs; the collection includes a goblet that belonged to Marshal Pétain. Next to this is the Panteón, which contains tombs of various kings of León and other nobles. There's also an immense retablo holding the cathedral's collection of relics; these include the head of the apostle Saint James Alpheus encased in a gilt bust, and a spine from the crown of thorns.

The other section of the museum, on the other side of the cathedral façade, is the Palacio de Xelmírez, interesting for being a Romanesque civil building (it was built as an archbishop's residence), although it was heavily modified in the 16th century. Features of it include an attractive patio and large kitchen and two beautiful halls.

Praza de Obradoiro

The other buildings on the Praza do Obradoiro are also interesting. To the left as you face the cathedral is the massive **Palacio de Xelmírez**, built as a pilgrims' hostel by Ferdinand and Isabella. After the rigours of the road, it must have been blissful to stay in such a building. Now a parador, pilgrims still have the right to three days' worth of free meals here on presentation of their *compostela*. The meals are served in a canteen around the back rather than in the restaurant, but the food's still pretty nice. The hotel has four pretty courtyards named after the evangelists and several elegant halls. Access is limited to non-residents, but the bits you are allowed to wander around are worthwhile.

Opposite the cathedral, the **Ayuntamiento**, is housed in an attractive neoclassical building, while the fourth side, opposite the parador, is partly taken up by the **Colegio de San Jerónimo**, a 15th-century building now part of the university, with a nice little patio and a portal that looks distinctly Romanesque; perhaps the architects didn't want to clash with the Pórtico de la Gloria of the cathedral. Next to it, the **Colegio de Santiago Alfeo** is a Renaissance construction used by the local government.

Monasterio de San Martín Pinario and around

① *Tue-Sun 1130-1330, 1600-1800, €2.* North of the cathedral, the San Martín Pinario monastery is half restricted to students, but you can still enter the church and museum from around the back. The door is high and slightly scary; it's reached via an attractive downward staircase. The interior is lofty and fairly bare, with a massive dome. In contrast to the sober architectural lines is the huge altarpiece, accurately described by the 19th-century traveller Richard Ford: *"In the retablo, of vilest Churrigueresque, Santiago and San Martín ride together in a fricasee of gilt ginger bread."* Similarly tasteless retablos decorate the side chapels. Of more interest is the *coro* behind the altar: see if you can find the hidden door that the monks used to enter through. The museum has some old printing presses, but little else of interest (until access to the old monastery pharmacy is re-established).

Near to the monastery is the **Convento de San Francisco**, founded by Saint Francis in person when he made the pilgrimage here in the early 13th century, and the newish **Museo das Peregrinacións** ① *Tue-Fri 1000-2000, Sat 1030-1330, 1700-2000, Sun 1030-1330, free*, a three-floor display about the pilgrimage to Santiago, images

and iconography of the saint, the Pórtico de la Gloria, and the medieval life of the town. It's reasonably interesting, more so if you're a pilgrim, but ducks a few crucial Saint James issues, perhaps wisely.

Around Porta do Camino

At the eastern end of town, opposite the Porta do Camino where pilgrims enter the city, are two more museums. **Museo do Pobo Galego** ① *Mon-Sat 1000-1300, 1600-1900, free*, was originally founded by Saint Dominic (again, in person) as a monastery. Inside is a monumental cloister and many ethnographic exhibits relating to Galician life. It's worth a look just for the architecture. There's also a chapel where the poet Rosalía de Castro, see page 578, is buried.

Next to the museum, the **Centro Galego de Arte Contemporánea** ① *Tue-Sun 1100-2000, free, good bookshop and café/restaurant*, is a modern building whose attractive white spaces can provide a good break from the timeworn granite. There's no permanent collection, but exhibitions tend to be of high international standard.

Colegiata de Santa María de Sar

① *Mon-Sat 1000-1300, 1600-1900, €0.60*. Colegiata de Santa María de Sar is a Romanesque church a 15-minute walk south from the centre. Built in the 12th century, on insecure ground, it is remarkable chiefly for the alarming lean its interior columns developed over the centuries, to the point that, after the Lisbon earthquake of 1755, massive buttresses had to be added to stop it falling down altogether. Pilgrims can get their pilgrim passports examined here and their *compostela* certificate on the first floor, Rúa do Vilar 1 – there are queues in summer. There's a small **museum** with a tiny bit of Saint Peter in a reliquary, and a cloister, of which one side survives with carvings attributed to Master Mateo of cathedral fame. To reach the church from the Rúa Fonte de San Antonio off Praza de Galicia, take the second right down Rúa Patio de Madres and follow it down the hill. The church is on your right after the railway bridge.

● Sleeping

Santiago *p574, map p577*
There are dozens of places to stay in Santiago; many restaurants in the centre have a few cheap rooms. Rooms can be hard to find in summer, be persistent.
LL Parador de los Reyes Católicos, Praza do Obradoiro 1, T981582200, www.parador.es. Santiago's top place to stay: the pilgrims' hostel built by the Catholic monarchs is a luxurious place to lie up. Built around 4 beautiful courtyards, it's something of a snip at around €160 a night for a double. It's located on the cathedral square, and the rooms lack nothing of the class that pervades the building.
A Hotel Airas Nunes, Rúa do Vilar 17, T981569350, www.pousadasdecompostela. com. Right in the thick of things, this new hotel has excellent facilities and plenty of attractive charm in a 17th-century building. Rooms are on the small side but comfy.
B Hotel San Clemente, Rúa San Clemente 28, T981569260, www.pousadasde

compostela.com. An excellent option located in the old town below and close to the cathedral. The charm of the old house still shines through.
C Costa Vella, Porta da Peña 17, T981569530, www.costavella.com. A smart, comfortable hotel with a top location and good rooms with trimmings, some with cathedral views.
C Hotel Entrecercas, Rúa Entrecercas 11, T981571151, F981571112. A central and charming option with courteous and helpful management. Breakfast included.
D Hostal 25 de Julio, Av Rodrigo de Padrón 4, T981582295, F981589695. A good option with friendly staff and very nice soft comfy rooms.
E Suso, Rúa Vilar 65, T981586611. A central pilgrims' favourite, often fully booked. Its ensuite rooms are pretty good value and there's a friendly vibe.
E Forest, Callejón de Abril Ares 7, T981570811. An excellent quiet option featuring decent rooms with shared bathroom and hospitable owners.

E-F **Hospedaje Noya**, Rúa Vilar 13.
A very central option, clean and friendly.
F **El Rápido**, Rúa Franco 22, T981584983.
Foolishly cheap rooms above a restaurant in
seafood central. The bathrooms are basic,
but ensuite, and the beds fine for the price.
F **Hospedaje Mera**, Porta da Pena 15. A
good quiet, and cheap option on a pedestrian street in the centre of town. Some of
the rooms have balconies and views.

Camping
As Cancelas, T981580266. A good campsite,
frequently served by city bus number 9.
Camping Monte do Gozo, Ctra Aeropuerto
s/n, T981558942. A massive summer-only
campsite on the hill 2 km east of town with
regular public transport.

⊕ Eating

Santiago *p574, map p577*
Seafood is the thing to eat here. Scallops
(*vieiras*) are an obvious choice, served in a
bacon and onion sauce, but they're
expensive at about €5 per scallop. *Percebes,*
are also popular here. *Tarta de Santiago* is a
tasty almond cake often engraved with a
sword. One of the main streets, Rúa Franco,
is something of a tourist trap (although
locals eat here too); prices are high and
quality variable.
€€€ **Toñi Vicente**, Av Rosalía de Castro 24,
T981594100. Galician nouvelle cuisine is the
order of the day at this top restaurant;
lampreys available in season, and some
superbly delicate fish creations.
€€ **Asesino**, Praza Universidad 16,
T981581568. Almost unmarked, this
restaurant opposite the university opens
when it chooses, and offers excellent
homestyle food accompanied by
appropriately familiar bric-a-brac decor.
€€ **Casa Marcelo**, Rúa das Hortas 3,
T981558850. Offers a set meal only, a
delicious *menú de degustación* for €29;
the food is rich but full of delicate flavours,
and abundant.
€€ **Don Gaiferos**, Rúa Nova 23,
T981583894. A dark and moody but modern
establishment that offers some good fish but
even better fancy steak-based options.

€ **Entre Ruas**, Ruela de Entreruas 2. A good
hidden spot to sit outside and have a drink,
or indulge in the very acceptable *menú del
día* for €7.80.
€ **Jamonería Ferro**, Rúa República de El
Salvador 20. A deli that's also a popular bar,
with generous free nibbles and some good
raciones, especially of the hammy kind.
€ **La Bodeguilla de San Roque**, Rúa San
Roque 13. A good bar, popular with students
for its cheap and filling *raciones*.
€ **La Crêpe**, Praza Quintana 1, T981577643.
Although it's a (small) chain, this place does
good pancakes, sweet and savoury.
€ **Marte**, Av Rodrigo de Padrón 11,
T981584905. A no-nonsense family-run
place much patronized by the police station
opposite. The *menú del día* is superb value
for €10 (there's an even cheaper one for
€6) and doesn't hold back on the seafood;
there's turbot, monkfish, and plenty more.
€ **O Cabaliño do Demo**, Porta do Camiño,
T981588146. Good vegetarian option with a
wide variety of dishes and a relaxing vibe.

Tapas bars and cafés
Cachimba, Rúa San Roque 7. A popular
meeting point for students; its window is
also a good place to look for a flatshare.
Café Casino, Rúa de Vilar 35. A massive
smart space popular with young and old for
evening coffee.
Café Garigolo, Rúa da Algalia de Arriba 38. A
good café and bar, which has regular live
music and cultural events.
Café Jacobus, Rúa Calderería 42,
T981583415. Big and busy café with heaps of
types of coffee and some excellent cakes.
Café Literarios, Praza Quintana s/n. Good
spot on this attractive and unusual square,
named after the redoubtable student
batallion of this granite city.
25 de Julio, Av Rodrigo de Padrón 4,
T981582295. A charming little spot, well
decorated, ideal for a midmorning coffee hit.

⊕ Bars and clubs

Santiago *p574, map p577*
The student nightlife kicks off around Rúa
Nova de Abaixos near Praza Roxa; try some
of the small bars in the arcades. They may

⬤ *For an explanation of sleeping and eating price codes used in this guide, see inside the*
● *front cover. Other relevant information is found in Essentials, see pages 47-56.*

look dead, but be assured they'll spark up some time after midnight, even on weekdays. Get the free newspaper *Compostelán or 7 Días Santiago* for bar, club events and venues listings.

Alamique, Rúa Nova de Abaixo 17. A good bar for pre-dance drinking and chat, always reasonably busy and cheery.

A Novena Porta, Rúa Cardenal Payá 3. The 9th door is a modern, bright bar popular for evening drinks with white-collar folk.

Cervecería Jolgarria, Rúa da República Arxentina 41, T981596210. A cross between a fastfood restaurant and a student bar, this massive joint is a basic and popular place to start an evening's drinking in this lively zone.

La Beixa, Rúa de Tras Salomé 3. A popular student haunt playing 70s music in a cosy and friendly environment.

Liberty, Rúa Alfredo Brañas 4. Santiago's students don't get going until the wee hours, and neither does this large *discoteca*, which is busy even on weeknights and doesn't let up until well after dawn.

N-VI, C Santiago del Estero s/n. It's rare that you get to drink in an underground car park, so take the opportunity. At the old-town end of Rúa Nova de Abaixo.

Rockinblues, Rúa das Rodas 7.

Septimo Cielo, Rúa da Raiña 20. Late opening bar near the cathedral playing Spanish chart hits to a cheery crowd.

Traveso, Rúa Travesa 11. A good spot for house music with regular guest DJs.

⊛ Entertainment

Santiago *p574, map p577*

Auditorio de Galicia, T981552290. Modern building a fair way to the north of town, with classical concerts and opera.

Teatro Galán, T981585166, www.teatrogalan.com.

Teatro Principal, Rúa Nova 21, T981586521. A council-run venue for theatre and occasional cinema festivals.

Sala Yago, Rúa Vilar 51, T981589288. Some good shows here for a very low entry price starting at about €4; there's also occasional quality cinema.

Cinesa Area Central, Rúa Fontiñas, T902333231.

Compostela, Rúa Ramón Piñeiro 3, T981560342.

⊛ Festivals and events

Santiago *p574, map p577*

Santiago's main fiesta is the day of the saint himself on **25 Jul**. When this day falls on a Sun, it's known as a **Holy Year** (this year, 2004). Apart from the usual partying, there's a solemn mass attended by thousands, and a spectacular pyrotechnic display the night before.

⊘ Shopping

Santiago *p574, map p577*

Santiago is a good place to buy *azabache* (jet) but shop around; many places near the cathedral make a living preying on tourists.

Books Librería Universitas, Rúa Fernando III el Santo 3, T981592438; **Librería San Pablo**, Rúa Vilar 39, which is slightly heavy on religion but still has a decent selection.

Food and drink Mercado de Abastos is a lively food market that's well worth a visit. It's in the old town on Praza de Abastos.

O Beiro, Rúa da Raiña 3, is a good place to buy (and drink!) Galician wines.

⊖ Transport

Santiago *p574, map p577*

Buy a copy of the newspaper *El Correo Gallego* for a complete list of transport times.

Air There are daily international flights to **London**, **Brussels,** and **Amsterdam**, as well as many internal ones to **Madrid** and **Barcelona** and, less frequently, **Bilbao** and **Seville**; there are also several flights to the **Canary Islands**, and the odd transatlantic one to **Buenos Aires** and **Washington**. Buses connect the airport with the city centre, stopping at Av General Pardiñas; they run approximately hourly.

Bus Buses run hourly to **A Coruña**; if you're in a hurry, make sure you get the *autopista* one. Three a day travel to **Fisterra** and **Camariñas**. 8 buses go to **Lugo**, hourly ones to **Pontevedra** and **Vigo**, and 7 to **Ourense**. Buses run hourly to **Ribeira**, and 6 times a day to **Vilagarcía**, **Cambados**, and **O Grove**. Long-distance bus services connect with **Bilbao** 3 times a day, **Ponferrada** and **Astorga** 4 times a day, **Zaragoza** once a day, **Madrid** 3 times a day, **Oviedo** and **Gijón**

twice, **Burgos** once, and **Zamora** and **Salamanca** twice.

Car hire Autos Brea, C Gómez Ulla 10, T981562670, is a reasonably central agency. There are several multinationals at the airport.

Train Trains run regularly to **A Coruña**, **Vigo**, and **Ourense**; there's a sleeper and a day train to **Madrid**, and 1 to **Bilbao**.

① Directory

Santiago *p574, map p577*
Hospital Hospital Xeral is fairly central on Rúa das Galeras, T981950000.
Internet Cyber Nova 50, Rúa Nova 50.
Mundonet, Rúa República de El Salvador 30.

Laundry Lavandeira, Av Rosalía de Castro 116, T981942110. A self-service laundromat with plenty of machines.

Post The main post office is on Travesa de Fonseca a block from the cathedral.

Telephone There's a *locutório* on C Bautizados 15, but only use it for very quick calls, as they charge about five times the going rate. There are several better ones in the streets around Praza Roxa.

Useful addresses and numbers
Dial T112 for any sort of emergency. T092 contacts the municipal police. The handiest **police station** is the massive one on Av Rodrigo de Padrón around the corner from the post office.

East of Santiago

The pilgrim route follows a windswept, mountainous path offering bleak but atmospheric moments along the way. Lugo, the provincial capital, is low-key and relaxed surrounded by some impressive city walls. Just a short drive from Lugo is a rural area lost in time, which is well worth visiting. ►► *For Sleeping, Eating and other listings, see pages 586-587.*

Pilgrim route to Santiago

Piedrafita → *Colour map 1, grid B4.*

The most spectacular approach into Galicia is via the pass of Piedrafita, a wind and rainswept mountain location which can be bleak in the extreme. Sir John Moore and his ragtag British forces were pursued up here by the French army, and many died of cold. Not much further, they found themselves without explosive to mine a bridge, and were forced to ditch all their gold over the edge so that they could travel faster and avoid being set upon from behind. At the pass, Piedrafita has banks, other services and lodging options, but many pilgrims and travellers prefer to move on further down a side road to O Cebreiro.

O Cebreiro

In many ways, this tiny village of attractive stone buildings is where the modern Camino de Santiago was reborn. The church and former pilgrim hostel were rebuilt in the 1960s and the energetic parish priest, Elías Valiña, found suitable people to run hostels in other waystations and began to popularize the notion of the pilgrim way once again. The area is famous for its mountain cheese. Although O Cebreiro can be incredibly bleak as the winds, rains and snows roll in and the power fails, it's atmospheric and friendly. The church has a reliquary donated by Ferdinand and Isabella to accompany the chalice known as the 'Grail of Galicia', after the host and communion wine became real flesh and blood one day as a skeptical priest went through the motions at mass. In high summer, pilgrims can outnumber locals (there are 31) by 30 or 40 times, and the army comes in to set up an outdoor canteen.

Portomarín → *Colour map 1, grid B3.*

At first glance you wouldn't know it, but this village is only 40-odd years old. The original lies underwater, submerged when the river Miño was dammed. Hearteningly, the villagers were helped to move the historic buildings to the new site, and Portomarín escaped becoming the sad and soulless concrete shambles that many such relocated villages in Spain are. The main street is attractive, with an arcade and whitewashed buildings, and the Romanesque parish church is well worth a look for its rose window and beautifully carved tall portals.

Further along the Camino, it's worth taking a short detour to see the church at **Vilar de Donas**, see Around Lugo page 586.

Lugo and around → *Phone code: 982; Colour map 1, grid B4; Population: 88,901.*

The Romans weren't ones for half measures, so when they decided their main Galician town Lucus Augusti needed walls, they didn't hang around. Still in top condition today, the wall impressively circles the old town and is the most obvious feature of what is a small and remarkably pleasant inland provincial capital. Attractive architecture within the perimeter adds to the appeal, and there are several good bars and restaurants. The area southwest of Lugo is out of the ordinary; a sort of microcosm of Galician rural life that seems to have changed little over the decades.

Ins and outs

Getting there and around ALSA, www.alsa.es, run buses all over Northern Spain. Lugo's bus station is conveniently located just outside the walls near the Praza Maior, while the train station isn't too far away from the eastern side of the old town. ⏵ *For further details, see Transport page 587.*

Tourist information The tourist office ① *in an arcade off the Praza Maior, Mon-Fri 0930-1400, 1630-1830,* is efficient.

History

Lugo was founded in 15BC as Lucus Augusti, named after Augustus, the emperor of the time. It rapidly became an important outpost; the Roman province that contained Galicia had its capital in distant Tarragona, so the city had an important local administrative role. The main streets in the town still follow the Roman axes. Today, Lugo is a busy little place, a centre for the surrounding farming districts and capital of Galicia's largest province.

Sights

Lugo's **walls** were erected in the third century AD and built to last. Made of slabs of schist, they are still almost complete and run over 2 km right around the centre of town at a height of some 10 m. Their width is impressive too; you could race chariots along the top, where the walkway is some 4-5 m wide. The wall has been shored up over the years, and most of the 82 towers that punctuate its length are of medieval construction. Walking around the walls is the best way to appreciate their construction, and walking along them is the best way to see the town. There are six points of access and 10 gates, of which the most authentically Roman is **Porta do Carme** (also called Porta Minha).

The 19th-century traveller George Borrow must have been having a bad day when he described Lugo's **cathedral** ① *1100-1300, 1600-1800,* as "a small, mean building"; although it's not the finest cathedral in Northern Spain, it's a reasonably

⬤ *If you feel a bit exposed on the top, that's because the upper portions of the towers were*
⬤ *removed during the Napoleonic wars because it was thought they wouldn't withstand cannon fire and would topple into the town's centre.*

large and interesting place. It was first built over earlier remains in the 12th century,
but its big twin-towered Baroque façade is what dominates today. Inside, some
Romanesque features remain, such as the distinctive *ajedrezado jaqués* chessboard
patterning associated with the Camino de Santiago. The town was granted the right to
have the consecrated host permanently on view; an honour seldom granted by the
Catholic church, and still a source of some pride. Galicia's coat-of-arms depicts the
host and the chalice for this reason. The altar itself is unattractive, being over-
silvered. In the apse is a famous and much-venerated statue of *La Virgen de los Ojos
Grandes*, the Virgin with the Big Eyes, an accurately titled Romanesque wood carving.
The cathedral museum and treasury is set around the small cloisters.

Nearby, the **Praza Maior** is large and attractive, and guarded by fierce stone lions.
At its top end is the Casa Consistorial (town hall), an attractive 18th-century building
in Galician Baroque, a style that (whisper it) might owe something to Portuguese
architectural traditions. **Museo Provincial** ① *Mon-Sat 1030-1400, 1630-2030 (2000
Sat), Sun 1100-1400, Jul/Aug Mon-Fri 1100-1400, 1700-2000, Sat 1000-1400, free*,
includes the **Iglesia de San Pedro**, with a curious 15th-century door and a strange
tower. There's an eclectic display, ranging from Roman pottery and coins to sundials,
Celtic jewellery, Galician painting, and ethnographic displays.

Lugo's **Roman baths** were built shortly after the city was founded, taking
advantage of the natural hot spring by the river. What's left of them is within the spa
hotel complex by the **Miño**. A walkway over the warm waters lets you see the ancient
changing rooms, with alcoves in the wall to stash your toga; another room nearby is of
uncertain function. The bridge across the river nearby is also of Roman origin.

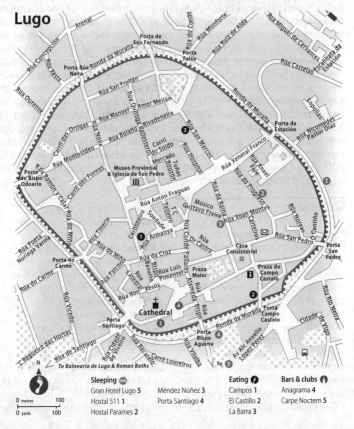

Lugo

Sleeping		Eating	Bars & clubs
Gran Hotel Lugo **5**	Méndez Núñez **3**	Campos **1**	Anagrama **4**
Hostal 511 **1**	Porta Santiago **4**	El Castillo **2**	Carpe Noctem **5**
Hostal Parames **2**		La Barra **3**	

0 metres 100
0 yards 100

To Balneario de Lugo & Roman Baths

One of Lugo's pleasures apart from strolling the walls is exploring the small streets within their sturdy circle. **Rúa Nova** is a centre for tapas bars and restaurants, while the shopping streets are in the eastern end of the old town.

Around Lugo → *Colour map 1, grid B4.*

This area southwest of Galicia is web of tiny roads connecting a series of hamlets where tractors are still outnumbered by mulecarts and villagers still bear loads on their heads.

There are two excellent churches. The first ① *guided tour only; Tue-Sat 1100-1400, 1530-1700 (1630-2030 summer), Sun 1100-1400*, in the tiny settlement of **Santa Eulalia de Bóveda**, is something of an enigma. Originally a Celtic and Roman temple, the mystery centres around an atrium and a small chamber with columns surrounding a basin. Very well-preserved paintings of birds and trees decorate the walls. Perhaps used for baptism, there can be no doubt that it dates to early Christian times, perhaps while rural religion was still heavily intertwined with pagan rites. Santa Eulalia can't be reached by public transport; get an Orense or Santiago-bound bus to drop you off at the turnoff and hitch (it's a good 1½-hour walk). If you have your own transport, take the Orense road (N540), turn right after 4 km, left about 1 km further on, then right about 6 km down that road. It's all signposted.

More accessible is the church ① *1100-1300, 1600-1800, admission by donation, the knowledgeable and kindly warden lives nearby and may come and open it outside these hours if you hang around*, at **Vilar de Donas**; it's also only a shortish detour off the Camino de Santiago. It's worth the trouble; it's one of Galicia's most interesting buildings. Built in the 12th century, it was modified at the behest of the Knights of Santiago to serve as a place of burial for the prestigious members of that order. The tombs line the walls after you've passed through the excellent Romanesque doorway with zigzag patterning. One of the finest tombs dates from 1378 and is mounted on two lions who are squashing a boar, representing wrath, and a wolf, symbolizing evil. In the apse are some excellent frescoes commissioned by John II, king of Castilla and father of Isabella, the Catholic monarch. Dating from 1434, the paintings depict the Annunciation and Pantocrator as well as shields with the devices of Castilla y León and the order of Santiago. In the transept is a *baldacchino*, an ornate carved canopy commonly used over altars in Galicia; this one is made of stone. it's easily reached by public transport; take any Santiago-bound bus from Lugo and get off at the turnoff on the main road; it's 500 m up a side road from here. If you're getting the bus back to Lugo, signal it very vigorously or it may sail on by.

◉ Sleeping

Pilgrim route to Santiago *p583*
D Hospedería O Cebreiro, O Cebreiro, T982367125, next door to the church. It is an excellent place to stay, with spacious woodbeamed rooms and a restaurant serving an incredibly generous dinner *menú* for €8. The food is cooked by the sister of Elías Valiña, who is buried next door. Nearby are 4 reconstructed *pallozas*, a circular dwelling of stone walls and straw roofs originating in Celtic pre-Roman Galicia; 2 house an ethnographic exhibition; the other 2 provide accommodation for pilgrims.
E Casa Carolo, O Cebreiro, T982367168, is

another good option serving meals.
E Casa García, Piedrafit, is a reasonable and friendly choice.
F Mesón de Rodríguez, Portomarín, T982545054, on the main street, is a good place for a bed and/or a meal; the rooms are clean and good value, and the food generously proportioned.
F Posada del Camino, Plaza del Conde de Fersosa s/n, Portomarín, is a cheap but acceptable option.

Lugo and around *p584, map p585*
AL Gran Hotel Lugo, Av Ramón Ferreiro 21, T982224152, F982241660. Lugo's top option, modern place, many facilities including pool.

C **Balneario de Lugo**, Barrio del Puente s/n, T982221228, F982221659. Although the atmosphere is staid, and it's a wee walk from the walled town, this spa hotel is well priced, right by the Miño river, and on the site of the old Roman baths.

C **Hotel Méndez Núñez**, C Reina 1, T982230711, F982229738. Very central, this old-style hotel is a little stuffy but reasonably good value.

F **Hostal 511**, Ronda Muralla 36, T982227763. Good, clean rooms just outside the walls between the Porta San Pedro and Porta Estación gates.

F **Hostal Parames**, Rúa Progreso 28, T982224816. Within the walls, and excellent for the price, with faultless rooms with TV and bathroom for very little cash.

F **Porta Santiago**, Ronda Muralla 176, T9822 52405. A good cheap *fonda* just outside the walls, a little noisy but otherwise OK.

🍴 Eating

Lugo and around *p584, map p585*
€€€ **La Barra**, C San Marcos 27, T982252920. A sleek, stylish seafood restaurant widely considered Lugo's best.
€€ **Campos**, Rúa Nova 4, T982229743. A top range of seafood can be had at this place, which does a *menú* for €14.50.
€ **El Castillo**, Praza do Campo Castelo 12. A cheap and simple place doing good *bocadillos* and a set lunch for €7.

🍺 Bars and clubs

Lugo and around *p584, map p585*
Lugo's lively and late bar scene is centred in the small streets around the cathedral.

Anagrama, Praza Alférez Provisional 5, nightly from about 2400 on. A lively bar by the side of the cathedral with some very cool interior pseudo-Roman design.
Carpe Noctem, Rúa Dois Clérigos 17, Thu-Sat from 2300. Atmospheric bar in the cathedral zone, one of the better bars in Lugo. Good range of people and a variety of music.

🛍 Shopping

Lugo and around *p584, map p585*
Books There are 2 good bookshops on Rúa Bispo Aguirre; **Aguirre**, at No 8, T982220336, with a good selection of maps; and **La Voz de la Verdad**, at No 17.

🚆 Transport

Lugo and around *p584, map p585*
Bus Within Galicia, there are 13 daily buses to **A Coruña**, 4 to **Ferrol**, 8 to **Orense**, 10 to **Santiago**, 5 to **Viveiro** and the north coast, 6 to **Ribadeo**, and 1 to **Vilalba**. Two buses run eastwards to **Ponferrada** via **Sarria**.
Long-distance **ALSA** services: there's 1 a day to **Zamora** and **Salamanca**, 2 to **Barcelona** via **Zaragoza**, 5 to **Madrid**, 2 to **Santander**, and a couple to **Oviedo** and **Gijón** via the **Asturian coast**.
Train There's 1 overnight train to **Madrid**, 3 a day to **A Coruña**, 1 to **Bilbao**, 5 to **Monforte**, and 1 overnight to **Barcelona**.

🗂 Directory

Lugo and around *p584, map p585*
Post Lugo's main post office is in the old town on Rúa San Pedro near the Praza Maior.

Rías Altas

The north coast is an interesting part of Galicia, not as overdeveloped as the west coast but still featuring some interesting fishing towns and a few cracking beaches. The inlets of the Rías Altas are deep, making perfect natural harbours and sheltered (if chilly) swimming spots. Of the two major ports on the north coast, Ferrol is an earthy industrial centre that makes few concessions to tourism, while A Coruña is a jewel set on a promontory with a harbour on one side, a great beach on the other, and a lively seafood tapas scene in between. ➤➤ *For Sleeping, Eating and other listings, see pages 596-600.*

Ribadeo and around → *Colour map 1, grid A4.*

Ribadeo faces its Asturian counterpart Castropol across the broad expanse of the inlet at the mouth of the river Eo; thus the town's name. It's a nice place, with a waterside promenade by the harbour at the bottom of the steep streets leading down from the old centre. The views across to Asturias a mile away across the water are picturesque, and the modern bridge over the *ría* impressive despite the thundering traffic. Past the bridge there's a small fort, the **Forte de San Damián**, to protect the town from seaward invasion. The old centre is pleasant too, with a good square with plenty of palm trees. There are many *indiano* houses, attractive structures built by Galicians returned from the Americas. There's a tourist office in the centre where you can gather information on Galicia if just arriving from Asturias.

Some of Galicia's best **beaches**, all within a 20-minute walk of the main road west of Ribadeo. **As Catedrais** (The Cathedrals) is a pretty little stretch named for its prettily eroded cliffs and rocks lying in the water. It all but disappears at high tide. Nearby **Reinante** is a superb stretch of whitish sand, as is **Arealonga**, while a little further, **Praia de Lóngara** and adjacent Fontela are the best options for surfing.

Foz and around → *Colour map 1, grid A4.*

The best feature of Foz is its attractive working fishing port, where the fishermen's families come down to wave at the boats heading out to sea in the late afternoon. The rest of the town is friendly but not particularly interesting. A good excursion is the walk or drive to **San Martín de Mondoñedo**, a hamlet whose church ① *1100-1300, 1600-1900 but the keyholder lives nearby*, was once a cathedral; the bishop must have been the least stressed of primates. It's about 8 km from town along a pleasant road heavy with the scent of eucalyptus. Although the church's origins are ninth century, most of what is visible is later Romanesque. It's on soft ground and is heavily buttressed; the apse features Lombard arching, a feature of the Romanesque of Catalunya. There's an attractive *cruceiro* outside, and the portal features the Lamb. Inside are some excellent Romanesque wallpaintings, good carved capitals, and the tomb of Gonzalo, yet another Galician saint.

The coast continuing west, becomes a little more rugged, but there are still some decent beaches. A multitude of rivers flow down to the sea from the Galician high country, and are good spots for trout fishing. The straggling village of **Xove** is less impressive than its name, which derives from the Latin *Iovii*, meaning 'of Jupiter'. Few places appeal as a stopover until you reach **Ría de Viveiro**. Near the town of Celeiro is the excellent patrolled beach of **Area**, a duney stretch that looks across to an islet.

Viveiro → *Colour map 1, grid A4.*

Viveiro is a curious place, which makes the best stop on this stretch of coast. Right at the tail of the *ría*, its small boats get marooned on mudflats at low tide. Viveiro is reasonably lively in summer, when there's a small but steady flow of holiday-makers, but it's strangely lifeless for the rest of the year. Viveiro is particularly known for its Easter festival, a serious event with a candlelit procession enacting the stations of the cross. The old town is interesting, and still preserves fragments of its walls as well as a couple of gates, one a very tight squeeze at the top of the town. Built in the 12th century, the Romanesque **Iglesia de Santa María del Campo** is in the centre of the old town. Inside is a pretty processional cross dating from the 16th century, as well as a sculptural assembly that used to adorn one of the gates of the

create it is inexplicable, but locals seem to trust it; there's many an offering of plastic
body parts, soliciting intervention for physical ailments.

Ortigueira to Ferrol → Colour map 1, grid A2/3.

There's no reason to stop in Ortigueira; a quick look at its gardened port will suffice. A
short distance west of Ortigueira, the main road cuts inland, but it's worth exploring
the headland, a wild and rugged landscape battered by some of Galicia's worst
weather. Apart from the dull sprawl of **Carriño**, it's a bleak and lonely place populated
mainly by wild horses. North of Carriño, the pretty **Cabo Ortegal** has a lighthouse and
good views; it's a nice walk along the green clifftops. Further west, the **Garita de
Herbeira** is an atmospheric and desolate arch of high granite cliffs 600 m high, and
pounded by waves and weather.

Back on the coast, the **Sanctuario de San Andrés de Teixido** is in a sturdy stone
hamlet. It's a simple chapel that was established by the Knights of Malta, who
brought a relic of Saint Andrew here back from the Holy Land. The saint is much
venerated along this understandably superstitious coast, and there's always a good
pile of *ex voto* offerings that range from representations of what intervention is being
sought for, such as models of fishing boats or plastic body parts to simple gifts of
pens and cigarettes. There's a well-attended *romería* (pilgrimage procession) to the
sanctuary on 8 September; some of the pilgrims make the journey in coffins to give
thanks for narrow escapes, mostly at sea.

South of the sanctuary of San Andrés de Teixido, and back on the main road is
Cedeira, a pleasant town on a nice *ría*. There are some excellent **beaches** around,
although the town beach isn't the best of them; try **A Magdalena**, a shallow-watered
strip of sand a couple of kilometres further along the coast. The two halves of Cedeira
are linked by a bridge; the old town is across it from the main road, and is a warren of
steep and narrow streets.

West of Cedeira is some of the nicest coastline in these parts, heavily wooded
and studded with excellent beaches, particularly **Villarube**, and **Do Rodo**, one of
Galicia's best surf beaches. **Da Frouxeira** is another excellent strip of sand, two miles
long, and backed by a lagoon that is an important haven for waterfowl.

Ferrol → Colour map 1, grid A3.

Although some 155,000 souls live in Ferrol and its suburbs, it's not a place of huge
interest. While Ferrol's glory days as a naval harbour ended abruptly (along with most
of Spain's fleet) during the Peninsular War, it's still an important port, and the navy
very much in evidence. Although poor, and with high unemployment, Ferrol has not
been shorn of its dignity; the streets around the harbour are lined with once-noble
terraced houses, and locals are proud of their city and its hardworking heritage.
Perhaps Ferrol's greatest claim to fame, however, is seldom mentioned these days: in
the winter of 1892 an uptight little boy was born to a naval family in a house near the
harbour. Francisco Franco y Bahamonde went on to rule Spain with a concrete fist for
the best part of four decades, see box page 590.

Hurry through Ferrol's outskirts and modern expansions; some of the most
depressing urban landscapes in Spain are to be found here. In some of the poorer,
high-density areas, the council inexcusably hasn't even bothered to give the streets
proper names; just letters. The city has a major traffic problem too.

Although the **waterfront** is mostly taken up by naval buildings and dockyards, it's
well worth strolling along: from the **Paseo de la Marina** at the western tip of the old

Dedicated follower of Fascism

"a less straightforward man I never met" John Whitaker, American journalist.

Franciso Franco y Bahamonde looms over 20th-century Spanish history like the concrete monoliths he was so fond of building, and, like them, his shadow is long. Born in 1892 in the Galician naval port of Ferrol, this son of a naval administrator wanted to join the navy but was forced to choose the army due to lack of places at the academy. Sent to the war in Morocco at 20, he excelled, showing remarkable ability and bravery. As commander of the new Foreign Legion, he was largely responsible for the victory achieved there in 1925; this success saw him made Spain's youngest ever general at 33.

The authoritarian Franco was just the man the government needed to put down the rebellion of the Asturian miners in 1934 which he achieved brutally. Sent to a command in the Canaries, out of harm's way as the government thought, he agreed to join the conspiracy against the Republic late. He took command of the army in Morocco, which was transported across to the Spanish mainland with German assistance, an intervention crucial in the context of the war. Franco's advance was successful and rapid – he soon manoeuvred his way into the Nationalist leadership, reluctantly being given supreme power by his fellow generals. He assumed the title of Caudillo, or 'head' and installed himself in Burgos.

Throughout the war, he was known for his ruthlessness, never more so than when the German Condor Legion razed Gernika from the air on market day, killing 1,500 civilians. After the Nationalist victory, the Generalísimo showed no signs of giving up power, although in 1949 he declared himself as a regent pending the choice of a king. He ensured that there was to be no leniency for those who had supported the former Republic. A cruel purge followed.

After the war Franco's dictatorship was shunned by the western democracies until Cold War politics made the USA adopt him as an ally, betraying the governments-in-exile they had continued to recognize. A massive aid package in exchange for military bases gave Franco the cash required to begin modernizing a country that had been crippled by the Civil War, but for much of his rule parts of Spain remained virtually Third World. Franco was recognized by other countries, and Spain was accepted into the United Nations, but remained politically and culturally stagnant. Separatism was not countenanced; Franco banned Euskara and even Galego, the tongue of his native Galicia. He never forgot an enemy; the regions that had struggled to uphold democracy were left to rot while he conferred favours on the Nationalist heartlands of Castilla and Navarra. The ageing dictator appointed Juan Carlos, grandson of the former king, as his successor in 1969.

Franco's waning powers were dealt a bitter blow when ETA assassinated his right-hand man Admiral Carrero Blanco, to whom he had delegated much authority in his latter years. Franco died in 1975; "Españoles", the Spanish people were solemnly informed, "Franco ha muerto". The man described as "a sphinx with no mystery" was no more: those who mourned the passing of this plump, shy, suspicious, authoritarian general were comparatively few, but Francoism is still alive within the political right, and memorial services on the anniversaries of his death are still held.

town, you can get a good idea of just how large Ferrol's excellent natural harbour (the Ría do Ferrol) is. Near here is one of the twin forts defending the port. Most of Ferrol's character is in the five or six parallel streets back from here. The elegant balconied buildings tell of days of prosperity, as do the several *indiano* buildings. The whitewashed neoclassical church and post office show some of these influences; nearby is the busy modern market. Franco was born on Rúa María, four streets back from the shore at No 136 (although the street was called Frutos Saavedra when he was a nipper).

Pontedeume and the Caaveiro Valley

→ *Colour map 1, grid A2.*

South of Ferrol, the rivermouth town of Pontedeume is a prettier and more relaxed place to hang out despite the almost constant line of traffic through town. Its main features are its long bridge across the Eume and an impressive 14th-century tower. Both were originally built by the Andrade family, local lairds, *bon viveurs*, and boar hunters, see Betanzos page 595. A weathered stone boar faces across the bridge. The tower holds the tourist office, which can advise on things to see in the area.

"The valley of Caaveiro", wrote Richard Ford in the mid-19th century, "is one of the most secluded in Spain". Not much has changed. The valley is a refuge of much wildlife; there are many otters – mostly further up, above the hydroelectric station – boar, ermine, and birds. Fishing has been suspended on the river to allow the salmon and trout levels to restabilize. Some 10 km up the valley is an atmospheric ruined monastery, **Monasterio de San Xoán de Caaveiro**. It was founded by the boy-bishop San Rosendo in the 10th century. The remaining Romanesque walls look over the river; it's a lovely setting. Nearby, a rapid watercourse feeds the Eume with yet more water. Don't be put off by the unlikely figure who may meet you at the information panel; he has chosen to live up here self-sufficiently, and is an excellent source of knowledge about the area and its nature. From here, you may want to strike off for a walk; the GR50 long-distance path crosses the bridge at the monastery. The whole walk is recommended; it stretches from Betanzos to Cabo Ortegal at the top of Galicia, and can be done comfortably in four days, or strenuously in two.

A Coruña/La Coruña → *Phone code: 981; Colour map 1, grid A2.*

Don't even think about seeing Santiago and slipping out of Galicia without coming to A Coruña. A superb city where, at least when it's not raining, everyone seems to stay outdoors enjoying the privileged natural setting, Coruña has a bit of everything; a harbour, a good beach, top seafood, great nightlife, high-quality budget accommodation, Romanesque architecture, entertaining museums, quiet corners, and a football team that came from nowhere and took Europe by storm. It's one of the most enjoyable cities in the north of Spain but still an important working port and commercial centre. ►► *For Sleeping, Eating and other listings, see pages 596-600.*

Ins and outs
Getting there and around A Coruña is connected with Madrid, Barcelona, and Bilbao by air, as well as Paris and Lisbon. It's a major railhead and bus terminus, well connected with the rest of Northern Spain. ►► *For further details, see Transport page 599.*
Getting around Most of A Coruña is easily explorable on foot. The coastal *paseo* around the headland is a long one, but a tram covers the route half-hourly.
Tourist information A Coruña's tourist office ① *Av de la Marina, Mon-Fri 1000-1345, 1700-1845, Sat/Sun 1000-1345*, will bend-over-backwards.

"She belongs more to the sea than to the stony mass of mainland behind her" is how Dutch writer Cees Nooteboom has described the city; this remains the case.

Such a fine natural harbour as Coruña's was pounced upon early; it was used by the Celts and Phoenicians before becoming an important Roman port, Ardobicum Coronium. It was said that the foundations were laid by Hercules himself. The city remained, and remains, a significant port; it was the westernmost member of the Hermandad de las Marismas, a trading league formed in 1296 along Hanseatic lines.

In 1386 John of Gaunt, son of Edward III decided to avenge the murder of his father-in-law, Pedro I, and landed here with an army. After a farcical progress through Galicia, a peace was finally brokered whereby John's daughter would marry the heir to the Castilian throne. The Castilian king compensated him for the expenses occurred in the invasion and he went home, honour satisfied.

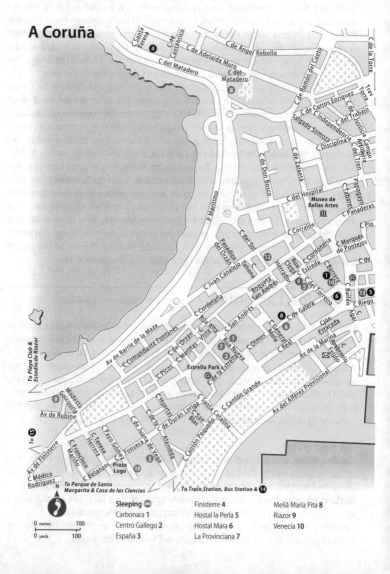

A Coruña

Sleeping

Carbonara 1	Finisterre 4	Meliá María Pita 8
Centro Gallego 2	Hostal la Perla 5	Riazor 9
España 3	Hostal Mara 6	Venecia 10
	La Provinciana 7	

0 metres 100
0 yards 100

When John's great-grandaughter, the Catholic monarch Isabella, died, Philip the Fair of Flanders landed here in 1506 to meet with Ferdinand and claim the Castilian throne. His grandson Philip II had plenty to do with Coruña too; while still a prince, he embarked from here to England, where he married Mary at Winchester. Some 34 years later he assembled his Armada, whose 130 ships put out from the harbour here with 30,000 men. In 1507 Francis Drake sailed here and set fire to the town but was thwarted by the town's heroine María Pita, who saved Coruña by seizing the British standard and rallying the townsfolk to repel the buccaneers.

In 1809 a dispirited and indisciplined British army were relentlessly pursued by the Napoleonic forces of Marshal Soult. Having abandoned all their baggage and gold, the army made for Coruña where a fleet was stationed, but Soult was hard on their heels. To save as many men as possible, the Scottish general, Sir John Moore, faced the French with a small force while 15,000 troops embarked Dunkirk-like on to

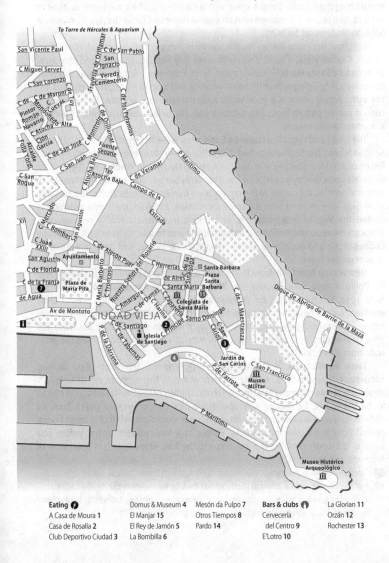

Eating 🍴
A Casa de Moura 1
Casa de Rosalía 2
Club Deportivo Ciudad 3

Domus & Museum 4
El Manjar 15
El Rey de Jamón 5
La Bombilla 6

Mesón da Pulpo 7
Otros Tiempos 8
Pardo 14

Bars & clubs 🍸
Cervecería
   del Centro 9
E'Lotro 10

La Glorian 11
Orzán 12
Rochester 13

the ships. Moore was killed and the force defeated, but the majority of the army got away thanks to the sacrifice. Compared to other Spanish cities, Coruña thrived in the 19th and 20th centuries; its close ties to northern Europe and its flourishing port seemed to save it from stagnation.

Sights

One of the best ways to take in A Coruña's sights is a walk starting in the old town by the port and continuing anticlockwise around the headland. It's a long stroll, but you can hop on the tram that circles the route about every half-hour.

Avenida de la Marina is a good place to start. It's a very elegant boulevard lined with attractive old houses with trademark *galerías* or *miradores*, windowed balconies that look out over the water. Off here is the Praza María Pita, named after the city's heroine. This elegant arcaded square is centred on a statue of María herself, defiantly brandishing the standard and a spear with a couple of Drake's mercenaries dead at her feet. She is commemorated with an eternal flame and faces the Ayuntamiento, a Galician Modernista building.

East from the Praza María Pita, the square is a very attractive network of old town streets, **Ciudad Vieja**, a quiet place with some fine houses, squares, and churches. **Colegiata de Santa María** ① *Tue-Fri 0900-1400, 1700-1900, Sat 1000-1300*, is a wide Romanesque building with solid barrel vaulting and a small museum of religious art. The 13th-century portal is a good work, as is the later rose window. In the eaves, a curious carved pattern looks like dripping wax. The side portal also features elegant Romanesque stonework.

The small and evocative **Jardín de San Carlos** is the final resting place of General Sir John Moore, the Scot who turned "like a lion at bay" to engage the superior French forces of Marshal Soult to give his dispirited army time to embark on the waiting ships. He was killed by a cannonball and hurriedly buried. "Not a drum was heard, not a funeral note, as his corpse to the ramparts we hurried." Charles Wolfe. The soldier's grave was later marked with a granite monument; in Spain, the Peninsular War is named the War of Independence, and British involvement fondly remembered, although the redcoats' behaviour and discipline was frequently atrocious. Poems by Charles Wolfe and Rosalía de Castro commemorate Moore, and fresh flowers often appear on the grave.

Descending from here down to the **marina**, the fort that juts into the bay was built by Philip II and now houses the **Museo Histórico Arqueológico** ① *Mon-Sat 1000-1930, Sun 1000-1430, €2*, the highlight of which is a number of pieces of Celtic jewellery. East of here, the massive glass cuboids of the port authority's control tower cut an impressive figure. From here, you might want to get the tram around to the Torre de Hércules, as it's a 20-minute walk with little of interest; apart from the great waterfront views, that is.

Torre de Hércules ① *Oct-Mar 1000-1745; Apr-Jun, Sep 1000-1845; Jul/Aug 1000-2045 (2345 Fri/Sat), €2*, stands very proud at the northern tip of Coruña's peninsula. It was originally built in the second century AD by the Romans, and claims to be the oldest lighthouse still operational. Its current exterior dates from an 18th-century reformation and, in truth, there's not much Roman left of it, apart from a central core and some foundations, visible in a low-ceilinged space before you ascend. It's worth climbing the 234 steps to the top, where there's a good view of A Coruña and the coast.

● *Coruña's northward orientation is historically linked with Britain, whose sailors referred to it as 'the Groyne'. British pilgrims used to disembark here en route to the tomb of Saint James. The 'camino inglés' was the easiest of the pilgrim routes to Santiago, at least when the Bay of Biscay was in clement mood.*

Not far beyond the lighthouse is the new **aquarium** ① *Mon-Fri 1000-1900, Sat/Sun 1000-2000, 2200 in summer, €6; €7 for combined ticket to here*, is a good one, with a large amount of Atlantic fish and some decent displays and temporary exhibitions.

The ark-like **Domus** ① *1000-1900, 2100 summer, €2, combined ticket with aquarium and Casa de las Ciencias €7, good restaurant*, looks like the hull of a boat and has become something of a city emblem since Japanese architect Araa Isozaki knocked it up. There's a very strange statue of a tubby Roman soldier out the front, but inside it's a good entertaining modern museum of humankind, dealing in all aspects of how we function physically and mentally.

Beyond the Domus, the curve of the city's excellent beach sweeps around the bay. It's a top stretch of sand, slightly marred by poor waterfront architecture. Although there's plenty of space, in summer it can be packed out. At its far end is the **Estadio de Riazor**. The city's football team, **Deportivo La Coruña**, tiny by European standards, rose to the top division in 1991 after decades of second and third division obscurity. They rapidly flourished, playing an exciting brand of attacking football, and in 1994 defender Djukic missed a penalty that would have given them the league title. A decline might have been expected, but Depor kept challenging the giants and finally captured the league in 2000, the first club to wrest the title from Barcelona or Madrid for 16 years. They have become one of the most feared clubs in Europe, particularly here at home, where they are almost unbeatable.

Excursions

The town of **Betanzos** makes a good day-trip from A Coruña. The site of a Celtic settlement, and a significant Roman port, it's an attractive, if slightly faded town that was dealt a bitter blow in the 17th and 18th centuries when the port silted up and Betanzos gradually became an inland town, although it's still a junction of the two pretty rivers that are to blame for the fiasco. In summer you can take a boat trip on them. The tourist office is behind the church on the plaza on the main road through town.

Betanzos's main attraction is its steep streets lined with trademark Galician housing. There are a couple of nice plazas and four churches, of which the absolute highlight is the **Iglesia de San Francisco**, a monastery church built in the 14th century. It was paid for by the count Fernán de Andrade, lord over most of this region, and dubbed 'O Bóo', or The good; it's not clear, probably himself. He had the church built with his own soul in mind: he intended to rest in peace in it, but wasn't prepared to compromise on things too much. His earthly love was boarhunting, and the number of carved boars both outside and in the church is noteworthy. The top attraction, though, is his tomb (although he's not actually in it). It's carved with excellent hunting scenes, all dogs, horns, and tally-ho's, and is mounted on the back of a large stone boar and a rather brainless-looking bear. There are many other tombs of lords and ladies, as well as some bad representations of saints; the coloured wood San Nicolás certainly wouldn't pass muster in these days of paedophilia hysteria. The apse is big and light and holds a simple sculpture of Saint Francis and the Crucifixion behind the altar. The vaulting is elaborate, but the pigs still pull focus.

Iglesia de Santa María del Azogue dates from the 14th century and has a pleasant spacious interior with some slightly skewed columns with good carved capitals. The retablo is dark and is centred on an icon of the Virgin. The façade features the elders of the Apocalypse around a scene of the Adoration on the tympanum. Strange animals adorn the capitals.

Iglesia de Santiago dates from the 15th century and has an excellent carved portal of Santiago Matamoros and the Pantocrator. The capitals on either side of the door are carved with scary beasts. The interior is simple, with a triple nave. In the **Praza Constitución** there's a small museum devoted to modern prints.

Ribadeo and around p588

A Parador de Ribadeo, Rúa Amador Fernández 7, T982128825, www.parador.es. The top place to stay in Ribadeo is this modern and not the most characterful of its brotherhood but with good views across the *ría* and a reasonable seafood restaurant.
B Hotel Mediante, Praza de Espanha 8, Ribadeo, T982130453, F982130578, is on the square and has good rooms slightly overpriced in Jul and Aug but top value at other times.
D Casa Guillermo, Vista Alegre 3, Santiago de Reinante, T982134150, is a good place to stay if you've got kids; it's near to the beach and has a large garden. Comfortable rooms.

Camping

There are several campsites to the west of town and along the coast.
Nosa Casa, Reinante beach, T982134065, Open all year round.
Ribadeo, west out of town, T982131167, which boasts a swimming pool and has bungalows (open Jun-Sep only).

Foz and around p588

A Hotel Ego, Area, T982560987, F982561762, wins more plaudits for its restaurant and excellent views than its name.
C Hostal Leyton, Av Generalísimo 6, Foz, T982140800, F982141712, is a good accommodation option with slightly garish decor. Outside Jul and Aug, it falls into the **E** category.

Viveiro p588

C Hotel Orfeo, Av García Navia Castrillón 2, T982562101, F982560453, is an excellent choice on the water, with comfortable, modern rooms, many of which come with a balcony and a view at no extra cost.
F Fonda Nuevo Mundo, Rúa Teodoro de Quirós 14, T982560025, is a good friendly budget option if you don't mind the odd pealing of churchbells.

Camping

Camping Vivero, T982560004, is across the estuary from the heart of town and on a popular patrolled beach with greyish sand.

Ortigueira to Ferrol p589

D Río da Cruz, T981428057. In the middle of the headland, some 9 km inland from Garita de Herbeira, is a lovely old stone farmhouse with cosy pinewood rooms. Nice meals, which can be eaten on an outdoor terrace.
E Chelsea, Praza Sagrado Corazón 9, Cedeira, T981481111, an acceptable place on a nice little square.

Camping

There's a good (if slightly pricey) campsite at Valdoviño, on the main road near Da Frouxeira beach, T981487076. It's open from Easter to Sep and has bungalows and many facilities.
Fontesín, T981485028, near the Praia do Río, simple campsite which also has good surf nearby; it's open Jun-Sep only.

Ferrol p589

Ferrol has a parador, an unlikely choice that probably had something to do with it being the dictator's hometown.
B Parador de Ferrol, Rúa Almirante Fernández Martín s/n, T981356720, www.parador.esferrol@parador.es. Situated in a good spot, at the end of the old town near the water. Comfortable rooms, many with views. One of the cheapest paradores.
F Hostal Magdalena, Rúa Magdalena 98, T981355615, is clean and cheap, and not as seedy as some of the options around.

Pontedeume and the Caaveiro Valley p591

There are several lodging options in Pontedeume.
B Hotel Eumesa, Av de A Coruña s/n, T981430925, F981431025, has a garish neon front, but good rooms, many overlooking the rivermouth.
E Allegue, Rúa Chafaris 1, T981430035, is a good little place with clean and comfortable rooms with simple bathrooms; it's on a square dominated by an old convent with an attractive patio. There are a couple of other options on this plaza.

A Coruña p591, map p592

There is plenty of quality budget accommodation, concentrated in around Av de la Marina. All categories are significantly cheaper outside Jul and Aug.

LL **Hotel Finisterre**, Paseo del Parrote 22, T981205400, www.hotelfinisterre.com. Superbly located on the headland, this is the nicest place to stay in A Coruña. Recently renovated, the rooms are smallish but bright, and many have superb views over the harbour and sea.

LL **Meliá María Pita**, Av Pedro Barrié de la Maza 1, T981205000, www.solmelia.es. A tasteless, glassy building, this hotel has an excellent location on the city beach. Businesslike in feel, there are significant discounts often offered.

A **Hotel Riazor**, Av de Pedro Barrié de la Maza 29, T981253400, F981253404. A big but pleasant beachfront hotel, near stadium.

C **Hotel España**, Rúa Juana de Vega 7, T981224506, F981200279. A good, bright, clean hotel handy for beach and harbour.

D **Hostal Mara**, C Galera 49, T981257962. In tapas bar heartland, this is a sound option with good, clean ensuite doubles at the quiet end of the street.

D **Hotel Los Angeles**, C Angeles 11, Betanzos, T981771511, F981776459, is a dull, modern choice with an attitude problem.

D **La Provinciana**, R Nueva 7, T981220400, F981220440. An excellent spot to stay off-season, as the rooms are good and drop to a very low price. Can be a little noisy.

E **Carbonara**, R Nueva 16, T981225251. A very good spot with friendly management and good rooms with bathrooms. One of the better choices.

E **Centro Gallego**, C Estrella 2, T981222236. Very good option above a café with excellent modern bathrooms in the rooms.

E **Hostal Barreiro**, C Rollo 6, Betanzos, T981772259, is the best option and has a friendly restaurant, **Os Arcos**. Try the swordfish or king crab (*buey*).

E **Hostal La Perla**, C Torreiro 11, T981226700. Not a bad option; some rooms are better than others.

F **Venecia**, Praza Lugo 22, T981222420. A very cheap option on a square a couple of blocks from the main bar zones. There are rooms with or without bath available.

Camping

El Rasoares. Betanzos, a campsite just outside the town.

🍴 Eating

Ribadeo and around *p588*

€€ **Solana**, C Antonio Otero 41, T982128635, is a good seafood restaurant; try the oysters if they're on, as Ribadeo is known for them.

Foz and around *p588*

€ **Restaurante O Lar**, Rúa Paco Maañon s/n. A good, solid seafood choice by the harbour, and cheap too.

Viveiro *p588*

€€ **O Asador**, Rúa Meliton Cortiñas 15, T982560688, is the best restaurant in Viveiro, a friendly upstairs spot looking over the narrow lane below. The fish, octopus, and service are superb.

€€ **O Muro**, C Margarita Pardo de Cela 28, T982560823, is a popular local *pulpería* with cheap bar snacks and an upstairs restaurant.

€ **The Galicia Café**, Av García Navia Castrillón 5, is another good spot for a drink and a fishy snack.

Ferrol *p589*

€€ **Casa Rivera**, Rúa Galiano 57, T981350759. This well-priced restaurant has excellent seafood and land-based dishes.

A Coruña *p591, map p592*

A Coruña has a superb tapas scene, with octopus (*pulpo*) the excellent local speciality. It's usually served boiled, simply garnished with paprika, olive oil, and salt, and accompanied by *cachelos* (boiled spuds). If you don't mind the texture, it's superb. The best zone for tapas is the long stretch of Calles Franja, Galera, and Olmos stretching westwards from Praza María Pita.

In Betanzos the bars with outdoor seats on the big Plaza Mayor do decent tapas.

€€€ **Domus**, Tue-Sun lunch, Fri/Sat dinner, T981201136. In the Domus museum, this restaurant has superb views out to sea and good if slightly pretentious food.

€€€ **Pardo**, C Novoa Santos 15, T981280021. Coruña's finest restaurant treats its fish just right and is far from overpriced. Good salads too.

Galicia Rías Altas: listings

● *For an explanation of sleeping and eating price codes used in this guide, see inside the*
● *front cover. Other relevant information is found in Essentials, see pages 47-56.*

€€ **Casa de Rosalía**, C del Principe 3, T981214243. Attractively set in an old-town house once lived in by Rosalía de Castro, see box, p578. Recommended is the rich, home-made duckliver *foie*, or the scrambled eggs with sea-urchin eggs. The fish is good too.

€€ **El Manjar**, C Alfredo Vicenti 29, T981251885. A cosy restaurant with excellent oldtime decor near the stadium.

€ **A Casa de Moura**, C Barrera 9. A long, cheery bar with decent cheap tapas.

€ **El Rey de Jamón**, C de la Franja 45. Don't like seafood? The ham in this bar is good: that's why there are about a thousand hams hanging on the ceiling.

€ **La Bombilla**, C Galera 7. A popular bar in the tapas zone that leaks on to the street.

€ **Mesón do Pulpo**, C de la Franja 11. The name says it all; on this street of octopus, this place does some of the best.

€ **Otros Tiempos**, C Galera 54, T981229398. A friendly bar deservedly popular with visitors for its generous and delicious *raciones*. Go for tapas portions if you're not seriously hungry.

Tapas bars and cafés

See also the € category above for places serving tapas in addition to other dishes.
Club Deportivo Ciudad, Rúa Tinajas 14, T981212302. A good, sleek, modern café near the Jardin de San Carlos. Ideal for morning coffees or for watching Deportivo games among fans.
Playa Club, Anden Riazor s/n, T981250063. An airy café with a superb location and views down the beach. Serve a good range of *platos combinados* and tapas.

🌓 Bars and clubs

Ferrol *p589*

As you'd expect from a naval town, Ferrol has a lively bar scene, mostly centred in the old town. One of the pleasanter spots is **Vétula**, Rúa Cantón de Molíns 6, T981354712, facing the park, and a friendly place for a drink or a coffee.

A Coruña *p591, map p592*

After tapas time is over, folk move on to one of two areas. A smarter scene best described as *pijo* (a slightly derogatory slang term for rich young Spaniards) goes on in the streets

around Praza España and the Museo de Bellas Artes. A more alternative crowd hangs out in the bars and clubs around C del Sol and C Juan Canalejo de Corralón between the tapas zone and the beach. At weekends it's as lively as anywhere in Northern Spain.
Cervecería del Centro, Rúa Torreiro 21. A good, cheap spot to drink and snack.
E'Lotro, C Barrera 5. A lively bar with three sections and good ham *pintxos* on the bar.
La Glorian, C Don Francisco 12. An intimate bar in the old town with a relaxed vibe and fishing-fleet-meets-Indian-bazaar-style decor.
Orzán, C/Orzán, is a good, cosy bar that has a cheerful and late scene. One of many top options in this area.
Rochester, C Franja 53. OK, it's an Irish pub, but it's cosy and has moody Belgian Grimbergen cheap on tap.

🎭 Entertainment

A Coruña *p591, map p592*
Centro Rosales, Rosales, T981128092. A very big cinema complex in a shopping centre.
Cine Equitativa, Av Emilia Pardo Bazán s/n, T981120153.
Palacio de la Opera, T902434443. As well as being an opera venue, it is the home ground of the Galician symphony orchestra. Tickets are extremely cheap, ranging from €7-21.

🎉 Festivals and events

A Coruña *p591, map p592*
Coruña's main festival is in honour of **María Pita** and lasts the whole month of **Aug**, with all sorts of cultural events and a mock naval battle. The main week, **Semana Grande**, is in the middle of the month.

🛍 Shopping

A Coruña *p591, map p592*
C del Real, one street back from Av de la Marina, is the handiest shopping street.
Librería Colon, R Riego de Agua 24, bookshop.

⛰ Activities and tours

Viveiro *p588*
You can rent canoes on the Praia de Covas beach just across the *ría* from town.

Roq Sport, T646514602, arrange activities including guided hikes, mountain biking, and archery.

⊖ Transport

Ribadeo and around *p588*
Bus Ribadeo is well supplied with buses, with 8 daily to **Lugo**, 7 along the coast to **Oviedo**, 4 to **Santiago**, and several running to **A Coruña** along the coast. Other destinations include **Vigo**, **Pontevedra**, **Santander**, and **Madrid**. 2 buses head inland to **Vilalba** and **Mondoñedo**.
Train The coastal FEVE train line stops here on its way between **Ferrol** and **Oviedo**. It's a good way to access some of the smaller coastal towns.

Viveiro *p588*
Buses run from here both ways along the coast and inland to **Lugo** and **Santiago**. The bus station is by the water 200 m north of the old town.

Ortigueira to Ferrol *p589*
Buses are the only way to access the coast on public transport, as the FEVE line has cut inland by this point.

Pontedeume and the Caaveiro Valley *p591*
Train Services between **Ferrol** and **A Coruña** call in at Pontedeume, as do buses on the same route.

Ferrol *p589*
FEVE station, RENFE station, and bus station are close together near Praza de España a short way north of the old centre. The new city tourist office is inconveniently located east of here on Estrada de Castela, on a concrete island at a freeway junction; you'd be better off getting information on Ferrol from wherever you're coming from.
Boat A launch service zips across the *ría* to Mugardos from Paseo de la Marina. You get a good view of the port, and Mugardos is a pretty little fishing town; you might want to stay for lunch and try the famed local recipe for octopus.
Bus Santiago, Pontevedra, Vigo, Betanzos, and the north coast are also regularly serviced by bus.

Train Four FEVE trains a day head eastwards towards **Oviedo**; 2 only make it to **Ribadeo**. RENFE trains connect **Ferrol** with **A Coruña**, to where there are also very frequent buses.

A Coruña *p591, map p592*
Air A Coruña's airport lies to the south of the city. There are international flights to **Lisbon** and **Paris** as well as national ones to **Madrid**, **Barcelona**, and **Bilbao**.
Bus The bus station is to the south of town, on C de Caballeros. Frequent buses connect it with the city centre. City bus number 1 runs from the main road between the bus and train stations into town. There are 6 buses a day to **Betanzos** from Coruña, and a couple to Santiago. The buses stop on the road across the river from the old town. Further afield, **Ourense** is served 8 times daily, **Lugo** 11 times, **Santiago** hourly, **Pontevedra** and **Vigo** 9 times, **Betanzos** 6 times, and **Ferrol** hourly. Five buses daily go down the **Costa da Morte** to **Camariñas**. Long-distant services include **Gijón/Oviedo**, serviced 3 times a day, **Santander/Bilbao/ San Sebastián** twice, **Madrid** 6 times, **Salamanca** 3 times, **León** twice, **Valladolid** and **Burgos** once, and **Zaragoza/Barcelona** once. On Fri and Sun a bus leaves at 1400 bound for **Porto** and **Lisbon** in Portugal.
Cycle hire There's a municipal bike rental shed on Paseo de la Dársena by the leisure harbour. Open 0900-2100 summer; 0900-1400, 1600-2100 winter. A 2-hr rental is €6; a whole day costs €21.
Train The train station is just across the main road from the bus station. **Santiago** is serviced 18 times daily, **Vigo** not much less at 16. There are also trains to **Lugo**, **Monforte**, **Ourense**, **Madrid** (3), **Barcelona** (2) and **Ferrol.**

A Coruña *p591, map p592*
Hospital Hospital Juan Canalejo T981178000.
Internet Unnamed copyshop at R Angel 19 and **Estrella Park**, C Estrella 12, has coin-op machines; €1 gets you 40 mins.
Post The main post office is on Av de la Marina opposite the tourist office.
Laundry Express, C de San Andrés; **Clean and Clean**, C Juan Florez; **Self Service**, Paseo Marítimo s/n, near big glass control tower is.

Telephone The sweet shop at C Estrella 14 has a couple of booths and some excellent international rates.

Useful addresses and numbers
Police T092, **General emergency number** T112.

The west coast

Costa da Morte → *Colour map 1, grid A1.*

The rugged coast west of A Coruña is named the 'coast of death', and has an interesting and dark history of marine disasters, wreckers, and 'four and twenty ponies trotting through the dark' smuggling. There are some excellent beaches and some fairly authentic towns, who get on with their fishing and farming as the majority of tourists zip straight down to Finisterre. ▸▸ *For Sleeping, Eating and other listings, see pages 609-615.*

Malpica

The first stop of interest along from A Coruña is Malpica, a lively, unadulterated fishing town ruled by a pack of large and brazen Atlantic seagulls. There's a offshore nesting sanctuary for less forceful seabirds on the **Islas Sisargas** opposite. There's no scheduled boat service to visit the islands, but on a fine day, you can find a boatowner who'll be happy to take you out for a fee. Malpica also has a good beach, which can get pretty good surf.

Ponteceso

Ponteceso has a bridge of medieval origins that crosses the marshy river. If it's beaches you want, stop at **Laxe**, which has a top strand of white sand, and an even better one to the west; peaceful **Praia Traba**. The town itself isn't great apart from that.

Camariñas

The coast continues to be impressive; Camariñas, the next worthwhile place from Ponteceso, makes a good place to stop. It's famous for lace; possibly of more interest is its location, on a pretty inlet stocked with pines and eucalyptus. It looks across the *ría* to Muxía on the other side. The port is small but serious, with some biggish boats heading far out to sea.

The best thing to do in Camariñas is explore the **headland** to the north. There's a series of dirt roads that are just about driveable, but it's nicer on foot with the smell of pine in your nostrils. **Cabo Vilán** is about an hour's walk, a dramatic spot with a big lighthouse building and high, modern windmills, which work pretty hard in these parts. Further east, there are a couple of small **beaches** and an English cemetery, with the graves of some of the dead when a vessel of the British navy was wrecked on the coast in 1890, at a cost of 170 lives. **Museo do Encaixo** details the history and practice of lacemaking; they make it bobbin-style here.

Muxía

The counterpart of Camariñas on the other side of the *ría*, Muxía isn't as charming. It's worth visiting though, to see the **Sanctuario de Nuestra Señora de la Barca** on a headland just past the town. With the waves beating the rocks to a pulp around the chapel, it's an atmospheric place; it's not hard to see why fisherfolk who brave the stormy seas have a healthy religious and superstitious streak around here. The Virgin Mary herself performed an impressive feat of navigation; she sailed from Palestine to this very spot in a stone boat. If you don't believe it, take a look inside the church: various fragments of the vessel are venerated in the sloping interior.

At the foot of the Finisterre peninsula, the fishing ports of Corcubión and Cée have grown into each other, stretching around the bay. It's a fairly serious fishing spot, but the old port in Corcubión is nice, and there are plenty of hotels and restaurants.

Fisterra

Further west from Cée, the town of Fisterra makes a better place to drop anchor for the night. It's an attractive if slightly bleak fishing port, and there are plenty of facilities catering to the passing tourists heading for Cabo Finisterre a couple of kilometres beyond. There's the remains of a small fort and good views across the bay.

Cabo Finisterre and around

The most westerly point in mainland Europe is not Cabo Finisterre. It's in Portugal, and the most westerly point in Spain is a little further up the coast, but Finisterre has won the audience vote. Part of its appeal comes from its name, literally derived from the Latin for 'end of the earth', part from its dramatic location; a small finger of land jutting into the mighty Atlantic. Gazing westwards from the rocks around its scruffy lighthouse is a magical enough experience, particularly at sunset; imagine what it would have been like if you believed the world literally ended out there, dropping off into a void. The cape is 2 km uphill from Fisterra, accessible by road. There's a small bar at the top and a hotel, see Sleeping.

In the middle of the headland, the village of **San Salvador** harbours another excellent place to stay, see Sleeping.

Carnota

Moving south towards the Rías Baixas, the village of Carnota is set 1 km back from a magnificent and wild beach 7 km long and rolling with enormous dunes. Carnota itself has a tourist office at the top of town and a hotel. It also boasts the longest *horréo* in Galicia, for what it's worth, the ridiculous 18th-century structure is 35 m long.

Rías Baixas → *Colour map 1, grid B2.*

The Rías Baixas are a succession of large inlets extending down the west coast of Galicia almost as far as Portugal. The sheltered waters are used to farm much of Spain's supply of shellfish, and the towns still harbour important fishing fleets. It's one of Galicia's prime tourist destinations, which fact has spawned a few myths that it's worth clearing up. Firstly, the *rías* are not 'fjord-like' – the coast is mostly low hills, and the inlets mostly fairly shallow, retreating over mudflats at low tide. They bear more resemblance to certain Scottish firths than Norway's dramatic serrations. Secondly, while there are some decent beaches here, they are generally not as good as those of the Costa da Morte or north coast. Lastly, they are not remote; much of the coast is a continuous ribbon of ugly strip development. That said, there are many spots worth visiting, and much good wine and seafood to be consumed. The cities of Pontevedra and Vigo are fascinating places to discover, and there are several villages and peaceful spots that merit exploration. ▶▶ *For Sleeping, Eating and other listings, see pages 609-615.*

Muros

The small town of Muros sits on the north coast of the northernmost *ría* of the Rías Baixas, which is named after it and Noia, its counterpart across the water. Muros has considerable charm, with a small but atmospheric old town, and a large fishing harbour. The Gothic church contains a Christ crucified that has a head of real hair; there's a lovely market reached by a double staircase, and a curious stone reptile

Galicia Rías Baixas

Shipwrecks and smugglers

The indentations and rocks that abound on Galicia's coastline , while impressive to look at also have a darker side. For it is a sobering fact that in the last 100 years some 140 ships have gone down with the loss of 500 lives. The scandalously mismanaged *Prestige* oil disaster of late 2002 is just one of a long series of shipping incidents on this coast.

Local legend attributes many of these wrecks to the activities of *raqueiros* or land pirates, who would lure ships onto the rocks by attaching lights to the horns of cattle. More likely though it is the combination of sea-surges and savage rocks that make passage along this coast so hazardous.

The natural features of the coast which make it so dangerous for shipping have made it a haven for smugglers down the years. During the last 20 years Galicia's smugglers have moved away from more traditional products towards drugs, especially cocaine. This has had the predictable effect of increasing problems of corruption and violence. The town of O Grove saw its former mayor facing drugs related charges and in Vilagarcia the local Chamber of Commerce Director was the victim of a professional hit. Recently heavy police activity has seen many smugglers relocate to Viana in northern Portugal.

slithering over a fountain. Apart from that, it's just strolling the seafront, and watching boats come and go.

Noia to Padrón

On the other side and further up the estuary, Noia isn't as attractive a place as Muros, being a busier centre for the area. The Gothic **Iglesia de San Martín** is the town's highlight. Fronted by a good *cruceiro*, it's got an excellent carved portal featuring the Apostles and the Elders of the Apocalypse; and a beautiful rose window above. Another church, the **Iglesia de Santa María**, is full of the tombstones that were salvaged from a recent tidy-up of the graveyard. Rough slabs of granite dating from the 10th to 17th centuries, they are carved with simple symbols and figures that seem to fall into four distinct types: marks of profession, rebuses of family names, heraldic motifs, and full figures of the deceased. Noia's tourist kiosk is opposite its town hall, built around a small, attractive atrium.

Continuing south, the coast is a pretty one, with some decent, if sometimes wild-watered, beaches. One of the better ones is **Ornanda**, just short of the decent village of **Portosín**. At **Baroña** there is a Celtic *castro*, a fort-cum-village well situated on an exposed point. A couple of kilometres from the town of Axeitos down a peaceful country lane is one of the nicer of Galicia's many dolmens; it sits in a dappled glade among pinecones. Near here a winding road leads up to a mirador, **La Curota**. If the day is good, the view is absolutely breathtaking, taking in all the *rías*, with their shellfish platforms looking like squadrons of U-boats in harbour. You can see north to Finisterre and south to Baiona, just short of Portugal.

Santa Uxia de Ribeira is the main town in this region, an important fishing port that's a fine enough place but has no real allure. This is the beginning of the next inlet, the **Ría de Arousa**, the largest of this coast. **Cambados** is the most attractive place to stay on this *ría*.

● *It's claimed that the Noia's name derives from that of Noah, because this was the spot the dove found the olive branch; the ark came to rest on a nearby hill. Folk here believe it too, and the event features on the coat of arms of the town.*

Cela Vida

Camilo José Cela was a hard-living author born on the outskirts of Padrón who was known in Spain as much for his flamboyant lifestyle as for his novels. Awarded the Nobel prize in 1989, Cela was a friend of Hemingway and the two shared a robust masculine approach to both life and writing.

Cela's first novel *La Familia de Pascual Duarte* (The Family of Pascual Duarte) had to be published in Argentina in 1942 because its was consided too violent and crude for the the Spain of the time. The story of a murderer, its uncompromising language was unlike anything else that was being produced in Spain. The book inspired many imitations and is said to be the most popular Spanish novel since Cervantes. He published over 70 works including *La Colmena* (The Hive), a novel about the denizens of 1950s Madrid cafés and their lives and loves. The Nobel citation praised his work for its "rich and intensive prose" and its "restrained compassion."

Although he fought for the nationalists in the Civil war Cela later published an anti-Franco magazine which became a forum for opposition to the Spanish dictator. His success as an author enabled him to pursue a colourful lifestyle which among other things saw him touring his native land in a vintage Rolls Royce. He died in 2002.

Galicia Rías Baixas

Padrón

A busy road junction, Padrón at first glance seems fairly unappealing, but it's got several interesting associations. It was a Roman town, and tradition has it that the followers of Saint James landed here after bringing his body back from Palestine. The parish church by the bridge over the river displays the mooring-stone (*el pedrón*) under the altar. There's a small tourist kiosk on the main road.

Padrón is also famous for its peppers, which have denomination of origin status. *Pimientos de Padrón* are seen all over Spain: small green jobs with bags of flavour and usually mild and slightly sweet. They are cooked in hot oil.

Padrón also has a strong literary connection. It was the longtime home of Galicia's favourite poet, Rosalía de Castro, see page 578. Her pretty gardened house has been turned into a museum, the **Casa Museo de Rosalía** ① *opposite the station, Tue-Sat 1000-1330, 1600-1900 (2000 in summer), Sun 1000-1330, €1.20.* In it are various personal possessions and biographical notes. Padrón's other writer was the Nobel prizewinning novelist Camilo José Cela, see box page 603, born on the town's outskirts. A former **canon's residence** has been turned into a museum displaying various manuscripts of his work and personal possessions, including a yellowing newspaper collection. Across the road is the collegiate **Iglesia de Santa María de Iria Flavia**, where the writer was baptized; it claims to have been the first church dedicated to Mary in the world (and therefore the beginning of Spanish polytheism).

Vilagarcía de Arousa and around

Vilagarcía de Arousa is a wealthy, brash place where drug-smuggling money pays for flash cars and tasteless modern villas. It's not a huge town, but with a multiplex cinema and a McDonald's, what more do you need? A much better option can be found just to the north in **O Carril**, a pretty little fishing harbour with several top-quality restaurants; there's also an excellent beach nearby, **Praia Compostela**, that is mobbed in summer.

South of Villagarcía, Illa de Arousa is an island linked to the mainland by a long modern bridge. It's not especially touristy, but not especially characterful here. The main town, Illa de Arousa, is a fishing port that reputedly pulls in more cocaine than crustaceans from its lobster pots. The beaches are sheltered but hardly appealing.

Cambados

This noble old town is by far the nicest place to stay on this *ría*. The highlight is the huge granite-paved square, flanked by impressive buildings and a noble archway, and only slightly marred by the cars zipping across it. Other attractive houses line the narrow lanes of the town. The crumbling **Iglesia de Santa Mariña de Dozo** is now used only as a cemetery; its 12th-century ruins are an atmospheric place.

Cambados is also the centre of the Rias Baixas wine region, which has D.O. (denomination of origin) status. Most of the land under vines is given over to the Albariño grape, which produces highly aromatic whites, fruity and flowery but crisp-finished, somewhat reminiscent of dry German or Alsacien wines; indeed one theory of the variety's origin is that Benedictine monks brought it to the region from the Rhine. It tends to be made in small quantities, and is fairly pricey. Of several *bodegas* in the area, one of the finest is **Martín Codax** ① *5 km east of town, T986524499, it's open for visits by prior appointment Mon-Fri 1100-1300, 1600-2000.* **Expo Salnés** is a tourist board-style exhibition about this area of the Rías Baixas.

O Grove

The resort town of O Grove enjoys an excellent natural setting at the tip of a peninsula at the southern mouth of the *ría*. No doubt it was once a charming fishing port, but the curse of overdevelopment has robbed it of much appeal. Still, it's not wholly spoiled, and could make a venue for a relaxed waterside family holiday, with its large number of hotels and seafood eateries. The most interesting sight in the area is **Acquariumgalicia**, 5 km to the west near the village of **Reboredo**. It's a large and excellent display; of most interest for its detailed coverage of the sealife of the *rías* and North Atlantic, although perennial favourites like piranhas and angelfish are also to be seen. There are some 15,000 creatures spread among the 20 large tanks. From here, you can also sally forth in a glass-bottomed boat to see fish and shellfish at liberty, although the visibility can be a little murky.

The area around O Grove is also good for watching waterbirds; many species can be seen patrolling the muddy edges of the *ría*. The main focus for life in the town is the waterfront promenade where you can find glass-bottom boats tours, see page 613.

A Toxa

It's a sobering thought that A Toxa was described by Georges Pillement in 1964 as "an earthly paradise". A lover of getting off the beaten track, the French travel writer would be appalled at his little island now. It's linked to O Grove by a short bridge, and although it's still attractively wooded, most of the atmosphere has been removed by the construction of several no-holds-barred luxury hotels, ugly apartments, and a casino. If you can beat off the old women selling seashells, stroll around the western half of the island, which is still undeveloped and fragrant with pine. Otherwise, while the hotels lack no comforts, the island reeks of people with more money than sense; in their paranoid wish to keep the rest of society at a healthy distance, they've even installed an armed security guard at the bridge to the outside world.

Praia A Lanzada

The best beach around this region is Praia A Lanzada, on the seaward side of the narrow neck of the peninsula. Its an excellent sandy stretch whose waters are said to boost female fertility. There's a small chapel at the southern end of the beach.

Sanxenxo

The resort of Sanxenxo lies on the northern edge of the Ría de Pontevedra and is something of a focus for the area's nightlife. The nicest bit of it is its high headland, while the waterfront is packed with cafés and bars. There are dozens of hotels; see Sleeping page 609.

Pontevedra → *Phone code: 986; Colour map 1, B2; Population: 75,864.*

In contrast to its overdeveloped *ría*, Pontevedra is a very charming place; its beautiful old town and relaxed street life make it a top place to visit. It's the most attractive town to base yourself in to explore the Rías Baixas; its good bus and train connections make daytrips an easy prospect. Its only downside is the occasionally nostril-searing odour from the massive paper mill a couple of kilometres down the *ría*. ►► *For Sleeping, Eating and other listings, see pages 609-615.*

Ins and outs

Getting there and around Pontevedra's bus station is a 20-minute walk southeast of the town centre on Avenida Calvo Sotelo. There are frequent connections within

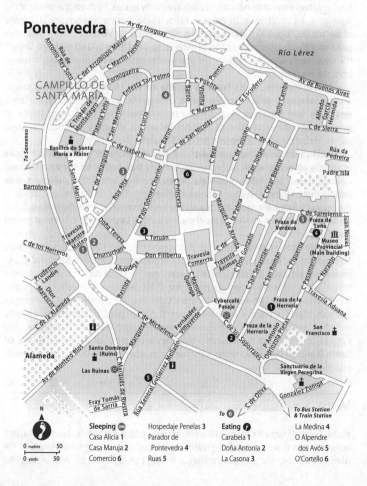

Pontevedra

Sleeping	Hospedaje Penelas 3	Eating	La Medina 4
Casa Alicia 1	Parador de	Carabela 1	O Alpendre
Casa Maruja 2	Pontevedra 4	Doña Antonia 2	dos Avós 5
Comercio 6	Ruas 5	La Casona 3	O'Cortello 6

(side tab) Galicia Pontevedra

Galicia and regular long-distance services. The train station is next door. ➤➤ *For further details, see Transport page 614.*

Tourist information Pontevedra's tourist office ⓘ *Rúa Xeneral Gutierrez Mellado s/n, Mon to Fri 0945-1400, 1630-1830, Sat 1030-1230*, is just outside the old town. There's also a kiosk nearby ⓘ *Alameda, 1030-1330, 1700-1900, Sun 1030-1330*. Guided tours of the town leave from the tourist office in summer at 1100 and 1800.

History

Like several inland Galician towns, Pontevedra was formerly an important seaport but was left stranded by its river, which deposited large quantities of silt into the *ría*, handing Vigo the initiative for maritime activity. It's said that Pontevedra was founded by Trojan colonists that left the Mediterranean after the defeat by the Greeks; though there's little evidence, it's not the most unlikely of the tall stories along this coast. Pontevedra declined in the 17th and 18th centuries, but on being appointed capital of this economically important Galician province a measure of wealth returned, and it's now a fairly prosperous administrative centre.

Sights

Pontevedra's endearing old town is built mostly of granite, and preserves a real medieval feel around its network of postcard-pretty plazas. Perhaps the nicest of the squares is the small, irregular **Praza da Leña**, ringed by attractive houses. Like many of the plazas, it contains a *cruceiro*. The bigger **Praza da Verdura** nearby is another good space with arcades and coats of arms on some of the grander buildings. There's the usual tacky tourist train doing the Pontevedra circuit, with commentary. It leaves from the Plaza de España.

Around the large, social **Praza da Ferrería** are two churches, the curious round, domed **Sanctuario de la Virgen Peregrína**, another Marian cult centre; and the larger **Igrexa de San Francisco**, with some attractive stained glass, carved tombs of goggle-eyed nobles and a fine rose window, as well as an array of unattractive carved saints, including some of the less popular stalwarts.

Basílica de Santa María a Maior is Pontevedra's finest church, which looks especially attractive when bathed in the evening sun. Dating mostly from the 16th century, it has particularly elaborate ribbed vaulting, late Gothic arches, a dark *retablo* that predates the church, and a sloping floor. The fine Plateresque façade is the work of a Flemish master and depicts scenes from the life of the Virgin Mary. In the gardens on the old town side of the church is a stone marking the location of the old Jewish cemetery.

Museo Provincial ⓘ *winter Tue-Sat 1000-1330, 1630-2000, Sun 1100-1400, summer Tue-Sat 1000-1415, 1700-2045, free to EU passport holders, otherwise €1.20,* covers five separate buildings, with the main one on Praza da Leña. It's one of the better such museums in Spain's north; the Celtic jewellery is a definite highlight; there's also a large 19th-century silverware collection and a replica of a 19th-century Spanish frigate admiral's onboard quarters. Some good paintings are present, including works by Goya and Zurbarán among many Galician, Aragonese, and Catalan artists. One of the museums buildings is the atmospheric ruined **Iglesia de Santo Domingo** by the Alameda; it contains a number of tombstones from different historical periods.

Vigo → *Phone code: 986; Colour map 1, grid B2; Population: 287,282.*

Vigo is Galicia's largest city and still a very important Spanish fishing, commercial, and industrial port that supplies huge quantities of sardines, among other things, to the whole of Europe; it's the world's largest fishing port after Tokyo. With a beautiful

location spread along its wide bay, it's a working place and wholly down-to-earth. Traffic problems, urban decay, and poverty are all present and evident, but it still recalls its golden days as an important steamer port bustling with passengers bound for London, Portugal, and South America. Faded but proud old buildings line the streets descending to the harbour, and the fresh seafood on offer here is as good as anywhere in Europe. If you're looking for a quiet, restful stop you may hate Vigo; if you're the sort of person who finds busy ports and earthy sailors' bars a little romantic it's an intriguing and likeable place. ➤➤ *For Sleeping, Eating and other listings, see pages 609-615.*

Ins and outs

Getting there Vigo's airport is Galicia's second most important. The airport is east of the centre, and connected with the city by bus. There are daily flights to several Spanish cities in addition to European and intercontinental connections. The bus station is a good distance south of the city centre, serviced by city buses from Praza Puerta del Sol (No 12 or 7). There are dozens of local buses within Galicia and regular connections to cities throughout Spain. Vigo's train station at the eastern end of town. There are good connections throughout the region. ➤➤ *For further details, see Transport page 614.*

Tourist information Vigo's new tourist office ① *Rúa Cánovas del Castillo, Mon-Fri 0930-1400, 1630-1830, Sat 1000-1200,* is opposite the passenger terminal at the heart of the waterfront.

History

Vigo's top natural harbour was used by the Phoenicians and Celts before the city as we know it was founded by the Romans, who named it Vicus Spacorum. Vigo's curse was often its pretty offshore islands, the Islas Cíes, which were used throughout history as cover and a supply base for a series of swashbucklers, raiders, and pirates, including Vikings, Corsairs, and Britons; Sir Francis Drake spent a couple of years

Vigo

Sleeping	La Nueva	Cre-Cotte **3**	**Bars & clubs**
Bahía de Vigo **1**	Colegiata **5**	Don Gregorio **4**	Edra **9**
Compostela **2**		Don Quijote **5**	La Abadia de
Hostal Puerta	**Eating**	El Corral **6**	Santos **10**
del Sol **3**	Bitacora **1**	El Mosquito **7**	Pedramola **11**
Hostal Savoy **4**	Café Laxe **2**	La Trucha **8**	Pergola **12**

0 metres 100
0 yards 100

menacing Vigo on and off. In 1702 a passing British fleet of only 25 ships heard that the treasure fleet from South America was in the port with a French escort. Their surprise attack was a success; they sank 20 and captured 11 of the fleet. The gold and silver was still on board because at that time only Cádiz had official permission to unload bullion from the colonies. Rumour has it that most of it was dumped into the sea; numerous diving expeditions have been mounted over the last couple of centuries, but no success had been reported. In the late 19th century, as the golden age of the steamer began, Vigo grew massively and became prosperous on the back of this and increasingly efficient fishing methods; nearly all its public buildings date from 1860-1890. Decline set in in the 20th century, particularly during the stultifying Franco years, when Spain lagged far behind other European powers. Pontevedra's status as provincial capital continues to annoy Vigo; there has never been much love lost between the two cities, and locals feel their city doesn't get a fair slice of the pie from the provincial administration.

Sights

Vigo's main sight is its busy **waterfront**. There are kilometres of it to wander if you're so inclined, and even the commercial docks are mostly easily accessible. Right in the centre is the passenger terminal where steamers used to dock; next to it is where the ferries leave for the ports of **Cangas** and **Moaña** across the bay, as well as the **Islas Cíes** in summer. The terminal still gets the odd cruise ship in, and many a yacht still puts in at the marina just to the east, which is backed with expensive bars.

To the west, it's worth having a look at the fishing port, where boats of all sizes and nationalities drop in on their way to and from the Atlantic fisheries. Further round are repair docks and shipwrecking yards, and the **Puerto de Bouzas** beyond is the customs-bonded dock where commercial goods are unloaded. When the fishing boats come in at dawn, *marisqueiras* still sell fresh shellfish around the streets; for a bigger selection, head for the market on **Rúa da Pescadería** near the marina.

The main attraction in the town itself is the elegant architecture on the streets leading back from the passenger terminal, very faded but a poignant reminder of golden days. Just to the west, the narrow streets are the oldest part of the town; it's known as **Berbés**, and is fairly quiet and seedy except at weekends when dozens of bars seem to mushroom from nowhere; it's as lively and hard-drinking a scene as you'd expect.

The new **Museo do Mar de Galicia** ① *Tue-Sun 1000-2100*, is on the waterfront a fair way west of the centre. It's an interesting display of Spanish maritime history and includes an exhibition on the treasure fleet disaster of 1702 and the importance of trade with the New World colonies.

Islas Cíes offshore are a complete contrast to Vigo and the overdeveloped *rías*; an unspoiled natural paradise of excellent beaches and quiet coves, and an old pirates' haunt. During summer, ferries run to the islands from the passenger dock; you'll have to return the same day unless you simultaneously purchase a voucher for the islands' campsite, which has a shop and bar/restaurant. There are four boats a day and a return ticket is €12.

Baiona → *Colour map 1, grid B1.*

Heading south, the elegant port and resort of Baiona is the main destination of interest. On the way, **Playa América** is a long, narrow, popular, and adequate beach with a well-equipped campsite, **Playa América**.

Baiona is a pleasant spot, built behind a large, walled fort on the headland, now a parador ① *€0.60 is haphazardly levied*. It was mostly built by the counts of Andrade, who bossed most of Galicia in their day, but the headland was earlier

inhabited by Celts, Phoenicians, and Romans. Take the 3-km stroll around the impressive walls, reinforced with cannon, and have a drink at the terraced bar; it's a superb spot, even if you can't afford to stay in the parador itself.

Baiona was agog in 1493, when the *Pinta* ① *Wed-Mon 1000-1930, €0.75*, of Columbus's small fleet, appeared at the port entrance with confirmation that the Atlantic could be crossed. There's a replica of the staggeringly small vessel in the port here, enlivened by a dummy crew.

On the hill above town is a giant and appallingly tasteless statue of the Virgin; you can, however, climb it for good views of the town and coast. Baiona has a small tourist office by the entrance to the parador.

A Guarda → *Colour map 1, grid B1.*

The last Spanish town on the Atlantic coast is A Guarda, a fairly uninspiring spot but worth visiting for the Monte Santa Trega high above town. Occupying the headland between the sea and the mouth of the Miño that marks the border with Portugal, it's a long but worthwhile climb (or drive). There's a €0.70 admission charge, but it's well worth it. As well as great views over the town, rivermouth, and out to sea, you can pace the impossibly narrow streets of the ruins of a large Celtic town. One of the round stone dwellings has been reconstructed; the palloza, its direct descendant, was still a feature of many Galician villages until fairly recent years. At the top, there's a chapel and a small museum with some finds from the site.

● Sleeping

Costa da Morte *p600*

There are several options in Camariñas, which gets a fair few tourists in summer.

A Pousada O Semáforo, Estrada do Faro s/n, Cabo Finisterre, T981725869, F981740807, which is situated in a former observatory and telegraph station, and offers considerable comfort and meals above the wild and endless sea.

C Hotel Miramar, Praza Generalísimo 2, Carnota, T981857016, a comfortable place in the centre of town with a restaurant.

D Dugium, San Salvador, T981740780, F981740795, a small and peaceful rural hotel with excellent rooms, a tranquil garden, and a good restaurant.

D Hostal Bahía, Av Generalísimo 24, Ponteceso, T981728207, is a clean and decent year-round option if you're staying.

D Hostal Mariquito, Rúa Santa Catalina 42, Fisterra, T981740375, F981740084, is in the centre and has rooms with views (some), bathroom, and heaters above a pub.

D Hostal Scala, Tras Playa 6, Camariñas, T981737109, is the sort of building that planning permission was invented to stop, but the structure craning to get a glimpse of the water has good, clean rooms.

D Hotel La Cruz, Av López Abente 44, Muxía, T981742084, the best accommodation option in Muxía, a big building with adequate comfort and little character.

D Panchito, Praza Villar Amigo 6, Malpica, T981720307, on the convivial square in the centre of town.

E Cabo Finisterre, Rúa Santa Catalina 1, Fisterra, T981740000, is another decent option, although the rooms can be a little chilly.

E Hostal Dársena, Rúa Alcalde Noguera Patiño 21, Camariñas, T981736263, perches above the far end of the harbour and is another decent option. There are several cafés and seafood restaurants.

E Hostal JB, Calle Playa 3, Malpica, T981721906, is even better, with good rooms overlooking the beach.

E Hostal Marina, C Miguel Freijó 3, Camariñas, T981736030, is on the waterfront and has good, clean rooms with views. There's a small horse-riding operation outside Camariñas, T981737279.

Rías Baixas *p601*

In Muros, there are several options for accommodation along the waterfront avenue. There are so many hotels in O Grove that getting a room is never a problem, even

in summer, although finding a bargain is trickier. There are better places to stay on the *rías* than Noia, but it's not a bad stop.

LL Gran Hotel La Toja, Isla de la Toja, A Toxa, T986730025, F986730026, is the top hotel; it's even got a golf course; the

AL Hotel Sanxenxo, Av Playa de Silgar 3, Sanxenxo, T986724030, F986723779, modern with pleasant rooms, many with views, and good off-season rates (**B**).

AL Louxo, Isla de la Toja, A Toxa, T986730200, F986732791, is no hovel either, and offers the smartest off-season rates (**B**).

A Parador de Cambados, Paseo de Cervantes s/n, Cambados, T986542250, cambados@parador.es. This is a nice place to stay, in a traditional Galicial *pazo* (country mansion), with a good garden and just-renovated rooms.

A Pazo O Rial, El Rial 1, Villagarcía, T986507011, F986501676, a hillside *pazo* (lordly mansion) in a walled garden off the main road. It's well priced for what you get, and it's even got a long *horréo* and *cruceiro*.

B Hotel Maruxia, Prolongación Luis Casais, O Grove, T986732795, F986730507, is a reasonable choice and open year-round.

B Hotel Nueva Lanzada, Praia A Lanzada, T986728232, is a decent beachfront hotel with a restaurant

B Playa Compostela, Av Rosalía de Castro 134, O Carril, T986504010, F986503341, an unremarkable modern hotel that is pricey in summer but fairly reasonable (**D**) at other times.

C Casa Mariñeira Lourdes, Av A Pastora 95, Cambados, T/F 986543985, one of several *casas rurales* in Cambados, of which the nicest is this one, with big bedrooms that feel quite homely.

C Hotel Muradana, Av Castelao 99, Muros, T981826885, is the smartest option in Muros.

D Casa Román, Rúa Carlos Casas 2, Sanxenxo, T986720031, is a more moderately priced alternative.

E Elisardo, C General Franco 12, Noia, T981820130, is near the shallows of the *ría*, and has good, clean rooms with bathroom.

E Hostal Maria Aguiño, R de Pablo Iglesias 26, O Grove, T986731187, is a friendly offering better value than most. Open all year.

E Hostal Pazos Feijóo, Rúa Curros Enríquez 1, Cambados, T986542810, is a decent *hostal* in the southern part of town.

E Hotel Benalua, Rúa Méndez Núñez s/n, Illa de Arousa, T986551335. On the other side of Villagarcía, this is a classy place to stay and a good-value option.

E Hotel Jardín, R Salgado Araujo 3, Padrón, T981810950, which offers excellent value in a big old house by the Jardín Botánico.

E Ría de Muros, Av Castelao 53, Muros, T981823776, F981823133, is a likeable place with a lounge facing waterwards. The best bedroom, also at the front, has a curious bedroom/bathroom annexe.

F Hospedería A Vianda, Av Castelao 49, Muros, has cheap but decent rooms above a café.

Camping

There are 3 summer campsites in Praia A Lanzada, of which the best equipped is: **Cachadelos**, T986745592, which has a pool and bungalows. Open Apr-Sep.
There are a couple of campsites in Illa de Arousa; **Salinas**, T986527444, has the most facilities. It's open Jun-Sep.

Pontevedra *p605, map p605*

For information on paradors in Spain, check out www.parador.es

AL Parador de Pontevedra, R Barón 19, T986855800, pontevedra@parador.es. A lovely parador in the heart of the old town, set in a *palacio* on a pretty square; there's a lovely terrace.

B Hotel Ruas, R Padre Sarmiento 20, T986846416, F986846411. Very well, located hotel in the liveliest area of the beautiful centre. It's **D** off-season.

D Hotel Comercio, R González Besada 3, T986851217, F986859991. A dull but central option with decent ensuite rooms.

F Casa Alicia, Travesía Maestro Mateo 1, T986857079. A cosy spot to stay, this small *pensión* is near the church of Santa María and has good little rooms with shared bath.

F Casa Maruja, Av Santa María 2, T986854901. Good cheap rooms, clean and with TV; some are ensuite. Well located in the old town.

For an explanation of sleeping and eating price codes used in this guide, see inside the front cover. Other relevant information is found in Essentials, see pages 47-56.

F Hospedaje Penelas, R Alta 17.
A lovely cheap option in the old town, clean and comfy.

Vigo *p606, map p607*
Vigo is full of accommodation of all types.
L Bahía de Vigo, Av Cánovas del Castillo s/n, T986226700, F986437487. Grab a room with a view if you're going to stump up for this sprawling hotel, perfectly placed on the harbour.
C Compostela, R García Olloqui 5, T986228227, F986225904. A quality mid-range hotel near the harbour, spruce and comfortable.
C Hostal Puerta del Sol, Puerta del Sol 14, T/F986222364. Can be a bit noisy, but this is a good, well-looked after place at the top of the old town, with a good number of house plants and comfy rooms.
E Hostal Savoy, Rúa Carral 20, T986432541. This was once a fairly grand Vigo hotel, but nothing has changed here since the 1950s. The beds in the bare, high-ceilinged rooms are comfortable enough, though the shower is confrontingly placed alongside. There's bags of character though, and the gentle old Cuban on night duty is the soundest of people.
F Don Quijote, C Laxe 4, T986229346. This good restaurant has some decent, cheap rooms available.
F La Nueva Colegiata, Plaza de la Iglesia 3, T986220952. A decent, cheap option in the old town with modernized facilities and adequate heated rooms.

Baiona *p608*
L Parador de Baiona, Monterreal s/n, T986355000, www.parador.es. One of the chain's finest, this hotel is superbly set among grassy gardens within the impressively walled fort on the headland. The rooms lack no comfort, and many have great views out to sea.
A Pazo de Mendoza, C Elduayen 1, T986385014, F986385988. In the dean's house in the centre of town, this is a classy option.
C Hotel Pinzón, C Elduayen 21, T986356046. A reasonable option on the waterfront, much better value off-season.
E Hospedaje Kin, Rúa Ventura Misa 27, T986355695. Small rooms in a good location

on the main pedestrian street, focus for tapas and restaurants.

Camping
Camping Baiona Playa, Praia Ladeira, T986350035, is a year-round campsite with cabins, a pool, and all the trimmings on a long beach east of the town.
Playa América, T986365404, with bungalows and a swimming pool; it's open mid-Mar to mid-Oct.

A Guarda *p609*
B Convento de San Benito, Praza San Benito s/n, T986611166, is a good option in a restored monastery with a pretty cloister.
F Bar Arturo, Av Rosalía de Castro 3, offers much simpler rooms for a low price.

⊘ Eating

Costa da Morte *p600*
There are some excellent restaurants in Fisterra.
€€ A Pedra do Abalar, Rúa Marina 35, Muxía, is the best restaurant in town; good seafood served.
€€ O Centolo, Paseo del Puerto s/n, Fisterra, T981740452. The classiest of Fisterra's restaurants, O Centolo, serves an excellent range of fish and seafood, and also organizes dinner cruises on the bay in summer.
€€ Casa do Arco, Praza Ramón Juega 1, Ponteceso, T981706904, has a good seafood restaurant.
€€ Casa Velay, Paseo da Ribeira s/n, Fisterra, T981740127, also does seafood and has a terrace by the beach.
€ O Tres Golpes, Rúa das Hortas 2, Fisterra, T981740047. The Three Blows has a distinctly nautical feel, and specializes in good fish stews.

Rías Baixas *p601*
€€€ Loliña, Praza Muelle s/n, O Carril, T986501281. Best of the restaurants here, a superb ivy-swathed place with characterful *gallego* decor. The house speciality is monkfish (*rape*).
€€ Beiramar, Paseo Marítimo 28, O Grove, T986731081, is one of the better seafood restaurants on the waterfront (closed Nov).

Casa Bóveda, Paseo La Mariña 2, O
Carril, T986511204, is a good choice, again
dealing in the fruits of the sea.

€€ **Don Bodegón**, R de Rosalía de Castro
22, Muros, has a good range of seafood and
a half-smart atmosphere.

€€ **María José**, Paseo de Cervantes
s/n,Cambados, is a decent 1st-floor
restaurant opposite the parador.

€€ **O Pementeiro**, C del Castro s/n, Padrón,
is a good spot to try the peppers when in
season (summer). There's also a cheap *menú
del día* for €6.50.

€€ **Posta do Sol**, Ribeira de Fefiñans s/n,
Cambados, T986542285. A good seafood
restaurant housed in a traditional former bar.

€ **A Capela**, R Hospital 37, Cambados,
T986524001, is a good choice for tapas.

€ **A Dársena**, Av Castelao 11, Muros,
T981826864, is a bright and friendly spot
that does decent pizzas and good *raciones* of
pulpo and other seafood.

€ **Finisterre**, Praza Corgo 2, O Grove, T9867-
30748, treats its fish superbly (closed Feb).

€ **Mesón Senra**, R Escultor Ferreiro 18, Noia.
A characterful restaurant that does excellent
zamburiñas (mini scallops).

Pontevedra *p605, map p605*

€€€ **Casa Solla**, Av Sineiro 7, San Salvador
de Poyo, T986873198. An excellent seafood
restaurant showing great innovation in its
dishes, 2 km west of Pontevedra on the way
to Sanxenxo.

€€€ **Doña Antonia**, Soportales de la
Ferrería 4, T986847274. Some excellent
gourmet dishes, including game in season,
can be found at this upstairs restaurant in
the old centre.

€€ **La Casona**, R Tetúan 10, T986847038. A
friendly restaurant that makes an excellent
choice. The food is generally traditional
Galician fare prepared with style; the
lenguado al albariño is a good dish of sole
cooked in the aromatic local white wine.

€ **Carabela**, Praza da Estrela s/n. A café with
a nice outdoor terrace on the largest square,
where you can watch Pontevedra's kids
feeding pigeons.

€ **La Medina**, Praza da Leña s/n. A good
friendly tapas bar with outdoor seating on
this pretty plaza.

€ **O Alpendre dos Avós**, C Gutiérrez
Mellado 6, T986896228. A fairly traditional

scene at this restaurant apart from the dishes
on offer, which include tapas of kangaroo
and ostrich.

€ **O'Cortello**, Rúa Isabel II 36, T986840443.
One of Pontevedra's best tapas options for
typical *gallego* dishes like *xoubas* (sardines).
Cheerful and popular.

Vigo *p606, map p607*
Despite the comic restaurant war between
two *marisquerías* on the waterfront of
Berbés, better value can be found around
C de Carral a little further east, opposite
the passenger terminal. There's excellent
cheap seafood on Rúa Pescadería by the
fish market.

€€€ **El Mosquito**, Praza da Pedra 2,
T986224411. This cheery restaurant in
the old-town streets above the port has
a deserved reputation for its seafood.
Recommended.

€€€ **La Trucha**, R de Luis Taboada 2. A
good corner eatery very popular with a
wealthy set for a small selection of good fish
and seafood.

€€€ **Restaurante Bitacora**, R Carral 26.
Good *raciones* of seafood in this smartish
tapas bar. The *zamburiñas* in garlic are
especially good.

€€ **Restaurante Don Quijote**, C Laxe 4,
T986229346. This restaurant on a steep
street above the passenger terminal is
excellent, particularly its wooden outdoor
tables. There's a full restaurant menu, but
you're as well going for the well-priced
raciones and tapas; the *mejillones* (mussels)
are particularly good.

€ **Cre-Cotte**, R da Oliva 10. A pretty
good *crêperie* with a few restaurants
through Galicia. The savoury and sweet
pancakes are well complemented by
good salads.

€ **El Corral**, R García Ollaqui 36. If you fancy
a change from seafood, head here for some
good ham.

Tapas bars and cafés
Café Laxe, C Laxe 11, T986225081. Very
good pastries and coffees at this popular
workers' café.
Don Gregorio, Plaza Puerta del Sol s/n.
A popular café with a big terrace at the top
of the old town. Good free snacks with
your drinks.

Baiona *p608*

€€€ **Abeiro**, R Ventura Misa 30, T986358375. This smart modern restaurant with excellent *pulpo* (octopus) has a good *menú del día* for €10. Closed Nov.

€€ **Entre Redes**, C Lorenzo de la Carrera 11, for smart seafood *raciones*.

€ **Jaqueyvi**, Rúa Xogo da Bola 1. This is a great spot for ham and cheese tapas.

A Guarda *p609*

€ **Casa Valladeiro**, Paseo Marino 8, has good seafood *raciones*.

🍸 Bars and clubs

Rías Baixas *p601*
Café Theatre is a decent café and bar in the old Mercedes Theatre on the plazaMuros.
Camelot, C del Castillo s/n, Muros, is built into bedrock and has comfy seats to enjoy a drink or 2.

Pontevedra *p605, map p605*
Praza del Teucro is the old-town centre for evening drinking. After hours the *marcha* moves out a little; many people head for Sanxenxo in summer.
Carabás, C Cobián, a typical Spanish *discoteca*.
D'Koña, C Marqués de Aranda 4, is a Latin-flavoured bar among many in the area.

Vigo *p606, map p607*
The bars of Berbés around C Real are seedy but interesting; however they only really get going at weekends. The classier joints around the marina see more midweek action, but are very pricey, particularly if you sit on the terrace. Most of the later *discoteca* action is around the train station.
Edra, Praza de los Pescadores 6. A no-frills little bar tucked in the old town, where locals come to sit outside on the wall and drink beer.
La Abadia de Santos, off C Victoria. A bar with an outdoor terrace unusually located in a side alley that's the entrance to a church. Good beers available.
Pedramola, R Real 25. A good bar if you like your music loud, dark, and metallic.
Pergola, C Pablo Morillo 7. One of the cheaper and better bars in this expensive zone, decorated with orange and Dionysiac wallpaintings.

🎭 Entertainment

Pontevedra *p605, map p605*
Pontevedra has a good cultural programme; look for the monthly guide *BIPO*. The main theatre is the **Teatro Principal**, R Charino 6, T986851932. There are two adjacent cinema complexes on Rúa Barco Porto are **ABC**, T986860392, and **Multicines Pontevedra**, T986860392.

Vigo *p606, map p607*
Multicines Centro, C María Berdiales 7, T986226366, is Vigo's main central cinema.

❋ Festivals and events

Costa da Morte *p600*
On the first Sun after 8 **Sep**, there's a big *romería* to the sanctuary; part of the ritual is a claustrophobic crawl under a huge rock

Rías Baixas *p601*
O Grove's famous seafood festival takes place in early **Oct**.

⊘ Shopping

Pontevedra *p605, map p605*
La Navarra, R Princesa 13. A no-frills place to buy a good selection of Galician wines at decent prices.

▲ Activities and tours

Rías Baixas *p601*
Acquavision, T986731246, and **Pelegrín**, T986730032, also run hourly glass-bottomed boat excursions in summer. The trips take about an 1½ hrs and are about €10 per head. There's most to be seen on and around the shellfish-breeding platforms, and the trip includes a tasting.

Vigo *p606, map p607*
Football Vigo's have-a-go football team, *Celta*, have done well in the Spanish league and Europe in recent years. They don their sky-blue tops at Balaidos, to the southwest of town, normally on a Sun evening. Tickets are available at the stadium for a couple of days before; the booths also open a couple of hours before the game.

● Transport

Costa da Morte *p600*
The excellent **Arriva** service, T902277482, www.arriva.es, covers the Costa da Morte thoroughly. There are at least 5 buses daily to every destination mentioned on the Costa da Mort. Services run to both A Coruña and Santiago.

Rías Baixas *p601*
There are 3 daily buses to **A Coruña** from **Muros**. In case of any confusion, the main avenue along the waterfront has only very recently changed its name from Calvo Sotelo to Castelao. There's a tourist kiosk on the waterfront promenade; from near here buses leave almost hourly for **Santiago** via **Noia**.

There are hourly buses to **Santiago** and **Muros** from **Noia**. Regular buses and some trains connect **Padrón** with **Santiago**.

Buses from Pontevedra visit **Illa de Arousa** a couple of times a day, otherwise it's not too far to walk across to the mainland, where buses along the main road are frequent.

Pontevedra *p605, map p605*
Bus Within Galicia, **Ourense** is served 8 times a day, **A Coruña** about 10 times, and **Santiago** even more often. There are hourly buses to **O Grove**, and even more to **Sanxenxo**. 10 a day go to **Cangas** and buses leave every half-hour or so for **Vigo** (some also go from Calle Arenal). 2 a day go to **Padrón** and **Noia**, and 4 to **Tuy** and **Valença** (Portugal). Hourly buses head north to **Vilagarcía**, some taking in the island of **Illa Arousa**, and 8 go to **Cambados**. 6 buses cross **Galicia** to **Lugo** every day. There are 6 long-distance buses to **Madrid**, 2 to **Bilbao** via **Benavente**, **Burgos**, and **Vitoria**, 1 or 2 to **Barcelona** and **Zaragoza**, 1 to **Salamanca**, **Gijón**, and **Valladolid**. On Fri and Sun there's a bus to **Lisbon** at 1600.
Train There a frequent connections to **Vigo** and **A Coruña** via **Santiago**.

Vigo *p606, map p607*
Air There are daily flights to several Spanish cities, mostly operated by **Spanair**. There are European flights to **Frankfurt**, **Copenhagen**, **Paris**, and **Stockholm**, and intercontinental ones to **Buenos Aires** and **Washington**.

Boat Vigo's days as a passenger port are just about over, but there are still ferries hourly to **Moaña** and half-hourly to **Cangas**, across the bay. In summer boats go to the **Islas Cíes**, see p608.
Bus There are frequent buses to **Pontevedra**, leaving both from the bus station and also from C Arenal 52. Buses to **Santiago** leave half-hourly, and there are about 10 daily to **Ourense**. Buses leave half-hourly for **Baiona**, and for **Tui** and **A Guarda**. There are about 5 daily buses to **Lugo**. There are 6 buses to **Madrid**, 2 to **Bilbao** via **Benavente**, **Burgos**, and **Vitoria**, 1 or 2 to **Barcelona** and **Zaragoza**, 1 to **Salamanca**, **Gijón**, and **Valladolid**. 2 daily buses at 0900 and 1830 leave for **Porto**, **Lisbon**, and the **Algarve**.
Train Galician destinations include **A Coruña** almost hourly, **Ourense** 5 times daily, and **Santiago** via **Pontevedra** about 15 times a day. There are good long-distance connections. There is a **Barcelona** sleeper, a day train to **San Sebastián** and the **French border**, and a day and night train to **Madrid**. There are 2 trains daily to **Porto** (Portugal), and 4 a day to **León**.

Baiona *p608*
Buses run half-hourly between **Baiona** and **Vigo**.

A Guarda *p609*
Buses leave for A Guarda from **Vigo** and **Tuy** half-hourly (fewer at weekends).

● Directory

Pontevedra *p605, map p605*
Hospital Clínica San Sebastián is a medical centre on R Benito Corbal 24, T986867890, with 24-hr attendance.
Internet Cybercafé Pasaje, Rúa dos Soportais 6. An upstairs location with coin-op machines at 40 mins per euro. **Las Ruinas**, C Marqués de Riestra 21, is another option.
Telephone There are cheap *locutórios* on the edge of the old town at C de la Marquesa 1 and C Marqués de Riestra 21.
Useful addresses and numbers Dial T112 for any emergency; T092 gets the local police (T986833080); while 061 is straight to the ambulance service.

Vigo *p606, map p607*
Internet There's a café on R Principe just
above the old town.

Post The central post office is on R da
Victoria.

615

Miño Valley

Rising northeast of Lugo, the Miño sweeps through much of Galicia in a southwesterly direction and forms part of the border between Spain and Portugal before it meets the Atlantic near A Guarda. Its lower sections run through a little-explored region of vineyards, monasteries, and hidden valleys, watering the pleasant provincial capital of Ourense on the way.

Tui/Tuy → *Colour map1, grid B1.*

Perched on a rocky hill high above the north bank of the Miño, Tui doesn't have the scurvy feel of most border towns. Tui is another attractive ancient Galician town that has exchanged growls through history with its counterpart fortress town Valença, across the water in Portugal. A former Celtic settlement, it was inhabited by Romans, then Sueves and Visigoths; briefly serving as capital of the boy-king Wittiza in the early eighth century. It was mentioned by Ptolemy, who named it Toudai and attributed its founding to Diomedes, son of Tydeus. ►► *For Sleeping, Eating and other listings, see pages 619-620.*

Tui has a solid assembly of attractive historic buildings, of which the highlight is the **cathedral** ① *0930-1330, 1600-1900, cloister, tower, and museum €1.80*, which doubled as a fortress for so long. This function influenced the building's architecture, which has a military simplicity. It was started in the early 12th century and has both Romanesque and later Gothic features. There's a door of each type; the Romanesque portal has a simple geometric pattern, while the Gothic door and porch features an excellent sculptured Adoration, an early work with traces of colour remaining. It's flanked by later statues of the Elders of the Apocalypse. Inside are striking wooden beams; the church has a lean and has had to be reinforced through history, especially after the 1755 Lisbon earthquake. The tomb of San Pedro González is here; he was a local Dominican who lived in the 13th century and cared for sick sailors, who dubbed him San Telmo after their patron. There's also an attractive cloister with a walkway above it that gives excellent views, as does the tower. There's a small museum too.

There are several other churches in town, and plenty of narrow lanes and fine old houses. It's a popular place with visiting Portuguese, and the town is well stocked with bars. There's a narrow, attractive road bridge from Spain to Portugal 1 km below the town; it was built by Gustave Eiffel in 1884. Although there's a depressing little border-bargain shopping area nearby, the town of **Valença** itself is a lovely place, well worth ducking across to see.

Ribadavia → *Colour map 1, grid B2.*

Following the Miño upriver, the next place of major interest is Ribadavia, an attractive small town that is the centre of the **Ribeiro wine region**. Ribeiro wines come both in a crisp white and a slightly effervescent red; both resemble Portuguese *vinho verde* and are produced from the same grape varieties.The area was also notable for having been a profitable tin-mining zone.►► *For Sleeping, Eating and other listings, see pages 619-620.*

66 99 The chief object of veneration in the cathedral is the Santísimo Cristo, a similar spooky Christ to the one of Burgos's cathedral. Made of fabric, the figure has real hair and a purple and gold skirt.

Ribadavia is famous for having maintained a sizeable Jewish population from the 12th to 16th century, even after the expulsion order of 1492. There are still some traces of the **Jewish quarter**; the old synagogue still preserves many features despite its conversion into a church and the narrow streets remain, although nearly all the buildings postdate the era. A few Hebrew inscriptions and a Jewish pastry shop evince the town's pride in this part of their history.

The 12th-century **Iglesia de San Xuán** ① *Mon-Sat 0930-1430, 1600-1830, Sun 1030-1500*, has a Romanesque apse and curious portal of Mozarabic influence. The nearby Plaza Mayor is a fantastic long space, which harbours the tourist office. The massive **Convento de Santo Domingo** ① *1000-1300, 1700-2000*, was once lived in by kings; the Gothic church and cloister is worth a look. The Museo do Ribeiro is a fairly unenlightening display on the region's winemaking.

Ourense/Orense → *Phone code: 988; Colour map 1, grid B2; Population: 109,051.*

Traffic-choked Ourense is the capital of Galicia's inland and least interesting (a relative term) province, a rural zone crisscrossed by rocky hills and pastured valleys where much wheat is farmed and cheese and wine are made. The town itself is a prosperous centre with active streetlife. Once you get away from the busy roads and into the pedestrianized old town, it's a pleasant place indeed, and well worth a visit.
▶▶ *For Sleeping, Eating and other listings, see pages 619-620.*

Ins and outs
Getting there and around The train station is across the river to the north of town; from Parque San Lázaro dozens of city buses go in this direction. The bus station is even further in the same direction; buses 6 and 12 make it out there.
Tourist information The tourist office ① *close to the Parque San Lázaro, 1000-1400, 1630-1830 (1700-2100 summer)*, has plenty of information on the city and surrounding region.

History
Although tradition claims that the city's name derives from ouro, meaning gold, it actually comes from the hot springs; the Roman town was named Aquae Urentes, or "warm waters". It was later an important city of the Suevish kingdom, and later of the Visigoths. As an important linking point between Galicia and the rest of Spain, Ourense flourished after its repopulation during the Reconquista. After the decline that seemed to affect almost every city in Spain at some point, it is now a prosperous place, thriving as capital of this significant agricultural province.

Sights
Casco Vello, Ourense's old quarter, is its most interesting part, and a good spot for wandering about. **Catedral de San Martiño** ① *museum 1130-1300, 1630-1900,*

€0.90, was started in the 12th century; most of its features are Transitional in style, ie late Romanesque/early Gothic. The nicest portal is well carved with scalloping and 12 good apostles below a headless Christ. The interior is long and gloomy, with many tombs of prelates carved into the walls; the attractive galleried cupola is a later early Renaissance work. There's an impressive version of Santiago's Pórtico de la Gloria, preserving much of its bright paintwork. Off the cloister is the cathedral museum.

Praza Maior is just by here, a nice arcaded space. It's overlooked by the **Museo Arqueolóxico**, the provincial museum, very attractively set in the former bishops' palace. It's currently undergoing significant renovation, but is due to open again in

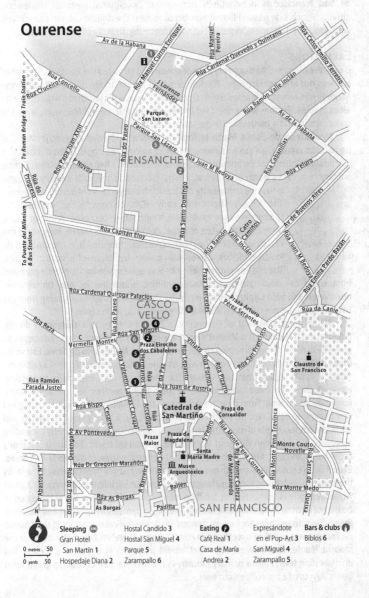

Ourense

Sleeping	Hostal Candido **3**	Eating 🍴	Expresándote	Bars & clubs 🍸
Gran Hotel	Hostal San Miguel **4**	Café Real **1**	en el Pop-Art **3**	Biblos **6**
San Martín **1**	Parque **5**	Casa de María	San Miguel **4**	
Hospedaje Diana **2**	Zarampallo **6**	Andrea **2**	Zarampallo **5**	

0 metres 50
0 yards 50

late 2003. It contains many Celtic finds as well as sculpture and paintings.

The pretty little **Praza da Magdalena** is off the main square and dominated by the cathedral and the Iglesia de Santa María Madre, an attractive Baroque church built from the ruins of the 11th-century original; some Romanesque columns and capitals are preserved.

The main pedestrian streets to stroll down of an evening are the **Calle Santo Domingo** and the **Rúa do Paseo**. Fans of cream and brown should check out the latter; at No 30 the **Edificio Viacambre** looks like a Chinese puzzle-box gone horribly wrong. Ourense isn't known for its liberal politics; on Rúa Capitán Eloy you can check out a memorial to the young Fascist who gave his name to the street. The cloister of **Iglesia de San Francisco** is a beautifully harmonious Transitional piece of stonework, although each side has a different number of arches. The double columns are carved with good capitals, many vegetal, but some featuring an array of strange beasts.

Excursions

Below the old town, **As Burgas** is the hot spring that attracted the Romans. The water streams out at a healthy 65°c. The Romans built a high bridge over the flood-prone Miño; it was rebuilt in medieval times, and is still in use; it's worth the walk to see its elegant lines. Further along the river is the writhing Puente del Milenium, a recent construction that's particularly impressive when floodlit.

Monasterio de Santa María la Real de Oseira ① *guided tour only; Mon-Sat 0930-1230, 1500-1730 (1830 summer), Sun 1230 only, €1.20,* is often dubbed the 'Escorial of Galicia' for its immense size and harmonious Renaissance lines. Sitting solitary in a valley north of Ourense, it was founded in the 12th century and still houses a community of Cistercian monks in archtectural splendour. The façade, from the early 18th century, is of monumental Churrigueresque style; the Virgin Mary occupies pride of place underneath a figure of Hope. Below is Saint Bernard, founder of the Cistercian order. The most interesting thing inside is the Claustro de los Medallones, carved with quirky depictions of historical figures.

❖ *As well as Ribadavia, there are many good things to see within daytrip range of Ourense.*

The austere church belies its Baroque façade and is of little joy apart from some colourful 17th-century wallpaintings. Worth the journey on its own, however, is the Sala Capitular, with beautiful vaulting flamboyantly issuing from the twisted barbers-pole columns; it's like a fireworks display in stone.

Of the main road east of Ourense is a beautiful gorge, the **Gargantas do Sil**, running up a tributary of the Miño. It's worth exploring by car or foot; viney terraces soon give way to rocky slopes dropping steeply into the river. **Monasterio de Santo Estevo de Ribas de Sil** stands out like a beacon with its pale walls and brick-red roof against the wooded valley. Apart from the setting, the monastery isn't especially interesting, although there are three cloisters, one of them huge; another still preserves some Romanesque arching. From near the monastery, the GR56 long-distance trail is a good way to explore some remote areas of Ourense province. It heads along the gorge and takes in another couple of monasteries along its 100-km route, before finally ascending steeply to the mountain village of **Manzaneda**, a small ski resort. The N120 continues León-wards and bids farewell to the Miño just before the town of **Monforte de Lemos**. Even if you've got a car, it's worth making a return train journey from Ourense to here, as the route is spectacular, running along the river and cutting into the Sil gorge for a short while. Monforte is dominated by a hilltop monastery and medieval tower that used to be part of a castle. Near Monforte are the amusingly named towns Sober and Canabal. Beyond Monforte, there are several ruinous castles in the valley, including the **Castelo de Torrenovaes** looming over the road near Quiroga. There's a Roman tunnel near the road at Monferado. The last major settlement in Galicia is O Barco, a friendly but uninteresting town whose primary industry is the manufacture of orujo, a grape spirit better flavoured or in coffee than neat.

● Sleeping

Tui *p615*
See www.parador.es for information on Spain's paradors.

A Parador de San Telmo, Av de Portugal s/n, T986600309, tui@parador.es. Below the town, in a modern replica of a Galician *pazo*, the San Telmo offers good views of the town and river. The best lodging option.

F Hostal Generosa, Av Calvo Sotelo 37, T986600055. A simple choice with shared bathrooms.

F O Cabalo Furado, Praza Generalísimo s/n, T986601215. Decent rooms by the cathedral, and also home to one of the better restaurants around, with cheerful and generous mid-range priced Galician *cocina de siempre*.

Ribadavia *p615*
E Hostal Plaza, Plaza Mayor 15, T988470576, is the nicest place to stay; a clean, modern choice right on the beautiful main square.

Ourense *p616, map p617*
Ourense's accommodation is very well priced.

AL Gran Hotel San Martín, Curros Enríquez 1, T988371811, F988372138. Looming over the park, this hotel has comfortable modern rooms, many of them with good views of the town.

D Hotel Parque, Parque de San Lázaro 24, T988233611, F988239636. A clean and proper Spanish hotel, not particularly memorable, but a comfortable spot overlooking the park.

D Hotel Zarampallo, R San Miguel 9, T988220053. An attractive central option above a good restaurant. Rooms with or without bathroom are available.

F Hospedaje Diana, C Santo Domingo 47, T988231256. Clean and well-located simple *pensión* on a pedestrian street near the Parque San Lázaro.

F Hostal Candido, R Hermanos Villar 25, T988229607. Good location on a quiet square; the ensuite rooms have big windows and balconies.

F Hostal San Miguel, R San Miguel 14, T988239203, F988242749. Good cheap

rooms with or without bath (**G**), very well located in a quiet corner of the old town.

● Eating

Ourense *p616, map p617*
€€€ **San Miguel**, R San Miguel 12, T988221245. An excellent choice for seafood, with superb sardines and a good wine list.

€€ **Casa de María Andrea**, Praza Eirociño dos Cabaleiros 1. An excellent option with a great location overlooking a pretty little square. The interior is modern and stylish; the upstairs dining area is arrayed around the central atrium and there's an excellent *menú del día* for €10.

€€ **O Grelo**, Rúa Chantada 16, Monforte de Lemos, T982404701. This is an excellent spot for lunch. Friendly traditional food cooked with a sure touch.

€€ **Zarampallo**, R San Miguel 9, T988220053. One of Ourense's better choices for a meal, with smart Galician fish and stews and a set *menú del día* for €8.

Tapas bars and cafés
Café Real, R Coronel Ceano Vivas 3. A nice, old-style café, very spruce and traditional.

Expresándote en el Pop-Art, C Santo Domingo 15. With a name that means 'expressing yourself via pop-art', this was never going to be anything other than a lively, relaxed café and bar.

● Bars and clubs

Ourense *p616, map p617*
There are many good modern bars in Ourense, but the 'CLUB' signs in the southern end of the old town indicate brothels, not *discotecas*, which are around Praza del Corregidor, C Pizarro, and Rúa Viriato.

Biblos, C Santo Domingo 10, is a lively modern bar, one of many interesting such spots in Ourense.

● Entertainment

Ourense *p616*
Teatro Principal, R da Paz 11, has regular theatre and occasional arthouse cinema. Tickets are cheap.

● For an explanation of sleeping and eating price codes used in this guide, see inside the
● front cover. Other relevant information is found in Essentials, see pages 47-56.

✹ Festivals and events

In early **May**, there's a **wine festival** in the Ribadavia.

✸ Transport

Tui *p615*
Boat There are crossings at A Guarda, and the village of **Goián**, which has a fort and an excellent place to eat in friendly **Hostal Asensio**, R Tollo 2, T986620152, where superb dishes include lamprey (in season) and other seafood; there's also a *menú del día* for €8.
Bus There are half-hourly buses from **Tui** to **Vigo** and **A Guarda**, and some across the river to **Valença**. From A Guarda, the road follows the north bank of the Miño to Tui, and the first bridge into Portugal.
Train The station, north of the centre, has 2 trains a day to **Vigo** and to **Porto**; it's easier to walk across to **Valença**, where there are more trains. Guillarei station, ½ hr to the east, has connections inland to **Ribadavia** and **Ourense**; a lovely trip.

Ribadavia *p615*
There are frequent **buses** and **trains** to and from **Ourense**.

Ourense *p616, map p617*
Bus There are 6 or 7 buses daily to all of **Santiago**, **Lugo**, **Pontevedra**, and **A Coruña**, and about 10 to **Vigo**. Buses run very regularly to **Ribadavia**, and twice daily to **Celanova**. There are several buses to **Verín** and the Portuguese border at **Feces**, and one daily to **Porto**. Buses run westwards to **León** 4 times daily, **Burgos** 3 times daily, **Madrid** 5 times, **Zamora** and **Salamanca** 3 times.
Train There are a few trains daily heading east to **León**, **Madrid**, and also further destinations. Several go to **Vigo** and **A Coruña**, stopping in **Ribadavia** among other places.

✹ Directory

Ourense *p616, map p617*
Laundry **Lava Express**, R Marañon 17.

621

Castilla-La Mancha and Extremadura

✴ Footprint features

Introduction

These provinces are about as far off the beaten track as you can hope to get in Spain. Castilla-La Mancha is vast and much of it is frankly uninspiring: the flat, monotonous heartland of La Mancha was made famous by Cervantes in his classic novel Don Quijote, and every village has sought a connection with the author or his imaginary knight in order to raise their profile. However there are places worth travelling to. Westwards is the spectacular city of **Cuenca**, with its famous 'hanging houses' clamped vertiginously above a gorge, and the rosy medieval town of **Sigüenza**. Eastwards, wander around graceful, Renaissance **Pastrana** or explore the wild mountains and valleys of the **Alcarría region**. If you are heading south to Andalucía, stop off at the bodegas of **Valdepeñas**, or visit the oldest theatre in Europe in delightful whitewashed **Almagro**. Your own transport is virtually essential throughout this sparsely populated and little visited region.

Extremadura is finally beginning to emerge from a long, long sleep. It has always been one of the poorest and emptiest corners of Spain, and the conquistadores were just the first in a long line of Extremaduran exiles who have been forced to find a better life elsewhere. Things are finally looking up, thanks in part to the burgeoning tourist trade: the perfect Renaissance cities of **Cáceres** and **Trujillo**, built with silver and gold from the Americas, and ancient **Mérida**, which contains one of the finest collections of Roman monuments in all of Europe, are beginning to feature on tourist itineraries. But much of the region remains incredibly unspoilt: the remote valleys of the mountainous north, scored with rivers and gorges, are scattered with stone hamlets where outsiders rarely penetrate, and the whitewashed villages of the sun-baked south have all the charm of their Andalucían counterparts with none of the tourist flummery.

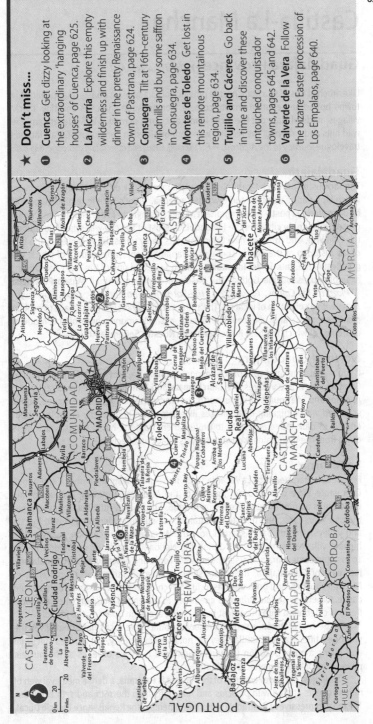

★ **Don't miss...**

① **Cuenca** Get dizzy looking at the extraordinary 'hanging houses' of Cuenca, page 625.

② **La Alcarría** Explore this empty wilderness and finish up with dinner in the pretty Renaissance town of Pastrana, page 624.

③ **Consuegra** Tilt at 16th-century windmills and buy some saffron in Consuegra, page 634.

④ **Montes de Toledo** Get lost in this remote mountainous region, page 634.

⑤ **Trujillo and Cáceres** Go back in time and discover these untouched conquistador towns, pages 645 and 642.

⑥ **Valverde de la Vera** Follow the bizarre Easter procession of Los Empalaos, page 640.

Castilla-La Mancha

Guadalajara Province → *Colour map 5, grid A1/2.*

Like much of Castilla-La Mancha, the province of Guadalajara boasts unappealing big towns but some beautiful remote corners. Romanesque churches and tiny 'black' villages made of slate dot the rocky landscape north of medieval Sigüenza, and the wild hills and valleys of the Alcarría were immortalised in Camilo José Cela's famous travelogue *Journey to the Alcarria*. ▸▸ *For Sleeping, Eating and other listings, see pages 635-638.*

Guadalajara

The lacklustre provincial capital of Guadaljara sits just off the NII/E90 motorway which zips northeast of Madrid towards Zaragoza. There's little to remind visitors of its once glorious past – as an important Muslim stronghold in the Middle Ages, and a prosperous, noble city after the Reconquista. Most of the city was wiped out during the Civil War, and much of new Guadalajara is sadly uninspiring. However, the tiny *casco histórico* at the centre contains a handful of enjoyable sights, of which the grandest is the **Palacio del Infantado**, built in 1483 and one of the most flamboyant examples of Isabelline Gothic. The basement contains a small **Museo Provincial** ① *Plaza de los Caídos, T949212773, Tue-Sat 1030-1400 and 1615-1900, Sun 1030-1400*, with a collection of local art. The 19th-century **market** is a good place to pick up picnic supplies, and you could also take a stroll around some of the Mudéjar churches, of which the best is the **Iglesia de Nuestra Señora la Antigua**.

North of Guadalajara

If you've got time (and your own transport), explore the little-visited region north of Guadalajara, where villages like **Marchamalo** and **Yunquera de Henares** still boast *palacios* and fine squares. Further north, the landscape becomes more rugged, and is scattered with intriguing little villages like **Campillejo** and nearby **El Espinar**, built entirely of dark stone and slate to protect them from the harsh winds which blow down from the mountains (known locally as 'black architecture').

La Alcarría

Few people had heard of La Alcarría, until nobel-prize winning author Camilo José Cela wrote *Viaje a la Alcarria* (Journey to the Alcarria), a moving account of his wanderings on foot through the region in 1946. Surprisingly little has changed more than 50 years later, and remote mountain roads still meander through wild forests and valleys. Already battle-scarred from the Wars of the Succession, many of the highest villages were deserted during the Nationalist advance on Madrid in the 1930s, and some remain sparsely populated. **Torija** and **Aldeanueva de Guadalajara**, just east of Guadalajara, have handsome arcaded squares and a smattering of Mudéjar chuches, and **Brihuega** has a clutch of crumbling *palacios* and a battered old castle. Otherwise sedate Brihuega goes mad at the end of October, when the local fiesta is celebrated with the oldest bull-running events in Spain. is the friendly

To the east of **Durón**, a series of reservoirs built in the 1950s have been given the grandiose title, **Mar de Castilla**; they are not especially pretty, but families still swim and picnic around **Sacedón** (apparently unfazed by news of leaks at the nuclear power reactor near Almonacid de Zorita).

The largest and loveliest town of the Alcarría is **Pastrana**, a dense medieval web of narrow streets stuffed with *palacios* and mansions from the 16th and 17th centuries. The most impressive of Pastrana's many monuments is the Renaissance **Palacio Ducal**,

where Felipe II's favourite, the Princess d'Eboli, was imprisoned by her husband during the last five years of her life. She was allowed to appear at the window for just one hour a day, which gave the square below its name: the **Plaza de la Hora**.

Sigüenza

Dreamily set on a hilltop in the northeastern corner of Castilla-La Mancha, Sigüenza is a tranquil pink-and-ochre medieval town. With a strategic location on the banks of the Río Henares, it became by turns a Celtic-Iberian settlement, a Roman and Visigothic military post, and was taken by the Muslims in the eighth century who held it until the 1120s and crowned it with a fortress. After the Reconquista, Sigüenza was eventually given to the Church, and was ruled by powerful archbishops until the end of the 18th century.

The first archbishop of Sigüenza ordered the construction of the city's extraordinary Gothic **cathedral** ① *Tue-Sat 0930-1330 and 1630-1930, Sun 1130-1300 and 1630-1730, guided visits of the chapels €1.80 Tue-Sat at 1100, 1200, 1630 and 1730*, which looms magnificently over the cobbled Plaza Mayor. Built of soft, rosy stone, it was begun in 1123, and completed more than three centuries later. Its austere lines and crenellated towers betray its dual function as a place of worship and front-line fortress in the continuing battles with the Muslim armies. Deep in the sombre interior is the tomb of Doncel Martín Vázquez de Arce, a 25-year-old page to Isabella the Catholic, who died in a battle against the Moors in 1486. In the Sacristía de las Cabezas, the roof erupts with hundreds of sculpted heads by Covarrubbias – Moors, knights and angels emerge in giddy profusion. Opposite is the 16th-century Capilla de los Reliqarios, with an enchanting cupola and an *Annunciation* by El Greco. There are illuminated hymn books and Flemish tapestries in the Sala Capitular, off the tranquil Gothic cloister, but most of the cathedral treasures, including a painting by Zurbarán, can be found next door in the **Museo Diocesano** ① *Tue-Sun 1100-1400 and 1600-1900, €1.80*.

The arcaded **Plaza Mayor**, recobbled after being destroyed in the Civil War, is surrounded by 15th- and 16th-century mansions, some still pocked with bullet holes and shrapnel. From here, the Calle Mayor head up past the Mudéjar Iglesia de Santiago to the Alcazaba, a castle-palace built for the Archbishops on the ruins of the Moorish fortress. Heavily restored in the 1970s, it's now a luxurious parador.

North to Atienza

Northwest of Sigüenza, the Ruta del Románico Rural follows a string of small villages with an impressive array of Romanesque churches, but you'll need your own transport. The route culminates in Atienza, perched high on a crag, where five Romanesque churches survive to administer to a population of just 500 souls – incredibly, more than 10,000 people lived here at the time of the Reconquest. Atienza's striking castle, complete with moats and turrets, seems to erupt from the rock above the village, and its impregnability even merited a mention in the *Song of El Cid*. The oldest of the churches is **Santa María del Rey**, on the outskirts of the village, with a charming, time-worn sculpted portal.

Cuenca and around

→ *Phone code: 969; Colour map 5, grid B3; Population: 4,2817; Altitude: 1001 m.*

Cuenca, clamped improbably to a sheer rock, is one of the most startling cities in all Spain. When the medieval builders ran out of room, they, like their 20th-century counterparts, decided to expand vertically. But unlike Chicago or New York, their buildings headed downwards to create the city's signature 'Hanging Houses', suspended precipitously over the gorges. Surrounded by the dramatic peaks of the

Serranía de Cuenca, it's no wonder that the city is so popular with weekending Madrileños and Valencianos – come during the week if you can to avoid the crowds. ▸▸ *For Sleeping, Eating and other listings, see pages 635-638.*

Ins and outs

Getting there The bus and train stations are next to each other in the new part of the city: take bus No 1 up to the top of the old city. There is a taxi stand outside the train station (or call Radio Taxi T969233 343). There are regular direct bus and train connections with Madrid and other major cities. ▸▸ *For further details, see Transport page 638.*

Getting around The main sights in Cuenca are clustered in the old part of the city at the top of the hill; if you can't face the hike up, take bus No 1 or 2.

Best time to visit Cuenca is a popular summer retreat from the heat, and it's best to come mid-week. Easter is a good time to visit, for the celebrations of Semana Santa and the international music festival, but book accommodation well in advance.

Tourist information The office ① *Plaza Mayor 1, T969232119, www.cuenca.org*, is hard to spot but it's just by the entrance archway.

Sights

Sinuous **Calle Alfonse VIII**, with its spindly houses painted ochres, yellows and blues, winds steeply uphill from the modern town to reach the hub of old Cuenca, the expansive **Plaza Mayor**. Flanked by a flamboyant 18th-century triple archway, and an uneven string of narrow, multicoloured townhouses, it's dominated by the vast bulk of the **cathedral** ① *Tue-Fri 1100-1400 and 1600-1800, Sat 1100-1400 and 1600-2000, Sun 1100-1400, admission to Tesoro €1.50.* Behind the jarring neo-Gothic façade (tacked on a century or so ago) lies a soaring 13th-century Gothic interior, softly lit by contemporary stained glass windows. The spacious ambulatory is the most attractive section of the cathedral, with a series of small chapels and a flamboyant 18th-century Transparente under which the apparently uncorrupted remains of San Julién lie in a silver casket. The **Tesoro Catedralico** is stored in the elaborately vaulted and gilded 16th-century sacristy. There's not much to see besides a collection of reliquaries and Baroque statuary, but the adjoining Sala Capitular has a beautiful carved wooden door (by Alfonse Berruguete) surrounded with Plateresque stucco work. Inside is what must once have been an exquisite artesonado ceiling, unfortunately painted a sickly shade of pink in the 18th century.

Calle Obispo Valero winds around the back of the cathedral and past the enormous Archbishop's Palace, part of which has been converted into the **Museo Diocesano** ① *C/Obispo Valero 3, T969224210, Tue-Sat 1100-1400 and 1600-1900, Sun 1100-1400, €1.80/.90.* Past the medieval virgins and fragments of old carpets, a stairway leads to an underground gallery where the real treasures are kept: among the glittering gold and silver is the exquisite staff of San Julien, and a shimmering 13th-century Greek diptych dripping with precious stones. There are two small El Grecos, and a remarkable *Crucifixion* by Gerard David. Almost opposite the Museo Diocesano is the engaging **Museo de Cuenca** ① *Tue-Sat 1000-1400 and 1600-1900, Sun 1100-1400, €1.20/.60*, which displays finds discovered at Roman Segóbriga (see below), including statuary and some gruesome-looking medical instruments, and a thin collection of Visigothic and Mozarabic ceramics.

At the end of this street are Cuenca's most emblematic sights, the **Casas Colgadas (Hanging Houses)**, dramatically clamped to the steep rock. They have been completely restored to house a fine restaurant (see below) and the excellent **Museo de Arte Abstracto** ① *C/Casas Colgadas, T969212983, Tue-Sat 1100-1400 and 1600-1900, €3/1.50*, now run by the Fundación Juan March. A series of whitewashed galleries provide a sleek setting for some of the best known Spanish abstract artists of the 1950s and onwards. Outside the museum, a small square offers fantastic views across the gorge to the vast **Monesterio de San Pedro**, now the parador. You can head down the

vaulted passage to arrive at the spindly **footbridge of San Pedro**, where some
fantastic walks begin along the banks of the narrow river.

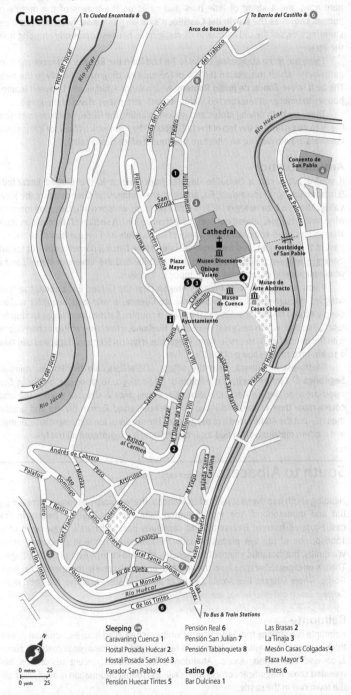

Cuenca

To Ciudad Encantada & 1

To Barrio del Castillo & 6

Arco de Bezudo

C del Trabuco

Río Júcar

C Hoz del Júcar

Ronda del Júcar

San Pedro

8

Río Huécar

Pilares

1

Julián Romero

San Nicolás

3

Severo Catalina

Almas

Convento de
San Pablo

4

Carretera de Palomera

Cathedral

Plaza
Mayor

Museo Diocesano

Obispo
Valero

Footbridge
of San Pablo

5 3

Clavel

Colmillo

4

Museo
de Cuenca

Museo de
Arte Abstracto

Casas Colgadas

Fuero

Ayuntamiento

C Alfonso VIII

Santa María

Alcázar

M Diego de Valera

C Alfonso VIII

Balada de San Martín

Paseo del Huécar

Bajada
al Carmen

2

Andrés de Cabrera

Palafox

Sto
Domingo

F Muelas

Peso

Artículos

M Viejo

Bajada Santa
Catalina

Retiro

T Retiro

Glez Francés

M Cano

Moreno

Solera

2

Olivares

Canaleja

Paseo del Huécar

C de los Tintes

Pósito

Gral Santa Coloma

7

Av de Ojeba

La Moneda

Río Huécar

Tintes

C de los Tintes

6

To Bus & Train Stations

Paseo del Júcar

Río Júcar

0 metres   25

0 yards   25

N

Castilla-La Mancha & Extremadura Cuenca & around

Calle San Pedro leads uphill from the Plaza Mayor to the **Arco de Bezudo**, a stone gateway which is all that remains of the castle. There's a big car park here now, and a string of little bars and cafés on the fringes of the huddle of houses known as the **Barrio del Castillo**; it's lacking in atmosphere, but you'll get stunning views of the old town with its vertiginous houses apparently erupting from the rock.

There are more staggering views to be had from the **Rondas** – narrow roads or pathways – which run around the rim of the old city, clinging perilously to the rock. The best is the **Ronda de Julián Romero**, which winds whimsically between leaning houses to emerge at unexpected moments with vertiginous views of the gorge.

There are both driving routes and walks (including the GR66, which departs from the Arco de Bezudo at the top of the hill) around the town which allow for glimpses of Cuenca's gravity-defying architecture (the tourist office has details).

Around Cuenca

If you've got a car, a favourite day-trip from Cuenca is the **Ciudad Encantada** (Enchanted City) ① *1000-dusk, €2*, about 12 km northeast of Cuenca along the Júcar Valley. This is a bizarre region of limestone outcrops whipped into fabulous forms by wind, rain and time, spread out over more than 20 km². A section of the most unusual shapes has been enclosed (with plenty of restaurants and even a *hostal* by the car park at the entrance), and they have all been given fanciful names. Look out for the 'Struggle between the Elephant' and the Crocodile and the 'Lovers of Teruel', and a whole menagerie of creatures from hippos to tortoises.

If you are heading west towards Aragón from the Ciudad Encantada, the road wriggles through the dramatic **Serranía de Cuenca**, a wild and beautiful region, deeply scored by the Júcar Gorge. There are a couple of attractive villages to stop for lunch, like **Uña**, which has great views, and **Huélamo**, a tumbling whitewashed village with the ruins of an Arab castle. From **Tragacete**, a typical Sierran village, you can take a 10 km-hike to the source of the Júcar river.

Southwest of Cuenca, near the village of Saelices, are the Roman ruins of **Segóbriga** ① *Ctra de Saelices a Villamayor de Santiago, T679090444, 15 Apr-15 Sep 0900-2100, 16 Sep-14 Apr 1000-1800, €2*. It was once a sizeable town – the area covers more than 10 ha², and includes a well-preserved Roman theatre and amphitheatre – but the Arabs razed it to the ground. The history of the settlement is recounted in a modern museum. You need a car to get there; it's signposted off the NIII.

South to Albacete → *Colour map 5, grid B3/C3.*

Heading south into the vast plain of La Mancha, the landscape becomes increasingly flat and monotonous. The much-vaunted Ruta del Don Quijote begins in the castle-topped town of Belmonte, and continues past Dulcinea's home town of El Toboso, one of the few places actually mentioned by name in Cervantes' story. Windmills, the romantic giants of La Mancha, stand in clumps next to dusty villages. There's unexpected respite from the endless, arid landscape in the spectacular Júcar Gorge, where villages like Alcalá Del Júcar are piled steeply above the river. ▸▸ *For Sleeping, Eating and other listings, see pages 635-638.*

Belmonte

Belmonte is a striking fortified village of whitewashed, tiled houses, hemmed in with thick 14th-century walls and dominated by a magnificent hexagonal castle ① *1000-1400 and 1600-1900, €1.80*. Abandoned for centuries, recent restoration has revealed some magnificent *artesonado* ceilings. Tourist information is available from the town hall in the castle.

Alarcón

Heading east of Belmonte, the lofty, fortified village of Alarcón is almost completely encircled by a loop of the río Júcar. Rising steeply on a rocky outcrop, it's a dramatic sight, and is topped by an impressive castle (now a parador). It's another popular weekend jaunt for Madrileños, who have restored the old stone mansions as holiday homes, and the streets – especially around the central Plaza de Don Juan Manuel – are surprisingly lively on summer weekends.

Mota del cuervo and around

Some 16 km southeast of Belmonte, the sweetly dilapidated town of Mota del cuervo has one of the biggest collections of windmills in La Mancha. Thanks to Cervantes' deliberate vagueness, no one knows whether these are the famous windmills which Don Quijote mistook for giants (and plenty of other towns have put in rival claims), but they are certainly a romantic sight, particularly in motion (which happens on 3 March). There is a long ceramic tradition in town, curiously carried out almost exclusively by women, and there are plenty of places to pick up souvenirs. To the south, the **lake of Manjavacas** is home to several species of waterbird, and is located on an important migration route. There's a visitors' centre, walking trails, and hides for dedicated birdwatchers.

El Toboso

This tiny, typical whitewashed Manchegan village, a few kilometres west of Mota del cuervo, is where Dulcinea, the object of Don Quijote's courtly attentions, supposedly lived. The house is now a small museum, the **Casa-Museo de Dulcinea** ① *C/Don Quijote, 1 T925197288, Tue-Sat 1000-1400 and 1600-1830, Sun 1000-1400, €0.70*, filled with 16th-century period furnishings.

Alcázar de San Juan

West of El Toboso is the city of Alcázar de San Juan, an industrial centre and major transport hub that has little to attract visitors. The tiled train station is very pretty – luckily, as you'll probably have to change here at some point. Close by, there's another group of windmills at **Campo de Criptana**, a dusty, nondescript little town that likes to claim a Don Quijote connection.

Albacete and around

The provincial capital of Albacete (from Al-Basite, meaning 'the plain' in Arabic), must be one of the dullest towns in Spain. But, as the major transport hub of the region, you may find yourself with an hour or two to kill. Interminable wars and plain neglect have virtually wiped out the old city, and the only real survivor is the **cathedral**, begun in the 16th century and completed less than a 100 years ago. It's not particularly interesting, but the square and surrounding streets are always pretty lively, with plenty of shops, bars and restaurants. Although now a modern, industrial city, it's had a colourful past, which can be discovered out in the park Abelardo Sánchez at the **Museo de Albacete** ① *Tue-Fri 1000-1400 and 1630-1900, Sun 0900-1400, mornings only in summer €1, free at weekends*. Highlights include the Sphinx of Haches-Bogarra, and a collection of exquisite, articulated Roman dolls made of ivory or amber.

Heading east towards Valencia, you might consider stopping at **Chinchilla de Monte Aragón**, 13 km southeast of Albacete, a relaxed market town crowned with another castle, it's long been famous for pottery and you can see the best of it – with pieces from all over Spain – in the local museum ① *weekdays by prior arrangement, Sat 1700-1900, Sun and holidays 1300-1400 and 1700-1900, €070*.

Just before the border with Valencia, there's another striking Arab castle at **Almansa**, with a tiny but charming old quarter hidden behind the urban sprawl. It's famous for making shoes, for those in the mood to shop.

An unhappy ending

Cervantes' famous novel begins with the words "In a little place in La Mancha, whose name I do not care to recall". Some 400 years later, the mayors of dozens of La Mancha towns quietly curse this vagueness under their breath. Unable to compete with seaside resorts, or pert hill towns in more impressive landscapes, the only enticement for the lucrative tourist trade in this flat, empty corner of Spain, is a Don Quijote connection. The roads are littered with signs advertising the Ruta del Don Quijote, heavily promoted by the tourist offices. Argamasilla del Alba, south of Alcázar de San Juan, has placed an emphatic signpost at the town entrance: 'This is THAT town in La Mancha'. It claims that Cervantes conceived his picaresque tale while incarcerated in the town jail, and plenty of romantic fools have locked themselves up in search of inspiration: in 1869, the Baron Hartzenbausch even set up a printing press and produced an edition of the novel.

The life of Cervantes was as adventurous and dramatic as any he could have cooked up for his hapless hero. Born in Alcalá de Henares, he came to Madrid as a young man, then left for Italy where he joined the army and fought at the famous Battle of Lepanto, where his left hand was seriously injured, earning him the nickname *El Manco del Lepanto* (The One-Handed Man of Lepanto). After more than five years of military service, he was sailing home when his ship was captured by Algerian pirates and he was held hostage for another five years. His family almost bankrupted themselves trying to raise the money for his ransom, and his release was eventually secured by two Trinitarian monks. Back once again in Spain, luck continued to elude him. By the time *Don Quixote* was published, he was a broken, penniless old man. The book was a sudden dazzling success, and seven editions were published within the first year, but, whoever was making money from it, it certainly wasn't Cervantes. He remained beset with financial problems until his death on 23 April 1616.

Hoz del Júcar

To escape the dreary monotony of the plains, head for the dramatic Hoz del Júcar (Júcar Gorge) in the northeastern corner of Albacete Province. A small road twists crazily along the riverside, passing steep lovely villages like La Requeja and Jorquera before arriving at **Alcalá del Júcar**. Perched mightily above the gorge, this is one of the most beautiful villages of Castilla-La Mancha. From the Roman bridge medieval streets twist up to the lofty castle, originally an Arabic fortress, but rebuilt after the Reconquest. From here, you'll have giddy views across the rooftops and the great loop of the river which almost completely circles the town. Some of the houses are burrowed deep into the rock – and in some cases, passages cut straight through it and emerge on the other side. Known as *cuevas* (caves), some are now café-bars and can be visited. Each year on 8 August, there's bull-running in the almost vertical streets – only for the very brave – which kicks off the two-week summer festival, with fireworks, pilgrimages, bull fights and lots of serious eating and drinking. The tourist office ① T/F967473090, runs guided tours of the town and has lists of casas rurales in the area.

Heartland of La Mancha

Setting off into the flat plain of La Mancha, you might feel at first the thrill of adventure in the empty, endless landscape. After a short distance of unrelieved monotony, delirium sets in, and it seems entirely unsurprising that Don Quijote would confuse windmills with giants. Don Quijote may be the major draw of this little-visited region, but birdwatchers will enjoy the marshy wetlands of La Mancha Humeda (Wet La Mancha). There is a smattering of handsome, historic towns, which have barely changed since this territory was ruled by the warrior-monks of the Order of Calatrava; Ciudad Real forms the heartland of La Mancha, another provincial capital with an exciting past and little to show for it, while Almagro is a beguiling old Manchegan town surrounded by endless plains. Campo de Calatrava is notable for its spectacular fortress ruins. ›› *For Sleeping, Eating and other listings, see pages 635-638.*

Ciudad Real → *Colour map 4, grid C6.*

The 'Royal City' of Ciudad Real is set deep in the monotonous heart of La Mancha. It's a modern, industrial city that has prospered since the arrival of the high-speed AVE train. It has the best transport connections in the region and the big student population ensures that it remains a buzzier place than many in this empty corner of Spain.

Ciudad Real was founded in 1255 by Alfonso X 'the Wise' to check the power of the military orders which ruled much of La Mancha (see below). Almost nothing remains of the old walled city, except a few gates, of which the 13th-century Mudéjar Puerta de Toledo is the most impressive. The city's few old monuments are mainly clustered in what remains of the *casco histórico*, centred around the Plaza Mayor. Here you'll find the Gothic **cathedral of Sant María la Mayor** ① *Tue-Sat 1000-1400 and 1700-2000*, with a Renaissance retablo, and the 15th-century Casa del Arco, now the Ayuntamiento (Town Hall) which also house the tourist office. The city's history is displayed close by in the modern **Museo Provincial**, with discoveries from archaeological digs including Roman mosaics, and a collection of local paintings and sculpture.

Ciudad's Real newest museum is the excellent **Museo de Don Quijote** ① *Ronda de Alarcos 1, T926200457, 1000-1400 and 1800-2100, Sun 1000-1400, free,* which was inaugurated in 2002, and houses a magnificent library of Cervantes' works. There are some great audio-visual exhibits, guaranteed to appeal to kids, which bring the book to life, and another gallery contains a series of bronze sculptures depicting Don Quijote with some of his constant companions.

Daimeil and La Mancha Humeda → *Colour map 4, grid C6.*

There's no escaping Don Quijote in these parts: scenes from the book even decorate the town fountain in **Daimiel**, 30 km northeast of Ciudad Real. An attractive market town surrounded by flat fields and pastures, it's also the gateway to the **Parque Nacional De Las Tablas De Daimiel** ① *summer 0900-2100, winter 0830-1830,* another 10 km away. These extensive wetlands are formed by the meeting of the Guadiana and Ciguela rivers, and are flecked with lagoons and islands which provide a habitat for almost three hundred species of birdlife. Wet La Mancha (La Mancha Humeda) dried up in the early 1980s, partly because local farmers were diverting more water for irrigation than could be replenished, and the area remains under threat because of illegal damming, particularly during the summer. You can get lists of the flora and fauna encountered in the park, as well as maps of the various trails and hides from the visitors' centre at the end of the track leading to the park. The **Lagunas de Ruidera**, 100 km east of Manzanares, are a popular summer picnic destination, with attractive walks and natural swimming holes.

Castilla-La Mancha & Extremadura Heartland of La Mancha

During the 13th century, Almagro was an important seat of the Knights of the Order of Calatrava, and then came under the protection of the Fuggers, bankers to the Habsburg king, Carlos I (Charles V). Briefly the capital of La Mancha in the 18th century, it remains a quietly prosperous and cultured town with a long theatrical tradition.

The Plaza de España, a long, rectangular square edged with porticoes, has been the heart of the town's life since the 13th century. Just off it is the 17th-century **Corral de las Comedías**, the oldest surviving theatre in Europe, with a cobbled floor, rickety wooden galleries and a double-decker stage. An **International Theatre Festival** ① *T926861490*, is held here every summer. Admission prices include entry to the nearby, bijou 19th-century **Teatro Municipal** ① *C/San Agustín, Tue-Fri 1000-1400 and 1700-2000, Sat 1000-1400 and 1700-1900, Sun and holidays 1100-1400 and 1700-1900, €1.80/0.90*, which has a collection of theatrical costumes on the upper floor.

Across the Plaza, the absorbing **Theatre Museum** ① *Tue-Fri 1000-1400 and 1600-1900, Sat 1000-1400 and 1600-1800, Sun and holidays 1100-1400, €1.20/0.60*, contains portraits of famous Spanish thespians, with enormous moustaches and smouldering glances, intricate models for stage sets, and all kinds of bizarre mementoes and keepsakes donated by performers – including the heart of the tenor José (Giuseppe) Anselmi, which he left to the theatre in his will. The brand new peach-coloured building on the corner of the square will be the vast, new home of the theatre museum, but work has been held up because of financial problems.

Almagro's neat streets of perfectly kept whitewashed houses contain several reminders of its illustrious past: there are dozens of churches and convents, including the pale, lofty **Iglesia de Madre de Dios** with its distinctive columns, and the **Almacén de los Fúcares**, a 16th-century factory owned by the influential Fuggers.

Campo de Calatrava

Calzada de Calatrava, 25 km south of Almagro, is another typical Manchegan market town in the heartland of the Campo de Calatrava. A few kilometres to the south lie the magnificent ruins ① *Tue-Sun 1000-1400 and 1600-1900, 1700-2000 in summer, free*, of the fortress where the Knights of the Order of Calatrava was founded (see box page 633), still deeply evocative of the battle-torn Middle Ages. Although almost nothing remains of the fortress itself, the adjoining church, which probably served as a prison for Moorish prisoners, has been immaculately restored. The ruins are signposted off the CR504.

In the continuous tug-of-war between the Christian and Muslim armies, the fortress was retaken by the Arabs, and, when the Knights eventually won it back, they prudently decided to build themselves a new castle 8 km away which would be harder to take. The result was **Salvatierra**, also ruined, but still an atmospheric place to ponder the fate of the soldier-monks.

Valdepeñas and beyond

Valdepeñas provides most of Spain's table wine: if you ask for the *vino de casa* in a Madrid restaurant, the chances are you'll end up with a bottle of this. It's not all plonk though: in the last 10 or 15 years, local producers have begun to take their wines more seriously and there are some very interesting new quality wines to try at one of the many *bodegas* running guided visits. You can discover the history of wine-making in the region at the **Museo del Vino** ① *C/Princesa 39, T926347927, www.vinoybod egas.com/museodelvinovaldepenas, winter Tue-Sat 1000-1400 and 1700-1900, Sun and holidays 1200-1400, summer 1030-1400 and 1800-2030, Sun and holidays 1200-1400*. The tourist office ① *Plaza de España, T926312552*, has a complete list of *bodegas* in the region.

⦂ Soldiers of Christ

In 1158, Spain's oldest military order, the Knights of the Order of Calatrava, was founded at the former Arab fortress of Calatrava La Vieja (now in ruins). At that time, the plains of La Mancha were the frontline in the battle against the Muslim armies, and, in a reversal of the usual order – knights taking on religious vows – Cistercian monks under Raymond de Fitero swore to defend the Christian lands against the Moors. They kept the vows of poverty, chastity and obedience, slept in their armour, and fasted regularly. Spectacularly successful in battle, the Order was granted vast swathes of land in recompense, gaining enormous riches and influence. Independent, wealthy and accountable only to the Cistercian Abbot of Morimond and the Pope, it was only a matter of time before the kings of Spain determined to check their power. Alfonso X established the Royal City of Ciudad Real to keep watch over them, and the title of Grand Master finally passed to the Castilian Crown in 1499, marking the end of their influence. The region is still known as the Campo de Calatrava, a testament to the power and prestige they once enjoyed. More than one writer has mused that if these knights had been as incompetent as Don Quijote, Spanish history might have taken a very different turn.

South to Andalucía

Wine is what otherwise nondescript Valdepeñas does best: if that holds no appeal, keep on driving. The NIV/E5 shoots down to Andalucía, entering it at the narrow gorge of the **Desfiladero de Despeñaperros**, once a famous bandit haunt. You could make a diversion to **Villanueva de los Infantes**, 20 km east of Valdepeñas, an elegant old town spread around the arcaded Plaza Mayor. It was the birthplace of the satirical poet Quevedo, the author of *La Vida del Buscón* (The Swindler), a classic novel which relates the adventures of Don Pablos with malicious brilliance. The house where he was born is now an attractive hotel, see Sleeping.

Toledo Province

Toledo – covered in Madrid and around chapter, see page 133 – is an enchanting city and one of Spain's most visited tourist attractions. But, surprisingly close to such a popular tourist destination, lie the wild, sparsely populated Montes de Toledo and ancient villages overlooked by castles and windmills. Heading west towards Extremadura, the vast forests of the Parque Nacional de Cabañeros are a birdwatcher's paradise. ▸▸ *For Sleeping, Eating and other listings, see pages 635-638.*

Southeast of Toledo

The ever-changing border between old Al-Andalus and Castilla was guarded by a series of castles. One of the most impressive – although now ruined – stands on a nubby hill on the outskirts of the little village of **Almonacid de Toledo**, and there's another just south in **Mascaraque**. The town of **Mora**, surrounded by endless olive groves, is famous for crafts – from cowbells to carpets – and the defiant remains of the castle of Peñas Negras sits loftily on a reddish outcrop to the east. The Count

● *A group of windmills line a crest above the village of Consuegra, which are set in motion*
● *during the saffron festival – four of them still use their 16th-century cogs.*

of Orgaz, immortalized in El Greco's masterpiece, see page 133, resided in the immaculate castle of **Orgaz**, originally a 12th-century Arabic fortress.

The Arabs introduced the cultivation of saffron to Spain, and in early autumn the fields around **Consuegra** glow with Crocus sativa. The town holds a **Fiesta de Azafrán** on the last weekend of October, with traditional dancing, lots of eating and drinking, and a prize for the fastest stigma-plucker. It takes about 100,000 blossoms to produce just one pound of saffron, and the finest is the deep-red *Mancha Superior*.

Montes de Toledo

The Montes de Toledo spread massively across the southern border of Toledo province and west into Extremadura. It's a wild, mountainous, sparsely populated region famous for hunting (the results of which show up in the local restaurants). The little village of **Cuerva**, in the foothills, has another 15th-century castle, and the little town of **Ventas Con Peña Aguilera** gets its name from two inns (*ventas*) and a tiny 16th-century hermitage to the Virgin of the Eagle built high on a rocky outcrop.

Heading deeper into the hills, **San Pablo de los Montes** is the highest village in these parts, huddled steeply around a fine Plaza Mayor, and famous for a peculiar local festival held each year on January 25, when people from out of town are 'herded' into the Plaza Mayor. A small track leads to the **Baños del Robledillo**, where you can take the waters at a small spa-hotel. The remnants of what was once a spectacular Templar castle survive close to **San Martín de Montalbán**, northeast of Ventas Con Peña Aguilera on the C403. A track splinters off to the right, for the ancient but much restored fortress-church of Santa María de Melque, an enchanting site strewn with Roman remains.

Parque Nacional de Cabañeros → *Colour map 4, grid C5.*

Another route will take you south of **Navahermosa** through the mountains to **Retuerta de Bullaque**, where a small road heads straight through the **Parque Nacional de Cabañeros**. The most extensive Mediterranean forest in Spain, it's home to more than 200 species of bird, including eagles, vultures and other raptors, along with deer, wild boar and a huge variety of trees and shrubs, who are largely left to their own devices, the park is little visited.

To Extremadura

The NV/E90 sweeps rapidly but monotonously from Madrid towards the Extremaduran border. Along this route, **Talavera De La Reina** is famous for ceramics, but it's not attractive, only worth a stop to pick up some souvenirs. **Oropesa** is quieter and prettier, topped with a castle, now a parador. **El Puente de Arzobispo,** 10 km to the south, was named, according to local legend, for a 14th-century archbishop who refused to build a bridge across the river Tajo. He got so annoyed with the pestering villagers that he threw his ring into the water and declared that he would build the bridge when the ring was returned to him. Three days later, he cut into a fish at dinner and discovered the ring inside. It's a pretty place, embellished with the local ceramics, on sale at numerous souvenir shops. Close by are the Roman ruins of Vascos, where you can pick out the outlines of the baths and forum. Almost at the border, Navalmoral de la Mata is a bleak town, but an important transport hub, on the main Madrid-Extremadura train line, and with bus services to the Valle de la Vera, see page 640.

● Sleeping

Guadalajara Province *p624*

Guadalajara tourist office has a full list of rural accommodation in the region of La Alcarría. Sigüenza has plenty of good places to stay.

A Parador, Plaza de Castillo, Sigüenza, T949390100, siguenza@parador.es. Set in the luxuriously converted castle, with a pool and excellent, and pricey, restaurant.

A-C Hotel Salinas de Imón, C/Real 49, Imón, T949397311, www.salinasdeimon. com. Midway between Sigüenza and Atienza, set in a lovingly restored country house, there is also a pool and good, mid-range priced restaurant.

C Hospedería Real de Pastrana, Ctra Pastrana-Zorita, Pastrana , T949371060, F949371026, set in a convent founded by the Princess d'Eboli 2 km out of town, with gardens, and a good, mid-range restaurant. A good central choice is

D Casa don Gonzalo, C/Estrella 7, Briheuga, T949280071, this 18th-century house in the centre of town is one of the best places to stay in La Alcarría. Friendly.

D Hostel El Doncel, C/General Mola 1, Sigüenza, T949390827, good central option.

D Hostel Moratín, C/Moratín, Pastrana, T949370628, with an English-style pub, and spotless rooms.

D Hotel España, C/Teniente Figueroa 3, Guadalajara, T949211303, in a turn-of-the-century mansion, with blandly modern rooms.

E Hostal El Mesón, C/Román Pascual 14, Sigüenza, T949390649, offers basic rooms right by the cathedral.

F Pensión Galicia, Paseo San Roque 16, Guadalajara, T949220059, basic place with a good, cheap little restaurant.

Cuenca and around *p625, map p627*

There are plenty of modern places to stay in the new part of Cuenca, but there's more atmosphere in the old city. Book as early as possible, especially if you are coming at a weekend.

L Parador San Pablo, Paseo Hoz Del Huécar s/n, T969232320. This sleek parador is set in the much-renovated old monastery of San Pablo, with perfect views of the hanging houses and a very fine restaurant.

AL Hotel Cueva Del Fraile Ctra, Cuenca-Buenache Km.7, T969211571, www.hotelcuevadelfraile.com. Set in a 400 -year-old monastery 5 km from Cuenca, this is a beautiful, tranquil place to stay, surrounded by gardens, with a pool and good, mid-range restaurant. There are a range of rooms, all with beams and antique furnishings, including special suites for families.

C Hostal Posada San José, C/Julián Romero 4, T969211300. An utterly delightful, rambling hotel set in a converted convent clamped to the side of the rock in the heart of the old city. Simple, tasteful whitewashed rooms, and an excellent tapas bar. Rooms without bathroom are cheaper (**D**).

E Hostal Posada Huécar, Paseo del Huecar 3, T969214201. A charming old inn overlooking the Río Huécar, with great views, and comfortable rooms.

E Pensión Huecar Tintes, C/Tintes 29, T969212398. At the cusp of the old town and the new, this is good value, with airy, spotless rooms and friendly owners.

E Pensión Tabanqueta, C/Trabuco 13, T969211290. In the upper reaches of the old town, this little pensión has rooms over-looking the gorge and a bar with a terrace.

F Pensión Real, C/Larga 39, T969229977. At the very top of the old city in the Barrio del Castillo, with just 4 rooms in a modernized old house.

F Pensión San Julian, C/Las Torres, 1, T969211 704. A slightly battered and atmospheric old pension at the bottom of the hill which leads up to the old city.

Camping

Caravanning Cuenca, Ctra Cuenca-Tragacete 8, T969231 656. The closest campsite to the city, but you'll still need your own transport. With a shady riverside location, pool, bar-restaurant, and a few bungalows. Open Mar-Dec.

South to Albacete *p628*

If you get stuck overnight in Albacete, there are several options, mostly catering to business clients.

● *For an explanation of sleeping and eating price codes used in this guide, see inside the*
● *front cover. Other relevant information is found in Essentials, see pages 47-56.*

L **Parador**, Avda Amigos de los Castillos, Alarcón, T969330315, alarcon@parador.es. Up in the castle, this is the plushest place to stay and eat.

C **Palacio Buenavista Hospedería**, C/José Antonio González 2, Belmonte, T967187580, F967187588, in a 16th-century mansion with the town's best restaurant serving mid-range priced cuisine.

C **San José**, C/San José de Calasanz 12, Albacete, T967507402, www.hotelsan jose-albacete.es. Large, functional rooms close to the Parque Abelardo Sánchez.

D **Posada del Infante**, C/Dr Tortosa 6, Alarcón, T969330323, posadadelinfante @hotmail.com. A charming, family-run choice, set in an immaculate whitewashed old townhouse.

E **Hermanos Plaza**, Hoz del Júcar, T967473029. One of the three simple *hostales* with cheap restaurants.

E **Hostal Rambla**, Av de los Robles, Hoz del Júcar, T967474064. One of the three simple *hostales* with cheap restaurants.

E **Júcar**, Hoz del Júcar, T967473055, are both on C/Batán. The prettiest of the three simple *hostales* with cheap restaurants.

F **Hostel La Muralla**, C/Osa de la Vega, Belmonte, T967171047. Simple but charming and also has a good, cheap traditional restaurant.

G **El Berrocal**, Ctra Tolosa s/n, Hoz del Júcar, T967473232, on the banks of the river just outside town (open year-round). A shady campsite with two pools.

Heartland of La Mancha *p631*
There are plenty of bland hotel geared towards business travellers in Ciudad Real.

AL **Parador**, Ronda de San Francisco, Almagro, T926860150, almagro@parador.es. Set in a Franciscan convent, this is a swanky option with an expensive restaurant.

A **Santa Cecilia**, C/Tinte 3, Ciudad Real, T926228545, F926228618, has all the 4-star trimmings at surprisingly reasonable prices.

C **Alfonso X**, C/Carlos Vázquez 10, Ciudad Real, T926224281, F926224264, is a sleek new hotel behind an historic façade right on the Plaza Mayor.

C **Hospedería Museo Valdepeñas**, C/Unión 104, Valdepeñas, T926310795, F926310882. A delightful choice.

D **Hospedería Real El Buscón de Quevedo**, C/Frailes 1, Villanueva de los Infantes, T/F9263 61788, www.hosteriasreales.com, which keeps one room as a shrine to his memory.

D **Hostal Las Brujas**, on the edge of Daimiel, Ctra N420 km 231, T926852289, with a popular, cheap, local restaurant.

D **Hostal Valdepeñas**, C/Gregorio Prieto 47, Valdepeñas, T926322328. A simple place.

D **Hotel Navarro**, Avda Pío XII 18, Ciudad Real, T926214377, is also modern, but reasonably central and good value.

D **La Posada de Almagro**, C/Gran Maestre s/n, Almagro, T926261201, www.laposada delal magro.com. The best place to stay in town is set in a beautifully converted 16th-century inn with an excellent, mid-range restaurant and popular tapas bar. Welcoming. Highly recommended.

E **Hospedería Almagro Convento de la Asuncíon**, Almagro, T926882087, F926882122. A good cheap option.

E **Pensión Escudero**, C/Galicia 48, Ciudad Real, T926252309, is cheapest of all and has spotless, basic rooms with or without bathrooms.

Toledo Province *p633*
There are few places to stay in the little-visited Parque Nacional de Cabañeros, but you'll find a complete list incuding *casas rurales* on the useful website www.montes detoledo.org (Spanish only).

D **Hostal Baños del Robledillo**, T925415300, Parque Nacional de Cabañeros, www.balneariorobledillo.com, offers simple rooms and a restaurant for those staying to take 'the cure' (and those who aren't).

D **Hostal El Álamo**, C/Cueva 5, Parque Nacional de Cabañeros, T926775198. One of plenty of options in Horcaja de las Montes, on the edge of the national park.

D **Las Provincias**, Consuegra, T925482000, F925460847. Modern roadside hotel with a pool and restaurant.

E **Casa Rural Casilda**, C/Urda 26, Consuegra, T677394872 (mob). Delightful.

Camping
G **Camping Navahermosa**, Camino de Hontanar s/n, T/F 925429036, info@camp ing-navahermosa.com, an attractive, shady campsite in Navahermosa.

AL Oropesa parador Plaza de Palacio, Oropesa, T925430000, oropesa@parador.es, is the grandest place to stay.

C-D La Hostería, Plaza del Palacio 5, Oropesa, T925430875, is a delightful, friendly place set around a lovely courtyard where you can dine on delicious local specialities.

🍴 Eating

Guadalajara Province *p624*

Sigüenza is surprisingly lively in the evenings thanks to a long-standing tapeo tradition. La Alcarría is famous for honey, especially around Brihuega; you'll get plenty of Castillian specialities in the local restaurants.

€€€ **Amparito Roca**, C/Toledo 19, Guadalajara, T949214639, one of the best restaurants in Castilla-La Mancha and certainly the fanciest place to eat in Guadalajara.

€€ **Calle Mayor**, Sigüenza, C/Mayor 21, T949391748, imaginative dishes.

€€ **Minaya**, C/Mayor 23, T949212253, is romantically set in a converted palacio and serves good traditional, Castillian dishes.

€€ **Sierra Ministra**, C/Valencia 51, Sigüenza, T949391758. Traditional Castilian cuisine at this old-fashioned option. Does a great, cheap, *menú del día*.

€ **Casino**, C/Mayor 22, T949226167, where you can eat cheaply in the café-bar downstairs or in more formal, and pricey, surroundings upstairs.

€ **El Figón**, C/Bardales 9, T949211588, a traditional spot with a terrace which does a great *menú del día*.

€ **Fonda Molinero**, C/Héctor Vázquez 11, Atienza near Sigüenza, T949399017, is an excellent, *muy típico* cheap local restaurant with a few basic rooms (**F**).

€ Snack on tapas in Sigüenza around Plaza Mayor or at any of the myriad bars along the C/Humilladero.

Cuenca and around *p625, map p627*

€€€ **Mesón Casas Colgadas**, C/Canónigas 3, T969223509. One of the finest restaurants in Castilla-La Mancha, set in the 14th-century Casa de la Sirena, and famous for its roast meats and local specialities.

€€ **Las Brasas**, C/Alfonso VIII, T969213 821. A good traditional restaurant, specializing in meats – especially lamb – grilled over charcoal.

€ **Plaza Mayor**, Plaza Mayor 1, T969211496. The best of several *mesones* on the Plaza Mayor, serving a good value *menú* for €12, and with a terrace out on the square.

€ **Tintes**, C/Tintes 7, T969214161. A student favourite on an attractive street, this serves up a great, plentiful *menú del día* for less than €5.

Tapas bars and cafés

Bar Dulcinea, C/San Pedro 6, T969233385. Classic little bar with blue and white tiles, which serves good tapas as well as a reasonably priced lunchtime *menú*.

Café Liceo, C/Colon 77, T969235410. Cheerful, old-fashioned café on a busy shopping street.

La Tinaja, C/Obispo Valero, 4, just off the Plaza Mayor, is a relaxed neighbourhood bar with a good range of tapas and tables outside.

Posada San José, Ronda Julián Romero 4, T969211300. One of the best tapas bars in Cuenca, set in the beautifully restored surroundings of an old convent.

South to Albacete *p628*

€€ **Marlo**, Plaza de Gabriel Lodares 3, Albacete, T967506475, you'll eat well at this fashionable restaurant.

€ **Nuestra Bar**, C/Alcalde Conangla 102, Albacete, T967244484, famously offers more than 80 different kinds of tapas and *raciones*.

€ **Rincón del Cordero**, C/Cura 5, Albacete, T967524465, simple and small which does a cheap *menú del día*.

Heartland of La Mancha *p631*

All the hotels listed in Almagro, see Sleeping, have restaurants, or you could drop in at any of the tapas bars on the Plaza de España. The tourist office has a small map outlining a tapas route in Almagro. In Valdepeñas there are several good restaurants and tapas bars on Plaza de España.

€€ **Restaurante Cúchares**, C/Palme 3, Ciudad Real, T926330697, is a classic local favourite, serving traditional, cuisine in a plush setting.

€ **España**, Plaza del Pilar 10, Ciudad Real, T926211349, overlooks a delightful square and offers a good *menú del día* for €8.

♠ Bars and clubs

Cuenca and around *p625, map p627*
Cuenca has a vibrant nightlife, thanks to the heavy student presence, mainly concentrated in the new town at the bottom of the hill. There are several streets which seem to be lined with nothing but bars; a good starting point is C Doctor Galíndez. For more relaxed bars, try around the Plaza de Hispanidad and the C San Francisco.

✪ Festivals and events

Cuenca and around *p625, map p627*
Holy Week is a big event in Cuenca, with the biggest processions taking place on the night of Maundy Thursday and Good Friday. Worth being in town for.
International Music Festival is held at the same time, with concerts on the square and in locations across the city.
Fiesta de San Mateo commemorates the conquest of the city by Alfonso VIII in 1177, and is celebrated with traditional parades and plenty of dancing and carousing in the streets. Good fun.

✪ Shopping

Guadalajara Province *p624*
Sigüenza has plenty of craft and antique shops to pick up souvenirs. Other good buys include local *embutidos* (cured meats), and honey from La Alcarría.

Cuenca and around *p625, map p627*
There are plenty of places to pick up souvenirs, especially ceramics, around Plaza Mayor in Cuenca.

✪ Transport

Guadalajara Province *p624*
Guadalajara is well connected by bus and train (although the train station is 2 km from the centre) to **Madrid**, **Sigüenza**, and **Zaragoza**. There are very few local buses to outlying villages, and your own transport is virtually essential.

Cuenca and around *p625, map p627*
There are 4 direct trains daily from **Madrid** and 6 from **Valencia**. Buses to **Madrid** (T969227087) are more frequent, and there are also buses to **Toledo**, **Valencia** and **Alcázar de San Juan** as well as infrequent services to surrounding villages, this is especially true at the weekends.

South to Albacete *p628*
There are bus connections from **Madrid**, **Cuenca**, **Albacete** and **Valencia** to **Belmonte**.

Heartland of La Mancha *p631*
Ciudad Real is well connected by train to **Seville** and **Madrid** (AVE and regional trains) and **Almagro**, and there are buses to **Toledo**, **Madrid**, **Seville**, **Córdoba**, **Valdepeñas**, **Jaén** and surrounding villages (T926211342).
   Valdepeñas is easily reached by bus or train from Ciudad Real, Madrid, and Almagro. For bus information, call T962322862.
   There are buses to **Daimiel** from **Ciudad Real**, but there's no public transport from Daimiel to the national park.
   There are several trains daily from **Almagro**, and infrequent buses to other towns in the region, T926860250.

Toledo Province *p633*
There are bus links between **Toledo**, **Ciudad Real**, **Alcázar de San Juan** and **Consuegra**, and infrequent buses to some local villages.

To Extremadura *p634*
Talavera de la Reina, **Oropesa** and **Navalmoral de la Mata** are all on the main **Madrid-Extremadura** train line, and are also served by local buses.

♻ Directory

Cuenca and around *p625, map p627*
Internet Cyber Viajero, Avda República Argentina 3, T969236696, www.cyberviajero.com. Internet access (€2 per hr).
Post On the corner of C/Parque del Parque de San Julián and C del Dr Fleming.

Extremadura

Plasencia → *Phone code: 927; Colour map 4, grid B3; Population: 36,060; Altitude: 352 m.*

Plasencia is a likeable little place, which is nonetheless the biggest town of empty northern Extremadura. Prettily located amid rivers and hills, behind the ugly modern outskirts there's a lively old quarter, with a smattering of noble mansions and narrow streets radiating from the delightfully eccentric cathedral. ▸▸ *For Sleeping, Eating and other listings, see pages 654-662.*

Ins and outs

Getting there There are regular train and bus connections throughout Extremadura and less frequent services to other major Spanish cities, including Madrid. ▸▸ *For further details, see Transport page 662.*

Getting around The train station is a couple of kilometres outside town and you'll need to call a taxi if you can't face the unattractive walk through factories and apartment blocks. Otherwise, the main sights are clustered in the old town and can easily be seen on foot.

Tourist information ⓘ *Plaza de Catedral, T927423843, Mon to Fri 0900-1400 and 1700-1900, Sat, Sun and holidays 1700-1900.*

Sights

The arcaded **Plaza Mayor** with its buzzy shops, bars and cafés is the hub of the town, and quickly fills up after the traditional evening *paseo*. A market has been held here every Tuesday since medieval times, with the biggest one (*Martes Mayor*) held on the first Tuesday of August.

Plasencia's biggest monument lies just off the Plaza Mayor (down Calle de las Claras); the **Catedral Vieja y Nueva**. The Old and New Cathedral got its name predictably enough because one half is 'old' (mainly 12th century) and the other half is 'new' (mainly 16th century). The new half is the one currently used for worship and the one which presents two dizzying Plateresque façades, densely carved with stone garlands and fabulous creatures. A lovely Romanesque cloister links the new cathedral with the old, its slender columns decorated with simple capitals of pale stone. The Old Cathedral (with strange faces oozing from the vaulted ceiling) has become a museum, with a few gems hidden away among a rag-bag collection of religious ornaments and statuary.

There are a handful of fine old palaces clustered around the cathedral: opposite is the 17th-century **Casa del Déan**, with a wrought iron balcony wrapped around one corner, and across the square is the **Palacio Episcopal** with a Romanesque doorway and the 14th-century **Hospital Provincial**. Just off the square is the oldest palace in Plasencia, the **Palacio de los Monroy**, better known as the 'Palace of Two Towers', even though one was lopped off in 1913. Just beyond the Plaza San Nicolas is the Renaissance **Palacio Mirabel** (now a luxurious parador), and around the corner from it is the **Puerta de las Berrozanas**, one of the few gateways in the old city walls to have survived.

⬤ *The classic Extremaduran landscape – rolling fields scattered with oak trees – is known as*
⬤ *dehesa, and is famous for rearing the pata negra pigs which feed on acorns and provide*
the much-prized local delicacy, jamón Iberico.

Wanted: Royal Retirement Home

The story goes that when Carlos V was thinking about packing in his royal duties, he asked a Flemish courtier where his favourite place in the world was. The courtier replied: 'The best place in the world is Spain; the best place in Spain is La Vera; and the best place in Vera is Jarandilla; the best place in Jarandilla is the *bodega* of Pedro Acedo de la Berrueza. That's the best place in the world. I'd like to be buried there and go to heaven, because they have the best wine in the region'. He seems to have sold it to Carlos V, who handed over the reins of the world's largest empire and retired here with a retinue of 50 (including his personal barber and clock-maker) until his death in 1558.

Valle de la Vera and the Monesterio de Yuste

The undulating Valle de la Vera northeast of Plasencia is one of the greenest corners of sun-bleached Extremadura. When Carlos V was looking for somewhere to hang up his imperial crown in the 16th century he had most of Europe to choose from, but selected a beautiful, wooded site in a fold of these hills. The area is famous for its steep mountain villages of gabled wooden houses, and dense forests criss-crossed with a network of rivers and waterfalls, many of which form natural swimming pools. It's a paradise for walkers, with plenty of well-marked trails striking out into the hills.
▶▶ *For Sleeping, Eating and other listings, see pages 654-662.*

Jarandilla and around

The biggest town in the Valle de la Vera is Jarandilla, slightly run down but still rather charming. Carlos V lived here (the mansion is now a parador) while his apartments were being prepared at the Monesterio de Yuste. From the tiny village of **Guijo de Santa Barbara**, there's a beautiful hour-long walk to a magical natural swimming pool with waterfalls. Time it right – mid-week is best – you could have it completely to yourself.

The hills and countryside east of Jarandilla are gentler, and the countryside less dramatic, but the villages strung out along the EX 203 are often very attractive. Furthest east is **Madrigal de la Vera**, with lots of Madrileño holiday homes and natural swimming pools. Heading west, **Villanueva de la Vera** is prettier and quieter, with a charming Plaza Mayor at the centre of a medieval labyrinth of streets. Carnival (February-March) is a riot – literally: a wooden figure known as *Pero Palo* is paraded around the street, giving the townspeople a good excuse to pass around leather *botas* of local wine and indulge in some serious partying. West again is **Valverde de la Vera**, the loveliest of the villages in the eastern reaches of the Vera valley, which also has a famous festival. *Los Empalaos* is a strange, penitential religious procession in which a volunteer is tightly bound with rope to a crucifix, crowned with a ring of thorns, and processed in agony around the town on the night of Maundy Thursday.

Monesterio de Yuste

① *Daily except Sun 0930-1230 and 15301800 (until 1830 in summer), €1, by guided tour only (in Spanish).* West of Jarandilla is **Cuacos de Yuste**, a whitewashed town of tiny streets clustered around a quiet old church topped with storks' nests. Two kilometres north is the **Monesterio de Yuste**, the hushed, monastic retreat of Carlos V. The (compulsory) guided tour takes you around the royal apartments, draped funereally in black. Carlos V ensured that his bed was placed in an alcove with a view into the church below so that even in his last sickness he would never miss a mass.

There are two graceful cloisters, one Gothic and one Plateresque, and the magnificent main altar in the church is the work of Felipe II's favourite architect, Juan de Herrera.

Jaraíz de la Vera and Garganta la Olla

West of Cuacos de Yuste, Jaraíz de la Vera is a sizeable if unremarkable village with several *casas rurales* and two horse-riding centres: **La Magdalena** ① *T927194118*, and **El Pasil** ① *T927170843*, which both offer treks through the valley. To the north is **Garganta la Olla**, perhaps the prettiest village of the Vera, with crooked houses piled chaotically around a Gothic church. Look out for the **Casa de la Muñecas**, still painted the traditional blue that once indicated a brothel.

Coria, Las Hurdes and the Sierra de Gata

Las Hurdes, the remote northern tip of Extremadura, is a wild, mountainous region of rivers, gorges and waterfalls scattered with tiny villages of squat, slate-roofed houses. Rumours of witchcraft still haunt it, but the poverty which Luis Buñuel exposed in his bleak 1932 documentary *Las Hurdes: Tierra Sin Pan* (Land without Bread) is no longer so apparent. Sierra de Gata borders it to the southwest, another little-visited corner with spectacular granite mountains and untouched villages. ▶▶ *For Sleeping, Eating and other listings, see pages 654-662.*

Coria → *Colour map 4, grid B2.*

Coria, south of Las Hurdes and the Sierra de Gata, may be surrounded by a dull modern sprawl, but it has a peaceful whitewashed core hemmed in by Roman walls. Narrow streets spiral tightly towards its grandest monument, the austere 14th-century **Catedral de la Asunción**. There's a tourist information office ① *Avda Extremadura 19, T927501351, www.coria.org.*

Las Hurdes

pinofranqueado is the gateway to Las Hurdes and one of its largest and most accessible villages. In August, the whole town explodes for the three-day festival of **La Enrammá** and there's a trail out to the **Cascada El Chorritero**, a famous waterfall with a natural swimming pool. **Nuñomoral** makes a good base in the northern Hurdes, with excellent walking in the surrounding mountains and gorges, and close to a smattering of remote, picturesque villages like **Martilandrán, Fragosa**, and **El Gasco**, which has another beautiful waterfall. To the east, the vast **Embalse de Gabriel y Galán** has become a centre for watersports, overlooked at its southern end by the abandoned fortified village of **Granadillo** (although the view is blighted by a power station). You'll pass dozens of roadside stands selling the delicious local honey.

Sierra de Gata

Hoyos, still crammed with noble mansions from the 15th and 16th centuries, is also one of the few places which hasn't lost its younger generation to the big cities. As a result, it has more life than many of its quieter neighbours, especially on the vibrant Plaza Mayor. **San Martin de Trevejo**, to the northwest, has a crumbling castle from its days on the front line between Spain and Portugal, and a handsome porticoed Plaza Mayor. **Gata**, to the north, is another good base, with a charming central square overlooked by the 13th-century Iglesia de San Pedro with a fine retablo. There's a natural swimming pool and picnic spot on the edge of the town. **Santibañez El Alto**, is a beautiful whitewashed village with the ruins of an Arabic fortress piled high on a hill overlooking the Embalse de Borbollón. Tiny **Robledillo de Gata** is surrounded by tightly terraced hills which produce the local *pitarra* wine, and has more excellent walking trails.

Parque Natural de Monfragüe

The main highway south of Plasencia towards Cáceres sweeps across an empty, watery landscape formed by two enormous reservoirs, created in the 1960s when the Rio Tajo was dammed. To the east is the craggy, forested Parque Natural de Montfragüe, home to more than 200 species of wildlife, including the extremely rare Spanish lynx and a wide variety of birds. Among the protected species of bird which nest here are the black stork, the Spanish Imperial eagle, and the black vulture – to see them, come between March and October as they spend the winter in Africa. The hills are stark in parts, part of a new programme to replace the eucalyptus trees that were planted in the 1960s with indigenous species like holm oak. The red trail partly follows the road (EX208) through the park, from where shorter trails lead up to the ruins of the Castillo de Monfragüe and a tiny hermitage which contains a venerated statue of the Virgin of Mon- fragüe. From here, you'll get incredible views out over the Peña Falcón, a rocky outcrop inhabited by a colony of black vultures which wheel slowly overhead. The park information office ① *Villareal de San Carlos, T927199134, www.monfrague.com*, has leaflets describing three colour-coded itineraries around the park. ▶▶ *For Sleeping, Eating and other listings, see pages 654-662.*

Cáceres → *Phone code: 927; Colour map 4, grid B2; Population: 84,702; Altitude: 439 m.*

Old Cáceres, an immaculate ensemble of palaces and churches linked with cobbled streets, sits as though charmed behind a ring of high, defensive walls. Almost nothing has changed since the elaborate mansions of honey-coloured stone were first built for conquistadors in the 16th century, their pockets bulging with gold from Spanish colonies in the Americas. The rest of Cáceres is resolutely modern and lively, with a big student population and the best nightlife in Extremadura. ▶▶ *For Sleeping, Eating and other listings, see pages 654-662.*

Ins and outs

Getting there There are direct trains and buses to Madrid and major Spanish destinations. Both bus and train stations are a 20-30 minute walk from the old city. Take bus No 4 down Avenida Alemania, or a taxi (Tele Taxi T927232323). ▶▶ *For further details, see Transport page 662.*

Getting around The Parte Vieja (the old city) is tiny and easily negotiable on foot. Don't try driving; the streets are very narrow and many are pedestrianised or one way.

Best time to visit Womad festival in May is excellent, but there's a full calendar of other events. ▶▶ *For details, see Festivals and events page 660.*

Tourist information The provincial tourist information office ① *Plaza Mayor 7 T927010834, Mon-Fri 0900-1400 and 1700-1900, Sat, Sun and holidays 0945-1400.* The municipal tourist office ① *Plaza Mayor*, runs excellent walking tours of the city, €4, Spanish only.

Background

Cáceres really took off from the 16th century when '*fiebre americana*' – American fever – took hold. The conquistadores returned from the Americas dripping with unimaginable wealth which they flaunted by building grand mansions and churches. But when the money dried up, so did Cáceres' political influence. By the 19th century, it was a poverty-stricken backwater. Ironically, the Renaissance gem of an old city was preserved through neglect. But Cáceres has been back on the map for at least half a century, and with the establishment of the university and the region's increasing prosperity, it is now one of the most dynamic cities in Extremadura.

The appealing Plaza Mayor sits at the main gateway to the walled city. Fairs, bullfights and hangings were held here from the Middle Ages onwards, and it's still the place to find the city's action. There are dozens of cafés to choose from, most with terraces out on the square, and it's one of the main venues for the summer Womad festival. A flight of steps sweeps up to the 18th-century **Arco de la Estrella**, an archway through the massive city walls.

As you pass through the archway, a dome covered with an untidy fringe of storks' nests can be glimpsed on the left; this is the **Casa de los Toledo Moctezuma**, a magnificent palace built for Juan Cano who married the daughter of the Aztec Emperor.

The Calle Arco de la Estrella leads to the graceful **Plaza de Santa María**, named after the cathedral. The **Concatedral de Santa María** was begun in the 13th century, and you can just make out the seams around the doorway where the original Romanesque church was picked apart and enlarged in the 15th and 16th centuries. Right opposite the church is the **Palacio Episcopal**, decorated with two medallions carved with the figures of a Philippino and an Aztec respectively, and a nod to both

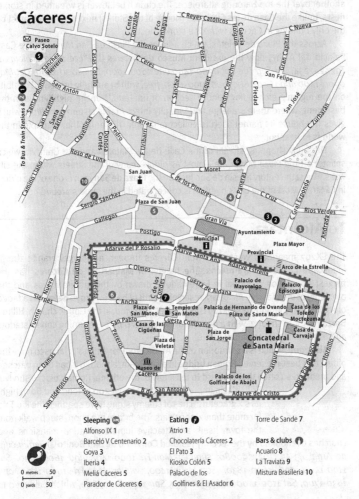

Cáceres

Map labels: Paseo Calvo Sotelo · C Cmte González · C Fco Paniagua · C Reyes Católicos · C García Holguín · C Nueva · Alfonso IX · C Pérez · Casas Coradilo · C Ceres · Sánchez Herrero · San Antón · C Sánchez · C Busquet · Pedro Corbacho · C Piedad · San Felipe · C José · San Vicente · Santa Paloma · San Pedro · C Parras · E Ulibarri · C Zurbarán · Santa Bárbara · Clavellinas · Donoso Cortés · Roso de Luna · Camino Llano · San Juan · C Moret · C de los Pintores · C Caneras · C Cruz · Canal Exponda · Ríos Verdes · Andrada · Sergio Sánchez · Plaza de San Juan · Gallegos · Postigo · Gran Vía · Ayuntamiento · Plaza Mayor · Adarve del P Rosalio · Adarve Santa Ana · Municipal · Provincial · Adarve Estrella · Arco de la Estrella · Puerta de Mérida · C Olmos · C de los Condes · Cuesta de Aldana · Palacio de Mayoralgo · Palacio Episcopal · Cornudillas · Fuente Nueva · Sierpes · C Ancha · San Pablo · Plaza de San Mateo · Templo de San Mateo · Palacio de Hernando de Ovando · Casa de los Toledo Moctezuma · Casa de las Cigüeñas · Cuesta Compañía · Plaza de Santa María · Casa de Carvajal · Torremochada · Petrolos · Plaza de Veletas · D Álvaro · Plaza de San Jorge · Concatedral de Santa María · C Damas · Museo de Cáceres · Palacio de los Golfines de Abajo · B de San Antonio · Amargura · Obra Pía de Roco · C Horrillo · San Ildefonso · Consolación · Adarve del Cristo

0 metres 50
0 yards 50

Sleeping
Alfonso IX **1**
Barceló V Centenario **2**
Goya **3**
Iberia **4**
Meliá Cáceres **5**
Parador de Cáceres **6**

Eating
Atrio **1**
Chocolatería Cáceres **2**
El Pato **3**
Kiosko Colón **5**
Palacio de los
  Golfines & El Asador **6**

Torre de Sande **7**

Bars & clubs
Acuario **8**
La Traviata **9**
Mistura Brasileria **10**

the extent of Spain's burgeoning empire and the *conquistadors* who were rebuilding Cáceres with their gold. The Bishop's Palace is flanked on one side by the **Palacio de Hernando de Ovando** and on the other by the **Palacio de Mayoralgo,** two of the largest and grandest palaces in the city. The latter is under restoration and work on the interior patio has just revealed some unsuspected Roman ruins, so plans for a visitors' centre are underway.

One of the few palaces that can be entered is tucked away behind the Concatedral, the **Casa de Carvajal,** which belongs to the city and holds a temporary exhibition space, and a small model of 16th-century Cáceres. The most magnificent palace of the whole city is on the other side of the Concatedral: the **Palacio de los Golfines de Abajo,** which is where the Catholic kings came to stay when they were in town, and is covered with sumptuous Plateresque decoration.

‡ *Almost all palaces and mansionsare still in private hands; only those noted can enter.*

The next square is the **Plaza de San Jorge,** which looks as though it has been here as long as everywhere else, but in fact is only 30 years old. A flight of steps leads up to the **Plaza de San Mateo,** named for the 16th- to 18th-century **Templo de San Mateo,** which also bears the scars of its enlargement. Inside is another over-the-top Baroque altarpiece. The church belltower is wreathed in storks' nests, unlike the **Casa de las Cigüeñas** (House of the Storks) next door which must be the only building in Cáceres *without* a stork's nest.

Across the Plaza de Veletas, which adjoins the Plaza de San Mateo, is the Casa Palacio del Aljibe, now the excellent **Museo de Cáceres** ① *Plaza de las Veletas 1, T924247234, Jun-Sep Tue-Sat 0900-1400 and 1600-1900, Sun 1000-1400, Oct-May 0900-1400 and 1600-1800, Sun 1000-1400, free,* with beautifully presented exhibits on the region's archaeology and a section of fine arts. But the highlight is in the basement, where there's a large and virtually intact Arabic cistern (or *aljibe,* which gives the house its name) used to collect rainwater. The only other example in the world is in Istanbul.

The busy shopping streets of the Calle de los Pintores and the Gran Vía which splinter off the Plaza Mayor are almost as old as many of the streets within the city walls. The 14th-century Iglesia de San Juan on the **Plaza de San Juan** is one of the oldest in Cáceres. Most of the city's nightlife is concentrated in the streets around here.

To Alcántara

The EX207 meanders westwards from Cáceres through a strange, granite-strewn landscape called **Los Barruecos.** The hamlet of **Malpartida de Cáceres** has the biggest population of storks in Extremadura, drawn by the granite ridges and the proximity of the massive Alcántara reservoir. North of here is **Arroyo de la Luz,** a faded old town with a famous retablo by Luis Morales, *El Divino,* in the Gothic church. Hilltop **Brozas** is more striking, with a handful of mansions built by returning conquistadors and a crumbling 17th-century castle.

Alcántara, which is a corruption of the Arabic word for 'bridge', claims to have the oldest and best-preserved **Roman bridge** in all of Spain, although it has been patched and mended so often that it's hard to tell if any of the original Roman blocks survive.

‡ *Accommodation is scarce in this rarely visited region.*

Still, it's an impressive sight: almost 200 m long and 60 m high, its six graceful arches of creamy stone have spanned the Río Tajo for more than 2,000 years. The bridge is a short, steep walk from the town itself, an attractive jumble of faded mansions and churches overlooked by the recently restored **Convento de San Benito** ① *Regimiento de Argel 43-45, T927390080, summer Mon-Fri 1000-1400 and 1600-1830, Sat 1100-1400 and 1600-1830, Sun 1100-1400, winter Mon-Fri 1000-1400 and 1630-1700, Sat 1100-1400 and 1630-1700, Sun 1100-1400, free,* which belonged to

The convent's triple-decker Renaissance gallery makes a striking backdrop for musical and theatrical performances held here in August.

Trujillo → *Phone code: 927; Colour map 4, grid C3; Population: 9,000.*

Trujillo is a pearl, a beautiful little city still stuffed full of Renaissance mansions and churches from the golden years, set around one of the loveliest squares in Extremadura. One of the most important conquistador towns in the 16th century, Trujillo was home to Pizarro, who discovered Peru, and Orellana, who explored the Amazon. The city has become a prosperous and popular tourist destination in recent years and, unlike its picture-postcard big sister, Cáceres, Trujillo exudes a ramshackle, lived-in charm, with its skyline of battered spires topped with storks' nests, and its meandering cobbled streets. Trujillo's tiny centre is easy to get around on foot.▶▶ *For Sleeping, Eating and other listings, see pages 654-662.*

Sights

Little has changed over the last five centuries in Trujillo's Plaza Mayor, with its narrow arcades, church spires and mansions. Still the centre of the town's life, restaurants and bars spread their tables out on to the square, and families gather to gossip by the central fountain. The equestrian statue of Trujillo's most famous *conquistador*, Francisco Pizarro, looks towards the flamboyant **Palacio de los Marqueses de la Conquista**, (long closed for restoration), built for Francisco's brother, Hernando Pizarro, and covered in Plateresque frills. Down a passage just off the Plaza Mayor, the **Palacio de Juan-Pizarro de Orellana**① *1000-1300 and 1600-1800, Sat, Sun and holidays 1100-1400 and 1630- 1900, free,* is one of the grandest noble mansions. It's now a school, but you can still visit its elaborate Plateresque patio, one of the finest in Extremadura. At the opposite end of Plaza Mayor, the **Palacio de los Duques de San Carlos** ① *0930-1300 and 1630-1830, Sun and holidays 1000-1230, €1.20,* now houses a closed order of Hieronymite nuns who make cakes and biscuits. Pull the bellrope for admission to the interior patio and wide marble staircase, overlooked by an enormous fresco of a double-headed eagle. The brick chimneys deliberately echo the architecture of the Incas, Aztecs and other cultures which were being discovered – and destroyed – in the Americas.

Castilla-La Mancha & Extremadura Trujillo

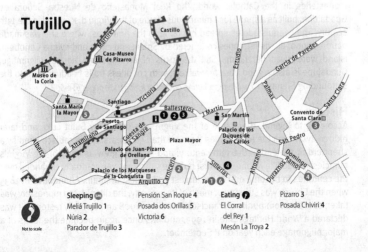

Trujillo

Castillo

Casa-Museo de Pizarro

Museo de la Coria

Santa María la Mayor

Santiago

Puerto de Santiago

Victoria

Ballesteros

San Martín

Convento de Santa Clara

Palacio de los Duques de San Carlos

Plaza Mayor

Palacio de Juan-Pizarro de Orellana

Palacio de los Marqueses de la Conquista

Arquillo

Mártires

Estudio

García de Paredes

Palmar

Santa Clara

San Pedro

Domingo Ramos

Sillerías

Altozano

Carnicería

Cuesta de la Sangre

Altamirano

Albercа

N
Not to scale

Sleeping	Pensión San Roque **4**	**Eating**	Pizarro **3**
Meliá Trujillo **1**	Posada dos Orillas **5**	El Corral	Posada Chiviri **4**
Núria **2**	Victoria **6**	del Rey **1**	
Parador de Trujillo **3**		Mesón La Troya **2**	

Nearby, the 14th- to 16th-century **Iglesia de San Martín** ① *0930-1400 and 1630-1930 (closed Sun morning and mornings of religious festivals for mass)*, €1.25, is the grandest of Trujillo's churches; kings and *conquistadors* have worshipped here and town councils were once held at the Gothic Puerta de las Limas on its western side. Some of the most famous *conquistador* families are buried in its Gothic interior.

Calle Ballesteros curves up behind the church of San Martín towards the old, walled city. Enter though the Puerta de Santiago, next to the little church of the same name. **Iglesia de Santiago** ① *1000-1400 and 1600-1900 (Oct-May), 1000-1400 and 1700-2030 (Jun-Sep)*, €1.25, is one of Trujillo's oldest, first built in the 13th century and once the burial place of Trujillo's aristocracy.

Close by, the **Iglesia Santa María la Mayor** ① *1000-1400 and 1600-1900*, €1.20, is the grandest church within the city walls, built over the remnants of a mosque. Predominantly Gothic, the highlights are a Plateresque choir and a gilded 15th-century altarpiece by Fernando Gallego. Look out for the tomb of Diego Gardia de Paredes, the Extremaduran Samson (Sansón extremeño), whose strength and bravery were legendary: he even gets a mention in *Don Quixote*. You can climb the dilapidated Romanesque tower for fabulous views.

There are more views across the empty plain from the battered old **Castillo** ① *1000-1400 and 1600-1900 (Oct-May), 1000-1400 and 1700-2030 (Jun-Sep)*, €1.25, which crowns the hill. Almost nothing remains of the original ninth-century Arab castle, but you can saunter around the 15th-century battlements (best at dusk) and pay your respects to Trujillo's patron saint, the Virgen de la Victoria, in the hermitage.

Near the castle, Francisco Pizarro's birthplace has been turned into the **Casa-Museo de Pizarro** ① *1000-1400 and 1600-1900 (Oct-May), 1000-1400 and 1700-2030 (Jun-Sep)*, €1.25, a disappointingly sparse collection of odds and ends that sheds little light on his exploits in the Americas.

More informative is the **Museo de la Coria** ① *T927321898, Sat, Sun and holidays 1130-1400, free*, housed in the beautiful semi-abandoned ruins of a former convent, which has exhibits covering the Spanish expeditions in the Americas, presented with some consideration for the cultures which were crushed and lost in the process.

Guadalupe → *Phone code: 927; Colour map 4, grid C3; Population: 2,507; Altitude: 640 m.*

Tucked away in the folds of the Sierra de Guadalupe is one of the most important monasteries in the Catholic world, the Real Monasterio de Nuestra Señora de Guadalupe, built as a shrine for a miraculous statue of the Virgin discovered in the 13th century. The conquistadores spread her fame to the Americas, where she was made patron saint of all the territories conquered by Spain, and cities and even a Caribbean island were given her name. Still the focus of an important annual pilgrimage, Guadalupe is also a good base for walkers, with countless trails heading out into the surrounding Sierras. ▸▸ *For Sleeping, Eating and other listings, see pages 654-662.*

History

According to legend, the statue of the Virgin was carved by Saint Luke and later hidden away from the Arab armies for more than 500 years. It was rediscovered by a shepherd at the end of the 13th century, and its fame grew as word of the Virgin's miracles spread like wildfire. The first humble sanctuary was gradually expanded over the centuries to become one of the largest and richest in Spain. Abandoned in 1835 when the Church was stripped of much of its property, the dilapidated monastery was taken over by a community of Franciscan monks in 1908 and carefully restored. It was declared a World Heritage Site in 1993, and has once again become the focus of a major pilgrimage each year on 8 September.

66 99 The spectacular monastery
dominates the little whitewashed village
that grew up at its feet and is dramatically
set against densely wooded hills...

Sights

The vast fortified **Real Monesterio de Nuestra Señora de Guadalupe** ① *Plaza Mayor, T927367000, 0930-1300 and 1530-1830, free, guided tour €2*, dominates the little village at its feet. Countless enlargements over the centuries have resulted in a mish-mash of architectural styles including Gothic, Mudéjar, Renaissance and Baroque, but the result is surprisingly harmonious. A flight of steps leads to the Gothic portal at the entrance to the Basílica itself, where the Virgin is enthroned on a golden dais above the altar. Admission is free, but you'll need the guided tour to visit the rest of the monastery and to see the Virgin in her 'boudoir' (*camarín*). At the heart of the complex is the beautiful Mudéjar cloister, with an upper gallery of delicate horseshoe-shaped arches, and a unique lacy 15th-century pavilion with a shallow fountain hidden among the fruit trees at the centre. The monastery's museums are set around the cloister: the Museo de las Bordados displays exquisitely embroidered religious vestments; in the Museo de Miniados, you'll find leather-bound illuminated texts dating back to the 14th century; and the Museo de Esculturas y Pinturas contains works by Zurbarán, Goya and a miniature alabaster crucifix attributed to Michelangelo. The florid Baroque Sacristy is one of the few places in Spain where you can see Zurbarán's works in the place for which they were designed; the eleven paintings depict the life of St Jerome. Every inch of the ornately decorated Relicario (Reliquary) is stuffed full of bits of elaborately packaged bone and hair, and also holds some of the Virgin's fabulous wardrobe including a cape stitched with 200,000 pearls. In the Gothic Basilica, where the Virgin floats above the altar on her golden throne, there's also a magnificent 18th-century choir and an elaborate Renaissance wrought-iron grille. From here, a monk will take you up a flight of marble steps to the Camarín, a tiny octagonal side chapel where the Virgin's ingenious throne is ceremoniously revolved to reveal the tiny, dark statue almost hidden under the weight of her elaborate robes.

The entrance to the Basilica overlooks the Plaza Mayor, crammed with cafés and handicraft shops – Guadalupe is well known for wickerwork and copper. Close by is the former hospital of **San Juan Bautista**, now a parador, with a beautiful 16th-century courtyard. There are plenty of walking trails leading from the village out into the surrounding hills (the tourist office has leaflets), including one to the **Ermita del Humilladero**, a tiny Mudéjar hermitage about 5 km from Guadalupe which was built to give pilgrims their first glimpse of the monastery itself.

Mérida → *Phone code: 924; Colour map 4, grid C2; Population: 40,005; Altitude: 218 m.*

Mérida contains an extraordinary collection of Roman monuments, liberally scattered around the otherwise rather ordinary modern city. Nowhere else in Spain manages to convey the might of the Roman Empire with such vividness, from the marble pillars of its beautiful theatre, to the remarkable bridges and aqueducts which span the river Guadiana. Modern Mérida is still only half the size of Roman Augusta Emerita, but the continuing work on the restoration of its archaeological heritage is going hand-in-hand with improvements to the modern city, including new parks along the

river banks and spectacular contemporary bridges. ▸▸ *For Sleeping, Eating and other listings, see pages 654-662.*

Ins and outs

Getting there A good network of bus and train services connect Mérida to most major Spanish cities. The bus and train stations are located about a 10-15 minute walk to the centre. ▸▸ *For further details, see Transport page 662.*

Getting around The centre of old Mérida is small and it's easy to make your way around on foot.

Tourist information The tourist office ① *C/Suarez Somonte (by the entrance to the Roman Theatre) Mon-Fri 0900-1445 and 1700-1915, Sat and Sun 0930-1345, T924009730, www.turismoextrema dura.com.* The main sights in Mérida can be visited with one combined ticket (€7.20 /3.60 concessions) which includes entrance to the Teatro and Anfiteatro complex; the Casa Anfiteatro; Basílica Santa Eulalia; Alcazaba; Casa Mitreo; and the Zona Arqueológico de Morerías. Individual entrance to each of these sites costs €2.50, except entrance to the Teatro and adjoining Anfiteatro which costs €5.10. The combined ticket price also includes a comprehensive guide to the sights in English.

History

The Roman colony of Augusta Emerita (Mérida is a corruption of its Roman name) was founded here in 25BC and rapidly developed into one of the most important cities on the Iberian peninsula, richly endowed with bridges, aqueducts, temples and theatres. Succeeding rulers barely tinkered with the Roman city, but it suffered badly during the interminable wars of the 17th and 18th centuries. It wasn't until the mid-20th century that work finally began on recovering Mérida's extraordinary archaeological heritage, and it was declared a World Heritage Site in 1993.

Sights

The star attraction in Mérida is undoubtedly the spectacular **Teatro y Anfiteatro Romanos complex** ① *entrance at the corner of C José Ramon Melida and Suárez Somonte, T924312024, Jun-Sep 0915-2015, Oct-May 0915-1345, €5.10 or combined entrance ticket,* which make a sublime setting for the summer festival of classical music and drama, see Festivals and events, page 660. The amphitheatre provided the bloodthirsty citizens of Roman Mérida with its best night out, when wild animals were pitted against each other, or, better yet, against gladiators. Next to the Amphitheatre is the Theatre, easily the grandest of all 18 of Spain's surviving Roman theatres. It accommodated 6,000 spectators, who faced one of the most beautiful stages in the Empire, adorned with a double tier of marble columns and liberally decorated with statues of gods and members of the Imperial family. The Imperial statues were no accident: the theatre was largely used as a means of spreading Rome's propaganda, although this was all considered a bit dull by ordinary people, who much preferred the bloody spectacles of men being torn apart by wild animals next door.

Close to the theatre is the **Casa Romana del Anfiteatro** ① *C/Octavio Augusto, T924318509, Jun-Sep 0930-1355 and 1700-1915 daily, Oct-May 0930-1345 and 1600-1815 daily €2.50 or with combined ticket,* discovered in the 1940s, and given its name purely because of its proximity to the Amphitheatre. Among the dusty ruins of what was once a fabulous mansion are several beautiful mosaics, including one of three pudgy revellers gleefully treading grapes.

Very close to the entrance to the theatre is one of Mérida's newest buildings, the **Museo Nacional de Arte Romano** (MNAR) ① *C/José Ramon Melida s/n, T924311690,*

● *Almost nothing remains of the Roman Circus on the fringes of modern Mérida, although it is just possible to trace the dusty remnants of the enormous oval track. It was once one of the largest Circuses of the Roman empire with capacity for 30,000 spectators.*

designed by Rafael Moneo in 1986. The ground floor is devoted to the most impressive finds from the Amphitheatre, Theatre and Forum, including a beautiful statue of Ceres which once graced the Theatre's main stage, and the elaborate main portico from the Forum. There are some enormous mosaics which have been hung so that they can be viewed section by section from each of the three levels of the museum, which, unfortunately, is a very dissatisfying way of seeing them. Still, you can make out some heated hunting scenes and Bacchic revelry. There are coins, jewellery, glassware, pottery and other domestic items on the second floor and the third floor explores themes such as the arts in Roman Mérida. Down in the spooky crypt, you can cross the old Roman road and poke about in the remains of more Roman houses.

Calle Sagasta leads from MNAR towards the river, passing the **Forum** and the **Templo de Diana** (once part of the forum complex but access is not permitted to either). The forum's portico has been reconstructed here (the original is in MNAR), complete with medallions depicting Jupiter. The Templo de Diana was one of the first buildings to be raised after Augusta Emerita's foundation, and was devoted to the imperial cult. It is the best preserved of the city's religious buildings, largely

Castilla-La Mancha & Extremadura Mérida

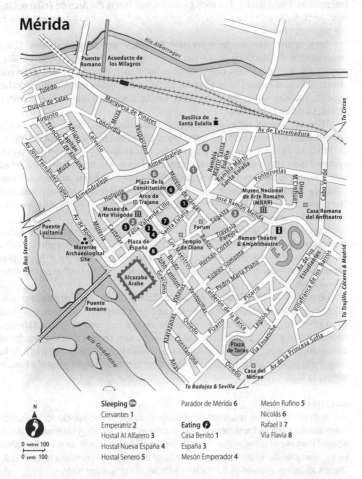

Mérida

Sleeping 😊
Cervantes **1**
Emperatriz **2**
Hostal Al Alfarero **3**
Hostal Nueva España **4**
Hostal Senero **5**

Parador de Mérida **6**

Eating 🍴
Casa Benito **1**
España **3**
Mesón Emperador **4**

Mesón Rufino **5**
Nicolás **6**
Rafael II **7**
Via Flavia **8**

N
0 metres 100
0 yards 100

thanks to its incorporation into a Renaissance palace. Set into the walls at the end of the Calle Sagasta is the **Alcazaba Árabe** (Arabic citadel) ① *entrance on C/Graciano, but hard to* spot, T924317309, Jun-Sep 0930-1355 and 1700-1915 daily, Oct-May 0930-1345 and 1600-1815 daily €2.50 or with combined ticket, built in AD835. There's not much to see here, although you can just about pick out the shape of the rooms in the old fortress and it's possible to walk into the old cistern (*aljibe*). Best of all is the access to the city walls: from up here you can enjoy panoramic views of the Puente Romano (Roman bridge). **Puente Romano** is still used, although now it's for pedestrians only, and stretches magnificently across the River Guadiana. From the bridge, you can see the gleaming white arc of the modern Puente Lusitania, and the riverside parks which have been created on the islands which dot the river and are being extended around the rim of the city.

Plaza de España (up Calle Puente) is where all the action is in Mérida nowadays. This attractive square was laid out in the 18th century, and has been added to ever since with a motley collection of bustling shops, tapas bars and cafes. Just off the Plaza de España is the dusty little **Museo de Arte Visigoda** ① *T924300106, Tue-Sat 1000-1400 and 1700-1900, Sun 1000-1400, free*, housed in the former convent of Santa Clara, which displays a few carved capitals and inscriptions dating back to the sixth century. Close to it is the **Arco de Trajano**, long mistakenly believed to be a triumphal arch, but in fact a monumental entrance to the provincial forum.

Back along the riverfront is the **Morerías archaeological site** (Zona Arqueológica de Morerías) ① *Jun-Sep 0930-1355 and 1700-1915 daily, Oct-May 0930-1345 and 1600- 1815 daily, €2.50 or with combined ticket*, where several streets of Roman houses have been excavated in the former Morería, the Moorish quarter. You can watch the excavations taking place and admire the surviving mosaics and wall paintings.

There are several sights on the fringes of the town. Next to the immaculately painted Plaza de Toros (bullring) at the top of Calle Graciano is the **Casa del Mitreo** ① *C/Oviedo, T924301504, Jun-Sep 0930-1355 and 1700-1915 daily, Oct-May 0930-1345 and 1600-1815 daily, €2.50 or with combined ticket*, which may have been linked with a temple to Mithras discovered beneath the bull ring. Some mosaics and wall paintings survive, including the fabulous Cosmological Mosaic (Mosaico Cosmólogico), one of the most detailed and best preserved Roman mosaics anywhere in the world.

If you arrived in Mérida by train, you won't have missed the vast triple-decker **Acueducto de los Milagros** (Aqueduct of the Miracles), which brought water to the city from the Roman-built reservoir of Proserpina. Close to it is another Roman bridge, smaller and more battered than its famous big brother on the other side of town.

Near here is the **Basílica de Santa Eulalia** ① *Av de Extremadura s/n, T924303407, Mon-Sat Jun-Sep 1000-1355 and 1700-1915, Oct-May 1000-1345 and 1600-1815, €0.50 or with combined ticket, closed Sun and religious holidays*, dedicated to the city's patron saint and built in the 14th century over the remains of a Visigothic church. The lavish 17th-century temple in front of the church was built to mark the exact spot of Santa Eulalia's martyrdom and incorporates parts of a Roman temple to Mars.

Excursions

The Romans built two reservoirs to ensure a steady water supply for Augustus Emeritus: the **Lago de Proserpina** (known locally as 'La Charca'), 5 km from Mérida, is a popular weekend jaunt, with a campsite and small beach. The reservoir at **Cornalvo**, 16 km from Mérida, is surrounded by forests of holm oak and is now a natural park. There's an information office by the lake with details of walking trails.

Badajoz and the Portuguese frontier towns

→ *Phone code: 924; Colour map 4, grid C1; Population: 124,616; Altitude: 186 m.*

Badajoz, just 4 km from the Portuguese border, is Extremadura's biggest city and one of Spain's poorest. A shanty town has grown up on its outskirts and even the old centre is depressingly dilapidated. After centuries of interminable battles on the front line between Spain and Portugal, Badajoz is trying to forget its bloody past in a new drive to modernize itself. Unfortunately, most of the new development is functional at best, and quiet whitewashed frontier towns like Olivenza, which still retain an alluring blend of Portuguese and Spanish influences, are much more attractive stop-overs.
▶▶ *For Sleeping, Eating and other listings, see pages 654-662.*

Ins and outs

Getting there There are frequent train and bus connections with Madrid and other major Spanish cities; bus information, call T924258661. Both bus and train stations are a good 30-minute walk from the city centre: take bus No 6 from the bus station to the centre, or bus Nos 1 and 2 from the train station. To get into town from the airport, it is necessary to take a taxi.▶▶ *For further details, see Transport page 662.*

Getting around Once you've made it into the centre from the bus and train stations, the main sights are all within easy walking distance of each other.

Tourist information Provincial office ① *Plaza de la Libertad 3, T924222763, otbadajoz@bme.es, Mon-Fri 0900-145 and 1700-1915, Sat and Sun 0930-1345.* Municipal office① *Pasaje de San Juan s/n, T924224 981.*

Background

The small Roman settlement at Badajoz became increasingly important under the Visigoths and enjoyed a brief period of glory in the 11th century when it became the capital of a small Aftasí kingdom. It was all downhill from there, endless battles culminating in some of the most notorious atrocities of the Civil War. Now the capital of Spain's largest province, it has begun the slow work of restoring its monuments but, for the moment at least, it remains one of Spain's least alluring large cities.

Sights

An 11th-century Arabic fortress at the peak of the hill, the **Alcazaba** ① *Plaza José Álvarez, T924222314, Tue-Sun 1000-1500, free,* has survived countless sieges to become modern Badajoz's most emblematic sight. Stretches of the walls, gateways and turrets still survive, and the ruins of the former mosque and a couple of churches are now surrounded with (slightly threadbare) gardens. There are great views from the walls over the río Guadiana. Within the grounds of the Alcazaba, the fortified palace of the Dukes of la Roca houses the city's rather old-fashioned archaeology museum, with more than 20,000 exhibits stretching back to pre-Roman times. The streets around the entrance to the Alcazaba are run-down and slightly sinister; the Plaza de San José, almost enclosed and ringed with arcades, is completely in ruins but there are plans for its restoration.

The Plaza de España is a nondescript little square which has disappeared behind a wall of scaffolding for renovation. It's overlooked by the pale bulk of the **Catedral de San Juan** ① *Plaza de España, T924223999, Tue-Fri 1100-1300 and 1800-2000, Sat 1100-1300, church free, museum, €1.20,* begun in the early 13th century, and gleaming after its recent restoration. The original Gothic interior was remodelled during the early 18th century, when it gained a florid Churrigueresque altarpiece, and there's a small museum just off the cloister with works by Luís Morales and Zurbarán, both natives of Extremadura.

Just east, the Plaza de la Soledad is overlooked by a dainty copy of Sevilla's famous tower, **La Giralda**, and close by is the pretty pink-and-yellow **Museo de Bellas Artes** ① *C/Duque de San Germán, 1000-1400 and 1800-2000, 1000-1400 and 1600-1800, free*, with works by Dalí and Picasso, more paintings by Morales and a series of panels by Zurbarán, all arranged around the marble halls of a former palace.

Heading down towards the river, the twin-towered **Puerta de las Palmas** was the monumental entrance through the walls to the old city in the 16th century. It overlooks the elegant **Puente de las Palmas,** or Puente Vieja, which was designed by Juan Herrera, Felipe II's favourite architect, and swoops gracefully across the río Guadiana.

Lost among the dreary offices and apartment blocks which ring old Badajoz is its most striking building: a 16th-century bastion, long used as the municipal prison, has been dramatically converted to house the **Museo Extremeño e Iberoamericano de Arte Contemporaneo** ① *C/del Museo 2, T924260384, Tue-Sat 1000-1330 and 1700-2000, Sun 1000-1330*. The extensive and absorbing collection of contemporary art from Extremadura and the Americas includes painting, sculpture, photographs and installations, handsomely set in curving galleries.

Excursions

Olivenza, some 25 km south of Badajoz, still doesn't seem to have got used to the idea that it has belonged to Spain for the past 200 years. Passed back and forth between Spain and Portugal for centuries, its character has remained distinctly Portuguese no matter where the border is marked on official maps. It's a tranquil, whitewashed town set in olive groves with a clutch of noble mansions, convents and Gothic churches tucked in behind the remnants of the medieval walls. At the centre is the 15th-century tower, all that remains of a castle which gave its name to the town's most elaborate church, the Iglesia de Santa María del Castillo, an elegant example of the Portuguese Manueline style. The Palacio de los Duques de Cadaval (now the town hall) has a beautiful Manueline portal, with swooping curves and rich decoration.

Zafra and south to Andalucía → *Phone code: 927; Colour map 6, grid A6.*

Whitewashed Zafra is tucked beneath a craggy outcrop, overlooked by its famous castle and a smattering of belltowers topped with untidy storks' nests. Its peaceful 16th-century squares and narrow streets have made it a popular weekend escape for stressed-out Madrileños and Sevillanos. Further south, Jerez de los Caballeros is a sleepy town which sees few tourists but has a gentle charm. ▸▸ *For Sleeping, Eating and other listings, see pages 654-662.*

Ins and outs

Getting there There are regular train connections from all major Spanish cities to Zafra. The train station is 3 km from the town centre. The bus station is close to the central Plaza de España and has regular services from major cities as well as local services to surrounding villages. ▸▸ *For further details, see Transport page 662.*

♣ *A web of pedestrianized streets span out from Plaza de España, good for cafés and tapas bars.*

Getting around The centre of old Zafra is tiny and you could easily cross it in 15 minutes, so you won't need public transport. There is a taxi stand on the Plaza de España.

Best time to visit Semana Santa is vigorously celebrated with colourful, solemn processions but the best time to visit is during the cattle fair (Feria de San Miguel) in early October which is also an excuse for lots of partying and cultural activities.

Tourist information The provincial tourist office ① *Plaza de España, T924551 036, www.zafraturismo.com, Mon-Fri 0930-1400 and 1600-1900, Sat, Sun and holidays 1000-1400*. The municipal tourist office ① *Casa del Aljimez, C/Botica, just off the Plaza*

Background

Each year in early October, Zafra holds its famous *Feria de San Miguel* (a cattle fair), a tradition which stretches back more than a thousand years. When the Arabs arrived in the 11th century, they called their new settlement 'Safra' meaning June, after the month when the cattle fairs were historically held. The Arabs were ousted in the 13th century, and Zafra became an important commercial town right up until the early 20th century, when it went into decline. It mouldered away, poor and half-forgotten, until the 1970s, when its dilapidated squares and mansions were restored and newly whitewashed, and Zafra blossomed again into one of Extremadura's prettiest and most engaging towns.

Sights

The old part of Zafra is a small egg-shaped cluster of tiny streets which begin right next to the **Plaza de España**, a big rather nondescript square. Head down **Calle Sevilla**, the busiest street in the old town, lined with all kinds of shops and constantly bustling. To the right is Zafra's storybook **castle**, complete with towers and crenellations. Built as a fortress and palace for the Dukes of Feria in 1443, it is now a very fine parador which has retained an elegant double-tiered patio of gleaming white marble, attributed to Juan de Herrera, architect of El Escorial, see page 119. To admire all the detailing – *artesonado* ceilings and Mudéjar decoration – you'll have to book a room.

Nearby is the **Convento de Santa Clara** ① *T924551199, daily except Wed, Jun-Sep 1800-2000, Oct-May 1700-1900, free*, begun in 1430 as a burial place for the first Lord and Lady of Feria, whose alabaster tombs are next to the main altar. There's a reliquary built into one wall, stuffed with the bones and hair of saints and martyrs, but unfortunately it's rarely open. A community of nuns still live here, and are famous for their *dulces* (sweets and cakes) – but don't count on finding a nun to sell you any.

The Calle Seville opens out into the heart of the old city, the **Plaza Grande**, a delightful, arcaded square surrounded with crooked whitewashed houses and shaded by the odd palm tree. Laid out in the 16th century, the Plaza Grande was built to allow the merchants to carry out their business underneath the arches. One half of it is marred by a car park, but the other half is full of cafés, stone benches and fountains.

A tiny archway, the **Arquillo del Pan**, leads to the **Plaza Chica (Little Square)**, a miniature version of the Plaza Grande and even prettier. It's also got its fair share of cafés and bars and buzzes until late on summer evenings. The grandest of the whitewashed buildings which surround the square used to be the Town Hall (now it's the **Palacio de Justicia**, private), a graceful mixture of neoclassical and Renaissance elements.

From the Plaza Chica, narrow Calle Boticas leads to the **Casa Ajimez** ① *C Boticas, Mon-Sat 1030-1330, free*, a beautifully restored Mudéjar house with characteristic horseshoe shaped arches, shallow brick vaulting and brilliant ceramic (*azulejo*) decoration. The house has an interesting audio-visual display in both English and Spanish giving the history of the city.

Calle Boticas culminates at the **Puerta del Cubo**, one of the original entrance points to the city, which has a little statue of a knight prancing on a charger – the first Lord of Feria. Opposite is the hulking white-and-ochre **Convento del Rosario** ① *0830-1330 and 1630-2030, free*, which houses a striking, tortured 17th-century statue of Christ (Christo del Rosario), the most venerated religious icon in Zafra.

Zafra's most important church is the **Iglesia de la Candelaria** ① *entrance on C/José, Jun-Sep 1030-1300 and 1830-2030, Oct-May 1030-1300 and 1730-1930, free*, with a fine portal. Inside, it's rather gloomy, in need of a paint job, and some birds are nesting in one corner. The retablo which dwarfs the main altar is a gilded,

Churrigueresque fantasy, but the highlight is a retablo containing some panels attributed to local boy, Zurbarán.

Jerez de los Caballeros and around

Surrounded by an endless landscape of parched *dehesa* close to the Portuguese border, the serene whitewashed town of Jerez de los Caballeros ('of the Knights') is named after the Knights Templar who established themselves here after the Reconquista. The town has produced several *conquistadors*, including Vasco Núñez de Balboa, who discovered the Pacific, and Hernando de Soto, who led one of the first expeditions up the Mississippi. According to legend, the Knights Templar held out against royal troops before being slaughtered in the Torre Sangrienta – 'the bloody tower', part of the Templar fortress. From the battlements, you can gaze down across the town and its distinctive skyline of frilly Baroque spires which deliberately echo Sevilla's La Giralda. The loveliest is the tower of San Bartolomé, covered in dazzling blue and gold azulejo tiles, and the church of San Miguel which overlooks the Plaza de España has delicate Mudéjar brickwork.

Fregenal de la Sierra and Llerena

Heading towards the Andalucían border and the mountains of the Sierra Morena, the little town of Fregenal de la Sierra has another restored Templar castle and a delightful Plaza Mayor surrounded with medieval arcades. The agricultural town of Llerena, further east, has another particularly charming Plaza Mayor, with a fountain designed by Zurbarán, and the curious 16th-century church of Nuestra Señora de la Granada with a frilly Mudéjar tower and a Renaissance cloister.

● Sleeping

Much of Extremadura's best accommodation is in *casas rurales* (see p47), which can range from simple rooms in tiny villages to whole apartments, or even beautifully converted country mansions full of antiques. For information, check out www.parador.es.

Plasencia *p639*
A **Alfonso VIII**, C/Alfonso VIII 32, T927410250, www.hotelalfonsoviii.com. A recently renovated luxury hotel close to the Parador with modern well-equipped rooms and excellent service.
A **Parador de Plasencia**, Plaza San Vicente s/n, T927425870, plasencia@parador.es. Housed in a 15th-century convent, this has elegant rooms set around a pretty cloister and plenty of extras including a pool and an excellent restaurant.
D **Rincón Extremeño**, C/Vidrieras 6, T927411150, F927420650. Just off the Plaza Mayor, with simple rooms and an excellent restaurant (mid-range) serving regional specialities, and a cheaper café-bar on the square.

F **Hostal La Muralla**, C/Berzocana 6, T927413874. This old-fashioned basic *hostal* is a great cheap option, just off the Plaza Mayor with a good bar and terrace.

Valle de la Vera and the Monesterio de Yuste *p640*
There are plenty of places to stay around Cuacos de Yuste. The few places to stay in the eastern part of the valley are mainly in *casas rurales*.
L **Parador de Jarandilla**, Av García Prieto 1, Jarandillo, T927560117, jarandilla@parador.es. Sleep like a king in the antique-furnished rooms set around a palm-shaded stone patio, and the restaurant is the best in the area but expensive.
B **Colmenarejo**, C/Almendro 1, Cuacos de Yuste, T927460300, www.casaruralcolmenarejo.com. A gorgeous old stone house 3 km outside Cuacos de Yuste; a path leads through woods to the monastery.
C **Antigua Casa del Heno**, Finca Valdepimienta, Losar de la Vera, T927198077, is a traditional, stylishly decorated stone farmhouse with a small restaurant just for guests.

● *For an explanation of sleeping and eating price codes used in this guide, see inside the*
● *front cover. Other relevant information is found in Essentials, see pages 47-56.*

C **Mansión El Abuelo Marciano**, Ctra Jaraíz-Garganta La Olla km 2.2, T927460426, a magnificent country house with beamed ceilings, and a roaring fireplace in winter.

D **Casa del Pozo**, C/Real 69, Villanueva de la Vera, T927566262, in a restored townhouse with a patio, garden and good, mid-range priced restaurant.

D **Jaranda**, Soledad Vega Ortiz, Jarandillo, T/F927560206, hoteljaranda@retemail.es. The rooms are modern and well-equipped and there is a popular local restaurant with stunning views.

E **Casa de Tía Emilia**, Vilar de Plasencia, T927489028, a pretty *casa rural* with a canopy of vines over the door which is run by a kindly family. Highly recommended.

Camping

G **Campamento de Turismo Carlos I**, Cuacos de Yuste, T927172092, also rents bungalows. Open all year.

Coria, Las Hurdes and the Sierra de Gata *p641*

C **El Puente**, Paseo de Extremadura 40, Las Hurdes, T927674028, immaculate with a restaurant on the terrace.

C **Maire**, C/Humilladero 66, Gata, T927672079, a traditional *casa rurale* near the hermitage of Humilladero, best option in Gata, comfortable rooms and fine views.

D **Casa Vieja**, Hoyos, Sierra de Gata, T927514138, a *casa rurale* in a traditional old house with kitchen facilities.

E **Montesol**, Puente de Hierro s/n, Coria, T927501049, a modern building by the river on the edge of town with 70s-style sketches of naked ladies in every room.

F **Pensión Avenida**, Avda Almeranar 12, T927672271, is a good budget option.

F **Pensión El Hurdano**, Nuñomoral, T927433012, small, basic rooms, café-bar.

F **Pensión El Redoble**, Plaza de La Paz 14, Hoyos, Sierra de Gata, T927514018. Basic. One of two options in Hoyos.

Camping

El Pino, Ctra de Salamanca, Las Hurdes, T927674141, for camping by the river .

Parque Natural de Monfragüe *p641*

There are no hotels in Villareal, but there are several *casas rurales* in nearby Torrejón el

Rubio or Malpartida de Plasencia (the park information office has a complete list) and many of them can organize excursions into the park.

La Posada de Amonaria, Malpartida de Plasencia, T927459446, set in a 19th-century traditional farm.

Posada El Arriero, Torrejón, T927455050, stone-built, with a restaurant.

Cáceres *p642, map p643*

L **Parador de Cáceres**, C/Ancha 6 T92721-1759. Beautiful parador set in a Renaissance mansion and the only place to stay within the walls of the old city. The excellent restaurant is surprisingly reasonable.

AL **Barceló V Centenario**, Urba. Los Castellanos, Ctra de Plasencia, T927232200, vcentenario@barcelo.com. A bland chain hotel in the suburbs which deserves a mention for its pool – a necessity in searing summer heat.

AL **Meliá Cáceres**, Plaza de San Juan s/n, T927215800, melia.caceres@solmelia.com. A big hotel chain, but still one of the most elegant hotels in the city set in an elaborately restored 16th-century palace. Light and well-equipped rooms and a popular bar.

C **Alfonso IX**, C/Moret 20, T927246400, F927247811. A modest, friendly option with a/c rooms and a café-restaurant. It's popular with weekending Spaniards, so book ahead.

C **Goya**, Plaza Mayor 33, T927249950, F927213758. A charming, rickety hotel right on the Plaza Mayor. Ask for a room with views of the 16th-century square – and bring ear plugs.

D **Iberia**, C/Pintores 2, T927247634, F927248200. Just off the Plaza Mayor on a shopping street, a newly renovated 17th-century building offering attractive, en-suite rooms (best are on the top floor).

To Alcántara *p644*

D **Casa Candi**, C/Cuatro Calles 8, Alcántara, T927390028, this delightful *casa rurale* in the old town is the best option in town.

D **La Posada**, Plaza de Ovanda 1, and in Brozas, T927373030, simple, friendly with an excellent, cheap restaurant.

D-E **Hostal Kantara al Saif**, Av de Mérida s/n, T927390246, F927390833, is modest but has a decent, and cheap, restaurant.

E **Hostal Divino Morales**, Arroyo, T927270257, basic.

Trujillo *p645, map p645*
AL **Meliá Trujillo**, Plaza de Campillo 1, T927458900, www.solmelia.com. A restored Baroque convent with plush rooms, a pool, and a restaurant set in what was the nuns' refectory.

A **Parador de Trujillo**, T927321350. Trujillo's parador is set in another restored convent, with an excellent restaurant. The rooms are arranged around a Renaissance patio, but all austerity has been banished.

A **Posada dos Orillas**, C/Cambrones 6, Trujillo, T/F927659079, www.dosorillas.com. An ancient, beautifully converted inn in Trujillo's old quarter, with a pretty breakfast patio, a good restaurant (mid-range), and a tiny outdoor pool.

C **Victoria**, Plaza Campillo 22, T927321819 F927322084. A converted 19th-century mansion with comfortable rooms, a pool and a restaurant, 5-min walk from the centre.

E **Hotel Núria**, Plaza Mayor 17, T927320907. Perfectly located on the plaza, a classic, old-fashioned hotel with immaculate rooms above a café-bar with a terrace on the square.

F **Pension San Roque**, C/Domingo Ramos 30, T927 32 31 55. Tucked down a quiet back street, this is a simple little *pensión* run by Margarita who runs the souvenir stall by the tourist information office on the Plaza Mayor (where you'll have to go to get the keys). She has some crisp new rooms overlooking the Plaza Mayor which are slightly more expensive (€30) but equipped with a/c, bathrooms and perfect views – highly recommended.

Guadalupe *p646*
B **Parador de Guadalupe**, Marqués de la Romana, T927367075, guadalupe@para dores.es. A luxurious parador housed in a 16th-century hospital, with a patio full of orange trees and an elegant restaurant.

C **Hospedería del Real Monesterio**, T927367000, F927367177. For the authentic pilgrim experience, stay in the monastery itself: simple accommodation (unless you want to splash out on the Royal Suite, full of paintings and antiques) in rooms once occupied by the monks. The refectory is now a restaurant, offering good local specialities.

D **Hostal Alfonso XI**, C/Alfonso Onceno 21, T927154287, juanplaza@bme.es. A modern hostal on Guadalupe's main street, with a good little restaurant and comfortable if functional en-suite rooms.

F **Isabel**, Plaza de Santa María de Guadalupe 13, T927367126. A simple pensión opposite the monastery on the main square.

Mérida *p647, map p649*
AL **Parador de Mérida**, Plaza de la Constitución 3, T924313800, merida@para dor.es. A former convent overlooking a quiet square, with a pool, gardens and plenty of old-fashioned charm. The mid-range priced restaurant is excellent.

B **Emperatriz**, Plaza de España 16, T924313111, hoteles@teleline.es. One of Mérida's oldest hotels, set in a 16th-century palace where the Catholic kings used to stay. It has a prime location overlooking the Plaza de España, a fine interior courtyard and a pretty garden.

C-D **Cervantes**, C/Camillo José Cela 10, T924314961, www.hotelcervantes.com. A modern hotel with small but well-equipped rooms and a good restaurant and old-fashioned bar downstairs. Friendly staff.

D **Hostal Al Alfarero**, C/Sagasta 40, T924300006, F924303183. A very pretty *hostal* set in an old yellow-painted house close to the Teatro and most main sights.

E **Hostal Nueva España**, T924313356, F924313211. Close to the train station, this modern *hostal* offers good-value, functional rooms. Short on charm, but convenient.

F **Hostal Senera**, T924317207, hostalsenero @oem.es. Close to the main sights, a small, modern *hostal* with simple en-suite rooms and accommodating staff.

Camping
Mérida, T924303453, 3 km out of town, just off the busy main road to Trujillo but is open all year, unlike the more attractive **Lago de Plasencia**, by the lake (5 km from Mérida), T924124055, which is open May to Sep only.

Badajoz and the Portuguese frontier towns *p651*
Badajoz has few places with charm: choose between modern hotels catering mainly to business people (usually excellent weekend deals) and battered hostels in the centre.

AL Rocamador, Ctra Nal.Badajoz-Huelva km 41, Almendral, T924489000, www.roca mador.com. This is one of the best hotels and restaurants in all Extremadura, located 15 km southeast of Olivenza in Almendral. Stylish and original this hotel is set in an idiosyncratically refurbished convent. Some rooms are built into the rock, which has been left atmospherically bare. There's an excellent Michelin-starred restaurant too.

B Barceló Zurbarán, Paseo de Castelar s/n, T924223741, zurbaran@barcelo.com. This huge, concrete chain hotel is the most luxurious that Badajoz has to offer. Prices are very reasonable at weekends, and amenities include a pool and gym.

C La Toja, Av de Elvas, T924273477. One of the city's best known restaurants (see below) has recently opened a delightful little *hostal* with just 10 prettily decorated rooms in a quiet neighbourhood on the edge of Badajoz.

D Heredero, Carretera Comarcal 426 km23, Olivenza, T924490835, a bland roadside hotel which offers plenty of comforts – including a restaurant and even a disco – for a very reasonable price.

D Río, C/Adolfo Diaz Ambrona 13, T924272600, hotelrioa@hotelrio.net. Another big, modern hotel with 90 identical rooms on the fringe of the old city. Prices are good for the facilities which include a pool and garden.

E Cervantes, C/Trinidad 2, T924223710, F924222935. The only one of Badajoz's city centre hotels which can lay claim to any charm, set in a 19th-century townhouse just off a pretty square. There's a modern annexe, but the rooms aren't as nice.

F Los Amigos, Av Chile 1, Olivenza. T924491001, which is small and old-fashioned but has a great café-restaurant.

F Niza I and Niza II, T924223173, F924223881. Two simple *hostales* on the same street with basic rooms all equipped with a/c and TVs. **Niza I** is older and a bit cheaper, but facilities are shared.

Zafra and south to Andalucía *p652*
AL Parador de Hernán Cortes, Plaza Corazón de María 7, Zafra, T924554540, F924551018. Set in Zafra's emblematic castle, this is a romantic place to stay. The

excellent restaurant – with a terrace on Herrera's white marble patio – is open to non-guests. Look out for special deals, including a 'youth' package, which offers rooms for less than €40.

A-C Huerta Honda, C/Lópes Asme 80, Zafra, T924554100, www.hotelhuertahonda.com. This traditional, ochre-painted hotel is a favourite with visiting bullfighters. Rooms are individually decorated, and there's a pool out in the gardens, and a very good restaurant. Prices become very reasonable (dropping 2 categories) in low season.

C Los Templarios, Ctra de Villanueva s/n, T924731636, is a modern roadside hotel in Jerez de los Caballeros with a restaurant, pool and all mod-cons.

D Hotel El Ancla, Plaza de España 8, Zafra, T924554382. A big blue anchor marks this centrally located hotel, which has large and airy marine-themed rooms set around a patio. Interior rooms are very quiet.

D Hotel Las Palmeras, Plaza Grande 14, Zafra, T924552208. Set right in the middle of the action in an old whitewashed mansion overlooking the Plaza Grande – the best rooms have balconies overlooking the square, but it's best for night owls who don't mind the noise from the restaurant-bar downstairs.

D Oasis, El Campo 18, Jerez de los Caballeros, T924731836, has a decent inexpensive restaurant.

E Hostal Carmen-Rogelio, Av Estación 9, Zafra, T924551439. The best value option with functional, en-suite rooms and a cheap restaurant.

F Hostal Arias, Ctra Badajoz-Granada km 72, Zafra, T924664855,The cheapest place to stay, a basic *hostal* with a decent budget restaurant on the outskirts of town (about a 10-min walk to the centre). It also offers good value apartments.

● Eating

Plasencia *p639*
To push the boat out in plush surroundings, you can't do better than the restaurant at the parador, see Sleeping.

€€ **Casa Juan**, C/Arenillas 2, T927424042. Closed Thu. Tucked away in a narrow street in what was once Plasencia's Jewish quarter, this classic restaurant serves regional

specialities, and has a lovely garden where you can dine in summer.

€€ **La Catedral**, Ave Calvo Sotelo, T927418579. Just a few steps from the cathedral, this is lined with bottles from its excellent *bodega*, and specializes in oven-roasted beef, suckling pig and kid.

€ **La Taberna Extremeña**, C/Vidrieras 2, T927421863. A rustic tavern serving good tapas, local wines and a reasonable *menú del día* for about €8.

Tapas bars and cafés

There are dozens of bars serving cheap *platos combinados* and tapas on the Plaza Mayor, including the café-bar at the **Hotel Rincón Extremeño**, see Sleeping. Most offer a lunchtime *menú* for around €6, as well as a range of tapas.

Valle de la Vera and the Monesterio de Yuste *p640*

See also Sleeping above.
Abadía, Av Constitución 73, Cuacos de Yuste, T927172241. For lunch, you won't do better, or much cheaper, than this option.

Parque Natural de Monfragüe *p641*

See also Sleeping above.
In Villareal, there are a couple of bars and restaurants, including the **Casa Paqui**, T927199002, which does a good value *menú del día*, but there's nowhere to shop to buy picnic stuff.

Cáceres *p642, map p643*

€€€ **Atrio**, Av de España 30, Bloque 4, T927242928. Closed Sun night. Despite the unpromising setting, this is the finest restaurant in Extremadura and the place to sample classic regional dishes – if you've got bags of cash. There's a *menú degustación* (tasting menu) at around €45.

€€€ **Torre de Sande**, C/de los Condes 3, T927211147. A romantic restaurant with a summer terrace in an ancient stone mansion in the old city; pricey, but worth it.

€€ **Figón de Eustaquio**, Plaza de San Juan 12, T927248194. A classic, stuck in a 1950s timewarp, serving old-fashioned Extremaduran cooking and justifiably proud of its reputation for excellent *migas*.

€€ **Palacio de los Golfines**, Adarve padre Rosalio 2, T927242414. Closed Sun night and

Mon. Tucked away into part of a 16th-century palace, an elegant restaurant with beamed ceilings which serves fine regional cuisine.

€ **El Asador**, C/Moret 24, T927213609. A busy bar serving up delicious *raciones* (including a selection of fine hams), or you can sit down in the *comedor* and enjoy the house dish of the day.

€ **El Pato**, Plaza Mayor 14, T927248736. The cheapest option on the Plaza Mayor, with tapas and a good value *menú del día* for about €8.

€ **Kiosko Colón**, Avda de España s/n, Paseo Calvo Sotelo, T927215052. On a popular tree-lined park, this delightful café has a terrace, a busy bar, and a plusher dining area serving up tapas and a good value *menú del día* for €13.

Tapas bars and cafés

Chocolatería Cáceres, Plaza Mayor 16, T924249763. One of dozens of café-bars with a terrace on the Plaza Mayor, this does very tasty *churros con chocolate* for breakfast.

To Alcántara *p644*

See also Sleeping above.
€ **Mesón San Pedro**, Plaza de España 6, T927390364, is central and has a good, cheap, *menú* of Extremaduran classics.

Trujillo *p645, map p645*

€€€ **Parador de Trujillo**, (see above) is perhaps Trujillo's finest, if you are looking to splurge.

€€ **El Corral del Rey**, Plazuela Corral del Rey 2, T927321780. Big, popular local restaurant serving Extremaduran specialities with a good range of home-made desserts.

€€ **Pizarro**, Plaza Mayor 13, T927320355. Probably the best of the restaurants surrounding the Plaza Mayor, the *Pizarro* serves imaginative variations on local classics.

€ **Mesón La Troya**, Plaza Mayor 10, T927321364. Reasonable prices and a prime Plaza Mayor location have made this place a local institution.

€ **Posada Chiviri**, C/Sillerias 7, T27322919. Tucked away down a side-street, the cosy *Chiviri* serves hefty *raciones* to a packed bar full of locals.

Guadalupe p646

Most of the hotels and *hostales* have decent restaurants, see Sleeping above. Another good option is the **Mesón El Cordero**, C/Alfonso Onceno 27, T927367131, which has wonderful views of the surrounding sierras to go with its fine, mid-range priced regional cooking. There's a good value lunch *menú*, too. Closed Mon and Feb.

Tapas bars and cafés

Atrium, C/Alfonso Onceno 6. Delicious *churros y chocolate* for breakfast.

Mérida p647, map 649

€€ **Mesón Rufino**, Plaza de Santa Clara 2, T924312001. Another local favourite, with huge windows overlooking the square. Try the house speciality, *cabrito al horno* (oven-baked kid) but save room for the homemade desserts.

€€ **Restaurante del Parador** (see above).
Nicolás, C/Félix Valverde Lillo 13, T924319610. Perhaps the best-known restaurant in Mérida, this is stylish and traditional. It offers classic regional cuisine including wild boar and pheasant accompanied by a good local wine list.
€ **El Briz**, C/Félix Valverde Lillo 5, T924319307. A relaxed local bar with a small *comedor* at the back. Good tapas and lunchtime *menús* at rock-bottom prices.
€ **Rafael II**, C/Santa Eulalia 13, T924318752. A local favourite with a few tables on a pedestrianized shopping street serving good tapas and a well-priced *menú del día*.
€ **Via Flavia**, Plaza del Rastro 9, T924301590. Right on the Plaza de España, you can eat tapas or *boccadillos* out on the terrace or in the bar, or head to the upstairs restaurant for good views and a cheap *menú del día*.

Tapas bars and cafés

The Plaza de España has dozens of tapas bars and cafés with terraces – good bets include the **España** and the **Mesón Emperador**. Most restaurants also serve tapas and raciones – the **Mesón Rufino** (see above) does very tasty *raciones* of local hams. The **Casa Benito**, Plaza de la Calatrava, is stuffed with bullfighting memorabilia and serves up local *pitarra* wine and ham.

Badajoz and the Portuguese frontier towns p651

€€€ **Aldebarán**, Av de Huelva T924274261. One of the most famous restaurants in Extremadura, chef and local celebrity Fernanco Bárcena creates exquisite Basque and Spanish dishes accompanied by a thoughtful and extensive wine selection.
€€€ **Los Monjes de Zurbarán**, in the Hotel Barceló Zurbarán, see above. Badajoz's most prestigious restaurant, serving creative regional cuisine accompanied by an excellent wine list. Unfortunately, it lacks much atmosphere.
€€ **El Tronco**, C/Muñoz Torrero 16, T924222076. A delightfully old-fashioned local favourite, with tasty Extremaduran dishes and enormous breakfasts. It's a great spot for tapas too, with a wide variety of local hams. Highly recommended.
€€ **Al Cañices**, C/Colón 3, Olivenza, T924491570, is probably Olivenza's best mid-range restaurant, with simple decor but fantastic food.
€ **Mesón Los Monteros**, Plaza de Santo Domingo, T924221515. Cosy, traditional restaurant with local dishes like *perdiz estofada* – stewed pheasant – and pears cooked in wine for dessert.
€€ **La Toja**, Av de Elvas, T924273477. A mixture of Gallego and Extremaduran dishes are on offer at this elegant restaurant in a quirky yellow and white building in a quiet suburb of Badajoz.

Tapas bars and cafés

Gran Café Victoria, Pasaje de San Juan (opposite the tourist office). Huge, belle époque-style café with a good selection of cakes, tapas and big windows overlooking the street. A few tables outside in summer.
La Tetería, C/Meléndez Valdés 14, T924239729. An Arab-style tea house with low, cushion-covered benches and hangings, offering a vast selection of teas and plenty of magazines to flick through.

Zafra and south to Andalucía p652

In Zafra the restaurants at the **Parador de Hernán Cortés**, and the **Huerta Honda**, see Sleeping above, are the places to go to splash out on an expensive dinner; the parador has the edge in terms of cuisine and setting.

€€€ **Barbacana**, Huerta Honda, Zafra, does an excellent value *menú del día* (€15) at lunchtimes.

€€ **Josefina**, Trav López Asme 1, Zafra. T924551701. Closed Sun night and second fortnight of Aug. Josefina is a local legend, and you'll taste some of her delicious local specialities including stuffed aubergines, grilled meats and fish, with a delicious *tocinillo* (a kind of flan) to finish up. The emphasis is purely on the food – the setting is functional and very plain.

€€ **The Ermita**, C/Dr Benítez 8, Jerez de los Caballeros, T924731476. This mid-range priced restaurant is set in a converted chapel and serves classic Extremeño dishes and local wines.

€ **Rogelio**, Avda Estación 9, Zafra, , T924551439. Good-value café and restaurant which is a favourite with local workers for its cheap *menú del día* (around €7).

Tapas bars and cafés

Bar Monreal, Plaza Chica 2, Zafra, T924553023. An excellent choice right on the Plaza Chica, this old stone tapas bar is well-known for its home-made ham *croquetas*.

Café Romero, Plaza de España 28, Zafra. One of the best-known bars on the Plaza de España, stuck in a 1950s time-warp and the most popular neighbourhood local. Good, cheap food and a great atmosphere.

🔾 Bars and clubs

Plasencia *p639*

Plasencia does well for bars, mostly concentrated on the Plaza Mayor and on the surrounding streets, particularly the little streets between the square and the Puerta Talavera. There are a couple of attractive bars on the Plaza de Santa Ana, including the **Café de Santa Ana**, where you can nurse a beer on the terrace.

Cáceres *p642, map p643*

There's always plenty going on in the Plaza Mayor, but most of the liveliest bars are clustered in the Calles Pizarro, Donosa Cortés and Sergio Sánchez close to the Plaza San Juan. They are all pretty good, but you could try **Mistura Brasileria**, C/Pizarro 7, T927244040, or **La Traviata** at C/Sergio

Sánchez 8, T927211374. The clubs are on the edge of town; best known is **Acuario**, Ave de España 6, T927220614.

Trujillo *p645, map p645*

Not a lot goes on in Trujillo, but there are a few bars along the streets which radiate off the Plaza Mayor. Try C/Carniceria or C/Ballasteros. Nothing beats a drink on the terrace of the Plaza Mayor itself, where the whole town seems to gather on summer nights.

Mérida *p647, map p649*

Head for the C John Lennon, where nearly every doorway belongs to a bar (names seem to change almost weekly) and the action doesn't stop till dawn.

Badajoz and the Portuguese frontier towns *p651*

Most of the bars concentrated on or around the Plaza de España and nearby C Zurbarán are traditional tapas bars, but many have terraces in summer to sit out and sip a beer. The liveliest nightspots are around the Av Sinforiano Madroñero on the outskirts – try the **Café Habana** at No 19.

Zafra and south to Andalucía *p652*

Zafra is a bit too sleepy too have much in the way of serious nightlife. The bars of the Plazas Grande and Chica are the best option in Zafra, with tables out on the square and a buzz which carries on until late. Try the **Bar Rey de Copas** or the **Pub Alibe** which has a 16th-century Arabic cistern, both on the Plaza Grande. In summer, there's a daily disco on the Ctra de la Puebla s/n, with the usual mix of *bacalao* and Spanish pop; **Factoría**, Pasaje de Feria s/n, is open at weekends throughout the year.

🟤 Festivals and events

Plasencia *p639*

Plasencia's local festival is held on the second weekend in **Jun**, with live music on the squares, and lots of eating and drinking. Don't miss the big annual market in **Aug**.

Cáceres *p642, map p643*

Womad in the first half of **May** (www.womadlatino.com). **Semana Santa**,

Fiesta de San Jorge (**22 and 23 Apr**), the city's patron saint. In **Jun**, there is the **Fiestas Medievales** and **Festivales de Cáceres** with parades, traditional dancing and carousing.

Trujillo *p645, map p645*

Holy Week processions are well known throughout Spain and are celebrated in style in Trujillo, culminating in **El Chíviri** on Easter Sunday, when families converge on the Plaza Mayor for plenty of eating, drinking and dancing. Other popular festivals include the **National Cheese Festival** at the beginning of May; the **Fiesta Mayor** dedicated to the town's patron saint the Virgin of Victory around 15 Aug.

Guadalupe *p646*

The pilgrimage to the Virgin of Guadalupe takes place on **Extremadura Day**, the **8 Sep** – when thousands of pilgrims from all over the world descend on the village. Book accommodation well in advance.

Mérida *p647, map p649*

The celebrated **Festival de Teatro Clásico** takes place in **Jul** and **Aug**. Holy Week and Carnaval (**Feb-Mar**) are also celebrated with gusto.

Badajoz and the Portuguese frontier towns *p651*

Carnaval in **Feb** is celebrated wildly in Badajoz, and the **Fiesta de San Juan**, at the end of **Jun**, sees plenty of flamenco performances and horse parades.

Zafra and south to Andalucía *p652*

Feria de Sant Miguel – early **Oct**. Romería de Nuestra Señora de Belén – Easter Sunday.

O Shopping

Plasencia *p639*

Tue is market day and is always lively. Local specialities include the fine (and pricey) ham for which Extremadura is known throughout Spain, as well as olive oil from the Sierra de Gata. You can pick some up at the appropriately named **Casa del Jamón**, C/Sol 18, T927414271.

Cáceres *p642, map p643*

To get a taste of what's on offer in Extremadura, visit the **Centro de Cultura Tradicional y Promoción de la Artesanía**, C/San Antón s/n, which has exhibitions and demonstrations of local crafts, including ceramics, leather goods and woodwork.

Trujillo *p645, map p645*

Trujillo's nuns bake delicious cakes: you can get them from the convent of Santa Clara next to the parador or from the nuns at the Palacio de los Duques de San Carlos.

Guadalupe *p646*

Guadalupe is stuffed full of touristy shops selling local crafts: wickerwork, ceramics and plenty of copper and brass. Lovers of religious kitsch shouldn't miss the monastery shop, where you can get a Virgin of Guadalupe snowshaker.

Mérida *p647, map p649*

Confitería Gutiérrez, C/Santa Eulalia 70, for a box of the local sweets, *caramelos de Santa Eulalia*, which has been in business since 1827.

Ultramarinos Zancada, C/Santa Eulalia 38, prettily covered with century-old advertisements in *azulejo* tiles, for local wine.

Badajoz and the Portuguese frontier towns *p651*

The main shopping streets are concentrated in the centre of the old city. The **Pastelería La Cubana**, C/Francisco Pizarro 9, sells traditional local cakes.

Zafra and south to Andalucía *p652*

Pick up some of the excellent local ham and wine at **La Fiambrera**, C/Sevilla 8, T924554211. Across the street at No 11b, you can pick up some serious riding boots or have them made specially for you at the old-fashioned leather shop **Cayetano**.

⊖ Transport

Transport connections in Extremadura are excellent between the major towns, but infrequent and erratic in the remoter areas. Your own transport is recommended.

Bus The bus station (T927425872) has frequent connections to **Madrid**, **Seville**, **Salamanca**, **Cáceres**, **Mérida** and **Badajoz**, and less frequent services to **Trujillo**, the **Parc Natural de Montfragüe** and the main villages of **Las Hurdes** and the **Valle de la Verde** – but check times in advance if you don't want to get stranded.

Train There are regular trains (T902240202) to **Cáceres**, **Mérida** and **Badajoz** and less regular connections to **Madrid** and **Salamanca**.

Valle de la Vera and the Monesterio de Yuste *p640*

The towns and villages along the EX 203 which crosses the valley are served by infrequent local buses, but a car is virtually essential to explore properly the Valle de la Vera. The nearest train stations are at **Plasencia** and **Navalmora** de la Mata, transport hubs for the region.

Coria, Las Hurdes and the Sierra de Gata *p641*

Your own transport is essential in the northern reaches of Extremadura. There is a once-daily bus between **Plasencia** and the larger villages of **Las Hurdes** like **Nuñomoral**, **pinofranqueado** and **Caminomorisco**, with less frequent services from those towns to **Caceres** and **Salamanca**. There's another infrequent service from **Plasencia** to **Hervás** in the Sierra de Gata.

Parque Natural de Monfragüe *p641*

The park is not easy to get to without your own transport, but guided tours and coach trips are arranged by the tourist office. There's a twice-weekly bus service between **Plasencia** and **Cáceres** via **Villareal de San Carlos**, and a daily bus between **Torrejón el Rubio** and **Plasencia**, but the times are rarely convenient. The nearest train station is at **Palazuelo-Empalme/Monfragüe**, a good 12 km from Villareal.

Cáceres *p642, map p643*

Cáceres has direct trains and buses to **Madrid**, **Seville**, **Barcelona**, **Mérida**, **Zafra**, **Badajoz** and **Plasencia**.

Trujillo *p645, map p645*

For **bus** information call T927320500. There's no **train** station in Trujillo but there are regular buses to **Cáceres**, **Mérida** and **Badajoz**, twice-weekly services to **Plasencia**, and daily services to **Madrid**.

Guadalupe *p646*

There are daily **buses** to **Trujillo** and **Cáceres**, and less regular services to **Madrid** (which sometimes require a change). The Trujillo tourist office organizes 1-day excursions to Guadalupe.

Mérida *p647, map p649*

Mérida is well connected by **train** and **bus** to **Madrid**, **Ciudad Real**, **Seville**, **Cáceres**, **Badajoz** and **Zafra** and most major Spanish cities. Taxis are rare: call **Tele Taxi** T924315756 or **Radio Taxi** T924371111.

Badajoz and the Portuguese frontier towns *p651*

Trains and **buses** connect **Badajoz** with **Lisbon**, **Madrid**, **Ciudad Real**, **Seville** and **Cáceres**, **Badajoz** and **Zafra**. There are twice-daily **flights** to Badajoz airport from **Madrid** (for information, T924210440). To get into town from the airport, you'll have to call a taxi (*Radio Taxi* T924243101) as there is no public transport and it's a good 10 km from the city centre.

Zafra and south to Andalucía *p652*

Trains to major Spanish cities including **Barcelona**, **Valencia**, **Madrid** and **Seville** at least once a day, plus more regular services to **Cáceres** and **Mérida**. To get from the town centre to the train station, 3 km, call a taxi on T924551024 or T924551041. For bus services to other Spanish cities and local villages, check departure times in advance as local buses usually cater for workers commuting to the town and leave early and late.

● Directory

Cáceres *p642, map p643*
Post Avda Primo de Rivero, T927225071.
Internet Internet Ciber Cáceres, C/Leon Leal, or **Ciber-just**, C/Diego María Crehuet.

❗ Footprint features

Introduction

The two Mediterranean autonomous communities of Valencia and Murcia are usually known collectively as **El Levante**. They may be next-door-neighbours, but they couldn't be more different. Green, fertile Valencia is famous for its orange groves and rice fields, yet much of Murcia is virtual desert. Valencia city is rapidly becoming one of the most dynamic and stylish cities on the Mediterranean, while Murcia's delightful little capital is much more low-key, but a great place to enjoy authentic Spanish traditions like tapas out on flower-filled squares.

The two provinces do share the Mediterranean coastline, however, with all the attendant worship of sun, sea and sand. Don't give up hope of finding a secret cove: the closer you get to the Andalucía border, the more wild and remote the coastline becomes. Inland is a different story altogether. In Valencia, **El Maestrat** is a mountainous region of castle-topped towns. Beautiful historic towns like **Xátiva**, **Gandía** or **Orihuela** are a welcome respite from the giddy seaside resorts. Ancient traditions still linger, and these are best appreciated during the fiestas: **Las Fallas** is one of the biggest and best in Spain, but almost as well known are Alcoy's **Battle of the Moors and the Christians**, and Alicante's **Las Hogueras**. Murcia´s interior is surprisingly green: the wild natural park of the **Sierra de Espuña** is still studded with traditional stone well used until less than a century ago. There is also a string of lovely towns to explore, like **Lorca**, with lavish Baroque architecture,or monumental **Caravaca de la Cruz**.

★ Don't miss...

1. **Las Fallas** Don't miss Valencia's fiery festival, page 675.
2. **Modernista market** Pick up picnic supplies at Valencia's fabulous market, page 669.
3. **Morella** Cool off in this medieval walled city, page 683.
4. **Benicàssim** Take in this town's famous festival of alternative music, page 679.
5. **Xàbia** Go diving in the rocky coves around here, page 689.
6. **Alicante** Go wild in this vibrant city, which has some of the best nightlife in the region, page 691.
7. **Alcoy** See the famous Battle of the Moors and the Christians, page 686.
8. **Murcia** Relax in the affluent little baroque city, page 698.
9. **Murcia's southern coast** Find a secret cove on this coast, page 704.
10. **Sierra de Espuña** Seek out the deer and wild boar in this remote sierra, page 701.

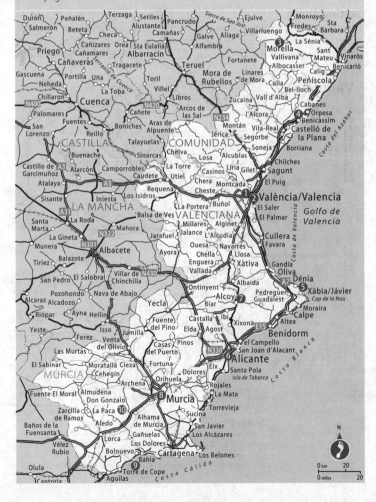

València/Valencia city

→ *Phone code: 96; Colour map 5, grid B5; Population: 74,574.*

Valencia was never one of the big players in the Spanish tourist stakes, and it's hard to understand why. The old town is a delightfully compact little maze boasting palaces, markets, beaches, nightlife and restaurants. But Valencia's days as a wallflower are over. The city is rapidly becoming one of the coolest places on the Mediterranean, partly thanks to a revamp which has seen the construction of the futuristic new Ciudad de las Artes y Las Ciències. Not everything is being modernized; the local festival of Las Fallas remains a classic, one of the biggest and wildest parties on the Spanish calendar. » For Sleeping, Eating and other listings, see pages 673-677.

Ins and outs

Getting there

Valencia airport, T961528500, www.aena.es, is in Manises, 14 km west of the centre. Airport bus into the centre every 10-15 minutes from 0630-2300, €0.90. Taxis are outside the departures hall and cost €15-18 to the city centre. The pretty Modernista

Valencia

Related map
A Valencia centre, see page 670.

Sleeping	Parador El Saler 4	Barocco 3
Consul del Mar 1	Patilla 5	Bodega Montaña 4
Hostal Tres Cepas 2		Casa Roberta 6
Jardín Botánico 6	**Eating**	Ca Sento 5
Las Arenas Youth	Albacar 1	El Ángel Azul 7
Hostel 3	Baiando al Sur 2	Joaquín Schmidt 8

train station is on the edge of the old city with regular connections to major cities. The bus station is on the edge of town at Avenida de Menéndez Pidal 3, T963497222, take bus No 8 or 79 for the city centre. ▸▸ *For further details, see Transport page 677.*

Getting around

The narrow streets of the old city (about 4 km from the seafront) are best explored on foot and most of the main sights are clustered within easy walking distance of each other. Local buses will take you to places further afield like the City of Arts and Sciences (about 2.5 km west of the old town), the port and the Albufera. The metro system is aimed at commuters, but Line 4 (a tramline above ground) is handy for the beach at Malvarossa. Taxis are easy to hail.

Best time to visit

Las Fallas, see box page 675, in March is one of the best festivals in Spain, but book accommodation months in advance. Otherwise, come in early autumn when the rice fields turn gold.

Tourist information

ⓘ *Plaza de Ayuntamiento, T963510417, Mon-Fri 0830-1415 and 1630-1815, Sat 0915-1245; C/Paz 48, T963986422, Mon-Fri 1000-1830, Sat 1000-1400, www.comunitat-valencia.com; Estación del Norte, C/Játiva 24, T963528573, Mon-Fri 0900-1830.*

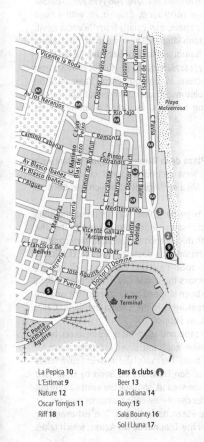

La Pepica **10**
L'Estimat **9**
Nature **12**
Oscar Torrijos **11**
Riff **18**

Bars & clubs ⏺
Beer **13**
La Indiana **14**
Roxy **15**
Sala Bounty **16**
Sol i Lluna **17**

History

Valencia's coastline had been settled by traders long before the Roman city of Valentia was founded here in 138BC. It was a modest settlement compared to Saguntum up the coast, and it wasn't until the 12th century that it began to prosper. Under Abd al-Aziz ibn Abi Amir, it became one of the mightiest cities of Al-Andalus. Briefly conquered by El Cid in 1094, it finally fell to the armies of the Reconquista, who resettled the land with Catalan and Aragonese families.

The 15th century was Valencia's Golden Age, a time of prosperous economic growth, vast building projects and excellence in the arts. But the expulsion of the Moors in 1609 heralded financial disaster; at a stroke, the city lost almost 40 per cent of its population. It wasn't until the 19th century that Valencia made a comeback, making its fortune with silk, agricultural produce, and ceramics. It was briefly the headquarters of the Republican government during the Civil War, and is now the seat of the Autonomous Community of Valencia.

Sights

Plaza de Ayuntamiento and around

The tree-lined Plaza de Ayuntamiento is filled with flower kiosks and overlooked by the 18th-century **City Hall**. It was completed in 1756 and given a frivolous façade in 1915. There's a small museum, **Museu del Historia de la Ciutat/Museo Histórico Municipal** ① *T963525478, Mon-Fri 0830-1430, free*, where you can potter through a thin but entertaining collection of odds and ends from Roman times to models of Valencia's ambitious new projectfs for the city.

Anyone arriving by train will already have seen Valencia's delightful Modernista **train station**, just west of the City Hall, with its whimsical mosaics and elaborate ticket booths. Next door is the **Plaza de Toros** (bull ring), which sees plenty of action, particularly during the summer festival held in July, and contains a small **Museo Taurino** ① *Pasaje Doctor Serra 16, T963883738, Tue-Fri 1000-1400 and 1600-2000, Sat 1100-1300, free*.

Valencia is famous for its wealth of ornate Baroque architecture, but the 18th-century **Palacio del Marqués de Dos Aguas** (to the north of the Plaza de Ayuntamiento) out-Baroques the lot. Every inch of this giddy, marble-encrusted palace is carved in swirls and curlicues, and it will come as no surprise that the architect, Hipólito Rovira, died insane shortly after completing it. It's now the **Museo Nacional de Cerámica** ① *C/Rinconada Garcia Sanchís s/n, T963516392, Tue-Sat 1000-1400 and 1600-2000, Sun and holidays 1000-1400, €2.40/1.20*, with a huge collection of ceramics gathered from all over Spain, particularly from Valencia itself. The top floor contains a typical tiled Valenciano kitchen. There are more tiles, along with paintings and sculpture, in the nearby Baroque church of **San Juan de la Cruz**.

Colegio del Patriarca ① *C/Nave 1, T963514176, 1100-1330, €1.20*, is a rare and elegant example of Renaissance architecture in Baroque-crazy Valencia. The cloister, enclosed by ranks of slim marble columns, is particularly beautiful, and the small museum contains some outstanding artworks, including paintings by El Greco and Ribalta.

Cathedral and around

North of the Plaza de Ayuntamiento is the **Plaza de la Reina**, an elegant square with terrace cafés and palm trees. Valencia's vast cathedral looms over one end, surmounted by the octagonal belltower, El Micalet (Miguelete), which has become the city's symbol.

Valencia's **cathedral** ① *0715-1300 and 1630-2015, free*, was begun on the ruins of a Mosque in the 13th century. Baroque craftsmen decided to tinker with it in the 18th century, and added the florid façade with thickly encrusted sculptural decoration and swooping lines. Just inside the main entrance, a doorway leads to **El Micalet** ① *1000-1230, 1630-1830, Sun and holidays 1000-1300 and 1700-1930, €1.20/.80*, which you can climb for staggering views across the whole city. The interior is light and elegant, and later embellishments have been stripped away to reveal the original Gothic features. The cathedral's greatest treasure is in the Capilla del Santo Cáliz, supposedly the golden chalice used at the Last Supper.

Museo de la Catedral ① *Mon-Sat 1000- 1300 and 1630-1900, €1.20/0.60*, has a collection of religious art, including a massive gold and silver Custodia, used for religious processions on the feast of Corpus Christi. The tour of the museum culminates in a small chapel containing two portraits of San Francisco de Borja by Goya (see Gandía, page 689). Both are dated 1788, but the second, showing the saint casting out sharp-toothed demons, prefigures Goya's later deeply unsettling *pinturas negras*.

Puerta del Apóstoles leads out to the Plaza de la Virgen. The extravagantly sculpted doorway is the theatrical setting for the **Tribunal de las Aguas**, which takes

place here every Thursday at 1230. Eight representatives from different parts of the city gather to discuss the city's water laws, just as they have since the custom was established by the Caliph of Córdoba in 960. The tribunal is held solely in Valenciano and fines are still meted out in the medieval currency.

The graceful Plaza de la Virgen is the most beautiful of Valencia's squares, and is named for the **Basílica de Santa María de los Desamparados** – Mary of the Helpless, the city's patron saint ① *0700-1400 and 1600-2100, free*. It's been undergoing restoration for years, but you can still visit the image of the Virgin surrounded by a sea of candles. Her feast day is celebrated on the second Sunday of May, when the whole square is covered with a carpet of flowers.

Palacio de la Generalitat ① *T963863461, weekdays 0900-0200, free, admission by appointment only*, just off the Plaza de la Virgen on Calle Caballeros, was built in 1510, an austere Gothic building with a graceful courtyard. The palace is now the seat of the Valencian government, but guided tours of the sumptuous Gothic interior can be arranged. The Salón Dorado contains a spectacular artesonado ceiling, and the Salón de Cortes is richly decorated with azulejo tiles and frescoes.

A narrow lane snakes behind the Basílica to the **Plaza del Almoina**, where Roman baths, forum, and bits of the Via Augusta are currently being excavated (closed for works). Just off the square is **Museo de la Ciudad** ① *Oct-Mar Tue-Sat 0930- 1400 and 1630-2000, Apr-Sep Tue-Sat 0930-1400 and 1730-2100, Sun and holidays all year 0930-1400*, set in the 19th-century Palacio del Marqués del Campo. The main galleries contain minor artworks from the middle ages onwards, and a modern annexe holds a bizarre collection of ethnographical curiosities. Almost opposite the museum is the **Cripta San Vicente** ① *T963941417, Tue-Sat 1000-1300 and 1700-2000, Sun and holidays 1000-1400, audio visual show Tue-Sat at 1000, 1130, 1300, 1800, 1900, Sun and holidays 1030, 1130, 1230, 1330, free*, a Visigothic burial chapel which was probably part of an early cathedral. It's displayed in the basement of an ultra-modern building, and a high-tech audio-visual tour outlines the history of the chapel.

Plaza del Mercado and around

Valencia's **market** ① *Mon-Thu 0800-1430, Fri 0800-2030, Sat 0800-1500*, is one of the prettiest in all of Spain, a vast Modernista concoction of wrought iron and stained glass surmounted with whimsical weather-vanes. Valencia isn't known as 'Spain's Orchard' for nothing and you'll find a breath-taking array of fresh produce. The market is always buzzy, but get there early to catch it in full swing – breakfast at one of the counter bars is an institution.

Facing the market is **La Lonja** ① *Tue-Fri 0915-1400 and 1730-2100, Sun 0900-1330, free*, the former Silk Exchange, which was built in the 15th century when Valencia was booming and is one of the finest examples of civic Gothic architecture in Europe. It's best visited on Sunday mornings when the stamp and coin market gives the place a little of the commercial buzz which would have animated it 500 years ago. Upstairs, the offices of the Consulado del Mar are reached by a spiral staircase and contain a magnificent artesonado ceiling.

A low-key market spreads around this slightly dilapidated neighbourhood on most mornings. It's biggest on Sundays, when toothless old men offer puppies for a song in the narrow, run-down streets which splinter off from the **Plaza Redonda**.

Barrio del Carmen

Barrio del Carmen, usually simply known as El Carmen, is the hippest neighbourhood in Valencia, stuffed with arty little cafés, shops, galleries, bars and restaurants, and the best place in the city for an aimless wander. The little Plaza de Carmen, with a charming Gothic church topped with a winsome angel, is a good place to start.

Valencia's excellent **Instituto Valenciano de Arte Moderno** (IVAM) ① *C/Guillem de Castro 118, www.ivam.es, T963863000, Tue-Sun 1000-2200, €2.10/1.60*, is

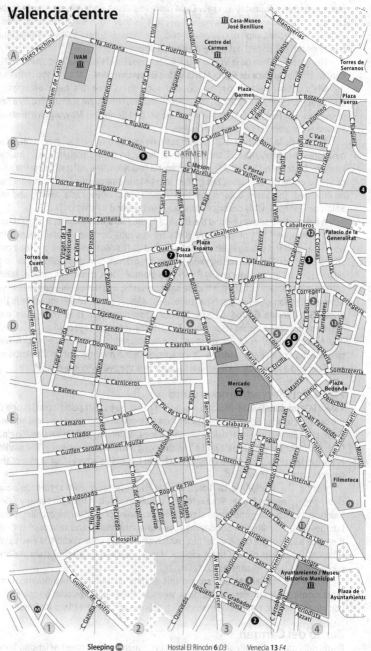

Valencia & Murcia Valéncia/Valencia city

Casa-Museo
José Benlliure

Centre del
Carmen

Torres de
Serranos

Plaza
Fueros

Plaza
Garmen

EL CARMEN

Meson
de Morella

Plaza
de Portal
de Valldigna

Torres de
Cuart

Plaza
Esparto

Plaza
Tossal

Palacio de la
Generalitat

La Lónja

Mercado

Plaza
Redonda

Filmoteca

Ayuntamiento / Museu
Historico Municipal

Plaza de
Ayuntamiento

IVAM

Paseo Pechina

C Guillem de Castro

C Na Jordana

C Lliria

C Salvador Giner

C Blanqueries

C Huertos

C Museo

C Sogueros

C Marqués de Cáio

C Beneficencia

C Ripalda

C San Ramón

C Corona

C Doctor Beltran Bigorra

C Pintor Zariñena

C Virgen de la Misericordia

C Cañen

C Quart

C Pinzon

C Palonar

C En Plom

C Murillo

C Tejedores

C En Sendra

C Pintor Domingo

C Lope de Rueda

C Cañas

C Villena

C Carniceros

C Balmes

C Recado

C Viana

C Camaron

C Triador

C Guillem Sorolla Manuel Aguilar

C Bany

C Maldonado

C Horno del Hospital

C Horno Hospital

C Recaredo

C Hospital

C Maldonado

C Guillem de Castro

C Gandia

C Pozo

C Palma

C Fos

C Atta

C Santo Tomas

C Santa Cristina

C San Miguel

C Atta

C Baja

C En Borras

C Pintor Fenol

C Roteros

C Cruz

C Palomino

C Vall de Crist

C Serranos

C Caballeros

C Alvarez

C Catalava

C Cocinas

C Curtias

C Valencians

C Cadrers

C Danza

C Bolseria

C Carda

C Valeriola

C Exarchs

C Bolseria

C Danzas

C Purisima

C Bou

C Clos

C Zurradores

C Trapinería

C Zapatería

C Sombrereria

C Mantas

C Trench

C Derechos

C Pie de la Cruz

C Calabazas

C En Gil

C Mallorquins

C Hiedra

C Musico Peydio

C Churers

C Linterna

C Linterna

C Editor Cabrero

C Viñatea

C Actors Riveiles

C Roger de Flor

C Beata

C Torno del Hospital

C Escolano

C Maestro Clave

C Rumbau

C En Llop

C les Garrigues

C Musica Peydio

C En Sanz

C Padilla

C Quevedo

C Grabador Selma

C Requena

C Arzobispo Mayoral

C Periodista Azzati

C Sangre

C San Vicente Martir

C San Vicente Martir

C Moratin

C San Fernando

C Av Maria Cristina

0 metres 100
0 yards 100

N

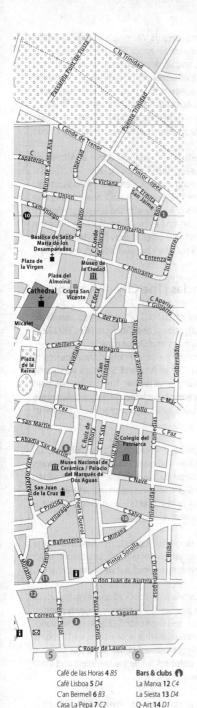

housed in a vast, uncompromisingly modern building on the edge of El Carmen. The museum of modern art houses 19th-century artworks and changing displays of Valenciano crafts and exhibitions by local artists. The centrepiece of the permanent collection is an extensive array of sculpture by Julio González. Other highlights include ethereal seascapes by Joaquin Sorolla, some edgy blockish reliefs by Lucio Fontana, a delicate mobile by Alexander Calder, several boxy sculptures by Eduardo Chillida, and paintings by Antoni Tàpies. The museum holds excellent temporary exhibitions.

Not far from IVAM, you can step back in time at the **Casa-Museo José Benlliure** ① *C/Blanquerías 23, T962911662, Tue-Sat 0915-1400 and 1730-2100, Sun and holidays 0915-1400, free*, the former home of the famous 19th-century Valenciano painter, which has been filled with period furniture and fittings. The highlight is the magical little garden at the back. Filled with tiles, fountains and shady palms, it's a delightful and utterly unexpected oasis in the middle of the city. At the end of the garden is Benlliure's light-filled studio, which contains his magpie collection of ceramics, swords and artworks.

This section of the city is scattered with the remnants of the 14th-century walls and towers which once enclosed the old city of Valencia. **Torres de Cuart** are impressive, but the most spectacular are a few hundred metres downriver. **Torres de Serranos** ① *Plaza de los Fueros, T963919070, Tue-Sat 0915-1400 and 1730-2100, Sun and holidays 0914-1400, free*, two sturdy crenellated towers guarding a narrow gateway, are a popular symbol of the city and visitors can climb up for panoramic views.

Along the River Túria

River Túria was prone to flooding and has long since been diverted. The empty riverbed has been converted into attractive gardens (still a 'work-in-progress' in parts), which extend for several kilometres.

Café de las Horas 4 *B5*
Café Lisboa 5 *D4*
C'an Bermell 6 *B3*
Casa La Pepa 7 *C2*
La Edad de Oro 8 *D4*
La Lluna 9 *B2*
Seu-Xerea 10 *B5*

Bars & clubs 🌑
La Marxa 12 *C4*
La Siesta 13 *D4*
Q-Art 14 *D1*

Puente del Real crosses the Túria riverbed towards Valencia's **Museo de Bellas Artes** ⓘ *C/San Pío V s/n, T963605793, Tue-Sun 1000-2000, free.* It claims to be the largest art museum in Spain after the Prado, and work is underway to make it even bigger, although this means that many of the artworks are uncomfortably crammed together in temporary galleries. While the museum has plenty of dull but worthy works by local artists, it also boasts a sizeable collection of treasures by El Greco, Ribera, Murillo, Van Dyck, Velázquez and Bosch. Just beyond the Museo de Bellas Artes, the leafy **Jardines del Real** ⓘ *0600-2200 (zoo 1000-2100), free*, are a good place for a picnic, and contain a small zoo.

Carry on walking to the end of the riverbed and you will arrive at **Museo de História de Valencia (Mhv)** ⓘ *C/Valencia s/n, T963 701 105, Apr-Sep Tue-Sat 0915-1400, 1630-2000, Sun and holidays 0915-1400.* Valencia's enthusiasm for shiny new museums with all the latest interactive gadgets hasn't abated: this one opened in May 2003 and presents 22 centuries of history with the latest 21st-century technology. Audio-visuals, computer simulations and even a Time Machine bring the past to life: you can see what the city looked like when it was founded, how the cathedral was built in the Middle Ages. It is a bit of a trek but well worth it, especially if you have kids in tow.

La Ciudad de las Artes y Las Cièncias (The City of Arts and Sciences)

ⓘ *You can buy individual tickets to each of the attractions or a combined admission for two sights (prices vary according to the attractions) or a City Pass (€25.85/18.18) for admission to Hemisfèric, Museu De Les Ciències and Oceanogràfic.*

Valencia couldn't fail to see how new architecture had revitalised the fortunes of Barcelona up the coast, and the glossy new City of Arts and Sciences was partly commissioned in order to raise the city's international profile. The gamble has paid off: the futuristic complex designed by local celebrity architect Santiago Calatrava is an overwhelming success, and you'll need to book well in advance to get into some of its attractions.

Museu de las Ciències ⓘ *Mon-Thu 1000-2000, Fri-Sun 1000-2100, €6.01/4.21, temporary exhibitions cost extra.* The vast, white and glassy Museu de las Ciències looks like a hangar for spaceships, and the chirpy staff in turquoise uniforms add to the sense of a 23rd-century airport. It's a brilliant science museum, with excellent interactive exhibits and all kinds of gimmicks to teach kids – and everyone else – about everything from how the body works to what electricity is.

L'Hemisfèric ⓘ *Mon-Thu 1000-2030, Fri-Sun 1100-1015, €6.61/4.81.* Next door to the museum is the vast eyeball-shaped Hemisfèric, which contains a planetarium, IMAX cinema and laserium – note that shows are regularly booked out weeks in advance.

L'Oceanogràfic ⓘ *weekdays 1000-1800, weekends 1000-2000, €19.80/12.80.* Housed in a series of beautifully sculpted pale pavilions, it is already a hugely popular attraction. It's the biggest aquarium in Europe, and the second-largest in the world. The aquarium recreates the world's most important marine ecosystems and is home to 45,000 fish and marine mammals. The biggest attraction by far is the massive dolphinarium, with a school of 20 bottlenose dolphins, while the creepiest and most popular is the moving walkway through the vast shark tank.

Palau de les Arts ⓘ *Av Autopista al Saler 1-7, T902100031, www.cac.es.* The final element of the complex is the stunning Palau de les Arts, which looks like a cross between a ship in full sail and a whale, and is devoted to the performing arts when it finally opens.

Playa Malvarrosa is where everyone in Valencia comes to party during the summer months. It is the closest city beach, a long golden strand lined with bathing huts and excellent seafood eateries and is a perfectly good place to sunbathe but the water suffers from pollution. At the end of the Playa de Malvarrosa is the low-key suburb of **Alboraya**, the birthplace of *horchata* (orxata in Valenciano), a refreshing drink made from tiger nuts.

Excursions

Llac Albufera sits about 8 km south of Valencia. The lake and surrounding area must have been beautiful once – it still is at dusk – but it's hard to block out the surrounding factories and even harder to ignore the contamination of the water by local factories. Despite the pollution, the area is still well known for its rice, used in the famous paella, and these marshy wetlands are also home to several species of water bird. There's information on walking trails at the park information office ① *Racó de l'Olla, T961627345, near the attractive village of El Palmar.*

🛏 Sleeping

Valencia city *p666, maps p666 and p670*
Accommodation isn't Valencia's strong point. A seafront place is a nice option though, see below.

LL Parador El Saler, Playa del Saler, T961611186, www.parador.es. A modern parador overlooking sand dunes and surrounded by pine forest, with an 18-hole golf course, pool and restaurant.

LL Inglés, Marqués de Dos Aguas 6, T963516426, F963940251. Set in a former palace overlooking the flamboyant ceramics museum. It's part of the Meliá chain, but doesn't feel like it. Rooms comfortable but lack indivuduality given its palatial setting. Service is attentive and friendly and the excellent restaurant is a place to be seen.

L Jardin Botánico, C/Doctor Peset Cevera 6, T963154012, www.hoteljardinbotanico.com. A modern hotel but refreshingly different from the run-of-the-mill chains. Stylish and modern rooms – sleek, pale wood and big flower prints – but a bit small for price. Most rooms have a terrace and all have hydro-massage baths tubs. Business facilities, café-restaurant and short walk from Old City.

L-A Consul del Mar, Avda del Puerto 39, T963625432, www.hotelconsuldelmar.com. The charming, whitewashed Modernista former consulate's residence has delightful, beautifully decorated rooms retaining some of the original plasterwork and fittings. There

is a tiny pool, gym and sauna. Prices tend to drop 50% at weekends. Overlooks busy street but not too far from beaches or City of Arts and Science.

L-A Reina Victoria, C/Barcas 6, T9635204 87, www.husa.es. Reina Victoria's heyday has long past, but, if it's faded glamour you're looking for, this handsome turn-of-the-century hotel has it in spades. Bland rooms are a disappointment, but the art deco salon is a treat.

AL Ad Hoc, C/Boix 4, T963919140, adhoc@adhoteles.com. An utterly charming, chic little hotel in a converted 19th-century mansion. Exposed brickwork and beams are complemented with a mixture of modern and antique furnishings. The restaurant (expensive) has become a very fashionable haunt – and the lunchtime fixed menu is excellent value.

A Venecia, C/El Llop 5, T963524267, www.hotelvenecia.com. A grand, turn-of-the-century mansion overlooking the Plaza de Ayuntamiento, this offers immaculate a/c rooms and a fabulous roof terrace with views.

B Continental, C/Correos 8, T963535282, continental@contitel.es. A reasonable modern hotel in a central location with good-sized rooms with all mod cons, including a/c. Lobby has a chic, boutique feel, the rooms are more functional.

C Florida, C/Padilla 4, T/F963511284. A large, nondescript *hostal* with reasonable, 70s-style rooms (lots of leatherette and fake wood).

● *During the summer months – June, July and August – air conditioning throughout the*
● *night is essential. If you have to economize, economize on something else!*

Prices are very good value for the facilities including a/c.

D Antigua Morellana, C/en Bou 2, T/F963915773. A delightful *hostal* housed in an 18th-century house just a step from the Lonja and the Mercado Central. Clean, well-equipped rooms (all with bathrooms and TVs), plus a little sitting room. Location couldn't be tter for sights and nightlife.

D Hostal Tres Cepas, Paseo Neptuno, T963715111. One of several moderate seafront hotels along the Paseo Neptuno, with a decent café-bar.

D Londres, C/Barcelonina 1, T963512244, F963521508. Right opposite the Ayuntamiento, this is set in a fine old building, with 60 modern, newly renovated but plain rooms. Best ones have a sea view. Look out for good weekend discounts.

E Hostal Moratín, C/Moratín 14, T/F963521220. Friendly little *pensión*, offering basic but recently renovated rooms at low prices. Cheerful owner can provide breakfast – and will even cook you up some dinner if you ask in advance. Recommended but there are no fans so hot in summer.

F Hostal El Rincón, C/Cardá 11, T963916083. Very close to the market – so expect to be woken up early – this is a good budget choice, with spotless rooms with stone floors and welcoming owners.

F Pensión Universal, C/Barcas 5, 2º, T963515384. A friendly, family-run *pensión* with good value, spotless rooms in an excellent location. They also run the **Pensión París**, C/Salvá 12, which is cheaper but plainer, and offers triples and quadruples.

G Hôme International Youth Hostel, C/de la Lonja 4, T963916229, www.likeahome.net. A new youth hostel in an elegant old building behind the Lonja, with accommodation in brightly painted dorms or a couple of twin rooms.

G Las Arenas Youth Hostel, C/Eugenia Viñes 24, T963564288. Valencia's youth *hostal* is right on the beach; dormitory beds cost a mere €5 with a discount flyer from the tourist office. It's out of town (take the metro to Las Arenas, or bus No 32 from the station), but the beachside location more than makes up for it.

Eating

Valencia city *p666, maps p666 and p670*

€€€ Albacar, C/Sorni 35, T963951005. A smart, traditional restaurant with a pretty interior garden, which serves fresh, modern interpretations of classic Mediterranean recipes accompanied by an excellent wine list. Closed Mon, Easter and Aug.

€€€ Ca Sento, C/Méndez Núñez 17, T963301775. One of the most talked-about restaurants in the city, where classic regional recipes have been given a creative new twist.

€€€ El Ángel Azul, C/Conde de Altea 33, T963745656. Romantic and very, very chic, the 'Blue Angel' is famous for its exquisite and highly imaginative Mediterranean cuisine. Interesting wine list, and fabulous desserts. The lunchtime *menú del día* is a reasonable €23, and there's a fantastic tapas bar. Closed Sun, Mon, Easter and Aug.

€€€ Joaquín Schmidt, C/Visitación 7, T963401710. Quirky and highly original, both in decor and cuisine, this is another fashionable favourite in Valencia. There's no traditional a la carte menu, but a variety of ever-changing set price menus (€40-55) offer distinctive variations on Mediterranean and international cuisine.

€€€ Oscar Torrijos, C/Dr Sumsi 4, T963732949. A classic, traditional restaurant serving superb local specialities, including a variety of rice-based dishes, seafood and game. Closed Easter mid-Aug to mid-Sep.

€€€ Riff, C/Comte d'Altea 18, T963335353. Newest project of Bernd Knoller, one of the most celebrated chefs in Valencia. A sleekly designed modern restaurant serving excellent contemporary Valenciano cuisine. Closed Mon.

€€ Beluga, C/del Arzobispo Mayoral 16, T963528876. A sleek, unusual restaurant serving organic, macrobiotic and vegetarian Mediterranean dishes with an Oriental twist. It's also open for breakfast or tea.

€€ C'an Bermell, C/Santo Tomás 18, T963910288. A well-known, traditional restaurant in the heart of the Old City which dishes up classic local dishes, and has a hugely popular tapas bar.

● *For an explanation of sleeping and eating price codes used in this guide, see inside the*
● *front cover. Other relevant information is found in Essentials, see pages 47-56.*

⁞ Fun at the fiesta

Valencia's festival of Las Fallas is one of the fieriest and most important fiestas in Spain. It dates back to the Middle Ages, when carpenters used to light a bonfire in honour of Sant Josep, their patron saint. Gradually, effigies were thrown into the fire, often depicting rival organizations.

Now, the vast creations made of papier-mâché, wood and wax take a year to build and are paraded through the streets from the 13th to 19th March. They can be of anything – cartoon characters, politicians, buxom ladies, animals – and each neighbourhood organization vies to create the best. They are accompanied by mini-versions, called *Ninots*, and the winning *Ninot* is the only one to escape the flames. Each day, firecrackers blast out over the Plaza de Ayuntamiento at 1400 (*La Mascletá*), bullfights are held in the afternoons, and the evenings culminate with a massive firework display. On the 18th, the *Virgen de los Desemperados*, patron saint of the city, is honoured with a spectacular offering of flowers. The fiesta culminates on the 19th, when the fallas are thrown into an enormous pyre, *the Cremá*. Prize-winning *fallas* are kept till last – but none escapes the flames.

You can see the prize-winning Ninots and find out more about the history of the event at the engaging Museo Fallero, *Plaza Monteolivete 4, T963525478, Tue-Sat 0915-1400 and 1730-2100, Sun and holidays 0915-1400, €1.80/.60*. To find out how the *fallas* are built, visit the Museo del Gremio Artistas Fallero, *Mon-Sat 1000-1400 and 1600-1900, Sat 1000-1400, €1.80/.90 OAPs/.60 children*.

€€ **Casa Roberta**, C/Maestro Gozalbo 19, T963951361. Pictures of famous bullfighters set the scene in this traditional stalwart, a great place to try an authentic paella. Closed Mon and Aug.

€€ **L'Estimat**, Avda de Neptuno 16 (Playa de las Arenas), T963711018. Pretty, tile-covered seafood restaurant on the seafront. Closed Tue, mid-Aug to mid-Sep.

€€ **La Pepica**, Paseo de Neptuno 6, T963714111, F963714200. Large, lively, perennially popular seafood restaurant overlooking the seafront that has been going for decades.

€€ **Seu-Xerea**, C/Conde de Almodóvar 4, T963924000. A super-hip restaurant serving unusual dishes with a Far Eastern flavour: try the strawberry gazpacho.

€ **Bajando al Sur**, C/Doctor Monserrat 32, T963925086. All kinds of sandwiches, crêpes and salads, including plenty of vegetarian options. Evenings only, closed Sun.

€ **Bar Pilar**, C/Moro Zeit 13, T963910497. A timeless old bar just off the Plaza del Esparto, where you should eat mussels (*clòtxines* in Valenciano, *mejillones* in Castellano) and toss the shells in the buckets under the table.

€ **Barocco**, C/Artes Graficas, T963613643. A big student favourite near the university, this serves Mediterranean home-cooking at very reasonable prices.

€ **Casa La Pepa**, C/Conquista 8 bajo, T963925447. A charming, old-fashioned place decorated with bullfighting posters and old photos.

€ **La Lluna**, C/San Ramón 23, T963922146. A sweet, stylish place in El Carmen which serves a good range of veggie and vegan dishes. Closed Aug.

€ **The Nature**, C/Ramon y Cajal 36, T9639-40141. A cheap and cheerful vegetarian canteen-style place which does a good Chinese buffet lunch or dinner for just €6.

Tapas bars and cafés

Bodega Montaña, C/José Benlliure 69, T963672314. This traditional, buzzy tavern opened its doors in 1836 and offers an excellent range of quality wines and tapas.

Bodeguilla del Gato, C/Catalans 10. T963918235. A brick-lined tapas bar

decorated with bullfighting posters with good, old-fashioned tapas and *raciones*.

Café de las Horas, C/Conde de Almodóvar 1, T963917336. Just off the Plaza de la Virgen, this is a relaxed little café with theatrical drapes to keep customers cosy.

Café Lisboa, Plaça Del Dr Colledo 9, T963919484. A big favourite in the old centre, this looks out over a pretty square and serves great sandwiches and salads as well as cocktails in the evenings. There's a big screen to watch the football at weekends.

La Edad de Oro, C/Don Generoso Hernandez 1, T963924724. Laid-back café in El Carmen, with changing art exhibitions and special events, serving good tapas and sandwiches. Closed Sun and Mon evenings.

Bars and clubs

Valencia city *p666, maps p666 and p670*
Valencia's nightlife is concentrated in different 'zones' around the city, but the best place to start is the hip Barrio del Carmen in the heart of the old city, where stylish restaurants, clubs and bars are nudged up against each other in the narrow streets. In summer, everyone piles down to the big bars and clubs near the Malvarrosa beach.

Beer, C/Salamanca, 4, T963741431. This calls itself '*el museo de la cerveza*', with a massive range of local, Spanish and imported beers. A lively, studenty hang-out with a popular summer terrace.

La Indiana, C/San Vicente 97, T963820891, www.laindiana.es. Ultra-slick club full of Valencia's beautiful people. Three dance floors with three different vibes – funk and acid jazz on one floor, salsa and dance on the others – and an aquarium to pose around.

La Marxa, C/Cocinas 5, T963917065. 2300 until late. Loud, buzzy, and massively popular nightclub in the Carmen, with a mixed crowd of tourists and locals.

Q-Art, C/Guillem de Castro 78-80, T963916115. A mellow cocktail bar and restaurant (serving good, cheap Mediterranean food), Q-Art also manages to pack in a bewildering number of activities, including theatre events, comedy nights, art exhibitions and classical music at weekends.

Roxy, C/San Vicente 200, T963803852. Massively popular disco on 2 floors – house and techno downstairs, chill-out sounds

upstairs – with guest DJs from around the world and a young, studenty crowd.

Sala Bounty, C/José Iturbi 4, T963342640. This small club is hard to find but worth it. Good house, electronica and theme nights (1970s, soul and funk).

Sol i Lluna, C/del Mar 29, T963922216. Another great, relaxed bar in the Carme neighbourhood with a spacious terrace for those hot summer nights and a good restaurant attached.

Entertainment

Valencia city *p666, maps p666 and p670*
To find out what's on, pick up the Friday edition of the local paper *El Levante* which has a listings supplement, or get a copy of the free *Hello Valencia* magazine from the tourist office. *Cartelera Turia* (€1.20) has the most extensive listings, and covers the whole of the Comunidad Valenciana. Other options incude *Qué y Dondé* and *Valencia Seminal*, all available from news kiosks.

Bullfighting Plaza de Toros, T963519315. Bullfighting is not as popular in Valencia as in other parts of Spain, but you can still see a *corrida* during **Feria de Julio** (July festival).

Cinema Films shown in their original language are listed as VO (versión originale).

Filmoteca, Plaza de Ayuntamiento 17, T963519130. Film seasons featuring cult classics, foreign films and special events.

Live music Jimmy Glass, C/Baja 28. A dim, photo-lined jazz bar with fortnightly gigs.

Black Note, Avda Poly y Peyrolón 15, T963933663. Live music nightly in El Carme – everything from jazz, blues and flamenco to rock, soul and funk.

Football FC Valencia, C/Artes Gráficas 44, T963600550, are a big, popular football team, but it's not impossible to get tickets for a match.

Theatre and classical music Teatro Principal, C/Barcas 15, T963510051. Most established, varied drama, opera, and ballet.

Palau de la Música, Jardines del Turia, T962275020. Huge glassy building overlooking the Túria for classical music opera, ballet and occasionally pop and jazz.

Palau de les Arts, Ciuadad de las Artes y las Ciencias, T902100031, www.cac.es. Calatrava's stunning new Palace of the Arts is looks like a futuristic galleon. With an aim to

'democratize' the arts and provide a dynamic mixture of classical and contemporary theatre, opera, dance and music.

✪ Festivals and events

Valencia city *p666, maps p666 and p670*
Valencia's biggest festival, **Las Fallas** is held in **mid-Mar**. **Feria de Julio** is held in **Jul**, with outdoor parades and concerts, a 'Battle of the Flowers', and bullfighting.

○ Shopping

Valencia city *p666, maps p666 and p670*
Valencia is a great place for shopping. The Old City throws up trendy, quirky fashion (Barri del Carme mainly) as well as the cool and contemporary. Around Plaza Redonda is the place to find timeless old-fashioned shops.
Abanicos Carbonell, C/Castellón 21, T962415395. This shop has been making exquisite handmade fans for almost a century.
Blanco, C/Correus 14, T963512885. Affordable fashion for young, hip women. Sexy style and a decent collection of shoes and accessories to match.
FNAC, C/Guillem de Castro 9. Books, CDs, city maps, with a good selection in English.
Momparler Baviera, C/Periodista Azzati 7. Plenty of local ceramics for souvenirs.
Las Añadas de España, C/Játiva 3, T963533-845. An excellent wine merchant and deli.
Studio, C/Purisima 8, T617952635. Retro furniture and knick knacks for the home, with a particularly good selection of lighting.
VIPS, Gran Vía Marqués del Túria 49, T96352-8499. A useful 24-hr convenience store.

▲ Activities and tours

Valencia city *p666, maps p666 and p670*
There's a swimming pool and sailing school

at the **Real Club Náutico de Valencia**, Camino Cardenal s/n. The local tennis club, **Club Tenis Valencia**, C/Botánico Cavanilles T961523804. Golf fans can try out the **Campo de Golf El Saler**, Ctra Saler km18, T961611186, one of the finest Spain.

⊜ Transport

Valencia city *p666, maps p666 and p670*
Air There are flights to **Madrid**, **Ibiza**, **Barcelona**, **Málaga**, **Bilbao** and **Sevilla**.
Boats Ferries for the **Balearics** leave from the port, T963670704, 4 km from the city centre; for details, **Trasmediterránea**, T902454645, and **Balnearia**, T902160180.
Bus There are services for **Barcelona** with Alsa, T902422242, www.alsa.es; **Madrid** with Auto Res, T915517200, and connections to most major Spanish and international cities.
Taxi Radio Taxi Valencia, T963703333, Radio Taxi Manises, T961521155 (airport).
Train To **Barcelona**, **Tarragona**, **Alicante** and **Murcia**, plus an hourly high-speed service to **Madrid** (between 0700-2000). Regional trains to **Castellón**, **Xàtiva**, **Gandia**, **Buñol**, **Requena** and **Utiel**.

❶ Directory

Valencia city *p666, maps p666 and p670*
Hospital Hospital Clínico, Av de Blasco Ibáñez 17, T963862600.
Internet There many places offering internet access. **Ono**, C/Sant Vicent Màrtier 22. Mon-Fri 0900-0100, Sat-Sun 1100-0100. A big, excellent internet centre just off the Plaza de Ayuntamiento. Broadband. From €1.50-2 per hr. **Cyber-pub Andromeda**, C/Salamanca 37, costs around €2 per hr and is open until late.
Post The main post office is on the Plaza de Ayuntamiento.

Costa del Azahar

A fertile plain covered with orange groves stretches north of Valencia, scarred by ugly ceramic factories puffing smoke. The beaches are popular with Spanish families, and particularly good around Benicàssim (which has an excellent music festival). The main city, Castelló, is no great shakes, but there are Roman ruins at Sagunto, and the remarkable papal city of Peñiscola piled on a rock. ▸▸ *For Sleeping, Eating and other listings, see pages 680-683.*

El Puig → *Colour map 5, grid B5.*

Heading northwards from Valencia, there's little to see until El Puig, 18 km north of Valencia, where the forbidding **Real Monasterio de El Puig de Santa María** ⓘ *T961470200, winter Tue-Sun 1000-1300 and 1600-1730, summer Tue-Sun 1000-1300 and 1600-1930; museum Tue-Sun 1000-1300 and 1600-1900, €1.80*, looms above the little town. Although it is still home to a community of monks, it's possible to visit the cloisters, salons and beautiful Gothic church. The eastern wing contains the **Museo de Artes Gráficas y La Imprenta**, devoted to print and graphics, which counts the world's smallest book (look at it through a magnifying glass) among its treasures.

Sagunt/Sagunto → *Colour map 5, grid B5.*

Sagunt (Sagunto in Castellano), north of El Puig, is a sleepy little town piled on to a hillside under a ruined castle. It's hard to imagine anything exciting ever happening here, but Sagunt made it into the history books in 218BC when the Iberian villagers held out against Hannibal and his army for more than eight months, finally throwing themselves on to a burning pyre rather than capitulate. The Romans rebuilt the city, and the most impressive surviving monument in modern Sagunt is the **Roman theatre**ⓘ *C/Castillo s/n, T962665581, museum opens winter Tue-Sat 1000-1400 and 1600-1800, Sunday and holidays 1000-1400, summer Tue-Sat 1000-2000, Sun 1000-1400, free*. It has been completely restored and is now used to host concerts in summer, but purists still don't think much of the concrete seating areas. A dull archaeology museum is attached, with a smattering of ceramics discovered during local excavations.

The lofty **castle** ⓘ *T962661934, Mon-Sat 1000-2000, Sun and holidays 1000-1400, free*, is mostly in ruins, but part of it now contains an exhibition of inscriptions, with monuments dating back to pre-Roman times. A stretch of walls, squares and watchtowers still snakes impressively along the ridge for several kilometres, and offers stunning views across the old town and out to sea.

Inland from Sagunt → *Colour map 5, grid B5.*

In **Vall d'Uixò**, 20 km north of Sagunt, boats wend along Europe's longest underground stream in the **Grutas de San José**ⓘ *Paraje San José s/n, T964696761, www.riosubterraneo.com*. It's a big tourist attraction, with all the attendant paraphernalia – snack kiosks, pool, playground.

Some 31 km northwest from Sagunt is the old walled town of **Segorbe**, surrounded by forested hills. There are several walking trails, including the GR10 in the nearby **Sierra Calderona**. It's a quiet, sleepy little place – except in early September, when bulls are chased through the streets for the wild festival of the **Entrada de Toros y Caballos**. The pretty old town is piled chaotically around the Catedral de la Asunción ⓘ *1100-1300*, originally built in the 12th century but subsequently given a showy Baroque makeover. The second storey of the cloister contains the cathedral museum, with medieval altarpieces, paintings by Ribera and Ribalta, and some fine sculpture.

Deeper into the hills, about 35 km northwest of Segorbe is the little spa town of **Montanejos**, where you can take the waters at the **Fuente de los Baños** or lose yourself in the surrounding sierra which has good hiking and mountain-biking trails along spectacular gorges.

Grain in Spain

Valencia is the birthplace of paella. Paella is not the unnaturally yellow dish advertised in five languages on laminated menus across the world, but an umbrella term for a vast array of rice-based dishes. The definitive paella is a chimera – most Spaniards claim they have the recipe, but it's never the same as anyone else's – but some things remain constant.

The dish is flavoured with garlic and saffron, cooked in a large flat pan, and the heat is turned up just before completion to ensure a thin crust on the rice called the 'soccarat'. Paella can be made with meat – traditionally it was made with rabbit or snails – or with seafood (*paella de mariscos*), or occasionally just with vegetables (*paella de verdura*).

Castelló de la Plana/Castellón de la Plana

→ *Colour map 5, grid B6.*

Castellón is a modern provincial capital, with little in the way of sights or monuments but some decent beaches spread out around the port (called the 'Grao'). What remains of the old town (most of it was blasted to smithereens during the Civil War) is set back about 5 km from the Grao and the beaches, but there are shuttle buses from the Plaza Borrull. The few sights, and all the shops and services, are all in the old town, but there are restaurants and tapas bars by the port.

Museo de Belles Artes ① *Av Hermanos Bou 28, T964727500, Tue-Sat 1000-2000, Sun and holidays 1000-1400, €2.10/1.20, free on Sun and holidays*, is set in an 18th-century mansion, one of the few buildings to have survived the Civil War in Castellón, and contains works by Ribera, Ribalta, Sorolla and Benlliure. There's a small archaeological section, but it's best known for its extensive collection of ceramics from the 16th to the 19th centuries.

Espai de'Art Contemporani de Castelló (EACC) ① *C/Prim s/n, T964723540, Tue-Sun 11100-2000, guided visits Sat 1900 or Sun 1200, free*, is one of the city's newest and slickest museums, with a changing programme of temporary exhibitions featuring both established and rising new artists.

A lesser known diversion is the **Convento Capuchinas** ① *C/Nuñez de Arce 11, T964220641, 1600-2000, free*, which owns a small collection of paintings by Zurbarán, depicting the establishment of several religious orders.

Benicàssim/Benicasim and around → *Colour map 5, grid B6.*

Benicàssim is a family seaside resort, famous for the massive outdoor music festival held each year in August (www.fiberfib.com). The little village has been swallowed up by apartment blocks and restaurants, and there's nothing much to do but catch some rays. Before the tourist boom, Benicàssim was known for the production of a sweet white wine, which can be tasted at the **Bodegas Carmelitano** ① *Avda Castellón s/n, T964300849, summer 0900-1330 and 1530-2000 (winter 1900), free*.

The seaside resort of **Oropesa**, a couple of kilometres north of Benicàssim, is not as chi chi as its neighbour and offers equally good beaches and cheaper accommodation. Lost in wooded hills a few kilometres inland from Benicàssim is the tranquil Carmelite **monastery of the Desierto de las Palmas** ① *T964300950, www.desiertodelaspalmas.com, church 1000-1300 and 1600-1900 (until 2000 in Jul and Aug); museum open Sun 1200-1400*. Established three centuries ago as a place of retreat it

still hosts workshops and meditation weekends. The church is open for visits and services, and there's an interesting museum of paintings and religious objects.

The surrounding hills are still scarred by forest fires which ravaged the area more than a decade ago, but the region has been designated a **natural park**, and is criss-crossed with walking trails and picnic spots. There's a park information office at La Bartola① *Carretera del desert, km. 8, T964760727*. You'll need your own transport, or else take a taxi (about €10).

Peníscola/Peñíscola to Vinaròs → *Colour map 3, grid C2.*

Peníscola

Peníscola is best seen from a distance. A tight mass of whitewashed houses piled on a rocky promontory and topped with a castle, it looks like a movie set – and movie buffs might recognize it from the film *El Cid*. Close up, the spell is quickly broken: the pretty cobbled lanes are gorged with coachloads of day-trippers, and the little whitewashed houses have been converted into cheap cafés and souvenir shops. Still, as tourist towns go, Peníscola is as pretty as any on the Valencian coast. The tourist office① *Paseo Marítimo, T964480208*.

Perched high above the tiled rooftops is the town's landmark, the 14th-century **Templar fortress**① *T964480021, summer 0930-1430 and 1630-2130, winter 0930-1300 and 1515-1800, €2*, which was later converted into a residence for pope Benedict XIII. During the Great Schism, the Church was split between Pope Urban VI in Rome and the rival Pope Clemente VII in Avignon. Benedict XIII succeeded Clemente, but during his reign the Schism was resolved in favour of Rome, and he found himself out of a job. He retired to Peníscola to create a third Papal City, but his successors failed to maintain it after his death. The castle is now a history and art museum, with frankly little to see, but fabulous views.

The narrow isthmus which reaches out to Peníscola is lined with thoughtless modern development, but the beaches are long and sandy (if jam-packed in high season). The town still has a small fishing fleet, and the return of the brightly painted boats (around 1630) to the harbour is a beautiful sight.

Benicarló

The next coastal resort along from Peníscola is Benicarló, where the ranks of apartment blocks haven't quite wiped out the character of this former fishing village. The fishing fleet now sits alongside glossy yachts in the marina, and there's a pretty Baroque church with a blue-tiled dome in the old town. The beach is small and popular with Spanish families, and the local speciality is artichokes – so prized that they have even been given their own denominación de origen, just like wines.

Vinaròs

A few kilometres further north from Benicarló is another fishing village-cum-seaside resort, Vinaròs. It's small and low-key, with the usual rash of concrete development along the beaches, but the port is still a hive of activity. The *langostinos* are famous throughout Spain, and the day's catch are auctioned off early each morning. Try them at one of the fancy seafood restaurants. The tourist office ① *Paseo de Colón s/n, T964453334, F964455625*.

● Sleeping

Sagunt *p678*
There are only a couple of places to stay in the old town, both on the main road.

C Azahar, Avda País Valencia 8, T962663368. Swishest option just outside the old town.
E Buenavista, C/Buenavista 4, T962672725, Popular *hostal* by the beach.
E Carlos, Avda País Valencia 43, T962660902,

is the budget option in the old town. It is pretty plain and modern.

E **Pensión California**, C/Buenavista 35, T962670701. Another popular *hostal* by the beach.

Inland from Sagunt *p678*

C **Rosaleda de Mijares**, Ctra Tales 28, Montanejos, T964131079. Next to the spa, this is the poshest place to stay in town. Bland.

C-D **Hospedería El Palen**, Segorbe, T964710740, F964712410, is the most central hotel, set in an old beamed townhouse with a good, mid-range priced restaurant.

C-D **María de Luna**, Avda Comunidad Valenciana 2, Segorbe, T964711313, mariadeluna@redestb.es, is modern and functional but the mid-range priced restaurant is recommended by locals.

D-E **Hostal Xauen**, Avda Fuente Banos 26, T964131151, xauen@hotelxauen.com, and **Hostal Gil**, T964131063. Both in Montanejos.

Castelló de la Plana *p679*

Virtually all Castellón's hotels are modern and geared towards business travellers. This can mean good weekend discounts.

A **Castello Center**, Ronda Mijares 86, T964342777, www.hotelcastellon center.com. Huge, white, modern chain hotel with a gym, pool and restaurant. Weekend deals can bring the prices down by up to 50%.

C **Doña Lola**, C/Lucena 3, T964214011, F964252235. Modern and comfortable with a good restaurant and business facilities.

D **Los Herreros**, Avda Del Puerto 28, T964284264, F964282736. Close to the port, with simple rooms painted an institutional pale green, and a very popular bar-restaurant downstairs.

E **La Esperanza**, C/San Jaume 40, T964131062. Basic, old-fashioned *hostal* run by a charming older couple with a simple restaurant downstairs.

Benicàssim and around *p679*

Accommodation is surprisingly expensive in Benicàssim, and many places require half-board during Jul and Aug.

A **Intur Bonaire**, Avda Gimeno Tomás 3, Benicàssim, T964392480, www.intur.com, is a huge modern complex overlooking the beach with pool, mini-golf, gym and tennis facilities.

C **Hotel Neptuno Playa**, Paseo La Concha 1, Oropesa, T964310040, F964310075, big, modern, right on the beach front with a pool and all mod-cons.

D **Hotel Eco Avenida**, Avda Castellon 2, Benicàssim, T964300047, F964300079, is a good moderate option, with a pool and plant-filled courtyard.

D **Hs Oropesa Sol**, Avda Madrid 11, T9643-10150. Simple, only open from Easter-Sep.

E **Garamar** and E **Garamar II**, both in Benicàssim near to the station and beach. Both are basic.

Camping

There are several campgrounds all along the beachfront, including the well-equipped.

G **Camping Bonterra**, Avda de Barcelona 47, T964300007, F964300060, which also rents out chalets.

Península to Vinaròs *p680*

There are plenty of options to stay in Peníscola, but book well in advance in Jul or Aug when prices jump.

AL **Parador de Benicarló**, Avda Papa Luna 3, Benicarló, T964470100, benicarlo @parador. es. The grandest place to stay in Benicarló is this modern option, with an excellent restaurant and pool.

AL-C **Hostería del Mar**, Avda Papa Luna 18, Peníscola, T964480600, www.hosteriadel mar.com. One of the dozens of big hotels along the isthmus. Upmarket with a pool, restaurant and medieval-style banquets.

B-D **Mare Nostrum**, Avda Primo de Rivera 13, Peníscola, T96481626, is right on the seafront, and the prettiest rooms have balconies overlooking the beach or the port.

D **Chiki**, C/Mayor 3, Peníscola, T964480284, is a well-kept, moderate option in the old town with a good cheap restaurant.

D **Hotel Marynton**, Paseo Marítimo 5, Benicarló, T964465030, F964460720. Pristine near the seafront.

D **Hotel Miramar**, Paseo Blasco Ibáñez 12, Vinaròs, T/F964451400, on the seafront, family run with a cheap restaurant.

D **Hotel Roca**, Avda San Roque, Vinaròs, T964401312, www.hotelroca.com. Modern,

For an explanation of sleeping and eating price codes used in this guide, see inside the front cover. Other relevant information is found in Essentials, see pages 47-56.

excellent value, with pool and tennis. Recommended.

E Hostal Belmonte, C/Pío XII 3, Benicarló, T964471239. Budget option.

E Hostal del Duc, C/Fulladosa 10, Peñíscola, T964480768. Best of the budget choices, in a ramshackle mansion in the old town (Apr-Sep).

Camping

G Camping El Eden, Avda Papa de Luna, Peñíscola, T964480562. One of several campsites, central and well-equipped with a pool, café and supermarket.

🍴 Eating

Sagunt p678

€€€ L'Armeler, Subida al Castillo 44, T962664382. The best place to eat in Sagunt, set in a pretty, traditional townhouse.

€€ Coll-Verd de Corinto, Avda Danesa 43, T962609104. Tasty seafood and rice dishes on a terrace overlooking the Playa de Corinto.

€ Mesón Casa Felipe, C/Castillo 21, T9626-60959. This popular choice has a simple menu of cheap sandwiches and light meals.

Castelló de la Plana p679

€€€ Delmónico, Plaza Cometa Halley 7, T964260044. The most original and creative cuisine in Castellón – the most fashionable spot in town.

€€ Brisamar, Paseo de Buenavista 26, T964283664. Tasty seafood served up on the terrace right on the seafront.

€€ Peñalen, C/Fola 11, T964234131. Creative, Mediterranean cuisine prepared with the freshest local ingredients in elegant surroundings.

€€ Tasca del Puerto, Avda del Puerto 13, T964236018. A popular local restaurant by the port serving good rice dishes, seafood and home-made desserts.

€ Aral, C/Río Júcar 12, T964247112. Aral's tasty home-cooking and cheap menús mean it's crammed with workers during the day and with students in the evening.

€ Restaurante Navarrete, C/Maestro Bretón 3, T964207560. Typical Spanish restaurant, complete with blaring TV and kids running riot. Friendly staff and a great selection of local rice dishes.

Tapas bars and cafés

There are dozens of good cafés and tapas bars around the Plaza Santa Clara (next to the Plaza Mayor), where all of Castellón seems to turn out for the evening paseo and for the summer concerts.

Benicàssim and around p679

There are lots of places along the seafront.

€€€ The Plaza, C/Cristóbal Colón 3, T964300072, has the best reputation in town. Offers an excellent €9 lunch menu, or a fancier €24 tasting menu in the evenings.

€ Villa del Mar, Paseo Maritimo, T96430-2852, good inexpensive seafood on the front.

Peñíscola to Vinaròs p680

There's a daily market in Vinaròs for picnics.

€€€ Casa Pocho, C/Sant Gregori 49, Vinaròs, T964451095. Another elegant seafood restaurant. Cheaper dishes available.

€€€ El Langostino de Oro, C/San Francisco 3, Vinaròs, T964451204. Classic seafood dishes. Mid-range options too.

€€€ Parador de Benicarló, see Sleeping, Benicarló. This parador has the best restaurant in town.

€€ Casa Jaime, Avda Papa Luna 5, Peñíscola, T964480030, which serves delicious fresh seafood on the terrace.

€€ El Cortijo, Avda Méndez Núñez 85, Benicarló, T964475038, also enjoys a good reputation for its seafood. The daily market is a good place to pick up picnic supplies.

€€ El Peñon, C/Santos Martires 22, Peñíscola, T964480716, which does a cheap menú del día for €6.

🍸 Bars and clubs

Castelló de la Plana p679

Castellón's students ensure that the nightlife is better than many towns of its size.

Dr. Slump, Poligona Castalia 42, 0230-0730. The maddest club in Castellón with resident DJs playing the best in house and techno to a packed, euphoric crowd.

🚌 Transport

Inland from Sagunt p678

Segorbe is on the main train line from **Valencia** to **Zaragoza**, with several daily train connections.

Castelló de la Plana *p679*
The new combined **bus** and **train** stations are located on the edge of the town, with frequent connections to **Barcelona**, **Valencia**, **Madrid** and most major Spanish cities. It's about a 15-min walk to the town centre, and there's a local bus from outside the arrivals hall of the train station.

Benicàssim and around *p679*
Benicàssim is on the train line between **Barcelona** and **Valencia**, with frequent connections to towns along the coast.

Península to Vinaròs *p680*
The **train** station, with connections along the coast between **Barcelona**, **Valencia** and **Alicante**, is set back 7 km at **Benicarló**. In summer, there are shuttle buses from **Vinàros** and **Benicarló** every 30 mins with AMSA, T964220054, but out of season you'll have to call a taxi (T964460505). There are **buses** directly to the town centre from **Barcelona** and **Zaragoza** with HIFE, T977440304, or from **Madrid** with Auto-Res, T964481888.

Inland Valencia

From the top of the province to the bottom there are some beautiful places to visit. At the top of is the historic and wild region of El Maestrat where hiking and other activities can be enjoyed. To the west of Valencia are vineyards where bogedas can be visited and then there are the mountainous villages belying their position just behind the often hectic action on the Coast Brava.

El Maestrat/El Maestrazgo → *Colour map 5, grid A6.*

Behind the Costa del Azahar is the wild and mountainous, El Maestrat – a region of castle-topped villages which date back to the time of the Templars, is a world away from the coastal fleshpots. There are excellent opportunities for hiking and adventure sports in the ravines and forests, but the region is difficult to explore without your own transport. The walled town of Moralla is the only place which is well set up for tourists.
➤➤ *For Sleeping, Eating and other listings, see pages 687-688.*

Morella
Morella, surrounded by forested hills and surmounted with a lofty castle, is a heart-stopping sight. Hemmed in behind fortified walls bristling with towers, it's a beautiful old town of steep, cobbled streets, and the cool mountain air makes it a popular weekend destination in summer.

Morella's main street, the Calle Blasco de Alagón, is lined with cafés and craft shops, and winds up steeply towards the lofty castle. Entrance is through the **Convento de Sant Francesc** ① *T964173128, 1030-1930, €2.80/1.20*, built in the 13th century but it hasn't been used as a place of worship for a long time and the decoration has long been stripped away. The main church contains fragments of Romanesque capitals and archways in the shallow chapels, and there's a pretty overgrown cloister gently tumbling into ruins. It's a long, hot climb up to the main square of the ruined castle, but the views are spectacular, sweeping across the hills and forests and looking out over a Gothic aqueduct below. East of the Convento de Sant Francesc is Morella's grandest church, the Gothic **Basílica de Santa María la Mayor** ① *Plaza Arciprestal, 1200-1400 and 1600-1800, free*, topped with a huge dome covered with deep blue tiles. It contains a beautiful 15th-century choir, and a gigantic Baroque organ which features in the Festival of Baroque Music held in August. There's a small museum of religious art with a serene Madonna by Sassoferato.

Seeing red

No one really knows how La Tomatina started – stories range from a food fight at a wedding which got out of hand, to a tomato attack on a bad musician – but it's been going since the 1940s. Now it's one of the best known festivals in Spain, attracting around 30,000 people every year.

On the last Wednesday of August, everyone converges on the main square just before 1100 and starts yelling 'to-ma-tes, to-ma-tes', clapping and stamping their feet. Finally, an ear-splitting blast signals the arrival of trucks bearing thousands of tons of tomatoes. For a second or two, the crowd looks sheepish but suddenly a bacchanalian frenzy takes hold and all hell breaks loose. Within minutes, the ground is a slithering mess and everyone is red from head to toe, clothes hanging off them in rags. At the height of the frenzy, the siren sounds again and, miraculously, everyone obediently downs tomatoes. The fire brigade hose down the buildings and the grateful, panting participants. The canny ones have packed clean clothes and stashed them somewhere safe, but there's always the odd tourist who has to head back on the train soaked in tomato juice.

Check exact dates and get more information from www.lahoya.net/tomatina.

Three of the towers have been turned into a miniature museum, each devoted to a different aspect of local history.① *All museums open daily 1100-1400 and 1600-1900, €1.80/1.20 each or combined ticket.* **Museo Tiempo de Imagen** (Torre Beneito) has some evocative black and white photographs, and **Museu del Historia** (Portal de la Nevera) contains exhibits and plans recounting the town's history since the time of the Templars. The most interesting is the **Museo Tiempo de Dinosaurios** in the Torre de Sant Miquel with bones, fossils and models of the Maestrat's prehistoric inhabitants.

The former **Iglesia de San Nicolás** is home to a delightful **museum** ① *C/San Nicolás s/n, 1100-1400 and 1600-1900, €1.80/1.20 or combined ticket*, devoted to Morella's famous festival, the **Sexenni**, which is held every six years (the next one is in 2006). It began as a festival of thanksgiving to the Virgen de Vallivana, who saved the town from the plague in 1672. It's a wild nine-day affair, with parades, folk-dancing, a pilgrimage to the sanctuary where the image of the Virgin is kept, and mad confetti battles in the streets. Each street makes incredibly elaborate decorations from crêpe paper – recent versions have included a copy of Picasso's *Guernica* – and there's a prize for the best one.

West of Morella

Some 10 km west of Morella is **Forcall**, a modest village on the banks of the river, which is famous for its crafts and fine cuisine. Just beyond it is pretty whitewashed **Todolella** with a medieval bridge and a boxy castle, which is well-known for its blood-curdling traditional dance, the Danza Guerrera which you can see at the summer festival in August.

Northern Maestrat

The northern Maestrat is wilder and more mountainous than the south, and towns and villages are clamped to sudden rocky outcrops. This region is known as Els Ports, referring to the mountain passes, and some villages are uninhabited in winter. To explore it, you'll need your own car and probably your own provisions as there are very few places to stay or eat, although you can usually find rooms above a bar. The

Tinença de Benifassà is the collective name for a group of small villages that once belonged to the abbey of Benifassà, which sits on a tranquil hillside near **Bellestar**. From here, the road wriggles northwards towards tiny **Fredes**, with just two streets and a Romanesque church, and south to **La Pobla de Benifassà**, the largest of the villages in these parts, with sturdy stone houses still bearing the old wooden balconies typical of the region. **Embalse de Ulldecona** is a popular summer picnicking spot, and the forests and ravines offer endless scope for walks and bike rides.

South of Morella

Catí has a twisting medieval core dotted with fine palaces, including the 15th-century Ajuntament. The landscape gets more rugged and mountainous as you head west towards the villages of the Alt Maestrat. Some, like tiny **Benasal**, are picturesque spa towns, and others, like striking **Vilafranca del Cid**, recall the legendary exploits of El Cid.

Sanctuaries of El Maestrat

El Maestrat is scattered with sanctuaries which still draw in pilgrims from across Spain. Perhaps the most extraordinary is the lofty **Santuario de La Balma**, about 15 km north of Forcall, which is thickly hung with dolls' clothes and all kinds of other mementoes which have been left here in thanks for the Virgin's intercession. From here, the road squiggles madly towards Mirambel and Teruel in the Aragonese Maestrazgo.

There are more sanctuaries in the small towns which line the N232 between Morella and Vinarós including one at **Vallivana**, where the image of the Virgin responsible for saving Morella's inhabitants from the plague (see above) is kept. Perhaps the most famous of all is the **Santuario de La Mare de Déu de la Font de la Salut**, near the ceramic-producing village of Traiguera. Celebrated visitors to this 15th-century church, hospital and palace have included Cervantes and several Spanish monarchs. Southwest of Traiguera, **Sant Mateu** was once the capital of the region, and retains vestiges of its medieval grandeur.

West of Valencia

West of Valencia are the wine towns of Requena and Utiel, modest little places which are probably only worth visiting if you are on your way to Aragón or Madrid. Buñol is the setting for **La Tomatina**, an ecstatic battle with thousands of tons of squashed tomatoes. ▸▸ *For Sleeping, Eating and other listings, see pages 687-688.*

Buñol → *Colour map 5, grid B5.*

Every year, thousands descend on Buñol for the world's biggest food fight, **La Tomatina** (see box page 684). The other 364 days of the year, it remains a tranquil little village, caught in a steep cleft in the hills, out of sight of the ugly concrete factories that squat next to the highway. The town is guarded by the ruins of an old Arab fortress, now a small archaeological museum, and tiny cobbled passages twist sharply downhill to the blue-domed 18th-century **Iglesia de San Pedro**. If it's been raining, there's a stunning waterfall at the nearby Cueva Turche, a popular local swimming and picnicking spot.

Requena and and Utiel → *Colour map 5, grid B4.*

Requena and Utiel are in the heart of Valencia's **wine country**, with vines snaking off as far as the eye can see. Requena's **Fiesta de la Vendimia**, celebrated at the end of the grape harvest in late August/early September, is one of the oldest in Spain. The town itself is a prosperous little place, with plane-shaded avenues radiating out from a sinuous medieval core, the Barrio de la Villa. Originally settled by the Arabs, only a single tower, the **Torre del Homenaje**, remains of the original fortress which gave the

⁝ Moor the merrier

According to local legend, the costumed parades and mock battles between the Moors and the Christians began when Felipe II and the Princess Isabel Clara Eugenia stopped off at Dénia's castle and were subjected to a fake ambush by men in Turkish costume. Suddenly, an army kitted out in Christian attire appeared from nowhere to chase the marauders away. The King thought it was a good joke and mock battles are now an intrinsic part of the local festivals of the Costa Blanca.

town its name (Rakkana, meaning 'secure'). It now contains two museums, one devoted to archaeology and the other to wine. There is a smattering of 15th- and 16th-century palaces, an old warehouse that recalls the days when Requena was one of the largest silk-producing centres in Spain, and a fine Gothic church. In the Plaza de la Villa, you can visit underground caves, **Las Cuevas**, used for wine storage.

Utiel, 13 km west, is less attractive, but you can visit some of the local **bodegas** for tours and tastings. Information is available from the tourist office ① *C/Puerta Nueva 9, T962171103, www.utiel-turistico.com.*

Inland from the Costa Blanca → *Colour map 5, grid A5.*

There are some engaging mountain towns in Valencia's interior to withdraw to if you fancy a break from the coast. Guadalest is the most striking, but also the most touristy, but lovely Xàtiva provides a welcome respite from the heat and bustle. Every village celebrates its local fiesta, but the best-known is Alcoy's **Battle of the Moors and the Christians.**⁇ *For Sleeping, Eating and other listings, see pages 687-688.*

Guadalest

Guadalest is a beautiful medieval village perched alarmingly on a pinnacle. The rock is a natural fortress, accessed via a tunnel, and the views from the lofty Plaza de Castillo are staggering. Its proximity to Benidorm – less than 30 km – means that tour buses disgorge thousands of visitors in an unending stream. Catch it out of season, or as early in the day as possible, as the mist lifts from the valley below. If you've got your own transport, stop off for a swim at the Fuentes del Algar, a string of waterfalls and natural pools hidden away in the forest near the small town of Callosa d'en Sarrià.

There's nowhere to stay in Guadalest itself, although there are a couple of *pensiones* in the nearby village of **Benimantell**. See Sleeping page 687.

Xàtiva/Játiva

Xàtiva, a tranquil town surrounded by olive groves and vines, has a sprinkling of old stone mansions and is topped with a castle. Set about 60 km south of Valencia, and about 30 km inland from Dénia, it's a popular weekend retreat. The town is the birthplace of two Borgia popes, **Calixtus III** and his nephew **Alexander VI**, as well as the painter **José de Ribera** (1591-1652).

It's a hot and dusty climb up to the castle① *Subida de Castillo s/n, mid-Mar to mid-Oct Tue-Sun 1000-1900, mid-Oct to mid-Mar Tue-Sun 1000-1800, €1.80,* but worth it for the stunning views. On the way stop off at the Romanesque **Capel de Sant Feliu**, with some striking medieval paintings inside. Just a few stones survive of the Castell Menor, but the Castell Major is largely intact. This is where the Bishop of Urgell, a pretender to the throne of Aragon, was imprisoned by Ferdinand I. You can stroll along the battlements and old walls which snake across the peak.

Back down in the old town, there are still a handful of noble mansions (mainly in private hands and closed to visitors), but much of Xàtiva was destroyed by Felipe V. The townspeople have punished him posthumously in the **Museo de Almudín** ① *C/Corretgería 46, T962276597, 15 Jun-15 Sep Tue-Fri 0930-1430, Sat-Sun 1000-1400, 16 Sep-14 Jun Tue-Fri 1000-1400 and 1600-1800, Sat-Sun 1000-1400, €1.80*, by turning his portrait upside down. The museum also contains Arabic ceramics and a beautiful artesonado ceiling, and works by Ribera.

Alcoi/Alcoy

Alcoi is a nondescript working town, but each year on the feast of **Saint George** (Sant Jorge, 23 April), it hosts the biggest and most dramatic enactment of the battle of the **Moros y Cristianos**, see page 686. St George came to the rescue during the Battle of Alcoy in 1276, and the festival has been celebrated ever since. The best costumes make it into the town museum, the **Casal de Sant Jordi** ① *C/San Miguel 60, Tue-Sat 1100-1300 and 1700-1930, Sun and holidays 1030-1400, free*, which has lots of exhibits, models and videos if you miss the real thing.

⊜ Sleeping

El Maestrat *p683*
Tourist information offices have lists of *casas rurales* in the region There is usually at least one bar in most of the villages of the Maestrat, some of which will rent rooms.
A-B Palau dels Osset-Miro, Plaza Major 16, Forcall, T964177524, F964177556, in a beautifully restored 16th-century palace. Recommended.
C Hotel Cardenal Ram, Cuesta Suñer 1, Morella, T964173085, F964173218, is set in a beautifully converted 16th-century palace, and the rooms are decorated with heavy wooden antiques and brightly coloured, locally made prints. Highly recommended.
C Molí l'Abad, Ctra Pobla de Benifassá km 7, La Pobla de Benifassá, T977713418, www.molilabad.com, is set in a converted mill by the river with a pool and camping area. It also rents apartments.
E Aguilar, Avda 3er centenario 1, Forcall, T/F964171106. A decent option.
E Hostal La Muralla, C/ Muralla 12, Morella, T964160243, is spotless and charmingly old-fashioned.
F Fonda Moreno, C/San Nicolás 12, Morella, T964160105, has simple rooms above a good, cheap little café-bar.

West of Valencia *p685*
D Hotel Avenida, C/San Agustín 10, Requena, T962300480, a modest affair.
D Hostal El Vegano II, Utiel, T962172355, F962170124. The only central place to stay here, a simple affair.

E Alojamiento Turístico La Villa, C/del Cristo 21, Requena, T962300374, www.incitur.com/lavilla. An old-fashioned place in the Barrio de la Villa. It also has a good, cheap restaurant which features the underground caves used for wine storage.
E Venta Pillar, Avda Pérez Galdós 5, Buñol, T962500923. This classic Spanish roadside hotel and restaurant 4 km from the centre, is the only hotel in Buñol.
Casa Castillo, T962502533, www.lahoya.net /casacastillo, is a charming *casa rural* in the heart of the old town (sleeps up to 10 people).

Inland from the Costa Blanca *p686*
L Hostería de Mont Sant, Carretera de Castillo s/n, Xàtiva, T962275081, www.servidex.com/montsant. For a real treat, stay here. Set in a former monastery with pool, gardens and a fine restaurant.
D El Trestellador, Benimantell, T965885221, which also has a good cheap restaurant.
D Hotel Murta, C/Angel Lacalle s/n, Xàtiva, T962276611, F962276550, is a modest choice near the football stadium. The
F Fonda Margollonera, Xàtiva, T962276677, has a fantastic location on the market place, but avoid the interior rooms if you can. Great cheap restaurant, too.

❷ Eating

El Maestrat *p683*
There are dozens of good restaurants in Forcall.
€€€ Hotel Cardenal Ram, Morella, see Sleeping, is very good.

€€€ **Palau dels Osset-Miro**, Forcall, see
Sleeping. A wonderful treat.

€€ **Casa Roque**, Cuesta San Juan 1,
Morella, T964160336, a traditional
establishment which specializes in truffles
(a celebrated local delicacy) and does a
good *menú* for €9.

€€ **Mesón de la Vila**, Plaza Mayor, Forcall,
T9641711125, which also does a cheap
menú del día.

€€ **Mesón del Pastor**, Cuesta Jovani 7,
Morella, T964160249, they serve tasty local
specialities in the mid-range price category,
including *croquetas Morellanas*.

€ **Fonda Moreno**, Morella, see Sleeping,
is good for a cheap snack.

€ **Vinatea**, C/Blasco Alagón, T964160744,
with tables out on Morella's porticoed main
street, traditional cuisine and great tapas.

West of Valencia *p685*

€€ **La Cueva**, C/Santísima Trinidad 21,
Utiel, T962170597, which is set in a cave, and
offers a good range of local wines.

€€ **Mesón del Castillo**, C/Gómez Ferrer 10,
Forcall, T962501231, which does good meat
and seafood cooked over charcoal.

€€ **Mesón del Vino**, Avda Arrabal 11,
T962300001. Head here to try the best local
wines which also offers excellent regional
dishes along a lengthy wine list.

€ There are plenty of old-fashioned
café-bars in Buñol along the main street
near the Iglesia de San Pedro, which all
offer a cheap *menú del día*, or for something
more upmarket.

☋ Activities and tours

El Maestrat *p683*
Tourist office, Plaza San Miguel, Morella,
T/F964173032, www.morella.net. Leaflets of
a well-marked network of walking paths

around the town are available from the
tourist office and are details of other
activities from pot-holing to mountain-
biking. You can also get combind entry
museum tickets here for €6.

Aula Muntanya, Plaza San Miguel 3, Morella,
T964173117, aulamuntanya@morella.net.
Have details of many adventure sports.
You can walk to the ancient settlement of
Morella La Vella, T964173051, 6 km from
Morella, where cave paintings have been
discovered. To see them, call in advance.

⊖ Transport

El Maestrat *p683*
There are **buses** with Autos Mediterráneo
(T964220536) from **Castellón** (2 daily
Mon-Fri, one on Sat) and **Vinarós** (2 daily
Mon-Fri) for **Morella** (about €8 for a return
ticket), but the times are not usually
convenient for a day-trip.

Sant Mateu and **Vallivana** are on the bus
routes from the coast to **Morella** (see above)
but there's no public transport to the
smaller villages.

West of Valencia *p685*
There are **buses** with Alsina, T963497230,
between **Requena**, **Utiel** and **Valencia**.

Requena and **Utiel** are on the regional
train line from **Valencia** with connections
to **Madrid**, **Cuenca**, **Ciudad Real** and
Albacete.

Inland from the Costa Blanca *p686*
From **Xàtiva** bus services travel to **Gandia**
and **Valencia**. There are regular train services
from Xàtiva to **Valencia** (at least 8 daily, about
1 hr), **Alicante**, **Murcia** and **Cartagena**.

The easiest way to get to **Guadalest** to
take a tour (information at the Benidorm
tourist office).

Costa Blanca → *Colour map 5, grid A5/6.*

*The Costa Blanca, along with the Costas Brava and Sol, is devoted to package tourism
on a grand scale. But it's not all skyscraper hotels and 'tea like your mum makes' –
some resorts remain refreshingly Spanish, not least among them the energetic city of
Alicante.* ▸▸ *For Sleeping, Eating and other listings, see pages 694-698.*

South of Valencia

Cullera

The Costa Blanca proper doesn't start until Denía, but there are a couple of big seaside towns south of Valencia. The first is Cullera, curled around the steep crag of the Monte del Oro and overlooking a vast, natural bay. The old town has been virtually swallowed up by a bland sprawl of modern apartment blocks but there are 14 km of beaches to compensate. Tourist information office ① C/Riu 38 and beachside at Plaza de la Constitución, www.cullera.com.

Gandía

The graceful old town of Gandía is surrounded by orange orchards. Its history is bound up with the fortunes of the Borjas, better known by their Italian name, the Borgias. In 1485, Ferdinand the Catholic gave the town to Rodrigo Borja, who would later become the notorious Pope Alexandro VI. The Spanish branch of the family was less Machiavellian, and the fourth Duke of Gandía, Francisco Borja (1510-1572) was canonised and is the town's patron saint. The town's most famous sight is the 15th-century **Palacio Ducal de los Borja** ① C/Santo Duque 1, T962276597, winter Mon-Sat 1100-1700, summer Mon-Fri 1000-1330 and 1730- 2030, closed Sun and holidays, €2.50/1.50, where San Francisco was born. It's currently occupied by Jesuits and is open for guided visits only. The original building was remodelled between the 16th and the 18th centuries, and only the patio retains its original Gothic splendour. The salons are decorated with ornate ceilings, azulejos and marble floors, and one boasts a beautiful frieze depicting the four elements made with ceramics from Manises. Unfortunately, some of the original tiling can't be reproduced as the plants used to make the original Arabic dyes have long been extinct. The tourist information office ① Avda Marqués de Campo, T962877788, www.gandiaexcelencia.com, has leaflets on various attractive walking and cycling routes around Gandía.

Regular shuttle buses depart from outside the train station in the centre of Gandía for its lively port, **Grao**, 4 km away. **Gandía-Playa** is a big, popular resort with a buzzy nightlife and famously manicured beaches (they get combed by tractors every day).

Around the Cape

The rocky cape which juts out between Dénia and Altea has some of the prettiest beaches of the Costa Blanca. Many of them are hard to get to without your own transport, which means – at least in terms of the brash Mediterranean Costas – they are comparatively unspoilt. ▸▸ For Sleeping, Eating and other listings, see pages 694-698.

Dénia

Dénia is a relaxed family resort dotted with colourful villas, and blessed with long sandy beaches. There's a ruined **castle** above the town (which is about to be converted into a theatre and cinema complex despite a local outcry) and you make the long scramble up to the top of the peak of Mongó for fantastic views. This wild, windswept area around the peak has been designated a natural park, and there are plenty of hiking trails. The local festival in early July is celebrated with the **Bous A La Mar** (Bulls By The Sea), in which the bulls are chased to the water's edge. Tourist office ① Plaza Oculista Buigues 9, T966422367, www.denia.net.

Xàbia

Xàbia (Jávea in Castellano) is a delightful old village set on a hilltop a couple of kilometres back from the sea. The peaceful seaside resort spreads gently around a

rocky horseshoe bay cut off by cliffs at either end. It's a low-key place, where, thankfully, high-rise hotels and apartment blocks have been banned. Scores of British and German families have set up home here, and you can pick up *Marmite* in the supermarket or an English book at the friendly bookshop. The tourist information office ① *Plaza Almirante Basterreche 24, T965790736, www.xabia.org*, runs hiking trips and guided tours in English.

The old pueblo is an immaculate little maze of whitewashed houses and pretty squares. Like most villages of this region, it celebrates its local festival (held in July) with a battle between the Moors and the Christians, which culminates with a spectacular firework show on the seafront. It's a good base for hiking in the **Natural Park of Montgó** (the tourist office has a series of excellent leaflets describing the various trails) and the Cape of San Antonio has been declared a marine reserve to prevent further development and the diving is excellent. The tourist office has lists of schools offering diving trips.

Calpe

Calpe, around the tip of the cape, is a big, blowsy resort in a stunning natural setting with excellent beaches. The extraordinary rock, the **Peñón de Ifach**, which juts sheerly

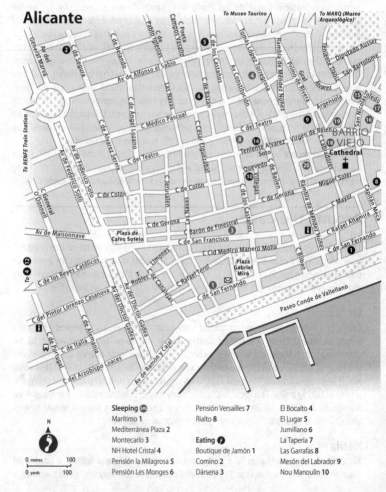

Alicante

Sleeping
Marítimo 1
Mediterránea Plaza 2
Montecarlo 3
NH Hotel Cristal 4
Pensión la Milagrosa 5
Pensión Les Monges 6
Pensión Versailles 7
Rialto 8

Eating
Boutique de Jamón 1
Comino 2
Dársena 3
El Bocaíto 4
El Lugar 5
Jumillano 6
La Tapería 7
Las Garrafas 8
Mesón del Labrador 9
Nou Manoulin 10

N

0 metres 100
0 yards 100

from the sea, was declared a natural reserve to preserve it from the onslaught of tourists. A tunnel has been bored up to the summit, but only 150 visitors are allowed at a time (it's a stiff climb and takes about two hours).

Altea

Altea is a picture-postcard village overlooking the sea. 'Discovered' by artists and hippies in the 70s, it's still got a mellow atmosphere and craft shops and galleries line its narrow streets. The village is crowned with a rosy church topped with a blue-tiled dome, which overlooks a buzzy square filled with tapas bars. The beach is pebbly and narrow, but still a favourite with families, and there's a craft market along the promenade on Tuesdays.

Benidorm

Benidorm, despite recent efforts to moderate its image, is still the king of package tourism, a mini New York of towering skyscrapers, flashing neon and crammed, sweaty beaches. The only reason to visit is for a hedonistic holiday of sun, sea and dodgy sangría. Its often seen as a mecca for northern Europeans and it's easy to forget that half the tourists who come here are Spanish.

O'Pote Galego **11**
Piripi **12**
Rincón Gallego **13**
Yale **14**

Caliu **16**
Callejón Pub **17**
Celestial Copas **18**
Cienfuegos **19**
Habana **20**

Bars & clubs
Armstrong **15**

Alicante → *Phone code: 965; Colour map 7, grid A5; Population: 265,473.*

Alicante, Valencia's second largest town, is the main gateway for package tours to the Costa Blanca. The coastline is dense with the ugly paraphernalia of hard-core tourism, but the town itself remains authentically and pleasingly Spanish. Elegant, palm-lined boulevards stretch along the seafront, decorated with colourful azulejo tiles and the old town, 'El Barrio', is an atmospheric huddle of narrow streets. It's packed with buzzy bars and restaurants, and Alicante offers some of the best shopping and nightlife in the whole region. ►► *For Sleeping, Eating and other listings, see pages 694-698.*

Ins and outs

Getting there Alicante's airport is 12 km from the centre at El Altet (see also Essentials, page 34). For airport information, call T966819000, www. aena.es. RENFE train station is on Avda Salamanca. The main bus station is on C/Portugal, T965130700. ►► *For further details, see Transport page 698.*

Getting around Local buses run between the beaches and the centre of town. Routes are clearly marked at bus stops. The old centre is small and easy to get around on foot. Taxis are usually easy to hail.

Best time to visit Alicante gets especially crowded in August, when accommodation can be hard to find, but the summer nightlife is hard to beat. The excellent local festival Las Hogueras is held in late June.›› *For further details, see page 697.*

Tourist information There are branches at the bus station, airport, train station, and the Ayuntamiento and summer kiosks at the beaches of San Juan and Postiguet as well as the principal office ① *Rambla de Méndez Núñez 23, T965200000, www.alicanteturismo.com.*

Sights

Alicante's biggest monument is the **Castillo Santa Bárbara** ① *grounds winter 0900-1900, summer 1000-2000. T965263131; Capa collection winter 1000-1400 and 1600-1900, summer 1000-1400 and 1700-2000, closed Mon and Sun pm, T965152969; lift costs €2.50,* an enormous medieval fortress clamped high on a cliff. The gardens and squares are strewn with sculptures, and the ancient walls offer tremendous views out to sea. There is more sculpture in the old stone halls of the castle, part of the extensive Capa collection. The best way to reach the castle is by the lift, which creaks up 205 m (entrance from Aveñida Jovellanos, behind the Playa de Postiguet) and saves the long, dusty climb via the road.

Alicante's old town is known simply as **El Barrio**, and is a cheerfully chaotic scramble of winding passages, stone mansions with flower-filled balconies, and a smattering of churches.

Baroque **Concatedral de San Nicolás de Bari** ① *Plaza Abad Penalva 1, T965212662, winter 0730-1230 and 1730-2000, summer 0730-12000 and 1730-2030, donation requested,* is restrained and elegant, with a single soaring nave below a lofty dome and a quiet cloister. It's dedicated to Alicante's patron saint, but, despite major restoration, it remains a gloomy and oddly unwelcoming place.

Iglesia de Santa María ① *Plaza Santa María, T965216026, 1030-1300 and 1800-1930, donation requested,* the oldest church in Alicante, is brighter and prettier. Its twin belltowers and exuberant Baroque portal overlook a handsome little square, but the whole lot is currently a building site while the church undergoes major restoration. Close by, Alicante's best art museum is located in the 17th-century Casa de la Asegurada. The light and airy **Museo de Arte Moderno** ① *Plaza Santa María, T965140959, Oct-May Tue-Sat 1000-1400 and 1600-2000, Sun 1030-1430, Jun-Sep Tue-Sat 1000-1400 and 1700-2100, Sun 1030-1430, free,* contains works by Dalí, Picasso, Miró, Tàpies, Chillida and other great Spanish artists of the 20th century, as well as excellent changing exhibitions of contemporary art.

The **Ayuntamiento** (City Hall) ① *Plaza de Ayuntamiento 1, T965149110, Mon-Sat 0900-1400,* is a splendid, Baroque building topped with tiled domes. You can tour the sumptuous apartments inside.

One of Alicante's quirkiest museums, the little **Museo de Belenes** ① *C/San Agustín 3, T965202232, Nov-Mar Tue- Fri 1000-1400 and 1630-1930, Sat 1000-1400, Oct-Apr 1000-1400 and 1700-2000, Sat 1000- 1400, free,* is devoted to the figurines which decorate nativity cribs. **MARQ** (Museo Arqueológico Provincial de Alicante) ① *Plaza del Doctor Gómez Ulla s/n, T965159006, Tue-Sat 1000-2000, Sun and holidays 1000-1400,* is a glossy new archaeology museum stacked with interactive exhibits and high-tech presentations of local history, including the Ibero-Roman city of Lucentum which is being excavated behind the Playa de la Albuferata. Finally, bullfighting afficionados could visit the **Museo Taurino** ① *next to Alicante's bullring, Tue-Fri 1030- 1430 and 1700-2000, Sat 1030-1330.*

The main town beach is the crowded, occasionally grubby, Playa del Postiguet. Next up along the coast is the **Playa de la Albuferata**, with the ruins of the old Roman settlement of Lucentum behind it. The **Playa de la Almadraba** is next, at the foot of the cape, with lots of rocky coves (one is a nudist beach). The **Playa San Juan** is a vast, gleaming sandy beach backed by hundreds of hotels, restaurants and discos. There's

South of Alicante

South of Alicante, there are more resorts and (slightly) quieter beaches along the coast. Inland, the palm forests and gardens of Elche offer shade and tranquility, and the little town of Orihuela hides a beautiful Baroque core.

Santa Pola and Isla de Tabarca → *Colour map 7, grid A5/B5.*

Santa Pola is another overgrown fishing village with a ring of bland apartment blocks. The attractive port has a small fishing fleet, and offers ferry links to the tiny island of Tabarca, 3.5 km out to sea. The island belongs to Alicante, but more ferries make the short trip from Santa Pola. It's a favourite with birdwatchers and divers, but in summer it can get horribly crowded. The former **Casa del Gobernador** (Governor's House) is now a simple little hotel.

Elx/Elche → *Colour map 7, grid A5.*

Elche, in a fertile plain 22 km southwest of Alicante, is a pristine modern city of broad avenues with a tiny old core. It's famous for three things: palm trees, a medieval mystery play and an ancient sculpture of a woman. The palm trees were first planted by the Phoenicians, and are still the city's biggest industry. The palms produce dates, but the cultivators make even more of a profit from their fronds, which form the crosses used throughout Spain on Palm Sunday (and often kept as charm against lightning). The beautiful gardens of the **Huerto del Cura** ① *0900-2100, free*, which spread to the east of the town contain some of the oldest palm trees, including one that's more than 150 years old.

Elche's medieval mystery play, the *Misteri d'Elx*, is held each year on 14-15 August in the 18th-century **Basílica de Santa María**. If you miss it, there's a small museum① *C/Major de la Vila 25, T965453464, winter Tue-Sat 1000-1300 and 1630-2030, Sun 1000-1300, summer Tue-Sat 1000-1300 and 1700-2100, Sun 1000-1300, €3, free on Sun, dedicated to its history with an audio visual show close by on C/Major de la Vila.*

In 1897, the **Dama de Elche** was discovered in La Alcudia, 2 km south of the town centre. It's probably the most famous piece of ancient art in Spain, and the sculpture of the woman with the inscrutable gaze (Elche's answer to the Mona Lisa) now has pride of place in Madrid's archaeological museum, see page 98. There's a copy of it, along with finds from prehistoric, Phoenician, and Roman times, in the **Museo Arqueológico**① *Palacio Altamira, T965453603, Tue-Sat 1000-1330 and 1630-2000, Sun 1030-1330, free*, just north of the cathedral.

It's also possible to visit the **excavations** of La Alcudia, where there's a small museum ① *Ctra Dolores 2 km, T966611506, Apr-Sep Tue-Sat 1000-1400 and 1600-2000, Sun 1000-1400, Oct-Mar 1000-1700, Sun 1000-1400, €2.80/1.80*, devoted to the history of the settlement

Orihuela → *Colour map 7, grid B4.*

Orihuela is one of those Spanish towns which don't look much on the outskirts but blossom on a closer viewing. It has an immaculate medieval centre stuffed full of reminders of its glorious past. In 1488, it was important enough for the Catholic Kings to hold court here, and mansions, churches and bridges attest to its former affluence.

The 14th-century **cathedral**① *Mon-Fri 1000-1330 and 1700-1930, Sat 1000-1330, free, €2 for the museum*, is small but perfectly formed in the Catalan Gothic tradition, with twisting columns and a pretty cloister (moved here brick by brick from an old convent in 1942). The small museum contains a suprisingly rich collection of religious

paintings, including works by Ribera, Velázquez and Morales.The tourist office is housed in the elaborately tiled Palacio de Rubalcava ① *C/Francisco Diez 25, T965302747, Tue-Fri 1000-1400 and 1700-2000, Sat-Sun 1000-1400, free,* filled with period furniture, ceramics, sculpture and paintings.

Almost opposite is the charming **Iglesia de Santiago**, which bears the emblems of the Catholic Kings who founded it above the portal, and contains sculptures by the Murcian artist Salzillo. Look out for the whimsical **Iglesia de Santa Justa y Rufina**, with a belltower topped with a fleet of gargoyles.

The most elaborate monument in Orihuela is the **Iglesia de Santo Domingo** ① *Tue-Sat 0930-1330 and 1700-2000, Sun and holidays 1000-1400, free,* which became a university in 1569, and is set around two graceful cloisters. There's a charming old refectory, decorated with faded azulejo tiling, and the main church is a breathless, gilded swirl of Baroque cherubs and ornamentation.

There are two small museums dedicated to Orihuela's biggest festivals: the **Museo del Semana Santa**, with exhibits on the Holy Week processions, and the **Museo de la Reconquista**, with costumes and photos from the annual **Battle of the Moors and the Christians** which takes place every July. Peek into the pretty little **Teatro Circo**, a recently restored 19th-century theatre, and take a stroll around Orihuela's cool palm grove, **El Palmeral**, on the outskirts of the town.

● Sleeping

South of Valencia *p689*

A-B Don Ximo Club Hotel, Partida de la Redonda, T962845393, www.hoteldonximo. com, a luxury resort hotel in Gandía-Playa with tennis, golf and pool (excellent off-season deals drop the price considerably).

C Riviera, Paseo de Neptune 28, T962840066, F962840062, is a big, family-run place on the seafront (closed Nov-Easter).

E El Nido, C/Alcoy 22, T962844640, which has a cheap restaurant. In the old town of Gandía, a good budget choice.

E Hostal Duque Carlos, C/Ducque Carles de Borja 34, T962872844. Adequate.

F Pensión Alberto, C/Doctor Fleming 2, T962860086. Simple.

Camping

La Naranja, T962840470, is closest to the beaches.

Around the Cape *p689*

LL Hotel Buena Vista, Partidal Tossalet 82, Dénia, T965787995, www.hotel-buenavista. com, this gorgeous hotel is set in beautiful gardens with a stunning terrace and an excellent, expensive, restaurant.

LL Melia Altea Hills, C/Suecia s/n, Altea, T966881006, www.solmelia.com. The most luxurious place to stay is this glossy modern complex on a hillside overlooking the sea, with health and beauty treatments.

L-B Casa Cecilia, Dénia, enquires@villa.shad bolt.net. A detached villa with 3 rooms and 2 bathrooms (can sleep up to 6) with access to a large pool within landscaped gardens. The mountain views are wonderful and it is convenient for central Dénia and beaches.

AL Parador, Avda del Mediterráneo 7, Xàbia, T965790200, F965790308, this modern parador is in a magnificent cliff-top location and has a fine restaurant.

A-B El Rodat, Carretera Cano de la Nao s/n, Xàbia, T966470710, www.todoesp.es/ el-rodat. A group of bungalows set in gardens around a split-level pool. It's popular with families and has other facilities including a sauna, gym, tennis and a café.

A-B Roca Esmeralda, C/Ponent 1 (Playa de Levante), Calpe, T965836101, www.rocaesmeralca.com. New beachside development with modern rooms (the best have sea views), plus gym, beauty centre, pools, sauna and dozens of sports.

B Hotel Rosa, C/Marinas 197, Dénia, T965781573, F966424774, is a seaside family hotel with 2 pools (one for kids) and a restaurant.

C Hotel Javea, C/Pío X 5, T965795461, F965795463, is a classic Spanish seaside hotel just back from the port. Friendly.

C-D Venta La Chata, Carretera N-232 km 172, Calpe, T965830308, F965830308, is a pretty 18th-century villa on the outskirts of Calpe. It could do with a lick of paint – but at least it's a bargain.

D **Hotel Castillo**, Avda del Cid 7, Dénia, T966421320, has unexceptional rooms but great views.

D **Pensión Marina**, Avda de la Marina Española 8, T965793139, has bright rooms right on the beachfront.

D **Hotel San Miguel**, C/La Mar 65, T965840400, is a delightful spot on the seafront. Look out for special offers.

E **Hostal Fornet**, C/Beniardá 1, T965843005. One of plenty of budget options in the old village near the church.

E **Hostal Llacer**, Avda del Mar 37, Dénia, T965785104, F965781849. Cheap option.

Alicante *p691, map p690*

L **Hotel Mediterránea Plaza**, Plaza del Ayuntamiento 6, T965156185, www.hotelmediterraneaplaza.com. Handsome, luxury hotel in a converted 18th-century mansion with gym and sauna. Rooms are stylish but a tad impersonal.

B **NH Hotel Cristal**, C/ López Torregrosa 9, T965143659, nhcristal@nh-hoteles.es. Crisp, modern chain hotel with a striking glassy façade; look out for special deals at weekends and in the off season.

C **Hotel Rialto**, C/Castaños 30, T965206433. A typical Spanish resort hotel with well equipped a/c rooms in a central location.

D **Hotel Marítimo**, C/Valdés 13, T965219985. Simple, modern hotel with spacious rooms decorated in nautical blue and white. Handily placed for the beaches and the nightlife.

D **Montecarlo**, C/San Francisco 20, T965206722. Another good budget choice, with no frills but spotless rooms convenient for the beaches and the nightlife.

E **Pensión Les Monges**, 1st floor, C/Monjas 2, T965215046. A gem of place, this quirky pensión has stylishly decorated rooms (with a/c for a bit extra), lots of artwork (including a sketch by Dalí), and a great location. Rooms with jacuzzi and sauna also available (**C**). Highly recommended.

E **Pensión Versailles**, C/Villavieja 3, T965214593. A good family-run budget choice, with spotless rooms set around a plant-filled courtyard in the heart of the buzzy Barrio Viejo.

F **Pensión la Milagrosa**, C/Villavieja 8, T965216918. Similar to the above but even more basic. Some rooms look out over the

church of Santa María, and there's a delightful breakfast terrace.

South of Alicante *p689*

L **Huerto del Cura**, Porta de la Morera 14, Elche, T966610011, F965421910, is linked to the parador network, and has bungalows scattered around the beautiful Heurto del Cura palm grove. It has fantastic sports facilities and offers excellent weekend deals.

D **Hostal Candilejas**, C/Dr Ferrán 19, Elche, T965466512, F965466652, is unexceptional but adequate.

D **Hostal Rey Teodomiro**, Avda Teodomiro 10, Orihuela, T966743348. The only place to stay in town is this slightly institutional hotel but with friendly management.

F **Pensión Faro**, Camis dels Magros 24, Elche, T965466263, a spotless, friendly little place on the edge of town.

⦿ Eating

South of Valencia *p689*

€€€ **L'Ullal**, C/Benicanena 12, T962877382, in Gandía-Playa this is best restaurant here.

€€ **La Gamba**, Ctra Nazaret-Oliva s/n, T962841310, has a terrace and excellent fresh seafood.

Around the Cape *p689*

Dénia produces some of the best prawns in the world.

€€€ **El Poblet**, Ctra Las Marinas km 2, El Poblet 43, Dénia, T965784179, a very fancy, expensive restaurant with a celebrated chef. Try some of the world's best prawns here.

€€€ **El Negro de Altea**, C/Santa Bárbara 4, Altea, T965841826, is a traditional restaurant, set in an elegantly restored mansion, with a beautiful panoramic terrace. Cheaper dishes also available.

€€€ **La Cambra**, C/Delfín s/n, Calpe, T966830605, a romantic spot serving delicious Mediterranean cuisine. Some cheaper dishes.

€€ **Bahía**, C/La Mar 141, Altea, T965840011, serving delicious fresh seafood on a terrace with views of the bay.

€€ **Bitibau**, C/San Vicente del Mar 5, Dénia, T966422574, serves imaginative Mediterranean cuisine .

€€ **Los Zapatos**, C/Santa María 7, Calpe, T965831507, which does imaginative North

African dishes, and has an excellent wine list. *Menú del día* for €18. There are lots of cheaper places along the Avda Gabriel Miró.

€€ **Oligarum**, C/Las Barcas 9, Xàbia, T966461714, is a converted fisherman's house on the beach with a terrace, and delicious, and pricey, local specialities.

€€ **Santajordi**, C/Salelles 6, Dénia, T962878177, is a hip little place with good cheap to mid-range Mediterranean cuisine.

€ **Café Tentación**, Xàbia, with tables out on the Plaza Mayor, in the old village, has great salads and sandwiches and cocktails in the evening.

€ **El Jamonal de Ramonet**, Passeig del Salader 106, Dénia. For tapas.

Tapas bars and cafés

You can get a coffee and check your email nearby at the **Café Internet** on the Ronda Norte, Xàbia, T965796017. There are lots of tapas bars with tables out on the Paseo Marítimo in Xàbia, and a couple of relaxed bars on the beach.

In Altea there are lots of good tapas places on the Plaza de la Iglesia, including **La Capella**, C/San Pablo 1, T966680484.

Alicante *p691, map p690*

€€€ **Dársena**, Pso del Puerto, T965207589, www.darsena.com. There are more than a hundred different rice-based dishes to choose from in this elegant, classic restaurant overlooking the port.

€€€ **Comino**, C/Segura 14, T965213214. Smart, stylish restaurant serving exquisitely prepared local cuisine, including game and wild mushrooms when in season. Closed Sat afternoon in summer and Sun all year.

€€ **El Lugar**, C/García Morato 4, T965141131. Relaxed neighbourhood restaurant serving substantial portions of home cooking. It specializes in stews, but you'll also find ultra-fresh seafood, grilled meats, and home-made desserts.

€€ **Nou Manoulin**, C/ Villegas 3, T965200368. An enormously popular, brick-lined restaurant with classic regional dishes and a good value *menú del día* at around €12. If you don't want to go the whole hog, there's an excellent, permanently crowded tapas bar.

€€ **Jumillano**, C/César Elguezábal 62-64, T965212964. A classic, traditional restaurant which was founded in 1941 and is decorated with paintings by local artists and plenty of taurine memorabilia. Great tapas, or delicious local dishes in the restaurant. Closed Jul, Aug, Sep and Sun.

€€ **O'Pote Galego**, Pza Santísima Faz 6, T965208084. A charming Gallego restaurant overlooking a pretty little square behind the Ayuntamiento. The emphasis is on fish, either simply grilled over charcoal, or served with different sauces.

€€ **Piripi**, C/Oscar Esplá 30, T965227940. Dine on traditional Levante cuisine prepared with the freshest local ingredients, or just sit at the bar for a fabulous range of tapas and wines. The lunchtime *menú del día* is a great bargain.

€ **La Taperia**, Plaza Santa Faz 3, T965206102. This informal, neighbourhood tapas bar also does good, cheap meals including some great desserts. Great value.

€ **Rincón Gallego**, C/Pórtico Ansaldo1. T965219616. Tasty Gallego specialities – lots of seafood, especially *pulpo* (octopus), washed down with sharp white wine.

Tapas bars and cafés

The tapas bars at the **El Nou Manolín** and **Piripiri** (run by brothers) are popular and very good.

Other options include: **Boutique de Jamón**, Paseo Explanada de España 7, T965208069. Every kind of ham under the sun, including the much-prized *jamón Iberico* produced from acorn-fed pigs. There's a great range of regional cheeses, too.

l Bocaíto, C/Isabel La Católica 22. T965227237. This fancy restaurant also has an upmarket tapas bar, a local favourite.

As Garrafas, C/Mayor, 33. With more bullfighting pictures and posters, and a bar thickly covered with tapas and *montaditos* – mini-rolls with all kinds of fillings.

Mesón del Labrador, C/Labradores19. T965201951. A classic on the Alicantino tapas scene, a traditional old stalwart serving a great range of tapas and *raciones*.

Yale, C/Teniente Alvárez Soto, 6. T965204344. Just a handful of tables, but a wonderful array of tapas and *montaditos*.

● *For an explanation of sleeping and eating price codes used in this guide, see inside the*
● *front cover. Other relevant information is found in Essentials, see pages 47-56.*

South of Alicante *p689*

€€€ **Huerto del Cura**, Elche, see Sleeping, has one of the best restaurants in town, if you've got plenty of cash to blow.

€€€ **Restaurante Parque Municipal**, Passeig de l'Estació s/n, Elche, T965453415, is set under palm trees in the pretty municipal park and serves good local rice-based dishes in the mid-range price category.

€ **Mesón El Tozal**, C/Arbres 22, Elche. There's a tasty *menú del día*.

€ There are plenty of cheap places to eat in Orihuela around the Avda Teodomiro, and the student population ensures that the nightlife is always lively.

❶ Bars and clubs

Alicante *p691, map p690*

Nightlife in Alicante is concentrated in two main areas. 'La zona' (behind Explanada on the streets around Avda de Ramón y Cajal) is most popular with teenagers and students. But the wildest, noisiest nightlife is in El Barrio, the old part of town around the Cathedral of San Nicolas. In summer, head for the beaches, especially Playa San Juan, for countless outdoor bars and clubs. Many disco-bars are open Thu-Sat only.

Armstrong, Plza Virgen del Carmen, 12. Open Fri and Sat nights, 2300-0430. Jazz bar, decorated with pictures of famous musicians, live bands – soul, jazz, funk.

Celestial Copas, C/San Pascual 1, A wacky, kitsch decor, and flamenco, rumba and sevillanas played for an older crowd.

Caliu, C/Monteglón, 8. A noisy, buzzy student favourite, which does cheap drinks and has guest Djs.

Callejón Pub, Plaza Quijano, 6, T965143727. Open Thu-Sat. One of the stalwarts of Alicante's nightlife, with plenty of Spanish and Latino pop from resident DJ Raul.

Cienfuegos, C/Cienfuegos, 8, T965217299. Another classic, this is a loud, fun disco-bar playing upbeat house and techno to an up-for-it young crowd.

Directo Café, Muelle de Levante, s/n, T965202310. Restaurant, bar and club with magnificent sea views.

Habana, Rambla Mendez Nuñez, 26, T965216926. Latin rhythms, salsa and Spanish pop on the dance floor, Cuban cocktails at the bar.

❸ Festivals and events

Alicante *p691, map p690*

Alicante's biggest and best festival is **Las Fogueras**, held on the feast of San Juan, **24 Jun**. Most of Spain celebrates the midsummer solstice with bonfires, but Alicante's are the biggest and best. The *Fogueras* are the massive sculptures which, despite taking months of hard work to build, end up in the flames. Picasso, Dalí and Miró have designed them in the past – all turned to ashes along with the rest.

❷ Transport

South of Valencia *p689*

Cullera is a 20-min train journey from Valencia. **Gandía** is also on the train line from Valencia, with connections to **Alicante** and **Murcia**.

Around the Cape *p689*

Bus There are frequent buses (about 6 daily) from Alicante and Valencia along the coast. It takes about two hours from one city to the other (€10 single). **Xàbia** is connected by local bus to **Dénia**, 6 times daily during the week but there is no service at weekends.

Boat More expensive, but a great way of seeing the cape is to take the sightseeing/ferry service in a glass-bottomed boat from **Dénia** to **Altea** via **Xàbia** and **Calpe** (Mundo Marino, T966423066, return from **Denia** to **Altea** costs €24, return to Xàbia costs €10). The port is the departure point for ferries to the **Balearics** (Trasmediterranea, T902454645, www.trasmediterranea.com or Balearia www.balearia.com T902160180).

Train **Dénia** is on the main train line south from **Valencia** and on the narrow-gauge train line (FGV) from **Alicante** (see below), which stops at **Altea** and **Benidorm** .

Alicante *p691, map p690*

Bus For the **Playa de San Juan**, take bus Nos 21 23, 30 31, 38; for the **Playa de Alburefeta**, take bus Nos 9, 21, 22, 38. Buses run at least every 15 mins and on summer weekends buses serve the string of discos north of Alicante all night. For information call T965140936, www.subus.es.

Car hire There are plenty of places offering car rental, both at the airport and in town. Try **Avis**, Explanada de España 3, T965144666; **Budget**, at the airport, T965683465, and **Atesa**, at the airport, T965682526.

Taxi Tele Taxi T9655101611, or Radio Taxi T9655910123.

Train The FGV train (see above) links **Alicante** with **San Juan**, stopping at all the beaches along the way. It runs a night service from late Jul to end Aug, with a stop at 'Discotecas' where the summer nightlife is concentrated. The narrow gauge railway run by FGV ('El Trenet') runs along the **Costa Blanca** between **Alicante** and **Dénia**, stopping at the popular beaches at **San Juan**, **Benidorm**, **Altea**, **Calpe**, **Gata** and **Dénia**. Www.fgv.es, T965262233. There are high-speed trains to **Valencia**, **Barcelona** and **Murcia**. Local trains connect **Alicante** with **Elche**, **Orihuela**, **Xátiva**, and **Murcia**.

Tram A line runs between the Plaza Puerta del Mar and the FGV station at the northern end of the bay, stopping at the **Playa del Postiguet** and **Playa del Alburefeta**. There are bus services along the **Costa Blanca**, and

to **Granada**, **Almería**, **Barcelona**, **Jaén**, **Málaga**, **Sevilla**, **Madrid** and **Valencia**. International services to **London**, **Paris** and many other destinations with **Eurolines**.

South of Alicante *p689*
From **Elche** there are regular trains and bus services to **Alicante** and **Murcia**, and local buses to the beaches at **Santa Pola**.

From **Orihuela** there are regular buses and trains from **Alicante** and **Murcia**, and a local bus links the town to the municipal beaches at **Orihuela Playas** and the resort of **Torrevieja**.

❶ Directory

Alicante *p691, map 690p*
Internet Pick up your email at tiny **Zippo's Bar**, C/Labradores 1, which has a couple of terminals at the bar, or **UP Internet**, C/Angel Lozano10, T965200577, www.upinternet.net.
Post There are post offices at C/Alonso Cano 40 and at C/Asturias 8.
Embassies and consulates Several consulates are based in Alicante, including **UK**, Plaza Calvo Sotelo 1-2, T965216022.

Inland Murcia

The autonomous Community of Murcia is often overlooked in the race for the more glamorous resorts of Andalucía or Valencia, and it's regularly the butt of jokes by other Spaniards. Although poor and arid in parts, with the rising popularity of 'rural tourism', Murcia's long neglected interior is finally opening up to visitors. The handsome towns of Lorca and Caravaca de la Cruz brim with opulent monuments to their illustrious past, but there are scores of sleepy, castle-topped villages with unusual local fiestas that are just beginning to feature on tourist itineraries. Best of all are the green slopes of the Sierra de Espuña, a natural park popular with hikers and bird-watchers. Not to mentioin the capital, a prosperous, engaging little city with a striking Baroque cathedral and great nightlife. ►► *For Sleeping, Eating and other listings, see pages 702-704.*

Murcia city → *Colour map 7, grid B4; Population: 318,688.*

Murcia is a truly delightful, deeply Spanish little city, where the paseo and the tapeo are an intrinsic part of everyday life. The superb Baroque cathedral is its grandest monument, but the city is best appreciated sitting out on one of the numerous flower-filled squares, tucking into tapas or enjoying a drink.

Ins and outs
Getting there and around Murcia airport is at San Javier, near the Mar Menor, 48 km from the city. There is no public transport from the airport, and a taxi costs around

€30, www.aena.es. There are direct trains and bus services from major cities, including Barcelona and Madrid and a network of regular local services. The bus station is to the east of the centre. The centre of Murcia is small and easy to negotiate on foot. ►► *For further details, see Transport page 704.*

Tourist information The tourist offices are ① *Plaza Cardenal Belluga, T968358600, www.murciaciudad.com and Palacio de Almudí, T968358720.* Provincial information from www.murcia-turismo. com. Tourist information line T902101070.

History
Murcia was founded in 831 by Abd-Al-Rahman on the banks of the Río Segura, which irrigated the surrounding *vega*, or pastureland, ensuring the city's prosperity. In 1243, it fell to Alfonso X, but reached the height of its influence in the 17th- and 18th-centuries, when many of its most splendid Baroque monuments were built.

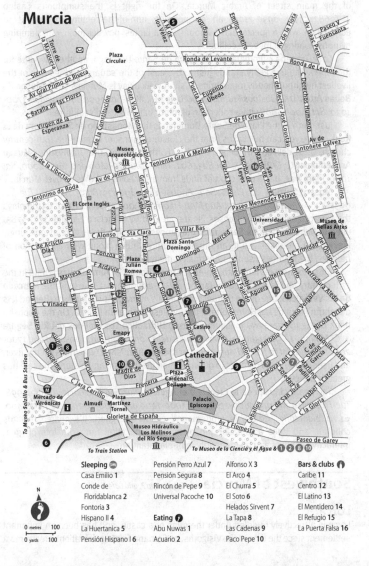

Murcia

Sleeping	Pensión Perro Azul 7	Alfonso X 3	Bars & clubs
Casa Emilio 1	Pensión Segura 8	El Arco 4	Caribe 11
Conde de	Rincón de Pepe 9	El Churra 5	Centro 12
Floridablanca 2	Universal Pacoche 10	El Soto 6	El Latino 13
Fontoria 3		Helados Sirvent 7	El Mentidero 14
Hispano II 4	Eating	La Tapa 8	El Refugio 15
La Huertanica 5	Abu Nuwas 1	Las Cadenas 9	La Puerta Falsa 16
Pensión Hispano I 6	Acuario 2	Paco Pepe 10	

Murcia's **cathedral** ① *Plaza Cardenal Belluga 1, T968221371*, was begun in 1394 on the ruins of the mosque, and is built in a surprisingly harmonious hotch potch of styles. The Gothic Puerta de los Apóstoles is the oldest surviving portal, but the façade was transformed in the 18th century and is covered in exuberant Baroque sculpture, topped with an elaborate belltower (which you can climb for tremendous views). Inside, the Capilla de los Vélez is encrusted with florid Plateresque decoration, and an urn contains the heart of Alfonso X 'the wise'. There's a museum, with paintings and sculpture, a frieze from a Roman sarcophagus, and an enormous gilded monstrance used in the Semana Santa processions.

The cathedral overlooks the Plaza Cardenal Belluga, a great place for tapas on the terrace, flanked on the opposite side by the elegant 18th-century **Palacio Episcopal**. On the other side of the cathedral, narrow Calle Trapería follows the route of the main street of Arabic Murcia. On the right is the sumptuous **Casino** ① *T968215399, 0930-2100*, an eye-popping turn-of-the-century monument to eclecticism, with a spectacular ballroom and a ladies' powder room with primping nymphs floating across the ceiling.

Calle Trapería culminates in the Plaza de Santo Domingo, another favourite for the *tapeo*. The university stands just to the east of the square, and it's one of the liveliest neighbourhoods for nightlife. A short walk away is Murcia's stuffy **Museo de Bellas Artes** ① *C/Obsipos Frutos 8, T968239346, Mon-Sat 0900-1400, winter 1700-1930, Sat 1100-1400*, with a collection of minor paintings and sculpture.

Just north of the Plaza de Santo Domingo is the **Monasterio de Santa Clara de la Real**, where you can buy cakes from the cloistered nuns, or admire the 18th-century church and delicate Mudéjar cloister. Further north, the interesting **Museo Arqueológico** ① *C/Alfonso X, T968234602, Mon-Fri 0900-1400 and 1600-2000, Sat 1000-1330, free*, has a collection of finds from archaeological digs all over Murcia.

Museo Salzillo ① *Plaza San Augustín 3, T968291893, Sep-Jun Tue-Sat 0930-1300 and 1600-1900. Jul-Aug Mon-Fri 0930-1300 and 1600-1900, €3*, displays the extraordinarily detailed *pasos* (floats) created by Francisco Salzillo (1707-1783) used in Murcia's famous **Semana Santa** processions. The figures are astonishingly lifelike and are displayed in an ornate Baroque church along with a collection of *belenes*, the figurines used in Christmas Nativity scenes.

Close to the Ayuntamiento, an Arabic grain house, or **Almudí**, was rebuilt in the 17th-century and is now used for temporary art exhibitions. Close by is the **Mercado de las Verónicas**, one of the prettiest of Murcia's many produce markets. Behind it is delightful Plaza de las Flores, one of the liveliest squares in Murcia. On the opposite bank of the river are two museums. **Museo Hidráulico Los Molinos del Río Segura** ① *C/ Molinos 1, T968358600, www.molinosdelrio.org, Mon-Sat 1100-1400 and 1700-2000, closed Sat in Jul and Aug*, is set in slickly refurbished watermills on the river, and uses multi-media exhibits to describe their mechanism and history. The café has great river views.

The nearby **Museo de la Ciencia y el Agua** ① *Plaza de la Ciencia, T968211998, Tue-Fri 1000-1300 and 1600-2000, Sat 1000-1400 and 1700-2000, Sun 1100-1400, €1.20,.planetario, €0.60*, is modern and crisply designed. It's geared towards children, and does a fantastic job of making education fun, with lots of great interactive exhibits and a kid-friendly mini-planetarium.

Southwest of Murcia → *Colour map 7, grid B3/4.*

Lorca

Lorca is attractively huddled under the ruins of a castle, and has been an important settlement since the time of the Visigoths. Its **Semana Santa** celebrations are the most

lavish in Murcia, and it's a lively little place all year round. Baroque churches and mansions dot the narrow streets, and the elegant squares are perfect for an indolent long lunch or some tapas in the evenings. The heart of the town is the **Plaza de España**, presided over by the Ayuntamiento (formerly a prison which explains the allegories of Charity and Justice which surmount it) and the exuberantly Baroque **Colegiata de San Patricio** ① *Mon-Fri 1100-1300 and 1630-1830, Sat-Sun 1100-1300, free.*

One of the most eye-catching of Lorca's many mansions is the **Palacio de los Guevara**, which now houses the tourist office, and is better known as the 'House of Columns' for the ornate twisting pillars at the entrance. Lorca was an important craft centre for centuries, and the **Centro de Artesanía** next door displays some of the finest. There's another extravagant Renaissance mansion on the corner of the Plaza Vicente, which is attached to a single Roman column, a former marker on the old Roman Via Herculea.

It's a long, hot climb up to the **castle**, built on the ruins of the Moorish fortress after the Reconquest. It's only open once a year on 23 November, the day when Alfonso X finally took the town from the Arabs, but the views over the rooftops are magical.

Totana

Totana, 40 km southwest of Murcia, is a prosperous ceramic-producing town in the foothills of the Sierra de Espuña. In the surrounding hills are the curious *pozos de nieva*, the stone snow wells which were used right up until the beginning of the 20th century. The tourist office ① *Ayuntamiento (Town Hall), Plaza de la Constitución, T968420003.*

Northwest of Murcia

Sierra de Espuña

The Sierra de Espuña is Murcia's most dramatic natural park, a surprisingly lush wilderness of pine-clad mountains watched over by eagles and vultures. It's a paradise for hikers and climbers, and the Centro de Interpretación① *inside the park, Casa Forestal de Huerta Espuña, T968431430*, has maps and leaflets describing walking routes and the park's flora and fauna.

The best base for the park is the little town of **Alhama de Murcia**, about 2.5 km from the park border, which has a ruined Arabic castle and plenty of tour operators running walking, biking, horse riding and nature trips into the park (information from the tourist information office).

Caravaca de la Cruz → *Colour map 7, grid A3.*

Caravaca de la Cruz is an impressive sight, a golden city set against pale mountains. High above it looms the dramatic 15th-century Templar castle, which contains the city's greatest treasure: the **Santuario de la Vera Cruz** ① *admission by guided visit only, 1100, 1200, 1300, 1630, 1730, 1830 daily in Aug, closed Mon the rest of the year €2.40.* According to legend, a cross borne by two angels appeared to the Moorish king of Valencia in 1231. The ornate Baroque chapel was built to house the relic, but it was lost during the Civil War, and the Vatican sent a sliver of the True Cross to replace it. The miracle is commemorated annually on the 3 May, when the Cross is processed through the streets and 'bathed'.

Caravaca also celebrates its local festivals (early May and August) with a **Battle of the Moors and the Christians**, but a special event, the **Caballos del Vino**, recalls another castle-related legend. The Templar knights were under siege, but made a desperate dash to search for water. All they came up with was wine, and this event is now recalled in a procession of costumed horsemen.

Moratalla is a sleepy, whitewashed mountain town in the northwestern Sierras. Steep streets scramble up towards the sturdy 15th-century **castle** erected by the Knights of the Order of Santiago and the fortress-like 16th-century **Iglesia de la Asunción,** with spectacular views across the valley. The town celebrates some unusual festivals, including the **Fiesta del Cristo del Rayo** (Christ of Lightning) in mid-July, when heifers are let loose on the streets. It's also well known for the **Tamborada,** when a thousand drums are thumped ceaselessly on Maundy Thursday and Good Friday during **Semana Santa.**

● Sleeping

Murcia city *p698, map p699*
Murcia's hotels are overwhelmingly geared towards business travellers, offering much in the way of charm; look out for excellent weekend deals.

AL Hotel Conde de Floridablanca, C/ Corbalán 7, T968214626, www.hotelescata lonia.es. Big, central hotel in an 18th-century townhouse with a modern annexe. Prices can drop by a third at weekends (**B**).

AL Rincón de Pepe, C/Apóstoles 34, T968212239, F968221744. Large, stylish rooms and an excellent bar (see below) and fine, classically elegant, expensive restaurant. It also offers excellent weekend deals (**B**).

B Hotel Fontoria, C/Madre de Dios 4, T968217789, F968210741. Modern, functional hotel close to the cathedral.

C Hispano II, C/Radio Murcia 3, T968216152, www.hispano.com. Smart, modern, central hotel with a popular restaurant serving mid-range priced dishes.

C La Huertanica, C/Infantes 5, T968217668, F968212504. An immaculate, modern hotel with good-sized rooms and large well-stocked bathrooms. Very good value.

D Hotel Casa Emilio, C/Alameda Colón 9, T968220631, F968213029. Simple, prettily decorated rooms close to the Jardín de Floridablanca.

D Pensión Hispano I, C/Trapería 8, T968216152, F968216859. A big, rambling old-fashioned *hostal* (linked to the posher option above) which is dire need of renovation but has adequate rooms in a good central location.

D Hotel Universal Pacoche, C/González Cebrián 9, T968217605. A reasonable, old-fashioned choice across the Puente Viejo from the old centre.

E Pensión Perro Azul, C/Simon Garcia 19, T968221700. The most characterful budget choice, 'the blue dog' is painted a startling shade of blue. Rooms are a bit battered, but there's a lively reggae bar downstairs and cheerful, laid-back staff.

E Pensión Segura, Plaza de Camachos 19, T968211281. Across the river, this is a plain and simple budget option with rooms decorated with brown chintz and friendly staff.

Southwest of Murcia *p700*
C-D Alameda, C/ Musso Valiente 8, Lorca, T968406600, is bland but central, good value.

D Hotel Plaza, Pza de la Constitución 5, Totana, T968423112, is central and well-equipped.

E Pensión Camioneros, Ctra N340 km 287, Totana, a truck-drivers' favourite on the edge of town (which can be noisy).

E Pensión del Carmen, Rincón de los Valientes 3, Lorca, T968466459, is central, spotless but basic.

Northwest of Murcia *p701*
AL-C Hotel Barceló Cenajo, Embalse del Cenajo, Moratalla, T968721011, www.bar celo.com, this option outside town is the plushest place to stay. Huge rooms and three pools. It offers good weekend deals.

C Hospedería Molino de Argos, Camino Viejo de Archivel, Caravaca de la Cruz, T606 3014 09. This is best place to stay, a luxuriously converted mill 10 km from the town.

D Hotel Los Bartoles, C/Alfonso X El Sabio 1, Alhama de Murcia, T968631671. A modern option handy as a base for the Sierra de Espuña.

F Pensión Reyes, C/ Tomas el Cura, Mora-talla, T968730377, has simple rooms above a local bar in town.

For information on *casas rurales,* contact **Noratur,** T902106600, who have lists of accommodation throughout Murcia.

🍴 Eating

Murcia city *p698, map p699*

Many of Murcia's best and best-known restaurants are attached to hotels.

€€€ **Acuario**, Plaza Puxmarina 1, T96821-9955. Pick out your victim from the aquarium, or choose good, roast meats. There's a reasonable *menú de degustación* for €24.

€€€ **Alfonso X**, Avda Alfonso X El Sabio 8, T968231066. Decorated in medieval style, serves classic roast meats, fresh local veggies. Excellent tapas and terrace in summer too.

€€€ **Rincón de Pepe**, see Sleeping, is considered the finest in town.

€€ **El Churra**, Avda Marqués de los Vélez 10, T968238400. Tasty Murcian dishes, including plenty of fresh fish from the Mar Menor, a good *menú* at €12 and a popular tapas bar.

€€ **Hispano** and the **Huertanica**, see Sleeping, both have good restaurants.

€€ **Las Cadenas**, C/Apóstoles 10. T968220924. Good home-cooking (and great desserts) made with the freshest local produce.

€ **El Soto**, Paseo de Malecón 14, T968296816. Laid-back, local restaurant with charming staff serving traditional meat and fish dishes.

€ **Paco Pepe**, C/ Madre de Dios 15, T968219276. Small, neighbourhood restaurant popular with local workers which serves a good *menú del día* at around €7.

Tapas bars and cafés

La Muralla, at the hotel **Rincón de Pepe** (see Sleeping above). Incorporating part of the old Moorish walls, this is easily the fanciest tapas bar in the city.

El Arco, C/Arco de Santo Domingo. T96821-9767. A relaxed arty café with tables on the square for lingering over coffee or breakfast.

La Tapa, Plaza de las Flores 13, T968211317. One of many tapas bars on the delightful Plaza de las Flores, this is always jam-packed. Good *croquetas*.

Pacopepe, C/Madre de Dios 14, T968219587. A great range of tapas and a buzzy crowd of locals.

Helados Sirvent, C/Trapería 30. Popular café with a few tables on the street, serving superb home-made ice-cream, plus refreshing *horchata* and *granizados*.

Abu Nuwas, C/Ruipérez 8,T968222042. Arab-style tea room, with Arabic pastries, and cushioned corners to sink into. Unusually, there's even a no-smoking area.

Southwest of Murcia *p700*

There are lots of good restaurants in Lorca including local favourite **Cándido**, C/Santo Domingo 13, T968466907 and **El Lorca**, Plaza de Colón 12, T968469909, which offers creative regional cuisine. **Rincón de los Valientes**, C/Rincón de los Valientes 13, T968466459, with good home-cooking and a cheap *menú del día*.

In Totana, try the elegant **Casa Mariquita II**, C/Cánovas de Castillo 8, T968422554, or the simpler **Plaza**, Plaza de la Constitución 5, T968423114.

🍸 Bars and clubs

Murcia is pretty lively for a city its size. Most of the action takes place around the university; check out the bars along C/Doctor Fleming and around the Plaza Universidad. There are more bars along C/Alfaro, near the Plaza Julian Romea.

Caribe, C/González Adalid 13. T968266886. Popular salsa bar, with live bands and plenty of dancing.

Centro, Calderón de la Barca, s/n. T968227196. *Discoteca* playing Spanish pop, with six bars and a chill-out area.

El Latino, C/Vitorio 9. T968215356. Live bands (mainly rock and blues), poetry readings, and photography shows.

El Mentidero, C/Saavedra Fajardo 3. T968223533. A swish, airy local bar with a huge range of whiskies and a smart, well-heeled crowd.

El Refugio, Plaza de las Balsas, 3. T606073136. One of the best-known bars on the Murcia scene with great cocktails and a terrace.

La Puerta Falsa, C/San Martín de Porres 5. T968200484. Classy jazz bar, with live acts, tertulias, and a laid-back atmosphere.

🛍 Shopping

Murcia city *p698, map p699*

Murcia is an affluent little city and there are plenty of fancy fashion and interior shops all over town. For one-stop shopping, the

department store **El Corte Inglés** has two vast premises opposite each other on the Gran Via Salzillo. To see what local crafts are on offer, visit **El Centro de Artesanía**, C/Francisco Rabal 8, T968284585.

⊖ Transport

Murcia city *p698, map p699*
Bus The bus station is on the east of the city centre. There are regular services to **Barcelona**, **Madrid**, **Málaga**, **Granada**, **Córdoba** and **Seville** and most other major Spanish cities, plus local buses to **Águilas**, **Lorca**, **Totana**, **Moratalla**, **Cartagena** and **Mazarron**. T968292211.
Train There are direct Euromed trains down the coast from **Barcelona** via **Valencia** and **Alicante**. Regional trains from **Alicante** are cheaper and almost as fast. There are direct trains to **Madrid** (about 4 a day), and local services to **Cartagena** and **Lorca**. The train station is 2 km from the city centre; take bus Nos 9, 11, or 17.

Southwest of Murcia *p700*
The bus and train stations in **Lorca** are next to each other on the edge of the old town, with regular services to **Murcia**, **Cartagena** and some of the smaller villages. There's also a daily bus service to **Granada**.

From Totana there are regional trains to **Murcia** and **Águilas** and local buses to **Murcia**, **Mazarrón** and **Lorca** (for bus information, call T968425427).

Northwest of Murcia *p701*
There are buses and trains (including Talgo to Barcelona) from **Murcia** to **Alhama de Murcia** for Sierra de Espuña; an hourly bus service to **Caravaca de la Cruz** from **Murcia**; and 3 buses a day from **Murcia** to **Moratalla**.

❶ Directory

Internet **La Red**, C/Antony Puig 1, and **Emapy**, C/Frutos Baeza 2, €2.50 per hr.
Post The main post office is on the Plaza Circular.

Coastal Murcia

The rocky coastline is pocked with quiet coves, places to relax, swim and enjoy fresh seafood. Most of the coast is refreshingly undeveloped with the exception of around the horribly built-up La Manga and the Mar Menor. Cartagena has a glorious past – unfortunately it has rather fallen from grace and these days offers little for the tourist.

Cartagena → *Colour map 7, grid B4.*

Cartagena is one of the oldest cities on the Iberian Peninsula, set around a natural bay and scattered with monuments from several ancient civilisations. Its glory days are long over, and it remains more interesting for what it once was, than what it is now: a rather shabby port town, which is only just beginning to dust itself off for the tourists. ▸▸ *For Sleeping, Eating and other listings, see page 706.*

Ins and outs
Getting there and around There are regular bus and train connections with Murcia and other major cities in the region. All the sights in Cartagena are concentrated in the area around the port and are easily seen on foot. ▸▸ *For further details, see Transport page 706.*
Tourist information ① *Puertas de San José, Plaza Almirante Bastarreche, T968506483, www.ctv.es/cartagena.*

History
The first settlement on this spectacular natural bay was founded by Hasdrubal Barca in 227BC. It became a prosperous commercial port and naval base, made rich by local

their own capital. Later an important Roman settlement, its fortunes declined under the Visigoths and subsequent rulers – the next time Cartagena made the history books was when it was sacked by Francis Drake in 1585. In 1873, it revolted against Spain's First Republic, and was viciously bombarded as a result. Worse was to follow during the Civil War, when the city was virtually flattened. Despite this, it remains Spain's most important naval base, arsenal and shipyard, and its finances are finally improving thanks to the proximity of the tourist resorts of the Mar Menor.

Sights

Cartagena's old town is dominated by the forlorn ruins of the **Castillo de la Concepción**, which contains the remnants of an Arabic lighthouse, and is surrounded by pretty gardens full of strutting peacocks (Parque de Torres). It offers great views out to sea. Below it are the remnants of the **Teatro Romano (Roman theatre)**, built in the first century BC, and only discovered in 1987. **Catedral de Santa María la Vieja** ① *Mon 1000-1400 and 1800-2030, Tue-Sat 1000-1400 and 1700-2030, Sun 1000-1400*, was built on top of the stalls which formed part of the theatre, and the site is still being excavated. There are Roman ruins scattered throughout the old town – part of the old **walls** are visible near the theatre, and remnants of the **Roman road** are clearly visible on Calle Duque (near the delightfully frivolous Modernista **Palacio Aguirre**).

The grim, forbidding 18th-century **Arsenal** (still in use and closed to the public) dominates Cartagena's port. Behind it is the **Museo Nacional de Arqueología Marítima** ① *Dique de Navidad s/n, T968121166, Tue-Sat 0930-1500, until 1400 in summer, free*, with an eclectic collection of amphorae and all kinds of bits and bobs salvaged from shipwrecks. The nearby **Museo Naval** ① *C/Menéndez y Pelayo 8, T968127138, Tue-Sun 1000-1330, free*, has some fascinating maps, and replicas of ancient seacraft. The port, a proper working port with massive cranes and no time to look pretty for the tourists, is overlooked by a big, white torpedo, which is actually a prototype submarine designed by local engineer Isaac Peral in 1884.

The Plaza de Ayuntamiento is overlooked by the florid Modernista **Palacio Consistorial** (now the city hall), and the Calle Mayor which leads off the square has more Modernista architecture, including the prettily tiled **Casa Llogestera**, and the city **Casino**. The street comes alive in the early evening, when families come to take the *paseo*, and pause for a drink at a terrace café. **Museo Arqueológico** ① *C/Ramón y Cajal 45, T968539027, Tue-Fri 1000-1400 and 1700-2000, Sat-Sun 1100-1400, free*, is in the new part of town (a good 20-minute walk from the centre). It's built on top of the late Roman necropolis of San Antón, and offers an interesting introduction to Cartagena's history.

La Costa Cálida → *Colour map 7, grid B5.*

La Costa Cálida lives up to its name (the warm coast) with average temperatures that rarely drop below 18ºC, and entice thousands of visitors every year, particularly around the built-up Mar Menor. For wilder, emptier beaches and less built-up resorts, head down to the Golfo de Mazarrón, which is less accessible, but you might find a beach all to yourself.

Mar Menor and La Manga

Most of Murcia's tourist development is concentrated around the Mar Menor, a vast saltwater lagoon which is divided from the Mediterranean by a narrow isthmus, called La Manga ('the sleeve'). In the 1960s, this area was completely unspoilt, but indiscriminate building since the tourist boom began has meant that it's now clogged

with unsightly development, particularly along La Manga itself. A popular package resort, the Mar Menor offers sun, sea and sand at a cheap price, with good sports facilities and spa centres.

There are several resorts around the Mar Menor. The largest are **Santiago de la Ribera** and **Los Alcázares**, where smart Murcians from the city have their summer apartments. **Lo Pagán**, at the northern end of the lagoon and surrounded by salt flats, is the least developed and most attractive. The black mud from the salt pools reputedly soothes all ails, particularly rheumatism, and people have been coming to slather themselves for centuries. The narrow Manga is an unbroken line of grim high-rise hotels and apartment blocks, but the beaches are all long and sandy, and packed with sailing and sports facilities.

Golfo De Mazarrón

Southern Murcia is a dry, scrubby virtual desert – perfect tomato-growing country. The dusty land is swathed in vast tents stretching as far as the eye can see, where tomatoes are grown under ghostly plastic covers. The coastline is barely built up, except for the two modest resorts of **Águilas** and **Puerto de Mazarrón**, and, with your own transport, it's possible to discover remote rocky coves without a soul on them. Best beaches are around the **Ciudad Encantada de Bolnuevo**, south of Mazarrón, where the rocks have been whipped into strange shapes by wind and time.

There are tourist offices ① *Águilas, Pza Antonio Cortijo s/n, T968493285, www.aguilas.org and at Puerto de Mazarrón, Avda Dr Meca 20, T968594426, www.serconet.com/mazarron.*

● Sleeping

Cartagena *p704*
D **Los Habaneros**, San Diego 60, T968505250. Right at the entrance to the old city, with well-equipped rooms and a popular restaurant serving traditional cuisine.
D **Hotel Cartagenera**, C/ Jara 32, T968502500. Modern and unexceptional, but with a good central location near the Plaza Tres Reyes.
F **Pensión-Hospedaje Oriente**, C/Jara 27, T968502469. Simple budget option with shared purple bathrooms and kindly owners.

● Eating

Cartagena *p704*
€€ **Emilio Marín**, C/Cartagena de Indias 15, T968500015, a quietly elegant restaurant which serves excellent regional dishes prepared with originality.
€€ **Mare Nostrum**, Paseo de Alfonso XII, T9689522131, a simple seafood restaurant in the port.

€ **La Tartana**, C/Mayor 5, T968500011, where you can enjoy tasty dishes made with local produce at very reasonable prices. There's also a popular tapas bar.

● Transport

Cartagena *p704*
The bus and train stations are conveniently located close to the town centre. There are regular regional and Talgo trains from **Murcia** to **Cartagena**, but the regional train is almost as fast and costs considerably less (about €4 one-way as opposed to €14).

La Costa Cálida *p705*
There are 3 bus services a day (€4) to **Los Nietos** on the **Mar Menor**. The narrow-gauge FEVE train also runs there every 15-30 mins. **Águilas** and **Puerto de Mazarrón** are both are reached by local buses from Murcia and Cartagena, but you'll need your own transport to find the lesser known coves.

Andalucía

☃ Footprint features

Introduction

Ask someone to conjure up images of Spain and the smart money is that most of the things they name will be Andalucían. Flamenco, sherry, beaches, olives, bullfights, orange trees, tapas; it's all here in spades. Andalucía was the heartland of the Moorish nation that occupied much of Spain for centuries and preserves much more of its Muslim heritage than any other part of the peninsula.

The cities of **Granada**, **Sevilla** and **Córdoba** are famous for their Moorish monuments, but just as much character can be found in the smaller towns, many of which wholly retain their street plan and narrow whitewashed feel of the times. The hill villages of **Alpujarras** are one good example and prime walking territory too but there are many other lesser-known destinations for some of Spain's best hiking: **Sierra de Cazorla** near Jaén, **Sierra Morena** that divides Andalucía from the rest of the peninsula, or the beautiful rainy hills around **Grazalema**. And of course, as if Granada wasn't quite beautiful enough, there's always the ski-slopes of the **Sierra Nevada**, dramatically visible as a backdrop to the city.

Many visitors to Andalucía don't get past its beaches. While this is in some ways understandable, there are certainly good ones and bad ones. The windy stretches of the **Costa de Luz** offer the best coastal scenery. The rest of the Cádiz Province is fascinating too, with the restrained Anglophilia of **Jerez** and its sherry bodegas and the capital itself with as rowdy a Carnaval as anywhere in Spain. Elsewhere in the region, seek out a bullfight in the cloven town of **Ronda**, the superb bird life of the **Coto Doñana** park, the scary terraformed **Rio Tinto Mines** and the superb Renaissance architecture of **Úbeda** and **Baeza**. The common factor? The gregarious Andalucíans who live at half pace in the sun and double the pace after dark.

709

Andalucía

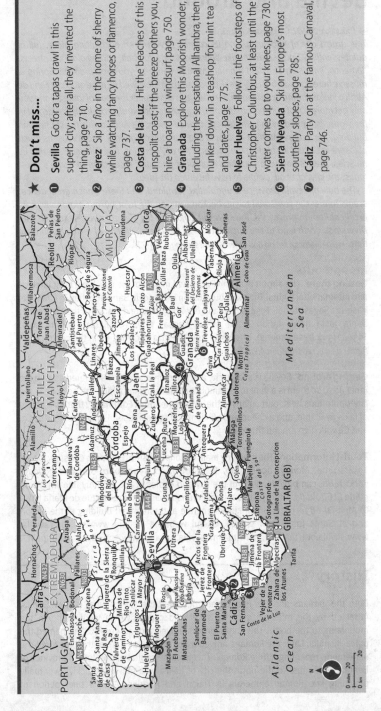

★ **Don't miss...**

❶ **Sevilla** Go for a tapas crawl in this superb city; after all, they invented the thing, page 710.

❷ **Jerez** Sip a *fino* in the home of sherry while watching fancy horses or flamenco, page 737.

❸ **Costa de la Luz** Hit the beaches of this unspoilt coast; if the breeze bothers you, hire a board and windsurf, page 750.

❹ **Granada** Explore this Moorish wonder, including the sensational Alhambra, then hunker down in a teashop for mint tea and dates, page 775.

❺ **Near Huelva** Follow in the footsteps of Christopher Columbus, at least until the water comes up to your knees, page 730.

❻ **Sierra Nevada** Ski on Europe's most southerly slopes, page 785.

❼ **Cádiz** Party on at the famous Carnaval, page 746.

Sevilla and around

→ *Population: 701,927; Colour map 6, grid B3.*

The largest city of Andalucía, and its capital, Sevilla is an enchanting place, full of quintessentially Spanish things like bullrings, tapas, football, narrow old-town streets, flamenco, imposing Christian monuments and dance-till-you-drop nightlife. Spring is massive here: the sombre Holy Week processions are followed by the exuberant Feria de Abril, a fantastic time to be in town, but the city creaks under the load of tourists, and you may get more out of a visit at other times. The Gothic cathedral, technically the largest in the world, is topped by the emblematic Giralda tower; it's Andalucía's finest Christian building; the nearby Mudéjar Alcázar is another major highlight. There's just as much pleasure to be had in strolling the streets of the city's barrios, and if the sun's flexing its muscles, there's always a cool bar, a glass of fino, and a selection of Spain's finest tapas; the city, after all, claims to have invented the idea.

The bulk of Sevilla province is undulating farmland, and there's not a great deal of scenic interest. A few small towns beckon through the heat haze; Carmona with its excellent Roman graveyard, the spires of Écija, and the elegant ducal seat of Osuna. Diversions north lead to the ancient town of Marchena, worthy of a visit if you have time. ►► *For Sleeping, Eating and other listings, see pages 721-729.*

Ins and outs

Getting there The airport is at San Pablo, 12 km east of the city, have both **internal** and international flights. The main bus station is Prado de San Sebastián in C Manuel Vásquez Sagastizabál, T954417111, and is within walking distance of the city centre. Santa Justa train station is on Av de Kansas City, T954414111 (information), T954421562 (reservations). Bus No 32 runs to Plaza Encarnación in the centre. ►► *For further details, see Transport page 728.*

Getting around Sevilla is a large city and the monuments are scattered around the inner area, so there is a limit to the amount of foot-slogging which can be done in the city's notorious heat, particularly in the summer months. Fortunately there are plenty of taxis available, and a cheap and efficient bus system. Useful buses are C1, C2, C3, and C4 which go around the road.

Tourist information The grudging main regional turismo ① *Av de la Constitución 21, T954221404, Mon-Fri 0900-1900, Sat 1000-1400, 1500-1900, Sun and holidays 1000-1400,* can provide maps of the city and copies of the monthly free what's-on guide *El Giraldillo*. There is also a smaller turismo close to the Parque de María Luisa ① *Mon-Fri 0830-1830*. Small kiosks operate at the terminal building at the airport and at Santa Justa train station. Useful websites include www.sol.com/sevilla, www.sevilla.org/tur.html, www.turismosevilla.org and www.spa.es/turismo/spain.

History

Both the Iberians and the Phoenicians occupied the site of what is now Sevilla, attracted by the minerals such as silver and copper which were found in the mountains to the north. The Carthaginians arrived around 500 BC and named the place Hispalis. Later the Romans arrived and under Julius Caesar they captured the settlement, renaming it Julia Romula. This became capital of the Roman province of Baetica, while just to the north the city of Itálica was growing quickly, eventually providing two Roman emperors in Trajan and Hadrian. After a brief period of

occupation by the Visigoths, Sevilla was taken by the Moors under Musa in 712. They changed the name to Ishbiliyya and also renamed the river Wadi El Kabir ("big river", which remains as the present Guadalquivir). The town, despite its own great wealth and status, became subject to the Caliphate of Córdoba, but in 1023 following the disintegration of the Caliphate, Sevilla took the opportunity to declare itself an independent *taifa*, (small kingdom).

Sevilla eventually fell in the Reconquest in 1248 to Ferdinand III and thereafter became a favourite residence of the Spanish monarchs. With the discovery of the New World, Sevilla entered a new age of splendour. The gold from the Indies poured in and by the 1500s it had an estimated population of 150,000, making it one of the most important cities in Europe and a magnet for painters and writers. It is during this period that many of the city's monuments were constructed.

Then followed a period of decline, which began with the silting up of the river, so that the port activities and trade with the Americas moved downstream to Cádiz. Sevilla was later affected by plagues, earthquakes and floods, to say nothing of decadence, while it was unaffected by the Industrial Revolution.

The post-Franco era saw a number of developments in Sevilla, helped by the fact that both the long standing premier, Felipe González, and his deputy were both Sevillanos. 1992 was marked by the Fifth Centenary of the Discovery of the Americas and by Expo 92, giving the city a year of wonderful publicity along with vast improvements in its infrastructure, including the AVE high speed train link with Madrid.

Sights

Catedral

① *T954214971, Mon-Sat, 1100-1800, Sun 1000-1330 for Giralda, 1430-1900 for Giralda and cathedral, last entry an hour before closing, €6, students and pensioners €1.50, free on Sun, a combined ticket secures entry to the cathedral and the Giralda.*

After Sevilla fell to the Christians in 1248, the existing mosque was retained for a while for Christian worship. In 1401, however, a decision was made to build a new cathedral on the site, designed by Alonso Martínez and on such a scale that people in the future would 'think its architects mad'. It was always thought to be the third largest cathedral in the world after St Pauls in London and St Peters in Rome, but latest calculations based on volume put it in first position; if you don't believe it, look in the *Guinness Book of Records*. Based on the rectangular plan of the mosque (116 m long and 76 m wide), extra height has been added, with the central nave rising to 42 m and even the side chapels looking like small churches. It is late Gothic in style and took four centuries to complete. The mosque's minaret, known today as the Giralda, was retained as the belltower, while the Patio de los Naranjos, the Moorish ablutions area, has also survived.

The exterior of the cathedral probably has more merit than the rest of the Andalucían cathedrals put together, with some superb stonework and crocketing on its doorways and windows, sturdy flying buttresses and some stained glass of interest. There are, in fact, seven exterior doors, varying in age, from the Moorish Puerta del Perdón leading into the Patio de los Naranjos to the Puerta Principal, built in the 19th century. The interior is magnificent, combining grandeur, space and solemnity. In the central area of the main nave, the *coro* or choir leads to the Capilla Mayor, notable for its huge retablo. It was the life work of the Flemish carver Pieter Dancart, although many others contributed before its completion in 1526. Depicting the life of Christ, the screen contains a vast number of figures and scenes, all dripping with gold leaf, but look particularly for the Virgin of the Sea and the scale model of Sevilla as it would have been in the 15th century.

To La Isla Mágica

LA CARTUJA

C Américo Vespucio

Av Carlos III

Monasterio
de Santa María
de las Cuevas
🏛

Camino de los Descubrimientos

Pasarela de
la Canuja

C Torneo

C Teodosio

C Santa Clara

C Juan Rabadán

Plaza San
Lorenzo

Miguel de Cid

C Baños

Río Guadalquivir

Related maps
A Seville centre, page 716.

To Huelva

Chapina

Paseo Nuestra Señora de la O

Av Cristo de la Expiación

Puente del
Cachorro

C Tejares

C Manuel Arellano

Pages del Corro

C San Vicente de Paul

Av Coria

Av Alvar Núñez

C López de Gómara

C Manuel Arellano

Plaza
Callao

C San
Jorge

C Alfonso XII

Avenida 5
Cines

Museo de
Bellas Artes
🏛

C Monsalves

C San Roque

C San Eloy

Plaza
de Armas

Taxis

Gravina

C Bailén

C Murillo

Taxis

Méndez Núñez

C Canalejas

C Marqués de Paradas

C Albuera

C Aljona

C Julio César

C Pablo

C Zaragoza

C Pastor y Landero

C Castelar

C Granizo

C Arfe

Taxis

C Reyes Católicos

Puente
Isabel II

Paseo

Plaza de Toros de
la Real Maestranza/
Museo Taurino
🏛

C Antonio Díaz

EL
ARENAL

C Cristóbal Colón

C Dos de Mayo

Teatro de la
Maestranza

C San
Jacinto

C Alfarería
Campos

C Betis

C Pureza

C Rodrigo de

C Pelay Correa

TRIANA

C Pureza

7

5

2

3

C Evangelista

C Pages del Corro

C José María Martínez

C Terra

Torre del
Oro Museo
Marítimo
🏛

6

Puente
San Telmo

Plaza
Virgen C Génova
Milagrosa

Taxis

Plaza
Cuba

C Juan Sebastián Elcano

Av República Argentina

C Niebla

C Asunción

LOS REMEDIOS

C Turia

C Santa Fe

C Virgen de Luján

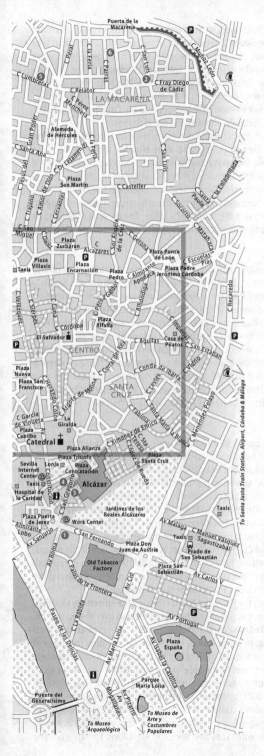

Andalucía Sevilla & around

N

0 metres 200
0 yards 200

Sleeping 🛏
Alfonso XIII **1**
Hostal Macarena **2**
Hostal Picasso **3**
Hostal Van Gogh **4**
Patios de la Cartuja **5**
San Gil **6**

Eating 🍴
Antigua Abacería de
  San Lorenzo **2**
Bodega Siglo XVIII **3**
Mariscos Emilio **5**
Río Grande **6**
Taberna Miami **7**

There are no fewer than 20 chapels located around the naves, of which the most important is the Capilla Real or Royal Chapel. Here are the remains of Ferdinand III in an urn, while his sword is kept in the chapel treasury. On either side of the domed chapel are tombs containing the remains of Ferdinand's wife, Beatrice, his son Alfonso the Wise, Pedro the Cruel and Pedro's mistress María de Padilla. Other chapels worth looking at, mainly because of their artwork, are the Capilla de San Antonio, which contains Murillo's *Vision of St Anthony* and the Capilla de San Pedro, with a clutch of paintings by Zurburán showing the life of St Peter.

In the southeast corner of the cathedral is a fascinating complex of rooms. The Sala Capitular has a superb domed ceiling, and more Murillos, while the Sacristía contains a vast array of art works, books and silver work, including in the centre a huge four-tier monstrance, said to be nearly 4 m high and weighing 475 kg.

Finally, don't miss the 19th-century Monument to Christopher Columbus, on the south side of the cathedral. It displays the figures of four kings, representing Aragon, Castile, León and Navarra, carrying the navigator's coffin. The remains of Columbus are supposed to be in the crypt below, but the tomb may or may not contain his body.

La Giralda

ⓘ *See cathedral for admission information*. The spectacular belltower of the cathedral, La Giralda, is constructed from patterned brick and stone and is Sevilla's most famous landmark. It dates from the 12th century and was the main minaret on Sevilla's mosque, the second largest in the world at that time. It is 100 m high and built on a Visigothic base. In Renaissance times balconies were added and a belfry of four diminishing storeys. Atop the tower is a *giraldilla* or weather vane, representing Faith, from which the tower's present name has been derived. Unusually, access to the summit is via 35 (seemingly endless) ramps, rather than steps, apparently designed to be sufficiently wide to allow two mounted horsemen to pass. The view from the top is well worth the toil, giving superb views over the pinnacles, buttresses and domes of the cathedral itself, as well as rooftop vistas of the city.

Alcázar

ⓘ *T954560040, Apr-Sep Tue-Sat 0930-2000, Sun and holidays 0930-1800; Oct-Mar Tue-Sat 0930-1800, Sun and holidays 0930-130, €5, children under 16, OAPs and registered disabled free, office shuts 1 hr before closing time.*

The Alcázar is one of the best surviving examples of Mudéjar architecture in Spain and has always been a popular place of residence for Spanish royalty when visiting the area. Work on a Moorish fortress in the Plaza del Triunfo originally began in 712 following the capture of Sevilla. In the ninth century it was transformed into a palace for Abd-Al-Rahman II. During the prosperous rule of the Almohads, the palace was extended further. The Patio del Crucio and Patio del Yeso are remnants of this period, but the fortress was vast, stretching right down to the Guadalquivir. However, much of the existing Alcázar was built in the 14th century for Pedro I (unfairly nicknamed the Cruel), who employed Moorish architects to undertake the work.

Entry to the Alcázar is from the Plaza del Triunfo through the splendidly Moorish, red coloured, **Puerta del León**, named after a tiled heraldic lion over the main arch. This leads into the **Patio del León**, a caged lion once guarded the entrance, and then into the **Patio de la Montería**, or Royal Guard, which has 14th-century buildings at each end with galleries and marble and brick columns. This is pure Mudéjar and sets the scene for the interiors to come. At the side of the patio is the Sala del Justicia, where Pedro dispensed his summary rulings. Firstly, however, the route goes through the **Salón del Almirante** , built by Isabel to administer the expeditions to the Americas. The best part of Isabel's complex is undoubtedly the Sala de Audencia, or **Capilla de los Navegantes**, with a fine *artesonado* ceiling. Above the altar is a large painting, *La Virgen de los Mareantes*, by the Sevillano artist Alejo Fernández.In the

painting, the Virgin spreads her protective mantle over, on her left, Columbus and the Pinzón brothers, while on her right is Carlos I and his retinue. In the foreground is a collection of boats, while in the background a selection of native people lurk, no doubt blessing their good fortune in having new-found Christian guardians. All very symbolic.

The tour of the Alcázar now moves into the main palace and from even the small entrance **vestibule, the combination of carved stucco work, horseshoe arches and** *azulejos* so typical of Moorish and Mudéjar architecture is immediately evident. A narrow passage now leads into the **Patio de las Doncellas** – the Patio of the Maidens – and here one immediately recognizes the influence of Granada's Alhambra. This was the main courtyard of the palace and was named after the maidens who would line the upper gallery when visiting ambassadors trooped in. The patio has double columned arches which, with the upper storey, were added by Carlos V and these seem to merge agreeably with the original Mudéjar work. The route passes through the **Salon of Carlos V** and the **chambers of María de Padilla**, the mistress of Pedro the Cruel and who was believed to have some magical hold over him – just as well because he has been described as "tall and handsome with a seductive lisp and an insatiable pursuer of beautiful women".

The route then leads to the **Salon de Embajadores** – Salon of the Ambassadors – which has more echoes of the Alhambra in Granada and a domed roof that resembles half an orange. Its arcades of horseshoe arches were inspired by the palace of Medina Azahara, near Córdoba. Unfortunately, Carlos V, in his usual way, made 'improvements' by adding balconies and panels of royal pictures to mark his marriage on this spot, to Isabel of Portugal. Nevertheless, the room is the highlight of the Alcázar.

Leading off is a small dining room which then brings us to a modest apartment built for Felipe II. After this is the last of the classic rooms of the Alcázar, the **Patio de la Muñecas** – Patio of the Dolls – named after two tiny faces carved in one of the arches and reputed to have been built as a playroom for King Pedro's daughter and her maids. But it was also the scene of some dirty deeds. It is probable that it was here that Pedro murdered his brother Fadrique in 1358. It was also the place where the visiting Abu Said of Granada was murdered for his jewels.

The Alcázar gardens are a somewhat rambling area, the result of several centuries of alterations and additions, which also provide welcome coolness and shade. The gardens were often used for balls. One, in 1350, was in honour of the Black Prince, who was greatly impressed by the Moorish dances performed by the Sevillian ladies. When he returned home, the dance became fashionable in England, giving rise, it is claimed, to the Morris Dance. Features of the garden include an unusual myrtle maze, a small pavilion built by Carlos V and some vaulted baths where María de Padilla was said to have bathed (and courtiers subsequently drank the water).

The Lonja

The Lonja, one of Sevilla's numerous palaces, on Avenida de la Constitución next to the cathedral, was designed for Felipe II by Juan de Herrera and completed in 1598 in pure Renaissance style. Today it houses the **Archivo General de Indias**, comprising some 38,000 files, documents, letters and manuscripts concerning the discovery and colonization of the Americas. Here you can see Columbus's diary and the Mapa Mundi by Juan de la Cosa.

Torre del Oro

① *T954222419, Tue-Fri 1000-1400, Sat-Sun 1100-1400, €1, Tue free.* This 12-sided defensive tower on Paseo Colón was built in the early 13th century by the Almohades. It used to be linked by chain to a similar tower on the west bank of the river, being part of the city's fortifications, which once included 166 towers and 12 gates. It gained its name from the gilded tiles that originally decorated it. It houses a small Maritime museum.

Sevilla centre

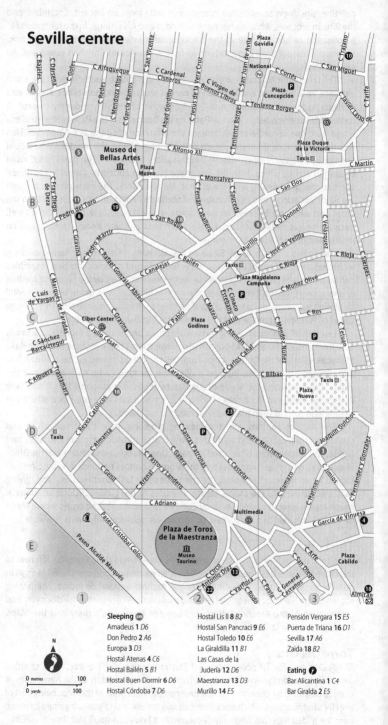

Sleeping
Amadeus **1** *D6*
Don Pedro **2** *A6*
Europa **3** *D3*
Hostal Atenas **4** *C6*
Hostal Bailén **5** *B1*
Hostal Buen Dormir **6** *D6*
Hostal Córdoba **7** *D6*

Hostal Lis II **8** *B2*
Hostal San Pancraci **9** *E6*
Hostal Toledo **10** *E6*
La Giraldilla **11** *B1*
Las Casas de la
  Judería **12** *D6*
Maestranza **13** *D3*
Murillo **14** *E5*

Pensión Vergara **15** *E5*
Puerta de Triana **16** *D1*
Sevilla **17** *A6*
Zaida **18** *B2*

Eating
Bar Alicantina **1** *C4*
Bar Giralda **2** *E5*

N

0 metres   100
0 yards   100

717

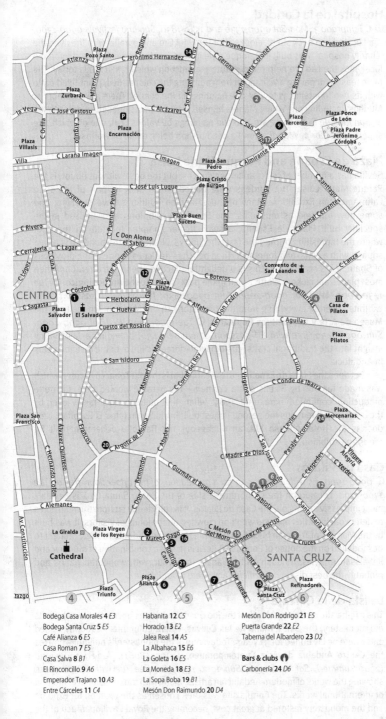

Bodega Casa Morales 4 *E3*
Bodega Santa Cruz 5 *E5*
Café Alianza 6 *E5*
Casa Roman 7 *E5*
Casa Salva 8 *B1*
El Rinconcillo 9 *A6*
Emperador Trajano 10 *A3*
Entre Cárceles 11 *C4*

Habanita 12 *C5*
Horacio 13 *E2*
Jalea Real 14 *A5*
La Albahaca 15 *E6*
La Goleta 16 *E5*
La Moneda 18 *E3*
La Sopa Boba 19 *B1*
Mesón Don Raimundo 20 *D4*

Mesón Don Rodrigo 21 *E5*
Puerta Grande 22 *E2*
Taberna del Albardero 23 *D2*

Bars & clubs 🕤
Carbonería 24 *D6*

Hospital de la Caridad

ⓘ *C Temprado 3, Mon-Sat 0900-1330 and 1530-1830, Sun and festivals 0900-1300, €3*. Located in a back street, close to the Torre del Oro and parallel with the river, the 'charity hospital' was built in Baroque style in 1676 by Miguel de Manera, a reformed local 'Jack the Lad', to help the destitute – a function which it still fulfils today. The main reason for paying a visit, apart from admiring the colonnaded, plant-filled patio with its two fountains, is to view the paintings in the chapel. There are a number of Murillos, including one where Manera himself (who commissioned the works) posed as *San Juan de Dios*. There are also two paintings by Valdés Leal, one of which, the superb *Finis Gloriae Mundi*, shows a dead bishop being eaten by worms.

Plaza de España and Parque María Luisa

Sevilla has a number of parks and open spaces, but the best, without doubt, is the Parque María Luisa. The gardens were turned into a park as part of the 1929 Latin-American Exhibition. Many of the exhibition buildings have survived, and some now function as museums. The Spanish exhibitions were housed in the specially built Plaza de España, a semi-circular complex located on the spot where the Inquisition burned the last witch in 1781. In front of the building is a vast square, with a canal and fountains. Tiled benches depict each one of the provinces of Spain. If it's not too hot, this is a delightful place to spend the afternoon when most places are closed. Worth a visit in the park is the **Museo Arqueológico**, ⓘ *Tue 1430-2000, Wed-Sat 0900-2000, Sun 0900-1430, free with EU passport*, with exhibits covering everything from the prehistoric to the Moorish. Opposite is the **Museo de Arte y Costumbres Populares**, ⓘ *Tue 1500-2000,Wed-Sat 0900-2000, Sun 0900-1430, free with EU passport otherwise €1.50*, providing a fascinating insight into the traditional crafts, customs and domestic life over the last 300 years in Andalucía.

Between the Plaza de España and the cathedral is the old **Tobacco Factory**, which was made famous by Bizet's opera *Carmen* – the heroine worked here. Cigarette production continued here until 1965, when the building was taken over by the university. It remains the second largest building in Spain (after El Escorial). Next door is the **Hotel Alfonso XIII**, an outrageous neo-Baroque behemoth built for the 1929 exhibition.

Casa de Pilatos

ⓘ *0900-1900, €5 with a further €3 for a guided tour of the upper floor, free on Tue 1300-1700*. Located on the far northwest side of the Barrio Santa Cruz is Sevilla's most impressive mansion, the Casa de Pilatos. It is sufficiently far from the main sites to deter coach parties and you won't be crowded out by loads of visitors. It was built by the Marquis of Tarifa on his return from the Holy Land and was wrongly thought to be modelled on the house of Pontius Pilate. It is in fact a combination of Mudéjar and Renaissance styles, Moorish and Italianate in flavour, with wonderful patios and probably the best display of *azulejos* anywhere in Andalucía.

La Isla de la Cartuja

This 215-ha site on the west bank of the Río Guadalquivir was once notable only for its old monastery, the **Santa María de las Cuevas**, where Columbus frequently visited and where he lay buried for 37 years. Today, one of the monastery's buildings houses the **Centro Andaluz de Arte Contemporáneo**, ⓘ *T954480611, Tue-Fri 1000-1930 (2300 summer), Sat 1100-1930, Sun 1000-1430, €3, free Tue with EU passport*, showing the works of modern Andalucían artists, along with the occasional exhibition of international works. The Cartuja site was then chosen as the location for Expo 92 and the monastery restored at great cost, becoming the Royal Pavilion. Much of the Expo site has now been taken over by the university and hi-tech industry. The area

amusement park. Its theme is claimed to be the 16th-century Spanish Empire,
although this is tenuous. Isla Mágica is, however, highly popular with children.

Museo de Bellas Artes

① *Plaza de Museo 9, T954221829Tue 1500-2000, Wed-Sat 0900-2000, Sun 0900-1400, Mon and holidays closed, free with EU passport otherwise €1.50.*

This museum is located in a renovated former convent in an attractive square, where the scene is set with a statue of Murillo. The museum concentrates on the religious art of its local Sevillan stalwarts, Zurburán, Murillo and Valdés Leal. Certainly, the small 19th and 20th century collection is uninspiring. A highlight, however, is Room 5, which is the convent's former church, where the light is exceptionally good. Here the vaulting and dome have been restored showing the 18th-century work of local artist Domingo Martínez. In the apse of the church are some of Murillo's best paintings, superbly set off by the surroundings. Some of Zurburán's work was produced rapidly on contract, but his hauntingly powerful crucifixions here place him in the very top tier. The museum also has some outstanding sculptures, including works by Montañes and Pedro Millan.

Real Maestranza

① *0930-1400, 1500-1900 daily, on bullfighting days 0930-1500, €4.* The famous Real Maestranza is one of the oldest bullrings in Spain; it contains a good taurine museum.

Barrios of central Sevilla

Around the central monumental area of Sevilla are a number of districts or barrios, each with their own distinct character. Close to the cathedral, and much visited, is the Barrio Santa Cruz, a maze of narrow streets (many of which are pedestrianized), whitewashed houses, small squares and flower festooned patios. A stroll around this atmospheric barrio, with frequent stops at its plethora of bars, is one of the delights of a visit to Sevilla. This was the site of the **judería,** a thriving Jewish quarter; a gateway marking the former entrance to a synagogue is all that survives.

Located across the river to the southwest, **Triana** was the centre of the city's *gitano* community until they were relocated throughout the city. It was the same gypsies who made Sevilla the home of flamenco. Triana today is well worth a wander to see its striking architecture, including famous *azulejos* covering house façades and its wrought iron balconies, as well as numerous great tapas bars, and good nightlife along the river.

Around Sevilla

Itálica

① *T955996583, summer Tue-Sat 0900-2000, Sun 0900-1500, winter Tue-Sat 0900-1730, Sun 1000-1600, free with EU passport, otherwise €1.50.*

The Roman ruins of Itálica are some 9 km north of Sevilla next to the village of Santiponce. The original city was founded in 206 BC by General Publius Cornelius Scipius as a convalescent area for his soldiers wounded in the Battle of Ilipa. Trajan, the first Emperor to hail from a Roman province, was born in Itálica. His successor, Hadrian, although born in Rome, received much of his education here and whilst he was Emperor he richly endowed the city, building a large new section. At its peak, Itálica had a population of over 500,000.

❖ *If visiting in the summer, beware of the heat, as there is little shade.*

What has been uncovered from the farmland is quite remarkable. Most astonishing of all is the huge amphitheatre estimated to have had a capacity of 25,000, believed to be the third largest in the Roman Empire. To the west of the amphitheatre is the city, which is laid out on a rough grid plan. Most of the houses have yet to be excavated, but those that have been uncovered have revealed an amazing collection of mosaics. Frequent buses run from the Plaza de Armas station taking about 20 minutes.

Carmona → *Colour map 6, grid B3; Population: 25,326.*

Carmona overlooks the Guadalquivir basin, with its fertile farmland devoted to olives and cereals, and has much of historic interest as a result of its active past. While settlement goes back to Palaeolithic times, it was the Carthaginians who set the town on its way during the third century. The Romans then conquered the town in 206 BC, naming it Carmo. It became one of the major fortified towns of the Baetica province of the Roman Empire, when most of Carmona's ancient walls were built. The town achieved its greatest splendour under the Moors. After the collapse of the Córdoba Caliphate, Carmona became capital of its own *taifa* (or small kingdom), until its capture by Ferdinand III during the Reconquest in 1247. It was later a favourite residence of Pedro the Cruel, who built a country palace within the castle. Today there are two Moorish alcázares (one now a parador), a unique Roman necropolis and a string of interesting churches and palaces.

Alcázar de Abajo (Lower Palace-Fortress) ① *T954190955, www.andal.es/carmona, Mon-Sat 1000-1800, Sun 1000-1500, €2, EU residents free*, includes the Puerta de Sevilla, a double archway with both Roman and Moorish elements that's the entrance to the old town. Today there is an audio-visual room, after which visitors can make self-guided tours with the aid of brochures. There is a small museum in the Alcázar. Running north from here is a sizeable stretch of the old walls of Carmona.

Alcázar de Arriba (Upper Palace-Fortress) was extended by both the Almoravids and the Almohads before the building of Pedro's palace. A large part of the structure was destroyed in the earthquakes of 1504 and 1755, leaving only the entrance gate and three towers. In 1976 it was tastefully rebuilt as a parador in the style of a Moorish palace.

On the corner of Calle Santa María and Calle San José is the Gothic 15th-century **Iglesia de Santa María de Mayor** ① *Mon-Fri 1000-1400, 1700-1900, €2.40*. Built over the Moors' Great or Friday Mosque, which itself is believed to have been built over a Roman Temple of Hercules, it retains the Patio de los Naranjos, with some fine horseshoe arches. Note also the superb 16th-century high altar and the Visigoth calendar marked on a pillar.

Located to the west of the town outside the walls (as was the custom in Roman times) is the **Roman necropolis** ① *T954140811, Tue-Fri 0900-1700, Sat and Sun 1000-1400, free with EU passport, otherwise €1.50*. This burial ground is unique in Spain and comparable only with some examples in Italy. Excavation of the site, which began in 1881, has revealed over 1,000 tombs dating from the second to the fourth centuries. Some 250 remain in their subterranean chambers and are often decorated with such motifs as birds and flowers. The larger tombs are massive. The most impressive is the Tumba de Servilia, named after the separate spaces for servants of the family. The Tumba del Elefante is named after a stone-carved elephant and has a number of ante rooms which may well have been kitchens among others, for use at funeral banquets. There is also a small museum with statues, urns and mosaics. To get to the necropolis take Calle San Pedro from the Puerta de Sevilla and proceed along Calle Enmedio for some 500 m. It is on the left-hand side of the road.

The *turismo* is located inside the ancient gateway of the Puerta de Sevilla ① *Casa de Cultura, T954190955, Mon-Sat 1000-1800, Sun 1000-1500*.

Écija → *Colour map 6, grid B4; Population: 37,113.*

Sandwiched between the Río Genil and a range of hills, Ecija is known as the 'City of Sun and Towers'. Records show that it is the hottest spot in the region, earning the description *La Sentenilla de Andalucía* – the frying pan of Andalucía; while a forest of spires and towers thrust up above the general level of white houses. All the major churches and palaces can be reached within minutes from the central, shady **Plaza de España**. **Ayuntamiento** is also located here with the tourist office inside, as well as a fine Roman mosaic. Worth a look is the **Iglesia de San Juan Bautista**, which has an ornate belfry in white stone – one of the few towers not capped with coloured tiles. Amongst the palaces, the most impressive is the huge **Palacio de Peñaflor**, with a pink marble portal and a curving balcony running the full length of the façade.

Marchena → *Colour map 6, grid B4; Population: 18,018.*

North of Morón and some 7 km north of the A92 is the ancient town of Marchena. Although going back to prehistoric times, it was the Moors who built its great walls and four gates, including the Puerta de Sevilla, the Arch of the Rose. After the Reconquest, the town was distinguished by the family of the Dukes of Arcos (which included the *conquistador* Ponce de León) who made Marchena a centre for artistic patronage. Don't miss the **Iglesia de San Juan Bautista**, which dates from 1490. The remarkable retablo contains 14 panels by Alejo Fernández and an alabaster head of St John the Baptist dating from 1593. The church's museum has no fewer than nine paintings by Zurburán, plus the usual books, gold and silver.

Osuna → *Colour map 6, grid B4; Population: 17,306.*

The charming town of Osuna is located a further 35 km along the A92. As with the neighbouring towns, it has an Iberian past, when it was known as Urso. In the 16th century it came into the hands of the Dukes of Osuna, particularly the Téllez Girón family, who founded many of the buildings still to be seen in the town today, including churches, mansions, the university and the Ducal Palace.

The hilltop above the town is dominated by two buildings, the old university and the collegiate church. The **university**, which was founded in 1548 by Juan Téllez Girón, is a rather austere, rectangular building in Italian Renaissance style with towers at its four corners and a central atrium. Its chapel displays a good collection of paintings and the main hall has a Mudéjar coffered ceiling. **Collegiate Church of Santa María de la Asunción** ① *guided tours only, Tue-Sun 1000-1330 and 1530-1830*, was founded by the same man, who used some of the finest craftsmen in Sevilla for its construction. The cream stone building has five naves with round Renaissance arches. The main Plateresque door of the church, the Puerta del Sol, was damaged by French troops during the Peninsular War, but remains impressive. The church also has some fine sculptures and paintings, including a Crucifixion by Ribera. Next to the church is the gloomy Plateresque-style pantheon which contains the tombs of the various dukes of Osuna and their families. Down in the town are a clutch of other churches and convents worth a visit, including the **Iglesia de la Merced**, with a barrel-vaulted ceiling, the **Iglesia de Santo Domingo** and the **Convento de Santa Catalina**. There is also a small **Museo Arqueológico** ① *Tue-Sun 1130-1330 and 1600-1800, free with EU passport, otherwise €0.60*, based in the Torre del Agua, part of the original Almohad fortress, and containing largely local finds.

● Sleeping

Sevilla *p710, maps p712 and p716*
There's lots of choice for accommodation. Prices rise sharply during Semana Santa and Fería de Abril.

LL Alfonso XIII, C San Fernando 2, T954222850, F954216033. One of the priciest in Spain at over €400 for a double, this famous hotel close to the monumental quarter is a luxurious 1920s building.

LL Don Pedro, C Gerona 24, T954293333, www.hoteldonpedro.net. Beautifully restored Sevillano *palacio* with a superb patio containing a fountain and plants. Central.

LL Las Casas de la Judería, Callejón de Dos Hermanos 7, Plaza Santa María La Blanca, Barrio Santa Cruz, T954415150, www.ibernet. net/lascasas. This 17th-century mansion has luxurious rooms around a series of patios full of orange and banana trees and pot plants.

L San Gil, C Parras 28, T954906811, hsangil@arrakis.es. Magnificently restored former *palacio* dating from 1901, with elegant tiled reception area and tranquil leafy patio. Pool, solarium, bar, restaurant.

A Patios de la Cartuja, C Lumbreras 8-10, T954900200, www.patiosdesevilla. Superb value aparthotel around a long plant-filled patio, in a quiet location. Smartly decorated apartments have bedroom, living room, fully equipped kitchen, bath, a/c, TV.

B Amadeus, C Farnesio 6, Barrio Santa Cruz, T954501443, www.hotelamadeusse villa.com. As its name suggests, this hotel, set in a beautifully restored 18th-century building with antique furnishings, was designed with musicians in mind. Some rooms have stereos with classical music or a piano. Rooftop terrace with superb views.

B Europa, Jimios 5, T954214305, F954210016, www.hotel¤ pasevilla.com. Classy, traditional hotel in 18th-century building near the Cathedral. Excellent value; ask for room with balcony.

B Puerta de Triana, C Reyes Católicos 5, T954215404, F954215401, www.puerta detriana.com Tastefully modernized luxurious hotel. Price includes breakfast. Superb value for this category.

C Hostal Córdoba, C Farnesio 2, Barrio Santa Cruz, T954227498. On same quiet street as Hotel Amadeus and Hostal Buen Dormir. Attractive rooms, some with balconies, a/c, with central fern-draped central patio. One of the better hotels in this category. 0300 curfew.

C Hostal Picasso, C San Gregorio 1, T954210864, www.ventalia/hpicasso.com. Under same management and just round the corner from Hostal Van Gogh (see below). Refurbished house colourfully decorated with an attractive patio filled with plants trailing from inner balconies above.

C Maestranza, C Gamazo 12, T954561070, www.andalunet.com/maestranza. Near Plaza Nueva, immaculate rooms, some with view of Giralda (just), best ones at front of hotel.

C Murillo, C Lope de Rueda 9, Barrio Santa Cruz, T954216095, www.hotel murillo.com. Traditional hotel featuring a pseudo-medieval decor theme and stuffed with elaborately carved antique furniture, suits of armour and coats of arms. Comfortable rooms and a quiet street.

C Sevilla, C Daóiz 5, T954384161, F954902160. Charming, traditional hotel with beautiful plant-bedecked patio situated on tranquil, pretty square in front of San Andrés church; ask for a room overlooking the plaza.

C Zaida, C San Roque 26, T954211138, www.andalunet.com/zaida. 18th-century mansion located in a street near Museo de Bellas Artes with patio entrance area comprehensively refurbished in Moorish style. Compared with patio, rooms are rather plain.

D Hostal Atenas, C Caballerizas 1, T954218047, atenas@jet.es. On a quiet street near the Casa de Pilatos, entry down a plant-filled passageway to a beautiful old patio with a tiled staircase. Attractive rooms with bath, a/c.

D Hostal Van Gogh, C Miguel de Mañara 1, T954563727, www.ventalia/hvangogh.com. In the shadow of the Alcázar, restored *Sevillano* house with similar decor to Hostal Picasso. Ask for a room with a balcony, from where you can see the Giralda and surrounding area.

E Hostal Bailén, C Bailén 75, T954221635. Small, friendly *hostal* with basic rooms, some with bath, near Museo de Bellas Artes. The best room is on the top floor at the front. Cheapest end of category.

E Hostal Lis II, C Olavide 5, off C San Eloy, T954560228, www.sol.com/hostal-lisii. Moorish-style interior, pretty patio and plants trailing from balconies inside and out. Good value, friendly; rooms have fans, some with bath. Great location, in centre but down a quiet street. Internet available, €2.50 per hr.

● *For an explanation of sleeping and eating price codes used in this guide, see inside the*
● *front cover. Other relevant information is found in Essentials, see pages 47-56.*

E **Hostal Macarena**, C San Luis 91, T954370141. Tastefully refurbished family run *hostal* on Plaza Pumarejo, in heart of La Macarena barrio and near the Alameda. A/c, some with bath, TV. Excellent value for this category. Recommended.

E **Hostal Toledo**, C Santa Teresa 15, Barrio Santa Cruz, T954215335. Small, friendly *hostal* on Plaza Santa Cruz with simple rooms, all with bath.

E **La Giraldilla**, C Gravina, is an attractive renovated cheapie with friendly management and individual exterior bathrooms.

E **Pensión Vergara**, C Ximenez de Enciso 11, Barrio Santa Cruz, T954215668. Restored 15th-century building with individually decorated rooms around a pretty central patio with exposed beams, Moorish-style arches and plants.

F **Hostal Buen Dormir**, C Farnesio 8, Barrio Santa Cruz, T954217492. Family run *hostal* with plain rooms, some with bath, around a tiled patio with caged birds. Rooftop terrace.

F **Hostal San Pancracio**, Plaza de las Cruces 9, Barrio Santa Cruz, T954413104. Popular *hostal* with basic rooms and shared bath.

F-G **Albergue Juvenil Sevilla**, C Issac Peral 2, off Av de la Palmera, T954613150. Out of the centre but accessible from Plaza Nueva on bus No 34. Usually crowded.

Sevilla, Ctra Madrid-Cádiz, Km 534, T954514379, 12 km from city, near airport. Campsite with hot showers, pool, restaurant, bar. Because of the heat, camping in high summer can be uncomfortable.

Around Sevilla *p719*
There is a limited choice of accommodation in Écija.

LL **Casa de Carmona**, Plaza de Lasso 1, Carmona, T954143300, F954143752. Restored *casa-palacio* with antique furnishings, luxurious rooms, and a pool.

AL **Parador del Rey Don Pedro**, C Los Alcázares, Carmona, T954141712, www.parador.es. Stunning views from most of the rooms at this historic site. If you can't afford to stay here, you can still experience a bit of its sumptious interior with a drink in the bar – although prices are hardly in the budget range here, either.

D **Caballo Blanco**, C Granada 1, Osuna, T954810184. In the old town, 14 en suite

rooms, a/c, wheelchair access, renovated, good restaurant.

D **Pensión Comercio**, C Torre del Oro 56, Carmona, T954140018. Spruce option near the Puerta de Sevilla, noisy cockerel next door.

D **Platería**, C Garcilópez 1A, Écija, T/F954835010. Best hotel in town tucked away in a small quiet side road, with 18 rooms, a/c, wheelchair access, restaurant.

E **Las Cinco Puertas**, C Carrear 79, Osuna, T954811243. In the old town, best of the cheaper places with 15 rooms and a restaurant.

F **Santa Cruz**, C Practicante Romero Gordillo 8, Écija, T954830222. The only budget option in the centre which can be recommended is this attractive, but spartan *pensión* with 18 rooms, near the Plaza de España.

🍴 Eating

Sevilla *p710, maps p712 and p716*
Despite being the most touristy area in Sevilla, **Barrio Santa Cruz** has loads of restaurants offering a good-value *menú del día* for around €6-9.

Parts of **Centro and the Alameda** have the advantage of being a bit less touristy than Barrio Santa Cruz, so go there if you want a more authentic glimpse of Sevillano life.

In the last decade **Triana** has undergone a transformation with the opening of many new bars and restaurants, particularly along C Betís and the area near the river, attracting an increasingly upmarket clientele and more tourists. The further into Triana you go, away from the river, the more bars you'll find full of Triana residents only, like the bars along C López de Gómara.

€€€ **La Albahaca**, Plaza Santa Cruz, Barrio Santa Cruz, T954220714. This is the place to come if you can afford a splurge. Sumptuous food served in a choice of exclusive *salones*, with lavish furnishings to match the food. With delights like *ostras gratinadas al aroma el eneldo y cava*, (gratin of oysters in dill and *cava*) on the menu you can't go wrong – but don't forget your credit card.

€€€ **La Moneda**, C Almirantazgo 4, T954223642. Superb seafood restaurant by the main post office, specializing in fried fish and *guisos* (stews). Excellent tapas also available.

€€€ **Mesón Don Raimundo**, Argote de Molina 26, Barrio Santa Cruz, T954223355. Splendid restaurant in a restored 11th-century building with a rich and colourful history, reflected in its cornucopia of antiques, curiosities and religious artefacts. Extravagant prices match the luxurious surroundings, but the *menú del día* is only €12.

€€€ **Río Grande**, C Betís s/n, Triana, T954278371. Boasting the best views across the Río Guadalquivir to the Torre del Oro, this famous riverside restaurant specializes in fried fish and many other seafood dishes.

€€€ **Taberna del Albardero**, C Zaragoza 20, T954502721. This must be one of Sevilla's best offerings for dining out in sheer opulence, with prices to match. If you can't afford dinner upstairs, try the better value *menú del día* served downstairs, €10.

€€ **Horacio**, C Antonio Díaz 9, T954225385. Situated on a street next to the Real Maestranza bullring , this place is worth a stop for specialities like *pimientos de pico con bacalao* (spicy red peppers with cod) and *codillo de pato al oporto* (duck wings in port wine sauce). Tapas also available.

€€ **Kiosco de las Flores**, C Betís s/n, between Plaza Cuba and the C Duarte, Triana, T954274576. This legendary fried fish emporium has a superb new position right on the riverside with irresistible seafood smells emanating before you even step in the door. Try their plate of *fritura variada* (€16).

€€ **La Mandrágora**, C Albuera 11, T954220184. Many return to this small, friendly vegetarian restaurant because of its intimate atmosphere and imaginative and constantly changing menu of excellent dishes. A bit out of the centre, but worth the effort. Closed Sun and Mon.

€€ **La Sopa Boba**, C Bailén 34, T954564884. Well-presented and unusual dishes like *magret de pato con mango y salsa de frambuesas al Oporto* (Oporto-style duck with mango and rasberry sauce) served in a brightly decorated restaurant near the Museo de Bellas Artes. Closed Mon evening and Sun.

€€ **Mesón Don Rodrigo**, C Rodrigo Caro 8, Barrio Santa Cruz, T954563672. Original menu with a definite fruity note – *salmón a la parrilla con vinagreta de frambuesa* (grilled salmon with raspberry dressing) and *salmorejo de fresas* (chilled strawberry soup). Stylish decor.

€€ **Puerta Grande**, C Antonio Diaz 33. Opposite the bullring, this smart place does good mixed seafood, and a cracking swordfish steak.

€ **Ali Baba**, C Betís 5, Triana, a wonderful new Lebanese café-restaurante with specialities like shawarma kebabs, hommous and falafel.

€ **Bauhaus**, Marquéz de Paradas 53. Innovative and stylish DJ-bar/restaurant specializing in international dishes like crêpes, quiche and couscous. Also limited tapas (€1.80) and a *menú del día*, €8. DJs from 1600 onwards, playing mainly house music.

€ **Casa Salva**, C Pedro de Toro 12, T954214115. Good-value and cheerful place near the Museo de Bellas Artes with abstract paintings on walls and a Mediterranean menu that changes regularly. Open Mon-Fri lunchtimes only.

€ **Il Ilustre Víctima**, Doctor Letamendi 31. International bar-restaurant near the Alameda serving anything from shawarma kebabs to enchiladas in colourful surroundings.

€ **Jalea Real**, C Sor Angela de la Cruz 37, east of Plaza Encarnación, T954216103. Small, busy vegetarian restaurant with salads, pancakes, crêpes and tapas available. Excellent value *menú del día*, €8. Closed Sun.

Tapas bars and cafés

As Sevilla is the place which claims to have originated the tapa, it is no surprise to find tapas bars in profusion throughout the city. Many are bedecked with sherry barrels and hanging hams, and are full of atmosphere. A tapas crawl in Sevilla is one of the highlights of a trip to Spain.

The bars in the touristy area of Barrio Santa Cruz are generally still surprisingly excellent value. In Centro, Plaza Alfalfa and the streets around it are bursting with excellent and cheap tapas bars. Another fertile area is along C San Eloy and Plaza Duque de la Victoria.

Antigua Abacería de San Lorenzo, C Pureza 12, Triana. Charming wooden-floored *quesería* exuding mouthwatering cheese aromas, bursting with *jamones*, cheeses and

bottles of wine. Homemade patés including *castaña* (chestnut) and *setas* (wild mushroom) and *montaditos* also available.

Bar Alicantina, Plaza Salvador 2-3. Great spot in a bustling square by the Iglesia del Salvador to people-watch and enjoy some of the best (and most expensive) seafood tapas in town.

Bar Marigalante, C Baños 60. Opened in 2001, this great bar has internet access (€2.50 per hr), a pool table and art exhibitions. It serves *montaditos*, *quesadillas* and tapas, as well as an array of special coffees.

Bodega Casa Morales, C García Vinuesa 11. Wonderful famous *bodega* whose decor looks untouched since it opened in 1850, including an antique cash till. Standing only at tatty wooden bar or huge wine barrels. Limited tapas, closed Sun.

El Rinconcillo, C Gerona 40. Established in 1670, this is probably the oldest bar in Sevilla; ceiling-high shelves of bottles line the walls, while the flagstone floor, beautiful tiles and chunky wooden bar make this the most atmospheric bar in town for a drink and some no-frills tapas.

Emperador Trajano, C Trajano 10. Located near Plaza Duque de la Victoria, this split-level bar with bare-brick walls serves original tapas including delicious homemade *pasteles*, or patés, and *tapitas de la Abuela*. Also excellent breakfasts from 0800.

Entre Cárceles, near Plaza Salavador. Tiny atmospheric bar lined with bottles of sherry, with a tapas menu including goodies like *calamar relleno en salsa oporto* (stuffed squid in port sauce) and *habas con choco* (beans with squid).

Bar Giralda, C Mateos Gago, Barrio Santa Cruz. Long established bar in an attractive restored Moorish bathhouse just down from the Giralda with a good range of tapas – including *langostinos*, or king prawns.

Bodega Casa Morales, C García Vinuesa 11. Wonderful famous *bodega* whose decor looks untouched since it opened in 1850, including an antique cash till. Standing only at tatty wooden bar or huge wine barrels. Limited tapas, closed Sun.

Bodega Santa Cruz, C Rodrigo Caro, Barrio Santa Cruz. This is a busy and cheerful bar, largely because it does some of Sevilla's choicest tapas and *montaditos*. Sees plenty of tourists but still very authentic close to the Giralda. Highly recommended. Usually known as **Las Columnas**.

Bodega Siglo XVIII, C Pelay Correa 32, Triana. One of Triana's most stunning bars, this 18th-century *bodega* has splendid antique furnishings, Moorish tiles, an eclectic mix of paintings and a magnificently carved wooden bar and ceiling. Apart from its excellent tapas, the **Bodega**'s most memorable feature is its somewhat incongruous Moorish patio.

Café Alianza, C Rodrigo Caro 9, Barrio Santa Cruz. Wonderful position in a small cobbled square shaded by orange trees and the Alcázar walls, with a glimpse of the Giralda.

Casa Roman, Plaza de los Venerables 1, Barrio Santa Cruz. Former grocers' shop beautifully decorated with antique lamps, oil paintings and the ubiquitous hanging *jamones*, the latter being the bar's speciality.

Habanita, C Golfo 3, off C Pérez Galdós, near Plaza Alfalfa, T606716456. Great little Latin café-bar dishing up a mix of Spanish and Cuban flavours, with lots of vegetarian and even some vegan options.

La Bodeguita de Santa Justa, Hernando Colón 1-3, Barrio Santa Cruz. Lots of fish choice (try the *albóndigas de chocos y langostinos*, squid and king prawn fish balls) and cheaper than bars closer to the cathedral, only a few mins' walk away. Mediocre *menú del día* for €7.

La Goleta, C Mateos Gago 22, Barrio Santa Cruz. Tiny bar with loads of character. Family-run since 1941, it specializes in a tasty orange wine.

Mariscos Emilio, C San Jacinto 39, Triana. Excellent seafood bar serving delights such as *ostras* (oysters) (€1.50 each) and sizzling *gambas al ajillo* (prawns with garlic).

Taberna Miami, C San Jacinto 21, Triana. Quails in whisky are among the more unusual offerings at this Triana watering hole.

Tequila Connection, C Bétis 41, Triana. A lively bar by night, this café has a soothing fountain, relaxing atmosphere, and internet access for €2.40 an hr.

Around Sevilla *p719*
In Carmona, look out for local specialities such as marinated partridge and spinach a la Carmona.

Rituals and riots

To be in Sevilla in Spring is a memorable experience, with two of the most extraordinary festivals in the whole of Spain, let alone Andalucía. It all begins with *Semana Santa* or Holy Week, when each of the parish churches of the city celebrate Easter. There are over 100 *cofradias* or brotherhoods who organize processions in which there are normally two *pasos* or floats, one of the Virgin Mary and the other of Christ, each carried by scores of *costaleros* or bearers. They are accompanied by bands that play deeply disturbing funereal tunes and march to the beat of drums, followed by members of the brotherhoods in their somewhat sinister, slit-eyed conical hats and accompanied by penitents, known as Nazarenes, who might be walking barefoot. Occasionally an onlooker, often from a balcony, will launch into an impromptu *saeta*, an eerie form of *cante hondo* or deep song in praise of the Virgin. Each procession eventually reaches the official route which leads along the pedestrianized Calle Sierpes and through the cathedral, accompanied throughout by the thunder of drums. The complete journey from and back to their own parishes can take as long as 12 hours, so it is hardly surprising that there are informal moments when the float is set down and a bearer takes the opportunity to nip into the nearest bar to use the toilet or to have a quick beer. The whole thing makes excellent street theatre.

The most popular procession is without doubt that of La Macarena, the goddess of the city, who incites an almost pagan adulation and whose *paso* is attributed to Luis Roldán. Indeed, many of the floats are considerable works of art in their own right and the brotherhoods (which include members from across the whole social range) spend much of the year in their preparation.

After the tense human emotion of Holy Week, it is almost inevitable that the Sevillanos will let off steam. Two weeks later the *Feria de Abril* takes place. Dating back to 1293, when Alfonso the Wise granted the city a charter to celebrate Pentecost, the *feria* is undoubtedly the largest and most vibrant in Andalucía. Since 1973 it has taken place at a permanent fairground in the barrio of Los Remedios. Here, large marquees or *casetas* are set up, many belonging to the more wealthy Seville families, while others are run by companies or political parties. The important thing is to have *enchufes* or the right connections – not to have access to the hospitality of a *caseta* means certain loss of face. The majority wear traditional costume, with the women in their colourful flamenco dresses and the whole city resounding to the wail of flamenco, the sound of guitars and the percussion of feet and hands. The climax comes when the great and good of Sevilla parade around in carriages or on horseback, while in late afternoon there are the traditional bullfights at the Maestranza bullring. The continual drinking, dancing, merry making and sheer exuberance of the *feria*, make it unique in Andalucía.

For more on Semana Santa, see www.semana santa.andal.es and www.hermandades-de-sevilla.org

€€€ **El Ancla**, C Bonifacio IV s/n, Carmona, upmarket option serving excellent seafood.
€€ **Molino de la Romera**, Puerta de Marchena, Carmona, T954190084.

Halfway between San Pedro Church and the Alcázar. Local dishes served in this old olive oil mill. Superb views from its terrace.

€ **El Tempranillo**, C Prim 7, Carmona, does good cheap meals, and also has occasional flamenco.

Tapas bars and cafés

The local tourist office in Carmona have produced a guide describing the town's best bars – ideal for those fancying a tapas crawl. Plaza San Pedro is one of the busier zones.

🌓 Bars and clubs

Sevilla *p710, maps p712 and p716*

As elsewhere in Andalucía, Sevilla's nightlife doesn't get going until past midnight, and once it does, there is loads of choice – particularly for flamenco (see Entertainment), jazz and blues and dance music. There are concentrations of late-night bars, or *bares de copas*, between Plaza Alfalfa and Plaza Salvador in the centre (including the lively C Pérez Galdós); C Betís, C Castillo and Plaza Chapina near the river in Triana; or around the Alameda de Hércules in the centre. Also see the excellent monthly free what's-on publication, *El Giraldillo*, available from bars, restaurants, hotel and *turismo*, or see www.elgiraldillo.es.

Bars

Antigüedades, C Argote de Molina 10, Centro. Larger-than-life figures hang from the ceiling and walls and the original decor gets a regular makeover. Cocktails and good selection of malts. Open 2100 until late.
Bar Betís 29, C Betís 29, Triana. Laid-back atmosphere with good music, 2100-0330 Mon-Thu (opens 1600 at weekends).
Bauhaus, Marqués de Paradas 53, Centro. Stylish dance music bar with DJs from 1600 onwards, with occasional video, DJ perfor-mances and exhibitions. Food served until 2400 (see Tapas bars above); open until 0400.
Blue Moon, C Antonio Cavestany 10. One of the best places to see live jazz Tue-Sat at 2400.
Café del Mar, C Jesús del Gran Poder 83, near Alameda de Hércules. Stylish bar playing mainly house music, with DJs from midnight onwards. Thu-Sat. Open 1600-0300, until 0500 Fri-Sat.
El Barón Rampante, C Arias Montano 3, next to the Centro Cívico in the Alameda de Hércules. Buzzing bar with a great atmosphere and a mixed crowd. 1600-0400.

Garlochi, C Boteros 26. Unusual and long-established cocktail bar with the most original decor in Sevilla – stuffed with religious paraphernalia, paricularly from Semana Santa, and gilt mirrors. Music – classical or religious – and drinks – *Sangre de Cristo*, or Blood of Christ – to match the surroundings.
La Otra Orilla, Paseo de la O s/n, Triana. Behind **Bar Las Niñas** next to the river, this great bar with summer *terraza* has live jazz and blues. Open every night in summer, Thu-Sat in winter, until 0600.
Si Rocco, C Betís 57, Triana. Music bar that gets more alternative after 0300, more a mixture of foreigners and Spanish than other bars along C Betís. Open 2200-0630.

Clubs

An area with several popular clubs, like **Antique**, is between Puente de la Barqueta and Palenque, in front of Isla Mágica.
Boss, C Betís 67. Upmarket *discoteca* with Spanish pop concerts and record launches. Expensive drinks. Thu-Sat only 2200-0800.
Catedral, C Cuesta del Rosario 12. Club playing mainly house, featuring video DJs. Wed-Sat only 2400-0700. €9 (some nights free for women), drinks €6. Closed Aug.
Itaca, Amor de Dios 25. Mainly gay club between the Alameda and Plaza Duque de la Victoria.
Weekend, C Torneo 43. Formerly the **Salamandra**, this club is somewhat with a Sevillano institution, staging a wide range of music concerts and DJ nights. Thu-Sat.

🎭 Entertainment

Sevilla *p710, maps p712 and p716*

Bullfights These are held Apr-Oct in the Plaza de Toros de la Real Maestranza, Paseo de Cristóbel Colón, T954210315 , www.realmaes tranza. com, one of the largest bullrings in Spain. Tickets are bought directly from the bullring and also from a kiosk in C Sierpes.
Cinema For details of the many other cinemas in Sevilla, see the newspapers *El Correo* or *El Diario de Sevilla*; the free monthly what's-on guide, *El Giraldillo*; www.cineciudad.com or ring T954380157.
Avenida 5 Cines, Marquéz de Paradas 15, near the Marquéz de Paradas bus station, T954293025. Unlike most cinemas which

dub foreign films in Spanish, this place shows foreign films in the original language, with Spanish subtitles. Bus Nos C1, C2, C3.
Cine Club UGT, Salón de Actos de UGT, Av Blas Infante 4, T954273003, union@sevilla.ugt.org. Art house cinema. Buses Nos 6, 42, C1 and C2.

Flamenco Due to the spontaneous nature of this art form, it can be remarkably difficult to find. Many visitors only see a *tablao*, which are overpriced shows put on for tourists.
Los Gallos, Plaza de Santa Cruz 11, T954216981, 2130-0130, is probably the best of the these.
The following are recommended for their mainly more impromptu nature:
La Abacería, Rosario Vega 3-4. Lively in informal, young Triana bar with drinks served in bottles only and tapas on paper plates.
Carbonería, Levíes 18, T954214460. Long-established, popular sprawling bar, a former coal yard where flamenco is performed at 2230 every night. It's very touristy, but there's a strong gypsy presence too, and some of the flamenco is very good. There's also a late-running tapas counter. Free (but the drinks are slightly pricier than normal), open until 0330.

Football Currently, Sevilla has two teams in the Primera Liga, both of whom are among the few clubs to have won the title.
Real Betis, a team with a blue-collar tradition, play at the Benito Villamarín Stadium in the south of the town, Av Heliópolis, T954610340. **Sevilla FC** are at the Sánchez Pizjuan stadium in the eastern suburbs, Av Eduardo Dato, T954489400.
Theatre Teatro Central, C José Gálvez s/n, T902400222, www.teatrocentral.com. In Isla de la Cartuja, with a varied programme of dance, drama, jazz and flamenco.
Teatro de la Maestranza, Paseo Colón 22, T954226573, www.maestranza.com. Impressive building near the bullring on the river, staging mainly opera, dance and classical music.

⊛ Festivals and events

Sevilla *p710, maps p712 and p716*
Mar-Apr Semana Santa celebrations in the week leading up to Easter are arguably the best in Spain, with effigies of Christ and the Virgin Mary being paraded through the streets by the brotherhoods; solemnity is replaced 2 weeks later by the riotous **Feria de Abril**, marked by bullfights, fireworks, dancing and general merrymaking lasting for a week (see also box).
15 Aug see the **Virgen de los Reyes** which celebrates the patron saint of Sevilla.

◎ Shopping

Sevilla *p710, maps p712 and p716*
The main shopping street is the pedestrianized C Sierpes, Sevilla's famed heart of the commercial area and packed with stylish shops. Alternatively, try the handicraft markets held on Thu, Fri and Sat on Plaza Duque and nearby Plaza Magdalena. For *azulejos* and other *cerámica*, go to C Antillano Campos in Triana.
Branches of **Librería Beta** (Av Constitución between the Cathedral and Plaza Nueva and off C Sierpes) have a good selection of maps and guidebooks on Sevilla and Andalucía, as well as books in English.

▲ Activities and tours

Sevilla *p710, maps p712 and p716*
Sevirama and **Sevilla Tour** run hop-on/hop-off multi-lingual city tours in open-topped buses, lasting 1 hr. Departures from the Torre del Oro. An all-day ticket costs €10. River cruises also run from the dock here. Walking tours of the city leave from the statue in Plaza Nueva Mon-Sat 0930 and 1130; the cost is €10; the same people also do guided tours of the cathedral and Alcázar.
Usit Unlimited, Av de la Constitución (opposite cathedral), T902252575, www.usitunlimited.es. Specialists in youth and student travel for longer trips.

⊖ Transport

Sevilla *p710, maps p712 and p716*
The city's infrastructure underwent many improvements for EXPO '92.
Air The airport is 12 km east of the city for both internal and international flights. For information T954449023. An **Amarillos** bus, T902210317 (24 hr), runs every 30 mins (less frequently on Sat, Sun and holidays) between the airport and the city centre at Puerta de Jerez, via the train station, costing €2 and

taking 30 mins. Taxis are available, but watch out for fiddled fares. The set fares can be seen in the airport and are currently €15.
Bus Sevilla has a cheap and efficient bus system. A map of routes covered by the city bus company, **Tussam**, is available from a kiosk (0900-1345, 1700-1900 Mon-Fri) on Plaza Nueva, €0.30. Also available are special tourist tickets, *tarjeta turística*, €6.50 for 3 days, €9.60 for 7 days. A *bonobús* for 10 bus trips costs €4.70 and is available from kiosks and tobacconists. A single ticket costs €0.90. For long-distance buses, the main station is Prado de San Sebastián in C Manuel Vásquez Sagastizabál, T954417111. From here there are frequent services to **Granada** (9 daily), **Córdoba** (12 daily) and **Málaga** (10 daily), among other destinations. **Jaén** is hit 4 times a day, **Jerez** 8 times, and **Cádiz** and **Algeciras** 9 to 10 times. There are 6 daily buses to **Ronda** via **Arcos de la Frontera**. Buses to **Carmona** leave hourly from the corner of C Carlos de Borbón and C Diego de Raño. The other station is at Plaza de Armas, T954907737, next to the Puente del Cachorro. Buses leave from here to **Madrid**, destinations in **northern Sevilla** province, as well as the provinces of **Huelva** – including **Aracena** (2 daily) – and **Extremadura**. For **Lisbon** connections, take the **Casal** bus to **Rosal del la Frontera** on the Portuguese border. The C4 bus runs between the 2 stations, or it's a 30-min walk. Both bus stations have luggage lockers. Bus company telephone numbers are published in the Cartelera section of *El Correo* newspaper.
Train The new Santa Justa train station (with exchange facilities) is on Av de Kansas City, T954414111 (information), T954421562 (reservations). There are 2 trains a day from **Algeciras**, 13 from **Cádiz**, 12 from **Córdoba**, 3 from **Granada**, 7 from **Huelva**, and 3 from **Málaga**. Nine daily trains from **Madrid** include the new AVE high speed service which makes the 340-mile trip in just under 2 hrs. There is a RENFE ticket office at C Zaragoza 29, T954211455, which can also provide timetables. See also www.renfe.es.

Around Sevilla *p719*
Casal bus company runs an hourly service to **Carmona** from **Sevilla**, stopping outside the rather dingy Bar La Parada on the main street. Timetables are available at the bar and nearby ice-cream kiosk.#

🛈 Directory

Sevilla *p710, maps p712 and p716*
Hospitals **Cruz Roja**, Av de la Cruz Roja, T954351400. **Hospital Universitario**, Av Doctor Fedriano s/n, T954378400. **Hospital General**, Av Manuel Siurot, T954558100, emergencies T954558195. **San Lázaro**, Av Fedriani s/n, T954378737. **First aid**: **Casa de Socorro**, T954411712.
Internet Sevilla has loads of internet places, particularly in the central areas. The following is a selection: **Work Center**, C San Fernando 1, opposite the Alfonso XIII, open 24 hours, **Multimedia Center**, C Adriano 7, **Sevilla Internet Center**, C Almirantazgo 2 on the corner of Avenida de la Constitución a block from the tourist office, **CiberCenter**, C Julio César 8.
Laundry **Lavandería Aguilas**, C Aguilas 21, with self-service and bag washes. Mon-Fri 1000-2030, Sat 1000-1400.
Post **Correos**, Av de la Constitución 32, Mon-Fri 0830-2030, Sat 0900-1300.
Telephone Locutorio in Plaza de Gavidia, open 1000-1400 and 1730-2200.

Huelva and around

→ *Colour map 6, grid B1; Population: 139,991.*

There is a saying in Spain which, roughly translated, means that once you have been to Huelva there is no need ever to return. An understandable sentiment, particularly if the city is approached from the southeast through the stench of interminable oil refineries and chemical works alongside the lifeless Río Tinto, polluted by centuries of mining in the area to the north. But penetrate this desolation, however, and you will find a surprisingly pleasant, friendly city, albeit without outstanding monuments.

The area around the city also has its fairshare of average, surrounded by some pleasant pastures, unremarkable villages and some reasonably interesting monuments to Christopher Colombus. However, there are two exceptions: one of Europe's best wetland reserves, Parque Nacional Coto Donaña, rivalled only by the Camargue and the Danube Delta, and the most beautiful section of the Sierra Morena, Sierra de Aracena.►► *For Sleeping, Eating and other listings, see pages 735-736.*

Ins and outs

Getting there The main bus company serving Huelva is Damas, Av de Portugal, T959256900. There are also small bus stations in Av de Italia, Av Alemania and Av Federico Molina. The Moorish-style train station is in Av de Italia on the southwest side of the town, T959266666; www.renfe.es.►► *For further details, see Transport page 736.*

Tourist information The provincial tourist office is located at① *Av de Alemania 14, T/F959257403, Mon-Fri 0900-1900, Sat 1000-1400.* There is also a municipal tourist office① *Plaza de las Monjas, Mon-Fri 1000-1400 and 1700-2000, Sat 1000-1400.*

Sights

Huelva is a port of some antiquity, having been founded by Phoenician traders over 3,000 years ago, when it was known as Onuba (its citizens are still known as *onubenses*). The Romans used it as a port for minerals, which they extracted from the Río Tinto mines to the north, as did the Moors who knew it as Guelbah. Much of the town was destroyed by the 1755 Lisbon earthquake.

Museo Provincial ① *Tue-Sat 0900-2000 (1800 winter), Sun 0900-1500, free,* some would say, is the only thing worth looking at in Huelva and it is certainly not to be missed. Housed in a pleasant modern building on Alameda Sundheim, the museum's ground floor consists of sections on archaeology and mining while the upper floor has a fine arts collection. The huge Roman water wheel in the entrance hall was found at the Río Tinto mines, one of a series used by slaves to raise water from flooded parts of the underground works. The archaeological section is excellent, with artefacts from the Bronze Age through to Moorish times. The displays devoted to mining are also outstanding, particularly the items of Roman origin.

There are one or two churches and convents of interest in Huelva. **Catedral de la Merced** dates from 1605 and was once a convent. **Iglesia de la Concepción** in Calle Concepción was first constructed in the 14th century, then rebuilt after the 1755 earthquake, retaining the richly decorated choir stalls. It also has paintings by Francisco de Zurburán. Of most interest, however, is the **Santuario de Nuestra Señora de la Cinta,** a simple white walled affair where Columbus is said to have prayed before setting out on his first voyage. To get here take bus No 6 from the Plaza de las Monjas.

Some 35 km along the coast is **Mazagón**, a more pleasant and low-key coastal resort than nearby **Matalascañas**. Mazagón has several *hostales*, campsites and a parador (T959536300, mazagon@parador.es), in case you wish to stay a night, as well as many excellent fish restaurants and tapas bars.

In the footsteps of Columbus

The area immediately east of Huelva has rich connections with **Christopher Columbus** and his quest to find the New World. At the narrow tip of land between the mouths of the Río Tinto and the Río Odiel, the **Punta del Sebo**, is the imposing monument to Columbus known as the **Spirit of Exploration**, completed by the American sculptor, Gertrude Whitney, in 1929. The caped figure stares resolutely out to sea, ignoring the towers of the petrochemical plant that provide a backdrop.

Monesterio de la Rábida

① *Guided tours (in Spanish) every 45 mins 1000-1300 and 1600-1815, at most stops there are plaques with brief comments in English, donations welcome.* Across the river, on a small hill, this Franciscan monastery was dedicated soon after the Reconquest. Columbus came here in 1491, after failing to gain royal approval for his plans. He met two friars, Antonio de Marchena and Juan Pérez (the latter having formerly been the Queen's confessor) and they took his case to court, gaining permission for his venture. Friars guide visitors around the complex. The church survived the 1755 earthquake and is in Gothic-Mudéjar style. Columbus' right-hand man, Martín Alonzo Pinzón, is buried here. There are many other commemorative objects relating to the voyages around the complex.

Muelle de las Carabelas

① *T959530597, winter Tue-Sat 1000-1700, summer Mon-Fri 1000-1400 and 1700-2100, Sun 1100-2000, €3, children €1.20.* Lying between the river and the bluff on which the monastery stands is the Muelle de las Carabelas. At this point, close to where Columbus's flotilla sailed in 1492, are accurate replicas of the *Niña*, the *Pinta* and the *Santa María* caravels, which were built for the 500th anniversary celebrations in 1992. The replicas, frighteningly small for such a voyage, give a realistic idea of the shipboard discomforts of the time. Lying along the jetty are artefacts from the age of Columbus, such as anchors and capstans, while at craft stalls artisans make rope and tar to the background noises of birds and animals from the Americas. There is a small museum and a restaurant with fine views out over the estuary.

Moguer → *Colour map 6, grid B1; Population: 13,749.*
Seven kilometres up river is the attractive town of Moguer, with its delightful square, Baroque mansions and a handful of convents. Moguer provided many of the crew members of the caravels and Columbus frequently visited the town. A tour of Moguer should certainly include the **Convento de Santa Clara** ① *guided tours only, every 30 mins, Tue-Sat 1100-1400 and 1700-2000, Sun 1700-2000, €1.50,* which was founded in the 14th century and surrounded by high walls and battlements. The convent's church is in Gothic-Mudéjar style and has a number of interesting features. Columbus often came to the convent and was in correspondence with the abbess, Doña Inés Enriquez. When he returned from his first voyage he spent a night in prayer here, fulfilling a vow he made on surviving a fearsome storm off the Azores. The convent is now a museum.

Moguer was also the birthplace of **Juan Ramón Jiménez** (1881-1958), the poet and winner of the Nobel Prize for Literature in 1956. The house in which he was born, Calle Jiménez 5, is now a museum to his memory, ① *€0.60.*

Parque Nacional Coto Doñana → *Colour map 6, grid B2.*

This superb national park consists of a variety of habitats; being above all a wetland, its largest habitats are the *marismas*, marshland which is inundated each winter and spring by the flood waters of the Río Guadalquivir. These various wetland habitats attract birds in huge numbers and more than 250 species have been recorded. ► *For Sleeping, Eating and other listings, see pages 735-736.*

Ins and outs

Getting there and around Large areas of the Coto Doñana have restricted access, but the official locations around the fringe of the reserve will satisfy all but the most fanatical birdwatchers. There is a 3-km trail with a series of hides overlooking a freshwater lake and marsh known as the Charco de la Boca. It is possible to book a

⦂ Under threat

Despite being one of only five national parks on mainland Spain and being designated a UNESCO Biosphere Reserve, the Coto Doñana has been under threat in recent years. Firstly, there have been several proposals for large-scale development in the park's surrounds, which would put extra demands on water supply, threatening the water table levels on the reserve. Locals in this impoverished region are understandably keen for anything that would bring more employment, and environmentalists equally understandably concerned to protect one of Europe's finest wetland habitats. A series of controversial clashes have dogged attempts at serious discussion of the issues at stake. A further threat to the Coto Doñana came in 1998 when a mining dam burst its banks releasing a flood of toxic chemicals into the Guadiamar River, which runs through part of the park. Considerable amounts of wildlife were killed, but the long-term damage is still difficult to assess.

bus tour of the reserve from El Acebuche (see below). These trips of three-hours leave twice a day at 0800 and 1500 or 1700, depending on the time of year, and cost e20. It's advisable to book well in advance. It is also possible to visit the southern edge of the reserve by boat from Sanlúcar and Sevilla.

Tourist information Centro de Visitantes or park's main visitors' centre (and the Coto Doñana headquarters) are at El Acebuche, 3 km north of Matalascañas and 12 km south of El Rocío on the A483 ① *T959448711, 0800-1900/2000/2100 depending on the time of year*. The centre has an audio visual room, an exhibition room, a restaurant and shop, which sells maps. There is a 5-km trail from the centre. La Rocina sub centre is located 500 m from El Rocío on the road to Matalascañas ① *T959442340, 0900-2100*, and has rooms for exhibitions and audio visual presentations.

Wildlife

Winter wildfowl from Northern Europe include some 60,000 grey lag geese and over 250,000 ducks and coots. Spring and autumn see much passing traffic of migrating wading birds such as godwit, ruffs, stints and sandpipers. It is the breeding birds in the spring and early summer that are the most spectacular. There are a number of large heronries with several types of heron and egret, Ibis, spoonbills, flamingoes, and storks are also common. The reed beds and scrub are alive with the calls of nightingales, cettis warblers, great reed warblers and savis warblers. The reeds are also the home of the purple gallinule – the emblem of the Coto Doñana. The sky is full of raptors, including red kites, booted eagles, short toed eagles and hundreds of black kites. There are an estimated 15 pairs of the rare Spanish imperial eagle nesting within the reserve. Mammals on show include mongoose, deer, boar and otters, and there are also some 25 pairs of the rare pardel lynx. Late February and mid May is the most rewarding time in terms of the maximum number of bird species. In summer, the *marismas* dry out, the heat is intense and the mosquitoes are out in force. Avoid the Whitsun *romería* at El Rocío (see below).

El Rocío

The centre of the Parque Nacional Coto Doñana is the remarkable town of El Rocío, which, with its sand-covered streets and houses with verandahs, looks like a set from a Wild West film. The town is the venue of the famous Whitsun *romería* to the sanctuary of the image of the Virgen del Rocío, held in the Iglesia de Nuestra Señora

lining up along the bridge and the *paseo* with their telescopes trained on the *marismas*. There is an information centre on Avenida Canaliega, T/F959443808, elrocio@infodonana.es.

Minas de Río Tinto → *Colour map 6, grid B6.*

① *Daily 1030-1500 and 1600-1900 (closed 1 Jan, 6 Jan and 25 Dec); €2.50. Corta Atalaya: Excellent guided tours in Spanish only are available from the Museo, 1200, 1300, 1400 and 1700 (also 1800 Apr-Oct), €2.45.*

Huge open-cast copper mines may not be everyone's cup of tea, but the sheer scale of the operations and the way the landscape has been desecrated has a certain horrific fascination and most people find the detour well worthwhile. Minerals have been extracted here since the time of the Phoenicians. The iron content of the rock has stained the waters and bed of the Río Tinto red and yellow and given it its name. The Romans deepened the mines in an effort to find silver, but this led to flooding problems, which were resolved by the use of a complicated system of slave-driven wheels to bring the water to the surface.

The **Museo Minero** is an absolute gem and has already established itself as one of the major theme museums in Andalucía. A superb geological section has display of fossils, rocks and minerals in abundance. The latest addition to the museum, opened in mid-2001, is a reproduction of a Roman mine. The most delightful exhibit is the Maharajah's railway carriage, which was built for Queen Victoria's visit to India. She never went and the carriage was sold to Río Tinto, who used it for the visit to the mines by King Alfonso XIII. There's almost no information in English, and the tours are in Spanish, but it's worthwhile even if you don't speak the language.

The museum is also the starting point for tours around the largest of Rio Tinto's five open-cast mines, Corta Atalaya, which at 1,200 m long, 900 m wide and 335 m deep, is Europe's largest open-cast copper mine. It is also one of the oldest, having been worked since Phoenician times. Standing on the edge of the mine is like peering down into a huge man-made volcano.

There is also a 22-km round trip taking two to three hours in a restored train dating from the early 20th century. The train travels along a refurbished line that follows the course of the Río Tinto towards Huelva.

Sierra de Aracena

Huelva contains the most beautiful part of the Sierra Morena, which forms the northern boundary of the province. It consists of wooded gently rolling hills, subdivided into a number of lesser sierras. The most scenic is the Sierra de Aracena. With a myriad of mule tracks linking the villages, this is also excellent walking country. ▸▸ *For Sleeping, Eating and other listings, see pages 735-736.*

Aracena → *Colour map 6, grid A2.*

An attractive market town set in the heart of the Sierras, Aracena makes a good base to explore the area. Dominating the town is the hill to the south capped with a church and a ruined **castle**. The view from the castle over the town is spectacular. The church, the **Iglesia de Nuestra Señora de los Dolores**, was built by the Knights Templar in the 13th century. The **Mudéjar tower** is decorated with brickwork reminiscent of Sevilla's Giralda. Inside are some elaborately carved alterpieces and fine ironwork doors. Dating from Moorish times, the castle above was built by the Portuguese on the remains of an Andalucían fortification.

Below the hill is **Plaza Alta**, a large cobbled sloping square around which most of Aracena's oldest buildings are located. Here is the excellent visitors' centre for the Parque Natural de la Sierra de Aracena ① *T/F959128825, winter 1000-1400, 1600-1800, summer 1800-2000.* It sells books and maps and has excellent premanent displays on all aspects of *serrano* life from food and fiestas to flora and fauna. The helpful staff speak some English. See also the useful website www.sierrade aracena.net, which details history, fiestas, walks, hotels, restaurants and more.

Gruta de las Maravillas → *Colour map 6, grid A2.*

① *T959128355, Plaza San Pedro, guided tours only (in Spanish), expect a wait in summer, €6.* Most people come to Aracena to see the Gruta de las Maravillas (the Cave of the Marvels), an impressive maze of 12 caves of over 2 km (half of which are open to the public) and six incredibly beautiful lakes that lie deep below the castle on the hill. Its stalagmites, pillars and organ pipes and tufa screens are lit with orange lighting giving them a somewhat surreal glow. The caves were discovered by a boy looking for a lost pig and were opened in 1914. The last of the caverns, known as the 'Chamber of Nudes', has some extraordinary rounded features resembling various parts of the human anatomy. If you fancy a dip after a hot day's hiking, try the municipal pool or the huge Embalse de Aracena a few kilometres out of town.

Around the sierra

There are many pretty villages to seek out, both for themselves and the walking options around. **Fuenteheridos** is named after its magnificent fountain, the Fuente de Doce Caños, or 12-piped fountain, situated in the plaza. There's not a great deal to see, but it makes a fairly peaceful base in the sierra, with a few good places to stay and a botanical garden to wander about just outside the village.

The village of **Castaño del Robledo** lies 4 km from Fuenteheridos along a beautiful road lined with the sweet chestnut trees that give the place its name. It seems not to have changed for centuries. One good reason to come here is for the walk to **Jabugo**, one of the Sierra's most beautiful. Leaving Castaño on the Fuenteheridos road, you go past a bar on your left and 100 m later is a track leading to a picnic area and a whitewashed shrine. The path starts to the right of the shrine, where there is post marked with two red arrows; take the wider track, to the left of the post. The trail goes through a shaded area, past a few fields of Iberian pigs snuffling around for acorns, before opening out with wonderful views across the sierra towards **Jabugo**.

Santa Ana la Real, one of the smallest villages in the Sierra, is perched on top of a hill with glorious views over the sierra. A good walk from here is to the waterfall at **Los Chorros de Ollarancos**; with a 50 m drop, this is the highest waterfall in the Sierra. To get there, walk out of Santa Ana on the Alájar road for 1 km and around the Km 17 sign, next to a bend in the road and a bridge, is a track to the Chorros.

It's not hard to see why **Alájar**, surrounded by olive and pine trees, has become increasingly popular over the last decade, with its narrow cobbled streets radiating from two small attractive plazas, perfect places to stop for wine and tapas. However, the village can also get very crowded on summer weekends.

Almonaster la Real is still dominated today by the 10th-century *mezquita*, or mosque, on the hill to the south of the town. If possible, time your visit to coincide with the **Fiesta de las Cruces de Mayo**, held during the first weekend in May and one of the best in Andalucía.

Other towns worth visiting in the Sierra include **Galaroza**, where the inhabitants soak each other with water every 6 September; **Cortegana**, with a dramatic hilltop setting under its castle (there's an excellent medieval fiesta here on the first weekend of August) and **Jabugo**, a famous centre for the production of *jamón serrano* ham. It's interesting to wander around the various piggy shops and curing places, but it's otherwise not a thrilling place.

● Sleeping

Huelva *p729*

Most of the *pensiones* are located in the area to the southeast of the attractive main square, Plaza de Monjas.

A Tartessos, Av Martín Alonzo Pinzón 13, T959282711, F959250617, is a centrally placed, comfortable modern option.

C Los Condes, Av Sundheim 14, T959282400, is another central option.

E Pensión Las Delicias, C Rascón 42, T959248392, has a pleasant patio and decent rooms.

F Calvo, C Rascón 33, T959249016, is basic but adequate and currently the cheapest place in town.

Parque Nacional Coto Doñana *p731*

Accommodation in El Rocío is scarce and impossible to find during the *romería*.

AL Puente del Rey, Av de la Canaliega s/n, El Rocío, T959442575, F959442070. Elegant, large new hotel close to the bridge, with pool and restaurant. Excursions arranged.

D Doñana Tour, Plaza Real 29, T959442468, El Rocío, 44 rooms.

D Isidro, Av los Ansares 59, El Rocío. 14 rooms, a/c.

F Las Marismas, C Baltasar III 4, El Rocío. 23 rooms.

The nearest campsite is **Rocío Playa**, Ctra Huelva-Matalascañas, Km 45, beachside, second category site.

Minas de Río Tinto *p733*

C Santa Bárbara, Cerro de los Embusteros, T959591852, sta.barb@teleline.es. Situated on the top of a hill with great panaramic view of Río Tinto and environs, is this newish upmarket hotel with comfy balconied rooms. For some strange reason the hotel's ostriches are made a feature.

E Hostal Los Cantos, Nucleo Residencial Los Cantos, left after **Hostal Galan**, T959591689. Basic and rather characterless a/c rooms with bath, above restaurant and bar.

Sierra de Aracena *p733*

Since the options are rather limited within Aracena, it's worth looking outside the town for something a bit different.

AL Finca Buen Vino, Km 95 on the

N433, Los Marines, T/F959124034, buenvino@facilnet.es. English-run farmhouse converted into an elegant and beautifully furnished guesthouse with 4 rooms, set in woodland 6 km west of Aracena. Fabulous views and outstanding food. Price includes breakfast and dinner. Recommended.

C Finca Valbono, Ctra de Carboneras, Km 1, T959127711, F959127576. Located 2 km from Aracena, Finca Valbono is a 20-ha farm with a luxurious 6-room hotel and 20 cottages to rent in a beautiful setting. Each cottage sleeps 3-5 and has a/c and TV. Horseriding, cycle hire, swimming pool, restaurant and volleyball court are some of the activities available.

C Los Castaños, Av de Huelva 5, Aracena, T959126300, F959126287. Reasonable but nothing special, with 33 comfortable rooms, garage, restaurant, a stone's throw from the caves. Not the quietest hotel; disco across the road can get a bit noisy late at night.

D La Posada, C Médico Emilio González 2, Alájar, T/F959125712, hotel.laposada@ navegalia.com, has 6 comfortable en-suite rooms, some with balcony. Horse riding, walking trips and mountain bike hire available amongst other tours.

E Casa Manolo, C Barbero 6, Aracena, T959128014. The only budget hotel in town. Central, some shared bath.

E Hostal Carballo, C La Fuente, Fuenteheridos, T/F959125108, hostalcarb allo@latinmail.com, is a small friendly hotel; the front rooms have a balcony overlooking a quiet cobbled street while the back ones, along with an upstairs terrace, have great views over the village rooftops and surrounding countryside.

Camping Aracena Sierra, Ctra Sevilla-Lisboa Km 83, T959501004. Just off the N433, 3 km from Aracena towards Sevilla, is this campsite, with some shaded areas, a pool and bar/restaurant. Next to it is a picnic and barbecue area.

● Eating

Huelva *p729*

For eating, head for the Plaza de las Monjas and the streets around. As Huelva is a fishing port it is no surprise that some good seafood is available.

€€ **Doñana**, Av Martín Alonso Pinzón 13, T959242773. Local seafood specialities include sardines with peppers, skate in paprika and clams in saffron sauce.
€ **Las Marismas**, C Padre Laraña 2, T959245272. Another good seafood spot with an economical menu.

Tapas bars and cafés

Try **Bar Berdigón** in C Berdigón, **Bar Agmanir** in C Carasa or **Marisquería Huelva** in C Cisneros – all have good seafood possibilities and local specialities.

Sierra de Aracena *p733*

The best eating options in Aracena are the tapas bars around the main plaza.
€€ **José Vicente**, Av Andalucía, Aracena, if you want to splash out, locally produced pork and ham at its best. Huge portions served in a/c and pampered comfort, but no fish or vegetarian options. A *menú* will set you back €15, but you won't need to eat for a week.

❶ Bars and clubs

Huelva *p729*

The liveliest scene is at Puerto Umbría in the summer, but in Huelva itself the best spot is **Alameda**, Alameda Sundheim.

✤ Festivals and events

Huelva *p729*

Late Jul-early Aug sees **Fiestas Colombinas**, the Columbus Festivals, which commemorate the departure of the caravels and is marked by bullfights, sports events and regattas.
On **8 Sep** is **Virgen de la Cinta**, the feast day of Huelva's patron saint.

▲ Activities and tours

Huelva *p729*

Football Real Club Recreativo de Huelva is the oldest club in Spanish football, founded when the sport was introduced to the area by British workers of the Rio Tinto mining company. The team struggles in the shadows of the 2 Sevillan giants, but made a surprise return to the Primera División in 2002; their stay is likely to be a brief one but has been a source of much pride to the little club. The football stadium is located in the north of the city, on Ctra de Sevilla.

❷ Transport

Huelva *p729*

There is a **boat** service between **Huelva** and the resort of **Punta Umbría** operating Jul-Sep between 0930 and 2130.
Daily **bus** services run to **Aracena** (2), **Ayamonte** (6), **Granada** (1), **Málaga** (1), **Matalascañas** (1) and **Sevilla** (12).
There are daily express **trains** from **Sevilla**, linking with the **Madrid** high speed AVE and other Andalucían regional centres. There are also 2 daily trains north to **Almonaster** and **Zufre**.

Sierra de Aracena *p733*

The sierra is 104 km north of Huelva and 89 km northwest of Sevilla.
Bus Many villages in the sierra are accessible by public transport, but because bus services are not always frequent, travelling by bus requires a certain amount of pre-planning. Two companies serve Aracena, **Damas** (for **Huelva**) and **Casal** (for **Seville** and **Aroche** via intermediate villages).

❶ Directory

Huelva *p729*

Internet Ciberforo, C Mackay y Macdonald 4.
Post Correos, Av Tomás Domínguez 1, T959249184.
Telephone No locutorios but plenty of cabins.

Sierra de Aracena *p733*

Internet Ar@NEt, Plaza de Abastos (in the market), T629118254. Friendly internet café/bar serving drinks and sandwiches, some outside seating, internet €2.75 per hr, open daily 1000-1500 (Sun 1200-1500), 1730-2400.

Jerez de la Frontera

→ *Colour map 6, grid C2; Population: 181,602.*

The name Jerez is synonymous with sherry and the town is famed for its numerous bodegas, which are all close to the town centre. These have mostly been taken over by multinational companies, but the sherry dynasties remain and continue to ape the British upper classes with their tweeds, polo horses and public school education. But Jerez has much more to offer: there are a number of historical monuments and museums, all within easy reach the town centre, while in the suburbs there is the world famous Equestrian School. It also has a sizeable gypsy population mainly living in the Barrio de Santiago and providing some of the most authentic flamenco in Andalucía. ►► *For details of Sleeping, Eating and other listings, see pages 739-742.*

Ins and outs

Getting there and around Conveniently the train and bus stations are close to each other a few blocks to the east of the city centre. Bus No 10 runs to the town centre. The airport is 7 km out of Jerez near the NIV and surprisingly there is no bus service to the city, so a taxi is needed and this will cost around €10. It is a compact city and so most of the sights can be visited on foot. ►► *For further details, see Transport page 742.*

Tourist information The municipal *turismo* ① *Plaza del Arenal s/n, T956355654 and C Larga 39, T956331150, F956331150, both open Mon-Fri 09301500 and 1630-1830 (1700-2000 summer), Sat/Sun 0900-1430.* They have a good range of brochures and maps. See also www.diariodejerez.com and www.jerez.org.

Background

The city was known as Ceret in Roman times, but renamed Scherish by the Moors. This later changed to Xeres and finally Jerez. The 'de la Frontera' element of the city's name, as with many other towns in the area, dates from around 1380 when it marked a Moorish frontier and also reflects the fact that Jerez changed hands numerous times during the course of the Reconquest.

The white, chalky soil in the area, known as *albariza*, has proved ideal for cultivating the Palomino grapes which produce the sherry for which Jerez has been famed for centuries, although, curiously, its vineyards are found many kilometres out of town. Many of the powerful sherry families were originally English, some having been involved in sherry production since the time of England's Henry VII. Today the town presents deep contrasts, with sterile high-rise suburbs and a fascinating ancient centre, with a close knit gypsy barrio and the upper-class villas of the sherry barons.

Sights → *Many tour companies combine a horse show with a bodega visit.*

Alcázar

① *May-Sep 1000-2000, Oct-Apr 1000-1800, €1.50 (extra for the camera obscura show).* Just to the south of the Plaza del Arenal is the Alcázar, which dates back to the 11th century; it was once the residence of the Caliphs of Sevilla. It has been heavily restored and consists mainly of walls and the 12th-century octagonal tower. The interior contains a mosque that was transformed into the Iglesia de Santa María la Real by Alfonso X when he recaptured the town. Within the grounds is the 18th-century Palacio de Villavicensio, which has a *camera obscura* show.

Catedral de San Salvador

ⓘ *1730-1800 during Mass*. Located on the Plaza de la Encarnación, the cathedral, although sited on a mosque, dates only from the 18th century and is baroque in style. Amongst its treasures are a 14th-century figure of Christ, *Cristo de la Viga* and Zurbarán's painting *La Virgen Niña* (Our Lady as a Child).

Bodegas

The buildings themselves are of considerable interest as each has a unique character. There is usually a demonstration by a vintner who dips a *venencia*, a silver cup on the end of a long pole, into a barrel and pours the sherry into the four glasses in his or her left hand without, of course, spilling a drop. Most sherry cellars offer guided tours and free tastings. It is best to phone beforehand as the largest *bodegas* may be fully booked with organized tours. The tourist office will supply a full list of bodegas. Be aware that some *bodegas* may close late August/early September when the grape harvest, or *vendimia*, takes place; a marvellous festival in itself.

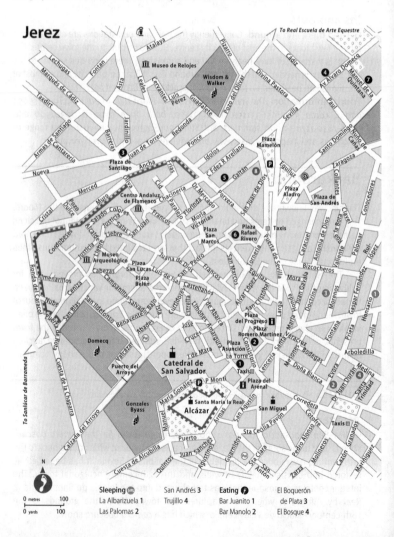

Jerez

Sleeping
La Albarizuela 1
Las Palomas 2
San Andrés 3
Trujillo 4

Eating
Bar Juanito 1
Bar Manolo 2
El Boquerón
de Plata 3
El Bosque 4

González Byass, ① *C Manuel María González, T956357016, www.gonzalez byass.es, 1-hr visits at 1100, 1200, 1300, 1400, 1700 and 1800 in Spanish, 1130, 1230, 1330, 1400, 1530, 1630 and 1730 in English (German and French tours also), €6,* conveniently located next to the Alcázar, is one of the largest *bodegas*. The tour used to feature a drunken mouse until he was devoured by a snake. There are now two equally inebriated replacement rodents.

Sandeman, ① *C Pizzaro 10, T956151700, www.sandeman.com, Mon-Fri 1030-1330, Sat Mar-Oct,* is one of the smaller bodegas and is highly recommended.

Museums

The museums are situated in the northwest of town. **Centro Andaluz de Flamenco**, ① *Mon-Fri 0900-1400, free,* has a collection of musical instruments and the offers the history of the art of flamenco, which *Jerezanos* claim began in their town. Video presentations are shown every hour on the hour; you can also watch videos from their archive of famous flamenco performers. **Museo del Vino** traces the history of sherry making, and the attractive **Museo Arqueológico** and the clock-filled **Museo de Relojes** are other museums that might appeal.

To Museo del Vino & Airport

Real Escuela de Arte Equestre

① *T956319635, www.realescuela.org, visits Mon, Wed and Fri 1000-1300, €6, OAPS, students and children €3; shows 1200 Thu and 1200 Tue Mar-Oct, from €12, students and OAPs €7.20.* The Royal Andalucían School of Equestrian Art is located in the Palace of the Cadenas, a 19th-century mansion built by Garnier, the architect of the Paris Opera. You can see training sessions and have a tour of the stables, an equestrian ballet is performed also by the Dancing Horses of Andalucía.

◉ Sleeping

Jerez de la Frontera *p737, map p738*
There are a number of luxury hotels in Jerez, and plenty of cheap *pensiones* near to the town centre, conveniently close to both the bus and train stations.
A La Albarizuela, C Honsario, 6, T956346862, F956346686. A brand spankingly new hotel, all white minimalism (a nod of respect for the white chalky soil known as *albariza,* natural Palomino grape habitat) with friendly management and interestingly shaped, light and airy rooms.
B Trujillo, C Medina, 36, T956342438. A more unusual hotel in a late 18th-century building with Moorish-style staircase and carved wooden ceilings. A bit crumbly, but

Gaitán **5**
La Abacería **6**
La Mesa Redonda **7**

Bars & clubs ⚫
La Cubatería **8**

Of Sherry and other Andalucían nobles

James Bond Pity about your liver, sir. Unusually fine Solera. '51, I believe.
M There is no year for sherry, 007.
Diamonds Are Forever

Sherry wines are produced in the area around Jerez de la Frontera, from which their English name derives. The region has a long winemaking history; the wines of Jerez were popular in Britain long before Shakespeare wrote about Falstaff putting away quarts of 'sack' to drown his sorrows or keep out the cold. The country is still the biggest consumer, and there's a distinctly British air to the region's wine-making culture.

The two principal grapes used for the production of sherry wines are the white Palomino Fino (the majority) and Pedro Ximénez. The region's soils have a massive influence on the final product; the chalky albariza tends to produce the finest grapes.

There are two principal styles of sherry, but no decision is taken on which will be produced from each cask's contents until a couple of months after the vintage. This decision is taken by the head *capataz* (cellarperson), who tastes the wines, which are poured using the distinctive long-handled *venencia*, designed so as not to disturb the yeast on the wine's surface.

Those destined to become rich, nutty, **olorosos** are fortified to about 18% to prevent yeast growth; these wines are destined for aging and may later be sweetened and coloured to produce styles such as cream or amoroso. The best olorosos may be aged 25 years or more.

Finos, on the other hand, are fortified to a lower level and nurtured so as to try and optimize the growth of the naturally occurring local yeast, flor. This produces a wine which is pale and dry, with a very distinctive clean finish, a perfect tapas accompaniment. **Manzanillas** are finos that have been aged in the seaside environment of Sanlúcar de Barrameda; the salty tang is perceptible. **Amontillados** are finos aged longer than normal so that some oxidation occurs after the protective layer of yeast has died away. Some of these are sweetened for the British market.

Another curiosity of sherry production is the use of the solera. This is a system of connected barrels designed to ensure the wine produced is consistent from one year to the next. The wine is bottled from the oldest barrels, which are in turn refilled from the next oldest, until the last are filled with the new wine. While the wine produced has no vintage date, the age of the solera is a matter of pride, and there are many around that are well over a century old.

Other similar Andalucían wines are **Montilla**, from Córdoba Province. Much like a sherry in style, the difference lies in the fact that they are rarely fortified. Málaga wines are fortified and mainly sweet; those from the highest grade, lágrima, is pressed using only the weight of the grapes and can be very good indeed.

Also made in Jerez, and also a common girl's name, is **brandy**. Although connoisseurs of French brandies usually sniff at the oaky nature of these Marlons, there are some good ones produced, and even the cheaper varieties are rarely bad. The spirit is produced using sherry casks, and the same solera system is employed.

with considerably more character than most of the hotels in Jerez. A very good deal in low season (**D**).

E San Andrés, C Morenos 12 y 14, T956340983. Undoubtedly the best option in this price range, this is a delightful place to stay, with balconied rooms, a beautiful tiled tropical courtyard and garden that is the owner's pride and joy.

F Las Palomas, C Higueras 17, T956343773. Quiet location, cheap, but not too friendly.

🍴 Eating

Jerez de la Frontera *p, map p738*
As in nearby El Puerto, it is the local habit to buy fresh fish and shellfish from *freidurías* and *marisquerías* and take them to a bar to eat with a drink. One of the most popular *freidurías* is **El Boquerón de Plata**, Plaza de Santiago.

€€ **El Bosque**, Av Alvaro Domecq, T956303333. Traditional Andalucían specialities served in this popular Jerez restaurant.

€€ **Gaitán**, C Gaitán 3, T956345859. Modern and traditional cuisine, with especially good seafood, this is another classic place, popular with locals; closed Sun.

€€ **La Mesa Redonda**, C Manuel de la Quintana 3, T956340069. More local cuisine in an established and traditional Jerez restaurant which has gained a well-deserved reputation for itself. Well worth the few extra ¤s you will have to shell out for it.

Tapas bars and cafés
There are a multitude of tapas bars to choose from, with the local fino the obvious accompaniment.

Bar Juanito, C Pescadería Vieja 4 (just off the Plaza del Arenal), a great introduction to Jerez. If you arrive at lunchtime head straight for this bar and your first impressions of Jerez will never leave you. Delicious *carne* and *jamón* dishes as well as *gambas*.

Bar Manolo, C Consistorio 6, is a friendly uncomplicated sort of place to enjoy a *fino* and a tapa.

La Abacería, Plaza Rafael Rivero s/n, is another gem, where you can sit outside at lunchtime in a pretty square and eat *boquerones con pimiento* (anchovies with pepper), delicious patés and *tostados* and sip

a decent *fino* or beer. In the evening it is a lively meeting place for young locals.

🍸 Bars and clubs

Jerez de la Frontera *p, map p738*
Much of the club nightlife of Jerez goes on in the area around and to the north of the bullring, especially C Nuño de Cañas. Another place worth a shout is the low key **La Cubatería**, Plaza Mamelón 9, a small, slick looking bar with a down-to -earth owner who enjoys a chat.

🎭 Entertainment

For flamenco, go to the Barrio Santiago and **La Taberna Flamenca**, C Angostillo de Santiago 3, which is a reasonable place to start. Performances here are highly regarded, but it is a considerably less spontaenous affair than you may find elsewhere in this district. For the real thing, try the *peñas* (flamenco clubs) of **Peña la Buena Gente**, C Lucas 9; **Peña Antonio Chacon**, C Salas 2; or **El Laga de Tío Parilla**, Plaza del Mercado.

🎉 Festivals and events

Jerez de la Frontera *p, map p738*
In **May** is **Feria del Caballo**. This impressive horse fair has races, shows and competitions featuring the locally bred Cartuja horses and 17th-century traditions.

The week before 24 **Aug** sees **Fiesta de la Vendimia**. This is the celebration and blessing of the grape harvest.

In **Sep**, during the first fortnight, is the **Fiesta de la Bulería**, a festival of song and dance. The month ends with the feast day of the patron saint of Jerez, **La Virgen de la Merced**.

🛍 Shopping

Jerez de la Frontera *p, map p738*
The *fino* and brandy for which the town is renowned can be bought direct from the *bodegas* (see above) or from supermarkets, alternatively go to the specialist sherry shop, **La Casa Del Jerez**, C Divina Pastora, 1, opposite the Escuela de Arte Equestre, T956335184, where you can sample before you buy.

☺ Transport

Air The airport, T956150083, is 7 km east of Jerez near the NIV. **Iberia**, T956150009, flies to **Madrid** and **Barcelona** and **Ryanair**, flies to Stansted, UK.
Bus The bus station is on C Cartuja, 1 km from the centre, T956345207. Buses go to **Cádiz** hourly between 0700-2200 Mon-Fri, with 9 buses a day on Sat and Sun; **El Puerto de Santa María** (12 daily); **Ronda** (4 daily); **Málaga** (1530). There are also buses to to **Sanlúcar de Barrameda** (30 mins) and 18 daily to Sevilla (1-hr). **Los Amarillos**, T956347844, go to **Arcos de la Frontera** and **Ubrique**.

Car Hire available at the airport: **Atesa** T956150014; **Avis** T956150005; **Europcar** T956150060; **Hertz** T56150038.
Train The station is southeast of the bus station, at Plaza de la Estación, C Cartuja, T956342319. There are frequent trains to **Cádiz** and **Sevilla**.

❶ Directory

Jerez de la Frontera *p, map p738*
Internet **Kerenet**, C Zaragoza, T956348598. Cheap.
Post Correos, C Veracruz, off C Santa María. Mon-Fri 0800-2100, Sat 0900-1400, T956349295.

Pueblos Blancos and Parque Natural Sierra de Grazalema

'Oh, white walls of Spain!' wrote Federico García Lorca in one of his deeply felt poems, presenting this colour as one of the most personal characteristics of the popular architecture of Spain. Andalucía typifies this architecture and the classic pueblo blanco *– more like a village than a town – is best seen in the triangle of land between Málaga, Sevilla and Algeciras including Ronda (see page 762). The area is firmly given over to tourism but despite this, the* pueblos blancos *have managed to retain their Moorish character and the Grazalema park offers some excellent walking.* ▶▶ *For Sleeping, Eating and other listings, see pages 744-745.*

Ins and outs

All the villages below are serviced by Los Amarillos buses. There are services from Jerez, Cádiz, Sevilla, Ronda, Málaga and between each village. More frequent services are from Jerez and Cádiz; between villages, buses are sometimes only once daily and not on Sun. ▶▶ *For further details, see Transport page 745.*

Arcos de la Frontera → *Colour map 6, grid C5; Population: 27,897.*

Arcos, the most westerly of the *pueblos blancos*, has an unrivalled position sitting on a long ridge above a steep limestone cliff dropping down to the Río Guadalete. There is a sprawl of white houses, comparing dramatically with the brown sandstone of the castle and the churches. The town goes back to Roman times, when it was known as Arco Briga, but it was during the Moorish occupation that it began to assume importance.

The **Barrio Antiguo** or old part of the town is a maze of narrow streets that retain their Moorish pattern and is more suitable for donkeys than cars. The centre of the old quarter is the Plaza del Cabildo, with a mirador looking out over the cliff to the rolling countryside to the south. On the west side of the square is the 11th-century **Castillo** established by the Ben Jazrum Dynasty and now privately owned and closed to the public. Also in the square is the **Iglesia de Santa María de la Asunción** ① *1000-1300*

66 99 Grazalema has a remarkable micro-climate. Just 8 km from the town, villages receive just a quarter of the rainfall.

and 1600-1900, €0.90. It was built on the site of a mosque in Gothic-Mudéjar style. The original belltower fell during the 1755 Lisbon earthquake and the replacement was never completed, giving a certain asymmetry to the overall effect. The Plateresque south side is impressive. The interior is rather dismal, although the magnificent choir stalls carved in a variety of woods by Roldán should not be missed.

It is well worth being in town for a fiesta, Holy Week is impressive as the **Feria de San Miguel.**➤➤ *For further details, see page 745.*

Ubrique → *Colour map 6, grid C5; Population: 17,960.*

Some 12 km south of the A372 on the A374 this white town spreads along the valley of the Río Ubrique. Ubrique is a friendly, urban base for exploring the Sierra de Grazalema. With its thriving traditional leather industry, the town has a busy working community and less of a boutique feel than some of the villages in the area. The **Castillo de Fátima** is Ubrique's only remnant of its Moorish past. The **Casco Antiguo**, or old town, is mainly 18th century, but there are some interesting examples of 16th- and 17th-century Christian architecture in the churches of **Jesús** and **San Juan de Letrán**. In the 19th century the town, prospering as a result of its newfound wealth from the fledgling leather industry, expanded down towards the river, where you will find most of the shops and **leather factories**. At the helpful and informative tourist office ⓘ *Av Dr Solís Pascual 19, T956464900, www.ayuntamientoubrique.es,* you can arrange guided visits to Occuris or the leather factories for €4.25.

Parque Natural Sierra de Grazalema → *Colour map 6, grid C5;*
Population: 2,256; Altitude: 823 m.

The gem of all the *pueblos blancos*, **Grazalema** is notorious as the wettest location in Spain. The rain ensures lush vegetation throughout the year. It is the main centre for the Parque Natural Sierra de Grazalema, a UNESCO biosphere reserve which supports a wide range of birds, flowers, and mammals.The traditional industry in Grazalema is the making of blankets and ponchos (they are even exported to Argentina) and woodwork. The British sociologist Pitt-Rivers wrote a classic study of the town called *People of the Sierra*. The village has become an important tourist centre over the last decade and many come to walk in the park and explore the varied flora and fauna, especially during summer. But with its two beautiful 17th-century churches, cottage industry and sensitive development, the town still has a strong community feel about it and makes an excellent base for visiting the park.

Ins and outs
Best time to visit Grazalema receives more rainfall per square inch than anywhere else in Spain. Don't let this put you off coming to walk. The rainfall is markedly seasonal – November, April and May tend to be the wettest months – and at other times of the year the chances are that of the weather will be good.

Tourist information The park representative ⓘ *C Piedras 11, T956132225, Tue-Sun 1000-1400 and 1600-1900 (winter), 1800-2000 (summer),* issues permits for the

restricted areas of the park and has a map of the park explaining the various walking routes from the town. There's a good range of walking information; the tourist office stocks an excellent 1:50000 map of the area.

Walks

The area around Grazalema and Ronda offers some of the most beautiful and varied walking in Spain. In spite of this – with the exception of holidays – you'll meet with few walkers and it's not unusual to spend a whole day in the hills without meeting another soul. The terrain is extraordinarily varied. Jagged formations of karst give way to poplar-lined valleys, thick stands of cork and evergreen oaks alternate with old groves of olives and almonds and with fields of wheat and barley.

Grazalema to Benaocáz via El Salto del Cabrero Distance 11-14 km; Time 4-4½ to 5½-6½ hours; Difficulty medium (short route) – medium/difficult (long route).
This is one of the Sierra's most beautiful walks. There are constant changes of terrain, great views to the west across the rolling countryside that leads down towards Jerez, and on clear days, to the Atlantic. You'll have a steep climb first thing if you leave from Grazalema (longer route) but you can avoid this by taking a taxi up to the Puerto del Boyar (call Rafael at the Casa de las Piedras, T956132014). Due to its popularity this walk is best undertaken on a weekday. Get going by 0930 to allow plenty of time for stops and a picnic along the way and to make the 1540 bus from Benaocáz back to Grazalema (Monday-Saturday). You could have a late lunch in Benaocáz. Beautiful stands of ancient oaks, interesting karst formations, exceptional flora and plentiful birds of prey make this an exceptionally varied excursion.

Sendero de la Garganta Verde Allow approximately four to five hours from the road for a round trip; only 30 people are allowed access at any one time.
Near the pleasant village of Zahara, north of Grazalema, is another excellent walk: the restricted Sendero de la Garganta Verde, starting 3 km from Zahara up the road to Grazalema. Within minutes of leaving the car park you enter a pristine, almost prehistoric, valley with no sign of human interference. After about 30 minutes of gentle walking the path descends rapidly, passing a cliff where you can see vultures nesting , into a canyon with sheer rock faces rising above, up to 400 m in some areas. The air becomes cooler as you follow the old river bed filled with huge boulders and unusual rock formations and descend deeper into the canyon. The route becomes slightly more hazardous at this point as you are required to clamber over rocks to a large cave called the Cueva de la Pileta. It is well worth the effort; the cave is made of an unusual pink rock with stalagmites and stalactites and is some 30 m high and approximately 75 m wide. Rock climbing equipment and a special permit are required to continue beyond this point as the route along the canyon becomes increasingly steep. The return journey is almost entirely uphill.

● Sleeping

Arcos de la Frontera *p742*
AL Parador Casa de Corregidor, Plaza del Cabildo s/n, T956700500, F956701116. The usual comfort you'd expect from a parador. Attractive, light and airy rooms with terrace-balconies with spectacular views over the cultivated, fertile plain below. A good but expensive restaurant.

B Cortijo Faín, Ctra de Algar, Km 3, T/F956701167. A small luxury alternative on the southeast outskirts of the town, in a converted 17th-century *cortijo*.
C El Convento, C Maldonado 2, T956702333. Atmospheric option in the old 17th-century convent at the back of the parador. 8 rooms.
E Callejón de las Monjas, C Deán Espinosa 4, T956702302. A simple and cosy *pensión* with 8 rooms in the centre of the old town.

● *For an explanation of sleeping and eating price codes used in this guide, see inside the*
● *front cover. Other relevant information is found in Essentials, see pages 47-56.*

Ubrique p743

E Pensión Rosario, C José Antonio Primo de Rivera 3, T956461046. Small *hostal* with basic double rooms in the old town up the hill near the main plaza – definitely the best option in terms of location.

Parque Natural Sierra de Grazalema and Grazalema p743

AL Puerta de la Villa, Plaza Pequeña 8, Grazalema, T956132376, F956132087. A large, swish, modern hotel that has recently appeared and seems out of place with its surroundings, although it's very comfortable and luxurious. An expensive restaurant serves hearty mountain fare and the bizarre sounding 'frugal octopus salad'.

C El Tejar, Montecorto, T/F952184053. If you're wheeled, this is a top base from which to explore the park. Picnics can be prepared and the owners have unparalleled knowledge of local walks and are well used to walkers. They also have 4 horses.

C Peñon Grande, Plaza Pequeña 7, Grazalema, T956132434, F956132435. A modern hotel built in keeping with the village architecture. Rooms, although not huge, have pretty views of main square and church or the sierra. A good mid-range option with restaurant.

D Marqués de la Sierra, C San Juan, 3, T/F956123061. An old, refurbished, family run inn. If you fancy staying in Zahara (and there's every reason to).

E Casa de las Piedras, C Las Piedras 32, Grazalema, T956132014. Pleasant family run hotel with a relaxed atmosphere, restaurant and a pretty courtyard at the heart of Grazalema. Good value: no-frills place, rooms have tiny shower rooms but are comfortable.

F Los Tadeos, Paseo la Fuente, T956123086, basic rooms in a small *hostal* with bar and restaurant. Also in Zahara, a good option.

Tajo Rodillo, Ctra C344 Km 49 (follow C Las Piedras to the end), T956132063. Camping costing €5.75 for 2 adults and car.

❶ Eating

Arcos de la Frontera p742

To splash out on a meal, try **El Convento**, C Marqués de Torresoto 7, the classy but low key restaurant of the hotel of the same name, local game dishes a speciality.

Los Faraones, C Debajo del Corral, T956700612, is a genuine Turkish restaurant with regular belly dancers to aid the digestion; *menú del día* €8.

Ubrique p743

€€ Casa Juan, Av de España 28B, in the new town, T956464077, a good place for a feed, an old fashioned and established unpretentious restaurant serving good grilled meat and *revueltos*.

Parque Natural Sierra de Grazalema and Grazalema p743

Several *bares de copas* on and near the main square serving basic tapas (try the goats' cheese in the spring and early summer).

€€ El Pinsapar, C Doctor Mateos Gago, Grazalema. A decent wine list to go with a simple, mid-ranged priced menu on which grilled trout is a good option.

€ Circulo de la Unión, Grazalema, a more modern saloon-type bar (with wide-screen TV) which gets lively with hikers needing a beer after a hard day's walking.

❸ Festivals and events

Arcos de la Frontera p742

The Holy Week processions are impressive and the floats have to be specially customized to negotiate the narrow streets. On 29 Sep is the Feria de San Miguel, when fighting bulls rampage through the streets. The locals run before them, dodging into doorways and jumping up on street signs and balconies to evade the horns.

❍ Shopping

Ubrique p743

Editorial Tréveris, C San Sebastián, T956463370, www.treveris.es. A multimedia, book and map shop, they sell large-scale maps of the area. Also a mine of information generally about the area. Internet access in addition (€0.5 for 15 mins).

❸ Transport

Arcos de la Frontera p742

Comes **buses** run regularly to **Cádiz**, **Jerez** and **Ronda**. The bus station is in the newer part of the town, in C Corregidores.

Cádiz and around

→ *Colour map 6, grid C3; Population: 143,129.*

With a proud and long maritime history stretching back to the Phoenicians, it comes as no surprise that Cádiz can seem less conservative and more outward looking than many Andalucían cities; geographically it's not far off being an island, and culturally it's typified by its riotous Carnaval. Earthquakes and buccaneering have deprived it of a significant collection of monuments, but it's a very likeable place with the sea seemingly at the end of every narrow street.

The area north of Cádiz as far as the estuary of the Río Guadalquivir consists of rolling farmland given over largely to the production of grapes. Along the attractive coastline are a series of fishing ports and holiday resorts, the latter being very popular with Sevillanos, many of whom own villas along the shore.

South from Cádiz along the Atlantic coast is known as the Costa de la Luz and remains mercifully underdeveloped, containing fine beaches, flower-strewn meadows, salt flats, rolling farmland, mountains and a number of small, but fascinating villages. It's by far the nicest part of the Andalucian coast. ▸▸ *For details of Sleeping, Eating and other listings, see pages 751-754.*

Ins and outs

Getting there and around The two main bus companies are Comes and Los Amallosri, both of whose stations are conveniently centred in the old part of the city. The train station is close to the entrance of the old part of the town. Fortunately, all the worthwhile features of Cádiz are contained within a very small area of the old part of the city and most can easily be covered on foot. Transport connections with attractions along the coast, both north and south, of the city are good. ▸▸ *For further details, see Transport page 753.*

Tourist information The tourist office① *Av Ramón de Carranza, near Plaza San Juan de Dios, www.infocadiz.com, Tue-Fri 0900-1900; Mon and Sat 0900-1400, 1700-2000.*

History

Cádiz has a long and fascinating history, claiming to be the oldest continuously occupied urban settlement in Western Europe. In Phoenician times it was known as Gadir, the port exporting minerals from the interior. Its strategic position also attracted the Romans, who called it Gades (the inhabitants of Cádiz are still known as *Gaditanos*) and Julius Caesar was given his first public office here. The Moors, whilst occupying the area, were not great seafarers, and there followed a period of decline until the 16th century when Spain became an important maritime power. With the colonization of the Americas Cádiz was ideally placed to benefit and when the river to Sevilla began to silt up, it became a great sea port once again. This strategic importance inevitably attracted the attentions of rival seafaring nations such as England, France and Holland, who regularly came to sack, pillage and "singe the King of Spain's beard", as Sir Francis Drake supposedly did. Much of the wealth from the Americas ended up in Cádiz, and a large area of the older part of the city, including the cathedral, dates from the 18th century. In the early part of the 19th century, during the Peninsular War, some of the radical citizens of Cádiz set up the first Spanish Parliament or Cortés. It was shortlived, but was the blueprint for the Spanish democracy of today, which ironically took more than 150 years to evolve.

Sights

Catedral

① T956259812, Tue to Fri 1000-1400 and 1630-1930, Sat-Sun 1000-1300, €3, free Wed and Fri 1900-2000,Sun 1100-1300. Known officially as the **Catedral Nueva** because it replaced the earlier Cathedral of Santa Cruz, which was largely destroyed by fire in 1596, it was begun in Gothic style in 1722. It was not until 1853, however, that it was finally completed, with the construction of the two towers at the western end. The 'gold' dome is in fact composed of yellow glazed tiles. The interior is plain and rather severe but well lit and lacking in the ornate gilding of many Andalucían cathedrals. The carved cedar **choir** stalls are the highlight. Many of the side chapels contain impressive images by the sculptor Ignacio Vergara, while a glance towards the roof will show areas of wire netting – the limestone has been affected by the salt air and

❧ *The city's most prominent landmark, the cathedral, is best viewed from the shore to the south where the gold dome contrasts with a row of colour-washed houses.*

pieces of the rock have been known to fall on worshippers. The museum is dominated by a 3-m high silver monstrance, said to contain a million jewels. Steps from the Presbytery lead down to the circular crypt, which holds the tomb of Manuel de Falla, the composer, born in Cádiz in 1870.

Museo de Cádiz

① Wed-Sat 0900-2000, Tue 1430-2000, Sun 0930-1430, free with EU passport otherwise €1.50. One of the best museums in Andalucía, housed in a restored mansion in the Plaza de Mina, this fine arts and archaeological museum has excellent lighting and information. Its ground floor has a magnificent collection of archaeological remains from the Cádiz region. There are some significant Phoenician artefacts from the necropolis at Gadir, but it is the Roman rooms which are absolutely outstanding. The fine arts collection is on the first floor, where the most important paintings are the 18 by Zurbarán, including a series of panels from the Carthusian monastery at Cartuja, near Jerez. The faces of the saints were painted from monks whom Zurbarán had met. Also here is Murillo's *Los Desposorios de Santa Catalina*, his last work; he fell to his death from scaffolding and the painting was completed by a pupil.

Torre Tavira

① C Marqués del Real Tesoro 10, T956212910, Jun-Sep, 1000-2000, Sep-Jun 1000-1800, €3.50. This tower, the tallest of over 60 watchtowers in Cádiz, is built in baroque style and was part of the Palace of the Marquis of Recano, whose first watchman, Antonio Tavira, gave it its name. In 1778, this tower was appointed the official watchtower for the town. Today, above the reception area, there are two exhibition halls. Well worth a visit is the camera obscura room, where a moving image of the spectacular rooftop view of the city is projected.

Playa de la Caleta and Playa de la Victoria

The north side of the town borders the harbour, but the full length of the south side of the town consists of Atlantic beaches. The original town beach is the Playa de la Caleta, which is tightly sandwiched between the ruined defensive castles of Santa Catalina and San Sebastián, and backed by two enormous fig trees, but this is really a beach only in name. Most *gaditanos* prefer to use the longer Playa de la Victoria, which extends the full length of the newer part of the city. It has plenty of sports facilities, beach bars, hotels, apartments and restaurants and can get very crowded in the summer.

Andalucía Cádiz & around

La Isla de León

In the bay just north of Cádiz, the peninsula town of La Isla de León is an interesting excursion; it's most famous for having been the home of one of the greatest of flamenco artists, Camarón "de la Isla".

Around Cádiz

El Puerto de Santa María → *Colour map 6, grid C2; Population: 73,728.*

Immediately across the Bahía de Cádiz is El Puerto de Santa María. A likeable place, this was the port from which Columbus's flagship the *Santa María* came. One of the

Cádiz

Bahía de Cádiz

N

0 metres 100
0 yards 100

Sleeping 🛏
Cuatro Naciones **1** *B5*
Francia y París **2** *A3*
Hostal Carlos I **3** *B6*

Hostal Colón **4** *C4*
Hostal del Duque **5** *B3*
Hostal Fantoni **6** *B5*
Parador Atlántico **7** *B1*

Pensión Bahía **8** *B5*
Quo Qádis **9** *C2*

three towns making up the so-called sherry triangle, it is also a fishing and
commercial port as well as being a resort, with some good beaches nearby.

There are few outstanding sights; look for the superb southern façade of the
Iglesia de San Francisco in Plateresque style, and check out the 13th-century **Castillo
San Marcos**. Familiar sights in El Puerto are the huge **sherry warehouses** lining the
riverfront. It is possible to visit some of the *bodegas* by reserving first ① *C Toneleros
sin número, T95685700/956855211, open for visits between 0900-1300 Mon-Fri, €3.*

The tourist office ① *C Luna 22, T956542413, summer 1000-1400 and 1800-2000
and winter 1730-1930*, runs free guided tours of the town at 1100 on Tuesday and
Saturday in summer and on Saturday only in winter.

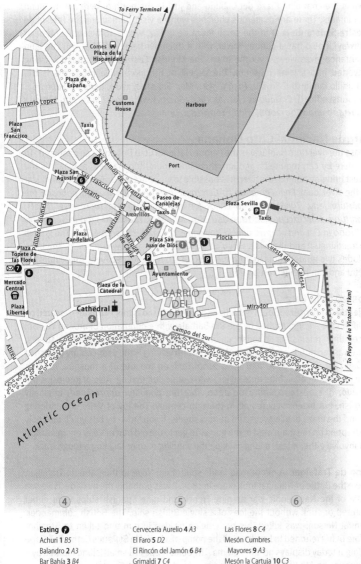

Eating 🍴

Achuri **1** *B5*
Balandro **2** *A3*
Bar Bahía **3** *B4*

Cervecería Aurelio **4** *A3*
El Faro **5** *D2*
El Rincón del Jamón **6** *B4*
Grimaldi **7** *C4*

Las Flores **8** *C4*
Mesón Cumbres
  Mayores **9** *A3*
Mesón la Cartuja **10** *C3*

The road, with its accompanying railway line, now runs along the estuary of the Río Guadalquivir to the town of Sanlúcar de Barrameda, the third point of the so-called sherry triangle, specializing in *manzanilla*; an excellent dry style given a salty tang by the sea breezes. Sanlúcar has Roman origins and the Moors built a defensive fort here, while later under the Christians it became an important port. Columbus left here on his second Atlantic crossing and it was Magellan's last port of call before his attempt to circumnavigate the world.

The town is divided into the older **Barrio Alto**, occupying the higher ground and containing most of the monuments, and the newer **Barrio Bajo** towards the river, the two being linked by a tree lined avenue, the Calzada de Ejército. The centre of the old town is the charming **Plaza del Cabildo** and just to the north of here are the main monuments. There are numerous churches worth a visit, particularly the **Iglesia de Nuestra Señora de la O** in the small Plaza de la Paz, with a 16th-century Mudéjar doorway. It also has a curious tower, with a three-tier belfry, which if you can gain admittance gives views over the town. The Moorish **Castillo de Santiago** is being converted into a wine museum. The largest of the *manzanilla* producers is the Barbadillo family ① *C Sevilla, T956385521, Mon-Sat 1200, 1300, tours available, €3.* The tourist office ① *Calzada de Ejército, T956366110, www.aytosanlucar.org, summer 1000-1400 and 1800-2000, winter 1600-1830.*

Parque Nacional Coto Doñana

Across the river from Sanlúcar is the Parque Nacional Coto Doñana (see page 731). To get there by car, requires a 150 km, three-hour round trip via Sevilla, which is the lowest bridging point of the river. It is possible to visit the Coto Doñana from Sanlúcar on the river boat *Real Fernando* ① *Centro de Interpretación located opposite the departure jetty, T956363813 to check for any changes and to reserve tickets, departures daily except Mon 1000 and 1600 Mar-May, 1000 and 1700 in Sep, 1000 and 1600 in Oct and at 1000 only in Nov and Feb €13.25, children €6.25.* The guides are multilingual and there is a video on the Coto Doñana shown on board. The price includes two guided tours around the park; of 1½ hour, respectively. Binoculars are useful and can be hired on board.

Costa de la Luz

Vejer de la Frontera South of Cádiz and slightly inland is this hill village, located on a cliff above a gorge eroded by the Río Barbate with a population of around 12,700. It certainly retains its Moorish character, with its labyrinth of narrow streets, whitewashed patios and a ruined Alcázar. Worth visiting is the 13th-century **Church of El Salvador** ① *1100-1300 and 1900-2100.* Built on the site of a mosque, it has a strange mixture of architectural styles, with Gothic dominating. Also of interest is the **Castillo,** ① *1100-1400 and 1700-2200, free but donation appreciated,* originally Moorish, but extensively rebuilt in the 15th century. The joy of Vejer is wandering around the maze of alleyways and narrow streets. If you arrive by bus you'll probably be dropped on the main road in the gorge. To get to the old part of Vejer on the clifftop will involve either a taxi, a long walk up the winding road or tackling a rough track.

Cabo de Trafalgar A minor road leads south from Vejer to the Cabo de Trafalgar, where the Battle of Trafalgar took place in 1805. It was probably the most decisive sea battle of the Napoleonic war as nine French and nine Spanish ships were either captured or sunk without the loss of a single British ship. The British commander, Admiral Nelson, was killed, his body being pickled in rum and taken to Gibraltar before being returned to London and the pomp of a burial in St Paul's Cathedral. Cape Trafalgar today displays no such drama. The actual cape is a small island marked by a lighthouse and linked to the mainland by a road along a sandy spit.

Zahara de los Atunes One of the most interesting little stops on the coast is Zahara de los Atunes, a sunny village blessed with an excellent sandy beach. The place name literally means 'Blossom of the Tuna Fish' and the village is part of this coast's important tuna fishing industry; the annual ambush of the massive migrating fish is a spectacular, bloody, and hazardous endeavour. The Almadabra is the town's major landmark; it's the massive fish market.

Playa de los Lances Approaching Tarifa, the coastal road nears the beach. This is the Playa de los Lances, the best of the many fine sandy beaches along the Costa de la Luz. It is highly popular with windsurfers, but the same wind which makes this sport so thrilling here also means that anyone just wanting to loaf around on the beach will have to put up with an element of sand blasting.

● Sleeping

Cádiz *p746, map 748*
You need to book well in advance for accommodation during Carnaval in Feb. The most characterful accommodations are the *pensiones* of the old town, but the quality varies significantly; make sure you see the room first. Keep an eye out for *camas* (beds) signs in windows; these can be a real bargain.
AL **Parador Atlántico**, Av Duque de Nájera 9, T956223908, www.parador.es. Located at the point of the isthmus, this modern, rather squat concrete block has great views over the Atlantic and the Bahía de Cádiz, but its rooms are pretty soulless.
B **Francia y Paris**, Plaza San Francisco 2, T9562223498, F956222431. Characterful hotel in charming square in a quiet, old part of city. A more stylish option than the more expensive 'luxury' places.
C **Pensión Bahía**, C Plocia 5, T956259061. Just off the main plaza, this is a good option. Its good value rooms, some with a/c and TV, are welcoming and the service is friendly.
C **Hostal Carlos I**, Plaza de Sevilla s/n, T956286600. 30 rooms. This is another good place to stay and good value for money. A/c, good facilities, very near the train station.
E **Hostal Colón**, C Marqués de Cádiz, 6, T956285351. On a street with several *hostal* options (all in the same price bracket), this is a good deal. Clean rooms, some with balconies overlooking the street. Some rooms have bath.
E **Hostal del Duque**, C Ancha, 13, T956222777. A more interesting location to stay in away from the other main *hostal* area, just off Plaza San Antonio, this place has big, light rooms with balconies overlooking the street, but is pretty basic.

E **Hostal Fantoni**, C Flamenco 5, T956282704. Good central *hostal* with a pleasant patio and renovated rooms, some with bath (**D**).
F **Cuatro Naciones**, C del Boquete 3, is a cheap and well-run *casa de huespedes* just off Plaza San Juan de Dios.
F **Quo Qádis**, C Diego Arias 1, T/F956221939. An innovative and excellent youth hostel with courses (from language to flamenco) and excursions. Breakfast included in price. Double rooms (**E**) or dorms from €10. There are no campsites around Cádiz itself, but plenty near Puerto de Santa María, Puerto Real and Rota.

Around Cádiz *p748*
There are few budget accommodation options in Sanlúcar de Barrameda and everything is likely to be taken in Jul and Aug. If you fancy staying in Zahara de los Atunes, there are several options.
L **Puerto Sherry Yacht Club**, Av de la Libertad s/n, El Puerto de Santa María, T956812000, F956853300. Top of the range in every respect is this exclusive hotel with every possible facility (and prices to match).
A **Convento de San Francisco**, Plazuela s/n, Vejer de la Frontera, T956451001, F956451004. Unique accommodation at a restored 17th-century monastery with 25 atmospheric rooms. The hotel was previously occupied by Franciscan monks. Good restaurant in the former refectory.
B **Gran Sol**, C Sánchez Rodriguez s/n, Zahara de los Atunes, T956439301, F956439197, with spotless rooms in a beachside location and an excellent restaurant.
B **Tartaneros**, C Tartaneros 8, Sanlúcar de Barrameda, T956385378, F956385394. A smaller and considerably more pleasant

Andalucía Cádiz & around: listings

option than some of the resort hotels, this place has simply decorated rooms in a 19th-century building in the town centre and an outside central patio in which to eat lunch.

D Hostal MonteMar, C Peñón 12, Zahara de los Atunes, T956439047, a cheap bet.

E Las Marismas, Plaza La Salle 2, Sanlúcar de Barrameda, T956366008. A small *pensión* close to the bus station, this is probably the best place to stay in town with a very pretty courtyard with rooms looking on to it and a roof terrace. Very good value.

E Manolo, C Jesús de los Milagros 18, El Puerto de Santa María, T956857525. Simple rooms over a delightful patio. The Esperanza opposite is also a good deal.

F Blanca Paloma, Plaza San Roque 9, Sanlúcar de Barrameda, T956363644. Small, economical *pensión* in the older part of town.

F La Posada, C Los Remedios 21, Vejer de la Frontera, T956450258. Simple rooms above a restaurant.

Camping

Las Dunas, Playa Puntillo, El Puerto de Santa María, T956872210. First category camp site on the beach with excellent facilities (including pool, restaurant, bar, tennis, fishing and launderette) and within walking distance of the Cádiz ferry, but can get very crowded in the high season.

There are 3 campsites in Vejer de la Frontera including **Camping Vejer**, Ctra N340, Km 39, T956450098. Good range of facilities including pool.

Eating

Cádiz p746, map 748

Unsurprisingly, fish is top of the menu in Cádiz. The city boasts 2 of the most outstanding (and pricey) fish restaurants in Andalucía:

€€€ Achuri, C Plocia 15, T956253613. An established favourite and it's worth shelling out for some of the freshest and best prepared seafood you'll eat in the city. Book ahead; and

€€€ El Faro, C San Felix 15, T956211008, has some excellent house specialities including a delicious and locally renowned paella, also a moderately priced *menú del día*.

€€ Balandro, Alameda Apodaca 22, T956220992, is an upmarket *tapas* bar and restaurant with a comfy dining area looking out across the water.

€€ Grimaldi, C Libertad, 9, on the Plaza de Topete , T956228316. The rather bizarre faux bodega interior, decorated with old photographs of Cádiz shouldn't put you off this reasonably priced, predominantly seafood, restaurant. Specialities include *pimientos rellenos con gambas* (prawn stuffed peppers) and other seafood.

€€ El Rincón del Jamon, Plaza San Augustín, 5, T956250183. A busy, down-to-earth tapas bar and restaurant. Delicious *gambas* and a good grilled *dorado* are particularly recommended. The house wines (both white and red) are also very good.

€ For inexpensive seafood, try the *freidurías*, of which **Las Flores**, Plaza las Flores, is one of the best. **Mesón La Cartuja**, Calle Abreu s/n, has good seafood *tapas* and cheap meals.

Tapas bars and cafés

For a tapas crawl head for C Zorilla, which runs from Plaza de la Mina to the northern shore and has several small tapas bars.

Mesón Cumbres Mayores, C Zorilla 4, T956213270, where you can eat great tapas surrounded by a forest of *jamones* hanging from the ceiling. Don't go there first, as you won't want to leave. Try the *diablillos*, an unusual snack of dates wrapped in bacon.

Bar Bahía, Av Ramón de Carranza 30, is a friendly place with a terrace, good service, and a tasty range of tapas.

Cervecería Aurelio, also on Zorilla, is the place to come in Cádiz for seafood tapas. You can smell the freshness of the *gambas* halfway down the street. There are plenty of other tapas bars in the Plaza de San Juan de Dios and the surrounding alleyways.

La Manzanilla, C Feduchy 9, is a serious sherry bar offering over 100 types of manzanilla.

Around Cádiz p748

El Puerto de Santa María is famous for its *marisquerías* which line the river front on the

Ribera del Marisco. Select your seafood, which is then weighed and given to you in a paper bag. The largest of the *marisquerías* in El Puerto de Santa María is:

€€€ **Casa Bigote**, Bajo de Guía s/n, SanLúcar de Barrameda, T956362696. One of several excellent fish restaurants along the same road, one back from the river. Others in this town include **Casa Juan**, **Marisquería**, **Poma** and **Arante Claro**.

€€ **Bar Ropiti**, C María Luisa 6, Zahara de los Atunes, T956439344, with a cool covered patio; they do good tuna steaks and *carpaccios* in the mid-range price category.

€€ **Romerijo**, T956541254, which also does good sit-in seafood platters

€ **Bar del Puerto**, opposite the Muelle del Vapor in El Puerto de Santa María, worth trying.

✪ Bars and clubs

Cádiz *p746, map 748*
Playa Victoria has a lively if tacky summer scene; try the following:
Las Pergolas, Paseo Marítimo 11, T956280949, and **Holiday**, Nereidas, Paseo Marítimo, T956273775.

In the **old town**, the bars and clubs are more small scale, but this does not stop things from going on well into the early morning hours, in summer and winter. There are several bars around Calle Manuel Raices and Calle Antonio López; **Woodstock**, at the corner of those 2 streets, is a decent bet.
Plaza España and around is a good bet for live music bars and late night drinking, including **Popart House Club**, Plaza España s/n, a good underground venue with DJs playing themes from rap to dance.
Poniente, C Beato Diego de Cádiz, a fun and lively gay club with drag shows most nights. Nearby, the area around Plaza Mina also stays lively until late. One of the best music bars in town, **Persígueme**, is on the corner of C Tinte and Sagasta, playing jazz and blues live later on in the week and at weekends; it's a firm local favourite.

☺ Entertainment

Cádiz *p746, map 748*
See local press or www.infocadiz.com, for details of what's on where.

Cinema There are no fewer than 7 cinemas in Cádiz, 2 of which are multiscreen.
Flamenco La Cava, C Antonio López, T956211866, is a popular flamenco taberna where you can eat, drink, and watch a spectacular show at very close quarters. Phone to check which nights have live shows.
Theatres Cádiz has 3 excellent theatres: **Teatro Andalucía**, C Londres 2, T956223029; **Teatro José Pemán** (open-air theatre in Parque Genovés, summer only), T956223534; and **Gran Teatro Falla**, Plaza de Falla s/n, T956220828.

✿ Festivals and events

Cádiz *p746, map 748*
In **Feb** is **Carnaval**. Cádiz is famous for its 10-day fiesta. Dating from the 19th century, even Franco was unable to suppress it. It is a riot of eating, drinking, dancing, singing and masquerades with a certain South American flavour. A distinctive feature are the bands – groups of people who parade around the city in fancy dress making music with any instruments they can lay their hands on, singing satirical songs, particularly about politicians. The large gay element in the city plays an important part and prizes are awarded for the most original and outrageous presentations.
Mar/Apr sees the celebration of **Semana Santa**, the week leading up to Easter. A much more devout affair but nevertheless a busy time in the city.
Early Aug is time for **La Velada de los Angeles**, a popular fair which has been revived in recent years.
On **7 Oct** is **La Virgen del Rosario**, celebrations for the city's patron saint.

⛰ Activities and tours

Cádiz *p746, map 748*
¤**tur** run guided tours of the town, €3 including visits to sights and a *bodega*; contact the tourist office for more details.

☻ Transport

Cádiz *p746, map 748*
Boat The port is next to Plaza de España. There's a ferry to the **Canary Islands** every

Tue at 1900. Tickets are available from travel agents or **Transmediterránea**, Av Ramón de Carranza, T902454645. There is a local ferry service to and from **Puerto de Santa María**; a leisurely *vapor* that takes 45 mins or a faster catamaran (see below).

Bus The main company is **Comes**, Plaza de Hispanidad, near Plaza de España and the port, T956807059. **Comes** has frequent buses to **Algeciras** (10 daily), **Jerez** (at least every hour, 45 mins), **Sevilla** (13 daily) and **Tarifa** (5 daily). There are also services to **Almería** (2 daily), **Córdoba** (1 daily), **Granada** (2 daily, 8 hr), **Huelva** (1 daily), **Málaga** (6 daily, 5 hr) and **Ronda** (3 daily). Los Amarillos terminal is on Paseo de Canalejas, T956285852. It runs frequent buses to **Sanlúcar** and **El Puerto de Santa María** (40 mins), as well as 3 daily buses to **Arcos** and **Ubrique**. Timetables are available at the tourist office.

Train There are 20 trains, T902240202, a day to **Jerez** (including El Puerto de Santa María), 12 to **Sevilla** and 3 to **Granada**.

Around Cádiz *p748*
Boat A pleasant way to arrive at **El Puerto de Santa María** is to take the *vapor* from **Cádiz**. It leaves Cádiz at 1000, 1200, 1400 and 1830 daily; departs from El Puerto at 0900, 1100, 1300 and 1530. On Sun and holidays there are supplementary services leaving **Cádiz** at 1630 and **El Puerto** at 1730. No sailings Mon, except holidays. The 10 km trip takes 45 mins and costs €2. The speedier catamaran *Rápido del Puerto* has 8 sailings daily each way; single €3.

Bus There are frequent services to and from **El Puerto de Santa María** for **Cádiz**.

◑ Directory

Cádiz *p746, map 748*
Internet El Navigante, C Doctor Marañón, south of Gran Teatro. €2 per hr; **Ciber C@i**, C Abreu 9; and **Ciber San Rafael**, C Benjumeda 38, near the Teatro Falla.
Post office The main correos is in Plaza Topete, T956211878.

Around Cádiz *p748*
There's **internet** access and **phone** booths at **Locutorio El Público**, C Palacios 39, El Puerto de Santa María.

The southern tip

This area is a real hotpotch. The Costa de la Luz ends as you reach Tarifa which, just 14 km from Morocco, has a distinct North African flavour with its narrow Moorish alleyways leading into mysterious cave-like houses, bars and shops. Many of the tourists that arrive in the town do so with a surfboard. The exfoliating levante wind, which in addition to leaving many of the beaches around comparatively undeveloped, creates great waves. Further down the coast is Algerciras, a container port and petro-chemical centre, with very little to offer the tourist. A short leap across the Straits and you are in Gibraltar, a small corner of Britain.

Tarifa → *Colour map 6, grid C3; Population: 15,118.*

Outpost town Tarifa occupies the most southerly tip of the Iberian peninsula. The strong winds, until recently, kept Tarifa as a backwater, but have now transformed it into one of the world's major windsurfing sites; the influx of north Europeans and Americans has given the town a cosmopolitan air enhanced by its main function as a ferry port linking Spain with Tangiers. Despite a rather shockingly rapid and haphazard development over the last decade, the old town of Tarifa is an intriguing place to explore and there is a relaxed and friendly atmosphere in the town's many bars, although you may be overwhelmed by windsurfers and tourists in the summer. On the hills to the northeast of Tarifa, thousands of wind farms take advantage of the conditions.➤➤ *For Sleeping, Eating and other listings, see pages 758-761.*

Tarifa has both Carthaginian and Roman origins It was named after Tarif Ibn Malik who in 710 led the first Moorish exploratory raid across the straits with 500 Berbers, returning the next year with a force of 12,000 men. The town was recaptured from the Moors in 1292 by Sancho IV, but their attempt to regain it two years later is more memorable. During the siege, the Moors threatened to murder the young son of the Christian commander, Alonso de Guzmán, unless Tarifa surrendered. Guzmán's response was to throw down his own dagger preferring 'honour without a son to a son without honour'. Nobody apparently asked the opinion of the son who was duly murdered, while Guzmán acquired the title of *El Bueno* (the Good) and extensive lands that later formed the dukedom of Medina Sidonia.

Sights

Castillo de Guzmán el Bueno ① *Tue-Sun 1000-1400 and 1800-2000, €1.20*, was built between 950 and 960 when the Caliph of Córdoba, Abd Al-Rahman III, decided that the area needed defending against any invasion from North Africa. The tower known as the **Torre de Guzmán** is more modern. There are superb views from the tower and battlements.

Iglesia de Santa María stands in a delightful square of the same name adjacent to the castle. Also in the square is the Ayuntamiento and a small, free museum. East of the square is a charming promenade with a mirador looking out towards North Africa. Following the success of Gibraltar's dolphin and whale watching trips, Tarifa can now offer two of its own. See page 759.

The tourist office is at the northern end of the Paseo de la Alameda ① *T9566 27027, Mon-Friday 1000-1400, 1700-1900 and 1000-1400 Sat all year, and Sat pm and Sun during summer.*

Just outside of Tarifa – along the N340 eastwards – you reach 340 m at the Puerto de Cabrito, surrounded by the ubiquitous wind farms. Just past this point is a mirador, with a small kiosk, giving fine views of North Africa. On clear days, individual buildings and minarets can easily be picked out on the Moroccan side of the straits.

Algeciras → *Colour map 6, grid C3; Population: 101,972.*

The N340 continues eastwards dropping quickly down to the city of Algeciras. A busy container port with an important petro-chemical industry, Algeciras can hardly be called an attractive place and few would think of lingering, unless they were waiting for a ferry. Pollution frequently hangs over the town and its high-rise suburbs are dreary. As a major embarkation point for Tangier and Ceuta with frequent daily ferries to both, Algeciras becomes congested during the summer months as migrant Algerians and Moroccans return home from France, Belgium, Germany and the Netherlands. ▶ *For further details, see Transport page 760.*

Gibraltar → *Colour map 6, grid C3; Population: 30,000.*

Whatever your views on its political status, this little corner of Britain perches on the coastline of the country its citizens are determined not to join. Although it's known as The Rock, most folk would refer to the massive pointy slab of stone as a mountain; the settlement sits at its feet like a toddler clutching the boots of a giant. This was one of the famed Pillars of Hercules; the gateposts to the unknown for the ancient Mediterranean civilizations. Although packed with duty-free shops to cater for the hordes that descend on the colony every day for cheap booze and fags, the town is surprisingly pleasant, and very British in feel. There is plenty to see, including a

Moorish Castle and the best preserved Arab Baths in the southern Iberia. There are many fortifications and gateways, a legacy of the sieges that have taken place over the centuries. The Upper Rock area has the impressive St Michael's Caves, with its nearby troops of Barbary Apes. The Upper Rock is also a good place to spot migrating birds of prey in spring and autumn. At a lower level, there are some fine botanic gardens. ▸▸ *For Sleeping, Eating and other listings, see pages 758-761.*

Ins and outs

Getting there No bus services cross the border from Spain, but Portillo buses run from towns and cities in Andalucía to La Linea on the Spanish side of the border. If arriving at Gibraltar by car for a short stay leave it in a carpark in La Linea, and walk through. This avoids the customs delays and the problem of finding a parking space on the Rock. A passport is required for entry into Gibraltar. ▸▸ *For further details, see Transport page 760.*

Getting around Regular buses (some double-deckers) run from the Gibraltar side of the border to the centre, but it's not far to walk, although you may be delayed if there's a plane landing, as the runway crosses the main road! Driving is on the right, the same as in Andalucía.

Tourist information The main tourist office, and home of the Gibraltar Tourist Board, is at Duke of Kent House in Cathedral Square, next to the Anglian Cathedral. There are also sub-offices at the airport, in the market place and in John Mackintosh Hall. Their staff are very helpful ① *Mon-Fri 1000-1800, Sat 1000-1400.*

Background

Gibraltar was inhabited in the prehistoric era as long as 100,000 years ago. In later times the Phoenicians knew Gibraltar as Calpe and in Greek mythology it formed, along with Mount Ablya on the other side of the Straits, the twin pillars of Hercules.

Moorish influence in the area began in 711 AD, when Tarik Ibn Zeyed invaded the mainland to start his campaign against the Visigoths. He named the Rock Gibel Tarik (or Tarik's Mountain), which has corrupted over time into Gibraltar. The Christians and Moors swapped possession a couple of times before the latter were finally evicted from the Rock in 1462 by forces led by the Duke of Medina Sedonia. They were to stay for a further 240 years until the War of the Spanish Succession. Although Britain supported the Spanish against the French, Gibraltar was taken by a combined Anglo-Dutch fleet in 1704 led by Admiral Rooke. Britain gained formal sovereignty over the Rock in the Treaty of Utrecht in 1713 and has remained there ever since, despite Spain's diplomatic and military attempts to regain it.

Gibraltar played an important strategic role in both world wars, but particularly the Second, when *The Rock* became honeycombed with passages and caverns (augmenting the existing caves) for the storage of ammunition and other arms, making a formidable fortress guarding the western entrance to the Mediterranean. Most of the inhabitants of Gibraltar were evacuated during the Second World War. The majority returned when hostilities ceased.

In the post-war period, Franco continued to try to persuade the British to give up the Rock, but in a number of referendums the Gibraltarians have always staunchly wished to remain British. Franco eventually closed the border in 1965; however, this only served to make the *llanitos* even more anti-Spanish. After the death of Franco and the entry of Spain into the Common Market, the borders were re-opened in 1985. In recent years, since the departure of the British forces, Gibraltar has made attempts to create some economic independence by forming a sort of financial paradise in the Mediterranean, with mixed results. Over 75,000 financial institutions now have a base in Gibraltar and the EU has accused many of drugs money laundering and harbouring Russian mafia money.

❖ *The oldest buildings and monuments in Gibraltar are Moorish.*

Of its 30,000 inhabitants, 20,000 are native Gibraltarians, 6,000 are expatriate Britons and the remainder guestworkers from Morocco or EU countries. The Gibraltarians themselves come from a variety of backgrounds – Spanish, British, Maltese, Jewish, Moroccan and Genoese – and while English is the official language, they will often mix English and Spanish (even within the same sentence) in a curious dialect known as llanito.

Sights

The castle The most obvious Moorish monument, but not the best location, is the castle. It was built in 1333, probably on the site of an earlier fortress. Entry, however, is not permitted as the castle functions today as Gibraltar's prison.

Gibraltar Museum ① *Mon-Fri 1000-1800, Sat 1000-1400, €2, children €1.* Rooms 1 and 2 consist of archaeological material covering the Paleolithic to the Moorish periods. In Room 7, a superb scale model of the colony in 1850 is a highlight, but the most interesting aspect is the superbly preserved Moorish baths underneath. In the Main Hall there is a central dome over a series of horseshoe arches, the columns of which are of particular interest, four being Moorish, one Roman and the other three Visigothic. The hall originally contained private cubicles for changing and relaxing. Next is a Cold Room, with higher ceilings to retain the cooler temperatures, and containing shallow cold and tepid baths. The next room to the east is the Hot Room, which is entered through a large round arch. It is believed that the steam bath was located at the north end and the hot plunge bath on the southern side. Some of the original lead piping may still be seen and the whole area is in a good state of preservation. The museum is also the main tourist information office. There is a small restaurant.

Upper Rock To view the features of the Upper Rock, it is best to take the **cable car**. ① *0930-1715, last trip down 1745, closed Sun, €5/€8.40 return, with a stop at the Apes Den, €7/12 includes all sites, €11.70 includes lunch at the upper terminal restaurant.* When the conditions are right, the view from the top of the rock can be superb with vistas of the Costa del Sol, Algeciras Bay and the mountains of Morocco. The lower station is located in Rosia Road close to the Alameda Botanical Gardens and the Bristol Hotel.

The so-called **Barbary Apes** (*Macaca sylvanus*) are in fact a species of tailless monkey, the only ones on the mainland of Europe. Legend has it that they arrived in Gibraltar via an underground tunnel from Morocco, but the truth is that they were imported for pets by British soldiers and some inevitably escaped. They used to live in two packs, one at the Apes Den and the other living on the steep slopes of Middle Hill. Today they are breeding so enthusiastically that they number around 260 and live in seven packs of around 40-50 in each. As they are causing damage to the natural vegetation and increasingly coming down into the inhabited areas to scavenge for food, it has been decided that their numbers are to be culled. The Apes Den near the middle cable car station is the best place to see them, but visitors are warned not to feed the apes or make sudden movements, as they are not as loveable as they look. Take care also of valuables such as cameras, which the apes take great delight in stealing.

A short walk from either the upper station or the Apes Den leads to **St Michael's Cave**, a huge cavern containing stalagmites, stalactites, pillars and flow structures. This cave is just one of a whole maze of natural and manmade caves which honeycomb the Rock.

Dolphin watching This has become increasingly popular in recent years. The Straits are rich in sea mammals; in addition to common dolphins, the striped and

● *During the Second World War, Sir Winston Churchill made a special effort to maintain the*
● *apes' numbers, as legend said that the British Empire would fall if the apes ever left the Rock.*

Andalucía Gibraltar

bottlenosed varieties can be seen, along with occasional whales, such as the fin, sperm, pilot and orca. **Fortuna** runs dolphin tours on an 80-year-old sailing boat, operating from Queensway Quay Marina. *MV Lochlan* has an underwater camera and video monitor and provides excellent food, see page 760.

● Sleeping

Tarifa *p754*
It is very difficult to find cheap accommodation in Tarifa; even basic *pensiones* have inflated prices due to the massive influx of tourists during peak season, 3 km west of town on the highway is the excellent.

A Hurricane Hotel, Ctra N340 Km77, T956684919, with a beachfront location, pleasant garden, swimming pool, and many activities on offer.

C Casa Amarilla, C Sancho IV El Bravo, T956681993, F9566- 27130, in town this is an excellent apartment- style hotel with refreshing Art Nouveau and North African interiors and top rooms equipped with kitchen; it's cheaper off-season (**D**).

C Casa del Comandante, C Alcalde Juan Núñez 8, T956681925. Attractive and colourful rooms in this modern *hostal* near the port.

C Posada La Sacristía, C San Donato 8, T956681759, is an excellent option, a cool whitewashed place with plenty of style around a pretty patio.

D Hostal Alborada, C San José, 52, T956681140, www.hotelalborada.com. A light and popular *hostal* outside the centre of town. All double rooms with bath or shower set around an attractive courtyard.

E Correo, C Coronel Moscardó 9, T956680206. Located opposite the post office, the best room in this popular *pensión* is at the top with great views (and costs slightly more).

E Fonda Villanueva, Av Andalucía 11, T956684149. Some rooms with bath; basic, secure and modern.

Camping

There is plenty of choice of campsites on or near the beach to the north of Tarifa. One of the best is **Paloma**, Ctra N340, Km 70, T956684203, www.tarifa.net/paloma. Bungalows, pool, windsurfing, horse riding, mountain biking, rock climbing and hang gliding available.

Gibraltar *p755*
Hotels in Gibraltar are generally more expensive than comparable hotels in Spain. There is little availability at the cheaper end of the range and those looking for budget accommodation should consider the *pensiones* in La Linea on the Spanish side of the border.

AL Whites, Governors Pde, T70700, F70243. Luxury hotel with a rooftop leisure area with pool, sauna, mini gym. Good restaurant and fine views.

B-C Bristol, 10 Cathedral Sq, T76800, F77613. A good place with recently refurbished rooms. Central location near the cathedral and museum, with garden and pool.

D Queens, 1 Boyd St, PO Box 99, T74000, F40030. 62 rooms. Conveniently placed for the cable car, Botanic Gardens and shopping. Some rooms with shared bath (**E**).

D-E Cannon, 9 Cannon Lane, T51711, cannon@gibnet.gi. Recently opened Swedish owned small hotel in the town centre. Rooms with or without bath.

E-F Emile Youth Hostel, Montagu Bastion, Line Wall Rd, T51106. Communal TV lounge and rooms. Continental breakfast included in the €12 a night. Singles and doubles.

● Eating

Tarifa *p754*
There are some good places to eat in Tarifa, but the nightlife is fairly seasonal.

€€€ Alameda, Paseo de la Alameda, has great seafood and *platos combinados*.

€€ Mandrágora, C Independencia 3, T956681291, is a chilled, low-lit Moroccan restaurant, serving delicious dishes such as kid with quince and cous cous for around €12, accompanied by an excellent CD collection of jazz and north African music.

Tapas bars and cafés

Café Central, C Sancho IV El Bravo, has another good terrace and cheery service; it's a Tarifa veteran at more than 100 years old.

Café Continental, Paseo de Alameda s/n, is a friendly spot for tapas or a drink in the sun.

El Barrilito, opposite **Café Central**, is tiny does excellent tapas and *bocadillos*.
El Tribú, C Nuestra Señora de la Luz 7, is a good spot for a drink.

Gibraltar *p755*
Pubs are excellent value (see below).
€€€ **Bunters**, 1 College Lane, T70482. International fare plus traditional English desserts, evenings only.
€€€ **Strings**, 44 Cornwalls Lane, T78800. International food, including Moroccan, closed Mon, booking advisable.
€€ **Country Cottage**, 13-15 Giros Passage, T70084. English cuisine including roast lamb and Aberdeen Angus steak.
€€ **Little Mermaid**, Marina Bay. Recently opened Danish restaurant with typical Scandinavian specialities.
€€ **Maharaja**, 21 Turnbulls Lane, T75233. The best Indian food on the Rock.
€ **Casements Fishery** on the 2nd floor of the International Commercial Centre, takeaway or eat in. For cheap fish and chips.

🍸 Bars and clubs

Tarifa *p754*
Far out, a 10-min walk on the main road heading towards Cádiz, is the latest and biggest club to hit town, and it's open all year round (although only on Fri and Sat during the winter). International DJs play house, techno, trance and funk.

Gibraltar *p755*
There are numerous **pubs**, most of which serve some sort of food, usually with an English flavour. The main pub zone is Main St; the **Horseshoe**, at no 193, is a sound choice for a pie and a pint.
The Clipper in Irishtown and **Sir Winston's Tavern** in Cornwalls Pde are equally good. For **nightclubs**, try **Sax**, 1st floor of the ICC, open until 0200, or **Penelope**, 3 West Pl of Arms, T70462, which is set in one of the old town walls.

🎭 Entertainment

Gibraltar *p755*
Cinema Queens, next to the hotel of the same name in Boyd St. Recently refurbished. Open daily, except Wed; admission €3-4.

⚙ Festivals and events

Tarifa *p754*
On **16 Jul**, **Fiesta del Carmen** sees the statue of the Virgen del Carmen taken out to sea to bless the waters.
First fortnight in **Aug**, **National Folk Music Festival**.
Early Sep, is the **Fiesta de Nuestra Señora de la Luz Fair** and pilgrimage in honour of Tarifa's patron saint.

Gibraltar *p755*
Gibraltar is sales-tax free and therefore has considerable attractions, not only to expatriates on the Costa del Sol, but also to Spaniards living over the border who flock in for their petrol and cigarettes. Be warned that there are limits on the goods you are permitted to import back into Spain and there are often long customs delays. You're allowed 1 litre of spirits and 200 cigarettes as the duty-free allowance. Shopping hours tend to resemble those of the UK rather than Spain. The official currency is the Gibraltar pound and the colony issues its own notes and coins, but ¤s and US dollars are widely accepted in all commercial establishments. Gibraltar notes are not exchangeable outside the Rock.

⛰ Activities and tours

Tarifa *p754*
Horse riding Hotel Dos Mares, T956684035, or **Hotel Balcón de España**, T956684326.
Windsurfing There are 21 recognized spots locally requiring varying degrees of expertize. There are numerous windsurfing schools and many shops in the town devoted to windsurfing gear.
Spin Out Surf Base, Casa de Porro, Ctra N340, Km 75, T/F956680844, beach T956236352, T639139060 (mob), info@tarifaspinout.com. Lessons from €48 for 2 hrs tuition. Board rental €28 for 2 hrs. Also arranges surf safaris to Essaouira in Morocco.
Whale Watch, T956627013, www.whale watchtarifa.com, and **FIRMM**, T956627008. Both claim to be non-profit making organizations. Early booking is essential.

Norafrica Tours, Estación Marítima, T956681830, www.tarifa-tanger.com. Excursions to Tangiers, for 1-2 days (1 night in Morocco) from €48 per person.

Gibraltar *p755*
Fortuna, T47333, operates from Marina Bay. Most sailings last around 2 hours. Booking is essential. **Dolphin Safari**, T71914, established over 30 years ago, runs a small catamaran with the emphasis on touchy-feely encounters with the dolphins. **Nautilus VI**, T73400, is a luxury semi-submersible offering underwater views of dolphins.

⊖ Transport

Tarifa *p754*
Boat Ferry tickets for **Tangiers** are available from **Marruecotur**, C Batalla del Salado 57, T956684751. Catamarans leave daily at 0930, 1130, 1300, 1600 and 1830 in summer and at 1130 and 1800 in winter. The journey takes 35 mins and costs about €21 single.
Bus The station is in C Batalla del Salado. There are frequent **Comes** buses, T9566-84038, to **Algeciras** and **Cádiz**, as well as 2 to **Málaga**, 4 to **Sevilla** and 1 to **Almería**.
Cycle Hire available at Hotel Dos Mares, T956684035.
Ferry **FRS**, run a fast ferry with passenger and car service from **Tarifa** and **Algeciras** to **Tangier** (35mins) with several daily departures. Contact **FRS**, Estación Marítima, PO/Aptdo de correos, 13 11380 Tarifa-Cádiz, T956681830, www.frs.es.

Algeciras *p755*
Boat There are frequent daily ferries to **Tangiers** (2 hrs, €45 return) and **Ceuta** (45 mins, €36.90 return) from 0700, with seasonal hydrofoils to both of these ports. FRS, run a fast ferry with passenger and car service from **Algeciras** to **Tangier** (35 mins) with several daily departures. Note that the hydrofoils may not run in rough weather, which is a not infrequent occurrence. Tickets can be purchased from kiosks all round the Campo de Gibraltar and travel agents in Algeciras. For more details, contact **Transmediterránea**, T902454645.
Bus The main bus station is on C San Bernardo. There are frequent buses to **Cádiz**,

Sevilla, and **Tarifa**, as well as 4 daily to **Madrid**. There are many buses to **La Linea**, the access point for Gibraltar. 7 buses hit **Málaga** daily, while 6 head for the hills of **Granada** and **Jaén**.
Train The station is on C San Bernardo. There are 2 daily trains to **Madrid**; 3 to **Granada**; 6 to **Ronda**; 3 to **Sevilla**.

Gibraltar *p755*
Air Gibraltar Airport was built in the Second World War on reclaimed land and a feature of the road into town is that it passes over the runway, which is shared with the RAF, and traffic is stopped as each plane lands and takes off. It is only served by 2 airlines: **GB Airways**, (a subsidiary of BA) and **Monarch**. It is worth considering routes via **Málaga**, which give greater choice and cheaper fares and less expensive car hire.
Boat Gibraltar has become an important ferry port with links to **Morocco**. *MS Estrella*, T77666, runs to and from **Tangiers** 3 days a week. Foot passengers pay €18 single and €30 return, vehicles €40 and €80. The crossing takes approximately 2 hrs. There is now a daily catamaran service to and from **Tangiers**, T79200. Tickets cost €30 for a period return and €25 for a day trip. The crossing takes 1¼ hrs. A hydrofoil service, the *Hanse Jet*, operated by FRS Maroc runs 2 return trips to **Tangier** daily and takes 1 hr.
Car Spanish customs are usually awkward in view of the widespread smuggling of cigarettes and drugs, so delays for re-entering Spain are common and can last from 15 mins to 5 hrs. Most of the inter-national car hire firms are based at the airport including **Avis**, T75552, **Budget**, T79666, **Hertz**, T42737 and **Europcar**, T77171. **Cycle, scooter and motorcycle hire** Rent a bike, T70420.

ⓘ Directory

Tarifa *p754*
There's **internet** access at **Ciber-Papelería Pandor@'s**, C Sancho IV el Bravo 5, T956681645. Expensive at €3.50/hr, but central. Further up the street is **El Navegante**, slightly cheaper but with a poorer connection.

Banks Branches of all the main British and Spanish banks, plus some from other European countries, are mainly based around the Main St/Line/Wall Rd area.

Internet Access at **Cyber Room**, on Bedlam Court just off Main St.

Post The main branch is located at 104 Main St, open 0900-1300 and 1400-1700, Sat 1000-1300. Gibraltar issues its own postage stamps.

Telephone When telephoning out of Gibraltar, the international prefix is 00 (except for Spain). To call Gibraltar from Spain dial first 9567 (except in Cádiz province where the code is 7). From outside Spain, the code is +350. Telephone cabins in Gibraltar are the traditional British red version.

Costa del Sol and inland trips

The stretch of coast west from Gibraltar to Malaga is a narrow coastal strip of ribbon development that since the late 1960s has grown into a collection of resorts, urbanizaciones and leisure complexes which on first sight can be quite a shock to the uninitiated. It is difficult to explain the success of the costa. It is certainly not the quality of the beaches, which are generally gritty or rocky; nor is it the access provided by the coast road, which is one of the most dangerous in Europe; it cannot be the cultural background, which, with a few notable exceptions, is sparse. The climate, however, particularly in winter, is the best on mainland Europe, attracting thousands of northern Europeans in the colder months. Many of the worst architectural features in the form of tower blocks were put up in the 1960s and 1970s; since then the main trend has been to build low rise urbanizaciones, which in the 1980s and 1990s have been dominated by the time share business. The highlights of the area are without a doubt away from the coast into the hills.

Estepona → *Colour map 6, grid C4.*

The most Spanish of the Costa resorts, Estepona has an attractive sea front with a promenade backing a shingle beach, with a few low rise apartment blocks. The town itself has some interesting corners, including two attractive squares, the Plaza Arce and the Plaza las Flores. The main restaurants and tapas bars are along Calle Terraza.

Casares → *Colour map 6, grid C4.*

Three kilometres west of Estepona, a winding road leads inland for 18 km to Casares, which claims to be the 'most photographed village in Spain'. Its whitewashed houses clothe the side of a hill which is capped by the ruins of a 13th-century Moorish fortress on Roman foundations built in the time of Ibn al Jatib. The fort was a centre of resistance against the French during the Peninsular War. Next to the fort is the Church of the Incarnación. It was built in 1505 and has a brick Mudejar tower (the remainder of the church is constructed of brick and stone, partly covered in plaster). The interior has three naves and a small chapel, but as it was partially destroyed during the Civil War, it is nowadays boarded up. The castle and church share their hilltop position with the local cemetery, which is meticulously kept (the view from the hill top shows a new one built on the outskirts). On the cliff below is a breeding colony of Lesser Kestrels, while there are spectacular views down to the coast towards Gibraltar and North Africa.

● *Casares is said to have derived its name from Julius Caesar, who may have been cured of*
● *his liver complaints by the sulphur springs at nearby Manilva.*

The 17th century Church of San Sebastián, which can be visited on the way to the fortress, is a simple whitewashed 17th-century building containing the image of the Virgen del Rosario del Campo. In the adjacent square is a statue of Blas Infante who was a native of Casares and leader of Andalucías nationalist movement. He was executed by Franco's supporters. There are possibilities for eating in the square, with **Bar Restaurant Claveles** having walls festooned with farming implements and specializing in game dishes such as rabbit, partridge and quail. Across the road is Bar los Amigos, busy with locals and providing a good range of tapas. There is another decent restaurant and craft shop at the entrance to the village. From their terrace there are fine panoramic views of Casares.

Ronda → *Colour map 6, grid C4; Population: 33,806.*

This charming, historic town is located on a limestone plateau in the Serranía de Ronda mountains, astride a spectacular gorge – El Tajo – some 120 m deep. Ronda is divided into two contrasting districts on each side of the gorge. To the south is La Ciudad, the old town containing many Moorish remains including its haphazard street plan. To the north of El Tajo is El Mercadillo, a largely modern district graced by what is claimed to be the oldest bullring in Spain. It's very touristy, but still a pleasant place. ➤➤ *For Sleeping, Eating and other listings, see pages 764-766.*

History

Ronda has a long and fascinating history. The Iberians named it Arunda; the Romans' name for Ronda was probably Arundo. The Moors' fortification of Ronda, their regional capital, was legendary but, due to internal divisions, it took a Christian army of 13,000 cavalry and 25,000 infantrymen only seven days to capture it in 1485. What remained of the Moorish Alcazaba was almost totally destroyed by the French during the Peninsular War in 1809. Ronda also saw plenty of action in the Civil War, when representatives of both sides were thrown into the Tajo. Now the coachloads roll in from the Costa, but this does not seem to spoil the essential charm of the town.

Sights

Around El Tajo Photogenic El Tajo is spanned by three bridges, and makes for excellent birdwatching, with rock doves, choughs and crag martins whirling through the gorge. A series of beautifully terraced gardens known as **La Mina**, give stupendous views of the gorge.

La Ciudad Cross the Puente Viejo bridge and pass under the arch of the **Puerta de Felipe V.** From here the distinctive roof of the **Baños Arabes** ① *T952873889, Tue 0900-1330 and 1600-1800, Wed-Sat 0930-1530, free*, can be seen with its cupolas and star-shaped roof windows. The building is made of brick and inside are octagonal columns supporting typical Moorish arches.

Return to the arch and climb up the steep hill of Calle Santo Domingo. Further up the hill to the right is the **Casa del Rey Moro** (House of the Moorish King), ① *T952187200, 1000-2000, €2.60*, an 18th-century mansion built on Moorish foundations. At the rear of the house is a stairway cut into the rocky side of the gorge, said to have been used by Christian slaves to bring water to their Moorish masters. Take care with the 365 steps, which are steep and often slippery. The stench of the river at the bottom, and the thought of climbing back, may make you conclude that the entrance fee is as steep as the steps.

The focal point of La Ciudad is the leafy square of the **Plaza de Duquesa de Parcent,** which is dominated by the **Iglesia de Santa María Mayor** ① *1000-1800, €1.50*. Originally a 13th-century mosque, it was rebuilt by the Christians but retains

much of the Moorish architecture. It has a late Gothic nave and heavily carved wooden Baroque choir stalls and an impressive retablo. There is also a *tesoro* – a museum of church treasures. In the entrance porch are some Moorish arches covered with Arab calligraphy; the balcony facing the square provided a position for dignitaries to watch bullfights before the main ring in the Mercadillo was built.

Leave the Plaza Duquesa de Parcent via the narrow Calle Manuel Montero and head for the **Casa de Mondragón**, undoubtedly the most important civil monument in Ronda. It was believed to be the residence of Abomelic, son of the Sultan of Morocco in the early 14th century. When Ronda fell to the Christians, Fernando and Isabel adapted the palace for their use. The outer façade of the building dates from the 18th century, but much of the interior is Moorish or Mudéjar, with filligree work and horseshoe arches and mosaics. There are a number of patios with fountains and stunning views over the Tajo. Much of the Casa de Mondragón is taken up with the reasonable **Museo Arqueológico** ① *Mon-Fri 1000-1800, Sat, Sun and holidays 1000-1500, €2, children under 14 free*, which includes ethnographic and environ- mental sections. Back in Calle Armiñán at Number 29 is the newly opened **Museo de Bandolero** ① *1030-1800, €2.50*. Ronda is an apt place for such a museum to be located as the mountains around the town abounded with Robin Hood characters in the 18th, 19th and even the 20th centuries. Some of the great figures of banditry are illustrated; the forces of law and order are also not forgotten.

The pueblos blancos, or white towns, including Grazalema, the gateway to the Sierra de Grazalema, with excellent walks, are easily reached from Ronda, see page 743.

El Mercadillo This part of the town has less in the way of monuments, but is not without interest. It is dominated by the **Plaza de Toros**, or bullring, built in 1785 and claimed to be the oldest in Spain. It holds 5,000 people and was used as the setting for the film *Carmen*. Under the bullring is a small **Museo de Toros** ① *1000-1800 (2000 in summer), €4*, but the most interesting thing about the visit is the bullpens at the back.

Marbella → *Colour map 6, grid C4; Population: 98,377.*

Marbella has a huge cachet as a classy resort with the so-called 'international jet-set' as well as Spaniards; virtually every A through D-list celebrity pops in here during the summer, and magazines such as *¡Hola!* virtually base themselves here at that time, hoping to spot an indiscreet snog or a glimpse of cellulite. Despite an attractive pedestrianized old town and some top restaurants, Marbella is largely hideous, with tacky mansions jostling for space on the busy boulevards, nowhere more so than at vaunted **Puerto Banús**, where luxury yachts dock and plastic surgeons and panelbeaters can retire at 30.

Marbella's saving grace is its old town, a maze of narrow alleyways, small squares and whitewashed houses festooned with flowers, centred around the beautiful **Plaza de los Naranjos** (Orangetree Square). **Museo de Bonsai**, ① *Parque Arroyo de la Represa, T952862926, 1030-1330 and 1700-2000, €3, children €1.50*, is an absolute gem and has become very popular. Housed in a modern building surrounded by landscaped gardens and lakes, the miniature trees are imaginatively displayed on a wooden raft-like structure over water containing turtles and fish.

Fuengirola → *Colour map 6, grid C5; Population: 44,924.*

The thriving resort of Fuengirola is quieter than Torremolinos to the east and has fewer 'beautiful people' than Marbella to the west. It is basically a family resort, which appeals to Northern European retirees in the winter and attracts large numbers of

Spanish visitors. Dominated by Sohail Castle, it is very much a working town, with a thriving fish dock and light industry in the suburbs to the north. The municipal tourist office ① *Av Santos Rein, T952467457, Mon-Fri 0930-1400 and 1600-1900, Sat 1000-1300*, has helpful multi-lingual staff. Other attractions include a zoo and several aquatic amusement parks. A popular boat trip ① *€4.80 (return €9), children under 10 €2.40 (return €3.65)*, runs from Fuengirola harbour to the marina at Benalmádena near Torremolinos. *Joven María II* runs approximately hourly in each direction.

There is a vast and cosmopolitan range of restaurant choices in Fuengirola, varying from simple Spanish seafood through to Indian, Chinese and exotic Indonesian. July is a good time to be in town for the **Fiesta de la Virgen del Carmen**, one of the best of its type along the coast. The statue of the virgin is carried from the church in Los Boliches in a two-hour procession to the beach and into the sea. An amazing spectacle, with half the inhabitants on the beach and the other half in the sea, either swimming or in boats.

Mijas → *Colour map 6, grid C4.*

Mijas is geared to catering for the tourist, with donkey rides, garish souvenirs and English-run restaurants. Despite all this, Mijas has a certain charm. It has a long history, certainly going back to Roman times, while the Moors built the defensive walls which partially remain today. The picturesque village is located at the foot of pine-covered mountains, with superb views along the coast from the well-kept gardens above the cliffs. Foreign residents outnumber the Spanish by two to one.

Torremolinos → *Colour map 6, grid C5; Population: 37,235.*

The nearest resort west of Málaga, Torremolinos was also the earliest to be developed, with a thriving hippie scene in the 1970s. It is loud, brash and dedicated to hedonistic culture. Many might be appalled by its vulgarity, but out of season it is far less offensive. It's heavily visited by Spaniards too, and there are many good places to eat among the tack. The local authorities are working hard to raise the image of Torremolinos and dispel its largely undeserved 'lager lout' reputation.

A promenade links Torremolinos' four beaches, packed in summer. The nicest part of town is around the **Playa de Carihuela**, the old fishermen's quarter, where there are some good beachfront eateries and some low-key tapas bars in the back streets.

● Sleeping

Ronda *p762*

Most of the cheaper places are located in the heart of the Mercadillo area.

AL Parador de Ronda, Plaza de España, T955590069, F952878080. Built within the original façade of the old town hall with spectacular views over the gorge.

B Alavera, C San Miguel s/n, T952879143, www.andalucia.com/alavera. Delightful small hotel with a restaurant, located between the town walls and the Baños Arabes. Tasteful rooms and good food.

B En Frente Arte, C Real 40, T952879088, www.enfrentearte.com. A combined hotel, art school and gallery. Converted house with 11 rooms, one in a 13th-century tower, in the old part of town. Price includes breakfast (served until 1500), lunch, internet and 24-hr bar. Great views, beautiful patios, pool, sauna, games and music rooms, restaurant.

E Andalucía, Av Martínez 19, T952875450. Opposite railway station, clean, with bath. Highly recommended.

E Aguilar, C Naranja 28, T952871994. Modernized *hostal* with good clean rooms.

Camping

A number of campsites have sprung up in the Ronda area in recent years. The best is the highly recommended:

Camping El Sur, just out of town on the Algeciras road, T952875939. Open throughout the year. Pool, bar, restaurant and bungalows.

Marbella *p763*
Most of Marbella's hotels are in the outskirts. Cheaper accommodation is mainly located around the fringes of the old town, particularly in C Luna.

🍴 Eating

Ronda *p762*
The better restaurants in Ronda serve the traditional food of the area, including *cocidos* and game dishes.
€€€ **Don Miguel**, Plaza de España, T952871090. Probably the best food in Ronda, certainly the best view, with its terraces overlooking the bridge and gorge.
€€€ **Tragabuches**, C José Aparicio 1, T952190291. Often claimed to be one of the best restaurants in Andalucía. Sophisticated ambience and complex cuisine.
€€ **Hermanos Andrades**, C Los Remedios 1. Good value.
€€ **Mesón Santiago**, C Marina 3, T952871367. Traditional Ronda restaurant with local dishes.
€ **Casa Santa Pola**, C Santo Domingo 3, T952879208. Diners greeted with free sherry, view over gorge, *menú del día* €7.25. Worth it for situation alone.
€ **Relax**, C Los Remedios 27. A friendly vegetarian café serving good food in a relaxed atmosphere.

Tapas bars and cafés
The best tapas bar in town is unpretentious **Bar La Viña**, C Lorenzo Borrego Gómez 9, while **Hermanos Macias**, C Pedro Romero 3, T952874238, has a formal, old-style atmosphere and good food. The terrace at **Atrium**, C José Aparicio 7, by the bullring, is a great spot for a coffee or a drink.

Marbella *p763*
€€€ **La Hacienda**, Urbanización Las Chapas, T952821267, was inaugurated by the late Paul Schiff, the famous Swiss chef. The menu is very unique, but pricey.

€€€ **La Meridiana**, Camino de la Cruz, Las Lomas, T952776190, is a modern restaurant with inventive international cooking. It's one of Marbella's top eating spots and is very expensive.

Torremolinos *p764*
Excellent fish restaurants include La Lonja and Los Pescadores, both right on the beach. Try also La Langusta and La Cantana on the Paseo Marítimo.

🍸 Bars and clubs

If you are looking for a lively night out on the costa, then Torremolinos is the place to be. Lager is the preferred tipple.

🎉 Festivals and events

Ronda *p762*
24 Jan Fiesta de la Virgen de la Paz
Patron saint of Ronda.
Early Sep Pedro Romero Festival with *corridas goyescas* (bullfights in Goyaesque attire).
There is also an **International Folk Festival** in **Sep** and a flamenco festival on the last Sat in **Aug** as part of the **Feria de Ronda**.

🚌 Transport

Ronda *p762*
Bus Portillo runs frequent services to **Marbella**, 4 coaches a day to **Málaga**, 1 to **La Linea** and 3 to **Cádiz** (one of which proceeds to **Jerez**). Comes and Lara serve the *pueblos blancos* to the north and west of Ronda.
Cycle Bicycles can be hired from **Biciserranía**, opposite the bus station.
Train The town is on the **Algeciras** to **Bobadilla** railway line and 5 trains a day run in each direction. The train journey from **Algeciras** runs through a number of picturesque towns and villages including **Gaucín**, **Castellar de la Frontera** and **San Roque** and is a highly recommended way of reaching Ronda.

Marbella *p763*
Local **buses** run every 30 mins along the coast in each direction.

● For an explanation of sleeping and eating price codes used in this guide, see inside the ● front cover. Other relevant information is found in Essentials, see pages 47-56.

Andalucía Costa del Sol & inland trips: listings

Fuengirola *p763*
Portillo **buses** every 30 mins along the coast road and also to Míjas. **Trains** for Málaga leave at 15 and 45 mins past.

Torremolinos *p764*
Regular Portillo **buses** run along the coast road between Málaga and Fuengirola every 15 mins. Torremolinos is on the Fuengirola-Málaga electric railway, with trains every 30 mins in each direction.

❶ Directory

Ronda *p762*
Internet Post office Correos, Virgen de la Paz 20, T952872557. Mon-Fri 0800-1500, Sat 0900-1300.
Telephone *Locutorios* on C de la Bola and C El Niño. Access at **Central Corner**, C Villanueva.

Málaga and around

→ *Colour map 6, grid C5; Population: 528,079.*
Spotted on the Costa del Sol: lively unspoiled town with a decent sandy beach, good seafood and tapas, an attractive centre, heaps of sun, and a real Spanish feel. Yes, it's Málaga, no more than an airport for millions of sunseekers but an important Spanish port and city with plenty to offer, perhaps more than the rest of the province's coast put together. While its port area and outer suburbs are in need of a facelift, its extensive pedestrianized old town is well-stocked with bars, teahouses and restaurants, and its cathedral and Alcazaba add weight to what is Spain's sixth largest city. The long town beach is clean despite the slightly unattractive colour, and there's plenty of good-value accommodation. Málaga is particularly proud of its two most famous 20th-century figures; Pablo Picasso and Antonio Banderas.

Around Málaga are some worthy attractions: Nerja, to the east, a coastal town which has escaped the brash development that characterizes the west coast; the ancient town of Antequera, strewn with religious buildings; and, a stone's throw from there, limestone sculptures and pink flamingoes. ⟩⟩ *For Sleeping, Eating and other listings, see pages 771-775.*

Ins and outs

Getting there

Málaga's busy airport, which handles seven million passengers a year, is located about 7 km west of the city centre and 4 km east of Torremolinos. There is a bus which runs between the aiport and Málaga every 30 minutes. If you're heading for Málaga or the nearer coastal resorts, the best option is the Fuengirola-Málaga train which runs every 30 minutes from 0711 to 2345 and stops in Torremolinos and Benalmádena. If you are going to Málaga, stay on until the final Centro-Alameda stop. Tickets are obtained from a machine on the platform or on the train. Málaga's main bus station is conveniently close to the RENFE train station (five minutes north on Paseo de los Tilos). There are bus connections to all the major Andalucían cities and towns. It is a 20-minute walk to the centre from here, but local buses cover the route. ⟩⟩ *For further details, see Transport page 774.*

Getting around

Most of the monuments and museums of Málaga are located within a compact area and can be conveniently visited on foot. For trips around Málaga, public transport is good, particularly along the coast.

The main regional tourist office ① *Pasaje Chinitas 4, T952213445, Mon-Fri 0900-2000, Sat 1000-1400.* The municipal tourist office is housed in a wonderful old building ① *Av de Cervantes 1, just off the Paseo del Parque, Mon-Fri 0800-1500, 1630-1930 (closing 30 mins earlier in winter), Sat 0930-1330.* There are smaller tourist offices at the airport and bus station, plus several information kiosks in the centre. See also the city's website, www.malaga.com.

History

Málaga has a long history dating back to the Phoenicians who are credited with planting the area's first vineyards and who founded a settlement called Malaka, a word derived from *malac*, meaning to salt fish. The city became a busy trading port during Roman times, exporting minerals and agricultural produce from the interior. From the eighth century Málaga was occupied by the Moors, when it was the main port for the province of Granada. The city fell to the Catholics in 1487 after a long and violent siege. The Moorish population was subject to considerable persecution, which led to a revolt in 1568. This was brutally put down and the remaining Moors expelled. Deprived of its most able citizens, the fortunes of Málaga declined. It was not, in fact, until the 19th century, when an agricultural based revival began, that things began to look up. During the Civil War, Málaga, Republican territory, saw a considerable amount of vicious fighting. Italian planes bombed the city, destroying part of its ancient centre.

Sights

Málaga has an impressive range of parks and gardens; the Paseo del Parque is a particularly Mediterranean inner-city space, while the Jardín Botánico three kilometres north of the city is an excellent spot for a sunny afternoon.

Alcazaba

① *T952216005, Tue-Sun 083-1900 €1.80/€3 combined with Castillo.* This former fortress and palace was started by the Moors in the 700s, but most of the structure dates from the mid-11th century. The site was originally occupied by both the Phoenicians and the Romans, and in fact there is a considerable amount of Roman masonry in the walls. The Alcazaba suffered badly during the Catholic Reconquista, but was carefully restored in the 1930s. Today, it rises impressively above the cramped streets below with a series of terraced, fortified walls and fine gateways, laid out with gardens and running water in typical Moorish style. Below the Alcazaba, a Roman theatre is being excavated, while from the terraces of the fort there are fine views over the port and the city.

Castillo

① *0830-1900, €1.80/€3 combined with Alcazaba.* The **Castillo Gibralfaro** (Lighthouse Hill) is a ruined Moorish castle built by Yusef I of Granada in the early 14th century. It offers easily offers the best views of the city from the top. It is linked to the Alcazaba below by parallel walls. A path leads up to it from the side of the Alcazaba, but this is a stiff walk and in the summer heat it's better to approach it by the road. Alternatively, take the No 35 bus from the Paseo del Parque.

Cathedral

① *1000-1845, closed Sun, €2.* Málaga's cathedral, as with many others in Andalucía, was built on the site of a mosque and dates from the 16th century, with numerous

modifications at later dates. One of its two towers was never completed, giving it a lopsided appearance, leading to the nickname of la Manquita, variously translated as 'the cripple' or 'the one-armed lady'. The cathedral has recently undergone considerable restoration after a massive fundraising effort. A large, somewhat gloomy building, its interior has also benefited recently from more imaginative lighting. The highlight of the cathedral is, without doubt, the Choir. Behind the stalls are some superb carvings of saints, 42 of which are attributed to Pedro de Mena around 1662. The Capilla de San José has a stone altarpiece with a superb triptych of the Annunciation by the Italian painter Cesere Arbassia. At the east end, behind the High Altar, is the Capilla de la Encarnación. Probably the most delightful chapel of all is that of Santa Bárbara, which is dominated by a superb retablo, festooned with saints and dating from the mid-16th century. The admission fee to the cathedral also

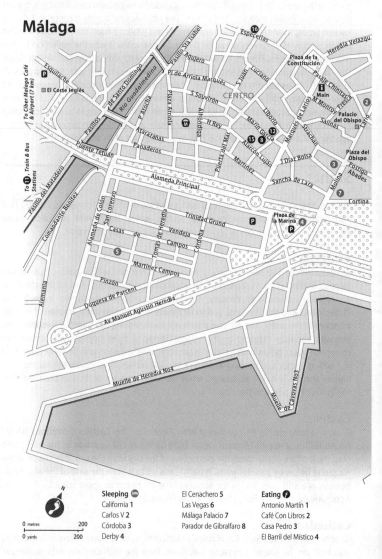

Málaga

Sleeping 🛌
California **1**
Carlos V **2**
Córdoba **3**
Derby **4**

El Cenachero **5**
Las Vegas **6**
Málaga Palacio **7**
Parador de Gibralfaro **8**

Eating 🍴
Antonio Martín **1**
Café Con Libros **2**
Casa Pedro **3**
El Barril del Místico **4**

0 metres 200
0 yards 200

includes entrance to the **museo**, a rundown affair near the entrance door containing the usual vestments, copes and silver.

Adjacent to the cathedral on Plaza del Obispo is the 18th-century **Palacio del Obispo**, or Bishop's Palace, which has one of the most beautiful façades in the city.

Museo Picasso

Málaga hasn't made as much of its most famous son as might be expected. The Museo Picasso has been long-awaited. The Picasso family sold 182 of the artist's works to the city at a knockdown price, and more acquisitions are in the pipeline.

The artist's birthplace on Plaza de la Merced, which is primarily a research facility, has several early paintings and sketches on display.

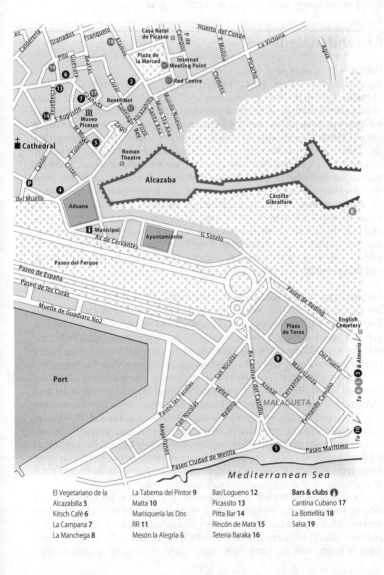

El Vegetariano de la Alcazabilla **5**	La Taberna del Pintor **9**	Bar/Logueno **12**	**Bars & clubs**
Kitsch Café **6**	Malta **10**	Picassíto **13**	Cantina Cubano **17**
La Campana **7**	Marisquería las Dos	Pitta Bar **14**	La Bottellita **18**
La Manchega **8**	RR **11**	Rincón de Mata **15**	Salsa **19**
	Mesón la Alegria &	Teteria Baraka **16**	

ⓘ *Mon-Fri 0900-1700, Sat-Sun 0900-1100, free but donation appreciated.* This beautiful spot dates from the days when 'infidels' (ie non-Catholics) were buried on the beach, making gruesome reappearances due to storms or hungry dogs. In the mid-18th century a British consul persuaded the authorities to allow him to start an English cemetery. Look for the small Church of St George, a block past the bullring on Paseo de Reding. From here a path leads into the leafy walled cemetery, a haven of peace in the noisy city. The inscriptions on the gravestones make absorbing reading; there are graves of many nationalities, the earlier ones covered in shells. The writer Gerald Brenan is buried here alongside his wife, the poet Gamel Woolsey; he had wanted his body to be donated to medical science, but was so well respected by the Malagans that none of the anatomy faculty could bring themselves to touch him; he finally arrived here in 2000, some 14 years after his death.

Around Málaga

Nerja → *Colour map 6, grid C6; Population: 15,326.*
Some 50 km from Málaga, Nerja is situated on a low cliff littered with sandy coves. Sheltered by the mountains, Nerja has a mild winter climate. Despite tourist development, Nerja has been spared the excesses of the western Costa del Sol, most of the buildings being low rise and the *urbanizaciones* tastefully designed. The tourist office ⓘ *Mon to Fri 1000-1400, Sat 1000-1300,* has very helpful staff who will provide a useful town plan. The main attraction is the **Balcón de Europa**, a tree-lined promenade jutting out into the sea with fine views along the coast and to the mountains inland. On the east side of the Balcón is the small, former fishermen's beach of Calahonda. There are a few token fishing boats left, but it has now been largely taken over by tourists.

Cuevas de Nerja ⓘ *T952529520, 1000-1400 and 1600-1830, €5, children over 6 €2.50,* were discovered in 1959 by a group of local schoolboys on a bat hunting expedition and are now a national monument. The most important finds were the wall paintings, probably Upper Palaeolithic in age but not on public view. However, the limestone features are genuinely awe-inspiring. There are regular buses from Nerja, and Málaga-Nerja buses stop at the caves too.

Antequera → *Colour map 6, grid B5; Population: 40,239.*
Some 45 km north of Málaga, the ancient town of Antequera lies at the junction of the Sierra de Torcal and the highly productive agricultural land to the north. It has always been a religious centre and has numerous convents and churches, plus prehistoric dolmens and a Moorish castle. It is a good base for exploring El Torcal, the fascinating limestone plateau to the south. The municipal tourist office is at Plaza San Sebastián.

Antequera's strategic position as a focus of routes has resulted in a long and important history. The clutch of dolmens to the east of the town show that the area was occupied in prehistoric times, while recent excavations to the west demonstrate that Antikaria, or the Ancient City, was an important Roman settlement. The Moorish past is evident in the hilltop Alcazaba, which dominates the town. In 1410, Antequera was the first major stronghold of the kingdom of Granada to be captured and held by the Christian armies, and was later an important base for the attacks on other Moorish bases. During the next two centuries Antequera built up its wealth, and many of its churches and other monuments date from this time.

Castillo de Santa María ⓘ *Mon-Fri 1030-1400, 1630-1830, Sat 1030-1400,* is a Moorish Alcazaba built in the 14th century over the remains of a Roman fort. The most impressive features are the two towers, the 13th-century Torre de Homenaje, or keep, and the earlier Torre Blanco (White Tower). Near the Castillo is the church of **Santa María la Mayor**, with an ornate Plateresque façade and recently restored Mudéjar

ceilings. Stripped of all its religious paraphernalia, the church has a wonderful simplicity that gives the visitor a chance to appreciate its basic architecture.

Ancient mansions are much in evidence in Antequera, including the Renaissance-style **Palacio de Nájera** on Plaza Coso Viejo, which now houses the **Museo Municipal**① *Tue-Fri 1000-1330, Sat 1000-1330, Sun 1100-1330, €1.20, hourly guided visits*. Although many of the displays are uninspiring, the museum is worth visiting for two remarkable exhibits. A bronze Roman statue – a life-size figure of a boy, El Efebo – was ploughed up in a field in the 1950s and is believed to date from the first century. The other exhibit is a wood carving of St Francis of Assisi, variously attributed to either Alonso Cano or Pedro de Mena.

Antequera's **Megalithic dolmens** ① *Tue 1500-1730, Wed-Sat 1000-1400 and 1500-1730, Sun 1000-1400, free (if closed you may be approached by some local pensionistas who will show you around for a small tip)*, on the northeast outskirts of the town off the road to Granada, are some of the best preserved prehistoric burial chambers in Europe. **Cueva de Menga**, the oldest, dates back to 2500 BC with huge, roughly cut stone slabs, believed to weigh 180 tonnes. The gallery leads to an oval burial chamber. Nearby **Cueva de Viera** is smaller and slightly less ancient, but has better cut stones, while the domed ceiling of **Cueva de Romeral**, circa 1800 BC, 3 km north, is regarded as one of the earliest examples of Spanish architecture. Menga and Viera can be reached on foot from the town by following the signs for Granada for 1 km. The local bus also runs this way. Romeral is 3 km further along the main road.

Parque Natural el Torcal → *Colour map 5, grid B6.*

This upland limestone block is 16 km south of Antequera and covers 1,171 ha. The grey limestone has been weathered into fantastic shapes giving an eerie atmosphere. The thin alkaline soil supports stunted trees and bushes such as elder, maple and hawthorn. There are a huge variety of wild flowers, including over 30 species of orchids, dwarf irises, peonies, rock roses and many more. To appreciate the abundant wildlife, it's best to avoid crowded times at weekends and in early summer when school parties visit. Centro de Visitantes has excellent displays and audiovisual presentations, 1000-1700. Near the centre is a terrace with exceptional views. From the visitors' centre there are three circular **walks** marked with arrows.

‡ *Spring and early summer are the best times to visit, but there are flowers to see at all times of the year.*

Laguna de la Fuente de Piedra

The saline Laguna de la Fuente de Piedra, located close to the town of the same name, lies just off the A92 to the west of Antequera. It is one of only two regular breeding sites for greater flamingoes in southwest Europe. Until the 1950s it was used as a *salinera* producing salt commercially; by 1982, the importance of the lagoon was officially recognized. The lagoon now has an information and display centre ① *1000-1500 and 1600-1900*, with panels, audio visual and computer displays regarding the way of life of the flamingoes and the other wildlife of the reserve. Next to the centre is a mirador located under a tree giving perfect viewing of the unlikely pink creatures. The best time to visit Fuente de Piedra is between January and June and try to arrive before 1100 as the heat haze and sun shining from the south make watching difficult later in the day.

● Sleeping

Málaga *p766, map p768*
There are many options, including some rather squalid ones. Book ahead in summer.
LL Málaga Palacio, C Cortina del Muelle 1, T/F952215185, www.ac-hoteles.com. An imposing hotel of 225 rooms opening on to a tree-lined esplanade. Conveniently close to the cathedral, city centre and nightlife. Rooftop pool.
AL Parador de Gibralfaro, Paseo García del Olmo, T952221902, www.parador.es. A superb traditional parador near the castle.

⁝ Coastal cuisine

One of the joys of a beach holiday in Andalucía is to have a lunch *al fresco* in a beach bar or *chiringuito*. In the early years of tourism, the *chiringuitos* were often owned by people who had their main restaurant in the town and just opened up their beach bar for the summer. They were just wooden shacks that blew down in the winter or were destroyed by storm waves and had to be rebuilt again for the following season. Nowadays they are much more permanent structures with impeccable hygiene, but many still have a traditional atmosphere with straw roofs and a colourful fishing boat in which to roast sardines on a spit. Invariably fresh fish figures prominently on the menus with paella and shellfish always popular. Some have become extremely well-known, others are still fairly rustic and temporary; everyone has their favourite.

The rooms have private entrances and sun terraces with panoramic views of the city and sea and a swimming pool. There are just 12 rooms, so reservations are essential.
A Las Vegas, Paseo de Sancha 22, T9522-17712, F952224889. Large traditional place with pleasant leafy garden, near bullring. Tropical gardens, pool and restaurant.
B Hotel California, Paseo de Sancha 17, T952215164, hcalifornia@spa.es. Near the beach at the eastern end of town, this is a friendly hotel with unremarkable but spacious rooms despite the ominous name.
C Carlos V, C Cister 10, T952215120. Located in the shadow of the cathedral with an interesting façade decorated with wrought-iron balconies. Parking.
D Derby, C San Juan de Dios 1 No 4, T952221302. This 4th floor *hostal* is excellent value, located in the heart of town overlooking the port. Recommended.
D El Cenachero, C Barroso 5, T952224088. This clean, no-frills *hostal* has 14 rooms, some with bath. Recommended.
F Córdoba, C Bolsa 9-11, T952214469. Small family-run *hostal* with shared bath. Although some rooms are a bit poky, it's a nice place.

Camping
Balneario del Carmen, Av Pintor Sorolla on the coast road west of Málaga, T952290021.

Around Málaga *p770*
In Nerja, there is a good choice of accommodation to suit all pockets. Antequera has some decent options too.

AL La Posada de Torcal, in Villanueva de la Concepción, Parque Natural El Torcal, T952031006, laposada@mercuryin.es. A small but luxurious and beautifully furnished place with a pool, facing the limestone mass of El Torcal.
AL Parador de Nerja, C Almuñécar 8, Nerja, T952520050, nerja@parador.es. Relatively modern parador set on cliff top with attractive gardens, lift to the beach, pool, tennis. All that one would expect from a parador.
A Parador de Antequera, C García del Olmo s/n, T952840901, www.parador.es. An understated modern parador surrounding a garden and swimming pool.
D Colón, C Infante Don Fernando 29, T952844516. A good modernized central option with a popular local restaurant.
E Manzanito, Plaza de San Sebastián 5, T952841023. Sizeable *hostal* with rooms with showers, in the main square.
E Miguel, C Almirante Ferrándiz 31, Nerja, T952521523. 8 rooms. Good ambience in the older part of town, close to the Balcón.

Camping
Camping Torcal, T952703582, Río de la Villa on the slopes of El Torcal, which has good facilities, including a pool.
La Laguna de Fuentepiedra, Camino de la Rábita s/n, T952735294. In the village close to the lake. Open throughout the year with pool, bar and restaurant.
Nerja Camping, on N340 4 km east of Nerja, T952529696. Located near Maro and the beach, this campsite has a pool and bar.

🍴 Eating

Málaga *p766, map p768*

There are some superb restaurants and tapas bars in Málaga where you can enjoy traditional local specialities such as *fritura malagueño* (fried fish), washed down with Malaga's famous wine, a sherry-like drink that comes in sweet and dry varieties. There are some excellent seafood restaurants and *chiringuitos* on the sea in the suburb of Pedregalejo.

€€€ **Antonio Martín**, Paseo Marítimo, the most celebrated fish restaurant. Popular and pricey with a sea view terrace, this traditional restaurant is frequented by matadors from the nearby bullring.

€€€ **La Taberna del Pintor**, C Maestranza 6. Arguably the best meat restaurant in Málaga, but pricey.

€€ **Casa Pedro**, C Quitapeñas 4, an enormous no-frills fish restaurant which is full of Spanish families on Sun.

€€ **El Vegetariano de la Alcazabilla**, C Pozo del Rey 5, near the Roman Theatre. One of several vegetarian restaurants. This one is excellent.

€€ **La Cónsula**, Churriana, T952622562. Restaurant of a well-known cookery school, specializing in Andalucían dishes. Located in an impressive 19th-century mansion where the writer Ernest Hemingway used to stay.

€€ **Marisquería Las Dos RR**, C Carpio 4, in the Huelin district. Another favourite, this one specializes in *pescado frito*, mixed seafood fried in batter.

€€ **Rincón de Mata**, Esparteros 8. An atmospheric small restaurant with interesting house specialities.

€ **Picassito**, C Echegaray 3, has cheerful Mediterranean cuisine and a *menú del día* for €6.50.

€ **Tintero**, in El Palo on the Playa del Dedo, is this remarkable place where the dishes are auctioned as they leave the kitchen. The bill is totted up according to the number of plates left on your table. For sheer entertainment value, this restaurant is hard to beat.

Tapas bars and café

There's a good tapas scene in Málaga, with many bars specializing in all manner of fried fish and seafood. The streets around the back of the cathedral are good for a prowl. One of the best areas is along the pedestrianized C Marín García.

Bar Logueno, C Marín García, the most famous bar. There's no number, but you can find it by the people milling outside sipping their glasses of *fino* (sherry). There is a tantalising choice of 75-plus tapas here, including many *Logueno* originals.

Café con Libros, C Granada 63, T952204717, is another good place that does exactly what it says on the cover.

El Barríl del Místico, Plaza Aduana 2, near the Alcazaba, is a nice underground bar with barrels of wine and tapas.

Kitsch Café, C Granada 44, T952608378, is a relaxed café-bar where the gaudily-coloured furniture and tigerskin screens live up to the name.

La Campana, C Granada 35, T952227566, a standout for its no-frills atmosphere and good fishy snacks.

La Catedral del Pescaíto, C Duque de Victoria 8, is another good spot for the fruits of the sea.

La Manchega, C Marín García No 4, great atmospheric.

Malta, C Keromnes s/n, is a spacious microbrewery that does good food and a refreshing homemade lager.

Mesón La Alegria, C Marín García 15, noted for its *jamón serrano*.

Pitta Bar, C Echegaray 8, near the Picasso Museum, has great Lebanese and Arab plates and tapas at knockdown prices.

Moroccan-style teashops

Increasingly popular, particular among students, are Moroccan-style teashops, or *teterias*. They are usually cosily cushioned with low tables and oriental rugs and serve dozens of different teas. Two of the most popular are situated on C San Agustin near the cathedral, while the largest is **Teteria Baraka**, housed in a former Arab bakery on the tiny C Horno, a few streets west of the Plaza de la Constitucíon.

● *For an explanation of sleeping and eating price codes used in this guide, see inside the*
● *front cover. Other relevant information is found in Essentials, see pages 47-56.*

Seafood restaurants in Nerja are moderately priced. For tapas bars in Antequera try around Plaza Abastos.

€€ **Hermanos Pulguilla**, C San Pablo 6, Nerja, T952521892. Seafood.

€€ **La Espuela**, Ctra de Córdoba s/n, Antequera, T952702633. Newish restaurant inside the bullring, local dishes with a good *menú del día*.

€€ **Marisquería la Familia**, C Diputación 17, Nerja, T952520046.

€ **El Angelote**, Plaza Coso Viejo, Antequera, T952703456. Local cuisine in an old mansion facing an attractive small square.

Madrona, C Calzada 31, Antequera, T952840014. Good pensión restaurant serving local dishes and tapas.

€ Those on a tight budget could try the lunchtime offerings of fish and shellfish in the *chiringuitos* on Burriana beach.

🍸 Bars and clubs

Málaga *p766, map p768*
Nightlife in summer spills out towards El Palo and its beachside discos. *Malagueños* love the *juerga* (a good night out), so nightlife is not hard to find, particularly in the summer. **ZZ Pub**, C Tejón y Rodríguez, has live music on Mon and Thu. Close by the **Warner Bar** on Plaza de los Martínez has a good atmosphere, as does **La Botellita**, C Alamos 38, and **El Cantor de Jazz**, C Lascano. For a Latino sound **Salsa**, C Méndez Nuñez, has live salsa on Wed and **Cantina Cubano**, C Granada, has good taped music and piña coladas. There are a host of disco bars in the Malagueta area, south of the bullring, where **Ragtime**, Paseo de Reding 12, is a favourite venue with blues, jazz or flamenco, depending on the night. **H20**, C Fernando Camino, is another throbbing club in this area. The bohemian crowd focus on **Café Teatro**, C Afligidos 8.

🎬 Entertainment

Málaga *p766, map p768*
Cinema Films are shown in the original language (versión original) at **Albéniz Multicines**, C Alcazabilla, T952128860.
Football Málaga is a competent Primera side; games are held at the **Estadio de**

Futbol La Roselada, P Martirincos, T952614374.
Theatre **Teatro Cervantes**, C Ramos Martín 2, T952224100, was restored in 1987 and stages opera, theatre and dance.

🎉 Festivals and events

Málaga *p766, map p768*
Málaga is noted for its fiestas.
In late **Feb**, is **Carnaval**.
Easter sees Semana Santa when local brotherhoods mount processions each day and a prisoner is released from Málaga jail. The ceremonies rival those of Sevilla and are arguably the best in Spain. See www.semanasanta.tv.
In **Aug** is **Feria**, an annual fair, which commemorates the incorporation of Málaga into the kingdom of Castille by the Catholic kings who entered the city in Aug 1487. More than an estimated million people come to the city to enjoy the bullfights, flamenco, processions, children's theatre and fireworks.

Around Málaga *p770*
During the **third week of Aug** Antequera sees **Real Feria de Agosto** (Royal August Fair) marked by bullfights and flamenco.

🚍 Transport

Málaga *p766, map p768*
Air For airport information, see p39.
Boat There are regular daily sailings to Melilla, the Spanish enclave in North Africa. The crossing takes around 10 hrs and costs €26.31 one-way. For information, contact **Transmediterránea**, C Juan Díaz 4, T9024-54645. Tickets from the Estación Marítima.
Bus The main bus station is on Paseo de los Tilos, T952350061. A complete timetable is available from the tourist office; buses leave every 15 mins to **Torremolinos** from the port; **Marbella** is served half-hourly. There are 7 daily buses to **Madrid** and to **Barcelona** via **Valencia**. There are 5 buses daily to **Córdoba**, 6 to **Cádiz**, hourly ones to **Granada**, 10 to **Sevilla**, 8 to **Almería**, 4 to **La Linea** by **Gibraltar** and hourly buses east to **Nerja** and the caves. There are 14 buses daily to **Antequera** and to **Ronda** in the north of the province.

Car Hire is most conveniently arranged at the airport, where all the main international firms have their offices. The following firms have offices in the city: **Avis**, C Cortina del Muelle, T952216627; **Hertz**, Alameda de Colón 17, T952225597; **Málaga**, Paseo Marítimo, T952210010; **Miramar**, Av Pries, T952226933.

Scooter and motorcycle hire Victoria Racing, C Victoria 6, T952220483.

Train RENFE station is on C Cuarteles, T952360202, but tickets can be obtained from many travel agencies. There are 8 daily trains to **Madrid**, 2 of which take only 4 hours, the others 6-8 hours.The same trains stop at **Córdoba**, while there is also a direct link with **Sevilla**. Other Andalucían destinations involve a change at **Bobadilla** junction. **Fuengirola-Málaga** stops at the main train station (RENFE) before the final stop, almost opposite El Corte Inglés department store. Tickets may be purchased on the train.

Around Málaga p770
In Antequera the bus station is on Paseo García del Olmo, near the town centre. There are 14 daily services to **Málaga** as well as the odd one to **Córdoba**, **Sevilla**and **Granada**.

The train station is 3 km from the town centre in Av de la Estación, T952843226. You can take a taxi to the centre (€3) or it's a 30-min walk. Few trains, however, visit Antequera, the main station being at Bobadilla, several kilometres away.

To reach **El Torcal** by car, take the C3310 from **Antequera** towards **Villanueva de la Concepción**, turning off after about 12 km towards the visitors' centre. Buses towards **Villanueva de la Concepción** are infrequent and drop you at the turn off with several kilometres still to walk. The best options are hitchhiking or a taxi.

❶ Directory

Málaga p766, map p768
Internet Ciber Málaga Café, Av de Andalucía 11. 1000-late. €2.5 per hr.
Internet Meeting Point, Plaza de la Merced 20. 1000-2400. €2 per hr.
Red Center, Plaza de la Merced 5. 1000-2000. € 2 per hr.
Rent@net, C Santiago 8. Open 1000-2400. €1.50 per hr.
Post office The main correos can be found in the Av de Andalucía, almost opposite El Corte Inglés, T952359008.

Granada → Colour map 6, grid B6; Population: 241,471; Altitude: 685 m.

"Give him alms, woman, for there is nothing in life so cruel as being blind and in Granada" Francisco de Icaza

Few who visit the city would disagree; Granada should not be missed. The Alhambra, regarded by many as the most dramatic and evocative monument in Europe, was the palace-fortress of the last Muslim kingdom in Spain and represents Moorish building and art at its sublime peak. The setting is magnificent. Built on a low hill between the rivers Genil and Darro, the Alhambra has the lofty Sierra Nevada as its backdrop. But there is much more to see in Granada. Opposite is the Albaicín, an old Moorish ghetto of atmospheric alleyways and squares, which straggles up the hill to the gypsy caves of Sacromonte. Down in the city, the Renaissance Cathedral has a Royal Chapel containing the tombs of Los Reyes Católicos, Ferdinando and Isabel. There are also many links with the Granadino writer and poet Federico García Lorca throughout the city, while the blend of students, tourists, conservatism and North African culture makes it an interesting place all year round. ►► For Sleeping, Eating and other listings, see pages 782-785.

Ins and outs
Getting there and around The national airport is 17 km to the west of the city, T958245200. José Gonzalez company runs five buses daily connecting the airport to the centre, stopping at the Palacio de Congresos and the Gran Vía (30 minutes,

€2.50). Taxis cost €15. The nearest international airport is at Málaga. The main bus station is on Ctra de Jaén, 3 km northwest of the town centre. A No 3 bus will bring you into the city. The train station is on Avenida de Andaluces, T958271272, reached by the No 11 bus, which follows a circular route. The city is best explored on foot. ▶▶ *For further details, see Transport page 785.*

Tourist information The main tourist office is tiny in the atmospheric Corral de Carbón ① *C Libreras 2, Mon-Sat 0900-1900, Sun 1000-1400, T958221022.* The municipal tourist office is larger and more people friendly ① *Plaza de Mariana Pineda 10, T958247128, Mon-Fri 0930-1900, Sat 1000-1400.* Both can provide city maps, accommodation lists and a free *¿Qué Hacer?* What's On? booklet.

History

Historical records go back to the Iberian tribe known as the Turdulos, who made coins on which Granada is named Iliverir. Then came successively the Phoenicians, the Greeks, the Carthaginians, and the Romans. The settlement grew in importance under the Visigoths, at which time a Jewish suburb, named Garnatha Alyehud, became established on the southern slopes of the Alhambra. This was significant, because it is believed that the Jewish population assisted the Moors in their invasion of the city.

The Moors gave Granada the name Karnattah (both names mean pomegranate, the fruit which has now been adopted as the city's symbol). For three centuries it was under the control of the Caliphate of Córdoba, but when this declined the capital was moved in 1013 to Granada where it was to remain for fourth and a half centuries until it was ended by the Catholic Monarchs in 1492. Its most affluent period came during the reigns of **Yusef I** (1334-1354) and **Muhmmed V** (1354-1391), the rulers who were largely responsible for the construction of the Alhambra. Towards the end of the 15th century, however, things changed for the worse. Firstly, in 1479, the Christian forces became united with the marriage of Ferdinand and Isabel and their combined armies had, within 10 years, taken Almería, Ronda and Málaga. At the same time the Moors were weakened by internal strife which led to civil war between rival supporters of the Sultan Muley Hassan's two most influential wives, Ayesha and Zoraya. The feud caused Ayesha to flee to Guadix with the heir Abu Abdullah (better known as Boabdil). He was proclaimed king there in 1482. Known as *El Rey Chico*, Boabdil eventually overthrew both his father and his uncle to become the last king of Granada. The Catholic Monarchs began to make impossible demands on **Boabdil**, who tried in vain to rustle up support from the Islamic world. War was declared and Granada quickly laid to siege. After seven months Boabdil gave in and formally ceded the city to the Catholic Monarchs in 1492, thus completing the Christian Reconquest. With the expulsion of the Jews and Moors, the city was deprived of many of its craftsmen, traders and merchants, and decline set in. As with many parts of Andalucía, the Peninsular War was a disaster for the city, with Napoleon's troops using the Alhambra as a barracks, causing untold damage. Granadinos have always had a reputation for being staid, middle class and right wing (a distinct contrast with neighbouring Córdoba) and during the Civil War the local fascists slaughtered literally thousands of left wingers and liberals, including the writer Federico García Lorca – a blemish which the city still struggles to live down.

Sights

Alhambra

The Alhambra, now the pleasure ground of stray cats rather than Moorish rulers, comprises four separate groups of buildings. The **Alcazaba** is a ruined 11th-century

fortress, which was the only building on the hill when the Nazrids made Granada their capital. The **Casa Real** or Royal Palace was built much later during the 14th century, mainly during the reign of Muhammad V. The **Generalife** on the northeast side of the hill was the extravagant pleasure palace of the Nasrid rulers, recreated today as a series of beautiful flower-filled terraces, cool fountains and pools. Finally, there is the **Palace of Carlos V**, a Renaissance building that would stand as an impressive structure on its own, but is a grandiose intrusion amongst the Moorish surroundings.

Ins and outs Only 8,800 visitors a day are allowed into the Alhambra so it's advisable to book in advance. There's a ticket office at the entrance, but in summer you'll be lucky to get in unless you turn up early. The ticket office opens at 0800. The vast majority of tickets are sold up to a year in advance through Banco Bilbao Vizcaya (BBVA), at a branch, or on T902224460 or T34 913465936 if abroad. Alternatively, see www.alhambra tickets.com, choosing the day and time you wish to visit. Pick up your tickets at the entrance to the Alhambra. In an effort at crowd control, the tickets to the Alhambra will have a 30-minute time slot for entry to the Casa Real (once in you can stay as long as you like) and as this is likely to be some time after your initial entry to the Alhambra, there will be time to see first the Generalife and the Alcazaba. Mar-Oct 0830-2000 (floodlit visits Tue-Sat 2200-2330); Nov-Feb 0830-1800 (floodlit visits Fri-Sat 2000-2130); €7, (€7.88 in advance), under 8s and disabled free.

> ◆ The Alhambra is best avoided during the heat of summer when it is most crowded, although it's better to see it in the summer than not at all.

Alcazaba The Alcazaba is the oldest part of the whole complex, but most of it was destroyed by Napoleon's departing troops. The **Torre de la Vela** gives magnificent views over the city and the snow-capped hills of the Sierra Nevada.

Casa Real The Casa Real (Royal Palace) is the source of the Alhambra's renown. Although its exterior is simple, the interior is highly intricate with a variety of ornamented ceilings and walls made of tiles, carved plaster work and Arabic inscriptions. There is clever use of light and space, with courtyards and delicate archways set off with fountains and water channels drawn off the nearby rivers. Water is skilfully used as the central theme throughout the palace, with many pools mirroring the surrounding carvings.

The entrance to the Casa Real leads into the **Mexuar**, the place where the Moorish kings held court with their subjects and dispensed justice. At the far end is a small **Oratorio**, set at an angle to Mecca. This leads to the **Cuarto Dorado** (Golden Room) which was re-vamped by Carlos V, although originally Mudéjar.

The first section of the Serallo, where guests were received, is the **Patio de los Arrayanes**, named after the neat myrtle hedges alongside the sizeable pool with its simple fountain. Notice here the beautifully carved filigree plaster work. The route now moves into the **Sala de la Barca**, which has an exceptional, restored *artesonado* wooden ceiling. Just beyond here is the **Torre de Comares**, the most impressive of the Alhambra's towers, 45 m high with walls 2 m thick. Inside is the **Salón de Embajadores**, by far the largest room in the palace with a ceiling soaring to a height of 20 m. The carved walls here are quite stunning, set off by a large number of windows, doorways and arches, complementing the cedarwood ceiling. The room has a strong sense of history, for it was here that Boabdil signed the document handing the city over to the Christians.

The Harem section of the Casa Real is the much-photographed **Patio de los Leones** (Court of the Lions). This beautiful courtyard represents a symbolic Islamic paradise with a central fountain supported by 12 small grey lions from which four rivers of paradise flow into four restful pavilions. The patio is surrounded by arches resting on a marble forest of 124 pillars, each with a different capital.

Granada

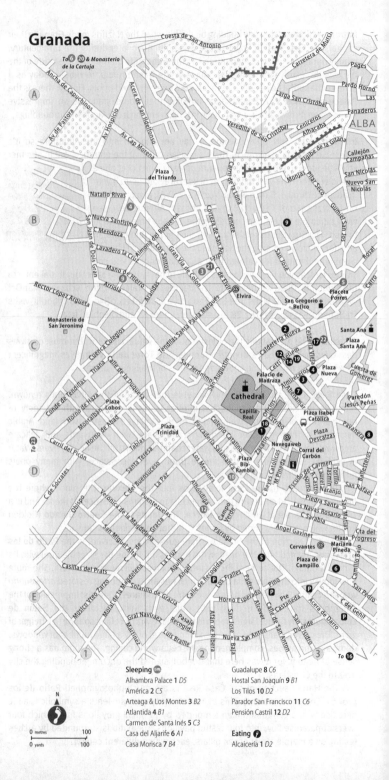

Sleeping 🛏
Alhambra Palace **1** *D5*
América **2** *C5*
Arteaga & Los Montes **3** *B2*
Atlantida **4** *B1*
Carmen de Santa Inés **5** *C3*
Casa del Aljarife **6** *A1*
Casa Morisca **7** *B4*

Guadalupe **8** *C6*
Hostal San Joaquín **9** *B1*
Los Tilos **10** *D2*
Parador San Francisco **11** *C6*
Pensión Castril **12** *D2*

Eating 🍴
Alcaicería **1** *D2*

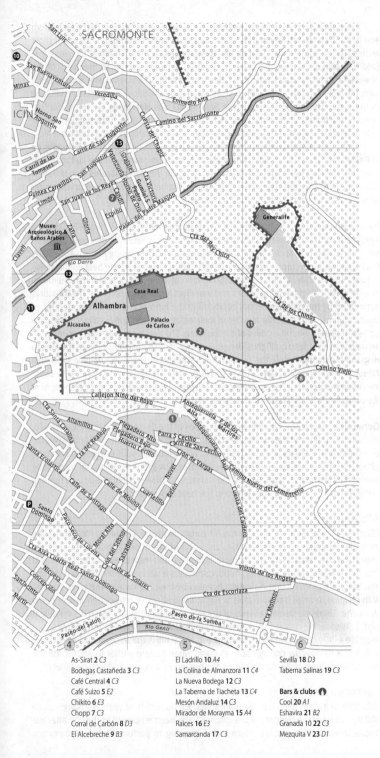

SACROMONTE

San Luis
San Buenaventura
Minas
ICIN
Horno San Augustín
Carril de las Tomases
Guinea Carreillos
Limón
San Augustín
Grajates
Manzuela Pedro Horno de Olio
San Juan de los Reyes
Carril
Espino
Zafra
Gloria
Museo Arqueológico & Baños Arabes
Clavell
Río Darro
Veredilla
Cta del Chapiz
Enmedio Alta
Camino del Sacromonte
Carril de San Augustín
Cta Victoria Gomels
Paseo del Padre Manjón

Generalife

Cta del Rey Chico

Casa Real
Alhambra
Alcazaba
Palacio de Carlos V
Cta de los Chinos
Camino Viejo

Callejón Niño del Royo

Cta Santa Catalina
Allamillos
Cta del Realejo
Plegadero Alto
Plegadero Bajo
Huerto Cecilio
Santa Escolástica
Calle de Santiago
Calle de Molinos
Paco Seco de Lucena
Moral Alta
Calle del Señor
Salvador
Cta Alta Cuarto Real Santo Domingo
Nicuesa
Concepción
San Jacinto
Mártir
Calle de Solares
Cuartelillo
Belén
Cuesta del Caidero
Vistilla de los Ángeles
Cta de Escorlaza
Cta Molinos
Paseo de la Somba
Paseo del Salón
Río Genil

Antequeruela Alta
Antequeruela Baja
P de los Mártires
Parra S Cecilio
Carril de San Cecilio
Cñon de Vargas
Nover
Camino Nuevo del Cementerio

Santo Domingo

As-Sirat **2** *C3*	El Ladrillo **10** *A4*	Sevilla **18** *D3*
Bodegas Castañeda **3** *C3*	La Colina de Almanzora **11** *C4*	Taberna Salinas **19** *C3*
Café Central **4** *C3*	La Nueva Bodega **12** *C3*	
Café Suizo **5** *E2*	La Taberna de Tiacheta **13** *C4*	**Bars & clubs**
Chikito **6** *E3*	Mesón Andaluz **14** *C3*	Cool **20** *A1*
Chopp **7** *C3*	Mirador de Morayma **15** *A4*	Eshavira **21** *B2*
Corral de Carbón **8** *D3*	Raíces **16** *E3*	Granada 10 **22** *C3*
El Alcebreche **9** *B3*	Samarcanda **17** *C3*	Mezquita V **23** *D1*

There are a number of rooms leading off the Patio de los Leones. At the far eastern end is the **Sala de los Reyes** (Hall of the Kings), entered by three porches with triple arches. To the south is the **Sala de los Abencerrajes**. In the fountain at its centre it is said that Abu al-Hassan, the father of Boabdil, beheaded some 16 members of the Abencerraj family whose leader had fallen in love with his favourite wife Zoraya. Don't miss the ceiling in this room with 16 sides, each lit by a window, and stalactite vaulting to the sides. On the north side is the **Sala de las dos Hermanas** (Room of the Two Sisters); the honeycomb of stucco work on the dome is dazzling. This room opens out onto a mirador, known as the 'eyes of the sultana', with a tranquil garden patio below.

Continuing along a rather tortuous route you eventually arrive at the **Peinador de la Reina**, the Queen's Pavilion, which was originally an oratory for the sultanas, but later the dressing room for Carlos V's wife. Next are the **Baños Reales** (Royal Baths) which are in the Roman style rather than Arabic. The baths are only open to visitors on specific days which change throughout the year.

Palacio de Carlos V This building was begun in 1526 after Carlos V had pulled down a significant part of the Casa Real to make way for it. The palace was designed by Pedro Manchuca, who was once a pupil of Michelangelo, and is in strong Renaissance style, but has never been completely finished. Although claimed to be the best Renaissance palace outside Italy, it sits uncomfortably amongst the delicate Moorish buildings around it, with its giant stone blocks and iron rings lending it a punk air. The interior is dominated by the massive central courtyard in the form of a circle surrounded by 32 Doric columns, with a similar number of Ionic columns in the upper gallery, which is a pattern repeated on the exterior of the building. The courtyard was often used as an arena and even staged bullfights. The ground floor of the palace now houses the **Museo Hispano-Musulmán**, while the upper floor is the site of Granada's **Museo de Bellas Artes**. ① *Both museums open Tue 1430-1800, Wed-Sat 0900-1800, Sun 0900-1430, the Alhambra entrance fee does not cover the museums and tickets must be bought at the door, free with EU passport, otherwise €1.50.*

Generalife Above the Alhambra on the slopes of the Cerro del Sol is the Generalife, the summer palace of the monarchs of Granada. The name is derived from the Arabic *Gennat-al-Arif* (Garden of the Architect). It was probably built in the 13th century, although it has since been altered several times. The grounds consist of a soothing interplay of pathways, gardens and fountains, with clever use of shade and running water, ideal for a relaxing hour or two in the heat of summer.

Albaicín

Clinging to the hillside across from the Alhambra on the far side of the Río Darro is the evocative Moorish *barrio* of Albaicín, once one of the busiest areas of Al-Andalus, shown by the remains of 30 or more mosques and numerous water tanks and fountains. Flanking the winding, narrow streets are villas with Moorish decoration and beautiful gardens tantalisingly concealed by their high walls. The air is scented with jasmine, orange blossom and, at night, the distinctive musky perfume of *dama de noche*. There are stunning views of the Alhambra (particularly when it's floodlit at night). Wandering around this area is definitely one of Granada's highlights, but exercise a little caution at night. Near the top of the hill is the Mirador de San Nicolás, which is a deservedly popular spot at dusk, when people gather to appreciate the magnificent views of the Alhambra, accompanied by buskers and fortune tellers.

Sacromonte

This area of gypsy caves has been inhabited for hundreds of years. Although some still do live here the majority of the *gitanos* have been rehoused in the city after the floods in 1962. The gypsies return in the evening to perform contrived flamenco

shows to coachloads of tourists, who are outrageously fleeced with over-the-top prices for drinks and tatty souvenirs, often with a spot of professional pick-pocketing and amateurish fortune telling. Nevertheless, Sacromonte has plenty of atmosphere and you can have a good, if pricey, evening out.

There are also a number of interesting sights in the valley, including the **Church of Santa Ana**, a brick church in Mudéjar style, which seems to rise out of the side of the Río Darro. Dating from the 16th century and located just above the point where the river disappears under the city, it was built in 1537 by Diego de Siloé and has a strong Mudéjar influence. Look, in particular, for the dazzling ceiling in the main chapel ① *Tue-Sat 1000-1400, free*. Nearby, the **Baños Arabes** (Arab baths), and the city's **Museo Arqueológico** are also worth a visit.

Catedral and Capilla Real

① *Mon-Sat 1045-1330 and Mon-Sun 1600-1900, €2.50, entry is along an alleyway from C Gran Vía de Colón*. Granada's cathedral is sometimes claimed to be one of the finest Renaissance churches in Spain; while it certainly wasn't knocked up on the cheap, it struggles to live up to this description. Next to it, however, is the Capilla Real, which contains the tombs of the Catholic Monarchs and their daughter Juana la Loca. It's an evocative experience to witness the last resting place of these rulers, who had such a profound impact on the course of the world's history. The Cathedral is located in the centre of the old Moorish city, or *medina*. Begun shortly after the reconquest, the construction was directed by a number of people, the most notable of whom was Diego de Siloé, between 1528 and 1563. Squat, towerless and hemmed in by other buildings, the exterior, which is made of brown sandstone, is dull, with only the main façade by Alonso Cano of some merit. The interior, however, has some redeeming features, being light, airy and possessing some fine stained-glass windows at higher levels by Theodore of Holland. The overall impression is somewhat cold; the frigid triumph of knowledge over faith. There are many side chapels containing ornate Baroque retablos; one of these holds a small fragment of the True Cross; not a fact much publicized in these cynical times. There is also a small museum, with the usual vestments, silverware and tapestries.

Capilla Real, ① *Mar-Sep Mon-Sat 1030-1330 and Sun 1100-1300, Mon-Sun 1600-1900, Oct-Feb daily 1030 (1100 Sun) -1300 and 1530-1830, €2.50*, enter from Calle Oficios, begun in 1506 and completed in 1521, was designed as a sepulchre for the Catholic Monarchs. Isabel died in 1505 and Ferdinand 11 years later, both being buried at the Alhambra, but in 1521 their remains were brought here.The tombs are found in the transept enclosed by a fine Plateresque *reja* by Maestro Bartolemé of Jaén. The tombs are carved from Carrara marble and the Catholic Monarchs are flanked by their daughter Juana la Loca (the Mad) and her unfaithful husband Felipe el Hermoso (the Fair). Unless you're a basketball player, it's a bit tricky to actually get a good view of the whole figures. The actual coffins are in the crypt underneath, but whether they still contain the monarchs' bodies is debatable as they were desecrated by Napoleon's troops during the Peninsular War. Other features of note are the retablo containing a wealth of figures and scenes including the handing over of the keys of the city by Boabdil, and the Sacristy which contains Ferdinand's sword, Isabel's crown and her personal art and jewellery collection, including some notable Flemish paintings.

Monesterio de San Jerónimo

① *Mon-Sat 1000-1330 and 1500-1830, Sun 1100-1330, €2.10*. This monastery was founded by the Catholic Monarchs in 1492 and the building was completed in 1547, much of the work directed by Siloé. Of exceptional importance are the cloisters, with a double layer of 36 arches, and the church, which has some 18th-century frescoes and a magnificent gold retablo.

① *1000-1300 (1200 Sun) and 1600-2000 Mar-Sep; 1030-1300 (1200 Sun) and 1530-1800 Oct-Feb, €2.50.* Not far from the university on the northwest side of the city on Calle Real de Cartuja is this impressive Carthusian monastery. It's a mixture of styles resulting in an overall impression of jumbled opulence, with Baroque dominant. Entry is through a Plateresque porch, with an arch bearing the coat of arms of Spain, over which is a vaulted niche with a 16th-century wooden statue of the Virgin. Within, there is a large courtyard full of orange trees and box hedges, with the monastery on one side and the church on the other. The church's wealth is almost overwhelming, but note in particular the 18th-century sacristy in brown and white marble and rich decorations. The Sagrario is almost as impressive. The monastery is a good 30 minutes' walk from the centre, but bus No 8 bus passes nearby.

Excursions

Located some 58 km east of Granada on the Río Guadix in a fertile farming region is the town of **Guadix**. Thousands of people in Guadix still live in well furnished caves dug out of the soft tufa rock of the hillside. It is thought that this troglodyte community, in the Barrio Santiago, was established following the Christian Reconquest of Spain, when fear of Felipe II caused local Moors to seek safety underground. There is a **Cave Museum**, ① *Mon-Fri 1000-1400 and 1600-1800, Sat 1000-1400*, in the barrio showing traditional implements and furniture. While the caves are interesting, the rest of the town is workaday and has little appeal beyond its ruined Moorish Alcazaba, built of red sandstone and offering great views towards the Sierra Nevada on a clear day.

Some 15 km from Granada and close to the airport, a minor road leads north to the village of **Fuente Vaqueros**, the birthplace of Federico García Lorca, the poet and dramatist who was shot by right-wing Nationalists in 1936. He was born in June 1898 in the house of the village schoolmistress, his mother. The house is now a museum ① *T958258466, summer Tue-Sun 1000-1300 and 1800-2000 and winter 1000-1230 and 1600-1830, €1*, and the neighbouring granary turned into an exhibition and cultural centre. The building is located in Calle Poeta García Lorca, just off the main square, and is full of Lorca memorabilia. Ureña buses come here from Granada approximately hourly from Avendia Andaluces by the train station.

Perched on a cliff top overlooking a deep gorge created by the Río Alhama, **Alhama de Granada** gets its name from the Moorish *Al Hamman* meaning thermal waters or baths. Both the Romans and the Moors valued Alhama highly as a spa and the baths are still in operation today. The town itself is a delight and one can appreciate Muley Hacen's cry of sorrow '*Ay di me Alhama*', when he lost the battle here against Christian forces in 1482. Most of the places to see are near to the Plaza de la Constitución, close to which is the **Barrio Arabe**, with a maze of alleyways following the original street plan. The Moorish **castle** is largely ruined and privately owned. Close by is the 16th-century **Iglesia del Carmen**, which looks out over the gorge. The church which dominates the town, however, is the **Iglesia de la Encarnación**, a 15th-century Gothic building with a Mudéjar pulpit and an *artesonado* ceiling, which the ubiquitous Siloé had a hand in designing. See also page 785.

● Sleeping

With over 50 hotels and around 100 *pensiones,* there is certainly loads of choice. Most are located in the district to the southeast of the cathedral. Granada's high season is spring and autumn, whereas during Jul and Aug most hotels drop their prices considerably.

LL Parador San Francisco, T958221440, granada@parador.es. Magnificent and luxurious accommodation inside the

Alhambra complex, within a former convent, although there is a more modern annexe. Try and get a room in the older section but book well in advance, especially in summer, as this is the most famous parador in Spain.

LL Alhambra Palace, C Peña Partida 2, T958221468, www.alhambrapalace.es. Luxury in pseudo-Moorish style complete with crowning dome and Arabian Nights decor. Try for a room with a balcony overlooking the city; stunning at sunset.

L Casa Morisca, Cuesta de la Victoria 9, T958221100, casamorisca@terra.es. On a steep hill in the Albaicín with Alhambra views, this 15th-century converted house has Moorish-inspired decor with a pretty central patio, stucco-work arches, multicoloured tiles and wooden ceilings embellished with arabic calligraphy.

AL Carmen de Santa Inés, Placeta Porras 7, T958226380, sinascar@teleline.es. A delightful intimate hotel with small walled garden complete with bubbling fountain, lemon tree, vines, roses and goldfish. Rooms are individually furnished with lovely tiles, modern art and fine fabrics.

A América, Real de la Alhambra 53, T958227471, F958227470. 13 rooms. Delightful small hotel, formerly a hostal, close to the parador, with a shady patio. Booking essential, expensive for the facilities but well worth it. Closed Jan-Mar.

A Guadalupe, Av de los Alijares s/n, T958223423, guadalupeh@infonegocio.com. A comfortable old-fashioned hotel close to the Generalife car park with good views from some rooms, so check in advance.

A Casa del Aljarife, Placeta de la Cruz, Verde 2, Albaicín, T/F958222425. Idyllic location in tiny square in the heart of the Albaicín with views of the Alhambra from the rooftop terrace. The 4 small rooms in this 17th-century house are individually furnished with lots of charm.

C Los Tilos, Plaza de Bib-Rambla 4, T958266712, www.hotellostilos.com. Excellent value, no-frills hotel with comfortable, modern interior overlooking pleasant square where there is a daily flower market. Good views from small 4th-floor terrace.

D Atlantida, Gran Vía 57, T958280423. Good value *hostal* on the main road a few blocks from the cathedral.

E Hostal San Joaquín, C Mano de Hierro 14, T958282879. A cosy rambling *hostal* with 2 shady patios and spacious rooms.

E Arteaga, C Arteagaa 3, T958208841. Just off Gran Vía, this is a good cheapie with clean shared bathroom and comfortable rooms. **Los Montes**, in the same building, is cheaper and also good value (**F**).

F Pensión Castril, Darrillo de la Magdalena 1, T958259507. Central, clean, friendly, shared bath. Recommended.

Camping
Los Alamos, Ctra A92, Km 290, 5 km from city, T958275743. Pool, open Apr-Oct.
Granada, Peligros, 3 km from city, T958340548. Both sites are on bus routes.

● Eating

Eating out is no problem in Granada, where there are restaurants and bars to suit all tastes and pockets. The Alhambra and Plaza Nueva areas have the inevitable tourist rip-off establishments. There are some excellent restaurants with North African and Middle Eastern flavours. Many bars in Granada give out free tapas with drinks; these often have a lot of effort put in to them and are delicious.

€€€ La Colina de Almanzora, C Santa Ana 16, T958229516. Next to the new Baños Arabes with sensational views of the Alhambra and Albaicín. Dishes include eggplant with honey and stewed partridges with chestnuts.

€€€ Corral de Carbón, Mariana Pineda 8, T958223810. Fabulous 14th-century *mesón* with brick and beam interior specializing in game dishes.

€€€ Mirador de Morayma, C Pianista García Carrillo 2, T958228290. Marvellous location overlooking the Albaicín and the Alhambra – a must for all romantics, specialities include *tortilla de Sacromonte*.

€€ Alcaicería, C Oficios 8, T958224341. Atmospheric location in the old Arab market close to the cathedral, good regional specialities.

€€ El Alcebreche, Plaza San Miguel El Bajo 6, T958273101. Pretty square in the Albaicín

● *For an explanation of sleeping and eating price codes used in this guide, see inside the*
● *front cover. Other relevant information is found in Essentials, see pages 47-56.*

where Moroccan owner dishes up healthy, tasty dishes with no preservatives and plenty of veggie choice. Closed Jan.

€€ **Chikito**, Plaza Campillo 9, T958223364. Attractive historical restaurant in a central location east of the cathedral with a medium priced *menú del día*.

€€ **Raices**, Pablo Picasso 30, T958120103. The longest established vegetarian restaurant in Granada (quite possibly in Spain!), with a daily changing menu, and imaginative desserts.

€€ **Samarcanda**, Calderería Vieja 3, T958210014. Excellent Lebanese restaurant with all the predictable favourites, as well as a few international dishes.

€€ **Sevilla**, C Oficios 12, T958221223. Open since the 1930s with 4 picturesque dining rooms and an outdoor patio overlooking the Capilla Real. Dishes are traditional *Granadino* with a *menú del día* of around €16.

€ **El Ladrillo**, Placeta Fátima. Lively restaurant with outside terrace specializing in seafood. If you don't care if you're unable to identify all the tentacles on your plate, order the vast seafood platter *barcos* for €8, which is easily enough for 2.

€ **La Nueva Bodega**, C Cetti Meriem 9, T958225934, is a no-frills spot with good tapas and a cheap restaurant.

€ **Mesón Andaluz**, C Cetti Meriem 10, does a *menú del día* that's as good as you're ever going to get for under €8.

Tapas bars and cafés

The best zone for tapas in central Granada is in the streets around C Elvira near Plaza Nueva, but there are local favourites in every corner of the city.

Bodegas Castañeda, C Almireceros 1 y 3, T958223222. This long-established and classy joint serves classic tapas dishes simply, as well as baked potatoes with a tasty choice of fillings. Try the *calicasa*, a potent blend of vermouth and other goodies.

Taberna Salinas, C Elvira 13, has an old-fashioned cavernous *bodega* atmosphere with hams hanging over the bar, dimly lit, cosy with delicious traditional tapas.

Chopp, C Abenamar 4, has a cosy atmosphere and nice tapas and *bocadillos*.

La Taberna de Tiacheta, Puente Cabrera s/n, is a new bar by the river with a friendly feel and excellent tapas; try the *morcilla*.

Café Central, C Elvira 3, near Plaza Nueva, has honest prices and some good food.

Café Suizo, Acera del Darro 26, is particularly good for breakfast, lots of coffees and teas.

Moroccan-style teashops

Teterias first emerged in Granada. The only catch is that they can be expensive, so do check the price of your cuppa before you order. Several of the most atmospheric are on C Calderer a Nueva.

As-Sirat, C Calderer a Nueva, one of the best. Also does excellent fresh dates.

Hammam Baños Arabes, C Santa Ana 16, T958229978, is a truly 5-star *teteria*. On the top floor, it has dreamy views and you can truly pamper yourself and have a bath, aromatherapy session or massage in the adjoining baths afterwards.

🟠 Bars and clubs

Like all Andalucían cities, Granada has a lively nightlife, powered by students and tourists. For live music, head towards the Gran Vía where jazz fans will enjoy **Eshavira**, Postigo de la Cuna 2, where there is also the occasional impromptu flamenco evening. **Mezquita V**, C Pinto López Mezquita 5, in the centre, is a laid-back bar with music at weekends. **Sala Trolls**, C Rodriguez de la Fuente, is a little way from the centre and has frequent heavy music nights. In Albaicín nightlife centres around Carrera del Darro: **Fontana**, opposite the Puente de Carrera, is a lively café by day and bar by night. **Unsettler**, a few doors down at number 7, is a cool place with a ragga and reggae vibe. *Discotecas* mainly flourish in university term time, when some of the lower Sacromonte caves are turned into lively discos. There are a couple of large discos: **Granada 10**, C Cárcel, opposite the cathedral, and **Cool** on C Dr Guirao, which is the city's largest with 3 dance floors.

🟠 Entertainment

Cinema Cine Club Universitario at the university occasionally screens original soundtrack films, T958243000.

Flamenco Popular and reliable flamenco theatre run by noted dancer at **Jardines Neptuno** on C Arabia from 2200 daily, book in advance, entrance includes drink, €21,

T95851112. The shows in the caves of Sacromonte are heavily tourist orientated; however, the Fri and Sat show at **Los Tarantos**, Sacramonte 9, is more authentic than most, €25. T958224525.

Theatre Concerts, dance and theatre productions take place in a number of venues, pick up a *Guía de Granada* at the tourist office to check what's on where.

☻ Festivals and events

The first 2 days in **Jan** is the fiesta which celebrates the end of the Reconquista and the arrival of the victorious Ferdinand and Isabel in Granada.

Early Feb sees **Romería Popular de San Cecilio**, a celebration of the city's patron saint, with a pilgrimage to Sacromonte Abbey.

In **Jun** is **Corpus Cristi**, a major festival with bullfights and other celebrations.

In **late Jun or early Jul** the **International Music and Dance Festival** is held. Highly recommended, it takes place in the Palacio de Carlos V; information from the tourist office.

☻ Transport

Bus Free bus maps and timetables are available from the tourist office and *bonobus* tickets for 10 journeys can be bought from tobacconists and kiosks for €3. There are daily buses to **Almería** (10), **Almuñecar** (6),

Córdoba (9), **Guadix** (11), **Jaén** (12), **Madrid** (10), **Málaga** (17), **Salobreña** (7), **Sevilla** (10) and **Ubeda/Baeza** (8). Buses marked *directo* are slower and cost slightly less. There are also daily buses to the Sierra Nevada, €5.50 return. A full set of timetables can be obtained from the tourist office.

Car Hire is available from **Atesa**, Plaza Cuchilleros 1, T958224004; **Autos Fortuna**, Infanta Beatríz 2, T958260254; **Autos Gudelva**, Pedro Antonío de Alarcón 18, T958251435; and **Ital**, Plaza Cuchilleros 12, T958223524.

Train There is a RENFE office at C Reyes Católicos 63, T958223119. Daily trains run to **Algeciras** (4), **Almería** (3), **Antequera** (4), **Cádiz** (4), **Córdoba** (3), **Guadix** (3), **Madrid** (2), **Málaga** (1), **Ronda** (4), and **Sevilla** (6).

☻ Directory

Hospital Cruz Roja (emergencies), C Escoriaza 8, T958222222; **Hospital General**, Av Coronel Muñez, T958292856.
Internet There are dozens: **Cervantes**, Plaza del Campillo 5, T958228583, Mon-Sun 1000-2300, €1.5 per hr; **Internet Elvira**, C Elvira 62, €1.50 per hr; **Navegaweb**, C Reyes Católicos 55, daily 1000-2300. Cheap rates.
Post Correos in Puerta Real, Mon-Fri 0800-2100, Sat 0800-1400.
Telephone There is a public call centre at C Reyes Católicos 55, Mon-Sat 0900-1400 and 1700-2200.

South of Granada

The Sierra Nevada's snow-capped peaks and fresh mountain air can come as a huge relief, especially during the summer, from the searing heat and constant activity of the surrounding cities and towns. Skiing, hiking, climbing are possible amoungst these peaks. The Alpujarras, at the bottom of the slopes of the sierra, are next stop. An area of outstanding beauty, it is a firm favourite for those wanting to walk, horse ride or just relax. To round it all off, the Costa Tropical awaits, offering a dip in the ocean in an area that is far less spolit than its neighbour, the Costa del Sol. ▸▸ *For Sleeping, Eating and other listings, see pages 791-792.*

Sierra Nevada → *Colour map 7, grid B/C1.*

The Sierra Nevada has several unique features. It is the most southerly ski centre in mainland Europe, but also one of the highest. This means that it has a long season, often lasting until late May, but also long hours of sunshine. It is exposed to high winds, but it also has excellent views, even to Africa on clear days. Three peaks rise

above the general level, **Alcazaba** (3,366 m), **Veleta** (3,398 m) and **Mulhacén** (3,481 m). The latter is the highest mountain on the Iberian Peninsula. A trip to the Sierra Nevada in summer makes a pleasant change from the oppressive heat in Granada. Summer activities include mountain walking, hang gliding and horse riding.

The Sierra Nevada is a national park covering nearly 170 000 ha. Despite this status and having been declared a Biosphere Reserve by UNESCO in 1983, there's still been substantial degradation of the alpine terrain as developers in the ski industry have run roughshod over the conservation interests. The park information centre ① *Ctra de Sierra Nevada, Km 23, T958340625, 1000-1400 and 1600-1800*, sells maps and guidebooks of the area and has a bookshop and cafeteria.

Wildlife
There are some 2,000 species of plants, of which around 70 are unique to the area; there's also a fine range of butterflies, birds, and mammals in the park, the Spanish ibex, once almost extinct in the area, has now recovered to number over 3,000. In the woodlands of the lower slopes are wildcats, beech martens and badgers.

Skiing and snowboarding
Prior to the second half of the 20th century, few Granadinos would have had any reason to go to the Sierra Nevada, particularly in winter. An exception were the 'icemen' who would toil up to the snowline and bring down blocks of ice on mules to sell in the streets of Granada. Things have changed. The purpose-built resort, Solynieve, is not an attractive place by alpine standards but this is made up for by the excellent skiing facilities. There are some 2,500 ha of skiable area with 19 lifts (cabins, chairlifts and t-bars), capable of carrying 30,000 people an hour, reaching 54 km of marked slopes. There are additionally six off-piste itineraries and a skiable vertical drop of 1,300 m. A total 3-km are floodlit for night time skiing at weekends. Snowboarding has its own circuit. Cross country skiing is also catered for, but is less popular than in other areas. Equipment hire is no problem and costs around €17 a day, €55 for six days. A lift ticket costs between €15 and €21.50 per day according to the season and up to €86 a week. Lifts operate 0900 to 1615-1700, according to conditions. Lift tickets can be obtained from kiosks in the Plaza de Pradollano and in the lower Al-Andaluz gondola terminal.There are around 20 ski schools, including one for infants. The best times for skiing are between 0900 and 1100 and 1300 to 1500, when the slopes are almost deserted. For a recorded daily update in both Spanish and English of ski conditions, T958249119. A useful website is www.sierranevadaski.com.

Walking and climbing
The upper reaches of the Sierra Nevada give some scope for mountain walking and scrambling during July and August, when most of the snow has gone. A dirt road runs from near the parador down to Capileira in the Alpujarras, but it is best to have a four-wheel drive vehicle for this journey. The ascent of Veleta begins from this road and should take about three hours to the summit. The ascent of Mulhacén normally starts from Trevélez in the Alpujarras and you should allow six hours for this climb. Although expert rock climbing skills are not required for these routes, walkers should obviously be well kitted out; get an up to date weather forecast, T958249119, and have a detailed map – there is a 1:50,000 map produced by the *Federación Española de Montañismo* which can be bought in bookshops in Granada and in Solynieve.

Las Alpujarras → *Colour map 7, grid C1.*

This area stretches across the southern slopes of the Sierra Nevada. It is a region of superb natural beauty, with deeply eroded valleys, lush meadows, terraced slopes

and villages of great character. The air is clear and the backdrop of the Sierra Nevada
is snow capped for much of the year. The Alpujarras undoubtedly provide the best walking and hiking opportunities in Andalucía. There are pensiones in most of the villages, as well as a good network of casas rurales. Advance booking is recommended for summer and fiestas.

Ins and outs

Getting there and around The road south from Granada towards Motril, the N323, leaves the vega and climbs steadily to a height of 860 m at the Puerto del Suspiro del Moro – the Pass of the Moor's Sigh, named after Boabdil the last Moorish king of Granada, who paused here for a last look at the city before his exile. The road continues south for 20 km before the A348 leads east to Lanjarón, the gateway to the Alpujarras. From Granada, there are three daily buses to Pitres that stop in Lanjarón, Órgiva, Pampaneira, Bubión and Capileira. Two of these go beyond to Pórtugos, Trevélez and Bérchules. Buses also run to Motril.

Best time to visit The scenery and clear air of the Alpujarras means that the region receives a steady stream of visitors throughout the year. Spring and early summer are undoubtedly the best times, with flowers at their best, birds in full song and plenty of snow on the peaks.

Background

This remote area is bordered to the north by the Sierra Nevada and to the south by a series of lower ranges. The silt laden valleys are extremely fertile, so that agriculture thrives, helped by a equable climate due to the mountains keeping out extreme cold from the north and extreme heat from the south. When Granada fell to the Christians, many of the Moors fled to the Alpujarras. They terraced the valley sides and left their stamp on the landscape, with street patterns in the villages unchanged over the centuries. The domestic architecture, too, is distinctive. The roofs are flat and constructed of blocks of the local schist. This is covered with a depth of several inches of slate shards. After the banishment of the Moors, the area fell into rural poverty. It was not until the second half of the 20th century that the fortunes of the Alpujarras began to revive. This recovery is based largely on tourism and on the influx of new Northern European residents. The popularity of Chris Stewart's best selling book *Driving Over Lemons*, which tells of an expat's life in the Alpujarras, has attracted even more visitors.

Órgiva → *Population: 5,039; Altitude: 450 m.*

Some 10 km east of Lanjarón, the gateway to the region, is Órgiva, the administrative centre of the region, which was made capital of the Alpujarra by Isabel II in 1839. It is also an important market town. It was frequently mentioned by the Arab chroniclers but there are few remains of its Moorish heritage around today.

North from Órgiva are three villages of the High Alpujarras, Pampaneira, Bubión and Capileira, which cling to terraces on the side of the Poqueira Valley.

Pampaneira → *Population: 337; Altitude: 1,058 m.*

Pampaneira is approached through the **Poqueira Gorge**, cut by the river of the same name which rises on the slopes of Mulhacén. It's one of the best places in the region, and makes a good base. There is a pleasant square next to the bricky Baroque church. Look for the *retablo* and the Mudéjar coffered ceiling. The Plaza de Libertad has bars, craft shops and the Sierra Nevada Natural Park Visitors' Centre. Here there is a small display showing the natural history, geology and wildlife of the Alpujarras, while there is also a comprehensive collection of books and pamphlets.

Just outside the village, perched on the side of the gorge, is the incongruous **Tibetan Buddhist Monastery of Clear Light** ① *T958343134, visits 1500 to 1800 daily,*

⁚ An Englishman in Yegen

On the wall of a house, just off a small square in the Alpujarran village of Yegen, is a tiny plaque which proclaims in blue letters that the English writer Gerald Brenan lived here in the 1920s and 1930s. This is a modest tribute to someone whom many consider to be the greatest English Hispanist.

Brenan was born in 1894 and after a public school education (where according to his biographer he developed most of his hang-ups), he fought in the First World War, gaining a Military Medal and the French Croix de Guerre. After the war he settled in Spain, mainly it seems because of the cheap wine and cigarettes, which were lifelong addictions.

He ended up in the then remote village of Yegen, with his collection of over 2,000 books, having married the American poetess Gamel Woolsey. It was here that he had a steamy relationship with a 15-year-old peasant girl, resulting in his only

daughter Miranda – who the long-suffering Gamel agreed to bring up. Don Gerardo, as he was known to the locals, was quite wealthy owing to a number of legacies which came his way, so he did not need to publish work to survive. Study and scholarship were more important and it was not until he was 40 that his first book was published. This was *South From Granada*, a perceptive insight into everyday life in an Andalucían *pueblo* (village) and since regarded as a sociological masterpiece, and recently made into a decent film. Then followed the scholarly *The Spanish Labyrinth* and the *Literature of the Spanish People*. Meanwhile, Brenan had developed a strong Andalucían dialect and a love for the Spanish, admiring their dignity in poverty and their emotions which they carried on their sleeves. It was a two-way rapport and his passionate writing found an appreciative readership in Spain.

also known as O Sel Ling, the birthplace of the young Osel, who is supposed to be the successor to the Dalai Lama.

Bubión → *Population: 376; Altitude: 1,300 m.*
In a stunning position backed by the snows of the Sierra Nevada, this is the next village along the valley. It is rapidly acquiring the trappings of tourism, but it has a long way to go to catch up with nearby Capileira.

Capileira → *Population: 560; Altitude: 1,436 m.*
This village at the head of the valley marks the start of the summer dirt road that climbs up to the upper slopes of Mulhacén and Veleta and down to Solynieve. It is also an excellent centre for walking and horse trekking holidays. **Church of Nuestra Señora de la Cabeza** has a carving of the Virgin, which was a gift from Ferdinand and Isabel.

The Taha
Returning south to the main east/west high road there is a cluster of villages, including Pitres, Pórtugos, Mecina Fondales, Ferreirola and Busquistar, which collectively make up what in Moorish times was known as the *Taa* or *taha* group (a word derived from the Arabic word for obedience). All five villages show the typical domestic architecture of the area, with the gallery-like *tinaos* and walls and roof made of *launa*. There are two good accommodation possibilities in Pórtugos, which makes

a convenient centre for exploring the area. In the tiny, unspoiled village of Ferreirola,
close to Bubión and Capileira, is a wonderful place to stay.

Trevélez → *Population: 793; Altitude: 1,476 m.*

The next valley has been cut by the Río Trevélez and with terraces lining the valley
sides, this is not so dramatic as the Poqueira. A road leads up one side of the valley to
the village of Trevélez, returning down the other side. Trevélez's main (but false) claim
to fame is that it is the highest village in Spain. Legend has it that Rossini was once
prepared to swap his Stradivarius for a Trevélez ham! Certainly the small square reeks
with the aroma of hams and sausages that hang in profusion from the ceilings of
every house and shop. The mountain air is perfect for curing them; a Fiesta de los
Jamones is held every year in August.

East of Trevélez

The high road continues through the unremarkable, but pleasantly attractive villages of
Juviles and **Bérchules**. In the north, the town of **Válor** is worth a visit. Surrounded by
well-wooded farmland, the village is characterized by its steep winding streets with the
houses covered by the dark grey *launa*. The nearby village of **Yegen** was the home for of
the British writer Gerald Brenan, who wrote the observational study *South of Granada*.
His house, **El Casa del Inglés**, can be found in the upper part of the village.

Walking in las Alpujarras

Thanks to the isolation of the Alpujarras and the comparatively recent arrival of paved
roads, the footpaths linking the villages are mostly intact and make for some
wonderful walking. Most routes have some steep climbing involved – there is no such
thing as a gentle *barranco* or ravine – but the walking is varied and often spectacular.
The best place to pick up maps and guidebooks is in the Centro de Visitantes in
Pampaneira where the excellent Nevadense guides are based, see page 787. The
amount of assembled literature and maps is really impressive.

Trevélez Circuit Distance: 14-km; Time: 7/8 hours; Difficulty: medium/difficult. One
of the most spectacular walks in the region is this long climb that takes you up to the
beautiful high cirque (2,900 m), which lies just beneath mainland Spain's highest
peak, the Mulhacén (3,479 m). From Trevélez you have a climb of nearly 1,500 m so to
enjoy this walk you should be reasonably fit and get going at a reasonable hour. The
path is steep and loose in parts; if in doubt you can simply make this an up-and-down
walk for as far as the mood takes you. Map 1:50000 Sierra Nevada General Map or
1:50000 Lanjarón (1042) and 1:50000 Güéjar-Sierra (1027).

The walk begins in the square at the bottom of Trevélez in front of **Bar Rosales**. Go
up the hill to Mesón La Fragua. Here bear left, pass **Hotel La Fragua**, turn right beneath
an archway then turn right into Calle Horno. After 40 m, at a yellow arrow on a
telegraph pole, go left. When the path divides (20 minutes) go straight on following
red and white marker posts. About 200 m after passing a threshing circle the path
divides. Bear left and climb: a rock with a white arrow points the way. At a small cairn
(45 minutes) bear left following red dots. You now follow cairns up across looser
terrain, with Trevélez visible way down below. The path climbs steeply through pine
forest and then zigzags; eventually red dots lead you to a flat area and a ruined farm:
Cortijo La Campiñuela (two hours 15 minutes). The path bears right between the farm
and a threshing circle then climbs past a tumbledown corral. Where it divides go left,
continuing up over looser shale. Cairns and red dots mark the path. The path
eventually descends and crosses the Río Culo de Perro (dog's arse). On the other side
bear left: the path is indistinct at first but soon cairns lead you slightly to the right,
away from the stream. After climbing for about 15 minutes the path divides. Bear left
and climb the Culo de Perro's steep, rocky right bank, marked on some maps as

'Chorreras Negras' – literally, the small, dark waterfalls. You cross the rocky river bed just before the top of the ridge and reach the beautiful glacial cirque of Siete Lagunas (three hours 45 minutes) which lies between Alcazaba (3,360 m) and Mulhacén (3,479 m), both of which can be climbed from here. This walk finishes here, at 2,900 m, on the flat, grassy area between the Siete Lagunas, or Seven Tarns, which is a perfect picnic spot.

Costa Tropical → *Colour map 6/7, grid C6/C1.*

The 60 km coastal stretch of Granada province is known as the Costa Tropical. It's a pleasant area, with two decent resort towns, Almuñecar and Salobreña, and less spoiled than most parts of the Andalucian coast. The shoreline consists largely of tall cliffs with the occasional small cove or fishing village.

Motril

Motril, set slightly inland, is the main town of the area, but has little appeal beyond its transport connections.

Salobreña

Some 4 km west of Motril is the small resort of Salobreña. It is in two parts, an old hill village and a modern beach development, both surrounded by sugar cane fields. The older part has the most spectacular location on the Granada coast. Salobreña has a long and interesting history. Founded by the Phoenicians in the eighth century as a trading post, it was later occupied in turn by the Carthaginians and the Romans. Under the Moors it was one of Granada's 30 districts and an area of some agricultural importance and a summer destination for royalty.Modern Salobreña is a reasonably well-planned tourist resort; the beach is divided in two by a large rock. The Moorish castle was once the most important bastion in these parts; it has been remodelled over the years but is still atmospheric. The tourist office is in Plaza de Goya.

Almuñécar → *Population: 21,500.*

Some 13 km west of Salobreña lies Almuñécar, the largest resort on the Costa Tropical. It was founded by the Phoenicians some 3,000 years ago and later occupied by the Romans, who left behind an aqueduct and the rather improbable name of Sexi Firmun Julium. The Moors wisely dropped that name and called it Al-Munnakkah.

Laurie Lee in *As I Walked Out One Midsummer Morning* described Almuñécar in withering terms at the start of the Civil War, when he was rescued from its rather stony beach by a British destroyer. Today, he would be surprised at Almuñécar's development as a holiday resort. A headland, the **Peñon del Santo**, divides the coastline into two, with the Playa de San Cristóbal to the west and the Playa de Puerta del Mar to the east. Both beaches are of stone or shingle, but backed by attractive *paseos* with a number of tapas bars.

It is well worth visiting the small **Museo Arqueológico** ① *Plaza de la Constitución, Tue-Sat 1030-1330 and 1600-1800, Sun 1030-1330, €2 including entry to castle.* Known as the Cuevas de las Siete Palacios (Cave of the Seven Palaces), the place is thought to have been a cellar of Roman construction, probably used for water storage. Local artefacts are displayed from Phoenician, Roman and Moorish periods, but the star exhibit is an inscribed Egyptian vase dating from the reign of the Pharaoh Apophis I.

Castillo San Miguel ① *see Museo Arqueológico above*, is perched on the headland that separates Almuñécar's two main beaches. The Castillo was built in the reign of Carlos V on the site of a Roman fort and a later Moorish Alcazaba. For years it was the town's cemetery, until quite recently when its inhabitants were dug

town **museum**. Beneath the walls of the Castillo is the site of a newly excavated Roman fish factory making *garum*, a kind of fish sauce, in similar style to that at Baelo Claudia in Cádiz Province.

The municipal **tourist office**① *Palacete de la Navarra, T958631125, www.almune carctropical.org, 1000-1400, 1600-1900*, is in an interesting Neo-Moorish building at the coastal end of Avenida Europa.

● Sleeping

Sierra Nevada *p785*
During the skiing season accommodation is quite expensive, many of the hotels close from Jun to Nov. The few which stay open all the year may halve their prices during the summer and include:
L Kenia Nevada, Pradollano s/n, T958480911, F958480807. 67 rooms. Garage, pool, sports. **C** in summer.
AL Parador Sierra Nevada, Ctra de Sierra Nevada, Km 34, T958480400, F958480458. Small and modern. **B** in summer.
E Albergue Universitario, Carretera de Veleta Km 36, T/F958480122, with 83 beds. Open all year round. Basic.

Las Alpujarras *p786*
There are many options in Órgiva, but basing yourself in a smaller village will give a better feel for the area.
B Alpujarras Grill, C Empalme s/n, Órgiva, T958785549. 22 a/c rooms and a garage.
D El Molino, on the main street, Órgiva, which is a friendly bed and breakfast.
D Hostal Ruta del Mulhacén, Av de la Alpujarra 6, Pampaneira, T958763010, which has attractive rooms with bath and balcony.
D Hostal Pampaneira, C José Antonio 1, Pampaneira, T958763107, opposite **Hostal Ruta del Mulhacén**, with a friendly owner and clean spacious rooms. It also has a good value *menú del día*.
A-B Villa Turística de Bubión, Barrio Alta sin número, Bubión, T958763111, F958763136, has apartments (no kitchen) for 2 to 4 people, as well as hotel facilities including a restaurant and pool.
B Nuevo Malagueno, Ctra Órgiva-Trevélez sin número, The Taha, T958766098, F958857337, with stunning views from rooms, a garage, bar and restaurant.
C Finca Los Llanos, Bubión, T958763071, an attractive place at the top of the village off the side of road to Sierra Nevada with pool.

C Mirador de Pórtugos, Plaza Nueva 5, The Taha, T958766014. A *pensión* sited on a terrace at the entrance to the Trevélez valley, with, as its name suggests, some marvellous views. Good restaurant too.
D Hostal Fernando, Trevélez Alto, Trevélez, T958858565; a small establishment with friendly staff. Good budget option. Recommended.
D Hostal Ruta de las Nieves, Carretera Sierra Nevada sin número, Bubión, T958-763106, with great views from its terrace. There are plenty of restaurants in town.
D Hotel La Fragua, Trevélez, T958858626, which is a fairly basic, small hotel at the top of the village with an excellent restaurant just a few yards away.
D Las Terrazas, Plaza del Sol, Bubión, T958763034, F958763252. Simple, good value accommodation and friendly owners, with mountain bikes available to hire.
D Sierra y Mar, Ferreirola, T958766171, F958857367. A delightful guesthouse but often fully booked. Owners José and Inge have exceptional knowledge of walks and the area. If this is full there are rooms and apartments to rent in the village from Fernando of **Nevadense**, based at the Centro de Visitantes in Pampaneira, T958766253.

Camping
There are 3 official campsites, all mid-range.
Camping Órgiva, Valle de Guadalfeo, Órgiva, T958784307.
Camping Trevélez, Haza de la Cuna, 1 km from the village, T958858735.
Balcón de Pitres, Carretera Órgiva-Ugíjár Km 51, T958766111.

Costa Tropical *p790*
There are many accommodation options in Salobreña and plenty of rented apartments available in Almuñécar.
D Tropical, Av Europa s/n, Almuñécar, T958633458. 11 rooms. Small, comfortable and central. Recommended.

D **Victoría II**, Plaza Damasco 2, Almuñécar, T/F958631734, hotelvictoria@teleline.es. 40 rooms with bath and TV in central location. Recommended.

E **Palomares**, C Fábrica Nueva 44, Salobreña, T958610181, is a friendly spot with clean, good value rooms. There's a decent campsite on the waterfront.

🍴 Eating

Sierra Nevada *p785*
See Sleeping for options.

Las Alpujarras *p786*
See Sleeping for further options.
€ **Casa Julio**, Pampaneira, is a top place to eat, with a terrace, views, and a welcoming family atmosphere.
CiberMonfi, is at C Alcalde Pérez Ramón 2, Bubión, an attractive and friendly Moroccan style internet café, with a pleasant garden and belly dancing on some Sat nights.
€ **Mesón la Bodega**, Plaza de Goya, Salobreña, has ambience along with sherry from the barrel and a reasonable *menú del día*.

Costa Tropical *p790*
€ Chiringuitos on the beach, such as **Flores** and **Tres Hermanos**, provide good, inexpensive fish dishes.

⊖ Transport

Sierra Nevada *p785*
Bus Autobús Viajes Bonal, T958273100, runs a daily bus service from **Granada** to the **Sierra Nevada**, leaving at 0900 from the Palacio de Congresos, on Paseo del Violón on the east bank of the Río Genil, returning at 1700, with tickets available at the **Bar El Ventorillo** beside the Palacio.
Car Wheel chains can be rented at garages on the Granada-Sierra Nevada road.
Taxi T95815146. A taxi from **Granada** to the **Sierra Nevada** costs around €40.

Costa Tropical *p790*
Buses stop at the town entrance, just off the coast road. There are 8 local buses in each direction, hourly to **Motril**, 7 buses a day from **Almería**, **Málaga** and **Granada**, with less frequent connections with **Sevilla**.

Almería

This is the most easterly of the provinces of Andalucía. It is the hottest, sunniest, driest and least populated province. Tourism has not made much progress here compared with the Costa del Sol. Almería has a semi-desert landscape with low rainfall, under 100 mm annually. Today, brief spring showers encourage a plethora of wildflowers to briefly bloom. The arid landscape, near constant sunshine, and the clear light have attracted film producers, with spaghetti westerns made by the score. Some of the sets have been preserved at Mini Hollywood, 12 km north of Almería. East of the provincial capital, Almería, there is an ever-changing coastline of towering cliffs, remote coves and occasional dunes. Further east, the ancient hilltop village of Mojácar has spilled down to the coast to form the modern resort of Mojácar Playa. The west of the province is marred by vast areas of plasticultura centred on the town of El Ejido, with market gardening produce supplied both to Spain and much of northern Europe.

Almería city → *Colour map 7, grid C2; Population: 168,025.*

Further south than both Algiers and Tunis, this busy seaport has a strong African flavour; the bristly Moorish Alcazaba, which looms over the city, adds to this feeling. Not as image-conscious as some places, the rest of the old centre and seafront could do with some loving care. The attractive Paseo de Almería is the focus of the town, but unless you get waylaid by the city's lively nightlife, you're unlikely to want to stay for days. ▶▶ *For Sleeping, Eating and other listings, see pages 796-798.*

Getting there Almería has its own international airport, just off the N344, 8 km to the east of the city, T950221954. Bus no 14 runs from the airport to the town every 30 mins Mon-Fri 0700-2130 and every 45 mins Sat and Sun. If returning to the airport, catch the bus outside Pizza Hut on Av de Federico García Lorca. The bus station is a few minutes' walk away at Plaza de Barcelona. Trains arrive at the station on Ctra de Ronda, about 20 minutes' walk from the centre, T902240202 for information. ▸▸ *For further details, see Transport page 797.*

Tourist information The tourist office ⓘ *Parque Nicolás Salmerón, on the corner of C Martínez Campos, T950274355, almeria@andalucia.org*, is opposite the port.

History

The city was probably founded by the Phoenicians and later occupied by the Romans. A major expansion came in Moorish times, when it was known as Al-Mariyat (the mirror of the sea). Under Abd ar-Rahman III the magnificent **Alcazaba** was built. Later, after the collapse of the caliphate at Córdoba, it became capital of a separate *taifa*. By the 14th century it had a population of over 300,000, with prosperity based on ship building and silk weaving. This period of affluence ended with the Christian Reconquest in 1490 and the expulsion of the Moors. Decline set in, not helped by the earthquake of 1522, which destroyed much of the town and the castle. By the 17th century the population had fallen to under 600. Recovery came in the 20th century with the construction of the railway line and a new harbour to export minerals such as iron and lead from the interior. During the Civil War, it was staunchly Republican, which led to the bombardment of the harbour by German warships in 1937. It was not until the last two decades of the 20th century that prosperity returned to Almería, spurred on by horticulture and tourism.

Sights

The Alcazaba ⓘ *Tue-Sun 0900-1830 (2000 in summer), Tue-Sun, free with EU passport otherwise €1.50*. The Alcazaba is the largest Moorish castle in Andalucía and its hill site dominates Almería. The Alcazaba has had a chequered history reflecting that of the town itself. Work on the building started in 955 under Abd ar-Rahman 111 of Córdoba, but its most glorious period was during the 11th century during the reigns of Jayran, Zuhayr and Almotocin. It has also experienced periods of total neglect. Although a residence of governors and kings, it was always first and foremost a military base. This use, combined with the effects of the earthquake in 1522, plus subsequent renovations, has substantially altered the original appearance.

It consists of three defensive compounds, all containing construction from different periods of history. The **first compound**, the largest of the three, is approached through an exterior gate, then up a zig-zag ramp (a defensive ploy common in Moorish fortifications) before arriving at the **Puerta de Justicia**, overlooked by the **Torre de Espejos** which was added in the 15th century. The mirrors were apparently used to contact ships approaching the harbour. The massive walls recall China as they stretch away to the northeast spanning a deep valley and up to the hill of San Cristóbal. The **second compound** served as a residence for the Muslim kings and governors and also housed their guards and servants. You can only wonder at its former magnificence, for there are only scant remains today. Archaeological work is continuing in this compound, concentrating on the ruins of the **Palacio de Almotacín** and the **Ventana de la Odalisca** in the north wall. There is a poignant tale concerning the latter. Apparently a prisoner fell in love with a Moorish slave girl who tried to help him escape, but the plot was discovered and he jumped to his death from the window, the girl inevitably dying from a broken heart some days later. The **third compound** is entirely post-Muslim. After the Reconquest of Almería, the Catholic Monarchs, seeing the earthquake wreckage, ordered the construction of a castle with

thicker walls in the westernmost and highest part of the Alcazaba. Entrance was by a bridge over a moat protected by three semi-circular towers. The interior **Patio de las Armas** is dominated by the **Torre del Homenaje** (keep). There are excellent views from the towers over the port and the gypsy area below the castle known as **La Chanca**.

Cathedral ① *Mon- Fri 1000-1700, Sat 1000-1300, €2.* The Cathedral was built for defence against attacks by Berber pirates as well as for worship. It consequently has massive stone walls and small high windows, while its corner towers had positions for cannons. Built on the site of the old mosque, it's got a distinct whiff of the desert about it. The only exterior feature of note is the strange Renaissance doorway; inside, amongst the severity, look for the paintings by Alonso Cano.

La Plaza Vieja With only one access road, it is easy to miss this delightful pedestrianized square, also known as the Plaza de la Constitución, with its late 19th-century Ayuntamiento. One block away to the north is the 17th-century **Church of Las Claras**.

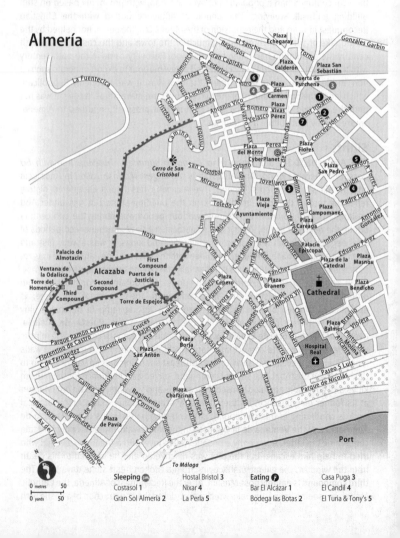

Almería

Sleeping 🛏
Costasol **1**
Gran Sol Almería **2**
Hostal Bristol **3**
Nixar **4**
La Perla **5**

Eating 🍴
Bar El Alcázar **1**
Bodega las Botas **2**
Casa Puga **3**
El Candil **4**
El Turia & Tony's **5**

0 metres 50
0 yards 50

Around Almería

Paraje Natural del Desierto de Tabernas → *Colour map 7, grid C2.*

On the A92 heading north, the road runs through the Paraje Natural del Desierto de Tabernas, a fascinating area of semi-desert, the bare treeless mountain slopes showing the rock structure, dried up river beds and flat topped plateaux. This is probably the only area of true semi desert on mainland Europe. The desert area now has no fewer than three spaghetti western theme parks.

Mini Hollywood → *Colour map 7, grid C2.*

ⓘ *1000-1900 in summer, weekends only in winter, €16, children €9. The car park is equally expensive at €3.50.* Some 12 km along the A92 and just past a junction with the N340, almost immediately on the right hand side of the road, is Mini Hollywood, the oldest and the best of the three theme parks, although tacky and overpriced. This is a relic of the golden age of

‖ *The successful Spanish comedy 800 Balas is worth seeing; based on the lives of unemployed extras from the spaghetti western era.*

spaghetti western films, such as *A Fistful of Dollars* and *The Good the Bad and the Ugly* (also *Indiana Jones*) which were made in this area in the 1960s and 1970s. The film makers were attracted by the arid scenery, reminiscent of the American Midwest, plus the clear air and almost unbroken sunshine, all of which were ideal for shooting. The film makers have now moved on but the sets remain, with bars, a bank, stables and Red Indian encampments. At noon and 1700, 'cowboys' enact shoot-outs and stunts. There is also a rather depressing zoo.

Cabo de Gata and Las Salinas → *Colour map 7, grid C2.*

It's worth heading east, away from the main road to the undeveloped Cabo de Gata peninsula, covered in desert plants, sand dunes, and saline wetlands which are an important breeding place for a number of birds. There are also a few reasonable beaches around, reached by few tourists.

Carboneras → *Colour map 7, grid C3; Population: 6,312.*

Relaxed Carboneras has an ugly cement factory, but the village centre is nicer, dominated by the sturdy 17th-century **Castillo de San Andrés** surrounded by landscaped gardens. There is a broad beach with a large number of fishing boats, backed by a collection of bars and *pensiones* and one unusual hotel, **El Dorado**, see Sleeping.

Map street names: Rambla del Obispo Orbera, C del Dr Gregorio Marañón, Av de Federico García Lorca, To Bus & Train Stations, García Alix, Navarro Rodrigo, Valero Rivera, Zaragoza, Minero, de los Reyes, Javier Sanz, Eguilior, Méndez Núñez, Carrera, Plaza del Ecuador, Padre Santaella, Paseo de Almería, C de Rueda López, Católicos, Rambla de Belén, Conde Ofalia, Dalía, Marqués de Comillas, Tamayo, Plaza Alfonso XIII, Plaza Pablo Cazard, General, Segura, Gravina, Martínez, Álvarez, General, Plaza Emilio Pérez, Real, C de Gerona, Campos, Santísima Trinidad, López Falcón, Plaza López Falcón, de Castro, Puerta del Mar, Salmerón, To Train Station, Airport (8 km), Cabo de Gata, Níjar & Mojácar, Av Reina Regente, Estación Marítima

Mediterranean Sea

Ríncon de Juan Pedro **6**
Valentín **7**

Bars & clubs ●
Molly Malone **8**

From Carboneras the road towards Mojácar is one of the most spectacular coastal drives in Andalucía, winding along the cliff top with hairpin beds and tantalizing views of isolated coves, some with access along rough tracks.

Mojácar → *Colour map 7, grid B5; Population: 4,525.*

A settlement at Mojácar goes back to Iberian and Roman times. The Moors defended Mojácar stoutly against the armies of the Catholic Monarchs, who eventually allowed them to keep their customs provided they swore allegiance to the Christian crown. Mojácar prospered in the early years of the 20th century and in the 1920s it had a population of 9,000, but after the Civil War and the years of emigration, it fell as low as 400. Its recovery began in the 1960s when it was discovered by an intellectual set of artists and writers. Later a travel company developed the resort of Mojácar Playa below.

There are two parts to Mojácar – the Old Mojácar Pueblo and the new Mojácar Playa 3 km below on the sea. The old part is the more interesting as it is a hill village with a distinctly Moorish flavour, with its sugar lump, whitewashed houses and original Moorish street pattern. It's solely given over to tourism and expat life though, and despite the picture postcard views, Old Mojácar is a little disappointing. At the entrance to Old Mojácar, is the very helpful tourist office ① *T950475162, Mon-Fri 1000-1900, Sat 1000-1330*. There's also a kiosk opposite the Centro Comercial on the beachfront. Mojácar Playa spreads for several miles along a mediocre sandy beach, densely packed with hotels, pensións, discos and restaurants.

Half of Mojácar's population are foreign residents, mainly British, with a significant number of artists and potters. A busy place in season, there's little going on in winter. Until quite recently, the women half-covered their faces with *cobijas* (triangular shawls) and drew *indalos* on their doors to keep away bad luck. *Indalos* are stick-like figures holding an arc above their heads, thought to have originated in Neolithic times. Although no longer seen over doorways, the *indalo* sign figures on just about every souvenir in the town's shops.

● Sleeping

Almería city *p792, map p794*

L Gran Sol Almería, Av Reina Regente 8, T950238011, F950270691. Traditional, comfortable, Andalucían city centre hotel with swimming pool, located between the town and the port.

B Costasol, Paseo de Almería 58, T/F950234011. Well-located hotel which offers good value on the Paseo, Almería's nicest part of town.

C La Perla, Plaza del Carmen 7, T950238877, F950275816. The city's oldest hotel, just off the Puerta de Purchena. Recently redeveloped with attractive a/c rooms.

E-F Nixar, C Antonio Vico 24, T950237255, F950237255. Probably the best of the *pensiones*, with rooms with and without bath available.

Around Almería *p795*

El Dorado, Playa de Carboneras, Carboneras, T950454050, info@eldorado-carboneras.com, with 17 rooms. Different parts of the hotel are decorated as film sets, such as *Dr Zhivago* and *Three Musketeers*. Pool and a restaurant.

AL Parador Reyes Católicos, Playa s/n, Mojácar, T950478250, F950478183. Modern building on seafront in landscaped grounds, with swimming pool and tennis court.

A Continental, Playa de Palmeral, Mojácar, T950478225. Smaller than most and one of the only hotels on the beach side of the road.

B Río Abajo Playa, Playa de Mojácar, Mojácar, T950478928. Small beach front hotel with pool.

C Mamabels, C Embajadores 1, Mojácar, T950475126. In the Pueblo, only 4 rooms, but good sea views and a decent restaurant.

E Pensión El Torreon, C Jazmin s/n, Mojácar, T950475259. Attractive place in the village with sea views, relaxing atmosphere, and friendly owners.

Camping

Camping El Quinto, Mojácar, T950478704. For campers looking for a little peace, on the Ctra Mojácar- Torre and within walking distance of Old Mojácar.

🍴 Eating

Almería city *p792, map p794*
The best restaurants are either on, or just off, the Paseo de Almería. Local specialities to look for including *gachas* (a hot clam stew), *trigo* (a stew with grains of wheat, pork, beans and herbs), *choto al ajo y en ajillo* (kid with garlic or garlic sauce) and spiced sardines.
€€-€ **Rincón de Juan Pedro**, Plaza del Carmen 5. A friendly spot with a good list of local specialities and has a *menú del día* for €7.50.
€€ **Valentín**, C Tenor Iribarne 17, one of several good seafood options on this street just off Paseo del Almería.
€ **El Turia**, C Ricardos 8, T950263768, and € **Tony's**, C Ricardos 7, both have cheap *menús*; the former is more traditional, the latter trendier.

Tapas bars and cafés
Bar El Alcázar, Paseo de Almería 4, has good seafood tapas.
Bodega las Botas, C Fructuoso Pérez 3, has a good atmosphere with sherry barrels and legs of *serrano* ham hanging from the ceiling.
Casa Puga, C Jovellanos 7, is a great old tapas bar with excellent snacks, lots of atmosphere, and grumpy service.
Montenegro, Plaza de la Catedral 3. Unglamorous but worth a stop for its superb *cigalas*.

Around Almería *p795*
All these listed are in Mojácar's. The vast range reflects Mojácar's international character. Most restaurants shut in winter.
€€€ **Bistro Breton**, Playa Mojácar, T950478008. French cuisine, closed Thu.
€€€ **La Lubina**, Pueblo Indalo, T950458376. Terrace, fish dishes.
€€€ **Palacio**, Plaza del Cano, in old town. Nouvelle cuisine and traditional dishes.
€€€ **Tito's**, Playa de Ventanicas, T950478711. Beachside fish restaurant.
€€ **El Bigote**, Mojácar Pueblo. International and Spanish food.
€€ **Estrella de Mar**, Rambla de Cantal. Excellent seafood restaurant, with tapas.

Tapas bars and cafés
For cheap tapas, try those round the main square in Mojácar Pueblo, such as **Bar**

Indalo. **Pavana**, below the plaza, is a decent bar with a pool table open year-round.

🍸 Bars and clubs

Almería city *p792, map p794*
Plaza de Urrutia is the zone for nightlife; the web of small streets behind the post office are packed with bars; very lively at weekends.
Molly Malone, Paseo de Almería 56, is a cut above most Irish bars, with a massive terrace and busy attractive interior.

🎉 Festivals and events

Almería city *p792, map p794*
Last week in **Aug** sees **Feria**, marked by sports events, bullfights and dancing.
Late **Dec-early Jan** are the **Winter Festivals**. These culminate in the **Romería de la Virgen del Mar** when the virgin of the sea is taken to Torre García beach.

Around Almería *p795*
The highlight of the year in Mojácar is the **Fiesta Moros y Cristianos**, on the weekend closest to **10 Jun**, a mock battle between the Moors and Christians, lasting 3 days and accomp- anied by fireworks, music and giant paellas. One of the best on the coast.

🚍 Transport

Almería city *p792, map p794*
Boat Ferries to **Melilla** are run by Transmediterránea, Parque Nicolas Salmerón 19, near the port, T902454645. Ferries run daily except Sat, leaving at 2330 and arriving in Melilla at 0800; €25.15.
Bus The station is in the Plaza de Barcelona, T950210029. There are services to Mojácar via **Carboneras** (8 daily, 1¼ hrs), and several to the **Cabo de Gata**. Up to 5 buses head to **Tabernas** north of town, passing the Mini Hollywood theme park. There are 10 buses to **Granada** daily, half going via **Guadix**, and 8 to **Málaga**. 3 buses head for **Sevilla** and 1 to **Córdoba**.
Train There are 4 *talgos* a day from **Madrid** and other connections from **Barcelona**, **Granada** and **Valencia**. Overnight trains come from **Sevilla** and **Córdoba**. RENFE have an office in the town centre, C Alcalde Muñoz, T950231207.

❶ Directory

Almería city *p792, map p794*
Internet CyberPlanet, C de las Tiendas 20; good connection; €2 per hr.
Post office Correos, Plaza J Casinello 1, Paseo de Almería, T950237207.

Telephone *Locutorio* in C Navarro Rodríguez 9. Open Mon-Sat.

Around Almería *p795*
Internet Access at the friendly **Digital United**, at the back of the Centro Comercial on the seafront in Mojácar; €3 per hr.

Jaén

The landlocked province of Jaén in northeastern Andalucía is one of the region's least visited areas, yet it has some interesting cities and protected areas. In its city architecture, it is more like central Spain, with which it is linked to by the Despeñaperros Pass. Like Baeza and Úbeda, the capital city, Jaén, has some fine Renaissance buildings, including the cathedral.

Two of Andalucía's finest Moorish castles are found in Jaén province – at Baños de la Encina in the north, guarding the Despeñaperros Pass, and at Alcalá la Real in the south. The mountainous east of the province is dominated by the Parque Natural de Cazorla, a series of limestone ridges running northeast-southwest, forming the largest protected area in Andalucía. ▶▶ *For Sleeping, Eating and other listings, see pages 804-806.*

Jaén city → *Colour map 6, grid B6; Population: 107,184; Altitude: 574 m.*

The self-styled 'olive oil capital of the world' is a busy provincial centre little visited by tourists. It's not a wildly interesting place but its lack of self-consciousness comes as a relief after the coastal excesses. The attractive streets and plazas are dominated by its cathedral, which appears to have bulked up on steroids in an effort to upstage the castle, which is perched on a rock and surrounded by seas of olive groves.

Ins and outs

Getting there and around The nearest airport is at Granada, and the nearest international airport is at Málaga. The city's bus station is at Plaza de Coca de la Piñera in the centre, T953255014. The RENFE train station is in Plaza de la Estación, T902240202, which is 20 minutes walk from the centre. You can visit most of the worthwhile monuments on foot as they are clustered to the northwest of the cathedral. Castillo bus company runs regular services around town from the bus station, stopping at Plaza de la Constitución. ▶▶ *For further details, see Transport page 806.*

Tourist information The municipal office ① *C Maestra 13, T953242624, Mon-Fri 1000-1900, Sat and Sun 1000-1300*, near the cathedral.

Background

The Moors took the former Iberian and Roman city in 712 and called it Yayyan, turning it into a strategic centre along local caravan routes. After the battle of Las Navas de Tolosa, Jaén became part of the Nasrid Kingdom of Granada, and was ceded to Fernando III by Muhammad Ibn Nasr in 1246, After the Reconquista, decline set in, a situation which was not helped by the steady emigration of its citizens to the colonies of the New World. Today, Jaén is the poorest of the provincial capitals of Andalucía, with chronic unemployment both in the city and the surrounding agricultural area.

Catedral ⓘ *0830-1300 (Sacristy Museum 1000) and 1600-1900 (1700-2000 summer), €1.80, €3.00 (for both cathedral and museum).* Jaén's outsize cathedral was built on the site of the Great Mosque. It was begun in 1492, but was not completed until the early years of the 19th century. The exterior is dominated by the west front in Baroque-style with Corinthian columns and twin-towers capped with small domes. The architecture elsewhere is undistinguished. The Renaissance interior is typically gloomy, due to the lack of windows. Kept behind the high altar, in a glass case, is a a cloth with which St Veronica is reputed to have wiped the face of Christ. The Sacristy Museum has a few sculptures and other items of interest.

Palacio de Villadompardo ⓘ *Tue-Fri 0900-2000, Sat and Sun 0930-1430, free with EU passport, otherwise €0.60, visits to the baths guided tour only, every 30 mins.* The palace was built in the 16th century over the **Baños Arabes**, which have now been re-opened. They are Andalucía's largest surviving Moorish baths. The site consists of an entrance hall and rooms for cold, tepid and hot baths. The floors are largely of marble, with brick walls and stone pillars supporting brick horseshoe arches. The ceilings are either cupolas with star-shaped windows or half-barrel vaults. The building also contains the **Museo de Artes y Costumbres Populares** and the **Museo Internacional de Arte Naif**.

Andalucía Jaén city

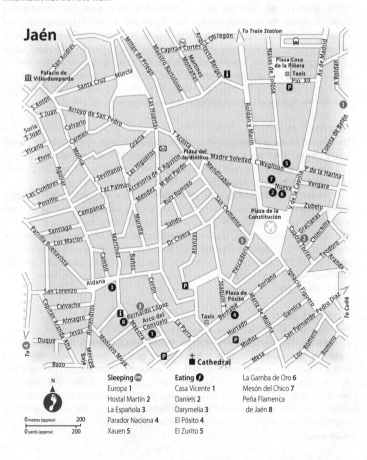

Jaén

To Train Station

Sleeping 🛏
Europa **1**
Hostal Martín **2**
La Española **3**
Parador Naciona **4**
Xauen **5**

Eating 🍴
Casa Vicente **1**
Daniels **2**
Darymelia **3**
El Pósito **4**
El Zurito **5**

La Gamba de Oro **6**
Mesón del Chico **7**
Peña Flamenca
 de Jaén **8**

N

0 metres (approx) 200
0 yards (approx) 200

Castillo de Santa Catalina ⓘ *15 Jun- 15 Sep Mon-Sun 1030-1330, rest of the year 1000-1400 and 1530-1930, closed Mon.* This castle stands on the hill overlooking the town. It was once an Arab palace built by Ibn Nasr, but, after its capture from the Moorish King Al-Hammar during the Reconquest, it has been much altered and restored. Some secret passages have been discovered leading down to the *barrio* of La Magdalena in the town below, which still has its winding Moorish street plan. The castle is now a parador and a path from its car park leads along to a mirador, giving magnificent views of the city below.

Museo Provincial ⓘ *Paseo de la Estación 27 , Tue 1500-2000, Wed-Sat 0900-2000, Sun 0900-1500, free for EU citizens.* This museum contains a fine collection of archaeological exhibits, the most important of which are the Iberian fifth-century stone-sculptures which were found in the west of the province. The Moorish room has a good collection of coins and ceramics, the latter in the green style that is still prevalent in the pottery of today. The Fine Arts section of the museum is upstairs, but is hardly worth the walk.

Around Jaén

The highlights of Jaén province are to be found in its eastern reaches. About 50 km from the capital, the neighbouring towns of Baeza and Úbeda are treasure-troves of Renaissance architecture; there's an incredible number of elegant golden buildings to justify a day of anyone's time. Beyond here, the Sierra de Cazorla is a rugged range of limestone mountains, much of which is encompassed by Spain's largest natural park. There's some superb walking to be done, but take your waterproofs: it is one of the wettest areas in Spain with an annual rainfall of over 2,000 mm which ensures that the headwaters of the Guadalquivir are well supplied.

South of Jaén

The town of **Alcalá la Real** was a Moorish stronghold (known as Al-Kalaat Be Zayde*)* with its peak of influence coming in the 12th and 13th centuries when it was an independent *taifa*. It changed hands several times during the Reconquest, finally falling to Alfonso X, who added the suffix *Real* to the place name.

The hilltop castle, the **Castillo de la Mota** and the adjacent church of **Santa María la Mayor**, covers some 3 ha, with rocky cliffs forming part of the external walls. The views from the castle over the town and the surrounding olive groves and mountains are stupendous. There were seven gates to the fortress, one of which, the Puerta de la Imagen, is now the main entrance. The walls were supported by a series of watchtowers, of which 15 still exist – six Christian and the remainder Arab. The keep now houses a small archaeological museum, with Roman, Moorish and Christian remains.

North of Jaén

The area north of Jaén is largely agricultural, with a rolling landscape covered with olive groves. The highlight is the superb, wonderfully preserved, Moorish castle of **Baños de la Encina**. The castle, composed of golden, sandy conglomerate and shaped like a ship, is in an excellent state of preservation, despite the fact that it was won and lost six times by the Christians. Entry is through a double horseshoe arch. The walls, with their crenellated tops, have restored battlements and no fewer than 14 towers. The viewing hours are informal and depend entirely on the ancient guardian and his equally antique key. If he is not around, enquire at the Ayuntamiento in the main square.

Baeza gives an overwhelming impression of sleepy Renaissance charm, set off by the honey-coloured sandstone of its buildings. The charmingly old-fashioned **tourist office** is located in the 16th-century former law courts, an attractive Plateresque building called Casa del Pópulo ① *T953740444, Mon to Fri 0900-1430, Sat 1000-1300.*

Delightful little **Plaza del Pópulo** (also known as the Plaza de los Leones) is at the entrance to the old town. In the centre of the square is the **Fuente de los Leones** (fountain of the Lions), which is believed to have been built with stones from the Roman ruins of Castulo. Dominating the nearby Plaza de Santa María is the 13th-century **Cathedral** ① *1000-1300 and 1600-1800 (1700-1900 in summer)*, which was built on the site of a mosque, but comprehensively updated by Andrés de Vandelvira 300 years later. The oldest part of the cathedral is the Puerta de la Luna (Door of the Moon) in 13th-century Gothic-Mudéjar, while the other door, in the south wall, is the 15th-century Puerta del Perdón, from which an alleyway leads to a mirador giving fine views over the rolling landscape of olive groves to the southeast.

Next to the cathedral is perhaps the most beautiful building in Baeza, the **Casa Consistoriales Altas**, also known as the Palacio de los Cabreras and once the upper Town Hall. Now a national monument, the walls display the coats of arms of Juana the Mad and her husband Felipe the Fair. Romanesque churches are like hens' teeth in Andalucía, but the **Iglesia de Santa Cruz** ① *Mon-Sat 1100-1330, 1600-1800, Sun 1200-1400*, is one, although with later additions. The simple white-walled interior has some 16th-century frescoes.

On the opposite side of the road and joined to the Seminary is the 15th-century **Palacio de Jabalquinto**, undoubtedly the most splendid of the palaces in the town but currently under long-term renovation.

Turn left into Calle Beato Avila by the **Antigua Universidad**. This old university was opened in 1542 and classes were held for over three centuries, but it was closed down in 1824. Since then it has been a high school ;the famous Spanish poet Antonio Machado gave French grammar lessons here from 1912 to 1919 and many of his best works come from this period of his life. 'I dream of you when I can no longer see you', he wrote of Baeza. Also worth a look is the Mudéjar ceiling in the main hall and the superb patio.

Úbeda → *Colour map 7, grid B1; Population: 32,524; Altitude: 757 m.*

Despite its large area of modern suburbs, Úbeda's delight is its large and architecturally outstanding old quarter, full of Renaissance richness. The extensive section (Conjunto Histórico), contains all of 46 classified historical buildings! It is a mildly prosperous market town, producing agricultural machinery, along with the more traditional olive oil, esparto and ceramics.

History Built on the foundations of a Roman settlement, the Moorish townwas walled in 852 and later occupied by both the Almoravids and the Almohads. It was during Moorish times that the craft industries of pottery and esparto work were developed, which still survive today. It was eventually conquered by Ferdinand III in 1234. Úbeda's heyday came in the 16th century, during the times of Carlos I and Fellipe II, when the area's textiles were traded throughout Europe, bringing great wealth to the town. Decline set in, however, in subsequent centuries.

Sights Head straight for the Plaza Vásquez de Molina which, flanked by a collection of honey-coloured Renaissance buildings, must be one of the most attractive squares in Spain. **Sacra Capilla del Salvador** is at the northeast end. Ordered by Francisco de la Cobos and originally designed by Diego de Siló́e (who was responsible for Granada and Málaga cathedrals), it was built by Vandelvira and the stonemason Alonso Ruíz. The church was originally the chapel of Cobos' mansion, which later burnt down. The

main west-facing façade is a mass of ornate Plateresque detail. Inside, the single nave has Gothic ribbed vaults and is dominated by the *retablo*, the work of Michelangelo's pupil Alonso de Berruguete.

Plaza del Primero de Mayo is easily reached from the Plaza de Vásquez de Molina by heading northwest along either of the streets on each side of the parador. Near the plaza, at the end of Calle San Juan de la Cruz, is the **Oratorio de San Juan de la Cruz**. St John of the Cross was a small friar (reputed to be only 1½ m tall) who was a writer, poet and mystic. He came to Úbeda in 1591, from the Convent of La Peñuela, for treatment to a cut on his foot, but died a painful death from gangrene. The Oratory has a small museum ⓘ *Tue-Sun 1100-1300 and 1700-1900, €1.20*, in which the cell where he died can be visited. Various relics and personal objects are on display.

The **tourist office** can be found in the elegant Palacio del Marqués del Contadero ⓘ *C Baja del Marqués 4, T953750897, Mon-Fri 0800-1900, Sat-Sun 1000-1400*. There are maps available from the tourist office. For guided tours of the city, contact Artificis, T953758150, or ask at the tourist office.

Parque Natural de Cazorla → *Colour map 7, grid B1.*

Southeast of Ubeda, this superb natural park merits much exploration. Heavily wooded, the whole area is a naturalist's delight, with some 1,300 flowering species including some 30 endemics such as the Cazorla violet. There is a lot of game – many were introduced when the park was a shooting reserve. The bellows of the rutting red deer are a typical sound in autumn. Ibex, boar, badgers, otters, polecats, martens, and the occasional lynx are also about. The park is a haven of birds of prey; there are vultures, four varieties of eagle, honey buzzards and peregrines. There is also a wide range of woodland birds, including crossbills and firecrests. Butterflies are outstanding in spring and early summer. Reptiles and amphibians include three species of snake and several lizards and skinks.

Ins and outs There are two daily buses from Jaén to Cazorla via Baeza and Úbeda into the park. There is very little public transport in the park, and no petrol stations within the park boundary. Signposting is also poor. For the most abundant flowers and birdlife the best time to visit the park is May and June. Avoid summer weekends and July and August, when the park is saturated with visitors. In Cazorla, the municipal tourist office ⓘ *Paseo del Santo Cristo 17, north of Plaza de la Constitución, T953710102, summer only*. Also Quercus Turismo ⓘ *C Juan Domingo 2, T953720115, www.excursionquercus.com*, for maps, guidebooks and tours of the park.

Cazorla The main tourist centre of the park, Cazorla stands at a height of 900 m beneath a steep limestone cliff, the **Peña de los Halcones**. The town has a long history, with both Iberians and Romans living here. It was the Moors who recognized its strategic position and originally built the two castles which dominate the village.

On **Plaza de la Corredera**, known locally as Plaza del Huevo because of its egg shape, is the Ayuntamiento in a Moorish-style palace. **Plaza Santa María** is the most lively square and is named after the ruined church, destroyed by Napoleon's troops in the Peninsular War. The square is overshadowed by **La Yedra**, the tower of one of the Moorish castles. Also in the square is the small **Museo de Artes y Costumbres** ⓘ *Tue-Sat 1000-1400*, which gives a glimpse of local history crafts and folklore. These two squares, as well as Plaza de la Constitución, have a wealth of tapas bars.

❖ *Most folk use the slightly dull town of Cazorla as their base; with your own transport, you may prefer to head further into the sierra to some of the smaller villages.*

Walking in the park The area immediately to the east of Cazorla contains some of the park's most dramatic scenery. If you don't have your own transport you'll need to rely on taxis or buses. The start of the Río Borosa walk below is a fair drive from town.

Best of the bunch

In Córdoba and Jaén provinces rolling olive groves stretch for endless hectares. Olive trees were first introduced to Andalucía by the Romans, who shipped the product back to Rome. The Moors extended the cultivation and called the oil az-zait, meaning 'juice of the olive'.

Today, Spain is the world's largest producer of olive oil and Andalucía accounts for 20% of this amount, producing some 550,000 tonnes of oil annually. Andalucíans are proud of their 1,000-year-old trees, which are very fire- and drought-resistant. Methods of harvesting and processing have barely changed since Roman times. The tree blossoms in spring and the green, unripe olives are harvested around September. Ripe olives turn black and are harvested later. Some 10% of the harvest is picked for consumption as a fruit and widely used, often stuffed with pimiento or anchovies. The remaining 90% is used for the production of oil. These olives will be taken to local factories where they are washed and then ground under cone-shaped stones. The resulting pulp is spread on esparto mats and pressed, so that the oil flows out; it is then filtered through a series of settling tanks, giving pure virgin olive oil. Selecting a bottle of olive oil from the supermercado shelf, is not so simple. It's important to check the percentage of acidity. The best oil, virgen extra, comes from olives which are picked ripe and milled immediately and which can contain a maximum 1% acidity. Fino is allowed 1.5% and corriente 3.3%. The higher the acidity, the stronger the flavour and the lower the price.

For **maps**, the Pentathlon 1:50000 Plano Topográfico de las Sierras de Cazorla, Segura y Las Villas, based on the IGN series 'L', covers the whole of the area in just one map but it is rather unwieldy. Other good maps easily found in Cazorla are the Alpina 1:40000 series.

Río Borosa Gorge Distance: 19 km; Time: 7-7½ hours; Difficulty: medium/difficult. The Sierra's best-known walk takes you along a beautiful section of the impressive gorge of the Río Borosa. You follow a dirt track and then a spectacular wooden walkway eastwards through the gorge which opens out into a huge, natural ampitheatre of soaring limestone crags. From here a steep climb takes you to a high reservoir which you reach by following the course of a mill race, tunnelled out of the mountainside. The walk can be as far up and down as you like but remember you'll climb for 600 m should you do the whole lot. It is best done on a weekday out of holiday season. Remember that the upper section of the walk is sometimes impassable in winter; check with the park rangers at Torre de Vinagre centre (see above) or with one of the agencies in Cazorla. Take a torch for negotiating the tunnels and in the warmer months remember your bathing costume – there are lovely river pools for swimming. **Map:** Alpina 1:40000 map: Sierra de Segura I or Penthalon 1:50000 Plano Topográfico de las Sierras de Cazorla, Segura y Las Villas.

To get to the start of the walk from Cazorla take the road that leads via La Iruela then Brunchel, up into the park, then turn left for Coto Ríos/Embalse del Tranco on the A319. When you reach the Centro de Interpretación Torre del Vinagre, turn right and follow signs for 'Central Eléctrica', the electricity generating station. Cross the river and leave your car in the park to the left of the road just before the *piscifactoría*, or trout farm.

Cazorla circuit Distance: 16 km; Time: 7-7½ hours; Difficulty: medium/difficult. This circular walk from Cazorla, mostly along high mountain trails, is one of the Sierra's

'classic' itineraries and is well worth its reputation. A long climb of nearly 900 m up from the village leads you to a high pass from where the peak of El Gilillo (1,848 m) is easily climbed: the views on a clear day of the distant Sierra Nevada alone make this walk worth the effort. From here a beautiful high mountain trail brings you back to Cazorla in a long, lazy loop – a wonderful reward for your efforts earlier in the day. If you find the long climb intimidating, you can avoid the initial 3 km of mountain road above Cazorla by taking a taxi to the barrier by the Hotel Ríogazas. **Map** Alpina 1:40000 map: Sierra de Segura I or Penthalon 1:50000 Plano Topográfico de las Sierras de Cazorla, Segura y Las Villas. You should be prepared for cold conditions on the higher, often windy section of this walk. If climbing Gilillo add an hour to the timings below.

Circular route by car If you only have one day in the park and have your own transport, the route below is recommended. Leave Úbeda eastwards on the N322, bypassing **Villacarillo** after 32 km. After another 6 km, a side road leads north to the hill village of **Iznatoraf**, which is well worth a diversion. There is a pleasant square, an imposing Renaissance church, a ruined Moorish castle above some narrow alleyways and some spectacular views from a mirador on the north side of the village. Back on the main road turn right just before Villanueva del Arzobispo on a minor road which leads to the park. The scenery improves dramatically and after about 10 km the road enters a spectacular wooded gorge, eventually arriving at the hamlet of **Tranco**, scattered around the dam of the Tranco reservoir. There are a number of bars and restaurants here, many of which have some accommodation, set amongst the trees overlooking the reservoir. To follow the reservoir southeast, you need to cross the dam, but another recommended diversion is to carry straight on northeast to the hill top village of **Hornos**, perched on a crag dominated by a castle, which, though mostly in ruins, makes an excellent viewpoint over the reservoir. The village has a strong Moorish flavour, with narrow streets and a small stretch of the original walls, complete with a horseshoe arch.

To go southeast into the park, return to Tranco, cross the dam and pass through the park gates. The road now continues along the north side of the Tranco reservoir, giving spectacular views of the island in the centre of the lake, the **Isla Cabeza de la Viña**. The road continues past the end of the reservoir, now following the Río Guadalquivir towards its headwaters, passing through the hamlet of **Coto Ríos**, before arriving at the Torre de Vinagre Interpretation Centre.

The main route through the park now leaves the Guadalquivir valley and climbs over the **Puerto de las Palomas** (Doves Pass), where a mirador gives superb views back through the valley. The road then drops down past the park boundary and into the villages of, firstly, **La Iruela** and then to **Cazorla**.

● Sleeping

Jaén city *p798, map p799*
AL **Parador Nacional**, Castillo de Santa Catalina, T953230000, F953230930. 45 a/c rooms, restaurant, pool, in restored section of the castillo, quiet with stunning views.
A **Europa**, Plaza de Belén 1, T953222700, F953222692. Comfortable and fairly stylishly modernized hotel reasonably centrally located off Av de Granada.
C **Xauen**, Plaza de Deán Mazas 3, T953240789, www.hotelxauenjaen.com. A central hotel with strange management

but comfortable standard rooms in an attractive building. May give a discount.
E **Hostal Martín**, C Cuatro Torres 5, T953191431, F953243678. Clean and simple option near the Plaza de la Consistución.
E **La Española**, C Bernardo López 9, T9532-30524. The faded charm is very faded. Some of the rooms are scruffy, particularly those without bath. The location near the cathedral is excellent though. Chilly in winter.

Around Jaén *p800*
In Úbeda, stay in the old quarter if you can afford it; otherwise staying in Baeza is

preferable to hanging out in Úbeda's ugly new town. There are, however, some stunning palaces to stay at in the old quarter, listed below. If you wish to stay in in Parque Natural de Cazorla, book accommodation well ahead in the park, especially during the summer months.

AL Parador Nacional Condestable Dávalos, Plaza Vásquez de Molina 1, Úbeda, T953750345, F953751259. This luxurious and atmospheric parador is undoubtedly the best place to stay in Úbeda. 31 a/c rooms and restaurant.

A María de Molina, Plaza de Ayuntamiento, Úbeda, T953795356, F953793694. Friendly hotel overlooking the plaza, very close to the major sights, in a smart building with slightly heavy decoration.

A Palacio de la Rambla, Plaza del Marqués 1, Úbeda, T953750196, F953750267. The present Marquesa de la Rambla lets out some of the rooms in her sumptuous mansion in the historic quarter. All rooms have TV, minibar, some with their own fireplace, family antiques and old-fashioned bath with legs; one even has its own patio.

A Parador El Adelantado, Sierra de Cazorla, in Parque Natural de Cazorla, T/F953727075, cazorla@parador.es. 33 rooms, pool, restaurant, functional building in hunting-lodge style in a superb setting.

B Confortel Baeza, C Concepción 3, Baeza, T953748130, F953742519. Newly-decorated hotel in central location, with a patio and restaurant. Price includes breakfast.

C Molino la Farraga, Cazorla, T953721249. A beautiful converted mill just outside of the town and by far the nicest place to stay in Cazorla; wonderful food and welcome.

C Palacete Santa Ana, C Santa Ana Vieja 9, Baeza, T/F953741657. Recently renovated, crammed full of Renaissance-style furniture, a little over the top. There's a huge restaurant with a roof terrace up the road that gives discounts to its guests.

C Río, Paraje de la Teja, La Iruela, in Parque Natural de Cazorla, T953720211. 21 rooms, most with delightful views.

C-D Apartamentos Reiza, Hornos de Segura, in Parque Natural de Cazorla, T953495106. Small well-equipped

apartments at the edge of the village which sleep from 2-6.

D Hostal Guadalquivir, Cazorla, T953720268. A friendly, family-run *hostal* close to Cazorla's main square. Popular with walking groups from the UK. Rooms are basic, but clean.

D La Finca Mercedes, just outside of Cazorla on the road to La Iruela, T953721087. Excellent rooms with views, food available. Good value. The owners have another 6 rooms in a farm just 5 minutes away. Pool and garden.

D Victoría, C Alaminos 5, Úbeda, T953752952. The best of the *pensiones*, closer to the sights in a better part of town. Small, a/c, all rooms with bath.

E Hostal Betis, Plaza de la Corredera 19, Cazorla, T953720540. Some rooms looking over the square but can be noisy.

F Hostal El Patio, C Conde Romanones 13, Baeza, T953740200, F953748260. An old Renaissance mansion built around a covered patio with potted plants and a fountain. A good budget option.

Camping

There are 3 sites in the Sierra de Segura and 6 in the Sierra de la Cazorla in Parque Natural de Cazorla. Most are well-equipped and in unspoilt surroundings.

Camping Cortijo, 1 km from Cazorla, T953721280.

Fuente de la Canalica, Ctra las Acebeas, Siles, T953491004. There are also a number of *camping libre* sites which are free, but have no facilities.

● Eating

Jaén city *p798, map p799*
Jaén's eating options are a little disappointing. There are plenty of cheap eats to be found in the tiny streets near the cathedral, especially C Arco del Conselo.

€€€ **Casa Vicente**, C Arco del Consuelo 1, T953262816. Priciest restaurant in town, in old mansion specializing in game and other local dishes.

€€€ **El Porche**, C Redonda de Santiago 7, Úbeda, T953757321, which has an attractive covered patio.

● *For an explanation of sleeping and eating price codes used in this guide, see inside the*
● *front cover. Other relevant information is found in Essentials, see pages 47-56.*

€€**Darymelia**, C Maestra 15, has a decent restaurant and some tasty bar snacks.

€€ **El Seco**, C Corazón de Jesús 8, Úbeda, T953791472, is opposite a pleasant plaza.

€€ **Gallo Rojo**, C Ramón y Cajal 3, Úbeda, T953752038, has good regional dishes.

€€ **Mesón Navarro**, Plaza de Ayuntamiento 2, Úbeda, T953790638, is a friendly place with excellent seafood; more atmosphere in the front tapas bar than the restaurant.

Tapas bars and cafés

Tiny C Nueva is the best tapas zone; **La Gamba de Oro**, at No 5, T953261613, has excellent no-frills seafood; **Daniels**, No 11, T953242041, is a cheery modern *cervecería* with a good range of interesting eats, and **Mesón del Chico**, No 12, T953228502, has a decent upstairs restaurant (mid-range priced) as well as a basement bar. Nearby, **El Zurito**, C Correa Weglison 4, is a cosy old bar which gives tasty free snacks with your wine. Another good place with irregular opening is **Peña Flamenca de Jaén**, C Maestra 11, T953231710, with good eats and atmosphere and occasional lovely flamenco music. **El Pósito**, Plaza de Pósito 10, is a relaxed spot for a drink, as is **Oppidum**, C Federico de Méndez 5.

Around Jaén *p800*

€€ **El Arcediano**, C Barbacana, Baeza, T953748184. Good value *menú del día*. Recommended.

€€ **La Góndola**, Portales Carbonería 13 (on main plaza), Baeza, T953742984. Bargain *menú del día*, which you can have on their pleasant summer terrace. Recommended.

Tapas bars and cafés

Generally most places in Baeza serve excellent tapas, like the bars on C San Pablo or on the main plaza. The liveliest *terraza* is **Cafetería Mercantil**, Plaza de España, Baeza. It is somewhat of an institution among the locals; word has it that this is the place for buying or selling a mule or tractor. It serves tasty *raciones* and ice cream.

Good tapas options in Úbeda are **El Estudiante**, Av Cristo del Rey 8, T953754402, and **Puerta Graná**, next to Puerta de Granada to the south of Úbeda. Trendy bar serving good tapas and *raciones* on a lovely patio. Recommended.

🕭 Bars and clubs

Jaén city *p798, map p799*

Nightlife in Jaén is poor by Andalucían standards. There are a few lacklustre discos, mainly along the Av de la Estación.

🕭 Festivals

Jaén city *p798, map p799*

11 Jun is when **Fiesta de Nuestra Señora de la Capilla** is held, a celebration for Jaén's patron saint; flowers, processions and dances. **12-20 Oct** is Feria de San Lucas, Jaén's most important fair, with bullfights and sports events.

Around Jaén *p800*

On **1 May** in Úbeda is **Romería**: a pilgrimage to the Virgen of Guadalupe. The day of the patron saint, San Miguel, is celebrated with a large fair, fireworks and flamenco.

🕭 Transport

Jaén city *p798, map p799*

There are at least 12 **buses** daily to **Baeza/Úbeda** (1 hr), 2 going onto **Cazorla** (2½ hrs), 4 to **Córdoba** (2 hrs), 14 to **Granada** (1 hr), 4 to **Málaga** (4 hrs) and 3 to **Sevilla** (5 hrs). There are also buses to **Madrid**. Few **trains** service Jaén. Possible destinations include **Madrid** (3 daily, 4 hrs), **Cádiz**, **Córdoba** and **Sevilla**.

Around Jaén *p800*

From **Baeza** there are buses to **Úbeda** (14 daily, 15 mins) and **Jaén** (12 daily, 45 mins. For **Úbeda**, there are frequent bus services from Jaén and connections with other major cities in the region. There are 12-14 daily services to and from **Jaén** via **Baeza**. There are also services to **Granada**, **Sevilla** (2 daily, 4½ hrs), **Córdoba** (2 daily, 2½ hrs), **Málaga** (1 daily, 2½ hrs), and **Madrid** (2 daily, 4 hrs). The nearest train station in **Úbeda** is Linares-Baeza, T953740444.

🕭 Directory

Jaén city *p798, map p799*
Internet Cu@k, C Adarves Bajos.
Post office Correos, Plaza de Jardinillos, T953191112. Mon-Sat 0900- 1400.

Córdoba → *Colour map 6, grid B5; Population: 309,961.*

Jaca negra, luna grande y aceitunas en mi alforja
Aunque sepa los caminos Yo nunca llegaré a Córdoba
A black horse, a full moon
There are olives in my pack
Though I know the roads I never will reach Córdoba

This, from one of Lorca's most haunting and perfect poems, captures some of the mystique surrounding this ancient Moorish city. The zenith of Córdoba's influence came in the 10th and 11th centuries when it was the western capital of the Islamic empire rivalling Baghdad in culture, sophistication and power. Although it is little more than a minor provincial capital today, the Moorish legacy lives on in the winding alleys of the old quarter. This area encompasses the equally fascinating Judería (Jewish quarter), and flows seamlessly into the new part of town. Dominating the lot is the Mezquita, probably the most stunning mosque ever built by the Moors and still an extraordinary place, despite the fact that a Christian cathedral has been built slap in the middle of it. Although it houses a sizeable population, Córdoba feels like a small town, unlike buzzing Granada and Sevilla. ➤➤ *For Sleeping, Eating and other listings, see pages 810-812.*

Ins and outs

Getting there
From the bus station, buses run to the centre every 15 minutes and a taxi costs approximately €5. The train station is on Avendia de América, on the north edge of the town, a 30-min walk from the old town via the commercial centre. Taxis and local buses connect the station with the old town. ➤➤ *For further details, see Transport page 812.*

Getting around
Fortunately, most of the monuments are located in a compact area on the north bank of the river and can easily be reached on foot.

Tourist information
The main tourist office is alongside the Mezquita ① *C Torrijos, T957471235, F957491778, summer Mon-Sat 0930-2000 (1800 winter), Sun 1000-1400.* Ask for a free copy of the monthly what's on guide, *Welcome Olé.*

History

The history of Córdoba is thought to date back to Neolithic times, but it was during Roman times that it sprang to prominence. In late 711, Córdoba was captured by Moorish troops led by Mugueiz El Rumí. By 756 Córdoba had become the capital of Moorish Spain and for several centuries it was the main centre of Muslim culture and learning. Much of the Iberian Peninsula was ruled from the city which was the capital of the western Caliphate from 929 to 1031 following independence from Baghdad. By now the city was the largest in western Europe with as many as 500,000 inhabitants and an estimated 3,000 mosques. Internal disputes and a revolt by the Berbers began to weaken the Ommayyads, and the Caliphate of Córdoba then split up into a number of minor *taifas* (kingdoms), while the city itself came into the hands of first the Almoravides in 1094 and subsequently the Almohades in 1149. Córdoba was

captured by the Christians led by Fernando III in 1236 and with the Reconquest the decline soon set in. Little of the wealth from the New World found its way to Córdoba, and by the time the French occupied the city during the Peninsular War, the population had dropped dramatically.

During the Civil War, Córdoba was captured by the Nationalists, who perpetrated some appalling atrocities. The Córdobeses proved, however, to have long memories and in the first post-Franco elections voted for a communist local authority; the only major city in Spain to do so. Today the city is once again, a prosperous centre of learning with a large university and a centre devoted to the study of Muslim history and culture.

Sights

The Mezquita

① *Mon-Sat 1000-1930 (1800 in winter), Sun and festivals 1400-1900 (1800 in winter), last admission half an hour before close, enter from C Magistral González Francés, euro 6.50, under 10 years free, 10-14 year olds half price.*

The mosque is Córdoba's most famous example of Muslim architecture. Although not as remarkable as Granada's Alhambra, it is in its own way an equally significant remnant of Spain's Moorish heritage. A visit is a bit frustrating; as impressive as the forest of pillars and arches is, the cathedral parked in the middle of it has ruined what must once have been a truly awe-inspiring place.

The building began in 785 in the time of Abd Al-Rahman I on the site of a Visigoth church and a Roman temple, with the intention of building Islam's most grandiose mosque. To save time the west-facing wall was retained, but this meant that the *mihrab* does not exactly face Mecca. The pillars were brought from a variety of other sites, meaning the longer ones had to be buried in the floor to match the height of the shorter ones, while a second row of pillars and arches were constructed to support the roof, a design that resembles a Roman aqueduct. A distinctive feature of the arches is the striped red and white pattern produced by using red brick and white stone. Abd Al-Rahman II and Al Hakkim both extended the mosque in the ninth and 10th centuries, and the legendary Al-Manzur brought it to its current massive size of 23,000 m².

❣ *The Mezquita can be crowded with visitors. Go in the late afternoon for a more peaceful tour.*

To the north of the mosque is the **Patio de los Naranjos**, a courtyard of orange trees and fountains where the ritual ablutions took place before prayer. Set into the north wall of the patio is the **bell tower**, built at the same time as the cathedral. You can climb it for city views.

After Córdoba was captured by Fernando III in the Christian Reconquest, the mosque was gradually converted into a church. The most drastic alterations took place in 1523 under Carlos I (Charles V) who sanctioned the building, despite local objections, of a **Capilla Real** (Royal Chapel) and the **Cathedral Coro** in Renaissance style. On inspecting the finished work he did have the decency to comment: "You have built what you or others might have built anywhere, but you have destroyed something that was unique in the world." The cathedral is not without its worth, however, and of particular interest are the mahogany choir stalls, looking like a fantasy of dark chocolate. There are also some items of interest in the Christian side chapels. In the *Tesoro* (treasury) is a monstrance by Enrique de Arfe, which was first seen in the Corpus Cristi procession of 1518. It is more than 2-m high, weighs 200 kg and is a mass of jewels, crosses and relics. Nevertheless, you are left yearning for a glimpse of what the Mezquite must have been like before its awkward lodger moved in.

Alcázar de los Reyes Cristianos

ⓘ *Tue-Sat 1000-1400 and, 1630-1830, Sun 0930-1430; €2, Fri free. Gardens open all day Tue-Sun.*

Also known as Nuevo Alcázar, work was started here in the 13th century for Alfonso X and was later enlarged and used as a palace by the Catholic kings. Ferdinand and Isabel received Columbus in this building, before he departed on his first voyage to the New World, while it was also the prison of Boabdil El Chico, the last of the kings of Moorish Granada. Along the riverside, opposite the palace, were a series of water wheels which are said to have infuriated Isabel as they prevented her from sleeping. One reconstructed wheel remains today. The Alcázar became a centre for the Inquisition from 1490 until 1821. Even as late as the mid-20th century, the building was functioning as a prison, so it is perhaps not surprising that there is little to see from its golden age. There is now a small municipal museum here, in which the locally-discovered Roman mosaics are the most important exhibit. Most enjoyable is wandering around the gardens to the south of the building, with its pools, fountains and rose beds, which are illuminated during the summer evenings.

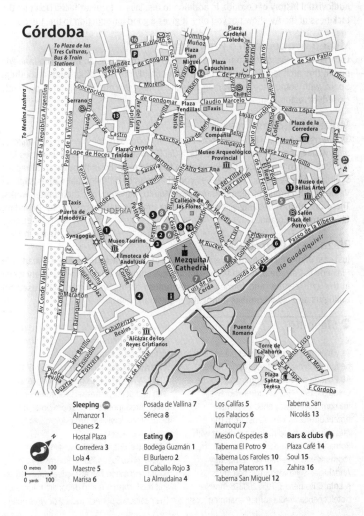

Córdoba

Sleeping	Posada de Vallina 7	Los Califas 5	Taberna San
Almanzor 1	Séneca 8	Los Palacios 6	Nicolás 13
Deanes 2		Marroquí 7	
Hostal Plaza	Eating	Mesón Céspedes 8	Bars & clubs
Corredera 3	Bodega Guzmán 1	Taberna El Potro 9	Plaza Café 14
Lola 4	El Burlaero 2	Taberna Los Faroles 10	Soul 15
Maestre 5	El Caballo Rojo 3	Taberna Platerors 11	Zahira 16
Marisa 6	La Almudaina 4	Taberna San Miguel 12	

0 metres 100
0 yards 100

① *Tue-Sat 1000-1400 and 1530-1730, Sun 1030-1330, free to EU citizens or €0.30.*
Córdoba's old Jewish quarter, between the Mezquita and the city walls to the west, is a warren of narrow lanes and alleyways, sadly overdosed with souvenir shops. However you can still find some delightful corners, such as the flower-filled Callejón de las Flores. This street sets the scene for the rest of Córdoba, which maintains the patios from the Romans and the Moors – from the humblest cottage to the grand *palacios*. The best approach to the *judería* is via the 14th-century Puerta de Almodóvar. From here turn right into Calle Judías, which leads to the **Synagogue**, one of only three in Spain. Built in 1315, this tiny building has some fine Mudéjar plasterwork of Hebrew texts and retains its women's gallery.

Torre de Calahorra

① *1000-1800, last entry an hour before, €4, €5.20 with full audiovisual programme, which runs on the hour from 1100-1600.* Located on the south side of the Roman Bridge, this defensive tower is now an Interpretation Centre, giving a high-tech audiovisual history of Córdoba in addition to displays of local artifacts. Don't let the tackiness of the AV show put you off – it gives a good introduction to the Mezquita.

Museo Arqueológico Provincial

Located in the Plaza de Jerónimo Páez in a Renaissance mansion with an Italian-style porch, this archaeological museum is undoubtedly the best of its kind in southern Spain, with some excellent Roman mosaics among the highlights, but is presently closed for restoration.

Museo de Bellas Artes

① *Tue 1500-2000, Wed-Sat 0900-2000, Sun 0900-1500, free to EU citizens, otherwise €1.50.* On the attractive Plaza del Potro is the Museo de Bellas Artes in a building which was once the Hospital de la Caridad. Entry is through an attractive sculpture-filled garden. The galleries contain works by all the usual names such as Valdés Leal, Zurburán, Alonso Cano and Murillo, although not their better works. There are also, refreshingly, some works by modern painters, such as Benedito, Chicharro and Solana.

Plaza de la Corredera

Just east of the Museo Arqueológico and north of the Plaza del Potro is the remarkable Plaza de la Corredera, which is an extraordinary colonnaded square. It was enclosed in the 17th century and formed a multi-purpose arena, which has been used for bullfights and even burnings during the Inquisition.

● Sleeping

As you would expect, cheaper places tend to be further away from the historic quarter.
AL Posada de Vallina, Corregidor Luis de la Cerda 83, T957498750, hotel@hotelvall ina.com. Recently opened as a small hotel-cum-restaurant across from the Mezquita, the building is magnificent with Roman columns and an ancient well. The 15 rooms are decorated in contemporary Andalucían style with small balconies.
A Lola, C Romero 3, T957200305, hotel@ hotelconencantolola.com. A charming, cosy

new hotel with individually decorated rooms and a home-from-home salon with plants, pictures and sink-into sofas.
B Marisa, C Cardinal Herrero 6, T957473142, F957474144. Fabulous neo-Moorish lobby with traditional arches sets the tone for the decor throughout this 36-room hotel in the heart of the Jewish quarter. A/c, garage, wheelchair access.
C Maestre, C Romero Barros 4/6, T957472410, F957475395. Rooms are positioned around an attractive inner patio and the furnishings and decor are traditional. The position is perfect, tucked down a quiet

cul-de-sac close to the Plaza del Potro. The management also runs a cheaper *hostal* next door, which is similarly good value.

E-F Almanzor, C Cardenal González 19, T957485400. In the centre of the historic quarter, this simple hostel is a real find. Comfortable and well-furnished rooms; several with balconies.

E Deanes, C Deanes 6, T957293744. Good-value choice in typical Córdoban house with plenty of old-fashioned charm. A large central patio has comfortable appeal and the tapas bar is popular with locals and serves some highly original specialities, like thistles in almond sauce!

E Séneca, C Conde y Luque 7, T957473234. Excellent value at lower end of this price category with stunning patio, complete with original Moorish pavement.

F Hostal Plaza Corredera, Plaza Corredera 1, T957470581. Friendly refurbished place with good rooms looking out over the pretty plaza. Recommended.

Camping
Campamento Municipal, Av del Brillante 50, T957278481. First category site, pool, 1 km north of town; take bus No 11 or 12 from centre.

🍴 Eating

Typical *cordobés* dishes to try are *salmorejo*, a much thicker version of *gazpacho* made with more garlic and bread and *cordero a la miel* (lamb in honey).

€€€ El Caballo Rojo, C Cardenal Herrero 28, T957475375. The oldest restaurant in Córdoba, just behind the Mezquita tucked down a cul-de-sac flanked by potted geraniums. It prides itself on a Moorish inspired menu. Try the lamb with honey, fish with raisins and pine nuts and their particularly tasty dessert, *canutillo de almendra* (almond pastry).

€€€ La Almudaina, Campo Santo de los Mártines 1, T957474342. A former 15th-century palace in an unbeatable location, facing the river in the old Jewish quarter. Formal dining in lace-curtained rooms or al fresco in a glass-roofed central patio. Specialities include hake with shrimp sauce and pork loin in wine sauce. Booking is essential.

€€ El Burlaero, Calleja de la Hoguera 5, T957472719. Famous throughout Spain for its game dishes, this restaurant is spread over several rooms with low, beamed ceilings and a typical Córdoban patio.

€€ Los Califas, C Deanes 3, T957471320. Great atmosphere and popular with locals. Warm limestone decor with brilliant blue tiles and old brick, plus outside terrace with stunning Mezquita views. Traditional Córdoban cuisine, as well as several Moroccan-inspired dishes.

€€ Marroquí, C Ronda de Isasa 6, T957492871. New Moroccan restaurant with colourful ethnic decor, outside tables and popular dishes including cous cous, and *tajine* (stew).

€€ Mesón Céspedes, C Céspedes 12, T957483229. Bright, cheery restaurant with a choice of 4 daily *menú del días*, priced €7-12, plus a daily special for just €5.

€ Taberna Plateros, San Franciso 6, T957470042. Opposite **Hotel Maestre**, this 17th-century bar and restaurant has a large patio decorated with colourful tiles and several small rooms, including one dedicated to the late, local bullfighter Manolete. The food is solid homestyle cooking with the starters a meal in themselves.

Tapas bars and cafés
There are many excellent tapas bars in the old part of Córdoba. The local tipple is *Montilla*, an unfortified mellow, dry sherry-like wine, which according to the locals, is less likely to lead to a hangover – or so they say.

Bodega Guzmán, close to the synagogue, is this cavernous option, frequented by crusty old men in flat caps and bullfight aficionados, hence the small *taurino* museum in the back. Great authentic atmosphere.

Los Palacios on C Amparo is a small bar at the back of the **Paseo de Ribera** restaurant, serving good snacks, including a great *salmorejo*.

Taberna El Potro, C Lineros 2, is a little heavy on the super-kitsch art reproductions of Julio Romero de Torre but serves wonderful tapas.

Taberna Los Faroles, C Velázquez Bosco, has a vast central patio, and is a great place to hang out while enjoying excellent tapas

and raciones, including *boquerones en vinagre* (anchovies in vinegar) and wedges of *tortilla*.

Taberna San Miguel, Plaza San Miguel 1, is a popular local haunt commonly known as 'El Pisto'; tapas here include *callos en salsa picante* (tripe in spicy sauce) and *patatas a lo pobre* (fried potatoes with onion and garlic).

Taberna San Nicolás, next to the Plaza de San Nicolás, a fine old bar serving up a superb range of tapas and *raciones*, including all kinds of fried fish.

◑ Bars and clubs

Nightlife in Córdoba, particularly during the summer, is centred in El Brillante. Av Gran Capitán is throbbing with late-night action.

Pub DSO, Llanos del Pretorio 1, has a large terrace and live music most weekends.

Gallery, C Molinos Alta 7, hopping from dawn to dusk on Sat.

Plaza Café, Plaza Mármol de Bañuelos 4, is an attractive modern bar near the Plaza Tendillas.

Soul on Alfonso XII (next to the Ayuntamiento) attracts a vibrant, arty crowd.

Zahira, C Conde de Robledo 3, in the centre of town, has Thu party nights and plays mainly latin and rock.

◉ Entertainment

Baths Hammam, C Corregidor Luís de la Cerda 51, T957484746, is a bathhouse in Moorish style. A 90-min session, including a massage, costs €18; sessions start every 2 hrs from 1000-2400; booking is advisable.

Cinema Filmoteca de Andalucía, C Medina y Corella 5, T957472018. Regular screenings of subtitled foreign films.

Flamenco One of the best venues with an authentic ambience and delightful patio is **Tablao Cardenal**, C Torrijos 10, T957483112. Flamenco starts 2230, closed Sun.

✪ Festivals and events

Feb sees **Carnaval**.

Easter Semana Santa involves some 28 traditional Easter processions.

5-12 May is the week of **Fiesta de la Patios** marked by concerts and flamenco, as well as a competition for the best decorated patio. The tourist office will have a map of the patios open to the public, or you'll notice 'patio' signs in the streets, which means you are invited to enter.

Fiesta de Nuestra Señora de la Fuensanta Celebrations for Córdoba's patron saint.

◉ Transport

Bus The main bus station is at Plaza de las Tres Culturas, T957404040. There is a daily bus to **Cádiz** at 1900 and several daily to **Madrid**, **Málaga**, **Jaén** and **Sevilla**.

Train The RENFE office is at Plaza de las Tres Culturas, T957400202. There are frequent connections from many destinations, with 27 trains daily to **Sevilla** and to **Madrid** (some are high- speed AVE train), 2 to **Algeciras**, 1 to **Jaén**, 3 to **Ronda**, 10 to **Málaga**, and 5 to **Cádiz**.

◉ Directory

Internet Ch@t, C Claudio Marcelo 17. 1000-2200, Sun 1600-2200, €1.80 per hr. **Ciberplanet**, Centro Comercial, El Arcangel. Open 1000-2200, €1.50 per hr. **Salón Internet**, Hostal El Pilar del Potro, C Lucano 12. 1000-2400. €2.40 per hr. **Serrano**, C Eduardo Dato 9. 1000-2200. €2.10 per hr. **Post** Correos, C Cruz Conde 15. Mon-Fri 0800-2100, Sat 0900-1400. **Telephone** Locutorio, Plaza Tendillas 7. Mon-Fri 0930-1400 and 1700-2300, Sat 0930-1400.

Background

History

Hominids

While Northern Spain was a stamping ground for dinosaurs (literally; their footprints are found all over the region), the peninsula was almost certainly the scene of the first upright walking in Europe. Fragments of hominid bone found near Granada are probably over a million years old. A valley just east of Burgos has yielded more substantial remains of *homo heidelbergensis*, which are of an incredible age, at least 400,000 years, and quite possibly double that in some cases. *Homo heidelbergensis* is seen as the ancestor of the Neanderthals, of whom extensive remains have been found. Many caves in the north and south of Spain bear evidence of their presence; tools and remains of occupation stretching back to 60,000 odd years ago until their extinction around 27,000 years ago. The famed skull of 'Gibraltar Woman' is one such remnant.

Upper Palaeolithic period

Some of the same caves and others, particularly in Cantabria and Asturias, have produced the first signs of *homo sapiens* in the peninsula. Dating from the Upper Palaeolithic (18,000BC onwards), these hunter-gatherers produced fairly sophisticated stone and bone tools including arrows and spears. They also experimented with art, and found it to their liking; primitive whittling of deer bones and outlines of hands on cave walls suddenly gave way to the sensitive, imaginative and colourful bison, deer, and horses found in several locations but most famously at Altamira in antabria, where the work is of amazing artistic quality. This so-called Magdalenian culture seemed to extend across Northern Spain and into southern France, where related paintings have been found at places such as Lascaux.

A more settled existence emerged in the sixth millennium BC, initially around Almería, where waves of migrants arrived from North Africa and the Levant, bringing significant technological advances that gradually spread across the region and propelled Spain into the Neolithic era. The most striking archaeological remnants from the period are a great number of dolmens, large stone burial chambers which were modish across much of Europe at the time. These are found principally along the north coast, particularly in the Basque lands and Galicia, but also in the south, most notably at Antequera.

Metalworking culture apparently first emerged at Los Millares in Almería Province. Working of copper from local deposits was followed by the emergence of the Bronze Age in the region in the early second millennium BC.

Early inhabitants

Vast amounts have been written about the inhabitants of the peninsula leading into the historical periods, and few of the many theories have much evidence to support or sink them. The principal inhabitants of the region are known as Iberians by default, but little is known of their origins apart from the fact that they spoke languages that are not from the Indo-European group that unites the vast majority of European and western Asian languages under its umbrella. The Basques, too, seem to have been around in those days. Their language isn' t Indo-European either, but no convincing evidence has been found that can link them and the Iberians (or anyone else for that matter). The Basques like to say that God created Adam from bones he found in a Basque cemetery. Certain genetic peculiarities in the Basque population have led to theories that they are directly descended from the Palaeolithic inhabitants of the region.

Celts

The third important group were the Celts, who descended from the north in waves in the late second millennium BC. They spoke an Indo-European tongue and settled mostly in the north and west of the peninsula. Their influence is very apparent in place names, language, and culture. There are still very close parallels between European areas settled by Celts; sitting over a cider while listening to bagpipes in Asturias you might want to ponder just how old these traditions are. The principal architectural remnant of the early Celts is the castro, a fortified hilltop fort and trading compound of which there are very many in Asturias and Galicia. While the mountainous terrain of the north meant that distinct groups developed separately in remote valleys, the flatter lands of the centre encouraged contact. The Celts and Iberians seemed to mingle in the centre of Spain and form a single culture, rather unimaginatively labelled Celtiberian.

Phoenicians and Carthaginians

This was a time of much cultural interaction, for in the early first millennium BC those master sailors and merchants from the Levant; the Phoenicians, set up many trading stations, mostly on the Andalucían coast. These included Cádiz, Huelva and Málaga, but they had plenty of contact with the north, and may have established a few ports on the Atlantic coast. There was also cultural contact with the Greeks, who established settlements on the Catalan coast. These trading alliances enabled the locals to make vast leaps forward, and Iberian kingdoms started issuing coins and developing writing.

The heirs and descendants of the Phoenicians, the Carthaginians, came to Spain in the third century BC and settled widely in the south, particularly at Cádiz, and at Cartagena, which they named after their hometown of Carthage. While there was contact with the north, and Hannibal campaigned in western Castilla, the biggest effect on the peninsula was as a direct consequence of his disputes with Rome. Bent on ending Carthaginian power in the Mediterranean, the Romans accurately realized that Spain was a 'second Carthage', and set out to change that. Once they realized the potential wealth in the peninsula, they set out to conquer it entirely.

Roman Conquest

It was the Romans that first created the idea of Spain, Hispania, as a single geographical entity, a concept it has been struggling with ever since. The Romans were given a tough time in the north, which it took them two centuries to subdue. The Celtiberian towns resisted the legions in a very spirited manner. Numancia, near Soria, resisted Roman sieges for many years, and was the centre of resistance that lost Rome tens of thousands of troops. Problems with the Cantabrians and Asturians lasted until Augustus and Agrippa finally did for them in the late years of the first century BC. The Romans gave up trying to impose their culture on the northern fringes; the Basques and Galicians were extremely resistant to it, and a 'live and let live' stance was eventually adopted in those areas.

The south of Spain, by contrast, became a real Roman heartland, the most Roman of the Roman colonies, with all the trappings of Imperial Rome. The peninsula was divided into three provinces; Baetica in the south, administered from Córdoba; Lusitania in the west, administered from Mérida, and Hispania Citerior in the north and east, run rather inconveniently from Tarragona. It was generally a time of peace and wealth; wine and olive oil, fish-sauce, gold and silver poured from the colony back to Italy. Mérida was the pre-eminent Roman city and still preserves the best Roman remains in Spain; while Itálica, near Sevilla, produced two Roman emperors in Trajan and Hadrian. Córdoba was the home of the Seneca family, while Martial penned epigrams out of modern Calatayud, near Zaragoza.

Christianity spread comparatively rapidly into Spain. The diocese of Zaragoza was founded as early as the first century, while Córdoba and León were other important early Christian centres. Christianity was certainly spread out to fit over existing religious frameworks; the Basques had few problems with the Virgin Mary considering their own earthmother figure was named Mari, and here as elsewhere the Christian calendar was moulded around pagan festivals. The fourth century Priscillian from Avila drew many followers with his austere teachings until declared a heretic and killed.

Visigoths

As the Roman order tottered, the barbarian hordes streamed across the Pyrenees and created havoc. Alans, Vandals, and Sueves capitalized on the lack of control in the early fifth century AD to such an extent that the Romans enlisted the Visigoths to restore order on their behalf. This they succeeded in doing, but the Sueves hung around and established themselves in the northwest of the peninsula, establishing capitals at Mérida and Astorga. Returning as they lost control of their French territories, the Visigoths finally put an end to their small kingdom. After a period of much destruction and chaos, a fairly tenuous Visigothic control ensued. A literary beacon of the time was San Isidoro, writing in Sevilla, see box.

Comparatively little is known about the couple of centuries that followed. A handful of Visigothic churches still exist in Northern Spain; these evidently draw on Roman architectural models but add some local features, and some iconography from the Visigoths' Germanic roots. After having based themselves primarily in Sevilla and Mérida, the Visigoth rulers established a capital at Toledo, and there's plenty of evidence to suggest that they managed to maintain high levels of education and public order despite ongoing dynastic struggles among the ruling families.

Despite King Reccared's conversion to Catholicism in AD587, and ongoing integration with the local Romanized inhabitants, the Visigothic state was vulnerable, largely because of these upheavals, and in AD711 the event occurred that was to define Spanish history for the next eight centuries. The teachings of Mohammed had been carried like a whirlwind across North Africa, and, after crossing the Straits of Gibraltar, the Moors had taken most of Spain before the prophet had been dead for even a century.

In 711, Tarik, governor of Tangier, and his force of Berbers, defeated the Visigothic king Roderic near Tarifa and the Muslim invasion swept easily across Spain, which became part of an empire known as Al-Andalus.

The Moors: Al-Andalus

Under Arab leadership, most of the invaders were native north African Berbers, but there was a substantial mercenary element, many of them from eastern Europe. The Moors swept on into France, where they were stopped by the Franks at Poitiers.

Geography breaks Spain into distinct regions which have tended to persist through time, and it was one of these, Asturias, that the Moors had some trouble with. They were defeated in what was presumably a minor skirmish at Covadonga, in the far northern mountains, in 717. While the Moors weren't too rattled by this at the time, Spain views it today as an event of immense significance, a victory against all odds and a sort of mystical event where God proved himself to be on the Christian side. Think the deliverance from Egypt meets Die Hard and that's something like the picture. It was hardly a crippling blow to the Moors, who were on the autoroutes of southern France before too long, but it probably sowed the seeds of what became the Asturian monarchy.

A curious development in many ways, this line of kings emerged unconquered from the shadowy northern hills and forests. Whether they were a last bastion of Visigothic resistance, or whether they were just local folk ready to defend their lands,

San Isidoro

"no one can gain a full understanding of Spain without a knowledge of Saint Isidore"
Richard Ford

Born in AD560 Isidoro succeeded his brother Leander as Bishop of Seville. Without doubt one of the most important intellectual figures of the Middle Ages, his prolific writings cover all subjects and were still popular at the time of the Renaissance. His *Etymologiae* was one of the first secular books in print when it appeared in 1472. The first encyclopedia written in the Christian west, it was the primary source for the 154 classical authors that Isidoro quoted. He also wrote on music, law, history, and jurisprudence as well as doctrinal matters.

Isidoro is also recognized as an important Church reformer and was responsible for the production of the so-called Mozarabic rite, which is still practised in Toledo Cathedral today. His writings were an attempt to restore vigour and direction to a Church that was in decline following the Visigothic invasions. His emphasis on educational reforms was to put the Church in Spain on foundations that were to last centuries. This was recognized by contempories when the Council of Toledo in 653 called him "the extraordinary doctor, the most learned man of the latter ages, always to be named with reverence, Isidore".

Another important element to Isidoro's writings was his prophesies, which were based both on the Bible and classical references. This element of his writings appealed to later generations living in the shadow of the Muslim conquests and was to be the source of many stories and legends. Following the expulsion of the Moors it seemed to some that an ancient prophecy was about to be fulfilled. Ferdinand was the hidden king of legend. The Ponce de León wrote in 1486 "there will be nothing able to resist his might because God has reserved total victory and all glory to the rod, that is to say the Bat, because Ferdinand is the encubierto [hidden one]… he will be Monarch of all the world."

Isidoro died in Seville in 636 and his writings continued to inspire Spain for the next 900 years. His body is now in León, moved there by Ferdinand I of Castile who repatriated it from Muslim control around 1060. This act of national piety was carried out with the help of a mystic whose skill revealed the previously lost location of the Saint's remains.

they established an organized monarchy of sorts with a capital that shifted about but settled on Oviedo in 808. Their most lasting legacy has been a number of churches and royal halls; beautifully proportioned stone buildings that show some Visigothic characteristics but are also a very original style. A style far more graceful than the name it has been saddled with, Asturian Pre-Romanesque.

Meanwhile, the Moors were establishing a fairly tolerant rule over most of Spain. Although turned back in France, they remained easily strong enough to repulse Charlemagne in northeast Spain in 778. After failing to take Zaragoza, he returned huffily to France but had his rearguard ambushed by Basques in the Navarran pass of Roncesvalles. The Basques were infuriated that he'd taken down the walls of Pamplona on his way through; the defeat suffered in the pass became the basis for the fanciful epic poem Chanson de Roland, which attributes the attack to Muslims.

The prince Abd al-Rahman of the Umayyad dynasty came to Spain in the mid-eighth century after the Umayyad overthrow by the Abbasids in the Middle East

⁞ Victor of God

Ibn-abu-amir was born to a poor family in Cordoba around 950. Known to later generations as Almanzour, or 'Victor of God' he is one of the most remarkable figures of the Middle Ages representing both the strength of Muslim Spain and its ultimate failure. A lawyer, he succeeded in reforming the administration of the Caliphate and in modernizing its army. Nominally the regent, he was content to let formal power reside with the Sultan but by 996 had assumed the title King.

With his power consolidated he launched a series of lightening raids across the North of Spain. His army, made up of mercenary Slavs, Christian renegades, and North African Berbers, sacked Zamora and Simancas in 981, Barcelona in 985, and León in 987. The Leonese king Bermudo had broken an agreement to pay tribute and was forced to flee to the Asturian Mountains. The only opposition to a total takeover of Spain now lay in Asturias and remote Galicia.

Almanzour was not however a blood-thirsty tyrant. Under his guidance a university was established in Córdoba and he was a great patron of the arts and science. On his many military campaigns both in Spain and North Africa he took a library of books. Respected and feared by his enemies he was merciful to those he defeated.

In 997 he embarked on his final campaign to extinguish Christian opposition. He took A Coruña and the holy city of Santiago where he removed the bells of the cathedral to the mosque of Córdoba. On encountering a lone priest protecting the shrine of Saint James he is said to have ordered his men to leave the holy relics of the city untouched.

After an inconclusive battle in 1002 at Calatañazor in Castille, Almanzour died of natural causes. The relief of the Christians was immense. A commentator wrote "In 1002 died Almanzour, and was buried in Hell". With his death the Caliphate fragmented into a number of small warring states, allowing the Christians to regroup. Never again were the Moors to be so united and his death marked a significant turning point in the history of Spain.

and North Africa. He and his successors ruled Al-Andalus as emirs from Córdoba, which became the pre-eminent city in western Europe. In 929 Abd al-Rahman III declared himself caliph, making the city the western equivalent of Baghdad. Although there was constant campaigning against the growing Christian north, it was a time of great cultural achievement in the south of Spain. The Umayyads were reasonably benevolent rulers (although it was far from the multicultural utopia often portrayed), and Jews and Christians were largely allowed freedom of religion and trade. The Jews, most of whom had arrived in Spain in Roman times, had been harshly treated by the Visigothic rulers (urged by the Church) and flourished in the cities of Al-Andalus. Many Christians converted to Islam during this period (some for tax reasons); those that didn't became known as Mozárabes. Huge advances were made in the sciences, in literature, agriculture and engineering; Muslim buildings such as Córdoba's Mezquita reached new heights of beauty and harmony.

In the north things were a bit different. While the Covadonga defeat was insignificant, the Asturian kingdom began to grow in strength and the process of the Reconquista, the Christian reconquest of the peninsula, began. The northmen took advantage of cultural interchange with the south, which remained significant throughout the period despite the militarized zone in between, and were soon strong

enough to begin pushing back. The loose Moorish authority in these lands certainly helped; the northern zone was more or less administered by warlords who were only partially controlled by the emirs and caliphs in Córdoba. Galicia and much of the north coast was reclaimed, and in 914 the Asturian king Ordoño II reconquered León; the capital shortly moved to here, and the line of kings took on the name of that town. As the Christians moved south, they re-settled many towns and villages that had often lain in ruins since Roman times.

Asturias/León wasn't the only Christian power to develop during this period. The Basques had been quietly pushing outwards too, and their small mountain kingdom of Navarra grew rapidly. Aragón emerged, and gained power and size via a dynastic union with Catalunya. The entity that came to dominate Spain, Castilla, was born at this time too. In the middle of the 10th century a Burgos noble, Fernán González, declared independence from the kingdom of León and began to rally disparate Christian groups in the region. He was so successful in this endeavour that it wasn't too long before his successors labelled themselves kings.

But the Moors weren't finished by any means. A formidable bloke named Al-Manzur managed to sack almost every Christian city in Northern Spain within a couple of decades (see box); surely one of the greatest military feats of the Middle Ages. Both sides were made painfully aware of their vulnerability and constructed a series of massive fortresses that faced each other across the central plains. The Muslim fortresses were particularly formidable; high eyries with commanding positions, accurately named the 'front teeth' of Al-Andalus. There are around three thousand forts and castles in various states of repair in Spain; a huge number of them are to be found in this area.

It was just after Al-Manzur's death that things began to go pomegranate-shaped for the Moors, as kinstrife and civil war over succession fatally weakened the caliphate while the Christian kingdoms were gaining strength and unity. The king of Navarra Sancho III ('the Great') managed to unite almost the whole of Northern Spain under his rule in the early 11th century; although this inevitably dissolved, the rival kingdoms at least had a common goal. The caliphate fragmented into numerous taifa states in 1031. Pitted against each other as well as the north, they were in no state to resist, and were forced to pay protection money to the Christian armies, enriching the new kingdoms. The big beneficiary was Castilla; the king Alfonso VI, with the help of his on-off mercenary El Cid, see box page 190, conquered swathes of Muslim territory, reaching Toledo in 1085.

Alfonso must have dreamed of reconquering the whole peninsula at that point, but he was stopped dead by the Almoravids, a by-the-book Islamic dynasty that quickly crossed from Morocco, appalled by the 'decadence' of the taifas, which they felt had strayed far from the teachings of Mohammed. They inflicted a heavy defeat on Alfonso near Badajoz and re-established the caliphate along stricter lines, based in Sevilla.

Tempted by big lunches, tapas, siestas and free-poured spirits, the Almoravids soon lapsed into softer ways though, and much of modern Andalucía was lost to the Moors: Alfonso VII had taken Córdoba, a significant prize, in 1146, and Almería in 1147, before a similar Moroccan group, the Almohads, crossed the Straits and took control back. They didn't last long either, and a heavy defeat at Las Navas de Tolosa (near Jaén) in 1212 at the hands of the Castillian king Alfonso VIII had the fat lady warming up in the wings. Once re-taken, Córdoba fell again in 1236 and Sevilla went down in 1248. Al-Andalus was reduced to the emirate of Granada, which held out for another two and a half centuries.

The Reconquista

The nature of the Reconquista was very similar to that of the Crusades; a holy war against the enemies of the faith that at the same time conveniently offered numerous opportunities for pillage, plunder and seizure of land. Younger sons, not in line for any

inheritance under customs of the time, could fight for the glory of God and appropriate lands and wealth for themselves at the same time. Knightly orders similar to those of the Crusades were founded in Spain; the three principal ones being the Knights of Calatrava, Alcántara, and Santiago.

Santiago (St James), although he had been dead for a millennium or so, played a major role in the Reconquista. The spurious discovery of his tomb at Compostela in the 9th century had sparked ongoing pilgrimage; it effectively replaced the inaccessible Holy Land as a destination for the devout and the penitent. The discovery came in time to resemble some sort of sign from God, and St James took on the role of Matamoros, Moor-slayer, and is depicted crunching hapless Andalusi under the hooves of his white charger in countless sculptures and paintings; quite a career-change for the first-century fisherman. With an apostle risen from the dead onside, it's little wonder that Christians flocked to the Reconquista banners.

Another factor in the success of the Reconquista was the organization of Christian Spanish society, in which the first-born son, meek or no, inherited the earth and the rest were left to fend for themselves. The 'holy war' against the Moors was a way for younger sons, as well as those of poorer birth, to gain wealth, prestige, and above all the land which was up for grabs.

By the mid-12th century Northern Spain was effectively secured under Christian rule. For largely geographical reasons, it had been the fledgling kingdom of Castilla who ended up with the biggest slice of the pie, since which time it has been Spain's most powerful political entity. It had already frequently been united with the Leonese kingdom by dynastic marriages, and this was confirmed in 1230, when Ferdinand III inherited both crowns (a fact still lamented in León today).

While Navarra was still going up in the mountains, it was Aragón who was the other main beneficiary from the reconquest. Uniting with Catalunya in 1150, it began looking eastwards to that great trading forum, the Mediterranean. Catalunya became a major power in the region, with an industrious mercantile society and prosperous agricultural interior. In the 13th century they took Sicily, Sardinia and Malta as trading bases; in time they would have a major foothold in the Italian mainland.

Post-war years

With the flush of war fading from faces, the north settled down to a period of prosperity. Castilla became a significant producer of wool and wheat, and the towns of the north coast established important trading links with northern Europe to distribute it. In 1296 the Hermandad de las Marismas, an export alliance of four major ports (A Coruña, Santander, Laredo and San Sebastián) was formed to consolidate this. The Basques were doing very nicely at this time. Demand for Vizcayan iron was high, and Basque sailors explored the whole Atlantic, almost certainly reaching north America a century or more before Columbus sailed.

These times were the Age of Towns. Places like Burgos and Medina del Campo became powerful centres controlling the distribution of goods to the coastal ports. Guilds and societies became increasingly important in the flourishing urban centres. Meanwhile the Castillian kings still pursued military aims. Becoming an increasing anachronism in an increasingly urban society, these crusading kings came to rely heavily on the towns for political and financial support. In order to keep them onside, they began to grant fueros, or exemptions from certain taxation and conscription duties. The towns stubbornly defended their fueros, and proto-democratic assemblies, the cortes, began to assemble to keep the kings honest.

The peace and wealth of this period provided a platform for important advances in art and architecture, helped by ideas from the rest of Europe diffusing via trade and pilgrimage. Towns spent vast sums in constructing soaring cathedrals, symbols of faith in architectural principles as much as Christianity. Alfonso X, based in Toledo, wisely promoted Castillian (Spanish) above Latin as the official language of Castile.

Meanwhile, the Nasrid rulers of Granada continued the age of Moorish splendour; this was the time of the Alhambra, the supreme surviving achievement of Moorish art and architecture.

But already in Castilla's time of prosperity the seeds of decline were sprouting. Cities that had forged the Reconquista, Oviedo and León, became insignificant country towns as populations moved southwards in the wars' wake. The massive numbers of sheep being grazed in migratory patterns across the land caused large-scale degradation and erosion of the soil; in many ways, the 'war on trees' was to prove as significant as any that had been waged against Moors. The barren landscapes of today's Castilla are a direct result of these post-reconquest years. The fueros that were so indiscriminately handed out meant that later kings were barely able to govern the towns, who understandably were reluctant to concede their privileges. The glory of the soldiering years rubbed off on Castillian attitudes too. Sons of minor nobles (hidalgos, from hijos d'algo, 'sons of somebody') yearned for the smell of battle, and scorned the dull attractions of work and education, an attitude that has cost Spain dear over the centuries and was memorably satirized in Cervantes' Don Quijote. The church, too, was in a poor state. Bled of funds by successive crusading kings, it developed a hoarding mentality and was in no condition to act as a moral light for the young Christian kingdoms.

Furthermore, it was far from being a peaceful pastoral and urban golden age. The nuggety walled towns of the Reconquista battle lines provided perfect bases for power-hungry nobles; civil strife was exacerbated by the fact that most kings openly kept mistresses outside their arranged dynastic marriages, and illegitimate children were a dime-a-dozen.

The 14th century

This was one of the most troubled periods in the country's history. Spain was drawn into the Hundred Years War when the bastard Henry of Trastámara waged war with French help on his English-backed brother Pedro I (the Cruel). After Pedro was murdered, his son-in-law John of Gaunt, Duke of Lancaster, claimed the Castillian throne. Landing in Galicia, he waged an inconclusive war with Henry before agreeing to marry his daughter to the king's son. He returned to England happy enough with this outcome and a substantial retirement package from Castillian funds.

Such marriage ties were of vital political importance, and it was one, in 1469, that was to have a massive impact throughout the world. The heir to the Aragonese throne, Ferdinand, married Isabel, heiress of Castilla, in a top-secret ceremony in Valladolid. The implications were enormous. Aragón was still a power in the Mediterranean (Fernando was also king of Sicily), and Castilla's domain covered much of the peninsula. The unification under the Reyes Católicos, as the monarchs became known, marked the beginnings of Spain as we know it today. Things didn't go smoothly at first, however. There were plenty of opponents to the union, and forces in support of Juana, Isabel's elder (but assumed illegitimate) sister waged wars across Castilla.

Religious persecution

The reign of the Catholic Monarchs was full of incident, particularly the year 1492, when Columbus sailed the Atlantic under their patronage, they completed the Reconquista by taking Granada, and thought they would celebrate the triumph by kicking the Jews out of Spain. Spain's Jewish population had been hugely significant since the 12th century, heavily involved in commerce, shipping, and literature throughout the peninsula, but hatred against them had begun to grow in the fourteenth century, and there had been many a pogrom. Many converted during these years to escape the murderous climate; they became known as conversos. The decision to expel those who hadn't converted was far more that of the pious Isabel than the pragmatic Fernando and has to be seen in the light of the paranoid

Christianizing climate. The Jews were given four months to leave the kingdom, and even the conversos soon found themselves under the Inquisition's iron hammer (see box). The kingdom's Muslim population was tolerated for another decade, when they too were given the choice of baptism (converts became known as moriscos) or expulsion. Finally, the moriscos too were expelled (in 1609); Spain still has not wholly recovered from this self-inflicted purge of the majority of its intellectual, commercial, and professional talent (particularly areas such as Aragón and Andalucía), and the lack of cultural diversity led to longterm stagnation. The ridiculous doctrine of limpieza de sangre (purity of blood) became all-important; the enduring popularity of ham and pigmeat surely owes something to these days, when openly eating these foods proved that one wasn't a pork-eschewing Muslim or Jew.

Conquest of the Americas

In the wake of Columbus' discovery, the treaty of Tordesillas in 1494 partitioned the Atlantic between Spain and Portugal, and led to the era of Spanish colonization of the Americas. In many ways, this was an extension of the Reconquista as young men hardened on the Castillian and Extremaduran meseta crossed the seas with zeal for conquest, riches and land. Spain was both enriched and crippled by this exodus; while the cities and Andalucía flourished on the New World booty and trade, the countryside of the centre and north was denuded of people to work the land. The biggest winner proved to be Sevilla, which was granted a monopoly over New World trade by the Catholic Monarchs in 1503. It grew rapidly and became one of Western Europe's foremost cities.

Isabel died in 1504, but refused to settle her Castillian throne on her husband, Ferdnando, to his understandable annoyance, as the two had succeeded in uniting virtually the whole of modern Spain under their joint rule. The inheritance passed to their mad daughter, Juana la Loca, and her husband, Felipe of Burgundy (el Hermoso/the Fair), who came to Spain in 1506 to claim their inheritance. Felipe soon died however, and his wife's obvious inability to govern led to Fernando being recalled as regent of the united Spain until the couple's son, Charles, came of age. During this period Fernando completed the boundaries of modern Spain by annexing Navarra. On his deathbed he reluctantly agreed to name Charles heir to Aragón and its territories, thus preserving the unity he and Isabel had forged.

Charles inherited vast tracts of European land; Spain and southern Italy from his maternal grandparents, and Austria, Burgundy and the Low Countries from his paternal ones. He was shortly named Holy Roman Emperor and if all that power weren't enough, his friend, aide and tutor, Adrian of Utrecht was soon elected pope.

Under the Habsburg monarchy, Carlos I (Charles V) and then his son Philip II relied on the income from the colonies to pursue wars (often unwillingly) on several European fronts. It couldn't last; Spain's golden age has been likened by Spanish historian Felipe Fernández-Armesto to a dog walking on its hind legs. Although over the centuries many indianos returned from the colonies to their native provinces with newfound wealth, the American expansion sounded a grim bell for northern Castilla. With Sevilla and Cádiz now the focus for the all-important trade with the colonies, Castilla had turned southwards, and its northern provinces rapidly declined, hastened by a drain of its citizens to the new world across the sea. The comunero revolt of the early 16th century expressed the frustrations of a region that was once the focus of optimistic Christian conquest and agricultural wealth, but had now become peripheral to the designs of a 'foreign' monarchy. A plague in the early 17th century didn't help matters any, wiping out about a tenth of the Castillian population.

Aragón, meanwhile, had become a backwater since civil strife in the 15th century had deprived it of Catalunya and therefore much of its Mediterranean trade. Above all regions, it suffered most from the loss of the Muslims and Jews; many of its cities had thrived on the cultural mixture. The union with Castilla had also eventually deprived it of

political significance. As an important focus of Spanish naval and maritime power, the north coast continued in a better vein. Much of the shipbuilding for exploration, trade, and war took place here, and many of the ships were crewed by Basques and Galicians.

For a brief time Spain and Portugal were united, as Philip II claimed the throne of his western neighbour in 1580. Much of the world was at his disposal, but he was bankrupt, mortgaged to the hilt to Genoan bankers, and over-dependent on the yearly treasure-fleets bringing booty from the gold and silver mines of the Americas. The disaster of the Armada in 1588 was a further blow to this pious king, wracked with anxiety for his people but hated by many of them.

The growing administrative requirements of managing an empire had forced the previously itinerant Castillian monarchs to choose a capital, and Philip II picked the small town of Madrid in 1561, something of a surprise, as Sevilla or Valladolid were more obvious choices. Although central, Madrid was remote, tucked away behind a shield of hills in the interior. This seemed in keeping with the somewhat paranoid nature of Habsburg rule. And beyond all other things they were paranoid about threats to the Catholic religion; the biggest of which, of course, they perceived to be Protestantism. This paranoia was costly in the extreme.

The decline of the monarchy

The struggle of the Spanish monarchy to control the spread of Protestantism was a major factor in the decline of the empire. Philip II fought expensive and ultimately unwinnable wars in Flanders that bankrupted the state; while within the country the absolute ban on the works of 'heretical' philosophers, scientists, and theologians left Spain behind in Renaissance Europe. In the 18th century, for example, the so-called 'age of enlightenment' in western Europe, theologians at the noble old university of Salamanca debated what language the angels spoke; that Castillian was proposed as a likely answer is certain. Philip II's successors didn't have his strength of character; Philip III was ineffectual and dominated by his advisors, while Philip IV, so sensitively portrayed by Velásquez, tried hard but was indecisive and unfortunate, despite the best efforts of his favourite, the remarkable Conde-Duque de Olivares. As well as being unwillingly involved in several costly wars overseas, there was also a major rebellion in Catalunya in the middle of the 17th century.

The decline of the monarchy paralleled a physical decline in the monarchs, as the inbred Habsburgs became more and more deformed and weak; the last of them, Charles II, was a tragic victim of contorted genetics who died childless and plunged the nation into a war of succession. 'Castilla has made Spain, and Castilla has destroyed it,' commented Ortega y Gasset. Despite these misfortunes, the 17th century had been a time of much inspiration in the arts; Spanish Baroque was a cheerful façade on a gloomy building, and painters such as Velásquez, Zurbarán, and Murillo hit the heights of expression.

The death of poor heirless Charles II was a long time coming, and foreign powers were circling like vultures to try and secure a favourable succession to the throne of Spain. Charles eventually named the French duke Philip of Bourbon as his successor, much to the concern of England and Holland, who declared war on France. War broke out throughout Spain until the conflict's eventual resolution at the Treaty of Utrecht, at which Britain received Gibraltar, and Spain also lost its Italian and Low Country possessions. Catalunya and Aragón, who had sided with the Austrian pretender, were harshly treated by the new regime, having their privileges revoked in 1707, bringing to an end the separate status of the old kingdom and reducing Aragón at least to minor status in peninsular affairs.

The 18th century: Bourbon Dynasty

The Bourbon dynasty succeeded in bringing back a measure of stability and wealth to Spain in the 18th century. They recovered possessions in Italy but turned most of their

attentions to the New World, skirmishing with Britain in the Seven Years' War and the American War of Independence. While this period brought significant prosperity to the south, particularly Cádiz, the north of Spain continued its decline more or less headlong. The Catholic church was in a poor state intellectually, and came to rely more and more on cults and fiestas to keep up the interest of the populace; a dogmatic tradition that is still very strong today. The Jesuits, an order that had its origins with the Basques, and a more enlightened lot than most, were expelled in 1767. The 18th century ended with a Spanish-French conflict in the wake of the French revolution. Peace was made after two years, but worse was to follow.

The 19th century

The 19th century was an unmitigated disaster for Spain from start to finish, an almost continuous period of brutal wars and political strife. First up was a heavy defeat for a joint Spanish-French navy by Nelson off Cape Trafalgar near Cádiz. Next Napoleon pulled a fast one on Charles IV. Partioning Portugal between the two of them seemed like a good idea to Spain, which had always coveted its western neighbour. It wasn't until the French armies seemed more interested in Madrid than Lisbon that Charles IV got the message. Forced to abdicate in favour of his rebellious son Fernando, he was then summoned to a conference with Bonaparte at Bayonne with his son, wife, and Manuel Godoy, his able and trusted advisor (who is often said to have been loved even more by the queen than the king). Napoleon had his own brother Joseph (known among Spaniards as Pepe Botellas for his heavy drinking) installed on the throne. On May 2 1808 (still a red-letter day in Spain), the people revolted against this arrogant gesture, and Napoleon sent in the troops in late 1808. The ensuing few years are known in Spain as the Guerra de Independencia (War of Independence). Combined Spanish, British, and Portuguese forces clashed with the French all across the north, firstly disastrously as General Moore was forced to retreat across Galicia to a Dunkirk-like embarkation at A Coruña, then more successfully as Wellington won important battles at Ciudad Rodrigo, Vitoria, and San Sebastián. The behaviour of both sides was brutal both on the battlefield and off. Marshal Soult's long retreat across the region saw him loot town after town of their treasures; his men robbed tombs and burned priceless archives. The allied forces were little better; Wellington described his own men as 'scum of the earth' who sacked the towns they conquered with similar destructiveness.

Significant numbers of Spaniards had been in favour of the French invasion, and were opposed to the liberal republican movements that sprang up in its wake. In 1812 a revolutionary council in Cádiz, on the point of falling to the French, had drafted a constitution proclaiming a democratic parliamentary monarchy of sorts. Liberals had high hopes that this would be brought into effect at the end of the war, but the returning king, Fernando, revoked it. The rest of the century was to see clash after clash of liberals against conservatives, progressive cities against reactionary countryside, restrictive centre against outward-looking periphery. Spain finally lost its empire, as the strife-torn homeland could do little against the independence movements of Latin America. In 1823 the French put down a democratic revolution and restored Fernando VII to the throne. When he died, another war of succession broke out, this time between supporters of his brother Don Carlos, and his infant daughter Isabella.

The so-called Carlist Wars of 1833-1839, 1847-1849 (often not counted as one) and 1872-1876 were politically complex. Don Carlos represented conservatism, and his support was drawn from a number of different sources. Wealthy landowners, the church, and the reactionary peasantry, with significant French support, lined up against the loyalist army, the liberals and the urban middle and working classes. The Carlist stronghold was Navarra and the rural Basque region; liberal reforms were threatening the two pillars of Basque country life; the church, and their age-old

fueros. In between and during the wars, a series of pronunciamientos (coups d'etat) plagued the monarchy. During the third Carlist war, the king abdicated and the shortlived First Spanish Republic was proclaimed, ended by a military-led restoration a year later. The Carlists were defeated but remained strong, and played a prominent part in the Spanish Civil War. There's still a Carlist party in Navarra and a pretender to the throne.

Despite all the troubles, industrialization finally began to reach Spain, and several of the ports of the north coast thrived. Vigo, A Coruña and Santander all flourished; Barcelona was thriving on its textile and engineering industries. Bilbao, on the back of its iron ore exports, grew into a major industrial and banking centre, and Asturias mined quantities of poor-quality coal. Basque nationalism as it is known today was born in the late 19th century.

The 1876 constitution proclaimed by the restored monarchy in the wake of the third Carlist war provided for a peaceful alternation of power between liberal and conservative parties. In the wake of decades of strikes and pronunciamientos this was not a bad solution, and the introduction of the vote for the whole male population in 1892 offered much hope. The ongoing curse, however, was caciquismo, a system whereby elections and governments were hopelessly rigged by groups of 'mates'.

Spain lost its last overseas posessions, Cuba, Puerto Rico and the Phillippines, in the 'Disaster' of 1898. The introspective turmoil caused by this event gave the name to the '1898 generation', a forward thinking movement of artists, philosophers and poets among whom were numbered the Granadan poet García Lorca, the Basques Unamuno and Zuloaga, and the Sorian poet Antonio Machado. It was a time of discontent, and strikes began to occur more and more regularly in the towns and cities of the north, particularly in Catalunya and Asturias, although Spanish industry profited from its neutrality in the First World War. The Semana Trágica in Barcelona was a week of church-burning and rioting sparked by the government's decision to send a regiment of Catalan conscripts to fight in the 'dirty war' in Morocco. Reprisals were brutal, further alienating Catalunya from Madrid.

The Republican period

The early years of the 20th century saw repeated changes of government under King Alfonso XIII. A massive defeat in Morocco in 1921 increased the discontent with the monarch, but General Miguel Primo de Rivera led a coup and installed himself as dictator under Alfonso in 1923. His rule was fairly benign as these things go, but growing discontent eventually forced the king to dismiss him. Having broken his coronation oath to uphold the constitution, Alfonso himself was soon toppled as republicanism swept the country. The anti-royalists achieved excellent results in local elections in 1931, and the king drove sadly out of the country. The ill-fated Second Republic was joyfully proclaimed by the left.

Things moved quickly in the short period of the republic. The new leftist government moved fast to drastically reduce the church's power. The haste was ill-advised and triumphalist, and served to severely antagonize the conservatives and the military. The granting of home rule to Catalunya was even more of a blow to the establishment and their belief in Spain as an indissoluble patria, or fatherland.

Latifundismo

Through this period, there was increasing anarchist activity in Catalunya and Andalucía, where land was seized as a reaction to the archaic system of latifundias, where nearly all arable land was part of huge estates owned by absentee aristocrats, and prospects for the workers, who were virtually serfs, were nil. Squabbling among leftist factions contributed to the government's lack of control of the country, which propelled the right to substantial gains in elections in 1933. Government was eventually formed by a centrist coalition, with the right powerful enough to heavily influence lawmaking.

A sad state

Although many Spaniards refuse to distinguish between the two, Basque nationalism and ETA are two very different things. The overwhelming majority of Basque nationalists, ie those who want more autonomy for the region, are firmly committed to a peaceful and democratic solution. ETA, on the other hand, are pessimistic about the possibility of achieving these aims in this manner, and seek by planned violent action to force the issue.

To probe the wrongs, rights and history of the issue would require volumes. Viewed in the context of the changing Europe, Basques have a strong case for independence, being culturally and ethnically distinct to Spaniards. The issue is muddied by the large number of Spaniards in the region, but the real sticking point is that Spain has no intention of giving up such a profitable part of the nation. Economics don't permit it, old-fashioned Spanish honour doesn't permit it, and, cleverly, the constitution doesn't permit it.

The nationalist movement was born in the late 19th century, fathered by Sabino Arana, a perceptive but unpleasant bigot, and master of propaganda. He devised the ikurriña (the Basque flag), coined terms such as Euskadi, and published manifestos for independence, peppered with dubious historical interpretations.

The tragically short-lived breakthrough came with the Civil War. The sundered Republic granted the Basques extensive self-government, and José Antonio Aguirre was installed as lehendakari (leader) at Gernika on 7 October 1936. A young, intelligent and noble figure, Aguirre pledged Basque support to the struggle against Fascism. The government was forced into exile a few months later when the Nationalists took Bilbao, but Basques fought on in Spain and later in France against the Nazis.

The birth of ETA can be directly linked to the betrayal of the Basque government by the western democracies. At the end of the Second World War, supporters of the Republic had hoped that a liberating invasion of Spain might ensue. It didn't, but Franco's government was ostracized by the USA and Europe. The Basque government in exile was recognized as legitimate by the western powers. However, with the Cold War chilling up, the USA began to see the value of the anti-Communist Franco, and granted a massive aid package to him. Following suit, France and Britain shamefully recognized the Fascist government and withdrew support from the horrified Basques.

ETA was founded as ATA by angry Basque youth shortly after this sordid political turnabout. Its original goal

Falange

The 1933 elections also saw the son of the old dictator, José Antonio Primo de Rivera, elected on a fascist platform. Although an idealist and no man of violence, he founded the Falange, a group of fascist youth that became an increasingly powerful force, and one which was responsible for some of the most brutal deeds before, during, and immediately after the Spanish Civil War.

The new government set about reversing the reforms of its predecessors; provocative and illegal infractions of labour laws by employers didn't help the mood among the workers. Independence rumblings in Catalunya and the Basque country began to gather momentum, but it was in Asturias that the major confrontation took

826

Background History

was simply to promote Basque culture in repressive Spain, but it soon took on a violent edge. In 1959 it took the name ETA (after realizing that *ata* meant duck in a dialect of Euskara), which stands for Euskadi Ta Askatasuna, the Basque Country and Freedom. They conducted their first assassination in 1968, and since then have been responsible for over 800 deaths, mostly planned targets such as right wing politicians, Basque 'collaborators', and police. The organization is primarily youthful, and uses extortion and donations to fund its activities. Their current demands are autonomy for the Basque region, the union of Navarra with the region, and the transfer of all Basque prisoners to prisons within the region (this is not just an ETA goal, and posters calling for this, with the appeal 'Euskal Presoak Euskal Herrira' is visible everywhere you go).

Despite the slogans, there's nothing noble or honourable about ETA's normal *modus operandi*. Many of those assassinated have been people with families with little or no power within the régime. In many cases it seems that the central leadership has little control over its trigger-happy thugs. This said, there's certainly an element of hypocrisy in the public's attitude. In 1973, when Franco's right hand man Admiral Carrero Blanco was sent

sky-high by an ETA car bomb (literally: the car was sent over a six-storey building and into its patio), the terrorist group were liberationist heroes to many. Now, in more cuddly times, such actions are seen as appalling. Tragically, the government and police have let themselves be drawn into a cycle of violence. Whenever ETA strike, their support drops dramatically in Euskadi. A few days later, when a mystery retaliatory killing of Basques occurs, anti-government feeling rises again.

The Socialist government of the early 1990s was scandalously found to have been funding a 'death squad' aimed at scaring Basques out of supporting nationalism and ETA. Basque prisoners are routinely tortured in Guardia Civil jails. The escalationist attitude of the Madrid government continued in 2002, when the parliament overwhelmingly passed legislation specifically designed to ban Batasuna, the political party often (and probably accurately) linked with ETA. The party was then banned by the courts; while the move may well help curtail ETA activity, the alarmingly undemocratic and heavy-handed step outraged Basques and their governing PNV (no friends of Batasuna) as well as many international observers.

place. Unlike the rest of the left, the Asturian miners were fairly united, with anarchists, socialists and trade unionists prepared to co-operate; they went on strike in protest against the entry of the rightwing CEDA into the vacillating centrist government. Proclaiming a socialist republic, they seized the civil buildings of the province. The arms factories worked 24-hour shifts to arm the workers; the army and Civil Guard were still holding out in Oviedo. The government response was harsh. Sending in the feared Foreign Legion and Moroccan troops under Generals Goded and a certain Franco, they swiftly relieved the garrison, defeated the insurrection, and embarked on a brutal spree of retribution for which they are rightly unforgiven in the province.

The left were outraged, and the right feared complete revolution; the centre ceased to exist as citizens and politicians were forced to one side or the other. The elections of February 1936 were very close, but the left defeated the right unexpectedly. In an increasingly violent climate, mobilized Socialist youth and the Falange were clashing on a daily basis, while land seizures continued.

Spanish Civil War

A group of generals began to plan a coup, and in July 1936 a military conspiracy saw garrisons throughout Spain rise against the government and try to seize control of their towns and provinces. Within a few days battlelines were clearly drawn between the Republican (government) and the Nationalists, a coalition of military, Carlists, fascists and the Christian right. Most of Northern Spain was rapidly under Nationalist control, while Madrid and the south remained Republican. The major resistance in the north was in Asturias, where the miners came out fighting once again, Cantabria, and the Basque provinces. These latter were in a difficult position; the Basques were democratic in outlook but Catholic, and the Catholic church was on the Nationalist side for its own protection from the anticlerical Republic. A 1927 catechism claimed that it was a mortal sin for a Catholic to vote for a liberal candidate. Carlist-oriented Navarra sided with the Nationalists, as did Álava, but the majority of Euskadi came out fighting on the side of democracy. Catalunya was Republican, as was much of Andalucía, although the cities of Córdoba, Cádiz, Sevilla, Huelva, and Granada were taken by the Nationalists.

In the immediate aftermath of the rising, frightening numbers of civilians were shot 'behind the lines', including the Granadan poet, Federico García Lorca. This brutality continued throughout the war, with some chilling atrocities committed on both sides, never condoned by the Republican government, unlike their Nationalist counterparts.

With battle lines drawn, the war began, and the most crucial blow was struck early. Francisco Franco, one of the army's best generals, had been posted to the Canary Islands by the government, who were rightly fearful of coup attempts. As the rising occurred, Franco was flown to Morocco where he took command of the crack north African legions. The problem was to cross into Spain; this was achieved in August in an airlift by German planes. Franco swiftly advanced; his battle-hardened troops met with little resistance. Meanwhile, the other main battle lines were north of Madrid, and in Aragón, where the Republicans made a determined early push for Zaragoza.

At a meeting of the revolutionary generals in October 1936, Franco had himself declared generalísimo, the supreme commander of the Nationalists. Few could have suspected that he would rule the nation for nearly four decades. Although he'd conquered swathes of Andalucía and Extremadura with little difficulty the war wasn't to be as short as it might have appeared. Advancing on Madrid, he detoured to relieve the garrison at Toledo; by the time he turned his attention back to the capital, the defences had been shored up, and Madrid resisted throughout the war.

A key aspect of the Spanish civil war was international involvement. Fascist Germany and Italy had troops to test out, and a range of weaponry to play with; these countries gave massive aid to the Nationalist cause as a rehearsal for the Second World War, which was seeming increasingly inevitable. Russia provided the Republicans with some material, but inscrutable Stalin never committed his full support. Other countries such as Britain, the USA, and France disgracefully maintained a charade of 'international non-intervention' despite the flagrant breaches by the above nations. Notwithstanding, thousands of volunteers mobilized to form the International Brigades to help out the Republicans. Enlisting for idealistic reasons to combat the rise of fascism, many of these soldiers were writers and poets such as George Orwell and WH Auden.

● Franco wasn't exactly a relaxed and charismatic prankster; after meeting him at Hendaye
● in 1940 to discuss possible Spanish involvement in Second World War, Adolf Hitler said he
"would rather have three or four teeth out" than meet him again.

There was long fighting on fronts in Aragón, but the prize, Zaragoza, stayed in rebel hands throughout the war. Meanwhile, the Republican government approved a statute of autonomy for the Basques, and a Basque government was sworn in under the oak tree in Gernika, long a symbol of Basque government and fueros. The young and able leader, José María Aguirre, assured the Republic that 'until Fascism is defeated, Basque nationalism will remain at its post'. It did, with Basques fighting Nazi forces right through World War Two, but the government was forced into exile when Bilbao fell in June 1937. This came in the wake of the appalling civilian bombings of Durango and Gernika, when German and Italian planes rained bombs on the country towns, killing almost 2,000. Franco claimed the Basques had done it themselves as a publicity gesture.

Although Republican territory was split geographically, far more damage was done to their cause by ongoing and bitter infighting between anarchists, socialists, Soviet-backed communists, and independent communists. There was constant struggling for power, political manoeuvring, backstabbing, and outright violence which the well-organized Nationalists must have watched with glee. The climax came in Barcelona in May 1937, when the Communist party took up arms against the anarchists and the POUM, an independent communist group. The city declined into a mini civil war of its own until order was restored. Morale, however, had taken a fatal blow.

Cities continued to fall to the Nationalists, for whom the crack German Condor legion proved a decisive force. Málaga fell in early 1937; fleeing refugees were massacred by tanks and aircraft. Separated from the rest of the Republic, Asturian and Cantabrian resistance was whittled away; Santander fell in August of the same year, Asturias in October. Republican hopes began to rest solely in the outbreak of a Europe-wide war. Franco had set up base appropriately in deeply conservative Burgos; Castilla was a heartland for Nationalist support and the venue for many brutal reprisals against civilians perceived as leftist, unionist, democratic, or owning a fertile little piece of land on the edge of the village. Republican atrocities in many areas were equally appalling although rarely sanctioned or perpetrated by the government.

The Republicans made a couple of last-ditch efforts in early 1938 at Teruel and in the Ebro valley but were beaten in some of the most gruelling fighting of the Civil War. The Nationalists reached the Mediterranean, dividing Catalunya from the rest of Republican territory and putting Barcelona under intense pressure; it finally fell in January 1939. Even at this late stage, given united resistance, the Republicans could have held out a while longer, and the World War might have prevented a Franco victory, but it wasn't to be. The fighting spirit was largely gone, and the infighting led to meek capitulation. Franco entered Madrid and the war was declared over on 1 April 1939.

If Republicans were hoping that this would signal the end of the slaughter and bloodshed, they didn't know the generalísimo well enough. A vengeful spate of executions, lynchings, imprisonments, and torture ensued and the dull weight of the new regime stifled growth and optimism. Although many thousands of Spaniards fought in the Second World War (on both sides), Spain remained nominally neutral. After meeting Franco at Hendaye, Hitler declared that he would prefer to have three or four teeth removed than have to do so again. Franco had his eye on French Morocco and was hoping to be granted it for minimal Spanish involvement; Hitler accurately realized that the country had little more to give in the way of war effort and didn't offer an alliance.

The Basques held out high hopes as the Second World War reached its end. Their government-in-exile was officially recognized by the Allies, and many hoped that Franco would soon be deposed and an independent Basque state be established. The UN imposed a trade boycott on Spain after the war, and things looked bright, but their hopes were dashed when the USA decided that the new enemy was communism. If Franco was anything, he was anti-communist, and the Americans under Eisenhower granted Spain a massive aid package (in return for four US bases on Spanish soil) and

resumed diplomatic relations. This betrayal of the Basques, followed by that of Britain and France, was a bitter pill to swallow, and led in no small way to the establishment of ETA. The USA's acceptance of the regime paved the way for Spain to join the United Nations in 1955 and the long process of modernization began.

Franco never forgave the Catalans, Basques or Asturians, and the regions were treated harshly during his oppressive rule. Development was curtailed, and use of the Catalan and Euskara languages was banned (as was Galego, although Franco himself was Galician). Navarra and Castilla, on the other hand, were rewarded for their roles, if being blessed with a series of concrete crimes against architecture in the name of progress can be called a reward.

Transitions to democracy

Spain boomed in the 1960s as industry finally took off, and the flood of tourism to its southern coasts began in earnest. But dictatorship was no longer fashionable in western Europe, and Spain was regarded as a slightly embarassing cousin. It was not invited to join the European Economic Community and it seemed as if nothing was going to really change until Franco died.

That, in fact, proved to be the case, but ETA, see box page , gave the government many anxious moments through the 1960s and 1970s. They had their most popular moment when they assassinated Franco's right-hand man, Admiral Carrero Blanco in 1973. The ageing dictator died two years later and his appointed successor, King Juan Carlos I, the grandson of Alfonso XIII, took the throne of a Spain burning with democratic desires.

The king was initially predicted to be just a pet of Franco's and therefore committed to maintaining the stultifying status quo, but he surprised everyone by acting swiftly to appoint the young Adolfo Suárez as prime minister. Suárez bullied the parliament into approving a new parliamentary system; political parties were legalized in 1977 and elections held in June that year.

The return to democracy was known as la transición; the accompanying cultural explosion became known as La Movida (Madrileña). Suárez' centrist party triumphed and he continued his reforms. The 1978 constitution declared Spain a parliamentary monarchy with no official religion; Franco must have turned in his grave, and Suárez faced increasing opposition from the conservative elements in his own party. He resigned in 1981 and as his successor was preparing to take power, the good old Spanish tradition of the pronunciamiento came to the fore again. A detachment of Guardia Civil stormed parliament in their comedy hats, and Lt Col Tejero, pistol waving and moustache twitching, demanded everyone hit the floor. After a tense few hours in which it seemed that the army might come out in support of Tejero, the king remained calm, and dressed in his capacity as head of the armed forces, assured the people of his commitment to democracy. The coup attempt thus failed, and JC was seen in an even better light.

In 1982, the Socialist government of Felipé González was elected. They held power for 14 years and oversaw Spain's entry into the EEC (now EU) in 1986, from which it has benefited immeasurably, although rural areas remain poor by western European standards. González was disgraced, however, when he was implicated in having commissioned 'death squads' with the aim of terrorizing the Basques into renouncing terrorism, which few of them supported in any case.

Regional autonomy

The single most important legislation since the return to democracy was the creation of the comunidades autónomas, in which the regions of Spain were given their own parliaments, which operate with varying degrees of freedom from the central government. This came to bear in 1983, although it was a process initiated by Suárez. The majority of regional Spaniards are happy with the arrangement, but there are still

Significantly, and perhaps foolishly, the new constitution specified that no further devolution could occur; Spain was 'indissoluble'. This means the topic can barely be raised in parliament as it is unconstitutional.

In 1996 the rightist PP (Partido Popular) formed a government under the young ex-tax inspector José María Aznar, and were re-elected in 2000. Economically conservative, Aznar has strengthened Spain's ties with Europe and taken strong action against ETA. In 2002, the democratically elected party, Batasuna, widely seen as linked to the terrorist group, was banned by the courts after a purpose-built bill was resoundingly passed in parliament. The governing Basque nationalist party (PNV), wholly against terrorism, denounced the move against their political opponents as 'undemocratic' and 'authoritarian', which it undoubtedly was. Whether the crackdown on ETA will have an effect remains to be seen. The early signs suggest it has worked, but such a heavy-handed approach has raised new questions about just how Francoist the PP is.

Spain is still divided along political lines. Catalunya still pursues its own agenda, the Basques have their PNV, and large parts of Asturias remain firmly leftist in orientation. On the other side, Galicia's president is a dinosaur that served in Franco's cabinet, and one suspects plenty in Spain's centre and Andalucía would vote for the man himself if he were still alive (and in democratic mood). Nevertheless, in most urban areas, Fascist street names have been changed and statues and memorials pulled down. The era is rarely discussed; neither is the Civil War, which remains a sensitive issue with combatants and war-criminals still alive and sipping wine in the corner of local bars. No judicial investigation of events of the war or the dictatorship has ever been undertaken; there's a sort of consensus to let sleeping dogs lie, understandable given the turbulent history of the 19th and 20th centuries.

Regional rejuvenation

Most of the cities of Spain have shaken off the torpor of the Franco era and the preceding centuries of decline and are prosperous, attractive places once more, best symbolized by Bilbao's astonishing urban renewal and also that of Sevilla. EU funding has helped to rejuvenate their superb architectural heritage, and the lively social life remains what it always has been, although with a freedom to party that wasn't smiled upon by Franco. In some rural areas, though, particularly Castilla and Galicia, depopulation is a serious issue. Many villages are populated only by pensioners, if at all, as the young seek employment and fulfilment in urban areas.

On a more positive note, the years since the return to democracy have seen a remarkable and accelerated reflowering of regional culture. The banned languages Catalá, Galego and Euskara are ever-more in use, as is Bable in Asturias; local artists, writers and poets are being keenly promoted by the regional governments. Museums are mostly free, not so much to lure tourists away from the beaches as to encourage their own population to visit and learn. Salamanca's enthusiastic year as a European Capital of Culture in 2002 is an example of this spirit; the great university town of the Middle Ages was back in the spotlight; whether the angels speak Castillian or Euskara these days is of little importance.

Contemporary Spain

Anchored firmly into the European Union and enjoying a period of growth and stability, contemporary Spain is a tolerant modern democracy. The aim of catching up with its European neighbours has been the central policy of all Spanish governments since the restoration of democracy; by and large they have succeeded admirably.

After the sleepwalking decades of the Franco dictatorship, the region has been saved with the return to democracy. Entry to the EEC/EU in 1986 has provided a massive boost both economically and mentally; the nation is looking outwards for the first time since the loss of the empire. Funding from the Community has been a godsend for the architectural heritage of the area, has spruced up its urban areas, and finally brought a degree of modernization to an ailing agricultural sector.

That said, not all is rosy. While there are few material reminders of the dictatorship itself, the scars of 40 years of isolation run deep. The fact that there was virtually no money for investment means that the housing stock in some parts of Spain is in need of urgent modernisation as fascist concrete crumbles and old electricity cables fray. Much has been done to rebuild Spain's cities but much remains to be done. Both during and since the dictatorship the emphasis in housing has often been on speed rather than quality. While much public housing is of high standard, nearly every Spanish city is ringed by developments that do nothing to inspire or impress. The worst, like those surrounding Málaga or Madrid, are depressingly awful and present a future store of social problems.

The housing shortage is one reason for the fact that many younger Spanish people seek to move abroad. Caught between the rock of unemployment and the hard place of being unable to leave the parental home for want of accommodation, temporary emigration is often seen as an attractive option. The phenomenon of young people living with their parents until their mid- thirties and beyond is one that surprises a lot of visitors. Spain's low birthrate can be partly attributed to the fact that couples are unable to find suitable accommodation until they are in the mid-thirties. Combined with a lack of substantial benefits, the costs of having a child can be prohibitively high. The need for people to be able to find affordable housing is becoming something of a demographic crisis.

Apart from the EU, the single most important step since the return to democracy was the creation of the *comunidades autonomas*, or semi-autonomous regional governments, a modern solution to Spain's age-old problems in administering its diverse parts. Without the deadening effect of centralization, the regions have largely flourished, and are in a much better position to care for their diverse natural environments and promote cultural growth. That said, some have benefited more than others.

The striking success stories are undoubtedly Catalunya and Euskadi, both badly repressed during the dictatorship. The industrious Basques have forged ahead on the back of their strong and ancient cultural unity, their significant industrial and commercial centres, and their high levels of education. Optimism in the region is high, although outside perceptions of the area continue to be clouded by the ETA issue (see box page). While the governing party, the PNV, seeks full independence from Spain, it is committed to achieving it by political means, although they face an uphill task, as the Spanish constitution doesn't allow for discussion of such an issue. Legally, Spain is 'indissoluble'.

Meanwhile, Catalunya is also thriving. Tourism, services and manufacturing combine to give the province a healthy and prosperous existence. Despite occupying only some 6 per cent of the country's area, Catalan industry accounts for 25 per cent of production. Like Euskadi, there has been an astonishing rebirth of language and culture since democracy, and the region is one of the most forward-looking and innovative in Spain.

Asturias has had a similarly go-ahead approach after it too suffered under Franco. Although it's far from well-off, and has high unemployment, an enlightened environmental programme, has secured protection for its superb natural mountains and forests, while putting in place an impressive and ecologically sound structure for tourism. Much of central Spain is still feeling the historical impact of the Reconquista,

population drain to Madrid, Barcelona and the coast.

Rural depopulation continues to be a problem; villages that were once important stops between cities are now bypassed by traffic, and young people flood to the provincial capitals, leaving the agricultural zone undermanned. Andalucía's vast latifundia farms provide almost no regular employment for its rural population, while travelling across the frighteningly dry meseta, it's a sobering thought that the region used to be forested and densely peopled. With the EU's Common Agricultural Policy discouraging farmers from using low-productivity land without a more committed environmental policy, the region is in danger of becoming an eroded wasteland.

Spain's comparative inexperience in dealing with environmental issues was cruelly exposed on 13 November 2002. The 26 year-old single-hulled tanker Prestige began to leak some of its cargo of 70,000 tonnes of heavy fuel oil off the coast of Galicia. The regional and national governments dithered, and rather than towing the stricken vessel into the nearest port, they culpably chose to tow the vessel further out to sea, into international waters. If the politicians thought they could thus wash their hands of the problem, they were wrong; the stricken vessel sank on the 19th and, at time of writing, had leaked some 25,000 tonnes of its cargo into the Atlantic. Much of this has washed up on the Galician and Asturian coasts, but oil has reached France and Portugal too. Volunteers streamed to the area from all over Europe to help clean the chapapote up and popular anger formed the Nunca Maís movement. The words mean 'never again' in Galego and the biggest target of outrage has been the Madrid government, who have been slow to admit their responsibility in the affair and incompetent in organizing the cleanup.

The full environmental effects will not be known for some time. Galicia is one of Spain's poorest regions, with half the GDP per capita of the Basque lands and virtually its whole economy (unfortunately) rests on fishing, shellfish cultivation, and tourism. Thousands of livelihoods have already been seriously affected, and it remains to be seen just how long marine stocks will take to recover; some estimates say 20 years.

The Partido Popular (PP) currently enjoys a large majority in both chambers of the central parliament. The party was formed from several rightist groups as Alianza Popular on the return to democracy. The party first came to power in 1996 and were re-elected in 2000. The Presidente del Gobierno (Prime Minister) is the moustached José María Aznar, a young but wily operator from a staunchly conservative background. Aznar's period in office has been characterized by rightist economic reform, conducted with the initial aim of making Spain a successful and integral part of the single currency zone. Under the present government the emphasis is very much on tax reduction and labour flexibility. Although there is a minimum wage there is no real aim of reducing poverty through taxation. Critics have warned that the country is over-reliant on EU subsidy and that the honeymoon will end once the EU incorporates poorer nations from Eastern Europe.

Another of Aznar's priorities has been to crack down on ETA terrorism. Typically for a Madrid government, this hasn't been conducted in a particularly sensitive manner. While a huge majority of Basques deplore terrorism, both the PP government and its Socialist predecessor have alienated many people in the region with their uncompromising anti-dialogue stance. A woeful record of human rights abuses of Basque prisoners has also caused massive concern. In 2002 the parliament overwhelmingly passed legislation specifically designed to ban Batasuna, the political party often (and probably accurately) linked with ETA. The party was then banned by the courts; while the move may well help curtail ETA activity, the

Population 40 847 371; Area 504 783 km²; Literacy 97%; Religion Catholic 94%; Life
expectancy, female 82.8 and male 75.6; Unemployment 13%; Population growth: +0.09%.

alarmingly undemocratic and heavy-handed step outraged Basques and their governing PNV (no friends of Batasuna) as well as many international observers. Closing down a democratically elected regional party is a worrying sign that Madrid will only respect regional autonomy when it suits it.

Aznar's popularity in recent times has been rocked both by the Prestige disaster and also his hawkish stance on the invasion of Iraq. Demonstrations in February 2003 brought millions on to the Spanish streets in opposition to a war; the grinding concrete sound heard near Madrid was Franco turning in his grave. The next election is due in 2004.

One of the government's pressing problems is Spain's unemployment rate, which by EU standards is sky-high, particularly in impoverished regions such as Andalucía and Galicia. Some market economists have targeted Spain's system of high employer contributions to pension schemes as a cause, but government proposals to change the scheme have met with widespread concern – understandably, as Spain's old people have one of the best lifestyles in Europe. As well as receiving generous pensions there is a nationwide system of leisure clubs that ensures that even those living in the smallest villages can enjoy an active social life. It is a common sight in most Spanish towns to pass the window of these pensioner super clubs and be deafened by the noise of gossip and card playing. Compared to the chronic isolation affecting older people in Northern Europe the position of older citizens in Spain is something to be greatly admired. The old folks themselves certainly seem to thrive on it; Spain's average life expectancy is Europe's second-highest.

It remains to be seen what effect the emphasis on the private sector will have on Spanish society. Mostly Spain's middle classes retain a certain social solidarity with their poorer neighbours. There are differences in class but without any of the pernicious distinctions to be found in other countries. Whether this will continue to be the case is an open question. Already in even modest sized towns there are housing developments that literally build a wall round their middle class residents. With no real crime problem it seems the main force behind such developments is a desire to be separate from poorer people. Although only a small proportion of new houses are built in this form, if it were to become more widespread Spain would definitely lose something valuable.

Spain's university system is excellent but remains difficult to access for students from poorer backgrounds. Students rely on their families for support, as there are few grants and scholarships, while wealthier parents tend to compensate for a substandard state school system with private tutoring. Most students attend their nearest university but for some subjects only a few universities offer courses. The cost of subsidizing one or two children while living in a different city is prohibitively expensive for most people and therefore some professions are still totally in the grip of the wealthy. It remains to be seen whether the political will exists to address this situation or whether it will continue to be a feature of Spanish society.

One of the most widely reported social issues in Spain is illegal immigration, which while not unique to Spain has some peculiarly Spanish features. Chief among these are the deaths among those who attempt to reach Spain in small boats from Morocco. Bodies are regularly found along the southern Spanish coast and also in the Canary Islands. Not all the people attempting this journey are Moroccans. Many countries of West Africa contribute to the group of people willing to risk their lives for an uncertain future in Spain. Many end up working in unregulated jobs under atrocious conditions.

Given the transformation of Spanish society since the restoration of democracy and considering how deep these changes have been it seems more than likely that an answer to these problems will be found. That may mean that over time Spain will probably become more similar to other European countries in its habits as well as

Some things don't change. Regionalism is the key feature of modern Northern Spain, as it has been for centuries. Finally, however, it seems an overwhelmingly positive force. While through history the Spanish government has struggled to control its outlying areas, the opposite action of granting them autonomy has largely been a significant success, and one that has been noted by other nations with similar issues. Spain can only be stronger as a looser alliance of flourishing regions; given freedom of expression (under Franco, for example, many regional fiestas were banned), cultural differences become a healthy source of celebration and pride rather than festering resentment. While there's a strong argument that regions like Euskadi and Catalunya should at least be given the constitutional right to vote on secession, it is understandable that Madrid is anxious not to lose such valuable parts of the nation. Despite any separatist issues, optimism and renewal are the overpoweringly positive aspect of regional autonomy and European involvement. Previously moribund cities like Valladolid and Oviedo have been turned into prosperous European towns, while world events like the Barcelona Olympics and Sevilla Expo showed that it was possible to promote both regional differences and national achievement at the same time.

Economy

For many centuries, it seems, Spain has been 'catching up' with the rest of Western Europe, and to some extent this is still the case. As a member of the EEC/EU since 1986 the Spanish economy has made great strides forward, but many figures indicate there's some way to go. While GDP per capita is some 80% of that of the EU's economic 'big four', unemployment is the EU's highest, Spain's average salary level is only ahead of Greece's and Portugal's within the community, while the legal minimum monthly salary is less than half that of France or the USA. That said, the Spanish economy is the tenth biggest in the world and is currently enjoying a period of stability and growth. This has been achieved largely through membership of the European Union, a policy which was set in stone when Spain left the peseta behind for the euro on 1 January 2002.

It is the current Spanish government's strategy of enthusiastic participation in the Union allied to reforms aimed at improving the efficiency of Spain's labour market and industrial base that has led Spanish GDP per capita to approach EU averages. The big question for the government and millions of citizens is whether the policy will have any effect on Spain's biggest economic problem which is its chronically high unemployment rate, currently 13%.

The service sector dominates the Spanish economy as it does in all other advanced economies. In 2001 it accounted for 66 per cent of all GDP. The industrial sector accounts for 21%, construction for 9 per cent and agriculture for 3.5 per cent. Within the service sector the most important activities are tourism, banking, retailing and telecommunications. The tourist industry is particularly important for Spain and receives a great deal of government attention. The industry is well organized and has seen Spain develop into one of the largest markets in the world. In telecomm-unications Spain has followed a liberalising path with all sectors open to competition following the end of the partly state-owned Telefónica monopoly. This has led to Spain to becoming an important market for internet-related growth at a time when other countries' markets are stagnating.

Membership of the euro has encouraged growth in Spain's well-organized financial service industry. A series of mergers has led to the development of a few

home-based groups able to take advantage of opportunities in other European countries. With a widespread system of alliances and well-placed acquisitions these companies are continuing the trend towards the service sector, although the number of jobs created has been disappointing. In the industrial sector vehicle manufacturing is the most important accounting for around five per cent of GDP. Three million vehicles are produced every year, 80 per cent of them for export. Mostly based around Valencia the industry is modern and attracts a good deal of Spanish capital investment.

Spain has a relatively large construction sector which is accounted for by two factors; the need to modernize its infrastructure, and strong demand for tourist industry projects and second homes. The Government's hope that infrastructure improvements in road and rail will benefit the economy have largely been fulfilled and new projects are constantly being developed. The importance attached to this policy is underlined by the fact that there is a cabinet minister in charge of infrastructure. The continuing need to modernize the housing stock will ensure that this sector will see growth for many years.

The agricultural sector is still an important and profitable part of Spain's economy. The wine industry is particularly profitable and continues to see investment and modernization as exports move up the quality ladder. The production of fruit and vegetables for export to the rest of the EU is also an important sector. The enormous plastic greenhouses seen in Andalucía supply much of Europe with fruit and the area around Valencia supplies nearly all of Europe's oranges Fishing is also a big industry and the Spanish fleet is the largest in Europe. Concentrated around Vigo in Galicia, which is the world's second largest fishing port, the fleet is modern and, as well as supplying high domestic demand, also supplies a large food processing industry (see Modern Spain for the impact of the Prestige disaster).

In terms of its international trade Europe accounts for around 85 per cent of both imports and exports. Other important trading partners are the United States and Japan. The idea that Spain gains some benefit from trading with other Spanish speaking countries is true only up to a point. Spain's agricultural sector will face increasing competition from Morocco if the EU allows for a reduction in tariffs, but current policy suggests that this won't be any time soon.

Spain's biggest economic problem continues to be high unemployment which sticks stubbornly around the 13 per cent mark, making it the highest in the EU. Unemployment affects certain regions and sectors of the population dispro- portionately. Mostly it is the more rural regions that are worse affected. The present government's policy is to reduce unemployment by liberalizing the labour market and encouraging small business. Reforms to the pension system have encountered large scale resistance and although the trend in unemployment is downward it is at a painfully slow rate. The promise of new jobs from investment in the more productive sectors of the economy has been slow to have much effect. The hope that small businesses will create jobs has also been largely unfulfilled. Spain's entrepreneurial culture is still weak. Access to capital is difficult for those without large savings and the most sought-after jobs are still those in the public sector.

In the future the prospects for the economy seem to be reasonable. Continuing improvements to the infrastructure mean that those areas of the economy that are strong at the moment will continue to see new growth. The industrial base is also competitive compared with other parts of Europe, although as this is based almost totally on vehicle production competition is world wide and so growth cannot be guaranteed. Spain's biggest problem will be to develop new sources of employment through investment in non traditional sectors. With continuing unemployment driving many young people to other parts of Europe this is not going to be an easy task, but the changes in the economy since the restoration of democracy have shown that large scale restructuring is possible.

Culture

Architecture

Spain's architectural heritage is one of Europe's richest and certainly its most diverse, due in a large part to the dual influences of European Christian and Islamic styles during the eight centuries of Moorish presence in the peninsula. Another factor is economic; both during the Reconquista and in the wake of the discovery of the Americas, money seemed limitless, and vast building projects were undertaken. The post-Reconquista decline of Northern Spain, coupled with the bankruptcy of Imperial Spain, although not an ideal situation at the time, has at least had a good effect. The building sprees of the Middle Ages in Spain's north were succeeded by periods where there was hardly any money to fund new construction; the result is a land which has an incredibly rich architectural heritage. Nowhere in Europe has such a wealth of Romanesque and Gothic churches. In the south, entire treasure fleets were spent in erecting lavish churches and monasteries on previously Muslim soil, while relationships with Islamic civilization spawned some fascinating styles unique to Spain. The Moors themselves adorned their towns with incredibly sensuous palaces, such as Granada's Alhambra, and elegant mosques, as well as employing compact urban planning that still forms the hearts of most Andalucían towns. In modern times Spain has shaken off the ponderous monumentalism of the Franco era and become something of a powerhouse of modern architecture, with the Basque lands jostling Valencia at the front of the pack.

Prehistoric structures

There are some very early stone structures in the peninsula, with the greatest concentration in Álava and in Galicia, and the finest examples from around Antequera, in Andalucía. Dolmens, menhirs and standing stone circles are the most common remnants of the Neolithic (late Stone Age) era. The first two mostly had a funerary function, while the latter are the subject of numerous theories; some sort of religious/astrological purpose seems likely, but an accurate explanation is unlikely to emerge. The dwellings of the period were less permanent structures of which little evidence remains.

Celts and Iberians

The first millennium BC saw the construction of sturdier settlements, usually on hilltops. The sizeable Iberian town of Numancia, though razed after a Roman siege, remains an interesting example, and many of the cities of Northern Spain were originally founded during this period. The Celts, too, favoured hilly locations for the construction of castros. These fort/villages were typically walled compounds containing a large building, presumably the residence of the chieftain and hall for administration and trading, surrounded by smaller, circular houses and narrow lanes. These dwellings were probably built from mudbrick/adobe on a stone foundation with a thatched roof. The Galician palloza, still seen in villages, has probably changed little since these times. There are many preserved castros in Northern Spain, principally in Galicia and western Asturias.

Phoenicians, Greeks and Carthaginians

While the Phoenicians established many towns in Southern Spain, and probably a few on the north coast, their remains are few; the Phoenicians were so adept at spotting natural harbours that nearly all have been in continual use ever since, leaving only the odd foundations or breakwaters.

Greek trading presence has left a similarly scant architectural legacy but one site, Empúries, stands out. An important Mediterranean trading post (the name means 'market'), there are remains of a forum, a defensive wall, a harbour and a temple to Asklepeius, a standard arrangement for such a place.

There are also few Carthaginian remains of note. Their principal capital was Cádiz, but two millennia of subsequent occupation have taken their toll, and Cartagena, named for Carthage, preserves similarly scant remnants.

Roman period

The story of Spanish architecture really began with the Romans, who colonized the peninsula and imposed their culture on it to a significant degree. The Roman occupation of Hispania was largely administered from the south and east, and the majority of architectural remains are in that region. They founded and took over a great number of towns; most of the provincial capitals of Spain sit on Roman foundations. More significant still is the legacy they left; architectural principles that endured and to some extenet formed the basis for later peninsular styles.

There's not a wealth of outstanding monuments, the theatre and town of Mérida is the finest, while the Segovia aqueduct, the (modified) fantastic walls of Lugo and the bridge at Alcántara are imposing single structures. Itálica, Clunia and Numancia are impressive, if not especially well-preserved, Roman towns, as are Sagunto and Bilbilis. Tarragona and Zaragoza also were important towns, and preserve some decent ruins, while some fine villas are to be found in the south and also in Palencia province. While not exactly architecture, the awesome landscape of the mines of Las Médulas in western León province attest to the engineering prowess and single-mindedness of the Roman occupancy.

Visigothic Period

Although the post-Roman period is often characterized as a time of lawless barbarism, the Visigoths added Germanic elements to Roman and local traditions and built widely; in particular the kings of the period commissioned many churches. Most of these were heavily modified or destroyed in succeeding periods, but a few excellent examples remain; the best are San Juan de Baños (near Palencia), Quintanilla de las Viñas (near Burgos), San Pedro de la Nave (near Zamora). All these date from the seventh century and are broadly similar. Sturdy yet not unelegant, these churches are built around a triple nave with short transepts and square apses. Friezes on the outside depict birds, fruit and flowers with some skill. The interiors are particularly attractive, with treble arches, frequently horseshoe-shaped, and altarstones. These altarstones are found in many other churches of later date and are interesting for their iconography; early Christian symbols heavily borrowed from pagan traditions. Depictions of the sun, moon, and crops are often accompanied by Celtic-like circles with arched spokes. Mérida then Toledo were Visigothic capitals but preserve few remains of the period.

Moorish period

❧ *Muslim law forbids the representation of human or animal figures, so stylized calligraphy and intricate geometrical patterns were popular.*

The first distinct period of Moorish architecture in Spain is that of the Umayyads ruling as emirs, then as caliphs, from Córdoba from the eighth to 11th centuries. The massive arched Mezquita is the standout building from this period. Added to by different rulers, it's an amazing mosque flanked by the characteristic courtyard for ablutions. The exterior features several fine doorways, and the interior use of alternating red brick and white stone was an innovation. Other impressive buildings from this period and the taifa period that followed it include the palace complex at nearby Medina Azahara, the Aljafería palace at Zaragoza (although much modified subsequently) and the mosque of Cristo de la

Luz in Toledo. Many defensive installations were also put up at this time; the proud castle of Gormaz in Soria province, and several of the Alcazabas of Andalucían towns: Almería and Málaga being especially impressive. Architectural features of the period included use of the horseshoe arch, the multifoil arch, ornate raised brickwork, and inner courtyards. Highly elaborate plaster and tiled decoration was favoured:

Once the caliphate disintegrated, the Almohads brought their own architectural modifications with them. Based in Sevilla, their styles were not as flamboyant, and relied heavily on ornamental brickwork. The supreme example of the period is the Giralda tower that once belonged to the Mosque in Sevilla – it now forms part of the cathedral. The use of intricate wood-panelled ceilings began to be popular, and the characteristic Andalucían azulejo decorative tiles were first used at this time. Over this period the horseshoe arch developed a point.

The climax of Moorish architecture ironically came when Al-Andalus was already doomed and had been reduced to the emirate of Granada. Under the Nasrid rulers of that city the sublime Alhambra was constructed; a palace and pleasure-garden that took elegance and sophistication in architecture to previously unseen levels. Nearly all the attention was focused on the interior of the buildings, which consisted of galleries and courtyards offset by water features and elegant gardens. The architectural high point of this and other buildings is the sheer intricacy of the stucco decoration in panels surrounding the windows and doorways. Another ennobling feature is mocárabes, a curious concave decoration of prisms placed in a cupola or ceiling and resembling natural crystal formations in caves. The alcázar in Sevilla is also a good example of the period, albeit constructed in Christian Spain.

Christian architecture

In the eighth century, the style known as Pre-Romanesque emerged in the Christian redoubt of Asturias. While there are clear similarities to the Visigothic style, the Asturians added some elements and created a series of buildings of striking beauty, many of which are well-preserved today. The style progressed considerably in a fairly short period. There are both churches and royal halls extant. The buildings are generally tripartite, with triple naves (or nave and two aisles) and arches (some exterior) resting on elegantly carved pillars. The small windows reflect this in miniature, often divided by a bonsai column. The floor plan is rectangular or that of a cross, with wide transepts; the altar area is often raised, and backed by three small apses, divided from the rest of the interior by a triple arch. Small domes were used in later examples. Narrow exterior buttresses line up with the interior arches. Mural painting is well-preserved in many of the buildings; the Asturian (Latin) cross is a frequent motif. The capitals of the pillars are in some cases finely carved, in many cases with motifs presumably influenced by contact with Moorish and Byzantine civilization; palm leaves, flowers, and curious beasts.

During the Muslim occupation of Northern Spain a distinctly Moorish style was used by Christian masons, particularly in church construction. These traditions persisted even after reconquest, and were strengthened by the arrival of Christians who had lived in the Muslim south. Known as Mozarabic, it is characterized above all by its horseshoe arches but in some cases also by exuberant fan vaulting and ornate ribbed ceilings; some of the churches feel far more Muslim than Christian. The style persisted, and even some of the most sober of later cathedrals and churches have the odd arch or two that bends a little further in. Fresco-work is present in some Mozarabic buildings too, and in some cases, such as the Ermita de San Baudelio (Berlanga de Duero) presents a fusion of scenes; some from orthodox Christian iconography, and some influenced by time spent in Moorish company; elephants, camels, and palm trees.

Background Culture

Romanesque

The style that spread across the whole of Northern Spain in the 11th and 12th centuries, and is most dear to many visitors' hearts, is the Romanesque or románico. The 'Catalan' style, derived from contact with Italy, features the Lombard arch (blind exterior decoration in the shape of fingers) as a primary characteristic. In the rest of northern Spain, Romanesque can be traced back to French influences. Many monks from France arrived in the north of the peninsula in the 11th century and built monasteries along the same lines as the ones of their home country, but the biggest single factor in the spread of the style was the Santiago pilgrimage. News of what was being built in the rest of Europe was spread across Northern Spain and it is fitting that the portal of the cathedral at Santiago is widely considered to be the pinnacle of Spanish Romanesque.

The typical features of Romanesque churches are barrel-vaulted ceilings (stone roofs considerably reduced the number of churches that burned down) with semi circular arches; these also appear on the door and window openings. The apse(s) is also round. Geometic decoration is common, such as the chessboard patterning known as ajedrezado jaqués, first known in the Pyrenean town of Jaca, from where it spread along the length of the pilgrim route. Fine carvings, once painted, are often present on capitals and portals; the cloisters of Santo Domingo de Silos and San Juan de la Peña as well as the church San Martín in Frómista are excellent examples. The carvings depict a huge variety of subjects; Biblical scenes are present, and vegetable motifs recurring, but scenes of everyday life from the sublime to the ridiculous, the mundane to the erotic, are common (and often dryly labelled 'allegorical' in church pamphlets), as are strange beasts and scenes from mythology. This is part of the style's charm, as is the beautifully homely appearance of the buildings, often built from golden stone. Some of the towns with an excellent assembly of the Romanesque are Soria and Zamora, as well as all along the Camino de Santiago and in Catalunya, but the purest examples are often in the middle of nowhere; places where someone had the money to build a stone church in the 11th century, and no-one's had the cash to meddle with it since.

Transitional architecture

Austerity in monastic life ushered in the change from Romanesque to Gothic; a preference for elegant remote purity. The whimsical carved capitals disappeared, and voluptuous curves were squared off as church authorities began to exert more control within their dioceses. Cathedral such as those of Zamora, Salamanca (the old one), Tarragona, Avila and Sigüenza are all good examples; in many cases the religious buildings were heavily fortified.

Gothic

It seems unbelievable that the word Gothic was originally a pejorative term, applied to the pointed style during the Baroque period to mean 'barbarous'. Spanish Gothic architecture also owed much to French influence, although German masons and master builders also did much work, particularly in and around Burgos. Advances in engineering allowed lighter, higher structures than their Romanesque forebears, and the wealth and optimism of the rapidly progressing Reconquista saw ever more imaginative structures raised. The cathedrals of León and Burgos are beautiful examples of this. Other examples of Spanish Gothic are the cathedrals of Girona, Toledo and Sevilla, among many.

Gothic architecture changed over time from its relatively restrained 13th century beginnings to a more extroverted style known as Flamboyant, but many of the basic features remained constant. The basic unit of Gothic is the pointed arch, symbolic of the general enthusiasm for 'more space, less stone' that pervaded the whole endeavour. The same desire was behind the flying buttress, an elegant means of

supporting the building from the exterior, thus reducing the amount of interior masonry. Large windows increased the amount of light; the rose window is a characteristic feature of many Gothic façades, while the amount of stained glass in León seems to defy physics (to the regular concern of engineers). Elaborate vaulting graced the ceilings. The groundplan was often borrowed from French churches; as the style progressed, more and more side chapels were added, particularly around the ambulatory. A feature of many Spanish Gothic churches is the enclosed coro (choir, or chancel) in the middle of the nave, a seemingly self-defeating placement that robs the building of much of the sense of space and light otherwise striven for. Nevertheless, the choirstalls are often one of the finest features of Gothic architecture, superbly carved in wood.

Ornate carved decoration is common on the exteriors of Gothic buildings. Narrow pinnacles sprout like stone shoots, and the façades are often topped by gables. Portals often feature piers and tympanums carved with Biblican figures and scenes, circled by elaborate archivolts.

The late 15th century saw a branching-off: the Isabelline style, which borrowed decorative motifs from Islamic architecture to adorn a basically Gothic structure.

Mudéjar

As the Reconquista took town after town from the Muslims, Moorish architects and those who worked with them began to meld their Islamic tradition with the northern influences of Romanesque and Gothic. The result is distinctive and pleasing, typified by the decorative use of brick and coloured tiles, with the tall elegant belltowers a particular highlight. Another common feature is the highly elaborate wooden panelled ceilings, some of which are masterpieces. The word artesonado describes the most characteristic type of these. The style became popular nationwide; in certain areas, Mudéjar remained a constant feature for over 500 years of building. Aragón, which had a strong Moorish population, has a particularly fine collection of Mudéjar architecture; Toledo, Sevilla, the Duero valley and Sahagún are also well-stocked.

> ‡ Mudéjar is a style of architecture that evolved in Christian Spain, and particularly Aragón, from around the 12th century.

Background Culture

Renaissance

The 16th century was a high point in Spanish power and wealth, when it expanded across the Atlantic, tapping riches that must have seemed limitless for a while. Spanish Renaissance architecture reflected this, leading from the late Gothic style into the elaborate peninsular style known as Plateresque. Although the style originally relied heavily on Italian models, it soon took on specifically Spanish features. The word refers particularly to the façades of civil and religious buildings, characterized by decoration of shields and other heraldic motifs, as well as geometric and naturalistic patterns such as shells. The term comes from the word for silversmith, platero, as the level of intricacy of the stonework approached that of jewellery. Arches went back to the rounded, and columns and piers became a riot of foliage and 'grotesque' scenes. The massive façade of San Marcos in León is an excellent example of the style, as is the university at Salamanca, and several buildings in Toledo.

A classical revival put an end to much of the elaboration, as Renaissance architects concentrated on purity. Classical Greek features such as fluted columns and pediments were added to by large Italianate cupolas and domes. Spanish architects were apprenticed to Italian masters and returned with their ideas. Elegant interior patios in palacios are an especially attractive feature of the style, to be found across the country. Andalucía is a particularly rich storehouse of this style, where the master Diego de Siloé designed numerous cathedrals and churches. The palace of Carlos V in the Alhambra grounds is often cited as one of the finest examples, and the north has plenty too,

particularly in Salamanca, as well as Valladolid and smaller places such as Medina del Campo. The Escorial, the severe palace built for Philip II, is perhaps the ultimate expression of Spanish Renaissance architecture: grand yet austere, on a massive scale, it represents all the power and introversion of Imperial Spain.

Baroque

The fairly pure lines of this Renaissance classicism were soon to be permed into a new style; Spanish Baroque. Although it started fairly soberly, it soon became quite an ornamental style, often being used to add elements to existing buildings, with greater or lesser success. Nevertheless, the Baroque was a time of great genius in architecture as in the other arts in Spain. Perhaps the finest Baroque structures in Spain are to be found in Galicia, where masons had to contend with granite and hence dedicated themselves to overall appearances rather than obsessive and intricate twirls. The façade of the cathedral at Santiago, with its soaring lines, is one of the best of many examples. Compared to granite, sandstone can be carved as easily as Play-Doh, and architects in the rest of Spain playfully explored the reaches of their imaginations; a strong reaction against the sober preceding style. Churches became ever larger – in part to justify the huge façades – and nobles indulged in one-upmanship, building ever-grander palacios. The façades themselves are typified by such features as pilasters (narrow piers descending to a point) and niches to hold statues. On a private residence, large sculptured coats-of-arms were de rigueur. The cathedral at Cádiz is one of the few wholly Baroque churches.

Churrigueresque

The most extreme form of Spanish Baroque, Churrigueresque, which has been not too harshly described as 'architectural decay', was named for the Churriguera brothers who took Spanish Baroque to an extreme of ornamentation in the late 17th and early 18th centuries. The result can be hideously overelaborate but on occasion transcendentally beautiful, like Salamanca's superb Plaza Mayor. Vine tendrils decorate the façades, which seem intent on breaking every classical norm, twisting here, upside-down there but often straying into the realm of the conceited.

Neo-classicism

Neo-classicism was an inevitable reaction to such frippery, encouraged by a new interest in the ancient civilizations of Greece and Rome. It again resorted to the cleaner lines of antiquity, which were used this time for public spaces as well as civic and religious buildings. Many plazas and town halls in Spain are in this style, which tended to flourish in the cities that were thriving in the late 18th and 19th centuries, such as Madrid, Bilbao and A Coruña. The best examples use symmetry to achieve beauty and elegance, such as the Prado in Madrid, the worst achieve only narrow-minded lifelessness.

Modernista

The late 19th century saw Catalan modernista architecture break the moulds in a startling way. At the forefront of the movement was Antoni Gaudí. Essentially a highly original interpretation of Art Nouveau, Gaudí's designs featured naturalistic curves and contours enlivened with stylistic elements inspired by Muslim and Gothic architecture. Most of the most startling modernista works are in his home city of Barcelona, but there are examples throughout Spain, notably in Comillas on the Cantabrian coast. Gaudí's master work, the Sagrada Familia, is steadily being completed: although he spent half his life on the building, it was never going to be enough for such a deeply imaginative design. More restrained fin de siècle architecture can be seen in the fashionable towns of San Sebastián, Madrid, Santander, and A Coruña, as well as the industrial powerhouses of Gijón, Almería and Bilbao.

Background Culture

Art Nouveau and Art Deco

At roughly the same time, and equally a break with the academicism of the last century, Art Nouveau aimed to bring art back to life and back to the everyday. Using a variety of naturalistic motifs to create whimsical façades and objets, the best Art Nouveau works manage to combine elegance with fancy. Art Deco developed between the World Wars and was based on geometric forms, using new materials and colour combinations to create a recognisable and popular style. San Sebastián is almost a temple to Art Nouveau, while cities all over Spain have many good examples of Deco, as do many other cities, particularly in old cinemas and theatres.

Modern architecture

Elegance and whimsy never seemed to play much part in fascist architecture, and during the Franco era Spain was subjected to an appalling series of ponderous concrete monoliths, all in the name of progress. A few avant-garde buildings managed to escape the drudgery from the 1950s on – the Basque monastery of Arantzazu is a spectacular example – but it was the dictator's death in 1975 followed by EEC membership in 1986 that really provided the impetus for change.

The Guggenheim Museum is the obvious example of the flowering that has taken place in the last few years in Spain, but it is only one of many. San Sebastián's Kursaal and Vitoria's shining Artium are both excellent examples of modern Spanish works, while the much-admired Valencian, Santiago Calatrava, has done much work for his home city and elsewhere. Zamora is also noteworthy as a city that has managed to combine sensitive modern design with the Romanesque heritage of its old town, while Sevilla and Barcelona have both benefited from hosting major world events (Expo and the Olympics in 1992) to give themselves a sleek 21st-century facelift. Much of Spain, however, is still plagued by the concrete curse on the outskirts of its major cities and in coastal areas, where lax planning laws are taken full and hideous advantage of.

Architectural traditions

Other architectural traditions worth mentioning are in Euskadi, where baserriak are large stone farmhouses with sloping roofs, built to last by the heads of families: many are very old. Their presence in the green Basque hills gives the place a distinctly non-Spanish air. The square wooded *horréos* of Asturias and their elongated stone counterparts in Galicia are trademarks of the region and have been used over the centuries as granaries and drying sheds, although those in Galicia are of a less practical design and were to some extent status symbols also. Cruceiros in Galicia are large stone crosses, most frequently carved with a scene of the Crucifixion. Mostly made from the 17th to the 19th centuries, they stand outside churches and along roads.

Art

Spain's artistic traditions go back a long way; right to the Palaeolithic, when cave artists along the north and southeast coasts produced art that ranged from simple outlines of hands to the beautiful and sophisticated bison herds of Altamira.

In the first millennium BC, Iberian and Celtic cultures produced fine jewellery from gold and silver, as well as some remarkable sculpture and ceramics. La Dama de Elche and La Dama de Baza are particularly fine busts that demonstrate significant influences from the eastern Mediterranean; they are to be found in Madrid's Museo Arqueológico. These influences derive from contact with trading posts set up by the Phoenicians, Greeks and Carthaginians; all three cultures have left artistic evidence of their presence, mostly in the port cities they established. Similarly, the Romans brought their own artistic styles to the peninsula, and there are many cultural remnants, mostly found in the south; these include a number of fine mosaïc floors.

Contrary to their wild and woolly reputation, the Visigoths were skilled artists and craftspeople, and produced many fine pieces, notably in metalwork. Madrid's archaeological museum holds an excellent ensemble found at their capital, Toledo, and there are some good items in the city itself. The finest examples of Visigothic art are delicately adorned gold and silver pieces commissioned by rulers; the style reflects the Germanic roots of the people.

Moors

The majority of the artistic heritage left by the Moors is tied up in their architecture. As Islamic law forbids the portrayal of human or animal figures, tradition favoured intricate decoration with calligraphic, geometric and vegetable themes predominating. Superb panelled ceilings are a feature of Almohad architecture; a particularly attractive style being that known as artesonado, in which the concave panels are bordered with elaborate inlay work. During this period, too, glazed tiles known as azulejos began to be produced; these continue to be a feature of Andalucían craftsmanship.

Meanwhile, free from Islamic artistic strictures, monks in the north produced some illustrated manuscripts of beauty in which their cloistered imaginations ran riot, particularly when dealing with creatures of the Apocalypse. Copies of the works of Beatus of Liébana are particularly outstanding and created from a tangible fear of a very real Hell.

Religious architecture

Away from the scriptoria, the outstanding examples of medieval Spanish art come from churches, where some superb fresco work has been preserved in situ, and in museums. Asturian pre-Romanesque buildings preserve some decoration, but the best examples are from Romanesque and Mozarabic churches. The Panteón (royal burial chamber) in the basílica of San Isidoro in León is stunning, as is the Mozarabic chapel of San Baudelio near Berlanga del Duero, although scandalously plundered by an American art dealer in the 1920s. Other particularly impressive ensembles from the period can be seen in the cathedral museum at Jaca in the Aragonese Pyrenees, and at the museum of Catalan art in Barcelona.

Romanesque

Romanesque art also hit lofty heights in the field of sculpture. Master masons responsible for such gems as the cloisters of San Juan de la Peña and Santo Domingo de Silos are not known by name, but achieved sculptural perfection, above all on the decorated capitals of the columns. Arguably the finest of them all is Master Mateo, whose tour de force was the Pórtico de la Gloria entrance to the cathedral at Santiago.

Other elements of Romanesque art that have come down to us include retablos (altarpieces or retables) and painted (the endearing jargon term 'polychrome' is more common) figures. These tend to be rendered in bright colours – as was the majority of stone sculpture, although wind and weather has usually stripped it off – and despite being fairly rigid and stylized by convention, many examples achieve significant beauty.

Gothic period

The Gothic style in Spain, like the Romanesque, arrived on more than one front. The Mediterranean coast, especially Valencia, was handily placed to receive architectural and artistic influences from Italy, while the north, boosted by the pilgrim traffic to Santiago, looked to France and northern Europe for its initial inspiration. Catalunya was in a position to pick and choose from both regions.

Over time, Gothic sculpture achieved more naturalism in rendering than in earlier periods. The style became more ornate too, culminating in the superlative technical

mastery of the works of the northern Europeans resident in Castilla, Simón de Colonia, and Gil and Diego de Siloé, whose stunning retablos and tombs are mostly in and around Burgos. Damián Forment was a busy late Gothic sculptor who left his native Aragón to train in Italy, then returned and executed a fine series of retablos in his homeland. Saints and Virgins in polychrome wood continued popular, and there are some fine examples from the period.

As well as sculptors, there were many foreign painters working in the Gothic period in northern Spain. As well as retablos, painted panels on gold backgrounds were popular, often in the form of triptychs. Often depicting lives of saints, many of these are excellent pieces, combining well-rendered expression with a lively imagination, particularly when depicting demons, subjects where the artist had a freer rein. Some of the better painters from this period are Fernando Gallego, whose paintings grace Salamanca, Jorge Inglés, resident in Valladolid and presumably an Englishman named George, Juan de Flandes (Salamanca; Flanders), and Nicolás Francés (León; France). All these painters drew on influences from the Italian and Flemish schools of the time, but managed to create a distinctive and entertaining Spanish style.

Much of the finest Spanish Gothic art, however, came from the coastal portions of the kingdom of Aragón; Catalunya and Valencia, both of which gave their names to a school of Gothic painting. In the early 14th century, Ferrer Bassá was heavily influenced from Italy, particularly Siena. Notable later artists in these schools include Jaume Serra, Luis Borrassá, Pere Nicolau and Bernat Martorell, all of whom evolved towards a more Spanish style. Considered two of the greatest of the Gothic artists are Jaume Huguet and Bartolomé Bermejo, both of whom brought painting to new levels of realism, sensitivity and expression, the latter influenced by contemporary artists in Flanders.

Renaissance

The Renaissance in Spain, too, drew heavily on the Italian. The transitional painter Pedro Berruguete hailed from near Palencia and studied in Italy. His works are executed in the Gothic manner but have a Renaissance fluidity that was mastered by his son, Alonso, who learned under Michelangelo and was court painter to Carlos I (Charles V). His finest work is sculptural; he created saints of remarkable power and expression in marble and in wood. Juan de Juni lived in Valladolid and is also notable for his sensitive sculptures of religious themes.

The best-known 16th-century Spanish artist was actually born in Crete. After training in Italy, Domenikos Theotokopoulos got a commission in Toledo and stayed on because he liked the place. Known almost universally as El Greco ('the Greek'), he was a man somewhat ahead of his time. There's a haunted quality to much of his work, which uses misshapen faces and sombre colouring to create a sort of shadow-zone linking life and death. Some of his later works are almost surreal, while earlier in his career he was more conventionally Italian in style. His finest works are in Toledo and Madrid.

As the Renaissance progressed, naturalism in painting increased, leading into the 'Golden Age' of Spanish art. This was the finest period of Spanish painting; one of its early figures was the 16th-century Riojan painter Juan Fernández Navarrete, many of whose works are in the Escorial. He studied in Venice and his style earned him the nickname of the Spanish Titian; his paintings have a grace of expression denied him in speech by his dumbness.

Francisco Ribalta (1565-1628) learned tenebrism from his Italian contemporaries and brought it home with him to Spain; the majority of his work can be seen in his hometown of Valencia. His one-time pupil, José de Ribera (1591-1652), resident in the Spanish territory of Naples, also took plenty of Italian techniques on board. One of the foremost European painters of his day, he had a huge influence on those who came after, such as Velásquez and Murillo. He was prolific, but rarely compromised his

style, which often depicted fairly gruesome martyrdoms and the like with powerful characterization of the main protagonists.

As Sevilla prospered on New World riches, the city became a centre for artists, who found wealthy patrons in abundance. Pre-eminent among all was Diego Rodríguez de Silva Velásquez (1599-1660), who started his career there before moving to Madrid to become a court painter. A consummate portraitist, he was far more a realist than any of his predecessors, and in some cases seems almost to have captured the subject's soul on canvas, such as in his depictions of the haunted Habsburg Philip IV. His most famous work, Las Meninas, depicts the young princess Margarita surrounded by courtiers, including a dwarf, always favourite companions for the Habsburgs. The artist himself appears, brush in hand, as does a reflection of the watching king. The perspective puzzles that Velásquez poses, as well as the sheer mastery of execution, make this one of the most remarkable of paintings.

Another remarkable painter working in Sevilla was Francisco de Zurbarán (1598-1664). While he produced plenty of high-speed dross on commission, his best works are from the topmost drawer of European art. His idiosyncratic style often focuses on superbly rendered white garments in a dark, brooding background, a metaphor for the subjects themselves, who were frequently priests. His paintings can be seen throughout Spain, above all in Andalucía. His Crucifixions are particularly memorable, full of despair and anguish, even if, as in one Prado example, his patrons sometimes chose to appear in the painting at Christ's feet; perhaps so that at dinner parties they could tell their friends that they'd been there...

During Zurbarán's later years, he was eclipsed in the Sevilla popularity stakes by Bartolomé Esteban Murillo (1618-1682). While at first glance his paintings can seem somewhat heavy on the sentimentality, they tend to focus on the space between the central characters, who interact with glances or gestures of great power and meaning. The religious atmosphere of imperial Spain continued to dominate in art; landscapes and joie de vivre are in comparatively short supply. Juan Valdés Leal certainly had little of the latter; his macabre realist paintings include a famous Sevilla example, Finis Gloriae Mundi, which shows a dead bishop being devoured by worms.

A fine portraitist overshadowed by his contemporary Velásquez was the Asturian noble Juan Carreño de Miranda (1614-1685). Late in life he became court painter and is noted for his depictions of the unfortunate inbreed king Carlos II. Of the so-called 'Madrid school', the most worthwhile painter is Claudio Coello, who painted portraits for the court as well as larger figured tableaux; some of his works hang in the Escorial.

Gregorio Hernández was a fine naturalistic sculptor working in Valladolid at this time, while in Andalucía Juan Martínez Montañés carved numerous figures, retablos, and pasos (ornamental floats for religious processions) in wood. Alonso Cano was a talented painter and sculptor working from Granada. The main focus of this medium continued to be ecclesiastic; retablos became ever larger and more ornate, commissioned by nobles to gain favour with the church and improve their chances in the afterlife. As the Baroque period progressed, this was taken to ridiculous degree. Some of the altarpieces and canopies are immense and overgilded, clashing horribly with the sober Gothic lines of the churches they were placed in; while supremely competent in execution, they can seem gaudy and ostentatious to modern eyes.

Bourbon Art

The early 18th century saw fairly characterless art produced under the new dynasty of Bourbon kings. Tapestry production increased markedly but never scaled the heights of the earlier Flemish masterpieces, many of which can be seen in northern Spain. The appropriately-enough named Francisco Bayeu produced pictures for tapestries ('cartoons'), as did the master of 19th-century art, Francisco Goya.

Goya, see box page 378, was a remarkable figure whose finest works included both paintings and etchings; his fresco work in northern Spanish churches never

scaled these heights. His depiction of the vain Bourbon royals is brutally accurate; he was no fan of the royal family, and as court painter got away with murder. His etchings of the horrors of the Napoleonic wars are another facet of his uncompromising depictions. His nightmarish 'black paintings', painted on the walls of his cottage as an old man in a state of semi-dementia, are an unforgettable highlight of Madrid's Prado.

Generation of 1898

After Goya, the 19th century produced few works of note as Spain tore itself apart in a series of brutal wars and conflicts. The rebirth came at the end of the period with the '1898 generation' (see Literature below). One of their number was the Basque painter Ignacio Zuloaga (1870-1945), a likeable artist with a love of Spain and a clear eye for its tragic aspects. His best work is portraiture, often set against a brooding Castillian landscape. His contemporary, Joaquín Sorolla (1863-1923), is best known for his depictions of his native Valencian beaches, which enjoyably reflect the Spain in which he lived.

Modernism and surrealism

The early 20th century saw the rise of Spanish modernism and surrealism, much of it driven from Catalunya. While architects such as Gaudí managed to combine their discipline with art, it was one man from Málaga who had such an influence on 20th century painting that he is arguably the most famous artist in the world. Pablo Ruíz Picasso (1881-1973) is notable not just for his artistic genius, but also for his evolution through different styles. Training in Barcelona, but doing much of his work in Paris, his initial Blue Period was fairly sober and subdued, named for predominant use of that colour. His best early work, however, came in his succeeding 'Pink Period', where he used brighter tones to depict the French capital. He moved on from this to become a pioneer of cubism. Drawing on non-western forms, cubism forsook realism for a new form of three-dimensionality, trying to show subjects from as many different angles as possible. Picasso then moved on to more surrealist forms. He continued painting right throughout his lifetime and produced an incredible number of works. One of his best-known paintings is Guernica, a nightmarish ensemble of terror-struck animals and people that he produced in abhorrence at the Nationalist bombing of the defenceless Basque market town in April 1937. Juan Gris was another Spanish cubist whose fluid compositions are widely seen across European galleries.

While Catalonians tend to claim Picasso due to the Barcelona connection, the region produced two of the greats of 20th century art in its own right; Joan Miró and Salvador Dalí. Dalí (1904-1989) goes under the label of surrealism often enough, but in reality his style was completely his own. His best paintings are visions of his own dreamworlds, spaces filled with unlikely objects and strange perspectives, but created with the most precise of brushwork. Miró (1893-1983) was a cheerier type, a fan of bright colours and bold lines, the sort of bloke (Joan is the Catalan version of Juan) that grumblers complain 'my kid could do better' about.

The Civil War was to have a serious effect, as a majority of artists sided with the Republic and fled Spain with their defeat. Franco was far from an enlightened patron of the arts, and his occupancy was a monotonous time. One of the main lights in this period came from the Basque lands in the 1950s. Painters such as Nestor Barretxea, and the sculptors Eduardo Chillida and Jorge Oteiza, see box page , were part of a revival; all three are represented at the tradition-defying monastery of Arantzazu. Chillida (who died in 2002) and Oteiza have continued to be at the forefront of modern sculpture, and their works are widespread through Northern Spain and Europe. Other sculptors such as the Zaragozans Pablo Serrano and Pablo Gargallo are also prominent.

The 1950s also saw the rise of the Generación Abstracta, a single movement who based themselves in Cuenca. The overtly political Antonio Saura is the best of these;

his large black and white compositions are unmistakeable. Antoní Tàpies experimented with a wide range of materials.

The provincial governments of Spain are extremely supportive of local artists these days, and the museums in each provincial capital usually have a good collection of modern works, among which female artists are finally being adequately represented; even more than in other nations, the history of Spanish art is a male one.

Literature

The peninsula's earliest known writers lived under the Roman occupation. Martial was born near modern Calatayud and wrote of his native land, while the poet Prudentius was from Calahorra in the Rioja region. The Seneca family hailed from the province of Baetica, now Andalucía. After the Roman period, San Isidoro was an incredibly significant figure in Spain's literary history, see box page 817.

In Al-Andalus a flourishing literary culture existed under the Córdoba caliphate and later. Many important works were produced by Muslim and Jewish authors; some were to have a large influence on European knowledge and thought. The writings of Ibn Rushd (Averroes) were of fundamental importance, asserting that the study of philosophy was not incompatible with religion and commentating extensively on Aristotle. The discovery of his works a couple of centuries on by Christian scholars led to the rediscovery of Aristotle, and played a triggering role in the Renaissance.

Tucked away in his monastery in the Picos de Europa in the middle of the eighth century, the monk Beatus de Liébana wrote commentaries on the Apocalypse which became a popular monastery staple for centuries, see box page 534. In the 10th century a monk made notes in Castillian in the margins of a text at San Millán, in La Rioja; this is the earliest known appearance of the language in writing.

In the 12th century, *El Cantar de Mío Cid* was an anonymous epic poem recounting the glorious deeds of the strongman northern Spanish mercenary, El Cid; it's the earliest known work in Castillian. Another early author was the Riojan poet Gonzalo de Berceo, who wrote popular religious verses in the same language.

The Castillian king Alfonso X was accurately dubbed 'el sabio' – the wise. He changed the official language of the kingdom from a Latin that by this time was much bastardized to Castillian. He was a patron of scholars and writers, and was a poet himself, writing verses in Galego (Galician).

Juan Ruíz, the archpriest of Hita, writing in the first half of the 14th century, has been dubbed the 'Spanish Chaucer' for his main work, *El Libro de Buen Amor*, which is a diverse collection of tales and adventure stories. He also wrote thousands of verses, many of them more than a touch bawdier than might have been expected for a man of the cloth.

It wasn't unusual for the nobility to take up the pen; the 15th century saw the Marqués de Santillana dashing off verse, including the first Spanish sonnets, while the Ponce de León wrote on a variety of subjects. The popular form of the period was the romantic ballad, dealing in damsels and knights, Christians and Moors. On a more sober note, Jorge Manrique produced perhaps the masterwork of the 15th century, his poem *Coplas por la muerte de su padre*, written after the death of his father.

Spain's Imperial period produced a flourish in the literature of the nation. Garcilaso de la Vega was one of Spain's earliest Renaissance poets, and concentrated principally on love themes, using sonnets as a form. One of the finest Spanish poets of any period was the theologian Fray Luís de León, see box page 172, whose 16th-century works include moving personal reflections on religion; the poems *A Cristo Crucificado* and *En la Ascensión* are noteworthy.

The most famous poet of the period is Luís de Góngora, whose exaggerated, affected style doesn't appeal to all readers but has been widely appreciated, more so

after his death than during his life. Francisco de Quevedo y Villegas, writing in the century, wrote on a range of subjects, but his finest poems are bitingly satirical.

The anonymous work *Lazarillo de Tormes* appeared in 1554. One of the first of the genre known as picaresque (after the Spanish pícaro, a rogue), it dealt with a journey across Northern Spain by the guide of a blind man. It's frequently described as the first Spanish novel.

The extraordinary life of Miguel de Cervantes (1547-1616) marks the start of a rich period of Spanish literature. *Don Quijote* came out in serial form in 1606 and is rightly considered one of the finest novels ever written; it's certainly the widest-read Spanish work.

A frequently overlooked source of interest is the royal archives, particularly those of Philip II. A fascinating glimpse of the period can be had from reading his tenderly written letters to family as well as his policy decisions that affected half the world.

However, it was drama that experienced the fullest explosion of talent. The opening of public theatres in the 17th century confirmed the popularity of dramatists such as Lope de Rueda, who wrote comedies and paved the way for the 'big three'. Lope de Vega (1562-1635), a contemporary of Shakespeare, is said to have written over 1500 plays in his time; what is unquestioned is his skill and flexibility. Tirso de la Molina, arguably the greatest of the three, is famous for producing the archetype of *Don Juan* as well as for such dextrous comedies as *Don Gil de las Calzas Verdes*. Completing the trio, Calderón de la Barca was a patriotic Spaniard who produced a work of comedies and religious allegorical plays notable for their depth of vocabulary and agility of dialogue.

The 18th century was not such a rich period for Spanish writing but two figures based in Asturias stand out. The Galician priest Feijóo, a major Enlightenment figure, wrote important essays from his Oviedo base and the later Gaspar Melchior de Jovellanos, see box page 558, wrote significant historical-political and sociological works; both were pestered by the Inquisition for their liberal outlook.

Several of the 19th century's major writers emerged from the north. Born in Valladolid, José Zorrilla spent much of his life in Mexico; he's famous for his poems and a play about Don Juan, Don Juan Tenorio. The playwright Echegaray was of Basque descent, while Leopoldo Alas, known as Clarín, set his novel *La Regenta* in the fictional city of Vetusta, clearly his native Oviedo. It's a fantastic depiction of Spanish provincial life of the time, seen through the eyes of its heroine. At the same time, Galicia's favourite poet, Rosalía de Castro, was writing her soulful verses in Spanish and Galego, see box page 578. Gustavo Adolfo Bécquer died young having published just one volume of poetry, high-quality yearning works about love.

A watershed in Basque writing came in the late 19th century with the fiery works of Sabino Arana. Littered with inaccuracies and untruths, much of his writing reads more like propaganda than literature or non-fiction, but it created modern Basque nationalism; since then it has been a little tricky for Basque writers to avoid the issue.

The Canarian Benito Perez Galdós was a writer who set about writing a social history of 19th-century Spain in novel form. The strong characters of his forty-volume *Episodios Nacionales* make it a remarkable series of works indeed.

At the end of the 19th century, Spain lost the last of its colonial possessions after revolts and a war with the USA. This event, known as 'the disaster' had a profound impact on the nation and its date, 1898, gave its name to a generation of writers and artists who sought to express what Spain was and had been, and to achieve new perspectives for the twentieth century. One of the foremost was the scholarly Basque Miguel de Unamuno, whose massive corpus of writing ranged from philosophy to poetry and novels, but also included much journalism. His novel *A Tragic Sense of Life* is an anguished and honest attempt to come to terms with his faith and inevitable death.

The slightly later realist novels of Pío Baroja are image-filled and often deeply reflect Basque rural life and urban life in Madrid. He has a strong claim to being the

country's finest 20th-century novelist. *The Tree of Knowledge* is his best-known work. Other notable members of the '98 generation are the essayist, historian and critic José Ortega y Gasset, and the novelist and critic Azorín (José Martínez Ruiz).

Another of the '98 Generation was the poet Antonio Machado, see box page 153. His work reflects his profound feelings for the landscape of his homelands of Andalucía and of Castilla; he lived for a considerable period in Soria. Alongside Federico García Lorca, he is considered the greatest of Spanish poets of the 20th century. A committed Republican, Machado was lost to Spain as a direct result of the Civil War.

Federico García Lorca was a young poet and playwright of great ability and lyricism with a gypsy streak in his soul. His play *Bodas de Sangre* (Blood Wedding) sits among the finest Spanish dramas ever written and his verse ranges from the joyous to the haunted and draws heavily on Andalucían folk traditions. Lorca was shot by fascist thugs just after the outbreak of hostilities in the Civil War.

Other excellent poets of the time include Juan Ramón Jiménez, a Nobel Prize winner in 1956 for *El Platero y Yo*, a nostalgic look back at his childhood. His poetry is precise and refined, although tends to the pretentious. He encouraged the development of Miguel Hernández, a young country boy with a talent for verse, above all after his arrest by the Nationalists during the Civil War. Hernández's poems are simple, noble and direct. He perished of neglect in prison in 1942 aged only 31. Another notable poet, Blas de Otero, who had a complex love for his native Bilbao, spent most of his writing life overseas.

Two writers that stand out in post-Civil War Spanish literature are Delibes and Cela. Miguel Delibes is from Valladolid and his works range from biting satire to evocative descriptions of the Castillian landscape. Camilo José Cela (1916-2002), was a Galician realist who won the Nobel Prize for Literature in 1989. He is most famous for the novels *La Colmena* (The Hive) and *La Familia de Pascual Duarte*, see box page 603. Although Cela fought on the Nationalist side in the Civil War, both battled censors in postwar Spain as editors of anti-Francoist newspapers.

Worthwhile contemporary writers include Manuel Vásquez Montalbán, Arturo Pérez-Reverte (a journalist and popular novelist whose best work is the fine *El Club Dumas*), Julián Rios and Antonio Muñoz Molina.

Music

Musical heritage

Contemporary Spain has one of Europe's richest musical heritages and music plays a hugely important part in the social life of Spanish people. The figures of Romanesque musicians still seen playing on the portals of various churches are proof that music has always been central to the culture of Spain. With a variety of regional styles and significant non-native influences, Spanish musical culture has been able to adapt while at the same time retaining a distinctiveness which makes it such a rewarding part of a visit to the country. While it is true that from the classical period Spain has contributed only a few names to the pantheon of great composers this also reflects the fact that the most interesting aspect of Spanish musical culture is its popular forms. Flamenco is only the best known of a variety of regional styles.

Musical forms

The earliest recognized piece of Spanish music is the Codex calixtinus composed in Santiago around 1140. A piece for three voices it emerged out of a long tradition of musical studies in the various monasteries of Northern Spain. The crusading spirit of the reconquista encouraged bishops to commission various musical forms as a celebration of the power of the church. It was a period of great musical creativity in

liturgical chants and church plays or autos. Even the 13th century King Alfonso the Wise joined the party with his songs Cantias de Santa María. The church was the main patron of music and pieces composed for religious occasions were the dominant form.

Habsburg monarchy

Like other art forms music enjoyed something of a golden age under the early Habsburg monarchs. Victoria (1548-1611) was a relatively famous composer of devotional music and his contemporaries Francisco de Salinas and Fernando de las Infantes also made significant contributions. The organ was the instrument of choice for most church compositions while for secular songs and music for dancing the lute was popular. It was during this period that the five-string Spanish guitar came to be developed and the emergence of a separate repertoire for this uniquely Spanish instrument.

Zarzuela

In 1629 Lope de Vega wrote the libretto for the first Spanish opera, which was to become a popular form. A particular Spanish innovation was the zarzuela, a musical play with speech and dancing. It became widely popular in the 19th century and is still performed in the larger cities. Spain's contribution to opera has been very important and continues to present times, producing a number of world-class singers such as Montserrat Caballé, Placido Domingo, José Carreras and Teresa Berganza. The world-wide fame of these singers has brought opera a popularity it has not enjoyed for a while.

The 19th century

This was a time of great disruption in Spain and all artistic activity suffered. As in other European countries during the 19th Century there was great attention focused on national folklore and regional forms. Isaac Albéniz (1860-1909) wrote *Iberia*, Joaquín Turina wrote the *Sevilla Symphony*, but the most famous composer in this style was Manuel de Falla who wrote several popular pieces based on local songs and inspired by a romantic view of the Spanish peasantry. The best composer of the 19th century, though, was the Catalan Felipe Pedrell. He combined classical form with traditional tunes and was consided at the time to have been an inspiration for other musicians.

Regional expression

In many ways the most distinctive musical forms are those of the various regions of Spain. The northwestern provinces of Galicia and Asturias derive their musical traditions from Celtic origins. Traditional instruments include bagpipes (*gaitas*), accordions, fiddles and tin whistles; there is a fascinating bagpipe museum in Gijón. There are a variety of different vocal styles in each province. Industrial Asturias has a tradition of male voice choirs similar to that of Wales. The unaccompanied choirs sing traditional Asturian songs and songs of the industrial struggles of this century.

In Galicia songs have emerged from the largely agricultural sector, many of them sung exclusively by women. The group Leilía have produced two albums of these haunting traditional ballads (*Leilía and E Verdade I e mentira*). The songs are performed with the traditional *pandereta* (tambourine) an instrument associated with female musicians in Galician culture. Other traditional Galician instruments include the *caneveira* a kind of split cane used for making clapping sounds and the *zanfona*, a Galician hurdy-gurdy. The group Habas Verdes have used these instruments on their recording *En el jardín de la yerba buena*. Llan de Cubel are another interesting starting point. Galician immigrant history has meant that some musicians have incorporated Latin rhythms into traditional Galician songs. Noitebregos from Ourense are one such group. Bagpiper Carlos Núñez was probably the first to develop this trend. A veteran of the European circuit he has collaborated with a variety of musicians including Ry Cooder. Other recommended Galician bands are Na Lúa, Fia Na Roca and Dhais.

Traditional Basque music is mostly associated with the accordion or *trikitrixa*. Musicians associated with this include Josepa Tapia and Kepa Junkera. Traditional songs are an important part of Basque culture which has had to struggle continuously to exist. These songs are therefore an important part of Basque musicians' repertoire. On the other hand there is the desire to innovate within the traditional form in order to ensure that it remains a living tradition rather than one of concern only to musicologists.

● The tensions inherent in Basque culture are reflected in both the lyrical content and the forms which are performed.

Basque rock music is particularly important in the struggle for national identity. The first Basque band were Ez doz Amairu (It's not 13) who were part of the Kantaldi Garaia (It's time to sing movement). The aim of this movement was to give Basque culture a modern appeal and its effects continue to this day. Recently, younger Basque musicians have found the rock genre restricting and have tried experimenting in different modern forms. Hemendik At! have produced three albums of Basque language dance music. Their lyrics are concerned with the problems of young Basque people rather than on a romanticising of history.

Music in Catalunya has also been strongly influenced by the struggle for national identity with singers such as Lluís Llach becoming widely popular throughout Spain. Exiled for four years during the Franco era, his Catalan-language songs were censored by the dictatorship. Along with Joan Manuel Serrat – who also sings both in Catalan and Spanish – Llach's songs are based on the themes of freedom and the love of place. While not nationalistic, both singers have managed to bring Catalunyan cultural issues to their music and to inspire young Catalan songwriters. Within more traditional Catalan music the iconic sardana dance remains important in local festivals and is a focus for local musicians.

Flamenco

Barcelona is an important centre for flamenco music with a number of important musicians being based there. However, although flamenco has moved away from its Andalucían roots its heartland is still very much in Spain's southern region. Questions of origin both of the form and name are now the subject of angel-on-a-pinhead type of debates but what is fairly certain is that flamenco has been influenced by all three of the traditional minorities of Andalucía: Moors, Jews, and gypsies. Of these it is gypsies who have had the biggest influence. Until recently they were synonymous with its performance and some purists maintain that only gypsies summon up the emotional depth to deal with the subject matter of many traditional songs. But the opening up of Spanish culture has seen flamenco's influence spread and singers such as Paco de Lucia have shown that the flamenco style can be successfully combined with other forms. Sevillana is a popularized version of flamenco music designed for the mass markets. The most famous flamenco singer of recent years was El Camarón de la Isla, a remarkable artist who almost single-handedly re-popularized the form.

There are three essential elements to flamenco. Firstly there is the song or el cante, normally performed in an agonised, melancholic style that conveys both a sense of loss and struggle. The second element is the guitar or el toque which is used to accompany the singer and to ensure that the lamentations have a lighter backing in order that the audience does not become too alienated. Thirdly there is the dance element which has developed into an art in its own right. Within these basic elements a whole hierarchy of songs and performance has emerged, of which the casual listener may be blissfully unaware. Although there is no pure flamenco its history as a music of the gypsy people means that all of its elements combine to give the feeling of melancholy and defiance in the face of ill fortune.

The main centres of traditional flamenco are to be found in the cities and towns of Andalucía, with Sevilla, Córdoba and Jerez being particularly important. Here it is

performed at fiestas, in concerts and impromptu performances in bars where
aficionados gather. These are often the best places to see flamenco as the audience
will often be very knowledgeable and demanding. But to enjoy flamenco it is not
essential to have an insider's knowledge. When the three elements combine well the
result is moving and memorable, when set in an overpriced cave the result can be
similar to paying someone dressed as a gypsy to shout at you.

Dance

Dance is everywhere in Spanish life and it would be very difficult to visit Spain without
seeing, and perhaps participating in, some type of dance. Dancing is popular at
fiestas, in bars and in clubs. Indeed any time Spanish people gather together dancing
will usually be on the agenda. Drawing inspiration from the various regional
traditions, dancing is an essential and lively part of Spanish culture. Although
flamenco is the most widely recognized of Spain's regional dances there are other
traditions that are equally as strong. Some of these have fed through into modern
ballet and professional dance but dance culture in Spain is resolutely popular and
based on participation rather than watching.

Regional dances are mostly seen at fiestas and reflect the historical background
of each region. Thus in Galicia and Asturias the dances are Celtic in origin and are
similar to Scottish dances. Following the basic reel pattern these dances are easy to
learn and not too demanding on the visitor who may be lucky enough to find
themselves called upon to partner an Asturian or Galician host. In Catalunya it is the
sardana which is the centre of local fiestas. Based on participation rather than
individual skill, the dance has become emblematic of Catalan regional pride although
its survival owes more to its enduring popularity and easily learned steps than any
nationalistic reasons. The other great Catalan movement tradition is that of the
Castells who form daring human pyramids.

The dances of the Basque country are more complicated although the difficult
parts are usually left to the dantzari, or experts. Many of the dances are extremely
physical as may be judged by their names, for example Bolant Dantza or flying dance.
Perhaps the most famous of all Basque dances are the Espatas or sword dances.
Performed using interlocking swords these dances reflect their martial origins although
in contempary Basque culture they are performed more to impress than intimidate.

Castilla, the heartland of old Spain, has a number of sober dances. Chief among
these are the seguidilla and the paloteo which are both accompanied by the flute,
drum and tambourine. In recent years Castille has seen a number of itinerant Balkan
dance groups added to its fiesta season giving locals the chance to add the polka and
mazurka to their repertoire. Both dances are features of local fiestas. In Aragon locals
like to dance the night away with the jota, a kind of hopping and jumping dance
performed to stringed instruments. The instrument of choice for many dances is the
local form of bagpipe.

Flamenco is the most widely recognised of Spain's national dances with
its roots in the gypsy communities of Andalucía. For the outsider it is the most
difficult style to learn as it is based on individual interpretation of a traditional form.
For most people from Andalucía, flamenco moves are as much a part of life as tapas
or bullfighting.

As with music, the emphasis of Spanish dance culture is on popular performance
and participation. To visitors the level of participation can come as a surprise. Come
midnight dancing in bars becomes almost compulsory and is not confined to young
people. Dancing is perhaps the most accessible part of culture and because of the
various local traditions it is something that is uniquely Spanish. It is an unforgettable
introduction to the life-enhancing aspects of Spanish culture.

Cinema

After years under the cultural anaesthetic of the fascist dictatorship, Spanish cinema is belatedly beginning to make its mark on the world stage. With a world full of Spanish speakers and an enthusiastic home audience of cinema-goers, it's about time. With an average of five visits a year, Spaniards are among the world's keenest cinema-goers. One of the early pioneers of cinema was the Aragonese film maker Segundo de Chomón who was hired by the French film company Pathé in order for them to compete against the great Georges Méliès in the late nineteenth century. He was an innovator in trick photography and made one of the earliest colour films *Le scarabée d'or* (The Golden Beetle). However it was indicative that he had to work outside his homeland. A shortage of capital and an underdeveloped home market meant that it was extremely difficult to develop any indigenous production facilities. As public awareness slowly mounted, demand was mostly met by imported American films.

> ✦ Around 80 films are produced by Spanish companies each year and Spanish films make up around 15 per cent of the Spanish market.

One of the greatest figures in the history of cinema came from a small town in the underdeveloped province of Teruel. Luís Buñuel sprang to prominence in France, where he collaborated with Salvador Dalí in the late 1920s; he pioneered surrealism on the screen. Buñuel was sure that the critics were going to hate their first film, *Un chien andalou*, so he took some stones along to the première to lob at any that voiced their disapproval. Luckily, it went down a treat, and they followed it up with the successful *L'Age d'Or*; both produced images that are still iconic. Along with a whole generation of talented artists, Buñuel left Spain with the onset of fascism but did return shortly before his death to work on a number of collaborations. His work has influenced generations of directors.

The beginnings of the native Spanish Film industry came during the 1930s with the help of the Republican Government. Locally produced films such as *Paloma Fair* (1935) and *Clara the Brunette* (1936) proved to be immensely popular and produced the first Spanish language star, the unlikely named Imperio Argentina. Another important development in this period was the move to dub imported films into Spanish, a practice which continues to this day.

The Civil War and its lead-up saw numerous propaganda films made from all perspectives, then the establishment of the Franco dictatorship saw the end of progress and development in the Spanish film industry. For the next 40 years the film industry was to be made subservient to the goals of the state, all film production had to be approved, and censorship was strict. The emphasis was on films with a unifying message. Glorified histories, inoffensive comedies and chaste romances were the order of the day. Regional differences were not encouraged and the use of Catalan, Euskara and Galego was forbidden.

Despite this some film makers managed to get message across. The most important of these was Antonio Bardem. His films, especially *Death of a Cyclist* (1956) suggested that it was possible to introduce some elements of criticism into film making. He founded the film magazine *Objectivo* in 1953 which for the 15 issues that it was allowed to operate became a rallying point for crititics of the Franco regime. However Bardem was arrested on numerous occasions and it became increasingly difficult for him to produce in Spain. Luís Berlanga was another who risked persecution to satirize the state.

Carlos Saura was the standout figure of Spanish cinema in the 1960s and 1970s. Films such as *La Caza* (The Hunt, 1965), and *Ana y los lobos* (Ana and the Wolves, 1973) managed to use symbolism to attack the institutions of the dictatorship, which had become somewhat freer by these times. A similar approach was taken by Victor Erice and his *El espíritu de la colmena* (Spirit of the Beehive, 1973), a film of haunting beauty

set in post-war Castilla. Meanwhile, foreign filmmakers were still taking advantage of good weather and low overheads to shoot many films in southeastern Spain, where the desert landscape of Almería became the United States for films such as *A Fistful of Dollars*, *The Good, the Bad, and the Ugly*, and many other westerns.

Since the abolition of censorship after Franco's death, things have changed; Spanish cinema has witnessed the transformation mirrored in many aspects of life in the peninsula. Without a doubt, the best-known post-Franco director has been Pedro Almodóvar. Films such as *Atame* (Tie Me Up, Tie Me Down), *Mujeres al borde de un ataque de nervios* (Women on the Edge of a Nervous Breakdown), and the Oscar-winning *Todo sobre mi madre* (All About my Mother) explore the themes of desire and obsession in Madrid that have made Almodóvar one of the world's most popular and prominent directors. His films have propelled actors Antonio Banderas and Penélope Cruz to international stardom.

Another Oscar-winning director is Fernando Trueba, whose *Belle Epoque* (1993) is a romantic comedy set in the pre-Civil War republic, also starring Cruz. Bigas Luna explores the strange worlds of sex, the unconscious, and food in films such as *Jamón Jamón* and *La Teta y la Luna*. A very talented young director is the Basque Alex de la Iglesia, whose recent *800 Balas* (800 Bullets) followed on his success with films such as *El Día de la Bestia*. The film focuses on former stuntmen and extras from the golden days of the spaghetti western now reduced to doing shootouts for tourists near Almería. Carlos Saura is still directing; a good recent film of his was *Goya en Burdeos* (Goya in Bordeaux), while the Mexican Guillermo del Toro, a protegé of Almodóvar, made the superb *El Espinazo del Diablo* (The Devil's Backbone), a Spanish-made ghost story set in the Civil War. Fernando León is another up and coming director whose recent socially-aware comedy *Los Lunes al Sol* (Mondays in the Sun) focused on a group of unemployed friends in a north-coast fishing town. It starred Javier Bardem, one of Spain's most talented cinematic actors.

At the end of September each year, the film world turns its attention to San Sebastian and over 200,000 visitors turn come to view the enormous number of both Spanish and international films on offer. As well as awarding internationally prestigious prizes the festival also focuses attention on regional Spanish cinema and tries to ensure that it is seen outside the limited area of its production. Recently there has been a recognition that Spanish cinema has been too Madrid and Barcelona-focused, and that regional film-making has to be given inadequate support; it has only been the patronage of the regional governments and TV companies that have enabled a regional film culture to evolve at all. The establishment of a national film school in Ponferrada will undoubtedly help this situation.

Religion

In a land where Radio María gets plenty of listeners, religion is bound to be a significant factor. The history of Spain and the history of the Spanish Catholic church are barely separable but in 1978, Article 16 of the new constitution declared that Spain was now a nation without an official religion, less than a decade after Franco's right hand, Admiral Luís Carrero Blanco, had declared that 'Spain is Catholic or she is nothing'.

From the sixth-century writings of San Isidoro onwards, the destiny of Spain was a specifically Catholic one. The Reconquista was a territorial war inspired by holy zeal, Jews and Moors were expelled in the quest for pure Catholic blood, the Inquisition demonstrated the young nation's religious insecurities and paranoias, and Philip II bled Spain dry pursuing futile wars in a vain attempt to protect his beloved Church from the spread of Protestantism. Much of the strife of the 1800s was caused by groups attempting to end or defend the power of the church, while in the 20th century

❝❞ Faced with a census form in 2001, a massive 94 per cent of Spaniards claimed to be Catholics, but less than a third of them were regulars at their parish church...

the fall of the Second Republic and the Civil War was engendered to a large extent by the provocatively anticlerical actions of the leftists.

Although regular churchgoing is increasingly confined to an aged (mostly female) segment of society, and seminaries struggle to produce enough priests to stock churches, it's not the whole picture. *Romerías* (religious processions to rural chapels) and religious fiestas are well attended, and places of popular pilgrimage such as Santiago, Zaragoza, Lourdes, Loiola and Covadonga are flooded with Spanish visitors during the summer months. Very few weddings are conducted away from the church's bosom, and come Eastertime a huge percentage of the male population of some towns participates in solemn processions of religious *cofradías* (brotherhoods). Nevertheless, the church plays an increasingly minor role in most Spaniards' lives, especially the young, born after the return to democracy.

Although not involved to the same degree in education as it once was, the church runs some 15 per cent of Spanish schools and several universities. The church and the right wing remain closely connected in Spain; the governing Partido Popular is largely a Catholic party, and allegations of Opus Dei involvement are frequent, see box page 391.

One curious facet of Spanish Catholicism is its Marian aspect. Worship and veneration of the Virgin seem to far outstrip that of Christ himself, who is often relegated to a side chapel; María is still by far the most common name in Spain (even being used for boys in combination with another name eg José María).

The practice of Catholicism in Spain is far more dogmatic than liturgical. The devotions of the Via Crucis, or Stations of the Cross (which arose in the 17th century), the Sacred Heart (which became popular in the 16th) and the Rosary are the focus of a sentimental and far from robust approach to the religion; the Bible itself has historically not been widely available to, or read by, the people. Encouraging the performance of these ritualistic elements was a way for the church to keep a superstitious populace in regular attendance; indulgences were traditionally offered as a carrot. The number of fiestas in Spain, which are nearly all religious in origin, historically had a similar aim.

Language

Languages and dialects are always thorny political issues, and Spain has its fair share. Spanish, of course, is the major one. Known as español or castellano, the constitution states that all citizens have a duty to know it. Nearly all do, although if you get off the beaten track in Catalunya, Galicia, Aragón or Asturias you'll find the occasional old person who doesn't, and plenty of urban Catalans are rusty, or pretend to be.

Castellano

Castellano is Castillian, one of several tongues to emerge from the post-Latin melange. With Castile playing a major role in the Reconquista the language spread

rapidly and was adopted as the official one of the kingdom of Alfonso X, which encompassed most of northwest Spain. The fact that it is now spoken by some 360 million people worldwide is perhaps more than an accident of history; its accessibility and comparatively simple grammar may have aided its spread in the first place. In Spain, the most respected institution dealing with it is the Real Academia Española, a hoary old body whose remit is 'to purify, clarify, and give splendour' to the language.

There are many regional accents of castellano, and ease of comprehension for the outsider differs markedly from place to place. Many words are purely local; olives are called aceitunas in some places, and olivas in others; ordering buey in Castilla will get you an ox steak, in Galicia a large crab. Similarly, slang differs widely from city to city.

One entertaining story about Castillian is that the 'th' sound used for the letters z and c came about because courtiers were anxious not to offend a lisping Habsburg king. It's almost certainly not true – linguists point to the fact that not all /s/ sounds are converted to /th/ – but it's often used to poke fun at mainland Spain by Latin Americans, who don't do it (neither do Andalucíans).

Catalan

The second most spoken language in Spain is Català (Catalan), with some ten million first or second language speakers. It evolved separately from Latin and is broadly more similar to Italian than Spanish; the Aragonese kingdom's maritime forays mean it is still spoken to a small extent on the island of Sardinia, as well as in Andorra and southwestern France. Since Franco's death, Catalan has flourished, and it's in very wide official and public use throughout Catalunya. Valencian is a variant of the language.

Galego

Of the other regional languages, the one with the most speakers is Galego (Gallego in Spanish), with some three million in Spain. It's related to Portuguese and the two are highly mutually intelligible. Although banned under Franco (who was himself Galician), it remained strong and is now taught in schools again. It's broadly similar enough to Spanish not to cause visitors too much concern.

Euskara

Euskara, or Basque, is a different matter altogether. Although the first known document written in the language dates from the same time as Castillian, it's a far older tongue whose origins are as obscure as the Basques themselves. It's a difficult language with no known relatives. Like Finnish, it is agglutinative, meaning roughly that distinct bits are joined on to words for each element of meaning. Whereas in Spanish, the –é at the end of hablé, (I spoke) denotes the tense (past), the person (first), the number (singular), mood, mode, and aspect, in Basque these are all represented by distinct additions, which results in numerous variations of a single word. People struggle with the seven cases in Latin, but Euskara has a massive twenty. Franco banned this, too, and cracked down heavily on its use, but after decades of hiding it's back with a bang: an evergrowing number of people are learning and using it. You'll see it everywhere; on road signs, in bars, on posters. Some 800,000 people speak it in Spain, but the number is rapidly rising.

Bable

Bable, the Asturian tongue, is similar enough to Castillian to be labelled a dialect. In truth, though, it's probably more accurate to put it the other way, as Castillian was likely largely derived from the tongue spoken in the Christian mountain kingdom. It's still widely spoken in Asturias, unlike Leonese, which is similar, but spoken by few people in that province, although sporadic efforts are made to revive it.

Aragonese is a word with two meanings; it refers to the version of Castillian spoken in Aragón and to the native language of the region, more similar to Català than anything else and still used, especially in the more remote mountain regions. There are several variations of both this and Català throughout the Pyrenees.

Land and environment

Geography

Spain's area of half a million square kilometres makes it the fourth largest country in Europe and second largest in the EU after France. It's also high; the average altitude is second only to Switzerland. Geographically, Spain is divided into distinct areas; to a large degree these have corresponded with cultural and political boundaries over time.

Although if you arrive over the Pyrenees it may not seem it, Spain's central plateau, the *meseta*, is high, with an average elevation of some six to seven hundred metres. It covers most of the centre of the country, and is bounded by chains of hills and mountains. It covers nearly the whole of the regions of Castilla y León, Castilla-La Mancha and Extremadura. One mountain range, the Cordillera Central, runs through its middle, but it's generally a consistent, if not wholly flat, plain that slopes gently towards the west. It was once wooded, but the 'war on trees' that cleared the land for agriculture has left vast tracts of it eroded and arid; much of the meseta isn't arable and the landscape can be a bleak horizon of scrub and stones.

In a land of few half measures, Spain's mountain ranges are serious ones. The Pyrenees are its biggest and ruggedest, straddling the northern border like a hardman bouncer. The highest summit of the Pyrenees is Aneto (3404 m), one of many that top the 10,000 ft mark. Sierra Cantábrica is basically a westwards extension of it, and includes the Picos de Europa in its westwards run along the coast. Further west, at the corner of Spain, Galicia is fairly hilly with a wild coast indented with sheltered inlets.

In the south, the scene is dominated by the Sierra Nevada, part of the Cordillera Bética that includes the peninsula's highest peak, Mulhacén (3478 m). The Sierra Morena is a lower range that cuts Andalucía off from the meseta. In the east of Spain, the Sistema Ibérico is a muscly chain that runs through Aragón at a healthy height.

Some of the best cultivable land in Spain is in fertile Catalunya, la Rioja, and Andalucía. Fruit and vegetable production centres on the southeast coast, where even the desert province of Almería bears fruit in its seas of irrigated plastic greenhouses.

The scarcity of water on the meseta has dictated settlement patterns, with most towns and villages on or near rivers. The two great rivers of Northern Spain are the Ebro, rising in Cantabria and flowing eastwards to its Mediterranean destiny; and the Duero, flowing west right across the meseta and into Portugal, where it becomes the Douro. In the south, the Tajo and the Guadiana rise in southern Aragón and head westwards, the Tajo (Tejo, Tagus) reaching the Atlantic at Lisbon, and the Guadiana hitting the sea further south, where it forms part of the Portuguese border. The Guadalquivir flows through Andalucía and is the waterway of Cádiz and Sevilla, while Galicia's Miño is another major river; it also forms a long section of the border with Portugal. Most of Spain's rivers are extensively dammed; these projects have deprived the rivers of their former majesty and have been socially and environmentally extremely controversial in some cases. Natural habitats as well as towns and villages have been flooded by the embalses; enforced eviction and laughable compensation for property was a feature of these projects, particularly in Franco's later years. Nevertheless, the water is much needed, particularly in the parched summers of the centre.

Spain's northern coasts are generally green and rocky, with plenty of sandy beaches and sheltered fishing harbours. The Prestige oil spill in late 2002 damaged

fisheries. In the south and east, the coasts are more sheltered, and the beaches draw millions of tourists to the Costa Brava, Costa Blanca and Costa del Sol in particular.

Climate

Spain's geographical layout generates significant differences in weather patterns across the nation. The high central meseta, shielded by the mountains, is generally continental in climate; fairly dry (very dry in some parts) with cold winters and very hot summers. Adding to the winter discomfort is the biting wind, which 'can kill a man but can't blow out a candle' according to locals. The climate in places like Burgos and León is popularly characterized as 'nueve meses de invierno, tres meses de infierno' ('nine months of winter, three months of hell'). The green hills of the north coast are that way for a reason: it rains a hell of a lot. Parts of Galicia get two metres of rain a year, more than ten times the precipitation of some towns in Castilla. It's a typically maritime climate, with mild summers and winters, and the rain fairly constant through the year; up to 150 rainy days per annum. The mountains, too, receive high rainfall, particularly the coastal Cordillera Cantábrica in the north and Cordillera Bética in the south. Snow is usually there to stay from January on, and many of the higher passes can still be snowbound as late as June or July; this goes for the Pyrenees too. Skiing is usually reliable from January until mid-April. The south of Spain is its sunniest part, in fact one of Europe's sunniest regions. Winter temperatures on the coast are very forgiving, and the summers are hot but not overly so. Inland Andalucía, however, is a furnace in the summer months.

Wildlife

Spain has a good selection of wildlife, with a number of 'respect' species like bears and wolves still lurking in the mountains and forests. The best havens for wildlife in the peninsula are the mountainous parts of Asturias and the Pyrenees, where conservation is most advanced and the habitats less accessible. The Andalucían uplands are also an important zone. While the meseta can be good for birdwatching, deforestation and the Spanish passion for hunting have made most four-legged creatures larger than a mouse scarce.

In the mountains, a common sight are chamois or *isard* (rebeco or sarrío), a type of agile antelope that likes the high altitudes. Also common are *jabalí* (wild boar), but being nocturnal, they're harder to see. Extensively hunted, they tend to be extra-wary when people are about. Still present, but in smaller numbers, are brown bears, an Asturian conservation programme will hopefully ensure their survival in the wild, and wolves, which still howl in the Galician and Castillian hills. The Iberian lynx can still be spotted in the Coto Doñana national park in Andalucía. A variety of deer are present both in the mountains and on the plains, where their heads make popular trophies. The impressively horned (and protected) ibex has made a strong comeback and can be seen in the national parks of Andalucía, particularly Grazalema, and also in the Sierra de Gredos in Avila province.

Smaller mammals include the stoat/ermine, which changes colour in winter, the fox, pine marten, red squirrels, and several species of bat. Wildcats are also present, although interbreeding with feral domestic cats has created a debased population. Otters can be seen in many of Spain's quieter rivers, while some of Andalucía's scrublands and wetlands harbour the Egyptian mongoose. And don't forget Europe's only monkeys, the so-called Barbary Apes living on the rock of Gibraltar.

Other creatures you might spot are salamanders and many species of lizard and snake in the dustier lands of Castilla. Few of the snakes are poisonous, although there are a couple of species of viper. Frogs can create a deafening noise around some of Spain's rivers, particularly when their hind legs are on a local menú del día. In Andalucía you can see a couple of weird reptiles in the gecko and the chameleon.

Background Land & environment

Spain's birdlife is superb in some parts of the country, which is a popular destination for watching flocks of migrating species. The best area is the Coto Doñana National Park in southwestern Andalucía, but there are other worthwhile spots in that region as well as in the centre and north of the country.

Migrating birds of prey aren't really into doing much wing-flapping; they far prefer to soar on thermal currents. Crossing large stretches of sea therefore doesn't appeal, so they all head for the Straits of Gibraltar, making this spot a fantastic one for observing them. Several species of buzzards, kites, eagles, kestrels and hawks all make the journey twice a year, tending to move north between March-May and back to Africa again in September-October. They are joined on the route by storks, such an enjoyable and plentiful sight on the church roofs of Andalucía, Extremadura, and Castilla y León in the summer months.

Other good places to see birds of prey include the mountains of the Pyrenees and the Picos de Europa. One of the most dramatic species is the lammergeier, or bearded vulture. Known as 'bone-breaker' (*quebrantahuesos*) in Spanish for its habit of dropping bones on rocks to shatter them and get at the marrow, it's a superb sight, drifting up valleys on its massive wings. Smaller but far more plentiful is the endemic common or griffon vulture (*buitre*). Golden eagles (*águila real*) can also be spotted in the Pyrenees. Numerous other birds of prey are common sights both in the mountains or circling the endless horizons of the meseta.

Spain's wetlands harbour abundant species of waders and waterfowl. The majority of them occur along the south and eastern coasts, but even in mid-meseta small lakes can attract dozens of species. Galicia's tidal estuaries are another good spot to take the binoculars, while at Fuente de Piedra in Málaga province you can see thousands of flamingoes in season. Rare sights in the mountains include capercaillie (urogallo) and wallcreepers; woodpeckers, chough, and owls are more common. On the plains, larks, grouse, and doves are common sights, as are two species of bustard. In the south, hoopoes and bee-eaters add a splash of colour to the countryside.

There are butterflies and moths in abundance; clouds of them grace the Pyrenees, the Sierra Nevada/Alpujarras and the Picos in early summer. Many species are unique to the peninsula, while others migrate through from Africa or, in the case of the monarch, America. Swallowtails and the massive two-tailed pasha are the most spectacular; the peacock moth is another heavyweight. Hummingbird hawk moths are a fascinating sight as they hover about.

Whales and dolphins are spotted regularly off the Costa de Luz, while the rivers of Northern Spain have always been full of trout and salmon, although overfishing and hydroelectric projects have reduced their numbers in many areas.

Vegetation

The war on trees conducted in Castilla through the centuries is over, with the sinister trunked creatures successfully eliminated. Most of the arid plains of the meseta were once covered with Mediterranean forest, but systematic deforestation, combined with overgrazing and war, have left it barren and bare; some of it barely able to support the sparse scrubby matorral that covers the land deemed unfit for agriculture.

Reforestation schemes in Castilla have primarily been for logging purposes, and the region needs a more enlightened environmental programme such as that of Asturias, which preserves some superb stretches of ancient forest. The forest cover of the Northern Spanish coast and mountains is impressive in many parts, with chestnut, beech and holm oak at lower levels and Scots pine and silver fir higher up, among other species. In the southeast, grassland gives way to virtual desert near Almería, with cactus and many Saharan species in evidence.

The wildflowers of Spain are nothing less than superb; the diversity of the terrain supports an astonishing range, best seen in spring. The mountains of the Pyrenees,

Cordillera Cantábrica and the Sierra Nevada, in particular, are a goldmine, with many species unique to those areas. The southern coastline is also in colourful bloom at that time, while even the parched meseta comes good with fields of poppies and cultivated sunflowers bright under the big sky. A great range of orchids can be found throughout the country.

National parks

Spain has several national parks (*parques nacionales*); the first, established in 1918, were Covadonga (now part of the Picos de Europa national park) and Ordesa, in the Aragonese Pyrenees. Far more numerous, and covering a larger area, are *parques naturales* (natural parks) administered by the autonomous communities. Although protection for the species within these areas in some cases isn't absolute, it is significant, and crucial in many cases for survival. *Reservas de caza* are protected areas that also have significant coverage but for less noble reasons: so that there'll be plenty of animals to shoot when the hunting season comes around.

Most of the parks have good systems of information centres and access trails. The national parks are all superb; four are mountain areas (two in the Pyrenees, one in the Picos de Europa, and one in Granada's Sierra Nevada), and two are wetlands that support a huge range of bird and animal life (Coto Doñana in Andalucía and Las Tablas de Daimiel in Castilla-La Mancha). Of the natural parks, Asturias has the best-administered ones, with several in its forested hills and valleys: Muniellos and Somiedo are two of the finest. Andalucía has some standouts too, such as Grazalema and Cazorla, which offer superb hillwalking. There are many in Catalunya and all through the Pyrenees; Galicia's Illas Ciés are another especially worth noting. In most areas the parks have a good range of accommodation available, including *casas rurales* (rural homes), hostels, and *refugios* (walkers' hostels).

Further reading

Art and architecture

Gijs van Hensbergen *Catalonia's Son*. (Harper Collins, 2001). An illuminating biography of Barcelona's most famous architect, Gaudí.

Moffitt, John F *The Arts in Spain*. (Thames and Hudson 1999). Excellent, highly readable introduction to all aspects of the arts in Spain.

Páramo Arias, L *Guía del Arte Prerrománico Asturiano* (Trea 1994). The best book on Asturian pre-Romanesque architecture. Spanish, but with an English summary.

History and politics

Carr, R (ed) *Spain: A History (2000)*, OUP. A compilation of recent writing on Spanish history, with entertaining and myth-dispelling contributions from academics. *Modern Spain 1875-1980* and *The Spanish Tragedy; the Civil War in Perspective*. Well-written accounts of recent Spanish history.

Elliott, J *Imperial Spain* (1963), Edward Arnold. Precise, sympathetic, and readable.

Hughes, R *Barcelona* (Harvill Press, 1992). A highly personal, immensely entertaining history of the city by the outspoken art critic. One of the very best books on Barcelona.

Kurlansky, M *The Basque History of the World* (1999), Vintage Press. A likeable introduction to what makes the Basques tick, what they eat, what they've done, and what they're like. Informal, fireside style.

Richardson, P *Our Lady of the Sewers*. Thoughtful, entertaining descriptions of some of Spain's oddest traditions and fiestas.

Steer, G *The Tree of Guernica* (1938), Hodder & Stoughton. Written by a reporter, an eye-witness to the bombing. Of most interest for an evocative description of the event itself.

Thomas, H *The Spanish Civil War* (1961/77), Penguin. The first unbiased account of the war read by many Spaniards in the censored Franco years, this is long but always readable. A superbly researched work.

Zulaika, J *Basque Violence: Metaphor and Sacrament* (2000), University of Nevada Press. An academic but intriguing exploration of the roots of Basque nationalist feeling, and the progression to violence.

Fiction/reportage and autobiography

Alas, L *La Regenta* (1885). Good novel about small-town prejudices in Spain, set in mythical Vetusta, heavily based on Oviedo.

Atxaga, B *Obabakoak* (1994), Vintage Books. A dreamlike series of anecdotes making up a novel by a well-respected contemporary Basque author. Drawn from Basque heritage rather than about Basque culture. Individual and profound.

Cela, C *La Familia de Pascual Duarte/The Family of Pascual Duarte* (1942). Nobel Prize winning writer's first and best novel, a grimly realistic novel about postwar Spain.

Cervantes Saavedra, M de *Don Quijote* (1605/1615). Don Quixote is an obvious choice and a superbly entertaining read.

Hemingway, E *Fiesta/The Sun Also Rises* (1927), Jonathan Cape. An evocative description of the Pamplona fiestas and trout-fishing in the Pyrenees.

Hooper, J *The New Spaniards* (1995), Penguin. An excellent account of modern Spain and the issues affecting peoples' lives.

Marías J *Tomorrow In the Battle Think on Me* and *A Heart so White*. (1996, Harvill Press). A brilliant contemporary novel, beautifully translated by Margaret Jull Costa.

Montalbán Manuel Vázquez *South Seas*. (1998, Harvill). One of a series of amusing adventures of the gourmet detective, Pepe Carvalho, set in Barcelona.

Orwell, G *Homage to Catalonia* (1938), Secker & Warburg. About Orwell's experience of the Spanish Civil War, and characteristically incisive and poignant.

Pérez-Reverte, A *The Flanders Panel*. (1994, Harvill Press). A highly entertaining suspense novel set in Madrid by one of Spain's most popular contemporary authors.

Quevedo Francisco *The Swindler* (translated in *Two Spanish Picaresque Novels*, Penguin 1969). A classic picaresque tale of the rise and fall of the eponymous 'swindler'.

Travelogues

Borrow, G *The Bible in Spain* (1842), John Murray Press. Amusing account of another remarkable 19th-century traveller who travelled widely through Spain trying to distribute Bibles during the first Carlist War.

Ford, R *A Hand-Book for Travellers in Spain* (1845), John Murray Press. Difficult to get hold of but worth it; comprehensive and entertaining guide written by a 19th-century British gentleman who spent 5 years in Spain.

Ford, R *Gatherings from Spain* (1846), John Murray Press. Superb and sweeping overview of Spanish culture and customs; Richard Ford was something of a genius and has been surpassed by few if any travel writers since.

Jacobs, M *The Road to Santiago*, (Pallas Athene Publishers). One of the best guides to the architecture of the pilgrim route, happily piety-free.

Lee, L *A Rose for Winter*. A beatifully written account of the author's travels in southern Spain in 1936. The sequel – *As I Walked Out One Midsummer Morning* (1969, Penguin), is a poignant account of a romantic walk across pre-Civil War Spain.

Nooteboom, C *Roads to Santiago* (1992), The Harvill Press. An offbeat travelogue that never fails to entertain. One of the best travel books around, soulful, literary, and moving.

Other

Casas, P *Food and Wines of Spain*, (Penguin 1985). A good guide to cuisine and wines.

Cohen, J (ed) *The Penguin Book of Spanish Verse* (1988), Penguin. Excellent collection of Spanish poetry through the ages.

Farino, T & Grunfeld, F *Wild Spain*, (Sheldrake Press). Knowledgeable book on wildlife.

Hemingway, E *Death in the Afternoon* (1939), Jonathan Cape. Superb book on bullfighting by a man who fell heavily for it.

Read, J *Wines of Spain* (2001), Mitchell Beazley. Updated edition of this good in-depth guide to Spain's wines and wineries.

Basic Spanish for travellers

Spanish has been described as an easy language to learn. Certainly it is spoken more or less as it appears and travellers who have fluency in other Latin-based languages such as French or Italian should not find it difficult. Bear in mind that in Castellano or standard Spanish, *z*, and *c* before *e* and *i* are a soft *th*. Other points to remember are that *ll* approximates to the English *y*, the *h* is invariably silent, while *j* and *g* are pronounced like an *h* when they are at the start of a word. *R*'s, and especially double *r*'s are rolled, often to excess. When *ñ* has an accent or tilde above it, the pronounciation is similar to the English *ny*. When consulting a dictionary, remember that *LL*, *CH* and *Ñ* are considered as separate letters in Spanish. Emphasis is routine, with stress on the penultimate syllable unless there is an accent. Exceptions are when a word ends in *d*, *l*, *r* or *z*, when stress is on the final syllable.

Spaniards treat all attempts to speak their language with patience and good humour, so that the effort is well worthwhile.

Numbers

zero	*cero*
one	*uno (m) una (f)*
two	*dos*
three	*tres*
four	*cuatro*
five	*cinco*
six	*seis*
seven	*siete*
eight	*ocho*
nine	*nueve*
ten	*diez*
eleven	*once*
twelve	*doce*
thirteen	*trece*
fourteen	*catorce*
fifteen	*quince*
sixteen	*dieciséis*
seventeen	*diecisiete*
eighteen	*dieciocho*
nineteen	*die cinueve*
twenty	*veinte*
thirty	*treinta*
forty	*cuarenta*
fifty	*cíncuenta*
sixty	*sesenta*
seventy	*setenta*
eighty	*ochenta*
ninety	*noventa*
one hundred	*cien*
two hundred	*doscientos*
one thousand	*mil*

Days and months

Sunday	*Domingo*
Monday	*Lunes*
Tuesday	*Martes*
Wednesday	*Miércoles*
Thursday	*Jueves*
Friday	*Viernes*
Saturday	*Sábado*
January	*Enero*
February	*Febrero*
March	*Marzo*
April	*Abril*
May	*Mayo*
June	*Junio*
July	*Julio*
August	*Agosto*
September	*Septiembre*
October	*Octubre*
November	*Noviembre*
December	*Dicembre*

Greetings

Hello/Goodbye	*Hola/Adiós*
Good morning	*Buenos días*
Good afternoon	*Buenos tardes*
Good evening	*Buenos noches*
See you later	*Hasta luego*
How are you?	*¿cómo esta?*
Sorry	*Perdón/lo siento*
Yes/no	*Si/no*
Thankyou	*Muchas gracias*
OK	*Vale*
Excuse me	*Con permiso*
It's nothing/you're welcome	*De nada*
Do you speak English?	*¿Habla Inglés?*
Go away!	*¡Márchese!*
I don't understand	*No entiendo*
Good luck!	*¡Buena suerte!*

Accommodation

Air conditioning	*Aire acondicionado*
Apartment	*Apartamento (m)*
Bathroom (with)	*(Con) baño*
Bed/double bed	*Cama (f)/cama matrimonial*
Bill	*Cuenta (f)*
Credit cards	*Tarjetas de crédito*
Change	*Cambio (m)*
Country/Inn	*Albergue (m)*
Heating	*Calefacción (f)*
Hotel	*Hotel (m)*

Hostel	Hostal (m)
How much?	¿Cuánto es?
Laundry	Lavandería (f)
Money	Dinero (m)
Receptionist	Recepcionista (f)
Room	Habitación (m)
Shower	Ducha (f)
State-run hotel	Parador (m)
Telephone	Teléfono (m)
Toilet	Servicio (m)
View	Vista (f)
Water (hot)	Agua (caliente)

Eating out

Waiter/waitress	Camarero/a
Spoon	Cuchara
Lunch	Almuerzo
Menu	Carta
Dinner	Cena
Cup	Copa
Knife	Cuchillo
Bill	Cuenta
Breakfast	Desayuno
Set menu	Menú del día
Morning/afternoon snack	Merienda
Table	Mesa
Course, dish or plate	Plato
Napkins	Serviettas
Chair	Silla
High chair	Silla alta
Cup	Taza
Fork	Tenador
Glass	Vaso
I would like to reserve a table	¿Quiero reservar una mesa?
Do you have a table for two?	¿Tiene usted una mesa para dos personas?
Could I see the menu/wine list?	¿Podría ver la carta/la lista de vino?
What do you recommend?	¿Qué recomendería usted?
I'm a vegetarian	Soy vegetariano/a
Can I have another...?	¿Puedo tenir otro...?
Could I have the bill, please?	¿La cuenta, por favor?
Is IVA/service included?	¿Está incluido la IVA/ el servicio?

Travel

Airport	Aeropuerto (m)
Arrival	Llegada (f)
Bus	Autobus (m)
Bus station	Estación de autobuses (f)
Car	Coche (m)
Car hire	Alquilar de coches
Customs	Aduana (f)

Duty free	*Libre de impuestos*
Fare	*Precio del billete (m)*
Ferry (boat)	*Barca (f)*
Garage	*Taller (m)*
Left luggage	*Consigna (f)*
Papers (documents)	*Documentación (f)*
Parking	*Aparcamiento (m)*
Passport	*Pasaporte (m)*
Petrol	*Gasolina (f)*
Puncture	*Pinchazo (m)*
Railway	*Ferrocarril (m)*
Taxi	*Taxi (m)*
Taxi rank	*Parada de taxis (f)*
Ticket (single/return)	*Billete (m)(de ida/devuelta)*
Ticket (return)	*Billete de ida y vuelta (m)*
Train station	*Estación de trenes (f)*
Train	*Tren (m)*

Other common words and question/phrases

Big	*Grande*
Cheap	*Barato*
Cold/hot	*Frío/caliente*
Day/night	*Día (m)/noche (f)*
Doctor	*Médico/a*
Enough	*Bastante*
Evening	*Tarde (f)*
Expensive (too)	*Caro (demasiado)*
Forbidden	*Prohibido*
Good (very good)	*Bien (muy bien)*
House	*Casa (f)*
How much?	*¿Cuánto es?*
Is there/are there?	*¿Hay un ..?*
Key	*Llave (f)*
Later	*Más tarde*
Little	*Pequeño*
Market	*Mercado (m)*
More/less	*Más/menos*
Near	*Cerca*
Now	*Ahora*
Small	*Pequeño*
Today	*Hoy*
Toilet	*Servicio (m)*
Tomorrow	*Mañana*
Tyre	*Neumá tico (m)*
What?	*¿Qué?*
What time is it?	*¿Qué hora es?*
When?	*¿Cuándo?*
Where (is)?	*¿Dónde (esta)?*
Why?	*¿Por qué?*
Yesterday	*Ayer*

Footnotes Basic Spanish for travellers

Food glossary

It is impossible to be definitive about terms used. Different regions have numerous variants. See also Eating, page 48.

Albóndigas Meatballs
Alcachofa Artichoke
Alcaparras Capers
Almejas Name applied to various species of small clams
Alubias Beans
Anchoa Preserved anchovy
Angulas Baby eels
Bacalao Salted cod, an emblematic Basque food
Berberechos Cockles
Berenjena Aubergine/eggplant
Bistek Steak
Boquerones Fresh anchovies
Buey Ox, or in Galicia, a large crab
Cabracho Scorpionfish
Cabrales A delicious Asturian cheese
Cabrito Young goat, usually roasted
Caldereta A stew of meat or fish
Caldo A thickish soup
Cangrejo Crab; occasionally river crayfish
Cazuela A stew, often of fish or seafood
Cecina Cured beef; a speciality of León
Cerdo Pork
Chuletón A massive T-bone steak
Cochinillo/lechón/tostón Suckling pig
Codorniz Quail
Cordero Lamb
Embutido Any salami-type sausage
Empanada A savoury pie
Gambas Prawns
Higado Liver
Idiazábal Basque sheepmilk cheese
Jamón Ham
Judías verdes Green beans
Lechazo Milk-fed lamb
Lenguado Sole
Lentejas Lentils
Lomo Loin, usually sliced pork
Longaniza A long sausage, speciality of Aragón
Lubina Sea bass
Manchego Spain's national cheese made from ewe's milk
Marisco Shellfish
Morcilla Blood sausage, either solid or semi-liquid

Navajas Razor-shells
Natillas Rich custard dessert
Nécora Small sea crab
Orejas Ears, usually of a pig
Ostra Oyster
Parrilla A mixed grill
Pato Duck
Pechuga Breast (usually chicken)
Perdiz Partridge
Percebes Goose-neck barnacles
Pescado Fish
Picadillo A dish of spicy mincemeat
Pichón Squab
Pimientos Peppers
Pintxo/pincho Bartop snack
Pipas Sunflower seeds, a common snack
Pochas Young haricot beans, a Riojan speciality
Pollo Chicken
Puerros Leeks
Pulga Submarine-shaped rolls
Pulpo Octopus
Rabas Crumbed calamari rings
Rabo de buey Oxtail
Rana Frog; ancas de rana is frogs' legs
Rape Monkfish
Relleno/a Stuffed
Revuelto Scrambled eggs
Riñones Kidneys
Rodaballo Turbot. Pricy and toothsome
Salchichón A salami-like sausage
Salpicón A seafood salad with plenty of onion and vinegar
Sepia Cuttlefish
Setas Wild mushrooms, often superb
Solomillo Beef fillet steak cut from the sirloin bone
Ternera Veal or young beef
Tocino Pork fat
Trucha Trout
Txangurro Spider crab, superb
Vieiras Scallops, also called veneras
Vizcaína (à la) In the style of Vizcaya, Bilbao's province
Xoubas Sardines in Galicia
Zamburiñas A type of small scallop
Zanahoria Carrot

Index

M

Map index

Acknowledgements

Andy Symington
I would like to thanks all those have helped with information and advice along the way. I owe a huge debt of gratitude to David Jackson, for superb text contributions and sterling company; and many thanks to my parents for their constant support, to the excellent team at Footprint, and to Riika for constant companionship over long distances. I'd also like to thank those people who gave their all to help research bars and restaurants with me: Andrew, Steve, Jon, Martin, Theresa, Jochen, Janie, Toby, Chris, Sophie, Menchu, Reinhard, Ben, and Hugh. And lastly, with love, María, who captures the essence of Spain.

Mary-Ann Gallagher
A big kiss and huge thanks to Susannah, Ajo, Raquel, Andrea, Pep, Adolfo, José Ángel (Machote), Candido, Willie, Fernando, Yolanda, Matías, Samuel, Julio, Guillermo, Rosa, Ángel, Claire, Lucy, Peter, Linz, Patrick, Adriano, Tatjana, Olgo, Nuria, José, Andrew, mum, dad, Oscar and Rosie, and all the countless kind strangers who helped me out along the way. Special thanks to all the team at Footprint, especially Caroline for her saintly patience.

Map symbols

Administration

□ Capital city
○ Other city/town
 International border
Regional border
Disputed border

Roads and travel

—— National highway, motorway
— Main road
— Minor road
- - - Track
······ Footpath
 Railway with station
✈ Airport
🚍 Bus station
Ⓜ Metro station
- - - Cable car
++++ Funicular
⛴ Ferry

Water features

River, canal
Lake, ocean
Seasonal marshland
Beach, sand bank
💧 Waterfall

Topographical features

Contours (approx)
⛰ Mountain
🌋 Volcano
Mountain pass
Escarpment
Gorge
Glacier
Salt flat
Rocks

Cities and towns

Main through route
Main street
Minor street

Pedestrianized street
Ⴑ Ⴑ Tunnel
→ One way street
IIIIIII Steps
⌒ Bridge
▲▲▲▲ Fortified wall
Park, garden, stadium
● Sleeping
❷ Eating
❶ Bars & clubs
❷ Entertainment
Building
■ Sight
⛪ Cathedral, church
🏛 Chinese temple
🏛 Hindu temple
Meru
🕌 Mosque
△ Stupa
✡ Synagogue
ℹ Tourist office
🏛 Museum
✉ Post office
Ⓟ Police
Ⓢ Bank
@ Internet
☏ Telephone
🏪 Market
➕ Hospital
Ⓟ Parking
⛽ Petrol
⛳ Golf
Ⓐ Detail map
Ⓐ Related map

Other symbols

∴ Archaeological site
♦ National park, wildlife reserve
Viewing point
▲ Campsite
⌂ Refuge, lodge
🏰 Castle
Diving
Deciduous/coniferous/palm trees
Hide
Vineyard
Distillery
Shipwreck
✕ Historic battlefield

Complete title listing

Cusco & the Inca Trail
Dominican Republic
Ecuador & Galápagos
Guatemala
Havana (P)
Mexico
Nicaragua
Peru
Rio de Janeiro
South American Handbook
Venezuela

Footprint publishes
travel guides to over 150
destinations worldwide. Each
guide is packed with practical,
concise and colourful
information for everybody from
first-time travellers to travel
aficionados. The list is growing
fast and current titles are noted
below.
Available from all good
bookshops and online

www.footprintbooks.com

(P) denotes pocket guide

North America
Vancouver (P)
New York (P)
Western Canada

Africa
Cape Town (P)
East Africa
Libya
Marrakech & the High Atlas
Marrakech (P)
Morocco
Namibia
South Africa
Tunisia
Uganda

Middle East
Egypt
Israel
Jordan
Syria & Lebanon

Latin America and Caribbean
Argentina
Barbados (P)
Bolivia
Brazil
Caribbean Islands
Central America & Mexico
Chile
Colombia
Costa Rica
Cuba

Australasia
Australia
East Coast Australia
New Zealand
Sydney (P)
West Coast Australia

Footnotes Complete title listing

Credits

Footprint credits

Editors: Caroline Lascom and
Stephanie Lambe
Assistant editor: Laura Dixon
Map editor: Sarah Sorensen

Publisher: Patrick Dawson
Editorial: Alan Murphy, Sophie Blacksell,
Claire Boobbyer, Caroline Lascom, Felicity
Laughton, Davina Rungasamy
Cartography: Robert Lunn,
Claire Benison, Kevin Feeney
Series development: Rachel Fielding
Design: Mytton Williams and Rosemary
Dawson (brand)
Advertising: Debbie Wylde
Finance and administration:
Sharon Hughes, Elizabeth Taylor

Photography credits

Front cover: Alamy
Back cover: Powerstock
Inside colour section: gettyone Stone,
Robert Harding Picture Library, Susannah
Sayler, Eye Ubiquitous, Pictures Colour
Library, Claire Boobbyer, Alamy

Print

Manufactured in Italy by LegoPrint
Pulp from sustainable forests

Footprint feedback

We try as hard as we can to make each
Footprint guide as up to date as possible
but, of course, things always change. If
you want to let us know about your
experiences – good, bad or ugly – then
don't delay, go to **www.footprintbooks.com**
and send in your comments.

Publishing information

Footprint Spain
2nd edition
© Footprint Handbooks Ltd
April 2004

ISBN 1 90347196 6
CIP DATA: A catalogue record for this book is
available from the British Library

® Footprint Handbooks and the Footprint
mark are a registered trademark of
Footprint Handbooks Ltd

Published by Footprint

6 Riverside Court
Lower Bristol Road
Bath BA2 3DZ, UK
T +44 (0)1225 469141
F +44 (0)1225 469461
discover@footprintbooks.com
www.footprintbooks.com

Distributed in the USA by

Publishers Group West

Every effort has been made to ensure that
the facts in this guidebook are accurate.
However, travellers should still obtain
advice from consulates, airlines etc about
travel and visa requirements before
travelling. The authors and publishers
cannot accept responsibility for
any loss, injury or inconvenience
however caused.

BRITISH AIRWAYS

Spain. Covered.

oneworld

More Spanish destinations than any other airline. Alicante, Almeria, Girona –
Costa Brava, Gran Canaria, Lanzarote, Malaga, Menorca, Murcia*, Palma de
Mallorca, Seville, Tenerife, and Valencia. For our best fares book at ba.com
Services operated by GB Airways Ltd. *From May 2003.

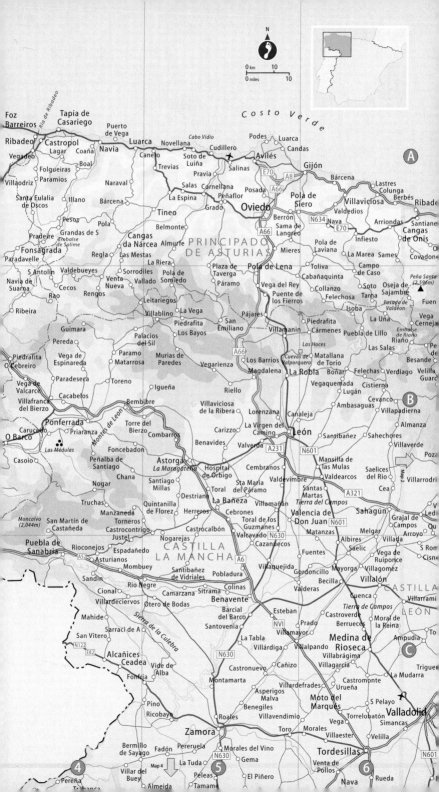

Bay of Biscay

N

0 km 10
0 miles 10

A

FRANCE

Cabo Billano
Baquio
Bermeo
Plencia
Mundaka
Mungia
Lekeitio
Ondarroa
San Sebastián/ Donostia
Pasaia/ Pasajes
Hondarribia
Irun
Basauri
Gernika
Zumaia
Getaria
Lasarte
Renteria
Markina
Deba
Zarautz
Usurbil
Hernani
Vera
Amorebieta
Berriz
Eibar
Azpeitia
Villabona
Andoain
Ceberio
Durango
Elorrio
Bergara
Errezil
Tolosa
Lizartza
Goizueta
Ventas
Sumbilla
Castillo y Elejabeitia
Arrasate-Mondragon
Zumárraga
Legazoi
Bessain
Betelu
Lecunberri
Echarri-Aranaz
Santesteban
Elizondo
Corbesa
Oñati
Berroeta
Murgia
Legutiano
PAÍS VASCO
Arantzazu
Altsasu/ Alsasua
Auza
Venta
Burguete/ Auritz
Roncesvalles/ Orreaga
Uchagavia
Escároz
Salvatierra
Eguilaz
Olazagutia
Huarte-Araquil
Olagüe
Erro
Arive
Embalse de Irabia
Vitoria/ Gasteiz
Gaceo
Larraona
Zudair
Echauri
Pamplona/ Iruña
Larrasoaña
Aburrea
Isaba
Roncal
Ustes
Peñacerrada
Arrai
Santa
Alqiza
Abarzuza
Astrain
Legarda
Aloain
Elorz
Agoitz
Artieda
Navascués
Burguí
Ansó
Hecho
Brinas
Bernedo
Elvillar
Acado
Estella
Puente la Reina
Obanos
Las Campanas
Monreal
N240
Lumbier
Tiermas
Sigüés
Berdún
Castie de Javier
Laguardia
Monasterio de Irache
Grauqui
Maneru
Mendigorria
Barasoain
Garinoain
Nardues
Liédena
Sangüesa
Ruesta
Santa Cilia
Cenicero
Viana
Los Arcos
Allo
Oteiza
Artazona
Lerga
Ujué
Cáseda
Monasterio de San Juan de la Peña
N24
Nájera
Logroño
Torres del Rio
Sesma
Larraga
Tafalla
Miranda de Arga
Olite
Sos del Rey Católico
Salinas
Navarrete
Mendavia
Lodosa
Lerin
Falces
Murillo El Fruto
Carcastillo
Uncastillo
Luesia
Biel
Baños Rio Tobia
Islallana
Ribaflecha
Ausejo
Cárcar
Andosilla
Persalta
Santacara
Caparossa
Sádaba
Farasdués
Luna
Ardisa
Ortilla
Anguiano
El Villar
Calahorra
Aldeanueva
Caparossa
Valareña
Ejea de los Caballeros
Erla
Embalse de la Sotonera
Torrecilla en Cameros
San Roman de Cameros
Arnedillo
Arnedo
Alfaro
Arguedas
Biel
Embalse de la Cuerda del Pozo
Montenegro
Pajares
Yanguas
Autol
Turruncun
Fitero
Cintruénigo
Tudela
Castejón de
Gurrea
Sierra de Luna
Torm
Vinuesa
Almarza
San Pedro Manrique
Baños de Fitero
Ventas
Cascante
Mallen
Tauste
Villaclervos
Cidones
La Rubia
San Felices
Magaña
Tarazona
Tulebras
Boria
Magallón
Remolinos
Esteban (744m)
Zuera
Leciñena
Numancia
Castilruiz
Agreda
Añon
Pozuelo de Aragón
Alagon
Villanueva de Gallego
Soria
Matalebreras
Olvega
Beraton
Sierra del Moncayo
ARAGÓN
Map 5
Villamayor
Lubia
Aldeapozo
Noviercas
Ciria
Calcena
Tabuenca
Zaragoza
Villafranc de Ebro
Matamala
Almenar de Soria
Gómara
Sauquillo
Mazaterón
Tierga
Cabarera (1,427m)
Epila
Maria del Huerve
Fuentes de Ebro
Almazán
Serón de Nágima
Deza
Villarroya de la Sierra
Ricla
Calátora
Muel
Mediana de Aragón
Quinto
Cobertélada
Villauenga
Ateca
Calatayud
Morata de Jalón
La Almunia de Doña Godina
Embalse de Mezaloche
Villasayas
Adradas
Monteagudo
Cariñena
Fuentedetos
Barahona
N11
Ariza
Cetina
Alhama de Aragón
N234
Codos
Villanueva de Huerva
Embalse de La Torcas
Azuara
Azaila
Medinaceli
Salinas de Medinaceli
Layna
Jaraba
Nuévalos
Mainar
Herrera
Lécera
Sigüenza
Alcolea del Pinar
Ciruelos
Maranchón
Campillo de Aragón
Milmarcos
Villafeliche
Daroca
Bádenas
Albalate del Arzobispo
Torremocha del Campo
Algora
Turmiel
Anquelo del Ducado
Cillas
Embid
Burbaguena
Ferreruela
Fonfria
Munesa
Hij
Saelices
Tornos
Retuerta
Segura de
Laguna de Gallocanta

4

5

6

B

C

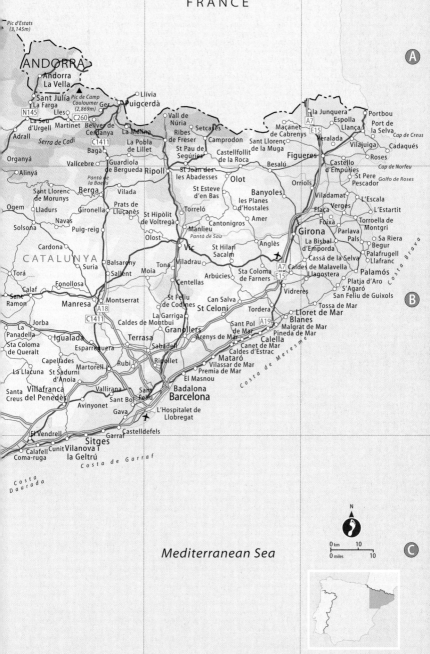

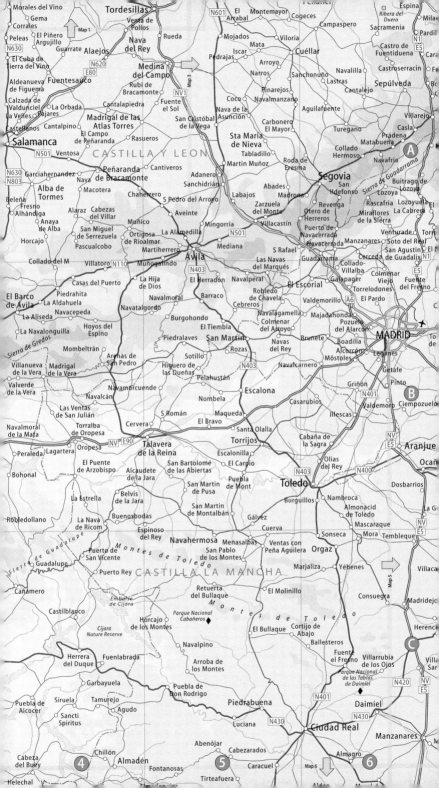

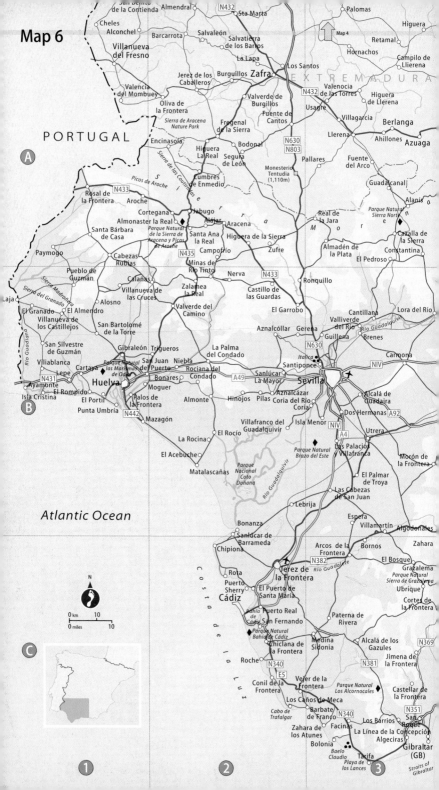

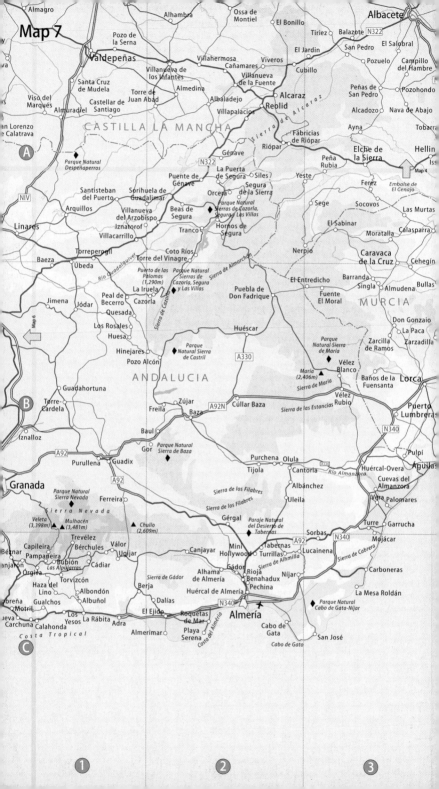

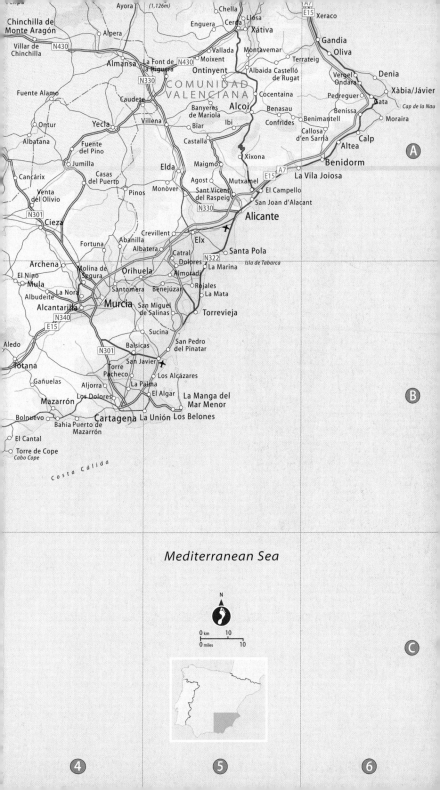

For a different view of Europe, take a Footprint

"" Superstylish travel guides – perfect for short break addicts.
Harvey Nichols magazine

Discover so much more...
Listings driven, forward looking and up to date. Focuses on what's going on right now. Contemporary, stylish, and innovative approach, providing quality travel information.